THE INTERNATIONAL ENCYCLOPEDIA OF DEPRESSION

Rick E. Ingram received his PhD in Clinical Psychology at the University of Kansas. The first part of his career was spent at San Diego State University where he was a professor of psychology and a core member in the joint San Diego State University–University of California at San Diego Doctoral Training Program in clinical psychology. He is currently a professor of psychology at the University of Kansas and serves as the editor of *Cognitive Therapy and Research* and as associate editor for the *Journal of Consulting and Clinical Psychology.* He has over 100 publications and over 175 conference presentations, mainly in the area of depression. He has authored or edited six books, the most recent of which are *Vulnerability to Psychopathology: Risk Across the Lifespan* (R. E. Ingram & J. Price, Eds., 2001) and *Cognitive Vulnerability to Depression* (R. E. Ingram, J. Miranda, & Z. V. Segal, 1998). He is a fellow of Division 12 of the American Psychological Association, and a founding fellow of the Academy of Cognitive Therapy. He is also the recipient of the Distinguished Scientific Award of the American Psychological Association for Early Career Contributions to Psychology, and earlier received the New Researcher Award from the Association for the Advancement of Behavior Therapy.

The International Encyclopedia of Depression

Rick E. Ingram, PhD

SPRINGER PUBLISHING COMPANY

New York

Springer Publishing Company, LLC
11 West 42nd Street
New York, NY 10036
www.springerpub.com

Acquisitions Editor: Philip Laughlin
Production Editor: Julia Rosen
Cover design: Mimi Flow
Composition: Apex CoVantage, LLC
Ebook ISBN: 978-0-8261-3794-4

09 10 11 / 5 4 3 2 1

Library of Congress Cataloging-in-Publication Data

The international encyclopedia of depression / [edited by] Rick E. Ingram.
    p. cm.
    Includes bibliographical references and indexes.
    ISBN 978-0-8261-3793-7 (alk. paper)
  1. Depression, Mental—Encyclopedias.   I. Ingram, Rick E.
    RC537.I573 2009
    616.85'27003—dc22   2008045866

Printed in the United States of America by Hamilton Printing Company.

EDITORIAL BOARD

CONTENTS

CONTRIBUTORS

John R. Z. Abela, PhD
Department of Psychology
McGill University
Montreal, Quebec
Canada
*Attributional Theories of
Depression, Diatheses-
Stress Models of
Depression*

Heather C. Abercrombie, PhD
Department of Psychiatry
University of Wisconsin
School of Medicine and
Public Health
Madison, Wisconsin
*Hypothalamic Pituitary
Adrenal Axis*

Emma K. Adam
Program on Human
Development and Social
Policy
School of Education and
Social Policy
Cells to Society Center,
Institute for Policy
Research
Northwestern University
Evanston, Illinois
Cortisol

Howard Aizenstein, MD, PhD
Western Psychiatric
Institute and Clinic
University of Pittsburgh
School of Medicine
Pittsburgh, Pennsylvania
*Computer Simulation
of Depression and
Depressive Phenomena*

George S. Alexopoulos, MD
Weill Medical College
Cornell University
Ithaca, New York
Director
Weill-Cornell Institute of
Geriatric Psychiatry
White Plains, New York
*Depression-Executive
Dysfunction Syndrome*

Nicholas Allen, PhD
University of Melbourne
Melbourne, Victoria,
Australia
*Childhood Depression:
Family Context*

Adam K. Anderson, PhD
Department of Psychology
University of Toronto
Toronto, Ontario, Canada
Affective Neuroscience

Bernice Andrews, PhD
Department of
Psychology
Royal Holloway
University of London
London, England
Shame

Jules Angst, MD
Zurich University
Psychiatric Hospital
Zurich, Switzerland
*Brief Recurrent
Depression*

Shelli Avenevoli, PhD
Division of Developmental
Translational Research

National Institute of
Mental Health
National Institutes of
Health
Bethesda, Maryland
*Continuity of Depression
Across Development*

R. Michael Bagby, PhD
Center for Addiction and
Mental Health
University of Toronto
Toronto, Ontario, Canada
*Personality Disorders and
Depression*

Michael J. Baime, PhD
Department of Psychology
University of Pennsylvania
Philadelphia, Pennsylvania
Attention

Ross J. Baldessarini, MD
Department of Psychiatry
Harvard Medical School
Boston, Massachusetts
*Bipolar Disorder
Treatment: Lithium*

Harriet A. Ball, MD
Medical Research Council
Social Genetic and
Developmental Psychiatry
Centre
Institute of Psychiatry
King's College
London, England
Twin Studies

Jacques P. Barber, PhD
Center for Psychotherapy
Research

Department of Psychiatry
University of Pennsylvania
School of Medicine
Philadelphia, Pennsylvania
Psychodynamic Therapy

Russel A. Barkley
Medical University of
South Carolina
Charleston, South
Carolina
SUNY Upstate Medical
University
Syracuse, New York
*Attention Deficit
Hyperactivity Disorder*

Alinne Z. Barrera, PhD
Department of Psychiatry
University of California at
San Francisco
San Francisco, California
Prevention

Steven R. H. Beach, PhD
Department of Psychology
University of Georgia
Athens, Georgia
Marital Therapy

Christopher G. Beevers, PhD
Department of Psychology
University of Texas at
Austin
Austin, Texas
*Cognitive Vulnerability:
Genetic Associations*

German E. Berrios, MD
Department of Psychiatry
University of Cambridge
Cambridge, England
History of Depression

Namgyal Bhutia, MD
Psychiatric Resident
UMDNJ-New Jersey
Medical School
Newark, New Jersey
Electroconvulsive Therapy

Antonia Bifulco, PhD
Lifespan Research Group
Royal Holloway,
University of London
London, England
Early Adversity

Steven L. Bistricky, MA
Department of Psychology
University of Kansas
Lawrence, Kansas
*Dysfunctional Attitudes
Scale, Minor Depression*

Rebecca E. Blanton, PhD
Department of Psychology
University of Southern
California
Los Angeles, California
Hormones

Sidney J. Blatt, PhD
Department of Psychology
Yale University
New Haven, Connecticut
*Anaclitic and Introjective
Depression*

Dan G. Blazer, MD, PhD
Department of Psychiatry
and Behavioral Sciences
Center for the Study
of Aging and Human
Development
Duke University Medical
Center
Durham, North Carolina
*Postmenopausal
Depression*

Carol Brayne, PhD
University of Cambridge
Parkinson's Disease

Patricia A. Brennan, PhD
Department of Psychology
Emory University
Atlanta, Georgia
*Family Transmission of
Depression*

Chris R. Brewin, PhD
Subdepartment of Clinical
Health Psychology
University College London
London, England
Intrusive Memory

Tabetha Brockman, MA
Department of Psychiatry
and Psychology
Mayo Clinic College of
Medicine
Rochester, Minnesota
Smoking

Caroline B. Browne, PhD
Department of Psychology
University of North
Carolina at Chapel Hill
Chapel Hill, North
Carolina
Peer Relations

Lisa D. Butler, PhD
Department of Psychiatry
and Behavioral Sciences
Stanford University School
of Medicine
Stanford, California
Cancer

Turhan Canli, PhD
Department of Psychology
Stony Brook University
Stony Brook, New York
*Genetic Transmission of
Depression*

Paul Carey, FCPsych, PhD
Department of Psychiatry
University of Stellenbosch
Stellenbosch, South Africa
*Human Immunodeficiency
Virus*

Robert M. Carney, PhD
Department of Psychiatry
Washington University
School of Medicine
St. Louis, Missouri
Heart Disease

Bernard J. Carroll, MBBS,
PhD, FRCPsych
Pacific Behavioral
Research Foundation
Carmel, California
*Dexamethasone
Suppression Test*

Christine Chang-Schneider,
PhD
Department of Psychology
University of Texas at
Austin
Austin, Texas
Self-Verification

Iwona Chelminski, PhD
Department of Psychiatry
and Human Behavior
Brown University School
of Medicine

Providence, Rhode Island
The Clinically Useful Depression Outcome Scale

Bruce F. Chorpita, PhD
Department of Psychology
University of Hawai'i at Manoa
Manoa, Hawai'i
Internalizing Disorders

Katherine H. Clemans, MA
Department of Psychology
University of Florida
Gainesville, Florida
Childhood Depression

Kimberly A. Coffey, MA
Department of Psychology
University of North Carolina at Chapel Hill
Chapel Hill, North Carolina
Positive Emotion Dysregulation

Sheldon Cohen, PhD
Department of Psychology
Carnegie Mellon University
Pittsburgh, Pennsylvania
Social Support

Jennifer Connolly, PhD
Department of Psychology
York University
Toronto, Ontario, Canada
Romantic Relationships

Jennifer K. Connor-Smith, PhD
Department of Psychology
Oregon State University
Corvallis, Oregon
Stress and Coping

Yeates Conwell, MD
Center for the Study and Prevention of Suicide
University of Rochester School of Medicine
Rochester, New York
Suicide in the Elderly

Rena Cooper-Kazaz, MD
Biological Psychiatry Laboratory
Department of Psychiatry
Hadassah-Hebrew University Medical Center
Jerusalem, Israel
Thyroid Function

E. Jane Costello, PhD
Department of Psychology
Duke University
Durham, North Carolina
Age of Onset of Depression

James C. Coyne, PhD
Abramson Cancer Center
University of Pennsylvania
Philadelphia, Pennsylvania
Marital Functioning and Depression

Jorden A. Cummings, MA
Department of Psychology
University of Delaware
Newark, Delaware
Cognitive Behavioral Therapy

Jill M. Cyranowski, PhD
Department of Psychiatry
Department of Psychology
University of Pittsburgh School of Medicine and Medical Center
Pittsburgh, Pennsylvania
Medical Conditions and Depression

Boldizsár Czéh, MD
Clinical Neurobiology Laboratory
German Primate Center
Göttingen, Germany
Hippocampus

Tim Dalgleish, PhD
Emotion Research Group
Cognition and Brain Sciences Unit
Medical Research Council
Cambridge, England
Differential Activation

Collin L. Davidson, MA
Oklahoma State University
Stillwater, Oklahoma
Stress Generation

Betsy Davis, PhD
Oregon Research Institute
Eugene, Oregon
Childhood Depression: Family Context

Asli Demirtas-Tatlidede, MD
Berenson-Allen Center for Noninvasive Brain Stimulation
Beth Israel Deaconess Medical Center
Harvard Medical School
Boston, Massachusetts
Transcranial Magnetic Stimulation

Elizabeth DeOreo, MD
Department of Psychiatry and Behavioral Sciences
Emory University School of Medicine
Atlanta, Georgia
Hypothalamic-Pituitary-Thyroid Axis

Richard A. Depue, PhD
Department of Human Development
Cornell University
Ithaca, New York
Dopaminergic Systems

Mary Amanda Dew, PhD
Department of Psychiatry
Department of Psychology
Department of Epidemiology
University of Pittsburgh School of Medicine and Medical Center
Pittsburgh, Pennsylvania
Medical Conditions and Depression

Guy Diamond, PhD
Children's Hospital of Philadelphia and University of Pennsylvania
Philadelphia, Pennsylvania
Family and Parent-Child Therapy

Sona Dimidjian, PhD
Department of Psychology
University of Colorado
Boulder, Colorado
Behavioral Models of Depression

Danielle S. Duggan, PhD
Department of Psychiatry
University of Oxford
Warneford Hospital
Oxford, England
Suicidal Cognition

Todd W. Dunn, MA
Department of Psychiatry
Southwestern Medical
Center
University of Texas
Dallas, Texas
Psychosocial Functioning

Yulia Chentsova Dutton, PhD
Department of Psychology
Georgetown University
Washington, D.C.
Culture and Depression

Kari M. Eddington, PhD
Department of Psychology
University of North
Carolina at Greensboro
Greensboro, North
Carolina
*Neuroimaging and
Psychosocial Treatments
for Depression*

Anne Farmer, MD
Medical Research Council
Social, Genetic, and
Developmental Psychiatry
Centre
Institute of Psychiatry
King's College
London, England
Genetics of Depression

Frank D. Fincham, PhD
Department of Psychology
Florida State University
Tallahassee, Florida
Marital Therapy

Philip A. Fisher, PhD
Oregon Social Learning
Center and Center for
Research to Practice
Eugene, Oregon
Maltreatment

Srnka J. Flegar, MD
Department of Psychiatry
and Mental Health
Observatory

Groote Schuur Hospital
University of Cape Town
Cape Town, South Africa
*Dermatology and
Depression*

Gordon L. Flett, PhD
Department of Psychology
York University
Toronto, Ontario, Canada
Perfectionism

Erika E. Forbes, PhD
Department of Psychiatry
University of Pittsburgh
Pittsburgh, Pennsylvania
Neural Systems of Reward

Joseph C. Franklin, MA
Department of Psychology
University of North
Carolina at Chapel Hill
Chapel Hill, North
Carolina
Peer Relations

Barbara L. Fredrickson, PhD
University of North
Carolina at Chapel Hill
Chapel Hill, North
Carolina
*Positive Emotion
Dysregulation*

Kenneth E. Freedland, PhD
Department of Psychiatry
Washington University
School of Medicine
St. Louis, Missouri
Heart Disease

Eberhard Fuchs, MD
Clinical Neurobiology
Laboratory
German Primate Center
DFG Research Center
Molecular Physiology of
the Brain
University of Göttingen
Department of Neurology
Medical School
University of Göttingen
Göttingen, Germany
Hippocampus

Daniel Fulford, MA
Department of Psychology
University of Miami

Coral Gables, Florida
Bipolar Disorders

Melinda A. Gaddy, BA
Department of Psychology
University of Kansas
Lawrence, Kansas
*Anger, Endogenous and
Reactive Depression,
Global Burden of
Depression*

Krauz Ganadjian, MD
Resident Physician
Department of Psychiatry
University of California at
San Diego
San Diego, California
Bereavement

Robert W. Garlan, PhD
Private Practice
San Jose, California
Cancer

Genevieve M. Garratt, PhD
Sacramento, California
Cognitive Meditation

Brandon E. Gibb, PhD
Department of Psychology
Binghamton University
(SUNY)
Binghamton, New York
*Developmental
Antecedents of
Vulnerability*

Paul Gilbert, PhD, FBPsS
Mental Health Research
Unit
Kingsway Hospital
Kingsway, Derby, England
Evolution

Omri Gillath, PhD
Department of Psychology
University of Kansas
Lawrence, Kansas
Attachment

Jane Gillham, PhD
Swarthmore College
Swarthmore,
Pennsylvania
University of Pennsylvania
Pittsburgh, Pennsylvania
*Family and Parent-Child
Therapy*

Michael J. Gitlin, MD
Department of Psychiatry
Geffen School of Medicine
at UCLA
Los Angeles, California
*Monoamine Oxidase
Inhibitors*

Layne A. Goble, PhD
Psychology Service
Veterans Administration
Connecticut Healthcare
System
Yale University
New Haven, Connecticut
Chronic Pain

Sherryl H. Goodman, PhD
Department of Psychology
Emory University
Atlanta, Georgia
Mothers and Depression

Araceli Gonzalez, MA
Department of Psychology
San Diego State University
University of California
San Diego
San Diego, California
*Childhood Depression:
Treatment*

Ian H. Gotlib, PhD
Department of Psychology
Stanford University
Palo Alto, California
Functional Neuroimaging

Julia A. Graber, PhD
Department of Psychology
University of Florida
Gainesville, Florida
Childhood Depression

John D. Guerry, MA
Department of Psychology
University of North
Carolina at Chapel Hill
Chapel Hill, North
Carolina
Peer Relations

J. Paul Hamilton, PhD
Department of Psychology
Stanford University
Palo Alto, California
Functional Neuroimaging

Nancy A. Hamilton, PhD
Department of Psychology
University of Kansas
Lawrence, Kansas
Insomnia

Benjamin L. Hankin, PhD
Department of Psychology
University of Denver
*Attributional Theories of
Depression, Diatheses-
Stress Models of
Depression*

Kate L. Harkness, PhD
Department of Psychology
Queen's University
Kingston, Ontario,
Canada
Stressful Life Events

Robert G. Harrington, PhD
Department of
Psychology and Research
in Education
University of Kansas
Lawrence, Kansas
Externalizing Disorders

Tirril Harris, MD
Department of Health and
Population Research
King's College
London, England
Loss

Lauren C. Haubert, PhD
Department of Psychology
University of Calgary
Calgary, Alberta, Canada
Behavioral Observations

Adele M. Hayes, PhD
Department of Psychology
University of Delaware
Newark, Delaware
*Cognitive Behavioral
Therapy*

Nicole Heilbron, MA
Department of Psychology
University of North
Carolina at Chapel Hill
Chapel Hill, North
Carolina
Peer Relations

Dirk Hermans, PhD
University of Leuven
Leuven, Belgium
Self-Esteem

Laura Hernangómez, PhD
School of Psychology
Complutense University
Madrid, Spain
*Automatic and Controlled
Processing in Depression*

Paula T. Hertel, PhD
Department of Psychology
Trinity University
San Antonio, Texas
Memory Process

Paul L. Hewitt, PhD
Department of Psychology
University of British
Columbia
Vancouver, British
Columbia, Canada
Perfectionism

**Jacqueline Hoare, MBChB,
DMH, MRCPsych, FCPsych**
HIV/Neuropsychiatry
Program
Groote Schuur Hospital
University of Cape Town
Cape Town, South Africa
*Human Immunodeficiency
Virus*

Jill M. Hooley, PhD
Department of Psychology
Harvard University
Cambridge, Massachusetts
Expressed Emotion

Jeffrey Horenstein, MA
Department of Psychology
Carnegie Mellon
University
Pittsburgh, Pennsylvania
Social Support

Steven S. Ilardi, PhD
Department of
Psychology
University of Kansas
Lawrence, Kansas
*Therapeutic Lifestyle
Change*

Rick E. Ingram, PhD
Department of Psychology
University of Kansas
Lawrence, Kansas
*Aaron Beck, Automatic
Thoughts, Causality,
Classification of
Depression, Cognitive
Distortion, Cognitive
Reactivity, Cognitive
Theories of Depression,
Cognitive Vulnerability,
Comorbidity, Depressive
Realism, Depressogenesis,
Gender Differences, High-
Risk Research Paradigm,
Internal Working Models,
Interpersonal Model of
Depression, Risk, Scar
Hypothesis, Schemas,
Self-Focused Attention,
Symptoms of Depression,
Vulnerability*

Lianna S. Ishihara-Paul, PhD
GlaxoSmithKline
Pharmaceuticals
WorldWide Epidemiology
Harlow, Essex
United Kingdom
Parkinson's Disease

Robin B. Jarrett, PhD
Department of Psychiatry
Southwestern Medical
Center
University of Texas
Dallas, Texas
Psychosocial Functioning

Amishi P. Jha, PhD
Department of Psychology
University of Pennsylvania
Pittsburgh, Pennsylvania
Attention

Sheri L. Johnson, PhD
Department of Psychology
University of Miami
Coral Gables, Florida
Bipolar Disorders

Thomas E. Joiner, Jr., PhD
Department of Psychology
Florida State University
Tallahassee, Florida
Suicide Theories

**John A. Joska, MBChB,
MMed (Psych), FCPsych (SA)**
HIV/Neuropsychiatry
Program
Groote Schuur Hospital
University of Cape Town
Cape Town, South Africa
*Human Immunodeficiency
Virus*

Cynthia Karlson, MA
Department of Psychology
University of Kansas
Lawrence, Kansas
Insomnia

Leslie Karwoski, PhD
Evidence-Based Treatment
Centers of Seattle
Seattle, Washington
*Eating Disorders,
Exercise, and Depression*

**Paul Keedwell, BSc, MB,
ChB, MRCPsych**
Department of
Psychological Medicine
Cardiff University
Heath Park, Cardiff,
Wales
Honorary Lecturer
Institute of Psychiatry
Decrespigny Park
London, England
Brain Circuitry

Charles Kellner, MD
Department of Psychiatry
UMDNJ-New Jersey
Medical School
Newark, New Jersey
Electroconvulsive Therapy

Robert D. Kerns, PhD
Psychology Services
Veterans Administration
Connecticut Healthcare
System
Yale University
New Haven, Connecticut
Chronic Pain

Ronald C. Kessler, PhD
Department of Health
Care Policy
Harvard Medical School
Boston, Massachusetts
Epidemiology

Cara J. Kiff, MA
Department of Psychology
University of Washington
Washington
Temperament

Hyoun K. Kim, PhD
Oregon Social Learning
Center and Center for
Research to Practice
Eugene, Oregon
Maltreatment

Cheryl A. King, PhD, ABPP
Departments of Psychiatry
and Psychology
University of Michigan
Depression Center
University of Michigan
Ann Arbor, Michigan
Suicide in Youths

Jason Klein, BA
Department of Psychiatry
University of Kansas
Lawrence, Kansas
Minor Depression

John P. Kline, PhD
Department of Psychiatry
University of South
Alabama
Mobile, Alabama
*Psychophysiology of
Depression*

Maria Kovacs, PhD
Department of Psychiatry
University of Pittsburgh
School of Medicine
Pittsburgh, Pennsylvania
*Children's Depression
Inventory*

Robert F. Krueger, PhD
Department of Psychology
University of Minnesota
Twin Cities
Minneapolis and St. Paul,
Minnesota
*Categorical and
Dimensional Models of
Depression*

Benji T. Kurian, MD, MPH
Department of Psychiatry
Southwestern Medical
Center

University of Texas
Dallas, Texas
*Combined
Psychological and
Psychopharmacological
Treatment*

Cecile D. Ladouceur, PhD
Department of Psychiatry
University of Pittsburgh
Pittsburgh, Pennsylvania
*Brain Function in
Depressed Children and
Adolescents*

Christine L. Larson, PhD
Department of Psychology
University of Wisconsin–
Milwaukee
Milwaukee, Wisconsin
*Hemispheric
Lateralization*

K. A. Lehman, PhD
Department of Psychology
University of Kansas
Lawrence, Kansas
Omega-3 Fatty Acids

Liliana J. Lengua, PhD
Department of
Psychology
University of Washington
Seattle, Washington
Temperament

Bernard Lerer, MD
Biological Psychiatry
Laboratory
Department of Psychiatry
Hadassah-Hebrew
University Medical Center
Jerusalem, Israel
Thyroid Function

Kenneth N. Levy, PhD
Pennsylvania State
University
State College,
Pennsylvania
*Psychodynamic Model of
Depression*

Peter M. Lewinsohn, PhD
Oregon Research Institute
Eugene, Oregon
*Behavioral Models of
Depression*

Alison R. Lewis, MA
Northwestern University
Evanston, Illinois
Anxiety

Cara C. Lewis, MS
Department of Psychology
University of Oregon
Eugene, Oregon
Adolescent Depression

Tzuri Lisfschytz, PhD
Biological Psychiatry
Laboratory
Department of Psychiatry
Hadassah-Hebrew
University Medical Center
Jerusalem, Israel
Thyroid Function

Carissa A. Low, MA
University of California at
Los Angeles
Los Angeles, California
Pittsburgh, Pennsylvania
Cytokines

David D. Luxton, PhD
Department of Psychology
University of Kansas
Lawrence, Kansas
*Insomnia, Posttraumatic
Stress Disorder*

Sarah D. Lynne, MA
Department of Psychology
University of Florida
Gainesville, Florida
Childhood Depression

Danielle J. Maack, MA
Department of Psychology
University of Wyoming
Laramie, Wyoming
Course of Depression

Christopher R. Martell, PhD,
ABPP
University of Washington
Seattle, Washington
*Behavioral Models of
Depression*

Eric J. Mash, PhD
Department of
Psychology
University of Calgary
Calgary, Alberta, Canada
Behavioral Observations

James P. McCullough, Jr.,
PhD
Department of Psychology
Virginia Commonwealth
University
Richmond, Virginia
*Cognitive Behavioral
Analysis System of
Psychotherapy*

Danyale McCurdy, MA
University of Kansas
Lawrence, Kansas
*Eating Disorders, Exercise
and Depression*

Joseph B. McGlinchey, PhD
Department of Psychiatry
and Human Behavior
Brown University School
of Medicine
Providence, Rhode Island
*Clinically Useful
Depression Outcome
Scale*

Peter McGuffin, PhD
Social Genetic and
Developmental Psychiatry
Centre
Institute of Psychiatry
Medical Research Council
King's College
London, England
Twin Studies

Caroline McIsaac, MA
Department of
Psychology
York University
Toronto, Ontario, Canada
Romantic Relationships

John R. McQuaid, PhD
Psychology Services
Veterans Administration
San Diego Healthcare
System
University of California
San Diego, California
Stress Assessment

Tiffany Meites
Department of Psychology
University of Kansas
Lawrence, Kansas
*Beck Depression
Inventory, Recurrence*

Gerald I. Metalsky
Department of Psychology
Lawrence University
Appleton, Wisconsin
Hopelessness

David J. Miklowitz
Department of Psychology
University of Colorado at
Boulder
Boulder, Colorado
*Bipolar Disorder
Treatment: Psychotherapy*

Joshua D. Miller
University of Georgia
Athens, Georgia
*Personality Disorders and
Depression*

Bethany H. Morris, MA
Department of Psychology
University of South Florida
Tampa, Florida
*Behavioral Activation
System, Behavioral
Inhibition System*

Michelle Moulds, PhD
School of Psychology
University of New South
Wales
Sydney, New South Wales,
Australia
Differential Activation

Ricardo F. Muñoz, PhD
Department of Psychiatry
University of California at
San Francisco
San Francisco, California
Prevention

Christy Nelson, MA
Department of Psychology
University of Kansas
Lawrence, Kansas
Insomnia

**Charles B. Nemeroff, MD,
PhD**
Department of Psychiatry
and Behavioral Sciences
Emory University School
of Medicine
Atlanta, Georgia
*Hypothalamic-Pituitary-
Thyroid Axis*

Arthur M. Nezu, PhD
Department of Psychology
Drexel University
Philadelphia, Pennsylvania
*Assessment of Depression,
Problem-Solving Therapy*

Christine Maguth Nezu, PhD
Department of Psychology
Drexel University
Philadelphia, Pennsylvania
*Assessment of Depression,
Problem-Solving Therapy*

Susan Nolen-Hoeksema, PhD
Department of Psychology
Yale University
New Haven, Connecticut
Rumination

K. Daniel O'Leary, PhD
Department of Psychology
Stony Brook University
Stony Brook, New York
*Cognitive Behavioral
Couples Therapy*

Roisin O'Mara, MS
Department of Psychology
University of Michigan
Ann Arbor, Michigan
Suicide in Youths

Gordon Parker, MD
Black Dog Institute
Prince of Wales Hospital
University of New South
Wales
Randwick, New South
Wales, Australia
Melancholia

**Alvaro Pascual-Leone, MD,
PhD**
Berenson-Allen Center
for Noninvasive Brain
Stimulation
Beth Israel Deaconess
Medical Center
Harvard Medical School
Boston, Massachusetts
*Transcranial Magnetic
Stimulation*

Christi A. Patten, PhD
Department of Psychiatry
and Psychology

Mayo Clinic College of
Medicine
Rochester, Minnesota
Smoking

Suzanna L. Penningroth, PhD
Department of Psychology
University of Wyoming
Laramie, Wyoming
Self-Regulation

Carolyn M. Pepper, PhD
Department of Psychology
University of Wyoming
Laramie, Wyoming
Course of Depression

Lukas Pezawas, MD
Division of Biological
Psychiatry
Medical University of
Vienna
Vienna, Austria
Molecular Genetics

Vicky Phares, PhD
Department of Psychology
University of South
Florida
Tampa, Florida
Fathers and Depression

Paul A. Pilkonis, PhD
Department of
Psychiatry
Department of Psychology
University of Pittsburgh
School of Medicine and
Medical Center
Pittsburgh, Pennsylvania
*Medical Conditions and
Depression*

Bruce G. Pollock, MD
Department of Psychiatry
University of Toronto
Toronto, Ontario,
Canada
Geriatric Depression

Robert M. Post, MD
George Washington
University School of
Medicine
Washington, D.C.
Penn State University
College of Medicine
Hershey, Pennsylvania

Bipolar Collaborative
Network
Bethesda, Maryland
Kindling

Mitchell J. Prinstein, PhD
Department of Psychology
University of North
Carolina at Chapel Hill
Chapel Hill, North
Carolina
Peer Relations

Rakesh Reddy, MD
Department of Psychiatry
Vanderbilt University
School of Medicine
Nashville, Tennessee
*Biological Models of
Depression*

Lynn Rehm, PhD
Department of Psychology
University of Houston
Houston, Texas
Behavior Therapy

Uzma S. Rehman, PhD
Department of Psychology
University of Waterloo
Waterloo, Ontario,
Canada
*Marital Functioning and
Depression*

Karen Reivich, PhD
Department of Psychology
University of Pennsylvania
Philadelphia, Pennsylvania
*Family and Parent-Child
Therapy*

John E. Roberts, PhD
Department of Psychology
State University of New
York at Buffalo
Buffalo, New York
Self-Esteem

Kathryn A. Roecklein, PhD
Psychology Services
Jackson Veterans Affairs
Medical Center
University of Mississippi
Medical Center
Jackson, Mississippi
*Seasonal Affective
Disorder*

Kelly J. Rohan, PhD
Department of Psychology
University of Vermont
Burlington, Vermont
*Seasonal Affective
Disorder*

Paul Rohde, PhD
Oregon Research Institute
Eugene, Oregon
*Adolescent Depression:
Treatment*

Paul D. Rokke, PhD
Department of Psychology
North Dakota State
University
Fargo, North Dakota
Self-Efficacy

Jonathan Rottenberg, PhD
Department of Psychology
University of South
Florida
Tampa, Florida
*Behavioral Activation
System, Behavioral
Inhibition System*

M. David Rudd, PhD
Department of Psychology
Texas Tech University
Lubbock, Texas
Suicide Warning Signs

Natalie Sachs-Ericsson, PhD
Department of Psychology
Florida State University
Tallahassee, Florida
*Postmenopausal
Depression*

Brenda Sampat, PhD
Department of Psychology
University of Kansas
Lawrence, Kansas
Reassurance-Seeking

Monica Z. Scalco, MD
Department of Psychiatry
University of Toronto
Baycrest Centre for
Geriatric Care
Toronto, Ontario, Canada
Geriatric Depression

Christine D. Scher, PhD
Department of Psychology
California State University
at Fullerton

Fullerton, California
Parenting

Walter D. Scott, PhD
Department of Psychology
University of Wyoming
Laramie, Wyoming
Self-Regulation

**Soraya Seedat, MBChB,
FCPsych (SA), PhD, MRC**
Unit on Anxiety and Stress
Disorders
Department of Psychiatry
University of Stellenbosch
Stellenbosch, South Africa
*Human Immunodeficiency
Virus*

Zindel V. Segal, PhD, CPsych
Center for Addiction and
Mental Health
University of Toronto
Toronto, Ontario, Canada
*Mindfulness-Based
Cognitive Therapy*

Emre Selcuk, MA
Department of Psychology
University of Kansas
Lawrence, Kansas
Attachment

Brian A. Sharpless, PhD
Center for Psychotherapy
Research
Department of Psychiatry
University of
Pennsylvania School of
Medicine
Philadelphia, Pennsylvania
Psychodynamic Therapy

Lisa Sheeber, PhD
Oregon Research Institute
Eugene, Oregon
*Childhood Depression:
Family Context*

Richard C. Shelton, MD
Department of Psychiatry
Vanderbilt University
School of Medicine
Nashville, Tennessee
*Biological Models of
Depression*

Greg Siegle, PhD
University of Pittsburgh
School of Medicine
Western Psychiatric
Institute and Clinic
Pittsburgh, Pennsylvania
*Amygdala, Brain Function
in Midlife Unipolar
Depression, Computer
Simulation of Depression
and Depressive
Phenomena*

Anne D. Simons, PhD
Department of Psychology
University of Oregon
Eugene, Oregon
Adolescent Depression

Lisa M. Sontag, MS
Department of Psychology
University of Florida
Gainesville, Florida
Childhood Depression

Susan C. South, PhD
Department of Psychology
University of Minnesota,
Minneapolis, Minnesota
*Categorical and
Dimensional Models of
Depression*

Kartik K. Sreenivasan, PhD
Department of Psychology
University of Pennsylvania
Pittsburgh, Pennsylvania
Attention

Nicole K. Starace, MA
University of Hawai'i at
Manoa
Manoa, Hawai'i
Internalizing Disorders

Dana Steidtmann, PhD
Department of Psychology
University of Kansas
Lawrence, Kansas
*Attributional Style,
Relapse*

Dan J. Stein, MD, PhD
Department of Psychiatry
and Mental Health
University of Cape Town
Cape Town, South Africa
*Human Immunodeficiency
Virus*

Laurence D. Steinberg, PhD
Department of Psychology
Temple University
Philadelphia, Pennsylvania
*Continuity of Depression
Across Development*

Cinnamon Stetler, PhD
Department of Psychology
Furman University
Greenville, South Carolina
Immune System

Natalie R. Stevens, MA
Department of Psychology
University of Kansas
Lawrence, Kansas
*Insomnia, Postpartum
Depression*

Daniel M. Stout, PhD
Department of Psychology
North Dakota State
University
Fargo, North Dakota
Self-Efficacy

Timothy J. Strauman, PhD
Department of Psychology
and Neuro Science
Duke University
Durham, North Carolina
*Neuroimaging and
Psychosocial Treatments
for Depression*

Natalie N. Stroupe, MA
Department of Psychology
University of Kansas
Lawrence, Kansas
Circadian Rhythms

William B. Swann, Jr.
Department of Psychology
University of Texas at
Austin
Austin, Texas
Self-Verification

Eva Szigethy, MD, PhD
Psychiatry and Pediatrics
University of Pittsburgh
School of Medicine
Department of
Gastroenterology
Children's Hospital of
Pittsburgh
Pittsburgh, Pennsylvania
Cytokines

June Price Tangney, PhD
Department of Psychology
George Mason University
Fairfax, Virginia
Guilt

Susan R. Tate, MA
Psychology Review
Veterans Administration
San Diego Healthcare
System
University of California at
San Diego
San Diego, California
Stress Assessment

Michael Terman, PhD
Professor, Department of
Psychiatry
Columbia University
Medical Center
New York, New York
*Seasonal Affective
Disorder: Light Treatment*

Julian F. Thayer, PhD
Department of Psychology
The Ohio State University
Columbus Ohio
Heart Rate Variability

Caitlin Thompson, PhD
Center for the Study and
Prevention Suicide
University of Rochester
Rochester, New York
Suicide in the Elderly

Leonardo Tondo, MD
University of Cagliari
Cagliari, Italy
*Bipolar Disorder
Treatment: Lithium*

Leandro Torres, PhD
Department of Psychiarty
University of California at
San Francisco
San Francisco, California
Prevention

Madhukar H. Trivedi, MD
Department of Psychiatry
Southwestern Medical
Center
University of Texas
Dallas, Texas

*Combined
Psychological and
Psychopharmacological
Treatment*

Jeanne Tsai, PhD
Department of Psychology
Stanford University
Palo Alto, California
Culture and Depression

Rudolf Uher, MD
Medical Research Council
Social, Genetic, and
Developmental Psychiatry
Centre
Institute of Psychiatry
King's College
London, England
Genetics of Depression

Amanda A. Uliaszek, MA
Department of Psychology
Northwestern University
Evanston, Illinois
Anxiety

Kimberly A. Van Orden, MA
Department of
Psychology
Florida State University
Tallahassee, Florida
Suicide Theories

Carmelo Vázquez, PhD
School of Psychology
Complutense University
Madrid, Spain
*Automatic and
Controlled Processing
in Depression*

**Bavanisha Vythilingum,
MBChB, FCPsych**
Groote Schuur Hospital
University of Cape Town
Cape Town, South Africa
*Dermatology and
Depression*

**Karen Dineen Wagner, MD,
PhD**
Department of Psychiatry
and Behavioral Sciences
University of Texas
Medical Branch
Galveston, Texas

*Childhood Depression:
Treatment With
Pharmacotherapy*

**Jerome C. Wakefield, PhD,
DSW**
Department of Psychology
New York University
New York, New York
Definition of Depression

Rachel H. Wasserman, MA
Department of Psychology
Pennsylvania State
University
State College,
Pennsylvania
*Psychodynamic Model of
Depression*

David Watson, PhD
Department of
Psychology
University of Iowa
Iowa City, Iowa
*Positive and Negative
Affect Schedule*

V. Robin Weersing, PhD
Department of
Psychology
San Diego State University
University of California at
San Diego
San Diego, California
*Childhood Depression:
Treatment*

Daniel R. Weinberger, MD
Genes, Cognition, and
Psychosis Program
National Institutes of
Health
Bethesda, Maryland
Molecular Genetics

Myrna Weissman, PhD
College of Physicians and
Surgeons
Mailman School of Public
Health
Columbia University
New York State
Psychiatric Institute
New York, New York
*Interpersonal
Psychotherapy*

Adrian Wells
Academic Division of
Clinical Psychology
University of Manchester
Manchester, England
Metacognition

Tony T. Wells, MA
Department of
Psychology
University of Texas at
Austin
Austin, Texas
*Cognitive Vulnerability:
Genetic Associations*

Thomas A. Widiger, PhD
Department of
Psychology
University of Kentucky
Lexington, Kentucky
*Diagnostic and Statistical
Manual of Mental
Disorders*

**Kay Wilhelm, AM, MB, BS,
MD, FRANZCP**
School of Psychiatry,
Faculty of Medicine
Black Dog Institute
University of New South
Wales
Randwick, New South
Wales, Australia
Psychiatry
St. Vincent's Hospital
Darlinghurst, New South
Wales, Australia
Serotonin

J. Mark G. Williams, PhD
Department of Psychiatry
University of Oxford
Warneford Hospital
Oxford, England
Suicidal Cognition

Paul Willner, DSc, FBPsS
Department of Psychology
Swansea University
Swansea, Wales
Dopamine

LaRicka R. Wingate, PhD
Department of Psychology
Oklahoma State University
Stillwater, Oklahoma
Stress Generation

Eddie J. Wright, MA
Department of Psychology
University of Kansas
Lawrence, Kansas
Adjustment Disorder,
Cyclothymia

Diane Young, PhD
Department of Psychiatry
and Human Behavior
Brown University School
of Medicine
Providence, Rhode Island
The Clinically Useful
Depression Outcome Scale

Mark Zimmerman, MD
Department of Psychiatry
and Human Behavior
Brown University School
of Medicine
Providence, Rhode Island
Clinically Useful
Depression Outcome
Scale

Richard E. Zinbarg, PhD
Department of Psychology
Northwestern University
Evanston, Illinois
Assessment of Depression

Sidney Zisook, MD
Department of Psychiatry
University of California at
San Diego
San Diego, California
Bereavement

David C. Zuroff, PhD
Department of Psychology
McGill University
Montreal, Quebec,
Canada
Anaclitic and Introjective
Depression

PREFACE

Depression touches virtually all of us. Millions of people worldwide experience clinical depression and many millions more experience subclinical depressive states. But the effects of depression reach well beyond those who are afflicted; people who are depressed have families and, to one degree or another, depression also takes a toll on the mothers and fathers, brothers and sisters, and sons and daughters of the depressed.

To mental health professionals, there is no more central concern than depression. Indeed, it is the rare psychologist, psychiatrist, or social worker who does not assess, treat, or counsel patients with primary or secondary depression. Mental health professionals, however, do not just diagnose and treat depression; numerous investigators have made depression the main focus of their research. In fact, few research programs are untouched by consideration of depression, either in conjunction with efforts to understand other mental health issues (e.g., anxiety research, treatment efficacy research), or in efforts to understand physical health (e.g., cardiovascular disorders, chronic pain, addictions). Not surprisingly, students in all of these areas have a keen interest in understanding depression.

The intense interest in depression is warranted. Depression is currently considered the second-most disabling disorder in the world and is predicted to be the most disabling disorder within the next two decades. Depression impairs functioning in all areas of life, from marital functioning to more general interpersonal functioning, and from occupation functioning to academic functioning. Depression can also have deleterious effects on physical health, and in the most extreme form is associated with earlier mortality compared to those who are not depressed, either from suicide or from damaged health. To state that depression is an enormous public health problem is something of an understatement.

Over the last few decades, knowledge of depression has grown rapidly. Although a number of antecedents to this explosion in depression theory and research could be identified, several developments in various scientific disciplines are key. From psychiatry, the introduction and now widespread use of antidepressant medications increased not only attempts to understand the efficacy of medication, but has also led to better knowledge of the underlying neurochemistry of depression. Developments in biology and genetics gave rise to a new understanding of the pathophysiology and heredity of depression, while innovations by cognitive researchers have led to neuroimaging advances that can provide a picture of brain functioning in depression. Finally, the development of cognitive therapy of depression revolutionized the psychological study of depression.

The wealth of information now available on depression is encapsulated in this encyclopedia. Experts from around the globe have contributed on everything concerning depression, from adolescent depression to HIV to vulnerability. In summarizing the vast amount of information on depression, the goal of the *International Encyclopedia of Depression* is to be an important resource for the public in general, and more specifically for clinicians, researchers, students, and patients and their families.

A number of people deserve acknowledgment and thanks. The encyclopedia would not have been possible without the help of an internationally esteemed editorial board composed of Chris Brewin, Ian Gotlib, Steve Ilardi, Robin Jarrett, Thomas Joiner, Scott Monroe, Susan Nolen-Hoeksema, Zindel Segal, Greg Siegle, Dan Stein, and Karen Rudolph. Their insights and suggestions went beyond superb. A special thanks also goes to Phil Laughlin at Springer Publishing, who initially approached me about the idea of doing this encyclopedia. Phil has been supportive and helpful at every step in the process. It has been a pleasure to work with him. Finally, I want to acknowledge the love and support of my family, Nancy Hamilton, and Suzanna Ingram, who graciously understood the long days and nights necessary to finish this encyclopedia. I am forever in their debt.

RICK E. INGRAM
LAWRENCE, KANSAS

LIST OF ENTRIES

A

Aaron Beck

Aaron T. Beck is the founder of cognitive therapy, arguably the most widely practiced psychotherapy in the world. Many psychologists and psychiatrists argue that he is the most influential figure ever in the field of depression. John Rush, a well-known depression researcher and professor of psychiatry at the University of Texas Southwestern Medical School, is quoted in the *Philadelphia Inquirer* as saying, "His work changed the paradigm—how we do things, how we think about things. . . . Somebody like him comes along every 50, 100 years."

Beck was born in 1921 in Rhode Island and received his undergraduate degree from Brown University and his MD from Yale University. He was trained as a neurologist but began to pursue a career in psychiatry, partly in response to the enormous mental health needs of veterans returning from World War II. Like most psychiatrists of the time, Beck pursued psychoanalysis as a way to treat patients. Dissatisfied by the lack of efficacy of traditional psychoanalysis, Beck began to consider alternative ways of conceptualizing psychological disorders, eventually recognizing the importance of the cognitive construction that individuals place on life events. This recognition led to the development of a cognitive theory of depression, which suggested that events were not responsible for the emotional turmoil that leads to depression as much as the way that individuals interpret these events.[1] This idea now reflects the core foundation for the understanding of not just depression, but of other psychopathological states as well.

Beck's 1967 book proposed the first modern cognitive theory of depression, and his 1987 book, coauthored with Rush, Shaw, and Emery, introduced cognitive therapy to a wide audience. Both books are considered landmarks, and the 1987 book remains the predominant manual today for the conduct of cognitive therapy.

Beck has published 18 books (and counting) and hundreds of journal articles. He founded *Cognitive Therapy and Research*, a thriving scientific journal, and the Beck Institute for Cognitive Therapy and Research. He is the recipient of numerous awards, including awards by the American Psychiatric Association and the American Psychological Association; he is the only psychiatrist ever to have received awards from both associations. In 2006 he was awarded the prestigious Albert Lasker Award for Clinical Medical Research, considered by many to be the "American Nobel Prize." In 2007 he was under consideration for the Nobel Prize.

Beck is currently a professor emeritus of psychiatry at the University of Pennsylvania and continues to write on cognitive theory and therapy.

RICK E. INGRAM

See also

Automatic Thoughts
Cognitive Behavioral Therapy
Cognitive Theories of Depression

Note

1. Around the same time, Albert Ellis (1913–2007) also developed cognitive ideas about emotional distress and a system of therapy known as rational emotive therapy. Ellis's contributions are recognized as extremely important, but because these ideas were not specific to depression, and because most cognitive therapy practiced today is inspired by Beck's work, most depression researchers credit Beck with the worldwide prominence of both cognitive theories of depression and cognitive treatment of depression.

References

Beck, A. T. (1967). *Depression*. New York: Harper and Row.
Beck, A. T., Rush, J., Shaw, B. F., & Emery, G. (1987). *Cognitive therapy of depression*. New York: Guilford Press.

Adjustment Disorder

Adjustment disorder is characterized by a psychological response to an identifiable stressor or stressors that result in clinically significant distress or functional impairment (American Psychiatric Association [APA], 2000). Though this diagnosis is common, its validity has been questioned and research is lacking. Adjustment disorder was initially conceptualized as a transient personality disorder in the first edition of the *Diagnostic and Statistical Manual of Mental Disorders* (*DSM-I;* APA, 1952) and a transient situational disturbance in the second edition. With the publication of the *DSM-III* (APA, 1980) came the term *adjustment disorder*, which was refined in subsequent editions.

Clinical Features

Adjustment disorder is a residual diagnostic category for stress-related emotional and behavioral disturbances that do not meet criteria for more specific disorders (APA, 2000). The *DSM-IV-TR* provides six subtypes: depressed mood, mixed anxiety and depressed mood, and mixed disturbance of emotions and conduct are relevant to depressive presentations. The remaining subtypes include anxiety, disturbance of conduct, and unspecified (APA, 2000). There is a dearth of research demonstrating the validity and clinical utility of these subtypes (Casey, 2001).

In contrast to posttraumatic stress disorder and acute stress disorder, the precipitating stressor in adjustment disorder can be of any magnitude (i.e., it does not have to be traumatic). Impaired occupational or academic performance and changes in social relationships are common manifestations of adjustment disorder (APA, 2000). Research suggests that individuals with the condition are younger and more likely to be impulsive or to have a personality disorder than those with certain other psychiatric illnesses (Jones, Yates, Williams, Zhou, & Hardman, 1999). While the disorder is associated with an increased risk of suicide behaviors, this risk appears to be substantially lower than that of other major psychiatric illnesses, such as major depressive disorder (Casey, 2001). Furthermore, suicidal ideation typically resolves rapidly following the dissolution of the stressful event (Casey, 2001). Adjustment disorder is further associated with substance misuse and somatic complaints (APA, 2000; Greenberg, Rosenfeld, & Ortega, 1995).

Adjustment disorders that develop into more specific psychiatric disorders are reclassified as such. For example, if the symptoms of an individual with adjustment disorder with depressed mood crystallize into a major depressive episode, then he or she would be diagnosed with the appropriate mood disorder (e.g., major depressive disorder). While depressive episodes often emerge from stressful life events, adjustment disorder is generally less severe than depressive illnesses (Casey, 2001). There is some evidence suggesting that adjustment disorder with depressed mood is a distinct condition from more specific depressive disorders (Jones et al., 1999). Considering the severity of adjustment presentations that warrant psychological or psychiatric attention (e.g., the presence of suicidal behaviors), however, this distinction may not be clinically useful (Casey, 2001). Furthermore, the lack of specific symptom profiles for adjustment disorder can make distinguishing it from normal stress reactions and problems of living difficult. The individual's cultural context is useful when clarifying such presentations.

Prevalence

Adjustment disorder is quite common, particularly in primary care and general medical settings (Casey, 2001). As the disorder can complicate medical illnesses (APA, 2000), addressing such issues is important. In clinical settings, adult women are twice as likely to be diagnosed with the disorder as their male counterparts, while it is equally distributed among male and female children and adolescents (APA, 2000). Jones and colleagues (1999) found that female outpatients were more likely to be diagnosed with a major depressive disorder or dysthymic disorder than adjustment disorder with depressed mood or mixed anxiety and depressed mood (73% vs. 57%). Prevalence rates vary depending on the population examined and the assessment methods employed. Adjustment disorder has been diagnosed in 10% to 30% of outpatients in mental health settings and up to 12% in general hospital inpatients referred for a psychological consultation (APA, 2000). A study concerning psychiatric inpatients found that 7.1% of the adults and 34.4% of the adolescents had an adjustment disorder diagnosis (Greenberg et al., 1995). Prevalence rates for community samples of children, adolescents, and the elderly range from 2% to 8% (APA, 2000). Despite these rates, most large-scale epidemiological studies of psychiatric disorders have neglected adjustment disorder (Casey, 2001).

Course

The diagnostic criteria for adjustment disorder state that the disturbance must occur within 3 months of the onset of the stressor and not persist longer than 6 months following its conclusion (APA, 2000). The diagnostic label, however, may be maintained beyond 6 months if the stressor is chronic or has enduring consequences. Research suggests a good prognosis for adjustment disorder. By definition, symptoms typically resolve with the passage of time, but severe symptoms (e.g., the individual is acutely suicidal) may require intervention. While the persistence of adjustment disorder or its development into more severe conditions may be more common in children and adolescents, this may be due to comorbid disorders or the possibility that the initial presentation represented a subclinical manifestation of the more severe condition (APA, 2000).

Andreasen and Hoenk (1982) observed individuals with adjustment disorder and found that 79% of the adults and 57% of the adolescents were well at 5-year follow-up, with 8% and 13%, respectively having an intervening problem. While most adults who remained ill developed major depressive disorder or alcoholism, adolescent illnesses included schizophrenia, schizoaffective disorder, major depression, bipolar disorder, antisocial personality disorder, and substance abuse. The chronicity of the disorder and the presence of behavioral symptoms were the strongest predictors of major pathology in the adolescent participants at follow-up (Andreasen & Hoenk, 1982). Another study found that both adult and adolescent inpatients had shorter initial hospitalizations but presented with more suicidal behaviors than comparison psychiatric inpatients (Greenberg et al., 1995). Although depressed mood and mixed disturbance of emotions and conduct were the most common subtypes applied at admission, they did not predict length of the stay or rehospitalization. Forty percent of the inpatients did not maintain a diagnosis of adjustment disorder at discharge (Greenberg et al., 1995).

EDDIE J. WRIGHT

See also

Classification of Depression
Diagnostic and Statistical Manual of Mental Disorders

References

American Psychiatric Association. (1952). *Diagnostic and statistical manual: Mental disorders*. Washington, DC: Author.

American Psychiatric Association. (1980). *Diagnostic and statistical manual of mental disorders* (3rd ed.). Washington, DC: Author.

American Psychiatric Association. (2000). *Diagnostic and statistical manual of mental disorders* (4th ed., text revision). Washington, DC: Author.

Andreasen, N. C., & Hoenk, P. R. (1982). The predictive value of adjustment disorders: A follow-up study. *American Journal of Psychiatry, 139*, 584–590.

Casey, P. (2001). Adult adjustment disorder: A review of its current diagnostic status. *Journal of Psychiatric Practice, 7*, 32–40.

Greenberg, W. M., Rosenfeld, D. N., & Ortega, E. A. (1995). Adjustment disorder as an admission diagnosis. *American Journal of Psychiatry, 152*, 459–461.

Jones, R., Yates, W. R., Williams, S., Zhou, M., & Hardman, L. (1999). Outcome for adjustment disorder with depressed mood: Comparison with other mood disorders. *Journal of Affective Disorders, 55*, 51–61.

Adolescent Depression

Adolescence is characterized by change. Indeed change during this stage of life is so ubiquitous, occurring across almost all possible domains from physical to interpersonal, that the word *adolescence* is almost synonymous with change. Many of these changes can be quite positive and usher in exciting opportunities for growth and development. Unfortunately, some of the changes in this developmental period can be quite negative and open the door for undesirable outcomes and life course. One such negative change is the dramatic increase in the probability of developing clinical depression, a psychological disorder characterized by low mood (or irritability) accompanied by a variable set of other symptoms (such as changes in appetite and sleep, loss of concentration, guilt, and suicidality) that persists for at least 2 weeks and impairs functioning. While estimates of *childhood* depression are quite low, with only 1% to 3% of children under the age of 12 experiencing an episode of depression, estimates of adolescent depression are quite high, with approximately 20% of teens experiencing an episode of major depression by age 18. These percentages are actually much higher when including adolescents who exhibit significant symptoms of depression that fall short of meeting the duration, frequency, or severity criteria for a *DSM* diagnosis of depression.

The likelihood of experiencing depression in adolescence is hardly inconsequential. While there is no opportune time to experience depression, it may be particularly disadvantageous during adolescence, a time that calls for the negotiation of critical life role transitions related to educational attainment, entry into the workforce, family and peer relationships, and romantic partnership. Depression can arrest these processes in their tracks and initiate a negative trajectory from which it can be difficult to recover. Longitudinal studies suggest that adolescent depression is associated with a long-term course characterized by recurrent depressions and adverse outcomes across a number of domains including other Axis I disorders (especially substance use but also anxiety and eating disorders), poor academic performance, pregnancy, problematic peer and family relations, and suicide.

The surge in depression in adolescence is especially notable for girls and leads to the well-known gender difference in adult depression. Epidemiology studies have reported female:male lifetime risk ratios ranging from 1.7:1 to 2.4:1, and such ratios have been found not just in the United States but in numerous other countries as well. The emergence of this difference begins sometime between the ages of 11 and 13 and is relatively firmly established by 15 years of age. Therefore, any model of adolescent depression has to be able to explain the spike in rates of depression for boys and girls, and the much higher rate of depression in girls (Hyde, Marzulis, & Abramson, 2008).

Prevailing models of depression are cast within variants of a diathesis-stress framework, a perspective that allows for a number of different vulnerabilities (e.g., neurobiologic, genetic, cognitive, and environmental) to interact with discrete or chronic life stressors (including those that occur early in life, e.g., abuse, as well as those that occur later, e.g., school transitions). The appeal of diathesis-stress models lies in their ability to unite two obvious classes of influence on psychopathology—individual vulnerability and environmental adversity—and their ability to explain why some, but not all, people become depressed in the face of the same environmental events or in the presence of the same vulnerability. The fundamental premise of a diathesis-stress model is that both the diathesis (also interchangeably referred to as vulnerability) and stress are necessary for the development of disorder; neither one alone is sufficient (Monroe & Simons, 1991). Contemporary models also recognize that vulnerabilities, life stress, and depression are not necessarily neatly independent. Rather, the nature of the interrelationships among these variables is likely reciprocal and dynamic over time. For example, early stress and adversity may result in subsequent vulnerability. Further, depressive symptoms themselves may generate negative life events (e.g., irritability may lead to family conflict) and/or may lead to the development of vulnerabilities (Hammen, 2005). In other words, stressors can lead to vulnerabilities and vulnerabilities can lead to stressors over time to produce depression.

We focus particularly on research that recognizes and includes the unique developmental features of adolescence (e.g., brain development, peer and family context) rather than simply applying a downward extension of adult models of depression. This reflects accumulating research that suggests there are important differences between adolescent and adult depression. Indeed, the prevailing diagnostic system recognizes that the symptom profile for depressed teens may be different than for depressed adults, by allowing irritability rather than sadness as the cardinal symptom. Adolescents with depression are also more likely than adults to have a comorbid disorder, especially anxiety, and are more likely to present with so-called atypical depression, characterized by increases, rather than decreases, in sleeping and eating, and by somatic symptoms. Interestingly, depressed adolescents are more likely to continue to be reactive to the social environment but are also more likely than depressed

adults to have suicidal ideation. In addition, adolescent depression is typically the first depression, whereas adult depression is often a recurrence of depression. This latter distinction is important to consider, as it has been observed that predictors of first onsets and later episodes often appear to be quite different. Finally, results from randomized clinical trials of different treatments for adolescent depression also indicate differences between adolescent and adult depression in terms of treatment response (Treatment for Adolescents With Depression Study Team, 2004).

To understand the etiology of adolescent depression, the following three questions are considered: (a) what are the developmental changes of adolescence that may confer vulnerability to depression; (b) what is the nature of the life stress that interacts with these vulnerabilities to produce depression; and (c) how might these stressors and vulnerabilities reciprocally influence one another? As we address these questions here, it is important to keep in mind not only the transactional nature of these relationships, but also the notion of equifinality, that is, the idea that many different diathesis-stress pathways may result in the same outcome (i.e., depression).

Puberty

The fact that the increase in depression coincides with the onset of puberty has led to the speculation that hormonal changes are involved. However, studies reveal only very weak associations between gonadal hormone changes and negative affect. Research has also examined the neuropeptide oxytocin, which is regulated by the female gonadal hormones, estrogen and progesterone, and consequently rises in adolescence. Oxytocin plays an important role in affiliative behavior and may explain the well-known increase in desire for interpersonal connection among adolescent girls. This desire for affiliation, however, may come to constitute a vulnerability for depression. For example, female teens may be sensitized to the disruption of relationship bonds, a class of negative events that has been shown to precede depression in teens (Monroe, Rohde, Seeley, & Lewinsohn, 1999) and is probably the most common trigger for suicide in teens.

Others have examined pubertal timing and found early-maturing girls have significantly elevated rates of major depression compared to girls who mature in synchrony with their peers. Interestingly, pubertal timing does not seem to make a difference for boys in relation to depression. Pubertal status (i.e., stage of development within puberty) has also been examined as a risk factor for depression, particularly for girls, with findings that rates of depression rise after reaching Tanner Stage III. It is important to note, however, that while pubertal status has been shown to predict depression in Caucasian girls, it does not predict depression in African American or Hispanic girls (Hayward, Gotlib, Schraedley, & Litt, 1999). This suggests that one must look at other factors operating in an adolescent's life to understand the effects of puberty and its possible relationship to depression (e.g., meaning of, and evaluation of, puberty-linked changes; skills required to deal with sexual attention).

Brain Development

Puberty-related physical changes are readily visible. Other biologic changes in brain structure and function, while less observable, may be more important for understanding adolescent depression. It has been stated that "puberty starts in the brain" (Davey, Yucel, & Allen, 2008), when the hypothalamus begins to release gonadotrophin-releasing hormone and continues with important changes, particularly in the prefrontal cortex. These changes include the selective elimination of unused synapses and the increase in myelination, resulting in a decrease in gray matter and an increase in white matter, thereby making the brain overall more efficient. This maturation of the prefrontal cortex is reflected in significant changes in cognitive functioning—the ability to think in more logical and abstract terms, to reflect on one's own thoughts, to understand the concept of extended time, and to anticipate the future. Davey and colleagues (2008)

argue that these emerging cognitive skills can double as vulnerabilities for an adolescent, as they also enable rumination, the generation of causal explanations (attributional style) for negative events, and frustration when anticipated rewards and goals are not forthcoming.

Genetic Factors

The literature suggests that postpubertal depression has a significant heritable component, with novel genetic influences emerging during this stage of development. Of note, one of the strongest predictors of childhood or adolescent depression is having one parent with a diagnosis of depression (Beardslee, Versage, & Giastone, 1998). Familial aggregation of depression has been examined through both top-down and bottom-up methodologies. The former method has found that children with a depressed parent have a 5:1 odds ratio of risk relative to controls and are approximately three times more likely to experience depression within their lifetime (Kaminski & Garber, 2002). The latter method of analysis has found elevated rates of depression in first-degree relatives of depressed children. However, regardless of this notable familial component, approximately one-third to one-half of teens develop depression in the *absence* of any familial history of the disorder. Another line of research that directly involves genetics has focused on a specific polymorphism, the short allele of the serotonin transporter gene (5-HTTLP-R). Partially replicating work done by Caspi and colleagues (2003) with young adults, Eley and colleagues (2004) found that this gene was a marker for the development of depression for adolescent girls, but not boys, who had experienced a recent negative life event.

Cognitive Factors

Cognitive factors have received considerable attention as risk factors for depression. A long list of cognitive factors, including attributional or inferential style, perfectionism, self-criticism, rumination, dysfunctional attitudes, and self-schema have all received at least partial support as conferring vulnerability to the development of depression (Abela & Hankin, 2008). There is also some suggestion of a gender difference in at least some of these cognitive factors (e.g., rumination), which might help to explain the higher rates of depression in girls. It is important to note that these cognitive factors most likely follow developmental trajectories and are likely to change in the weight they carry in the development of depression. In other words, the influence of cognitive factors on depression may change as individuals age. For example, it has been found that negative attributional style interacts with life events to predict depression in middle schoolers (sixth to eighth graders), but not in younger children (third to fifth graders). Although subject to consideration of research attention, cognitive factors as diatheses for depression have yet to be firmly established; this may be in part due to pooling different age groups, as well as to inconsistencies in the measurement of these variables.

Life Stress

All diathesis-stress models conceptualize stress as playing an important role in the development of depression. In adult samples overall, it has been shown that most episodes of major depression are preceded by negative life events. Interestingly, the converse is not true; the majority of people do *not* develop depression after a negative life event (Hammen, 2005). However, although stress is considered important in the development of adolescent depression, the research on adolescents in relation to life stress and depression has lagged far behind that of adults. There continues to be a wide range of definitions, conceptualizations, and assessment approaches to stress employed in research investigating this developmental period. Therefore, of the three major domains of relevance—vulnerabilities, stressors, and depression—the least is known about the role of stress.

For the purposes of this chapter, the definition offered by Grant, Compas, Thurm, McMahon, and Gibson (2004) is adopted: "*environmental* events or chronic conditions that objectively threaten the physical and/or psychological health or well being of individuals of a particular age in a particular society" (p. 449). This definition argues against the view of stress as being only what is *perceived* as distressing, taxing, or beyond one's coping capabilities. Rather, perceptions or appraisals of events and responses to events are seen as moderators of the impact of stress and/or mediators of the relationship between stressors and depression. This view suggests that interviews that can provide relatively objective assessments of what stressors have occurred, when they occurred, and how threatening they were, given the autobiographical circumstances of the adolescents, are preferable to self-report checklists. A review of the different studies purporting to examine the role of stress in teen depression, however, reveals that 45% of the studies constructed their own measures of stress, and fewer than 2% employed context-based interviews (Grant et al., 2004). While acknowledging the labor-intensive nature of administering and rating these interviews, lack of widespread use has likely prevented the acquisition of new knowledge about this important construct.

Environmental events may be especially potent in adolescence, given the pervasive social changes and role transitions that transpire during this time period. Family dynamics change as teens strive for more autonomy and the importance of peer groups becomes paramount. Not surprisingly, much attention has been given to interpersonal relationships and events such as family conflicts, peer rejection, bullying, relational aggression, and relationship breakups. In addition to specific events, the *themes* of events have been considered and have been shown to be important. In particular, the theme of loss, be it the loss of a person through death or the loss of a so-called cherished ideal (e.g., ideal of parental unity and intact family lost when parents divorce) or goal (e.g., school failure) appears to be especially salient. The number and severity of events, as well as whether the stressor is seen as dependent on the individual's own actions (e.g., a girl is dumped by her peer group for betraying confidences) or independent of the individual's behavior (e.g., a girl's grandmother dies from cancer), have been shown to be associated with increased risk for depression. In general, greater and more severe events, especially dependent events, carry greater risk for subsequent depression.

Events occurring early in life, such as child abuse, maltreatment, and neglect, deserve special mention. Brown, Cohen, Johnson, and Smailes (1999) discovered a three- to fourfold increase in the likelihood of developing adolescent depression in teens who had experienced child abuse. In particular, sexual abuse carries with it the most significant risk of depression and suicide, independent of the contextual risks that the literature has identified to accompany abuse (e.g., low parental involvement, low parental warmth, low family income). The increased risk for depression is especially notable in females: in a mixed adolescent and young adult sample, the odds ratio for depression in females who had experienced childhood sexual abuse was 3:8 (Molnar, Bukar, & Kessler, 2001). In addition to increasing risk for later depression, early adversity also appears to increase risk for later adverse events and stressors, especially interpersonal difficulties. Early adversity, too, may result in greater psychobiological sensitivity to later stressors. The pathways by which early adversity translates into stress sensitization, subsequent stressors, and depression are unknown at this time but are the focus of considerable current research. Our understanding of the pathways to depression in adolescence is still incomplete. However, the lines of research highlighted in this chapter are quite promising. A diathesis-stress perspective offers a potential fruitful framework to view the dynamic interrelationships among genetics, puberty, brain changes, cognitive factors, and stressors.

CARA C. LEWIS AND ANNE D. SIMONS

See also

Adolescent Depression: Treatment
Brain Function in Depressed Children and Adolescents
Childhood Depression
Childhood Depression: Family Context
Childhood Depression: Treatment
Childhood Depression: Treatment With Pharmacotherapy
Children's Depression Inventory
Family and Parent-Child Therapy
Family Transmission of Depression
Fathers and Depression
Mothers and Depression

References

Abela, J., & Hankin, B. (2008). The development of depression during the transition from early to middle adolescence: A cognitive vulnerability-stress perspective. *Journal of Affective Disorders, 107,* 111–112.

Beardslee, W. R., Versage, E. M., & Giastone, T. R. G. (1998). Children of affectively ill parents: A review of the past 10 years. *Journal of the American Academy of Child and Adolescent Psychiatry, 37,* 1134–1141.

Brown, J., Cohen, P., Johnson, J. G., & Smailes, E. M. (1999). Childhood abuse and neglect: Specificity of effect on adolescent and young depression and suicidality. *Journal of the American Academy of Child and Adolescent Psychiatry, 38,* 1490–1496.

Caspi, A., Sugden, K., Moffitt, T. E., Taylor, A., Craig, I. W., Harrington, H., et al. (2003). Influence of life stress on depression: Moderation by a polymorphism in the 5-HTT gene. *Science, 30,* 386–389.

Davey, C., Yucel, M., & Allen, N. (2008). The emergence of depression in adolescence: Development of the prefrontal cortex and representation of reward. *Neuroscience and Biobehavioral Reviews, 32,* 1–19.

Eley, T. C., Sugden, K., Corsico, A., Gregory, A. M., Sham, P., McGuffin, P., et al. (2004). Gene-environment interaction analysis of serotonin system markers with adolescent depression. *Molecular Psychiatry, 9,* 908–915.

Grant, D., Compas, B., Thurm, A., McMahon, S., & Gibson, P. (2004). Stressors and child and adolescent psychopathology: Measurement issues and prospective effects. *Journal of Clinical Child and Adolescent Psychology, 33,* 412–425.

Hammen, C. (2005). Stress and depression. *Annual Review of Clinical Psychology, 1,* 293–319.

Hayward, C., Gotlib, I. H., Schraedley, P. K., & Litt, I. F. (1999). Ethnic differences in the association between pubertal status and symptoms of depression in adolescent girls. *Journal of Adolescent Health, 25,* 143–149.

Hyde, J., Mezulis, A., & Abramson, L. (2008). The ABCs of depression: Integrating affective, biological, and cognitive models to explain the emergence of the gender difference in depression. *Psychological Review, 115,* 291–303.

Kaminski, K. M., & Garber, J. (2002). Depressive spectrum disorders in high-risk adolescents: Episode duration and predictors of time to recovery. *Journal of the American Academy of Child and Adolescent Psychiatry, 41,* 410–418.

Molnar, B. E., Bukar, S. L., & Kessler, R. C. (2001). Child sexual abuse and subsequent psychopathology: Results from the national comorbidity survey. *American Journal of Public Health, 91,* 753–760.

Monroe, S. M., Rohde, P., Seeley, J. R., & Lewinsohn, P. M. (1999). Life events and depression in adolescence: Relationship loss as a prospective risk factor for first onset of major depressive disorder. *Journal of Abnormal Psychology, 108,* 606–614.

Monroe, S. M., & Simons, A. D. (1991). Diathesis-stress theories in the context of life stress research: Implications for the depressive disorders. *Psychological Bulletin, 110,* 406–425.

Treatment for Adolescents With Depression Study Team. (2004). Fluoxetine, cognitive behavioral therapy, and their combination for adolescents with depression: Treatment for Adolescents With Depression Study (TADS) randomized control trial. *Journal of the American Medical Association, 292,* 807–820.

Adolescent Depression: Treatment

Given the high prevalence, negative sequelae, and significant public health burden of adolescent depression, a number of interventions designed to treat this condition have been developed and evaluated in randomized controlled trials. Current treatments for depressed adolescents include various psychosocial interventions, pharmacotherapy, and combination treatments (medication plus psychotherapy).

Psychosocial Treatments

Several randomized controlled studies have examined the efficacy of a variety of individual and group-based psychosocial interventions for depressed adolescents. Based on the available research, certain forms of psychotherapy appear to be an appropriate initial treatment recommendation for adolescent depression.

Cognitive behavioral therapy (CBT) focuses on the role of one's thoughts and actions in becoming and remaining depressed. CBT has been evaluated in the largest number of trials to date and has been shown to be superior to wait-list control, and generally more efficacious than alternative psychosocial treatments. Brent and colleagues (1997) contrasted individual CBT, systemic behavior family therapy, and individual nondirective supportive therapy for adolescent depression. Over the course of 12 to 16 weeks of acute treatment, response rates were significantly higher for CBT (60%) compared to either active comparison condition (39% for supportive therapy and 38% for family therapy), although treatment differences faded during the 2-year follow-up period. In the United Kingdom, an initial study of brief CBT (averaging six sessions) did not demonstrate superiority to an active comparison (nonfocused intervention), although a subsequent modification of brief CBT was superior to a different active comparison (relaxation training).

Peter Lewinsohn and colleagues found that the group-administered Adolescent Coping With Depression Course (CWD-A), a 7-week, twice-weekly intervention, was superior to a wait-list control condition. Clarke, Rohde, Lewinsohn, Hops, and Seeley (1999) conducted a larger replication of this study (N = 96) with treatment extended to 8 weeks and found similar results. In both trials, recovery rates for two forms of the CWD-A (one with just adolescents and the second consisting of an identical group for adolescents with a separate group for parents) were superior to wait-list, with nonsignificant differences between active treatments (e.g., 67% of treated adolescents no longer met criteria at posttreatment vs. 48% in wait-list in the second trial). More recent research with the CWD-A has included one of the first randomized controlled trials of a psychosocial intervention for depressed adolescents with current comorbidity (conduct disorder in that study) and the incremental benefit of augmenting standard care in a health maintenance organization (HMO) with the CWD-A. Although this group CBT resulted in greater reductions in depression measures compared to an active control condition, it did not confer a significant added benefit over usual HMO care.

These studies show that, for the treatment of depressed adolescents, CBT was superior to passive control or comparison conditions, and superior acutely to some but not all active comparison conditions. Follow-up assessments indicate that the relative superiority of CBT compared to other active interventions was attributable to more rapid effects, as other treatments "caught up" with CBT during the follow-up period. Although initial meta-analyses reported large effect sizes for CBT across studies (e.g., 0.97–1.27), the most recent meta-analysis (Weisz, McCarty, & Valeri, 2006) was far more sobering. Although CBT for depression continued to show a significant benefit for young people, the effect sizes were significantly smaller than those reported in earlier studies (mean ES = .34), and CBT was not significantly more effective than other psychotherapeutic approaches.

Current research in CBT includes applications of the recent reconceptualization of behavioral activation (BA) for the treatment of depressed adolescents. This approach focuses on the specific role of avoidance in depression, relying heavily on an examination of the consequences of depressotypic behaviors, particularly those that serve to avoid imminent distress at the cost of blocking access to future positive reinforcement.

Another psychosocial intervention, interpersonal psychotherapy for adolescents (IPT-A), which was developed by Laura Mufson and colleagues, is based on the theory that interpersonal conflicts or transitions maintain depression. IPT-A has been evaluated in an initial pilot study looking at pre-postchange, a randomized controlled trial comparing it to clinical monitoring, and an effectiveness study comparing IPT-A to treatment as usual (TAU) in school-based mental health clinics (Mufson et al., 2004), finding that depressed adolescents receiving IPT-A had significantly greater symptom reduction and improvement in overall functioning, compared to those receiving TAU. Most recently, IPT-A has been modified to be delivered in a group format, but this version of the intervention has not yet been empirically validated. Another version of IPT for adolescents has been compared to CBT and

wait-list control in Puerto Rican adolescents with major depression. The two active interventions were found to be comparable and superior to wait-list control in reducing depressive symptoms.

In addition to these individual and group-based psychosocial interventions, Guy Diamond and colleagues have developed and begun evaluation of an attachment-based family therapy for adolescent depression. This family-based intervention appears promising and suggests that forms of family therapy warrant further attention for the treatment of depressed adolescents.

Pharmacotherapy

The rationale for pharmacological treatments of depression in adolescents is based on data suggesting the continuity of adolescent mood disorders with depressive disorders in adults and the responsiveness of depressive disorders in adults to a wide range of antidepressant medications. While earlier studies evaluating the efficacy of tricyclic antidepressants provided no support for their use as a first-line treatment, recent findings for the serotonin-specific reuptake inhibitors (SSRIs) are more promising. A variety of medications (paroxetine, sertraline, citalopram) have been found to have at least some degree of efficacy for depression, although only fluoxetine has been approved by the U.S. Food and Drug Administration as both safe and effective for minors with depression, based on data from a single-site NIMH-funded trial (Emslie et al., 1997) and a large, multisite, industry-sponsored trial. Research by Emslie and colleagues also suggests that continued fluoxetine treatment may be effective in preventing depression recurrence in child and adolescent patients who initially responded to acute medication treatment, although no other published controlled studies are available evaluating the safety and efficacy of antidepressants beyond short-term acute treatment. The Treatment for Adolescents With Depression Study (TADS), described below, recently provided very strong support for the effectiveness of fluoxetine (Treatment for Adolescents With Depression Study Team [TADST], 2004).

Significant controversy has arisen regarding the safety of antidepressant therapy in adolescents, and close monitoring of young patients treated with antidepressant medications has been strongly suggested by both regulatory agencies and professional organizations. In conclusion, the current evidence-based treatment guidelines support the careful use of antidepressants in children and adolescents with significant mood disorders, although it is clear that a minority of patients suffer either nuisance or intolerable side effects that limit the utility or acceptability of pharmacotherapy.

Combination Therapies

The simultaneous emergence of (a) research suggesting that even our most empirically supported psychotherapies achieve smaller treatment effects than had previously been found, and (b) concerns regarding small, but real, increases in suicidality in adolescents treated with antidepressants has led to some confusion and concern regarding the recommended treatment for depressed adolescents. The combination of pharmacotherapy and psychotherapy may represent a choice that addresses the safety and efficacy concerns raised by using either intervention modality alone.

TADS was the first published study to look at combination of pharmacotherapy and psychotherapy as compared to monotherapies for adolescent depression, and this treatment package was found to be superior when considering both costs and benefits. The TADS project compared individual CBT, fluoxetine, combination CBT-fluoxetine, and a pill placebo with clinical management in 439 adolescents with major depression. TADS consisted of a 12-week acute treatment phase (after which, adolescents receiving pills only were unblinded), 6 weeks of graduated maintenance treatment, 18 weeks of maintenance treatment, and a one-year open follow-up. Results from the acute phase of therapy (TADST, 2004) used the Children's Depression Rating Scale–Revised as the primary

outcome and found a significant advantage for combination treatment compared to pill placebo ($p = .001$), which was not present for either fluoxetine ($p = .10$) or CBT ($p = .40$) monotherapies. Combined treatment also was superior to fluoxetine ($p = .02$) and CBT ($p = .01$); in addition, fluoxetine was superior to CBT ($p = .01$). Using a dichotomous measure of recovery (Clinical Global Impression Improvement score), rates of response were 71% for combination treatment, 61% for fluoxetine, 43% for CBT, and 35% for pill placebo. Regarding patient safety, the rates of harm-related adverse events were 12% for fluoxetine, 8% for combination therapy, 4% for CBT, and 5% for pill placebo.

Although the acute phase results in TADS were disappointing for CBT monotherapy, data from the Week 36 follow-up suggest that recovery rates for CBT monotherapy caught up to the recovery rates for fluoxetine and combination treatments, suggesting that CBT requires more time to be effective. Rates of response at Week 36 were 86% for combination therapy and 81% for both fluoxetine and CBT monotherapies. In summary, the TADS project found that treatment with either fluoxetine monotherapy or in combination with CBT accelerated the response for depression adolescents, and the addition of CBT enhanced the safety of pharmacotherapy. Balancing the benefits and risks of various interventions, the combination treatment appeared superior to either monotherapy as a treatment for adolescents with moderate to severe depression.

The other large trial of combination therapy, the Treatment of SSRI-Resistant Depression in Adolescents (TORDIA), was a randomized controlled trial of a clinical sample of 334 adolescents (ages 12–18) with a primary diagnosis of major depression who had not responded to an initial SSRI treatment. Participants were randomized to 12 weeks of (a) a second, different SSRI (paroxetine, citalopram, or fluoxetine); (b) a different SSRI plus individual CBT; (c) venlafaxine; or (d) venlafaxine plus CBT. At the end of 12 weeks, the combination of CBT plus either medication resulted in a higher response rate than either medication monotherapy (55% vs. 40%, $p = .009$). Differences across the four treatment conditions on continuous measures of depression change, suicidal ideation, and harm-related events, however, were nonsignificant.

Other, smaller studies comparing combination treatments versus monotherapy approaches have not found significant differences. Greg Clarke and colleagues (1999) found that the addition of a brief CBT intervention (mean of five sessions) as an adjunct to SSRI treatment delivered in an HMO failed to improve outcomes for depressed adolescents, although this may have been because the group randomized to CBT received a lower average medication dose. Glenn Melvin and colleagues found no significant benefit for combination therapy compared to either CBT or pharmacotherapy monotherapy for the treatment of mild-to-moderate depression in adolescents. In that study, youths receiving CBT monotherapy had a superior response compared to those receiving pharmacotherapy monotherapy, although this may have been due to a relatively low dosage of sertraline. Ian Goodyer and colleagues recently reported results from a British study comparing treatment with a combination CBT and fluoxetine to fluoxetine only in a study of depressed adolescents. This study failed to replicate findings from the TADS and TORDIA trials that superior outcomes are obtained from combination treatment. One possible explanation for the nonsignificant results could be that the fluoxetine monotherapy protocol in the Goodyer study actually included a number of psychosocial ingredients (e.g., problem solving, focus on family and peer relationships), which suggests that it may have been more similar to combination treatment than to the medication monotherapy protocols evaluated in TADS or TORDIA.

Conclusions

Depression in adolescents is a serious public health concern, with the costs including significant lifetime morbidity and even mortality. Fortunately, significant progress over the past 20 years has been made in the development and evaluation of evidence-based interventions for this population of vulnerable youths. Research studies are now available that support the use of both psychosocial and pharmacological treatments, alone or in combination, for adolescents with depressive illness. This developing field, however, has not been without controversy. Even the best-supported psychotherapy interventions have not consistently fared well in comparison to other active interventions. Medication treatment studies have not been universally positive, and in some studies, SSRIs have been associated with elevated rates of serious adverse events. From a risk-benefit perspective, findings from the most well-powered trials currently argue for the adoption of a combination of SSRI medication and CBT as the best-practice treatment of adolescent depression. Future research, however, needs to address whether the positive effects of combination treatment are specific to CBT or could be obtained with other, more broadly available forms of psychotherapy, and the optimal method of disseminating best-practice interventions to depressed adolescents being treated in community settings.

Paul Rohde

See also

Adolescent Depression
Brain Function in Depressed Children and Adolescents
Childhood Depression: Family Context
Childhood Depression: Treatment
Childhood Depression: Treatment With Pharmacotherapy
Children's Depression Inventory
Family and Parent-Child Therapy
Family Transmission of Depression
Fathers and Depression
Mothers and Depression

References

Brent, D. A., Holder, D., Kolko, D. J., Birmaher, B., Baugher, M., Roth, C., et al. (1997). A clinical psychotherapy trial for adolescent depression comparing cognitive, family, and supportive therapy. *Archives of General Psychiatry, 54,* 877–885.

Clarke, G. N., Rohde, P., Lewinsohn, P. M., Hops, H., & Seeley, J. R. (1999). Cognitive-behavioral treatment of adolescent depression: Efficacy of acute group treatment and booster sessions. *Journal of the American Academy of Child and Adolescent Psychiatry, 38,* 272–279.

Diamond, G. S., Reis, B. F., Diamond, G. M., Siqueland, L., & Isaacs, L. (2002). Attachment-based family therapy for depressed adolescent: A treatment development study. *Journal of the American Academy of Child & Adolescent Psychiatry, 41,* 1190–1196.

Emslie, G. J., Rush, A. J., Weinberg, W. A., Kowatch, R. A., Hughes, C. W., Carmody, T., et al. (1997). A double-blind, randomized, placebo-controlled trial of fluoxetine in children and adolescents with depression. *Archives of General Psychiatry, 54,* 1031–1037.

Goodyer, I., Dubicka, B., Wilkinson, P., Kelvin, R., Roberts, C., Bryford, S., et al. (2007). Selective serotonin reuptake inhibitors (SSRIs) and routine specialist care with and without cognitive behaviour therapy in adolescents with major depression: Randomised controlled trial. *British Medical Journal, 335,* 142–146.

Lewinsohn, P. M., Clarke, G. N., Hops, H., & Andrews, J. A. (1990). Cognitive-behavioral treatment for depressed adolescents. *Behavior Therapy, 21,* 385–401.

Melvin, G. A., Tonge, B. J., King, N. J., Heyne, D., Gordon, M. S., & Klimkeit, E. (2006). A comparison of cognitive-behavioral therapy, sertraline, and their combination for adolescent depression. *Journal of the American Academy of Child & Adolescent Psychiatry, 45,* 1151–1161.

Mufson, L., Dorta, D., Wickramaratne, P., Nomura, Y., Olfson, M., & Weissman, M. (2004). A randomized effectiveness trial of interpersonal psychotherapy for depressed adolescents. *Archives of General Psychiatry, 61,* 577–584.

Treatment for Adolescents With Depression Study Team (2004). Fluoxetine, cognitive-behavioral therapy, and their combination for adolescents with depression: Treatment for Adolescents With Depression Study (TADS) randomized controlled trial. *Journal of the American Medical Association, 292,* 807–820.

Weisz, J. R., McCarty, C., & Valeri, S. (2006). A meta-analysis of psychotherapy outcomes for depressed children and adolescents. *Psychological Bulletin, 132,* 132–149.

Affective Neuroscience

The term *emotion* most commonly denotes thoughts and feelings that combine to generate a specific experiential state. With the advent of modern functional neuroimaging, it is now possible to examine neural activity associated with the generation of emotional experience. The importance of such studies is, on the one hand, to uncover the functional neuroanatomy of emotions, that is, to associate emotional experiential states to specific brain substrates—mapping function to structure. In addition, affective neuroscience allows an addressing of the fundamental representational structures on which emotional experience depends. This latter approach can provide neural constraints on the traditional theoretical models used to examine and understand emotional experience.

Structure of Emotions: Theory

For better or worse, affective neuroscience research in humans is dominated by competing models of the structure of emotions originating from behavioral investigations (Murphy, Nimmo-Smith, & Lawrence, 2003). Basic emotions models argue all humans are evolutionarily endowed with a limited number of discrete emotions that are specific adaptations for coping with particular situations (e.g., anger, fear, sadness). Each basic emotion is postulated to have a distinct facial expression and pattern of peripheral physiological response, as well as a dedicated central nervous system representation. The varieties of emotional experience can then be understood as the recruitment of brain regions supporting these distinct emotion programs, as well as their combination to promote complex emotional states. This conception of emotion space has some direct support from studies looking at stimulus triggers with emotional value, such as social signals of emotional states. For example, the amygdala has been associated with comprehension of fear expressions, and the right anterior insula-caudate disgust (Murphy et al., 2003).

Dimensional models, on the other hand, maintain that distinct emotions are combinations of lower-order underlying dimensions. These dimensions can be related to hedonics (positive or negative valence, either as bipolar or separate unipolar dimensions), activation or arousal (low vs. high, tense vs. energetic), action tendencies (appetitive vs. defensive, approach and withdrawal), or peripheral nervous system representation and regulation (sympathetic vs. parasympathetic). Distinct emotions that have unique verbal labels and experiential correlates would then be subserved by a smaller number of common neural systems that represent the dimensionality of all emotional experience. This conception of emotion space has some direct support from studies looking at experiential states, such as finding that distinct regions of the orbitofrontal cortices are related to the subjective pleasantness and unpleasantness of sensory experience (Anderson et al., 2003).

Comparing and Contrasting Basic and Dimensional Models

The direct mapping of emotional functions to brain structures, although intuitively appealing, has many complexities. To illustrate some of these, I focus below on one of the brain structures most consistently associated with emotional functioning—the amygdala, a complex of multiple subnuclei that in nonhuman animals has been shown to play diverse roles. Numerous neuroimaging studies have shown amygdala activity varies with emotional experience in both healthy and affect-disordered populations, suggesting a central role in emotional phenomenology. However, the precise contributions of the amygdala remain a matter of ongoing study. It has been argued that the amygdala may play a specific role in fear and anxiety, supporting a modular basic emotions model for emotional experience. The amygdala has also been characterized as supporting a more dimensional role, related to overall negative affectivity, or more generally related to the intensity or arousing and/or activating nature of emotional experience (Anderson et al., 2003; Murphy et al., 2003). The difficulty in separating these models of amygdala function is highlighted by the fact that fearful or anxiety-evoking stimuli result in greater negative valence and experiential and sympathetic arousal, as well as many other variables, and as such amygdala recruitment can reflect any of these correlated experiential dimensions.

Studies in healthy samples that have matched emotional valence and intensity have shown the amygdala responds equally to carefully titrated pleasant and unpleasant experiences and correlates with the intensity of experience, consistent with a more primitive arousal response (Anderson et al., 2003). However, this arousal dimension may be tuned through normative or pathological experience to represent enduring traits, whereby the amygdala is hyperresponsive to fear or negative affect, or even positive affect. Manipulations of present valence focus (to consider the positive or negative values of objects) have been shown to tune the amygdala to be responsive to more short term negatively or positively valenced states (Cunningham, Van Bavel, & Johnsen, 2008). This online attentional shaping of amygdala response may be interpreted as reflecting some intrinsic valence dimensional representation, rather than a valence tuning of a more primitive amygdala arousal orienting response.

In contrast with the amygdala, the orbitofrontal cortices (OFCs) appear to more clearly support some form of pleasant and unpleasant valence dimensions (Anderson et al., 2003; Rolls, 2000). The OFCs are highly plastic and represent the dynamics of affective value, being less a representation of the stimulus and more an internal representation of changing values to the perceiver (Rolls, 2000)—a prerequisite for ascribing a valenced phenomenological state to brain substrates. In particular, the more medial portions of the OFCs have been associated with pleasurable experiences, from basic pleasant smells and tastes, to abstract monetary reward, to looking at attractive individuals. Whereas, more lateral OFC regions have been associated with negative affective experience. It has been argued on the basis of nonhuman primate anatomical connectivity that the medial and lateral OFCs represent largely independent networks with greater intra- than interregional connectivity (Rolls, 2000). Corroborating functional imaging findings suggests that valence is not neurally coded along a single bipolar dimension but is subserved by separate valence axes in the medial and lateral OFCs (Anderson et al., 2003).

This medial-lateral pattern, however, has not always been replicated using more complex stimuli that may engage more sophisticated cognitive and emotional appraisal processes. Indeed, meta-analyses collapsing across stimulus types do not clearly neurally demarcate such valence axes (Murphy et al., 2003). It may be that the brain does not support amodal valence dimensions, being sensory or stimulus specific, making the neural representation of emotional experience much higher in dimensionality and complexity than previously thought. In addition, emotional valence may better characterize linguistic conceptions of emotional states rather than their underlying neural bases. Emotions of similar negative valence such as anger and disgust may evoke different action tendencies (approach vs. withdrawal) and autonomic response (sympathetic vs. parasympathetic activation).

Neuropsychological Studies

Functional imaging research can demonstrate correlations between regional activity and emotional experience; however, these findings are often misinterpreted to reflect a causal relationship. Neural activity may represent any of diverse but correlated processes associated with emotions. Thus, neuropsychological studies remain critical to the study of affective neuroscience. For example, considering the mounting neuroimaging evidence associating the amygdala with emotional experience, there is little direct evidence of disordered emotional experience following amygdala damage. Patients with amygdala lesions provide reports of basic and valenced states of similar magnitude, frequency, and underlying covariance structure as healthy controls and, when asked to relive emotions, display remarkably intact emotional expressions including fear (see Anderson & Phelps, 2002). By contrast, more evidence supports the amygdala's role in altering information processing associated with emotional experience, including the emotional enhancement of mnemonic and attentional processes.

Self and Emotion

As the concept of "self" is central to human emotions, increased interest in the neural foundations of selfhood have important implications for affective neuroscience. Altered cortical midline activation, particularly in the ventromedial prefrontal cortices (VMPFCs), has been associated with judgments of self-relevance as well as appreciation of emotional valence (Phan et al., 2004), ranging from simple sensory to more complex and abstract events. As this region receives connections from all exteroceptive and interoceptive modalities, it has been viewed as a polymodal convergence zone (Rolls, 2000), supporting the integration of external and internal stimuli with judgments about their value to the self. These VMPFC representations are in contrast to lateral prefrontal regions that may support a more self-detached and objective analysis of events. Another important aspect of the self is how the afferents from the body are represented in the brain. Structural and functional imaging research has linked right anterior insular volume and activity with increased sensitivity to visceral awareness (Critchley, Wiens, Rothstein, Ohman, & Dolan, 2004). In conjunction with the somatosensory cortex, the right mid and anterior insula enable a cortical representation of feedback regarding the exteroceptive somatic and interoceptive physiologic condition of the body. The future of affective neuroscience is to more fully and precisely understand how these bodily and conceptual bases of self interact, giving rise to complex neural states that support emotional experience.

ADAM K. ANDERSON

See also

Amygdala
Behavioral Activation System
Behavioral Inhibition System
Brain Circuitry
Hemispheric Lateralization
Hypothalamic-Pituitary-Adrenal Axis
Hypothalamic-Pituitary-Thyroid Axis
Positive Emotion Dysregulation

References

Anderson A. K., Christoff, K., Stappen, I., Panitz, D., Ghahremani, D. G., Glover, G., et al. (2003). Dissociated neural representations of intensity and valence in human olfaction. *Nature Neuroscience, 6,* 196–202.

Anderson, A. K., & Phelps, E. A. (2002). Is the human amygdala critical for the subjective experience of emotion? Evidence of intact dispositional affect in patients with lesions of the amygdala. *Journal of Cognitive Neuroscience, 14,* 709–720.

Critchley, H. D., Wiens, S., Rotshtein, P., Ohman, A., & Dolan, R. J. (2004). Neural systems supporting interoceptive awareness. *Nature Neuroscience, 7,* 189–195.

Cunningham, W. A., Van Bavel, J. J., & Johnsen, I. R. (2008). Affective flexibility: Evaluative processing goals shape amygdala activity. *Psychological Science, 19,* 152–160.

Murphy, F. C., Nimmo-Smith, I., & Lawrence, A. D. (2003). Functional neuroanatomy of emotions: A meta-analysis. *Cognitive, Affective, and Behavioral Neuroscience, 3,* 207–233.

Phan, K. L., Taylor, S. F., Welsh, R. C., Ho, S. H., Britton, J. C., & Liberzon, I. (2004). Neural correlates of individual ratings of emotional salience: A trial-related fMRI study. *Neuroimage, 21,* 768–780.

Rolls, E. T. (2000). On the brain and emotion. *Behavioral and Brain Sciences, 23,* 219–228.

Age of Onset of Depression

There are several questions about when depression first occurs whose answer requires different research designs; for several, the research has still to be done. Here we review what is known about four key questions about the onset of depression: when do depressive disorders first appear; at what age are people most likely to experience the onset of depression; what factors are associated with early onset of depression; and does early onset predict a worse course of illness?

When Do Depressive Disorders First Appear?

The idea that children could suffer from depressive disorders is fairly recent. Until the 1970s it was believed that children were cognitively unable to experience many of the core symptoms of depression, such as hopelessness or feelings of worthlessness. Beginning in the 1970s, empirical studies began to establish that children and adults report very similar depressive symptoms. Recently, research on children as young as 2 years old has shown that mothers report similar syndromes even in the preschool years (Angold, Egger, & Carter, 2007). Epidemiological studies in the past 2 decades have shown that the population prevalence of depression is low before puberty but rises to adult levels in adolescent girls (Angold, Worthman, & Costello, 2003). From adolescence on, prevalence rates are in the same range as those seen in studies of adults.

But are child- and adult-onset depressions cases of the same disorder? Even when the same diagnostic criteria are used, might these symptoms reflect different neurobiological processes, just as symptoms such as fever or fatigue can be epiphenomena of many different underlying disorders? Some have argued there is too little evidence to conclude that childhood and adult depression are the same disorder, and much neurobiological evidence that they are different. One of the most important differences is response to tricyclic antidepressant medication. Unlike adults, children respond to tricyclics no better than to placebos (Geller, Reising, Leonard, Riddle, & Walsh, 1999). On the other hand, depression is common in the adult relatives of children who develop depression (Warner, Weissman, Mufson, & Wickramaratne, 1999), and childhood depression is a strong predictor of adult depression (Reinherz, Paradis, Giaconia, Stashwick, & Fitzmaurice, 2003). In short, it makes sense to treat childhood, adolescent, and adult depression as members of the same family until proven different.

At What Age Are People Most Likely to Experience the Onset of Depression?

Cases of depression may be diagnosable as early as 2 years of age, but the peak age at onset is somewhat later, especially for girls. Almost all epidemiological studies find that the prevalence rate of depression is considerably higher in adolescence than in childhood, which suggests that many adolescent cases are first-onset cases. In studies of adult samples that ask about age at onset of first episode, in people with a lifetime history of depression, the median age tends to be around 30, with an interquartile range of about 25 years. This means that, assuming everyone lives to age 75, half of those who ever had one or more major depressive episodes would have had their first episode by age 30, and half of these would have had their first episode by age 18 (Kessler, Berglund, Demler, Jin, & Walters, 2005).

A problem with these estimates is that they are based on retrospective recall of the onset of depression by people of all ages, including elderly people, who may have forgotten how early their problems began. The recent National Comorbidity Survey–Replication estimates that around 20% of an adult sample aged 18 and older had suffered from depression at some time in their lives (Kessler et al., 2005). Several studies of samples aged younger than 20 report similar rates. For example, in one birth cohort followed to age 32, over 50% of women and 30% of men had experienced at least one episode of depression (Moffitt et al., 2007). In another prospective longitudinal study, 11% of young people had experienced at least one episode by age 21. Reports such as this suggest that the evidence of older people may overestimate the peak age at which depression begins.

What Factors Are Associated With Early Onset of Depression?

The factor most widely publicized as predicting early onset of depression is date of birth. There is a widespread belief that, at least in the second half of the 20th century, there has been a dramatic fall in the age of onset of depression, accompanied by an increase in prevalence. However, a review of more than 30 studies published since the 1970s shows no evidence for either increased prevalence or earlier onset (Costello, Erkanli, & Angold, 2006).

There is more reliable evidence that comorbidity with other psychiatric disorders affects, and is affected by, the onset of depression. In the Great Smoky Mountains Study (Costello, Angold, & Sweeney, 1999), the mean age of onset of depression, in those who developed the full disorder by age 16, was 13.5 years (SD 2.1 years). The mean age at onset was a full year earlier (12.8, SD 2.4) in those who had a history of anxiety disorder than in those who did not (13.8, SD 1.8). It was also earlier in girls, but not boys, with oppositional disorder. Conversely, the mean age at onset of oppositional disorder and separation anxiety disorder were later in youths with a history of depression than in others with the disorders, while the onset of generalized anxiety disorder and attention deficit hyperactivity disorder were earlier in those with depression than in others with the disorders. In summary, the onset of depression may bring forward the emergence of some other psychiatric disorders.

Although gender is well known to increase the risk of onset of adolescent depression (Angold et al., 2003), the same study showed no difference in mean age at onset of depression by age 21. Family history of depression has been linked to earlier onset, however.

Does Early Onset Predict a Worse Course of Illness?

We lack the life-course longitudinal studies that would answer this question properly. There is evidence that, like adult-onset depression, early depression is likely to be recurrent, although the National Comorbidity Survey data suggest that, in both adolescents and adults, the excess of women with depression applies only to first episodes; thereafter the risk of recurrence is the same for both sexes (Kessler, 2003).

Conclusions

This brief survey of the literature on age of onset of depression concludes that (a) depression, as defined in the *Diagnostic and Statistical Manual of Mental Disorders,* fourth edition (American Psychiatric Association,

1994), can be diagnosed in children as young as 2; (b) there are many similarities, although some differences, when childhood- and adult-onset depressions are compared; (c) at least a quarter of people who experience depression during their lifetime had their first episode in childhood or adolescence; (d) the evidence on whether more people are having early-onset depression is equivocal; (e) the presence of other psychiatric disorders may increase the risk of early-onset depression; (f) early onset is more common in children from families with a history of depression; (g) childhood-onset depression is as likely as later-onset depression to be recurrent. Early-onset depression is a serious public health problem, not something that children will "grow out of."

E. JANE COSTELLO

See also

Adolescent Depression
Childhood Depression
Course of Depression
Epidemiology

References

American Psychiatric Association. (1994). *Diagnostic and statistical manual of mental disorders* (4th ed.). Washington, DC: Author.

Angold, A., Egger, H., & Carter, A. (2007). The measurement of psychopathology in children under the age of six. In W. Narrow, M. First, P. Sirovatka, & D. Regier D. (Eds.), *Age and gender considerations in psychiatric diagnosis: A research agenda for DSM-V* (pp. 177–189). Arlington, VA: American Psychiatric Association.

Angold, A., Worthman, C. M., & Costello, E. J. (2003). Puberty and depression. In C. Hayward (Ed.), *Gender differences at puberty* (pp. 137–164). New York: Cambridge University Press.

Costello, E. J., Angold, A., & Sweeney, M. E. (1999). Comorbidity with depression in children and adolescents. In M. Tohen (Ed.), *Comorbidity in affective disorders* (pp. 179–196). New York: Marcel Dekker.

Costello, E. J., Erkanli, A., & Angold, A. (2006). Is there an epidemic of child or adolescent depression? *Journal of Child Psychology and Psychiatry, 47*, 1263–1271.

Geller, B., Reising, D., Leonard, H. L., Riddle, M. A., & Walsh, B. T. (1999). Critical review of tricyclic antide-

pressant use in children and adolescents. *Journal of the American Academy of Child and Adolescent Psychiatry, 38*, 513–516.

Kessler, R. C. (2003). Epidemiology of women and depression. *Journal of Affective Disorders, 74*, 5–13.

Kessler, R. C., Berglund, P., Demler, O., Jin, R., & Walters, E. E. (2005). Lifetime prevalence and age-of-onset distributions of DSM-IV disorders in the National Comorbidity Survey replication. *Archive of General Psychiatry, 62*, 593–602.

Moffitt, T. E., Harrington, H., Caspi, A., Kim-Cohen, J., Goldberg, D., Gregory, A. M., et al. (2007). Depression and generalized anxiety disorder: Cumulative and sequential comorbidity in a birth cohort followed prospectively to age 32 years. *Archives of General Psychiatry, 64*, 651–660.

Reinherz, H., Paradis, A., Giaconia, R., Stashwick, C., & Fitzmaurice, G. (2003). Childhood and adolescent predictors of major depression in the transition to adulthood. *American Journal of Psychiatry, 160*, 2141–2147.

Warner, V., Weissman, M. M., Mufson, L., & Wickramaratne, P. J. (1999). Grandparents, parents, and grandchildren at high risk for depression: A three-generation study. *Journal of the American Academy of Child and Adolescent Psychiatry, 38*, 289–296.

Amygdala

Location and Structure

The amygdala (Latin for "almond") is an oblong limbic brain region located in the medial temporal lobe of reptiles and mammals. The human amygdala is conventionally thought of as being bounded posteriorly by the alveus of the hippocampus, anteriorly by the horn of the lateral ventricle, inferiorly by white matter, and superiorly by the subarachnoid space. It is bounded laterally by periamygdaloid cortex adjacent to white matter and medially by periamygdaloid cortex adjacent to the subarachnoid space.

The amygdala represents a collection of nuclei with different functions and structural connectivity to different regions of the brain. Its original definition incorporated what is currently termed the basolateral complex of the amygdala, including the lateral, basal, and accessory basal nuclei. Subsequently, additional adjacent but structurally and functionally heterogenous nuclei, including the central, medial, and cortical nuclei, have been included. Increasingly, a notion of the amygdala as extending even more superiorly toward the rostral extent of the bed nucleus of the stria terminalis has been embraced, having often been described the "extended amygdala."

Function and Connectivity

The amygdala, as a whole, is generally regarded as being important to recognizing emotional aspects of information and generating emotional reactions (for reviews, see Phelps, 2006; Zald, 2003). The different subnuclei of the amygdala appear to subserve different aspects of this overall functionality. The basolateral region is often considered the so-called input region of the amygdala, which, given incoming connections from sensory regions such as the thalamus, regions associated with memory retrieval such as the hippocampus, and higher associations in medial cortical regions, computes the salience, threat, or reward value of the stimulus. Outgoing connections to regions such as the orbitofrontal cortex, hippocampus, and striatum are hypothesized to influence subsequent cognitive consequences (e.g., memory formation) or behaviors (e.g., approach/avoidance) based on these computations. The basolateral amygdala appears to disinhibit neurons in the central nucleus via intra-amygdala intercalated cell masses. The central nucleus is often conceived of as the primary output region of the amygdala, involved in generating emotional reactions such as autonomic and cognitive aspects of fear and anxiety, emotion-relevant attentional allocation, and so forth, through connections to a variety of cortical and subcortical regions, including regions associated with autonomic regulation, such as the hypothalamus, nucleus ambiguous (which is involved in cardiac regulation), and facial motor nucleus. Thus, in anatomic studies, the amygdala is implicated as one of the most widely connected brain structures, having influences on, or being influenced by, nearly every functionally important region of the mammalian brain.

The amygdala has specifically been shown to react to low-level perceptual features associated with threatening or environmentally salient information, including low-spatial-frequency stimuli, the whites of eyes, and masked threat-related stimuli presented too quickly for conscious awareness. It also responds to higher-level emotional stimuli such as emotional pictures, films, personally relevant words, and expected monetary loss. The amygdala appears to activate proportionally to the intensity and arousal-content of emotional stimuli and as a function of prestimulus sad-mood priming. Thus, the amygdala has been implicated in a wide variety of human behaviors involved in emotional information processing, including emotion recognition, generation, emotional memory, emotional learning, the experience of sadness, and rumination.

Inhibition of the amygdala by the cortex has been described as a mechanism for emotion regulation and has been observed through both animal studies and human neuroimaging. In particular, inhibitory connections from the ventromedial prefrontal cortex (specifically the peri- and subgenual regions of the cingulate cortex) and orbital prefrontal cortex have been hypothesized to serve this function (for reviews, see M. L. Phillips, Ladouceur, & Drevets, 2008).

Functional Role of the Amygdala in Depression

Tonic Activity

Given the centrality of the amygdala in emotional reactivity, a strong role for this structure in the pathology of depression has long been hypothesized and observed (for reviews, see Davidson, Jackson, & Kalin, 2000; W. C. Drevets, 1999; W. C. Drevets, Price, & Furey, 2008; Mayberg, 2003; M. L. Phillips, Drevets, Rauch, & Lane, 2003; Whalen, Shin, Somerville, McLean, & Kim, 2002). As the amygdala is involved in detection of emotional features of information, observed increased tonic amygdala activity in unipolar depression is hypothesized to maintain negative affect, increase detection of emotional features in the environment, and create a predisposition toward affectively charged information processing. This activity is observed not only during waking but also in sleep. In support of the functional importance of tonic amygdala activity in depression, the severity of depression has been associated with tonic amygdala activity. Activity has been related to changes in the neurochemical milieu of the amygdala in depression (for review see W. C. Drevets, Price, & Furey, 2008); decreased serotonin binding and decreased mu-opioid binding potential during sad mood have been specifically implicated.

Reactivity

Increased amygdala reactivity is consistently observed in depression, to low-level stimuli such as faces, particularly those that are remembered, and to unattended emotional stimuli, suggesting that biases in amygdala reactivity are associated with early, automatic processing (for review consistent with this perspective, see Leppanen, 2006). Increased and sustained amygdala activity are often observed in depression in response to higher-level emotional stimuli such as negative words and thoughts, even during attempts at regulation of sad feelings. Increased and sustained amygdala reactivity have been associated with rumination and depressive severity. Increased activity of the extended amygdala during anticipation of aversive events in depressed individuals further attests to the potential role of this structure in the phenomenology of cognitive biases such as anticipation of negative outcomes. Amygdala reactivity in depression appears to be modulated by genes associated with serotonin function.

Functional Connectivity

Increasingly, examinations of amygdala function in depression acknowledge the importance of the greater network of brain function involved in the disorder. Thus, data suggest that amygdala activity across the hemispheres is more tightly coupled in depression, but that functional connectivity assessed via covariation with prefrontal regulatory regions is decreased in depressed individuals, particularly during mood regulation, though these effects may differ as a function of genetics and life stress.

Heterogeneity

Other research suggests considerable functional heterogeneity in the role of the amygdala in depression. For example, initial studies suggest that amygdala reactivity to emotional stimuli appears to be decreased in depressed postpartum women and children, and decreased in vulnerable youths by the presence of a task compared to passive viewing. As depressed children display increased amygdala activity for emotional information they remember, a general pattern of avoidance in childhood depression may be present. Thus, further investigation into the functional heterogeneity and causes of variation in amygdala function in depression may be necessary. Additionally similar patterns of increased amygdala activity and reactivity have been observed in a host of other related disorders such as social anxiety disorder, suggesting a potential lack of specificity for observed effects, though the presence of comorbid depression appears to be associated with decreased amygdala activity in posttraumatic stress disorder.

Structure

The functional importance of the amygdala in depression is echoed by data suggesting that amygdala shape and volume are also disrupted. The direction of effects in these studies is mixed, though, with studies showing increased, decreased, or no differences in amygdala volume in depression. Heterogeneity in the ways amygdala volumes are quantified (e.g., what boundaries are used for tracing the amygdala on an MRI) has been shown to moderate detection of group differences and may thus contribute to the lack of consistent results. Limited data suggest that decreased amygdala volumes are related to increased activity in response to emotional information but decreased biases toward remembering negative information in depression.

Involvement in Treatment

Significant evidence suggests a role for the amygdala in recovery from depression in evidence-based treatments such as cognitive therapy and antidepressant medications (for review, see DeRubeis, Siegle, & Hollon, 2008). Recovery is associated with reductions of tonic amygdala activity, increased functional coupling with prefrontal regions, and decreased reactivity to low-level stimuli, suggesting that amygdala function may be an index of the depressive state. Yet, other data suggest that upon induction of a depressive state, amygdala activity in formally depressed individuals serves roles seen in depression, such as increasing a predisposition to remember negative information, consistent with a diathesis-stress interpretation of the role of the amygdala. Consistent with this idea, depletion of serotonin in vulnerable individuals is also associated with increased amygdala activity in response to emotional stimuli. Furthermore, targeted interventions such as stimulation of subgenual cingulate regions with strong connectivity to the amygdala appear to better target depressive symptomatology than dorsal cingulate regions without this connectivity. Yet, the causal role of the amygdala in either the phenomenology or treatment of depression may be questioned in a report of a patient who had depressed mood and responded to antidepressant medications despite amygdala lesions.

The extent to which structural volume abnormalities resolve with treatment for depression is unclear and may be dependent on the modality. For example, an early study suggested that volumes normalize with electroconvulsive therapy, but other data have not found volumetric changes in recovered individuals.

Increased amygdala activity in response to cognitive and emotional stimuli appears to positively predict recovery in depressed individuals for treatments that target emotional functioning such as cognitive therapy, as well as interventions known to affect limbic function partial sleep deprivation, antidepressant medications, and unselected treatments.

GREG SIEGLE

See also

Affective Neuroscience
Behavioral Activation System
Behavioral Inhibition System
Brain Circuitry
Functional Neuroimaging
Hemispheric Lateralization
Hippocampus
Hypothalamic-Pituitary-Adrenal Axis
Hypothalamic-Pituitary-Thyroid Axis

References

Campbell, S., & MacQueen, G. (2006). An update on regional brain volume differences associated with mood disorders. *Current Opinion in Psychiatry, 19*(1), 25–33.

Davidson, R. J., Jackson, D. C., & Kalin, N. H. (2000). Emotion, plasticity, context, and regulation: perspectives from affective neuroscience. *Psychological Bulletin, 126*(6), 890–909.

DeRubeis, R. J., Siegle, G. J., & Hollon, S. D. (2008). Cognitive therapy versus medication for depression: treatment outcomes and neural mechanisms. *Nature Reviews Neuroscience, 9*(10), 788–796.

Drevets, W. C. (1999). Prefrontal cortical amygdalar metabolism in major depression. *Annals of the New York Academy of Sciences, 877*, 614–637.

Drevets, W. C., Price, J. L., & Furey, M. L. (2008). Brain structural and functional abnormalities in mood disorders: implications for neurocircuitry models of depression. *Brain Structure and Function, 213*(1/2), 93–118.

Konarski, J. Z., McIntyre, R. S., Kennedy, S. H., Rafi-Tari, S., Soczynska, J. K., & Ketter, T. A. (2008). Volumetric neuroimaging investigations in mood disorders: bipolar disorder versus major depressive disorder. *Bipolar Disordersm, 10*(1), 1–37.

Leppanen, J. M. (2006). Emotional information processing in mood disorders: a review of behavioral and neuroimaging findings. *Current Opinion in Psychiatry, 19*(1), 34–39.

Mayberg, H. S. (2003). Positron emission tomography imaging in depression: a neural systems perspective. *Neuroimaging Clinics of North America, 13*(4), 805–815.

Phelps, E. A. (2006). Emotion and cognition: insights from studies of the human amygdala. *Annual Reviews of Psychology, 57*, 27–53.

Phillips, M. L., Drevets, W. C., Rauch, S. L., & Lane, R. (2003). Neurobiology of emotion perception II: Implications for major psychiatric disorders. *Biological Psychiatry, 54*(5), 515–528.

Phillips, M. L., Ladouceur, C. D., & Drevets, W. C. (2008). A neural model of voluntary and automatic emotion regulation: implications for understanding the pathophysiology and neurodevelopment of bipolar disorder. *Molecular Psychiatry.*

Whalen, P. J., Shin, L. M., Somerville, L. H., McLean, A. A., & Kim, H. (2002). Functional neuroimaging studies of the amygdala in depression. *Seminars in Clinical Neuropsychiatry, 7*(4), 234–242.

Zald, D. H. (2003). The human amygdala and the emotional evaluation of sensory stimuli. *Brain Research, Rev, 41*(1), 88–123.

Anaclitic and Introjective Depression

Several investigators have noted marked limitations in studying depression from the categorical symptom-based approach articulated in the American Psychiatric Association's *Diagnostic and Statistical Manual of Mental Disorders* (*DSM-IV;* 1994) and have instead focused on differences in the experiences that lead to depression—a more person-centered rather than a disease- or symptom-centered approach.

Symptoms of depression are quite heterogeneous and include psychological symptoms (e.g., mood change and pervasive loss of energy and interest) and somatic or neurovegative symptoms (e.g., loss of sleep and appetite). This heterogeneity of symptoms has made it difficult to differentiate meaningful subtypes of depression in both clinical and nonclinical samples. Several research teams (Arieti & Bemporad, 1978; Beck, 1983; Blatt, 1974, 2004) over the past three decades, however, have differentiated subtypes of depression based not on symptoms but on differences in personality style and the life experiences that can lead to depression. These research teams have differentiated two major types of depression: a depression initiated by disruptions of interpersonal relationships such as interpersonal loss and feelings of abandonment and loneliness (an anaclitic or dependent [e.g., Blatt, 1974], sociotropic [Beck, 1983], or dominant other [e.g., Arieti & Bemporad, 1978] depression) from a depression initiated by disruptions of self-esteem, achievement, identity (an introjective or self-critical [e.g., Blatt, 1974; autonomous [Beck, 1983], or dominant goal [e.g., Arieti & Bemporad, 1978] depression).

Extensive research with both clinical and nonclinical samples (see summaries in Blatt, 2004) demonstrates that these two types of depression—a depression focused on interpersonal issues and one on issues of self-esteem and self-worth—derive from very different early life experiences, are precipitated by different types of current life events or stressors, have different clinical expression, and are responsive to different types of therapeutic intervention. An anaclitic-dependent, sociotropic, or a dominant-other type of depression that derives primarily from neglectful and depriving parenting is precipitated primarily by interpersonal stressors (e.g., experiences of loss and abandonment); is expressed in lethargy, feelings of helplessness and loneliness, somatic concerns and can involve suicidal gestures; and is responsive primarily to supportive types of therapeutic intervention. An introjective-self-critical, autonomous or a dominant-goal type of depression, in contrast, that derives primarily from harsh, punitive, judgmental parenting; is precipitated primarily by experiences of failure and criticism; is expressed in feelings of hopelessness, failure, intense self-criticism, and can involve serious suicidal risk; and is responsive primarily to more intensive, long-term, interpretive types of therapeutic interventions.

Evaluation of therapeutic response in long-term intensive treatment, in both inpatient and outpatient settings, indicates that anaclitic and introjective patients are differentially responsive to supportive-expressive psychotherapy and more intensive psycho-analysis (Blatt & Shahar, 2004) and change in different ways—in ways consistent with their basic personality organization (Blatt & Ford, 1994). While introjective patients are more responsive than anaclitic patients to intensive long-term treatment, they are significantly less responsive to brief manual-directed psychotherapy and antidepressive medication (e.g., Blatt & Zuroff, 2005).

Thus, a person-centered developmental approach to depression has been valuable in establishing a meaningful clinical distinction that has led to fuller understanding of some of the etiological factors that contribute to depression, as well as some of the processes involved in effective therapeutic intervention.

Extensive research has also been devoted to describing individual differences in vulnerability to the two forms of depression. Dependency is a personality dimension that confers vulnerability to anaclitic depression; self-criticism is a stable personality dimension that confers vulnerability to introjective depression (Blatt, 2004). The most widely used measure of dependency and self-criticism is the Depressive Experiences Questionnaire (Blatt, D'Afflitti, & Quinlan, 1979), which has been translated into over 15 languages spoken in North America, South America, Europe, the Middle East, and Asia.

Dependent and self-critical people differ in terms of their fundamental motivations, cognitions about themselves and others, patterns of interpersonal relationships, and affective experiences (Blatt, 2004). Individuals with high levels of dependency have a greater number of interpersonal goals involving affiliation and intimacy and fewer achievement and individualistic goals (Mongrain & Zuroff, 1995); dependent individuals' needs for nurturance and affection come at the expense of their own individuation. Individuals with high levels of self-criticism, in contrast, endorse a greater number of achievement goals, more self-presentation strivings, and fewer interpersonal strivings (Mongrain & Zuroff, 1995), indicating a relative disinterest in affiliative and warm exchanges with others.

Highly dependent individuals perceive themselves as weak and vulnerable, and needing the support and guidance of others. At the same time, they lack confidence in the emotional availability of others, and fear abandonment and the loss of supportive relationships. Self-critical individuals report negative representations of self and others, including parents, friends, and romantic partners. They are afraid of being rejected, are not comfortable with closeness, and do not feel they can rely on their partners (Zuroff & Fitzpatrick, 1995). Their negative models of self and others leave them distrustful, guarded, and avoidant of intimacy, seeking to protect themselves against anticipated rejection and criticism.

High dependency is associated with a mixed pattern of positive and negative interpersonal experiences. Highly dependent individuals describe themselves as experiencing more love and intimacy and having greater social support (Priel & Shahar, 2000), but not as more satisfied with their interactions or relationships (Zuroff, Stotland, Sweetman, Craig, & Koestner, 1995). The interpersonal experiences associated with self-criticism are consistently negative, with impairments reported in peer relationships, romantic relationships, child-rearing, and therapeutic relationships. Associated with these impairments are low levels of social support and high levels of stress (Dunkley, Zuroff, & Blankstein, 2003).

The characteristic emotional tones of individuals with high scores on dependency and self-criticism also differ (Zuroff et al., 1995). Self-criticism is associated with consistently high levels of negative emotions and consistently low levels of positive emotions. Dependency is also associated with high levels of negative emotions but is unrelated to levels of positive emotions, suggesting that positive emotions may fluctuate from low to high in those with high levels of dependency. In summary, highly dependent individuals value and seek relatedness, fear its loss, and, perhaps because of their fluctuating relationships, experience considerable variations in their emotional states. Self-critical individuals seek achievement and perfection rather than relatedness, fear being hurt by others, and, perhaps because of their impaired relatedness with others, experience little positive affect and much negative affect.

These findings about the nature of two types of depressive experiences and the characteristics of dependent and self-critical individuals suggest that other forms of psychopathology beyond depression, especially the personality disorders, may be more fully understood from a more person-centered approach in which psychopathology is understood as exaggerated distorted preoccupation, at different developmental levels, with issues of interpersonal relatedness or issues of self-definition. Thus, a person-centered approach would facilitate further understanding of the complex links between depression and personality disorders.

SIDNEY J. BLATT AND DAVID C. ZUROFF

See also

Attachment
Cognitive Theories of Depression
Cognitive Vulnerability
Internal Working Models
Psychodynamic Model of Depression
Psychodynamic Therapy

References

American Psychiatric Association. (1994). *Diagnostic and statistical manual of mental disorders* (4th ed.). Washington, DC: Author.

Arieti, S., & Bemporad, J. R. (1978). *Severe and mild depression: The therapeutic approach*. New York: Basic Books.

Beck, A. T. (1983). Cognitive therapy of depression: New perspectives. In P. J. Clayton & J. E. Barrett (Eds.), *Treatment of depression: Old controversies and new approaches* (pp. 265–290). New York: Raven Press.

Blatt, S. J. (1974). Levels of object representation in anaclitic and introjective depression. *Psychoanalytic Study of the Child, 29*, 107–157.

Blatt, S. J. (2004). *Experiences of depression: Theoretical, clinical, and research perspectives*. Washington, DC: American Psychological Association.

Blatt, S. J., D'Afflitti, J., & Quinlan, D. M. (1979). *Depressive Experiences Questionnaire (DEQ)*. Unpublished research manual, Yale University.

Blatt, S. J., & Ford, R. (1994). *Therapeutic change: An object relations perspective*. New York: Plenum Press.

Blatt, S. J., & Shahar, G. (2004). Psychoanalysis: For what, with whom, and how: A comparison with psychotherapy. *Journal of the American Psychoanalytic Association, 52*, 393–447.

Blatt, S. J., & Zuroff, D. C. (2005). Empirical evaluation of the assumptions in identifying evidence based treatments in mental health. *Clinical Psychology Review, 25*, 459–486.

Dunkley, D. M., Zuroff, D. C., & Blankstein, K. R. (2003). Self-critical perfectionism and daily affect: Dispositional and situational influences on stress and coping. *Journal of Personality and Social Psychology, 84*, 234–252.

Mongrain, M., & Zuroff, D. C. (1995). Motivational and affective correlates of dependency and self-criticism. *Personality and Individual Differences, 18*, 347–354.

Priel, B., & Shahar, G. (2000). Dependency, self-criticism, social context and distress: Comparing moderating and mediating models. *Personality and Individual Differences, 28*, 515–520.

Zuroff, D. C., & Fitzpatrick, D. A. (1995). Depressive personality styles: Implications for adult attachment. *Personality and Individual Differences, 18*, 253–265.

Zuroff, D. C., Stotland, S., Sweetman, E., Craig, J. A., & Koestner, R. (1995). Dependency, self-criticism, and social interactions. *British Journal of Clinical Psychology, 34*, 543–553.

Anger

The frequency with which anger is experienced in adult depression may not be adequately emphasized in current diagnostic criteria. In the fourth edition of the *Diagnostic and Statistical Manual of Mental Disorders* (*DSM-IV*; American Psychiatric Association [APA], 1994), sadness or "depressed mood" is the only affective symptom explicitly included in the diagnostic criteria for major depressive episode in adults. The subsequent revised edition (*DSM-IV-TR*; APA, 2000) acknowledges that irritable mood may contribute to a diagnosis of depression in children and appear alongside atypical features in adults. However, a substantial number of individuals presenting with major depressive disorder present with clinically relevant levels of anger.

Anger and the Nosology of Depression

Depressive syndromes characterized by anger or hostility are commonly highlighted in subtyping approaches to the classification of depression. Sometime ago, for instance, Paykel (1971) conducted a cluster analysis of both inpatients and outpatients and found four subgroupings of depression: psychotic, anxious, hostile, and young mildly depressed individuals with personality pathology. Similarly, a cluster analysis by Overall, Hollister, Johnson, and Pennington (1965) yielded three subcategories of major depressive disorder, labeled the hostile, anxious, and retarded depression types.

In 1990, Fava, Anderson, and Rosenbaum (1990) first introduced the concept of "anger attacks," in patients diagnosed with major depressive disorder. These anger attacks are similar to panic attacks in their temporal course and autonomic activation, but without the intense fear and anxiety that accompanies panic. These attacks are not viewed as ego-syntonic, rather, they are considered uncharacteristic by the person having the attacks. Several studies have been undertaken since 1990 to explore major depressive disorder with anger attacks in terms of response to antidepressant medications, physiological correlates, and clinical presentation.

Some researchers have suggested that anger in the context of unipolar major depressive disorder signifies a bipolar spectrum mood disturbance (e.g., Benazzi & Akiskal, 2005). In patients diagnosed with major depressive disorder, anger is related to markers of bipolar disorders, including younger age of onset, bipolar family history, higher rates of atypical depressive features, and hypomanic symptoms. There is also evidence, however, that depression with anger may be more closely aligned with unipolar depression. For example, antidepressant medications have been found to reduce anger and hostility, and individuals with major depressive disorder plus anger seem no more likely than their counterparts without anger attacks to experience a switch to bipolar I or II following treatment with antidepressant medications.

Demographic, Personality, Cognitive, and Biological Correlates

Prevalence estimates of clinically relevant levels of anger and hostility in samples of depressed individuals have ranged from nearly one-fifth to over one-third. Anger and hostility appear to be clinically relevant in a large portion of both inpatients and outpatients with major depressive disorder. Patients with major depressive disorder plus anger do not seem to differ in age compared to those with major depressive disorder but without anger attacks. Evidence suggests, however, that those experiencing significant irritability or hostility in the context of depressive episodes tend to be younger than those not experiencing irritability or hostility.

Findings regarding gender differences in hostile, angry, and irritable expressions of depression have been mixed. Where gender differences on a particular anger-related construct are found in some research, other research does not find these differences. Despite mixed findings regarding the relationship of gender to anger in depression, some have suggested that males tend to exhibit a unique depressive syndrome marked by irritability, anger, and low impulse control.

Little research has examined the personality and cognitive correlates of anger in the context of major depressive disorder. The presence of anger attacks in major depressive disorder may be indicative of Cluster B and/ or C Axis II pathology, and hostility is associated with low agreeableness and contentiousness. With regards to cognitive correlates, depression has been associated more strongly with cognitive as opposed to behavioral expressions of hostility. For example, depression with hostility may be associated with external and specific attributions for negative events.

Whereas research exploring the personality and cognitive correlates of anger in depression is sparse, studies examining the biological correlates have been many. For instance, research suggests that major depressive disorder plus anger is associated with hypofunctionality of the ventromedial prefrontal cortex and insufficient inhibition of amygdalar activity in anger inducing situations. In addition, dysregulated neurotransmitter functioning is associated with anger in depression. Diminished serotonergic activity has been linked to stable hostility and anger attacks, elevated dopamine neurotransmission has been associated with anger attacks, and low levels of GABA have been liked to overt hostility in depression. Finally, a genetic contribution to anger in depression is likely. Research has suggested links between anger in depression and polymorphisms in genes implicated in serotonergic functioning, hypothalamic-pituitary-adrenal axis functioning, and emotional reactivity (Wasserman, Geijer, Sokolowski, Rozanov, & Wasserman, 2007).

Clinical Presentation and Treatment Response

In general, hostility in the context of major depressive disorder seems to carry negative prognostic value, and is associated with greater time spent ill. Compared with less hostile forms, those experiencing major depressive disorder and notable hostility may experience greater obsessive worry, paranoia, psychotic symptoms, and/or appetite increase but also may experience fewer somatic symptoms. Although anger seems to exhibit a positive correlation with depressive symptom severity, research evidence is mixed regarding anger as a predictor of suicidality.

Researchers have yet to explore the relative efficacy of any forms of psychotherapy for depression with and without anger. Several studies, however, have explored response to pharmacological treatments. Research suggests that monoamine oxidase inhibitors are more effective than placebo in reducing hostility in hostile depressed patients, whereas evidence for the efficacy of tricyclics in these patients is mixed. The treatment of depressed outpatients with the serotonin reuptake inhibitors (SSRIs) has resulted in decreased hostility as well as improvement in depressive symptoms. Treatment with SSRIs also seems effective in reducing anger attacks, but it is unclear to what extent they are effective in reducing depressive symptoms in those with major depressive disorder plus anger. Finally, hostile-depressed nonresponders to antidepressant medication may respond when switched to treatment with mood stabilizers, but it is unclear whether mood stabilizers in combination with antidepressants would be beneficial in treating major depressive disorder with anger.

Conclusions

Anger in the context of depression seems to be an important construct in need of further exploration by researchers. Significant anger and/or hostility is experienced by about one-third of individuals presenting with an major depressive disorder. Although depression with anger seems to be related to certain personality features, biological correlates, and clinical features, it is not yet clear whether depression with anger or major depressive disorder plus anger would be better classified as a distinct subtype of major depressive disorder. Treatment research related to depression with anger is sparse, especially with regards to psychotherapy, but available evidence suggests some efficacy of certain antidepressant medications for reducing depressive symptoms and anger in those with angry or hostile depression.

It would be helpful for standard assessments for unipolar depression to also assess symptoms such as hostility and anger. However, there is little agreement in the literature about how to best define and measure these constructs. *Anger*, *hostility*, and *irritability* are used interchangeably by some to describe the same phenomena, whereas others reserve *anger* to indicate the affective construct that is distinct from, although related to, the cognitive construct of hostility and the behavioral construct of aggression. The lack of clarity in definitions of and instruments used to measure these constructs has caused confusion regarding the degree to which descriptions of "hostile" and "angry" depression overlap, and represents a significant roadblock to advancing our understanding of how anger and hostility affect clinical presentation and outcomes in depression with anger.

MELINDA A. GADDY

See also

Comorbidity

References

American Psychiatric Association. (1994). *Diagnostic and statistical manual of mental disorders* (4th ed.). Washington, DC: Author.

American Psychiatric Association. (2000). *Diagnostic and statistical manual of mental disorders* (4th ed., text revision). Washington, DC: Author.

Benazzi, F., & Aksikal, H. (2005). Irritable-hostile depression: Further validation as a bipolar depressive mixed state. *Journal of Affective Disorders, 84,* 197–207.

Fava, M., Anderson, K., & Rosenbaum, J. F. (1990). "Anger attacks": Possible variants of panic and major depressive disorders. *American Journal of Psychiatry, 147,* 867–870.

Overall, J. E., Hollister, L. E., Johnson, M., & Pennington, V. (1965). Computer classifications of depressions and differential effect of antidepressants [Abstract]. *Journal of the American Medical Association, 192,* 217.

Paykel, E. S. (1971). Classification of depressed patients: A cluster analysis derived grouping. *British Journal of Psychiatry, 118,* 275–288.

Wasserman, D., Geijer, R., Sokolowski, M., Rozanov, V., & Wasserman, J. (2007). Genetic variation in the hypothalamic-pituitary-adrenocortical axis regulatory factor, T-box 19, and the angry/hostility personality trait. *Genes, Brain, and Behavior, 6,* 321–328.

Anxiety

Though anxiety and depression are distinguishable, as we discuss in more detail below, they overlap to a considerable degree and share important features. Thus, no consideration of depression would be complete without also addressing anxiety disorders and the relationship between depression and the anxiety disorders. With an estimated 29% of people suffering from an anxiety disorder at some point in their lives, the anxiety disorders as a group are the single most common form of psychopathology within the general population. There are several different anxiety disorders, and what unites these problems is the central role of anxiety in each of them. In addition, they tend to share some common features, often involving some form of avoidance and a tendency to selectively focus on threatening information. What distinguishes the various anxiety disorders from one another

is the focus of anxiety involved in each (Barlow, 2002).

Panic disorder (PD) is characterized by recurrent unexpected panic attacks, discrete periods in which intense fear is accompanied by strong symptoms of physical arousal, and a fear of future panic attacks. A common complication of PD is agoraphobic avoidance of situations in which it might be difficult to escape or receive help should a panic attack occur.

Specific phobias involve circumscribed fears of particular objects or situations often leading to avoidance behavior. Subtypes include animal type, natural environment type, blood-injection injury type, situational type, and other type.

Social phobia involves anxiety about being evaluated in social or performance situations. Concerns may be confined to particular performance or social situations (such as public speaking) or may be triggered by many types of social interaction.

Obsessive-compulsive disorder (OCD) is characterized by repetitive and intrusive thoughts or images that provoke anxiety and/or the compulsive performance of overt or covert rituals that serve to neutralize anxiety or distress.

Posttraumatic stress disorder (PTSD) involves anxiety about a particular past event that provoked intense fear, horror, or helplessness. This anxiety is manifested by reexperiencing the traumatic event, avoidance of stimuli associated with the trauma, and hypervigilance.

Separation anxiety disorder (SAD) is a childhood disorder that involves excessive fear or anxiety concerning separation from the home or an attachment figure.

Generalized anxiety disorder (GAD) involves experiencing excessive and uncontrollable worry or anxiety about a number of different issues. This worry is also typically accompanied by several other symptoms of anxiety such as insomnia, muscle tension, and feeling restless, keyed up, or on edge.

Most anxiety disorders are more prevalent among women, although OCD is equally prevalent among men and women

(American Psychiatric Association [APA], 2000). In general, anxiety disorders tend to onset relatively early in life, typically manifesting before late adolescence (APA, 2000). PD is unusual in that it most frequently begins in early adulthood, although panic attacks often onset by midadolescence. PTSD may occur at any age, including in childhood, following the occurrence of a trauma.

In adults, untreated anxiety disorders tend to be relatively chronic, with only 12% to 30% of adults exhibiting spontaneous remission. Rates of recovery are somewhat higher in adolescents, and the majority of youth anxiety disorders remit by early adulthood. However, early anxiety disorders, particularly those that develop in late adolescence, are a major risk factor for the development of anxiety disorders in adulthood (Pine, Cohen, Gurley, Brook, & Ma, 1998). Many disorders, such as PD, social phobia, GAD, and OCD, frequently exhibit waxing and waning symptom courses in which the exacerbation of symptoms may relate to stress (*DSM-IV-TR;* APA, 2000).

Comorbidity Between Anxiety and Depressive Disorders: Overlapping and Distinctive Features

Comorbidity at the individual level refers to the co-occurrence of disorders; comorbidity at the group level refers to the co-occurrence of disorders across individuals at a rate that is greater than what would be expected by chance alone. Countless studies attest to the high frequency of comorbidity between depressive and anxiety disorders (see Mineka, Watson, & Clark, 1998). That is, research suggests that the frequent co-occurrence of depressive and anxiety disorders cannot be completely explained by the chance pairings of several highly prevalent disorders. Instead, the relationships between depressive and anxiety disorders are more nuanced. It has been consistently shown that anxiety disorders frequently precede depressive onset, but that depression rarely precedes anxiety. The complexity of the relationship between depressive and anxiety disorders has led many researchers to conclude that the presence of a common diathesis for both types of disorders best explains this relationship. This diathesis has been described in both phenotypic and genotypic analyses of depression and anxiety, briefly reviewed below.

At the phenotypic level, it is thought that depression and anxiety disorders consist of a common core of negative affect, along with factors that are more specific to each disorder. For example, a low positive affect or anhedonia factor is relatively specific to depression, while physiological hyperarousal is relatively specific to panic attacks (Mineka et al., 1998; Zinbarg et al., 1994). The common core of negative affect is believed to account for the high rates of comorbidity of anxiety disorders and depression. In contrast, the anhedonia specific to depression and the various factors specific to different types of anxiety may account for the fact that anxiety disorders and depression can be reliably diagnosed and distinguished from each despite their high comorbidity. Interestingly, it appears that one of the anxiety disorders, GAD, is more highly comorbid with major depressive episodes and dysthymia than it tends to be with the other anxiety disorders (Krueger, 1999).

Behavioral genetic research has yielded moderately consistent results, suggesting a genotypic model of depression and anxiety that is closely related to the phenotypic model described above. Results suggest that the genetic vulnerability for depression and anxiety consists of two separate, but related, factors. One of these genetic factors appears to be a vulnerability for major depression and GAD, which are genetically indistinguishable from one another. This genetic diathesis has been shown to be closely linked to neuroticism, the personality trait thought to make one vulnerable to negative affect—the common phenotypic core of depression and anxiety. PD, agoraphobia, and social phobia are related to this factor as well but are even more strongly related to a second genetic factor. This second genetic factor also underlies specific phobias, which are largely unrelated to the first genetic factor, and it may best represent a vulnerability to the somatic symptoms of panic attacks (Kendler et al., 1995). The evidence suggesting genetic indistinguishability of GAD and depression, together with the phenotypic evidence showing that GAD is even more highly comorbid with depression than it is with the other anxiety disorders, may lead to a reorganization of our current diagnostic system. In this reorganization GAD would be grouped together with the major depressive episodes and dysthymia rather than with the anxiety disorders.

Treatment of Anxiety Disorders

Earlier we stated that untreated anxiety disorders in adults tend to be relatively chronic. Fortunately, the anxiety disorders are among the most treatable of all the psychiatric disorders (Barlow, 2002). The two forms of treatment for anxiety disorders that have the greatest amount of empirical evidence to support them are cognitive behavior therapy and medications.

There are three primary cognitive behavior therapy techniques for anxiety that are often combined into a comprehensive treatment package: cognitive restructuring, relaxation exercises, and exposure therapy. Cognitive restructuring consists of teaching the patient to (a) better identify thoughts, beliefs, and/or images that might be contributing to excessive anxiety, (b) challenge these thoughts with existing evidence and more balanced thoughts, and (c) subject these thoughts to empirical tests. Relaxation exercises include progressive muscle relaxation, diaphragmatic breathing, guided imagery, and more recently, mindfulness meditation exercises. While there are several varieties of exposure therapy, all involve intentionally confronting anxiety-provoking triggers and situations and replacing avoidance behavior with approach behavior. Imaginal exposure involves confronting anxiety triggers in imagination, whereas in vivo exposure involves actual confrontation with anxiety triggers. Interoceptive exposure involves intentionally bringing on the sensations of anxiety, which can trigger further anxiety or fear, and is often used in the treatment of PD. Whereas cognitive behavior therapy does not always produce what might be considered a complete cure, the vast majority of people who complete a cognitive behavior therapy program for anxiety disorders experience substantial improvement.

Recent evidence has begun to suggest that the anxious patient's marital and marriagelike relationships and relationships with other close family members predict the patient's response to individual cognitive behavior therapy (e.g., Zinbarg, Lee, & Yoon, 2007). In particular, hostility expressed toward the patient by relatives or partners predicts higher rates of treatment dropout and poorer treatment outcome. In contrast, nonhostile criticism appears to predict better outcome. These results suggest that some form of family therapy may augment the effectiveness of treatment for at least some cases of anxiety disorders. Indeed, whereas the effects of family therapy remain largely untested in anxiety disorders, some forms of involvement of intimate partners in treatment for PD with agoraphobia has led to superior outcomes (Daiuto, Baucom, Epstein, & Dutton, 1998).

The most commonly prescribed medications for anxiety disorders currently include the selective serotonergic reuptake inhibitors and the benzodiazepines. Medications prescribed for anxiety are effective for many people and in most cases will begin to act more quickly than cognitive behavior therapy. Unfortunately, however, these medications sometimes have unpleasant side effects, and relapse rates are very high if the medications are withdrawn before the patient has had a course of cognitive behavior therapy. Moreover, cognitive behavior therapy is typically effective even in the absence of medications. Thus, many psychologists

researchers have developed specific assessment procedures to differentiate between these diagnostic entities. Examples include the Screening Assessment of Depression–Polarity, a clinician-administered instrument, and the Mood Disorder Questionnaire, a self-report inventory.

Cultural Differences

Of particular importance regarding interindividual differences is the influence of differing ethnic and cultural backgrounds. Sensitivity to this concern first involves ensuring that a depression measure has been competently back-translated into a foreign language when used with a non-English-speaking sample. In addition, for a depression measure to be valid within a given sample, research needs to demonstrate that it actually addresses constructs that have meaning within that culture of interest. Whereas some similarities exist in the expression of depression across various cultures, differences occur with regard to predominate symptom features. In the United States, depression is often detected by sad mood or decreased interest in activities, whereas predominant depression features in Latino and Mediterranean cultures include headaches and "nerves," fatigue and "imbalance" among Asian cultures, and "problems of the heart" in Middle Eastern countries (APA, 2000). Many measures of depression that were initially developed in Western cultures have, in fact, been demonstrated to be applicable across a variety of cultures and have been translated into numerous languages, such as the Beck Depression Inventory, the Patient Health Questionnaire, and the Zung Self-Rating Depression Scale. However, depression measures have also been specifically developed for non-Western cultures, including the Vietnamese Depression Scale and the Chinese Depressive Symptom Scale.

Future Directions

It is important to note that during the past several decades, the actual definition of depression has changed, as documented across the various *Diagnostic and Statistical Manuals for Mental Disorders*. As such, an important future concern involves the need for current measures of depression to be revised or new measures to be developed in order for them to be consistent with such definitional changes (Nezu et al., 2009).

In addition, future research should focus on improving the assessment of depression among (a) differing ethnic populations, (b) medical populations experiencing symptoms that overlap with depression, (c) individuals residing in rural areas, (d) persons in lower socioeconomic levels and poor literacy rates, (e) the elderly (especially those experiencing cognitive difficulties), and (f) the disabled.

ARTHUR M. NEZU AND CHRISTINE MAGUTH NEZU

See also

Beck Depression Inventory
Clinically Useful Depression
Outcome Scale
Diagnostic and Statistical Manual of
Mental Disorders

References

American Psychiatric Association. (2000). *Diagnostic and statistical manual of mental disorders* (4th ed., text revision). Washington, DC: Author.

Nezu, A. M., Nezu, C. M., Friedman, J., & Lee, M. (2009). Assessment of depression among mental health and medical patient populations. In I. H. Gotlib & C. L. Hammen (Eds.), *Handbook of depression* (2nd ed., pp. 44–68). New York: Guilford Press.

Nezu, A. M., Nezu, C. M., McClure, K. S., & Zwick, M. L. (2002). Assessment of depression. In I. H. Gotlib & C. L. Hammen (Eds.), *Handbook of depression* (pp. 61–85). New York: Guilford Press.

Attachment

In the third volume of his *Attachment and Loss* trilogy, Bowlby (1980) wrote about the way attachment insecurities may contribute to later development of depression. Bowlby argued that individuals who experience negative interactions with their attachment figures (close relationship partners—usually primary caregivers during childhood—who provide protection, comfort, and support), are more likely to develop psychopathologies in general and depression in particular.

According to attachment theory, human beings are equipped with an innate attachment behavioral system, which regulates proximity-seeking behaviors. When encountering threats or stressors, infants are motivated to restore their sense of security by seeking proximity to their attachment figures. Over time, the attachment figures and the interactions with them are internalized as mental representations or working models. These mental representations include knowledge about the self, the relationship partners, and the social world.

A sensitive and responsive parenting style is likely to lead individuals to internalize positive representations of the self (as worthy of love and support) and others (as dependable and likely to provide love and support). Individuals holding such representations are thought to have a secure attachment style. An inconsistent or rejecting parenting style, on the other hand, is likely to lead individuals to internalize negative representations of the self (as not worthy of love) and others (rejecting, neglecting, unreliable, and not helpful). Individuals holding such representations are said to have an insecure attachment style. Once formed, these attachment styles are thought to be relatively stable and tend to influence people's cognitions, emotions, and behaviors.

Individual differences in adult attachment are most commonly conceptualized in terms of two dimensions of insecurity. The first dimension, attachment avoidance, results from encountering consistent rejections from attachment figures. It is characterized by a strong preference for self-reliance, reluctance to get close or show emotions to relationship partners, as well as discomfort with letting others depend on oneself. Avoidantly attached people tend to downplay their emotions in an attempt to deactivate their attachment system.

The second dimension, attachment anxiety, is thought to result from encountering inconsistent and intrusive caregiving behaviors. It is characterized by a strong desire for closeness to—and protection from—relationship partners, and a hypervigilance toward cues of partner rejection or unavailability. Anxiously attached people tend to ruminate on negative experiences, be preoccupied with negative thoughts and emotions, and present themselves as helpless and needy.

Currently, there are two main approaches to measure individual differences in adult attachment styles. One approach, mainly used by social psychologists, is based on self-reports. As research on attachment progressed, self-report measures evolved from assessing attachment in terms of three or four types (e.g., secure, anxious, dismissing-avoidant, and fearful-avoidant) to assessing it along the above-mentioned anxiety and avoidance dimensions. The other approach, mainly used by clinical and developmental psychologists, is based on interviews. The most widely used of these measures is the Adult Attachment Interview (AAI). In the AAI, adults are asked to describe their parents and the relationships they had with them during childhood. The responses are scored primarily in terms of discourse coherence rather than the content. The coherency of the overall responses is assumed to reflect the interviewee's "state of mind with respect to attachment" and is used to assign the interviewee into one of the three major "state of mind" categories (autonomous—corresponding to a secure style, preoccupied—corresponding to an anxious style, and dismissing—corresponding to an avoidant style).

To date, hundreds of studies have shown that individual differences in attachment style, measured either via self-reports or interviews, are correlated with relationship satisfaction, well-being, forms of coping with stress and regulating affect, and mental health. One of the central findings coming out of this literature is that attachment security provides a resilience resource that reduces the likelihood to develop psychological disorders.

Early Attachment Experiences and Later Vulnerability to Depression

Bowlby (1980) suggested that depression may result from a failure to form secure, supporting bonds with one's primary caregivers. This lack of secure bonds might be either due to the actual loss of a caregiver (because of death or prolonged separation) or due to rejection or inconsistent care from a caregiver. Individuals who experienced such events (e.g., prolonged separation or rejection), are more likely to form negative perceptions of the self, which include feelings of being abandoned, unwanted, unlovable, and unable to form and maintain affectional bonds. As a result, these individuals are at a higher risk to develop depression.

Studies that tested the effects of caregiving quality or separation during early childhood on later depression provided empirical support for Bowlby's ideas. For example, individuals who lost one or both of their parents in childhood (due to either separation or death) were found to be more likely to show depressive symptoms in adulthood as compared to individuals who did not experience such loss. Likewise, individuals who reported receiving insensitive caregiving from their attachment figures in childhood were more likely to show depression in adulthood. Beyond this correlational evidence, there is also experimental evidence showing that individuals who reported low-quality maternal caregiving were more likely to show an attention bias toward negative stimuli (which can be interpreted as an index of vulnerability to depression), as compared to individuals who reported high-quality maternal caregiving.

Individual Differences in Adult Attachment Style and Depression

Cross-Sectional Studies

Numerous studies focusing on individual differences in adult attachment style have found positive associations between attachment insecurities and depressive symptoms. In a recent comprehensive review, Mikulincer and Shaver (2007) identified more than a hundred studies investigating this association in nonclinical samples, with most of them using self-reports to assess attachment style. Regardless of the attachment measure used, these studies consistently showed that anxious attachment was positively associated with depression in nonclinical samples. Results were more mixed with respect to avoidant attachment. Whereas some researchers reported positive associations between avoidance and depression, others reported null findings.

Mikulincer and Shaver (2007) noted that although anxiety seems to be more strongly associated with depression than avoidance, this discrepancy is less pronounced when researchers examined how anxiety and avoidance relates to different facets of depression. Thus, anxiously attached individuals' chronic preoccupation with emotional closeness and reassurance-seeking from relationship partners make them more vulnerable to interpersonal facets of depression, such as being overly dependent and lacking autonomy. Conversely, avoidant individuals' excessive preference for self-reliance makes them more vulnerable to intrapersonal facets of depression, such as perfectionism or self-criticism. Indeed, research has shown that attachment anxiety was positively correlated with dependency, concern about what others think, and pleasing others; whereas attachment avoidance was positively correlated with perfectionism, need for control, and defensive separation.

Studies conducted with clinically depressed individuals found similar positive associations between insecure attachment and depression. Using self-report measures, several studies found that fearful-avoidant individuals (those who are high on both attachment anxiety and avoidance) were more likely to suffer from major depression. Findings based on the AAI were less consistent. Whereas some researchers found individuals diagnosed with depression to be more often classified as having a dismissing state of mind, other researchers found that these individuals were actually more likely to be classified as having a preoccupied state of mind.

Various explanations were suggested to account for these conflicting findings. One of these explanations is related to the studies' inclusion criteria for the depressed sample. Dozier, Stovall-McClough, and Albus (2008) noted that studies excluding individuals with comorbid internalizing symptoms (such as symptoms of borderline personality disorder) found dismissing state of mind to be associated with depression. In contrast, studies excluding individuals with comorbid externalizing symptoms (such as symptoms of conduct disorder) found preoccupied state of mind to be associated with depression. Another explanation is the depression subtype. Research has shown that patients with bipolar disorder were more likely to be classified as dismissing as compared to patients with major depressive disorder or dysthymia.

Longitudinal Studies

In line with cross-sectional findings, longitudinal investigations also confirmed the hypothesis that insecure attachment predicts depressive symptoms. Using self-report measures, numerous researchers reported that during college years (a time of transitioning to young adulthood for many people), attachment insecurity prospectively predicts depressive symptoms assessed 6 weeks to 2 years later. Longitudinal studies conducted with participants experiencing other important life transitions also found a positive correlation of attachment insecurity and level of depressive symptoms. For example, women's attachment anxiety assessed prenatally was found to predict elevated postpartum depressive symptoms. Moreover, one's partner's attachment style was also found to affect one's own levels of depression. For example, husbands' attachment security predicted reduction in wives' depressive symptoms over a 6-month period; whereas husbands' avoidant attachment was found to be positively associated with the persistence of wives' depressive symptoms.

Direction of the Relationship

Although it is theoretically more plausible to expect that attachment insecurity leads to depression, it may also be the case that depression heightens attachment insecurity. Findings from recent experimental studies have favored the former hypothesis over the latter one. In one of these studies, participants were primed with either the phrase "Mommy and I are one" (a prime which might create a sense of closeness to an attachment figure) or an attachment-unrelated control phrase, and then their depressive symptoms were assessed using a self-report measure. The negative correlation between attachment security and depressive symptoms was found to be stronger among participants primed with the attachment-related phrase as compared to those primed with the control phrase. This finding provides some support for the hypothesis that a sense of security lowers depressive symptoms. One explanation for this finding can be that the security prime strengthens the association circuits in memory related to maternal closeness and security, and weakens the association circuits related to negative self views.

A different way to examine the direction of the link between attachment and depression is by investigating whether experimentally increasing depressive mood would lower the sense of attachment security. In studies using this strategy, participants were exposed to either a depressive, neutral, or happy mood induction, and then their attachment styles were assessed. Results of these studies revealed that there were no self-reported or interview-based attachment style differences between the different mood induction conditions (depressed vs. happy or neutral). Taken together, these studies provide two preliminary conclusions: (a) There might be a causal link between attachment insecurity and depression; and (b) the direction of the link seems to be such that changes in attachment insecurity are likely to bring changes in depressive symptoms. Before a more decisive conclusion could be drawn, however, more empirical evidence showing that elevation of the sense of attachment security can reduce depressive symptoms is needed.

Process Models

Recently, researchers have started to investigate the process underlying the relationship between attachment insecurities and depression. This line of research identified many mediating factors. Among cognitive factors, low self-esteem, dysfunctional attitudes about one's self-worth, low self-reinforcement (ability to value, encourage, and support oneself), and maladaptive perfectionism were found to mediate the relationship between both types of insecure attachment and depressive symptoms. When looking separately at each of the insecurities, changes in self-efficacy beliefs, self-concealment (predisposition to conceal intimate and negative personal information), and self-splitting (inability to integrate different images of oneself) were found to mediate only the relationship between attachment anxiety and depressive symptoms, whereas incoherency and low emotional intensity of autobiographical memories were found to mediate the relationship between attachment avoidance and depressive symptoms.

Among interpersonal factors, negative events in interactions with close others (family members, peers, and romantic partners), and inability to meet autonomy and relatedness needs were found to mediate the association between both types of attachment insecurities and depressive symptoms. Loneliness and need for reassurance were found to mediate the association between attachment anxiety and depressive symptoms, whereas discomfort with self-disclosure was found to mediate the association between attachment avoidance and depressive symptoms. Similarly, different emotion regulation strategies were found to mediate the links between each of the attachment insecurities and depressive symptoms. Thus, emotional reactivity (a strategy characterized by hypersensitivity to stimuli in the environment) was found to mediate the association between attachment anxiety and depressive symptoms, whereas emotional cutoff (a strategy characterized by distancing from others in times of intense emotional experiences) was found to mediate the association between attachment avoidance and depressive symptoms.

Unfavorable contextual factors were also found to moderate the association between attachment insecurities and depressive symptoms. Insecure people, who usually lack psychological resources to cope effectively with stress, would be expected to be more likely to develop depression when they face socioeconomic, environmental, or interpersonal stressors. In line with this reasoning, anxious women who experienced stressful life events were found to show higher levels of depressive symptoms as compared to anxious women who did not experience such stress.

Finally, dyadic factors may interact with attachment security to affect depressive symptoms. Thus, not only that one's attachment style may affect his or her partner's levels of depression (as mentioned above), but dyadic factors may moderate this link. For example, it was found in married couples that spouses' attachment insecurity was related to lower depressive symptoms when marital satisfaction was high than when it was low. Similarly, husbands' high social support and low anger weakened the effects of wives' attachment anxiety on their own postpartum depressive symptoms. When examining husbands' depressive symptoms, it was found that husbands' perceptions of their wives as unresponsive decreased the husbands' sense of attachment security, which, in turn, increased their depressive symptoms. Taken together, these findings indicate that having a secure and supporting partner mitigates the effects of having an insecure attachment style on depression; whereas having an insecure and unresponsive partner exacerbates these effects.

Attachment and Response to Treatment of Depression

Individual differences in attachment style were also found to be associated with responses to therapy aiming to alleviate depression. Studies conducted with people who participated in therapy programs for major depression found that fearful avoidance was negatively associated with remission and positively associated with time to stabilization (time to consistently obtain low-depressive symptom scores) among remitted individuals.

EMRE SELCUK AND OMRI GILLATH

See also

Anaclitic and Introjective Depression
Early Adversity
Internal Working Models
Maltreatment

References

Bowlby, J. (1980). *Attachment and loss: Vol. 3. Sadness and depression.* New York: Basic Books.
Dozier, M., Stovall-McClough, K. C., & Albus, K. E. (2008). Attachment and psychopathology in adulthood. In J. Cassidy & P. R. Shaver (Eds.), *Handbook of attachment: Theory, research, and clinical applications* (2nd ed., pp. 718–744). New York: Guilford Press.
Mikulincer, M., & Shaver, P. R. (2007). *Attachment patterns in adulthood: Structure, dynamics, and change.* New York: Guilford Press.

Attention

Distractions constantly challenge our ability to stay on task—a "New E-mail Message" note appears on your computer screen as you attempt to work; a ringing cell phone distracts your driving. The ability to achieve and maintain goal-focused behavior in the face of distraction is critical for surviving and thriving in our world. This highlights the importance of attention, which is the ability to select what is most relevant for current task goals. Attention developed to help the brain solve a computational problem of information overload. For example, during perception of natural scenes, there is a multitude of incoming sensory input, which cannot all be fully analyzed by a limited-capacity perceptual system within the human brain. Under these circumstances, attention serves to restrict sensory processing in favor of the most relevant subset of items in order to ensure that the behavior of the organism is guided by the most relevant information.

Attention is a multidimensional system known to be dysfunctional in depression (Ingram, 1990). Therefore, understanding the computational structure and neuroanatomical basis of attention is a crucial step in treating attentional dysfunction associated with depression. Here, we review what is known about attention from this body of research and introduce our work investigating the influence of mindfulness training on the attention system. Our initial studies suggest that mindfulness training may improve attention by improving the ability to select information. We explore the hypothesis that these attentional effects may contribute to the efficacy of mindfulness-based clinical interventions in the treatment of depression relapse.

The Human Attention System

Attention comprises three functionally and neuroanatomically distinct cognitive networks. These networks carry out the operations of alerting, orienting, and conflict monitoring. Alerting consists of achieving and maintaining a vigilant or alert state of preparedness; orienting restricts processing to the subset of inputs that are relevant for the current task goals; and conflict monitoring prioritizes among competing tasks and resolves conflict between goals and performance. Two basic paradigms have been used to investigate attentional subsystems: the attentional spatial cuing paradigm and the flanker paradigm (see Fan, McCandliss, Sommer, Raz, & Posner, 2002, for an overview).

Attentional spatial cuing paradigms provide a means to behaviorally index attentional alerting and orienting. In this paradigm, participants sit at a computer and perform a visual computer task similar to a simple video game. They are to attempt to detect a target that is presented after either informative or neutral spatial cues. Informative cues provide spatial information regarding the target location with high probability. Neutral cues signal the imminent appearance of a target but provide no spatial information regarding its location. Neutral cues confer an attentional advantage when compared to no-cue trials. This advantage in performance is thought to be due to *alerting*. The neutral, so-called warning cue increases arousal signifying that a target is forthcoming. Comparisons of performance on trials with informative cues versus neutral cues assess orienting. Performance is typically fastest and most accurate for targets whose location had been correctly predicted by an informative cue (valid cue) and slowest and least accurate for targets whose location had been incorrectly predicted by the cue (invalid cue). The advantage in performance for valid relative to neutral cues, referred to as the validity effect, is due to orienting of spatial attention as directed by the cue prior to the target's appearance. The disadvantage in performance for invalid relative to neutral cues, referred to as the invalidity effect, is due to the cost of recovery of attention after orienting to the wrong location. The validity and invalidity effects have been used to further characterize the orienting subsystem as comprising attentional engagement at the cue location, disengagement when the cue location is misleading, and moving of attentional focus (often referred to as a spotlight) to the appropriate location after disengagement.

Flanker paradigms provide a means to behaviorally index conflict monitoring by selectively manipulating the presence or absence of response competition while keeping other task demands constant. In this simple visual computer task, a target is to be identified by a two-alternative forced-choice method (e.g., determine if the arrow "<" is left or right facing). The target is surrounded by task-irrelevant flankers that are either of the same response category (<<<) as the target or of another response category (><>). Responses in trials in which the flanking stimuli indicate a different response than the central stimulus (incongruent condition) are significantly slower than those in trials in which all stimuli indicate the same response (congruent condition). Longer response times are attributed to the need for greater conflict resolution and monitoring during incongruent relative to congruent trials.

Recently, the Attention Network Test (ANT) has been devised to identify behavioral and neural indices of alerting, orienting, and conflict monitoring during a single task (Fan et al., 2002). The task manipulates attentional cuing (valid, neutral, and no-cues) as well as the type of target (congruent or incongruent flanker). Alerting is indexed by subtracting performance measures on neutral cue trials from no-cue trials. Orienting is indexed by subtracting performance measures on spatial cue trials from neutral cue trials. Conflict monitoring is indexed by subtracting performance measures on congruent from incongruent target trials. Our studies of the effects of meditation training on attention use this task (see below).

Attention With Mindfulness Training

While the attention system developed over evolutionary history as a means of solving information overload from the external environment, mindfulness or meditation practices may have developed over human history as a means of solving the overload suffered by the fragile internal environment of our mental landscape as it becomes easily flooded by sensations, thoughts, emotions, and memories.

Numerous meditation texts distinguish between two disparate forms of attention, described as *concentrative* and *receptive*, that can be trained (see Lutz, Slagter, Dunne, & Davidson, 2008, for a review). One meditation practice used to cultivate concentrative attention begins with instructions to maintain attention on the breath. If attention wanders from the breath, it is to be gently returned. Another meditation practice involves instruction to experience the present moment without orienting, directing, or limiting attention in any way. Practitioners are to be receptive to any stimulus (e.g., sounds, lights, tactile sensations, thoughts, memories, emotions) that engages attention while keeping awareness neutral and unreactive. This exercise is used to cultivate receptive attention. Thus, while attention to the present moment of experience is a critical aspect of meditation instruction, in general, the particular way in which this instruction guides practitioners to attend can differ across meditation exercises.

There are two dimensions along which meditation texts distinguish concentrative and receptive attention: (a) the aperture of attentional focus and (b) the intensity of attentional focus. Concentrative practices direct subjects to hold a very narrow focus on the contents of attention. Examples across meditation traditions include a repeated sound, an imagined image, or a specific body sensation such as the breath. These types of practices emphasize the narrowing of attention and are sometimes described as single-pointed practices, in that attention is to be focused very closely on a specific focus or a single point. Receptive practices, in contrast, direct subjects to hold a very broad aperture of attentional focus. For example, instruction may direct one to attend to "all sounds" without specifying the particular sound on which attention should be focused. The concept of an attentional aperture is akin to cognitive psychological discussion of the attentional "zoom lens" in which the spatial extent of attention is thought be modulated intentionally (see Eriksen & St. James, 1986). The second dimension of attention described in mindfulness texts is the intensity of the attentional focus. Some traditions encourage a more intense focus on the object of the meditation, while others emphasize an effortless engagement of attention. Typically, concentrative practices have a narrow attentional aperture and a higher intensity of focus. Concentrative training is associated with facilitated ease of attentional engagement. In contrast, receptive attention has the features of having a broad attentional aperture, akin to keeping attention ready for some unspecified event, and having low intensity of focus, which results in a less-intense engagement and greater ease of

disengagement from a stimulus. Importantly, each of these dimensions is considered to be along a continuum.

In our recent work (Jha, Krompinger, & Baime, 2007) we examined the influence of meditation training on the functioning of specific attentional subsystems. Participants receiving meditation training in the form of participation in an 8-week mindfulness-based stress reduction (MBSR) course or a 1-month meditation retreat (attended by experienced meditators) performed the Attention Network Test before and after training. Their performance was contrasted with the performance of control subjects who were also tested at two time points. We investigated two main hypotheses: (a) We hypothesized that prior experience with, and training in, concentrative meditation techniques would correspond to greater efficiency in the functioning of voluntary top-down attentional selection. Positive support for this hypothesis was observed on two counts. First, retreat participants, who were experienced with concentrative meditation prior to training, demonstrated better conflict monitoring (reduced flanker interference), compared to meditation-naïve subjects. Second, after meditation training, MBSR participants improved in their orienting performance relative to control participants. Since both conflict monitoring and orienting are forms of voluntary attentional selection, our results suggest that concentrative meditation may indeed alter functioning of voluntary response- and input-level selection processes. (b) We hypothesized that prior experience with concentrative meditation may allow for the emergence of receptive attention after training. Receptive attention corresponds to attentional readiness and alerting. We found that after training, not only did retreat participants differ in their alerting performance compared to control and MBSR participants, but the magnitude of their alerting scores after training was correlated with prior meditation experience. Greater experience corresponded with reduced alerting scores, indicating that attention was in a more readied state when no warning about target onset was provided. Thus, our results suggest that meditation training improves performance on specific conditions of the attention network test.

that might result in the best clinical outcomes.

AMISHI P. JHA, MICHAEL J. BAIME, AND
KARTIK K. SREENIVASAN

Attention, Mindfulness Training, and Depression

In recent years, a dysregulation of the attention system has been increasingly identified as a hallmark of clinical depression. Specifically, the attentional focus of depressed individuals tends to be inordinately self-related, and this self-focus may play a role in prolonging depressive symptoms such as rumination (Ingram, 1990). Rumination is also strongly associated with depression (Nolen-Hoeksema, 2000) and mindfulness trains individuals to refocus their attention in a manner that may counteract the tendency toward rumination (Ramel, Goldin, Carmona, & McQuaid, 2004). A related finding is that patients with depression appear to focus their attention on items in the environment with a negative emotional valence. These pieces of evidence have resulted in a focused effort to treat symptoms of depression with techniques designed to improve components of the attention system.

Mindfulness-based cognitive therapy (MBCT) has already been shown to reduce relapse and recurrence of depressive episodes in certain depressed populations (for a review see, Ma & Teasdale, 2004, and Segal, this volume). MBCT combines techniques from MSBR courses along with elements of cognitive behavioral therapy. As reviewed above, mindfulness-based techniques are known to modulate different aspects of the attention system, suggesting that the therapeutic effects of MBCT may arise from its ability to improve attention so that it is directed analytically at the self to improve awareness of negative thinking patterns. Future research on the interface of attention, mindfulness-training, and depression will better reveal the correspondence between changes in attentional engagement and disengagement tied to specific mindfulness-based techniques

See also

Memory Processes
Mindfulness-Based Cognitive
Therapy
Rumination
Self-Focused Attention

References

Eriksen, C. W., & St. James, J. D. (1986). Visual attention within and around the field of focal attention: A zoom lens model. *Perception and Psychophysics, 40,* 225–240.

Fan, J., McCandliss, B. D., Sommer, T., Raz, A., & Posner, M. I. (2002). Testing the efficiency and independence of attentional networks. *Journal of Cognitive Neuroscience, 14,* 340–347.

Ingram, R. E. (1990). Self-focused attention in clinical disorders: Review and a conceptual model. *Psychological Bulletin, 107,* 156–176.

Jha, A. P., Krompinger, J., & Baime, M. J. (2007). Mindfulness training modifies subsystems of attention. *Cognitive Affective and Behavioral Neuroscience, 7,* 109–119.

Lutz, A., Slagter, H. A., Dunne, J. D., & Davidson, R. J. (2008). Cognitive-emotional interactions: Attention regulation and monitoring in meditation. *Trends in Cognitive Sciences, 12,* 163–169.

Ma, S. H., & Teasdale, J. D. (2004). Mindfulness-based cognitive therapy for depression: Replication and exploration of differential relapse prevention effects. *Journal of Consulting and Clinical Psychology, 72,* 31–40.

Nolen-Hoeksema, S. (2000). The role of rumination in depressive disorders and mixed anxiety/depressive symptoms. *Journal of Abnormal Psychology, 109,* 504–511.

Ramal, W., Goldin, P. R., Carmona, P. E., & McQuaid, J. R. (2004). The effects of mindfulness meditation on cognitive processes and affect in patients with past depression. *Cognitive Therapy and Research, 28,* 433–455.

Attention Deficit Hyperactivity Disorder

Children, adolescents, and adults diagnosed with attention deficit hyperactivity disorder (ADHD) have considerably higher rates of comorbidity with certain other psychiatric disorders than would be expected from the base rates of those disorders in the population at large (Barkley, Murphy, & Fisher, 2008). At least 80% or more of ADHD cases have at least one other disorder, and 50% or more may have two other disorders (Barkley et al., 2008). Major depression is among those disorders having some relationship to ADHD, though the relative association of these disorders varies as a function of whether samples are children or adults and whether they are ascertained through clinic referrals or epidemiological samples.

Studies of Children

Symptoms of depression are often elevated among clinical samples of children with ADHD (Jensen, Martin, & Cantwell, 1997), with the highest levels occurring among those children having comorbid aggression (or oppositional defiant disorder/conduct disorder; ODD/CD). Symptoms reflecting low self-esteem, however, are chiefly associated with aggressiveness and particularly depression in ADHD samples and are otherwise not especially problematic when ADHD is found alone (Bussing, Zima, & Perwien, 2000).

A review of this association found between 15% and 75% of ADHD cases had depression as a comorbidity (Spencer, Wilens, Biederman, Wozniak, & Crawford, 2000). However, most studies reported rates of 9% to 32% of children with ADHD having major depressive disorder (Biederman, Newcorn, & Sprich, 1991). Up to 20% of children with ADHD seen in a pediatrics clinic and up to 38% of those seen in a psychiatric clinic may have comorbid major depressive disorder (Spencer et al., 2000). Pfiffner and colleagues (1999) studied clinic-referred boys with ADHD and a control group referred to the same outpatient clinic but not diagnosed as ADHD. They found that while just 5% of ADHD cases had depression alone (vs. 11% of boys without ADHD), another 21% had depression with an anxiety disorder (vs. 15% of the psychiatric control group). All of this suggests a clear risk of depression or frank major depressive disorder in 25% to 30% of children with ADHD.

Wilens et al. (2002) reported that dysthymia occurred in 5% of both preschool- and school-age groups, while major depressive disorder was diagnosed in nearly half of their samples, 42% and 47%, respectively—risks higher than found by most other researchers. Biederman, Mick, and Faraone (1998) have argued that this association reflects an overlap of two clinical disorders and that the depression evident in ADHD is not just a reflection of demoralization over failures in major life activities. Yet early longitudinal studies of children with ADHD followed to adulthood did not report significantly elevated rates of depression or other mood disorders (e.g., Spencer et al., 2000). A more recent follow-up study (Fischer, Barkley, Smallish, & Fletcher, 2002), in contrast, found that 27% of these children had major depressive disorder by young adulthood. This risk had dropped substantially by the age 27 follow-up, however, and its presence was mediated by CD in adolescence and young adulthood and the persistence of ADHD to age 27 (Barkley et al., 2008). However, Peterson, Pine, Cohen, and Brook (2001) found that ADHD was consistently related to depression across four follow-up periods from childhood to young adulthood.

The inverse relationship of ADHD risk in cases of depression in children is far less studied. But the weight of the available evidence suggests some elevated risk of ADHD among youths diagnosed with depression (Spencer et al., 2000). Early data suggest, however, that rates of ADHD were not significantly elevated, but levels of other disruptive behavior, such as oppositional and conduct problems were so.

Large studies of community samples can shed further light on the existence and nature of this comorbid relationship in children. In their meta-analysis of such studies, Angold, Costello, and Erkanli (1999) reported a median odds ratio of 5.5 for the comorbidity of ADHD and major depressive disorder, ranging from 3.5 to 8.4 and being significantly greater than that seen between ADHD and anxiety disorders, noted above. Undoubtedly, then, ADHD and major depressive disorder show a greater level of association than expected by chance alone. But depression is also strongly associated with ODD/CD and anxiety, raising the possibility that it is the presence of one of these latter disorders that mediates the relationship between ADHD and major depressive disorder, as was suggested in the follow-up study by Fischer and colleagues (2002), where lifetime CD predicted occurrence of major depressive disorder. This was also evident in evidence provided by Angold and colleagues (1999), where the association of ADHD with depression was greatly reduced when controlling for comorbidity of ADHD with ODD/CD and with anxiety. In other words, the relationship of ADHD and depression may be an epiphenomenon (Angold et al., 1999) that arises only because of the association of ADHD with ODD/CD and ADHD with anxiety—absent these other two disorders, ADHD may not have an association with depression.

The comorbidity of depression along with ADHD is often associated with a poorer outcome than either disorder alone (Spencer et al., 2000). This comorbidity is also a marker for a history of greater family and personal stress, and greater parental symptoms of depression and mood disorders (see Jensen et al., 1997, and Spencer et al., 2000, for reviews). Though not well established, this group of comorbid children may respond better to antidepressants than do those ADHD children without comorbidity for internalizing symptoms (Jensen et al., 1997). Unlike anxiety disorders, major depression does demonstrate a familial linkage with ADHD such that risk for one disorder in a child predisposes to risk for the other disorder not only in these children but also among biological family members of the comorbid children (Biederman, Faraone, & Lapey, 1992). Thus, ADHD and major depressive disorder may share underlying familial etiological factors (Spencer et al., 2000). As noted above, though, CD is also elevated among these comorbid children and among their family members and could, in part, explain the link of ADHD with major depressive disorder. Obviously the jury is not in yet on the reason why ADHD and depression share such an elevated comorbidity, but the overlap of both with CD provides one possible explanation.

Studies of Adults

Approximately 16% to 31% of adults meeting ADHD diagnostic criteria also have major depressive disorder (Barkley, Murphy, & Kwasnik, 1996). Indeed, one study of Norwegian adults with ADHD reported a lifetime prevalence of 53% and current prevalence of 9% for major depression (Torgersen, Gjervan, & Rasmussen, 2006), although its sample appeared to have quite severe ADHD, among other disorders. Dysthymia, a milder form of depression, has been reported to occur in 19% to 37% of clinic-referred adults diagnosed with ADHD (Murphy, Barkley, & Bush, 2002). Even so, a few studies comparing clinic-referred adults with ADHD to adults seen at the same clinic without ADHD did not find a higher incidence of major depression among the ADHD group (Barkley et al., 2008), questioning whether the link of ADHD and depression is partly an artifact of clinic-referral status. But most studies did find elevated ratings of depressive symptoms or even diagnosable dysthymia in ADHD adults relative to clinic and community control groups nonetheless, even if frank major depressive disorder was not present (Barkley et al., 2008). Thus, not only is the risk of major depression elevated in adults with ADHD, but this is even more so with its milder variant of dysthymia. Such an association of ADHD with risk for depressive symptoms and disorders was recently found in two large epidemiological studies of general population samples of adults, suggesting that there is true comorbidity between ADHD and these disorders (Kessler et al., 2006; Secnik, Swensen, & Lage, 2005). Rucklidge and Kaplan (1997) reported one of the few studies of women with ADHD and found them to report more symptoms of depression, anxiety, stress, and low self-esteem, and a more external locus of control than did women in the control group. But psychiatric diagnoses were not reported in this study, making it difficult to compare to earlier research using such diagnoses.

In a study of parents of ADHD children who also have ADHD, Minde and colleagues (2003) did not find a greater prevalence of major depression relative to a control group of parents (15% vs. 8%). The study, however, used small samples, limiting its representation of parents with ADHD and its statistical power to detect group differences. It also did not find elevated rates of antisocial personality disorder, which might be a potential moderator between ADHD and depression. In contrast, the much larger study of parents with ADHD who also had children with ADHD by McGough et al. (2005) did find greater mood disorders than in their comparison group.

There is a significant elevation in risk for suicidal thinking in children with ADHD, particularly during high school (see Barkley et al., 2008, for a review). But ADHD is especially associated with risk of a suicide attempt during this period if the individual has contemplated suicide, perhaps due to the marked impulsiveness associated with ADHD. The likelihood of suicidal thinking and attempts appear to decline by age 27, though suicidal thinking in particular remains somewhat elevated over that seen in control samples. The risk for suicidality in ADHD cases is largely a function of the presence of major depressive disorder, and to a lesser extent CD and severity of earlier or concurrent ADHD symptoms (Barkley et al., 2008).

What of the inverse relationship of ADHD in cases of depression in adults? A study of adults with major depressive disorder found that 16% self-reported symptoms from childhood sufficient to warrant a retrospective diagnosis of ADHD, while 12% reported persistence of these symptoms into adulthood (Alpert et al., 1996). Both figures for ADHD risk are greater than population prevalence estimates for either children or adults. But the relationship of ADHD in cases of depression seems to be considerably less striking than is the risk for depression in cases of ADHD.

In general, the weight of the evidence suggests a significant relationship between ADHD in adults and risk for depression, as it does in children with the disorder. This risk may be partly mediated by the comorbidity of both disorders with CD and antisocial personality disorder. While some genetic vulnerability to depression may exist in cases of ADHD and their biological family members, this may require exposure to repeated stress, social disruption, or other environmental disadvantage in order for depression to become manifest or to rise to the level of diagnosable major depressive disorder. These social factors are also associated with CD and antisocial personality disorder and could mediate this three-way linkage among disorders.

RUSSEL A. BARKLEY

See Also

Adolescent Depression
Childhood Depression
Externalizing Disorders
Internalizing Disorders

References

Alpert, J. E., Maddocks, A., Nierenberg, A. A., O'Sullivan, R., Pava, J. A., Worthington, J. J., et al. (1996). Attention deficit hyperactivity disorder in childhood among adults with major depression. *Psychiatry Research, 62,* 213–219.

Angold, A., Costello, E. J., & Erkanli, A. (1999). Comorbidity. *Journal of Child Psychology and Psychiatry, 40,* 57–88.

Barkley, R. A., Murphy, K. R., & Fischer, M. (2008). *ADHD in adults: What the science says.* New York: Guilford Press.

Barkley, R. A., Murphy, K. R., & Kwasnik, D. (1996). Psychological adjustment and adaptive impairments in young adults with ADHD. *Journal of Attention Disorders, 1,* 41–54.

Biederman, J., Faraone, S. V., & Lapey, K. (1992). Comorbidity of diagnosis in attention-deficit hyperactivity disorder. In G. Weiss (Ed.), *Child and adolescent psychiatry clinics in North America: Attention deficit disorder* (pp. 335–360). Philadelphia: W. B. Saunders.

Biederman, J., Newcorn, J., & Sprich, S. (1991). Comorbidity of attention deficit hyperactivity disorder with conduct, depressive, anxiety, and other disorders. *American Journal of Psychiatry, 148*, 564–577.

Bussing, R., Zima, B. T., & Perwien, A. R. (2000). Self-esteem in special education children with ADHD: Relationship to disorder characteristics and medication use. *Journal of the American Academy of Child and Adolescent Psychiatry, 39*, 1260–1269.

Fischer, M., Barkley, R. A., Smallish, L., & Fletcher, K. (2002). Young adult follow-up of hyperactive children: Self-reported psychiatric disorders, comorbidity, and the role of childhood conduct problems. *Journal of Abnormal Child Psychology, 30*, 463–475.

Jensen, P. S., Martin, D., & Cantwell, D. P. (1997). Comorbidity in ADHD: Implications for research, practice, and DSM-V. *Journal of the American Academy of Child and Adolescent Psychiatry, 36*, 1065–1079.

Kessler, R. C., Adler, L., Barkley, R. A., Biederman, J., Conners, C. K., Demler, O., et al. (2006). The prevalence and correlates of adult ADHD in the United States: Results from the National Comorbidity Survey Replication. *American Journal of Psychiatry, 163*, 716–723.

McGough, J. J., Smalley, S. L., McCracken, J. T., Yang, M., Del'Homme, M., Lynn, D. E., et al. (2005). Psychiatric comorbidity in adult attention deficit hyperactivity disorder: Findings from multiplex families. *American Journal of Psychiatry, 162*, 1621–1627.

Minde, K., Eakin, L., Hechtman, L., Ochs, E., Bouffard, R., Greenfield, B., et al. (2003). The psychosocial functioning of children and spouses of adults with ADHD. *Journal of Child Psychology and Psychiatry, 44*, 637–646.

Murphy, K. R., Barkley, R. A., & Bush, T. (2002). Young adults with ADHD: Subtype differences in comorbidity, educational, and clinical history. *Journal of Nervous and Mental Disease, 190*, 147–157.

Peterson, B. S., Pine, D. S., Cohen, P., & Brook, J. S. (2001). Prospective, longitudinal study of tic, obsessive-compulsive, and attention-deficit/hyperactivity disorders in an epidemiological sample. *Journal of the American Academy of Child and Adolescent Psychiatry, 40*, 685–695.

Pfiffner, L. J., McBurnett, K., Lahey, B. B., Loeber, R., Green, S., Frick, P. J., et al. (1999). Association of parental psychopathology to the comorbid disorders of boys with attention-deficit hyperactivity disorder. *Journal of Consulting and Clinical Psychology, 67*, 881–893.

Rucklidge, J. J., & Kaplan, B. J. (1997). Psychological functioning of women identified in adulthood with attention-deficit/hyperactivity disorder. *Journal of Attention Disorders, 2*, 167–176.

Secnik, K., Swensen, A., & Lage, M. J. (2005). Comorbidities and costs of adult patients diagnosed with attention-deficit hyperactivity disorder. *Pharmacoeconomics, 23*, 93–102.

Spencer, T., Wilens, T., Biederman, J., Woniak, J., & Harding-Crawford, M. (2000). Attention-deficit/hyperactivity disorder with mood disorders. In T. E. Brown (Ed.), *Attention-deficit disorders and comorbidities in children, adolescents, and adults* (pp. 79–124). Washington, DC: American Psychiatric Press.

Torgersen, T., Gjervan, B., & Rasmussen, K. (2006). ADHD in adults: A study of clinical characteristics, impairment, and comorbidity. *Nordic Journal of Psychiatry, 60*, 38–43.

Treuting, J. J., & Hinshaw, S. P. (2001). Depression and self-esteem in boys with attention-deficit/hyperactivity disorder: associations with comorbid aggression and explanatory attributional mechanisms. *Journal of Abnormal Child Psychology, 29*, 23–39.

Wilens, T. E., Biederman, J., Brown, S., Tanguay, S., Monuteaux, M. C., Blake, C., et al. (2002). Psychiatric comorbidity and functioning in clinically-referred preschool children and school-age youth with ADHD. *Journal of the American Academy of Child and Adolescent Psychiatry, 41*, 262–268.

Attributional Style

Attributional style, also called explanatory style, is a term used to describe the types of attributions, or causes, that people tend to give for events that happen to them. It is categorized along three dimensions: (a) internal-external (whether people tend to attribute the causes of things to themselves or others, (b) stable-transient (whether people tend to view the causes of events as remaining constant or as things that will change over time, and (c) global-specific (whether people tend to view the causes of situations as things that are present across situations or specific to individual situations.

Beck (1972) observed that when something negative happens "[a depression-vulnerable] individual interprets an experience as representing a personal defeat or thwarting; He attributes this defeat to some defect in himself. . . . He sees the trait as an intrinsic part of him. . . . He sees no hope of changing" (p. 278). Indeed, it has repeatedly been found that people who are depressed are more likely to make internal, stable, and global attributions for negative events than never-depressed people (see Sweeney, Anderson, & Bailey, 1986, for a review). For example, if a depressed person fails an exam, she might say that she failed the exam because she is stupid (internal), that she will always be stupid (stable), and that she is stupid in everything she does (global). However, in the same situation a nondepressed person might say that she failed the exam because her neighbors kept her up late the night before the exam (external), that this is unlikely to happen again (transient), and that it will not affect her performance in other courses or other exams (specific). Conversely, depressed people are more likely to make external, transient, and specific attributions for positive events than are never-depressed individuals. If a depressed person receives an *A* on an exam, she might attribute the *A* to getting lucky (external), just this once (transient) and in just this class (specific), whereas a nondepressed person might attribute the *A* to being smart (internal), most of the time (stable) in most things she does (global). A meta-analysis of attributional style in children and adolescents has revealed similar findings in that higher levels of depressive symptoms are associated with internal, stable, and global attributions for negative events, and external, transient, and specific attributions for positive events (Gladstone & Kaslow, 1995).

Attributional style is most commonly assessed in adults using the Attributional Styles Questionnaire (Peterson et al., 1982) and the Expanded Attributional Styles Questionnaire-Revised (Peterson & Villanova, 1988). In children it is measured using the Children's Attributional Style Questionnaire (Kaslow, Rehm, & Siegel, 1984), the Children's Attributional Styles Questionnaire–Revised (Thompson, Kaslow, Weiss, & Nolen-Hoeksema, 1998), and the Children's Attributional Styles Questionnaire Interview (Conley, Haines, Hilt, & Metalsky, 2001). The measures ask people to imagine that a variety of hypothetical situations have happened to them and then to imagine the causes of those events. After causes are identified, people rate the imagined causes along internal-external, stable-transient, and global-specific dimensions.

The findings that depressed people make internal, stable, and global attributions for negative events are quite robust within the research literature. Some researchers have suggested that the depressive attributional style is a causal factor in depression. In addition, it has been proposed that it may characterize a "hopelessness subtype" of depression, and a depressive attributional style is widely recognized as serving to maintain the length of depressive episodes.

There are several exceptions to the findings regarding depressive attributional style. Recent research suggests that flexibility of attributional style may be more predictive of depression than the types of attributions made (Fresco, Tytwinski, & Craighead, 2007). In another study of dysphoric participants, it was found that those with predominantly hostile mood tended to make external attributions, while those with predominantly sad mood evidenced the more typical internal, stable, and global depressive attributional style (Scott, Ingram, & Shadel, 2003). Thus, it is possible that even within depression, mood states are important to consider when assessing attributional style.

DANA STEIDTMANN

See also

Attributional Theories of Depression
Cognitive Theories of Depression
Hopelessness

References

Beck, A. T. (1972). *Depression*. Philadelphia: University of Pennsylvania Press.

Conley, C. S., Haines, B. A., Hilt, L. M., & Metalsky, G. I. (2001). The Children's Attributional Style Interview: Developmental tests of cognitive diathesis-stress theories of depression. *Journal of Abnormal Child Psychology, 29,* 445–463.

Fresco, D. M., Tytwinski, N. K., & Craighead, L. W. (2007). Explanatory flexibility and negative life events interact to predict depression symptoms. *Journal of Social and Clinical Psychology, 26,* 595–608.

Gladstone, T. R. G., & Kaslow, N. J. (1995). Depression and attributions in children and adolescents: A meta-analytic review. *Journal of Abnormal Child Psychology, 23,* 597–606.

Kaslow, N. J., Rehm, L. P., & Siegel, A. W. (1984). Social-cognitive and cognitive correlate s of depression in children. *Journal of Abnormal Child Psychology, 12,* 605–620.

Peterson, C., Semmel, A., von Bayer, C., Abramson, L. I., Metalsky, G. I., & Seligman, M. E. P. (1982). The Attributional Style Questionnaire. *Cognitive Therapy and Research, 6,* 287–299.

Peterson, C., & Villanova, P. (1988). An expanded Attributional Style Questionnaire. *Journal of Abnormal Psychology, 97*, 87–89.

Scott, W. D., Ingram, R. E., & Shadel, W. G. (2003). Hostile and sad moods in dysphoria: Evidence for cognitive specificity in attributions. *Journal of Social and Clinical Psychology, 22*, 234–253.

Sweeney, P. D., Anderson, K., & Bailey, S. (1986). Attributional style in depression: A meta-analytic review. *Journal of Personality and Social Psychology, 50*, 974–991.

Thompson, M., Kaslow, N. J., Weiss, B., & Nolen-Hoeksema, S. (1998). Children's Attributional Styles Questionnaire–Revised: Psychometric examination. *Psychological Assessment, 10*, 166–170.

Attributional Theories of Depression

According to both the reformulated learned helplessness theory (Abramson, Seligman, & Teasdale, 1978) and the hopelessness theory (Abramson, Metalsky, & Alloy, 1989) of depression, different individuals possess different attributional styles: habitual ways of perceiving the causes of negative events.

Reformulated Learned Helplessness Theory

The reformulated learned helplessness theory (Abramson et al., 1978) operationalizes a pessimistic attributional style as the tendency to attribute the causes of negative events to internal, global, and stable factors. In contrast, the theory operationalizes an optimistic attributional style as the tendency to attribute the causes of negative events to external, specific, and unstable factors. Individuals with a pessimistic attributional style are posited to be at risk for developing depressive symptoms following negative events because they are more likely than other individuals to make depressogenic attributions for such events. Making depressogenic attributions increases the likelihood of developing helplessness expectancies—the belief that one has no control over the occurrence of future events. Once helplessness expectancies develop, depression is inevitable, as helplessness expectancies are viewed as a proximal sufficient cause of depression by the theory.

Hopelessness Theory

According to the hopelessness theory of depression (Abramson et al., 1989), individuals with a pessimistic attributional style exhibit the tendency to attribute the causes of negative events to global and stable factors, whereas individuals with an optimistic attributional style exhibit the tendency to attribute such causes to specific and unstable factors. According to the hopelessness theory, individuals with pessimistic attributional style are more likely than individuals without such styles to make depressogenic inferences about the causes of negative events. Making such inferences increases the likelihood of developing hopelessness—the belief that bad events will occur and good events will not occur coupled with the belief that one can do nothing to change the likelihood of such outcomes. Once hopelessness develops, depression is inevitable, since hopelessness is viewed as a proximal sufficient cause of depression by the theory. Although the focus of this entry is on attributional style as a vulnerability factor to depression, it is important to note that the hopelessness theory elaborates on the reformulated learned helplessness theory by delineating two additional cognitive styles that play a role in the etiology of depression. Individuals with pessimistic cognitive styles about consequences and the self exhibit the tendencies to view negative events as having many disastrous consequences and to view the self as flawed and deficient following negative events. In contrast, individuals with optimistic cognitive styles about the self and consequences exhibit the tendencies to infer that negative consequences will not follow from negative events and to believe that the occurrence of negative events in their life does not mean that they are flawed in any way.

Assessing Attributional Style

Traditionally, most researchers examining the attributional vulnerability hypothesis of the reformulated learned helplessness and hopelessness theories of depression have used some variation of the Attributional Style Questionnaire (ASQ; Peterson et al., 1982) to assess attributional style. The ASQ is a self-report questionnaire that consists of 12 hypothetical life events: 6 negative events and 6 positive events. Participants are asked first to imagine that each event happened to them and next to write down a cause for each event's occurrence. Participants subsequently rate the cause on a 1 to 7 scale along three separate dimensions: internal versus external, global versus specific, and stable versus unstable. Separate composite scores are computed for attributional style for negative and positive events. For both composite scores, higher scores represent more internal, global, and stable attributional styles. As both the reformulated learned helplessness and the hopelessness theories of depression operationalize vulnerability to depression as consisting of the manner in which individuals tend to perceive the causes of negative events, the remainder of this entry focuses on attributional style for negative events. At the same time, it is important to note that although attributional style for positive events has not been implicated in playing a role in the initial development of depression, subsequent research and theory has suggested that it plays a role in the recovery from depression (Needles & Abramson, 1990).

In order to increase the reliability of the original ASQ, expanded versions of the measure containing 12 (Metalsky, Halberstadt, & Abramson, 1987) or 24 (Peterson & Villanova, 1988) hypothetical negative events have been developed. Similarly, to assess cognitive styles about consequences and the self, in addition to attributional style, Abramson, Alloy, and Metalsky (1988b) developed the Cognitive Style Questionnaire. Consistent with the etiological chains proposed by both the reformulated learned helplessness and hopelessness theories of depression, these newer measures only assess attributional style for negative events.

To date, the majority of research examining the attributional vulnerability hypothesis in youth has utilized the Children's Attributional Style Questionnaire (CASQ; Seligman et al., 1984). The CASQ is a forced-choice questionnaire containing 48 items, each consisting of a hypothetical positive or negative event and two possible causes of the event. Children choose the option that best describes the way they would think if that event happened to them. The two choices for each item hold constant two dimensions of attributional style while varying the third. In order to increase the reliability of the CASQ as well as its appropriateness for use with younger children, researchers have recently developed the Children's Attributional Style Interview (CASI; Conley, Haines, Hilt, & Metalsky, 2001). Similar to the ASQ, the CASI allows youth to generate their own causal attributions and then rate each attribution on continuous scales of internality, stability, and globality. In order to make the CASI appropriate for young children, events are illustrated pictorially, and children rate their attributions using a sliding pointer on large, colorful scales with icons representing the concepts of internality, stability, and globality.

Prospective Studies Examining the Association Between Explanatory Style and Depression

Initial research examining the reformulated learned helplessness and hopelessness theories of depression focused on examining either the cross-sectional association between attributional style and depressive symptoms or the main effect of attributional style on change in depressive symptoms over time. Critical reviews of the literature, however, argued that such early studies provided an inadequate examination of the theories, as they failed to examine the theories' central hypothesis: individuals with a pessimistic attributional style are only more likely than other individuals to experience increases in depressive symptoms in the face of negative events; in the absence of such events, individuals with a pessimistic attributional style are no more likely than others to exhibit depression

(Abramson, Alloy, & Metalsky, 1988a; Alloy, Hartlage, & Abramson, 1988). In response to such critiques, the field saw a major shift in methodologies used to test these theories, and prospective diathesis-stress designs became the gold standard. Recent comprehensive reviews of the literature have demonstrated that although inconsistencies exist in the findings of studies, the majority have provided support for the hypothesis that a pessimistic attributional style confers vulnerability to the development of depressive symptoms following the occurrence of negative events in children (Abela & Hankin, 2008), adolescents (Abela & Hankin, 2008), and adults (Abela, Auerbach, & Seligman, 2008).

JOHN R. Z. ABELA AND BENJAMIN L. HANKIN

See also

Attributional Theories of Depression
Cognitive Theories of Depression
Hopelessness

References

Abela, J. R. Z., Auerbach, R. P., & Seligman, M. E. P. (2008). Dispositional pessimism across the lifespan. In K. S. Dobson and D. Dozios (Eds.), *Risk factors in depression* (pp. 197–222). San Diego: Academic Press.

Abela, J. R. Z., & Hankin, B. L. (2008). Cognitive vulnerability to depression in children and adolescents: A developmental psychopathology perspective. In J. R. Z. Abela & B. L. Hankin (Eds.), *Handbook of child and adolescent depression* (pp. 35–78). New York: Guilford Press.

Abramson, L. Y., Alloy, L. B., & Metalsky, G. I. (1988a). The cognitive diathesis-stress theories of depression: Toward an adequate evaluation of the theories' validities. In L. B. Alloy (Ed.), *Cognitive processes in depression* (pp. 3–30). New York: Guilford Press.

Abramson, L. Y., Alloy, L. B., & Metalsky, G. I. (1988b). The Cognitive Style Questionnaire: A measure of the vulnerability featured in the hopelessness theory of depression. Unpublished manuscript, University of Wisconsin–Madison.

Abramson, L. Y, Metalsky, G. I., & Alloy, L. B. (1989). Hopelessness depression: A theory-based subtype of depression. *Psychological Review, 96,* 358–372.

Abramson, L. Y., Seligman, M. E. P., & Teasdale, J. (1978). Learned helplessness in humans: Critique and reformulation. *Journal of Abnormal Psychology, 87,* 49–74.

Alloy, L. B., Hartlage, S., & Abramson, L. Y. (1988). Testing the cognitive diathesis-stress theories of depression: Issues of research design, conceptualization, and assessment. In L. B. Alloy (Ed.), *Cognitive processes in depression* (pp. 31–73). New York: Guilford Press.

Conley, C. S., Haines, B. A., Hilt, L. M., & Metalsky, G. I. (2001). The Children's Attributional Style Interview: Developmental tests of cognitive diathesis-stress theories of depression. *Journal of Abnormal Child Psychology, 29,* 445–463.

Metalsky, G. I., Halberstadt, L. J., & Abramson, L. Y. (1987). Vulnerability to depressive mood reactions: Toward a more powerful test of the diathesis-stress and causal mediation components of the reformulated theory of depression. *Journal of Personality and Social Psychology, 52,* 386–393.

Needles, D. J., & Abramson, L. Y. (1990). Positive life events, attributional style, and hopefulness: Testing a model of recovery from depression. *Journal of Abnormal Psychology, 99,* 156–165.

Peterson, C., Semmel, A., von Baeyer, C., Abramson, L. Y., Metalsky, G. I., & Seligman, M. E. P. (1982). The Attributional Style Questionnaire. *Cognitive Therapy and Research, 6,* 287–300.

Peterson, C., & Villanova, P. (1988). An expanded Attributional Style Questionnaire. *Journal of Abnormal Psychology, 97,* 87–89.

Seligman, M. E. P., Peterson, C., Kaslow, N. J., Tenenbaum, R. L., Alloy, L. B., & Abramson, L. Y. (1984). Attributional style and depressive symptoms among children. *Journal of Abnormal Psychology, 93,* 235–241.

Automatic and Controlled Processing in Depression

John, a 37-year-old man, has suffered several depressive episodes throughout his life. After a problematical marriage, he and his wife, Anne, divorced. He worked as a receptionist when, 3 months ago, the last depressive episode took place. "I think the reason for this last episode was that I felt lonely and there were too many women working at my office. I used to see lots of women but I seemed invisible to them. Furthermore, while trying to work or to chat with any female colleague, I could not get rid of the scene of my last argument with Anne, and this happened over and over, invading my mind without my being able to do anything to avoid it." When asked about the meaning of this situation, John told us: *"It reminded me over and over what I will never be able to get: I will never have a wife, no woman likes me. . . . It's just impossible. My life has been a failure and will always be a failure. . . . It's obvious, I'm not good-looking, I look so miserable . . . pathetic, it's always been that way."*

In his cognitive model of depression, Aaron Beck (1976) suggested that depressed people generate negative products such as images (e.g., "the scene of our last farewell appeared over and over"), thoughts (e.g., "I'm not good-looking"), and inferences (e.g., "I will never have a wife") automatically. These automatic products, which are usually assessed via the verbalizations of the depressed person, would be the reflection of underlying automatic processes. Beck's ideas regarding the processes by which automatic products are generated paralleled the definitional criteria for automatic versus controlled processing developed by cognitive theorists in the 1970s. Automatic processes are operations that (a) take place without requiring attention or conscious awareness, (b) occur in parallel without interfering with other operations or stressing the capacity limitations of the cognitive system, and (c) occur without intention or control. However, effortful processes (a) require attention and thereby take place serially, inhibit other pathways, and are influenced by cognitive capacity limitations; (b) improve with practice; and (c) can be used to produce learning (Hartlage, Alloy, Vázquez, & Dyckman, 1993).

Different lines of empirical research have consistently found that, in fact, depressed persons have difficulty planning, initializing, and monitoring complex goal-directed behaviors in the face of distracting negative information (see Hartlage et al., 1993). Thus, in a broader sense, depressed individuals seem to show a reduced executive control, which leads them, for example, to being unable to control or adequately redirect their attention when negative thoughts or images appear (e.g., "I could not get rid of the scene of my last argument with Anne") or even to retrieve rather overgeneral negative autobiographical memories (e.g., "My life has been a failure").

Are automatic processes also affected in depression? Although the experimental evidence is less robust in this case, there is also empirical evidence suggesting that, in depressed persons as well as in depression-prone individuals, negative cognitions are more easily activated than in normal participants (Lau, Segal, & Williams, 2004). Although clinical observations are not a direct way to measure cognitive processes, John's description of his own mental experiences describes many instances in which negative cognitions seem to be easily activated, and, moreover, he also seems to have difficulties to inhibit those processes once initiated (i.e., problems with controlled or effortful processes). This distinction of a dual processing mechanism has proved to be a valuable tool to understand diverse findings in the literature on various cognitive processes in depression (attention, memory, thinking, etc.).

According to the differentiation of automaticity and control, the statement that biases in depression and anxiety operate on different processing levels that correspond to different cognitive tasks has become a dominant theme. Thus, it has often been stated that anxiety states are more closely related to biases in the automatic processing of threatening material (particularly reflected in attentional tasks), whereas depressive states are characterized by biases in operations of controlled processing (especially reflected in biases of memory; e.g., Matt, Vázquez, & Campbell, 1992). However, some caution is required when establishing a division of this kind. In fact, in most cognitive tasks, there are aspects that require both controlled and automatic processing. For example, although attention has traditionally been considered an automatic process, it also implies effortful processing, such as disengagement. Actually, depressed patients as well as recovered depressed patients seem to have difficulty moving attention away from negative information once it is presented (Joorman & Gotlib, 2007). Moreover, the data about this depression-versus-anxiety dichotomy reflecting different ways of processing are not as conclusive as has often been stated.

Vulnerability and Automatic and Controlled Processing

Frequently, the onset of a depressive episode is found to be associated with a stressful event; then again, people who have suffered depressive episodes in the past seem to be more sensitized to the appearance of stressors, so that minor events, of apparently little consequence, can be responsible for triggering a depressive episode. In the case of John, seeing women triggers a series of automatic thoughts about himself and his life, facilitating a depressive mood, which in turn fuels those negative cognitions in a perpetuating way. Segal, Williams, Teasdale, and Gemar (1996) invoked the concepts of kindling and sensitization to explain this heightened susceptibility to recurrence of previously depressed individuals. In the process of kindling, the continued reactivation of negative memory structures would produce dense interconnections, so that activation of one element in the array is likely to activate the entire structure; this means that only minimal cues are needed to activate the array of depressive constructs. In the process of sensitization, the repeated activation of depressotypic constructs during previous depressive experiences produces the lowering of the activation threshold for these structures. Hence, the phenomena of sensitization and kindling (see Monroe & Harkness, 2005) can be interpreted in terms of a decrease in the threshold of automatic activation of cognitive processes and, in parallel, a greater difficulty for the executive processes to counteract them, which can create escalating spiraling cycles of negative cognition-emotion.

Finally, although more investigation is needed about the precise role of the cognitive mechanisms in the onset and relapse of depression and its relation with the processes of kindling and sensitization, the distinction between controlled and automatic processes is probably a way to fruitful analysis. The results of some recent high-risk prospective studies show that the onset of depression is more likely when there is a confluence of negative cognitive schemas (about oneself, the world, and the future) together with a tendency to process information ruminatively (i.e., Alloy et al., 2006). Thus, more spontaneity in generating negative thoughts and more difficulty in controlling them and redirecting processes toward specific contents seem to be powerful candidates to explain the risk of onset, relapse, and recurrence of depression.

Implications for Therapy

The importance of working with automatic thoughts was emphasized by cognitive depression therapy from the beginning. The goal is, firstly, to make clients aware of the automatic thoughts that come into their minds and of the underlying dysfunctional beliefs. A common way of achieving this is to record automatic negative thoughts. Secondly, such thoughts are challenged with alternative, more adaptive and functional thoughts. The idea is to get clients to have "second thoughts" about thoughts that automatically come to their minds and that, following repeated and disciplined practice, these automatic thoughts will be countered. However, there are few data about the cognitive mechanisms involved in effective therapeutic interventions and, especially, whether there are real changes in the *ways* of processing (Beevers, 2005). Future research will have to show whether the efficacy of cognitive interventions in depression is based on the direct reduction of the automaticity of the negative cognitive processes, or on the teaching of metacognitive skills that serve to render this type of automatic processing more accessible to effortful reflection. Approaches such as mindfulness-based cognitive therapy for depression, or acceptance and commitment therapy help patients to deliberately monitor and observe their thinking patterns when they feel sad and to respond to these thoughts and feelings in a way that allows them to disengage from the cognitive consequences of automatically activated mood-related rumination (Segal, Williams, & Teasdale, 2002). Given that these automatic processes seem to be related to depressive relapse, effective prophylactic interventions should involve attempts to deautomatize such processes. Future investigation must attend to the cognitive mechanisms that underlie therapeutic improvement and determine the most feasible and effective ways (i.e., reducing automaticity vs. increasing executive control) to improve interventions and reduce the likelihood of relapse.

CARMELO VÁZQUEZ AND LAURA HERNANGÓMEZ

See also

Attention
Memory Processes
Mindfulness-Based Cognitive
Therapy

References

Alloy, L. B., Abramson, L. Y., Whitehouse, W. G., Hogan, M. E., Panzarella, C., & Rose, D. T. (2006). Prospective incidence of first onsets and recurrences of depression in individuals at high and low cognitive risk for depression. *Journal of Abnormal Psychology, 115*, 145–156.

Beck, A. T. (1976). *Cognitive therapy and the emotional disorders.* New York: International Universities Press.

Beevers, C. G. (2005). Cognitive vulnerability to depression: A dual process model. *Clinical Psychology Review, 25*, 975–1002.

Hartlage, S., Alloy, L., Vázquez, C., & Dyckman, B. (1993). Automatic and effortful processing in depression. *Psychological Bulletin, 113*, 247–278.

Joormann, J., & Gotlib, I. H. (2007). Selective attention to emotional faces following recovery from depression. *Journal of Abnormal Psychology, 116*, 80–85.

Lau, M. A., Segal, Z. V., & Wiliams, J. M. G. (2004). Teasdale's differential activation hypothesis: Implications for mechanisms of depressive relapse and suicidal behaviour. *Behaviour Research and Therapy, 42*, 1001–1017.

Matt, J., Vázquez, C., & Campbell, K. (1992). Mood-congruent recall of affectively toned stimuli: A meta-analytic review. *Clinical Psychology Review, 2*, 227–256.

Monroe, S. M., & Harkness, K. L. (2005). Life stress, the "kindling" hypothesis, and the recurrence of depression: Considerations from a life stress perspective. *Psychological Review, 112*, 417–445.

Segal, Z. V., Williams, J. M. G., & Teasdale, J. D. (2002). *Mindfulness based cognitive therapy for depression: A new approach to preventing relapse.* New York: Guilford Press.

Segal, Z. V., Williams, J. M. G., Teasdale, J. D., & Gemar, M. (1996). A cognitive science perspective on kindling and episode sensitization in recurrent affective disorder. *Psychological Medicine, 26*, 371–380.

Automatic Thoughts

Automatic thoughts are an important part of Beck's cognitive model of depression. Automatic thoughts, called self-talk by some theorists, reflect the subconscious mono-

logue in which individuals are constantly engaged. In addition to self-talk, automatic thoughts can also consist of images. The idea that these thoughts are subconscious suggests that individuals have little ongoing awareness of these thoughts, but that they easily can be brought into conscious awareness. In depression, automatic thoughts are negative in nature and reflect deeper levels of cognitive activity, such as the operation of cognitive self-schemas. Early in the process of cognitive therapy, individuals are taught to monitor these thoughts, and once they can be monitored, the therapist teaches the depressed patient to challenge, and presumably alter, automatic thoughts. Modifying such thoughts has therapeutic value in its own right, but another reason for focusing on such thoughts is to gain access to the negative cognitive schemas of the depressed patient, with the idea that these schemas can be modified in a more adaptive manner.

As a cognitive variable comprising self-statements, the assessment of automatic thoughts must rely on self-report questionnaires. The Automatic Thoughts Questionnaire (ATQ-N) was developed by Hollon and Kendall (1980) as a way to measure these thoughts. Examples of items include statements such as "I feel like I am up against the world" and "I've let people down." Individuals are asked not whether they believe these statements to be true or not, but rather to rate the frequency that these, and similar thoughts, occur over a period of time. The ATQ-N includes 30 such statements, with each statement rated on a 1 (never) to 5 (all time) scale, with scores ranging from 30 to 150. A variety of studies have shown that the ATQ-N is a valid and reliable measure.

The ATQ-P was developed by Ingram and Wisnicki (1988) as a counterpart to the ATQ-N, with a focus on the frequency of positive thoughts. Like the ATQ-N, the ATQ-P includes 30 statements (e.g., "My future looks bright") to which respondents rate the frequency of occurrence on a scale of 1 to 5. The ATQ-Revised (ATQ-R) was developed by Kendall, Howard, and Hays (1989), also as a way to examine positive thoughts. Unlike the ATQ-P, the ATQ-R adds 10 positive statements to the ATQ-N. Ingram, Kendall, Siegle, Guarino, and McLaughlin (1995) compiled data that showed the ATQ-P to be reliable and valid, and Burgess and Haaga (1994) reviewed data suggesting that the ATQ-P and the ATQ-R are roughly equivalent measures positive automatic thoughts.

RICK E. INGRAM

See also

Aaron Beck
Cognitive Behavioral Therapy
Cognitive Theories of Depression

Rumination
Self-Focused Attention

References

Burgess, E., & Haaga, D. (1994). The Positive Automatic Thoughts Questionnaire (ATQ-P) and the Automatic Thoughts Questionnaire-Revised (ATQ-PR): Equivalent measures of positive thinking. *Cognitive Therapy and Research, 18,* 15–23.

Hollon, S., & Kendall, P. (1980). Cognitive self-statements in depression. *Cognitive Therapy and Research, 4,* 383–395.

Ingram, R. E., Kendall, P. C., Siegle, G., Guarino, J., & McLaughlin, S. (1995). Psychometric properties of the Positive Automatic Thoughts Questionnaire. *Psychological Assessment, 7,* 495–507.

Ingram, R. E., & Wisnicki, K. S. (1988). Assessment of automatic positive cognition. *Journal of Consulting and Clinical Psychology, 56,* 898–902.

Kendall, P., Howard, B., & Hays, R. (1989). Self-referent speech and psychopathology: The balance of positive and negative thinking. *Cognitive Therapy and Research, 13,* 583–598.

B

Beck Depression Inventory

Currently in its third iteration, the Beck Depression Inventory (BDI-I, Beck, Ward, Mendelson, Mock, & Erbaugh, 1961; BDI-IA, Beck & Steer, 1993; BDI-II, Beck, Steer, & Brown, 1996) is a 21-item self-report inventory of depressive symptoms. Each item represents a component of a depressive symptom and is rated on a 0 to 3 scale, with lower scores representing either the absence or minimal presence of symptoms. Individuals' responses are summed across each of the questions for a total score ranging between 0 and 63. Scores from 0 to 9 are considered to represent nondepressed individuals, with dysphoric individuals typically scoring between 10 and 15, and depressed individuals scoring above 16. The BDI has been demonstrated to have acceptable test-retest reliability, internal consistency, and strong convergent and discriminant validity (see Beck, Steer, & Garbin, 1988, for a review). Coefficient alphas range from .76 to .95 for psychiatric populations and .73 to .92 for nonpsychiatric populations (Beck et al., 1988). Concerns over the relation between the BDI and the *Diagnostic and Statistical Manual of Mental Disorders* (*DSM-IV*) criteria (American Psychiatric Association [APA], 1994) for major depression, particularly regarding including individuals' increases in sleep, appetite, and weight, led to the development of the BDI-IA, followed by the revision of the BDI in 1996.

The BDI-II addressed these concerns while maintaining the original 21-item format and scoring method. Modified to be consistent with the *DSM-IV* criteria (APA, 1994), the BDI-II assesses depressive symptoms during the past 2 weeks, a change from the BDI, which assessed symptoms during the prior week only. Furthermore, the language was updated, leading to rewording of most of the 21 items. Score cutoffs for symptom severity were likewise modified, with 0 to 13 representing "minimal," 14 to 19 "mild," 20 to 28 "moderate," and 29 to 63 "severe" symptoms, respectively (Beck, Steer, Ball, & Ranieri, 1996). The BDI-II has acceptable 1-week test-retest reliability (.93 in one sample of psychiatric outpatients; Beck, Steer, Ball, et al., 1996), has high internal consistency (Steer & Clark, 1997), and is comparable to the BDI-IA in identifying mood disorders (Beck, Steer, & Brown, 1996). Factor analyses suggest that the BDI-II is composed of two factors: cognitive symptoms and somatic symptoms. Primarily used as a screening tool for depressive symptoms, the BDI-II, as with the BDI, is often used as a measure of treatment outcome for depressive symptoms.

The BDI-II has been translated into a variety of languages and used in a number of cultures with good reliability and validity, including Spanish, Chinese, and Persian. Acceptable psychometric properties have also been found with the BDI-II in college students of a variety of ethnicities and in geriatric inpatients. More recently a short form of the BDI (BDI-SF; Furlanetto, Mendlowicz, & Bueno, 2005) was developed and validated for use as a screening tool with medical inpatients. Overall, the BDI-II appears to be a valid and reliable tool for measuring depressive symptoms in a variety of populations.

TIFFANY MEITES

See also

Assessment of Depression
Cognitive Theories of Depression
Definition of Depression
Diagnostic and Statistical Manual of
Mental Disorders

References

American Psychiatric Association. (1994). *Diagnostic and statistical manual of mental disorders* (4th ed.). Washington, DC: Author.

Beck, A. T., & Steer, R. A. (1993). *Manual for the Beck Depression Inventory*. San Antonio, TX: Psychological Corporation.

Beck, A. T., Steer, R. A., Ball, R. B., & Ranieri, W. F. (1996). Comparison of Beck Depression Inventories-IA and II in psychiatric outpatients. *Journal of Personality Assessment, 67*, 588–597.

Beck, A. T., Steer, R. A., & Brown, O. K. (1996). *Beck Depression Inventory manual* (2nd ed.). San Antonio, TX: Psychological Corporation.

Beck, A. T., Steer, R. A., & Garbin, M. G. (1988). Psychometric properties of the Beck Depression Inventory: Twenty-five years of evaluation. *Clinical Psychology Review, 8*, 77–100.

Beck, A. T., Ward, C. H., Mendelson, M., Mock, J., & Erbaugh, J. (1961). An inventory for measuring depression. *Archives of General Psychiatry, 4*, 561–571.

Furlanetto, L. M., Mendlowicz, M. V., & Bueno, J. R. (2005). The validity of the Beck Depression Inventory-Short Form as a screening and diagnostic instrument for moderate and severe depression in medical inpatients. *Journal of Affective Disorders, 86*, 87–91.

Steer, R. A., & Clark, D. A. (1997). Psychometric characteristics of the Beck Depression Inventory-II with college students. *Measurement and Evaluation in Counseling and Development, 30*, 128–136.

Behavioral Activation System

The behavioral activation system (BAS) is a theorized neurophysiological system that mediates appetitive motivation. The BAS, along with the behavioral inhibition system (BIS), which mediates withdrawal-related motivation (see the Behavioral Inhibition System entry), comprises a two-part brain-based dimensional framework for understanding emotion and motivation. The BAS and BIS are each presumed to have functional evolutionary significance in a broad range of mammalian species. For instance, in the presence of food (or a food-related cue), the BAS operates via neural signals to facilitate approach and consumption of the food, as well as hedonic feeling states (e.g., pleasure) that support appetitive behavior. Thus, intact BAS activity supports the effective pursuit of important environmental opportunities (e.g., approaching a mate), and deficient BAS activity will lead to poorer adaptation (e.g., poor psychosocial functioning). In this entry, we briefly review the history and theoretical development of the BAS construct, discuss methods for measuring BAS-relevant activity, and overview research applications of the BAS construct in both nonclinical and clinical samples, including persons with affective disorders.

Two "Fundamental Emotion Systems": A Historical Overview

Jeffrey Gray's theory of reinforcement sensitivity (Gray, 1970, 1981; Gray & McNaughton, 2000), developed over 30 years, has had historical importance in the development of the BAS (and BIS) constructs. Originally, Gray applied findings from work on anxiety states in animal learning models to humans and, in doing so, offered a revised account of Eysenck's personality theory (see Gray, 1981). This account focused upon two dimensions of personality, impulsivity and anxiety, which were proposed as 30° rotations of Eysenck's extraversion and neuroticism constructs, respectively. Gray proposed that variations in trait anxiety were a result of individual differences in sensitivity to cues of punishment, nonreward, and novelty cues in the environment, which were based on activity of an underlying neurophysiological system (the BIS). Likewise, Gray proposed that a trait impulsivity dimension described individual differences in sensitivity to signals of reward and nonpunishment, which was governed by a separate physiological motivational system, the so-called behavioral approach system (also abbreviated BAS). Gray's BAS construct is conceptually related to the behavioral facilitation system proposed by Depue and Iacono (1989) and to Fowles's (1980) behavioral activation system, which has become the most commonly used title for the BAS construct.

Gray's work was pioneering in its conceptualization of neurophysiologically based emotion-motivation systems as the fundamental building blocks of affect states and adaptive behavior, which ultimately manifest as personality dimensions. Gray's theory viewed Eysenck's personality traits as products of the interaction of the BAS and the BIS. For example, Gray suggested that the extraversion-intraversion dimension was a result of the relative strength of the BAS to the BIS (e.g., higher extraversion results from BAS predominance), and that neuroticism resulted from their joint strengths (although later researchers separately mapped extraversion to the BAS and neuroticism to the BIS; see Watson, Wiese, Vaidya, & Tellegen, 1999). Gray's theory was widely influential in part because of its broad scope, linking the areas of emotion, motivation, and personality, and has generated abundant research in humans and nonhuman animals since the 1970s.

How Is BAS Activity Measured?

Because BAS activity by definition involves a neurophysiological-affective-behavioral network it is not surprising that multiple methods have been utilized to index correlates of BAS-relevant activity. Indeed, given the integrative nature of the BAS construct, it is natural that researchers measure multiple systems in order to capture BAS activity, with no single measurement providing a gold standard of the BAS.

For example, in work utilizing animal behavioral models of BAS-relevant activity, researchers often index BAS activity by assessing reward learning, goal-directed behavior, and consummatory behaviors (see Schultz, 2006). Likewise, studies of the reward system in humans have utilized a variety of behavioral tasks to index BAS-relevant activity, including reward learning, responsiveness to rewarding or pleasant stimuli, and both anticipatory and consummatory aspects of approach behavior.

The most commonly used self-report measure of trait reward sensitivity is Carver and White's (1994) BIS/BAS scales. This 20-item measure yields three subscale scores representing three proposed components of the theorized BAS trait: Reward Responsiveness, Drive, and Fun-Seeking. Extensive work in human and nonhuman animals has focused understandably upon the neurological correlates of BAS-related activity. In particular, Davidson and colleagues have examined hemispheric asymmetries in prefrontal brain regions as correlates of BAS and BIS. Importantly, greater relative left activation as assessed by electroencephalography correlates with self-reported levels BAS sensitivity (e.g., Sutton & Davidson, 1997). Other neurologically informed work on the BAS has focused upon measurement of neurotransmitters, specifically the dopaminergic system (e.g., dopamine receptor density and binding sensitivity). Finally, recent investigations have sought to elucidate the molecular genetic underpinnings of BAS activity.

Applications to Normal and Abnormal Functioning

The two-system emotion-motivation framework has been a generative research framework for understanding several aspects of psychological functioning. The BAS construct has been used extensively in personality research, including work examining the links between personality (i.e., trait-like BAS-relevant activity) and emotional responding. This work has often been in the area of positive emotionality, although other work has examined connections between the BAS construct and anger as well as aggression (see Harmon-Jones, 2003). This latter work has sparked a fruitful debate as to whether the BAS is exclusively limited to governing rewarding, positive affect generating approach behaviors, or whether the BAS also governs approach behaviors in the context of negative affect (i.e., aggression).

The BAS construct has also had broad utility in the context of psychopathology, where deficits in the ability to react and respond to rewarding opportunities (i.e., either underactivity or and overactivity in the BAS) have been demonstrated in several mental disorders. For example, BAS indices show overactivity in childhood externalizing disorders, attention deficit hyperactivity disorder, and alcohol and substance abuse; in turn, BAS indices show underactivity in schizophrenia and social phobia (see Beauchaine, 2001; Clark, 2005).

Application to Affective Disorders

Perhaps the most extensive body of work on BAS and psychopathology has been in the area of affective disorders. For example, overactivity of BAS indices has been implicated in bipolar mood disorders (e.g., Meyer, Johnson, & Winters, 2001), while underactivity in BAS indices has been associated with a poor course of unipolar depression (Kasch, Rottenberg, Arnow, & Gotlib, 2002). Findings linking depression to deficits in BAS-related activity appear to be robust and emerge with a variety of BAS indices. For example, depression has been associated with reduced behavioral responsiveness to reward, reduced physiological reactivity to pleasant stimuli, and reduced self-report of positive affect (see Kasch et al., 2002, for a review). Consistent with that the idea that depression is linked to deficient approach system activity, treatment strategies that specifically target approach and rewarding behaviors appear particularly promising in reducing clinical depression symptoms (see Jacobson, Martell, & Dimidjian, 2005). Thus, the BAS construct is likely to continue to be a useful framework for conceptualizing approach deficits in depression and has the potential to afford researchers with a better understanding of the etiology of affective disorders.

BETHANY H. MORRIS AND JONATHAN ROTTENBERG

See also

Affective Neuroscience
Behavioral Inhibition System
Brain Circuitry
Functional Neuroimaging

References

Beauchaine, T. (2001). Vagal tone, development, and Gray's motivational theory: Toward an integrated model of autonomic nervous system functioning in psychopathology. *Development and Psychopathology, 13,* 183–214.

Carver, C. S., & White, T. L. (1994). Behavioral inhibition, behavioral activation, and affective responses to impending reward and punishment: The BIS/BAS scales. *Journal of Personality and Social Psychology, 67,* 319–333.

Clark, L. A. (2005). Temperament as a unifying basis for personality and psychopathology. *Journal of Abnormal Psychology, 114,* 505–521.

Depue, R. A., & Iacono, W. G. (1989). Neurobehavioral aspects of affective disorders. *Annual Review of Psychology, 40,* 457–92.

Fowles, D. C. (1980). The three arousal model: Implications of Gray's two-factor learning theory for heart rate, electrodermal activity, and psychopathy. *Psychophysiology, 17,* 87–104.

Gray, J. A. (1970). The pyschophysiological basis of introversion-extraversion. *Behavior Research and Therapy, 8,* 249–266.

Gray, J. A. (1981). A critique of Eysenck's theory of personality. In H. J. Eysenck (Ed.), *A model for personality* (pp. 246–277). Berlin, Germany: Springer.

Gray, J. A., & McNaughton, N. (2000). *The neuropsychology of anxiety* (2nd ed.). New York: Oxford University Press.

Harmon-Jones, E. (2003). Anger and the behavior approach system. *Personality and Individual Differences, 35,* 995–1005.

Jacobson, N. S., Martell, C. R., & Dimidjian, S. (2005). Behavioral activation treatment for depression: Returning to contextual roots. *Clinical Psychology: Science and Practice, 8,* 255–270.

Kasch, K., Rottenberg, J., Arnow, B., & Gotlib, I. (2002). Behavioral activation and inhibition systems and the severity and course of depression. *Journal of Abnormal Psychology, 111,* 589–597.

Meyer, B., Johnson, S. L., & Winters, R. (2001). Responsiveness to threat and incentive in bipolar disorder: Relations of the BIS/BAS scales with symptoms. *Journal of Psychopathology and Behavioral Assessment, 23,* 133–143.

Schultz, W. (2006). Behavioral theories and the neurophysiology of reward. *Annual Review of Psychology, 57,* 87–115.

Sutton, S. K., & Davidson, R. J. (1997). Prefrontal brain asymmetry: A biological substrate of the behavioral approach and inhibition systems. *Psychological Science, 8,* 204–210.

Watson, D., Wiese, D., Vaidya, J., & Tellegen, A. (1999). The two general activation systems of affect: Structural findings, evolutionary considerations, and psychobiological evidence. *Journal of Personality and Social Psychology, 76,* 820–838.

Behavioral Inhibition System

The behavioral inhibition system (BIS) is a theorized neurophysiological system that governs withdrawal motivation. The BIS is one component of a two-system brain-based dimensional theoretical framework for understanding emotion and motivation, along with the behavioral activation system (BAS), which supports approach-related activity (see the Behavioral Activation System entry).

Together, the BIS and BAS offer a functional theoretical account of how the brain generates adaptive psychophysiological responses to environmental stimuli and, in turn, produces positive and negative emotions. (See the Behavioral Activation System entry for more detail on the two-system theory.) For example, when an animal encounters an aversive, nonrewarding, or novel stimulus, BIS activity inhibits movement toward that stimulus, motivates adaptive withdrawal behavior, and produces negative feeling states associated with increased vigilance and withdrawal behavior. According to evolutionary theories of emotion, organisms with intact BIS activity systems will be better prepared to perform adaptive action when an unfamiliar or potentially threatening situation presents itself (e.g., an unexplored environment, the scent of a predator). In turn, oscillations in BIS activity are considered adaptive responses to salient environmental cues, and deficits in this system are presumed to lead to maladaptive responses and poor outcomes (e.g., premature death). In this entry, we briefly review the history and theoretical development of the BIS construct, discuss the various methods used to measure BIS activity, and overview applications of the BIS construct in research with nonclinical and clinical samples, including persons with affective disorders.

A Brief History of the Behavioral Inhibition System

The BIS construct has its roots in Jeffrey Gray's theory of reinforcement sensitivity (Gray, 1970, 1981; Gray & McNaughton, 2000), which has significantly contributed to the two-system emotion motivation framework over the last three decades. Gray's original work focused on anxiety in animal learning models, which he eventually applied to humans in his revised account of Eysenck's personality theory (see the Behavioral Activation System entry). Gray proposed that trait anxiety results from individual differences in sensitivity to cues of punishment, nonreward, and novelty in the environment. The BIS represents the neurophysiological network that coordinates responses to these cues and promotes adaptive withdrawal and feelings of anxiety or increased vigilance (see Gray & McNaughton, 2000, for the most recent refinement of BIS theory).

How Is BIS Activity Measured?

Because the BIS integrates neurophysiological, affective, and behavioral responses, researchers have utilized multiple measures across a variety of response systems to index the correlates of BIS activity. There is a long history of research investigating BIS-relevant activity in animal models utilizing pharmacological intervention, lesion methods, and behavioral learning paradigms. These studies often index BIS-relevant activity by assessing learning related to aversive or nonrewarding stimuli, withdrawal behavior, and inhibition of goal-directed behaviors. Likewise, studies of the withdrawal system in humans have utilized a variety of behavioral tasks to index BIS-relevant activity, including learning and behavioral responsiveness to aversive or punishing stimuli, as well as tasks that require inhibiting behavioral responding. Importantly, no single index of BIS activity has emerged as the gold standard of measurement, and increasingly investigations of BIS activity in humans are utilizing multiple indices of the BIS (e.g., self-report, behavioral, neural activity), to understand the interaction and coherence of different facets of the BIS (e.g., Amodio, Master, Yee, & Taylor, 2007).

Studies examining the trait-like aspects of the BIS construct often utilize self-report measures of trait punishment sensitivity, the most widely used of which is Carver and White's (1994) BIS/BAS scales. This 20-item measure yields a total BIS subscale score representing the individual's sensitivity to punishment cues and proneness to experience negative affect and anxiety in response to them. Neural activity has also been used to assess traitlike aspects of BIS activity. Davidson and colleagues used electroencephalography to assess hemispheric asymmetries in neural activity and found that right-sided hemispheric activation in prefrontal brain regions predicted BIS scores as ascertained by self-report (e.g., Sutton & Davidson, 1997). Thus, hemispheric asymmetry in prefrontal activation favoring the right hemisphere has been used as an index of BIS activity.

It is important to note, however, that a large number of physiological correlates of BIS-relevant activity have been examined. These include autonomic nervous system activity (e.g., skin conductance responses), hormonal indicators, and neural activity in critical brain areas (see Fox, Henderson, Marshall, Nichols, & Ghera, 2005, for a review from a developmental perspective). In particular, a large literature exists linking amygdala activation to BIS-relevant behaviors, anxiety, and vigilance. Recent work by Gray has refocused the role of the BIS as a conflict-monitoring system (mediating between approach and fight-or-flight motivation) and implicates involvement of the neurotransmitter norepinephrine and the anterior cingulate cortex in BIS activity (Gray & McNaughton, 2000).

Application to Normal and Abnormal Functioning

The BIS construct has been studied extensively in the contexts of personality and psychopathology. For example, high levels of BIS activity have been linked to anxiety and social withdrawal (e.g., see Fox et al., 2005), while low levels of BIS activity are implicated in disinhibited and externalizing behaviors, and primary psychopathy (e.g., Newman, MacCoon, Vaughn, & Sadeh, 2005). Perhaps the most extensive work on BIS and psychopathology has been in the area of anxiety disorders. For example, social phobia, generalized anxiety, and panic have all been associated with overactivity on BIS-relevant indices. Finally, a large literature examines the developmental trajectory of temperamental behavioral inhibition from infancy to adolescence and risk for psychopathology in adulthood (e.g., Beauchaine, 2001). Findings in this area have highlighted the potential contribution of BIS underactivity to conduct disorder and attention deficit hyperactivity disorder.

Application to Affective Disorders

In the context of affective disorders, BIS activity has been investigated mainly among persons with major depressive disorder. Major depressive disorder has been associated with elevations in self-reported BIS and in negative affect, more generally. Major depressive disorder has also been associated with overactivity in brain regions implicated in BIS activity, such as the amygdala. There is also evidence from electroencephalography studies linking major depressive disorder to greater relative right resting hemispheric activity in prefrontal brain regions (see Thibodeau, Jorgensen, & Kim, 2006).

Though major depressive disorder has been associated with elevations in BIS activity, the significance of these deficits and their specificity to depression remain to be seen. For example, although elevations in BIS activity are concurrently related to depression symptoms, there has not yet been compelling evidence to suggest that BIS activity predicts future depression (e.g., Kasch, Rottenberg, Arnow, & Gotlib, 2002). Anxiety disorders, which are frequently comorbid with and commonly predate onset of major depressive disorder, are also associated with elevations in BIS activity, raising some question as to the extent elevated BIS activity in major depressive disorder is a function of comorbid anxiety symptoms. For example, behavioral inhibition during childhood appears to be more closely related to the development of anxiety disorders than to depression. In this regard, clarifying the etiological significance of the BIS in affective disorders remains a high priority for future research.

BETHANY H. MORRIS AND JONATHAN ROTTENBERG

See also

Affective Neuroscience
Behavioral Activation System
Brain Circuitry
Functional Neuroimaging

References

Amodio, D. M., Master, S. L., Yee, C. M., & Taylor, S. E. (2007). Neurocognitive components of the behavioral inhibition and activation systems: Implications for theories of self-regulation. *Psychophysiology, 44,* 1–9.

Beauchaine, T. (2001). Vagal tone, development, and Gray's motivational theory: Toward an integrated model of autonomic nervous system functioning in psychopathology. *Development and Psychopathology, 13,* 183–214.

Carver, C. S., & White, T. L. (1994). Behavioral inhibition, behavioral activation, and affective responses to impending reward and punishment: The BIS/BAS scales. *Journal of Personality and Social Psychology, 67,* 319–333.

Fox, N. A., Henderson, H. A., Marshall, P. J., Nichols, K. E., & Ghera, M. M. (2005). Behavioral inhibition: Linking biology and behavior within a developmental framework. *Annual Review of Psychology, 56,* 235–262.

Gray, J. A. (1970). The pyschophysiological basis of introversion-extraversion. *Behavior Research and Therapy, 8,* 249–266.

Gray, J. A. (1981). A critique of Eysenck's theory of personality. In H. J. Eysenck (Ed.), *A model for personality* (pp. 246–277). Berlin, Germany: Springer.

Gray, J. A., & McNaughton, N. (2000). *The neuropsychology of anxiety* (2nd ed.). New York: Oxford University Press.

Kasch, K., Rottenberg, J., Arnow, B., & Gotlib, I. (2002). Behavioral activation and inhibition systems and the severity and course of depression. *Journal of Abnormal Psychology, 111,* 589–597.

Newman, J. P., MacCoon, D. G., Vaughn, L. J., & Sadeh, N. (2005). Validating a distinction between primary and secondary psychopathy with measures of Gray's BIS and BAS constructs. *Journal of Abnormal Psychology, 114,* 319–323.

Sutton, S. K., & Davidson, R. J. (1997). Prefrontal brain asymmetry: A biological substrate of the behavioral approach and inhibition systems. *Psychological Science, 8,* 204–210.

Thibodeau, R., Jorgensen, R. S., & Kim, S. (2006). Depression, anxiety, and resting frontal EEG asymmetry: A meta-analytic review. *Journal of Abnormal Psychology, 115,* 715–729.

Behavioral Models of Depression

Behavioral models of psychological disorders, in general, are based on the premise that the emphasis for both the cause and cure lies in person-environment relationships. Behaviorism is particularly nonmentalistic and rejects hypothesized theories of mind and internal structures. Rather than attributing problems to an internal, hypothetical construct such as the mind, behaviorists focus on the person-environment interactions. Environment composes the current setting in which behavior occurs, as well as the setting in which behaviors have occurred over time. Behaviors are also defined broadly as those that can be observed by others (e.g., making a statement about how badly one feels about oneself), as well as those that are private and not observable to others (e.g., thinking to oneself that one is a bad person). The broad term *context* is often used to incorporate factors that are specific to a given individual—such as physical characteristics, intellectual capacity, and so forth—those that are "external" to the individual—such as the neighborhood in which one lives, number of siblings, and such—and the particular behaviors that are maintained as a result of the person-environment transactions. We put the word "external" in quotation marks, because behaviorists do not make distinctions between the principles that govern overt behavior and private behaviors and, therefore, see the separation between what is considered internal and external as an arbitrary one.

The specific foci of behaviorism are on processes of conditioning whereby neutral environmental stimuli take on properties of stimuli that are positive or aversive (classical conditioning) and processes whereby the actions of the individual operate on the environment in such a way that results in consequences that make the actions more or less likely to occur under similar circumstances in the future (operant conditioning). More recently, behaviorists have responded to criticism of reductionism and of inadequate accounting for complex processes of human cognition and learning that occurs without direct manipulation of contingencies through empirical evaluation of learning processes. The theory of relational frame theory has been proposed as a behavior analytic formulation of cognition (Hayes, Barnes-Holmes, & Roche, 2001). This theory has expanded the original formulation of Skinner (1957) and provides a theory of how the complexity of human language and cognition is learned in the absence of direct reinforcement. A discussion of relational frame theory is beyond the scope of this paper and interested readers are directed to the work of Hayes, Barnes-Holmes, and Roche (2001) for a comprehensive presentation of the theory. Basically, relational frame theory stresses the capability of human beings to develop verbal behaviors without direct training. When a human being is directly trained that A equals B, and that B equals C; the human can also recognize that A equals C without ever having received direct training that they do so. There are various types of relational frames that nonhuman organisms are not capable of learning which human beings do indeed learn. The relational frames can be extremely complex and are not limited to simple matching.

There is more research to be done on relational frame theory; however, the theory helps to explain the phenomena of the stereotypically negative, self-focused thinking seen in depression that plays so heavily in cognitive theory. Relational frame theory also helps to account for the level of distress experienced by depressed individuals, who are caught in a cycle of negative rumination, with an explanation that follows from observations in the experimental laboratory that are consistent with well-established learning theory.

Historically, behavioral models were first considered in the understanding of depression in the 1970s by Ferster (1973) and following the pioneering work of Peter Lewinsohn and colleagues (Lewinsohn, Biglan, & Zeiss, 1976). Simply stated, the basic behavioral theory of depression suggests that low levels of response-contingent positive reinforcement and high levels of aversive control result in depression (Lewinsohn, 1974). Punishment and unpleasant events are also correlated with depression and with decreased experience of pleasantness for formerly pleasant events (Grosscup & Lewinsohn, 1980).

The causes of decreases in response-contingent positive reinforcement can vary. Lewinsohn (1974) identified several factors that could result in low levels of positive reinforcement. First, the environment may not provide the necessary reinforcers. This is the case for individuals who have impoverished environments that are lacking in basic needs such as adequate housing, food, and so forth; however, the impoverished environment may also be social or interpersonal in nature. For example, children raised in the homes of depressed caregivers may experience this condition. The environment is impoverished because it offers little appropriate feedback to proactive behaviors on the part of the infant or young child. For example, a child gurgles and coos when it sees its mother's face, but the mother, in a depressed mood, simply grins and then looks away from the infant. In this way, the proactive attempt at social interaction, gurgling and cooing, has not been reinforced. Repeated instances of such interactions may result in an impoverished environment for the child. Thus, impoverished environments can consist of a variety of subtle contingencies that will have a negative impact on mood; they should not be understood only as actual "poverty" and can include genetically linked familial transmission.

Second, there may be a sudden change in an environment that once produced positive reinforcement such that reinforcers become unavailable. This situation would occur, for example, when a loved one dies. A less dramatic change may be the completion of high school or college, when a readily available network of friends that provided many instances of positively reinforced social interaction is no longer available as they move onto different settings. Third, the individual may lack the ability to access positive reinforcement in the environment. This is often the case when individuals have developed a repertoire of escape and avoidance behaviors that are reinforced negatively through the relief of aversive conditions but do not allow for engagement in the environment such that approach behaviors are reinforced. For example an individual that has experienced strong, negative reactions to perceived criticism of others may avoid social situations because socializing has been previously experienced as aversive. When invited to a birthday celebration for a friend, the individual politely turns down the invitation and feels immediate relief that there will not be a social obligation and potentially aversive experience. However, the person has also inadvertently reduced the possibility that the experience will be enjoyable and make it more likely that there will be more socializing in the future that will also be experienced as positive. This is also the case when an individual has specific skills deficits, for example, an extremely shy individual who lacks social flexibility may not interact comfortably with others and therefore lacks the repertoire to access positive reinforcement in social situations.

The behavioral model does not deny that some individuals are vulnerable to depression due to familial transmission or early learning experiences, and in these vulnerable individuals, the natural feelings that follow a less rewarding life lead to escape and avoidance behaviors that can be understood as attempts to cope with negative feelings but that subsequently become secondary problems in themselves.

Although behaviorism has been criticized as reductionistic, such criticism has often been based on misunderstandings of the model or the ways in which behavioral concepts have been communicated. Certainly, contemporary behavioral models are far from reductionistic. Although rejecting a medical model that assumes all psychological problems to be biologically based diseases, behaviorists postulate that the person's environment, learning history, and frequent patterns of person and environment interactions all have an impact on biology, and vice versa. The original model proposed by Lewinsohn and colleagues was expanded to an integrated model (Lewinsohn, Hoberman, Teri, & Hautzinger, 1985) that suggested a chain of events leading to the occurrence of depression. The chain begins by the occurrence of an evoking event that disrupts relatively automatic behavior patterns of an individual, and such disruptions and the emotional upset they engender can lead to a reduction in positive reinforcement or an elevated rate of aversive experience. The individual attempts to reduce the impact of these disruptions, and the inability of the individual to reverse the impact, results in a heightened state of self-awareness. Feeling increasingly self-aware and dysphoric leads to the cognitive, behavioral, and emotional changes that are correlated with depression. These changes reduce the individual's ability to cope with future depression-evoking events. The model also allowed for the possibility of feedback loops whereby becoming depressed, thinking and behaving in depressed ways, interferes with the individual's ability to problem solve and reverse the disruption, thus contributing to the cycle of depression.

Behaviorism is associationist. Human thoughts, behaviors, and emotions are all a part of a complex transaction between the individual and the environment. Classical conditioning demonstrates that a conditioned stimulus (such as the color blue) takes on the properties of an unconditioned stimulus (such as an electric shock) when they are paired. As a result, the organism may show fear (an un-conditioned response to electric shock) when in the presence of the color blue (the conditioned stimulus). Behaviorists also understand that stimulus generalization occurs in that variations in the color blue may occasion a similar fear response. Operant conditioning suggests that behavior is learned, maintained, or extinguished by its consequences. For example, if extending one's hand to a new acquaintance results in the individual taking one's hand, gently shaking it, and smiling, one will learn to greet people in this way, and the behavior is likely to be maintained across similar situations. On the other hand, if one extended one's hand and the other person turned away, it is less likely that extending one's hand in greeting will occur on the next meeting of a stranger. Also, human language allows us to learn rules that will govern behavioral responses so that human learning does not require repeated trials of direct experience. When one has learned to trust the direction of a parent (through both classical conditioning and operant conditioning), one will follow the instruction of the parent and learn rules of behavior that do not require direct consequences of the environment. For example, one can be told that "it is proper to shake another person's hand when greeting him." Nevertheless, direct consequences are still at work to shape behavior, thus in our example, if one follows the parent's rule to offer a handshake, and the stranger turns away or scowls, one may be likely to offer a hand in the presence of one's parents (because of their strong stimulus value for doing so) but not in their absence.

Behavioral models of depression incorporate these basic principles in the understanding that processes of conditioning and learning have affected an individual's experience of events. Thus, a song on the radio (a conditioned stimulus) that played when one was going through the painful demise of one's first love affair (an unconditioned stimulus) may occasion feelings of sadness and dysphoria (the conditioned response) even years after the breakup occurred. If one's response were to turn off the song and switch to a different radio station, therefore experiencing a slight lifting of the dysphoria, the avoidance behavior would be negatively reinforced, and one would be more likely to turn off the song immediately upon hearing it in the future. Responses to negative (dysphoric) feelings play a central role in the behavioral model of depression. Depressed clients are acting in ways that make sense when we recognize their behavior as conditioned responses and learned methods for dealing with negative feelings. However, when the depressed individual responds to aversive events in such a fashion as to lose contact with positive reinforcers, or when depressed behavior is reinforced through sympathy from others, the ability to successfully cope is diminished. Unfortunately, the means of coping can become secondary problems in themselves, since escape and avoidance behaviors, by being the occasions for passivity and withdrawal, may exacerbate depression.

Avoidance Behavior in Depression

An essential feature of the behavioral model of depression is the understanding of the impact of avoidance behavior on both the development and maintenance of depressive symptoms. Ferster (1973) was one of the early behaviorists who posited that much behavior observed in depressed patients serves an avoidance function. Depressed clients are often trying to escape from a negative affective state and may engage in behaviors such as sleeping, drinking alcohol, or watching endless hours of television that allow them to escape from feeling down. These behaviors may also allow them to avoid activities for which they no longer feel capable or out of fear that they will feel more depressed, and thus more hopeless. Such avoidance creates a downward cycle for the individual. While a person may experience immediate relief from the negative affect, following the urge not to act continues the cycle. The less individuals do, the more they feel depressed and problems in their life context are exacerbated. As a result, depression and hopelessness can reciprocally reinforce one another.

While avoidance has long been considered an essential feature in the anxiety disorders, there was substantially less emphasis on avoidance in cognitive behavioral therapy for depression. According to the behavioral conceptualization, emotional reactions such as feeling blue, sad, and lethargic are understandable responses to a lack of response contingent positive reinforcement or punishment—put simply "a less rewarding life." Earlier research suggested that depressed individuals were more sensitive to aversive stimuli than nondepressed controls (as measured by galvanic skin response to mild electric shock) and may, therefore, show greater tendencies to avoid or withdraw from unpleasant situations (Lewinsohn, Lobitz, & Wilson, 1973).

Helping clients to recognize these avoidance behaviors is the first step in modification of avoidance. A simple rule that avoidance feels good in the short run but often makes things worse in the long run is shorthand that clients can easily remember. Recognizing avoidance is the first step, the next step is more difficult: actually engaging in behavior that may require the client to approach situations that he or she finds aversive in some way. This can be done through activity scheduling, but it is essential here that clients can identify the barriers to action and how they will, at the present moment, overcome those barriers and approach rather than avoid.

The Role of Rumination

It is possible that activity may not have a positive impact on mood if a depressed individual is attending only to observable activity (e.g., building a treehouse with the children) and not to private activity (e.g., ruminating on how miserable life feels rather than concentrating on the activity of the moment). Research has suggested that a passive ruminative style is correlated with greater frequency, intensity, and duration of depressive episodes (Nolen-Hoeksema, Morrow, & Fredrickson, 1993).

This is also consistent with Lewinsohn's earlier understanding that depressed individuals can become self-focused in such a way as to interfere with problem solving.

Research Support

Behavioral models of depression have informed the development of behavioral treatments for depression, which have been an increasing focus of empirical attention. Lewinsohn and colleagues focused on reductions in pleasant events in the lives of depressed individuals and developed behavioral activation strategies for helping depressed individuals engage in behaviors that would bring pleasure into their lives and increase the possibility that active (i.e., nondepressed) behaviors would be positively reinforced. These behavioral activation techniques were also incorporated as an essential component of Beck and colleagues' cognitive therapy for depression (Beck, Rush, Shaw, & Emery, 1979). In this context, they were highlighted as particularly important in early therapy sessions to increase client experiences of pleasure or mastery and to lay the foundation for subsequent cognitive restructuring strategies.

Jacobson and colleagues proposed that these behavioral activation strategies were both necessary and sufficient in the treatment of depression (Jacobson et al., 1996). Behavioral activation was subsequently developed into a bona fide treatment for depression (Jacobson, Martell, & Dimidjian, 2001). Based on the functional analysis of behavior, behavioral activation was modified somewhat from the approach of Lewinsohn but is founded on the same principles, namely, that increases in behaviors that bring the client into contact with positive reinforcement and that break cycles of negatively reinforced escape and avoidance will serve an antidepressant function.

Decades of research have indicated that behavioral treatments for depression are better than no treatment or than the provision of simple support (Ekers, Richard, & Gilbody, 2008), and that behavioral activation in particular performs as well as or better than cognitive therapy for depressed adults (Dimidjian et al., 2005; Jacobson et al., 1996). Such findings are part of a larger resurgence in interest in behavioral and activation oriented interventions for depression (Hopko, Lejuez, LePage, Hopko, & McNeil, 2003; Martell, Addis, & Jacobson, 2001) and offer support for the behavioral model of depression. Continued research is needed to improve our understanding of the mechanisms of change in such behavioral treatments for depression.

There is current support for the premise originally proposed by Lewinsohn and colleagues that low levels of response contingent positive reinforcement plays a role in depression. Hopko, Armento, Cantu, Chambers, and Lejuez (2003) asked nondepressed and mildly depressed college students to record behaviors and activities at half-hour intervals for a week, and for each entry the student was to answer two questions: "How rewarding or pleasurable was the activity?" and "How likely is it that this behavior will lead to a future reward?" The results supported the hypothesis that there is a relationship between a lack of rewarding experiences and depression. Research on proposed appetitive and aversive motivational systems (the behavioral activation system and the behavioral inhibition system) have supported the hypothesis that negative daily events are correlated with negative affect and that positive daily events are correlated with positive affect (Gable, Reis, & Elliot, 2000). Nolen-Hoeksema, Morrow, and Fredrickson's (1993) study of rumination also support the model originally proposed by Lewinsohn and colleagues throughout the 1970s and 1980s.

CHRISTOPHER R. MARTELL, SONA DIMIDJIAN, AND PETER M. LEWINSOHN

See also

Behavior Therapy
Behavioral Observation
Cognitive Theories of Depression

References

Beck, A. T., Rush, A. J., Shaw, B. F., & Emery, G. (1979). *Cognitive therapy of depression.* New York: Guilford Press.

Dimidjian, S., Hollon, S. D., Dobson, K. S., Schmaling, K. B., Kohlenberg, R. J., Addis, M., et al. (2006). Randomized trial of behavioral activation, cognitive therapy, and antidepressant medication in the acute treatment of adults with major depression. *Journal of Consulting and Clinical Psychology, 74,* 658–670.

Ekers, D., Richards, D., & Gilbody, S. (2008). A meta-analysis of randomized trials of behavioural treatment of depression. *Psychological Medicine, 38,* 611–623.

Ferster, C. B. (1973). A functional analysis of depression. *American Psychologist, 28,* 857–870.

Gable, S. L., Reis, H. T., & Elliot, A. J. (2000). Behavioral activation and inhibition in everyday life. *Journal of Personality and Social Psychology, 78,* 1135–1149.

Grosscup, S. J., & Lewinsohn, P. M. (1980). Unpleasant and pleasant events, and mood. *Journal of Clinical Psychology, 36,* 252–259.

Hayes, S. C., Barnes-Holmes, D., & Roche, B. (2001). *Relational frame theory: A post-Skinnerian account of human language and cognition.* New York: Kluwer Academic/Plenum Press.

Hopko, D. R., Armento, M. E. A., Cantu, M. S., Chambers, L. L., & Lejuez, C. W. (2003). The use of daily diaries to assess the relations among mood state, overt behavior, and reward value of activities. *Behaviour Research and Therapy, 41,* 1137–1148.

Hopko, D. R., Lejuez, C. W., LePage, J. P., Hopko, S. D., & McNeil, D. W. (2003). A brief behavioral activation treatment for depression: A randomized pilot trial within an inpatient psychiatric hospital. *Behavior Modification, 27,* 458–469.

Jacobson, N. S., Dobson, K., Truax, P. A., Addis, M. E., Koerner, K., Gollan, J. K., et al. (1996). A component analysis of cognitive-behavioral treatment for depression. *Journal of Consulting and Clinical Psychology, 64,* 295–304.

Jacobson, N. S., Martell, C. R., & Dimidjian, S. (2001). Behavioral activation therapy for depression: Returning to contextual roots. *Clinical Psychology: Science and Practice, 8,* 255–270.

Lejuez, C. W., Hopko, D. R., LePage, J. P., Hopko, S. D., & McNeil, D. W. (2001). A brief behavioral activation treatment for depression. *Cognitive and Behavioral Practice, 8,* 164–175.

Lewinsohn, P. M. (1974). A behavioral approach to depression. In R. J. Friedman & M. M. Katz (Eds.), *The psychology of depression: Contemporary theory and research* (pp. 157–178). Washington, DC: Hemisphere Publishing.

Lewinsohn, P. M., Biglan, A., & Zeiss, A. S. (1976). Behavioral treatment of depression. In P. O. Davidson (Ed.), *The behavioral management of anxiety, depression and pain* (pp. 91–146). New York: Brunner/Mazel.

Lewinsohn, P. M., Hoberman, H. M., Teri, L., & Hautzinger, M. (1985). An integrative theory of unipolar depression. In S. Reiss & R. R. Bootzin (Eds.), *Theoretical issues in behavioral therapy* (pp. 313–359). New York: Academic Press.

Lewinsohn, P. M., Lobitz, W. C., & Wilson, S. (1973). "Sensitivity" of depressed individuals to aversive stimuli. *Journal of Abnormal Psychology, 81,* 259–263.

Martell, C. R., Addis, M. E., & Jacobson, N. S. (2001). *Depression in context: Strategies for guided action*. New York: W. W. Norton.

Nolen-Hoeksema, S., Morrow, J., & Fredrickson, B. L. (1993). Response styles and the duration of episodes of depressed mood. *Journal of Abnormal Psychology, 102*, 20–28.

Skinner, B. F. (1957). *Verbal behavior*. New York: Appleton-Century-Crofts.

Behavioral Observation

Behavioral observation is a method of assessment that involves recording of overt behaviors and emotions by human observers in research or clinical settings. Ideally, behavioral observation includes recording behavior when it occurs; using trained and impartial observers who follow clearly specified rules and procedures regarding when and where observations will occur; using previously designated, well-defined categories of behavior that require a minimal degree of inference; and using some procedure to assess interobserver agreement. These features distinguish behavioral observation from related procedures for assessing behavior, such as narratives, retrospective reports, and ratings (Hartmann, Barrios, & Wood, 2004).

Historically, behavioral observation has been associated with behavioral research and behavior therapy practice. Since its use in the ideal form typically requires more time and resources than other assessment methods, behavioral observation has been used much more extensively in research than in clinical practice (Mash & Foster, 2001). Nevertheless, although often not conforming to the ideal, the use of more informal methods of behavioral observation is ubiquitous in clinical practice, transcending all theoretical frameworks and methods of assessment involving face-to-face contact between therapist and patient. In the context of depression, behavioral observation can play an important role in several areas of clinical practice, including case formulation, diagnosis, treatment planning, monitoring of treatment progress, and assessing treatment outcomes. Behavioral observation may be particularly helpful in conducting a functional analysis of behavior, which is the identification of behaviors to be targeted for treatment and their potential controlling variables (antecedents and consequences).

Behavioral Observation in Research

Behavioral observation has been used in research to examine factors related to depression across a range of naturalistic and analog settings and populations. For example, research into family processes in depression has suggested that depression is inversely related to levels of support, attachment, and approval experienced by adolescents in their families. The Living in Family Environments (LIFE; Hops, Biglan, Tolman, Arthur, & Longoria, 1995) coding system represents one method designed to assess both behaviors characteristic of depressed individuals and the interactions between the depressed person and his or her family members. Observers record the affect and verbal content of interactions as they unfold in real time, and various behaviorally based constructs (e.g., aggressive and facilitative behavior) can then be derived from the coding system. In a similar vein, observational coding systems (Kerig & Baucom, 2004) have been used to examine multiple aspects of couples' problem-solving interactions (e.g., communication, specific affect, attachment), revealing that depressed couples display more negative communication and lower comprehension of each other's messages.

Behavioral Observation in Clinical Practice

Given the time and resources required for systematic behavioral observation, its use in clinical practice is typically less structured and more informal. In terms of assessment, a diagnosis of depression may involve establishing whether certain behavioral markers and symptoms of depression are present, including psychomotor agitation or retardation, frequent tearfulness, or difficulty with concentration. Direct observation of a patient and his or her behaviors (e.g., poor eye contact, low voice volume) may alert the clinician to problems that the patient may not wish to acknowledge or verbalize.

Patients themselves may also be asked to engage in some form of behavioral observation during the treatment process. For example, psychotherapy grounded in behavioral theory may conceptualize depression as being rooted in the antecedents and consequences of various target behaviors (e.g., rumination, withdrawal), and it would therefore be beneficial to collect information regarding these behaviors. The patient may be asked to collect data between sessions by observing his or her own behaviors (self-monitoring), in order to specify the factors associated with target behaviors and links to affect. For example, patients may also be advised to gather behavioral information by observing bodily sensations, activities in which they were engaging, and emotional and behavioral reactions to various life events.

As part of the assessment and treatment process, the clinician must also assess key symptoms that might influence treatment decisions and observe behavioral indicators that may indicate whether or not treatment outcomes are being achieved. By observing the degree of change in target behavioral symptoms and impairments, the clinician and patient may be able to determine whether interventions should be continued, changed, or terminated. In order to assess treatment outcome, the therapist may ask a patient to complete a daily log in which to note changes in certain symptoms and behaviors that may be relevant to the patient's treatment goals, such as assertiveness, engagement in social activities, episodes of tearfulness, or ruminative thinking. From a cognitive-behavioral perspective, the clinician may wish to use role-play activities during therapy as a tool for observing patterns and changes in a patient's response styles during the course of therapy. Treatment approaches placing a strong emphasis on interpersonal factors in depression (e.g., social skills and communication) can provide many opportunities for clinicians to incorporate behavioral observation into both individual and group modalities.

In addition to its use in psychological treatments, behavioral observation can also be useful in evaluating patient responses to antidepressant medications. For example, clinicians should remain attentive throughout the treatment process to various behavioral indicators that medications are having their desired effects for the patient, in addition to monitoring signs of problematic negative side effects. Behavioral observation may be helpful for monitoring change within the therapy session itself, and certain behaviors such as facial expressions, nonverbal behaviors, affect, and arousal may yield important information about improvement in depressive symptoms. Observation may also be used as a tool to assist the clinician in monitoring the therapeutic relationship, by directly monitoring both the patient's and his or her own behaviors and emotional responses.

Behavioral observation can be a particularly important tool for assessing depression in children. Depressive symptoms in young children frequently go undetected by adult caregivers because they are typically less disruptive to the child's environment than externalizing disorders (e.g., attention deficit hyperactivity disorder), and because young children are less able to spontaneously and/or directly report depressive symptoms. Observation of a child's enthusiasm or other positive and negative emotions and behaviors during a free play or structured task interaction with caregivers may be useful in identifying preschool children with depression, as well as in differentiating early depression from co-occurring externalizing disorders (Luby et al., 2006).

General Issues and Considerations

One of the major advantages of behavioral observation is that unlike self-report data, it is less subject to the biases of the patient who may lack accurate awareness or insight into his or her own depressive behaviors. Occasionally, patients wish to present themselves more or less favorably through self-report measures of depression and behavioral observation may allow the clinician or researcher to gather a more objective picture of the patient's presenting problem. Clinician rating scales for depression in adults, such as the widely used Hamilton Rating Scale for Depression (Hamilton, 1967), often involve observation of relevant behaviors and associated ratings of frequency and severity. Similarly, rating scales for depression in young children, such as the Preschool Feelings Checklist (Luby, Heffelfinger, Koenig-McNaught, Brown, & Spitznagel, 2004), are based largely on behavioral observations by parents or caregivers.

Several important issues relevant to behavioral observation should be considered, such as reliability and validity of behavioral observations, especially when using observational methods for research purposes. One of the key issues related to construct validity (i.e., the extent to which observations assess the domain of interest) involves specifying the construct or behavior to be observed, and how it will be operationalized. For example, the target behavior of "improved social involvement" may be operationalized in a number of ways, including less social withdrawal, participation in a greater number of social activities, or speaking more frequently to others when in social situations. Therefore, it is often useful to assess multiple indicators related to the behavior of interest.

Data gathered through behavioral observation are complex and are not without their own forms of bias including sampling and interpretive errors on the part of the observer. Systematic errors in observation may result from the observer's expectancies regarding the outcome of an intervention or research protocol. Obtaining observational data from multiple informants is best, in order to balance out expectancy effects and other interpretive errors. For example, obtaining observational data from both parents and teachers may provide a more complete picture of a child's depression. It is important to note, however, that interobserver agreement, or the extent to which different observers provide comparable scores or ratings when observing an individual's behaviors, is often only fair to moderate, particularly when observations are made in different settings. When including behavioral observation data in clinical and research reports, it should be clearly identified as such and references for the reliability and validity of observational tools used should also be provided (Hunsley & Mash, 2008). In the context of behavioral observation, collecting data at multiple time points and from multiple observers is generally the optimal approach.

LAUREN C. HAUBERT AND ERIC J. MASH

See also

Assessment of Depression
Behavior Therapy
Behavioral Models of Depression

References

Hamilton, M. (1967). Development of a rating scale for primary depressive illness. *British Journal of Social and Clinical Psychology, 6,* 278–296.

Hartmann, D. P., Barrios, B. A., & Wood, D. D. (2004). Principles of behavioral observation. In S. N. Haynes & E. M. Heiby (Eds.), *Comprehensive handbook of psychological assessment, Vol. 3: Behavioral assessment* (pp. 108–127). Hoboken, NJ: John Wiley and Sons.

Hops, H., Biglan, A., Tolman, A., Arthur, J., & Longoria, N. (1995). *Living in Family Environments (LIFE) coding system: Reference manual for coders.* Eugene: Oregon Research Institute.

Hunsley, J., & Mash, E. J. (2008). *A guide to assessments that work.* New York: Oxford University Press.

Kerig, P. K., & Baucom, D. H. (Eds.). (2004). *Couple observational coding systems.* Mahwah, NJ: Lawrence Erlbaum Associates.

Luby, J. L., Heffelfinger, A., Koenig-McNaught, A. L., Brown, K., & Spitznagel, E. (2004). The Preschool Feelings Checklist: A brief and sensitive screening measure for depression in young children. *Journal of the American Academy of Child and Adolescent Psychiatry, 43,* 708–717.

Luby, J. L., Sullivan, J., Belden, A., Stalets, M., Blankenship, S., & Spitznagel, E. (2006). An observational analysis of behavior in depressed preschoolers: Further validation of early-onset depression. *Journal of the American Academy of Child and Adolescent Psychiatry, 45,* 203–212.

Mash, E. J., & Foster, S. L. (2001). Exporting analogue behavioral observation from research to clinical practice: Useful or cost-defective? *Psychological Assessment, 13,* 86–98.

Behavior Therapy

Behavior therapy is an approach to psychological treatment that assumes that psychopathological behavior is learned and that it can be unlearned by the same learning principles. It is based on several traditions in psychology. First it is based on the philosophical position of behaviorism, which holds that the science of psychology ought to be concerned with observable, measurable behavior. This position rejects introspection and speculation about internal structures and mechanisms that were earlier studied from other philosophical approaches to psychological science. Second, behavior therapy is based on a tradition of learning theory derived from the laboratory study of humans and animals. Both the classical conditioning tradition of Pavlov and the operant approach of Skinner are represented in this work. Many of the assumptions about the nature of psychological disorders are derived from laboratory models of these disorders, and treatment is derived from laboratory models of eliminating the disordered behavior. Third, this laboratory tradition brings with it an experimental methodology concerned with controlled manipulation of variables and the measurement of effects. Behavior therapy with patients involves this methodology of hypothesis development and testing by the manipulation of relevant variables and assessing the effects of the manipulation on the targeted behavior. The term *behavior therapy* is almost synonymous with the term *behavior modification*, although the latter carries more or a connotation of being limited to operant methods.

Behavior therapy began with methods developed primarily to treat anxiety disorders. Following from the notion that anxiety could be a conditioned response, methods for reversing the process by counterconditioning were developed. This process is illustrated by Watson and Raynor's (1920) famous case of creating a conditioned fear in Little Albert. A conditioned fear was established by pairing a frightening noise with the presentation of a laboratory animal. Mary Cover Jones (1924) completed the intended study by subsequently treating a similar naturally occurring fear in Little Peter. She counterconditioned the fear by pairing the gradual introduction of the feared object while Little Peter was happily enjoying his lunch. In theory, the enjoyment of lunch inhibited the fear at each step of the gradient of introduction. The treatment of anxiety known as systematic desensitization came more formally into the field with the publication of Joseph Wolpe's *Psychotherapy by Reciprocal Inhibition*, in 1958. Relaxation was the typical inhibitor of anxiety presented in graded imagery scenes.

It was some time later that the behavior therapy approach was applied to depression. Charles Ferster (1973) wrote some speculative papers on the behavioral analysis of depression, but it was Peter Lewinsohn (1974) who developed a theoretical model and translated it into a program of treatment and treatment research. Lewinsohn theorized that depression represented a loss or lack of response contingent positive reinforcement. In other words, when people suffer a loss, such as a job or a loved one, they lose a source of reinforcement that organizes their behavior. In the absence of that source of reinforcement many related behavior chains may deteriorate. For example, the boy who breaks up with a girlfriend no longer looks forward to weekends and loses interest in reading the paper to find out what movies are playing. These formerly enjoyable experiences have lost the reinforcing value they had because they were connected with dating the girlfriend.

Lewinsohn expanded on this idea by saying that there are three primary ways in which people might suffer from insufficient reinforcement to maintain their behavior. First, the environment may lack the reinforcement due either to a loss of a reinforcer or to a deficient and unrewarding environment. Second, people may lack the skills (social, job, etc.) to obtain sufficient reinforcement. Third, people may suffer from anxiety that keeps them from experiencing the reinforcement that the environment offers. Each of these ways of not being reinforced leads to a different therapy strategy. For the first, activity scheduling is used to increase the person's rewarding activities. Often when people are depressed they do not engage in behavior that was formerly rewarding. This approach returns them to those behaviors. The second problem calls for social skill training, and the third for desensitization of the anxiety. Lewinsohn later developed a psychoeducational therapy approach that combined these therapy modules and added additional content.

Wolpe (1958) had suggested that depression was caused by a lack of assertiveness. Being unassertive puts people at a disadvantage in interpersonal relationships, leading to unrewarding experience. This thread of assertiveness training and various formats for improving social skills has been evaluated in a number of studies and has been demonstrated to be an effective form of behavior therapy for depression. A related idea is that depression results from a lack of problem-solving skills. Nezu, Nezu, and Perri (1989) published a therapy manual for problem-solving therapy for depression and reviewed the literature that demonstrates that depressed people tend not to view difficulties in their lives as problems to be solved, but as unfortunate situations to be endured. Thus, they have poorly developed problem-solving skills and benefit from a program that improves them.

The work of Martin E. P. Seligman (1981) represents another process of animal research leading to a behavioral model of depression with implications for strategies of behavior therapy. Seligman was doing research with dogs in an escape-avoidance learning paradigm. In this type of study the animal is in a shuttle box with two sides separated by a low barrier. A light comes on one side of the box, signaling that a shock will be presented through a grid on the floor in a few seconds. Typically the dog first learns by trial and error that the shock can be escaped by jumping to the other side of the box. Gradually the dog learns to avoid the shock by jumping to the other side when the light comes on before the shock. Seligman observed that when the animals had had an earlier experience with unavoidable shock, they were poor at

learning the escape and avoidance sequence. Some dogs just lay down and waited for the shock to be over. He termed this phenomenon *learned helplessness* and viewed it as an animal model for depression. When humans encounter uncontrollable aversive experiences they feel helpless and fail to make effective efforts to improve their lot. A number of parallels between learned helplessness and depression were cited. Seligman extended his research to humans and noted that following an experience with an unsolvable puzzle, they were less able to succeed at a solvable problem. Their behavior in this regard was similar to the behavior of the helpless animals and was also similar to the behavior of actually depressed individuals.

This theory evolved into a more cognitive form with the idea that humans are vulnerable to becoming helpless, and thus developing depression, if they have a depressive attributional style. A depressive attributional style involves making attributions that are internal, stable, and global for negative events and external, unstable, and specific for positive events. That is, they are prone to blame themselves for negative events and assume that the internal cause is a continuing and general tendency of theirs, and at the same time are prone not to take credit for positive events that are likely to be seen as transient and specific chance occurrences with no implications for the future or other circumstances. Seligman proposed that the learned helplessness model of depression leads to four possible treatment strategies. He termed these strategies (a) environmental enrichment, where therapy would make the person's environment more controllable; (b) personal control training, where therapy would teach social skills to make the person more effective and less helpless; (c) resignation training, in which therapy would be aimed at helping the person to give up an unrealistic goal that person is helpless to achieve; and (d) attributional retraining, where therapy is aimed at modifying depressive biases in making attributions about negative and positive events. The last strategy has been used as a depression prevention intervention.

Each of these behavior therapy approaches to depression is based on a different conception of the nature of the disorder. Each is formulated in behavioral learning terms and is based on models from experimental research. Each has been researched and tested as a model of depression and as a strategy or set of strategies for ameliorating depression.

In recent years behavior therapy has blended with the cognitive approaches to psychology and therapy. The cognitive perspective on the treatment of depression is best represented by Beck's (1967) cognitive therapy, which has behavioral components. Albert Ellis (1962) developed rational emotive therapy, but later renamed it rational emotive behavior therapy, in recognition that it also had behavioral components. Just as the cognitive therapies have behavioral components, most of the behavioral therapies have developed in ways that incorporate cognitive elements. Today these approaches together are termed cognitive behavior therapy and have both behavioral and cognitive elements.

LYNN REHM

See also

Behavioral Models of Depression
Cognitive Behavioral Therapy
Cognitive Theories of Depression

References

Beck, A. T. (1967). *Depression: Clinical, experimental, and theoretical aspects.* New York: Harper and Row.
Ellis, A. (1962). *Reason and emotion in psychotherapy.* Secaucus, NJ: Lyle Stuart.
Ferster, C. B. (1973). A functional analysis of depression. *American Psychologist, 28,* 857–870.
Jones, M. C. (1924). The elimination of children's fears. *Journal of Experimental Psychology, 1,* 383–390.
Lewinsohn, P. M. (1974). A behavioral approach to depression. In R. J. Friedman & M. M. Katz (Eds.), *Psychology of depression: Contemporary theory and research* (pp. 157–178). New York: Wiley.
Nezu, A. M., Nezu, C. M., & Perri, M. G. (1989). *Problem-solving therapy for depression: Theory, research and clinical guidelines.* New York: Wiley.
Seligman, M. E. P. (1981). A learned helplessness point of view. In L. P. Rehm (Ed.), *Behavior therapy for depression:*
Present status and future directions (pp. 123–141). New York: Academic Press.
Watson, J. B., & Raynor, R. (1920). Conditioned emotional reactions. *Journal of Experimental Psychology, 3,* 1–4.
Wolpe, J. (1958). *Psychotherapy by reciprocal inhibition.* Stanford, CA: Stanford University Press.

Bereavement

Bereavement has been described as one of the most disruptive and distressing events of anyone's life. Though most individuals mourn and ultimately return to their daily lives adequately, for a significant proportion of otherwise normally bereaved individuals, some aspects of the grieving process may never end. One investigator even stated: "One doesn't get over it—one just gets used to it." Like other major stressors, bereavement can precipitate complications such as depression and other psychiatric disorders and general medical conditions, especially when additional risk factors are present. In order to maximally help bereaved patients, clinicians must understand the normal grieving process, be able to recognize major depression and other complications, and become familiar with basic treatment principles in the presence of bereavement.

Definitions

Grief can be defined as the emotional, behavioral, social, and functional responses to a significant loss or even the anticipation of such event. The term *bereavement* is used when grief results from the death of a loved one. Complicated grief (a.k.a., traumatic, unresolved, or chronic grief) is the current designation for a syndrome of severe and unrelenting grief symptoms lasting beyond 6 months and causing substantial impairment in work and social functioning. Associated with negative long-term general medical and mental health consequences, including suicidality, complicated grief is characterized by a preoccupation with thoughts of the deceased, being upset by memories of the deceased, inability to accept the death, longings for the person, being drawn to places and things associated with the person, anger, disbelief, feeling stunned or dazed, difficulty trusting and/or caring about others, pain in the same parts of the body as the deceased, avoidance of reminders, emptiness, feelings of unfairness, bitterness, envy of others, and feeling excruciating loneliness. While these features are part and parcel of acute grief reactions, the hallmark of complicated grief is their intensity and unrelenting persistence beyond the socially and culturally sanctioned duration of what is considered normal grief, currently defined by several groups of investigators as 6 months.

Tasks of Grief

While some investigators have attempted to define discrete stages of grief, such as an initial period of shock, disbelief, and denial; followed progressively by anger, somatic and emotional distress, social withdrawal and depression; and finally culminating in a period of reorganization and recovery, most modern grief specialists recognize the limitations of such formulas for grief and emphasize instead the variations and fluidity of grief experiences that differ considerably in intensity and length among cultural groups and from person to person. No grief stage theory, to date, has been able to account for how people cope with loss, why they experience varying degrees and kinds of distress at different times, and how they adjust to a life without their loved one over time.

An alternate model of grief postulates several relatively independent tasks that challenge many, if not most, bereaved individuals: working through the intensely painful emotional and cognitive responses that accompany the loss of a loved one and accepting positive feelings that also permeate the grief process; finding healthy and adaptive ways of modulating emotional pain and limiting maladaptive coping; maintaining a psychologically and symbolically acceptable continuing relationship with the deceased loved one while coming to grips with the reality of the death; adjusting to a world in which the deceased is missing in a very real and concrete way by maintaining old roles and developing the capacity to master new ones as necessary; maintaining key relationships with friends and relatives and becoming available to form new intimate relationships as appropriate; and achieving a healthy and integrated self-concept and stable worldview.

Distinguishing Normal Grief From Major Depression

The *Diagnostic and Statistical Manual of Mental Disorders*, fourth edition, text revision (*DSM-IV-TR*; American Psychiatric Association, 2000), suggests the diagnosis of bereavement "when a focus of attention or treatment is the death of a loved one," even if the person meets criteria for major depressive episode and symptoms have been present for up to 2 months from the time of the loss. However, a major depressive episode should be strongly considered when there is guilt about things unrelated to actions at the time of the death, pronounced psychomotor retardation, morbid feelings of worthlessness, sustained suicidal ideation, or prolonged and marked functional impairment. Bereaved individuals may also be at risk for prolonged anxiety symptoms and panic and phobic disorders. Risk factors for developing depression and/or prolonged anxiety during bereavement include relative youth, substance abuse, serious medical illness, and past histories of psychiatric disorders. Once a psychiatric complication occurs, it tends to take on a life of its own and may be every bit as chronic and recurrent as a non-bereavement-related major depressive episode and anxiety disorders. Therefore, most grief theorists recommend treating the major depressive episodes and anxiety disorders that occur in the wake of bereavement as aggressively as any other non-bereavement-related major depressive episodes and anxiety disorders.

Treatment Considerations

Most bereaved individuals grieve and ultimately adapt to their loss without the need for treatment. On occasion, grief groups can provide support, education, and normative information that can help a struggling individual cope with his or her pain and suffering. This may be especially true after particularly traumatic losses, such as death of a child or after a suicide or homicide. The two situations for which there is substantial data that more formal treatment can be helpful are for (a) the syndrome of complicated grief and (b) a major depressive episode. For complicated grief, a specific form of short-term, focused psychotherapy, called complicated grief therapy (CGT), is a modification of interpersonal psychotherapy that adds elements derived from cognitive behavioral therapy and from motivational interviewing. Each session includes loss-focused grief work and restoration-focused attention. The loss-related work focuses on helping the bereaved accept the loss, talk comfortably about the death and surrounding events, take pleasure and comfort in memories of the loved one, and feel a deep sense of connection with the deceased. To accomplish these goals, it uses imaginal revisiting and other exercises that resemble the prolonged exposure techniques used for posttraumatic stress disorder. The restoration-focused work helps the person become free to pursue personal goals, engage in meaningful relationships with others, and experience satisfaction and enjoyment. This form of therapy has been found very effective in normalizing complicated grief symptoms even in situations of great severity, chronicity, and comorbidity (Shear et al., 2005). For major depressive episodes, it is important to consider bereavement-related depression just as real and potentially pernicious as any other non-bereavement-related major depressive episode. Research has found that more than one-third of the widows and widowers who meet criteria for major depressive episode 2 months after their spouse's death remain depressed at 12-month follow-up, suggesting that perhaps treatment as early as 6 to 8 weeks after the loss may minimize long-term difficulties. At present, no single form of psychotherapy and/or antidepressant medication has been found to be the most effective. It is not uncommon for clinicians to be concerned about the use of medications in the context of grief; some fear that such interventions will negatively disrupt the natural course of the grieving process. However, emerging data suggests that treating major depressive episode and with medications, if otherwise indicated, actually facilitates the grief process, allowing individuals to experience their emotions and reactions without interference. Guidelines for the use of antidepressant medications in the treatment of non-bereavement-related major depressive episode apply equally to the treatment of major depressive episode in the presence of bereavement (Zisook & Shuchter, 2001; Auster et al., 2008; Hensley, 2005).

Summary

Grief is a complex, highly individualized process involving immense turmoil and pain. In most circumstances, the pain subsides and the bereaved individual adjusts to the loss, getting on with life without need for professional intervention. However, for a minority, bereavement is a risk factor for onset of major depressive episode and other psychiatric complications. In turn, these conditions can be associated with diminished quality of life and increased medical morbidity and mortality unless treated. Unfortunately, the misconception that depression is an expected feature of grief often leads to underdiagnosis and undertreating of these patients. Existing data suggest that treating complicated grief and depression can facilitate grief. A model that includes education, support, individualized psychotherapy, and medication management, while addressing each patient's needs and preferences, maximizes the probability of successful treatment.

KRAUZ GANADJIAN AND SIDNEY ZISOOK

See also

Diagnostic and Statistical Manual of Mental Disorders
Interpersonal Psychotherapy

References

American Psychiatric Association. (2000). *Diagnostic and statistical manual of mental disorders* (4th ed., text revision). Washington, DC: Author.

Shear, K., Frank, E., Houck, P., & Reynolds, C. F. (2005). Treatment of complicated grief: A randomized controlled trial. *Journal of the American Medical Association, 293,* 2601–2608.

Zisook, S., & Shuchter, S. R. (2001). Treatment of the depressions of bereavement. *American Behavioral Scientist, 44,* 782–797.

Biological Models of Depression

Major depression is a leading cause of psychiatric morbidity, with a prevalence rate of 10% to 15% in the general population. Many neurobiological systems have been proposed as possible etiological pathways for depressive disorders, including monoamines, neurohormones, neuroplasticity or neurogenesis, and inflammation. The biological hypotheses of depression are bolstered by family studies showing a higher risk of depression in first-degree relatives of persons with depression (Kendler, Davis, & Kessler, 1997). However, the effects of moderating variables such as early trauma are known to influence the genetic risk for depression. Such variables may change the threshold for depression (i.e., increasing the likelihood of depression in a vulnerable population) (Rutter, Moffitt, & Caspi, 2006) as well as influence the manifestations of psychopathology, for example, determining the path to depression versus generalized anxiety disorder (Kendler, 1996). These gene-by-environment interactions also influence the presentation of specific neurobiological abnormalities within the depressed populations (Nemeroff, 2004). These abnormalities may, in turn, produce secondary effects that enhance risk for psychopathology.

Our contemporary views about the pathophysiology of depression have been heavily influenced by the discovery of effective antidepressant treatments beginning in the 1950s. For example, the monoaminergic theories of depression are directly related to the mechanisms of action of antidepressant drugs. This not only helped with improved understanding of pharmacodynamics of antidepressant drugs but also with better analyzing the pathophysiology of depression. Below, we present an overview of the different biological models of depression.

The Monoamines

Various behavioral and psychological functions such as mood, emotion, sleep, and appetite are known to be modulated by the serotonin system. After the discovery that many antidepressants act by increasing synaptic levels of serotonin and norepinephrine, it was proposed that depression is caused by a decrease in absolute concentrations of one or both of these transmitters. Although these early studies were overly simplistic in their conclusions, dysregulation of monoamines may play an etiological role in at least some forms of depression. This view is strongly supported by the observations of the effects of the depletion of monoamines on response to antidepressants. For example, Delgado and colleagues (1990) have used paradigms to acutely deplete serotonin by giving a tryptophan-free mixture of amino acids (which rapidly depletes brain tryptophan, a precursor of serotonin). Similarly, brain norepinephrine can be rapidly reduced by the administration of alpha-methylparatyrosine, which inhibits the enzyme tyrosine hydroxylase, the rate-limiting step in the synthesis of norepinephrine (Miller et al., 1996). These depletion methods have been given to patients effectively treated with either serotonin or norepinephrine selective reuptake inhibitors (SSRIs and NRIs, respectively). As predicted, rapid serotonin depletion quickly induces depression in many patients treated with SSRIs, while norepinephrine reduction reverses NRI effects. Alternately, the opposites are not true (Delgado et al., 1999). These data suggest that the maintenance of antidepressant effects of drugs requires continuous transsynaptic signaling with at least one of the transmitters. This, in turn, supports the view that these transmitters may be involved in central mood regulation.

The underlying pathophysiology of the serotonin system may relate to the distribution or responsiveness of specific serotonin receptors. For example, many studies have shown upregulation of cortical serotonin 2A receptors (5HTR2A) and a relatively decreased number or responsiveness of the 5HTR1A type in depression, especially when associated with suicide (Arango, Underwood, & Mann, 2002). Activation of 5HTR2A generates anxietylike responses in both animals and humans (Abrams et al., 2005), whereas 5HTR1A tends to attenuate anxious response (Klemenhagen, Gordon, David, Hen, & Gross, 2006). These and related studies suggest that cellular mechanisms that regulate the available of these receptors may be involved in the etiology of depression.

The serotonin transporter protein (5HTT) in cells is responsible for the termination of serotonin signaling in the synapse by taking up the available serotonin into presynaptic neurons. The 5HTT is a critical regulator of transsynaptic serotonin signaling. Specific polymorphic variants of the 5HTT gene significantly affect the efficiency of either the expression or function of this protein. Two common polymorphic variants of the promoter region of the 5HTT gene are known to significantly decrease expression of the protein. One of these, known as 5HTTLPR, is a tandem repeat sequence in short (s) and long (l) variants. The long variant has 16 repeats and is associated with normal expression of the gene, while the short variant has 14 repeats and results in decreased expression. Although it might be expected that the s allele would act like a built-in antidepressant, the opposite has been shown in both animals in humans. This is likely to be the result of the fact that poorly regulated serotonin signaling leads to abnormal serotonin innervation, with subsequent failures of serotonergic modulation of mood.

The s variant has been shown to have a slight overall influence on the risk for both anxious temperament and depression, although the results have been mixed. However, this variant shows a major gene-by-environment effect, which influences the threshold for depression risk. Caspi et al. (2003) studied a large cohort of adults in New Zealand who had been followed with regular systematic evaluations since early childhood. The sample was divided into definite, possible, or no abuse in childhood. In the nonabused sample, 5HTTLPR had no influence on risk of depression or suicide. However, among those who definitely had been abused this variant dramatically increased the risk for both depression and suicide, with the possibly abused group being intermediary. These data suggest that altered serotonin innervation in brain may enhance risk for depression, but that this risk is moderated by the presence or absence of early trauma.

The Hypothalamic-Pituitary-Adrenal Axis

The hypothalamic-pituitary-adrenal (HPA) axis is a key regulator of physiological responses to stress. Stress stimulates the release of corticotrophin releasing hormone (CRH) from the hypothalamus into the pituitary, which releases adrenocorticotrophic hormone (ACTH) into the systemic circulation. This, in turn, stimulates the adrenal glands to release cortisol, a major feedback inhibitor of stress responses. CRH release is stimulated by norepinephrine arising from the locus ceruleus (LC), primarily (Wong et al., 2000), a positive feedback loop system in which CRH also activates LC. The binding of cortisol to glucocorticoid receptors (GRs) provides feedback regulation to the system.

A prodigious literature implicates abnormalities of the HPA axis in depression (Gillespie & Nemeroff, 2005). These findings include increased 24-hour cortisol secretion, attenuated feedback inhibition by cortisol via GRs, and elevated CRH in the cerebrospinal fluid. In addition, the elevation of HPA axis activity is associated with increased norepinephrine in cerebrospinal fluid, which indicates a disinhibited or "free-running" stress-response system in the brain.

It is also clear that HPA axis dysregulation does not occur in all depressed people (Carroll, 1985). Elevated cortisol appears to occur primarily in the melancholic subtype of depression, which is characterized by signs of hyperarousal, including insomnia and anorexia (Wong et al., 2000). Moreover, excess HPA axis activity also appears to be significantly associated with early-life adversity such as physical or sexual abuse (Heim et al., 2002). This suggests that the central nervous system is sensitized by early stressors, which increases risk for subsequent depression.

Neuroinflammation

Recent interest in inflammatory factors such as cytokines, chemokines, acute phase proteins, and cellular adhesion molecules as possible mediators of depression has been kindled, in part, by the observation of severe depressive reactions in patients with hepatitis C who are treated with interferon (IFN; Raison, Capuron, & Miller, 2006). These depressive symptoms occur very acutely after IFN infusion and can be reversed or prevented with antidepressant treatment (Raison et al., 2007). There also have been a number of studies suggesting that some patients with depression have elevated serum levels of proinflammatory cytokines such as interferon gamma (IFN-γ), interleukin-1 (IL-1), interleukin-6 (IL-6), and tumor necrosis factor-alpha (TNF-α; Raison et al., 2006). Exogenous administration of cytokines such as IL-1 and TNF-α to humans or animals causes nonspecific "sickness behavior" very similar to depression, including loss of interest in usual activities, anorexia, and diminished grooming. Proinflammatory cytokines evoke neuroendocrine and brain neurotransmitter changes associated with stress and depression and may contribute to the onset of depression (Pace, Hu, & Miller, 2006).

Neurotrophins

Neurogenesis—the birth of new neurons—continues through the life span from infancy to old age. Neurogenesis occurs most prominently evident in two areas in the brain: (a) the subgranular zone of the dentate gyrus in the hippocampus and (b) the subventricular zone, which is susceptible to actions of trophic factors such as brain-derived neurotrophic factor (BDNF). Neurogenesis is associated with processes such as learning and memory and is part of neuroplasticity—that is, the remodeling of neural circuitry related to memory. These changes, then, reflect adaptations of the brain to a changing environment and the concomitant new learning that takes place over time.

Growing evidence implicates neurotrophins, especially BDNF (and its receptor, TrkB), in the pathophysiology of depression (Duman & Monteggia, 2006). It has been shown in animal models that stress suppresses BDNF, which is associated with atrophic changes, especially in paralimbic structures (Duman & Monteggia, 2006). Antidepressant drugs have been shown to enhance BDNF secretion in the brain and both prevent and reverse the atrophic effects of stressors (Duman & Monteggia, 2006).

Depression has been shown to be associated with reduced volume of the hippocampus, which is similar to the stress effects seen in rats (Sheline, Wang, Gado, Csernansky, & Vannier, 1996). Moreover, as in the rat model, antidepressant drugs appear to restore normal hippocampal architecture (Sheline, 1996; Sheline et al., 1996). In addition, cortisol hypersecretion must be factored into this model. For example, Sapolsky, Uno, Rebert, and Finch (1990) have shown hippocampal injury in primates exposed to high-dose corticosteroids, which mimics the hypercortisolemic state in some depressed patients. This is similar to the reduced volume of hippocampus in some depressed patients, which is restored with effective antidepressant treatment (Sheline et al., 1996). The loss of hippocampal volume with elevated corticosteroids may be due, in part, to the effects on BDNF (Kim et al., 2004). High corticosteroid exposure results in reduction in BDNF, with associated decreases in neurogenesis in the hippocampus (Kim et al., 2004). This suggests that the elevated HPA axis activity in depression may mediate hippocampal injury via suppression of BDNF activity. Moreover, antidepressant drugs may restore hippocampal function via two different but interrelated mechanisms: direct stimulation of BDNF and TrkB synthesis, and suppression of elevated HPA axis activity.

Conclusions

Clearly, the pathobiology of depression is complex and is influenced by phenotypic variations in the condition. Moreover, several neurotransmitter and hormonal pathways have been implicated in the pathophysiology of depression; the mechanisms fundamental to the pathogenesis of depression are not well understood. Various biological models described above suggest that stress and other types of neuronal insult can lead to depression in susceptible individuals, and they also indicate novel targets for the rational design of new therapeutic agents.

RAKESH REDDY AND RICHARD C. SHELTON

See also

Affective Neuroscience
Behavioral Activation System
Behavioral Inhibition System
Biological Models of Depression
Dopamine
Dopaminergic Systems
Genetics of Depression
Genetic Transmission of Depression
Hypothalamic-Pituitary-Adrenal Axis
Hypothalamic-Pituitary-Thyroid Axis
Molecular Genetics
Monoamine Oxidase Inhibitors
Neural Systems of Reward
Serotonin

References

Abrams, J. K., Johnson, P. L., Hay-Schmidt, A., Mikkelsen, J. D., Shekhar, A., & Lowry, C. A. (2005). Serotonergic systems associated with arousal and vigilance behaviors following administration of anxiogenic drugs. *Neuroscience, 133*, 983–997.

Arango, V., Underwood, M. D., & Mann, J. J. (2002). Serotonin brain circuits involved in major depression and suicide. *Progress in Brain Research, 136*, 443–453.

Carroll, B. J. (1985). Dexamethasone suppression test: A review of contemporary confusion. *Journal of Clinical Psychiatry, 46*, 13–24.

Caspi, A., Sugden, K., Moffitt, T. E., Taylor, A., Craig, I. W., Harrington, H., et al. (2003). Influence of life stress on depression: Moderation by a polymorphism in the 5-HTT gene. *Science, 301*, 386–389.

Delgado, P. L., Charney, D. S., Price, L. H., Aghajanian, G. K., Landis, H., & Heninger, G. R. (1990). Serotonin function and the mechanism of antidepressant action: Reversal of antidepressant-induced remission by rapid depletion of plasma tryptophan. *Archives of General Psychiatry, 47*, 411–418.

Delgado, P. L., Miller, H. L., Salomon, R. M., Licinio, J., Krystal, J. H., Moreno, F. A., et al. (1999). Tryptophan-depletion challenge in depressed patients treated with desipramine or fluoxetine: Implications for the role of serotonin in the mechanism of antidepressant action. *Biological Psychiatry, 46*, 212–220.

Duman, R. S., & Monteggia, L. M. (2006). A neurotrophic model for stress-related mood disorders. *Biological Psychiatry, 59*, 1116–1127.

Gillespie, C. F., & Nemeroff, C. B. (2005). Hypercortisolemia and depression. *Psychosomatic Medicine, 67 (Suppl. 1),* S26–S28.

Heim, C., Newport, D. J., Wagner, D., Wilcox, M. M., Miller, A. H., & Nemeroff, C. B. (2002). The role of early adverse experience and adulthood stress in the prediction of neuroendocrine stress reactivity in women: A multiple regression analysis. *Depression and Anxiety, 15*, 117–125.

Kendler, K. S. (1996). Major depression and generalised anxiety disorder. Same genes, (partly) different environments—revisited. *British Journal of Psychiatry Suppl., June* (30), 68–75.

Kendler, K. S., Davis, C. G., & Kessler, R. C. (1997). The familial aggregation of common psychiatric and substance use disorders in the National Comorbidity Survey: A family history study. *British Journal of Psychiatry, 170*, 541–548.

Kim, J. B., Ju, J. Y., Kim, J. H., Kim, T. Y., Yang, B. H., Lee, Y. S., et al. (2004). Dexamethasone inhibits proliferation of adult hippocampal neurogenesis in vivo and in vitro. *Brain Research, 19*, 1–10.

Klemenhagen, K. C., Gordon, J. A., David, D. J., Hen, R., & Gross, C. T. (2006). Increased fear response to contextual cues in mice lacking the 5-HT1A receptor. *Neuropsychopharmacology, 31*, 101–111.

Miller, H. L., Delgado, P. L., Salomon, R. M., Berman, R., Krystal, J. H., Heninger, G. R., et al. (1996). Clinical and biochemical effects of catecholamine depletion on antidepressant-induced remission of depression. *Archives of General Psychiatry, 53*, 117–128.

Nemeroff, C. B. (2004). Neurobiological consequences of childhood trauma. *Journal of Clinical Psychiatry, 65*, 18–28.

Pace, T. W., Hu, F., & Miller, A. H. (2006). Cytokine-effects on glucocorticoid receptor function: Relevance to glucocorticoid resistance and the pathophysiology and treatment of major depression. *Brain, Behavior, and Immunity, 21*, 9–19.

Raison, C. L., Capuron, L., & Miller, A. H. (2006). Cytokines sing the blues: Inflammation and the pathogenesis of depression. *Trends in Immunology, 27*, 24–31.

Raison, C. L., Woolwine, B. J., Demetrashvili, M. F., Borisov, A. S., Weinreib, R., Staab, J. P., et al. (2007). Paroxetine for prevention of depressive symptoms induced by interferon-alpha and ribavirin for hepatitis C. *Alimentary Pharmacology and Therapeutics, 25*, 1163–1174.

Rutter, M., Moffitt, T. E., & Caspi, A. (2006). Gene-environment interplay and psychopathology: Multiple varieties but real effects. *Journal of Child Psychology and Psychiatry, 47*, 226–261.

Sapolsky, R. M., Uno, H., Rebert, C. S., & Finch, C. E. (1990). Hippocampal damage associated with prolonged glucocorticoid exposure in primates. *Journal of Neuroscience, 10*, 2897–2902.

Sheline, Y. I. (1996). Hippocampal atrophy in major depression: A result of depression-induced neurotoxicity? *Molecular Psychiatry, 1*, 298–299.

Sheline, Y. I., Wang, P. W., Gado, M. H., Csernansky, J. G., & Vannier, M. W. (1996). Hippocampal atrophy in recurrent major depression. *Proceedings of the National Academy of Sciences, 93*, 3908–3913.

Wong, M. L., Kling, M. A., Munson, P. J., Listwak, S., Licinio, J., Prolo, P., et al. (2000). Pronounced and sustained central hypernoradrenergic function in major depression with melancholic features: Relation to hypercortisolism and corticotropin-releasing hormone. *Proceedings of the National Academy of Sciences, 97*, 325–330.

Bipolar Disorders

The *Diagnostic and Statistical Manual of Mental Disorders* (*DSM-IV-TR;* American Psychiatric Association, 2000) defines four bipolar spectrum disorders: bipolar I disorder, bipolar II disorder, cyclothymic disorder, and bipolar disorder not otherwise specified (NOS). Bipolar I disorder is defined by the presence of at least one lifetime manic or mixed episode. A manic episode is further defined as a period of abnormally elevated or irritable mood, accompanied by three additional (four, if the mood is irritable only) symptoms lasting at least 1 week. The 1-week duration criterion is not necessary if the mood disturbance results in hospitalization. Additional symptoms can include the following: increased talkativeness; racing thoughts or flight of ideas; distractibility; grandiosity or heightened self-esteem; psychomotor agitation or increases in goal-directed activities; significant decrease in the need for sleep (while still feeling rested); increased involvement in activities that may result in unfavorable consequences, such as spending money beyond one's means or risky sexual behavior.

It is important to note that each symptom must represent a marked change from what is usual for the person. Like other psychological disorders, these symptoms cannot be attributed to the effects of a substance (including antidepressants) or a general medical condition. Perhaps most importantly, the mood disturbance must cause severe impairment in functioning (i.e., occupational, social, or relationship problems; hospitalization; presence of psychosis). A mixed episode is defined by co-occurring symptoms of mania and depression that are present nearly every day for at least 1 week.

Bipolar II disorder involves the presence of at least one episode of a less severe form of mania: hypomania. The symptom criteria for a hypomanic episode are identical to those for mania, but hypomanic episodes can be diagnosed when symptoms last only 4 days instead of a week and do not cause impairment in functioning. Rather, hypomanic episodes are defined by a marked change in functioning that is noticeable to others. Unlike bipolar I disorder, a diagnosis of bipolar II disorder requires the presence of at least one lifetime major depressive episode.

While bipolar I and II disorders are defined by discrete episodes, cyclothymic disorder is unique in its rapidly fluctuating nature. According to the *DSM-IV-TR,* cyclothymic disorder presents as numerous periods of depressive symptoms that do not meet criteria for a major depressive episode, as well as numerous periods of hypomanic symptoms. These fluctuations in mood must be present for at least 2 years (1 year for children and adolescents), with no more than 2 months with the symptoms absent. In addition, during the first 2 years of the disorder, no major depressive episode, manic episode, or mixed episode may be present.

Bipolar disorder NOS includes conditions with manic features that do not meet full criteria for any of the above disorders. Examples listed in the *DSM-IV-TR* include rapidly alternating symptoms of depression and mania that do not meet the duration criterion for full-blown episodes; repeated hypomanic episodes without any symptoms of depression; symptoms of cyclothymic disorder that are too infrequent to meet criteria; or mania that results from a substance or general medical condition.

Identifying Bipolar Disorders

Bipolar disorders are difficult to diagnose and may persist for many years before being properly detected by a mental health professional. There is no biological test that can indicate presence of the disorder.

Several standardized interviews include modules designed to diagnose these disorders. Perhaps the most well-known standardized diagnostic interviews for bipolar disorders are the Structured Clinical Interview for DSM (SCID), the Schedule for Affective Disorders and Schizophrenia (SADS), and the Kiddie Schedule for Affective Disorders and Schizophrenia (K-SADS). The SCID includes a module for the diagnosis of mania using questions that directly mirror *DSM* criteria. That is, a trained interviewer asks the patient or research participant if he or she has experienced (a) a period of at least 1 week in which he or she felt extremely high, excited, or hyper and was not his normal self and/or got into trouble, and/or (b) a period of at least 1 week in which he or she felt extremely irritable. If either (a) or (b) is endorsed, then the interviewer continues by asking the person about the presence of the various symptoms of mania listed in the *DSM*. A diagnosis is provided if the person identifies an episode that meets *DSM* criteria.

Base Rates and Costs to Society

The prevalence of bipolar I disorder in the United States has been consistently estimated at approximately 1%. Estimations of the prevalence of bipolar II disorder, cyclothymic disorder, and bipolar disorder NOS are more variable, with estimates ranging from 1% to 5% (Kessler et al., 2006). Bipolar disorders are equally common among men and women. The typical age of onset for bipolar disorders is in the early to mid-20s, but it is increasingly recognized that the disorder can start during childhood.

Bipolar I disorder is an extremely costly disorder. Those diagnosed with the disorder tend to experience repeated relapses, which can result in hospitalizations, chronic unemployment, and even suicide. The costs of the other bipolar disorders are less known. The majority of consequences of bipolar II disorder are associated with recurrent major depression, while the presence of cyclothymic disorder puts one at increased risk for the development of future manic and depressive episodes. In addition, those with bipolar disorders are at an increased risk for the development of medical conditions such as cardiovascular disease, diabetes, and obesity (Kupfer, 2005).

Etiology

Although less is known about the cause of bipolar disorders in general, there is much evidence that bipolar I disorder is highly heritable, much more so than major depressive disorder. Twin studies have shown a 70% concordance rate among monozygotic (identical) and a 25% concordance rate among dizygotic (fraternal) twins (Kelsoe, 1997). Several studies have also identified specific genes linked to bipolar I disorder, but it is currently accepted in the field that the disorder has polygenetic links. That is, bipolar I disorder is not likely associated with one gene, but rather is associated with the interaction of multiple genes.

In addition to findings of heritability, much research has focused on the role of neurotransmitters in bipolar I disorder. More specifically, sensitivity of serotonin and dopamine receptors, as well as a set of other neurotransmitters, has been implicated in mania. Finally, brain imaging studies have been used to identify abnormalities in the brain structures of those with bipolar I disorder. Most of these studies have found abnormalities in the levels of activity of the amygdala, hippocampus, prefrontal cortex, and basal ganglia.

Treatment

Psychotropic drugs have been the mainstay for treatment of bipolar I disorder since the mid-20th century. Of these, mood stabilizers and antipsychotics have been the most widely used for bipolar I disorder. The most well-established treatment for bipolar I disorder is the mood stabilizer, lithium. Other medications, including antipsychotic and antiseizure medications, have been shown to be quite effective in managing the disorder. Antidepressant medications are often prescribed to help treat the depression associated with bipolar disorders. However, it must be advised that antidepressants, when used without a mood-stabilizing medication, may trigger a manic episode and, thus, should always be used in conjunction with a mood stabilizer. There is currently much debate about the use of antidepressant medications in bipolar disorder because of this issue. Although psychotropic drugs are highly effective in the treatment of mood episodes, enjoyment of the high energy and euphoria typically associated with mania often leads those with bipolar I disorder to have trouble adhering to their medications as prescribed.

Due to the difficulties associated with medication adherence and the way in which psychosocial variables can contribute to the course of disorder, various psychosocial therapies have been created to augment pharmacological treatment. Therapies include teaching patients about the nature of the disorder and the need for medication (psychoeducation), helping them maintain consistent lifestyle schedules (sleep-wake cycles and social relationships), challenging and helping restructure maladaptive beliefs that might intensify depressive or manic states (cognitive therapy), and working with relatives of those with the disorder to improve family functioning. Psychological treatment has been found to reduce rates of hospitalization and relapse and to be particularly helpful in relieving depressive symptoms of bipolar I disorder.

Daniel Fulford and Sheri L. Johnson

See also

Bipolar Disorder Treatment: Lithium
Bipolar Disorder Treatment: Psychotherapy
Classification of Depression
Diagnostic and Statistical Manual of Mental Disorders

References

American Psychiatric Association. (2000). *Diagnostic and statistical manual of mental disorders* (4th ed., text revision). Washington, DC: Author.

Kelsoe, J. R. (1997). The genetics of bipolar disorder. *Psychiatric Annals, 27,* 285–292.

Kessler, R. C., Akiskal, H. S., Ames, M., Birnbaum, H., Greenberg, P., Hirschfeld, R. M. A., et al. (2006). Prevalence and effects of mood disorders on work performance in a nationally representative sample of U.S. workers. *American Journal of Psychiatry, 163,* 1561–1568.

Kupfer, D. J. (2005). The increasing medical burden in bipolar disorder. *Journal of the American Medical Association, 293,* 2528–2530.

Bipolar Disorder Treatment: Lithium

Lithium bromide was used to treat mania in the mid-19th century by William Hammond of New York, and the carbonate form was used in Denmark at the end of the century by Carl and Fritz Lange to treat depression. Lithium carbonate was introduced into modern psychiatry by John Cade in Australia in 1949 and further developed by internist Mogens Schou in Denmark (Baldessarini & Tarazi, 2005). Cade first provided suggestive evidence of long-term, mood-stabilizing, or effects of lithium prophylactic, and the concept was better established by Schou. Lithium was the first of many psychotropic agents introduced in the 1950s, and its selective benefits supported then-emerging nosological separation of bipolar disorder from Emil Kraepelin's broader manic-depression syndrome of the 1890s. Lithium is not only the first mood-stabilizing treatment, but also continues to set clinical standards for modern alternatives, including anticonvulsants and antipsychotics. Molecular actions of lithium in the brain are extraordinarily complex, and a coherent theory of its critical mechanism of action in the treatment of bipolar disorder remains to be defined (Baldessarini & Tarazi, 2005).

Clinical Utility of Lithium

Lithium carbonate and other salt preparations are relatively specific for the treatment of mania. However, the onset of useful action over 5 to 10 days is impractically slow for currently brief psychiatric hospitalizations. For this reason, and due to its limited margin of safety or therapeutic index, lithium is best used following initial control of mania with antipsychotics, certain anticonvulsants (usually divalproex or carbamazepine), or potent sedatives. Lithium can then be added more safely in gradually increasing doses (Baldessarini & Tarazi, 2005).

Lithium is particularly valuable for continuation in the months following recovery from an acute episode of mania, and for long-term maintenance or prophylactic treatment aimed at minimizing risk of future recurrences of all phases of bipolar disorder (Baldessarini & Tarazi, 2005). In maintenance treatment for bipolar disorder, effectiveness of lithium appears clinically to rank hypomanic > manic > mixed > depressive phases. Treatment of bipolar II disorder is poorly studied, but lithium appears to be effective in the episodic major depressive and mixed dysphoric-excited states of this syndrome, as well as its hypomania (Baldessarini & Tarazi, 2005). Lithium is also useful adjunctively in nonbipolar recurrent major depression, including cases of apparent antidepressant unresponsiveness or loss of efficacy (Baldessarini & Tarazi, 2005). Less favorable response to lithium as well as to anticonvulsants is found among patients who present with mixed, agitated, or psychotic bipolar states, with rapid cycling (≥4 recurrences per year), and with depression that precedes mania (Baldessarini & Tarazi, 2005). Delay from illness onset to starting sustained, long-term treatment, with multiple recurrences, is typically several years but does not predict inferior

response to lithium maintenance treatment (Baldessarini et al., 2007). Moreover, there is evidence that the effectiveness of lithium has not declined appreciably since its initial introduction, despite broader inclusion of patients considered to have bipolar disorder in recent decades (Tando et al., 1997).

Mortality rates are elevated among bipolar disorder patients due to stress-sensitive cardiovascular and pulmonary diseases, especially in later years, complications of substance abuse and "accidents," and the extraordinarily high risk of suicide in bipolar disorders, especially early in their course (Baldessarini et al., 2006). Lithium is the only form of long-term treatment in recurring major affective disorders with substantial evidence of reducing suicidal risk. Lithium treatment is consistently associated with reduction of attempts and suicides by more than half (Baldessarini et al., 2006), and similar effects may extend to nonbipolar recurrent major depression (Guzzetta, Tondo, Centorrino, & Baldessarini, 2007). Moreover, several comparisons have found more protection against suicidal behaviors with lithium than with anticonvulsants in bipolar disorder patients. It is not clear whether this is a specific effect, such as against anger, aggression, or impulsivity, or a reflection of long-term protection against depression by lithium. Death by acute overdose of lithium is possible, but the rate of overdosing during long-term lithium treatment is low; vomiting typically limits acute intoxication, and dialysis is highly effective in removing lithium (Baldessarini et al., 2006). Indeed, the lethality of lithium overdoses is surprisingly low, and similar to that of divalproex, modern antidepressants, or antipsychotic drugs. There is some evidence that effective long-term treatment of bipolar disorder patients, including with lithium, may reduce overall mortality risk, and not only death from suicide (Angst, Stassen, Clayton, & Angst, 2002).

Long-term treatment of bipolar disorder patients with available mood-stabilizing agents leaves most patients unwell during more than 40% of weeks of follow-up, and at least three-quarters of residual morbidity is accounted for by depression and dysthymia (Goodwin

& Jamison, 2007). These poorly responsive components of the disorder are associated with substance abuse, disability, and suicidality. Such unsatisfactory response to treatment encourages excessive use of antidepressants, whose efficacy and safety for long-term use in bipolar disorder remain inadequately tested (Baldessarini et al., 2007). In addition, inadequate response to monotherapies for bipolar disorder encourages use of combinations of drugs, such as anticonvulsants, antidepressants, antipsychotics, or sedatives, with or without lithium, even though research supporting such plausible options is lacking for most combinations (Baethge et al., 2005). Although lithium is no longer used as often as other heavily marketed antimanic and mood-stabilizing agents, it remains the longest-sustained mood stabilizer once it is used, especially in nonotherapy (Baldessarini et al., 2007).

Psychoeducational, group, and other psychotherapeutic and rehabilitation-oriented interventions can enhance stability and treatment adherence in bipolar disorder patients in a cost-effective manner and are increasingly employed in the comprehensive, long-term care of such patients.

Dosing of Lithium

Dose-response relationships of lithium and other proposed mood-stabilizing agents have not been investigated extensively. Most studies have considered daily minimum or trough serum concentrations of lithium (ca. 12 hours after the last dose). Such measures were introduced to protect against overdosing with this potentially toxic agent. Morning blood levels of about 0.6 to 1.2 mEq/L cover the therapeutic range, levels below 0.5 mEq/L are less effective, and levels above 1.0 mEq/L provide limited additional benefit but increase adverse effects and are best reserved for acute mania, rapid cycling, or treatment-resistant cases in young, vigorous patients (Baldessarini & Tarazi, 2005). Tolerability and treatment adherence can be enhanced by long-term use of moderate doses of lithium providing levels at 0.6 to 0.8 mEq/L, as is standard in international clinical practice (Severus et al., 2008).

Many patients and some physicians are reluctant to accept lithium treatment owing to popular views of its alleged toxicity or lack of efficacy, as well as concern about social stigmatization, and as a manifestation of denial of illness. Moreover, adherence to long-term treatment with lithium and other mood-stabilizing agents is often variable and requires sustained encouragement in order to maximize protective benefits.

A strongly supported aspect of long-term treatment with lithium and many other psychotropic drugs is that abrupt or rapid discontinuation is followed by sharply increased, largely time-limited, risks of recurrences of mania and depression and also suicidal acts, to levels that are much greater than suggested by the natural history of the untreated disorder. Gradual discontinuation over at least several weeks can reduce this risk by half (Baldessarini & Tarazi, 2005), and retreatment is nearly as effective as initial treatment (Tondo, Baldessarini, Floris, & Rudas, 1997).

Adverse Effects of Lithium

Adverse effects of lithium include initial frequent urination and thirst and 10% to 20% risk of later persistent, but usually reversible, clinically significant diabetes insipidus, associated with elevated circulating levels of antidiuretic hormone and unresponsiveness to exogenous synthetic antidiuretic peptides (Baldessarini & Tarazi, 2005). High 24-hour urine volumes (≥5 L) have been associated with elevated risk of histopathological changes in renal biopsies suggestive of chronic granulomatous, nephron-distorting inflammation. Nevertheless, irreversible renal failure associated with long-term lithium treatment is uncommon and can be anticipated by quarterly monitoring of serum creatinine concentrations, watching for gradually rising trends (Baldessarini & Tarazi, 2005).

Acute overdoses resulting in serum concentrations of ≥5 mEq/L require urgent and intensive medical care and immediate dialysis. If slow-release preparations are involved, there is risk of secondary rises in serum concentrations that may require more prolonged dialysis, often over several days (Baldessarini & Tarazi, 2005).

Weight gain and dermatological disorders (severe acne, worsening of psoriasis, mild alopecia) are common reasons for discontinuing lithium. However, subtle neurological or cognitive effects are leading reasons to avoid or discontinue long-term lithium treatment. These include resting tremor and impaired handwriting, as well as varying degrees of subjective cognitive impairment, mental confusion, and even mild delirium, which can occur even at trough serum concentrations in a nominally therapeutic range, particularly in elderly or neurologically impaired patients and those given multiple psychotropic drugs (Baldessarini & Tarazi, 2005).

Reduced output of thyroid hormones, occasionally with clinical myxedema, is unusual during lithium therapy. Diffuse, nonprecancerous goiter can occur, sometimes with a lowering of serum thyroid hormone indices into the low-normal or subnormal range, with early elevation of serum levels of thyroid stimulating hormone (Baldessarini & Tarazi, 2005). Treatment options include use of an alternative mood stabilizer or adding exogenous thyroid hormone.

Risk of cardiovascular malformations during the first trimester of pregnancy appears to be moderately increased with exposure to lithium (Baldessarini & Tarazi, 2005). Most often Ebstein's tricuspid-septal cardiac malformations are found in newborns at 5 to 10 times above the spontaneous base rate of approximately 1 out of 20,000 live births. These risks are far lower and less ominous than the high risks of spina bifida (≥1/100) associated with divalproex and carbamazepine (Baldessarini & Tarazi, 2005). Lithium also can induce neonatal hypotonia (so-called "floppy-baby" syndrome). Soon after childbirth, elimination and tolerance of lithium can decrease sharply to increase risk of maternal intoxication. These risks, appropriately, strongly encourage patients and physicians to avoid lithium and other psychotropic medicines during pregnancy. However, recurrence risks among women with bipolar disorders in early pregnancy, and especially the neonatal period, are extraordinarily high when lithium is discontinued early in pregnancy (Viguera et al., 2007). Such risks and that of suicide are particularly high when treatment is discontinued abruptly or rapidly, as often occurs with pregnancy or medical complications of treatment, even among patients who have been euthymic for several years (Baldessarini et al., 2007).

Conclusions

Overall, lithium remains one of the most effective and versatile options for preventing recurrences of bipolar disorder, and its evident suicide-sparing effects appear to be unique among mood-altering treatments. Nevertheless, its potential toxicity requires close medical supervision during its long-term use for prophylaxis in bipolar disorder.

Ross J. Baldessarini and Leonardo Tondo

See also

Bipolar Disorders
Bipolar Disorder Treatment: Psychotherapy
Classification of Depression
Diagnostic and Statistical Manual of Mental Disorders

References

Angst, F., Stassen, H. H., Clayton, P. J., & Angst, J. (2002). Mortality of patients with mood disorders: Follow-up over 34–38 years. *Journal of Affective Disorders, 68,* 167–181.

Baethge, C., Baldessarini, R. J., Mathiske-Schmidt, K., Hennen, J., Berghofer, A., Müller-Oerlinghausen, B., et al. (2005). Long-term combination therapy vs. monotherapy with lithium and carbamazepine in 46 bipolar I patients. *Journal of Clinical Psychiatry, 66,* 174–182.

Baldessarini, R. J., Leahy, L., Arcona, S., Gause, D., Zhang, W., & Hennen, J. (2007). Prescribing patterns of psychotropic medicines in the United States for patients diagnosed with bipolar disorders. *Psychiatric Services, 58,* 85–91.

Baldessarini, R. J., & Tarazi, F. I. (2005). Pharmacotherapy of psychosis and mania. In L. L. Brunton, J. S. Lazo,

& K. L. Parker (Eds.), *Goodman and Gilman's the pharmacological basis of therapeutics*, Vol. 11 (pp. 461–500). New York: McGraw-Hill.

Baldessarini, R. J., & Tondo, L. (2005). Does lithium treatment still work? Evidence of stable responses over three decades. *Archives of General Psychiatry, 57*, 187–190.

Baldessarini, R. J., Tondo, L., Baethge, C., Lepri, B., & Bratti, I. M. (2007). Effects of treatment latency on response to maintenance treatment in manic-depressive disorders. *Bipolar Disorders, 9*, 386–393.

Baldessarini, R. J., Tondo, L., Davis, P., Pompili, M., Goodwin, F. K., & Hennen. J. (2006). Decreased risk of suicides and attempts during long-term lithium treatment: A meta-analytic review. *Bipolar Disorders, 8*, 625–639.

Goodwin, F., & Jamison, K. R. (2007). *Manic-depressive illness* (2nd ed.). New York: Oxford University Press.

Guzzetta, F., Tondo, L., Centorrino, F., & Baldessarini, R. J. (2007). Lithium treatment reduces suicidal risk in recurrent major depressive disorder. *Journal of Clinical Psychiatry, 68*, 380–383.

Severus, W. E., Kleindienst, N., Seemüller, F., Frangou, S., Möller, H. J., & Greil, W. (2008). What is the optimal serum lithium level in the long-term treatment of bipolar disorder? A review. *Bipolar Disorders, 10*, 231–237.

Tondo, L., Baldessarini, R. J., Floris G., & Rudas, N. (1997). Effectiveness of restarting lithium treatment after its discontinuation in bipolar I and bipolar II disorders. *American Journal of Psychiatry, 154*, 548–550.

Viguera, A. C., Whitfield, T., Baldessarini, R. J., Newport, D. J., Stowe, Z., & Cohen, L. S. (2007). Recurrences of bipolar disorder in pregnancy: Prospective study of mood-stabilizer discontinuation. *American Journal of Psychiatry, 164*, 1871–1824.

Bipolar Disorder Treatment: Psychotherapy

Bipolar disorder is typically treated with medications such as lithium, anticonvulsants, and the atypical antipsychotic agents. However, most patients have recurrences within 2 years even if they are maintained on optimal medications. One study estimated that patients spent an average of 47% of the weeks in their lives in states of illness (Judd et al., 2002). Studies find that only about half of patients recover fully in the first year after a manic or mixed episode, and that even when symptomatic recovery occurs, patients still experience notable impairments in work functioning or social relationships.

These limitations on the effectiveness of medications alone has led some investigators to examine the benefits of combining psychosocial interventions with pharmacotherapy, as a means of speeding recovery, delaying recurrences, and improving functioning. Most modern methods of psychosocial intervention are psychoeducational, meaning that they focus on helping the patient to understand the nature and causes of bipolar disorder and develop strategies for coping with eliciting stressors. They also emphasize adherence with medications and illness management or lifestyle strategies, such as learning to identify the earliest warning signs of new episodes or regulating sleep-wake cycles.

Psychoeducation

Several studies have found that the combination of medication with individual or group psychoeducation has beneficial effects on the 1- to 2-year outcomes of bipolar disorder. One study conducted in Barcelona, Spain, found that in a sample of 120 bipolar patients who had been recovered for at least 6 months, a 21-session psychoeducation group in combination with medication was more effective than a standard support group and medication on a broad array of symptom outcomes over 2 years (Colom et al., 2003). Multisite studies of psychotherapy effectiveness have found that group psychoeducation is particularly effective in stabilizing mania symptoms when given in the context of an overall systematic care intervention (e.g., Bauer et al., 2006). The effects of psychoeducation on depression symptoms have been less consistent.

Cognitive Behavioral Therapy

Cognitive behavioral therapy (CBT) of depression has as its basis the identification and challenging of dysfunctional cognitions and self-defeating behaviors. The CBT of bipolar disorder includes a focus on learning to identify prodromal symptoms of relapse and obtain early medical intervention; stabilizing and regulating sleep-wake cycles; and identifying and challenging overly optimistic thinking or excessive goal-striving during hypomania or mania. It is typically administered in 12 to 20 sessions. One randomized single-center study conducted in the United Kingdom ($N = 103$) found that CBT plus pharmacotherapy was more effective over 30 months in delaying depressive episodes and reducing days of illness than pharmacotherapy alone (Lam, Hayward, Watkins, Wright, & Sham, 2005). A five-site UK community effectiveness trial (N = 253) did not replicate this result, however. CBT and medication did not delay recurrences except within a subgroup of patients (identified post hoc) with fewer than 12 episodes (Scott et al., 2006). Thus, the effectiveness of CBT in community effectiveness studies is uncertain.

Interpersonal and Social Rhythm Therapy

An adaptation of the interpersonal psychotherapy of depression, interpersonal and social rhythm therapy (IPSRT) aims to resolve and prevent key interpersonal problems that contribute to episodes of mania or depression. These problems usually center upon grief, role transitions, interpersonal disputes, or interpersonal deficits. IPSRT also includes a substantial focus on stabilizing sleep-wake rhythms and daily and nightly routines (social rhythms), and identifying environmental factors that disrupt these rhythms and destabilize mood.

In a single-site randomized trial, 175 acutely ill bipolar patients were given pharmacotherapy and assigned to IPSRT or a comparison psychosocial intervention, intensive clinical management, which included clinical status monitoring, education, and problem solving. Once they stabilized from their acute episode, patients were rerandomized to IPSRT or intensive clinical management, so that four sequential treatment strategies were compared (Frank et al., 2005). The results of this trial, while complex, generally supported the efficacy of IPSRT. IPSRT given weekly immediately following the acute episode was associated with longer intervals of wellness prior to recurrences in the maintenance phase of follow-up; IPSRT during the maintenance phase, however, did not delay recurrences beyond what could be accomplished with intensive clinical management.

The IPSRT appeared to achieve its effects in part by regulating patients' social rhythms.

Family-Focused Treatment

Family-focused treatment (FFT) incorporates principles of family therapy, psychoeducation, and behavioral skills training. In a 9-month, 21-session protocol, patients and their parents or spouses learn about the symptoms, onset, course, treatment, and self-management of the disorder, including conducting a "relapse drill" in which participants develop strategies for family support and emergency intervention when new symptoms emerge. In later phases of treatment, patients and relatives learn skills for effective interpersonal communication and problem solving. These methods are designed to alleviate high expressed emotion within the family (high levels of criticism, hostility, or emotional overinvolvement in caregiver-patient relationships), given the well-replicated observation that high expressed emotion environments are associated with higher rates of recurrence in many forms of psychiatric disorder (Miklowitz & Goldstein, 1997).

In a sample of 101 patients who began treatment shortly after an acute episode, Miklowitz, George, Richards, Simoneau, and Suddath (2003) found that patients who received FFT and pharmacotherapy had longer delays prior to recurrences and less severe manic and depressive symptoms over 2 years than a group receiving three sessions of family psychoeducation and pharmacotherapy. FFT was also associated with better medication adherence and more positively toned family interactions after treatment than the brief psychoeducation. In a 2-year randomized trial involving 52 patients, Rea and colleagues. (2003) found that 21 sessions of FFT and pharmacotherapy were more effective than 21 sessions of individual psychotherapy and pharmacotherapy in delaying recurrences and rehospitalizations. In that study, families appeared to learn to recognize and intervene with prodromal signs of recurrence before hospitalizations were necessary.

A Comparison of Approaches: The STEP-BD Program

Only one published trial has compared two or more of these treatment models to each other. The Systematic Treatment Enhancement Program (STEP-BD) compared 30 sessions of FFT, IPSRT, or CBT to a 3-session psychoeducational control (called collaborative care) in 293 acutely depressed bipolar patients. Patients were treated with evidenced-based pharmacotherapy in 1 of 15 treatment centers across the United States. Being in any form of intensive psychotherapy was associated with a higher 1-year rate of recovery from depression (64.4%) than being in collaborative care (51.5%; Miklowitz et al., 2007). Patients in intensive treatment were also more likely to remain well during any given month of the 1-year study, and to have better psychosocial functioning than patients in the comparison group. The 1-year rate of recovery for FFT was 77%; for IPSRT, 65%; and for CBT, 60%; these rates did not statistically differ.

Conclusions and Future Directions

Psychosocial treatments for bipolar disorder have many common ingredients—teaching coping strategies to manage mood, intervening early with prodromal symptoms, enhancing patients' consistency with mood-stabilizing medications, and working toward resolution of key interpersonal or family problems. Successfully achieving these objectives may contribute to more rapid recoveries from mood episodes or to longer periods of stability. Future research should attempt to identify moderators of treatment outcome (i.e., subgroups who show greater or lesser benefit from different forms of psychotherapy) and mediators (change mechanisms) of treatment effects (e.g., increased acceptance of the disorder, leading to greater adherence with medications and reduced risk of mania; decreased family conflict and enhanced family support, leading to lower depressive symptom burden).

The results of multiple trials suggest that bipolar patients require more intensive psychotherapy than is typically offered in the community. Thus, in conjunction with pharmacotherapy, psychotherapy should be considered a vital part of the effort to stabilize episodes of the illness.

DAVID J. MIKLOWITZ

See also

Bipolar Disorders
Bipolar Disorder Treatment: Lithium
Classification of Depression
Diagnostic and Statistical Manual of Mental Disorders

References

Bauer, M. S., McBride, L., Williford, W. O., Glick, H., Kinosian, B., Altshuler, L., et al. (2006). Collaborative care for bipolar disorder: Part 2, Impact on clinical outcome, function, and costs. *Psychiatric Services, 57,* 937–945.

Colom, F., Vieta, E., Martinez-Aran, A., Reinares, M., Goikolea, J. M., Benabarre, A., et al. (2003). A randomized trial on the efficacy of group psychoeducation in the prophylaxis of recurrences in bipolar patients whose disease is in remission. *Archives of General Psychiatry, 60,* 402–407.

Frank, E., Kupfer, D. J., Thase, M. E., Mallinger, A. G., Swartz, H. A., Fagiolini, A. M., et al. (2005). Two-year outcomes for interpersonal and social rhythm therapy in individuals with bipolar I disorder. *Archives of General Psychiatry, 62,* 996–1004.

Judd, L. L., Akiskal, H. S., Schettler, P. J., Endicott, J., Maser, J., Solomon, D. A., et al. (2002). The long-term natural history of the weekly symptomatic status of bipolar I disorder. *Archives of General Psychiatry, 59,* 530–537.

Lam, D. H., Hayward, P., Watkins, E. R., Wright, K., & Sham, P. (2005). Relapse prevention in patients with bipolar disorder: Cognitive therapy outcome after 2 years. *American Journal of Psychiatry, 162,* 324–329.

Miklowitz, D. J., George, E. L., Richards, J. A., Simoneau, T. L., & Suddath, R. L. (2003). A randomized study of family-focused psychoeducation and pharmacotherapy in the outpatient management of bipolar disorder. *Archives of General Psychiatry, 60,* 904–912.

Miklowitz, D. J., & Goldstein, M. J. (1997). *Bipolar disorder: A family-focused treatment approach.* New York: Guilford Press.

Miklowitz, D. J., Otto, M. W., Frank, E., Reilly-Harrington, N. A., Wisniewski, S. R., Kogan, J. N., et al. (2007). Psychosocial treatments for bipolar depression: A 1-year randomized trial from the Systematic Treatment Enhancement Program. *Archives of General Psychiatry, 64,* 419–427.

Rea, M. M., Tompson, M., Miklowitz, D. J., Goldstein, M. J., Hwang, S., & Mintz, J. (2003). Family focused treatment vs. individual treatment for bipolar disorder: Results of a randomized clinical trial. *Journal of Consulting and Clinical Psychology, 71,* 482–492.

Scott, J., Paykel, E., Morriss, R., Bentall, R., Kinderman, P., Johnson, T., et al. (2006). Cognitive behaviour therapy for severe and recurrent bipolar disorders: A randomised controlled trial. *British Journal of Psychiatry, 188,* 313–320.

Brain Circuitry

Despite the fact that major depression is common and causes considerable disability, little is known about the functional circuits in the brain that mediate its symptoms. Neuroimaging work is beginning to define intermediated phenotypes, or endophenotypes, of depression, which could lead to earlier and more accurate diagnosis in vulnerable individuals, predict treatment response, or help provide targets for new treatments (such as transmagnetic brain stimulation, deep brain stimulation, and the new generation of pharmacotherapy). Knowledge of patterns of disordered brain function in depression could lead to a more sensitive and complex set of treatment options, tailored to the individual's unique set of brain responses to the environment (Figure B.1).

However, there are some pitfalls to avoid in this process: we must be sure that any abnormal functioning of the brain that we identify is seen more readily in depression than in healthy volunteers, that it is on the so-called disease pathway rather than being an epiphenomenon, leading to real insight in the etiology of the primary dysfunction, rather than representing a compensatory remote effect of some abnormality elsewhere in the body or brain.

It is worth considering how early research carried out prior to the development of modern imaging techniques gave us important clues about the neural correlates of depression. Lesion studies and neuropathological (postmortem) studies have guided the design of structural and functional imaging studies, and the interpretation of their findings.

Lesion-Deficit Studies

Lesion-deficit studies of neurologically depressed individuals have focused on three main clinical groups: individuals with discrete lesions, individuals with known neurochemical deficits such as Parkinson's disease, and individuals who have diseases with generalized or randomly distributed pathology, such as Alzheimer's disease or multiple sclerosis.

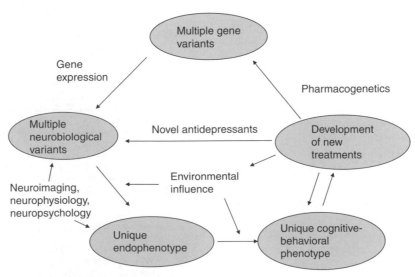

Figure B.1   The place of neuro-imaging in the development of new treatments for depression.

Frontal lobe lesions have long been implicated in depression. For example, research in poststroke depression in the 1970s and 1980s suggested a higher incidence of depression in left-hemisphere lesions, particularly if they were positioned near the frontal pole. Some studies of trauma cases and tumor patients have suggested that dorsolateral rather than ventral frontal lobe lesions are important for depressive mood change, but these are heterogeneous conditions and findings are inconsistent.

The importance of temporal lobe pathology in the genesis of organic depression is suggested by the link between depression and sclerosis of the hippocampus in temporal lobe epilepsy, the presence of temporal lobe lesions and/or atrophy in multiple sclerosis, and the extent of temporal involvement in those with Alzheimer's disease.

Cerebral blood flow asymmetries in the historically defined limbic cortex (cingulate gyrus, thalamus, hypothalamus, amygdala, hippocampus, and parahippocampus) have been implicated in depression associated with multiple sclerosis, and the basal ganglia have also been implicated in the pathogenesis of poststroke depression.

Disturbances in mood, including depression, are particularly common in Parkinson's disease. Mood changes can be seen early in the course of the illness, suggesting that depression in this context is part of the disease process rather than a reaction to disability. In Parkinson's disease, there is indirect evidence of degeneration in the ventral prefrontal cortex and ventral striatum in a number of imaging studies, including positron emission tomography measures of dopamine and noradrenaline binding, and a preclinical study of tyrosine hydroxylase depletion (an enzyme involved in the production of dopamine and noradrenaline). The ventral striatum may represent a confluence of pathology between the nigrostriatal pathway and the mesolimbic reward system. Below, I discuss studies of the dopaminergic reward system in primary depression.

The findings from lesion studies are summarized in a review by Helen Mayberg (2000), who suggests that the sum of knowledge points to depression occurring as result of disruptions in two functional pathways: the orbital-frontal-striatal-thalamic circuit and the basotemporal-limbic circuit, the former linking the prefrontal cortex (PFC; including the ventromedial PFC; VMPFC) to striatal-limbic structures (caudate, putamen, thalamus) through the middle of the brain, and the latter linking the frontal cortex to basal limbic structures (hippocampus, amygdala) via the anterior temporal cortex. The regions that are purported to be connected by these circuits are mapped in Figure B.2, with a summary of their relevant putative functions. Note the addition of the insula, a deeply embedded part of the temporal lobe, close to the putamen, which has also been implicated in subsequent imaging studies, as we shall see.

Lesion-deficit studies have two main problems, however. First, the lesioned or organically diseased brain may not behave in the same way as a brain with primary depression. Second, unpredictable compensations can occur in a lesioned brain, which could lead to erroneous conclusions about causality.

Postmortem Studies

Reduced numbers of glial cells and a reduced neuronal cell density have been found at postmortem examination in the dorsal anterolateral PFC, subgenual anterior cingulate gyrus (below the genu of the corpus callosum), orbitofrontal cortex (near the olfactory tracts), and ventrolateral PFC in individuals who had either major depressive disorder or bipolar affective disorder. In addition, reduced glial cell density has been observed in the amygdala and ventral striatum in patients with major depressive disorder and in the ventral striatum in bipolar affective disorder.

The main failing of neuropathological investigation, however, is that it is seldom possible to control for the independent effects of long-term medication use on brain biology. Also, dead tissue can give us only a limited insight into the dynamic disease state. Advances in structural and functional

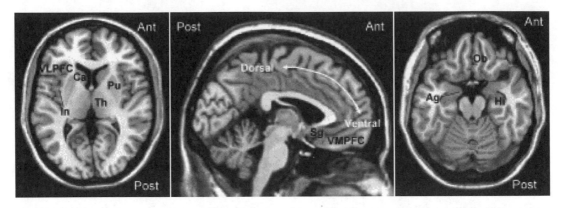

Ant = Anterior. Post = Posterior. Ca = caudate (part of the striatum, implicated in valence of feeling: pleasure or aversion); Pu = Putamen (part of the striatum, also implicated in processing pleasure or aversion); In = insula (a deep strip of temporal cortex, activity related to anxiety, autonomic function, disgust); Th = thalamus (subcortical structure which processes and coordinates sensory information); Sg = subgenual cingulate gyrus (the most ventral part of the anterior cingulate cortex, under the genu of the corpus collosum, thought to be important for integrating limbic/autonomic and prefrontal cortical inputs); Ag = amygdala (an almond shaped structure at the base of the temporal lobe, implicated in many functions, including reward processing, affect-laden memory, and the processing of fear); VMPFC = ventromedial prefrontal cortex (thought to be important in assessing the rewarding potential of stimuli, self referent processing, and voluntary emotional control, depending on the region); Ob = orbitofrontal cortex (ventral part of the VMPFC by olfactory tracts, important for more involuntary control of appetitive behaviour, 'intuitive' decision making, strong links to SG); Hi = hippocampus (at the base of the temporal lobe, proximate with the amygdala at the anterior end, implicated in processing affect-laden memories); VLPFC (ventrolateral prefrontal cortex) may be implicated in depressive rumination an processing negative outcomes; the dorsolateral and dorsomedial prefrontal cortices (not shown) demonstrate decreased activity in depression, which may contribute to difficulties with working memory and other executive functions)

Figure B.2 Anatomically and functionally connected cortical, striatal, and limbic structures implicated in the pathogenesis of depression.

imaging have made it possible to make detailed noninvasive examinations of the brain in vivo.

Structural Imaging

In support of the neuropathological data, structural MRI has demonstrated reduced left subgenual anterior cingulate cortex volumes in patients with familial major depressive disorder or bipolar affective disorder and reduced caudate, amygdala, and putamen volumes in patients with major depressive disorder.

However, reviews of structural imaging data conclude that, in general, findings are inconsistent both in terms of lack of agreement on regions of interest and in terms of consistency of findings of studies looking at the same brain regions. Hence, there are relatively few reports on the frontal cortex and striatum, whereas there are many more reports on the amygdala and the hippocam-

pus, and changes in amygdala volumes are inconsistently reported.

Nevertheless, findings in the literature are reasonably consistent with regard to diminished hippocampal volumes in depression, and this might relate to earlier age of onset and chronicity. Furthermore, limited data suggest that observed hippocampal shrinkage may be reversed by antidepressant treatment, which has been shown to inhibit dendritic atrophy and stimulate neurogenesis in the hippocampus in rat models of depression.

It is unclear whether any of these structural changes represent state or trait effects, and the effect of medication is difficult to exclude. Furthermore, it would be an error to assume that the size of an anatomical structure relates to its function. Given that there has been little evidence of actual neuronal cell loss in any of the regions described above (as opposed to glial or other cell loss), it is difficult to interpret the functional significance of macroscopic changes.

Hence, it is necessary to use anatomical- or structural-based studies as a general guide only to the regions we should be focusing on when investigating the neural markers of depression in functional studies. Accepting that functional specialization undoubtedly occurs in different regions of the human brain, it is also true that functional *circuits* are more important than discrete anatomical structures, especially when one considers that apparently discrete structures, such as the VMPFC, thalamus, or striatum, have been implicated in many different functions, including memory, sensory integration, learning, and motor control.

Functional Neuroimaging

The two most widely used methods of functional imaging are functional MRI (fMRI) and positron emission tomography (PET). The former uses the blood oxygen level dependent (BOLD) response as an analogue of neuronal activity. A close spatial and temporal relationship has been demonstrated between increases in local field potentials created by cortical neuronal activation and increases in the flow of oxygenated blood to these activated areas. Oxygenated blood is more paramagnetic than deoxygenated blood, and this difference is what fMRI is able to gauge. However, there is some debate about whether fMRI measures presynaptic or postsynaptic activity, excitatory or inhibitory activity, or all of these. PET, on the other hand, measures neuronal activation by using radiotracers. These can detect the rate of neuronal glucose metabolism (by using fluorine-18) or regional cerebral blood flow (using oxygen-15).

Resting-State Studies

The results of early resting-state PET studies of major depression seemed to be consistent with the neuropathological findings of reduced neuronal density in the PFC in major depressive disorder. They demonstrated reduced activation of parts of the PFC in depressed patients compared with healthy controls.

However, controlling for structural changes in brain regions helps to clarify the results of resting-state studies. Hence, after correcting for reduced gray matter volume, PET studies indicate an increase in metabolic activity in the subgenual prefrontal area, Brodman area 25 (BA25). Furthermore, when examining the neural correlates of treatment with the antidepressant fluoxetine, increased resting-state activity in the subgenual PFC of patients with major depressive disorder subsided with clinical improvement (Mayberg, 2000). Patients with persisting symptoms continued to have increased metabolism in this area.

The same research group had previously demonstrated increased activity in BA25 in healthy volunteers during experimentally induced sadness, suggesting that this was an analogue of depressive brain activity. Other studies had demonstrated increased activity in the VMPFC of healthy individuals during sad-mood induction, although not specifically in BA25. Conversely, *reduced* activity has been demonstrated in more dorsal prefrontal regions in depression. Persistently reduced activity in certain dorsolateral and dorsomedial areas has been shown to be indicative of poor antidepressant response, in the work of Helen Mayberg and colleagues cited above. These deficits may relate to problems with executive function in depression.

Complex relationships exist between the severity of depression and the cerebral blood flow in left ventrolateral PFC and anterior insula areas. Although the metabolism in these areas seems to be greater in patients with major depressive disorder than in the normal controls, neural activity correlates inversely with depression ratings. Drevets (2000) has argued that elevated activity in these areas is not essential for the production of depressive symptoms, but that it reflects endogenous attempts to "attenuate emotional expression, or interrupt . . . patterns of aversive, nonrewarding thought and emotion" (p. 819). However, without proper experimental control for such "endogenous attempts," it is difficult to accept such an interpretation.

Resting-state studies have also highlighted the role of limbic and striatal structures in the neural networks implicated in mood disorders, as suggested by the early lesion-based studies. Depressed individuals have demonstrated abnormally increased metabolism in the left thalamus and amygdala, and activity in the latter has been shown to correlate positively with depression severity. In contrast, metabolism in the caudate is abnormally *decreased* in patients with major depressive disorder.

In conclusion, the literature on resting-state imaging provides evidence of cortico-striato-limbic pathology in depression, mainly involving the VMPFC, dorsolateral PFC, ventrolateral PFC, insula, ventral striatum, amygdala, and thalamus (Table B.1). However, dynamic studies and connectivity analyses are welcome alongside these studies in order to clarify (a) the relative contributions of these regions to the pathogenesis of depression, (b) identify functional circuits, and (c) examine how regions interact within these circuits, including the order of effect (e.g., primary versus compensatory).

Dynamic (Task-Related) Studies

Although resting-state studies have provided important clues about the functional neuroanatomy of mood disorder, they are potentially more sensitive to the confounding effects of individual differences in arousal, mood, and cognitive state; independent metabolic and medication effects; and individual variation in terms of anatomy and hemodynamic response. It is necessary, for example, to control for variations in the size of smaller brain structures because this variation may have significant effects on radiation readings, which are independent of neural function.

Task-related designs have the potential to control to some extent for these independent variables because the hemodynamic response to each condition is compared with a baseline or comparison condition. The disadvantage is that, due to a high signal-to-noise ratio, tasks need to be repeated a number of times to provide sufficient power to detect a true signal change. Thus, in order to avoid unacceptably long experiments, tasks are necessarily brief events. Averaged responses are then compared between groups.

Again, the medial PFC has been a focus of much research, and cognitive tasks have been used in an attempt to demonstrate deficits. When compared with normal controls, patients with major depressive disorder have demonstrated reduced activation in the right mid-PFC and the anterior cingulate cortex while performing tasks that tap into the processes of selective attention, cognitive interference, and working memory (such as the continuous performance task and Stroop test). Further support is provided by performance in the Tower of London task, where a deficient neural response to positive or negative feedback on a depressed individual's performance was demonstrated in the medial caudate and VMPFC (Elliott et al., 1997). It

Table B.1   Activity in the Cortico-striato-limbic Circuit in Major Depressive Disorder

Level	Structure	
	Increased activity	Decreased activity
Cortex	Insula, ventrolateral prefrontal cortex, ventromedial prefrontal cortex,[a] subgenual anterior cingulate[b]	Dorsolateral prefrontal cortex[a]
Limbic system	Thalamus Amygdala	
Striatum/basal ganglia	Ventral pallidum	Ventral striatum[a,c]

[a]*Activity reversed in mania.* [b]*After correcting for volume changes.* [c]*Ventral striatum is defined here as nucleus accumbens and/or ventral aspects of caudate and putamen.*

has been argued that this abnormality of medial prefrontal function in major depressive disorder may lead to a deficient suppression of automatic subcortical and ventral cortical processes, which drive negative affect and thinking.

Positive Stimuli, Anhedonia, and the Reward System

Anhedonia (the diminished capacity to experience pleasure) is said to be a central feature of depression and thus has deserved some attention in the literature on the functional anatomy of depression. The putative reward-related system consists of mesolimbic dopaminergic neurons projecting from the ventral tegmentum into the ventral striatum–amygdala and thence to the medial PFC. The functional significance of the PFC in this system partly relates to its participation in the modulation of responses to aversive and appetitive stimuli. With regard to the ventral striatum, dopamine release has been shown to be tightly correlated with the euphoric response to dextroamphetamine in humans.

One might reasonably expect, therefore, that dysfunction in the reward system might be disturbed in depression, leading to the core depressive symptom of anhedonia (lack of pleasure). An emerging literature highlights positive and negative correlations between severity of anhedonia and responses to positive stimuli in VMPFC (BA10/24) and ventral striatum, respectively, in depression (e.g., Keedwell et al., 2005). This challenges the idea that depression is characterized by an inherent deficit in VMPFC control over subcortical structures per se but is consistent with resting-state data revealing reduced ventral striatum metabolism in depression. This underlines the importance in functional imaging in relating findings to the type of provocation used. In response to positive stimuli it is possible that the increase seen in VMPFC activity is a compensation for reduced ventral striatal sensitivity. However, VMPFC activity could well be increasing from a low baseline, and increased levels may still be lower than those seen in healthy volunteers.

There is increasing evidence, however, that responses in the striatum to reward are diminished in depression compared with healthy individuals. A study of adolescent depression and healthy individuals demonstrated relatively reduced ventral striatal responses in the depressed group in response to both anticipation and receipt of monetary reward (Forbes et al., 2006).

fMRI studies of depressed individuals employing a dopaminergic probe (dextroamphetamine, e.g., Tremblay et al., 2005) have demonstrated reduced responses in the ventral striatum to positive stimuli when compared with healthy individuals, despite the fact that depressed individuals had stronger euphoric responses. This suggests that although depressed individuals had greater postsynaptic sensitivity to presynaptic dopamine release (possibly due to an upregulation of postsynaptic receptors), they also had less dopamine release overall due to a smaller reserve of this neurotransmitter.

Recent work has demonstrated an increase in caudate and putamen responses to positive autobiographical memories following clinical recovery in depression. Also, negative correlations were demonstrated between Hamilton Rating Scale for Depression (HRSD, Hedlung & Vieweg, 1979) scores and caudate BOLD responses to happy stimuli (but not sad stimuli) at baseline. These preliminary findings are in keeping with depression reflecting a state of decreased striatal response to positive stimuli, which can be ameliorated upon recovery (Keedwell et al., 2008).

Physical anhedonia, which relates to somatic experience, has traitlike properties in the healthy population, leading to speculation that a high level of physical anhedonia might represent a vulnerability marker for the subsequent onset of depression. In common with findings for depressive anhedonia, this trait has been shown to be positively correlated with VMPFC responses to positive stimuli in nondepressed individuals, and there is a negative correlation with caudate volumes.

The precise functional relationship between elements of the reward system remains to be evaluated. Functional connectivity has been demonstrated between the ventral cingulate and amygdala, possibly mediated by variations in the serotonin transporter single-nucleotide polymorphism, but further studies are needed (see under Connectivity, below). Focus on this system might be more useful for severe depression, which features higher levels of anhedonia and psychomotor retardation. In fact, retardation has been shown to cosegregate with anhedonia in factor analyses of symptom scores, leading to attempts to demarcate a more endogenous or melancholic form.

Emotion Perception and Regulation: Corticolimbic Processes

Perceptual Bias

It is now well established that individuals with major depressive disorder demonstrate bias in emotion recognition away from happy stimuli and toward negative stimuli. This attentional bias compounds more general difficulties with executive function through an emotional Stroop effect and may help to maintain depression.

The neural basis of this bias has been explored using functional neuroimaging. In one study, fearful, neutral, and happy facial expressions were presented to depressed and healthy participants subliminally. The patients demonstrated increased left amygdala activation to all faces relative to normal controls but with a particularly strong response to fearful faces. A study measuring neural responses to neutral, positive, and negative pictures of the International Affective Picture System in 15 healthy individuals and 15 depressed patients revealed that the severity of depression correlated with responses to negative pictures in the left amygdala, bilateral inferior orbitofrontal areas, and left insula.

Research has shown that amygdala activation in response to negative words lasts for a significantly longer time in people currently experiencing episodes of depression than in normal controls. No such difference was demonstrated for neutral or positive words. Therefore the time course, rather than the intensity, of amygdala activation may mediate a perceptual bias toward stimuli with negative emotional meanings.

Overall then, evidence is converging to support the idea that increased amygdala activation could represent a biological substrate for the negative cognitive bias seen in depression. Elevated activity in this structure has been shown to persist after recovery from familial pure depressive disease, suggesting that this might be a trait marker of depression. The mechanism could involve increased access to emotionally negative memories, which drives perceptual bias and negative rumination.

In support of the trait-marker hypothesis for the amygdala, Hariri, Mattay, and Tessitore (2002) found that serotonin transporter genetic variation (which interacts with life events to influence the risk of depression) could modulate the amygdala response to emotional faces. This is supported by a more recent meta-analysis, although the effect size is smaller than that originally reported.

Ventral anterior cingulate responses have also shown to be important indicators of perceptual bias. A cross-sectional study (Gotlib et al., 2005) found that moderately to severely depressed patients had greater responses to the covert recognition of sad faces in the subgenual cingulate when compared to healthy volunteers. For happy stimuli, depressed individuals demonstrated greater responses in the pregenual cingulate.

A recent longitudinal antidepressant treatment study examining covert responses to sad and happy facial stimuli replicated these findings at baseline and demonstrated a decrease in right BA25 responses to sad stimuli over time, correlating with decreases in depression symptom score (Keedwell et al., in press). Consistent with other studies, there were also significant decreases in responses to sad facial stimuli in the visual cortex, bilateral amygdalae, and ventral striatum (caudate and putamen) by the end of the study period. In contrast, responses to happy facial expressions increased over time in the ventral striatum and visual cortex, consistent with previous work demonstrating attenuated overall responses in limbic-subcortical and visual cortical regions prior to treatment, which increased after antidepressant treatment (Fu et al., 2007).

The dissociated responses in visual cortex and striatum to sad and happy stimuli pre- and postrecovery are consistent with the findings showing a double dissociation of response in these regions to sad and happy stimuli in depressed and healthy individuals. In other words, visual cortical and subcortical responses tend toward normality with treatment.

Mood Provocation

Autobiographical memory prompts have been commonly employed in neuroimaging tasks that attempt to provoke sad mood. However, the neuroimaging research examining persistent abnormalities in remitted patients is sparse. In one study (Liotti, Mayberg, McGinnis, Brannan, & Jerabek, 2002) a unique effect of sad mood provocation in the pregenual cortex (BA24) was demonstrated in remitted depressed patients but not in depressed patients and healthy controls. It was suggested, therefore, that this might represent a trait marker, although scarring or treatment effects could not be ruled out.

A recent study of severely depressed individuals' responses to happy autobiographical memories over the course of antidepressant treatment, during which a large proportion went into remission (Keedwell et al., 2008), demonstrated an increase in caudate and putamen responses following clinical recovery. Further work is needed to determine if ventral striatal sensitivity returns to a level comparable to that of healthy individuals.

Ruminatory Circuits

A positive correlation has been demonstrated between degree of negative rumination and activity in the ventrolateral PFC, BA47 (Keedwell, Andrew, Williams, Brammer, & Phillips, 2005). Depressed individuals' responses to sad faces have been demonstrated

to have a greater response in BA47 after clinical improvement compared to before improvement (Keedwell et al., in press). These findings are consistent with previous work that has demonstrated that BA47 is not activated in the severely depressed in response to sad mood induction, whereas mild and remitted depressives do activate this area. It was concluded that partial or complete recovery appears to unlock ruminatory processes. A ruminative coping strategy in response to negative life events is a risk factor for depression. Hence, residual BA47 sensitivity to sad stimuli following an episode of depression might be a vulnerability marker for future relapse.

Changes Dependent on Treatment Modality

Functional imaging studies of major depressive disorder demonstrate response-specific regional changes following various modes of antidepressant treatment. For example, a resting-state PET study (Goldapple et al., 2004; Kennedy et al., 2007) examined the effects of cognitive behavioral therapy (CBT) and performed a post hoc comparison with an independent group of paroxetine-treated responders. Treatment response to CBT was associated with decreases in BA25, in common with the antidepressant group. However, there were increases in hippocampus and dorsal cingulate (BA24) and decreases in dorsal (BA9/46), ventrolateral (BA47/11), and medial (BA9/10/11) frontal cortex in the CBT group not seen in the antidepressant group, where prefrontal increases and hippocampal decreases were seen. Therefore, it appears that in CBT an active frontal area is required in order that patients may learn to recognize and change thought patterns that contribute to their depression. The patients who responded to CBT did so either because, by nature, they had more active frontal activity at baseline, or they were at an earlier stage of depression in which their frontal areas could still rise to the challenge of psychological treatment. Hence, initial high levels of frontal activity are thought to represent cognitive attempts to self-correct distorted (negative) thinking. When this attempt was successful, the frontal areas could deactivate.

To avoid the problems inherent in post hoc comparisons, further work has randomized depressed patients to antidepressant treatment with either CBT or venlafaxine and found that response to either treatment modality is associated with decreased activity in the left medial PFC (and bilateral orbitofrontal cortex). With regard to BA25, although reductions are seen in response to both treatment modalities, changes in metabolism in the anterior and posterior parts of the subgenual cingulate cortex differentiate CBT and venlafaxine responders.

Connectivity

We have seen that certain brain regions known to be implicated in emotion regulation (Figure B.2; see Phillips, Drevets, Rauch, & Lane, 2003) function abnormally in depression. However, we can not be sure how these regions are functionally related (influence each other) without some form of connectivity analysis.

It is assumed that reciprocal functional pathways link cortical (VMPFC/BA25) to subcortical (striatal and limbic) structures in order to influence autonomic activity, perception, learning, memory, motivation, and reward—core functions that are impeded in depressed patients. Functional connectivity is sometimes assumed because of the proximity or contiguity of structures within these regions or because of known white matter tracts connecting them. Diffusor tensor imaging (DTI) has helped to define white matter tracts in vivo by measuring fractional anisotropy (the tendency of radiolabeled water molecules to flow along fibers rather than across them). Hence, we are starting to obtain a more detailed picture of connections between regions of interest, which improve upon data obtained from the dissection of brains of higher-order mammals, lesions studies, and postmortem studies. For example, we can now define clear links between the VMPFC and limbic structures,

and in vivo human studies have shown that the cingulate gyrus and occipital cortex are connected by fast fibers of the inferior fronto-occipital fasciculus.

Although these anatomical data are welcome, we can not assume that anatomical connections translate to functional connections because (a) white matter connections may be more numerous and complex than DTI tractography suggests, (b) disturbance on the disease pathway can have remote effects in anatomically connected regions that are not directly influencing psychopathology, and (c) a single task will activate more than one circuit, while different tasks can activate the same circuit in different ways.

Hence, various attempts have been made to determine the *functional* connectivity between the regions implicated above using additional imaging and/or analysis techniques. One approach is to do a regression analysis of BOLD changes that occur in tandem with clinical improvement. For example, a recent study of clinical improvement during antidepressant treatment (Keedwell et al., in press) found that changes in BOLD responses to sad facial expressions in the right visual cortex (BA19) and the right subgenual cingulate were strongly correlated. Furthermore, BOLD changes in the following brain areas were also correlated with each other: BA17 and BA18 of the right primary visual cortex, and the right hippocampus and the primary visual cortex.

Alternatively, post hoc correlations can be examined between regions demonstrating different resting-state glucose metabolism in depressed patients versus healthy controls. For example, post hoc analyses of connectivity in depressed bipolar II patients demonstrate multiple limbic-cortical-striatal interactions in depressed individuals that are not evident in healthy individuals.

An fMRI study examining effortful elimination of negative mood through reappraisal, tested the hypothesis that depression was due to a failure of the vulnerable individual to engage cortical mood-regulating centers to control limbic mood-generating centers (Johnstone, van Reekum, Urry, Kalin, & Davidson,

2007). Their results indicated that a key feature underlying the pathophysiology of major depression was the counterproductive engagement of right PFC and the lack of engagement of left lateral-ventromedial prefrontal circuitry, purported to be important for the down regulation of amygdala responses to negative stimuli.

Anand and colleagues (2005) used a novel approach to assessing functional connectivity; they measured low-frequency BOLD-related fluctuations (LFBFs) in different corticolimbic regions of interest and then examined correlations between them. LFBFs, by definition, are not directly related to either the major BOLD response to the task, or physiological factors such as respiration. Rather, they seem to relate to an underlying trend in BOLD responsiveness. In order to establish regions of interest, they compared unmedicated unipolar depressed patients and matched healthy individuals' neural responses to negative and neutral pictures in a block design. Next, low-frequency blood oxygenation dependent (BOLD) related fluctuations (LFBF) data were acquired at rest and during steady-state exposure to neutral, positive, and negative pictures. Finally, LFBF correlations were calculated between regions of interest (anterior cingulate cortex) and limbic regions (amygdala, striatum, and medial thalamus), for resting and active conditions. The overall finding was that corticolimbic LFBF correlations were decreased in depressed patients compared to healthy individuals, whether at rest or in response to the pictures. This was consistent with the authors' hypothesis that decreased cortical regulation of limbic activation in response to negative stimuli may be present in depression.

Using the same technique, the same research group (Anand, Li, Wang, Gardner, & Lowe, 2007) proceeded to examine changes in connectivity in depression following treatment, testing the hypothesis that antidepressants act by increasing functional connectivity between the cortical mood-regulating regions and the limbic mood-generating regions. After 6 weeks of treatment with the antidepressant sertraline, resting-state, functional connectivity between the anterior cingulate cortex and limbic regions increased, while limbic activation in response to negative versus neutral pictures decreased. The results of this study are consistent with the hypothesis that antidepressant treatment reduces limbic activation by improving connectivity with the VMPFC.

Conversely then, refractoriness to treatment in depression might lead to persistent corticolimbic connectivity problems. A resting-state fMRI study (Greicius et al., 2007) of individuals with major depression and healthy controls examined functional connectivity within the default-mode network of regions highlighted in previous resting-state PET studies by Mayberg and other research groups. Independent component analysis was used to isolate connectivity in this network in each subject. Group maps of connectivity were then compared, revealing greater functional connectivity between the subgenual cingulate, thalamus, and rest of the network in the depressed individuals than in the control group. Within the depressed group, the length of the current depressive episode correlated positively with increased functional connectivity for these two regions.

One can conclude from these findings that overall there is mounting evidence of abnormal cortico-striato-limbic connectivity in depression (involving regions highlighted in Figure B.2). However, there are some inconsistencies in terms of the direction of effect, possibly dependent on methodological differences and specific regions of interest within the VMPFC (restricted to BA25 or more broadly defined). Further work is needed in this area, particularly the employment of connectivity analysis in tandem with task-related (provocation) approaches, and comparing clinical and nonclinical groups.

Therapeutic Implications

The finding of reduced BA25 activity during treatment for depression has been replicated in a number of dynamic or resting-state studies using a variety of treatment modalities, including antidepressant medication, vagus

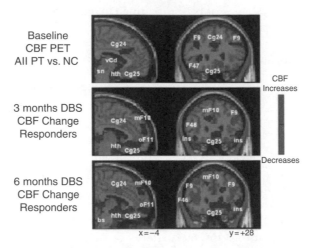

CBT, cognitive behavior therapy; DBS, deep brain stimulation. CBF, cerebral blood flow. PET, positron emission tomography. Cg24, cingulate gyrus, BA24; F9, dorsolateral prefrontal cortex, BA9; F47, ventrolateral prefrontal cortex, BA47; Cg25, subgenual cingulate, BA 25; Ins, insula; hth, hypothalamus; sn, substantia nigra; bs, brain stem; oF11, orbitofrontal cortex, BA11; vCd, ventral caudate.

Figure B.3   Changes in cerebral blood flow before deep brain stimulation and at 3 months and 6 months posttreatment in responders.

nerve stimulation, psychosurgery, CBT, and transmagnetic nerve stimulation. In response to this body of data, a recent approach to the management of treatment-resistant depression employed deep brain stimulation of the white matter tracts adjacent to BA25, demonstrating a 60% response rate (Figure B.3).

General Conclusions

Our ability to uncover clinically useful findings based on investigations of brain function is increasingly dependent on advances in structural and functional neuroimaging techniques, and careful synthesis of the data arising from these two sources.

Both resting-state and task-related fMRI studies implicate cortico-striato-limbic dysregulation in depression. This could be due to a deficit in top-down regulation of limbic structures such as the amygdala by the VMPFC (but not BA25), leading to overactivity in these areas. Antidepressants might increase VMPFC activity, which then leads to a reduction in limbic overactivity. Furthermore, there is increasing evidence from functional connectivity analysis that the junction between the VMPFC (particularly BA25) and subcortical structures (such as the ventral striatum, amygdala and thalamus) is disturbed but can be remediated with treatment.

The pattern is being complicated by findings for BA25 and the striatum in both resting-state and dynamic studies. BA25 activity is increased at rest and in response to the covert viewing of sad facial expressions in depression compared to healthy individuals. This dysfunction correlates with visual cortical sensitivity and contributes to the perceptual bias toward negative aspects of the sensorium observed clinically and empirically in depression (Figure B.4). Subcortical structures such as the amygdala and hippocampus may increase access to negative associations and memories, thereby facilitating negative cognitive biases and perpetuating depression. The response of the ventral striatum also appears to be interacting with other subcortical structures to perpetuate the depressive bias: longitudinal treatment

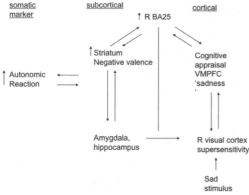

Model of Perceptual Bias In Depression (sad stimuli)

Figure B.4 Model of brain responses to sad stimuli in depression.

studies show that recovery from depression is associated with increased responses in the ventral striatum to positive stimuli and decreased responses to negative stimuli.

In conclusion, an improved knowledge of the functional neuroanatomy of depression, combined with advances in neurochemical investigation, pharmacological manipulation, and molecular genetics, will inform future models of diagnosis, etiology, prognosis, and treatment. Responses to positive and negative affective stimuli and reward-based decision-making tasks appear to be particularly promising as biomarkers of treatment response.

There is more work to be done on identifying trait markers of brain function that are not state-dependent but indicate vulnerability to depression. This will inform preventative and early intervention treatment programs. The study of depressive patients in remission is complicated by the confounding factors of possible scarring effects of illness, residual symptomatology, and treatment effects. The next generation of studies will focus on imaging young individuals determined to be at risk by virtue of their personality, family history, environment, and/or genotype. Neural markers of at-risk individuals may prove to be more sensitive predictors of subsequent depression and sensitivity to treatment than the clinical predictors we have at present.

PAUL KEEDWELL

See also

Affective Neuroscience
Amygdala
Biological Models of Depression
Brain Function in Depressed Children and Adolescents
Brain Function in Midlife Unipolar Depression
Cortisol
Cytokines
Dopamine
Dopaminergic Systems
Hormones
Hypothalamic-Pituitary-Adrenal Axis
Hypothalamic-Pituitary-Thyroid Axis
Kindling
Molecular Genetics
Neural Systems of Reward
Neuroimaging and Psychosocial Treatments for Depression
Transcranial Magnetic Stimulation

References

Anand, A., Li, Y., Wang, Y., Gardner, K., & Lowe, M. J. (2007). Reciprocal effects of antidepressant treatment on activity and connectivity of the mood regulating circuit: An fMRI study. *Journal of Neuropsychiatry and Clinical Neuroscience, 19,* 274–282.

Anand, A., Li, Y., Wang, Y., Wu, J., Gao, S., Bukhari, L., et al. (2005). Activity and connectivity of brain mood regulating circuit in depression: A functional magnetic resonance study. *Biological Psychiatry, 57,* 1079–1088.

Drevets, W. C. (2000). Functional anatomical abnormalities in limbic and prefrontal cortical structures in major depression [Review]. *Progress in Brain Research, 126,* 413–431.

Elliott, R., Baker, S. C., Rogers, R. D., O'Leary, D. A., Paykel, E. S., Frith, C. D., et al. (1997). Prefrontal dysfunction in depressed patients performing a complex planning task: A study using positron emission tomography. *Psychological Medicine, 27,* 931–942.

Forbes, E. E., Christopher May, J., Siegle, G. J., Ladouceur, C. D., Ryan, N. D., Carter, C. S., et al. (2006). Reward-related decision-making in pediatric major depressive disorder: An fMRI study. *Journal of Child Psychology and Psychiatry, 47,* 1031–1040.

Fu, C. H., Williams, S. C., Brammer, M. J., Suckling, J., Kim, J., Cleare, A. J., et al. (2007). Neural responses to happy facial expressions in major depression following antidepressant treatment. *American Journal of Psychiatry, 164,* 540–542.

Goldapple, K., Segal, Z., Garson, C., Lau, M., Bieling, P., Kennedy, S., et al. (2004). Modulation of cortical-limbic pathways in major depression: treatment-specific effects of cognitive behavior therapy. *Archives of General Psychiatry, 61,* 34–41.

Gotlib, I. H., Sivers, H., Gabrieli, J. D., Whitfield-Gabrieli, S., Goldin, P., Minor, K. L., et al. (2005). Subgenual anterior cingulate activation to valenced emotional stimuli in major depression. *Neuroreport, 16*, 1731–1734.

Greicius, M. D., Flores, B. H., Menon, V., Glover, G. H., Solvason, H. B., Kenna, H., et al. (2007). Resting-state functional connectivity in major depression: Abnormally increased contributions from subgenual cingulate cortex and thalamus. *Biological Psychiatry, 62*, 429–437.

Hariri, A. R., Mattay, V. S., & Tessitore III, A. (2002). Serotonin transporter genetic variation and the response of the human amygdala. *Science, 297*, 400–403.

Hedlung, J. L. & Vieweg, B. W. (1979). The Hamilton rating scale for depression. *Journal of Operational Psychiatry, 10*, 149–165.

Johnstone, T., van Reekum, C. M., Urry, H. L., Kalin, N. H., & Davidson, R. J. (2007). Failure to regulate: Counterproductive recruitment of top-down prefrontal-subcortical circuitry in major depression. *Journal of Neuroscience, 27*, 8877–8884.

Keedwell, P. A., Andrew, C., Williams, S. C. R., Brammer, M. J., & Phillips, M. L. (2005). The neural correlates of anhedonia in major depressive disorder. *Biological Psychiatry, 58*, 843–853.

Keedwell, P. A., Drapier, D., Surguladze, S., Giampietro, V., Brammer, M., & Phillips, M. (2008). Diminished caudate responses to happy mood triggers in depression increase with clinical recovery. Unpublished manuscript.

Keedwell, P. A., Drapier, D., Surguladze, S., Giampietro, V., Brammer, M., & Phillips, M. (in press). Neural markers of symptomatic improvement during antidepressant therapy in severe depression: subgenual cingulate and visual cortical responses to sad, but not happy, facial stimuli are correlated with changes in symptom score. *Journal of Psychopharmacology.*

Kennedy, S. H., Konarski, J. Z., Segal, Z. V., Lau, M. A., Bieling, P. J., McIntyre, R. S., et al. (2007). Differences in brain glucose metabolism between responders to CBT and venlafaxine in a 16-week randomized controlled trial. *American Journal of Psychiatry, 164*, 778–788.

Liotti, M., Mayberg, H. S., McGinnis, S., Brannan, S. L., & Jerabek, P. (2002). Unmasking disease-specific cerebral blood flow abnormalities: Mood challenge in patients with remitted unipolar depression. *American Journal of Psychiatry, 159*, 1830–1840.

Mayberg, H. S. (2000). Depression. In A. W. Toga, J. C. Mazziota, & R. S. Frackowiak (Eds.), *Brain mapping: The disorders* (pp. 458–507). San Diego: Academic Press.

Phillips, M. L., Drevets, W. C., Rauch, S. L., & Lane, R. (2003). Neurobiology of emotion perception. Part 1: The neural basis of normal emotion perception. *Biological Psychiatry, 54*, 504–514.

Tremblay, L. K., Naranjo, C. A., Graham, S. J., Herrmann, N., Mayberg, H. S., Hevenor, S., et al. (2005). Functional neuroanatomical substrates of altered reward processing in major depressive disorder revealed by a dopaminergic probe. *Archives of General Psychiatry, 62*, 1228–1236.

Brain Function in Depressed Children and Adolescents

Early-onset major depressive disorder is a recurrent and often familial disorder that affects approximately 5% of children and adolescents. It is marked by acute and chronic disruptions in functioning and tends to continue into adulthood. The risk of major depressive disorder increases dramatically across development, with a sharp increase in prevalence in early adolescence. Neuroimaging techniques are some of the tools that researchers are using to investigate the pathophysiology of early-onset depression, with the ultimate goals of elucidating the developmental mechanisms underlying the initial onset of depression and understanding the effects of depression on the developing brain. Unfortunately, efforts to understanding the pathophysiology of early-onset depression lag behind research currently underway in adult depression. Nevertheless, in the past few years, there has been an increasing number of neuroimaging studies providing evidence that early-onset depression is associated with abnormalities in neural regions implicated in the regulation of emotion. Below, I provide a brief review of the neuroimaging studies that have focused on early-onset depression.

Magnetic Resonance Imaging

MRI is a noninvasive neuroimaging technique that uses a powerful magnetic field, radio waves, and a computer to produce images of the brain. Abnormalities in brain structure related to depression in young people are assessed using MRI by examining differences in the volume of gray and white matter in the brain.

One line of research examining structural brain abnormalities in early-onset depression has focused on the frontal cortex, which plays an important role in the regulation of emotion and behavior. One study reported reduced frontal gray matter volumes in depressed adolescents compared to healthy controls (Steingard et al., 1996). Another set of more recent studies, however, reported increased gray matter volumes and reduced white matter volumes in the frontal cortex in depressed adolescents compared to healthy controls (Steingard, 2000; Steingard et al., 2002). Botteron and colleagues focused on a specific region of the frontal cortex, the subgenual

PFC, which plays an important role in mediating emotional and autonomic responses to socially significant or emotionally salient stimuli. They found that depressed young women with adolescent-onset depression had significantly reduced gray matter volume in the left subgenual PFC compared to healthy controls (Botteron, Raichle, Drevets, Heath, & Todd, 2002). Together these findings suggest that early-onset depression is associated with alterations in the development of the frontal cortex, which plays an important role in the regulation of emotion and modulation of autonomic stress responses.

Another line of research has focused on brain structure abnormalities in subcortical regions implicated in the perception and appraisal of emotional information. One study reported reduced bilateral amygdala volumes in depressed youths compared to healthy controls (Rosso et al., 2005), whereas another study found greater amygdala volumes associated with depression (MacMillan et al., 2003). Findings from the latter study, however, were no longer statistically significant once age and intracranial volume were taken into account. Differences in hippocampus volumes have also been reported. Some studies reported reduced hippocampus volumes in depressed youths compared to healthy controls (MacMaster & Kusumakar, 2004; MacMaster et al., 2008), whereas another study did not find any significant group differences (Rosso et al., 2005).

Overall, MRI studies in early-onset depression remain scarce, and findings from these studies are rather inconsistent, preventing us from drawing any firm conclusions about the nature of structural brain abnormalities related to depression in youths. Discrepancies in these findings may be attributed to small sample sizes, inconsistencies in the methods used to analyze the MRI data, differences in the medication status of the subjects, and presence of various comorbid disorders.

Functional MRI

Functional magnetic resonance imaging (fMRI) is a neuroimaging technique that uses magnetic resonance imaging to measure the small metabolic changes that take place in an active part of the brain. It is based on the increase in blood flow to the local vasculature that accompanies neural activity in the brain. Very few fMRI studies have been conducted in child and adolescent depression, compared to adult depression. Nevertheless, the few studies that have been conducted suggest that early-onset depression may be related to abnormalities in the functioning of certain subcortical neural regions.

One of the first studies conducted in depressed youths focused on the neural functioning of the amygdala, a subcortical structure located within the medial temporal lobe that plays an important role in the processing and memory of emotional reactions, particularly those related to threat. In this small study, authors reported reduced amygdala activation to fearful faces in girls with major depressive disorder (Thomas et al., 2001). Findings from a larger study, however, revealed greater amygdala activation in adolescents with major depressive disorder compared to healthy adolescents during a task that involved the incidental encoding of faces (Roberson-Nay et al., 2006). A recent study also found greater amygdala activation to the passive viewing of fearful faces in healthy adolescent offspring at high risk for major depressive disorder compared to offspring at low risk for depression (Monk et al., 2008).

Researchers are also beginning to examine abnormalities in neural systems that support the processing of positive stimuli or reward in childhood depression. The reasoning is that reduced activity in the neural systems that support the processing of positive emotional information or reward may explain the low positive affect and reduced motivation often present in early-onset depression (Davey, Yücel, & Allen, 2008; Forbes & Dahl, 2005). Findings from studies in adults suggest that depressed adults fail to display increased activation in neural regions implicated in processing positive or rewarding stimuli (e.g., ventral striatum) (Lawrence et al., 2004). One study in youths also reported altered neural responses to rewarding events in the context of a decision-making task in depressed youths compared to healthy controls (Forbes et al., 2006). Such reductions in the activation of neural systems implicated in processing positive emotional information were also found in healthy adolescent offspring at risk for major depressive disorder. Monk and colleagues (2008) reported that adolescents at risk for major depressive disorder exhibited less nucleus accumbens activation when passively viewing happy faces compared to adolescents at low risk for depression (Monk et al., 2008).

Although the amount of data is relatively sparse, these findings suggest that abnormalities in neural systems that support the processing of emotionally salient information are a key feature of early-onset depression. For example, neural regions implicated in processing threat-related information may be overactive, whereas neural regions implicated in processing positive emotions or reward may be blunted in children and adolescents diagnosed with depression compared to healthy children and adolescents. More studies are needed to elucidate the maturation of these subcortical structures in children and adolescents diagnosed with depression and whether abnormalities in the functioning of these neural regions represents a biological risk factor for depression. Furthermore, more research is needed to investigate the functioning of frontal cortical regions and their connectivity with subcortical neural systems as a way to better understand the nature of alterations in the regulation of emotion in early-onset depression.

Magnetic Resonance Spectroscopy

Magnetic resonance spectroscopy (MRS) is a noninvasive neuroimaging method used to examine concentration of major chemicals in the brain such as choline (Cho), creatinine (Cr), glutamate (Gl), and N-acetylaspartate (NAA). MRS studies have documented neurochemical abnormalities in adult depres-

sion. Findings from the few MRS studies conducted in depressed youths suggest significantly higher brain Cho/Cr and Cho/NAA ratios in left anterior medial frontal lobe (Steingard et al., 2000) and lower Gl in the anterior cingulate cortex (Rosenberg et al., 2005) in depressed adolescents compared to healthy adolescents. The increased Cho/Cr and Cho/NAA ratios could index overactivity of the cholinergic system and the decreased anterior cingulate glutamate may be indicative of altered neuronal and glial cell functioning in the anterior cingulate cortex. Overall, these findings parallel those found in adult depression.

Conclusions

Each of the neuroimaging techniques described above represents a different approach to investigating brain function in depressed children and adolescents. Overall, results from these studies suggest that early-onset depression is associated with both structural and functional abnormalities in frontosubcortical brain regions. Further research is greatly needed, however, to elucidate further the pathophysiology of early-onset depression and clarify the extent to which these abnormalities in brain function are the cause or the consequence of the disorder. For instance, longitudinal studies using a multimodel neuroimaging approach (MRI, fMRI, MRS, etc.) to investigate maturational changes in brain structure and function in children diagnosed with depression, in remission, and at risk of depression, would be most helpful. Furthermore, such studies could provide additional information with regard to the role of sex differences and pubertal maturation, given findings that the prevalence of major depressive disorder increases most drastically following puberty in anxious girls. Finally, knowing more about brain function in early-onset depression could eventually lead to studies investigating neural markers of response to various treatment approaches such as pharmacological and cognitive behavioral therapy.

CECILE D. LADOUCEUR

See also

Amygdala
Biological Models of Depression
Brain Function in Midlife Unipolar
Depression
Functional Neuroimaging
Hypothalamic-Pituitary-Adrenal Axis
Hypothalamic-Pituitary-Thyroid Axis
Neural Systems of Reward
Neuroimaging and Psychosocial
Transcranial Magnetic Stimulation

References

Botteron, K. N., Raichle, M. E., Drevets, W. C., Heath, A. C., & Todd, R. D. (2002). Volumetric reduction in left subgenual prefrontal cortex in early onset depression. *Biological Psychiatry, 51,* 342–344.

Davey, G. C., Yücel, M., & Allen, N. B. (2008). The emergence of depression in adolescence: Development of the prefrontal cortex and representation of reward. *Neuroscience and Biobehavioral Reviews, 32,* 1–19.

Forbes, E. E., & Dahl, R. E. (2005). Neural systems of positive affect: Relevance to understanding child and adolescent depression? *Development and Psychopathology, 17,* 827–850.

Forbes, E. E., May, J. C., Siegle, G. J., Ladouceur, C. D., Ryan, N. D., Carter, C. S., et al. (2006). Reward-related decision-making in pediatric major depressive disorder: An fMRI study. *Journal of Child Psychology and Psychiatry and Allied Disciplines, 47,* 1031–1040.

Lawrence, N. S., Williams, A. M., Surguladze, S., Giampietro, V., Brammer, M. J., Andrew, C., et al. (2004). Subcortical and ventral prefrontal cortical neural responses to facial expressions distinguish patients with bipolar disorder and major depression. *Biological Psychiatry, 55,* 578–587.

MacMaster, F. P., & Kusumakar, V. (2004). Hippocampal volume in early onset depression. *BMC Medicine, 2,* 2.

MacMaster, F. P., Mirza, Y., Szeszko, P. R., Kmiecik, L. E., Easter, P. C., Taormina, S. P., et al. (2008). Amygdala and hippocampal volumes in familial early onset major depressive disorder. *Biological Psychiatry, 63*(4), 385–390.

MacMillan, S., Szeszko, P. R., Moore, G. J., Madden, R., Lorch, E., Ivey, J., et al. (2003). Increased amygdala-hippocampal volume ratios associated with severity of anxiety in pediatric major depression. *Journal of Child and Adolescent Psychopharmacology, 13,* 65–73.

Monk, C. S., Klein, R. G., Telzer, E. H., Schroth, E. A., Mannuzza, S., Moulton III, J. L., et al. (2008). Amygdala and nucleus accumbens activation to emotional facial expressions in children and adolescents at risk for major depression. *American Journal of Psychiatry, 165,* 90–98.

Roberson-Nay, R., McClure, E. B., Monk, C. S., Nelson, E. E., Guyer, A. E., Fromm, S. J., et al. (2006). Increased amygdala activity during successful memory encoding in adolescent major depressive disorder: An fMRI study. *Biological Psychiatry, 60,* 966–973.

Rosenberg, D. R., MacMaster, F. P., Mirza, Y., Smith, J. M., Easter, P. C., Banerjee, S. P., et al. (2005). Reduced anterior cingulate glutamate in pediatric major depression: A magnetic resonance spectroscopy study. *Biological Psychiatry, 58,* 700–704.

Rosso, I. M., Cintron, C. B., Steingard, R. J., Renshaw, P. F., Young, A. D., & Yurgelun-Todd, D. A. (2005). Amygdala and hippocamus volumes in pediatric major depression. *Biological Psychiatry, 57,* 21–26.

Steingard, R. J. (2000). The neuroscience of depression in adolescence. *Journal of Affective Disorders, 61,* S15–S21.

Steingard, R. J., Renshaw, P. F., Hennen, J., Lennox, M., Cintron, C. B., Young, A. D., et al. (2002). Smaller frontal lobe white matter volume in depressed adolescents. *Biological Psychiatry, 52,* 413–417.

Steingard, R. J., Renshaw, P. F., Yurgelun-Todd, D. A., Appelmans, K. E., Lyoo, K. I., Shorrock, K. L., et al. (1996). Structural abnormalities in brain magnetic resonance images of depressed children. *Journal of American Academic Child Adolescent Psychiatry, 35,* 307–311.

Steingard, R. J., Yurgelun-Todd, D. A., Hennen, J., Moore, J. C., Moore, C. M., Vakili, K., et al. (2000). Increased orbitofrontal cortex levels of choline in depressed adolescents as detected by in vivo proton magnetic resonance spectroscopy. *Biological Psychiatry, 48,* 1053–1061.

Thomas, K. M., Drevets, W. C., Dahl, R. E., Ryan, N. D., Birmaher, B., Eccard, C. H., et al. (2001). Amygdala response to fearful faces in anxious and depressed children. *Archives of General Psychiatry, 58,* 1057–1063.

Brain Function in Midlife Unipolar Depression

This section focuses on understanding brain function in depression specifically using neuroimaging. Brain imaging complements information gathered through other technologies including animal models and pharmacological probes, described in sections, particularly including *Biological Models of Depression.*

Brain imaging affords the ability to assess brain structure, function, and neurochemistry, and how they differ in depressed and never depressed individuals. Hundreds of articles have employed such imaging technologies, to very different effects. Recent reviews of these studies have largely been bottom-up, focusing on findings from investigations of group differences in the activity, volume, or connectivity of specific brain structures. An alternate way of organizing findings involves understanding observed data from the standpoint of what aspects of the phenomenology of depression are addressed. This review selectively examines evidence from brain imaging for bases for the symptoms of depression, with an additional section relevant to the clinical utility of examined conclusions.

An important caveat to this approach is that very few studies have tried or been sufficiently powered to examine associations of depression with specific symptom clusters. Thus, a slightly different and clearly less well developed picture of the field will be revealed than is often portrayed in similar reviews. An additional caveat is that, to the extent that depression truly is a single syndrome, subserved by common underlying network of brain function, this approach may overemphasize slight differences between neural mechanisms associated with specific symptoms.

Depressed Mood

A core symptom of depression involves prolonged and sustained depressed mood. The literature on depressive mood and cognitions is necessarily conflated. That is, if the prevailing notion is adopted that emotional information processing affects mood in a longer term, the majority of brain imaging findings in depression relevant to brain function subserving cognition or emotion can be seen as supporting an understanding of this symptom. As brain imaging has been used so extensively to understand substrates of the core combination of negative feelings and thoughts in depression, rather than individual studies, reviews will be cited.

Brian Activity

Reviews of brain activity in depression have largely converged on a central set of findings involving increased activity and reactivity in ventral brain regions associated with tonic and early reactive automatic emotional functioning, such as the amygdala, and decreased control over these regions subserved by more dorsal regions such as the rostral and caudal anterior cingulate and the dorsolateral prefrontal cortex. Disruptions of connectivity between the dorsal and ventral systems, particularly through connectivity involving so-called gatekeeper regions, which implement proximal inhibition of ventral structures, such as the subgenual anterior cingulate cortex, have specifically been implicated. These same structures regularly emerge in analyses of group differences regardless of the imaging paradigm or technology, from resting-state studies of the brain's baseline activity or correlation structure during no-task instruction, to tasks involving nominally emotional or purely cognitive stimuli.

Using these notions, tonic activity of limbic structures such as the amygdala might predispose depressed individuals toward initial affectively laden interpretations of information. Increased and sustained affective reactions to emotional stimuli, which would not be adequately dampened by prefrontal regions could yield sustained negative emotional information processing, and thus sustained negative mood.

Structural, Neurochemical, and Genetic Imaging Correlates

Structural abnormalities in nearly all of these regions have regularly been detected. Similarly, attention has been paid to the extent to which relevant neurotransmitter systems, particularly monoamine systems, innervate these regions and may thus affect observed group differences in brain activity (Fossati, Radtchenko, & Boyer, 2004). Genetic factors that are associated with vulnerability to mood disorders and mediate relevant neurotransmitter function have further been associated with relevant brain mechanisms in the dorsal-regulatory and ventral-reactive networks, via imaging genomic methods (Kalia, 2005).

Anhedonia

Fewer studies have used neuroimaging with the goal of explicitly examining any symptom of depression other than anhedonia. Thus, for the remaining symptoms, reviews will be cited when possible and otherwise, collections of individual imaging studies will be cited.

Increasingly, data suggest that depression is characterized by decreased activity in reward systems such as the amygdala and ventral striatum, particularly toward positive and rewarding stimuli, though other studies have suggested that limbic correlates of depression are observed regardless of the valence of presented emotional information. These mixed results potentially suggest that specificity to positive or rewarding experiences may be dependent on the employed sample or paradigm.

Hyporesponsivity in the insula and rostral cingulate have also been repeatedly observed. Potentially such results are due to increased recruitment of regulatory regions in response to positive information. These deficits have been associated with dopamine dysfunction (Tremblay et al., 2005).

Weight Loss or Gain

Use of neuroimaging to understand the weight loss or gain aspect of depression is in its infancy. A literature review of the PubMed database (U.S. National Library of Medicine, n.d.) revealed no studies with the terms *depression* and *weight* or *eating* as well as imaging related terms in the title. That said, Mayberg (2003) has noted that many dorsal system structures (subgenual cingulate, anterior insula) as well as ventral system structures (amygdala, hypothalamus) as serve a so-called vegetative-circadian function, potentially suggest a role in such vegetative symptoms. A growing literature on imaging of eating disorders implicates reward systems, potentially suggesting a biological basis for this symptom.

Sleep Disturbances

Sleep researchers have long held that biological substrates of hyperarousal during wakefulness are associated with disordered sleep in depression (Thase, 1998). To the extent that sleep disturbances in depression reflect prolonged waking cognitive features of the disorder such as rumination, the same limbic features that are associated with rumination during waking in depressed individuals (e.g., amygdala activity) could predispose them to sleep disruption. Thus, depressed individuals display hypermetabolism in ventral system regions, including the amygdala, during waking and into sleep (Nofzinger et al., 2005). Given the strong innervation of the amygdala by the serotonin system, this theory would fit with the notion of serotonergic mediation sleep disruptions in depression (Thase, 1998).

Yet, the pattern of disruptions in brain function during sleep appears more pervasive, with depressed individuals often showing smaller decreases in dorsal system, particularly prefrontal function, from waking to sleep, larger decreases in ventral, especially limbic system activity, and an explicit thalamic role (Nofzinger et al., 2005), potentially suggesting the picture is more nuanced.

Psychomotor Agitation or Retardation

A recent review of imaging evidence associated with psychomotor symptoms in depression (Schrijvers, Hulstijn, & Sabbe, 2008) documents the association of psychomotor symptoms with resting blood flow in dorsal system components including the dorsolateral prefrontal cortex and cingulate subregions, as well as basal ganglia regions known to be associated with movement (caudate, striatum) but also potentially reflecting motivation. Schrijvers also notes the association of psychomotor disturbances with decreased dopamine (D2) binding, leading to his suggestion that a core disturbance of dopamine system function may underlie this symptom cluster.

Fatigue or Loss of Energy

Use of neuroimaging to understand the fatigue or loss of energy aspect of depression is in its infancy. A literature review of the PubMed database revealed no studies with the terms *depression* and *fatigue* or *energy loss* as well as imaging-related terms which did not revolve around comorbid medical conditions clearly associated with fatigue, such as multiple sclerosis, chronic fatigue syndrome, or treatment with agents that specifically increase fatigue, such as interferon-alpha. These literatures have not yet clearly converged on brain mechanisms specific to depression. To the extent that symptoms of fatigue are related to those of sleep disturbance, the same brain substrates described above may apply.

Feelings of Worthlessness or Guilt

The brain-imaging literature has largely conflated all domains of negative thought, potentially because it is so difficult to be sure that a depressed individual has encountered one aspect of negative thinking without having others. Thus, the current literature on feelings of worthlessness or guilt may be strongly associated with the literature on sadness. Thus, a literature review of the PubMed database revealed no specific papers with *worthless* or *guilt* and *depression*, and imaging terms.

But, a growing literature is examining the neural basis of moral and social emotional functioning including guilt. This literature has revealed associations of guilt with activity in regions specifically implicated in depression such as the subgenual cingulate, rostral cingulate, and amygdala. Other structures more uniquely associated with self-evaluation, such as the anterior ventromedial prefrontal cortex, and theory of mind, such as the temporoparietal junction and temporal sulcus, are also implicated.

Such data could suggest that guilt processes may arise in the context of depression, as the representations of these emotions are easily triggered by brain areas active in a variety of negative cognitions. As guilt has a broader pattern of neural correlates than

is typically found in depression, it may be a secondary consequence of these other aspects of depression rather than a primary manifestation of core biological processes in depression (Critchley, 2003).

Reduced Concentration

Reduced concentration has largely been examined in the context of neuroimaging investigations of executive functioning in depression, particularly with regard to the role of the dorsolateral prefrontal cortex. This region is consistently observed in studies of executive control associated with task-relevant focus. Tonically depressed individuals consistently display decreased dorsolateral prefrontal activity compared to healthy individuals, potentially contributing to a general lack of cognitive control. The neuroimaging literature on dorsolateral prefrontal recruitment in depression is mixed (Ottowitz, Dougherty, & Savage, 2002). Multiple studies have found increased dorsolateral prefrontal activity in depressed individuals during attention-demanding cognitive tasks and have interpreted this as an index of cortical inefficiency. Others have shown decreased dorsolateral prefrontal function on less-demanding cognitive tasks, potentially suggesting failure to recruit the structure. Potentially then, dorsolateral prefrontal function, a hallmark of task engagement, is inefficient in depressed individuals and is decreased when not absolutely necessary. That said, still other studies do not observe group differences in dorsolateral prefrontal function during cognitive tasks in which performance is preserved, potentially suggesting a need for further investigation.

Reduced concentration has also been attributed to thoughts and feelings in depressed individuals that are not inherently part of tasks at hand, such as ruminations or task-induced frustration. Indeed, increased activity in brain regions associated with emotional function and regulation have been observed during nominally cognitive tasks in depressed individuals.

Together, these data are consistent with an integrated role of dorsal and ventral mechanisms in both cognitive, nominally nonemotional aspects of depression, such as concentration, and more explicitly emotional aspects of depression, such as sad mood.

Suicidality

There is an increasing literature using neuroimaging to understand suicidality, particularly in depression. A recent review of this literature (Mann, 2005) specifically cites several imaging studies suggesting decreased serotonin function in suicidal individuals and decreased activity in associated areas of the dorsal system involved in emotion regulation, such as the anterior cingulate. Yet, a number of regions more specific to suicidality are also highlighted, particularly those that seem to be involved in impulsivity and aggression, such as the right lateral temporal cortex (BA21), right frontopolar cortex (BA10), and right ventrolateral prefrontal cortex (BA47) (Goethals et al., 2005). This literature has also found structural abnormalities in relevant regions of the dorsal system, particularly the orbitofrontal cortex, which has specifically been linked to potential decision-making deficits that could lead to suicidality. Thus, such data potentially suggest clinically important subtype differentiation in brain function for this symptom.

Clinical Implications: Toward Personalized Treatment

As structures implicated in the dorsal-ventral network highlighted in the discussion of sad mood recur throughout examinations of so many symptoms, this central network may be useful to consider in understanding and predicting response in the largest number of patients. Thus, reviews of brain imaging in treatment response have largely implicated these same systems (Mayberg, 2003). Yet, the specific roles of these regions in facilitating treatment outcome may differ between treatments.

For example a neuroimaging-informed understanding of the mechanisms engaged by interventions could lead to the development of algorithms that predict which treatment is more likely to benefit a given patient. To the extent that different interventions such as medications and therapy address abnormal ventral system function (e.g., directly, or through increasing dorsal system functioning), high levels of ventral system reactivity should predict recovery in such interventions. In fact, increased amygdala activity in response to cognitive and emotional stimuli appears to positively predict recovery in depressed individuals for treatments that target emotional functioning, such as cognitive therapy, as well as interventions known to affect limbic function—partial sleep deprivation, antidepressant medications, and unselected treatments. Recovery in psychotherapies such as cognitive therapy, which focus on helping depressed individuals to increase their emotion regulation skills, might best be predicted by low dorsal-system or gatekeeper functionality, which has been observed. In contrast, recovery in interventions that work from a more bottom-up level and do not depend on increasing dorsal system function might work best in conjunction with a better-functioning dorsal system. Thus, increased rostral cingulate activity, both in resting-state and reactivity studies, has predicted recovery with medications. These findings, taken together, suggest that amygdala activity may represent a general predictor of recovery. Decreased rostral and/or subgenual cingulate activity may predict good response to psychotherapy, whereas increased rostra and/or subgenual cingulate may predict better response to medications. Upon sufficient replication, such an algorithm might be used to aid in personalizing treatment.

Importantly, such treatments are expected to target the general mechanisms of emotional reactivity and cognitive control associated with disorders. To the extent that brain substrates of specific symptoms are observed, designing or employing interventions that more uniquely target these systems may be particularly important, for example, adjunctive agonists for specific neurotransmitters, or exercises that target specific brain regions involved in specific symptoms.

Conclusions

In summary, a dorsal-ventral system distinction, culled empirically from the imaging literature can be adopted to account for the expression of many symptoms of depression as well as clinical response. Yet, as it is well known that symptoms often do not co-occur, it stands to reason that additional brain mechanisms may be associated with individual symptoms. Examination of specific symptoms yields hints of such roles and the potential for frameworks in which to examine the neural basis for symptom clusters. For example, if mechanisms of disruptions in eating are related to those for reward, it could suggest common etiology for anhedonia and decreased appetite in depression. Considering symptoms separately also gives rise to the potential for constructing treatments, from a neuroscientific level, that target specific clusters of symptoms.

GREG SIEGLE

See also

Affective Neuroscience
Amygdala
Biological Models of Depression
Brain Function in Depressed Children and Adolescents
Functional Neuroimaging
Hypothalamic-Pituitary-Adrenal Axis
Hypothalamic-Pituitary-Thyroid Axis
Neural Systems of Reward
Neuroimaging and Psychosocial

References

Critchley, H. (2003). Emotion and its disorders. *British Medical Bulletin, 65*, 35–47.

Fossati, P., Radtchenko, A., & Boyer, P. (2004). Neuroplasticity: From MRI to depressive symptoms. *European Neuropsychopharmacology, 14 (Suppl 5)*, S503–S510.

Goethals, I., Audenaert, K., Jacobs, F., Van den, E. F., Bernagie, K., Kolindou, A., et al. (2005). Brain perfusion SPECT in impulsivity-related personality disorders. *Behavioral Brain Research, 157*, 187–192.

Kalia, M. (2005). Neurobiological basis of depression: An update. *Metabolism, 54 (Suppl 1)*, 24–27.

Mann, J. J. (2005). What does brain imaging tell us about the predisposition to suicidal behavior. *Crisis, 26*, 101–103.

Mayberg, H. S. (2003). Positron emission tomography imaging in depression: A neural systems perspective. *Neuroimaging Clinics of North America, 13*, 805–815.

Nofzinger, E. A., Buysse, D. J., Germain, A., Price, J. C., Meltzer, C. C., Miewald, J. M., et al. (2005). Alterations in regional cerebral glucose metabolism across waking and non-rapid eye movement sleep in depression. *Archives of General Psychiatry, 62*, 387–396.

Ottowitz, W. E., Dougherty, D. D., & Savage, C. R. (2002). The neural network basis for abnormalities of attention and executive function in major depressive disorder: Implications for application of the medical disease model to psychiatric disorders. *Harvard Review of Psychiatry, 10*, 86–99.

Schrijvers, D., Hulstijn, W., & Sabbe, B. G. (2008). Psychomotor symptoms in depression: A diagnostic, pathophysiological and therapeutic tool. *Journal of Affective Disorders, 109*, 1–20.

Thase, M. E. (1998). Depression, sleep, and antidepressants. *Journal of Clinical Psychiatry, 59 (Suppl 4)*, 55–65.

Tremblay, L. K., Naranjo, C. A., Graham, S. J., Herrmann, N., Mayberg, H. S., Hevenor, S., et al. (2005). Functional neuroanatomical substrates of altered reward processing in major depressive disorder revealed by a dopaminergic probe. *Archives of General Psychiatry, 62*, 1228–1236.

U.S. National Library of Medicine. (2008, June). *PubMed*. Retrieved from http://www.ncbi.nlm.nih.gov/pubmed/

Brief Recurrent Depression

Recurrent brief depression (RBD) is a relatively recent concept and is not well known. Brief episodes of depression persisting for a few days and occurring spontaneously or triggered by mild psychosocial stressors represent, however, a common psychiatric syndrome (Pezawas, Angst, & Kasper, 2005).

Historically, brief episodes of depression were described in 1852 by Pohl in Prague as periodic melancholia; they were later observed especially among subjects who had attempted suicide (Gregory, 1915; Head, 1901; Paskind, 1929). RBD as a specific disorder was first identified in a prospective community study as representing an important group of treated depressive subjects not meeting criteria for major depression, a group conventionally labeled by the *Diagnostic and Statistical Manual of Mental Disorders* as *not otherwise specified* (NOS) (Angst & Dobler-Mikola, 1985). Two-thirds of treated NOS patients turned out to be suffering from RBD.

RBD differs from major depression (whose diagnosis requires a minimum duration of 2 weeks) mainly in its temporal criteria. It is defined by brief episodes of depression which last 1 to 13 days, recur at least about monthly over 1 year, and are independent of the menstrual cycle. Most episodes last 1 to 3 days. As with major depression, at least five or more of the nine diagnostic symptoms must be present; in addition at least one episode has to be associated with work impairment (Angst, 1988). *DSM-IV* (American Psychiatric Association, 1994) introduced a slightly modified concept, requiring a minimum duration of 2 to 13 days with significant distress or impairment in functioning, and the *International Classification of Disease,* tenth edition (*ICD-10*) includes a broadened concept embracing mild (two or three of nine symptoms), moderate (four symptoms), and severe (five or more symptoms) depressive episodes, with a minimum duration of 1 to 13 days, and requiring no impairment (WHO, 1992–1994).

RBD is associated with major depressive episodes (combined depression) (Montgomery, Montgomery, Baldwin, & Green, 1989) in about one-third of cases; combined depression is a more severe illness than pure major depression and is comparable to double depression (major depressive episode plus dysthymia). RBD is not merely a prodromal or residual syndrome of major depressive episode. About 10% of major depressive episode cases later develop RBD, and about 20% of RBD cases later also develop major depressive episode. The diagnostic stability of the two diagnostic groups is similar. Like major depressive episode, RBD can also be seasonal with more episodes in autumn and winter (Angst, Kasper, & Weiller, 2000).

The lifetime prevalence of RBD is as high as that of major depressive episode (21% and more), and the two diagnostic groups are similar in family history of depression, age of onset, severity of distress, work impairment, and treatment rates. The symptom profile of RBD is the same as that of nonpsychotic major depressive episode. By definition major depressive episode is more severe in terms of days spent in depression over 1 year. Like major depressive episode, RBD is associated with increased suicide attempt rates: several general practice studies, including one conducted by the World Health Organization, found rates varying between 14% and 23% among RBD subjects. Suicide attempts are especially frequent in the combined group (MDE plus RBD). RBD has also been found to be common in the elderly.

Today RBD represents the prototype of a special, highly recurrent course pattern, often associated with three other brief psychiatric syndromes: recurrent brief hypomania, recurrent brief anxiety, and recurrent brief neurasthenia (Angst, 1997).

In contrast to major depressive episode, which is more prevalent among females, RBD has a gender ratio of about 1:1.

As many as 50% of RBD cases manifest as bipolar RBD. Bipolar RBD is more severe than its unipolar counterpart in terms of the number of symptoms, distress, treatment rates, and recurrence. In temperament, unipolar RBD patients do not seem to differ from other depressed individuals; bipolar RBD individuals share with bipolar I and bipolar II patients a similar cyclothymic temperament.

RBD is not significantly associated with dysthymia (defined as a chronic form of minor depression, with subjects spending at least half of their time depressed over 2 years). RBD subjects spend, cumulatively, only about 1 to 2 months per year in depressive episodes. Two-thirds of RBD subjects seek professional help during their lifetime, but RBD is very often treated in general practice or by psychotherapy without being recognized as a specific disorder.

The treatment of RBD represents a considerable and unsolved problem. Unfortunately there are no successful systematic randomized trials of modern antidepressants versus placebo. Some trials have dealt mainly with subjects diagnosed primarily as suffering from personality disorders. Trials also present a serious methodological problem in that the usual design for placebo-controlled studies may be unsuitable for the rapid recurring episodic course of RBD. The findings of some single-case analyses look more promising.

As a rapid cycling disorder, RBD is difficult to treat and guidelines are lacking. A first choice of treatment may be antidepressants; mood stabilizers may also be helpful. Longer delays of response have been reported as being characteristic of RBD (Pezawas et al., 2005). As a consequence of the lack of good treatment data, RBD is still insufficiently recognized and is often treated by psychotherapy without any study of efficacy. In view of its high prevalence and clinical significance (impairment, suicidality), RBD should be a major area of future depression research.

JULES ANGST

See also

Classification of Depression
Definition of Depression

Diagnostic and Statistical Manual of Mental Disorders

References

American Psychiatric Association. (1994). *Diagnostic and statistical manual of mental disorders* (4th ed.). Washington, DC: Author.

Angst, J. (1988). Recurrent brief depression. A new concept of mild depression (Abstract FR 04.05). In *16th CINP Congress, Munich Psychopharmacology, 96*, 123.

Angst, J. (1997). Recurrent brief psychiatric syndromes: Hypomania, depression, anxiety and neurasthenia. In L. L. Judd, B. Saletu, & V. Filip (Eds.), *Basic and clinical science of mental and addictive disorders* (pp. 33–38). Basel, Freiburg, Paris: Karger.

Angst, J., & Dobler-Mikola, A. (1985). The Zurich Study: A prospective epidemiological study of depressive, neurotic, and psychosomatic syndromes. 4. Recurrent and nonrecurrent brief depression. *European Archives of Psychiatry and Neurological Science, 234*, 408–416.

Angst, J., Kasper, S., & Weiller, E. (2000). Recurrent brief depression: A frequent syndrome in clinical practice. *International Journal of Psychiatry and Clinical Practice, 4*, 195–199.

Gregory, M. S. (1915). Transient attacks of manic-depressive insanity. *Medical Record, 88*, 1040–1044.

Head, H. (1901). Certain mental changes that accompany visceral disease. *Brain, 24*, 345–429.

Montgomery, S. A., Montgomery, D., Baldwin, D., & Green, M. (1989). Intermittent 3-day depressions and suicidal behaviour. *Neuropsychobiology, 22*, 128–134.

Paskind, H. A. (1929). Brief attacks of manic-depressive depressions. *Archives of Neurology and Psychiatry, 22*, 123–134.

Pezawas, L., Angst, J., & Kasper, S. (2005). Recurrent brief depression revisited. *International Review of Psychiatry, 17*, 63–70.

World Health Organization. (1992–1994). International statistical classification of diseases and related health problems: ICD-10. 10th rev. Geneva: World Health Organization.

C

Cancer

The belief that depression is an expected and normal reaction to receiving a cancer diagnosis is both widely held and mistaken, with the result that depression in this population is underresearched and frequently undertreated. This belief may also lead to the conclusion that treatment would be ineffective, and feelings of helplessness among treating physicians may result in avoidance rather than aggressive intervention.

As with any major life stressor or setback, depression *may* result; however, a majority of patients weather a cancer diagnosis without diagnosable depression. For those who do suffer from depression, or from subsyndromal depressive symptoms, treatment is typically as effective as it is in the general population. Indeed, much of what can be said about depression and cancer could be said about depression in general. This entry focuses on aspects of depression where cancer has a specific or characteristic bearing, cancer-specific issues related to depression assessment and treatment, and the effects of depression on cancer. References at the end can guide the reader to more detailed information and reviews of individual studies; we particularly recommend the materials available at the National Cancer Institute Web site. Much of the following is summarized from information available in these excellent resources.

From Diagnosis to Survivorship or Palliative Care

From the first suspicion that something may be wrong, a (future) cancer patient is confronted with the potential loss of control of his or her destiny, and with a diagnosis of cancer he or she faces a journey laden with emotional and physical challenges. A patient's experience with cancer, regardless of type, will typically progress through identifiable stages of varying lengths, each with characteristic emotional pitfalls and personal trials that may exacerbate distress for some patients and/or overwhelm his or her ability to adapt or cope.

At *diagnosis,* the typical response is disbelief, denial, and shock lasting for about 1 week, followed by 1 to 2 weeks of dysphoria and significant distress. Once *active treatment* begins, the patient must cope with side effects, fears of (or actual) painful procedures, and disruptions to everyday living and role functioning. *Posttreatment* is marked by the end of the active phase of treatment, and many patients feel a renewed sense of vulnerability and increased feelings of depressed mood that typically resolve in a couple of weeks. *Recurrence* and a transition to *palliative care* can bring a renewed sense of disbelief, denial, and shock yielding to considerable distress and many depressive symptoms (e.g., sadness and crying, withdrawal, thoughts of death) that differ from the clinical syndrome mainly in their shorter duration. These symptoms typically begin to resolve in a matter of weeks. With chronic or terminal conditions, the patient may also experience acute feelings of grief due to perceived losses and a deep sense of mourning. Some patients also report *anticipatory grief* regarding anticipated future losses. *Survivorship* refers to the extended period following the cessation of treatment without recurrence or to the phase that cancer is being managed as a chronic illness. During survivorship there is typically a gradual adjustment over many years during which patients cope with feelings of vulnerability, fears of recurrence, intrusive memories of treatment, feelings of estrangement from others, and concerns about body image and sexuality.

Risk Factors for Depression

Many risk factors for depression in cancer patients are the same as in the general population, including a history of depression (particularly with two or more episodes, one of which was early or late in life), alcoholism, or substance abuse; previous suicide attempts; family history of depression or suicide; lack of family support; concurrent stressors; concurrent illnesses that produce depressive symptoms (e.g., stroke); and past treatment for psychological problems. Specific risk factors associated with cancer include poor adjustment at the time of cancer diagnosis; poorly controlled pain or increased physical impairment or discomfort; an advanced stage or more severe cancer; having pancreatic cancer; being unmarried and having head and neck cancer; avoidant coping; and treatment with some chemotherapy agents (i.e., corticosteroids, procarbazine, L-asparaginase, interferon-alpha, interleukin, and amphotericin-B).

Factors indicating better adjustment include preservation of self-esteem; active involvement in daily life; minimization of disruptions to spousal, parental, and professional roles; acceptance of the illness such that treatment recommendations are followed; and the capacity to manage and tolerate anxiety and depressive feelings (hopelessness, helplessness, worthlessness, and/or guilt) associated with the illness. Family functioning also makes a tremendous contribution to patient adjustment. Patients with families that express feelings openly, convey information directly, and solve problems effectively, tend to have less depression and/or anxiety.

Prevalence of Depression

Although a cancer diagnosis can precipitate significant distress in most people—including sadness, grief, and reminders of one's mortality—it is not true that *depression* is the usual response to cancer for most people. Prevalence estimates of depressive conditions in patients with a variety of cancer types have ranged from 15% to 40%, with 15% to 25% as the best estimate for major depression. The most common diagnosis of depressive conditions in persons with cancer is as an adjustment disorder with depressed mood (sometimes referred to as reactive depression), which may involve dysphoria and impairment in normal functioning that exceeds a normal reaction but does not meet criteria for a major depressive episode. It is thought that depression affects males and females with cancer equally.

Identifying and Diagnosing Depression

A significant issue in the recognition and diagnosis of depression in cancer patients is the similarity between symptoms of cancer or side effects of treatment and the biological or physical symptoms of depression, particularly because neurovegetative symptoms (weight loss, sleep disturbance) and fatigue associated with depression may be mistakenly attributed to the medical condition. Therefore, cognitive symptoms such as guilt, worthlessness, hopelessness, thoughts of suicide, and particularly anhedonia and depressed mood, are probably the most useful in diagnosing depression in people with cancer. The overlap of symptoms and the expectation that it is "normal" to become depressed lead to clinical depression being underdiagnosed and undertreated. When symptoms are present but a diagnosis is not clear-cut, evaluation by a psychiatrist or other suitably trained professional is prudent. It should be noted that a cancer diagnosis can impact an entire family, and depression can afflict family members and caregivers even when the patient is coping well.

Suicide

Reported incidences of suicide in cancer patients range widely, from equivalence with general population levels to estimates 2 to 10 times higher. Cancer patients may be at increased risk for suicide within 2 years of diagnosis, particularly in the first few months, with males being at particular risk. Incidences are also elevated among patients with oral, pharyngeal, and lung cancers, and HIV-positive patients with Kaposi sarcoma. Other cancer-related risk factors for suicide include advanced stage, poor prognosis, confusion or delirium, inadequately controlled pain, and the presence of deficit symptoms (e.g., loss of mobility, loss of bowel and bladder control, sensory loss, amputation, paraplegia, inability to eat or swallow, and exhaustion or fatigue).

Treatment

Depression and related syndromes in cancer patients should be treated as depression is treated in other populations, using psychotherapy, pharmacotherapy, or a combination. Cancer, existential, and related themes may warrant some measure of insight-oriented therapy, and cognitive behavioral therapy has also been found to be effective. Some pharmacological agents used to treat depression may be contraindicated (or otherwise adjusted) where they interact or conflict with agents used to treat cancer or due to impaired organ function. Communication between the physician treating the depression and the physician treating the cancer is therefore important.

Supportive Care

In addition to traditional treatments for depression, a growing number of supportive care programs are being offered by cancer centers nationwide. Cancer supportive care centers frequently offer support groups, massage, seminars on sexuality, and adjunctive treatments that can help patients to manage pain and discomfort, as well as offer moral support and bolster patients' coping efforts.

Depression and Cancer Outcomes

The importance of aggressive treatment for depression in this population is underscored by its potential to improve psychosocial functioning, ability to cope with the illness, and the quality of life for cancer patients, as well as a suggestive body of evidence that persistent cancer-related distress may be associated with faster disease progression and/or shorter survival. Although the mechanisms are not well understood, there is evidence that chronic depression may interfere with both medical treatment adherence and hypothalamic-pituitary-adrenal function (particularly with respect to aspects of the circadian cortisol profile), which may in turn suppress immune function reducing resistance to tumor progression.

ROBERT W. GARLAN AND LISA D. BUTLER

See also

Comorbidity
Heart Disease
Medical Conditions and Depression

References

National Cancer Institute. (n.d.). *Depression: Health professional version*. Retrieved January 17, 2008, from http://www.cancer.gov/cancertopics/pdq/supportivecare/depression/HealthProfessional
National Cancer Institute. (n.d.). *Normal adjustment and the adjustment disorders: Health professional version*. Retrieved January 17, 2008, from http://www.cancer.

gov/ cancertopics/pdq/supportivecare/adjustment/Health Professional

Rodin, G. M. (2000). Psychiatric care for the chronically ill and dying patient. In H. H. Goldman (Ed.), *Review of general psychiatry* (pp. 505–511). New York: McGraw-Hill.

Rosenbaum, E. H., Spiegel, D., Fobair, P., & Gautier, H. (2007). Everyone's guide to cancer survivorship: A road map for better health. Kansas City, MO: Andrews McMeel Publishing.

Spiegel, D., & Giese-Davis, J. (2003). Depression and cancer: Mechanisms and disease progression. *Biological Psychiatry, 54,* 269–282.

Categorical and Dimensional Models of Depression

There has been a long and extensive debate as to whether depression is a categorically distinct disorder, or whether it is best conceptualized as a dimension of pathology. Although the standard nosology (*Diagnostic and Statistical Manual of Mental Disorders,* 4th edition, text revision [*DSM-IV-TR*]; American Psychiatric Association [APA], 2000) describes depression as a category, this conceptualization is not well supported by the data. Depressive disorders, like many other forms of psychopathology, are more accurately conceptualized in dimensional terms.

The major difficulty in conceptualizing depression as a category involves defining a nonarbitrary threshold at which symptoms are sufficient to infer the presence of a disorder (e.g., because they cause "significant impairment" in functioning). There is a longstanding debate as to whether people with subthreshold symptoms of depression are quantitatively or qualitatively distinct from people with major depressive disorder, that is, whether people with mild or moderate levels of depression differ in degree or in kind from those with severe depression. This debate is important not only for how we understand and conceptualize depression in a scientific sense, but also for how it should best be assessed and treated in applied clinical settings (Flett, Vredenburg, & Krames, 1997).

Evidence that depression is best characterized as a continuously distributed latent liability, not as a discrete category of disorder, comes from at least three interrelated lines of research. Phenomenological research examines whether individuals with varying levels of depression differ significantly on symptoms and associated features and generally supports a dimensional conceptualization, as people with subclinical levels of depression do not appear to vary significantly from people with diagnosable depression in terms of functional impairment (e.g., service utilization, work disability; Flett et al., 1997). Depression also seems to exhibit etiological continuity, as elevated yet subthreshold levels of depressive symptoms are a risk factor for a diagnosable major depressive disorder (Flett et al., 1997). Further support for a dimensional conceptualization comes from studies utilizing various types of statistical modeling to examine the latent structure of depression. For example, researchers have long studied the distinction between endogenous (biological, including melancholic symptoms of anhedonia, guilt, and somatic symptoms) and exogenous (reactive, nonmelancholic symptoms of depressed mood and helplessness) forms of depression, often using cluster analysis. Other studies have used factor, discriminant function, latent trait, latent class, and taxometric analyses. Generally speaking, there does seem to be greater support for a continuous rather than categorical model of depression using these approaches (Watson, 2005). Indeed, a recent item response modeling study of *DSM-III-R* major depression found that the symptoms form a single, coherent liability spectrum. A unidimensional liability scale was a better predictor of personality and future depressive episodes and also showed stronger genetic influences, when compared with a yes-no major depressive disorder diagnosis (Aggen, Neale, & Kendler, 2005).

Consider also research placing depression in the context of the broader structure of psychopathology. There is considerable comorbidity between depressive disorders and other disorders, which suggests that a categorical approach may not accurately represent the structure and etiology of depression as it exists in nature. By comorbidity, we mean that mental disorders are significantly correlated, such that a person is diagnosed with two (or more) disorders more often that would occur by chance. For example, evidence suggests extensive nonrandom co-occurrence between mood and anxiety disorders, particularly depression and generalized anxiety disorder. This phenotypic overlap also extends to causal influences; the overlap between depression and anxiety is so great that they are genetically identical (Kendler, 1996). Studies have attempted to explain the extensive comorbidity between different disorders (e.g., depressive and anxiety disorders) through multivariate quantitative modeling of psychopathology data from large-scale community samples. Across different samples that vary in age, ethnicity, and cultural background, a common hierarchical structure has emerged. A coherent dimension of internalizing pathology subsumes two lower order factors: distress, which includes depression, dysthymia, and generalized anxiety disorder; and fear, which encompasses panic disorder, agoraphobia, social phobia, and specific phobia (Krueger & Markon, 2006).

If depression is best conceptualized as a dimension rather than a category, this suggests the need for a revision of the current diagnostic system. Several different proposals have been suggested for how to incorporate a dimensional system of classification, varying from more minor changes to a major overhaul of the existing *DSM-IV-TR*. The current categorical system could be kept in place, with the addition of dimensional severity ratings of the existing categories. This type of system would be particularly justified for depression, as evidence indicates a continuum of severity from mild to severe depression. It also has the advantage of retaining a widely known set of constructs and could be implemented across both research and clinical settings (Brown & Barlow, 2005).

Other proposals entail altering the *DSM-IV-TR* to accommodate dimensional assessment of higher-order constructs, based on dimensions that emerge from structural models of psychopathology. In such a system, depression might become the label for the "form" of internalizing pathology a person exhibits. By focusing on dimensional measures of affect, behavior, and cognition, such an approach could better incorporate assessment of differences in intensity, chronicity, and symptom endorsement patterns. As Moses and Barlow (2006) suggest, this type of system might lead to an individual profile of scores similar to a Minnesota Multiphasic Personality Inventory personality profile. Dimensional, continuous scores also tend to have the advantage of higher levels of reliability and stability than categorical measures. Ultimately, any type of dimensional system that is implemented should provide greater information on etiology, biological correlates, and course and treatment, than the current categorical system (Brown & Barlow, 2005).

SUSAN C. SOUTH AND ROBERT F. KRUEGER

See also

Classification of Depression
Diagnostic and Statistical Manual of Mental Disorders
Symptoms of Depression

References

Aggen, S. H., Neale, M. C., & Kendler, K. S. (2005). DSM criteria for major depression: Evaluating symptom patterns using latent-trait item response models. *Psychological Medicine, 35,* 475–487.

American Psychiatric Association. (1987). *Diagnostic and Statistical Manual of Mental Disorders* (3rd ed., revised). Washington, DC: Author.

American Psychiatric Association. (2000). *Diagnostic and Statistical Manual of Mental Disorders* (4th ed., text revision). Washington, DC: Author.

Brown, T. A., & Barlow, D. H. (2005). Dimensional versus categorical classification of mental disorders in the fifth edition of the *Diagnostic and Statistical Manual of Mental Disorders* and beyond: Comment on the special section. *Journal of Abnormal Psychology, 114,* 551–556.

Flett, G. L., Vredenburg, K., & Krames, L. (1997). The continuity of depression in clinical and nonclinical samples. *Psychological Bulletin, 121,* 395–416.

Kendler, K. S. (1996). Major depression and generalized anxiety disorder: Same genes, (partly) different environments, revisited. *British Journal of Psychiatry, 168,* 68–75.

Krueger, R. F., & Markon, K. E. (2006). Reinterpreting comorbidity: A model-based approach to understanding and classifying psychopathology. *Annual Review of Clinical Psychology, 2,* 111–133.

Moses, E. B., & Barlow, D. H. (2006). A new unified treatment approach for emotional disorders based on emotion science. *Current Directions in Psychological Science, 15,* 146–150.

Watson, D. (2005). Rethinking the mood and anxiety disorders: A quantitative hierarchical model for DSM-V. *Journal of Abnormal Psychology, 114,* 522–536.

Causality

A central question in the study of depression is what causes the disorder. The answer to this question is exceptionally complex; the theories reviewed in this encyclopedia all stake a claim to describing at least a part of the causal processes at work in depression. Before understanding what causes depression, and before evaluating the validity of the causal claims of various theories, it is important to understand what causality means.

Necessary, Sufficient, and Contributory Causality

The first principle of causality is that the assumed causal variable must precede the occurrence of depression. As should be clear in the discussion that follows, a variable that follows the occurrence of depression cannot be responsible for its onset.

For variables that do precede depression, a number of researchers have distinguished between necessary, sufficient, and contributory causal variables. Necessary causes are those that *must* occur for symptoms to develop. If factors are necessary, then depression cannot occur in the absence of these variables. Sufficient factors are those whose presence *guarantees* that depression will come about. The converse of this is that if depression has not occurred, then the factor is not present. Contributory variables are those whose presence *augments* the possibility that depression will occur but are not by themselves either necessary or sufficient.

Combinations of necessary and sufficient factors are possible. For example, some psychological or biological process might be

both necessary and sufficient. The presence of these processes assures that depression will arise and cannot arise without them. Or, a process might be necessary but not sufficient; depression cannot arise without the factor being present, but in and of itself does not guarantee depression because other factors must come into play before the onset of the disorder. Finally, a variable might be sufficient but not necessary. That is, if it is present then depression will occur, but because it is not necessary, other cases of depression might arise for different reasons.

Concomitant and Consequential Variables

Like the ideas of necessary, sufficient, and contributory variables, investigators have also suggested the ideas of concomitant and consequential variables. In an influential paper, Garber and Hollon (1991) noted the idea of concomitant factors, which are not antecedents of depression, but instead occur concurrently with the onset of the disorder. This idea is important because it makes clear that although a given variable *may* play a role in the cause of depression, the mere presence of the variable does not assure any casual role at all. Likewise, consequential factors are the result of the processes that cause depression, or perhaps are due to the occurrence of depression itself, and therefore cannot play a role in the onset of depression. Hence, consequential variables are clearly correlated with depression but are the result, not the cause, of the disorder.

Distal and Proximal Causes

Causal variables can be proximal or distal. Proximal variables are those that precede depression but also occur temporally close to the onset of the disorder. For instance, if a cognitive theory posits that unrealistic interpretations of a life event causes depression, this would be an example a proximal factor; the process occurred just before the onset of depression. On the other hand, distal factors likewise occur before depression but are much further removed from the actual onset of the disorder. As an example, dysfunctional parenting might play a role in the cause of depression, but the effects of parenting occur well before depression arises. Of course, distal and proximal factors can be closely related; in this example, the distal factor, dysfunctional parenting, might lead to the proximal factor, the tendency to interpret life events in an unrealistically negative light. Depression research has tended to focus on proximal factors because the longitudinal research necessary to understand distal causes is time consuming and expensive.

Onset and Course of Depression

A final distinction in understanding causality pertains to differences between the cause of the onset of depression and cause of the course, or maintenance, of depression. It is natural to think of variables that cause depression as those that are linked to the onset of depression. It is important to understand, however, that depression is a disorder that persists over a long period of time, and it is arguably this extension that reflects the most damaging aspects of depression; a depressive episode that lasts for 2 out of 365 days would be uncomfortable but is no comparison to a depressive episode that lasts for 200 out of 365 days.

This distinction is unimportant for theories that propose that the same factor that leads to onset also leads to maintenance. However, few theories make such a distinction, although some make a case that different causes for onset and maintenance exist. For example, several models that feature rumination suggest that this process perpetuates depression rather than causes it (see Ingram, Miranda, & Segal, 1998).

Conclusions

Theories vary in which factors they propose to cause depression. It is not possible to evaluate such theories unless we understand the assumptions on which their concepts of causality are founded. As noted, causality can be construed in terms of necessary, sufficient, or contributory, and in terms of proximal or distal causality. How such concepts are applied within a theory allow researchers to more precisely test how well theories hold up against the data, as well as possibly pointing to areas where theories may need modification. It is also important to distinguish between causal agents as they apply to the onset of depression versus those that apply to the maintenance of the depressed state over a period of time. Such distinctions are insignificant if causal factors are assumed to be identical in these phases of the disorder, but few theories make such explicit distinctions. Ultimately a refined understanding of the different conceptualizations of causality should lead to better theories.

RICK E. INGRAM

See also

Cognitive Theories of Depression
Risk
Vulnerability

References

Garber, J., & Hollon, S. D. (1991). What can specificity designs say about causality in psychopathology research? *Psychological Bulletin, 110,* 129–136.
Ingram, R. E., Miranda, J., & Segal, Z. V. (1998). *Cognitive vulnerability to depression.* New York: Guilford Press.

Childhood Depression

Depression during the childhood years, like depression at other periods of the life span, is associated with significant psychosocial impairment and a period of illness that typically ranges from 8 to 13 months for a depressive episode. Despite this similarity, fewer studies have examined depression during childhood, in sharp contrast to the adult and adolescent literatures. In fact, many reviews of juvenile depression consider childhood and adolescence jointly. One challenge in discussing childhood depression is determining when childhood ends; hence, rather than focusing on age, several studies differentiate prepubertal (childhood) from postpubertal (adolescent) depression. At the same time, studies of depression in childhood have typically not examined children under the age of 8. The recent development of assessment protocols for diagnosing disorders in preschool and early school-age children have expanded our understanding of childhood depression.

The prevalence rate of major depressive disorder in school-age children is generally estimated to be between 1.5% and 2.5% (Garber, 2000; Hammen & Rudolph, 2003), with the experience of subclinical symptoms being more frequent. Notably, rates are comparable for boys and girls. This stands in contrast to the higher rates of depression in adolescent and adult females than in males. The *Diagnostic and Statistical Manual of Mental Disorders,* fourth edition (*DSM-IV*; American Psychiatric Association, 1994) diagnostic criteria for major depressive disorder in childhood is similar to that of adults, with the primary exception being that, in children and adolescents, the *DSM* allows the required mood disturbance to manifest itself as irritability as well as sadness. An adultlike depressive disorder is thought to be present if the appropriate *DSM* criteria are met by the child.

However, the extent to which children and adults or adolescents experience the same disorder has been debated. Early work suggested that children may not experience key symptoms of adult depression, such as hopelessness and self-denigration, due to less-developed cognitive capacities or limited abilities to adequately describe psychological symptoms to a parent, teacher, or clinician, regardless of whether the symptoms are present. In contrast, recent comparisons of symptoms reported by children and adolescents with major depressive disorder found very few differences between the two groups (Yorbik, Birmaher, Axelson, Williamson, & Ryan, 2004). Children with major depressive

disorder were more likely than adolescents with major depressive disorder to have experienced a specific preceding event and were less likely to report hopelessness, fatigue, weight loss, and suicidality. Across all other symptoms—depressed mood, irritability, concentration, social withdrawal, insomnia, weight gain—children and adolescents with major depressive disorder were comparable.

At the same time, childhood-onset depression may have different developmental outcomes than adolescent- and adult-onset depression. Traditionally, early-onset depression has been a risk factor for depressive episodes in adulthood. However, several researchers (e.g., Harrington, Fudge, Rutter, Pickles, & Hill, 1990) have found evidence that depression in childhood does not predict adult depression as strongly as adolescent-onset depression.

Overall, although depression, or at least major depressive disorder, appears to be the same illness in school-age children, adolescents, and adults, special concerns arise in the identification of depression in younger children, pediatric bipolar depression, and identifying comorbid or co-occurring disorders and problems.

Depression in the Preschool Years

As indicated, preschool depression (ages 3–6 years) has recently emerged as a distinct area of investigation, despite resistance to the idea of applying diagnostic criteria to young children. The assessment of depression in preschoolers poses increased difficulty due to the high rate of developmental changes experienced by young children, as well as the significant language constraints inherent in this age group. Because the cognitive and emotional barriers that may make it difficult for children to describe symptoms accurately are even more prevalent in this age group, diagnoses are heavily reliant on reports from parents and teachers instead of from the child. Diagnoses are generally made using *DSM-IV* criteria for childhood depression, with some adjustments: Emphasis is placed on the fact that negative feelings, such as worthlessness, excessive guilt, or preoccupation with death, may manifest themselves only in the child's play. In addition, mood dysregulation is required to be present, not persistent, to allow for the high variability in mood among preschoolers (Stalets & Luby, 2006). Preschool depression appears to be quite rare, with prevalence estimates ranging from 0.3% to 1.4% of the population. Early longitudinal research shows moderately strong stability of preschool-onset depression through middle and late childhood.

Pediatric Bipolar Disorder

Along with the increased awareness of childhood depression over the past 20 years, diagnoses of bipolar disorder in childhood have begun to increase markedly. Traditionally, bipolar disorder is characterized by dramatic mood swings from very high (i.e., mania) to very low (i.e., depression), typically with normal mood occurring between episodes of fluctuation. While there is a general consensus that cases of bipolar disorder are evident in prepubertal children, there is still controversy over developmentally appropriate diagnostic criteria. Very rarely do children manifest bipolar disorder according to *DSM-IV* criteria established for diagnosis in adults. In particular, children frequently do not display distinct manic episodes or periods of relatively good functioning between episodes. Rather, children generally exhibit chronic or rapid cycles of mood shifts (variation within a 24-hour period) which are frequently accompanied by irritability, rage, and aggression.

In fact, symptoms of bipolar disorder in childhood, such as hyperactivity, distractibility, racing thoughts, pressure to talk, and impulsivity, overlap with other disorders, in particular attention deficit hyperactivity disorder (ADHD; Hammen & Rudolph, 2003). In an attempt to distinguish pediatric bipolar disorder (P-BPD) from other disorders, Geller and colleagues (2002) have identified key symptoms of mania that more concretely differentiated manic episodes or chronic mania in childhood from symptoms of ADHD.

Specifically, elation, grandiosity, flight of ideas and/or racing thoughts, decreased need for sleep, and hypersexuality were unique to P-BPD. Symptoms of irritability, distractibility, hyperactivity, and accelerated speech were common to both P-BPD and ADHD.

In contrast, others have proposed that there may be broad versus narrow subtypes of P-BPD (Dickstein et al., 2005). The narrow definition required manic symptoms that did not overlap with symptoms of ADHD, whereas the broad definition of P-BPD was referred to as emotional dysregulation (ED) and included children with chronic, rather than episodic, irritability and hyperarousal without an elevated or expansive mood. Children diagnosed with narrow P-BPD typically reported a later age of onset of disorder (10 years of age) than those with a broad diagnosis of P-BPD (5–6 years of age).

Clearly distinguishing P-BPD has important implications for treatment of childhood problems; that is, behavioral therapies and prescribed medications differ for P-BPD and other disorders such as ADHD or major depressive disorder. As such, caution should be used in applying new diagnostic criteria that have only limited verification. In addition, it is important to point out that it is still unclear if and how prepubertal manifestations of bipolar disorder are associated with bipolar disorder in adulthood. Longitudinal evaluations from early childhood into adulthood are needed to clarify this association.

Comorbidity and Childhood Depression

Comorbidity refers to the occurrence of a second disorder in a child with an existing disorder. Accurately assessing comorbid disorders is important, as they influence the prognosis and treatment options for children who suffer from depression. Among the most common disorders comorbid with depression in childhood are childhood anxiety disorders, conduct disorder, oppositional defiant disorder (ODD), and ADHD. Rates of comorbidity with depression for children ages 11 and younger range from 43% to 71% for anxiety disorders, 14% to 79% for conduct disorder and ODD, and 14% to 57% for ADHD (Angold, Costello, & Erkanli, 1999). Gender differences in rates of comorbidity with childhood depression have also been observed. Girls tend to experience comorbid anxiety disorders more often than boys, whereas boys tend to experience higher rates of comorbid ADHD and disruptive behavior disorders.

As might be expected due to overlapping symptoms and the challenges of adapting adult criteria to children, cases of P-BPD are frequently comorbid with other disorders. Estimates across studies indicate that the most common comorbid diagnosis is ADHD (62%); however, other disorders such as ODD (53%), conduct disorder (19%), anxiety disorders (27%), and substance-use disorders (12%) also occur at rates higher than observed within the general pediatric population (Kowatch, Youngstrom, Danielyan, & Findling, 2005). Moreover, psychosis is not uncommon with P-BPD (42%).

Often, disorders that are comorbid with childhood depression precede depression in onset of symptoms (Hammen & Rudolph, 2003). Few studies have evaluated why this occurs. It has been suggested that childhood depression may reflect a general emotional or behavioral dysregulation that occurs due to the experience of the other disorder. It is also possible that there are direct causal relationships between childhood depression and comorbid disorders. Similarly, comorbidity may be accounted for by common risk factors such as parental depression or conflict. To address these issues, researchers must develop and evaluate longitudinal data sets that follow children from early childhood through adulthood, assessing rates and onset of psychopathology as well as risk and protective factors common across disorders.

Correlates or Causes of Depression in Childhood

Depression is often viewed as a function of the interaction between external stress and prior vulnerabilities to psychopathology. Depression in childhood, compared to depression in adolescence or adulthood, is most likely to occur among children who are genetically vulnerable or exposed to severe trauma, or to vulnerable children who experience serious stressors (Garber, 2000). For example, young children who tend to be highly reactive to new or challenging situations (a characteristic of temperament) may require a lower threshold of negative experiences to manifest emotional and behavioral problems compared to children who adapt more quickly to new challenges. Vulnerabilities to depression represent stable traits (temperament, cognitive styles, genetic risk, dysregulations in biological systems, etc.) that exist *prior* to the experience of the stressor. Development of vulnerabilities across childhood stems from a wide range of developmental factors, including normative maturational processes (e.g., neural development, maturation of the adrenal glands), environmental influences (e.g., parent-child and peer interactions), and genetic factors.

Child Psychological Characteristics and the Experience of Stress

Similar to depression in adults and adolescents, depression in children has been found to be significantly associated with both minor and major undesirable life events (Garber, 2000). A recent study examining a group of children (6–12 years of age) with an anxiety disorder, depression, or no diagnosis found that children diagnosed only with depression experienced significantly more stressful life events compared to the other children. Although it has been argued that depressed children may be more likely to attract stressful events due to more difficult personality or temperamental qualities, Williamson, Birmaher, and Dahl (2005) found that depressed children had significantly more stressful life events that were independent of the child's behavior (e.g., death of a family member) compared to anxious or healthy children.

Although exposure to negative events is associated with depression, not all individuals, including children, respond to the same negative events (in the same manner e.g., separation from a parent). For example, Wallerstein and Kelly (1980) found that preschool children (3–6 years) tended to have intensified fear and sleep disturbance in response to parental divorce, whereas elementary school children (7–8 years) showed declines in schoolwork, and 9- to 12-year-olds tended to manifest the full syndrome of depression. These findings suggest that the association between particular negative events and depressive symptoms might vary developmentally. In addition, research shows that how a child reacts to negative events or stressors may be dependent on prior vulnerabilities, such as poor emotion regulation skills or a difficult temperament. For example, the tendency to experience high levels of negative affect and concurrently low levels of positive affect (which maps directly onto symptoms of depression) is associated with higher rates of major depressive disorder in children (Compas, Connor-Smith, & Jaser, 2004). In these cases, the child exhibits a particular temperament or characteristic way of responding to situations that makes her or him more vulnerable to having negative experiences in interactions with others.

Mezulis, Hyde, and Abramson (2006) hypothesize that temperament is associated with depression via the development of cognitive vulnerabilities to depression. That is, children with temperaments high in withdrawal or inhibition (e.g., distress or avoidance of novel situations; easily upset, fearful, sad, or tearful; and highly sensitive to negative events), were more likely to develop cognitive interpretations of events that are associated with hopelessness and negative self appraisals. Thus, particular child temperaments confer vulnerability for developing cognitive styles; these cognitive styles in turn confer vulnerability for major depressive disorder and depressive symptoms when stressful events occur.

Stress and the Limbic-Hypothalamus-Pituitary-Adrenal System

Notably, temperament, cognitive styles, and other psychological vulnerabilities are intrinsically connected to the biology of stress. In particular, when stress or novelty is experienced, the limbic-hypothalamus-pituitary-adrenal (L-HPA) system typically responds with the secretion of cortisol from the adrenal glands. Once an individual has processed the stress or adapted to it, cortisol levels decline to resting levels (see Graber & Sontag, in press, for a review). Group differences in the functioning of the L-HPA axis have been found in adults (e.g., depressed adults have been shown to have higher cortisol levels upon waking). However, few of these group differences occur among children who are depressed. When group differences have been found, they tend to be subtle alterations in normal patterns of cortisol (Hammen & Rudolph, 2003).

On the other hand, recent findings examining physiological reactions to the administration of chemical stressors provide clear evidence of dysregulation of the L-HPA axis in depressed children. Specifically, cortisol levels typically decrease in response to the administration of the medication dexamethasone (this test is known as the dexamethasone suppression test or DST); however, if cortisol levels *do not* decrease, this is an indication of overproduction or dysregulation of cortisol. Recent studies have demonstrated that depressed children show similar tendencies for overproduction of cortisol on the DST as compared to depressed adults (Kaufman et al., 2001). Cortisol reactivity (that is, changes in response to stress) has also been shown to be dysregulated in preschoolers rated as depressed in comparison to other preschoolers; in fact, this cortisol reactivity was similar to what is typically seen in clinically depressed adolescent and adult populations (Luby et al., 2003). Whereas nondepressed preschoolers demonstrated decreased cortisol levels after separation from a caregiver and increased cortisol levels after frustrating tasks (both signs of normal, regulated system functioning), depressed preschoolers displayed a pattern of increasing cortisol levels after both stressors. These findings provide some of the first evidence of disruptions in stress processing in children as young as age 3 who are depressed.

Sleep Disruptions

Given that fatigue, not being able to sleep, and sleeping too much are included in the list of symptoms of major depressive disorder, it is not surprising that sleep disturbances may also be an indication of disrupted physiological functioning associated with depression. Research has shown that depressed adults may show many sleep abnormalities. Although some of these disturbances are paralleled in adolescence (such as difficulty getting to sleep or decreased sleep efficiency), researchers have yet to find similar patterns of disturbances in young children (Garber, 2000). A recent study examining subjective sleep complaints and laboratory measures of sleep disturbances found that depressed children and adolescents reported significantly worse sleep on the subjective scales compared to other children but showed no significant differences in brain wave patterns that would indicate poorer quality sleep (Bertocci et al., 2005). Dahl and Ryan (1996) suggested that the inability to find consistent parallels stems from the fact that the sleep of young children is very difficult to disrupt because they are such deep sleepers. When sleep disturbances *do* emerge, research has shown that the first form of sleep disruption observed is difficulty initiating sleep (Garber, 2000).

Genetic Factors and Family Aggregation

There is consensus that both depression and P-BPD are heritable. In fact, having a parent with major depression is one of the greatest risks for children to develop depression (Hammen & Rudolph, 2003). Interestingly, recent studies of genetic and environmental influences on depression have found stronger evidence of heritability in adolescents, whereas children's depressive symptoms were strongly associated with environmental factors (see Hammen & Rudolph, 2003, for a review). Unfortunately, many of the studies examining heritability of depression are cross-sectional in nature. As such, the results of these studies cannot rule out the influence of adverse psychosocial factors, such as poor caregiver attachment in infants and toddlers, disordered parent-child relationships during middle and late childhood, stressful life events and conditions, and parental or marital discord, which are common in families with depressed parents (Hammen & Rudolph, 2003). For example, parents who suffer from depression also tend to exhibit more maladaptive parenting behaviors, marital dysfunction, and stress. In turn, children who are exposed to these conditions early in development might be especially vulnerable to developing depressive disorders. Notably, advances in the study of genetics have identified gene-environment interactions that influence the development of depression (Caspi et al., 2003). Specifically, individuals with a variant of a gene associated with the neurotransmitter serotonin exhibited more depressive symptoms, higher rates of diagnosable depression, and more suicidality in relation to stressful life events than individuals with the more common variant of the gene. Unfortunately, this study demonstrated that childhood experiences and genetics are predictive of *subsequent* depression; less is known about gene-environment interactions during childhood.

Overall, it remains unclear exactly what is inherited. Is it temperament? Is it emotionality? These questions still remain and warrant further examination of the interaction between heritability and environmental risks for the development of depression.

Parent-Child Relationships

There has been much interest in understanding how early childhood experiences, such as attachment to caregivers, influence the development of depression. Attachment in infancy and early childhood refers to the child's desire to seek and maintain proximity with a caregiver; over time, the child learns whether the caregiver will be responsive to his or her behaviors (e.g., being fed or picked up when crying). According to Bowlby (1980), vulnerability to depression may arise in family environments in which the child's need for security, comfort, and acceptance are not met by the primary caregiver. However, most of the research supporting this notion stems from the adolescent depression literature (Garber, 2000). Two relationship dynamics of parent-child interactions may explain how early childhood experiences impact *childhood* depression.

Parent-Child Interactions: Depressed Parents

As mentioned previously, one possible explanation for the familial link of childhood depression is the impaired parent-child interactions of depressed parents. Overall, research has shown that depressed parents differ significantly from nondepressed parents, displaying more negative, disengaged, or hostile behaviors in combination with fewer positive behaviors toward their children (Hammen & Rudolph). These parenting behaviors in turn have been linked with depressive symptoms among children of depressed parents. In addition, depression in parents has been linked to cognitive vulnerabilities in older children, such as low self-worth, negative attribution styles, and hopelessness. These views of the self and the world may arise from modeling of parental cognitive styles, internalization of negative parental feedback, and reactions to maladaptive parenting styles (Hammen & Rudolph, 2003).

Parent-Child Interactions: Depressed Children

When examining parent-child relationships of depressed children with nondepressed parents, many types of family dysfunction are apparent, such as decreased parental emotional and psychological availability and acceptance, decreased family support, high levels of criticism and control, and insecure parent-child attachment (Garber, 2000; Hammen & Rudolph, 2003). Studies have also demonstrated that mothers of depressed children set higher standards for their children's success, are more dominant in parent-child

interactions, and show less support, validation, and positive behavior. In turn, depressed children demonstrate more problematic interpersonal skills, less-effective problem-solving skills, and less confidence in establishing autonomy during parent-child interactions compared to nondepressed children. In fact, mother-infant interactions associated with depression may influence the development of neural circuits for emotional expression and regulation (Goodman & Gotlib, 1999). Ultimately, the findings mentioned for both types of parent-child dynamics support the notion that maladaptive parenting is associated with the development of childhood depression.

Depression in young children is often associated with aspects of the parent-child relationship. However, as indicated, these experiences shape temperament and cognitive vulnerabilities for depression. Furthermore, these vulnerabilities and social skills typically result in more stressful social experiences at school and with peers. Peer rejection, as well as victimization by peers, are negative, stressful events that have been linked to increases in depressive symptoms during childhood. Thus, dynamic interactions between vulnerabilities and stressful events are likely to occur across childhood unless vulnerabilities are ameliorated.

Pharmacology and Treatment for Depressed Children

Typically, the first-line treatment for children with moderate to severe depressive symptoms is pharmacotherapy (i.e., medication), either alone or with therapy. In general, new medications that target the neurotransmitter serotonin (i.e., selective serotonin reuptake inhibitors or SSRIs) are effective for treating children with major depressive disorder (Singh, Pfeifer, Barzman, Kowatch, & DelBello, 2007). In fact, fluoxetine, an SSRI, better known as Prozac, is the only FDA-approved antidepressant to treat major depressive disorder in children younger than 7 years of age (Singh et al., 2007). Research has shown that SSRIs seem to relieve symptoms of depression by blocking the reabsorption or reuptake of serotonin, in turn leaving more serotonin available in the brain and improving mood. In contrast, other drugs that have been found to be effective in adults with depression (e.g., lithium and selective norepinephrine reuptake inhibitors) have not been effective when used with children. Although SSRIs produce decreases in depressive symptoms in children, the fact that many of the other drugs used to treat adult depression do not produce similar results in children suggests that the biology of depression (i.e., the role of neurotransmitters, dysregulations in neural processing) may not be the same for children and adults. As physical maturation, especially neural development, demonstrates dramatic changes over the course of childhood, such findings are not surprising and suggest that some aspects of depression may not be experienced until systems have matured (or approach maturation, as seen in postpubertal adolescents). Yet, it is important to remember that children still report many of the same emotional and physical symptoms of depression even if their bodies are not demonstrating the same disruptions when they are depressed.

It should also be noted that therapy with children is also a treatment option, either alone or in combination with medication. However, because few studies have evaluated effective psychotherapy techniques with young children, the number of science-based practices available for treatment is quite limited. For older children (8–12 years) who are cognitively capable of participating in the process, cognitive behavioral therapy (CBT) has been shown to be effective for the treatment of major depressive disorder. This form of therapy focuses on modifying cognitions, assumptions, beliefs, and behaviors as a way to reduce symptomatology and, compared to other therapeutic techniques, has resulted in greater reduction in depression, more rapid symptom relief, and higher remission rates. However, due to cognitive limitations of younger children, CBT is likely an inappropriate route for treatment. To date, no studies have been conducted examining the efficacy of psychotherapy treatment of preschool major depressive disorder; however, techniques such as play-based therapy or teaching parents to serve as more effective mood regulators are under investigation as effective forms of treatment (Stalets & Luby, 2006).

Conclusions

Throughout this discussion, we have noted the similarities and differences in the experience of depression in childhood versus other periods of the life span. Often, many similarities have been demonstrated. At the same time, the developmental experiences that lead to depression in children versus other points in development are not fully understood. Advancements in diagnostic protocols and studies that differentiate disorders more clearly have led to a greater understanding of early-onset bipolar disorder and preschool-age onset of depression. However, few treatment protocols have been adequately evaluated for either disorder. Moreover, the serious nature of depression and its length would suggest that the effects of experiencing depression during childhood are not solely in the prediction of subsequent depression, but also in disruptions of academic progression, peer interactions, and a broad range of developmental impacts that have yet to be fully documented. Hence, while we have moved substantially forward in understanding the causes and correlates of depression in childhood, we are far from preventing it or fully ameliorating its effects on child development.

LISA M. SONTAG, SARAH D. LYNNE, KATHERINE H. CLEMANS, AND JULIA A. GRABER

See also

Adolescent Depression
Adolescent Depression: Treatment
Brain Function in Depressed Children and Adolescents
Childhood Depression: Family Context
Childhood Depression: Treatment

Childhood Depression: Treatment With Pharmacotherapy Family and Parent-Child Therapy

References

American Psychiatric Association. (1994). *Diagnostic and statistical manual of mental disorders* (4th ed.). Washington, DC: Author.

Angold, A., Costello, E. J., & Erkanli, A. (1999). Comorbidity. *Journal of Child Psychology and Psychiatry, 40,* 57–87.

Bertocci, M. A., Dahl, R. E., Williamson, D. E., Iosif, A., Birmaher, B., Axleson, D., et al. (2005). Subjective sleep complaints in pediatric depression: A controlled study and comparison with EEG measures of sleep and waking. *Journal of the American Academy of Child and Adolescent Psychiatry, 44,* 1158–1166.

Bowlby, J. (1980). *Attachment and loss. Vol. 3: Attachment.* New York: Basic Books.

Caspi, A., Sugden, K., Moffitt, T. E., Taylor, A., Craig, I., Harrington, H., et al. (2003). Influence of life stress on depression: Moderation by a polymorphism in the 5-HTT gene. *Science, 301,* 386–389.

Compas, B. E., Connor-Smith, J., & Jaser, S. S. (2004). Temperament, stress reactivity, and coping: Implications for depression in childhood and adolescence. *Journal of Clinical Child and Adolescent Psychology, 33,* 21–31.

Dahl, R. E., & Ryan, N. D. (1996). The psychobiology of adolescent depression. In D. Cicchetti & S. L. Toth (Eds.), *Adolescence: Opportunities and challenges* (pp. 197–232). Rochester, NY: University of Rochester Press.

Dickstein, D. P., Rich, B. A., Binstock, A. B., Pradella, A. G., Towbin, K. E., Pine, D. S., et al. (2005). Comorbid anxiety in phenotypes of pediatric bipolar disorder. *Journal of Child and Adolescent Psychopharmacology, 15,* 534–548.

Garber, J. (2000). Development and depression. In A. J. Sameroff & M. Lewis (Eds.), *Handbook of developmental psychopathology* (pp. 467–490). New York: Kluwer Academic.

Geller, B., Zimerman, B., Williams, M., DelBello, M. P., Bolhofner, K., Craney, J. L., et al. (2002). DSM-IV mania symptoms in a prepubertal and early adolescent bipolar disorder phenotype compared to attention-deficit hyperactive and normal controls. *Journal of Child and Adolescent Psychopharmacology, 12,* 11–25.

Goodman, S. H., & Gotlib, I. H. (1999). Risk for psychopathology in the children of depressed mothers: A developmental model for understanding mechanisms of transmission. *Psychological Review, 106,* 458–490.

Graber, J. A., & Sontag, L. M. (in press). Internalizing problems during adolescence. In R. M. Lerner & L. Steinberg (Eds.), *Handbook of adolescent psychology* (3rd ed.). Hoboken, NJ: John Wiley and Sons.

Hammen, C., & Rudolph, K. D. (2003). Childhood mood disorders. In E. J. Mash & R. A. Barkley (Eds.), *Child psychopathology* (pp. 233–278). New York: Guilford Press.

Harrington, R. C., Fudge, H., Rutter, M., Pickles, A., & Hill, J. (1990). Adult outcomes of childhood and adolescent depression. *Archives of General Psychiatry, 47,* 465–473.

Kowatch, R. A., Youngstrom, E. A., Danielyan, A., & Findling, R. L. (2005). Review and meta-analysis of the phenomenology and clinical characteristics of mania in children and adolescents. *Bipolar Disorders, 7,* 483–496.

Luby, J. L., Heffelfinger, A., Mrakotsky, C., Brown, K., Hessler, M., & Spitznagel, E. (2003). Alterations in stress cortisol reactivity in depressed preschoolers relative to psychiatric and no-disorder comparison groups. *Archives of General Psychiatry, 60,* 1248–1255.

Mezulis, A. H., Hyde, J. S., & Abramson, L. Y. (2006). The developmental origins of cognitive vulnerability to depression: Temperament, parenting, and negative life events in childhood as contributors to negative cognitive style. *Developmental Psychology, 42,* 1012–1025.

Singh, M. K., Pfeifer, J. C., Barzman, D., Kowatch, R. A., & DelBello, M. P. (2007). Pharmacotherapy for child and adolescent mood disorders. *Psychiatric Annals, 37,* 465–476.

Stalets, M. M., & Luby, J. L. (2006). Preschool Depression. *Child and Adolescent Psychiatric Clinics of North America, 15,* 899–917.

Wallerstein, J. S., & Kelly, J. B. (1980). *Surviving the breakup: How children and parents cope with divorce.* New York: Basic Books.

Williamson, D. E., Birmaher, B., & Dahl, R. E. (2005). Stressful life events in anxious and depressed children. *Journal of Child and Adolescent Psychopharmacology, 15,* 571–580.

Yorbik, O., Birmaher, B., Axelson, D., Williamson, D. E., & Ryan, N. D. (2004). Clinical characteristics of depressive symptoms in children and adolescents with major depressive disorder. *Journal of Clinical Psychiatry, 65,* 1654–1659.

Childhood Depression: Family Context

A strong body of evidence has established that unipolar depressive disorders tend to run in families, for both youth- and adult-onset depression. A meta-analysis of well-conducted family studies indicated that individuals whose first-degree relatives included someone with a depressive disorder were nearly 3 times more likely to experience a depressive disorder than were individuals without a family history (Sullivan, Neale, & Kendler, 2000). In thinking about youths more specifically, children of depressed parents are also about 3 times as likely as their peers to experience a depressive disorder, with evidence suggesting that girls of depressed parents are particularly vulnerable. Parents of depressed youths, moreover, are more likely to have depressive histories than are parents of emotionally healthy children. It is also well established that the familial concordance has both genetic and environmental roots (Rice, Harold, & Thapar, 2002).

With regard to environmental influences, numerous studies have indicated that depressed children and adolescents are more likely than their peers to experience adverse family environments characterized by elevated levels of harsh and conflictual interactions and an absence of supportive and warm interactions (Sheeber, Davis, Leve, Hops, & Tildesley, 2007). Though the bulk of research has focused on mothers, data from existing studies indicate that both nurturant and harsh parenting behavior on the part of fathers relate to depressive symptomatology in a similar manner. The quality of parent-child interactions is also predictive of both the course of depressive episodes and response to treatment. These findings are consistent with evidence regarding the detrimental effect of chronic interpersonal stress on children's emotional well-being.

Notably, similar interactional patterns have been shown to characterize families of depressed parents (Sheeber, Davis, & Hops, 2002). Indeed, research suggests that the intergenerational transmission of depression is attributable, in part, to disruptions in parenting behavior associated with maternal depressive symptomatology. Parental depression is, moreover, associated with a host of additional life stressors (e.g., marital conflict and divorce) with implications for offspring's vulnerability to depression. As there are significant genotype-by-environment correlations (i.e., those with genetic vulnerability are also more likely to exposed to stressful family environments), offspring of depressed parents are often subject to dual sources of risk. Other biological risk factors are also likely to be correlated with adverse family environments. For example, a recent study reported that adolescents with larger amygdalae, brain structures associated with depressive phenomena, were also more likely to behave aggressively during family interactions (Whittle et al., 2008).

Increasingly, research has focused on the mechanisms by which adverse family processes create vulnerability to depression. A developing literature suggests that the association between family interactions and depression may be mediated, in part, by the young person's development of depressive cognitive styles. In particular, it appears that harsh parenting is associated with depressive cognitive styles including negative attributions, automatic thoughts, and opinions regarding oneself, the world, and the future. Supportive parenting, on the other hand, is protective. For example, adolescents' sense of self-worth has been shown to mediate the association between depressive symptoms and both parental behavior that conveys acceptance of the child and parental use of discipline strategies that induce guilt and anxiety in the child (e.g., Garber, Robinson, & Valentiner, 1997).

The association between family interactions and youth depression also appears to be partially mediated by their affective reactivity and regulation. Parent-child interactions comprise a primary environment in which children develop the capacity to regulate affect. For example, secure attachments to parents, warm parenting behavior, and parents' moderate and nonhostile expressions of emotion are associated with better affect regulation and indices of psychological adjustment, including lower levels of internalizing symptoms. Conversely, children from families characterized by difficulty in deescalating negative emotions may not develop effective skills for regulating affect.

In addition to the general affective climate of the home, the nature of parents' responses to adolescents' emotional behavior has implications for their affective reactivity and regulation (Gottman, Guralnick, Wilson, Swanson, & Murray, 1997). In particular, punitive and minimizing responses to negative affect are associated with elevations in children's and adolescents' negative emotionality and deficits in their strategies for dealing with negative affect, as well as with internalizing symptomatology. Conversely, accepting and coaching responses are associated with better emotional functioning. Though much less research has been directed at parental responses to children's positive emotions, recent findings suggest that punitive or dampening responses to expressions of positive emotions may also be associated with poor affect regulation and elevated depressive symptoms.

Overall, this literature suggests a clear association between the family environment, and adolescent affective functioning and disorder. However, it does not take into consideration evidence that individuals will differ in terms of their sensitivity to family contexts. An important focus of recent research has been on identifying and understanding interactions between biological risk factors and those posed by family processes. A developing literature suggests that the interaction of genetic risk and adverse family environments is predictive of depressive symptomatology and disorder in both youths and adults. In fact, it has been suggested that many genes exert their effects by influencing individual sensitivity to risk environments (Rutter, Moffitt, & Caspi, 2006). Literature is similarly emerging, indicating that family processes may interact with a range of biological characteristics, including physiological reactivity, brain structure, and peripheral levels of neurotransmitters to influence vulnerability to depression.

In conclusion, although the fact that depression runs in families is well established, this observation still leaves many questions unresolved. Recent research on the interplay between family environments and biological risk factors has highlighted the ways in which these aspects of vulnerability are likely to be correlated, and the ways in which they interact to drive the emergence of depressive disorders. Further exploration of these questions is likely to open up new avenues for prevention. For example, understanding how family environments can be modified in order to reduce risk among those with biological and other risk factors is likely to present important opportunities for targeted prevention and early intervention. Indeed, some models have proposed that sensitivity to the environment may confer benefits as well as risks. Those predisposed to have a maladaptive response to harsh environment may especially thrive in nurturing ones. As such, further understanding of these processes may have the potential to not only reduce risk, but also to enhance resilience.

LISA SHEEBER, NICHOLAS ALLEN, AND BETSY DAVIS

See also

Adolescent Depression
Adolescent Depression: Treatment
Brain Function in Depressed Children and Adolescents
Childhood Depression
Childhood Depression: Family Context
Childhood Depression: Treatment With Pharmacotherapy
Family and Parent-Child Therapy

References

Garber, J., Robinson, N. S., & Valentiner, D. (1997). The relation between parenting and adolescent depression: Self-worth as a mediator. *Journal of Adolescent Research, 12,* 12.

Gottman, J. M., Guralnick, M. J., Wilson, B., Swanson, C. C., & Murray, J. D. (1997). What should be the focus of emotion regulation in children? A nonlinear dynamic mathematical model of children's peer interaction in groups. *Development and Psychopathology, 9,* 421–452.

Rice, F., Harold, G., & Thapar, A. (2002). The genetic aetiology of childhood depression: A review. *Journal of Child Psychology and Psychiatry, 43,* 65–79.

Rutter, M., Moffitt, T. E., & Caspi, A. (2006). Gene-environment interplay and psychopathology: Multiple varieties but real effects. *Journal of Child Psychology and Psychiatry, and Allied Disciplines, 47,* 226–261.

Sheeber, L. B., Davis, B., & Hops, H. (2002). Gender specific vulnerability to depression in children of depressed mothers. In S. H. Goodman & I. H. Gotlib (Eds.), *Children of depressed parents: Mechanisms of risk and implications for treatment* (pp. 253–274). Washington, DC: American Psychological Association.

Sheeber, L. B., Davis, B., Leve, C., Hops, H., & Tildesley, E. (2007). Adolescents' relationships with their mothers and fathers: Associations with depressive disorder and subdiagnostic symptomatology. *Journal of Abnormal Psychology, 116,* 144–154.

Sullivan, P. F., Neale, M. C., & Kendler, K. S. (2000). Genetic epidemiology of major depression: Review and meta-analysis. *American Journal of Psychiatry, 157,* 1552–1562.

Whittle, S., Yap, M. B., Yucel, M., Fornito, A., Simmons, J. G., Barrett, A., et al. (2008). Prefrontal and amygdala volumes are related to adolescents' affective behaviors during parent-adolescent interactions. *Proceedings of the National Academy of Sciences U. S. A., 105,* 3652–3657.

Childhood Depression: Treatment

Depression in childhood is an impairing, distressing, and persistent problem that imposes a significant public health burden. In the literature, depression in children and adolescents tends to be collectively referred to as *youth depression*; however, there is evidence suggesting that child depression may manifest differently than adolescent depression. Prepubertal depression is less prevalent than adolescent depression (1%–2% vs. 4%–8%) and does not show the gender imbalance seen in adolescent and adult depression. In addition, child depression is more commonly comorbid with conduct problems and is characterized by negative mood, irritability, and angry outbursts. Risk factors for child depression include negative family environment, such as family discord, parental substance abuse, and maternal depression, and depressogenic patterns of thinking. For example, depression symptoms in children are associated with increased memory for negative emotional stimuli, greater distractibility by negative pictures, and decreased expectations of future positive events. Similarly, children at risk for depression exhibit reduced self-worth and negative attribution styles. Current treatment models have been developed to map onto these risk factors and onto the clinical presentation of depression in children.

Treatments

There currently are 15 published, randomized clinical trials of interventions targeting depression in children. Eight studies have assessed the effects of psychotherapeutic interventions, and seven studies examined the effects of antidepressant medications. Many of these studies have included a mixed sample of children and adolescents, and, notably, there are no published treatment studies focusing solely on children meeting diagnostic criteria for depression. Some investigations focus exclusively on children, but these studies have only been conducted with children selected for having significant symptoms of depression, and no information is available on the effects of treatment in more severe, diagnosed samples. To date, three treatment models have received the most empirical attention: cognitive behavioral therapy (CBT),

adjunctive family therapies, and antidepressant medication.

Cognitive Behavioral Therapy

CBT is the most widely tested psychotherapeutic model for treating depression in children. CBT theories of depression were developed to explain depression in adults and modified to fit child and adolescent populations. In CBT models, depression is hypothesized to be caused by an interaction between significant life stress and underlying cognitive and behavioral mood-regulation vulnerabilities. Cognitive vulnerability to depression is characterized by a pessimistic and bleak view of the world, the future, and one's ability to successfully cope with stress. Such individuals typically report low self-esteem and feelings of worthlessness and hopelessness. Behavioral vulnerability to depression is characterized by helpless and avoidant coping styles in response to stress. Social skill deficits and difficulty using pleasant activities to raise mood also may be observed. Under conditions of significant stress, these vulnerabilities are thought to deepen naturally occurring low mood and to prevent the individual from effectively coping and rebounding from adversity. Negative mood spirals may develop, and individuals sink into clinically diagnosable depressive states.

CBT treatment focuses on interrupting this negative cycle through a variety of cognitive restructuring (e.g., identifying and challenging negative thoughts) and behavioral activation (e.g., pleasant activity scheduling) and related skill-building exercises. In the treatment of children with depression, CBT interventions typically are modified to be made age-appropriate for younger children who may not yet have the abstract reasoning capacity to engage in cognitive restructuring. In this case, treatments may be adapted to emphasize behavioral activation (e.g., scheduling and engaging in fun activities to raise general mood, coping with negative feelings by doing things that bring pleasure or give a sense of mastery, such as riding a bike or completing chores), problem-solving, and stress-management skills. Cognitive techniques may be modified to focus on concrete examples and skills taught with the use of child-friendly cartoons. Additionally, CBT may be modified for younger children to include parental coaching in-session, assistance with out-of-session activities and homework, and reinforcement of behavioral principles.

Several studies support the benefits of CBT for children with depression symptoms compared to no treatment, waiting lists, or an attention-only control condition. Weisz, Thurber, Sweeney, Proffitt, and LeGagnoux (1997) developed a comprehensive CBT intervention for elementary school children with symptoms of depression. Children were randomized to eight sessions of a group program focusing on coping with negative affect through primary (e.g., active problem-solving, behavioral activation) and secondary (e.g., modification of negative thoughts, relaxation) control enhancement training or to a no-treatment control. Significantly more youths in the treatment group than the no-treatment group were in the normal range on clinical self-report measures at posttreatment and remained in the normal range at follow-up.

Wood, Harrington, and Moore (1996) compared CBT with relaxation training in the treatment of child and adolescent (ages 9 to 17) outpatients meeting diagnostic criteria for a depressive disorder. After five to eight sessions of individual treatment, more than half of the CBT group and approximately one-fourth of the relaxation group no longer met criteria for depression. In addition, youths in the CBT group showed improvement on measures of self-reported depressive symptoms, self-esteem, and general psychosocial functioning. Despite large between-group differences at posttreatment, the differences diminished at 6-month follow-up due to continued treatment gains for the relaxation group and high relapse for some youths in the CBT group.

Other investigators have tested components of the CBT treatment model rather than comprehensive, broad-based CBT packages. Stark, Brookman, and Frazier (1990)

tested elements of CBT by comparing the effects of self-control training and problem-solving skills training in a highly symptomatic school-based sample. The self-control treatment was more structured and didactic, while the behavioral problem-solving condition placed a greater emphasis on social relationships and in-group discussion. They found that children in the self-control condition were more improved than the children who received behavioral problem-solving, and both groups showed significant improvement over the wait-list group. Butler, Mietzitis, Friedman, and Cole (1980) found both role-play and cognitive restructuring to be effective in improving depression symptoms among school-aged children, with the role-play having stronger effects. In addition, Kahn, Kehle, Jenson, and Clark (1990) found CBT, relaxation, and self-modeling to have large effects on decreasing symptoms of depression in middle school children.

Alternatively, other investigators have not found effects of CBT or its components above and beyond those produced by an attention placebo control intervention. Liddle and Spence (1990) compared social competence training, an 8-week CBT intervention with problem-solving, cognitive restructuring, and social skills components, to an attention placebo control group and a no-treatment control group. All groups indicated a decline in depression; however, there were no significant differences between the CBT and the control groups at either posttreatment or follow-up. Similarly, Vostanis, Feehan, Grattan, and Bickerton (1996a) found positive effects for both CBT and a control treatment. This group of investigators compared CBT, consisting of self-monitoring, social problem-solving, and cognitive restructuring, to a nonfocused control intervention in treating depression in a sample of outpatient youths. Though slightly more youths in the CBT group than the control group no longer met criteria for depression at posttreatment, the difference was not statistically significant. At follow-up, approximately three-quarters of youths in each group were depression free (Vostanis, Feehan, Grattan, & Bickerton,

1996b). Both groups showed positive effects in improving symptoms of depression and anxiety, self-esteem, and social functioning; however, CBT did not outperform the control intervention.

Taken together, these studies support the benefits of CBT techniques in active treatments. Some evidence from meta-analyses suggests that specific cognitive techniques may not be needed to produce positive effects, as effects of treatments that do not alter cognitions are similar in magnitude to those that do (Weisz, McCarty, & Valeri, 2006).

Adjunctive Family Therapy

There is a growing body of literature supporting the role of family factors in childhood-onset depression. For example, family stress has been found to be associated with longer length of first-episode depression and poorer social competence in later years in both children and adolescents. Given the important role of family and environmental stress in child depression, researchers have augmented existing CBT interventions with family and parent elements. Asarnow, Scott, and Mintz (2002) developed a CBT intervention including a family component and found moderate effect sizes in improving depressive symptoms on a school sample of fourth to sixth graders. A recent nonrandomized pilot study using a similar treatment approach has thus far produced promising results (Tompson et al., 2007). It should be noted, however, that family components have been added onto existing cognitive behavioral treatment programs, making it difficult to disentangle intervention effects that may be due to CBT or to the family components.

Antidepressant Medication

Results of randomized clinical trials testing the effects of medication in children and adolescents have been mixed. Several studies have demonstrated efficacy with selective serotonin reuptake inhibitor (SSRI) antidepressants, with fluoxetine being particularly efficacious in children and adolescents. Though sertraline, citalopram, and escitalopram have demonstrated some benefits in treating depression in combined child and adolescent samples, analyses of age-related performance show that fluoxetine is the only agent to outperform placebo in depressed children. In addition, fluoxetine has been the most studied antidepressant and is the only antidepressant to receive Food and Drug Administration (FDA) and Medical and Health Research Association approval for use for the treatment of depression in children and adolescents. Paroxetine has demonstrated some efficacy on depressed adolescents, but not children. Though tricyclic antidepressants have been effective in adults in depression, this has not been shown in child samples. In general, these results should be viewed with caution. All studies of psychopharmacology in children have utilized combined child and adolescent samples and were not designed to address age-related efficacy of antidepressants. Nevertheless, there is evidence to suggest that children and adolescents may respond differently to medications, and further study is needed to examine these differences (Moreno, Roche, & Greenhill, 2006).

A recent FDA warning that antidepressant medication use in children and adolescents may be associated with increased suicidality has caused concern regarding the safety of SSRIs in youths. However, a recent meta-analysis suggests that the benefits of antidepressant medication (SSRIs and other second-generation agents) may outweigh the risks (Bridge et al., 2007). For example, it was estimated that the number of treated cases needed to produce 1 clinical recovery is 10 youths, whereas the number of treated cases needed to harm (via suicidal ideation, suicide attempt) 1 youth was 112 youths. This risk-to-benefit ratio appears favorable, however, more research is needed to examine whether this ratio is similar among children, specifically.

Conclusions and Future Directions

Depression in children is distressing, impairing, and predictive of negative outcomes in adolescence and adulthood. Fortunately, a number of different treatment interventions are available to help alleviate the negative effects of depression in prepubertal youths. CBT appears to be the most promising, though some study results have been mixed. Completed studies of psychotherapeutic interventions utilized highly symptomatic but undiagnosed child samples; the effects of such treatments on children diagnosed with depression are yet to be seen. There have been several studies testing the effects of antidepressant medication in combined child and adolescent samples, and results suggest that SSRIs hold the most promise but are more effective for adults and adolescents than for children. There is a growing interest in family-based approaches to treatment; however, more work is needed to examine whether the effects of family components provide benefits above those produced by CBT techniques. There are several intervention studies currently underway that may provide some clarification regarding some of these issues with more severely affected youths.

ARACELI GONZALEZ AND V. ROBIN WEERSING

See also

Adolescent Depression
Adolescent Depression: Treatment
Childhood Depression
Childhood Depression: Family Context
Family and Parent-Child Therapy

References

Asarnow, J. R., Scott, C. V., & Mintz, J. (2002). A combined cognitive-behavioral family education intervention for depression in children: A treatment development study. *Cognitive Therapy and Research, 26,* 221–229.

Bridge, J. A., Iyengar, S., Salary, C. B., Barbe, R. P., Birmaher, B., Pincus, H. A., et al. (2007). Clinical response and risk for reported suicidal ideation and suicide attempts in pediatric antidepressant treatment: A meta-analysis of randomized controlled trials. *Journal of the American Medical Association, 297,* 1683–1696.

Butler, L., Mietzitis, S., Friedman, R., & Cole, E. (1980). The effect of two school-based intervention programs on depressive symptoms in preadolescents. *American Educational Research Journal, 17,* 111–119.

Kahn, J. S., Kehle, T. J., Jenson, W. R., & Clark, E. (1990). Comparison of cognitive-behavioral, relaxation, and self-modeling interventions for depression among middle-school students. *School Psychology Review, 19,* 196–211.

Liddle, B., & Spence, S. H. (1990). Cognitive-behaviour therapy with depressed primary school children: A cautionary note. *Behavioural Psychotherapy, 18,* 85–102.

Moreno, C., Roche, A. M., & Greenhill, L. L. (2006). Pharmacotherapy of child and adolescent depression. *Child and Adolescent Psychiatric Clinics of North America, 15,* 977–998.

Stark, K. D., Brookman, C. S., & Frazier, R. (1990). A comprehensive school-based treatment program for depressed children. *School Psychology Quarterly, 5,* 111–140.

Tompson, M. C., Pierre, C. B., Haber, F. M., Fogler, J. M., Groff, A. R., & Asarnow, J. R. (2007). Family-focused treatment for childhood-onset depressive disorders: Results of an open trial. *Clinical Child Psychology and Psychiatry, 12,* 403–420.

Vostanis, P., Feehan, C., Grattan, E., & Bickerton, W. L. (1996a). Treatment for children and adolescents with depression: Lessons from a controlled trial. *Clinical Child Psychology and Psychiatry, 1,* 199–212.

Vostanis, P., Feehan, C., Grattan, E., & Bickerton, W. L. (1996b). A randomised controlled out-patient trial of cognitive-behavioural treatment for children and adolescents with depression: 9-month follow-up. *Journal of Affective Disorders, 40,* 105–116.

Weisz, J. R., McCarty, C. A., & Valeri, S. M. (2006). Effects of psychotherapy for depression in children and adolescents: A meta-analysis. *Psychological Bulletin, 132,* 132–149.

Weisz, J. R., Thurber, C. A., Sweeney, L., Proffitt, V. D., & LeGagnoux, G. L. (1997). Brief treatment of mild-to-moderate child depression using primary and secondary control enhancement training. *Journal of Consulting and Clinical Psychology, 65,* 703–707.

Wood, A., Harrington, R., & Moore, A. (1996). Controlled trial of a brief cognitive-behavioural intervention in adolescent patients with depressive disorders. *Journal of Child Psychology and Psychiatry, 37,* 737–746.

Childhood Depression: Treatment With Pharmacotherapy

Depression in children and adolescents is a serious disorder that is associated with significant impairment in a youth's academic, social, and family functioning. Although recovery rates from an episode of depression are high, relapse rates are up to 50%. Depression is also associated with a risk of suicide, particularly in the adolescent population. Given the morbidity and mortality of the disorder in youths, it is important to render evidence-based treatment for depression (Wagner & Pliszka, in press).

Selective serotonin reuptake inhibitors (SSRIs) are the only class of medication that has demonstrated efficacy in the treatment of depression in children and adolescents. Of this class only one medication, fluoxetine (Prozac), has Food and Drug Administration (FDA) approval for the treatment of major depression in youths, ages 7 years and above. Three double-blind placebo-controlled trials have shown superiority of fluoxetine to placebo in treating depression in children and adolescents. In these trials, which were 8 to 12 weeks in duration, response rates (much or very much improved) for fluoxetine ranged from 52% to 61% compared to that of placebo, which was 33% to 37%.

Other SSRIs that have shown efficacy in controlled trials for the treatment of depression in children and adolescents are sertraline (Zoloft) and citalopram (Celexa). SSRIs that have not been shown to be significantly superior to placebo on primary outcome measures in controlled studies include paroxetine (Paxil), escitalopram (Lexapro), and citalopram in one study with adolescents.

A meta-analysis of SSRI controlled trials in depressed children and adolescents has shown that the SSRIs are superior to placebo in treating depression, with overall response rates of 61% for antidepressants and 50% for placebo (Bridge et al., 2007).

In controlled trials of other classes of antidepressants for treating depression in children and adolescents, medication has not been significantly superior to placebo, including mirtazapine (Remeron), venlafaxine (Effexor), and nefazadone (Serzone). Given the lack of demonstrated efficacy and risk of cardiovascular side effects, tricyclic antidepressants are not currently used for the treatment of depression in children. To date there are no reported controlled trials of bupropion or duloxetine; the efficacy of these agents in treating depression in children and adolescents remains to be determined.

There has been considerable discussion about why antidepressants have not demonstrated efficacy in studies with youths, unlike with adults. In most studies with depressed children, placebo response rates have been high (e.g., up to 59%), which makes statistical separation from placebo difficult. It is noteworthy that in the positive trials of fluoxetine, the placebo response rate was lower, about 35% to 37%. Other considerations include study methodology and later maturation of the noradregeneric system compared to serotenergic system in youths (Emslie, Ryan, & Wagner, 2005).

The efficacy of antidepressant treatment compared to cognitive behavioral therapy (CBT) was investigated in a large controlled trial with depressed adolescents (March et al., 2004). Response rates (much or very much improved) for fluoxetine were 61% and for fluoxetine plus CBT 71%, both of which were superior to placebo. However, the response rate for CBT alone (43%) was not significantly superior to placebo (35%). It was also found that for those adolescents who had moderate to severe depression, the rate of improvement of depression was faster in the fluoxetine alone group and fluoxetine with CBT group compared to CBT alone.

Consensus guidelines for the use of antidepressant medications for major depression in children and adolescents have been developed, based upon scientific evidence and expert clinical consensus in the absence of scientific evidence (Hughes et al., 2007). It is recommended that medication treatment be initiated with an SSRI, (fluoxetine, citalopram, or sertraline). If a child fails to respond to treatment with one of those agents, then it is recommended that an alternative SSRI be selected (fluoxetine, sertraline, citalopram, escitalopram, paroxetine; adolescents only for paroxetine)). If a child fails to respond to this alternative SSRI, then it is recommended that medication be selected from a different class of antidepressant (bupropion, venlafaxine, mirtazapine, duloxetine). If a child fails to respond to this different class of antidepressant medication, then it is recommended that there be a reassessment of the diagnosis and that the clinician seek treatment consultation.

Dose ranges of antidepressants for youths are similar to those used with adults; however, lower initial starting doses of antidepressants are usually prescribed for children than for adults. Typically, doses are increased by 4 weeks if there is no symptom improvement. After 8 to 10 weeks if there continues to be no improvement, then switching to another antidepressant is recommended. It is generally recommended that antidepressants be continued for at least 6 to 12 months after depressive symptoms have resolved.

When treating a child with an antidepressant medication, it is important to weigh the benefit versus the risk of treatment. Side effects should be carefully monitored in youths. Common side effects of SSRIs are headaches, nausea, abdominal pain, insomnia, dry mouth, somnolence, and sexual dysfunction. In children, irritability, agitation, behavioral activation, and impulsivity may occur.

The FDA issued a warning about the risk of suicidality (suicidal thinking and behavior) in children and adolescents being treated with antidepressant medication. This warning was based upon a combined analysis of 24 short-term placebo-controlled trials of antidepressant medications in youths. It was found that the risk of suicidality was 4% in the antidepressant group and 2% in the placebo group. Of note, there were no suicides in any of these clinical studies. A black box warning has been added to the label of antidepressant medication regarding suicidality and the need for close monitoring of youths on antidepressant medications.

The black box warning on antidepressants in youths has raised considerable debate regarding whether there is an association between antidepressant use and youth suicide. Subsequent to the black box warning, there have been reports of decrease in the rates of diagnosis and treatment of depression in children and increase in suicide rates in youths. Carefully designed prospective studies are warranted to determine whether there is any causal link between antidepressant use and suicidality.

Based upon a number needed to treat (number needed to treat to get one positive response to medication) of 10 and a number needed to harm (number needed to get one event of suicidality) of 112, it has been suggested that the benefits of antidepressant treatment outweigh the potential risks of suicidality in youths (Bridge et al., 2007).

KAREN DINEEN WAGNER

See also

Adolescent Depression
Adolescent Depression: Treatment
Biological Models of Depression
Brain Function in Depressed Children and Adolescents
Childhood Depression
Childhood Depression: Family Context
Childhood Depression: Treatment
Dopamine
Dopaminergic Systems
Family and Parent-Child Therapy
Serotonin

References

Bridge, J. A., Iyengar, S., Salary, C. B., Barbe, R. P., Birmaher, B., Pincus, H. A., et al. (2007). Clinical response and risk for reported suicidal ideation and suicide attempts in pediatric antidepressant treatment: A meta-analysis of randomized controlled trials. *Journal of the American Medical Association, 297,* 1683–1696.

Emslie, G. J., Ryan, N. D., & Wagner, K. D. (2005). Major depressive disorder in children and adolescents: Clinical trial design and antidepressant efficacy. *Journal of Clinical Psychiatry, 66,* 14–20.

Hughes, C. W., Emslie, G. J., Crismon, M. L., Posner, K., Birmaher, B., Ryan, N., et al. (2007). Texas Children's Medication Algorithm Project: Update from Texas Consensus Conference Panel on Medication Treatment of Childhood Major Depressive Disorder. *Journal of the American Academy of Child and Adolescent Psychiatry, 46,* 667–686.

March, J., Silva, S., Petrycki, S., Curry, J., Wells, K., Fairbank, J., et al. (2004). Treatment for Adolescents With Depression Study (TADS) Team. Fluoxetine, cognitive-behavioral therapy, and their combination for adolescents with depression: Treatment for Adolescents With Depression Study (TADS) randomized controlled trial. *JAMA, 292,* 807–820.

Wagner, K. D., & Pliszka, S. R. (in press). Treatment of childhood and adolescent disorders. In A. F. Schatzberg & C. B. Nemeroff (Eds.), *Essentials of clinical psychopharmacology.* Arlington, VA: American Psychiatric Publishing.

Children's Depression Inventory

The Children's Depression Inventory (CDI) was designed in response to the need for a practical, easy-to-administer, reliable, and valid way to assess the severity of depressive symptoms among children and adolescents aged from 7 to 17 years (Kovacs & MHS Staff, 2003). Having been developed in the 1970s, it was the first self-report questionnaire of its kind and queried youngsters about their own depressive symptoms. The inventory items are written as declarative statements and exemplify various manifestations of depressive symptoms, several of them in contexts relevant to youngsters, such as at school. The CDI has the lowest reading-grade level of self-rated depression scales and has been noted to be the most widely used self-report depression questionnaire for pediatric populations (e.g., Liss, Phares, & Liljequist, 2001).

The items in both the original self-report inventory ("original CDI," 27 items) and the short version ("short CDI," 10 items) cover a range of depressive symptoms and complaints including sad and dysphoric mood, negative self-evaluation and pessimism, physical symptoms such as disturbed sleep or fatigue, impaired school functioning, and depression-related interpersonal concerns. Each item consists of three options (scored from 0 to 2) and the youngster selects the one that best describes him or her for the past 2 weeks. Completion time for the original CDI is about 15 minutes; for the short version it is about 5 minutes. The responses to the items are summed to obtain the total raw score, with higher scores indicating more depressive symptoms. In addition to the total raw score, the original CDI also yields a standardized total score as well as scores on five separate factors.

Both clinical and school-based samples had served to establish the instrument's initial psychometric properties, and separate norms were developed for boys and girls and for younger (aged 7–12) and older (aged 13–17) children. The option to convert raw scores into standardized T-scores enables the tester to compare the level of depressive symptoms of a given child with the symptom levels of same-sexed and similar-aged normative peers. The psychometric properties of the CDI have been extensively researched: its reliability and validity have been documented by many studies of diverse samples across more than three decades (Kovacs & MHS Staff, 2003), and the information continues to be updated as new research is published (e.g., Timbremont, Braet, & Dreessen, 2004). Importantly, while the CDI is a symptom severity scale and is *not* a diagnostic tool, recent findings converge in supporting its ability to distinguish youngsters with depressive and other psychiatric diagnoses (e.g., Liss et al., 2001; Timbremont et al., 2004), suggesting its potential usefulness as a prescreen for clinical depression.

The CDI has been officially translated into more than two dozen languages, and it has been used in hundreds of studies. Research conducted by many different investigators over the past 35 years has produced a compelling body of data that show the CDI's utility in a great diversity of samples, including community-based, school-based, and mental health treatment setting–based (both inpatient and outpatient) groups, pediatric groups with various medical disorders, and among children at risk for depression and other forms of psychopathology. The instrument also has been used extensively in treatment-outcome research, theory-driven research, and research looking at the heritability of childhood-onset depression. A sampling of these studies is provided in the manual for the inventory (Kovacs & MHS Staff, 2003).

To facilitate the multiperspective assessment of pediatric depression, pertinent items from the original inventory were used to derive a parent-rated version (CDI Parent) that includes 17 items, and a teacher-rated version (CDI Teacher) that includes 12 items. The items in the parent- and teacher-based versions of the CDI reflect only those depressive symptoms that are observable (including the target youngster crying or looking sad or verbalizing negative self-statements), as well as evident functional consequences of depression, such as worsening school performance (Kovacs & MHS Staff, 2003). Norms and standardized scores are available for the parent- and teacher-rated versions for boys and girls, and for the two age groups already noted above.

The availability of parent- and teacher-rated versions, along with the self-rated inventory, maximizes the likelihood of the accurate detection of children with elevated depressive symptoms. And the use of the suite of tools also can yield particularly useful information in educational and mental health treatment settings. For example, a child's own responses on the CDI, along with the responses of the parents about that child, can be used clinically by a therapist not only to identify particularly problematic depressive symptoms but, in the case of major differences in ratings, to explore family and contextual issues (reflected in divergent symptom ratings) that may have contributed to a child's difficulties. Finally, all versions of the CDI are available in paper-and-pencil format (designed for easy recording, scoring, and profiling of responses) and as computer-based and Web-enabled assessments.

MARIA KOVACS

See also

Adolescent Depression
Assessment of Depression
Beck Depression Inventory
Childhood Depression

References

Kovacs, M., & MHS Staff. (2003). *The Children's Depression Inventory (CDI). Technical manual update.* Toronto, Canada: Multi-Health Systems.

Liss, H., Phares, V., & Liljequist, L. (2001). Symptom endorsement differences on the Children's Depression Inventory with children and adolescents on an inpatient unit. *Journal of Personality Assessment, 76,* 396–411.

Timbremont, B., Braet, C., & Dreessen, L. (2004). Assessing depression in youth: Relation between the Children's Depression Inventory and a structured interview. *Journal of Clinical Child and Adolescent Psychology, 33,* 149–157.

Chronic Pain

Pain is defined by the International Association for the Study of Pain (1994, p. 210) as "an unpleasant sensory and emotional experience associated with actual or potential tissue damage, or described in terms of such damage." This definition underscores the inseparable relationship between the sensory and emotional components of pain. Pain may be considered either acute or chronic. Acute pain is a healthy response of the nervous system acting as an alert to possible injury and the need to enact behaviors to promote healing. It is thought that the sensory experiences of chronic pain are maintained beyond the course of natural healing; and chronic pain is often described as pain that continues for 6 months or longer. As a result, the sensations experienced with chronic pain no longer serve as adaptive and reliable warning signals to the body. While negative emotions are related to both acute and chronic pain, a particularly strong relationship between chronic pain and depression has been recognized.

It is difficult to determine the prevalence of chronic pain due to variation in the criteria for defining pain and the tools used to diagnose different types of pain. For example, the National Health and Nutrition Examination Study conducted by the U.S. Center for Health Statistics from 1974–1975 reported that 15% of the general population experienced chronic musculoskeletal pain. In the eight-year follow-up to this study a 32.8% prevalence was reported, although this figure was based on different criteria (Magni et al., 1993). In another epidemiological study conducted in Canada (Millar, 1996), it was estimated that 20% of women and 15% of men experience chronic pain. The prevalence of chronic pain in this study also increased with age; 10% among 15 to 24 year-olds, and 35% among individuals 75 years and older. Gallagher and Verma (2004) note, "Chronic pain is the most frequent symptom for which patients seek medical care and is associated with substantial economic and psychosocial costs."

A variety of diagnostic criteria and tools have also been used in studies of depression and chronic pain co-morbidity leading to a range of prevalence rates of depression among persons with chronic pain ranging from 20% to 80% (Gallagher & Verma, 2004). In a literature review by Bair et al. (2003), different prevalence rates are reported by setting: 52% in pain clinic or inpatient pain programs; 38% in psychiatric clinics or psychiatric consultation; 56% in orthopedic clinics or rheumatology clinics (excluding studies that focused on fibromyalgia or rheumatoid arthritis); 85% in dental clinics addressing facial pain; 13% in gynecology clinics addressing chronic pelvic pain; 18% in population-based settings; and 27% in primary care clinics. Banks and Kerns (1996) also provide evidence suggesting that depression rates appear to be higher among individuals with chronic pain compared to other chronic medical conditions.

Comorbid depression and pain aggravate one another across a variety of outcomes that suggest significantly worse functioning for these patients than for those who experience only depression or pain. These outcomes include more severe depression, more intense pain, more pain complaints, greater pain-related functional limitations, higher unemployment rates, decreased social functioning, and more frequent use of opioid analgesics and pain-related doctor visits (Bair et al., 2003). To date, research addressing the temporal relationship between depression and chronic pain suggests that depressive symptoms often develop after the onset of pain. Additional research examining neurochemical mechanisms shared by depression and chronic pain also suggest that both may occur simultaneously, rather than following any temporal sequence.

Clinicians and researchers recognize that many of the symptoms associated with clinically diagnosable depression, particularly somatic symptoms such as sleep difficulties, fatigue, and anergia, overlap with those associated with chronic pain and may occur in the absence of depression. Clinically, this overlap implies a high likelihood of misdiagnosis, either because pain symptoms are erroneously attributed to depression or because depressive symptoms are erroneously attributed to pain. This is a special concern in primary care settings where patients are more likely to present with physical complaints, the majority of which are pain related, that may interfere with the recognition of depression and with a timely intervention (Bair et al., 2003). Moreover, patients with more physical complaints are more likely to have subclinical or milder cases of depression, further complicating diagnosis and treatment.

Several cognitive and behavioral models of depression provide greater insight into how depression develops within the context of chronic pain (Banks & Kerns, 1996). Additional research examining a neurobiological pathway also provides additional insights into the high comorbidity of depression and chronic pain. Beck's cognitive distortion model suggests that the cognitive vulnerability for depression may become activated by the stressful experience of chronic pain. Negative schemas may become activated, eliciting negative thoughts about the self, world, and others (the negative triad). These negative thoughts are prone to include distorted perceptions and errors in logic that are extended to experience of chronic pain. The negative thought pattern of catastrophizing (anticipating the worst possible outcome for an event or misinterpreting an event as a catastrophe) has been specifically associated with increases in pain intensity, physical disability, and depression.

Seligman's model of learned helplessness also provides insight for a possible pathway for the development of depression in the context of chronic pain. Symptoms related to pain might be conceptualized as an uncontrollable negative event that is aversive, inescapable, and resistant to treatment. The extended experience of chronic pain may lead individuals to believe that there is nothing they can do to control the pain. An extension of the learned helplessness model includes a depressive attributional style where individuals prone to depression tend to make more internal, stable, and global attributions that may be generalized to the experience of chronic pain.

Fordyce applied a behavioral model of depression to chronic pain in which he describes reductions in positive reinforcement as behaviors that were once rewarding are now accompanied or followed by pain. Physical activity is decreased as the new associations with pain result in once-rewarding behaviors becoming punishing. Further restrictions in activities (i.e., social, recreational, vocational, and domestic) result from physical impairments or the fear of pain and further injury. In this behavioral model, individuals may become trapped in a cycle of reduced reinforcement and reduced activity, leading to depression and pain. Pain and depressive behaviors may also be reinforced by others, such as family members and medical providers.

A diathesis-stress hypothesis has been proposed by Banks and Kerns (1996) to specifically address the comorbidity of depression and chronic pain to provide an integrative model for the psychological theories presented above. While nonspecific stressors are related to depression, the stressors related to chronic pain are thought to be more specific. These stressors include aversive sensory and distressful emotional aspects of the pain symptom, impairment and disability, secondary losses across various domains, and the perception of nonvalidating responses from medical providers. The diathesis in this model is drawn from the theory of cognitive distortion (negative schemas resulting in negative thoughts about the self, the world, and the future), the theory of learned helplessness (the tendency to make internal, stable, and global attributions when confronted with a highly aversive outcome), and from the behavioral theory (deficits in instrumental skills).

Finally, a neurobiological hypothesis (Bair et al., 2003) posits that a depletion of serotonin and norepinephrine results in the amplification of minor signals from the body such as pain. Associated with this amplification is an increase in attention and emotion focused on these signals. This hypothesis is supported by the use of antidepressant medications that modulate pain signals through increasing the availability of serotonin and norepinephrine.

Despite patients' common attributions of their experience of depression to persistent pain and beliefs that pain relief will result in reduction or elimination of symptoms of depression, there is conflicting evidence that this is the case. A meta-analysis of psychological interventions for chronic low back pain, for example, revealed robust effects of these interventions on pain and functioning, but not depressive symptom severity (Hoffman, Papas, Chatkoff, & Kerns, 2007). Similarly, trials of analgesics have rarely demonstrated concurrent reductions in depressive symptoms. Therefore, treatment of concurrent depression and chronic pain should be one that targets both disorders in an integrative, multimodal, and interdisciplinary fashion that is informed by contemporary theories of these important comorbidities.

LAYNE A. GOBLE AND ROBERT D. KERNS

See also

Comorbidity
Medical Conditions and Depression

References

Bair, M. J., Robinson, R. L., Katon, W., & Kroenke, K. (2003). Depression and pain comorbidity. *Archives of Internal Medicine, 163,* 2433–2445.
Banks, S. M., & Kerns, R. D. (1996). Explaining high rates of depression and chronic pain: A diathesis-stress framework. *Psychological Bulletin, 119,* 95–110.
Gallagher, R. M., & Verma, S. (1999). Mood and anxiety disorders in chronic pain. In R. H. Dworkin and W. S. Breitbart, (Eds.), *Psychosocial Aspects of Pain: A Handbook for Health Care Providers* (pp. 139–178). Seattle: IASP Press.
Hoffman, B. M., Papas, R. K., Chatkoff, D. K., & Kerns, R. D. (2007). Meta-analysis of psychological interventions for chronic low back pain. *Health Psychology, 26,* 1–9.
International Association for the Study of Pain Task Force on Taxonomy. (1994). Part 3: Pain terms, a current list with definitions and notes on usage. In H. Merskey & N. Bogduk (Eds.), *Classification of chronic pain* (2nd ed., pp. 209–214). Seattle, WA: IASP Press.

Magni, G., Marchett, M., Moreschi, C., Merskey, H., & Luchini, S. (1993). Chronic musculoskeletal pain and depressive symptoms in the National Health and Nutrition Examination I. Epidemiologic follow-up study. *Pain, 53*, 163–168.

Millar, W. J. (1996). Chronic pain. *Health Reports, 7*, 47–53.

Circadian Rhythms

Numerous human functions, including the sleep-wake cycle, body temperature, hormone production, mood, attention, and cognition all follow a circadian pattern (McClung, 2007). The circadian timing system is governed by both endogenous and exogenous factors. Rhythms are generated by a master oscillator in the suprachiasmatic nucleus (SCN) of the hypothalamus, the function of which is governed by genes such as Clock, Bmal, Per, and Cry (McClung, 2007). Internal rhythms are entrained to the 24-hour light-dark cycle by sunlight via the retinohypothalamic tract, a direct projection from the eye to the SCN (Wirz-Justice, 2006). Sunlight also affects rhythms indirectly by suppressing production of melatonin, a pineal hormone synthesized and released at night that exerts its effects via receptors at the SCN (Pandi-Perumal et al., 2006).

Neurotransmitters associated with mood regulation, such as serotonin, have been shown to follow a circadian rhythm (Wirz-Justice, 2006). Decreases in amplitudes and changes in the cycles of circadian rhythms of body temperature, cortisol, norepinephrine, serotonin, and melatonin accompany major depressive disorder (Souetre et al., 1989; Wirz-Justice, 2006). Melatonin levels have been shown to be increased in some individuals with depression and decreased in others, suggesting potential subcategories of depression. Although findings regarding the levels of melatonin are discrepant, it appears that the phase of the melatonin rhythm is advanced in major depressive disorder, which may account for the prevalence of early insomnia among individuals with the disorder (Srinivasan et al., 2006). It has been suggested that double desynchronization—the combination of desynchronization of internal rhythms with respect to both each other and

to the external light-dark cycle—constitutes a chronobiological vulnerability for depression (Wirz-Justice, 2006).

Circadian changes are particularly pertinent in seasonal affective disorder (SAD), a subcategory of depression characterized by increased sleep, weight gain, decreased activity levels, and decreased interest in sex (Wehr et al., 2001). Notable seasonal changes to circadian rhythms in SAD include significant increase in nighttime temperature minima, phase delay of temperature rhythm, and increased melatonin production (Avery et al., 1997; Schwartz et al., 1997; Wehr et al., 2001).

Normal circadian rhythms lead to a body temperature increase a few hours prior to waking. Phase delays in these rhythms may explain why individuals with SAD experience difficulty waking in the morning, as they are waking closer to their temperature minima, when alertness and concentration are lower (Avery et al., 1997).

Individuals with SAD produce melatonin for a greater length of time during the night in winter compared to summer, a biological indicator of season change similar to that of other mammals. It has been hypothesized that individuals predisposed to SAD are either exposed to more natural light or that the retina and neural circuits in such individuals are less responsive to light, such that they only respond to stronger, natural light. Research examining these two hypotheses is mixed (Wehr et al., 2001).

Stabilizing circadian rhythms can have a positive impact on symptoms of depression. Bright light has been shown to increase the amplitudes of circadian rhythms, shift phase, and resynchronize internal and external cycles (Wirz-Justice, 2006). In addition to circadian effects, morning bright light has also been shown to be therapeutic for both seasonal and nonseasonal depression, producing effects equivalent to those of antidepressant medications in much less time (Terman & Terman, 2005).

Although exogenous melatonin administration impacts rhythms of sleep, temperature, and cortisol, it appears to have, at best, no impact on mood state in individuals with depression (Wehr et al., 2001; Wirz-Justice, 2006). However, preliminary trials of agomelatine, a melatonergic and serotonergic agonist, have suggested that it may positively impact both the endogenous pacemaker and mood symptoms of individuals with depression (Loo, Hale, & D'Haenen, 2002).

Social environments also shape human circadian rhythms; disruptions in social routines have been shown to impact rhythms and alteration of these external timekeepers may lead to the rhythm changes that accompany depression (Ehlers, Frank, & Kupfer, 1988). It is therefore unclear if depression is related to endogenous abnormalities of the circadian clock or to reactions to external factors (Healy & Waterhouse, 1995).

NATALIE N. STROUPE

See also

Insomnia
Seasonal Affective Disorder: Light Treatment

References

Avery, D. H., Dahl, K., Savage, M. V., Brengelmann, G. L., Larsen, L. H., Kenny, M. A., et al. (1997). Circadian temperature and cortisol rhythms during a constant routine are phase-delayed in hypersomnic winter depression. *Biological Psychiatry, 41,* 1109–1123.

Ehlers, C. L., Frank, E., & Kupfer, D. J. (1988). Social zeitgebers and biological rhythms: A unified approach to understanding the etiology of depression. *Archives of General Psychiatry, 45,* 948–952.

Healy, D., & Waterhouse, J. M. (1995). The circadian system and the therapeutics of the affective disorders. *Pharmacology and Therapeutics, 65,* 241–263.

Loo, H., Hale, A., & D'Haenen, H. (2002). Determination of the dose of agomelatine, a melatoninergic agonist and selective 5-HT(2C) antagonist, in the treatment of major depressive disorder: A placebo-controlled dose range study. *International Clinical Psychopharmacology, 17,* 239–247.

McClung, C. A. (2007). Circadian genes, rhythms, and the biology of mood disorders. *Pharmacology and Therapeutics, 114,* 222–232.

Pandi-Perumal, S. R., Srinivasan, V., Maestroni, G. J., Cardinali, D. P., Poeggeler, B., & Hardeland, R. (2006). Melatonin: Nature's most versatile biological signal? *FEBS Journal, 273,* 2813–2838.

Schwartz, P. J., Rosenthal, N. E., Turner, E. H., Drake, C. L., Liberty, V., & Wehr, T. A. (1997). Seasonal variation in core temperature regulation during sleep in patients with winter seasonal affective disorder. *Biological Psychiatry, 42,* 122–131.

Souetre, E., Salvati, E., Belugou, J. L., Pringuey, D., Candito, M., Krebs, B., et al. (1989). Circadian rhythms in depression and recovery: Evidence for blunted amplitude as the main chronobiological abnormality. *Psychiatry Research, 28,* 263–278.

Srinivasan, V., Smits, M., Spence, W., Lowe, A. D., Kayumov, L., Pandi-Perumal, S. R., et al. (2006). Melatonin in mood disorders. *World Journal of Biological Psychiatry, 7,* 138–151.

Terman, M., & Terman, J. S. (2005). Light therapy for seasonal and nonseasonal depression: Efficacy, protocol, safety, and side effects. *CNS Spectrums, 10,* 647–663.

Wehr, T. A., Duncan, W. C., Jr., Sher, L., Aeschbach, D., Schwartz, P. J., Turner, E. H., et al. (2001). A circadian signal of change of season in patients with seasonal affective disorder. *Archives of General Psychiatry, 58,* 1108–1114.

Wirz-Justice, A. (2006). Biological rhythm disturbances in mood disorders. *International Clinical Psychopharmacology, 21,* S11–S15.

Classification of Depression

Depression is classified in the *Diagnostic and Statistical Manual of Mental Disorders (DSM;* American Psychiatric Association, 2000) as a mood disorder. Mood disorder is a broad classification, however, and there are a number of mood disorders. These are divided into two broad categories: unipolar disorders and bipolar disorders.

Unipolar Disorders

A major depressive episode is classified as unipolar disorder. In addition to a major depressive episode, dysthymia is also a mood disorder in this category. Dysthymia differs from a major depressive episode in that the depressed mood must last for at least 2 years and must occur on most days during this period. Whereas a major depressive episode requires that at least five out of a possible nine symptoms be present, for dysthymia, only two out of a possible six symptoms are required. Major depressive episode and dysthymia are not mutually exclusive, and individuals can be diagnosed with both, a condition that is known as double depression.

Bipolar Disorders

Bipolar disorders is the second major category of mood disorders. Bipolar disorders are differentiated from unipolar disorders by the occurrence of either a manic state or a hypomanic state. A manic state is characterized by a period where the individual experiences a distinctly elevated and expansive mood or, in some cases, irritability. Among other symptoms, an elevated mood can be seen in grandiosity, a decreased need for sleep, and reckless behavior A hypomanic state is marked by a persistently elevated mood for at least 4 days that is distinctly different from a normal good mood. During this period, the person might be more talkative and have more energy than usual, and have an inflated sense of self-esteem. Bipolar disorders are divided into bipolar I and bipolar II disorders. Bipolar I is characterized by the occurrence of at least a manic episode whereas bipolar II is characterized by a hypomanic episode.

A sizable minority of bipolar patients may have never experienced a depressive episode. A mixed episode is where the criteria for a manic episode and a major depressive episode are both met. Sometimes the individual can rapidly cycle between mania and depression, although such cases are relatively rare.

Cyclothymia disorder is also a bipolar disorder and is defined as the occurrence over 2 years of numerous periods of hypomania that do not meet the criteria for mania, and periods of depressed mood that do not meet the criteria for a major depressive episode.

Other Subtypes and Classifications

Beyond the distinction between unipolar and bipolar disorders, a number of different subtypes and classifications have been proposed. Some of these subtypes are "officially sanctioned" by the *DSM*, whereas others reflect meaningful classifications that have not yet been formerly recognized for diagnostic purposes. For example, an officially recognized subtype is seasonal affective disorder, a seasonal pattern of mood disorder wherein the person experiences periods of depression in winter months that tend to lift with the end of winter.

There are also historical subtypes. An example is the distinction between neurotic and psychotic depression. While neurotic depression no longer exists in the official nomenclature, psychotic depression, more specifically a mood disorder with psychotic features, continues to be recognized. In the case of psychotic depression, the individual experiences delusions (false beliefs such as "I am dead") or hallucinations (false sensory experiences such as hearing voices).

More contemporary distinctions are also present in the mood disorders literature. One classification sometimes seen is that between reactive and endogenous depression. Reactive depression is that which is assumed to result from stressful life events, whereas endogenous depression (sometimes referred to as melancholia) is assumed to be less of a response to stress and more driven by the dysregulation of neurobiological processes. Endogenous depression is also seen as having more severe depressive symptoms such as psychomotor retardation.

RICK E. INGRAM

See also

Assessment of Depression
Categorical and Dimensional Models of Depression
Definition of Depression
Diagnostic and Statistical Manual of Mental Disorders
Melancholia

Reference

American Psychiatric Association. (2000). *Diagnostic and statistical manual of mental disorders* (4th ed., text revision). Washington, DC: Author.

Clinically Useful Depression Outcome Scale

The quantitative measurement of treatment outcome has long been the province of psychiatric researchers conducting investigations of the efficacy and effectiveness of care. Recently, some investigators have suggested that scales should be used to monitor the course of treatment in routine clinical practice (Trivedi et al., 2006). If the optimal delivery of mental health treatment depends, in part, on systematically assessing outcome, then precise, reliable, valid, informative, and user-friendly measurement is the key to evaluating the quality and efficiency of care in clinical practice. Clinicians are already overburdened with paperwork, and adding to this load by suggesting repeated detailed evaluations with such instruments as the Hamilton Rating Scale for Depression (HAMD) (Hamilton, 1960) is unlikely to meet with success. Self-report questionnaires are a cost-effective option because they are inexpensive in terms of professional time needed for administration, and they correlate highly with clinician ratings. To be sure, there are also limitations with self-report questionnaires, such as response-set biases, and their use may be limited by the readability of the scale and literacy of the respondent. However, self-report scales are free of clinician bias and are therefore free from clinician overestimation of patient improvement (which might occur when there is incentive to document treatment success).

Three consumers should be considered in the selection of a self-administered outcome questionnaire to be used in routine clinical practice: the patient, the clinician, and the administrator. Patients should find the measure user-friendly and the directions easy to follow. The scale should be brief, taking no more than 2 to 3 minutes to complete, so that upon routine administration at follow-up visits patients are not inconvenienced by the need to come for their appointment 10 to 15 minutes early in order to complete the measure. This would make it feasible to have the scale completed at each follow-up visit in the same way that blood pressure, cholesterol levels, and weight are routinely assessed in primary care settings for patients being treated for hypertension, hypercholesterolemia, and obesity.

The instrument should provide clinicians with clinically useful information and improve the efficiency of conducting their clinical evaluation; thus, the measure should have practical value to the practicing clinician. Of course, clinicians need to be able to trust the information provided by any instrument they use. Consequently, outcome measures of any kind should have a sound basis in psychometrics, demonstrating good reliability, validity, and sensitivity to change. Clinicians and clinics should also find the instrument user-friendly; it should be easy to administer and score with minimal training.

Clinic administrators likewise want measures to be both reliable and valid. To successfully implement an outcomes assessment program, administrators want measures to have high patient and clinician acceptance. Administrators are also concerned about the cost of an instrument, from the perspective of both the purchase price and the cost of labor to score the scale. Thus, an outcome measure, or outcome assessment program, should be inexpensive to purchase and implement.

As part of the Rhode Island Methods to Improve Diagnostic Assessment and Services project our research group developed the Clinically Useful Depression Outcome Scale (CUDOS) to attend to the concerns of these different stakeholders. Certainly, there is no shortage of self-report depression scales. However, other questionnaires are either too long, lack adequate coverage of the *Diagnostic and Statistical Manual of Mental Disorders* (DSM-IV; American Psychiatric Association, 1994) diagnostic criteria, are expensive to purchase, or are somewhat complicated to score. These factors reduce their appeal as outcome tools for use in routine clinical practice.

Description of the CUDOS

The CUDOS contains 18 items assessing all of the *DSM-IV* inclusion criteria for major depressive disorder as well as psychosocial impairment and quality of life. The 16 symptom items were derived from a larger pool of 27 items. Alternative wordings of items were written and the psychometric performances of the alternative items were compared to select the best-performing versions of the items. Compound *DSM-IV* symptom criteria referring to more than one construct (e.g., problems concentrating or making decisions; insomnia or hypersomnia) were subdivided into their respective components, and a CUDOS item was written for each component. The individual symptoms assessed by the CUDOS are depressed mood, loss of interest in usual activities, low energy, psychomotor agitation, psychomotor retardation, guilt, worthlessness, thoughts of death, suicidal ideation, impaired concentration, indecisiveness, decreased appetite, increased appetite, insomnia, hypersomnia, and hopelessness. The CUDOS also includes items assessing global perception of psychosocial impairment due to depression and overall quality of life.

On the CUDOS the respondent is instructed to rate the symptom items on a 5-point Likert scale indicating "how well the item describes you during the past week, including today" (0 = not at all true/0 days; 1 = rarely true/1–2 days; 2 = sometimes true/3–4 days; 3 = usually true/5–6 days; 4 = almost always true/every day). A Likert rating of the symptom statements was preferred in order to keep the scale brief. Scales such as the Beck Depression Inventory (BDI; Beck, Rush, Shaw, & Emery, 1979), Diagnostic Inventory for Depression (Zimmerman, Sheeran, & Young, 2004), and Inventory of Depressive Symptoms (Rush, Gullion, Basco, Jarret, & Trivedi, 1996) assess symptoms with groups of 4 or 5 statements and are thus composed of 80 or more statements. These scales take respondents 10 to 15 minutes to complete, and this was considered too long for regular use in clinical practice in which the scale would be routinely administered at follow-up appointments.

Patient Acceptability of the CUDOS as a Measure of Outcome in Clinical Practice

The feasibility and acceptability of incorporating the CUDOS into routine clinical practice was examined in two studies of depressed psychiatric outpatients who were in ongoing treatment (Zimmerman & McGlinchey, 2008). In the first study we examined the amount of time it took to complete the scale, and the perceived burden of completing the measure. In the second study, we asked patients to compare the burden imposed by two different self-report depression scales—the BDI and the CUDOS. We compared the acceptability of the CUDOS to the BDI because the BDI is the most widely used self-report measure of depression severity.

In the first study, the amount of time needed to complete the CUDOS during a follow-up appointment with a psychiatrist was recorded in a consecutive series of 50 depressed outpatients presenting for a follow-up appointment. The patients also completed a questionnaire assessing how burdensome it was to complete the scale during the visit (0 = very little burden; 3 = a large burden), and their willingness to complete the scale at every visit to help monitor the progress of their treatment (0 = not at all willing; 3 = very willing to fill it out at every visit).

All but 2 patients completed the scale in less than 3 minutes (mean = 102.7 seconds; *SD* = 42.7). Almost all patients considered questionnaire completion very little or a little burdensome (98.0%, *n* = 49), and no patient perceived it as moderately or very burdensome. More than 90% of patients indicated a willingness to complete the CUDOS at every visit in the future if their clinician believed that it was helpful (94.0%, *n* = 47).

In the second study of feasibility, a separate sample of 50 depressed outpatients completed both the CUDOS and the BDI during a follow-up visit. After completing the two questionnaires the patients completed a feasibility and acceptability questionnaire. Significantly more patients indicated that the CUDOS took less time to complete, was less of a burden to complete, and would prefer to complete the CUDOS at every visit in order to monitor the outcome of treatment.

Reliability and Validity of the CUDOS

Internal consistency coefficients were computed separately for the 1,475 psychiatric outpatients who completed the scale at intake and 100 depressed patients who completed it during a follow-up appointment (Zimmerman, Chelminski, McGlinchey, & Posternak, 2008). The CUDOS demonstrated excellent internal consistency in both samples (Cronbach's alpha at intake = .90; Cronbach's alpha at follow-up = .90). All item-scale correlations at baseline and follow-up were significant (mean at intake = .64; mean at follow-up = .57).

The test-retest reliability of the CUDOS was examined in 176 subjects at baseline and 33 subjects during follow-up. At both time points the test-retest reliability of the total scale was high (r = .92 and .95, respectively), and the test-retest reliability of each item was significant (mean at intake = .73; mean at follow-up = .81).

The convergent and discriminant validity of the CUDOS was examined in 204 patients who completed a package of questionnaires at home less than a week after completing the scale. The CUDOS was more highly correlated with the BDI (r = .81) than with measures of the other symptom domains (mean of correlations = .35). Moreover, the CUDOS was nearly as highly correlated with the HAMD (r = .69) and the Clinical Global Index (CGI) of severity (r = .71), clinician ratings of the severity of depressive symptoms, as with the self-rated BDI.

The ability of the CUDOS to discriminate between different levels of depression severity was examined with an analysis of variance on the CGI depression severity rating in 1,475 patients. CUDOS scores increased with increasing global severity ratings (nondepressed, 13.0 ± 10.4; minimal, 20.7 ± 10.4; mild, 27.9 ± 9.9; moderate 37.5 ± 9.1; severe, 44.2 ± 9.0), and the difference between each adjacent level of severity (e.g., nondepressed vs. minimally depressed; mild vs. moderate) was significant.

Patients with current *DSM-IV* major depressive disorder or bipolar depression scored higher than patients not in an episode of major depression. The diagnostic performance of the CUDOS was evaluated by comparing it to the results of the SCID interview. The sensitivity of the scale was 83.3%; its specificity was 72.1%; positive predictive value, 72.6%; negative predictive value, 82.9%; and chance-corrected agreement level, k = .55.

Fifty-five depressed patients completed the CUDOS and were rated on the Montgomery-Asberg Depression Rating Scale (MADRS), at baseline and 6 weeks after initiating antidepressant medication. The patients were divided into three groups using the MADRS to determine remission and response status. Patients scoring 10 and below at week 6 were considered to be in remission (n = 29); patients improving at least 50% on the MADRS but who scored above 10 at week 6 were considered responders (n = 7), and the remaining patients were considered nonresponders (n = 19). Remitters scored significantly lower than responders, and responders scored significantly lower than nonresponders.

The CUDOS as an Indicator of Remission

In another study, distinct from the large validity study of the CUDOS, 267 psychiatric outpatients who were being treated for a *DSM-IV* major depressive episode completed the CUDOS and were evaluated with the 17-item HAMD (Zimmerman, Posternak, & Chelminski, 2004). The goal of the study was to determine the score on the CUDOS that corresponded most closely with the 17-item HAMD score of 7, the most commonly used cutoff to define remission. We examined the ability of the CUDOS to identify

Table C.1   The Clinically Useful Depression Outcome Scale

INSTRUCTIONS

This questionnaire includes questions about symptoms of depression. For each item please indicate how well it describes you during the PAST WEEK, INCLUDING TODAY. Circle the number in the columns next to the item that best describes you.

RATING GUIDELINES

0 = not at all true (0 days)

1 = rarely true (1–2 days)

2 = sometimes true (3–4 days)

3 = often true (5–6 days)

4 = almost always true (every day)

During the PAST WEEK, INCLUDING TODAY:

1.	I felt sad or depressed	0 1 2 3 4
2.	I was not as interested in my usual activities	0 1 2 3 4
3.	My appetite was poor and I didn't feel like eating	0 1 2 3 4
4.	My appetite was much greater than usual	0 1 2 3 4
5.	I had difficulty sleeping	0 1 2 3 4
6.	I was sleeping too much	0 1 2 3 4
7.	I felt very fidgety, making it difficult to sit still	0 1 2 3 4
8.	I felt physically slowed down, like my body was stuck in mud	0 1 2 3 4
9.	My energy level was low	0 1 2 3 4
10.	I felt guilty	0 1 2 3 4
11.	I thought I was a failure	0 1 2 3 4
12.	I had problems concentrating	0 1 2 3 4
13.	I had more difficulties making decisions than usual	0 1 2 3 4
14.	I wished I was dead	0 1 2 3 4
15.	I thought about killing myself	0 1 2 3 4
16.	I thought that the future looked hopeless	0 1 2 3 4

17. Overall, how much have symptoms of depression interfered with or caused difficulties in your life during the past week?

    0) not at all

    1) a little bit

    2) a moderate amount

    3) quite a bit

    4) extremely

18. How would you rate your overall quality of life during the past week?

    0) very good, my life could hardly be better

    1) pretty good, most things are going well

    2) the good and bad parts are about equal

    3) pretty bad, most things are going poorly

    4) very bad, my life could hardly be worse

patients who were in remission according to the HAMD across the range of CUDOS cutoff scores by conducting a receiver operating curve (ROC) analysis.

The Pearson correlation between the HAMD and the CUDOS was .89. In the ROC analysis the area under the curve was significant (AUC = .95, p < .001). The sensitivity, specificity, and overall classification rate of the CUDOS for identifying remission according to the HAMD threshold of <7 was examined for each CUDOS total score. The maximum level of agreement with the HAMD definition of remission that provided the best balance of sensitivity and specificity occurred at a cutoff of <20 (sensitivity = 87.4%, specificity = 87.8%, total agreement = 87.6%, kappa = .75).

In a separate study, we examined the validity of the CUDOS as an indicator of remission amongst patients who responded to antidepressant treatment (Zimmerman et al., 2006). That is, psychosocial functioning was compared in treatment responders who were and were not in remission according to the CUDOS. In a sample of 371 depressed outpatients who were judged by their treating psychiatrists as having responded to treatment, 250 scored in the remission range on the CUDOS. Compared to treatment responders whose depression was not in remission, the patients who were in remission reported significantly less psychosocial impairment, reported significantly better quality of life, and were significantly more likely to assert that they were in remission from their depression. These findings thus supported the validity of the CUDOS as an index of remission status among treatment responders.

Conclusions

The CUDOS is a reliable and valid brief self-administered depression questionnaire tied to the *DSM-IV* criteria and is feasible to incorporate into routine clinical practice. On average the scale takes less than 2 minutes to complete, and more than 95% of patients were able to complete it in less than 3 minutes

(Table C.1). Patients do not find scale completion burdensome and are willing to complete it on a regular basis. The CUDOS achieved high levels of internal consistency and test-retest reliability and was more highly correlated with another self-report measure of depression than with measures of anxiety, substance-use problems, eating disorders, and somatization, thereby supporting the convergent and discriminant validity of the scale. The CUDOS was also significantly correlated with interviewer ratings of the severity of depression, and CUDOS scores were significantly different in depressed patients with mild, moderate, and severe levels of depression. The CUDOS was a valid measure of symptom change and distinguished patients whose episode had remitted, responded, or had not responded to treatment. And finally, the diagnostic properties of the CUDOS were adequate.

Mark Zimmerman, Iwona Chelminski, Joseph B. McGlinchey, and Diane Young

See also

Assessment of Depression

References

American Psychiatric Association. (1994). *Diagnostic and statistical manual of mental disorders* (4th ed.). Washington, DC: Author.

Beck, A. T., Rush, A. J., Shaw, B. F., & Emery, G. (1979). *Cognitive therapy of depression*. New York: Guilford Press.

Hamilton, M. (1960). A rating scale for depression. *Journal of Neurology, Neurosurgery, and Psychiatry, 23,* 56–62.

Rush, A. J., Gullion, C. M., Basco, M. R., Jarrett, R. B., & Trivedi, M. H. (1996). The Inventory of Depressive Symptomatology (IDS). *Psychological Medicine, 26,* 477–486.

Trivedi, M., Rush, A., Wisniewski, S., Nierenberg, A., Warden, D., Ritz, L., et al. (2006). Evaluation of outcomes with citalopram for depression using measurement-based care in STAR*D implications for clinical practice. *American Journal of Psychiatry, 163,* 28–40.

Zimmerman, M., Chelminski, I., McGlinchey, J. B., & Posternak, M. A. (2008). A clinically useful depression outcome scale. *Comprehensive Psychiatry, 49,* 131–140.

Zimmerman, M., & McGlinchey, J. B. (2008). Patient acceptability of the use of scales to monitor the outcome of depression in clinical practice. *Annals of Psychiatry, 20,* 125–129.

Zimmerman, M., Posternak, M., & Chelminski, I. (2004). Using a self-report depression scale to identify remission in depressed outpatients. *American Journal of Psychiatry, 161,* 1911–1913.

Zimmerman, M., Posternak, M., McGlinchey, J., Friedman, M., Attiullah, N., & Boerescu, D. (2006). Validity of a self-report depression symptom scale for identifying remission in depressed outpatients. *Comprehensive Psychiatry, 47,* 185–188.

Zimmerman, M., Sheeran, T., & Young, D. (2004). The Diagnostic Inventory for Depression: A self-report scale to diagnose DSM-IV for major depressive disorder. *Journal of Clinical Psychology, 60,* 87–110.

Cognitive Behavioral Analysis System of Psychotherapy

The cognitive behavioral analysis system of psychotherapy (CBASP; Keller et al., 2000; McCullough, 2000, 2006) is a psychological treatment program developed specifically for the chronically depressed patient. In the *Diagnostic and Statistical Manual of Mental Disorders* (*DSM-IV;* American Psychiatric Association, 1994), chronic depression is a unipolar affective disorder lasting a minimum of 2 years; without adequate treatment, the patient more often than not faces a lifetime of psychosocial disability. Early (prior to age 21) and late onset are the diagnostic descriptors indicating when the disorder began. The clinical courses among chronically depressed patients include several types of profiles. Two of the more common ones are (a) an early-onset of dysthymia beginning at 12 to 13 years of age, followed by a continuing course that includes one or more episodes of major depression—a clinical profile labeled *double depression*; and (2) a late-onset course exacerbated at age 25 to 26 with a major depressive episode that never fully remits. Approximately 23% of adults with late onset do not recover from their first episode, and the course becomes chronic. Without adequate regimes of medication and psychotherapy, prognosis for recovery for both types is poor, and even with treatment, the ever-present danger of relapse and recurrence remains a serious threat throughout the life span.

The long-standing course of chronic depression, often coupled with a developmental history characterized by maltreatment at the hands of significant others, results in clinicians facing entrenched and refractory emotional-cognitive-behavioral habit patterns. This means that the CBASP psychotherapist must address issues that denote more than just a cognitive or thinking disorder. Emotional abuse and trauma characterize the patient whose mood state is highly resistant to change. Refractory emotional patterns have to be resolved in addition to the individual's cognitive and behavioral problems; thus, a broad attack that tackles multiple intrapersonal and interpersonal problems is required. CBASP offers such a broad treatment approach, addressing the developmental-intrapersonal issues concomitantly with the interpersonal ones.

Patients enter treatment demoralized and with prominent helplessness and hopelessness symptoms. Both demoralization and the helplessness-hopelessness dilemma point to the core issue. Pervasive and chronic interpersonal avoidance patterns and a failure to perceive that one's behavior has predictable interpersonal consequences render these individuals socially isolated and perceptually alone. The interpersonal ripple effects of such a lifestyle are catastrophic and leave family members, caring friends, spouses, and work colleagues helpless to aid the individual. Patients begin therapy entrapped in an egocentric circle of helplessness and hopelessness with no exit.

Motivation to change at treatment outset is inhibited by a generalized outlook of despair that patients frequently express with such statements as, "It doesn't matter what I do, I stay depressed." The social skill deficits that originate from an extended history of interpersonal avoidance coupled with the fact that patients are unable to recognize that the way they behave literally drives others away make their despairing statement a valid self-diagnosis.

CBASP Techniques

CBASP psychotherapy seeks to accomplish two overarching goals: The first goal is to teach patients to recognize and identify the interpersonal consequences of their behavior. Situational analysis (SA; McCullough, 2000) is the technique used for this purpose. In SA, patients learn through repeated practice to focus on specific and problematical interpersonal encounters. Approaching interpersonal troubles in this specific manner helps clinicians countercondition the patient's tendency to talk in a general, global manner ("No one could ever care for me," "Nothing will ever work out," "I'll always fail," etc.). SA also makes explicit how one contributes directly to negative interpersonal problems. Over time, the consistent message of SA finally gets through to the patient: *if you tire of the interpersonal outcomes you describe in SA, then you must change your behavior!* Achieving a *perceived functionality* perspective denotes the point when patients understand that the negative interpersonal consequences they report are self-productions. Recognizing that one's behavior affects others in malevolent ways has another positive outcome—it motivates persons to learn to behave differently; reacting to others in more positive ways predictably results in more desirable situational outcomes, and best of all, it leads to patients feeling better.

The second overarching goal of CBASP is to socialize the patient through *therapist-disciplined personal involvement* (McCullough, 2000, 2006), which usually results in persons experiencing more positive emotions. The rationale for this goal arises from the severe social isolation and the trauma and abuse history many chronically depressed patients report. Disciplined personal involvement is a novel therapeutic role used in CBASP to deal with the person's idiosyncratic problems. An extensive description of the personal involvement role is found in McCullough's 2006 book.

Achieving the second goal requires CBASP practitioners to engage patients on personal interactive levels. This means that CBASP therapists become proactive, nonneutral participants in the treatment process and engage patients with Disciplined Personal Involvement (DPI; McCollough, 2006). For example, patients are taught to discriminate between the consequences received at the hands of maltreating significant others (caregivers), and the salubrious ones they experience with their psychotherapist. The Interpersonal Discrimination Exercise (IDE: McCullough, 2000, 2006) is the technique administered to accomplish this goal. The IDE does three things: (a) it insures that patients learn to discriminate between the person of the therapist and others who have hurt them; (b) the IDE heals early emotional trauma through the salubrious responsivity of the practitioner; and finally, (c) the IDE makes explicit the fact that growth possibilities are now possible because of the absence of the earlier toxic interactions that were previously so damaging. All of these outcomes lead patients to feel better about themselves and others.

CBASP practitioners utilize a second disciplined personal involvement technique called contingent personal responsivity (CPR; McCullough, 2006). Not infrequently, the patient's interpersonal behavior in the early sessions precludes clinicians from conducting CBASP therapy. Many patients come to treatment with interpersonal habits that compete with the work of therapy. For example, some persons make blatantly hostile comments about the practitioner's competence, the therapy model, the therapy setting itself, the clinic staff, or the therapist's integrity; others make overt sexual comments or overtures that are intended to detour the direction of treatment; withdrawn or disassociating patients often refuse to make eye contact; not infrequently, patients "talk over" the clinician, disregarding his or her comments; patients can be patently rude and inattentive; some actively refuse to answer the questions they are asked and change the subject at every opportunity. All of these behaviors inhibit the administration of CBASP therapy and require that the clinician personally address the problem with Personal Responsivity Behavior (CPR).

CBASP psychotherapists require two basic cognitive-behavioral skills from patients if they are to do their work: (a) therapists must be able to achieve some degree of verbal stimulus control over patient talk (e.g., patients must be able and willing to listen and answer the therapist's questions); and (b) the patient must be able to focus and concentrate on the subject matter or task at hand. Individuals who cannot generate these behaviors must be taught to do so before psychotherapy begins. CPR consequates and shapes up these "pretherapy behaviors," utilizing the personal reactions of the therapist as a direct interpersonal consequence for such prohibitive patterns.

The chronically depressed adult is challenging—to put it mildly. CBASP has been developed to deal specifically with the idiosyncratic and refractory lifestyle difficulties of this patient and to date has achieved some notable successes (e.g., Keller et al., 2000).

JAMES P. MCCULLOUGH, JR.

References

American Psychiatric Association. (1994). *Diagnostic and statistical manual of mental disorders* (4th ed.). Washington, DC: Author.

Keller, M. B., McCullough, J. P., Jr. Klein, D. N., Arnow, B. A., Dunner, D. L., Gelenberg, A. J., et al. (2000). A comparison of nefazodone, the cognitive behavioral analysis system of psychotherapy, and their combination for the treatment of chronic depression. *New England Journal of Medicine, 342,* 1462–1470.

McCullough, J. P., Jr. (2000). *Treatment for chronic depression: Cognitive behavioral analysis system of psychotherapy (CBASP).* New York: Guilford Press.

McCullough, J. P., Jr. (2006). *Treating chronic depression with disciplined personal involvement: CBASP.* New York: Springer.

Cognitive Behavioral Couples Therapy

Behavioral couples therapy began in the late 1960s and early 1970s with an initial conceptual emphasis on operant learning principles and their application to couples. Although the vast majority of the studies in the 1980s and 1990s were with married couples, the concepts also apply to individuals in long-term nonmarried relationships. More specifically, core concepts of behavioral couples therapy included positive reinforcement, reciprocity, and caring days. Based on several early

studies, it was clear that the ratio of pleasing to displeasing behaviors in happy relationships was much higher than in unhappy relationships. It was held that positive reinforcers are critical in maintaining a good marriage or relationship, and it was postulated that if positive reinforcement in a relationship could be increased, relationship satisfaction would improve. Reciprocity was also a concept of importance to early behavioral marital therapists because the behavior of partners is interdependent, and it was found that on average partners were equally positive to one another (and equally negative as well!). To improve a relationship, it was necessary to shift the balance from negative to positive exchanges. Therapists encouraged their clients to act in pleasing and positive ways with their partners via so-called caring days on which partners would be expected to do nice things for one another. Although there was evidence that the more partners engaged in such positive behaviors the more likely they were to be happy in their relationship, it also became clear that even the combination of positive and negative behaviors did not correlate with marital satisfaction at more than .40 to .55. Thus, as was the case in psychology in general, there was a shift in the 1980s from focusing exclusively on behavioral change to focusing more on cognitive and affective variables in dyadic interactions.

Attribution of fault or blame was a cognitive variable of importance because individuals who blame their partners are more likely to be discordant and they are less likely to improve in marital therapy. Distressed spouses also perceive their partners' communications as more negative than intended. When partners feel threatened, they often become angry and hostile rather than addressing their feelings of being hurt and unloved. Individuals in discordant relationships often attempt to enlist the aid of the therapist in getting their partner to change a long list of behaviors, rather than learning to accept some stylistic and personality factors that may not change. In short, after the 1980s, marital therapists became more cognitively and affectively oriented, and they helped spouses attend to their dysfunctional communication patterns and attitudes, convey their hurt and relationship fears, accept some things that may not change, and work on relationship patterns that likely could change.

Cognitive behavioral marital therapy has been successful in over a dozen treatment outcome studies in which husbands and wives report significant improvement in their marital satisfaction, and such results have been obtained in both the United States and in Europe. In addition, individuals who are assigned to nontreatment control groups show very little if any improvement. The differences between the treatment and no-treatment control groups has been so significant that there was a call to stop using wait-list controls (Baucom, Hahlweg, & Kuschel, 2003). On the other hand, the change seen in marital therapy is such that even if there is improvement in as many as two-thirds of a treatment group, about half of those treated do not reach a generally satisfied state of marriage. Such results have led to the successful development of marital treatments for specific types of relationship problems and coexisting problems such as depression; intimate partner violence, especially low-level forms of partner violence; affairs; and chronic pain. The next section focuses specifically on the treatment of relationship problems and coexisting depression, especially major depressive episodes.

It has been known for decades that having significant marital problems can lead some individuals to become depressed. In an early epidemiological study, individuals were 25 times more likely to be depressed if they were not getting along with their spouse. This association between marital discord and depressive symptomatology has been shown in a number of studies, and empirical reviews and meta-analyses have shown that there is a medium to large association (.35–.45) between marital discord and depressive symptoms for both men and women in community populations. Moreover, this association can be seen even more strikingly in populations of clinically depressed or maritally discordant

individuals (Whisman, 2001). Further, in longitudinal work in representative community samples, marital dissatisfaction showed a threefold increased risk of a subsequent diagnosis of depression. Finally, if a woman experiences a highly negative life event, such as a threat of separation or divorce or learning of a partner's affair, there is a strong likelihood that she will become clinically depressed almost immediately after experiencing the negative event. While it is now very clear that marital discord often can lead to depression, it has also been shown that relationships with a chronically depressed partner can become discordant. Thus, it has become equally important for marital therapists to develop interventions to help both the depressed and the nondepressed partner.

The need for couple-based treatments for the depressed person and his or her nondepressed partner is supported by the following documented characteristics of such couples that are living with depression: spouses of depressed individuals commonly express critical and hostile attitudes; there are more negative communications (e.g., blaming, criticism) than in couples where there is no depression; and spouses' expressions of criticism and hostility are highly predictive of having a slower recovery from depression or a relapse into depression. There is also a need to focus on helping the nondepressed spouse because of his or her inhibited communication, resentment, friction, and codependency. The nondepressed spouse often has significantly heightened psychological distress due to burdens associated with living with a depressed person. Further, there are diminished social and sexual relations, chronic rumination and worrying, and irritability, all of which have been shown to contribute to relationship deterioration.

Cognitive behavioral marital therapy was successfully used for the treatment of coexisting marital discord and depression by O'Leary and Beach (see Beach, Dreifuss, Franklin, Kamen, & Gabriel, 2008). In this treatment, in addition to emphases on changes like those already described, there also was an emphasis on providing support for the depressed patient. This treatment was successful not only in alleviating depression but also in increasing marital satisfaction and in minimizing relapses into depression. The treatment model seemed especially well suited to depressed individuals who attributed their depression to the marital problems. Fortunately, researchers in the United States and Europe have shown that variations of marital treatments can be used to alleviate depression and increase marital satisfaction. It is also now known that depressed individuals and their nondepressed spouses can be treated with intensive but relatively short-term therapy combined with psychoeducational information about depression. Such an approach includes empathy and support building, communication training, and tailored interventions to address individual and dyadic issues surrounding depression.

Cognitive behavioral marital therapy clearly is associated with reductions in depression, though individual therapy for depression has not demonstrated comparable improvements in marital satisfaction, or if there are changes in marital satisfaction associated with individual treatment or pharmacotherapy, they are relatively small. Given this pattern of change or lack thereof, one can wonder what mechanisms of change in depression occur when one receives marital therapy. Alternatively, does the change in marital satisfaction lead to the reductions in depression? In two different studies, it was shown that the effects of marital therapy are mediated or brought about by the changes in marital satisfaction. These results lead to another question, namely, "Can marital therapeutic modalities other than cognitive behavioral marital therapy lead to similar reductions in depression?" Interpersonally oriented psychotherapy in a partner-assisted couple format was associated with reductions in depression without an increase in marital satisfaction. Further, it appears that one can assist women in reducing their depression in a cognitive behaviorally based, couple-based format even if the women do not report significant marital distress at the outset of treatment. Thus, in addition to increases in

marital satisfaction, there appear to be other factors that can lead to reductions in depression in couple-based treatments. Such factors include increases in support of the depressed partner, reduced negativity of both partners, and reduced negative attitudes toward depression by the nondepressed partner.

K. DANIEL O'LEARY

See also

Cognitive Behavioral Therapy
Family and Parent-Child Therapy
Family Transmission of Depression

References

Baucom, D., Hahlweg, K., & Kuschel, A. (2003). Are waiting-list control groups needed in future marital therapy outcome research? *Behavior Therapy, 34,* 179–188.

Beach, S. R. H., Dreifuss, J. A., Franklin, K., Kamen, C., & Gabriel, B. (2008). Couple therapy and the treatment of depression. In A. S. Gurman (Ed.), *Clinical handbook of couple therapy* (pp. 546–566). New York: Guilford Press.

Whisman, M. A. (2001). The association between marital dissatisfaction and depression. In S. R. H. Beach (Ed.), *Marital and family processes in depression: A scientific foundation for clinical practice* (pp. 3–24). Washington, DC: American Psychological Association.

Cognitive Behavioral Therapy

Cognitive therapy (CT) for depression evolved from Beck's (1967) theory that depression is maintained by negatively biased information processing and dysfunctional beliefs. CT is a time-limited, problem-focused, directive therapy that typically includes 14 to 16 weekly sessions (50 minutes each), but it can last longer for more severe and chronic depression. It is usually conducted as an individual therapy, although CT with groups and other modalities of delivery also have demonstrated efficacy. We focus our review on the form of cognitive therapy developed by Aaron T. Beck and his colleagues and on recent developments that have a fairly direct historical lineage to this approach.

Over the past 40 years, CT has evolved to be one of the most widely practiced and researched psychotherapies for depression. Numerous randomized clinical trials have demonstrated the efficacy of CT as a front-line, acute-phase treatment with enduring prophylactic effects, even for recurrent depression. For example, in a multisite, randomized controlled trial of treatments for moderate to severe depression, CT had an enduring effect over a 12-month follow-up that was equivalent to maintaining patients on antidepressant medication (Hollon et al., 2005). CT responders were then followed without additional CT, and responders to the acute-phase pharmacotherapy were randomly assigned to placebo withdrawal or to continuation pharmacotherapy. DeRubeis and colleagues (2005) reported that CT responders were less likely to relapse (31%) than medication responders in the placebo-withdrawal condition (76%) and were no more likely to relapse than those who continued to receive medication (47%). CT also has been extended with good outcomes to low-income and ethnic minority populations and to geriatric populations.

Overview of the Cognitive Approach to Treating Depression

Beck (1967) proposed that distorted or dysfunctional thinking is central to depression and that the evaluation and modification of this negative thinking can facilitate improvement in mood and behavior. Those who are depressed or are prone to depression typically have negative thoughts about themselves, their world, and their future (the cognitive triad) that are often related to themes of personal worthlessness and inadequacy, helplessness, and loss. Automatic thoughts (and images) are considered a surface or manifest level of cognition that are easily triggered and often fleeting. Automatic thoughts can go unrecognized but can be brought into awareness when patients are taught to monitor them. These thoughts are hypothesized to arise from an intermediate level of irrational beliefs that include attitudes, assumptions,

and rules by which the person operates, and also from a deeper level of underlying dysfunctional schemata. Schemata are conceptualized as templates of the self and the world that guide attention, perception, information processing, and memory. Dysfunctional schemata can remain dormant until activated by emotional distress and life events. When activated, schemata can give rise to cognitive biases and distortions that filter and modify incoming information to fit the relevant schema, thereby exacerbating and maintaining negative emotional states. This biased processing becomes apparent at the level of automatic thoughts, which is often the starting point of cognitive therapy.

Early in the course of CT for depression (Beck, Rush, Shaw, & Emery, 1979) patients are taught to monitor their negative thoughts to become aware of how they spring up automatically, without careful deliberation and reasoning. Patients become aware of the dynamic interplay between cognitions and situations, feelings, physiology, and behavior. This monitoring of thoughts also serves to interrupt the automatic mode of negative thinking and rumination and to access a more deliberative mode of processing. In addition, this monitoring can reveal affectively charged or "hot" cognitions and important themes related to depression.

Patients learn skills in CT to evaluate the validity and utility of depressive cognitions, test them empirically, and change them to a more adaptive viewpoint. Patients also learn to identify, evaluate, and modify underlying assumptions and core dysfunctional beliefs that can predispose them to depressive reactions and increase their risk of relapse. In essence, patients are taught to decenter from their irrational thoughts and to view these thoughts as hypotheses to be tested. The patient learns to become an observer of the flow of depressive thoughts and to deliberately examine the validity of these thoughts, even if they emotionally "feel true" (Beck et al., 1979). CT can be conceptualized as attentional training that teaches patients to disengage from the automatic processes that narrow and bias perception and to broaden one's perspective to consider a more full range of information. Some recent iterations of CT place more emphasis on decreasing cognitive reactivity in the face of emotional distress and negative life events by focusing explicitly on attentional retraining, decentering, and unhooking from the toxic process of rumination.

Siegle, Ghinassi, and Thase (2007) are developing cognitive control therapy (CCT), a 2-week adjunctive intervention that teaches depressed patients to exercise executive control in the face of rumination and emotional arousal. The exercises in this program are thought to "jump start" prefrontal cortex inhibitory systems and to facilitate change in treatments for depression. These authors report exciting preliminary findings that CCT combined with treatment as usual is associated with more improvement in depressive symptoms and rumination than treatment as usual alone.

CT also includes a number of behavioral components that focus on teaching adaptive coping and problem-solving skills, increasing activity and engagement with potentially rewarding experiences, and assigning graded tasks to initiate behavioral change. Behavioral experiments are designed throughout the course of therapy to test patients' negative beliefs. Because of the importance of behavioral techniques, CT is sometimes referred to as cognitive behavioral therapy, but the emphasis throughout therapy is on facilitating cognitive change.

In a recent study on the extent to which a sample of 35 moderately to severely depressed patients used the skills learned in CT (behavioral activation, changing automatic thoughts, and schema change techniques), Strunk, DeRubeis, Chiu, and Alvarez (2007) found that both the development and independent use of CT skills predicted reduced risk for relapse 1 year later. Among treatment responders, both CT coping skills and in-session evidence of their implementation predicted lower risk for relapse, even accounting for symptom levels and change at the end of treatment. Although preliminary, these findings suggest that CT might teach patients a repertoire of specific skills to maintain their treatment gains and manage their symptoms of depression.

Implementation and Specific Techniques

Therapeutic Relationship

Beck (1967; Beck et al., 1979) refers to CT as a process of "collaborative empiricism" because the therapist and patient work together to establish goals, set an agenda for each therapy session, systematically gather and examine evidence for the patient's beliefs, and develop homework assignments that continue the work of CT between sessions. Hypothesis testing is facilitated by the use of Socratic questioning rather than direct disputation by the therapist. The patient is helped to make guided discoveries and to design behavioral experiments to test the validity of automatic thoughts and assumptions. The cognitive therapist also functions as an educator and skills trainer.

Beck et al. (1979) highlight the importance of establishing and maintaining a solid therapeutic alliance in CT for depression, especially with comorbid Axis II pathology. Safran and Segal (1990) introduced the idea that ruptures in the alliance are also important and that these problems present potent opportunities for CT therapists to examine and modify core interpersonal schemata and patterns. Consistent with this perspective, if alliance ruptures are repaired in CT, it appears that there is more improvement in personality symptoms and depression in patients with Cluster C personality disorders. Thus, a critical task for cognitive therapists is to develop and maintain a solid working relationship and a spirit of collaboration.

Case Conceptualization and Psychoeducation

The early sessions of CT are spent teaching the patient about depression and developing an individualized case conceptualization and specific set of target problems and goals. The patient is introduced to the cognitive model, using material from the patient's experiences and case conceptualization to illustrate how the CT model is relevant to his or her depression. This process lays the groundwork for the collaborative relationship between the therapist and patient and also begins to show the patient how he or she can participate in the recovery process. Once the CT model is taught to the patient, psychoeducation is less of a direct focus, but it is often integrated throughout the remainder of treatment.

Homework

Homework is employed extensively in CT, with the majority of sessions ending with a homework assignment. The purpose of homework is to practice and generalize the strategies learned during sessions into everyday life, as well as to further test the validity of negative thoughts or beliefs between sessions. Patients and therapists regularly design mini experiments outside of the context of therapy to test patients' depressive beliefs. For example, a depressed patient who thinks, "No one wants to spend time with me," might invite a number of people to spend time with him or her in order to evaluate how many people actually decline the invitation. Patients can also be given assignments to practice new skills between sessions and to increase engagement with their environment.

Behavioral Techniques

Behavioral techniques are employed throughout CT for depression to increase activation, teach important skills such as coping, problem-solving, relaxation, and social skills, and to introduce graded task assignments. As described above, behavioral experiments are also designed throughout the course of therapy to test negative beliefs related to one's depression.

An important behavioral technique, especially for severe depression, is behavioral activation. Behavioral activation exercises are concentrated in the early sessions of therapy to counter the lethargy, withdrawal, avoidance, and hopelessness associated with depression. Patients first record their daily activities on an hour-by-hour basis and rate the level of mastery and pleasure obtained from each activity. This baseline allows the patient and therapist to examine the patient's daily lifestyle and opportunities for reinforcement. Specific activities are then planned to elicit high levels of mastery and/or pleasure in order to increase the reinforcement received from the environment. This activity also helps the patient to understand the link between events, thoughts, moods, and behavior. For example, depressed patients often withdraw from friends and family, so a patient can be instructed to contact two friends and spend time with them over the course of the week as homework. This social engagement can increase the chances of positive social interactions, which can increase the likelihood of continued social involvement and the availability of social support. This activation can initiate an upward spiral of improved mood, behavior, and cognitions, and increase the resources for change. These techniques have evolved into a stand-alone behavioral activation treatment referred to in the section of this chapter on new developments.

CT often includes a variety of skill-building interventions related to emotion regulation and problem solving. When relevant, patients are taught general skills to improve their interactions with others and to decrease the probability of generating more negative events related to skills deficits and maladaptive attempts to cope with distress.

Another useful behavioral technique in CT is graded task assignments. At times, depressed individuals can see homework assignments as overwhelming and requiring too much effort. A homework task can be divided into smaller components and graded in difficulty. The patients can complete the homework task in portions, starting with tasks that require less effort and are likely to be met with positive outcomes. This teaches patients that although tasks can be more difficult or take longer during depression, they can still accomplish them.

Identifying and Modifying Negative Automatic Thoughts, Irrational Beliefs, and Core Beliefs

A central target of CT is negative automatic thoughts. During CT, patients are taught how to identify and change their own automatic thoughts, which can facilitate later cognitive restructuring and change the patient's negative emotions and behaviors. Therapists work to elicit negative automatic thoughts from their patients during sessions (e.g., "What were you thinking when you felt that way?"), often using Socratic questioning (e.g., "What would be the worst thing that would happen, if you did that?"). Automatic thoughts are also elicited as homework and reviewed in session. Early in therapy, patients are introduced to the daily thought record, which involves having them keep track of the moods, events, and negative automatic thoughts that they experience over the week. As treatment progresses, patients learn to identify specific cognitive errors associated with their thinking, develop rational alternatives to those negative automatic thoughts, and evaluate the impact of those alternative thoughts on emotions and behaviors. For example, patients rate the strength of each negative thought (i.e., how much the patient believes in its accuracy) at the time it occurred and again after it has been examined and replaced with an alternative, more adaptive cognition. This allows therapeutic progress to continue outside of therapy by allowing patients to collect their own information and review it with the therapist in the session.

By using the daily thought record patients learn to recognize the associations between events, thoughts, moods, and behaviors. Patients can identify intermediate beliefs that are composed of attitudes (e.g., "It is unacceptable not to know the answer to a question"), assumptions (e.g., "If I work very hard to cover everything, I will not be caught off guard"), and rules (e.g., "I should know everything and should always be at the top of my game") that link automatic thoughts to underlying core beliefs of schemata (e.g., "I am inadequate and incompetent"). Patients can also identify thoughts that are particularly "hot" or affectively laden and that have roots in early experiences to reveal underlying schemata that are targeted later in therapy. It is thought to be especially important to target schema-level change when patients have a history of childhood adversity and/or comorbid Axis II pathology that contributes to their depression (Beck et al., 1979). Underlying schemata also can be discovered by the vertical exploration or so-called downward arrow technique in which the consequences of a particular thought are repeatedly drawn out, and also in emotionally evocative imagery exercises, as described below.

Over time, the focus of therapy shifts from the level of automatic thoughts related to a specific event to more general themes related to core dysfunctional schemata, which are often characterized as global, overgeneralized, rigid, and absolute. Once such dysfunctional schemata have been identified, patients learn to examine when and under what conditions they become triggered, to monitor their ongoing reactions to these schemata, and to examine the validity of these dysfunctional beliefs.

To evaluate core beliefs, patients examine the childhood origins of the core beliefs related to their depression, how the beliefs have been maintained over the years, and how they contribute to current problems. The exploration of the past is brief and used only to better understand how dysfunctional schemata play out in current difficulties. Patients work with therapists to actively develop new, more realistic, and functional core beliefs. With repeated practice and restructuring, the depressive schemata can weaken and the more adaptive and accurate thinking and mode of processing strengthens.

Emotionally Evocative Techniques

It is becoming increasingly apparent that long-lasting cognitive change occurs best in a affectively charged context (Greenberg, 2002). Since our early appraisal of CT more than a decade ago (Robins & Hayes, 1993), emotionally evocative techniques have come to play a more important role in facilitating change in CT. Although Beck makes clear the importance of affective arousal in the original CT treatment manual for depression (Beck et al., 1979), there are now more specific techniques with which to enhance the affective charge of sessions. Most of these techniques, such as guided imagery and imagery-related role playing techniques, have been imported from Gestalt therapies. Therapists can help patients to develop a different understanding of the early traumatic or adverse experiences that relate to their depression by using guided imagery, Socratic questioning, dialogue, and role-playing exercises. The imagery and role-playing exercises can activate core dysfunctional schemata, and new corrective information can be introduced under this state of activation rather than talking about the schemata from a more intellectualized perspective. This work can be especially important when patients present with early childhood adversity and/or comorbid personality disorders. Both imagery and role playing also can be used to prepare for a homework assignment. For example, if a homework assignment involves a social interaction, the therapist and patient can role play the situation in session to prepare the patient for the interaction between sessions. If a client is concerned about how he or she will handle nervousness or awkwardness, imagery and role-playing exercises can be used to help activate these feelings and to work through the emotions before facing the real interaction.

In line with the theoretical importance of increasing affective arousal and exploring the developmental context of dysfunctional schemata, our research group (Hayes, Castonguay, & Goldfried, 1996) found that a more developmental focus in Hollon and colleagues's (1992) clinical trial of CT for depression predicted more change in depression at the end of treatment and was associated with less relapse. Hayes and Strauss (1998) subsequently found that this developmental focus was associated with more in-session arousal, destabilization of the depressive network, and the influx of corrective information.

Seeing the parallels with exposure-based therapies in anxiety disorders, Hayes and colleagues are developing an exposure-based cognitive therapy (EBCT), a cognitive approach that applies principles of exposure therapies for anxiety disorders to the treatment of depression. Consistent with principles of exposure therapy, cognitive and emotion theorists emphasize the importance of fully activating the cognitive, affective, behavioral, and somatic components of the depressive network, increasing tolerance to avoided emotions and thoughts, and increasing exposure to corrective information to facilitate cognitive restructuring and emotional processing. The first phase of EBCT integrates behavioral activation, stress management, and mindfulness meditation to help counter avoidance and rumination patterns and also teaches healthy lifestyle habits related to diet, exercise, and sleep. This phase is designed to increase the energy, stability, and resources for change. The second phase involves activating the core negative view of self and hopelessness and enhancing affective arousal and the exploration of developmental circumstances related to the core schemata. Throughout the course of therapy, patients write about their depression to facilitate processing, and the essays from the early phase of therapy are used to activate and explore the depressive network. Cognitive and emotional processing is facilitated by exploring this material without avoiding or ruminating and with less fear, so that the patient has more information available and can move to new meaning and perspective, much as patients do in exposure-based therapies for posttraumatic stress disorder. As in exposure therapies, this period of exposure and activation is associated with a transient worsening of symptoms that if conducted carefully, is therapeutic. The third phase focuses on similar exposure to avoided positive experiences and emotions and on strengthening the interconnections of a positive network that can compete with the depressive network and help prevent relapse.

There is preliminary evidence that such an approach may be helpful for the treatment of depression. In an initial open trial of EBCT, Hayes, Beevers, Feldman, Laurenceau, and Perlman (2005) reported that 83% of participants reported a 50% or greater reduction in symptom severity and no longer met diagnostic criteria for depression at the end of treatment. Process analyses (Hayes et al., 2005) indicated that higher levels of cognitive and emotional processing (i.e., exploring and questioning issues and material related to depression with some insight or perspective shift) during the second phase of therapy, when patients were taught to approach their sense of hopelessness, defectiveness, and failure, was predictive of treatment response, whereas processing in the first phase was not. Most of the therapeutic processing occurred during a period of high affective engagement that the authors call a *depression spike*. Whether EBCT enhances standard CT or reduces vulnerability to relapse has not yet been examined, but the process findings suggest that affective arousal and cognitive-emotional processing might be important in the change process.

Ongoing Developments and Future Directions

Consistent with the emphasis on empirical analysis, cognitive therapy has continued to evolve over the decades in the face of new data and theoretical challenges. CT is at such a point now, as it becomes apparent that the behavioral components of CT are more potent than originally realized and that behavioral activation performs well as a stand-alone treatment (e.g., Dimidjian et al., 2006). In addition, although there is mounting evidence that cognitive changes do occur in cognitive therapy (Garratt, Ingram, Rand, & Sawalani, 2007) and that these gains are maintained for up to 2 years (Jarrett, Vittengl, Doyle, & Clark, 2007), it is less clear that these changes are *specific* to cognitive therapy. For example, cognitive changes have also been reported in such noncognitive therapies as pharmacotherapy and behavioral activation therapy (Garratt et al., 2007). These data suggest that both behavioral and cognitive change can

facilitate recovery from depression and that cognitive change can occur through multiple pathways, even without a specific focus on cognitive change.

However, Beck (1967) proposed long ago that depressive schemata are less apparent after depression symptoms improve because they are dormant until triggered by life events and emotional distress. In order to examine this sort of cognitive change, it is imperative to examine the schemata under mood prime or other methods of activation, which many of the studies of cognitive change did not (Garratt et al., 2007). In contrast, studies that examine changes in cognitive reactivity, or the extent to which depressive cognitions are activated with a sad mood induction or with increases in naturally occurring fluctuations in dysphoric mood, reveal a different picture. The studies described below suggest that the extent of cognitive reactivity is an important predictor of relapse and that change in cognitive reactivity might be specific to CT. These advances in the study of cognitive change have spawned interesting offshoots of cognitive therapy, especially as related to relapse prevention.

Cognitive therapy specifically aims to decouple negative cognition from dysphoria and the symptoms of depression. Applying Post's (1992) concepts of *kindling* and *episode sensitization*, Segal and colleagues proposed that repeated episodes of depression may strengthen the associations between negative beliefs, information processing biases, and depressed mood. Over time, depressed mood can more easily activate a network of depression-related material, which then sets off negative information-processing biases and rumination, both of which decrease access to corrective information and deliberative, analytic thought and further worsen mood (Teasdale & Barnard, 1993). With repeated activation and episodes of depression, negative self-referent information becomes more highly interconnected and entrenched. As the depressive network is strengthened and generalizes to a range of different contexts, it is more easily activated (kindling) and can be activated by a wider range of stimuli (sensitization). Beevers, Wells, and Miller (2007) found that those with more previous episodes of depression reported more negative cognitions at pretreatment (even accounting for initial depression severity), and that these elevated negative cognitions fully mediated the relationship between history of depression and slower change in depression across inpatient and outpatient treatment. Cognitive therapy is particularly well suited to address these cognitive vulnerabilities.

In early writings, Beck and colleagues (1979) and Safran and Segal (1990) recognized that CT might have its effects by helping patients to step back and decenter from the automatic depressive cascade. By unhooking from the negative thoughts and the ruminative processes that exacerbate the negative cycle, patients would show less cognitive reactivity and could engage in more deliberative examination of their thoughts and interrupt the automaticity. Over time, this would contribute to a store of more accurate views of the self, world, and future. Ingram and Hollon (1986) posited that decentering might be the process by which CT has its long-term effects. Teasdale and colleagues (2001) further argued that CT prevents relapse by teaching patients methods to shift away from this automatic and ruminative processing mode more than by modifying the content of the negative thoughts.

From this perspective, cognitive reactivity at the end of treatment should predict relapse, decentering might decrease cognitive reactivity, and change in reactivity is likely to be specific to CT. In line with this argument, Segal, Gemar, and Williams (1999) demonstrated that although remitted depressed patients reported significant change in cognitions whether treated with CT or antidepressant (ADM) medication, those in the CT condition showed less cognitive reactivity to a laboratory mood induction than those in the ADM condition. In addition, lower cognitive reactivity predicted lower rates of relapse. In a replication study that added random assignment to treatment condition and an 18-month follow-up, Segal and

colleagues (2006) reported the same pattern of findings. Fresco, Segal, Buis, and Kennedy (2007) reported that patients in the Segal and colleagues (2006) trial who received CT showed significantly more improvement in decentering than those who received ADM. Decentering was a stronger predictor of lower relapse rates in CT than in ADM, particularly in conjunction with low cognitive reactivity. These findings begin to highlight a specific effect of CT and decentering as possible mechanism of change.

Relapse Prevention and Treatment for Chronic Depression

Another challenge to CT and to the treatment of depression in general is the increasing recognition of the chronicity of depression. Fifty percent of patients who experience depression will have another episode within 10 years. In addition, those experiencing a second episode have a 90% chance of experiencing a third, and individuals who experience three or more lifetime episodes of depression have a 40% chance of relapse within a month of completing treatment. Acute-phase CT has been demonstrated to have enduring prophylactic effects, even without the addition of continuation sessions. Sacco and Beck (1995) recommend that these effects can be enhanced by adding four to five booster sessions after acute phase treatment. However, approximately one-third of patients do not meet criteria for remission with the best treatments available, and the rates of relapse and recurrence are still high (Hollon, Stewart, & Strunk, 2006). Fortunately, a number of extensions of CT have been developed to begin to address the problems of relapse and recurrence and of chronic depression.

Continuation Cognitive Therapy

Continuation cognitive therapy (C-CT) has been developed by Jarrett and colleagues (Jarrett & Kraft, 1997) for patients at high risk for relapse, such as those with partial remission, early age of onset, and complications from early childhood adversity. C-CT is offered over an 8-month period following acute CT treatment and consists of 10 sessions. For the first 2 months, sessions occur every other week (four sessions total) and then once monthly for 6 months. Each session is 60 to 90 minutes long.

Mindfulness-Based Cognitive Therapy

Mindfulness-based cognitive therapy (MBCT; Williams, Teasdale, Segal, & Kabat-Zinn, 2007) is an eight-session relapse prevention program that combines mindfulness meditation with cognitive therapy techniques. This program is introduced after remission from depression to prevent its return, and it is most potent for those who have experienced three or more episodes of depression. There is also preliminary evidence that MBCT might also be applied to the treatment of residual depressive symptoms. Patients in MBCT engage in daily mindfulness practice and learn to pay attention to their dysfunctional thoughts, observe them, and recognize their transient nature. They learn tools with which to decenter from these thoughts and to shift out of an automatic and ruminative mode of processing to a mindful "experiencing-being" mode of processing that is more aware and controlled. MBCT significantly reduces depressive symptoms for those experiencing three or more episodes of depression, as compared to a treatment as usual condition. Moreover, relapse rates in the treatment as usual group were as high as 66% but were only 37% in the MBCT condition (Teasdale et al., 2000).

Well-Being Therapy

Clinicians and researchers are increasingly focusing not only on reducing symptoms, but also increasing overall mental health and well-being. Some researchers contend that not addressing wellness leaves patients vulnerable to relapse. Well-being therapy (WBT; Fava & Ruini, 2003) is based upon Ryff and Singer's (1998) model of psychological well-being, which includes six dimensions:

autonomy, personal growth, environmental mastery, purpose, positive relations, and self-acceptance. The treatment consists of eight sessions, although more sessions (e.g., 12–16) or fewer can be offered depending on patient need. Sessions are 30 to 50 minutes long and are conducted either weekly or bimonthly. Specific techniques involved in WBT are similar to those in CT and include self-observation, cognitive restructuring, activity scheduling, assertiveness training, problem-solving skills, structured diaries, and the use of interactions between patient and therapist. In initial sessions, WBT focuses on identifying moments of well-being and their situational context. Intermediate sessions focus on identifying thoughts and beliefs that lead to interruption of well-being, and the use of CT techniques to discuss the rationality of those thoughts and beliefs. Final sessions focus on identifying specific impairments on Ryff's six dimensions of well-being, progressively introducing each dimension into the patient's structured diary.

Well-being therapy seems to be a useful intervention for reducing residual symptoms and relapse after pharmacotherapy. In a study of patients randomly assigned after acute-phase treatment to either 10 sessions of WBT or to clinical management (and gradual taper off medications), patients who received WBT had a 25% relapse rate over the 2-year follow-up period, whereas those in the clinical management condition had a substantially higher 80% relapse rate (Fava, Rafanelli, Grandi, Conti, & Belluardo, 1998).

Cognitive Behavioral Analysis System of Psychotherapy

Cognitive behavioral analysis system of psychotherapy (CBASP; McCullough, 2000) is an integrative treatment for chronic depression that combines elements of several other therapies, including cognitive, behavioral, interpersonal, and psychodynamic approaches. According to this model, those with chronic depression experience disconnectedness from their environment and therefore have decreased access to important feedback on problematic interpersonal patterns and relationships. The therapeutic relationship is actively used to help patients generate empathic behavior, identify and change interpersonal patterns related to depression, and heal interpersonal trauma. CBASP consists of three techniques: (a) situational analysis, a problem-solving technique designed to help the patient realize the consequences of his or her behavior on others and modify it; (b) interpersonal discrimination exercises, examining past traumatic experiences with others and differentiating those from healthier relationships; and (c) behavioral skill training or rehearsal, such as assertiveness training, to further help depressed individuals modify maladaptive behavior. In a 12-site randomized clinical trial, patients were randomly assigned to one of three conditions: antidepressant (Nefazodone), CBASP, or the combination. Of those who completed therapy, about half of the patients responded to the pharmacotherapy and CBASP conditions alone, and 85% responded to the combination (73% in the intent-to-treat sample; Keller et al., 2000). Overall, the combination treatment was associated with a more rapid and greater reduction in symptom severity and with higher response and remission rates than either monotherapy (Keller et al., 2000).

Schema Therapy

Schema therapy (Young et al., 2007) is another integrative therapy that incorporates cognitive, behavioral, and emotion-focused components that can be used to address the problems associated with chronic depression. This approach is designed to address the particularly entrenched core schemata associated with chronic depression and comorbid Axis II pathology and can be a useful addition to acute-phase CT to help prevent relapse and recurrence. The therapy explores and attempts to modify patients' early maladaptive schemata related to unmet needs for safety, nurturance, autonomy, self-expression, and limits. The efficacy of schema therapy has not been examined in the treatment of chronic depression, but a clinical trial (Giesen-Bloo

et al., 2006) comparing it with a transference-focused therapy in the treatment of borderline personality disorder suggests that almost twice as many of those in schema therapy recovered (45%), as compared to 24% in the comparison condition. Young and colleagues (2007) suggest that this therapy might be a useful treatment for chronic depression because of the overlap of problems and engrained patterns in chronic depression and personality disorders.

Conclusion

Consistent with its empirical roots, Beck's cognitive therapy has evolved considerably over the four decades since its introduction, as new findings have emerged that challenge some of the original assumptions and emphases. These new developments are elaborations and extensions of the original work, and this spirit of open inquiry will undoubtedly yield further developments, as our understanding of the psychopathology and treatment of depression deepens.

ADELE M. HAYES AND JORDEN A. CUMMINGS

See also

Cognitive Behavioral Analysis System of Psychotherapy
Cognitive Behavioral Couples Therapy
Cognitive Distortion
Cognitive Mediation
Cognitive Reactivity
Cognitive Theories of Depression
Cognitive Vulnerability

References

Beck, A. T. (1967). *Depression.* New York: Harper & Row.

Beck, A. T., Rush, A. J., Shaw, B. F., & Emery, G. (1979). *Cognitive therapy of depression.* New York: Guilford Press.

Beevers, C. G., Wells, T., & Miller, I. W. (2007). Predicting response to depression treatment: The role of negative cognition. *Journal of Consulting and Clinical Psychology, 75,* 422–431.

DeRubeis, R. J., Hollon, S. D., Amsterdam, J. D., Shelton, R. C., Young, P. R., Saloman, R. M., et al. (2005). Cognitive therapy vs. medications in the treatment of moderate to severe depression. *Archives General Psychiatry, 62,* 409–416.

Dimidjian, S., Hollon, S. D., Dobson, K. S., Schmaling, K. B., Kohlenberg, R. J., Addis, M. E., et al. (2006). Randomized trial of behavioral activation, cognitive therapy, and antidepressant medication in the acute treatment of adults with major depression, *Journal of Consulting and Clinical Psychology, 74,* 658–670.

Fava, G. A., Rafanelli, C., Grandi, S., Conti, S., & Belluardo, P. (1998). Prevention of recurrent depression with cognitive behavioral therapy. *Archives of General Psychiatry, 55,* 816–820.

Fava, G. A., & Ruini, C. (2003). Development and characteristics of a well-being enhancing psychotherapeutic strategy: Well-being therapy. *Journal of Behavior Therapy and Experiential Psychiatry, 34,* 45–63.

Fresco, D. M., Segal, Z. V., Buis, T., & Kennedy, S. (2007). Relationship of posttreatment decentering and cognitive reactivity to relapse in major depression. *Journal of Consulting and Clinical Psychology, 75,* 447–455.

Garratt, G., Ingram, R. E., Rand, K. L., & Sawalani, G. (2007). Cognitive processes in cognitive therapy: Evaluation of the mechanisms of change in the treatment of depression. *Clinical Psychology: Science and Practice, 14,* 224–239.

Giesen-Bloo, J., van Dyck, R., Spinhoven, P., van Tilburg, W., Dirksen, C., van Asselt, T., et al. (2006). Outpatient psychotherapy for borderline personality disorder: A randomized trial of schema-focused therapy versus transference-focused therapy. *Archives of General Psychiatry, 63,* 649–658.

Greenberg, L. S. (2002). Integrating an emotion-focused approach to treatment in psychotherapy integration. *Journal of Psychotherapy Integration, 12,* 154–189.

Hayes, A. M., Beevers, C., Feldman, G., Laurenceau, J.-P., & Perlman, C. A. (2005). Avoidance and emotional processing as predictors of symptom change and positive growth in an integrative therapy for depression. *International Journal of Behavioral Medicine,* 111–122.

Hayes, A. M., Castonguay, L. G., & Goldfried, M. R. (1996). The effectiveness of targeting the vulnerability factors of depression in cognitive therapy. *Journal of Consulting and Clinical Psychology, 64,* 623–627.

Hayes, A. M., & Strauss, J. L. (1998). Dynamic systems theory as a paradigm for the study of change in psychotherapy: An application to cognitive therapy for depression. *Journal of Consulting and Clinical Psychology, 66,* 939–947.

Hollon, S. D., DeRubeis, R. J., Evans, M. D., Wiemer, M. J., Garvey, M. J., Grove, W. M., et al. (1992). Cognitive therapy and pharmacotherapy for depression: Singly and in combination. *Archives of General Psychiatry, 49,* 774–781.

Hollon, S. D., DeRubeis, R. J., Shelton, R. C., Amsterdam, J. D., Salomon, R. M., O'Reardon, J. P., et al. (2005). Prevention of relapse following cognitive therapy vs. medications in moderate to severe depression. *Archives of General Psychiatry, 62,* 417–422.

Hollon, S. D., Stewart, M. O., & Strunk, D. (2006). Enduring effects for cognitive behavior therapy in the treatment of depression and anxiety. *Annual Review of Psychology, 57,* 285–315.

Ingram, R. E., & Hollon, S. D. (1986). Cognitive therapy for depression from an information processing perspective. In R. E. Ingram (Ed.), *Information processing approaches to clinical psychology* (pp. 259–281). San Diego, CA: Academic Press.

Jarrett, R. B., & Kraft, D. (1997). Prophylactic cognitive therapy for major depressive disorder. *In Session, 3,* 65–79.

Jarrett, R. B., Vittengl, J. R., Doyle, K., & Clark, L. A. (2007). Changes in cognitive content during and following cognitive therapy for recurrent depression: Substantial and enduring, but not predictive of change in depressive symptoms. *Journal of Consulting and Clinical Psychology, 75,* 432–446.

Keller, M. B., McCullough, J. P., Klein, D. N., Arnow, B., Dunner, D. L., Gelenberg, A. L., et al. (2000). A comparison of nefazodone, the cognitive behavioral analysis system of psychotherapy, and their combination for the treatment of chronic depression. *New England Journal of Medicine, 342,* 1462–1470.

McCullough, J. P. (2000). *Treatment for chronic depression: Cognitive behavioral analysis system of psychotherapy (CBASP).* New York: Guilford Press.

Post, R. M. (1992). Transduction of psychosocial stress into the neurobiology of recurrent affective disorder. *American Journal of Psychiatry, 149,* 999–1010.

Ryff, C. D., & Singer, B. (1998). The contours of positive human health. *Psychological Inquiry, 9,* 1–28.

Sacco, W. P., & Beck, A. T. (1995). Cognitive theory and therapy. In E. E. Beckham & W. R. Leber (Eds.), *Handbook of depression* (2nd ed.) (pp. 329–351). New York: Guilford Press.

Safran, J., & Segal, Z. V. (1990). *Interpersonal process in cognitive therapy.* New York: Basic Books.

Segal, Z. V., Gemar, M., & Williams, S. (1999). Differential cognitive response to a mood challenge following successful cognitive therapy or pharmacotherapy for unipolar depression. *Journal of Abnormal Psychology, 108,* 3–10.

Segal, Z. V., Kennedy, S., Gemar, M., Hood, K., Pedersen, R., & Buis, T. (2006). Cognitive reactivity to sad mood provocation and the prediction of depressive relapse. *Archives of General Psychiatry, 63,* 749–755.

Siegle, G. J., Ghinassi, F., & Thase, M. E. (2007). Neurobehavioral therapies in the 21st century: Summary of an emerging field and an extended example of cognitive control training for depression. *Cognitive Therapy and Research, 31,* 235–262.

Strunk, D. R., DeRubeis, R. J., Chiu, A. W., & Alvarez, J. (2007). Patients' competence in and performance of cognitive therapy skills: Relation to the reduction of relapse risk following treatment for depression. *Journal of Consulting and Clinical Psychology, 75,* 523–530.

Teasdale, J. D., & Barnard, P. J. (1993). *Affect, cognition, and change: Re-modeling depressive thought.* Hillsdale, NJ: Lawrence Erlbaum Associates.

Teasdale, J. D., Segal, Z. V., Williams, J. M. G., Ridgeway, V. A., Soulsby, J. M., & Lau, M. A. (2000). Prevention of relapse/recurrence in major depression by mindfulness-based cognitive therapy. *Journal of Consulting and Clinical Psychology, 68,* 615–623.

Williams, M., Teasdale, J., Segal, Z., & Kabat-Zinn, J. (2007). *The mindful way through depression: Freeing yourself from chronic unhappiness.* New York: Guilford Press.

Young, J. E., Rygh, J. L., Weinberger, A. D., & Beck, A. T. (2007). In D. H. Barlow (Ed.). *Clinical handbook of psychological disorders: A step-by-step treatment manual* (4th ed.) (pp. 250–305). New York: Guilford Press.

Cognitive Distortion

The idea of cognitive distortion is important in many psychosocial models of depression. Beck's (1967) theory was the first to suggest that depressed individuals make errors in how they process information, which results in a negative distortion of that information. Such distortion is fundamental since it causes the depressed state to be maintained; continued access to negative information perpetuates the depressed state.

Although the concept of distortion may seem straightforward enough, different conceptualizations of this idea are possible. The overall idea is that distortion reflects beliefs, or the processing of information, that do not correspond to reality. In the original discussion of cognitive distortion, Beck (1967) offered what suggests *distortion by commission*. Using this definition, depressed individuals somehow "change" positive or neutral information into negative; what is actually positive or neutral information is interpreted as negative.

A different definition of distortion is a *distortion by omission* idea. In this scenario, depressed individuals may process negative information very accurately, but do not attend to or process positive information. Although some information is processed accurately, the overall effect of this processing would be a distortion, not because information was altered in some fashion, but rather because of an imbalance in the information that was processed relative to what was available. Such a conceptualization also suggests that cognitive distortion perpetuates depression, but the means for doing so are different from a distortion by commission process.

Kendall (1985) has also pointed out an important difference between cognitive distortion and cognitive deficiencies. In discussing child disorders, he argues that children who show cognitive deficiencies, such as a lack of impulse control, may reflect a different set of problems, and present different treatment challenges, than children who cognitively distort information.

Conclusions

Cognitive distortion is an important concept in many psychosocial models of depression. Yet, how distortion is conceptualized has important consequences for not only theories of depression, but for how relevant research questions are asked. A more detailed specification of how cognitive distortion is conceptualized by existing theories would help answer these questions and thus help move the field ahead in ways that may be important.

RICK E. INGRAM

See also

Aaron Beck
Automatic Thoughts
Cognitive Theories of Depression
Depressive Realism

References

Beck, A. T. (1967). *Depression: Causes and treatment*. Philadelphia: University of Pennsylvania Press.
Kendall, P. C. (1985). Cognitive processes and procedures in behavior therapy. In G. T. Wilson, C. M. Franks, P. C. Kendall, & J. P. Foreyt (Eds.), *Review of behavior therapy: Theory and practice, Vol. 11*. New York: Guilford Press.

Cognitive Mediation

In recent decades, cognitive models have been hugely influential to our understanding of many psychological disorders including depression. Cognitive models of depression emphasize that people become depressed primarily because of the way that they think. Specifically, these models propose that stress such as a negative life event (e.g., failing a class) is an important trigger for a depressive episode, but it is the perception of the situation that determines how one feels. Thus, cognitive models propose that cognition (e.g., perception) mediates the relationship between stress and depression (i.e., cognition is the link between them).

Cognitive models have generally stressed that maladaptive cognitions play a causal role in both the development and maintenance of depression. Therefore, these models have identified a potential mechanism for explaining why some people seem particularly prone to becoming and staying depressed. Numerous cognitive models have been proposed over the past several decades, but Beck's (1967, 1976) theory of depression is arguably the most influential of these models. Moreover, since its original proposal, substantial elaboration of the model has been suggested by Beck as well as others.

Beck's cognitive model emphasizes the role of depressogenic schemas in the onset and maintenance of depression. Schemas are conceptualized as cognitive structures that function like templates to facilitate the screening and evaluation of incoming information and, therefore, can help one make sense of their world more efficiently. Although everyone has schemas, Beck suggests that overly rigid and negative schemas (i.e., maladaptive) tend to characterize depression-vulnerable individuals. Specifically, his model proposes that depression is characterized by maladaptive schemas (also referred to as *core beliefs*) about the self, the world, and the future, which he refers to as the *cognitive triad* (Beck, 1970). The depressed person's schemas tend to reflect a view of the self as worthless, the world as filled with obstacles that are overwhelming and impossible to overcome, and the future as hopeless.

Beck's cognitive model also proposes that depressive schemas are latent (i.e., not active) until evoked by stressful circumstances. In fact, these depressive schemas are usually so fundamental and deep that the individual is not aware of them even when they are depressed. However, once the depressive schemas are evoked, they lead to a cascade of other more superficial maladaptive cognitions. For example, evoked depressive schemas bring about maladaptive information processing patterns, which are the pervasive biases in the perception, attention, and memory for negative information (e.g., only remembering past experiences with failure). Moreover, negative automatic thoughts emerge, which reflect the most superficial cognitions, and consist of the thoughts, decisions, and images that arise from the interaction of schemas with incoming information (e.g., "I must be stupid because I failed my exam"). Although Beck proposes that depressive schemas lie at the root of depression and are causally related to the onset of the depressive episode, these other more superficial maladaptive cognitions also have causal relevance because they help to maintain the depression. In other words, the biases for negative information and the negative automatic thoughts are significant to keeping one depressed. Taken together, these elements form the core causal features of the model and explain how maladaptive negative cognitions result in a "normal" sad mood spiraling downward into depression (Ingram, Miranda, & Segal, 1998).

It is worth noting that Beck developed a therapeutic intervention, cognitive therapy (or cognitive behavioral therapy), for the treatment of depression that is based on his theory. Cognitive therapy consists of a set of techniques that are intended to alter the function of the depressive schemas and the other maladaptive cognitions that serve to maintain the depression. Empirical support for the effectiveness of Beck's cognitive therapy in the treatment of depression is substantial. Moreover, data suggest that cognitive therapy helps to prevent future depressive episodes, whereas other treatments for depression (e.g., antidepressant medications) have not been shown to confer this benefit (Hollon, Stewart, & Strunk, 2006). Finally, findings from cognitive therapy outcome studies tend to support the development of more adaptive thinking as being critical to improvement in depression and, therefore, are at least consistent with cognitive mediation models.

Information-processing models of depression expand on Beck's model by elaborating on the negative biases in perception, attention, and memory that emerge and serve to maintain the depression. Many of these models utilize theories from cognitive science and computer science about how information is processed and stored. According to Ingram's (1984) information-processing model, the initial experience of depression results from the activation of a cognitive-affective network that consists of cognitive and affective components associated with depression. This model borrows from cognitive science theories on cognitive (and cognitive-affective) networks, which are conceptualized as the numerous connections between units of information that are embedded within the same network. Theories on cognitive networks propose that once a single unit of information is activated within a network, this results in a spreading of activation whereby other units of information within that network become activated as well. Ingram suggests that the cognitive-affective networks possess links to affective features of the respective emotion (e.g., action tendencies, physiological responses associated with feeling depressed) and to the respective cognitions (e.g., memories associated with feeling depressed). Once the cognitive-affective network for depression is activated, this results in a process of spreading activation throughout the network. The end result is heightened accessibility of the information embedded within the network that ultimately serves to maintain the depressed mood. Thus, when one feels depressed, one becomes more aware of negative information (e.g., memories, thoughts, and perceptions of incoming information), which further exacerbates the depressed mood.

Consistent with cognitive models examining information-processing patterns in depression, Nolen-Hoeksema (1991) suggests that depression is causally related to perseverative attention that is directed toward negative information (negative thoughts, negative aspects of the situation, etc.). Specifically, she proposes that an unrelenting negative focus in response to stress, referred to as rumination, exacerbates negative thinking and interferes with effective problem solving. Thus, more severe and prolonged periods of depression ensue. Moreover, consistent with

Beck's model, this general inclination to ruminate by depression-vulnerable individuals is often coupled with a tendency to engage in negative self-focused rumination (i.e., not just rumination about one's negative situation). Hence, depression-vulnerable individuals would be especially likely to ruminate on perceived negative aspects about the self when faced with a relevant stressor.

In addition to elaborations on Beck's cognitive model of depression, some theorists have focused on better understanding cognitive mediation in specific subtypes of depression. According to the hopelessness theory of depression (Abramson, Metalsky, & Alloy, 1989), the expectation that desirable outcomes are unlikely to occur, or that negative outcomes are very likely, and that there is nothing one can do to alter these outcomes is causally related to a specific subtype of depression—hopeless depression. Moreover, they propose that the specific attributions or explanations that people make about the causes of events contribute to the development of hopelessness. A tendency to make specific, unstable, external attributions for positive events and global, stable, and internal attributions for negative events renders one vulnerable to hopelessness. Thus, individuals who are vulnerable to hopeless depression generally assume that negative events will occur in every aspect of their life and will continue to happen, and that they hold responsibility for these events happening in the first place. Whereas positive events are assumed to occur in very specific situations, are unlikely to happen again, and are the result of things that are external to them and for which they have no control.

Although there are a number of other elaborations on cognitive mediation models for depression, the aforementioned models reflect some of the more eminent ones. One example of a widely recognized thinker on cognition and depression is Albert Ellis (1962) who developed a therapeutic approach that emphasizes the significance of negative thinking to depression. Ellis's rational emotive therapy, which he later referred to as rational emotive behavioral therapy, possesses many overlapping characteristics with Beck's cognitive therapy. However, Beck went to great lengths to articulate his cognitive model, and his theory and therapy have been widely researched. Moreover, as discussed earlier, many of the theorists who expanded on cognitive mediation models of depression elaborated on Beck's originally proposed model. Thus, this entry attempted to highlight some of the most influential cognitive mediation models that have been the most widely researched. Furthermore, although there are variations between the models described here, a cognitive conceptualization of depression (and depression vulnerability), whereby the relationship between stress and depression is mediated by cognition, is universal. Lastly, while the aforementioned models do not directly address the role of biological factors, each acknowledges their significance to depression. In the future, it is likely that cognitive mediation models will attempt to integrate biology with cognition and stress to explain how each of these factors interact in depression and contribute to depression vulnerability. In fact, research examining the relationships between biology, cognition, and stress, and how they interact with one another in depression, is already underway.

GENEVIEVE M. GARRATT

See also

Cognitive Reactivity
Cognitive Theories of Depression
Cognitive Vulnerability

References

Abramson, L. Y., Metalsky, G. I., & Alloy, L. B. (1989). Helplessness depression: A theory-based subtype of depression. *Psychological Review, 96*, 358–372.

Beck, A. T. (1967). *Depression: Clinical, experimental, and theoretical aspects.* New York: Harper and Row.

Beck, A. T. (1970). The core problem in depression: The cognitive triad. In J. H. Masserman (Ed.), *Depression:*

Theories and therapies (pp. 47–55). New York: Grune and Stratton.

Beck, A. T. (1976). *Cognitive therapy and the emotional disorders.* New York: International Universities Press.

Ellis, A. (1962). *Reason and emotion in psychotherapy.* New York: Lyle Stuart.

Hollon, S. D., Stewart, M. O., & Strunk, D. (2006). Enduring effects for cognitive behavior therapy in the treatment of depression and anxiety. *Annual Review of Psychology, 57*, 285–315.

Ingram, R. E., Miranda, J., & Segal, Z. V. (1998). *Cognitive vulnerability to depression.* New York: Guilford Press.

Nolen-Hoeksema, S. (1991). Responses to depression and their effects on the duration of depressive episodes. *Journal of Abnormal Psychology, 100*, 569–582.

Cognitive Reactivity

A major challenge to cognitive theories of depression was issued by a series of studies showing that the negative cognitive variables specified by these theories, and clearly present in the depressed state, could no longer be detected once depression remitted (for a detailed discussion of these studies see Segal & Ingram, 1994). One conclusion to be drawn from such studies was that negative cognition was either a consequence of the depressed state, or arose concomitantly with the depressed state and thus played no role in causing depression (e.g., Barnett & Gotlib, 1988).

These studies, however, did not test these variables within an appropriate diathesis-stress context. In particular, most cognitive theories of depression are diathesis-stress models that specify that cognitive variables will emerge in response to stressful situations; among individuals who are vulnerable to depression, cognitive variables are reactive to stress. The term *cognitive reactivity* has been used to refer to this process.

A number of studies, using an appropriate diathesis-stress framework, have now demonstrated cognitive reactivity (for a recent examination of these studies, see Scher, Ingram, & Segal, 2005). These studies have two common elements. The most theoretically relevant is the introduction of priming methods, intended to model the affective consequences of the depressed state. Because it would be unethical to introduce significant stress in study participants, priming methods endeavor to create a depressed mood that is mild and short-lived, but strong enough to detect cognitive reactivity if it is present. The most common way to prime participants is to have them listen to music that provokes some sad mood. The second common element is the nature of the participant sample. Although other methods are possible, typically a vulnerable sample composed of individuals who have previously experienced a depressive episode is employed in these studies. Clearly not all individuals in such a sample will again encounter a depressive episode, but as a group they are at risk.

Using such commonalities as template, numerous studies have now examined cognitive reactivity. Although an occasional failure to document cognitive reactivity is reported, the bulk of reported studies show reactivity using a variety of different measures. A common measure is the Dysfunctional Attitudes Scale, with a number of studies showing that formerly depressed individuals when induced into a mildly negative mood endorse more of these attitudes than do nonvulnerable people induced into the same sad mood. Other studies have employed information processing measures to examine cognitive reactivity. In a study reported by Ingram and Ritter (2000), for example, formerly depressed individuals induced into this mood paid more attention to negative information than did nonvulnerable participants.

In two intriguing studies that show perhaps the strongest evidence to date for cognitive reactivity, Segal and colleagues (Segal, Gemar, & Williams, 1999; Segal et al., 2006) primed participants who had been treated for depression and were now in remission. Two results are particularly noteworthy. First, patients who had been treated with cognitive therapy showed less evidence of cognitive reactivity than did those who had been treated with medication. Such a result suggested that cognitive therapy does indeed modify cognitive variables in a way suggested by cognitive theory (Garratt, Ingram, Rand, & Sawalani, 2007).

The second noteworthy result was that people who had shown the most cognitive reactivity immediately following treatment were also the most likely to relapse within a year and a half after treatment. This finding suggests that not only is cognitive reactivity present, but that its presence is related in a meaningful way to the causes of a subsequent depressive episode.

In sum, cognitive reactivity is theoretically in line with the diathesis-stress nature of contemporary cognitive models of depression, and in fact, empirical data have now shown consistent support for the idea that negative cognitive variables are reactive to stressful events in at least some people who are vulnerable to depression.

RICK E. INGRAM

See also

Causality
Diathesis-Stress Models of Depression
Dysfunctional Attitudes Scale
Vulnerability

References

Barnett, P. A., & Gotlib, I. H. (1988). Psychosocial functioning in depression: Distinguishing among antecedents, concomitants, and consequences. *Psychological Bulletin, 104*, 97–126.

Garratt, G., Ingram, R. E., Rand, K. L., & Sawalani, G. (2007). Cognitive processes in cognitive therapy: Evaluation of the mechanisms of change in the treatment of depression. *Clinical Psychology: Science and Practice, 14*, 224–239.

Ingram, R. E., & Ritter, J. (2000). Vulnerability to depression: Cognitive reactivity and parental bonding in high-risk individuals. *Journal of Abnormal Psychology, 109*, 588–596.

Scher, C. D., Ingram, R. E., & Segal, Z. V. (2005). Cognitive reactivity and vulnerability: Empirical evaluation of construct activation and cognitive diathesis in unipolar depression. *Clinical Psychology Review, 25*, 487–510.

Segal, Z. V., Gemar, M., & Williams, S. (1999). Differential cognitive response to a mood challenge following successful cognitive therapy or pharmacotherapy for unipolar depression. *Journal of Abnormal Psychology, 108*, 3–10.

Segal, Z. V., & Ingram, R. E. (1994). Mood priming and construct activation in tests of cognitive vulnerability to unipolar depression. *Clinical Psychology Review, 14*, 663–695.

Segal, Z. V., Kennedy, S., Gemar, M., Hood, K., Pedersen, R., & Buis, T. (2006). Cognitive reactivity to sad mood provocation and the prediction of depressive relapse. *Archives of General Psychiatry, 63*, 749–755.

Cognitive Theories of Depression

Cognitive approaches to the conceptualization, assessment, and treatment of depression marked their start with Beck's 1967 influential book, *Depression: Causes and Treatment*. As with cognitive approaches to psychopathology in general, the vitality of the cognitive view of depression is evidenced by innumerable research papers, books, and journals devoted extensively to the cognitive approach. Moreover, cognitive theories are tied to a cognitive approach to treatment, an approach that is effective in alleviating depression.

The fundamental assumption underlying cognitive models of depression is that certain cognitive processes are related to the onset, course, and/or alleviation of the disorder. Within this general context of definition, the degree of "cognitiveness" of a theory can vary substantially. Some theories that can be considered cognitive contain only minimal cognitive elements among a network of constructs. For example, Lewinsohn and colleagues (1985) offered a theory that accords a substantial role to self-focused attention, a cognitive construct, but this is virtually the only such construct in this model. For other cognitive theories the majority of conceptualization is accounted for by cognitive constructs.

Common Theoretical Ideas in Cognitive Models of Depression

A comprehensive understanding of cognitive theories requires some discussion of concepts and assumptions that are common to these theories. An obvious commonality, as just noted, is that any theory that is defined as a cognitive theory must incorporate at least some nontrivial cognitive elements within its conceptual framework. Aside from this defining feature of cognitive theories, several important ideas occur consistently across cognitive models of depression.

The Concept of the Self in Cognitive Models of Depression

Cognitive theories of depression are theories of cognition pertaining to the self. For instance, studies of cognition in depression have almost uniformly addressed the processing of self-related information, such as the occurrence of self-statements, or in research studies focus on understanding encoding of information as it pertains to descriptions of oneself. Of course, "the self" is not the only important cognitive construct in depression. The concept of internal working models, for example, represents an expansion of this idea. Even though this idea includes representations of the self, it also considers representations of significant others, and representations about potential interactions between the self and others; that is, internal working models represent a template based on past interactions, and that template is applied to expectations, perceptions, beliefs, and behaviors in future interactions.

Cognitive Distortion

The idea of cognitive distortion is integral to many models of depression. Beck (1967) was the first to suggest that depressed individuals perceive themselves, their future, and their world in a distortedly negative way—an idea known as the *cognitive triad*. Such distortion can function in different ways. It may be, for example, that depressed individuals take positive or neutral information and "twist it" into a negative direction. Or that depressed individuals actively interpret negative information but are inattentive to, and thus distort, positive information. Or perhaps as Kendall (1985) has noted, some individuals (e.g., children) have cognitive deficiencies (lack the processing necessary to control impulses), and that deficiency is thus a type of distortion. Regardless of how distortion is defined and measured, it is an important aspect of cognitive theories.

Cognitive Causality

Virtually all cognitive theories are causal theories, that is, the cognitive factors they specify are considered to be the primary causal agents. Thus, for example, structural models (discussed later) view constructs such as schemas as playing the key causal role in either the onset or maintenance of depression. Research has indeed begun to support the causal propositions of cognitive theories, in at least some kinds of depression (Garratt, Ingram, Rand, & Sawalani, 2007).

Categorization of Cognitive Theories

Cognitive theories can be considered in terms of the metaconstruct framework proposed by Ingram (1990) to help organize examination of cognitive models. In brief, this framework argues that theories can be categorized according to those emphasizing cognitive products (e.g., the thoughts and cognitions that are characteristic of depression), cognitive structures and propositions that underlie cognition (such as schemas), or those underscoring the primacy of cognitive processes in the depressed state.

Theories Focusing on Cognitive Products

Theories focusing on cognitive products emphasize the kinds of cognitions that individuals experience.

Cognitive Errors: Ellis

The earliest cognitive theories were relatively simple and tended to emphasize a linear association between thinking errors and the experience emotional distress; thinking X leads to emotion Y. The emphasis of these early approaches was almost completely on the development of effective therapeutic interventions, and less so elaborating the theoretical mechanisms. Consequently, the theoretical articulation of cognitive processes tended to be fairly limited and relied on straightforward assumptions about errors in thinking leading to the onset of emotional distress.

Although Ellis's approach was not specific to depression, it can nevertheless be applied to depressive disorders. Ellis's ideas are framed within the development of rational-emotive behavioral theory (REBT; Ellis, 1996) and proposed that irrational beliefs lead to psychological disorders such as depression. An example of an irrational belief proposed by Ellis is, "It is a dire necessity for adult humans to be loved or approved by virtually every significant other person in their community." Ellis also proposed the idea of *musturbatory thinking* to suggest that those vulnerable to emotional distress believe that some actions must occur to be happy, an expectation that sets the person up for failure. Hence, depression-prone individuals were proposed to hold rigid standards by which their life is judged, and as a consequence of these rigidly high standards, the individual expects too much of him- or herself, others, and life in general. Such irrational beliefs and unrealistic standards inevitably lead to disappointment and, ultimately, to depression.

Hopelessness Theory

Hopelessness theory followed the discovery of learned helplessness and the consequent development of the learned helplessness theory of depression by Martin Seligman (Seligman, 1975); Seligman observed that animals who were unable to control negative stimuli often developed behavior that looked like depression. Learned helplessness theory generated substantial research, some of which highlighted the shortcomings of the theory. As a result of these shortcomings, the theory was reformulated in 1978 by Abramson, Seligman, and Teasdale as a theory that focused on individuals' attributions about the causes of events. In particular, making specific, unstable, external attributions for positive events while making global, stable, and internal attributions for negative events was proposed to lead to depression.

Abramson, Metalsky, and Alloy (1989) presented a more recent iteration attributional theory, which they referred to as the hopelessness theory of depression. In so doing, they also proposed that this represents a subtype of depressive disorders, in particular, a subtype of depression that is characterized by hopelessness. Along with a negative attributional style, hopelessness depression is caused by the *expectation* that desired outcomes will not occur or that aversive outcomes will occur, and that no response the person can make will change the likelihood of these outcomes. Such expectations lead to hopelessness and in turn to depression.

Theories Focusing on Cognitive Structures and Propositions

In contrast to theories that emphasize some aspect of thinking, theories focusing on cognitive structures place emphasis on depressogenic cognitive structures, and the content that is represented within these structures. These theories incorporate other cognitive elements such as thoughts or cognitive processes, but the central organizing principle of these approaches is the structure embodied in the idea of a schema.

Dysfunctional Cognitive Schemas

The most widely known and cognitive theory of depression in this category is that which was proposed by Beck (1967, 1987). Beck's theory contended that dysfunctional cognitions are an important cause of depression. More specifically, the theory proposes that there are three "layers" of cognitions that are involved in precipitating depression. In one layer, negative thoughts (labeled as automatic thoughts) occur in depressed individuals throughout the day. Underlying the automatic thoughts at a deeper layer are irrational beliefs and cognitive errors ("If I do not get an *A* on a test, I am a failure"). These in turn are a function of the deepest layer, the depressogenic schema. Beck suggests that such dysfunctional thinking is triggered by

stress to which the individual has been previously sensitized. For instance, if during important developmental periods a child was sensitized to rejection, a rejection experience in adulthood will trigger the dysfunctional thoughts and underlying beliefs (e.g., rejection equates to worthlessness) that eventuate in depression.

Beck's theory contends that these depressogenic schemas are latent until they are activated by certain stresses and, when activated, provide access to a complex system of negative themes that lead to a pattern of negative self-referent information processing that precipitates depression (Segal & Shaw, 1986). Hence, the theory predicts that these structures are accessible only under certain conditions of stress. A recent review by Scher, Ingram, and Segal (2005) of studies assessing this idea suggest a good deal of support for this contention.

Sociotropic and Autonomous Cognitive Structural Subtypes

Beck (1987) refined his theory to include two types of individuals prone to depression because they have specific concepts represented within schemas. The first is more interpersonally focused and is referred to as *sociotropy*; individuals with this style predominantly value positive interchange with others, and focus on guidance from others, acceptance, and support. The second type is more achievement oriented and is called *autonomy*; these types of individuals tend to overvalue achievement, independence, and mobility. Stressors that are consistent with these themes are proposed to activate dysfunctional structures that bring about depression. For example, the person with the sociotropic style would be vulnerable to depression as a result of problematic interpersonal relations, while the autonomous person would be vulnerable as a result of perceived failures at work.

These ideas are similar to those proposed by Blatt's (1974) developmentally rooted model of depression in which he referred to two types of depression: anaclitic depression and introjective depression. Anaclitic depression is characterized by fears of abandonment and feelings of weakness, helplessness, and being unloved. Introjective depression is developmentally more advanced and is characterized by excessive demands for perfection, a tendency to assume blame and responsibility, and feelings of helplessness to achieve approval, recognition, and acceptance.

Cognitive Network Theories

Although quite similar to conceptualizations that feature cognitive schemas, cognitive network theories focus on somewhat different assumptions and accentuate information processing as the key factor for depression.

According to an early model proposed by Ingram (1984), the initial experience of depression results from the activation of affective structures that are associated with the experience of sadness (i.e., sadness nodes of the type proposed by Bower, 1981). Once activated, cognitions are proposed to recycle through cognitive networks that have previously been linked to sadness and depression. This not only initiates the depressive episode but, once fully activated, perpetuates depression until the affective and/or cognitive activity level eventually decays. Vulnerability is seen in this model as the availability of relatively well developed cognitive networks that are associated with sadness affective structures. When activated by any variety of events, sadness provides access to extensive and elaborate processing of depressive information, which generates the spiraling from the normative sadness experienced by non-vulnerable people into the more significant and debilitating depression experienced by those who are vulnerable. As these cognitive networks become larger and better articulated, the universe of events that can trigger depression becomes larger.

Interacting Cognitive Subsystems

John Teasdale and colleagues (Teasdale & Barnard, 1993) have proposed perhaps the most comprehensive information processing model of depression. Called the interacting cognitive subsystems (ICS) framework, it attempts to account for virtually all aspects of information processing in depression. According to this theory, various aspects of experience are represented by different patterns of mental codes. At a relatively superficial level, for example, experiences are coded in visual, auditory, and proprioceptive inputs. At deeper levels, sensory codes are represented by intermediate codes. At even deeper levels, mental codes are related to meaning that in turn reflects meaning that is linked to emotions. According to the ICS framework, emotional reactions are produced when patterns of low-level meanings and patterns produce emotion-related schematic models; the production of a depressed state occurs when depressogenic schematic models are synthesized, and depressed mood is maintained when these models are continually produced. When the production of such models stops, then depression lifts.

Theories Focusing on Cognitive Processes

Ruminative Response Styles

One cognitive theory has focused explicitly on factors maintaining rather than precipitating depressive mood. Nolen-Hoeksema (1987) argues that persons who maintain depressive mood states differ in their responses to depressive mood from persons who are able to cope effectively with depressive mood states. She has termed this approach the responses style theory of depression. In particular, she proposes that those who ruminate about depressive symptoms and the causes of those symptoms are more likely to maintain depression than are individuals who try to distract themselves. Thus, the ruminative response is seen as a factor that maintains the length and intensity of depression. An interesting aspect of this theory is its application to gender differences in depression. That is, Nolen-Hoeksema has proposed that women are more likely than men to ruminate, thus accounting for the well-established fact that women are twice as likely as men to be diagnosed with depression.

Self-Regulation

Pyszczynski and Greenberg (1987) also offered a theory highlighting cognitive processes in depression, specifically a self-regulatory perseveration model. They proposed that disruptions in important life domains (e.g., the dissolution of a relationship) lead to enhanced attention toward the self. While such an attentional process may be quite short-lived for those not vulnerable to depression, for those who are vulnerable this process is not easily escaped. As a result, depressed individuals are proposed in this theory to perseverate in a heightened state of self-focused attention. The exception to this is when positive events occur, at which point the depressed individual avoids a focus on the self and is thus unable to take full advantage of the mood lifting effects of positive life events.

Conclusions

One way to organize the numerous cognitive theories is to cluster them according to constructs suggested by a metaconstruct framework. According to the framework, models suggested by a number of theorists fall into the structural or propositional category. The most well known of these models is Beck's schema theory. Other models tend to emphasize the cognitive processes that operate in depression, while cognitive product models focus more on the cognitions that depressed people experience as important determinants of depression.

Despite the different emphases in these models, there are a variety of issues that occur across virtually all models. For instance, all extant cognitive models are essentially models of the self in dysfunction. The principle of the self remains an important construct, yet cognitive models need to include additional elements (see Gotlib & Hammen, 1992, for an early attempt to integrate cognitive and interpersonal theories) to fully maintain their viability and central place among psychological theories of depression.

Distortion or inaccurate information processing is also a construct that is central to cognitive models of depression. To the extent that individuals are prone to distorting information in a negative fashion, they are more likely to experience the onset of depression. Moreover, continued distortion of information also helps to maintain the depressed state.

Finally, the issue of causality is also an important consideration for cognitive models; cognitive models are inherently causal models. Studies evaluating the causal proposals of cognitive theories have been infrequent, but the data that have been reported tend to support these ideas. In an intriguing set of studies, for example, Segal and colleagues (Segal, Gemar, & Williams, 1999; Segal, Kennedy & Gemar, 2006) showed that the level endorsement of dysfunctional attitudes among treated depressed individuals predicted those who would relapse later. Hence, the fact that dysfunctional attitudes predict who will become depressed is very much in line with the causal predictions of cognitive theories. More data are needed to fully investigate the accuracy of theories in this regard, but the data that have been reported thus far are quite encouraging.

RICK E. INGRAM

See also

Aaron Beck
Anaclitic and Introjective Depression
Attributional Theories of Depression
Automatic Thoughts
Cognitive Distortion
Diathesis-Stress Models of
Depression
Hopelessness

References

Abramson, L. Y., Metalsky, G. I., & Alloy, L. B. (1989). Hopelessness depression: A theory-based subtype of depression. *Psychological Review, 96,* 358–372.

Abramson, L. Y., Seligman, M. E. P., & Teasdale, J. (1978). Learned helplessness in humans: Critique and reformulation. *Journal of Abnormal Psychology, 87,* 49–74.

Beck, A. T. (1967). *Depression: Causes and treatment.* Philadelphia: University of Pennsylvania Press.

Beck, A. T. (1987). Cognitive models of depression. *Journal of Cognitive Psychotherapy, 1,* 5–37.

Blatt, S. J. (1974). Level of object representation in anaclitic and introjective depression. *Psychoanalytic Study of the Child, 29,* 107–157.

Bower, G. H. (1981). Mood and memory. *American Psychologist, 36,* 129–148.

Ellis, A. (1996). *Better, deeper, and more enduring brief therapy: The rational emotive behavior therapy approach.* New York: Brunner/Mazel Publishers.

Garratt, G., Ingram, R. E., Rand, K. L., & Sawalani, G. (2007). Cognitive processes in cognitive therapy: Evaluation of the mechanisms of change in the treatment of depression. *Clinical Psychology: Science and Practice, 14,* 224–239.

Gotlib, I. H., & Hammen, C. L. (1992). *Psychological aspects of depression: Toward a cognitive-interpersonal integration.* Chichester, England: Wiley.

Ingram, R. E. (1984). Toward an information processing analysis of depression. *Cognitive Therapy and Research, 8,* 443–477.

Ingram, R. E. (1990). Self-focused attention in clinical disorders: Review and a conceptual model. *Psychological Bulletin, 107,* 156–176.

Kendall, P. C. (1985). Behavioral assessment and methodology. In C. M. Franks, G. T. Wilson, P. C. Kendall, & K. D. Brownell (Eds.), *Annual review of behavior therapy: Theory and practice, Vol. 10* (pp. 47–86). New York: Guilford Press.

Lewinsohn, P. (1985). A behavioral approach to depression. In J. C. Coyne (Ed.), *Essential papers in depression* (pp. 150–172). New York: New York University Press.

Nolen-Hoeksema, S. (1987). Sex differences in unipolar depression: Evidence and theory. *Psychological Bulletin, 101,* 259–282.

Pyszczynski, T., & Greenberg, J. (1987). Self-regulatory perseveration and the depressive self-focusing style: A self-awareness theory of reactive depression. *Psychological Bulletin, 102,* 1–17.

Scher, C. D., Ingram, R. E., & Segal, Z. V. (2005). Cognitive reactivity and vulnerability: Empirical evaluation of construct activation and cognitive diathesis in unipolar depression. *Clinical Psychology Review, 25,* 487–510.

Segal, Z. V., Gemar, M., & Williams, S. (1999). Differential cognitive response to a mood challenge following successful cognitive therapy or pharmacotherapy for unipolar depression. *Journal of Abnormal Psychology, 108,* 3–10.

Segal, Z. V., Kennedy, S., Gemar, M., Hood, K., Pederson, R., & Buis, T. (2006). Cognitive reactivity to sad mood provocation and the prediction of depressive relapse. *Archives of General Psychiatry, 63,* 749–755.

Segal, Z. V., & Shaw, B. F. (1986). Cognition in depression: A reappraisal of Coyne and Gotlib's critique. *Cognitive Therapy and Research, 10,* 671–694.

Seligman, M. E. P. (1975). *Helplessness: On depression, development, and death.* San Francisco: Freeman.

Teasdale, J. D., & Barnard, P. J. (1993). *Affect, cognition, and change.* Hillsdale, NJ: Erlbaum.

Cognitive Vulnerability

A cornerstone of cognitive theories of depression is the idea that cognitive variables play an important causal role in depression (see Ingram, Miranda, & Segal, 1998). These causal statements are easily translated into propositions about cognitive vulnerability. That is, to the extent that currently nondepressed individuals possess the capacity for sufficiently negative cognition, they are vulnerable to depression.

Another important point about these theories as they pertain to vulnerability is their diathesis-stress nature; cognitive variables (the diatheses) are proposed to be reactive to stressful life events; these events trigger the return of these negative cognitions that otherwise lay dormant. Hence, even though people who are not vulnerable will react with sadness and likely some negative cognition to a negative event, vulnerable individuals react with cognitions that are more negative and extensive. These negative cognitions intensify the effects of stress and begin what some theorists have described as a downward spiral into depression for the vulnerable person.

The themes embodied in these cognitions are ones of self-derogation; the individual views him or herself as unworthy and unlovable and accepts blame for negative events whether warranted or not. This last point illustrates the idea that the negative cognition that is bought to the surface is likely to be distorted in a dysfunctional way. Hence, individuals misinterpret information as more negative than warranted and are prone to a negative cognitive triad where the self, future, and world are seen in unrealistically negative terms.

In general, these negative cognitions pertain to beliefs about the self as unworthy and to blame for negative events. Within this general framework a fairly wide variety of negative cognitive variables have been examined as indicators of cognitive vulnerability. Each of the two major cognitive theories of depression focus on somewhat different vulnerability cognitions. The hopelessness theory (Abramson, Metalsky, & Alloy, 1989) focuses on attributional patterns that take responsibility for negative events and eschew responsibility for positive events. Hence, to the extent that individuals are prone to attribute negative events to the self, and positive events to external forces, they are thought to be vulnerable in the face of negative events.

The other major theory, Beck's (1967) theory, relies on the cognitive schema as the central organizing principle underlying cognitive vulnerability. Vulnerable individuals are believed to possess negative self-schemas that are activated in response to stress. Once activated, the schemas distort information in a negative way, give rise to negative automatic thoughts relevant to the self, and trigger dysfunctional beliefs about the self. Such dysfunctional thinking is sufficient to lead to a depressive disorder.

In sum, cognitive theories of depression also embody ideas about vulnerability that is cognitive in nature. These theories rely on diathesis-stress ideas wherein the cognitive vulnerability serves as the diathesis that is bought "on-line" in response to stress. Vulnerable people thus respond to negative events in a different way than nonvulnerable people, bringing negative cognitive patterns to bear on the assessment of the events and the assessment of the self. In some sense the distinction between cognitively vulnerable and nonvulnerable people is nicely illustrated by Freud's distinction between mourning and melancholia. In Freud's view, mourning is the normal sad state that accompanies a loss, whereas melancholia is viewed as a depressive disorder that is precipitated by loss. According to Freud, in mourning, the individual's self-statement about loss is, "This is terrible," whereas the statement of the melancholic individual is "I am terrible." Contemporary cognitive theorists do not have much in common with Freud, but in this instance they would view this as an accurate view of cognitive vulnerability.

RICK E. INGRAM

See also

Attributional Theories of Depression
Cognitive Behavioral Therapy

Cognitive Reactivity
Cognitive Theories of Depression
Diatheses-Stress Models of Depression
Hopelessness
Mindfulness-Based Cognitive Therapy
Schemas

References

Abramson, L., Metalsky, G., & Alloy, L. (1989). Hopelessness depression: A theory-based subtype of depression. *Psychological Review, 2,* 358–372.
Beck, A. T. (1967). *Depression.* New York: Harper and Row.
Ingram, R. E., Miranda, J., & Segal, Z. V. (1998). *Cognitive vulnerability to depression.* New York: Guilford Press.

Cognitive Vulnerability: Genetic Associations

Major depressive disorder is a common, recurrent, and impairing condition that predicts future suicide attempts, academic failure, interpersonal problems, and unemployment, among other negative outcomes. Cognitive theories (e.g., Beck, Rush, Shaw, & Emery, 1979) assert that negatively biased memory, attention, and interpretation of environmental stimuli play a critical role in the development of depression. Vulnerable individuals are expected to selectively attend to negative information, filter out positive information, and interpret neutral information as being more negative or less positive than is actually the case. Recall is also expected to be biased in a similar fashion. Further, these biases are expected to be especially pronounced among vulnerable individuals in the context of life stress. Indeed, cognitive vulnerabilities are more consistently observed in the presence rather than the absence of negative mood states (Scher, Ingram, & Segal, 2005).

Genes and Cognitive Vulnerability to Depression

Heritability studies estimate that depression has sizable genetic and environmental components. As a result, an effort is underway to identify specific genes that contribute to depression vulnerability. Research has primarily focused on genes that influence the serotonin system, as serotonin is a neurotransmitter that influences the generation, experience, and regulation of emotional states.

Serotonin Transporter

The 5-HTTLPR gene regulates the reuptake of serotonin from the synaptic cleft. There are two variants of the serotonin transporter: a short allele and a long allele (although recent findings suggest there are two versions of the long allele). The presence of one or two short alleles, rather than two copies of the long allele, is associated with significant decreases (approximately 50%) in serotonin reuptake, which presumably leads to less-efficient regulation of serotonin. The notion that 5-HTTLPR function is at least partly under genetic control is particularly interesting, as the 5-HTTLPR molecule is commonly found in brain regions critical for regulating emotional states.

Recently, Caspi and colleagues published a landmark study indicating that 5-HTTLPR genotype was associated with depression risk, but only in the context of life stress (Caspi et al., 2003). Specifically, among individuals who had experienced four or more stressful life events, people with two short 5-HTTLPR alleles had approximately twice the risk of experiencing a major depressive episode than people with two copies of the long 5-HTTLPR allele. In contrast, allele status was not significantly related to depression risk among people who experienced two or fewer stressful life events. Over the last few years, several studies have now replicated the finding that 5-HTTLPR genotype combines with life stress to predict depression onset.

This evidence suggests that 5-HTTLPR genotype does contribute to the development of depression, but less is known about *how* the 5-HTTLPR genotype imparts this risk. Considering the broad range of emotional, cognitive, and behavioral factors included in a diagnosis of depression, it is unlikely that a

single gene would impact all aspects of such a complex syndrome. Therefore, examining genetic associations with intervening factors (i.e., intermediate phenotypes) may help elucidate how genes contribute to a syndrome as complex as depression. This approach has been particularly promising for studying associations between the 5-HTTLPR and neural markers of depression vulnerability using brain imaging techniques (Hariri et al., 2002). Interestingly, brain imaging research suggests that the 5-HTTLPR gene is associated with greater reactivity and poorer connectivity within brain regions critical to the regulation of emotional states. Given these findings, research is now investigating whether the 5-HTTLPR gene is also associated with cognitive vulnerability to depression.

Although numerous studies indicate that the short 5-HTTLPR allele is associated with neuroticism, a personality trait (or temperament) associated with anxiety and depression, few studies have directly examined links between cognitive vulnerability and the 5-HTTLPR gene. Beevers and colleagues investigated the effects of 5-HTTLPR genotype on biased attention for emotional information within a psychiatric inpatient population (Beevers, Gibb, McGeary, & Miller, 2007). They found that short-allele carriers displayed a stronger attentional bias for anxious word stimuli than individuals with two copies of the long allele. This effect was observed even when stimuli were presented outside of conscious awareness. They also found no effect for 5-HTTLPR genotype on biased attention for dysphoric word stimuli. A limitation of this study is that the sample was a heterogeneous group of psychiatric inpatients. Additional research with individuals carefully screened for current and past psychiatric history is needed to more clearly identify the role of the 5-HTTLPR gene in the etiology of this particular cognitive vulnerability. Nevertheless, this study suggests that 5-HTTLPR genotype may influence how an individual attends to emotional stimuli.

Hayden and colleagues reported an association between 5-HTTLPR genotype and cognitive vulnerability to depression among seven-year-old children after a negative mood induction (Hayden et al., 2008). Children with two short alleles were more likely to describe themselves with negative adjectives and remember those adjectives than children with two long 5-HTTLPR alleles. This indicates that, after a negative mood induction, children with two copies of the short 5-HTTLPR allele were more likely to display cognitive vulnerability to depression than children with two copies of the long allele. Both the Hayden and colleagues and Beevers and colleagues studies involved small samples, so replication is clearly warranted before firm conclusions can be determined. Nevertheless, although sparse, this burgeoning literature suggests that the 5-HTTLPR genotype may have an important role in the etiology of cognitive vulnerability to depression.

Other Promising Genes

These studies represent the first investigations of a link between 5-HTTLPR genotype and cognitive vulnerability to depression. The results so far are intriguing but far from conclusive. Future research should continue to investigate associations between cognitive vulnerability and the 5-HTTLPR genotype. However, other genes likely influence cognitive vulnerability to depression. For instance, variants of the catechol-O-methyltransferase and tryptophan hydroxylase-2 genes have both been associated with abnormal neural responses during the regulation of emotional information. Further, the brain-derived neurotrophic factor genotype has been associated with rumination, a cognitive factor strongly associated with depression (Hilt, Sander, Nolen-Hoeksema, & Simen, 2007). These genes appear to be promising candidates for cognitive vulnerability studies. Ultimately, it is unlikely that a cognitive vulnerability will develop due to variability in a single gene. Investigating the unique and combined impact of several genes (perhaps in the context of stressful life environments) may ultimately be critical for developing a more comprehensive understanding of the genetic etiology of cognitive vulnerability to depression.

Conclusions

Given the level of impairment and human suffering associated with an episode of depression, it is imperative that we develop comprehensive etiological models for this disabling condition. Understanding the cognitive and genetic contributions to depression is an excellent place to start. However, there is much more work to be done. Additional research that integrates other etiological factors into this work, such as the role of the social environment, neural processes (e.g., brain function, structure, and connectivity), and emotion regulation, will be important for developing a comprehensive understanding of the disorder. Through a better understanding of how these factors work in concert to produce an episode of depression, it may be possible to design better diagnostic tests, implement novel treatments that more precisely target underlying pathophysiology, and potentially prevent initial onset through early intervention. The integration of cognitive and genetic models of vulnerability to depression represents a small but important step toward this ultimate goal.

CHRISTOPHER G. BEEVERS AND TONY T. WELLS

See also

Cognitive Vulnerability
Risk
Serotonin
Vulnerability

References

Beck, A. T., Rush, A. J., Shaw, B. F., & Emery, G. (1979). *Cognitive therapy of depression.* New York: Guilford press.

Beevers, C. G., Gibb, B. E., McGeary, J. E., & Miller, I. W. (2007). Serotonin transporter genetic variation and biased attention for emotional word stimuli among psychiatric inpatients. *Journal of Abnormal Psychology, 116,* 208–212.

Caspi, A., Sugden, K., Moffitt, T. E., Taylor, A., Craig, I. W., Harrington, H., et al. (2003). Influence of life stress on depression: Moderation by a polymorphism in the 5-HTT gene. *Science, 301,* 386–389.

Hariri, A. R., Mattay, V. S., Tessitore, A., Kolachana, B., Fera, F., Goldman, D., et al. (2002). Serotonin transporter genetic variation and the response of the human amygdala. *Science, 297,* 400–403.

Hayden, E. P., Dougherty, L. R., Maloney, B., Olino, T. M., Sheikh, H., Durbin, C. E., et al. (2008). Early-emerging cognitive vulnerability to depression and the serotonin transporter promoter region polymorphism. *Journal of Affective Disorders, 107,* 227–230.

Hilt, L. M., Sander, L. C., Nolen-Hoeksema, S., & Simen, A. A. (2007). The BDNF Val66Met polymorphism predicts rumination and depression differently in young adolescent girls and their mothers. *Neuroscience Letters, 429,* 12–16.

Scher, C. D., Ingram, R. E., & Segal, Z. V. (2005). Cognitive reactivity and vulnerability: Empirical evaluation of construct activation and cognitive diatheses in unipolar depression. *Clinical Psychology Review, 25,* 487–510.

Combined Psychological and Psychopharmacological Treatment

Major depressive disorder is a common and debilitating psychiatric illness that more often than not presents with a chronic, recurring course. Over two-thirds of patients presenting for treatment in the recently completed National Institute of Mental Health–funded STAR*D trial had chronic or recurrent major depression. In fact, 50% to 60% of patients who suffer a first-time major depressive episode will develop a second episode, and those with two or more prior episodes can almost be assured of having further episodes (American Psychiatric Association, 2000). Incomplete response to treatment is a common problem that can lead to the return of depressive symptoms (i.e., relapse). For this reason, full remission (i.e., absence) of depressive symptoms is the goal of acute-phase treatment.

The most common treatments for major depressive disorder fall among psychological (psychotherapy) and psychopharmacological (antidepressant medications) modalities. Among psychological modalities, cognitive, cognitive behavioral, and interpersonal therapies are all somewhat effective for acute treatment of major depressive disorder. Recent pharmacological developments have provided more options than at any other time in history for choosing an appropriate pharmaceutical treatment for major depressive

disorder. Despite these facts, based on recent real-world effectiveness trials in routine outpatient psychiatric and primary care clinics, remission rates following up to 14 weeks of a single standard antidepressant medication (citalopram) are modest, at 28% (Trivedi et al., 2006). As such, recent expert opinion advocates the use of combination treatments earlier in the course of treatment for patients with major depressive disorder (Fava & Rush, 2006). Many various psychopharmacological medication strategies are available; however, it is the combination of psychotherapy with pharmacotherapy that is the focus of this entry.

Depression is an illness that has been described in multiple phases: the acute phase, in which the goal is for the patient to achieve some level of remission of symptoms (full or partial) in the current major depressive episode; the continuation phase, in which the goal represents preventing a relapse of symptoms in the current major depressive episode; and the maintenance phase, in which the goal is to prevent a recurrence of major depressive disorder (i.e., prevent another major depressive episode from occurring). Combination treatment with psychotherapy and antidepressant medications has been described in each of these three phases, with varying results.

Combination Psychotherapy Plus Pharmacotherapy in the Acute Phase

The recommendations for psychotherapy used alone or in combination with antidepressant medications for the treatment of major depressive disorder are based on current evidence including cognitive, cognitive behavioral, and interpersonal therapies. Depending on the availability of well-trained therapists, each of these modalities may be used alone or in combination with antidepressant medications. Furthermore, treatment with psychotherapy alone or in combination should be guided by the patient's preference for treatment modality.

Cognitive therapy (CT) and cognitive behavioral therapy (CBT) for depression are treatments based on cognitive paradigms that focus on assisting patients with problems as they relate within their current depressive episode, rather than focusing on events from the past. In the acute treatment phase, combination therapy, consisting of medication and CBT, has been found to be superior to either medication or CBT used alone for patients with more severe, recurrent, or chronic forms of depression (Keller et al., 2000; Thase et al., 1997). In addition, cognitive therapy and CBT are recommended treatments for patients who do not respond to antidepressant medications or have difficulty tolerating them (Depression Guideline Panel, 1993; Schatzberg et al., 2005). In fact, next-step treatment with cognitive therapy (added on to the antidepressant citalopram) has been shown to posit the same probability of remission as does adding common pharmacological augmentation agents (i.e., bupropion or buspirone) (Thase et al., 2007). One limitation of augmenting an antidepressant with cognitive therapy may be that the time to achieve remission is generally longer (about 20 days) with cognitive therapy versus pharmacological treatments (Thase et al., 2007). Additionally, though the process by which CBT is effective in depression is not well understood, several studies have shown that CBT reduces residual symptoms in depression and can ultimately reduce the risk for relapse. In general the superiority of combination therapy (consisting of medication and CT or CBT) in the acute phase of major depressive disorder versus either used alone should be considered for patients with more severe, recurrent, or chronic forms of depression.

Interpersonal therapy (IPT), similar to CT and CBT, focuses on the depressed patient's current frame of mind, but as that relates to his or her interactions with other people. IPT has also shown efficacy for use in the acute phase of treatment for patients suffering from major depressive disorder, either alone or in combination with antidepressant medications. In fact, a seminal study performed by DiMascio and colleagues in 1979 showed that the combination of antidepressant medication (amitriptyline) and IPT was superior to either treatment alone. Furthermore, recent studies in depressed psychiatric inpatients have relayed benefits of IPT when added to standard antidepressant medications (Schramm et al., 2008). Additional benefits reported for combination treatment include benefits in health utilization and cost domains over monotherapies for major depressive disorder.

Combination Psychotherapy Plus Pharmacotherapy in the Continuation and Maintenance Phases

The continuation and maintenance phases are the next stages, respectively, in treating major depressive disorder. In order for patients to be classified in either of these phases they must have achieved remission of their depressive symptoms. Increasing evidence supports the efficacy of evidence-based psychotherapies in the continuation phase of treatment, both for reduction in the risk of relapse, as well as for the treatment of residual symptoms (Hollon et al., 2005; Jarrett et al., 2001). Additional studies have shown that CBT which sequentially follows a successful course of pharmacotherapy reduces rates of relapse of major depressive disorder. For instance, Fava, Rafanelli, Grandi, and Canestrari (2004) completed a 6-year follow-up assessment of 40 patients who had been successfully treated with antidepressants and divided into two groups, those who received CBT, and those who received standard clinical management (CM; Fava et al., 2004). All subjects were slowly tapered off their antidepressant medications. The effects of CBT on residual symptoms were evident at the 4-year follow-up, reducing the total number of recurrent depressive episodes, and CBT was shown to decrease the relapse rate of major depressive disorder. In addition, Fava and colleagues (2004) found that both CBT and a shorter version of CBT, well-being therapy, were associated with significant reductions in residual symptoms (Fava et al., 2004). Similar to hypertension or diabetes, major depression is a chronic illness with a relapsing-recurring course. With this in mind subjects with a history of recurrent depression who are in the continuation and maintenance phases of treatment for major depressive disorder require close monitoring and treatment. Sequential treatment with CBT (following pharmacotherapy) is an established treatment to reduce the number of residual depressive symptoms and prevent depressive episode recurrences in this population.

Conclusions and Summary

The disabling and recurring nature of depressive episodes necessitates that major depressive disorder be viewed as a chronic illness. In fact, the majority of patients suffering their first major depressive episode will have another in their lifetime. In this light, treatment for major depressive disorder focuses on extinguishing the acute symptoms of a given depressive episode, followed by a shift in focus to preventing a recurrence of depressive symptoms over time. The two most common treatments for major depressive disorder are pharmacological treatments (i.e., antidepressant medications) and psychological treatments (i.e., psychotherapies). Newer generations of antidepressant medications have conferred not only therapeutic benefits, but safety benefits as well. Meanwhile, two main schools of psychotherapy have proven effective for treatment in major depressive disorder: cognitive or cognitive behavioral psychotherapy and interpersonal psychotherapy.

There is substantial evidence that both pharmacotherapy and psychotherapy are effective treatments for patients suffering from major depressive disorder when used separately. The evidence for their use as combination treatments for patients suffering from major depressive disorder is relevant in both acute and long-term settings. Acutely, combination treatment appears effective for those suffering from chronic or recurrent forms of depression, whereas in long-term settings sequential treatment with psychotherapy following pharmacotherapy has proven efficacy in reducing the risk for recurrent major depressive episodes. Further research should focus to better delineate how treatments relieve depressive symptomatology. Ideally, this will allow for the identification of depressive treatment phenotypes and guide treatment among those that are likely responders to monotherapy with antidepressant medications, psychotherapies, or combination treatments.

MADHUKAR H. TRIVEDI AND BENJI T. KURIAN

See also

Childhood Depression: Treatment With Pharmacotherapy
Cognitive Behavioral Therapy
Dopamine
Dopaminergic Systems
Serotonin

References

American Psychiatric Association. (2000). *Diagnostic and statistical manual of mental disorders* (4th ed., text revision). Washington, DC: Author.

Depression Guideline Panel. (1993). *Depression in primary care, Vol. 2: Treatment of major depression.* Publication No. 93-0551. Rockville, MD: Agency for Health Care Policy and Research.

DiMascio, A., Weissman, M. M., Prusoff, B. A., Neu, C., Zwilling, M., & Klerman, G. L. (1979). Differential symptom reduction by drugs and psychotherapy in acute depression. *Archives of General Psychiatry, 36,* 1450–1456.

Fava, G. A., Ruini, C., Rafanelli, C., Finos, L., Conti, S., & Grandi, S. (2004). Six-year outcome of cognitive behavior therapy for prevention of recurrent depression. *American Journal of Psychiatry, 161,* 1872–1876.

Fava, M., & Rush, A. J. (2006). Current status of augmentation and combination treatments for major depressive disorder: A literature review and a proposal for a novel approach to improve practice. *Psychotherapy Psychosomatics, 75,* 139–153.

Hollon, S. D., DeRubeis, R. J., Shelton, R. C., Amsterdam, J. D., Salomon, R. M., O'Reardon, J. P., et al. (2005). Prevention of relapse following cognitive therapy vs. medications in moderate to severe depression. *Archives of General Psychiatry, 62,* 417–422.

Jarrett, R. B., Kraft, D., Doyle, J., Foster, B. M., Eaves, G. G., & Silver, P. C. (2001). Preventing recurrent depression using cognitive therapy with and without a continuation phase: A randomized clinical trial. *Archives of General Psychiatry, 58,* 381–388.

Keller, M. B., McCullough, J. P., Klein, D. N., Arnow, B., Dunner, D. L., Gelenberg, A. J., et al. (2000). A comparison of nefazodone, the cognitive behavioral-analysis system of psychotherapy, and their combination for the treatment of chronic depression. *New England Journal of Medicine, 342,* 1462–1470.

Schatzberg, A. F., Rush, A. J., Arnow, B. A., Banks, P. L., Blalock, J. A., Borian, F. E., et al. (2005). Chronic depression: Medication (nefazodone) or psychotherapy (CBASP) is effective when the other is not. *Archives of General Psychiatry, 62,* 513–520.

Schramm, E., Schneider, D., Zobel, I., van Calker, D., Dykierek, P., Kech, S., et al. (2008). Efficacy of interpersonal psychotherapy plus pharmacotherapy in chronically depressed inpatients. *Journal of Affective Disorders, 109,* 65–73.

Thase, M. E., Friedman, E. S., Biggs, M. M., Wisniewski, S. R., Trivedi, M. H., Luther, J. F., et al. (2007). Cognitive therapy versus medication in augmentation and switch strategies as second-step treatments: A STAR*D report. *American Journal of Psychiatry, 164,* 739–752.

Thase, M. E., Greenhouse, J. B., Frank, E., Reynolds, C. F., III, Pilkonis, P. A., Hurley, K., et al. (1997). Treatment of major depression with psychotherapy or psychotherapy-pharmacotherapy combinations. *Archives of General Psychiatry, 54,* 1009–1015.

Trivedi, M. H., Rush, A. J., Wisniewski, S. R., Nierenberg, A. A., Warden, D., Ritz, L., et al. (2006). Evaluation of outcomes with citalopram for depression using measurement-based care in STAR*D: Implications for clinical practice. *American Journal of Psychiatry, 163,* 28–40.

Comorbidity

Comorbidity refers to the co-occurrence of two or more disorders. In the present context this then refers to the presence of depression and another mental disorder. The various conditions with which depression is frequently or sometimes comorbid are discussed in various sections of this encyclopedia. What follows is a brief overview of comorbidity involving depression and conditions with which depression is comorbid. It is important to note, therefore, that what follows is merely an illustration of the idea of depression and comorbidity.

Anxiety

Anxiety is one of the most common states that is comorbid with depression. Some of this co-occurrence may be accounted for by overlapping diagnostic criteria. For instance, sleep disturbances, difficulty concentrating, and fatigue appear in the diagnostic criteria for both depression and generalized anxiety disorder. However, even when diagnostic overlap is taken into account, there is still substantial comorbidity between depressive and anxious states. The category of anxiety disorders contains a number of different disorders such as phobias and posttraumatic stress disorder, all of which have moderate to high rates of comorbidity with depression.

Other Psychiatric Disorders

Schizophrenia is frequently associated with depression; people diagnosed with schizophrenia have also 30 times greater odds of being depressed than do people without schizophrenia (Boyd et al., 1984). Likewise, many patients with eating disorders also have a diagnosis of depression, and if not a diagnosis, then a greater number of symptoms of depression than those without eating disorders.

Medical Disorders

Depression is associated with numerous medical disorders, particularly conditions that are chronic. For example, some research has suggested that approximately 1 in 5 diabetic patients have concurrent depression, and even higher rates of depression have been found among hospitalized medical patients, with between 22% and 33% reporting depression (for a review, see Katon & Sullivan, 1990). Research has also shown a high degree of comorbidity between depression and both osteoarthritis and rheumatoid arthritis (Smith, Wallston, & Dwyer, 1995).

Comorbidity between depression and medical illness is not limited to the chronic conditions; depression is also a common diagnosis in acute and severe medical problems. For example, some research has found that 20% to 30% of oncology patients report depression. Likewise, some research has found roughly 20% of patients report major depression following myocardial infarction. Clearly, both chronic and acute medical illnesses are linked with depression.

In examining comorbidity in depression and medical disorders, it is important to point out the problem of symptom overlap. For instance, if a cancer patient complains of loss of appetite, is this a symptom of the malignancy or depression? Other symptoms of depression that can overlap with medical symptoms include appetite or weight disturbance, psychomotor agitation or retardation, insomnia or hypersomnia, decreased libido, and fatigue. This overlap points to the need for the careful assessment of depression symptoms in medical conditions to ensure that they are symptoms of depression and not the medical illness.

Personality Disorders

There is a very high rate of comorbidity between personality disorders and depression. In an early study, for example, Shea, Glass, Pilkonis, Watkins, and Docherty (1987) reported that 75% of a sample of 249 persons with major depression had a probable or definite diagnosis of personality disorder. Pilkonis and Frank (1988) found that 48% of a sample of recurrent unipolar depressed patients who had responded to treatment had concurrent probable or definite personality disorders. Rates of co-occurrence are even higher for inpatients. Clearly, the presence of a personality disorder complicates depression.

RICK E. INGRAM

See also

Anger
Anxiety
Chronic Pain
Eating Disorders
Heart Disease
Parkinson's Disease
Posttraumatic Stress Disorder
Smoking
Thyroid Function

References

Boyd, J. H., Burke, J. D., Gruenberg, E., Holzer, C. E., III, Rae, D. S., George, L. K., et al. (1984). Exclusion criteria of DSM-III: A study of co-occurrence of hierarchy-free syndromes. *Archives of General Psychiatry, 41,* 983–959.

Katon, W., & Sullivan, M. D. (1990). Depression and chronic medical illness. *Journal of Clinical Psychiatry, 51,* 3–11.

Pilkonis, P., & Frank, E. (1988). Personality pathology in recurrent depression: Nature, prevalence, and relationship to treatment response. *American Journal of Psychiatry, 145,* 435–441.

Shea, T., Glass, D., Pilkonis, P., Warkins, J., & Docherty, J. (1987). Frequency and implications of personality disorders in a sample of depressed outpatients. *Journal of Personality Disorders, 1,* 27–42.

Smith, T. W., Wallston, K. A., & Dwyer, K. A. (1995). On babies and bathwater: Disease impact and negative affectivity in the self-reports of persons with rheumatoid arthritis. *Health Psychology, 14,* 64, 73.

Computer Simulation of Depression and Depressive Phenomena

Computational models use logical or mathematical rules to understand depressive phenomena through computer simulations. They provide novel insights and testable predictions about affective disorders by integrating our understanding of cognitive, affective, and biological aspects of depression. The use of computational models, particularly in conjunction with empirical testing, provides a number of unique benefits including the ability to rigorously generate predictions, test predictions in a model in ways that would be unethical to do in people (e.g., purposefully harm the sample or predispose it to catastrophic ends), integrate otherwise disparate theories via simulation of potentially interacting features, and test causal associations.

This review discusses models of individual symptoms commonly associated with depression. There are no published computational models of the full range of symptoms of unipolar depression. In addition, since there are relatively few models that address even conjunctions of symptoms found in affective disorders (most relevant models address specific cognitive or affective symptoms), focusing on individual symptoms allows this entry to survey the broadest cross-section of relevant literature. Attending to the nature and implications of individual symptoms can help inform our understanding of depression as a syndrome. Moreover, examining how models of differing etiologies lead to the expression of individual symptoms could inform our understanding of individual differences in the expression of depression.

Impaired Attention and Memory

Phenomenon

A common symptom of depression involves an inability to concentrate. Depressed individuals have increased reaction times on cognitive tasks as well as impaired performance on memory tasks (for a review see MacLeod & Mathews, 1991).

Models

A number of computational models address mechanisms that could be associated with impaired attention and memory. Random destruction of synapses in a neural network model has been associated with impaired recognition performance (Carrie, 1993) as well as decreased discrimination among category exemplars (Virasoro, 1988), which would affect both coding ability and reaction times on cognitive discrimination tasks. While such a mechanism would not be expected to resolve as depression resolves, random synapse destruction is formally equivalent in such models to any phenomenon that decreases the signal-to-noise ratio in the model. Such manipulations have been identified with decreased dopamine availability (Cohen, Servan-Schreiber, & McClelland, 1992). These results are consistent with both lesion and neurotransmitter disruption explanations for cognitive deficits in depression. Similarly, Wang and Ross (1990) suggest that change in a neuronal firing threshold can be used to tune connectivity in an attractor network, which they associate with variation in recognition performance as well as a tendency toward distraction (i.e., non-task-relevant association).

Aston-Jones, Raikowski, and Cohen (1999) provide a specific model of the role of the locus coeruleus (LC) in discrimination tasks. They show, through simulation, that the LC is likely to have tonic and phasic modes of activity; tonic activity is more associated with processing information from a variety of stimuli. Thus, more time in the phasic mode could lead to decreased performance on attentional tasks. Aston-Jones and colleagues further cite evidence that chronically decreased LC function could be associated with other affective symptomatology, suggesting links between attentional function and other hallmarks of depression such as flattened affect.

Some models of memory impairment simulate mechanisms that are intended to be specific to other pathologies such as Alzheimer's disease. For example Hasselmo (1994) shows that a process of "runaway synaptic modification" resulting in exponential growth in synaptic connectivity can lead to memory interference. Hasselmo demonstrates a likely differentiation of mechanisms in depression and Alzheimer's disease in a simulation of the orderly progression of expected deterioration in this mechanism; this progression is different from the more state-dependent disturbance in memory associated with depression.

Increased Early Attention to Negative Information

Phenomenon

In contrast to the findings of generalized attention and memory deficits, there is some evidence that depressed individuals pay *more* attention to negative information than never-depressed individuals. There is some support for the role of early attentional biases such as increased perception of negative words, and greater interference from negative content (see section *Attention*), though such biases appear to be more strongly associated with anxiety. Depressed individuals also display increased amygdalar responses to masked faces, suggesting a preconscious attentive bias (see section, *The Amygdala*).

Models

Models of increased early attentional processing of negative information implicate very different mechanisms. For example, Matthews and Harley (1996) extend a neural network model of the Stroop effect (delays in recognizing the color in which a word is printed, when the word is the name of another color) to account for emotional Stroop interference (delays in recognizing the color in which negative or threatening words are printed) by including structures in the model representing a task, which can be either color naming or attending to emotional information. The latter task is not an explicit goal but is presumed to represent a constant implicit task for individuals with affective disorders. They show that by increasing the activity in these structures, they can simulate biased attention toward emotional information, and thus cognitive interference effects. This manipulation presumably corresponds to increased activity in brain areas associated with threat detection, such as the amygdala, suggesting that individuals who display early attentional biases may have a hyperactive amygdala.

Similarly, Siegle (1999) has simulated simultaneous activation of brain areas that recognize affective and semantic aspects of information (potentially a hippocampal-amygdala loop). Increased exposure to negative information strengthens connections to the affective feature units, leading to greater cognitive interference (i.e., affective feature unit activity, which competes for activity with task-relevant semantic-feature units). This type of model is again consistent with the notion of increased amygdala activity (and consequent inhibition of prefrontal cortex), though it results from a different etiology than that proposed by Matthews and Harley. Simulations suggest this mechanism is less strongly associated with early attentional biases than sustained processing biases of negative information and is therefore discussed more in the next section.

Another general mechanism of decreased cognitive inhibitory mechanisms has also been explored in the context of anxiety.

Phaf, Christoffels, Waldorp, and den Dulk (1998) cite literature suggesting that attentional biases result from decreased inhibition of unattended material. They use a connectionist model of a nonemotional Stroop task (requiring naming the color in which words are printed; the words are the names of other colors) in which there is mutual inhibition between output units representing the color to be named. Through this formalism, they note that such decreased inhibition should affect both nonemotional as well as emotional task performance. Counterintuitively, Phaf and colleagues also demonstrate that increasing inhibition between the output units allowed greater interference from a nonattended stimulus, leading to increased simulated reaction times. Phaf and colleagues thus suggest that disorders of biased attention such as anxiety (and presumably, depression) should be associated with increased, rather than decreased, inhibition from non-task-relevant representations. This conclusion is consistent with the previously presented models in which interference effects are generated by strong activation from a representation of non-task-relevant information. This simulation is particularly important because it forces theorists who argue for decreased inhibition to move away from a notion of overall decreases to be more specific (e.g., decreased inhibition of just emotional aspects of information). This conclusion could argue for specifically decreased connectivity from brain regions associated with inhibiting emotional processing (e.g., from prefrontal cortex to the amygdala) rather than for a disturbance in a diffuse phenomenon (e.g., monoamine availability) associated with overall gain.

Elaborative Processing of Negative Information

Phenomenon

Despite the weak evidence for early attentional biases in depression, stronger evidence suggests that depressed individuals process negative information for *longer* than never-depressed individuals, in an elaborative or interpretive way (for a review see MacLeod & Mathews, 1991). Such elaborative processing of negative information has been proposed as an explanatory mechanism for both cognitive products of depression such as biased memory for negative information, interpretation of any situation or information as negative, and dysfunctional attitudes, and for affective aspects of depression such as prolonged sadness and feelings of worthlessness, and hopelessness and rumination on negative information (see sections *Cognitive Bias, Memory* and *Rumination*).

Models

Explanations for sustained and elaborative processing of negative information largely emerged from computational semantic network models popular in the 1970s in which spreading activation between nodes in a network leads to cognitive association. Semantic networks were theoretically augmented with the notion that emotions can be viewed as nodes in a semantic network. Ingram (1984) suggested that in depression, sad emotion nodes become especially active, leading to excessive spreading activation from them, yielding negative elaboration. The activity of sad emotion nodes are maintained by connections that feed back to them. This formulation has been used to explain not only negative elaboration but the onset and maintenance of depression, treatment response, and its potential recurrence.

Aspects of this type of model have been implemented as a computational neural network (Siegle, 1999) in which feedback between cognitive and affective representations of information is operationalized as feedback between brain structures responsible for processing cognitive and affective features of information (e.g., the amygdala and hippocampus). This model simulates high-level interactions between brain processes associated with affective and episodic determinations (e.g., as performed by the amygdala and hippocampus) and regulatory executive areas (e.g., as performed by the prefrontal cortex). Three potential mechanisms for depression were simulated with this model, including exposure to negative information, which increases weights from the affective feature units to the output units, increased feedback between affective and semantic representations, and decreased inhibition from the output units to affective feature units, which simulates decreased prefrontal cortex inhibition of the amygdala. Through simulation, depressed individuals are predicted to display increased processing of negative information if they experience increased exposure to negative information, which strengthens connections to specific negative representations in the amygdala, leading to excessive feedback with connected structures. Simulations further supported the idea that sustained processing of negative information could be augmented by decreased activity in structures that inhibit the amygdala, such as prefrontal cortex, though this mechanism is not sufficient to produce sustained processing of negative information (rather, it is associated with disregulation of all emotional processing regardless of valence in the model). This model has been shown to capture aspects of sustained processing of emotional information in depression such as sustained physiological reactivity as well as amygdala activity to negative information (e.g., Siegle, Steinhauer, Thase, Stenger, & Carter, 2002).

A number of arguments regarding the validity of models (e.g., whether they could account for thinking about an emotion but not feeling the emotion) have also emerged. In response, theoretical models have been proposed based on computational principles, but not implemented as computer programs. These reformulations provided novel predictive capabilities, often capitalizing on biological congruity associated with neural networks.

A different environmentally mediated approach to explaining elaborative processing of negative information allows simulation of many cognitive aspects of depression, including brooding rumination, decreased motivation, depressive realism, decreased self-esteem, low self-efficacy, and negative attributional style (Webster, Glass, & Banks, 1988). Webster's system attempts to adapt to change in a simulated environment and sometimes fails. Failure, in the simulation, results in punishment from the environment. The system adjusts in response to punishment by learning that its method for dealing with the environment is ineffective, resulting in a host of generalizations. For example, its reactions to the environment are predicated on knowledge of how to act; without confidence in how to act the system takes fewer actions, which Webster relates to low motivation. Similarly, it estimates its chances of subsequent success as low after learning from the punishment experience leading to low "self-esteem." The system is goal oriented and, thus, attempts to find new ways to interact with its environment, which leads to sustained and repetitive elaboration of the mechanism for its failure and consideration of its implications for future action, which Webster likens to rumination. Webster observes that such sustained processing, while temporarily causing an apparent increase in cognitive aspects of depression, could lead to increased performance on cognitive tasks (e.g., when adaptive adjustments are made in response to recognition of failures). Thus a continuum of potentially adaptive and maladaptive aspects of depression is highlighted. A further refinement of this model segments planning and adjustment to a simulated "left hemisphere" function and the monitoring of potential failure to a simulated "right hemisphere" and demonstrates the same behavioral outcomes in this division.

Park (1998) uses a similar approach to simulate environmental induction of depressive overgeneralization of negative responses. A network is initially trained to discriminate punishing and rewarding stimuli. Previously rewarding stimuli are then paired with punishment, and the network displays a generalized bias to name all stimuli as punishing or negative, which Park likens to a depressive state.

Dayan and Huys (2008) model a different aspect of "later" processing of emotional information involving decision-making biases following negative affective thoughts by showing that if serotonin serves to prune decision trees associated with possible decisions, the presence of negative thoughts in the presence of decreased serotonin availability could lead to biased decision making.

Impairments in Implicit and Explicit Learning

Phenomena

Learning is often divided into two types: explicit or declarative learning (i.e., learning with awareness, as when someone is asked to remember items, facts, or events) and implicit learning (learning without awareness, as in learning of skills, procedures, or emotional responses). Imaging and lesion studies suggest that explicit learning is highly dependent on the medial temporal lobe, whereas the implicit learning systems depend instead on the neocortex, the amygdala for emotional learning, and the striatum for sequence learning.

Distinctions between implicit and explicit learning are particularly relevant to models of depression. Because these systems are differentially affected by depression and primary cognitive impairment, they provide an opportunity to investigate the relationship between cognition and depression. For instance, in Alzheimer's disease, the most prevalent primary cognitive disorder, the medial temporal lobe memory system is prominently affected, whereas implicit learning is relatively preserved. In depression, however, implicit and explicit learning results are more mixed. Similarly, impairments in depression are more mixed than those found in subcortical disorders such as Parkinson's disease and Huntington's disorder (preserved explicit learning, impaired implicit learning), despite similarities in other symptoms such as psychomotor slowing. The disparate results may be secondary to subject selection and/or the specific learning task used. Similarly mixed results have been found with explicit learning performance in depression. A number of studies have found decreased performance on explicit tasks, such as the Wisconsin Card Sorting Task. However, it is not clear whether the explicit learning component is impaired on these tasks or if the impairment is driven by the attentional changes. That explicit recognition is generally preserved in depression suggests the impairment is more specific for attention than learning.

Models

Several computational models of implicit and explicit learning have been proposed. These models have in common representations of the input and output that are shared by both the implicit and explicit components of the model, with separate representations for the implicit and explicit learning components. In several of the models the model features responsible for the implicit learning aspect of the task are related to the basal ganglia, and those responsible for modeling explicit learning are related to the prefrontal cortex and the medial temporal lobe.

A particular aspect of sequence learning models (Berns & Sejnowski, 1998; Cleeremans & McClelland, 1991) is their sensitivity to the temporal relationship of the input stimuli. Models have been specifically developed for this purpose, capitalizing on the ability of models to use output of the network at one time to inform its input at the next time (recurrent neural networks). On each learning trial, the model is presented with an input pattern that is paired with the desired target output. For instance, in a standard serial reaction time task, which requires learning a 10-item repeating sequence, the input to the network is the previous stimulus and the output is the model's prediction of the current stimulus. In one simulation of mechanisms by which sequence learning could be impaired, Berns and Sejnowski (1998) model low levels of dopamine (simulating of aspects of Parkinson's disease) by decreasing the learning rate parameter of the model, which decreases performance on the task.

Ashby's model of implicit and explicit category learning has also been used to model aspects of performance by depressed subjects on learning tasks. In particular, Ashby models depression as a preferential attentional impairment on category learning, which leads to greater impairment on the explicit component rather than the implicit component of the task. As mentioned by Ashby there is a limitation in the assumption of preserved subcortical function in depression. Nevertheless, the model does capture some aspects of performance by depressed subjects on the category learning task. Of particular note, to model impairment in depression, Ashby and colleagues increase a model parameter representing a neurotransmitter that results in increased perseverative errors on categorization tasks.

Learned Helplessness

Phenomenon

When an animal is unable to avoid negative reinforcement, it exhibits a number of behaviors reminiscent of depression, including no longer trying to avoid punishment ("giving up"), acting frustrated, and increased arousal. Learned helplessness has been suggested as a potential mechanism for depression in humans. Of particular note for models described below, it has been shown that individuals low in a marker of norepinepherine feel as if their life is controlled by outside influences, a hallmark of learned helplessness (see section *Learned Helplessness*).

Models

Leven (1998) presents a series of successively more complex computational models of learned helplessness. Based on an earlier theoretical model he shows that different aspects of learned helplessness, including motoric aspects (e.g., perseveration), vegetative aspects (e.g., withdrawal), and more cognitive symptoms (e.g., anticipation of failure), can be manipulated independently in a model with different but interacting components for motoric, hypothalamic-pituitary-adrenal axis, and cortical functioning. This work spurred Leven to find empirical evidence for such independence between subconstructs. Subsequent revisions to the model specifically showed potential roles for norepinepherine disruptions in helplessness, and potential interactions between these systems. Leven thus began to account for the roles of interactions between prefrontal cortex, hippocampus, and the amygdala in expressions of learned helplessness.

Davis (2000) also simulated aspects of learned helplessness, as a way of testing predictions in a computational instantiation of Tomkins's (1963) affect theory framework. This extraordinarily broad and sophisticated undertaking allows Davis to represent a host of features relevant to cognition and affect, and to model interactions between them. Davis's system is capable of generating a host of simulated continuously valued affective responses to stimuli, including surprise/startle, fear/terror, interest/excitement, anger/rage, distress/anguish, and enjoyment/joy. Each affective response is generated in response to a pattern of neural firing. In the simulation of learned helplessness, distress is signaled based on a moderately dense but sustained level of stimulation, in this case, of a representation of efficacy—lower levels of perceived efficacy lead to higher and more sustained firing. To test his implementation, Davis simulates a traditional triadic design in which some simulated participants have control over the extent to which they receive punishment and other simulated participants with different reward-punishment contingencies are yoked to the first group's reaction (i.e., they have no control). As predicted by Tomkins's theory, the simulated subjects with little control experience decreased evaluation of their efficacy and a consequent increase in negative affect states. Modeled interactions between affective states and cognitive reactivity lead to other hallmarks of learned helplessness, such as decreased motivation and finally passivity. Davis's simulations also allow predictions regarding individual differences in vulnerability to learned helplessness, for example, individuals with decreased

neural activity in response to estimates of efficacy (i.e., who place less importance on efficacy) are predicted to be less susceptible to this substrate of depression.

Decreased Activity and Arousal

Phenomenon

A primary symptom of depression involves not taking pleasure in activities that generally cause pleasure (see section *Anhedonia*). More generally, depressed individuals are frequently unmotivated and have decreased levels of activity. Psychotherapy for depression often involves behavioral activation (see section *Behavioral Activation*), which involves helping depressed individuals to increase their levels of goal-directed behavior.

Models

Grossberg has created some of the most enduring computational models of motivated behavior, which have at their foundation the *gated dipole*, a circuit that produces sustained or transient responses to phasic and tonic arousing inputs. Grossberg (1999) shows that this circuit functions optimally at moderate levels of inputs associated with arousal; too high or too low levels of arousal lead the circuit to stop firing, leading to decreased behavior, states that Grossberg names underaroused depression and overaroused depression. Grossberg speculates on brain processes that could lead to such under- and overaroused depressive syndromes and implicates multiple possible brain processes including disruption in both amygdalar and prefrontal circuitry.

Aston-Jones and colleagues' (1999) model of locus coeruleus function also provides a continuous parameter that could represent switches between over- and underaroused states. Specifically, their model provides for a tonic state, which is associated with increased lability, and a phasic state, which is associated with more stable attention.

Normal functioning involves spending time in each state. The authors make the point that increased tonic-state activity could lead to instability in judgments, and potentially impulsivity. Decreased tonic-state activity could lead to unresponsiveness, which the authors associate with flattened affect.

Computational models of bipolar disorder have also included possible mechanisms for decreased arousal, in the course of implementing a mechanism that allows switching between depressed (underaroused) and manic (overaroused) states. In particular, Jobe, Vimal Kovilparambil, Port, and Gaviria (1994) use a computational model to suggest that acetocholine gating neurons in the forebrain are normally in a state in which a given threshold of activity is needed to make them fire. They show that small changes in a parameter of their model associated with dendritic conductance could make the neurons associated with acetecholine release fire too easily (associated with mania) or not easily enough (associated with depression).

Recovery

Phenomena

Many mechanisms have been associated with recovery from depression, including spontaneous remission and remission in treatment with antidepressants and psychotherapy. While particular treatments are often associated with recovery in approximately 60% of participants in controlled trials, little is known about which individuals are likely to recover in which treatments.

Models

A number of the previously discussed models implicitly allow inferences about recovery. For example, many of those models simulate aspects of depression by change in continuous parameters, which are often likened to the action of diffuse neurotransmitters. Trivially, returning these parameters to their premorbid values returns the network's functioning to its premorbid state. Though this type of change could be likened to an tidepressant effects, spontaneous variation, or downstream effects of psychotherapy, simulation of mechanisms by which these parameters could change is necessary for the models to be of practical utility. A few models have addressed these mechanisms.

Webster's models, described previously, operationalize depression as an adaptive reaction to prolonged or repetitive failure. Webster notes that when the models have learned enough from a failure experience to succeed in situations in which they had previously failed, the model ceases to display many of the simulated aspects of depression. This type of recovery could be likened to spontaneous remission of depression in response to positive life events, which are central to some theories of recovery from depression.

Siegle's models, described previously, incorporate three mechanisms for depression. One mechanism involves overtraining the network on negative information, which induces a biased and sustained processing of negative information. Siegle et al. have demonstrated that retraining the network on nonnegative stimuli is associated with decreases in information processing biases. This retraining may be likened to the recognition of positive information encouraged in cognitive therapy. The other two mechanisms involve changes in parameters governing feedback in the network, loosely corresponding to disruption in frontal inhibition of the amygdala system and amygdalar-hippocampal interaction. Retraining the network on positive information was possible only when these two continuous parameters were not very disrupted. That is, retraining involved successfully associating a stimulus with an adaptive nonnegative association. When feedback between areas responsible for affective and semantic association (i.e., hippocampal-amygdala interactions) was too strong, incoming positive stimuli would be associated with something negative before new nonnegative associations were learned. Similarly, since each of the simulated mechanisms was associated with different aspects of information processing biases, simply returning the parameters associated with frontal inhibition of the amygdala and amygdala-hippocampal feedback to their premorbid values is not expected to entirely ameliorate depressive information processing biases. These simulations may shed some light on the observed increase in efficacy of combined cognitive therapy and medication over either individual treatment.

Park (1998) also simulates recovery from depression as relearning to associate stimuli with activity in model outputs representing *reward* in a model (feed-forward neural network) that had been previously biased to make associations of both punishing and rewarding stimuli with only outputs representing only punishment. Parks further simulates processes associated with serotonin neurotransmission as affecting the baseline firing rate of feed-forward and feedback inhibitory interneurons in a pathway from the dorsal to median raphe nuclei by biasing the network's sigmoid activation function. Parks simulates the effects of tricyclic antidepressants as decreased activity in the feed-forward and feedback inhibition between these structures. Selective serotonin reuptake inhibitors are simulated as decreased feed-forward inhibition and increased feedback inhibition. Parks shows that both of these manipulations effectively decrease the time it takes the network to relearn positive or rewarding associations, specifically by reducing interference from previous associations.

One computational model has been used to predict aspects of recovery from depression under both cognitive therapy and antidepressant treatment (Luciano, 1996). The nominal goal of this work is to predict which patients will recover in which therapies. This model does not address mechanisms of recovery but, rather, performs statistical prediction using the neural network to compute a nonlinear regression. Yet, since Luciano uses a neural network platform for this work, she has proposed incorporating mechanisms as modules in the model and has begun to implement initial models of neurotransmitter pathways as well as functional connectivity from regions such as the locus coeruleus for inclusion in this type of model (Luciano, Cohen, & Samson, 1994). Such integrations promise to allow interaction between mechanistic accounts of depression and statistical prediction of recovery.

Conclusions

Different computational models have examined many central features of the phenomenology and biology of depression. Cognitive and affective aspects of the disorder are accounted for. Yet, accounting for the full phenomenon of depression is, at this point, difficult largely because a full model of a functioning human has not been created. Without such a substrate of normal functioning to begin with, modeling disturbances in this substrate is difficult and potentially impossible. Thus, a central challenge for models in the future will be understanding the extent to which symptoms and features of depression are related, and the extent to which these relationships are captured or predicted by models.

Note: Much of the text in this article has appeared in Siegle (2001), and also will appear in Siegel & Aizenstein (in press).

GREG SIEGLE AND HOWARD AIZENSTEIN

See also

Attention
Brain Circuitry
Memory Processes
Recurrence
Relapse Rumination

References

Aston-Jones, G., Raikowski, J., & Cohen, J. (1999). Role of locus coeruleus in attention and behavioral flexibility. *Biological Psychiatry, 46,* 1309–1320.

Berns, G. S., & Sejnowski, T. J. (1998). A computational model of how the basal ganglia produce sequences. *Journal of Cognitive Neuroscience, 10,* 108–121.

Cleeremans, A., & McClelland, J. L. (1991). Learning the structure of event sequences. *Journal of Experimental Psychology General, 120,* 235–253.

Cohen, J. D., Servan-Schreiber, D., & McClelland, J. (1992). A parallel distributed processing approach to automaticity. *American Journal of Psychology, 105,* 239–269.

Davis, M. (2000). *A computational model of affect theory: Simulations of reducer augmenter and learned helplessness phenomena.* Unpublished doctoral dissertation, Department of Psychology, University of Michigan.

Dayan, P., & Huys, Q. J. (2008). Serotonin, inhibition, and negative mood. *PLoS Computational Biology, 4,* e4.

Grossberg, S. (1999). Neural models of normal and abnormal behavior: What do schizophrenia, Parkinsonism, attention deficit disorder, and depression have in common? In J. A. Reggia, E. Ruppin, & G. L. Glanzman (Eds.), *Disorders of brain behavior and cognition the neurocomputational perspective* (pp. 375–406). New York: Elsevier.

Hasselmo, M. E. (1994). Runaway synaptic modification in models of cortex: Implications for Alzheimers disease. *Neural Networks, 7,* 13–40.

Ingram, R. E. (1984). Toward an information processing analysis of depression. *Cognitive Therapy and Research, 8,* 443–478.

Jobe, T., Vimal Kovilparambil, A., Port, J., & Gaviria, M. (1994). A theory of cooperativity modulation in neural networks as an important parameter of CNS catecholamine function and induction of psychopathology. *Neurological Research, 16,* 330–341.

Leven, S. (1998). A computational perspective on learned helplessness and depression. In R. W. Parks, D. S. Levine, & D. L. Long (Eds.), *Fundamentals of neural network modeling neuropsychology and cognitive neuroscience* (pp. 141–163). Cambridge, MA: MIT Press.

Luciano, J. S. (1996). *Neural network modeling of unipolar depression: Patterns of recovery and prediction of outcome.* Unpublished doctoral dissertation, University of Boston.

Luciano, S., Cohen, M. A., & Samson, J. A. (1994). *A neural model of unipolar depression.* Paper presented at the Irish Neural Network Conference, Ireland.

MacLeod, C., & Mathews, A. M. (1991). Cognitive experimental approaches to the emotional disorders. In P. R. Martin (Ed.), *Handbook of behavior therapy and psychological science: An integrative approach, Vol. 16* (pp. 116–150). MA: Allyn & Bacon.

Matthews, G., & Harley, T. A. (1996). Connectionist models of emotional distress and attentional bias. *Cognition and Emotion, 10,* 561–600.

Park, S. B. (1998). Neural networks and psychopharmacology. In D. Stein & J. Ludick (Eds.), *Neural networks and psychopathology* (pp. 34–56). Cambridge, UK: Cambridge University Press.

Phaf, R. H., Christoffels, I. K., Waldorp, L. J., & den Dulk, P. (1998). Connectionist investigations of individual differences in Stroop performance. *Perceptual and Motor Skills, 87,* 899–914.

Siegle, G. J. (1999). A neural network model of attention biases in depression. *Progress in Brain Research, 121,* 415–441.

Siegle, G. J. (2001). Connectionist models of psychopathology: Crossroads of the cognitive and affective neuroscience of disorder. *Cognitive Processing, 2,* 455–486.

Siegle, G. J., & Aizenstein, H. (in press). Computational approaches to understanding the neurobiology of major depression: Integration through simulation. In D. M. Barch (Ed.), *Cognitive and affective neuroscience of psychopathology.* Oxford, England: Oxford University Press.

Siegle, G. J., Steinhauer, S. R., Thase, M. E., Stenger, V. A., & Carter, C. S. (2002). Can't shake that feeling: fMRI assessment of sustained amygdala activity in response to emotional information in depressed individuals. *Biological Psychiatry, 51,* 693–707.

Tomkins, S. S. (1963). *Affect imagery and consciousness, Vol. 2: The negative affects.* New York: Springer.

Wang, L., & Ross, J. (1990). Interactions of neural networks models for distraction and concentration. *Proceedings of the National Academy of Sciences, 87,* 7110–7114.

Webster, C., Glass, R., & Banks, G. A. (1988). *Computational model of reactive depression.* Hillsdale, NJ: Lawrence Erlbaum.

Continuity of Depression Across Development

The notions of connectedness and continuity were inspired by Western history and philosophy and are deeply rooted in scientific inquiry. The underlying assumption of continuity in developmental science has generated research that has contributed broadly to knowledge of both adaptive and maladaptive functioning throughout the life span. Likewise, examinations of continuity of depression, an especially salient case of maladaptation, have been fruitful in elucidating its etiology and natural course. Although the very existence of depression during childhood was once denied, it is now widely recognized that depression that begins early in life significantly impacts later functioning and psychopathology. In addition, it is now known that adult depression is often rooted in childhood syndromes.

Continuity of depression has been defined in many ways in the psychological, psychiatric, and epidemiological literatures. Most commonly, continuity of depression refers to recurrence, persistence, or stability of depression over time or across development. More recently, there is growing recognition that continuity is not synonymous with behavioral stability. Rather, a fundamental premise in the study of developmental psychopathology is the notion that "continuity lies not in isomorphic behaviors over time but in lawful relations to later behavior, however complex the link" (Sroufe & Rutter, 1984, p. 21). This perspective is consistent with evidence of multiple pathways to depression as a function of individual differences in experience and vulnerability and acknowledges that emergent capacities in cognition, language, affect, and behavior contribute to differences in the expression of depression across development. A comprehensive approach to understanding continuity, therefore, includes examinations of both homotypic continuity (i.e., stability in the same or similar behavioral responses over time) and heterotypic continuity (i.e., stability of an underlying construct that is manifested differentially across development) (Avenevoli & Steinberg, 2001).

Whereas many previous studies of continuity were based on retrospective reports of adult samples, a number of well-designed, long-term longitudinal studies of clinical and community samples of youths now provide prospective estimates of continuity of depression across childhood and adolescence and into adulthood. Studies that begin early in childhood (i.e., during the toddler and preschool years) are currently underway but have yet to yield data that inform this issue.

Homotypic Continuity

Available evidence supports the homotypic continuity of depression from childhood to adulthood. Prospective studies show that youths who have experienced major depressive episodes are at high risk of recurrence within a few years, with a cumulative probability of approximately 40% to 70%. Studies assessing depression as a dimensional construct also report moderate stability and considerable predictive power of depressed mood and other symptoms over time. Major depression and dysthymia during childhood are associated with depression during adolescence, even after accounting for co-occurring anxiety and behavioral problems. Likewise, depression and subthreshold depressive symptoms that begin during adolescence are associated with adult depressive disorders. Depressed adolescents are at 2 to 7 times increased odds of recurrence in adulthood compared to adolescents without depression (Rutter, Kim-Cohen, & Maughan, 2006). While both child and adolescent depression are linked to adult depression, depression that has its onset prior to puberty may be less continuous with adult depression than depression that begins in adolescence. Although some evidence suggests that child-onset and adolescent-onset depression are heterogeneous conditions with qualitatively different profiles of risk and course, more research on this issue is needed.

Examinations of the childhood history of adults with depression also inform questions about the homotypic continuity of depression. Follow-back analyses using prospective studies report that young adults with depression are more likely than those without depression to have had depression in adolescence. They are also more likely to report a history of depression than any other disorder. Associations between adult depression and childhood history of depression (as measured in follow-back studies) are generally smaller than those between child depression and adult depression (as measured prospectively), suggesting heterogeneity in the pathways (either discontinuity or heterotypic continuity) to depression during different developmental periods.

Heterotypic Continuity

Available research also supports the existence of heterotypic continuity in depression across development. The many changes that take place during the transition from childhood to adulthood appear to influence, at least to some degree, the experience and expression of internal states across developmental periods. For example, there is limited evidence to suggest small age differences in the symptom expression of depression (e.g., somatic complaints decrease with age, hypersomnia increases during adolescence). Additionally, a growing literature highlights the significance of syndromes (e.g., minor depression) that fall below diagnostic thresholds for identifying adolescents in need of intervention and at risk for later depressive disorder. Thus, while most agree that the essential features of depression are similar among adults and older children and adolescents, insufficient attention to developmental differences in symptom expression may lead to the underestimation of continuity and limit our understanding of the etiology of depression and the identification of clinically meaningful cases.

In addition to defining heterotypy as differential manifestations of currently defined depressive symptoms, heterotypic continuity may also be defined by alternative forms of internalized distress. Clinical, high-risk family and community studies converge in suggesting that anxiety is an age-dependent expression of depression. Depression and anxiety are the most common concurrent mental health conditions among youths. More significantly, among those with both conditions, the onset of anxiety typically precedes that of depression. This sequential association is linked to development, with anxiety emerging in early to middle childhood and depression more commonly surfacing during adolescence.

Mechanisms of Continuity

Although a diverse literature documents genetic, biological, cognitive, psychosocial, and contextual correlates of depression, much less is known about factors that contribute to the continuity of depression across development. Studies assessing the influence of stressful life events on the stability of depression have yielded mixed results but generally suggest that adverse events contribute more significantly to the onset of depression than to its recurrence. Some evidence supporting the stress generation hypothesis, however, suggests that depressed individuals generate stressful events that likely trigger successive experiences of depression. Individual biological factors, such as genetic predisposition, dysregulation of the hypothalamic-pituitary-adrenal axis, and hormonal changes associated with puberty may contribute to both the stability and heterotypic continuity of depression (i.e., the association between anxiety and depression), though evidence is limited. Cognitive biases associated with depression are moderately stable over time but have not been clearly linked to the stability

of depression from childhood and/or adolescence to adulthood.

In sum, depression exhibits both moderate behavioral stability and heterotypic continuity across time and development. Further research is needed to better elucidate the mechanisms that contribute to this continuity and to describe the circumstances under which depression is stable, heterotypically continuous, or discontinuous.

SHELLI AVENEVOLI AND LAURENCE STEINBERG

See also

Adolescent Depression
Age of Onset of Depression
Childhood Depression

References

Avenevoli, S., & Steinberg, L. (2001). The continuity of depression across the adolescent transition. In H. Reese & R. Kail (Eds.), *Advances in Child Development and Behavior, 28*, 139–173.
Rutter, M., Kim-Cohen, J., & Maughan, B. (2006). Continuities and discontinuities in psychopathology between childhood and adult life. *Journal of Child Psychology and Psychiatry, 47*, 276–295.
Sroufe, A., & Rutter, M. (1984). The domain of developmental psychopathology. *Child Development, 55*, 17–29.

Cortisol

Dysregulation of the hypothalamic-pituitary-adrenal (HPA) axis, one of the bodies' major stress-sensitive physiological systems, is frequently implicated in the etiology of major depressive disorder. A primary product of the HPA axis in humans is the steroid hormone cortisol. Levels of cortisol can be quickly and noninvasively measured in small samples of human saliva; as a result, a large body of research relating HPA-axis activity to major depressive disorder has focused on this hormone. Robust cross-sectional associations have been found between the presence of major depressive disorder and aspects of cortisol activity, including elevated basal cortisol levels and impaired negative feedback control of cortisol (Ehlert, Gaab, & Heinrichs, 2001).

Basal (nonstress) cortisol levels exhibit a regular diurnal pattern, being high in the morning at awakening, then increasing, on average, 50% to 60% in the first 30 to 40 minutes after waking (called the cortisol awakening response, CAR). Cortisol levels then drop off rapidly over the next few hours and decline more gradually over the rest of the day, reaching a low point or nadir around midnight. Cortisol levels also increase acutely at any point in the day in response to either real or anticipated psychological threat. The cascade of physiological events in the HPA axis resulting in cortisol elevations includes the release of corticotropin releasing hormone (CRH) from the hypothalamus, which stimulates the pituitary gland to release adrenocorticotropin (ACTH) into general circulation. ACTH in turn stimulates the release of cortisol from the adrenal cortex. Most cortisol (95%) is immediately bound to corticosteroid binding globulin (CBG) and albumin, making it biologically inactive, while the rest remains active to affect a wide variety of processes in the body and brain. Negative feedback of cortisol to glucocorticoid receptors in hippocampus, hypothalamus, and pituitary help to contain HPA-axis activation, with high circulating levels of cortisol reducing further release of CRH, ACTH, and cortisol (Kirschbaum & Helhammer, 2000).

Stress-related increases in cortisol have a number of short-term effects on the body. A major role of cortisol in the stress response is to increase the energy resources available to cope with a threat by way of increased glucose production. Cortisol also helps to temporarily suppress the activity of systems that are typically useful only in the absence of threat, such as digestion, growth, and sexual behavior. It also serves to coordinate and contain immune and inflammatory responses. Cortisol and the central CRH component of the HPA response also influence mood and attentional and cognitive processes. While HPA-axis activation increases alertness, vigilance to, and memory for, fear- and threat-relevant stimuli, it inhibits

and impairs more complex and non-threat-relevant cognitive and memory processes. It is notable that the systems influenced by HPA activity overlap considerably with systems involved in the symptoms of major depressive disorder: alertness, vigilance, appetite, and mood as well as cognitive, metabolic, sexual, and memory processes (Gold & Chrousos, 2002).

About 20% to 40% of depressed outpatient adults and 60% to 80% of depressed inpatient adults show evidence of cortisol hypersecretion (higher basal levels of cortisol) compared to nondepressed adults (Thase, Jindal, & Howland, 2002). Depressed adults are also more likely than nondepressed adults to fail to reduce production of cortisol the morning after taking an oral dose of a synthetic hormone, dexamethasone (Ehlert et al., 2001). Associations between cortisol and depression are far less consistent in children and adolescents than in adults (Kaufman, Martin, King, & Charney, 2001). The most robust cross-sectional correlate of depression in adolescents is elevated cortisol levels in the evening hours, shortly before sleep onset, as compared to a more general basal hypercortisolism observed in adult depression. This pattern is found more consistently for inpatient populations and for suicidal adolescents than for depressed outpatient populations (Dahl et al., 1991). Impaired negative feedback control of the HPA axis, as measured by failure to suppress morning cortisol levels in response to dexamethasone, is also less consistently found in adolescents and adults but is again more common in inpatient populations (Birmaher & Heydl, 2001). It is not known why findings are less consistent in children and adolescents, but it seems likely that developmental factors such as pubertal development or the ongoing development of neurobiological processes related to mood, cognition, and HPA-axis regulation could play a role. Alternatively, a longer history of exposure to stress or degree of exposure to prior episodes of major depressive disorder in adults could alter the ways in which major depressive disorder and cortisol are related.

Surprisingly few studies have measured individual differences in cortisol prior to the onset of major depressive disorder, in order to establish that cortisol differences are risk factors, rather than just correlates or consequences of the disorder. The few studies that have taken a prospective longitudinal approach have converged upon similar findings. Although elevated cortisol levels across the full day and especially in the evening hours are the most frequent cross-sectional correlates of major depressive disorder, it is elevated *morning* cortisol that is most often found to be prospectively predictive of depression (Halligan, Herbert, Goodyer, & Murray, 2007). It has not yet been clarified whether it is size of the cortisol awakening response, or elevated morning cortisol levels more generally that are involved in increased risk for major depressive disorder.

What are the origins of individual differences in cortisol levels observed both in the presence of, and prior to the onset of major depressive disorder? There are clearly genetic contributions to individual differences in HPA-axis activity. Twin studies show strong genetic contributions to cortisol, particularly cortisol levels in the morning hours. In addition, several genetic polymorphisms (particularly those related to the functioning of the glucocorticoid receptor [GR] gene) have been identified that are related both to increased HPA-axis reactivity and to greater risk for major depressive disorder (Wüst et al., 2004).

On the other hand, extensive evidence exists, in both animal and human models, for alteration of HPA-axis activity and cortisol levels by experience, with social experiences playing a particularly prominent role (Adam, Klimes-Dougan, & Gunnar, 2007). Researchers have suggested that experiences during prenatal development and the first few years of life may be most important in setting up cortisol patterns that place individuals at risk for major depressive disorder (Halligan et al., 2007). It has also been suggested that a pathway from early life stress to depressive disorder by way of altered HPA-axis activity may be relevant to only a subset of individuals with major depressive disorder (Heim, Plotsky, & Nemeroff, 2004), which could help to account for why altered cortisol patterns are not evident in all major depressive disorder cases.

Other researchers suggest that several subtypes of HPA-axis dysregulation are evident, corresponding with subtypes of depressive symptoms, with hypercortisolism (elevations in basal cortisol) corresponding to the presence of melancholic depressive symptoms, and hypocortisolism (low basal cortisol) corresponding with atypical depressive symptoms. These chronically elevated or suppressed levels of cortisol, by way of their impact on metabolic, immune, and inflammatory processes, are thought to be one pathway by which major depressive disorder is related to later adverse physical health conditions, including cardiovascular disease (Gold & Chrousos, 2002).

New approaches to understanding the role of cortisol in major depressive disorder will involve a combination of genetic and environmental measures and will require observations of how cortisol levels change over time in relation to stress exposure and the emergence and course of depressive disorder. Prevention studies, which attempt to alter perceived stress and cortisol levels in the hopes of preventing the development of depression, or altering its course, will be another important new direction to pursue.

EMMA K. ADAM

See also

Hormones
Hypothalamic-Pituitary-Adrenal Axis
Hypothalamic-Pituitary-Thyroid Axis

References

Adam, E. K., Klimes-Dougan, B., & Gunnar, M. R. (2007). Social regulation of the adrenocortical response to stress in infants, children and adolescents: Implications for psychopathology and education. In D. Coch, G. Dawson, & K. Fischer (Eds.), *Human behavior, learning, and the developing brain: Atypical development* (pp. 264–304). New York: Guilford Press.

Birmaher, B., & Heydl, P. (2001). Biological studies in depressed children and adolescents. *International Journal of Neuropsychopharmacology, 4*, 149–157.

Dahl, R. E., Ryan, N. D., Puig-Antich, J., Nguyen, N. A., Al-Shabbout, M., Meyer, V. A., et al. (1991). 24-hour cortisol measures in adolescents with major depression: A controlled study. *Biological Psychiatry, 30*, 25–36.

Ehlert, U., Gaab, J., & Heinrichs, M. (2001). Psychoneuroendocrinological contributions to the etiology of depression, posttraumatic stress disorder, and stress-related bodily disorders: The role of the hypothalamus-pituitary-adrenal axis. *Biological Psychology, 57*, 141–152.

Gold, P. W., & Chrousos, G. P. (2002). Organization of the stress system and its dysregulation in melancholic and atypical depression: High vs. low CRH/NE states. *Molecular Psychiatry, 7*, 254–275.

Halligan, S. L., Herbert, J., Goodyer, I., & Murray, L. (2007). Disturbances in morning cortisol secretion in association with maternal postnatal depression predict subsequent depressive symptomatology in adolescents. *Biological Psychiatry, 62*, 40–46.

Heim, C., Plotsky, P. M., & Nemeroff, C. B. (2004). Importance of studying the contributions of early adverse experience to neurobiological findings in depression. *Neuropsychopharmacology, 29*, 641–648.

Kaufman, J., Martin, A., King, R. A., & Charney, D. (2001). Are child-, adolescent-, and adult-onset depression one and the same disorder? *Biological Psychiatry, 49*, 980–1001.

Kirschbaum, C., & Helhammer, D. (2000). Salivary cortisol. In G. Fink (Ed.), *Encyclopedia of Stress, Vol. 3* (pp. 379–383). San Diego: Academic Press.

Thase, M. F., Jindal, R., & Howland, R. H. (2002). Biological aspects of depression. In I. H. Gotlib & C. L. Hammen (Eds.), *Handbook of depression* (pp. 192–218). New York: Guilford Press.

Wüst, S., Federenko, I., Van Rossum, E., Koper, J. W., Kumsta, R., Entringer, S., et al. (2004). A psychobiological perspective on genetic determinants of hypothalamic-pituitary-adrenal axis activity. *Annals of the New York Academy of Science, 1032*, 52–62.

Course of Depression

Over the past 20 years, our understanding of the course of major depression has transformed. Once viewed as an acute, single-episode disorder, we now understand that for most individuals with depression this disorder follows a relapsing and remitting course over the lifetime. At least half of those who have one episode of depression will have a second episode. On average, those who have an episode of major depression will have at least five episodes over their lifetime (Burcusa & Iacono, 2007). We are beginning to understand risk factors that increase the likelihood for recurrence, and researchers have developed theories that predict how the relationship between depression and variables such as stressful life events may change over the course of the disorder.

Remission, Relapse, and Recurrence

Early research on the course of depression was hampered by inconsistent use of the terms *remission, relapse,* and *recurrence.* The MacArthur Foundation task force recommended change points to define these terms (Frank et al., 1991). *Remission* is the point when an episode has ended. In some cases, the symptoms of depression improve somewhat but continue to cause distress or impair functioning. This *partial remission* is found in 20% to 30% of cases. Those who experience partial remission in one episode are likely to experience the same pattern of remission in subsequent episodes (American Psychiatric Association [APA], 1994). *Full remission* is the point when an individual no longer meets criteria for the disorder and has no more than minimal symptoms. Full remission for a defined period of time, typically 8 weeks for depression, marks a *recovery.* A recovery can occur with or without treatment. A *relapse* occurs when the symptoms of the disorder return and meet diagnostic criteria before a full recovery has been made. If the symptoms of the disorder emerge after the 8-week remission period, this is viewed as a new episode of depression or a *recurrence.*

About 20% of patients who recover from an episode of major depression will have a recurrence within 1 year. The number of previous episodes of depression is the strongest predictor of recurrence. Other predictors of recurrence include older age, a history of other psychiatric disorders, and having comorbid dysthymic disorder or so-called double depression (Burcusa & Iacono, 2007).

The longitudinal Collaborative Depression Study provided the first long-term study of the recurrence of depression. After 2 years, 25% to 40% of cases recurred, with up to 60% recurring after 5 years. At 10-year follow-up, 75% of cases had recurred and

87% after 15 years. The rate of recurrence also increases with subsequent episodes (Boland & Keller, 2002). These data suggest that for the overwhelming majority of cases, depression is a recurrent disorder rather than a single-episode phenomenon.

Demographic Variables

Depression is more likely to occur in women than in men, with lifetime prevalence rates of 1 in 4 and 1 in 6, respectively (Kessler, Bergland, Demler, Jin, & Walters, 2005). This sex difference is eliminated in rates of recurrence; men and women do not differ in risk of recurrence nor in the number of recurrences experienced. Other demographic variables such as low socioeconomic status and not being married also are associated with increased likelihood of developing depression, but not recurrences of depression (Burcusa & Iacona, 2007).

Nature of First Episode

Major depressive disorder can begin at any age, with the average age of onset in the mid-20s. Late onset of depression has been associated with more frequent episodes and more severe symptoms (Sorenson, Rutter, & Aneshensel, 1991). Earlier age of onset may predict a worse course overall of depression, but studies have produced mixed results on this question (Burcusa & Iacona, 2007). The nature of the first episode appears to predict later outcome. In adult samples, initial episodes with more symptoms and more severe symptoms predict earlier relapses in the future. Severe symptoms such as suicidal ideation and attempts, as well as sleep disturbances, also predict relapses. The duration of the initial episode, however, has not been shown consistently to predict recurrences (Burcusa & Iacona, 2007).

Length of Episode

In addition to number of episodes, the length of an episode is a course variable. The duration of major depressive episodes is typically at least 6 months if untreated. In the majority of cases, the episode will end and the person will return to his or her normal mood and functioning. In 5% to 10% of cases, however, episodes endure for at least 2 years without a period of at least 2 months of normal mood (APA, 1994). These cases are called chronic major depression. For around 10% of cases, the episode continues for at least 5 years (Boland & Keller, 2002).

Comorbidity

A diagnosis of a psychiatric illness in addition to depression increases the risk of recurrence in adults and may affect the age of onset and course of depression (Rohde, Lewinsohn, & Seeley, 1991). Double depression (major depression and dysthymia occurring simultaneously) is by nature a chronic condition, as dysthymia must be present for at least 2 years. A diagnosis of comorbid dysthymia also has an effect on the course of major depression. Those with double depression recover more rapidly from their major depression, although they typically continue to experience dysthymia. However, they relapse to depression at twice the rate as patients who only have major depression (Boland & Keller, 2002).

Other comorbid clinical disorders also modify the course of depression. Those with comorbid anxiety disorders experience longer depressive episodes and are at increased risk for recurrence of major depression. In addition, comorbid anxiety in depressed individuals is characterized by an earlier age of onset and increased suicidal tendencies (Rhode et al., 1991). Patients with comorbid alcoholism are half as likely to recover from an episode of major depression as those without alcoholism. Alcohol and drug disorders also are associated with higher rates of recurrence. Surprisingly, in children and adolescents, only comorbid dysthymia is related to the course of major depression. Comorbid anxiety disorders and disruptive behavior disorders do not affect course of depression in children and adolescents and are not related to an increased risk for recurrence (Burcusa & Iacona, 2007).

Changes in Processes Over the Course of Depression

Numerous so-called scar theories have been advanced that suggest that there is something about the experience of having depression that changes an individual in a way that makes him or her more susceptible to future episodes of depression. There is little empirical support for scar models that suggest mechanisms of changes in social interactions, but it is unclear whether cognitive processes or personality changes after depression (Burcusa & Iacono, 2007). Scar theories are particularly difficult to test as they require data collected before and after the onset of the disorder.

Some evidence suggests that biological processes may change following a depressive episode in a way that lowers the threshold for subsequent episodes. For example, the relationship between stressful events and depressive episodes may change with subsequent onsets. The kindling hypothesis proposes that having a depressive episode increases the individual's vulnerability to become depressed again at the biological level (Post, 1992). Changes at the level of gene encoding occur at the time of the first depressive episode that make the individual more prone to recurrence of depression. In initial episodes of depression, the relationship between stress and depression is much stronger than in later episodes. Sensitization to life stressors occurs during early episodes, making a person more sensitive to even small stressors, thereby leading to later depressive episodes. In addition, sensitization to dysphoric moods occurs so that less-severe dysphoric moods lead to depression in later episodes. Eventually, episodes become independent of any external stressor. Some research support has been found for the kindling model, although there are inconsistencies in the literature.

The stress generation model, in contrast, predicts that depressed persons are more likely to have stressful life events to which they had contributed. These dependent events, particularly negative interpersonal events, set up the circumstances for future recurrences of depression (Hammen, 1991). Although proposed as a scar theory where the generation of stressful life events is a result of previous depressive episodes, it is currently not clear whether the stress generation process begins after the onset of depression or precedes the initial onset.

Conclusions

Major depressive disorder is best characterized as a relapsing and remitting condition. Some characteristics of first episodes, such as severity of symptoms, predict earlier time to recurrences. Other variables, such as age of onset, length of episode, sex, and marital status, have not consistently been shown to predict recurrences. Individuals with depression and comorbid dysthymia, anxiety disorders, or substance use disorders also have earlier recurrences than those with only depression. Some evidence suggests that kindling processes may sensitize individuals to stressful events such that less severe stressors are needed to trigger later events. Stress generation models predict that an individual's behavior while depressed may trigger interpersonal life events, thereby setting up subsequent depressive episodes. These models, while intriguing, will require further research.

CAROLYN M. PEPPER AND DANIELLE J. MAACK

See also

Causality
Recurrence
Relapse
Risk

References

American Psychiatric Association. (1994). *Diagnostic and statistical manual of mental disorders* (4th ed.). Washington, DC: Author.

Boland, R. J., & Keller, M. B. (2002). *Course and outcome of depression*. In I. H. Gotlib & C. L. Hammen

(Eds.), *Handbook of depression* (pp. 43–60). New York: Guilford Press.

Burcusa, S., & Iacono, W. (2007). Risk for recurrence in depression. *Clinical Psychology Review, 27,* 959–085.

Frank, E., Prien, R. F., Jarrett, R. B., Keller, M. B., Kupfer, D. J., Lavori, P. W., et al. (1991). Conceptualization and rationale for consensus definitions of terms in major depressive disorder. *Archives of General Psychiatry, 48,* 851–855.

Hammen, C. (1991). Generation of stress in the course of unipolar depression. *Journal of Abnormal Psychology, 100,* 555–561.

Kessler, R., Bergland, P., Demler, O., Jin, R., & Walters, E. (2005). Lifetime prevalence and age-of-onset distributions of DSM-IV disorders in the national comorbidity survey replication. *Archives of General Psychiatry, 62,* 593–602.

Post, R. M. (1992). Transduction of psychosocial stress into the neurobiology of recurrent affective disorder. *American Journal of Psychiatry, 149,* 999–1010.

Rohde, P., Lewinsohn, P. M., & Seeley, J. R. (1991). Comorbidity of unipolar depression, 2: Comorbidity with other mental disorders in adolescents and adults. *Journal of Abnormal Psychology, 100,* 214–222.

Sorenson, S., Rutter, C., & Aneshensel, C. (1991). Depression in the community: An investigation into age of onset. *Journal of Consulting and Clinical Psychology, 59,* 541–546.

Culture and Depression

The likelihood of developing major depressive disorder varies widely across cultures. Consider this: approximately 1 in 7 individuals living in Eastern or Western Europe, North America, and Australia will develop major depression in their lifetimes. In contrast, only about 1 in 25 individuals living in East Asian countries will be affected. Similarly, individuals of European descent in Western cultures (e.g., individuals of European descent in Europe, Australia, and North America) tend to fare worse than members of immigrant and ethnic minority groups living in the same cultures (e.g., East Asian and Hispanic immigrants, and African Americans) in their likelihood to develop major depressive disorder and experience depressive symptoms. The data show that despite enjoying higher standards of living, lower likelihood of discrimination, and better access to medical care, individuals in Western cultures shoulder a greater burden associated with major depression than their neighbors whose families immigrated from East Asian or Hispanic countries, or their counterparts living in Korea and Japan.

These differences are particularly striking when examined against the background of remarkable cross-cultural similarities in the prevalence of bipolar disorder (Weissman et al., 1996). Clearly, cultural factors play an important role in the etiology and expression of major depression. As we learn more about the interplay of biological and environmental factors in the etiology of major depression, we have something to gain from closer examination of cultural contexts that appear to confer protective benefits to their members. Over the last 40 years, research on culture and depression has not only documented cultural differences in the prevalence and manifestations of major depression, but also has examined some of the factors that account for these differences.

The causes of cross-cultural and within-culture differences in the prevalence of depression are complex. They include factors such as cultural differences in stress, standards of living, and reporting biases. People in some countries live harder lives than those in others. Exposure to stressors such as wars, civil unrest, crime, rapid political and economic changes, discrimination, and unemployment differs across cultural groups, as do standards of living, access to health care, and educational opportunities. There are also substantial cultural differences in the stigma associated with discussing one's mental health with others. Finally, clinicians in different cultures rely on different diagnostic heuristics, giving more or less weight to particular symptoms, such as reports of low energy or feelings of worthlessness. As a result, the likelihood that a case of major depression is recognized and diagnosed varies substantially across cultures.

All of these factors contribute to the variability in prevalence of major depression across cultural groups, but they do not fully account for the observed differences. Taking standards of living into account, and relying on standardized instruments to assess depression does not eliminate cross-cultural differences in the prevalence of depression. Thus, it is important to consider how culture (or a widely shared system of meanings, values, and norms transmitted across generations, and embodied in artifacts and behavioral patterns) affects vulnerability to depression and its manifestation. The considerable literature on culture and depression cannot be adequately summarized here; hence, we limit our discussion to three key areas of research: (a) cultural differences in positivity, (b) cultural differences in construals of self and social relationships, and (c) cultural differences in affective presentation of distress. Because most of the studies have compared samples of North American and East Asian individuals, we focus on this cultural contrast in our review.

Cultural Differences in Positivity

In Western cultures, and particularly in North American cultures, optimal emotional functioning is associated with the tendency to feel good about oneself, one's life, and one's future, and to feel in control of one's life (Heine, 2001). Parents and teachers in these cultural contexts strive to raise optimistic children with high levels of self-esteem, belief in their own uniqueness, motivation to excel, and an "I think I can" attitude. The goals of pursuing positive emotions, especially high-arousal positive emotions such as excitement and elation, are highly valued. Cultural emphasis on positivity appears to serve an important protective function against major depressive disorder in Western cultural contexts. Holding positive attributional beliefs (i.e., positive views about oneself, one's future, and one's life) in the face of stressors is predictive of high levels of emotional well-being (e.g., positive emotions, happiness) and the absence of depressive symptoms in these cultural settings. Conversely, a failure to fulfill the cultural imperative to make positive attributions makes one vulnerable to depressive symptoms.

If this is the case, why is it that individuals in Western cultural contexts are more, rather than less, vulnerable to depression than those in other cultural contexts? For many people, high levels of positive emotions and positive attributions are difficult to attain and sustain in the face of stressors and failures. This may be particularly true in cases in which an individual is temperamentally predisposed to experience high levels of negative affect, or when positive views about oneself, one's future, and one's life are inflexible and are not grounded in realistic assessment of one's effort or abilities. A failure to feel and think positively can be interpreted as a failure to live up to the culturally shaped ideal self—positive, successful, and in control. As a result, an individual may experience guilt, self-reproach, and social sanctions secondary to this failure, leading to further negative thoughts, negative mood, failure to persevere in one's efforts, and withdrawal.

At first glance, individuals in East Asian cultures appear more vulnerable to depression than individuals in Western cultures. They are reluctant to state that they feel happy, optimistic, and enjoy their lives, on self-reported inventories of depressive symptoms (Yen, Robins, & Lin, 2000). Moreover, individuals in these cultural contexts tend to hold more negative views of themselves, evaluate their performance more critically, engage in less self-affirmation, and hold less-positive views about their futures than their Western counterparts (Arnault, Sakamoto, & Moriwaki, 2005; Heine & Lehman, 1995; Kanagawa, Cross, & Markus, 2001). Yet they are less, rather than more, vulnerable to the syndrome of major depression. What factors account for this apparent discrepancy? East Asian cultures promote self-effacement, or the ability to critically assess and publicly acknowledge one's shortcomings. Consequently, negative information about the self does not serve an emotional blow; instead, individuals in East Asian cultures are prone to interpret their failures as indicative of insufficient effort on their part. Thus, failures are seen as important diagnostic tools that allow one to adjust one's behavior in pursuing important life goals (Heine et al., 2001). As a result, in the face of failure they are less likely to withdraw and are more likely to step up their effort to master the challenge. Because negativity does not violate cultural norms, it is less likely to be associated with shame or comparing oneself unfavorably to one's standards and with others. Because it does not make one stand out, it may be less likely to lead to social sanction. Thus, holding pessimistic and fatalistic beliefs about life events is less likely to be associated with symptoms of depression among individuals in East Asian cultures than among individuals in Western cultures.

In summary, studies on culture and depression suggest that the effects of negative views about the self on the symptoms of depression are dependent on the cultural context. Failure to maintain culturally normative levels of positive feelings and positive thoughts is associated with increased emotional distress. Future research needs to examine diverse cultural contexts more closely to understand the interplay between stress and cultural variability in positivity norms on the etiology and maintenance of major depressive disorder.

Another important factor that needs to be taken into account to understand cultural differences in depression is the role of close relationships in the individuals' models of the self. Research suggests that the way individuals maintain their relationships and think of themselves in the contexts of different relationships impacts their ability to withstand stressors.

Cultural Differences in Construals of Self and Social Relationships

Cultural models of the self differ in the extent to which social relationships are incorporated into one's self-construal, or model of the self (Markus & Kitayama, 1991). Western cultural contexts tend to be highly individualistic. They place an emphasis on personal autonomy and the ability to make individual choices in life. As a result, relationships are selected to fit individual goals. Relatively few adults live close to their extended families or childhood and college friends or become actively involved in these individuals' lives. Individuals in individualistic cultural contexts are more likely to move frequently throughout their lives in pursuit of their life goals. As a result, they tend to pursue more flexible and short-term relationships with diverse groups of friends, such as colleagues, reading group members, or neighbors. These relationship patterns are expected to change as the individuals' goals, interests, and choices of location and profession evolve over a lifetime.

In contrast, in collectivistic cultural contexts (such as East Asian and Eastern European cultures) there is an emphasis on connectedness and maintenance of relational harmony with close others, particularly with family members. Individuals in these cultural contexts tend to live their lives in proximity to their ingroup members, such as immediate and extended family and close friends, assume responsibility for ingroup members' well-being, and reacting emotionally to the successes and failures of ingroup members much as they would to their own. There is an expectation that important social relationships with ingroup members remain stable throughout life and require substantial investment of one's time and energy.

Research on social relationships and depression shows that across cultural groups, stable and supportive social relationships are protective against depressive symptoms in the face of stress (e.g., Calvete & Connor-Smith, 2006; Lehtinen et al., 2003; Plant & Sachs-Ericsson, 2004). Thus, a cultural imperative on the maintenance of stable close-knit social networks is one of the factors that may contribute to resilience to major depression. When relational harmony is achieved, individuals in collectivistic cultural contexts may be more protected from depression than their Western counterparts. On the other hand, interpersonal relationships can also become a burden. Severe interpersonal stressors, such as conflict with friends, divorce, separation from loved ones, or a family member's disgrace may be particularly distressing for individuals in collectivistic cultural contexts.

Similarly, due to the cultural emphasis on autonomy, individuals in individualistic cultural contexts tend to develop a sense of self that is stable, bounded, and independent of contextual cues. For example, an individual may think of herself as someone who is highly organized and shy in general, across her relationships and roles. In contrast, individuals in collectivistic cultural contexts tend to develop a sense of self that is flexible and context-dependent. In order to maintain interpersonal harmony, they need to be able to adjust to the situation and play different roles in different relational contexts. For instance, an individual in these cultural contexts may think of herself as someone who is highly organized and shy at work, but lively and dominant in her relationships with her friends. In the face of life changes or stressors, there may be significant emotional advantages to the flexible, context-dependent self that does not keep all of its emotional "eggs" in one basket (see Koch & Shepperd, 2004, for a review). For example, a student who experiences a stressor, such as a failure on an important exam in school, may cope with this stressor more effectively if she views herself differently in her roles as a student and as a friend. Her negative feelings about her academic failure may not affect her feelings about her ability to provide and obtain support from her friends. Thus, a culturally promoted tendency to develop a highly context-dependent sense of self may be protective of major depression, particularly when an individual feels in control of different aspects of herself.

In addition to the studies examining cultural differences in the models of self, studies on culture and depression have also focused on the cultural differences in acceptable ways of communicating emotional distress.

Cultural Differences in Affective Presentation of Distress

Cross-country differences in prevalence of major depression in part reflect cultural tendencies to describe distress in affective (i.e., emotional) versus somatic (i.e., bodily) terms. The *Diagnostic and Statistical Manual of Mental Disorders* criteria for major depressive episode include both affective and somatic symptoms, but greater importance is placed on the former rather than the latter. An individual cannot meet the criteria for major depressive episode without endorsing one of the key emotional symptoms (i.e., depressed mood or reduced pleasure or interest in formerly pleasurable activities). These criteria may not adequately capture presenting complaints reported in clinics around the world. Relative to individuals from Western cultural contexts, individuals from Asian, Middle Eastern, South American, and Eastern and South European cultural contexts tend to describe their distress in somatic terms, focusing on complaints such as headaches, sleep difficulties, and low energy rather than on feeling depressed, experiencing less pleasure than usual, or feeling worthless (e.g., Waza, Graham, Zyzanski, & Inoue, 1999). Because emotional symptoms are integral to the *DSM* diagnosis of major depressive episodes, these individuals' symptoms may fail to meet the criteria for diagnosis despite substantial impairment.

The differences in symptom presentation are due to cultural models of conceptualizing and communicating distress. Depressed individuals in non-Western cultural contexts may believe that it is inappropriate for them to reveal emotional distress, that their clinicians expect to hear reports of somatic, but not affective, symptoms, or that that the clinicians should be able to infer the existence of affective symptoms from the reports of somatic symptoms (e.g., Burr & Chapman, 2004). In addition, the tendency to emphasize somatic symptoms during initial presentation reflects the fact that in many parts of the world, physicians have little chance to develop ongoing relationships with their clients. Across cultures, depressed individuals do not feel comfortable sharing their emotional complaints with strangers, such as unfamiliar primary care doctors. They become more willing to report that episodes of major depression affect their emotional as well as physical well-being as they develop rapport with their clinicians (Simon, VonKorff, Picvinelli, Fullerton, & Ormel, 1999). In summary, cross-cultural differences in ways of communicating distress in clinical settings influence the likelihood that some symptoms will be emphasized at the expense of others, and, as a result, that individuals in some cultural settings will be less likely to meet the criteria for major depression.

Conclusions

Research on cultural differences in depression provides initial evidence that the widely shared cultural models of the self and ways to communicate distress allow individuals across cultural contexts to effectively cope with the stressors in their lives. Conversely, a failure to feel and think about the self in culturally normative ways is associated with higher vulnerability to major depression. At this point, it is still unknown whether such a failure places individuals at risk for developing major depression, or whether symptoms of major depression disrupt individuals' abilities to monitor and comply with the norms of their culture. Future research needs to employ longitudinal studies of individuals at risk for major depression and individuals with histories of major depressive disorder to begin to untangle these important questions.

As we learn more about cultural differences in depression and their causes, clinicians need to take these differences into account in order to provide effective treatment to individuals from diverse cultural contexts. Most empirically tested treatment approaches—both pharmaceutical and psychotherapeutic—have been designed for and tested on individuals with major depression in Western cultural contexts. Factors such as racial group differences in optimal dosage of antidepressants (Lin, 2001) and cultural differences in the value placed on emotional disclosure (Lawrence et al., 2006) can hinder efforts to disseminate empirically supported treatment approaches to non-Western populations. Additional studies can help us better understand how to adapt our efforts at alleviating distress in diverse cultural groups.

YULIA CHENTSOVA DUTTON

See also

Definition of Depression
Diagnostic and Statistical Manual of Mental Disorders

References

Arnault, D. S., Sakamoto, S., & Moriwaki, A. (2005). The association between negative self-descriptions and depressive symptomology: Does culture make a difference? *Archives of Psychiatric Nursing, 19,* 93–100.

Burr, J., & Chapman, T. (2004). Contextualizing experiences of depression in women from South Asian communities: A discursive approach. *Sociology of Health and Illness, 26,* 433–452.

Calvete, E., & Connor-Smith, J. K. (2006). Perceived social support, coping, and symptoms of distress in American and Spanish students. *Anxiety, Stress and Coping: An International Journal, 19,* 47–65.

Heine, S. J. (2001). Self as cultural product: An examination of East Asian and North American selves. *Journal of Personality, 69,* 881–905.

Heine, S. J., & Lehman, D. R. (1995). Cultural variation in unrealistic optimism: Does the West feel more invulnerable than the East? *Journal of Personality and Social Psychology, 68,* 595–607.

Heine, S. J., Lehman, D. R., Ide, E., Leung, C., Takata, T., & Matsumoto, H. (2001). Divergent consequences of success and failure in Japan and North America: An investigation of self-improving motivations and malleable shelves. *Journal of Personality Social Psychology, 81,* 599–615.

Kanagawa, C., Cross, S. E., & Markus, H. R. (2001). "Who am I?": The cultural psychology of the conceptual self. *Personality and Social Psychology Bulletin, 27,* 90–103.

Koch, E. J., & Shepperd, J. A. (2004). Is self-complexity linked to better coping? A review of the literature. *Journal of Personality, 72,* 727–760.

Koss-Chioino, J. D. (1999). Depression among Puerto Rican women: Culture, etiology and diagnosis [Special issue: The psychology of Latina women]. *Hispanic Journal of Behavioral Sciences, 21,* 330–350.

Lawrence, V., Murray, J., Banerjee, S., Turner, S., Sangha, K., Byng, R., et al. (2006). Concepts and causation of depression: A cross-cultural study of the beliefs of older adults. *Gerontologist, 46,* 23–32.

Lehtinen, V., Michalak, E., Wilkinson, C., Dowrick, C., Ayuso-Mateos, J.-L., Dalgard, O. S., et al. (2003). Urban-rural differences in the occurrence of female depressive disorder in Europe: Evidence from the ODIN study. *Social Psychiatry and Psychiatric Epidemiology, 38,* 283–289.

Lin, K. M. (2001). Biological differences in depression and anxiety across races and ethnic groups. *Journal of Clinical Psychiatry, 62,* 13–19.

Markus, H. R., & Kitayama, S. (1991). Culture and the self: Implications for cognition, emotion, and motivation. *Psychological Review, 98,* 224–253.

Plant, E. A., & Sachs-Ericsson, N. (2004). Racial and ethnic differences in depression: The roles of social support and meeting basic needs. *Journal of Consulting and Clinical Psychology, 72,* 41–52.

Simon, G. E., VonKorff, M., Picvinelli, M., Fullerton, C., & Ormel, J. (1999). An international study of the relation between somatic symptoms and depression. *New England Journal of Medicine, 18,* 1329–1335.

Waza, K., Graham, A. V., Zyzanski, S. J., & Inoue, K. (1999). Comparison of symptoms in Japanese and American depressed primary care patients. *Family Practice, 16,* 528–533.

Weissman, M. M., Bland, R. C., Canino, G. J., Faravelli, C., Greenwald, S., Hwu, H. G., et al. (1996). Cross-national epidemiology of major depression and bipolar disorder. *Journal of the American Medical Association, 276,* 293–299.

Yen, S., Robins, C. J., & Lin, N. (2000). A cross-cultural comparison of depressive symptom manifestation: China and the United States. *Journal of Consulting and Clinical Psychology, 68,* 993–999.

Cyclothymia

Cyclothymic disorder, or cyclothymia, is a chronic mood disturbance characterized by the presence of numerous periods of hypomanic symptoms and numerous periods of depressive symptoms (American Psychiatric Association [APA], 2000). In contrast to the bipolar disorders, these symptoms do not meet criteria for a manic episode or major depressive episode, respectively (APA, 2000). Cyclothymia was initially viewed as a personality disorder in the second edition of the *Diagnostic and Statistical Manual of Mental Disorders* (*DSM-II;* APA, 1968) but was reclassified as a mood disorder with the publication of the *DSM-III.* Despite this nosological shift, the diagnosis is uncommon in clinical practice, as such patients typically present with major depressive episodes, thus warranting a diagnosis of bipolar II disorder (Akiskal, 2001). Individuals can, however, be diagnosed with both cyclothymic disorder and bipolar II disorder if the major depressive episode occurs after the initial 2 years of cyclothymia (APA, 2000).

Prevalence

Studies suggest a lifetime prevalence of 0.4% to 1% for cyclothymia, with prevalence rates in mood disorder clinics ranging from 3% to 5% (APA, 2000). While women with the condition may be more likely to present to clinical settings than their male counterparts, research involving community samples suggests an equal distribution among men and women (APA, 2000; Howland & Thase, 1993).

Clinical Features

Cyclothymic disorder is quite heterogeneous. Its cycles of hypomanic and depressive symptoms range in duration from days to weeks and follow each other in an irregular and often sudden manner (Akiskal, 2001; Howland & Thase, 1993). Such rapid and unpredictable mood swings can undermine the individual's sense of self (Akiskal, 2001). The disorder can further be described via the biphasic nature of these mood shifts, such as jocularity versus tearfulness, people-seeking versus self-absorption, and mental sharpness versus mental confusion (Akiskal, 2001). Individuals with cyclothymic disorder may rarely experience periods of euthymic or, even, mood (Akiskal, 2001; Akiskal, Djenderedjian, Rosenthal, & Khani, 1977). Considering the often unpredictable nature of cyclothymia, symptom severity and functional impairment fluctuate.

While cyclothymic mood episodes impact functioning across a variety of domains, the onset of such episodes is often unrelated to external factors (Akiskal et al., 1977). Anger and irritability are common features of cyclothymia, and reactive anger outbursts may occur (Akiskal, 2001). During these periods, such individuals seem hostile and inconsiderate to the people around them, thus inciting interpersonal conflict. Individuals with cyclothymia may shift to periods of guilt, shame, and embarrassment following symptomatic periods involving interpersonal disputes and inconsiderate treatment of others (Akiskal, 2001). Furthermore, the unpredictable mood shifts encourage a history of inconsistent work and study behaviors. While some individuals perform better during hypomanic periods, others find that euthymic periods are more conducive to work productivity (Akiskal, 2001). Substance misuse is not uncommon in cyclothymia. Although drugs and alcohol may function as self-medication or self-indulgence, mood cycles continue to occur in the absence of such substances (Akiskal, 2001; Akiskal et al., 1977).

Course

Cyclothymia is a chronic condition that typically begins during adolescence or early adulthood and has an insidious onset (Akiskal et al., 1977; APA, 2000). Onset occurring in late adulthood may stem from a mood disorder due to a general medical condition (e.g., multiple sclerosis; APA, 2000). The clinical presentation of cyclothymia is more commonly dominated by depressive periods punctuated by euthymic, irritable, and occasional elevated and expansive periods (Akiskal, 2001). Individuals with the disorder often present to clinical settings because of brief but recurring episodes of depressive symptoms (Akiskal, 2001). By definition, however, these symptoms do not meet the symptom or duration criteria for a major depressive episode. While the seasonal pattern specifier is not diagnostically applied to cyclothymic disorder, as it can be in major depressive disorder and the bipolar disorders, winter groupings of depressive periods are not uncommon (Akiskal, 2001). Furthermore, the fluctuating mood cycles generally persist for years without the long symptom-free periods that occur in the bipolar disorders (Howland & Thase, 1993).

Certain presentations of cyclothymic disorder may represent an early manifestation of other mood disorders, particularly those in the bipolar spectrum (APA, 2000; Howland & Thase, 1993). Individuals with cyclothymia have a 15% to 50% risk of subsequently developing a bipolar disorder (APA, 2000). The condition may be more closely related to bipolar II than bipolar I disorder, which is reasonable considering that cyclothymia is essentially defined as a subthreshold version of the bipolar II disorder. Research, such as family history, biological, and treatment studies, however, has yet to provide a clear link between these disorders, and clinical heterogeneity makes such associations difficult. Considering treatment implications, studies examining the relationship between cyclothymia and other psychiatric illnesses (e.g., which manifestations tend to crystallize into bipolar disorder) are important.

EDDIE J. WRIGHT

See also

Classification of Depression
Diagnostic and Statistical Manual of Mental Disorders

References

Akiskal, H. S. (2001). Dysthymia and cyclothymia in psychiatric practice a century after Kraepelin. *Journal of Affective Disorders, 62,* 17–31.

Akiskal, H. S., Djenderedjian, A. H., Rosenthal, R. H., & Khani, M. K. (1977). Cyclothymic disorder: Validating criteria for inclusion in the bipolar affective group. *American Journal of Psychiatry, 134,* 1227–1233.

American Psychiatric Association. (1968). *Diagnostic and statistical manual of mental disorders* (2nd ed.). Washington, DC: Author.

American Psychiatric Association. (2000). *Diagnostic and statistical manual of mental disorders* (4th ed., text revision). Washington, DC: Author.

Howland, R. H., & Thase, M. E. (1993). A comprehensive review of cyclothymic disorder. *Journal of Nervous and Mental Disease, 181,* 485–493.

Cytokines

Cytokines are intracellular signaling proteins that play an integral role in orchestrating the inflammatory response throughout the body. Immune cells at the site of infection and injury release a cascade of different cytokines that rely on complex feedback mechanisms to initiate, sustain, amplify, and attenuate inflammation. Cytokines also mediate systemic responses between immune, endocrine, autonomic, and central nervous systems. An imbalance between proinflammatory (e.g., interleukin [IL]-1, IL-6, and tumor necrosis factor [TNF]-α) and anti-inflammatory cytokines (e.g., IL-10) can result in infections, autoimmune disorders, atherosclerosis, and other medical morbidities.

Converging lines of evidence implicate cytokine-mediated pathways connecting the immune system and brain in the pathophysiology of depression (Raison, Capuron, & Miller, 2006). Empirical support for the relationship between cytokines and depression includes the following: (a) exogenous administration of pro-inflammatory cytokines or agents that activate the inflammatory cascade induces depressionlike sickness behaviors in healthy animals and humans; (b) depressed individuals who are otherwise medically healthy exhibit increased levels of circulating inflammatory mediators; (c) cytokine immunotherapy for medically ill patients can elicit major depression; and (d) depression is prevalent among patients with inflammatory medical conditions (Pollak & Yirmiya, 2002).

Cytokines and Sickness Behavior

In the context of an acute infectious threat, cytokines help coordinate a complex set of local and systemic changes to remove the pathogen, including fever and leukocytosis. Peripheral cytokines also act on the brain to produce behavioral changes including hypersomnia, anorexia, and reduction in exploration, social interaction, aggression, and sexual behavior (Dantzer, O'Connor, Freund, Johnson, & Kelley, 2008; Maier & Watkins, 1998). These motivated "sickness behaviors" are hypothesized to serve protective evolutionary functions by prioritizing recuperation and allocating metabolic resources to fighting the infection (Hart, 1988). Interestingly, many components of sickness behavior overlap considerably with symptoms of depression.

Relevant to their mediation by pro-inflammatory cytokines, sickness behaviors can be experimentally induced in a dose- and time-dependent manner by administering either exogenous cytokines (e.g., IL-1β and TNF-α) or inflammatory stimuli (e.g., endotoxin, *Salmonella typhi* vaccine). For example, mice injected with cytokines reduce motor activity, withdraw socially, increase slow-wave sleep, exhibit hypothalamic-pituitary-adrenal (HPA) axis activation, and reduce food and water intake. They also exhibit increased immobility in a forced swim test and reduced preference for sweet-tasting solutions, behaviors interpreted as animal models of helplessness and anhedonia. These depressionlike behaviors are attenuated by pretreatment with cytokine antagonists and acute administration of antidepressants (Maier & Watkins, 1998). Other factors, such as prenatal stress exposure, gender, and the estrus cycle may also affect the magnitude of cytokine-induced effects in rodents.

In healthy humans, exogenous stimulation of the inflammatory response transiently increases self-reported depressed mood (Reichenberg et al., 2001). Moreover, increases in depressed mood are significantly and positively correlated with circulating levels of pro-inflammatory cytokines. Taken together, these experimental findings suggest that cytokines mediate the observed behavioral response to acute infectious threats, including depressed mood and depressionlike behaviors.

Cytokines and Endogenous Depression in Humans

In addition to mediating adaptive behavioral responses to acute infection, cytokines may also contribute to some cases of depression in physically healthy individuals. Across multiple studies, patients with major depression exhibit elevated levels of circulating inflammatory mediators relative to nondepressed participants, including pro-inflammatory cytokines (e.g., IL-6, TNF-α), acute phase proteins (e.g., C-reactive protein), and chemokines and adhesion molecules (e.g., soluble intracellular adhesion molecule–1) (Raison et al., 2006). In several of these investigations, depressive symptom severity was also positively correlated with plasma concentrations of inflammatory markers. In some studies, antidepressant treatment was demonstrated to suppress the observed cytokine hypersecretion among depressed patients. Specific cytokines have also been found to be elevated in the postmortem brains of suicide victims and showed gender specificity (IL-4 and TNF-α in women and IL-13 in men) compared to normal controls (Tonelli et al., 2008).

Although these findings are suggestive of a connection between cytokines and the etiology of depression, it is important to note that this literature is not without inconsistencies. For example, some investigators have reported no association between depression and inflammatory markers when controlling for body mass index, gender, or personality. The observational and cross-sectional nature of much existing research also limits causal inference, as psychological stress has been linked to increased production of pro-inflammatory cytokines in laboratory studies of both animals and humans. In summary, additional longitudinal and experimental research is required to determine causal relationships between inflammation and psychological distress.

Cytokines and Physical Illness-Related Depression in Humans

The neuropsychiatric effects of cytokine immunotherapy provide a useful quasi-experimental model to study cytokine-induced depression. Cytokine therapy (i.e., IFN-α and IL-2) is used for the treatment of immune-mediated medical illnesses including certain cancers and chronic hepatitis C. Patients undergoing cytokine therapy frequently report sadness, loss of interest, cognitive disturbances, appetite loss, fatigue, and altered sleep during the course of treatment (Capuron et al., 2002). Indeed, these therapies have been demonstrated to elicit major depression in up to 50% of patients (Musselman et al., 2001). Immunotherapy-induced depressive symptom scores have been significantly correlated with increased production of pro-inflammatory cytokines (Loftis, Huckans, Ruimy, Hinrichs, & Hauser, 2008). In a majority of patients, the neurovegetative symptoms of major depression (e.g., fatigue, anorexia, altered sleep patterns) develop within the first 2 weeks of IFN-α therapy, whereas mood and cognitive symptoms (e.g., irritability, difficulties with memory and attention) usually develop between the first and third month of cytokine therapy in vulnerable patients only. Furthermore, mood and cognitive symptoms appear to be highly responsive to prophylactic treatment with selective serotonin reuptake inhibitors, while the neurovegetative symptoms are not responsive to antidepressants (Capuron et al., 2002).

The fact that cytokine system activation induces mood symptoms less frequently than neurovegetative symptoms points to the existence of vulnerability factors for cytokine-induced depression. Cancer patients who develop significant depressive symptoms during cytokine therapy displayed elevated pretreatment scores on a depressive symptom inventory relative to those who do not develop depressed mood (Musselman et al., 2001). They also exhibited greater HPA responses to the first cytokine injection (Capuron et al., 2003). Preliminary data indicate that other risk factors for development of cytokine-induced depressive symptoms include sleep difficulties and poor social support (Capuron & Dantzer, 2003). Future studies focused on the role of genetic polymorphisms in cytokines as well as gene-environment interactions in mediating cytokine-induced behavioral symptoms will also be critical in identifying individuals vulnerable to cytokine-mediated depression.

Results from studies of patients receiving cytokine immunotherapy must be interpreted with caution, as the doses of cytokines administered in these protocols are in excess of circulating levels of cytokines. However, endogenous inflammation may also underlie the significant comorbidity between medical illness and depression. Depression is highly prevalent in inflammatory disease, both infectious (e.g., influenza, gastroenteritis, hepatitis C, HIV) and noninfectious (e.g., diabetes mellitus, cardiovascular disease, rheumatoid arthritis, systemic lupus erythermatosus, inflammatory bowel disease, multiple sclerosis) (Gold & Irwin, 2006; Szigethy et al.,

2004). Although depression was previously viewed as a psychological response to the stress of physical illness or as a premorbid risk factor for disease, pro-inflammatory cytokines may also represent a shared etiological pathway between depression and various medical conditions. For example, in a murine model of colitis, early life stress was associated with both depressionlike behavior and vulnerability to intestinal inflammation in adulthood that was reversed by antidepressant treatment (Varghese et al., 2006). Preliminary treatment studies in humans have yielded promising results, with data suggesting that psychotherapy and antidepressants may reduce both depressive symptoms and inflammatory markers in patients with multiple sclerosis and inflammatory bowel disease, and that cytokine antagonists can have both anti-inflammatory and antidepressant effects.

Pathways Linking Cytokines to Depression

Pro-inflammatory cytokines circulating in the periphery do not freely cross the blood brain barrier but are hypothesized to signal the brain via vagal and trigeminal afferent nerves, specific transport mechanisms, and gaps in the barrier (e.g., circumventricular organs and choroid plexus; Bluthe et al., 1994; Raison et al., 2006). Once in the brain, microglial cells produce cytokines to mirror the peripheral immune response. Cytokine receptors have been localized to both neurons and nonneural cells in the brain (Dantzer et al., 2008).

These central cytokines act to increase levels of corticotrophin-releasing hormone (CRH), stimulating the HPA axis. Hypersecretion of CRH in the hypothalamus and amygdala has also been implicated in the links between psychological stress and depression, and patients with major depression exhibit disruption in glucocorticoid sensitivity. Moreover, glucocorticoids have anti-inflammatory effects. Thus, reductions in central or peripheral glucocorticoid receptor number or function represent one pathway by which cytokines and depression may be linked, such that cytokine-induced depression may be associated with increased glucocorticoid resistance, resulting in reduced glucocorticoid-mediated suppression of both CRH production and pro-inflammatory cytokine production.

Cytokines may also affect neurotransmitter metabolism (Dunn, 2006; Tracey, 2002). For example, cytokine immunotherapy has been demonstrated to deplete concentrations of tryptophan, an essential precursor of serotonin, and to induce release of norepinephrine. The cytokine-mediated activation of the enzyme indoleamine-2,3-diosygenase is gaining attention as a metabolic pathway that reduces the bio-availability of tryptophan and consequently the synthesis of serotonin (Dantzer et al., 2008). Cytokine-induced sickness behaviors have also been linked to alterations in metabolism of norepinephrine and dopamine.

A nascent neuroimaging literature exploring the circuitry of cytokine-mediated depression suggests that IFN-α patients demonstrate greater activation of the anterior cingulate cortex, an important structure in emotion regulation. Positron emission tomography also suggests that cytokine therapy alters metabolism in the hippocampus, amygdala, hypothalamus, and frontal lobes. Cytokines have been associated with basal ganglia–related reward circuitry and motor slowing (Capuron et al., 2007).

Conclusions

While depression is a heterogeneous, multidetermined disorder, growing evidence suggests that pro-inflammatory cytokines are associated with depressive symptoms in some cases. Cytokines mediate adaptive depressionlike sickness behaviors in the context of acute infection and may also contribute to depression in healthy individuals. In patients with chronic medical illnesses, both exogenous cytokine immunotherapy and endogenous disease-relevant inflammation may lead to depression in vulnerable individuals. Fortunately, preliminary clinical research suggests that inflammation-associated depression is responsive to psychotherapy, antidepressant treatment, and cytokine antagonists. Although the extant literature is not without inconsistencies, with a reliance on cross-sectional methodology that precludes causal interpretations, the association between cytokines and depression is an exciting and evolving area of research. Further longitudinal, experimental, and clinical treatment research will be necessary to disentangle bidirectional relationships linking the immune system and the brain and to elucidate biobehavioral moderators and mechanisms of these relationships.

EVA SZIGETHY AND CARISSA A. LOW

See also

Biological Models of Depression
Hypothalamic-Pituitary-Adrenal Axis
Hypothalamic-Pituitary-Thyroid Axis
Serotonin

References

Bluthe R. M., Walter V., Parnet, P., Laye, S., Lestage, J., Verrier, D., et al. (1994). Lipopolysaccharide induces sickness behaviour in rats by a vagal mediated mechanism. *Comptes rendus de l'academie des sciences III*, 317, 499–503.

Capuron, L., & Dantzer, R. (2003). Cytokines and depression: The need for a new paradigm. *Brain, Behavior, and Immunity*, 17, 119–124.

Capuron, L., Gumnick, J. F., Musselman, D. L., Lawson, D. H., Reemsnyder, A., Nemeroff, C. B., et al. (2002). Neurobehavioral effects of interferon-alpha in cancer patients: Phenomenlogy and paroxetine responsiveness of symptom dimensions. *Neuropsychopharmacology*, 26, 643–652.

Capuron, L., Pagnoni, G., Demetrashvili, M. F., Lawson, D. H., Fornwalt, F. B., Woolwine, B., et al. (2007). Basal ganglia hypermetabolism and symptoms of fatigue during interferon-alpha therapy. *Neuropsychopharacology*, 32, 2384–2392.

Capuron, L., Raison, C., Musselman, D. L., Lawson, D. H., Nemeroff, C. B., & Miller, A. (2003). Association of exaggerated HPA axis response to the initial injection of interferon alpha with development of depression during interferon-alpha therapy. *American Journal of Psychiatry*, 160, 1342–1345.

Dantzer, R., O'Connor, J. C., Freund, G. G., Johnson, R. W., & Kelley, K. W. (2008). From inflammation to sickness and depression: When the immune system subjugates the brain. *Nature Reviews Neuroscience*, 9, 46–57.

Dunn, A. J. (2006). Effects of cytokines and infections on brain chemistry. *Clinical Neuroscience Research*, 6, 52–68.

Gold, S. M., & Irwin, M. R. (2006). Depression and immunity: Inflammation and depressive symptoms in multiple sclerosis. *Neurologic Clinics*, 24, 507–519.

Hart, B. L. (1988). Biological basis of the behavior of sick animals. *Neuroscience and Biobehavioral Reviews*, 12, 123–137.

Loftis, J. M., Huckans, M., Ruimy, S., Hinrichs, D. J., & Hauser, P. (2008). Depressive symptoms in patients with chronic hepatitis C are correlated with elevated plasma levels of interleukin-1beta and tumor necrosis factor-alpha. *Neuroscience Letters*, 430, 264–268.

Maier, S. F., & Watkins, L. R. (1998). Cytokines for psychologists: Implications of bidirectional immune-to-brain communication for understanding behavior, mood, and cognition. *Psychological Review*, 105, 83–107.

Musselman, D. L., Lawson, D. H., Gumnick, J. F., Manatunga, A. K., Penna, S., Goodkin, R., et al. (2001). Paroxetine for the prevention of depression induced by high dose interferon alpha. *New England Journal of Medicine*, 344, 961–966.

Pollak, Y., & Yirmiya, R. (2002). Cytokine-induced changes in mood and behaviour: Implications for depression due to a general medical condition, immunotherapy, and antidepressive treatment. *International Journal of Neuropsychopharmacology*, 5, 389–399.

Raison, C. L., Capuron, L., & Miller, A. H. (2006). Cytokines sing the blues: Inflammation and the pathogenesis of depression. *Trends in Immunology*, 27, 24–31.

Reichenberg, A., Yirmiya, R., Schuld, A., Kraus, T., Haack, M., Morag, A., et al. (2001). Cytokine-associated emotional and cognitive disturbances in humans. *Archives of General Psychiatry*, 58, 445–452.

Szigethy, E., Levy-Warren, A., Whitton, S., Bousvarous, A., Gauvreau, K., Leichtner, A. M., et al. (2004). Depressive symptoms and inflammatory bowel disease in children and adolescents: A cross-sectional study. *Journal of Pediatric Gastroenterology and Nutrition*, 39, 395–403.

Tonelli, L. H., Stiller, J., Rujescu, D., Giegling, I., Schneider, B., Maurer, K., et al. (2008). Elevated cytokine expression in the orbitofrontal cortex of victims of suicide. *Acta Psychiatrica Scandinavica*, 117, 198–206.

Tracey K. J. (2002). The inflammatory reflex. *Nature*, 420, 853–859.

Varghese, A. K., Verdu, E. F., Bercik, P., Khan, W. I., Blennerhassett, P. A., Szechtman, H., et al. (2006). Antidepressants attenuate increased susceptibility to colitis in a murine model of depression. *Gastroenterology*, 130, 1743–1753.

D

Definition of Depression

Depressive disorders, involving pathologically severe or persistent states of sadness and associated experiences, have been recognized since the origins of medicine in ancient Greece. Indeed, Hippocrates defines depressive disorder essentially as excessively prolonged sadness. The disorder was initially thought to be caused by an imbalance in black bile (one of the four bodily humors of ancient medicine) and thus was labeled *melancholia* (black bile disorder); in contrast, normal sadness and negative moods in response to circumstances or due to a generally negative temperament were referred to as *melancholy*. This terminology still lives on, but as the belief in the black bile theory waned, *melancholy* and *melancholia* were largely replaced by the all-purpose and etiologically neutral descriptive term *depression*, both for the disorder and for normal moods and temperament. This terminological switch was already evident, for example, in Samuel Johnson's *Dictionary* of 1755 and was popularized in the United States in the early 20th century by the psychiatrist Adolph Meyer. After some initial comments about normal depression, the primary focus here is on depression as disorder, so to avoid confusion between normal and disordered depression, the phrase *depressive disorder* is used to refer specifically to the medical condition.

Depression—literally, the state of being pushed down—is commonly used to refer to emotional states of sadness, despair, numbness/ emptiness/deadness/hopelessness, and related "down" or "blue" moods that often involve a depletion of normal levels of energy, interest, mental focus, pleasure, social engagement, and appetite. However, atypically, such reactions can also involve agitation and overeating, and traditionally often were said to include anxiety and fear. Such emotional reactions can be perfectly normal—and have always been recognized as such by physicians. Normal sadness or depression generally involves an emotional response that is proportionate in intensity to the severity of some major negative life event that triggers the feelings; it does not include severe symptoms such as psychotic ideation, suicidality, or total immobilization; and unless the triggering stressor is chronic, in normal depression the initial feelings are generally followed by a gradual trajectory of coping, in which a new set of meanings or behaviors is constructed to allow reengagement with, and renewed enjoyment of, life.

Such experiences are common during ordinary bereavement after loss of a loved one. But the same experiences frequently occur after a variety of losses and disappointments, especially those in which a sense of humiliation or hopelessness is involved, such as loss of a job, loss of financial resources, loss of valued possessions, betrayal by a lover or friend, end of a romantic relationship, marital separation, diagnosis of a serious illness in oneself or in a loved one, humiliation or other loss of status, or deep disappointment due to failure to achieve some major life goal. When used in such contexts, *depression* simply describes a certain kind of emotional experience or mood. Evidence from cross-cultural, primate, and infant studies converges to suggest that such reactions are to some extent part of the biological inheritance of the human species and were naturally selected to serve some purpose. However, the functions of grief and sadness that led to their natural selection remain controversial. Such functions are thought to potentially include, for example, such adaptive effects as allowing time to rethink one's meaning system when one's situation radically changes; encouraging withdrawal under dangerous circumstances of status loss or loss of a conflict, where continued engagement might prove harmful; and prevention of premature commitment to new projects or attachments when current ones are lost.

Depression also refers to a pathological condition that is one of the commonest mental disorders. Indeed, at the time of this writing, major depressive disorder has become the signature diagnosis of psychiatry, with 40% of all psychiatric diagnoses being of depressive disorder, up from about 20% a few decades ago, and roughly 8% of the American population taking antidepressant medication at any one time. In depressive disorder, the very same experiences that can occur normally in response to grief and loss become pathologically severe and persistent. These experiences are often immobilizing, unremitting, and recurrent and may involve suicidality. The symptoms, although they may be initially triggered by some negative event as in normal sadness, have a duration or intensity that is unrelated in any proportionate way to such environmental events, and continue even if the triggering situation is reversed.

The symptoms cited by medical and psychiatric writers to indicate depressive disorder have remained remarkably stable from ancient times to our own: sadness, despair, lack of pleasure, withdrawal from usual social interactions and roles, emotional numbness or deadness, slowness of thought and movement, feelings of worthlessness and guilt, distractedness and difficulty focusing attention, fatigue, insomnia (or sometimes oversleeping), lack of appetite (or sometimes overeating), thoughts about death and suicidality, and anxiety. It is such symptoms that are used today, both by the authoritative American Psychiatric Association's *Diagnostic and Statistical Manual of Mental Disorders,* fourth edition, text revision (*DSM-IV-TR;* 2000), as well as the World Health Organization's *International Classification of Disease* (*ICD*), tenth edition, to define which conditions are depressive disorders and which are not.

In addition to symptoms, the key distinction in ancient through 19th-century definitions of melancholia was between states of sadness *without cause* and those that had similar symptoms arising from actual losses; only the former were considered mental disorders. *Without cause* does not mean uncaused, for throughout history depression has been attributed to postulated physical or psychological causes such as excessive black bile, disturbances in the circulation of blood, or depletion of energy. Rather, *without cause* means that the symptoms of depression were not associated with the sorts of environmental events that would appropriately and normally lead to sadness, such as bereavement, rejection in love, economic failure, and the like. Conversely, traditional physicians would not consider symptoms of depression that occur *with cause* as signs of a mental disorder. The symptoms could be identical in the two conditions; the distinction lay in the relation of the symptoms to the context in which they appeared. Symptoms that arose in contexts that could be expected to produce them, and that abated in a reasonable period of time after the triggering events ended, indicated normal functioning. Comparable symptoms that arose without appropriate triggering events, or had greater duration or intensity than was appropriate to the triggering events, potentially indicated disorder.

But, because it was considered inadequately scientific, the reference to context has been largely abandoned in psychiatric diagnosis since the 1980s. In particular, the widely used *DSM* defines major depressive disorder essentially as a condition including five or more symptoms that lasts 2 or more weeks. *DSM* diagnosis of depressive disorder (called *major depressive disorder* and often referred to as *clinical depression*) requires that five symptoms out of the following nine be present during a 2-week period, where the five must include either depressed mood or diminished interest or pleasure: (a) depressed mood; (b) diminished interest or pleasure in activities; (c) weight gain or loss or change in appetite; (d) insomnia or hypersomnia (excessive sleep); (e) psychomotor agitation or retardation (slowing down); (f) fatigue or loss of energy; (g) feelings of worthlessness or excessive or inappropriate guilt; (h) diminished ability to think or concentrate or indecisiveness; and (i) recurrent thoughts of death or suicidal ideation or suicide attempt.

A further important clause in the definition—the only major reference to context—excludes from diagnosis those individuals whose symptoms are due to what the *DSM* defines as a normal period of bereavement after the death of a loved one, lasting no more than 2 months and not including especially serious symptoms such as psychosis or thoughts about suicide: "The symptoms are not better accounted for by Bereavement, i.e., after the loss of a loved one, the symptoms persist for longer than 2 months or are characterized by marked functional impairment, morbid preoccupation with worthlessness, suicidal ideation, psychotic symptoms, or psychomotor retardation" (American Psychiatric Association, 2000, p. 356). This limited "bereavement exclusion" is the definition's only acknowledgment that some instances of normal intense sadness might include the definition's symptomatic criteria. If an episode of bereavement that includes the five out of nine symptoms lasts longer than 2 months or contains one of the severe symptoms, then it is labeled *complicated bereavement* and diagnosed as major depressive disorder. Obviously, the definition thus fails to take into account all the many other situations of loss, stress, and disappointment that may trigger normal intense sadness.

In addition to the bereavement exclusion, there are several additional exclusions from diagnosis of those satisfying the symptom criteria, but none concern contextual explanations: (a) conditions that also include manic symptoms in the history, either in pure manic episodes or in episodes with mixed depressive and manic symptoms, are classified under bipolar disorders; (b) conditions that do not cause clinically significant role impairment or distress—that is, where the symptoms are so mild and minor that they cause no harm to the individual—are excluded; (c) conditions that are the direct result of a general medical condition or use of either an illegal substance or prescribed medication are diagnosed as depressive disorders, but when such causes are identified, the conditions are placed under separate categories of mood disorder due to general medical condition, or substance-induced mood disorder rather than major depressive disorder; and (d) the depressive episode is not better explained as a side effect or part of a psychotic disorder that is active at the time of the depressive feelings (e.g., schizophrenia, schizophreniform disorder, delusional disorder, or psychotic disorder not otherwise specified). Despite all these qualifiers, the vast majority of episodes that contain at least the five necessary symptoms for 2 weeks do not fall under the exclusions and are classified as major depressive disorders.

For this reason, the five-symptoms-out-of-nine-for-at-least-2-weeks criterion has become a common definition of depressive disorder. For example, symptom checklists are distributed to patients in some doctors' offices and to students in some high schools to test for depressive disorder, and the criterion is simply that the individual report at least five of the symptoms. (Under such circumstances of mass screening, the exclusions are often to some extent ignored.) As will be evident, this approach to defining depressive disorder, with no reference to the context or triggers of the sad feelings, allows for the misdiagnosis of intense normal sadness as a disorder (Horwitz & Wakefield, 2007).

The use of the symptom-based approach, and the abandonment of the traditional examination of context as an integral part of the definition of depressive disorder, could be responsible for the purportedly widespread nature of depressive disorder. For example, studies using the checklists in the community to identify depressive disorders suggest that by the mid-20s, almost half of all individuals experience at least one episode of depressive disorder. This seems to make more sense if in fact the symptom checklists are identifying normal intense sadness as well as depressive disorder. This suspicion is strengthened when one finds out that one of the most powerful predictors of a young adult experiencing such a depressive episode is that he or she recently experienced the breakup of a romantic relationship. Surely, temperamental differences anchored in genes as well as early experience of loss shape the intensity and reactivity of an individual to later loss, but much of the variation may well be normal.

When the nature of a disorder is known, the disorder is usually defined in terms of the internal pathological condition that is the cause of the manifest symptoms. However, there is no scientifically demonstrated theory of the etiology of depressive disorder. So, there is no way at present to define depression in terms of a specific brain or mental dysfunction that is its cause. In fact, it seems likely that what is currently labeled depression will turn out to encompass several different kinds of malfunctions that lead to similar symptoms of deep and relentless sadness.

Prior to the *DSM* definition in the 1980s, the situational context was used in definitions to distinguish normal from pathological sadness. With the abandonment of reference to context, psychiatry is thus reduced to defining depression by its symptoms. But, as noted, this can be misleading because the very same symptoms that can indicate a depressive disorder can also occur in a normal emotional response of sadness to severe loss. Further inquiry into the best way to define depressive disorder is thus needed for improvement in the validity of diagnosis and research.

I have focused on major depressive disorder, the most common form of depressive disorder. However, it should be noted that depressive disorder comes in many forms and can fall under many different diagnostic categories, not just major depressive disorder. Bipolar I and II disorders can contain depressive episodes but also contain manic episodes or symptoms. Dysthymia is a mild but chronic form of depressive disorder intended to capture the notion of "neurotic" depression, in which depressive symptoms are more moderate than in major depressive disorder but persist for very long periods of time, generally several years. Adjustment disorder with depression refers to a depressive reaction to some stressor that is time-limited and not at an adequate level of symptomatic intensity to qualify for major depression, and subsides within months of the end of the stressor. And finally, mood disorder not otherwise specified includes all forms of depressive disorder that do not fall under the other categories, including subthreshold or minor depressive conditions—not yet having their own category—that do not have the five out of nine symptoms but are judged nonetheless to be a disorder.

JEROME C. WAKEFIELD

See also

Categorical and Dimensional Models of Depression
Classification of Depression
Diagnostic and Statistical Manual of Mental Disorders
Symptoms of Depression

References

American Psychiatric Association. (2000). *Diagnostic and statistical manual of mental disorders* (4th ed., text revision). Washington, DC: Author.

Horwitz, A. V., & Wakefield, J. C. (2007). *The loss of sadness: How psychiatry transformed normal sorrow into depressive disorder.* New York: Oxford Press.

Depression-Executive Dysfunction Syndrome

Late-life depression is a heterogeneous syndrome that often occurs in the context of ill medical health and brain lesions. As a result, many depressed elderly patients have cognitive dysfunction, including executive dysfunction and poor retrieval, although recognition memory is rather preserved. We proposed that a depression-executive dysfunction syndrome exists and has distinct clinical presentation and course of illness (Alexopoulos, 2001).

Impairment in executive functions, including perseverative responses and disturbances in initiation of behavior and in inhibition of inappropriate responses, are common in geriatric depression. Observations from acute treatment trials and from longer-term follow-up of depressed elders receiving uncontrolled treatment suggest that impairment of executive functions remains even after amelioration of depressive symptoms and signs. Executive dysfunction is consistent with disruption of frontostriatal pathways. Studies using different methodology suggest that frontostriatal dysfunction predisposes to depression (Alexopoulos, 2005).

Clinical studies document that depression is frequent in patients with disorders of subcortical structures, including vascular dementia, Parkinson's disease, Huntington's disease, supranuclear palsy, and basal ganglia calcification. Moreover, development of depression is more likely to occur in Alzheimer's patients with subcortical atrophy.

Structural neuroimaging studies note that white matter hyperintensities (WMH) are common in geriatric depression and mainly occur in subcortical structures and their frontal projections. Stroke of the caudate head and the left frontal pole are the ischemic lesions most likely to lead to depression. Reduced basal ganglia volumes have also been observed in depression.

Functional neuroimaging at rest shows hypoactivity of the caudate nucleus as well as in the left or bilateral frontal regions, including the dorsolateral, inferior, and medial and/or anterior cingulate gyri in major depression. However, hyperactivity in some of these brain areas has also been reported. Studies using probes showed that frontal and limbic areas are abnormally activated in elderly and younger depressed patients. Depressed elderly patients showed reduced activation of the anterior dorsal cingulate and the hippocampus bilaterally during a word activation task. Younger patients with mood disorders, when challenged with the Stroop response inhibition task, demonstrated blunted activation of the left anterior cingulate and minimal activation of the right anterior cingulate gyrus compared to normal controls.

The Clinical Syndrome

Elderly patients with major depression and impairment in some executive functions had more pronounced psychomotor retardation, loss of interest in activities, and less agitation, guilt, and insight than patients without executive dysfunction. Depressed elderly patients with executive dysfunction have functional disability disproportional to the severity of their depression. Depression occurring in the context of vascular disease, a syndrome associated with frontostriatal impairment, has a clinical presentation consistent with that of depression with executive dysfunction. Taken together, these studies suggest that the depression-executive dysfunction syndrome of late life is characterized by psychomotor retardation, apathy, mild depressive ideation, and pronounced disability, a clinical presentation that resembles medial frontal lobe syndromes. However, it should be noted that patients with both major depression and executive dysfunction also have sad mood, hopelessness, helplessness, and worthlessness of similar severity to depressed patients without executive dysfunction. Therefore, patients with depression and executive dysfunction do not merely have a frontal lobe syndrome.

Course of Illness

Several studies documented that executive impairment predicts poor or delayed antidepressant response of geriatric major depression.

Clinical Studies

An early study observed that poor or slow antidepressant response is associated with reduced psychomotor activity and prolonged latency of the P300 auditory evoked potential, functions requiring integrity of prefrontal systems. Abnormal scores in executive function tested with Trails B and card sorting, perseveration predicted poor overall outcomes of geriatric depression. A recent geriatric study documented that elderly patients with major depression and impairment in initiation and/or perseveration and response inhibition tasks were less likely to achieve remission after treatment with a target dose of 40 mg of citalopram daily than patients without executive dysfunction (Alexopoulos et al., 2005).

In addition to chronicity, executive dysfunction (initiation and/or perseveration) has been associated with relapse and recurrence of geriatric major depression and with residual depressive symptomatology, although some disagreement exists. Unlike executive dysfunction, neither memory impairment, nor disability, medical burden, social support, or number of previous episodes has been shown to influence the course of geriatric depression. Therefore, the relationship of executive dysfunction to chronicity, relapse, and recurrence of geriatric depression appears to be specific to this disturbance. These observations suggest that abnormalities of specific striatofrontal systems may predispose or perpetuate depressive syndromes or symptoms in the elderly.

In addition to executive dysfunction, other frontostriatal abnormalities have been associated with poor outcomes of depression. Subcortical white matter hyperintensities have been found to predict chronicity of geriatric depression, although a negative study exists. In the elderly, white matter abnormalities were found associated with executive dysfunction, perhaps related to disruption of frontostriatal pathways. Basal ganglia lesions predicted failure to respond to antidepressant monotherapy with high sensitivity and adequate specificity. Lesions in subcortical gray matter predict poor outcome of geriatric depression over a period up to 64 months. Finally, microstructural white matter abnormalities lateral to the anterior cingulate have been reported to predict poor remission of geriatric depression and were correlated with abnormal scores in initiation and/or perseveration and response inhibition tests.

Processing abnormalities in frontostriatal pathways are associated with poor response of depression to treatment. Electromagnetic tomography in depressed young adults showed that hyperactivity in the rostral anterior cingulate predicts good response to nortriptyline. Large left frontal error negative wave amplitude following Stroop activation predicts limited or slow change in depressive symptoms in geriatric patients treated with citalopram. Finally, elderly patients with major depression who failed to achieve remission after 8 weeks of treatment with escitalopram had large error negative wave and small error positive wave following an emotional go/no-go task. The error negative wave is principally generated by the dorsal anterior cingulate during error detection, while the generators of the error positive wave are though to be at the rostral anterior cingulate.

Functional neuroimaging studies have shown that improvement of depression is associated with frontostriatal changes. Hypometabolism of the rostral anterior cingulate is a predictor of treatment resistance in younger depressives, while cingulate hypermetabolism predicts favorable response. Finally, increased metabolism of the left anterior cingulate has been found in young, depressed individuals who failed to respond to treatment. Remission of depression is associated with metabolic increases in the dorsal cortex (dorsal anterior cingulate, posterior cingulate, dorsolateral, and inferior parietal cortices) and decreases in ventral limbic and paralimbic structures, including the subgenual cingulate, the ventral medioposterior insula, the hippocampus, and the hypothalamus.

These observations suggest that metabolic changes occur during depression in cortico-striato-limbic systems and that remission is accompanied by restoration of the activation patterns occurring during depression. A potential explanation is that some of the observed microstructural abnormalities in cortico-striato-limbic networks interfere with the reciprocal regulation of dorsal cortical-ventral limbic structures and lead to a so-called disconnection syndrome associated with poor antidepressant response.

Research on Depression-Executive Dysfunction

Classical studies have demonstrated that the frontal lobes are connected with the basal ganglia through contiguous, nonoverlapping, parallel zones. Thus specific areas of the basal ganglia constitute domains for information from specific areas of the cortex. Five frontostriatal circuits with a similar basic structure have been described. Behavioral disturbances may occur after damage at any level of these pathways. The neurotransmitters of these circuits have been identified and include glutamate, GABA, and enkephalins, while dopamine and acetylcholine serve a modulating role. Assuming that predisposition to depression-executive dysfunction development is mediated by disturbances in one or more frontostriatal circuits, drugs enhancing the function of specific neurotransmitters of these circuits may have antidepressant action. Thus the depression-executive dysfunction can serve as a target for novel antidepressant interventions.

GEORGE S. ALEXOPOULOS

See also

Biological Models of Depression
Functional Neuroimaging
Geriatric Depression

References

Alexopoulos, G. S. (2001). The depression-executive dysfunction syndrome of late life: A specific target for D3 receptor agonists? *American Journal of Geriatric Psychiatry, 9*, 1–8.

Alexopoulos, G. S. (2005). Depression in the elderly. *Lancet, 365*, 1961–1970.

Alexopoulos, G. S., Kiosses, N., Heo, M., Murphy, C. F., Shanmugham, B., & Gunning-Dixon, F. (2005). Executive dysfunction and the course of geriatric depression. *Biological Psychiatry, 58*, 204–210.

Depressive Realism

Depressive realism is the idea that depressed individuals are actually more accurate in the processing of information than are nondepressed people. Such an idea contradicts an important component in many psychosocial models of depression, namely, that depressed people are actually prone to distort information in a negative way.

The idea of depressive realism stems from groundbreaking studies conducted by Lauren Alloy of Temple University and Lyn Abramson of the University of Wisconsin. A series of experiments they performed found that depressed college students showed evidence of more accurate information processing than did nondepressed control subjects (Alloy & Abramson, 1979, 1982). They suggested that depressed people were "sadder but wiser" and dubbed this phenomenon *depressive realism*. Moreover, they suggested that perhaps the distortion in information processing in depressed people is apparent only in comparison to nondepressed people who in fact distort their information processing in an unrealistically self-enhancing manner.

Summary

Subsequent research has shown that the depressive realism phenomenon may not be as robust as originally thought and may depend on the population studied; the finding seems less applicable to more seriously depressed people. At the very least it is clear that interactions between accurate information processing level and depression are determined by a complex set of factors that defy general conclusions (e.g., "depressed people process information accurately").

It may also be the case that cognitive distortion is evident based on what kinds of information are processed. If depressed individuals pay inordinate attention to negative information, but ignore positive information, then the overall effect of this process could be seen as distortion. Of course, the reverse might also be true for nondepressed people if they pay more attention to positive information, but less to negative. It may thus not be the case that depressed individuals do distort information and that nondepressed people do not, but rather that different groups evidence different kinds of cognitive biases.

RICK E. INGRAM

See also

Cognitive Distortion
Cognitive Reactivity
Cognitive Theories of Depression

References

Alloy, L. B., & Abramson, L. Y. (1979). Judgment of contingency in depressed and nondepressed college students: Sadder but wiser? *Journal of Experimental Psychology: General, 108*, 441–485.
Alloy, L. B., & Abramson, L. Y. (1982). Learned helplessness and the illusion of control. *Journal of Personality and Social Psychology, 42*, 1114–1126.

Depressogenesis

Two terms that are used frequently in the cognitive depression literature, but that apply to all theoretical domains, are *depressotypic* and *depressogenic*. Their semantic similarity and awkwardness have caused some confusion, particularly to individuals who are new to the field and to lay observers. Even some researchers inappropriately use the terms interchangeably. Yet they are different and

have potentially very different implications for theories of depression.

Depressotypic is the broader term and reflects any variable that is descriptive of depression. In the cognitive realm, an example of a depressotypic variable would be dysfunctional attitudes. Depressogenic, on the other hand, is a more specific term and refers to variables that play a casual role in depression; hence, they contribute somehow to the genesis of depression. Thus, to be depressogenic rather than depressotypic, dysfunction attitudes as an example, would need to contribute to the cause of depression.

As can be seen, the ramifications for a depression theory are substantial when a variable is depressotypic versus depressogenic. If a variable simply describes depression, then this is not informative about the causes of the disorder, whereas if the variable is depressogenic it has at least some relevance to the causes of depression. Of course, if a variable is depressogenic then it must also be depressotypic in that the variable that causes depression must also describe something about depression. In this sense, investigators can appropriately use these terms interchangeably if there is strong reason to believe that the variable is related to the causes of depression. On the other hand, a depressotypic variable may or may not be depressogenic, and lacking evidence of causality, then it is more accurate to refer to a variable as depressotypic.

RICK E. INGRAM

See also

Causality
Cognitive Theories of Depression
Risk
Vulnerability

Dermatology and Depression

The epidermis and central nervous system develop from the ectoderm of the trilaminar germ disc. It is therefore not surprising that depression occurs commonly in disorders of the skin. Indeed, psychiatric disorders among patients with skin diseases are frequent, with depressive illness accounting for 44% of referrals (Woodruff, Higgins, Du Vivier, & Wessely, 1997). We provide an overview of the links between dermatology and depression, covering the etiology and management of depression in the dermatological patient.

Etiology

There are several mechanisms that mediate the association between depression and dermatology.

Psychoneuroimmunodermatology: The Brain-Skin Axis

There is increasing evidence to support the notion that an inappropriate reactivity of the hypothalamic-pituitary-adrenal axis in its response to a stimulus may have an impact on an individual's defense against physical disease and severe and enduring psychological states. Studies of patients with psoriasis show hypocortisolic response to stress in those with comorbid depression and anxiety. The implication is that such patients may be primed to flares of their psoriasis.

Psychiatric Medication and Dermatology

Lithium is widely used for the prophylaxis and treatment of recurrent depression and bipolar affective disorder. Adverse effects tend to be directly related to plasma levels. Lithium aggravates or triggers cutaneous conditions that are characterized by the pathological findings of neutrophilic infiltration, in particular psoriasis and acne. Lithium use is not contraindicated in these patients, and a careful risk-benefit assessment may help to inform decisions regarding its use.

Lamotrigine is an anticonvulsant that is effective both as a treatment for bipolar depression and as prophylaxis against further episodes. Its use in treatment is complicated by the risk of developing a rash, which is associated with the speed of the dose titration. This is characterized by an exanthematous generalized rash that may lead to an exfoliative reaction and may involve mucous membranes. Fever, hepatitis with elevated liver enzymes, eosinophilia, and lymphadenopathy are systemic hallmarks of this syndrome. Although uncommon (1–10 cases per 10,000 exposures), this idiosyncratic drug reaction is potentially fatal.

Systemic Conditions Causing Depression and Skin Disorders

Systemic Lupus Erythematosus

Systemic lupus erythematosus (SLE) is a systemic autoimmune disease that primarily affects women of childbearing age. Prevalence rates for neuropsychiatric complications in SLE (including depressive and anxiety disorders) range from 15% to 75% (Kotzin & Kozora, 2001). Dermatological manifestations of SLE include a fixed erythematous malar rash and discoid rash (erythematous raised patches with adherent keratotic scaling). Corticosteroids are the mainstay of SLE management. Steroid use is associated with anxiety and mood symptoms. This represents another possible mechanism in the association of SLE with depression.

Human Immunodeficiency Virus

HIV is associated with a host of dermatological manifestations ranging from eczema to Kaposi's sarcoma. Furthermore HIV is a neurotrophic virus, with up to 85% of HIV-seropositive individuals reporting some depressive symptoms, and up to 50% experiencing a major depressive disorder (Stolar, Catalano, Hakala, Bright, & Fernandez, 2005). HIV should thus be considered as a differential diagnosis in patients presenting with both dermatological and depressive disorders.

Developmental Considerations

The onset of certain skin disorders, such as acne and psoriasis, during adolescence and young adulthood can have greater emotional impact in contrast to disease having a later onset. The effect of a skin disorder on body image should be assessed in the context of the patient's life and developmental stage, as adolescents and young adults may have greater difficulty adjusting to cosmetic problems imposed by skin disorders.

In the later stages of life, the cutaneous changes associated with photo damage and chronologic aging have important psychosocial implications, especially for women, socially and in the workplace.

Specific Dermatologic Disorders and Depression

Psoriasis

Psoriasis is a chronic inflammatory, currently incurable, skin disease affecting 2% to 3% of the population. Depressive symptoms in psoriasis may be primary or secondary to the impact of the disease on the quality of life of the patient. Studies investigating the prevalence of depression in patients with psoriasis have reported a range from 10% to 58%.

Pruritis is a particularly troublesome symptom of psoriasis. The severity of depression correlates with pruritis severity, and improvement in pruritis is associated with improvement in depression scores in psoriasis, suggesting that if depression is comorbid with pruritis, treatment of the depression may have a beneficial effect on the symptom of pruritis.

Acne

The topic of acne and depression needs to consider (a) the prevalence of depression and suicide among adolescents and young adults, and (b) the psychological impact of acne on depression, anxiety, and suicide.

Acne has a peak incidence during adolescence, a life stage when individuals are highly invested in their appearance and body image. Acne patients may experience problems with self-esteem, self-confidence, body image, social withdrawal, anxiety, and impaired social functioning, including poorer academic achievement, unemployment, and decreased dating and participation in sports.

Alopecia Areata

A survey of alopecia areata patients reports a 8.8% prevalence of major depression. Patients whose alopecia areata is exacerbated by stress also have higher depression scores, suggesting that comorbid depression may render the condition more stress reactive.

Atopic Dermatitis

Atopic dermatitis is a chronically relapsing skin disease characterized by dry and eczematous skin lesions, erythematosus papules, and intense pruritis. Moderate to severe atopic dermatitis in children attending school increases the risk for the development of psychological difficulties and can have a negative impact on social and academic development. Atopic patients report higher anxiety and depressive symptoms. Pruritis severity in atopic patients is correlated to severity of depressive symptoms.

Treatment

Selective serotonin reuptake inhibitors (SSRIs) are usually first-line options as they are better tolerated than tricyclic antidepressants. Choice of drug within this group is informed by individual patient factors (such as renal and liver functions, other medications being taken, agitated or retarded depression, and stated preference) and the drug profile in view of wanted and unwanted side effects.

Probably the only tricyclic antidepressant worth considering as a possible first-line antidepressant in dermatology is doxepin.

There also are two antidepressants with different mechanisms of action other than SSRIs that are worth keeping in mind when treating psychodermatologic patients who have depression: venlafaxine (Effexor) and bupropion (Wellbutrin).

Psychological Therapies

White (2001) has published a guide on the application of cognitive behavioral therapy (CBT) in the treatment of chronic medical problems such as skin conditions. Findings from controlled studies have shown that adjunctive CBT reduces psychological distress and clinical severity of the skin condition. Ehlers and colleagues employed CBT with patients with atopic dermatitis and found significant reductions in anxiety, frequency of scratching and itching, and cortisone use (Ehlers, Stangler, & Gieler, 1995).

Conclusions

The skin is the largest organ of the human body and shares its embryological origins with the central nervous system. Throughout life, the skin is important for social and sexual communication. Diseases of the skin and some of their treatments are associated with psychiatric disorders. Similarly, certain psychiatric disorders and their treatments present with dermatological manifestations. Multisystem infective or connective tissue disorders can present with both skin and psychiatric symptoms. The topic of depression and the skin is therefore relevant to the general practitioner, dermatologist, and mental health professional, who will often have to work together to provide comprehensive and effective management of patients.

SRNKA J. FLEGAR AND BAVANISHA VYTHILINGUM

See also

Comorbidity
Medical Conditions and Depression

References

Ehlers, A., Stangler, U., & Gieler, U. (1995). Treatment of atopic dermatitis: A comparison of psychological and dermatological approaches to relapse prevention. *Journal of Consulting and Clinical Psychology, 63,* 624–635.

Kotzin, B. L., & Kozora, E. (2001). Anti-DNA meets NMDA in neuropsychiatric lupus. *Nature Medicine, 7,* 1175–1176.

Stolar, A., Catalano, G., Hakala, M., Bright, R. P., & Fernandez, F. (2005). Mood disorders and psychosis in HIV. In K. Citron, M. J. Brouillette, & A. Beckett (Eds.), *HIV and psychiatry: A training resource manual* (Ch. 4). Cambridge, UK: Cambridge University Press.

White, C. A. (2001). *Cognitive behaviour therapy for chronic medical problems: A guide to assessment and treatment in practice.* West Sussex, UK: John Wiley & Sons.

Woodruff, P. W. R., Higgins, E. M., Du Vivier, A. W. P., & Wessely, S. (1997). Psychiatric illness in patients referred to a dermatology-psychiatry clinic. *General Hospital Psychiatry, 19,* 29–35.

Developmental Antecedents of Vulnerability

Vulnerability is defined as a relatively enduring, traitlike, possibly latent, characteristic that increases risk for a disorder. Theorists and researchers agree that vulnerability to depression is multifactorial and includes genetic, biological, psychological, and environmental risk factors. At the outset, it should be noted that the development of vulnerability to depression is a dynamic, transactional process that unfolds over time, and many of the factors implicated in the development of vulnerability to depression reciprocally influence each other. When examining the development of these vulnerabilities, the majority of theorists and researchers focus on childhood, during which time many of the vulnerabilities are hypothesized to exhibit the greatest plasticity. Given the significant role played by negative life events in contributing risk for depression, theories addressing vulnerability to depression tend to focus on factors that increase reactivity to environmental events.

According to cognitive models of depression (e.g., Abramson, Metalsky, & Alloy, 1989; Clark, Beck, & Alford, 1999), individuals' characteristic ways of attending to, interpreting, and remembering information may contribute vulnerability to depression. Although theorists suggest that various types of psychopathology are characterized by these *forms* of information-processing bias, the *content* of the biases is hypothesized to be disorder specific. In depression, the information-processing biases are hypothesized to be specific to themes of helplessness and loss. Cognitive theories provide vulnerability-stress models of depression risk because they suggest that these information-processing biases should contribute to the development of depression in the presence, but not absence, of negative life events, a hypothesis that has been supported in adults and children. Theorists (e.g., Clark et al., 1999; Rose & Abramson, 1992) have suggested that negative experiences in childhood may contribute to the development of a cognitive vulnerability to depression. To date, the majority of prospective research on the development of a cognitive vulnerability to depression has focused on individuals' attributional styles, or characteristic ways of interpreting the causes of negative events. In proposing a model for the development of these attributional styles, Rose and Abramson (1992) hypothesized that when negative events such as abuse occur in a child's life, the child initially makes hopefulness-maintaining explanations for the event's occurrence. With chronic and widespread abuse, however, these hopeful explanations are repeatedly disconfirmed, and the child may begin making more hopelessness-inducing explanations. Over time, these negative causal attributions may generalize to initially unrelated events and crystallize into a relatively stable cognitive vulnerability to depression. Supporting these hypotheses, research has suggested that causal attributions become more stable over the course of childhood, and there is evidence that negative events, particularly emotional abuse and verbal peer victimization, contribute to prospective changes in children's attributional styles (Abela & Hankin, 2008).

In terms of biological vulnerability, depression is known to be associated with dysregulation of the hypothalamic-pituitary-adrenal (HPA) axis. In normal functioning, a perceived stressor triggers the release of corticotropin releasing hormone (CRH) from the hypothalamus, which causes adrenocoricotropin to be released by the pituitary, causing glucocorticoids including cortisol to be synthesized and released by the adrenal cortex. HPA-axis reactivity to acute stressors is typically self-limiting, with cortisol downregulating production of CRH through a negative feedback loop. When stress is chronic, however, this negative feedback loop may be compromised, resulting in chronically elevated cortisol levels, heightened HPA-axis reactivity to new stressors, and hippocampal damage. These effects appear especially likely when chronic stress occurs early in life, and there is a growing body of research supporting the link between early negative life events, particularly childhood physical and sexual abuse, and dysregulation in HPA-axis functioning (for a review, see Harkness & Lumley, 2008). Thus, there is evidence that childhood abuse may contribute to the development of a biological vulnerability to depression in the form of heightened HPA-axis reactivity to future stress.

Finally, there is also growing evidence for specific genetic influences on the development of vulnerability to depression. Although the heritability of depression has long been recognized, the mechanisms by which genetic risk is conferred are just beginning to be uncovered. In terms of specific genetic risk factors for depression, the strongest evidence to date has been obtained for a functional polymorphism in the promoter region of the serotonin transporter gene (5-HTTLPR). There are two common variants in 5-HTTLPR, a short allele (S) and a long allele (L). Although more recent studies have suggested a triallelic variation (S, L_A, L_G), the majority of studies to date have focused on individuals carrying one or two copies of the short allele (SS or SL) versus those homozygous for the long allele (LL). There is increasing evidence that carriers of the short allele are more likely to develop depression following negative events than are individuals homozygous for the long allele, an effect that has been observed in both adults and children (Rutter, Moffitt, & Caspi, 2006). Although the precise mechanisms by which 5-HTTLPR increases risk in the presence of negative life events are not known, there is evidence that the 5-HTTLPR short allele is associated with greater amygdala activation to emotional stimuli (Munafò, Brown, & Hariri, 2008) as well as greater HPA-axis reactivity to stress (Gotlib, Joormann, Minor, & Hallmayer, 2008). More recently, research has suggested that individuals with one or two copies of the 5-HTTLPR short allele are more likely to exhibit a cognitive vulnerability to depression than are those who are homozygous for the long allele. Although preliminary, these findings suggest that 5-HTTLPR may play a role in the development of both biological and cognitive vulnerabilities to depression.

As noted above, the development of vulnerability to depression is a dynamic, transactional process that includes genetic, biological, psychological, and environmental influences. Researchers are beginning to understand how these multiple levels of influence may contribute to the development of a relatively traitlike vulnerability to depression. In combination, the research reviewed here suggests that negative events early in life may contribute to the development of both cognitive and biological vulnerabilities, which increase risk for depression by heightening reactivity to future stress. There is also growing evidence that a specific genetic risk factor—5-HTTLPR—is associated with heightened amygdala and HPA-axis reactivity and with the presence of a cognitive vulnerability to depression. More integrative research is still needed to determine how each of these factors may influence each other to predict prospective changes in vulnerability over time and to determine whether there are specific windows of heightened risk for the development of each form of vulnerability.

BRANDON E. GIBB

See also

Adolescent Depression
Childhood Depression
Cognitive Vulnerability
Risk
Vulnerability

References

Abela, J. R. Z., & Hankin, B. L. (2008). Cognitive vulnerability to depression in children and adolescents: A developmental psychopathology perspective. In J. R. Z. Abela & B. L. Hankin (Eds.), *Handbook of depression in children and adolescents* (pp. 35–78). New York: Guilford Press.

Abramson, L. Y., Metalsky, G. I., & Alloy, L. B. (1989). Hopelessness depression: A theory-based subtype of depression. *Psychological Review, 96*, 358–372.

Clark, D. A., Beck, A. T., & Alford, B. A. (1999). *Scientific foundations of cognitive theory and therapy of depression.* New York: Wiley.

Gotlib, I. H., Joormann, J., Minor, K. L., & Hallmayer, J. (2008). HPA axis reactivity: A mechanism underlying the associations among 5-HTTLPR, stress, and depression. *Biological Psychiatry, 63*, 847–851.

Harkness, K. L., & Lumley, M. N. (2008). Child abuse and neglect and the development of depression in children and adolescents. In J. R. Z. Abela & B. L. Hankin (Eds.), *Handbook of depression in children and adolescents* (pp. 466–488). New York: Guilford Press.

Munafò, M. R., Brown, S. M., & Hariri, A. R. (2008). Serotonin transporter (5-HTTLPR) genotype and amygdala activation: A meta-analysis. *Biological Psychiatry, 63*, 852–857.

Rose, D. T., & Abramson, L. Y. (1992). Developmental predictors of depressive cognitive style: Research and theory. In D. Cicchetti & S. L. Toth (Eds.), *Rochester symposium on developmental psychopathology, Vol. 4* (pp. 323–349). Hillsdale, NJ: Erlbaum.

Rutter, M., Moffitt, T. E., & Caspi, A. (2006). Gene-environment interplay and psychopathology: Multiple varieties but real effects. *Journal of Child Psychology and Psychiatry, 47*, 226–261.

Dexamethasone Suppression Test

The dexamethasone suppression test (DST) is a biomarker of melancholic or endogenous depression. This test is an outgrowth of the neuroendocrine research strategy in mood disorders. This strategy arose in the 1960s when it was appreciated that the limbic system sites that control mood and affective displays also modulate hypothalamically driven neuroendocrine activity, especially for the stress-responsive hormones. These brain regions include amygdala, hippocampus, orbital frontal cortex, and anterior cingulate cortex. Thus, patterns of dysregulated neuroendocrine activity may serve as proxy evidence of limbic system dysfunction in disordered mood states. Abnormal secretion patterns of the hormones in the hypothalamo-pituitary-adrenal (HPA) axis have been noted in mood disorders, and, conversely, clinical mood episodes commonly occur in some primary endocrine conditions in which central HPA-axis activity is increased, for example, secondary depression in Cushing disease and Addison disease. The main hormones implicated in HPA-axis (stress axis) function are corticotropin releasing hormone (CRH) and arginine vasopressin (AVP) released from the hypothalamus, adrenocorticotropic hormone (ACTH) released from the anterior pituitary gland, and cortisol released from the adrenal cortex.

The DST was first applied in clinical endocrinology. Several DST protocols were developed for the diagnostic workup of patients suspected of having cortisol overproduction syndromes. Dexamethasone is a synthetic corticosteroid drug that acts on glucocorticoid receptors (GR) in normal subjects to reduce the secretion of ACTH from the pituitary gland. Dexamethasone crosses the blood-brain barrier with difficulty, but when the drug is delivered into the brain it will also act on hypothalamic GR to reduce the secretion of CRH. AVP is comparatively resistant to suppression by dexamethasone. Low doses of dexamethasone suppress ACTH and cortisol production in normal subjects. Higher doses suppress these hormones in patients with ACTH-dependent Cushing disease, typically caused by a tumor of the anterior pituitary gland. For reasons having to do with the history of the laboratory assays, the clinically applied versions of the DST were standardized using plasma cortisol rather than plasma ACTH levels as the response measure. The higher doses of dexamethasone fail to suppress cortisol production in patients with adrenal tumors (these patients have ACTH-independent overproduction of cortisol, and their ACTH levels are already suppressed).

In the DST, the degree and duration of cortisol suppression depends on a balance among the amount of dexamethasone administered, its rate of clearance, its plasma half-life in a given subject, and the degree of that individual's hypothalamic drive on the HPA axis (reflecting primarily CRH and AVP secretion into the pituitary portal circulation). The most widely used low-dose protocol in mood disorders has been the administration of dexamethasone, 1 mg orally, at 11 p.m. or midnight, followed by plasma cortisol determinations at intervals over the following 24 hours. Early studies used 2-mg and 1.5-mg doses, but the compromise between sensitivity and specificity of the test is best with the 1.0-mg dose (Carroll et al., 1981). In 95% of normal individuals, plasma cortisol levels remain suppressed to low levels for the full 24 hours in response to this low-dose overnight DST protocol. In contrast, 40% to 70% of patients with major depression show cortisol nonsuppression or early escape from suppression (a positive DST) during the 24 hours following dexamethasone administration. This finding is taken to signify the degree of activation or "overdrive" of the HPA axis in the patient.

Positive DST results are found most often in patients with severe depression, especially those with psychotic features or melancholic features, and in cases of mixed bipolar disorder. When research diagnostic criteria are used, patients with the diagnosis endogenous depression have abnormal DSTs, whereas those with nonendogenous depression have a low rate of positive test results (Carroll et al., 1981; Rush et al., 1996). Longitudinal studies in rapidly cycling bipolar disorder show abnormal DST results during or slightly preceding the depressive phases and normal results in the manic phases.

Abnormal DST results are especially common in depressed patients who are incapacitated to the extent that they are unable to complete self-rated depression scales. Abnormal DST results have been reported in depressed children, and they are quite common in depressed adolescents. They are also common in the depressed elderly who have what is now termed vascular depression. Many studies suggest that only about 10%

of patients with depressive adjustment disorders, bereavement, and most other psychiatric illnesses show cortisol nonsuppression.

Abnormal DST results occur often in anorexia nervosa, and with intermediate frequency in demented and acutely psychotic patients. Certain drugs will produce false-positive DST results by accelerating the rate of dexamethasone metabolism and clearance. Valid testing is not possible if these drugs, such as carbamazepine or phenytoin, are continued. Major physiologic perturbations, especially those that cause release of AVP as well as CRH, also can cause the HPA axis to override low-dose dexamethasone suppression. Examples of these perturbations are acute stressful arousal, major surgery, electroconvulsive therapy, insulin-induced hypoglycemia, nausea and vomiting, alcohol withdrawal, dehydration-starvation ketosis, administration of CRH, and central cholinergic activation by physostigmine.

These examples clarify why patients should not be tested within the first few days after admission to hospital. These examples also clarify the occurrence of abnormal DSTs in acutely disturbed, psychotic patients with mania or schizophrenia or delirium. The frequency of abnormal DSTs falls markedly in such patients after 5 to 7 days in the hospital. In depressed patients, however, this hospitalization effect is minor. Similar disruptive effects of these physiologic perturbations are seen in other endocrine tests such as the glucose tolerance test.

In several early studies, low plasma dexamethasone levels did not appear to account for the abnormal DSTs found in depressed patients. Later evidence contradicted this view, and measurement of plasma dexamethasone levels is now recommended to confirm the validity of the test in individual patients. Plasma dexamethasone concentration windows have been proposed. Levels that are below the window are associated with false-positive DST results; levels that are above the window are associated with false-negative DST results. Because of this requirement, the DST now is seldom used in the routine clinical setting.

Soon after the standardized psychiatric DST protocol was introduced in 1981, psychiatrists began to use the DST as a screening test, rather than as an ancillary diagnostic test. The DST was used inappropriately as a marker in the *Diagnostic and Statistical Manual of Mental Disorders,* third edition (*DSM-III;* American Psychiatric Association, 1980), diagnosis "major depressive disorder," whereas it was developed primarily for the distinction of endogenous from nonendogenous major depressive disorder. This distinction had treatment implications: endogenous, DST-positive patients definitely required somatic antidepressant treatments, whereas nonendogenous, DST-negative patients did not necessarily require somatic treatments. The DST was never intended for the discrimination of major depressive disorder from the universe of nondepressive disorders. Its main value was as a confirmatory diagnostic test for "biologic" or endogenous or melancholic depressions. Even for this purpose, a negative DST result was never considered to override a clinical diagnosis of endogenous depression.

An abnormal DST is a state marker, not a trait marker of endogenous or biologic depressions. In one combined neuroendocrine-brain imaging study, resolution of depression was accompanied not only by HPA-axis normalization using a modified DST, but also by normalization of regional glucose metabolism in prefrontal cortical, limbic, and paralimbic regions. The most likely significance of an abnormal DST in depressed patients is that it signals limbic system noise in the emotion circuits associated with ongoing or developing depressive episodes. The DST is at best an indirect marker of disturbed limbic system activity in the brains of certain depressed patients, which may be the reason its sensitivity is rarely as high as 80% even in the most severe cases of psychotic depression and mixed bipolar disorder. There is no reason to think that the neuroendocrine disturbance is in any way etiologically responsible for the depressive episode. In repeated episodes of depression, consistent DST results are seen about 80% of the time. There are no systematic data on the heritability of DST results in mood disorder pedigrees.

With repeated testing, abnormal DST results usually convert to normal as patients improve (Carroll, Curtis, & Mendels, 1976). This conversion is a good prognostic sign. In the minority of patients who have persistently abnormal tests, even though they may show clinical improvement, early relapse is seen. This dissociation of DST status from active symptomatic status indicates that the neuroendocrine signal is not simply an epiphenomenon of psychological distress in depressed patients. That inference is confirmed also by the differential incidence of abnormal DSTs in endogenous versus nonendogenous depressions: both groups have very similar depressive symptom severity recorded by observer ratings and self ratings.

In patients with unipolar depression, an abnormal DST is associated with a large drug versus placebo response difference approximating 40%, whereas this difference is only about 10% in depressed patients with a normal DST (Brown, 2007). The corresponding numbers needed to treat are 2.5 and 10, respectively. These findings result from a low rate of response to placebo (about 20%) in patients with an abnormal DST, compared with a placebo response rate over 50% in depressed patients with a normal DST. The DST provides better discrimination of placebo responders and nonresponders than either clinically assessed depression subtype or depression severity. Similar differences appear to hold for response rates to psychotherapy alone in depressed patients: DST-positive patients do not do well with psychotherapy alone. Thus, the DST has the potential to maximize the efficacy signal in clinical trials of antidepressant treatments. Likewise, DST results can signal the homogeneity or heterogeneity of multicenter studies in depression: if the frequency of abnormal biomarker results varies widely among sites in multicenter studies, even though all centers use standard clinical diagnostic criteria, then this biological heterogeneity signals that dissimilar patients have been enrolled in different centers. Absent the biomarker, there would be no way to recognize this heterogeneity.

For longer-term prognosis, an abnormal DST during an index episode constitutes an approximately four- to eightfold risk factor for eventual suicide, for switch to bipolar disorder, and for rehospitalization after treatment of the index episode. The prediction of completed suicide by DST status appears strongest for inpatients with manifest suicidality. Death from all causes also is associated with DST status in the index depressive episode. On the other hand, the DST does not predict nonlethal suicidality, and it is not informative in nondepressed psychiatric populations at risk of suicide. The DST may be a more powerful predictor of completed suicide in depression than the customary clinical measures such as age, male sex, or past suicide attempts (Coryell & Schlesser, 2001). Notwithstanding the present desuetude of the DST in clinical practice, it remains a very informative biological marker and research tool in depression (Fink, 2005).

BERNARD J. CARROLL

See also

Biological Models of Depression
Cortisol
Hormones

References

American Psychiatric Association. (1980). *Diagnostic and statistical manual of mental disorders* (3rd ed.). Washington, DC: Author.

Brown, W. A. (2007). Treatment response in melancholia. *Acta Psychiatrica Scandinavica, 115 (Suppl 433),* 125–129.

Carroll, B. J., Curtis, G. C., & Mendels, J. (1976). Neuroendocrine regulation in depression. I: Limbic system-adrenal cortical dysfunction. *Archives of General Psychiatry, 33,* 1039–1044.

Carroll, B. J., Feinberg, M., Greden, J., Tarika, J., Albala, A. A., Haskett, R. F., et al. (1981). A specific laboratory test for the diagnosis of melancholia: Standardization, validation and clinical utility. *Archives of General Psychiatry, 38,* 15–22.

Coryell, W., & Schlesser, M. (2001). The dexamethasone suppression test and suicide prediction. *American Journal of Psychiatry, 158,* 748–753.

Fink, M. (2005). Should the dexamethasone suppression test be resurrected? *Acta Psychiatrica Scandinavica, 112,* 245–249.

Rush, A. J., Giles, D. E., Schlesser, M. A., Orsulak, P. J., Parker, C. R., Jr., Weissenburger, J. E., et al. (1996). The dexamethasone suppression test in patients with mood disorders. *Journal of Clinical Psychiatry, 57,* 470–484.

Diagnostic and Statistical Manual of Mental Disorders

The *Diagnostic and Statistical Manual of Mental Disorders* (DSM) is the classification of psychopathology developed under the authority of the American Psychiatric Association (APA). The current version of this diagnostic manual is *DSM-IV-TR* (APA, 2000), standing for the fourth edition, text revision (Frances, First, & Pincus, 1995). Included within are the diagnostic criteria for major depressive disorder and dysthymia, along with social phobia, nicotine dependence, schizophrenia, mental retardation, attention deficit hyperactivity disorder, mathematics disorder, stuttering, dissociative identity disorder, borderline personality disorder, narcissistic personality disorder, pathological gambling, frotteurism, nightmare disorder, and many other disorders.

Confusion reigned prior to its first edition (Salmon, Copp, May, Abot, & Cotton, 1917). Each major medical center had its own set of diagnoses. Even if two clinicians were using the same diagnosis, they might still differ substantially in the symptoms that guided their provision of this diagnosis. It was very difficult under these conditions for patients to receive a consistent diagnosis and for scientific research to accumulate.

However, as a common language of communication, *DSM-IV-TR* is a very powerful document. It provides the authoritative statement of the APA as to when particular behaviors, thoughts, or feelings are considered to be a mental disorder. Many important social, forensic, clinical, and other professional decisions are significantly impacted by this diagnostic manual, from deciding whether coverage will be provided for the treatment of a condition to mitigating criminal responsibility for the commission of an illegal act.

Persons think in terms of their language, and the predominant language of psychopathology is *DSM-IV-TR*, but *DSM-IV-TR* is not the final word. Work is in fact underway toward the development of *DSM-V*. Briefly discussed herein will be the definition of mental disorder, the threshold for diagnosis, and the categorical model of classification.

Definition of Mental Disorder

DSM-IV-TR includes a rather lengthy and cumbersome operational definition of mental disorder, originally developed to help resolve the controversy over the diagnostic status of homosexuality. Wakefield (2007) has provided quite thorough and compelling critiques of this definition, offering as an alternative his own *harmful dysfunction* conceptualization. Dysfunction is a failure of an internal mechanism to perform a naturally selected function as developed through evolution, and harm is a value judgment that the design failure is harmful to the individual.

Wakefield's harmful dysfunction definition has drawn considerable attention but has also received a number of compelling criticisms. One fundamental limitation is its conjoining with evolutionary theory, thereby limiting its relevance and usefulness to cognitive-behavioral, social-interpersonal, psychodynamic, and even neurochemical models of etiology and pathology that concern more proximate dysfunctions (McNally, 2001). In addition, it would be difficult for the authors of a diagnostic manual to effectively use harmful dysfunction as a basis for determining when something is a mental disorder, as the precise "intentions" of the ongoing process of evolution are not particularly obvious.

Missing from Wakefield's (2007) conceptualization is any reference to dyscontrol. Mental disorders are perhaps better understood as dyscontrolled impairments in psychological functioning (Widiger & Sankis, 2000). The concept of a mental disorder implies the presence of impairments to feelings, thoughts, or behaviors over which a normal (healthy) person is considered to have adequate control. To the extent that a person willfully, intentionally, freely, or voluntarily engages in harmful sexual acts, drug usage, gambling, or child abuse, the person would not be considered to have a mental disorder. It is when the person effectively loses control of these behaviors, and experiences clinically significant impairment, that a diagnosis of mental disorder becomes warranted.

Threshold for Diagnosis

One of the fundamental purposes of a diagnostic manual is demarcating the boundary between normal and abnormal psychological functioning. Most everyone will at some point have feelings of sadness and depression. At what point would these feelings become a mental disorder?

The *DSM-IV-TR* criterion set for major depressive disorder currently excludes most instances of depressive reactions to the loss of a loved one (i.e., uncomplicated bereavement). Depression after the loss of a loved one can be considered a mental disorder if "the symptoms persist for longer than two months" (APA, 2000, p. 356). Allowing only two months to grieve, though, is perceived by some as a rather arbitrary basis for determining when normal sadness becomes a mental illness. In addition, there are many other losses that lead to depressed mood (e.g., loss of job or physical health), yet these do not warrant a comparable reprieve from becoming classified as a mental illness (Wakefield, Schimtz, First, & Horwitz, 2007).

Wakefield and First (2002) have argued that the distinction between disordered and nondisordered behavior should require an assessment for the presence an underlying, internal pathology (e.g., irrational cognitive schema or neurochemical dysregulation), and not simply be based on the amount of time or impairment is associated with the depression. However, a limitation of diagnosing a disorder on the basis of pathology is the absence of agreement over the specific pathology that underlies any particular disorder. There is insufficient empirical support to prefer one particular cognitive, interpersonal,

neurochemical, or psychodynamic model of pathology relative to another.

The concern that the nomenclature is subsuming normal problems in living may itself be misguided. Persons critical of the *DSM* have decried its substantial expansion over the past 50 years. However, perhaps it would have been more surprising to find that scientific research and increased knowledge have failed to lead to the recognition of more instances of psychopathology. In fact, the current manual might still be inadequate in coverage. The most common diagnosis in general clinical practice is often *not otherwise specified* (NOS). The diagnosis of mood disorder NOS is provided when a clinician determines that a mood disorder is present (e.g., recurrent brief depressive disorder, minor depressive disorder, mixed anxiety-depressive disorder, or premenstrual dysphoric disorder), but the symptomatology fails to meet criteria for a major depressive disorder or dysthymia (APA, 2000). The frequency with which clinicians provide the diagnosis of NOS for mood disorders is a testament to inadequate coverage. Perhaps the problem is not that depression in response to a loss of a job or physical disorder should not be a disorder, analogous to bereavement (Wakefield, 2007); perhaps the problem is that bereavement should be a mental disorder when the depression is both impairing and dyscontrolled (Widiger & Sankis, 2000).

Categorical Model of Classification

"*DSM-IV* is a categorical classification that divides mental disorders into types based on criterion sets with defining features" (APA, 2000, p. xxxi). The intention of the diagnostic manual is to help the clinician determine which particular disorder is present, the diagnosis of which would purportedly indicate the presence of a specific pathology that would explain the occurrence of the symptoms and suggest a specific treatment that would ameliorate the patient's suffering (Frances et al., 1995). However, as expressed by the chair (Dr. Kupfer) and vice chair (Dr. Regier) of the forthcoming *DSM-V*, the classification system has not been particularly successful in meeting this goal (Kupfer, First, & Regier, 2002).

The existing diagnostic nomenclature does not appear to be identifying qualitatively distinct conditions. Most mental disorders appear to be the result of a complex interaction of an array of interacting biological vulnerabilities and dispositions with environmental and psychosocial events. The symptoms and pathologies of mental disorders appear to be highly responsive to a wide variety of neurochemical, interpersonal, cognitive, environmental, and other mediating and moderating variables that help to develop, shape, and form a particular individual's psychopathology profile. This complex etiological history and individual psychopathology profile are unlikely to be well described by a single diagnostic category that attempts to make distinctions at nonexistent discrete joints (Widiger & Samuel, 2005).

Conclusions

Nobody is fully satisfied with, or lacks valid criticisms of, *DSM-IV-TR*. Clinicians, theorists, and researchers will at times feel frustrated at being required to use *DSM-IV-TR*. It can be difficult to obtain a grant, publish a study, or receive insurance reimbursement without reference to a *DSM-IV-TR* diagnosis. The benefits of an official diagnostic nomenclature, though, do appear to outweigh the costs. Despite its significant flaws, *DSM-IV-TR* does at least provide a useful point of comparison that ultimately facilitates the development of new ways of conceptualizing and diagnosing psychopathology.

THOMAS A. WIDIGER

See also

Categorical and Dimensional Models of Depression
Classification of Depression
Definition of Depression
Symptoms of Depression

References

American Psychiatric Association. (2000). *Diagnostic and statistical manual of mental disorders* (4th ed., text revision). Washington, DC: Author.

Frances, A. J., First, M. B., & Pincus, H. A. (1995). *DSM-IV guidebook*. Washington, DC: American Psychiatric Press.

Kupfer, D. J., First, M. B., & Regier, D. A. (Eds.). (2002). *A research agenda for DSM-V*. Washington, DC: American Psychiatric Association.

McNally, R. J. (2001). On Wakefield's harmful dysfunction analysis of mental disorder. *Behaviour Research and Therapy, 39*, 309–314.

Salmon, T. W., Copp, O., May, J. V., Abbot, E. S., & Cotton, H. A. (1917). Report of the committee on statistics of the American Medico-Psychological Association. *American Journal of Insanity, 74*, 255–260.

Wakefield, J. C. (2007). The concept of mental disorder: Diagnostic implications of the harmful dysfunction analysis. *World Psychiatry, 6*, 149–156.

Wakefield, J. C., & First, M. B. (2002). Clarifying the distinction between disorder and nondisorder: Confronting the overdiagnosis (false positives) problem in *DSM-V*. In K. A. Phillips, M. B. First, & H. A. Pincus (Eds.), *Advancing DSM: Dilemmas in psychiatric diagnosis* (pp. 23–55). Washington, DC: American Psychiatric Association.

Wakefield, J. C., Schmitz, M. F., First, M. B., & Horwitz, A. V. (2007). Extending the bereavement exclusion for major depression to other losses: Evidence from the National Comorbidity Survey. *Archives of General Psychiatry, 64*, 433–440.

Widiger, T. A., & Samuel, D. B. (2005). Diagnostic categories or dimensions: A question for *DSM-V. Journal of Abnormal Psychology, 114*, 494–504.

Widiger, T. A., & Sankis, L. M. (2000). Adult psychopathology: Issues and controversies. *Annual Review of Psychology, 51*, 377–404.

Diatheses-Stress Models of Depression

Depression is one of the most commonly occurring of all the major psychiatric disorders. It has been rated as one of the leading causes of disability, burden, and morbidity, as it has profound effects on individuals' emotions, thoughts, behaviors, relationships, work, sense of self, physical functioning, biology, and life satisfaction. Given the clear public health importance of depression, significant research into the causes of depression has been conducted. Despite a substantial theoretical and empirical research literature, however, that has investigated etiologies of depression from various independent perspectives, including genetic, biological, emotional, interpersonal, cognitive, personality, and life stress perspectives, the precise underlying mechanisms and processes that contribute to the development of depression have remained elusive. Rather than studying the possible etiologies and developmental pathways to depression from disparate and independent, potentially competing perspectives (e.g., genetic versus interpersonal influences), a framework that incorporates vulnerabilities (we use the term *vulnerability* to mean the same thing that others have labeled as *diathesis*) along with stressful life events may prove more powerful in explaining why individuals are prone to exhibit elevated depressive symptoms or develop depressive episodes. The primary goals of this entry are to articulate the rationale why the vulnerability-stress model may provide additional explanatory power beyond a focus on either vulnerability or environmental stressors alone, to provide an overview of vulnerability-stress models to depression, and to review a couple of empirical examples of research investigating vulnerability-stress models.

Why a Diathesis-Stress Perspective?

A primary reason that a diathesis-stress model of depression has proven useful relates to the role that stressful life events, by themselves, play as predictors of future depression. The vast majority of individuals with a depressive episode have experienced at least one significant stressor in the month prior to their depressive disorder onset. At the same time, the majority of individuals who encounter at least one significant stressor do not progress to develop a depressive disorder. In fact, only between 20% and 50% of individuals who have experienced a severe stressful life event become clinically depressed. Thus, it appears that there is something about certain individuals that makes them particularly sensitive to the deleterious impact of negative events on depression. Hence, research examining the relations between life events and depression must include a focus on vulnerability factors to increase explanatory power.

A singular and exclusive focus on vulnerabilities, however, without considering the role of stressors, is likely to prove as equally ineffective in unearthing the causes of depression as an exclusive focus on life events. Indeed, of the vulnerabilities that have received the most empirical attention, such as genetic influences, cognitive factors, interpersonal factors, and personality and temperament traits, no single vulnerability factor has been able to, as a main effect, account for more than half of the variance in predicting future depressive symptoms (Hankin & Abela, 2005).

In sum, neither stressful life events nor vulnerabilities by themselves are necessary or sufficient for the development of depression. Therefore, including a single vulnerability, or multiple integrated vulnerabilities, in interaction with negative life events into an overarching vulnerability-stress model has been advanced as a framework for improving the predictive and explanatory power of models of the causes of depression. Next, an overview of the different ways in which vulnerability-stress models have been conceptualized is provided.

Types of Diathesis-Stress Models

Numerous formal models conceptualize and combine vulnerability and stress (Ingram & Luxton, 2005). First, an additive model represents the basic, linear association such that the likelihood that depression occurs depends upon the additive contribution of the effects of stress and the vulnerability loading. Second, an ipsative approach reflects an inverse relationship between vulnerability and stressors, such that less of one factor (e.g., negative events) the more of the other factor (e.g., the vulnerability) is needed to precipitate depression. Third, the traditional, or mega, vulnerability-stress model supposes that both the vulnerability and negative life event are needed for depression to develop. In this model, higher levels of stress combined with a greater dose of the vulnerability contribute to onset of depression.

Within these three broad conceptualizations and structures, there are additional, more-refined models that can be considered (Ingram & Luxton, 2005). First is the interactive model with dichotomous vulnerabilities, in which an individual either has or does not have the vulnerability. For a person with the vulnerability, the individual is hypothesized to develop depression in the face of stress. In contrast, an individual without the vulnerability will not become depressed regardless of the stress level he or she faces. Second is the quasi-continuous vulnerability model. Unlike the prior model, individuals are proposed to vary in their degree of vulnerability and their degree of stressor exposure. The likelihood of developing depression becomes stronger as a function of increases in both stress and vulnerability level. Third, the threshold model specifies that there is a synergistic relation between vulnerability and stress that is greater than their combined main effects. In addition, each person has a particular threshold at which he or she is likely to become depressed, and this individual difference in threshold is defined by the synergism of vulnerability and stress combined. Finally, risk-resilience models postulate that people possess protective factors—resiliencies, strengths, and competencies—as well as varying degrees of vulnerability. There is likely a continuum ranging from most invulnerable to most vulnerable across the population, and this distributed degree of vulnerability across individuals can interact with the varying amount of stress that people experience in their lives. A strength of this model is that it suggests that the severity of one's depression may be contingent upon one's level of invulnerability-vulnerability, such that a very resilient person may experience low levels of depressive symptoms under very high levels of stress.

In addition to these general principles of vulnerability-stress models (i.e., additive, ipsative, or traditional vulnerability-stress) and the particular kinds of vulnerability-stress models just reviewed (see Ingram & Luxton, 2005), there are other important issues to consider in conceptualizing vulnerability-stress models. First, most theories that contain a vulnerability-stress component implicitly assume, or explicitly specify, only one particular vulnerability (e.g., genetic, interpersonal, cognitive). It is clearly possible, however, that individuals have multiple vulnerabilities, and given this perspective, there are many ways to conceptualize how multiple vulnerabilities interact with stressful life events (Abela & Hankin, 2008). First, one approach is to add up the vulnerabilities into an overall risk loading, and this overall or additive vulnerability would interact with stressors to contribute to depression. Second, there could be higher-order interactions among the various vulnerabilities and stressors (e.g., genetic × cognitive × stress interaction). Third, the weakest-link approach hypothesizes that an individual may have multiple vulnerabilities that vary in magnitude, but that the most negative vulnerability is the determinant of an individual's degree of risk. For example, for an individual with low genetic risk, low temperamental risk, and high cognitive risk, the cognitive vulnerability would be considered the weakest link and would be the factor most likely to interact with stressful events to contribute to depression. Overall, these different structural conceptualizations of vulnerability-stress models make different predictions concerning the factors that would contribute to depression and the processes by which an individual would be hypothesized to become depressed.

A second important issue to consider is that most of these approaches presume that the vulnerability is an enduring, traitlike feature of the individual, and for several vulnerabilities this may be a perfectly reasonable assumption (e.g., DNA for genetic vulnerability does not change over time). For many psychosocial vulnerabilities (e.g., cognitive, interpersonal, personality), however, this is an assumption that has rarely been tested (but see Hankin, 2008; Hankin, Fraley, & Abela, 2005). Indeed, just as one's personality traits are not "fixed like plaster" from birth, it is likely that many of the psychosocial vulnerabilities are both somewhat stable and enduring but also exhibit some change, especially across childhood and early adolescence (e.g., Hankin, in press). The likely dynamic, nonstatic nature of these psychosocial vulnerabilities is captured by the vulnerability-transactional stress model (e.g., Hankin & Abramson, 2001), which is consistent with a developmental psychopathology approach. This conceptual model seeks to capture this dialectic of both stability and change in vulnerabilities over time by proposing that there is a dynamic, reciprocal, transactional set of relationships among vulnerabilities, life experiences, and depressive symptoms across development. In addition to explicitly positing that different psychosocial vulnerabilities may exhibit both stability and change over time, consistent with a transactional perspective, this model hypothesizes that various influences such as stressful life events, depressive symptoms, interpersonal relationships (e.g., parents, peers, romantic partners), temperament, genetics, and other factors may affect the development, consolidation, and stabilization of one's vulnerability level for different depression risks. As such, the vulnerability-transactional stress model is a dynamic, not a static, approach that seeks to understand and explain the developmental origins and trajectories of psychosocial vulnerabilities, as well as the degree of stability in these vulnerabilities over time.

Examples of Specific Diathesis-Stress Models and Associated Findings

Having covered some of the important structural and conceptual issues pertaining to vulnerability-stress models to depression, we now turn to two particular examples of vulnerability-stress models of depression that have garnered considerable theoretical and empirical attention. Examples of genetic vulnerability-stress and cognitive vulnerability-stress models are both described, and the empirical evidence supporting the utility and predictive power of these models is provided. These empirical illustrations make clear two points. First, the vulnerability-stress model is likely more powerful in understanding the etiology of depression than

is any particular vulnerability (e.g., genetics, cognitive risk) or stressors alone. Second, the specific form that the vulnerability-stress interaction takes is not always consistent across studies. Consequently, the pattern of the vulnerability-stress interaction observed across studies can be interpreted differently and be consistent with varying types of vulnerability-stress conceptual models (e.g., traditional mega vulnerability-stress or ipsative models). Thus, these recent empirical examples convey the importance of clearly identifying and understanding the various structures and forms that the vulnerability-stress model can take.

Genetic vulnerabilities, such as individual differences in specific candidate genes (e.g., allelic variation in the serotonin transporter gene 5-HTTLPR, typically the short allele), have been studied as a diathesis that may interact with the occurrence of stressful life events to predict individuals' propensity to experience depression. A bevy of studies has examined this genetic vulnerability by stress interaction for different candidate genes and different environmental stressors, and presently the evidence provides support for the genetic vulnerability-stress model predicting future risk for depression. Additionally, these studies show that the main effect of genetic risk typically does not predict depression, and the interaction of genetic vulnerability with stressors contributes to risk for future depression more than the main effect of stressful environments alone.

Finally, although the evidence clearly supports the predictive power of the genetic vulnerability-stress hypothesis, the specific form that the gene by stress interaction takes can differ across studies and, as a result, can be used to support different conceptual vulnerability-stress models. For example, Caspi and colleagues (2003) studied allelic variation in 5-HHTLPR gene interacting with self-reported major stressors to predict onset of clinical depression over 5 years and found evidence that conformed to the traditional, mega vulnerability-stress model: individuals with the short version of 5-HTTLPR who experienced more major negative life events were the most likely to be diagnosed with clinical depression. In contrast, Kendler, Kuhn, Vittum, Prescott, and Riley (2005) examined the same genetic risk (5-HHTLPR) in interaction with negative events, assessed via a stress interview, and found evidence consistent with the ipsative model: individuals with the short version of 5-HTTLPR who experienced more minor (but not major) stressors were the most likely to develop depression. Most studies have found data consistent with the traditional, mega vulnerability-stress model and Caspi and colleagues (2003) work, but the different set of results conforming to varying structural conceptual models of the vulnerability-stress model highlight the importance of clearly specifying which of the different vulnerability-stress models is being tested and the a priori rationale for evaluating each particular model.

Cognitive vulnerability theories of depression typically posit a vulnerability-stress component. According to one prominent theory, the hopelessness theory of depression (Abramson, Metalsky, & Alloy, 1989), individuals who tend to attribute negative events to global and stable causes, to catastrophize the consequences of the event, and to make negative inferences about their self after experiencing stressors are the most likely to develop depression. Numerous studies with adults and youths have investigated this cognitive vulnerability-stress hypothesis and have found supportive evidence for predicting future increases in depression. Despite the strong evidence base generally supporting this and other cognitive theories of depression, results from specific studies again illustrate that the specific form that the cognitive vulnerability-stress interaction takes can vary and can be interpreted to support different conceptualizations of vulnerability-stress models. For example, a 2-year longitudinal study showed that individuals with high levels of cognitive vulnerability who reported more stressful events over time were the most likely to be diagnosed with an episode of clinical depression across the 2-year follow-up (Hankin, Abramson,

Miller, & Haeffel, 2004). A similar pattern of results was recently found in a 2-year follow-up of a sample of early adolescents. The results from these studies, and indeed most investigations, are consistent with the traditional, mega vulnerability-stress model. However, a 1-year longitudinal study of high school adolescents found that individuals with depression were most likely when individuals experienced high levels of stress, regardless of cognitive vulnerability levels; yet, under low stress conditions, those youths with higher cognitive vulnerability were more likely to become depressed than youths with low cognitive vulnerability. This pattern of results is most consistent with the ipsative model.

Finally, in most studies examining the cognitive vulnerability-stress hypothesis, the particular types of cognitive vulnerabilities (e.g., negative inferences for causes, consequences, and self-implications) are averaged together to form an overall cognitive vulnerability composite. However, as the weakest-link model suggests, the different cognitive vulnerability profiles can be disaggregated and investigated separately in interaction with stressors to predict depression. Research (e.g., Abela & Sarin, 2002; Gibb et al., 2006) that has followed the weakest link approach has provided support for this conceptualization of the vulnerability-stress model underlying how cognitive risks interact with stressors to contribute to depression.

Conclusions

In sum, there are many theoretical frameworks to conceptualizing the general vulnerability-stress model, and these different approaches are not necessarily interchangeable and may be considered competing approaches which is the best model for understanding the etiology of depression. By clearly specifying theoretically and testing empirically the different forms and structures that the vulnerability-stress model can take (e.g., general mega vulnerability-stress model or ipsative model; weakest-link model or additive model), enhanced progress in understanding the etiological processes contributing to the development of depression can be made.

BENJAMIN L. HANKIN AND JOHN R. Z. ABELA

See also

Cognitive Theories of Depression
Cognitive Vulnerability
Risk
Vulnerability

References

Abela, J. R. Z., & Hankin, B. L. (2008). Cognitive vulnerability to depression in children and adolescents: A developmental psychopathology approach. In J. R. Z. Abela & B. L. Hankin (Eds.), *Handbook of depression in children and adolescents* (pp. 35–78). New York: Guilford Press.

Abela, J. R. Z., & Sarin, S. (2002). Cognitive vulnerability to hopelessness depression: A chain is only as strong as its weakest link. *Cognitive Therapy and Research, 26,* 811–829.

Abramson, L. Y, Metalsky, G. I., & Alloy, L. B. (1989). Hopelessness depression: A theory-based subtype of depression. *Psychological Review, 96,* 358–372.

Caspi, A., Sugden, K., Moffit, T. E., Taylor, A., Craig, I. W., & Harrington, H. (2003). Influence of life stress on depression: Moderation by a polymorphism in the 5-HTT gene. *Science, 301,* 386–389.

Gibb, B. E., Beevers, C. G., & Andover, M. S. (2006). The hopelessness theory of depression: A prospective multiwave test of the vulnerability-stress hypothesis. *Cognitive Therapy and Research, 30,* 763–772.

Hankin, B. L. (2008). Stability of cognitive vulnerabilities to depression: A short-term prospective multi-wave study. *Journal of Abnormal Psychology, 117,* 324–333.

Hankin, B. L., & Abela, J. R. Z. (2005). Depression from childhood through adolescence and adulthood: A developmental vulnerability-stress perspective. In B. L. Hankin & J. R. Z. Abela (Eds.), *Development of psychopathology: A vulnerability-stress perspective* (pp. 245–288). Thousand Oaks, CA: Sage Publications.

Hankin, B. L., & Abramson, L. Y. (2001). Development of gender differences in depression: An elaborated cognitive vulnerability-transactional stress theory. *Psychological Bulletin, 127,* 773–796.

Hankin, B. L., Abramson, L. Y., Miller, N., & Haeffel, G. J. (2004). Cognitive vulnerability-stress theories of depression: Examining affective specificity in the prediction of depression versus anxiety in three prospective studies. *Cognitive Therapy and Research, 28,* 309–345.

Hankin, B. L., Fraley, R. C., & Abela, J. R. Z. (2005). Daily depression and cognitions about stress: Evidence for a trait-like depressogenic cognitive style and the prediction of depressive symptoms trajectories in a prospective daily diary study. *Journal of Personality and Social Psychology, 88,* 673–685.

Ingram, R. E., & Luxton, D. D. (2005). Vulnerability-stress models. In B. L. Hankin and J. R. Z. Abela (Eds.), *Development of psychopathology: A vulnerability-stress perspective* (pp. 32–46). Thousand Oaks, CA: Sage Publications.

Kendler, K. S. Kuhn, J. W., Vittum, J., Prescott, C. A., & Riley, B. (2005). The interaction of stressful life events and a serotonin transporter polymorphism in the prediction of episodes of major depression. *Archives of General Psychiatry, 62,* 529–535.

Differential Activation

A key component of Beck's classic cognitive model of depression (see Beck, 2005) is the close reciprocal association between depressed mood, emotionally negative mental content, and a repertoire of cognitive processes that prioritize the processing of emotionally negative information. These cognitive-affective interactions are proposed to operate with vicious circularity such that exacerbation of depressed mood enhances the accessibility of negative mental content and primes negative processing biases, which in turn further augment the depressed mood (Teasdale, 1983). There is a wealth of empirical evidence to support these contentions in individuals currently suffering from depression (see Williams, Watts, MacLeod, & Mathews, 1997, for a review). However, Beck's classic cognitive model also supposes that such enhanced negativity of cognitive content and process will characterize currently nondepressed individuals who are nevertheless known to be *vulnerable* to depression (for example, they may have had several previous episodes), and indeed it is this cognitive signature that to a large extent is thought to confer their vulnerability. In contrast to the reliable findings involving currently depressed samples, empirical support for such cognitive differentiation along the lines of depression vulnerability in those who are not currently depressed has proved recurrently elusive. For example, previously depressed individuals (who are thus known to be vulnerable to future episodes) report levels of negative thoughts and beliefs that, to all intents and purposes, are indistinguishable from those who have never been depressed (and who are presumably less vulnerable). Similarly, cognitive processing biases such as mood-congruent memory that characterize those in a depressive episode appear to be largely absent in nondepressed vulnerable samples (Teasdale & Dent, 1987). How can this be? Is it the case that the negative cognitive content and process associated with depression develop as a result of the onset of a depressive episode and do not therefore contribute to vulnerability to such onset? Or is there some other means by which this cognitive profile confers vulnerability to depression?

A compelling answer to these questions was provided by Teasdale (1988) in his differential activation hypothesis (DAH). The DAH assumes that during early episodes of depression the close associations between depressed mood and the negative cognitive content and processing biases described above become established. When the individual recovers from depression, this negative cognitive profile becomes quiescent. However, by virtue of the close association between this profile and depressed mood in depression-vulnerable individuals, any subsequent downturn in mood has the capacity to activate the negative cognitions and processes again—what the DAH terms *cognitive reactivity*. In other words, downward fluctuations in mood differentially activate cognitive material in vulnerable versus nonvulnerable individuals. For the vulnerable, the toxic vicious circle of depressed mood exacerbating negative cognizing that, in turn, augments depressed mood, comes into play, and there is a risk of onset of a full depressive episode. For the less vulnerable, this cognitive-affective baggage from previous episodes of depression is absent, and downturns in mood consequently present far less of a threat. This intimate relationship between mood and negative cognition that characterizes those vulnerable to depression, the DAH proposes, becomes further consolidated with each additional depressive episode such that the necessary downturns in negative mood required to precipitate episode onset become progressively less severe.

Empirical support for the DAH to date is impressive (for a review, see Scher, Ingram, & Segal, 2005). Laboratory studies demonstrate that, although as noted above, recovered depressed patients and never-depressed controls do not differ on self-report of negative cognitions (e.g., "If I fail at my work, then I am a failure as a person") in neutral mood, following a sad mood induction designed to bring about differential activation, recovered depressed patients report elevated levels of such cognitions compared to controls (Miranda & Persons, 1988). Similar mood-related enhancements in cognitive reactivity in depression-vulnerable individuals exposed to a sad mood induction have also been demonstrated on non-self-report measures such as the encoding and retrieval of negative information. For example, Teasdale and Dent (1987) asked recovered-depressed and never-depressed participants, with or without a sad mood induction, to read a list of positive and negative trait adjectives, including global negative trait adjectives such as *stupid, pathetic,* and *worthless.* Participants had to indicate which adjectives described them and which did not. Subsequently, participants were given a surprise recall memory test. The rationale was that degree of recall of negative trait adjectives previously rated as self-descriptive would be an index of activation of those concepts. The results showed that formerly depressed and never-depressed groups did not differ on this activation index while in neutral mood. However, following a sad mood induction, the formerly depressed group recalled significantly more self-referred negative words relative to the never-depressed controls. This therefore suggests differential activation of negative self-concepts in the recovered-depressed group in tandem with the downturn in depressed mood following the induction. Similar demonstrations have been provided in other cognitive domains, for instance, capture of attention by negative material on a dichotic listening task (Ingram, Bernet, & McLaughlin, 1994) and associations between the self and negative cognitive content on the Implicit Association Test (Gemar, Segal, Sagrati, & Kennedy, 2001).

A further important validation of the DAH comes from studies examining the relationship between activation of dysfunctional cognitions following a mood induction and later depressive relapse in formerly depressed patients, in other words, studies assessing whether greater cognitive activation does indeed confer greater vulnerability. In two separate studies, Segal and colleagues (2006) asked patients who had recovered from depression, either through cognitive behavior therapy or with antidepressants, to complete self-reported ratings of depressive cognitions before and after a sad mood induction. In line with the predictions of the DAH, the results showed that the degree of increase in endorsement of negative cognitions following the mood induction, irrespective of type of treatment, independently predicted increased probability of depressive relapse.

Finally, there is support for the DAH's prediction of increasing consolidation of the association between negative cognition and depressed mood with each recurrence of depression. Specifically, whereas initial depressive episodes are typically precipitated by negative life events, the relationship between environmental stressors and depression progressively diminishes with recurrent episodes—a process referred to as *kindling* (Kendler, Thornton, & Gardner, 2000)—presumably to some extent reflecting the greater ease with which cognitive reactivity occurs as a function of downturns in depressed mood.

In summary, the DAH is an elegant theoretical proposal that accounts for why the negative cognitive content and processes associated with depression confer vulnerability to the disorder even when individuals are not in a depressed state. The theory is supported by an impressive magnitude and variety of clinical, self-report, and experimental data.

TIM DALGLEISH AND MICHELLE MOULDS

See also

Aaron Beck
Cognitive Theories of Depression
Cognitive Vulnerability

References

Beck, A. T. (2005). The current state of cognitive therapy: A 40-year retrospective. *Archives of General Psychiatry, 62,* 953–959.

Gemar, M. C., Segal, Z. V., Sagrati, S., & Kennedy, S. J. (2001). Mood-induced changes on the Implicit Association Test in recovered depressed patients. *Journal of Abnormal Psychology, 110,* 282–289.

Ingram, R. E., Bernet, C. Z., & McLaughlin, S. C. (1994). Attentional allocation processes in individuals at risk for depression. *Cognitive Therapy and Research, 18,* 317–332.

Kendler, K. S., Thornton, L. M., & Gardner, C. O. (2000). stressful life events and previous episodes in the etiology of major depression in women: An evaluation of the "kindling" hypothesis. *American Journal of Psychiatry, 157,* 1243.

Miranda, J., & Persons, J. B. (1988). Dysfunctional attitudes are mood-state dependent. *Journal of Abnormal Psychology, 97,* 76–79.

Scher, C. D., Ingram, R. E., & Segal, Z. V. (2005). Cognitive reactivity and vulnerability: Empirical evaluation of construct activation and cognitive diathesis in unipolar depression. *Clinical Psychology Review, 25,* 487–510.

Segal, Z. V., Kennedy, S., Gemar, M., Hood, K., Pedersen, R., & Buis, T. (2006). Cognitive reactivity to sad mood provocation and the prediction of depressive relapse. *Archives of General Psychiatry, 63,* 749.

Teasdale, J. D. (1983). Negative thinking in depression: Cause, effect, or reciprocal relationship? *Advances in Behaviour Research and Therapy, 5,* 3–25.

Teasdale, J. D. (1988). Cognitive vulnerability to persistent depression. *Cognition and Emotion, 2,* 247–274.

Teasdale, J. D., & Dent, J. (1987). Cognitive vulnerability to depression: An investigation of two hypotheses. *British Journal of Clinical Psychology, 26,* 113–126.

Williams, J. M. G., Watts, F. N., MacLeod, C., & Mathews, A. (1997). *Cognitive psychology and emotional disorders* (2nd ed.). Chichester, UK: Wiley.

Dopamine

The discovery of antidepressant drugs in the 1950s led, a decade later, to the monoamine hypotheses of depression, which attributed mood changes to changes in the availability of two neurotransmitters: the catecholamine noradrenaline (NA; also known as norepinephrine) and the indoleamine serotonin (5-hydroxy-tryptamine: 5HT). The evidence suggested that depression was associated with deficiencies in transmission at synapses utilizing these two monoamines, that depression was induced by drugs that decreased their availability, and that antidepressant drugs had the common property of increasing their availability. (All of the evidence was subsequently questioned, but, in modified form, both hypotheses remain current.) Dopamine (DA) was known at that time as the neurochemical from which nerve cells synthesize NA, but it had only recently been discovered that DA also functions as a neurotransmitter in its own right. This was one reason why a possible role of DA in depression was at first overlooked. A second was that, while most of the evidence pointing to a role for NA implicates DA equally well, antidepressant drugs did not, at that time, appear to alter transmission at DA synapses. As described below, antidepressant drugs do actually have important effects on the functioning of DA synapses. However, the main reason for the growth of interest in DA and depression was the explosion of research into DA systems that began in the early 1970s and still continues, and the realization that the emerging properties of DA systems could be very relevant to depressive disorders (Randrup et al., 1975).

The three monoamine neurotransmitters are located within discrete pathways that largely originate in quite small regions of the brain stem. Activation of these pathways results in the release of the transmitter at nerve terminals that are distributed across very wide areas of the forebrain, and, broadly speaking, this has the effect of modulating information transmission within the structures where they terminate. There are two major DA pathways. The larger nigrostriatal pathway is involved primarily in motor functions, and in the present context is of lesser interest. The smaller mesolimbic (or more properly, mesocorticolimbic) system innervates structures such as the nucleus accumbens, amygdala, ventral hippocampus, and prefrontal cortex, which are part of, or closely associated with, the limbic system, which has been known since the 1930s to be critical for the expression of emotional behavior (see Dunlop & Nemeroff, 2007).

The mesolimbic DA system supports a variety of behavioral functions related to motivation and reward, and these properties make it an obvious candidate for investigation in relation to affective disorders. The DA hypothesis of reward proposed that rewarding events, irrespective of their modality, shared the common property of activating the mesocorticolimbic DA system; conversely, inactivation of DA function would lead to anhedonia, the inability to experience pleasure (Wise, 1982). This was a particularly influential hypothesis, though subsequent research points more toward a motivational function (Salamone, Correa, Mingote, & Weber, 2005). More recently, this research perspective has broadened to include consideration of the wider brain circuitry within which the mesocorticolimbic DA system is embedded. In this approach, the major focus shifts to the role of DA in getting the flow of information through the nucleus accumbens, which serves as the major interface through which emotional information processing in limbic structures (amygdala, hippocampus, and prefrontal cortex) gains access to motor output systems. Consequently, the mesoaccumbens DA pathway plays a crucial role in the selection and orchestration of goal-directed behaviors—particularly those elicited by incentive stimuli—and in reward-related learning (Willner & Scheel-Kruger, 1991). These properties make a hypofunction of this pathway a prime candidate to mediate the inability to experience pleasure (anhedonia) and loss of motivation (lack of interest) that lie at the heart of major depressive disorder. (Conversely, manic hyperexcitability could readily result from a DA hyperfunction: this possibility has long been recognized [Randrup et al., 1975].) The neural pathways that bring information into the nucleus accumbens from other forebrain structures use glutamate as their neurotransmitter, and the interactions between glutamate and dopamine within the nucleus accumbens represent an exciting area of current research (e.g., West, Floresco, Charara, Rosenkranz, & Grace, 2003). The involvement of essentially the same circuitry in addiction could be an important factor in the strong comorbidity of addiction and depression (Markou, Kosten, & Koob, 1998).

Much of the evidence in support of the DA hypothesis of depression comes from studies in experimental animals (traditionally, rats, but increasingly, mice, because of their greater suitability for genomic studies). It was mentioned earlier that antidepressant drugs do not in general increase the availability of DA at synapses. However, the effect of antidepressants to increase functioning at NA and 5HT synapses actually creates a conundrum, because these effects occur immediately, whereas clinically, antidepressant action requires several weeks of treatment. Beginning in the 1970s, it has been established that long-term treatment with antidepressant drugs causes numerous slowly developing changes in synaptic functioning in a variety of brain systems. One of the most consistent effects, which is an almost-universal property of clinically effective antidepressants (both drugs and other nondrug treatments such as electroconvulsive therapy or rapid eye movement–sleep deprivation), is to increase the effectiveness of DA transmission in the nucleus accumbens. DA acts by interacting with two families of receptors, known as D1-like and D2-like, and the effect of antidepressants is to increase the functional responsiveness of D2 receptors (Gershon, Vishne, & Grunhaus, 2007).

A number of animal models have been developed to study neurobiological processes relevant to depression. These generally involve behavioral changes elicited by exposure to stressors (Willner & Mitchell, 2002). Perhaps the best known is the learned helplessness model, which is usually implemented as a decrease in escape learning ability following exposure to uncontrollable electric shock; perhaps the most valid is the chronic mild stress model, which is usually implemented as a decrease in responsiveness to rewards (anhedonia) following exposure to a variety of mild stressors. In both of these models, and in others, the induction of a depressive state is accompanied by a decrease in DA function in the nucleus accumbens, and behavior is normalized by long-term treatment with antidepressant agents. Furthermore, it can be demonstrated that antidepressants act in these models by sensitizing D2 receptors, because the depressive behavior can be reinstated by acute administration of drugs that block transmission at these receptors,

using a very low dose that is without effect in non-antidepressant-treated animals (Willner, 1997). A similar reinstatement of depression by a very low dose of a D2 antagonist has also been demonstrated in antidepressant-treated patients (Willner, Hale, & Argyropoulos, 2005). These effects are irrespective of the various primary actions of antidepressants in other forebrain regions and suggest that increased neurotransmission at DA synapses in the nucleus accumbens may serve as a final common pathway through which antidepressants influence behavior. Another exciting area of current research aims to elucidate the molecular mechanisms that underlie these slowly developing changes in DA receptor functioning, and the genes responsible for them.

The clinical pharmacology is broadly supportive of the DA hypothesis, but the results are less clear and less compelling than the preclinical studies. In general, drugs that directly stimulate the D2 family of DA receptors have been reported, in both open and double-blind studies, to have antidepressant effects comparable to those of conventional antidepressants. This includes older drugs such as piribedil and bromocriptine, and more recent studies of the very selective D2-family agonist pramipexole (Aiken, 2007). It is also notable that DA uptake inhibition (which prolongs the action of DA at the synapse) is a prominent feature of a number of newer drugs, including nomifensine, bupropion, amineptine, and minaprine that have been marketed for the treatment of depression (see Dunlop & Nemeroff, 2007). However, there are hazards in this approach: the most DA-selective of these drugs, amineptine, was withdrawn because of its abuse liability. There is some evidence that these drugs, which powerfully activate DA synapses, may be particularly effective in patients with evidence of DA insufficiency, such as psychomotor retardation or, particularly, Parkinson's disease (Mouret, Lemoine, & Minuit, 1987). Indeed, the very high incidence of depression in Parkinson's disease is supportive of the DA hypothesis, as is the high incidence of depression as a side effect of neuroleptic

(DA-antagonist) therapy in schizophrenia (Randrup et al., 1975). (However, this is a complex issue, with debates about whether neuroleptic-induced depression is a side effect of treatment, a part of schizophrenia, a secondary effect of having schizophrenia, or the unmasking of a preexisting depression when psychotic symptoms are brought under control.)

Contrary to expectations, given the antidepressant effects of DA agonists, there is also clear evidence that under certain circumstances, neuroleptic drugs are also active as antidepressants. This is another complex problem. In the case of the so-called atypical neuroleptics, the solution seems to be that antidepressant effects are seen at much lower doses than are neuroleptic effects; and while these drugs do antagonize DA function at higher doses, at low doses they act preferentially to increase the release of DA.

Psychostimulant drugs, such as amphetamine and methylphenidate, which increase the availability of DA at synapses, cause activation and euphoria in nondepressed volunteers; these effects are mediated via DA synapses, since they are antagonized by DA receptor blockers. Single doses of psychostimulants also cause a transient mood elevation in a high proportion of depressed patients. Indeed, there is some evidence that the rewarding effects of amphetamine are greater in depressed patients than in nondepressed controls, and that this difference increases with the severity of depression (Tremblay et al., 2005). These apparently paradoxical findings are usually interpreted as arising from a decreased DA release in depression, leading to compensatory changes that are engaged by amphetamine. While amphetamine has acute mood enhancing effects, psychostimulants are not considered to be efficacious as antidepressants with repeated use. Psychostimulants appear more effective in older people, but this is probably via psychomotor stimulation rather than a true antidepressant effect. Similarly, the DA precursor l-DOPA was reported to produce a modest global improvement, primarily in retarded patients, but the effect was largely one

of psychomotor activation with little effect on mood (see Dunlop & Nemeroff, 2007). It is not entirely clear why psychostimulant drugs lose their mood-elevating effects with repeated administration. However, following the success of, for example, amineptine, a new class of drugs, the so-called triple uptake inhibitors, has recently been developed that combines the action of psychostimulants (which enhance DA and produce a rapid but brief mood elevation) and tricyclic antidepressants (which enhance NA and 5HT, with slower but more long lasting benefits). These drugs appear to be effective as conventional antidepressants, and, it is claimed, may have a more rapid onset of action (Chen & Skolnick, 2007).

While there is a strong theoretical case that depression may be associated with impaired functioning of the mesocorticolimbic DA system, and this is reasonably well supported by clinical pharmacology, there is little evidence that is both directly supportive and clearly interpretable. Many studies have attempted to assess forebrain DA function in depressed patients by measuring levels of the DA metabolite homovanillic acid (HVA) in cerebrospinal fluid (CSF). Most of these studies have reported that CSF HVA levels are decreased in depressed patients. However, this decrease is strongly associated with psychomotor retardation—as seen also in Parkinson's and Alzheimer's disease (Wolfe et al., 1990); there is no decrease, and perhaps even an increase in patients with psychomotor agitation. Some studies have tried to look more directly at forebrain DA function by conducting postmortem assays of the brains of depressed patients, typically following suicide. These studies encounter numerous technical problems, and no clear picture has emerged from them. In vivo neuroimaging studies are less problematic, but the results are no clearer: there are several reports of differences in D2 receptor binding and DA transporter levels in depressed patients relative to controls, and of changes in D2 receptors during antidepressant treatment, but there is no consistency across studies in the direction of the changes reported (see

Dunlop & Nemeroff, 2007). Genetic studies are no more encouraging. They include studies of the genes for tyrosine hydroxylase (the main enzyme in DA synthesis), the DA transporter (which removes DA from the synapse), and all five DA receptors. There is a suggestion that particular forms of D3 and D4 receptors might increase the risk of depression (Lopez-Leon et al., 2005). However, most findings are negative, and with these possible exceptions, the occasional reports of abnormalities associated with depression have not been confirmed; this applies both to unipolar depression and to bipolar disorder, which is known to have a stronger genetic component (see Dunlop & Nemeroff, 2007).

While the failure to establish clear and unambiguous evidence of depression-related abnormalities in the mesolimbic DA system is disappointing, the technical problems involved in trying to evaluate the functioning of a single component of a very small brain region are formidable. And these are not the only problems: others reflect the immensely heterogeneous nature of depressed patients with respect to, for example, medication status, medication history, age, severity, and above all, symptomatology. So absence of evidence should not at present be interpreted as evidence of absence. For the future, a more productive strategy to discover direct evidence of DA abnormalities in depression may be to focus on a more homogeneous group of patients who display anhedonia, which is both the most promising endophenotype of depression (Hasler, Drevets, & Charney, 2004) and the aspect of depression in which DA is predicted from the preclinical evidence to be most strongly involved.

PAUL WILLNER

See also

Biological Models of Depression
Dopaminergic Systems
Parkinson's Disease
Serotonin

References

Aiken, C. B. (2007). Pramipexole in psychiatry: A systematic review of the literature. *Journal of Clinical Psychiatry, 68,* 230–236.

Chen, Z., & Skolnick, P. (2007). Triple uptake inhibitors: Therapeutic potential in depression and beyond. *Expert Opinion on Investigational Drugs, 16,* 1365–1377.

Dunlop, B. W., & Nemeroff, C. B. (2007). The role of dopamine in the pathophysiology of depression. *Archives of General Psychiatry, 64,* 327–337.

Gershon, A. A., Vishne, T., & Grunhaus, L. (2007). Dopamine D2-like receptors and the antidepressant response. *Biological Psychiatry, 61,* 145–153.

Hasler, G., Drevets, W. C., & Charney, D. S. (2004). Discovering endophenotypes for major depression. *Neuropsychopharmacology, 29,* 1765–1781.

Lopez Leon, S., Croes, E. A., Sayed-Tabatabaei, F. A., Claes, S., Van Broeckhoven, C., & van Duijn, C. M. (2005). The dopamine D4 receptor gene 48-base-pair-repeat polymorphism and mood disorders: A meta-analysis. *Biological Psychiatry, 7,* 999–1003.

Markou, A., Kosten, T. R., & Koob, G. F. (1998). Neurobiological similarities in depression and drug dependence: A self-medication hypothesis. *Neuropsychopharmacology, 18,* 130–174.

Mouret, J., Lemoine, P., & Minuit, M. P. (1987). Marqueurs polygraphiques, cliniques et therapeutiques des depressions dopamino-dependantes. *Comptes rendus de l'academie des sciences III, 305,* 301–306.

Randrup, A., Munkvad, I., Fog, R., Gerlach, J., Molander, L., Kjellberg, B., et al. (1975). Mania, depression and brain dopamine. In W. B. Essman & L. Valzelli (Eds.). *Current developments in psychopharmacology* (Vol. 2, pp. 206–248). New York: Spectrum Press.

Salamone, J. D., Correa, M., Mingote, S. M., & Weber, S. M. (2005). Beyond the reward hypothesis: Alternative functions of nucleus accumbens dopamine. *Current Opinion in Pharmacology, 5,* 34–41.

Tremblay, L. K., Naranjo, C. A., Graham, S. J., Herrmann, N., Mayberg, H. S., Hevenor, S., et al. (2005). Functional neuroanatomical substrates of altered reward processing in major depressive disorder revealed by a dopaminergic probe. *Archives of General Psychiatry, 62,* 1228–1236.

West, A. R., Floresco, S. B., Charara, A., Rosenkranz, J. A., & Grace, A. A. (2003). Electrophysiological interactions between striatal glutamatergic and dopaminergic systems. *Annals of the New York Academy of Sciences, 1003,* 53–74.

Willner, P. (1997). The mesolimbic dopamine system as a target for rapid antidepressant action. *International Clinical Psychopharmacology, 12*(Suppl. 3), S7–S14.

Willner, P., Hale, A., & Argyropoulos, S. (2005). Dopaminergic mechanism of antidepressant action in depressed patients. *Journal of Affective Disorders, 86,* 37–45.

Willner, P., & Mitchell, P. J. (2002). Animal models of depression: A diathesis-stress approach. In H. D'Haenen, H. Den Boer, & P. Willner (Eds.), *Biological psychiatry* (Vol. 2, pp. 703–726). Chichester, UK: Wiley.

Willner, P., & Scheel-Kruger, J. (Eds.). (1991). *The mesolimbic dopamine system: From motivation to action.* Chichester, UK: Wiley.

Wise, R. A. (1982). Neuroleptics and operant behaviour: The anhedonia hypothesis. *Behavioral and Brain Sciences, 5,* 39–88.

Wolfe, N., Katz, D. I., Albert, M. L., Almozlino, A., Durso, R., Smith, M. C., et al. (1990). Neuropsychological profile linked to low dopamine in Alzheimer's disease, major depression, and Parkinson's disease. *Journal of Neurology, Neurosurgery, and Psychiatry, 53,* 915–917.

Dopaminergic Systems

Historical Perspective: An Interaction of Two Research Trends

In 1965, the psychiatrist Joseph Mendels proposed the catecholamine hypothesis of affective disorders and later extended that hypothesis to include indoleamines. Catecholamines, such as norepinephrine (NE) and dopamine (DA), and indoleamines, such as serotonin (5-HT), function as neurotransmitters in the central nervous system (CNS) and play a direct role in modulating many behavioral processes. The cell bodies of these neurotransmitters are localized in the ventral portion of the brain stem, being distributed across the medulla, pons, and midbrain regions. Their afferents project widely across most regions of the brain. Thus, these neurotransmitter systems are evolutionarily old, integrate immense amounts of input information from higher and lower levels of the CNS, and, in turn, broadly provide excitatory or inhibitory modulatory influences over the flow of neural information throughout the brain. Their functional effects are therefore diverse and depend on the specific behavioral processes promoted by the brain region being innervated rather than on the nature of the neurotransmitter itself.

The remarkable, truly revolutionary aspect about Mendels's hypothesis is that it represented the first *organized* attempt to draw a link between the animal literature on the neurobiological underpinnings of normal behavior with the altered behavior of a psychiatric disorder. Mendels noted that catecholamines, with an emphasis on NE more than DA (indeed, it was not until the mid-1970s that DA was specifically posited to be involved in affective disorders), modulate normal behavioral processes that underlie behavioral manifestations of affective disorders, particularly mood, motivation, motor activity, and cognition. Thus, Mendels was suggesting a paradigm shift in the study of psychiatric disorders, where instead of almost random searching for disordered biological variables associated with

a disorder, one could now proceed logically from disordered behavioral manifestations back to the neurobiological underpinnings of related normal animal behavioral processes.

Problematically, psychiatry at the time (and even generally today) was not used to thinking along the lines of such a perspective on disorder, nor was it generally familiar with the animal brain-behavior literature. Accordingly, progress in understanding or supporting the catecholamine and/or indoleamine hypotheses has been slow and incomplete even to this date. Moreover, most attention until recently has focused on NE and 5-HT, particularly as they relate to the mechanisms of antidepressant drug therapies. A more detailed analysis of depressive behavior based on brain-behavior relations, however, would suggest that DA is strongly involved in at least a sizable subgroup of affective conditions.

In parallel to Mendels's analysis, psychology was making steady progress in understanding the neurobiological underpinnings of normal animal behavior. In the early 1970s, a significant development occurred in this area, when Jeffrey Gray of England proposed a categorization of behavior into motivational-emotional systems that should reveal separable, albeit interacting, underlying brain networks. From an evolutionary biology perspective, such systems represent behavior patterns that evolved to adapt to stimuli critical for survival and species preservation. Such behavioral systems are fundamentally emotional systems that incorporate a motivational state and emotional experience that is concordant with the reinforcement (positive or aversive) properties of critical stimuli. Furthermore, Gray suggested that these motivational-emotional systems formed the foundation of our major, higher-order traits of personality, that is, they define the structure of human behavior.

Integrating these two trends of thought represented by Mendels and Gray, I and others have suggested that many forms of psychiatric disorders, particularly the affective disorders of unipolar and bipolar depression and anxiety, and personality disorders, may represent either extreme variations along the behavioral dimensions associated with normal motivational-emotional systems, or dysregulations in motivational systems that arise from variant forms of genes in interaction with environmental influences (e.g., Depue, 2006, 2007; Depue & Collins, 1999; Depue & Iacono, 1989; Depue & Lenzenweger, 2005; Depue & Morrone-Strupinsky, 2005).

Using such an integrated model of psychiatric disorder, one could make a strong case for unipolar and bipolar affective disorders as being related to DA dysfunction, which we first suggested in 1989 (Depue & Iacono, 1989). Since then, DA has indeed become of increasing interest to researchers in affective disorders, culminating in several recent integrative reviews (Dunlop & Nemeroff, 2007; Gershon, Vishne, & Grunhaus, 2007; Leon et al., 2005; Southwick, Vythilingam, & Charney, 2005). I will outline the important findings of these reviews and other research below.

Dopamine and Normal Motivated-Emotional Behavior

Before addressing the major findings of these reviews, it is important to outline the normal function of DA in behavior that is relevant to the manifestations of depression. DA cell bodies in the ventral tegmental portion of the midbrain comprise what is referred to as the mesolimbic DA system. These cell bodies project densely to an area of the ventral basal ganglia known as the nucleus accumbens (Nacc), as well as to other limbic regions. In addition, DA cell bodies lying medial to the mesolimbic neurons project to most regions of the cortex, but most densely to prefrontal and temporal cortices, forming the mesocortical DA projection system. DA release from the latter projection system, specifically in prefrontal cortical regions, is important for the adequate functioning of working memory, which is a critical element to many cognitive processes. Mesolimbic DA release

in the Nacc facilitates a range of behavioral manifestations, which taken together comprise a basic mammalian behavioral system. Relevant to our discussion, one such motivational-emotional system evolved in order to promote positive motivated approach to and acquisition of critical primary rewards in our environment, such as food, sex, mates, other people, and safety, as well as acquisition of conditioned rewards associated with primary rewards, such as money. Thus, this behavioral system, which is highly relevant to DA and to depression, is activated by, and serves to bring a person in contact with, unconditioned and conditioned rewarding incentive stimuli. It is consistently described in all animals across phylogeny, and we define this system as *behavioral approach based on positive incentive motivation* (Depue & Collins, 1999; Depue & Morrone-Strupinsky, 2005).

Incentive stimuli are inherently evaluated as positive in valence and activate a behavioral approach pattern consisting of incentive motivation, increased energy, and forward locomotion as a means of bringing a person into close proximity to reward. Moreover, an incentive state is inherently rewarding but in a highly activated manner, and animals will work intensively to obtain that reward without evidence of satiety. In humans, the incentive state is associated with strong subjective feelings of desire, wanting, excitement, elation, enthusiasm, energy, potency, and self-efficacy that are distinct from, but typically co-occur with, feelings of pleasure and liking. In other words, a subjective state of positive affect and incentive motivation, and the belief that one has the capacity to obtain the reward, is facilitated. This subjective experience is associated with personality traits of social dominance, achievement, endurance, persistence, efficacy, activity, and energy—or what we more abstractly know as extraversion (Depue, 2006; Depue & Collins, 1999; Depue & Morrone-Strupinsky, 2005).

An important point about such a behavioral system is that, from a functional standpoint, it is unipolar in nature. That means that the above description refers to a heightened state of incentive motivation and positive affect. A reduced or deficient functional level of activation in this system is not characterized by negative affect, but rather by an absence of incentive motivation and positive affect, specifically, lethargy, fatigue, reduced facilitation of motor activity and cognitive processes, depressed mood characterized as an absence of positive reactivity to reward, and anhedonia (a lack of interest in, and inability to experience pleasure from, activities associated with reward). Thus, heightened levels of activation in the positive incentive system reflect extraverted behavior, while low levels of activation reflect an unengaged, nonmotivated absence of positive affect. The similarity of this latter behavioral profile to some forms of depression is impressive, while the behavioral features associated with a heightened activation of this system are qualitatively similar to those of hypomania (Depue & Iacono, 1989).

That the functioning of the incentive motivation-positive affect system is dependent upon DA release in the Nacc is supported by an extensive animal and human literature (Depue, 2006, 2007; Depue & Collins, 1999; Depue & Morrone-Strupinsky, 2005). DA agonists or antagonists administered in DA cell bodies or Nacc in rats and monkeys facilitate or markedly impair, respectively, a broad array of incentive-motivated behaviors. Furthermore, dose-dependent DA receptor activation in the Nacc facilitates the acute rewarding effects of stimulants, and the Nacc is a particularly strong site for intracranial self-administration of DA agonists (indicating strong rewarding effects). DA agonists injected in the Nacc also modulate behavioral responses to *conditioned* incentive stimuli in a dose-dependent fashion. In single-unit recording studies, these DA neurons are activated preferentially by appetitive incentive stimuli and respond vigorously in proportion to the magnitude of both conditioned and unconditioned incentive stimuli and in anticipation of reward.

In humans, incentive motivation is associated with both positive *emotional* feelings,

such as elation and euphoria, and *motivational* feelings of desire, wanting, craving, potency, and self-efficacy. DA-activating psychostimulant drugs induce both sets of feelings. Also, neuroimaging studies of the DA-agonist cocaine in cocaine addicts found that, during acute administration, the intensity of a subject's subjective euphoria increased in a dose-dependent manner in proportion to DA levels in the area of the Nacc. Moreover, cocaine-induced activity in the Nacc is linked equally strongly (if not more strongly) to motivational feelings of desire, wanting, and craving, as to the emotional experience of euphoric rush. And the degree of amphetamine-induced DA release in Nacc is correlated strongly with feelings of euphoria. Hence, taken together, the animal and human evidence demonstrates that DA release in the Nacc is a primary neural circuit for incentive motivation and its accompanying positive subjective state of reward.

Dopamine and Depression

The etiology of affective disorders is undoubtedly heterogeneous (i.e., there are many etiologies underlying the phenotypes of depression). First, there is the distinction between unipolar and bipolar depression, and, second, within each of these types there are likely many different etiologies, particularly in the unipolar depressions. Therefore, it is unlikely that DA will be a primary etiologic factor in more than a sizable subgroup of depressions, although other subgroups might manifest DA dysfunction secondary to other etiologic variables. This means that assessment of DA functioning or DA genetics in heterogeneous depressed patient groups may frequently reveal weak association between DA and depression. Therefore, it is critical to try to define subtypes that reveal stronger association with DA, either post hoc by analysis of subgroup patterns in the results or, better yet, beforehand on the basis of drug response, behavioral profile, and so forth.

Behavioral profile has not been used sufficiently in designing depression studies. Usually, it is noted post hoc that certain behavioral profiles do or do not relate to the biological variable of interest. However, the discussion above on the behavioral features of high and low levels of functioning in the incentive motivation system may be helpful in this respect. The behavioral features at the low end of functioning are clearly depressive in nature but with specific features: an absence of incentive motivation and positive affect, that is, lethargy, fatigue, reduced facilitation of motor activity and cognition, depressed mood characterized as an absence of positive reactivity to rewards, and anhedonia. In the psychiatric literature, these features would be summarized as anergia, psychomotor retardation (slow initiation and reduced production of speech, thoughts, cognition, and motoric processes), anhedonia (of the type where the patient has a deficit in positive experience associated with the activation of incentive motivation), and a lack of reactivity of positive affect to rewards. Not all forms of depression manifest with such features, but we showed previously that such features characterize most robustly depressions associated with classic bipolar affective disorder. Importantly, since about two-thirds of afflicted first-degree relatives of bipolar probands manifest with only depressed episodes, such unipolar depressions (i.e., behaviorally unipolar, genetically bipolar) may also appear with similar behavioral features as seen in bipolar depression. There also may be other forms of DA-relevant subgroups that do not have a bipolar genotype, such as severely anhedonic-psychomotorally retarded-anergic unipolar patients with no bipolar family history. In any case, such bipolar and unipolar groups could be predicted on behavioral grounds to be associated most closely with DA dysfunction, whether of primary or secondary etiology. Unfortunately, researchers have not assessed these distinctions carefully, and so their validity will require more specific studies of this issue. Yet this is important, because it has become progressively clear that the majority of depressed patients treated with drugs acting on 5-HT or 5-HT/NE neurotransmission (which do not strongly affect DA functioning), while

responding better than to placebo, still do not achieve full remission of symptoms.

The number of studies on the association of DA and depression is not substantial as yet, and there are many conflicting or non-replicated results. There are many potential reasons for this, including, among others, variations in (a) patient subgroups (i.e., heterogeneity), (b) the methods, reliability, and validity of different assessment techniques of DA functioning, (c) DA-specificity of pharmacological challenges, and (d) type of control groups. In particular, the lack of making subgroup distinctions in these studies prior to sampling is a major deficit in this research, since post hoc subgrouping typically yields very small subgroup samples and hence low statistical power. Readers interested in the details of the conflicting findings can see the reviews listed above. Here, I will highlight only promising trends in the literature.

A promising trend across various methods of assessing DA in depressed patients is the relative consistency of low DA functioning in patients with an anhedonic-psychomotor retarded-anergic behavioral profile. One means of assessing the functional properties of DA functioning is to measure the major metabolite of DA, homovanillic acid (HVA), in cerebrospinal fluid (CSF). Two spinal taps separated in time, during which HVA is pharmacologically inhibited from exiting CSF, yields an estimate of the accumulation of HVA and, hence, the turnover of DA across time. The majority of studies have not only found lower accumulations of HVA in depressed patients relative to controls, but this finding is particularly robust and consistent in patients with psychomotor retardation. While low pretreatment levels of CSF HVA generally have not robustly predicted treatment response to drugs that enhance DA functioning, they do so in both unipolar and bipolar patients with psychomotor retardation, and this effect is correlated positively with the degree of the drug's efficacy in enhancing DA.

Two neuroimaging strategies for assessing DA functioning may also relate to a psychomotor retardation profile. First, there are approximately five different types of DA receptors that transduct the effects of DA release to the postsynaptic cell, D2 receptors being one major type. Degree of binding to the D2 receptor can be imaged by use of a radioactively labeled agonist of the receptor. The number of such studies is small, and results are inconsistent. However, depressed patients with psychomotor retardation are more consistently found to have elevated D2 receptor binding in the striatum, which if characterizing the ventral striatum (Nacc), could reflect altered DA functioning that affects reward processing. Furthermore, where elevated D2 receptor binding has not been found, few of the patients had even moderate psychomotor retardation. It is not known whether an elevation in D2 receptor binding reflects increased numbers or affinity of D2 receptors, or reduced availability of synaptic DA. It is also possible that the latter—reduced availability of synaptic DA—could activate a compensatory increase in D2 receptor number and/or affinity.

Second, after DA is released into the synapse, the major means of inactivating synaptic DA is to transport it back across the presynaptic membrane, a process that requires active transport via a DA transporter (DAT). In conditions where DA release is decreased, compensatory feedback mechanisms can decrease DAT activity, which enhances DA's temporal availability at the postsynaptic receptor. Again, results of DAT uptake in depression are conflicting, although the largest study found reduced DAT binding (i.e., reduced uptake of DA from the synapse), and another study found reduced uptake in the striatum to be particularly the case in depressed patients with psychomotor retardation.

There are other indications that an anergic-anhedonic-psychomotor retardation profile is important in studies of DA functioning in depression. There are converging lines of evidence that indicate that different types of antidepressant treatments, including tricyclics (TCAs), selective serotonin-reuptake inhibitors, monoamine oxidase inhibitors (MAOIs), and electroconvulsive shock, have a common effect of increasing the sensitivity of D2 receptors in the Nacc (which increases the effects of DA postsynaptically), and that this effect is directly related to antidepressant efficacy (Gershon et al., 2007). Importantly, pharmacological treatments, such as TCAs and MAOIs, show greater efficacy in anergic depressed patients. In addition, the DA agonist piribedil was found to be efficacious in patients with low pretreatment CSF HVA, which itself is inversely related to psychomotor retardation. And reduction of the synthesis of DA by inhibition of its rate-limiting enzyme, tyrosine hydroxylase, rapidly elicits a marked increase in depressive symptoms, particularly anhedonia, inefficient cognition, and anergia.

There are several other approaches to studying DA neurotransmission in depression, but in each case, the results are conflicting, and subtypes of depression have been insufficiently studied. For details, the reader is referred to the above reviews. These approaches include analysis of the association of polymorphisms in genes that code for different types of DA receptors to depression, where the most promising finding to date is in the most polymorphic of DA receptors, D4 (Leon et al., 2005). Also, the efficacy of DA agonists to enhance acutely reward functioning in depressed patients has revealed a positive correlation between reward response to the agonist and severity of depression. This could mean that reduced DA release in depression may cause a compensatory upregulation of postsynaptic DA receptors and/or decreased DAT density, resulting in a net increase in DA signal transduction (and increased reward) elicited by the agonist-induced release of DA into the synapse.

One set of findings may be particularly significant with respect to DA functioning in affective disorders. When DA agonists are used to challenge the functioning of DA neurotransmission, and when some types of treatments for depression are administered, bipolar depressed patients and a subgroup of unipolar depressed patients experience a sudden, rapid shift into a hypomanic or manic state (Depue & Iacono, 1989; Miklowitz &

Johnson, 2006). Thus, enhancement of DA activity by increasing synthesis (l-dopa), release (amphetamine), or postsynaptic receptor activation (piribedil, methylphenidate, or bromocriptine) is associated with hypomanic, or less frequently manic, behavioral disturbance.

Rapid shifts are more frequent and intense in response to acute and chronic treatment with TCAs and MAOIs, an effect that is much more common in bipolar than unipolar depressed patients and in patients with a history of full manic episodes rather than only hypomanic episodes. The proportion of patients experiencing disturbance with TCA usage is approximately 9%, whereas for MAOIs it varies from 11% to 27% depending on type of MAOI. However, when polarity of the patients is verified, rates of shifting of 30% to 60% have been reported for bipolar patients for both treatment and prophylactic studies of TCAs and for treatment studies of MAOIs (Depue & Iacono, 1989). If finer gradations of activation of behavior are studied, as opposed to just full shifts into extreme clinical episodes, this proportion may be even larger. It has not been fully established that these effects are directly the result of alterations in DA functioning, but the fact that (a) as noted above, a common effect of antidepressant treatments is to enhance DA functioning via modification of D2 receptor sensitivity, and (b) MAOIs robustly increase DA functioning in preclinical studies, all support the possibility of DA involvement in the rapid-shift phenomenon.

Thus, a potentially large proportion of bipolar, and a subset of unipolar (with bipolar genotype?), depressed patients show a qualitatively similar increase in positive behavioral activation, as do controls, but this increase is quantitatively exaggerated, where the functional process set in motion by the DA-agonist may proceed until an extreme behavioral state opposite from the prechallenge level is achieved. This may indicate that some forms of bipolar disorder may be characterized by poorly regulated DA functioning underlying the incentive motivation-positive affect-behavioral approach system. This weak regulation could reflect a stable vulnerability factor in bipolar disorder, because, as clinically observed long ago by Schou, high behavioral variation in the incentive motivation-positive affect system also characterizes bipolar patients prior to first episode and in intermorbid periods between episodes.

Rapid shifts are most likely to become manifest under conditions of internal or external regulatory challenge. External challenges, as in stressful events, are known to increase the probability of rapid shifts from a euthymic state to depression or hypomania or mania, or from one clinical state to another. This may relate to the fact that psychosocial stress-induced elevations in glucocorticoid concentrations in blood may selectively facilitate DA transmission in the Nacc, an effect that may be particularly pronounced in people with poor early life maternal care—often associated with affective disorders (Pruessner, Champagne, Meaney, & Dagher, 2004). This raises the possibility that repetitive experience of stress-induced glucocorticoid secretion sensitizes DA functioning in the Nacc (Dunlop & Nemeroff, 2007), leaving the DA system oversensitive to subsequent challenges in individuals vulnerable to bipolar and some forms of unipolar disorder.

Conclusions

As this review indicates, several lines of study support an association between DA functioning and affective disorders. This is particularly the case in bipolar and unipolar patients with psychomotor retardation-anhedonic-anergic clinical features. The latter is supported by reduced accumulation of CSF HVA, elevated D2 binding in the striatum, reduced DAT activity, and the rapid behavioral shifts induced by DA agonists, TCAs and MAOIs. One promising line of future investigation is to analyze the nature of the instability reflected in these rapid shifts, whether they reflect a primary DA dysfunction, and the extent to which they reflect a trait vulnerability to bipolar and some forms of unipolar disorder. In any line of future research on DA and depression, patient heterogeneity needs to be defined and controlled beforehand in a much more rigorous manner. Otherwise, findings will continue to be conflicting or nonreplicable. And if a more comprehensive understanding of affective disorders is to be achieved, integration of animal and human neurobehavioral systems frameworks with psychiatric perspectives on disorders will be necessary.

RICHARD A. DEPUE

See also

Biological Models of Depression
Dopamine
Parkinson's Disease
Serotonin

References

Depue, R. A. (2006). Dopamine in agentic and opiates in affiliative forms of extraversion. In T. Canli (Ed.), *Biology of personality and individual differences*. New York: Guilford Press.

Depue, R. A. (2007). Neurobehavioral dimensions in personality and personality disorders. In S. Wood (Ed.), *The neuropsychology of mental illness*. New York: Cambridge University Press.

Depue, R. A., & Collins, P. (1999). Neurobiology of the structure of personality: Dopamine, facilitation of incentive motivation, and extraversion. *Behavioral and Brain Sciences, 22*, 491–569.

Depue, R. A., & Iacono, W. (1989). Neurobehavioral aspects of affective disorders. *Annual Review of Psychology, 40*, 457–492.

Depue, R. A., & Lenzenweger, M. (2005). A neurobehavioral model of personality disorders. In D. Cicchetti (Ed.), *Developmental psychopathology*. New York: Wiley-Interscience.

Depue, R. A., & Morrone-Strupinsky, J. (2005). Neurobehavioral foundation of affiliative bonding: Implications for a human trait of affiliation. *Behavioral and Brain Sciences, 28*, 313–395.

Dunlop, B. W., & Nemeroff, C. B. (2007). The role of dopamine in the pathophysiology of depression. *Archives of General Psychiatry, 64*, 327–337.

Gershon, A. A., Vishne, T., & Grunhaus, L. (2007). Dopamine D2-like receptors and the antidepressant response. *Biological Psychiatry, 61*, 145–153.

Leon, S. L., Croes, E. A., Sayed-Tabatabaei, F. A., Claes, S., Van Broeckhoven, C., & van Duijn, C. M. (2005). The dopamine D4 receptor gene 48-base-pair-repeat polymorphism and mood disorders: A meta analysis. *Biological Psychiatry, 57*, 999–1003.

Miklowitz, D. J., & Johnson, S. L. (2006). The psychopathology and treatment of bipolar disorder. *Annual Review of Clinical Psychology, 2*, 199–235.

Pruessner, J. C., Champagne, F., Meaney, M. J., & Dagher, A. (2004). Dopamine release in response to a psychological stress in humans and its relationship to early life maternal care. *Journal of Neuroscience, 24*, 2825–2831.

Southwick, S. M., Vythilingam, M., & Charney, D. S. (2005). The psychobiology of depression and resilience to stress: Implications for prevention and treatment. *Annual Review of Clinical Psychology, 1*, 255–291.

Dysfunctional Attitudes Scale

The Dysfunctional Attitudes Scale (DAS; Weissman & Beck, 1978) is a 40-item self-report inventory that is used to evaluate the presence of maladaptive thinking. The DAS measures the relative presence of pessimistic and maladaptive attitudes about evaluation and performance, attributional style, and beliefs about control. Using a 7-point Likert scale (1 = totally agree; 7 = totally disagree), participants rate the degree to which they agree or disagree with statements that reflect dysfunctional thinking. Scores range between 40 and 280. Studies have reported depressed group mean scores on the DAS ranging from 142 to 172 (Serfaty et al., 2002; Zuroff, Blatt, Sanislow, Bondi, & Pilkonis, 1999). In contrast, DAS mean scores for normative, nondepressed adult groups have ranged between 89 and 131 (Dozois, Covin, & Brinker, 2003). Adolescent normative samples have tended to score higher than adult samples, ranging between 123 and 137 (Ingram, Nelson, Steidtmann, & Bistricky, 2007).

Scale Development and History

The DAS was theoretically derived from Beck's cognitive theory of depression (1967) and was created with the intent of measuring attitudes that might predispose individuals to depression. The original 100-item scale was divided into two 40-item forms that exhibit good reliability and correlate highly with one another. Test-retest reliability for the DAS is strong. A DAS comprises overall affiliative (e.g., need for approval) and achievement (e.g., perfectionism) components.

The DAS and Cognitive Approaches to Studying Depression

The DAS is among the most frequently cited cognitive measures related to depression and has been utilized extensively in treatment outcome research. Although the DAS was developed for adults, it has been frequently utilized with adolescent samples. The DAS is often administered with other measures that assess depressive cognitions, including the Attributional Style Questionnaire (ASQ), Automatic Thoughts Questionnaire (ATQ), Hopelessness Scale (HS), Cognitive Checklist (CCL), Cognitive Style Questionnaire (CSQ), and Cognitive Bias Questionnaire (CBQ). Form A is more commonly used than Form B. The DAS has been modified for use with specialty populations and has been translated into many languages.

In keeping with the theory that depressed and depression-vulnerable individuals are characterized by dysfunctional cognition, the DAS correlates moderately with measures of depressive symptoms and can distinguish depressed from nondepressed groups. Additionally, the DAS has been found to correlate moderately with other measures of negative cognitive content, including the ASQ, ATQ, HS, CBQ, and CSQ. Aside from depression, DAS data suggest that dysfunctional attitudes correlate significantly with personality pathology (particularly cluster C disorders), anxiety, and self-consciousness.

DAS Findings and Implications for Theories of Depression

Use of the DAS in research has led to findings that influence the ongoing study of depression. An important theoretical debate has centered around whether dysfunctional attitudes are merely a symptom of depression or whether they are causally related to depression. In the absence of naturally occurring or experimentally induced stress, formerly depressed (i.e., depression-vulnerable) and never-depressed individuals do not appear to differ in endorsement of dysfunctional attitudes. Further, inducing a negative mood seems to increase dysfunctional attitudes regardless of whether individuals have experienced past depression. With respect to treatment outcome research, some data show that depressed individuals who respond favorably to cognitive behavioral therapy show a significantly larger reduction in dysfunctional attitudes than depressed individuals with minimal response. From these findings, it could be interpreted that dysfunctional attitudes are mood state dependent; however, other evidence suggests that dysfunctional attitudes are relatively stable, even after effective treatment for depression. Furthermore, negative mood induction tends to evoke higher levels of dysfunctional attitudes in formerly depressed individuals than never-depressed individuals, a difference that does not exist prior to the mood-prime. Additionally, evidence suggests that elevated levels of dysfunctional attitudes, when coupled with negative life stressors, lead to increases in negative thoughts and depressive symptoms in children and adults. Thus, dysfunctional attitudes may be depressogenic.

Dysfunctional attitudes have also been studied from a biological perspective. Elevated DAS scores have been associated with greater physiological arousal. Also, serotonin has long been thought to be involved in both mood and cognition, and studies in which serotonin has been manipulated support a link between serotonin and dysfunctional attitudes. A unidirectional interpretation may be premature, as a bidirectional relationship could exist, with dysfunctional attitudes also influencing changes in serotonin neurotransmission. This latter path of influence may be supported by certain studies in which selective serotonin-reuptake inhibitor antidepressants have failed to effect a reduction in dysfunctional attitudes. Whether dysfunctional attitudes are a product or producer of depressive biological phenomena remains unclear.

Though the number and complexity of cognitive theories of depression have increased since the initial development of the DAS, its widespread use and influence with respect to contemporary theories have continued.

STEVEN L. BISTRICKY

See also

Assessment of Depression
Cognitive Theories of Depression

References

Beck, A. T. (1967). *Depression: Causes and treatment.* Philadelphia, PA: University of Philadelphia Press.

Dozois, D. J., Covin, R., & Brinker, J. K. (2003). Normative data on cognitive measures of depression. *Journal of Consulting and Clinical Psychology, 71,* 71–80.

Ingram, R. E., Nelson, T., Steidtmann, D., & Bistricky, S. (2007). Comparative data on child and adolescent cognitive measures associated with depression. *Journal of Consulting and Clinical Psychology, 75,* 390–403.

Serfaty, M. A., Bothwell, R., Marsh, R., Ashton, H., Blizard, R., & Scott, J. (2002). Event-related potentials and cognitive processing of affectively toned words in depression. *Journal of Psychophysiology, 16,* 56–66.

Weissman, A. N., & Beck, A. T. (1978). *Development and validation of the Dysfunctional Attitude Scale: A preliminary investigation.* Paper presented at the annual meeting of the American Educational Research Association, Toronto, Ontario, Canada.

Zuroff, D. C., Blatt, S. J., Sanislow, C. A., Bondi, C. M., & Pilkonis, P. A. (1999). Vulnerability to depression: Re-examining state dependence and relative stability. *Journal of Abnormal Psychology, 108,* 76–89.

E

Early Adversity

There is substantial research evidence that negative experiences in early life have lasting impact on psychological disorders such as depression throughout the life course (Cicchetti & Carlson, 1989). Early formulations in psychoanalytic theory indicated that childhood maternal loss led to chronic mourning and thereby to lifetime depression. Subsequently, attachment theory argued that the disrupted relationship with the primary caregiver(s) led to impaired cognitive and emotional processes in relating styles (Bowlby, 1980). These approaches have been complemented by the parallel social psychiatry focus on adverse social environment, where maternal deprivation, institutional care, and social disadvantage in childhood serve as a basis for later disadvantage and disorder (Rutter, 1972, 1990).

Researchers investigating adult depression have shown that childhood adversity assessed retrospectively is a causal factor in later disorder (Bifulco & Moran, 1998). Key experiences are childhood neglect and abuse, which are indicative of family breakdown and social disadvantage. These experiences have negative impact on the psychological and social development of children, as well as leading to impoverished social contexts that increase risk of depression in teenage and later years (Parker, Hadzi Pavlovic, Greenwald, Weissman, 1995).

Definitions of Early Adversity

Adversity in early adolescence as well as childhood is critical, creating additional negative impacts on future life trajectories. While definitions of such adversity have been various, those targeted on the child and indicative of significant maltreatment are the most pertinent for depression (Bifulco & Moran, 1998):

- Neglect is defined in terms of parental indifference to the child's needs in terms of material care (feeding, clothing, health care), intellectual development (school work and attendance), socialization (friendships and leisure activities), and support (responsiveness to child's distress).
- Physical abuse is parental violence toward the child in terms of attacks using implements such as stick and belts, or punching, kicking, or burning.
- Sexual abuse is unwilling sexual contact usually by any older peer or adult, and also includes noncontact experiences such as being made to watch sexual activity.
- Psychological abuse is sadistic parental behavior involving coercive control and psychological manipulativeness, to terrorize, humiliate, and engender submissiveness.

Neglect or abuse is more common where there is adverse family context. Thus factors such as parental conflict, financial hardship, and parental loss are each associated with double the likelihood of neglect and abuse of children also present. While a wide range of prevalence figures are quoted, severe instances that would merit child protection service investigation show rates of neglect and physical abuse are each around 20% of inner city populations, with sexual abuse less common (12%). Psychological abuse involving sadistic coercive behavior is probably the most rare, although representative figures are not available. Rates are similar across gender apart from sexual abuse, which is more than double in females (May-Chalal & Cawson, 2005). Of cases referred to child protection services in the United Kingdom, neglect is the most common at 43% (in 2006), compared with physical abuse at 16%, emotional abuse at 21%, and sexual abuse at only 5%.

Definitions of Depression

Depression is one of the most common psychological disorders in the community, with rates of 15% yearly prevalence quoted in inner-city community samples of women. This is around double that found in men. Depression is at a peak at age 17, with a high rate of reoccurrence for teenage onset and with the gender differential marked at this age. Major depression is the most common form, although variants include dysthymia (fewer symptoms but more chronic), with psychotic depression rare in the general community (e.g., 1 in 1,000). Major depression includes depressed mood or loss of interest together with four other symptoms including weight loss or gain, insomnia or hypersomnia, agitation or retardation, fatigue or energy loss, feelings of worthlessness, diminished ability to think, concentrate, or make decision, and recurrent thoughts of death or suicide plans or attempts. Clinical episodes last a minimum of 2 weeks with significant distress or impairment to functioning.

Models of Adversity and Depression

While the causes of depression are recognized as biological, psychological, and social, social factors account for much of the variance. Adult social factors include severe life events and difficulties, lower social class position, and lack of marital and other support. Psychological factors include poor self-esteem and helplessness, ineffective coping, and insecure attachment style. Life-span causal models of depression emphasize how trajectories of negative social conditions interact with negative psychological states to bring about disorder.

Factors shown to mediate between childhood adversity and depression are both social and psychological (Bifulco, Kwon, Jacobs, Moran & Bunn, 2006). The former include teenage pregnancy, domestic violence and single parenthood. Research is now revealing that psychological mediation is shown by insecure attachment style. While biological factors are increasingly being identified in depression (e.g., genetic abnormalities in the serotonin transportation, and abnormal cortisol patterns), these are not yet integrated into life-span psychosocial models with childhood adversity.

While depression is 3 times more common among individuals with neglect and abuse, only around a third of those with such adversity develop depression. Studies of resilience identify a range of factors including positive parenting, good support from adult or peer, high intelligence, religious practice, and family cohesiveness. In particular, support in childhood has been consistently shown to protect against effects of neglect or abuse (Rutter, 1990).

Measurement of Childhood Adversity

There has been much debate on how to measure childhood adversity accurately, not only for research investigation of life-span causal models, but also for practice investigations where a history of neglect and abuse is used to inform intervention and treatment. Retrospective accounts are utilized because there are a number of difficulties in questioning children about abuse and obtaining reliable accounts. This is due to children's poor capacity to develop time frames for experience, their limited understanding of abusive behavior, and potential conflict of loyalty in reporting when the abuser is a close figure. Thus, while it is important to develop suitable child measures, it is also important to utilize retrospective assessment in adolescents and adults.

Potential problems with retrospective accounts of childhood can involve bias from symptoms of depression. However, the use of detailed, factual interview measures, which question chronologically and use probes to develop focused narrative accounts, can overcome this. Methods such as the Childhood Experience of Care and Abuse Interview used with adults have been validated by comparing accounts of sisters raised together, and against relevant contemporary records (from child psychotherapy case reports, parental death certificates, etc.) (Bifulco & Moran, 1998). Studies controlling for depression at time of reporting and in test-retest have shown good reliability of such instruments. Given both ethical and measurement problems of interviewing children directly for research, using retrospective measurement has proved very important in developing the field.

Treatment and Interventions

Definitions of neglect and abuse are now enshrined in child care policy. The lifetime negative impact of childhood neglect and abuse has led to social policies in Western countries to try to eradicate abuse and to improve parenting. Preventative action is undertaken on a population basis for poor parenting (e.g., lax supervision, harsh or variable discipline, critical or hostile parenting) through family interventions and parenting programs. The aim is to ensure that such parental behaviors do not develop into maltreatment under stress conditions and to provide support as a protective factor for parents. This has led to nationwide interventions such as Sure Start as a preventive measure of improving parenting and development in young children. Educational and promotional campaigns have been used to increase knowledge of abuse among the public, with teachers and others involved with children. Thus official rates show decline in those requiring child protection services. As well as aiming to prevent childhood adversity, there are also successful treatments for individuals with depression. These include pharmaceutical and cognitive behavior therapy interventions, which are becoming more available as the scale of depression prevalence is becoming recognized (Allen, 2005). Thus a range of health and social care interventions has emerged directly as a result of the research on childhood adversity and adult depression.

ANTONIA BIFULCO

See also

Maltreatment
Parenting

References

Allen, J. G. (2005). *Coping with trauma: A guide to self-understanding* (2nd ed.). Washington, DC: American Psychiatric Press.

Bifulco, A., Kwon, J.-H., Jacobs, C., Moran, P., & Bunn, A., & et al. (2006). Adult attachment style as a mediator of childhood neglect/abuse and adult depression and anxiety. *Social Psychiatry and Psychiatric Epidemiology, 41,* 796–865.

Bifulco, A., & Moran, P. (1998). *Wednesday's child: Research into women's experience of neglect and abuse in childhood and adult depression.* London: Routledge.

Bowlby, J. (1980). *Attachment and loss, Vol. 3: Loss, sadness, and depression.* New York: Basic Books.

Cicchetti, D., & Carlson, V. (Eds.). (1989). *Child maltreatment: Theory and research on the causes and consequences of child abuse and neglect.* New York: Cambridge University Press.

May-Chahal, C., & Cawson, P. (2005). Measuring child maltreatment in the United Kingdom: A study of the prevalence of child abuse and neglect. *Child Abuse and Neglect, 29,* 969–984.

Parker, G., Hadzi Pavlovic, D., Greenwald, S., & Weissman, M. (1995). Low parental care as a risk factor to lifetime depression in a community sample. *Journal of Affective Disorders, 33,* 173–180.

Rutter, M. (1972). *Maternal deprivation reassessed.* Harmondsworth, England: Penguin.

Rutter, M. (1990). Psychosocial resilience and protective mechanisms. In J. E. Rolf and A. S. Masten (Eds.), *Risk and protective factors in the development of psychopathology* (pp. 181–214). New York: Cambridge University Press.

Eating Disorders

Although first described in the psychological literature over a hundred years ago, clinicians and researchers are still struggling to understand the etiology, neurobiology, and treatment of eating disorders. Their high comorbidity with major depression has led researchers to investigate their shared psychobiological underpinnings and evaluate the use of treatments developed for depression with patients with eating disorders. This entry will focus on the relationship of depression to anorexia and bulimia nervosa in terms of comorbidity, biology, and treatment among women. Although men do suffer from eating disorders, 90% to 95% of those with an eating disorder are female, and the majority of research has been done with females. Consideration will be given to the role of depression in eating disorders generally, and in anorexia and bulimia specifically.

Approximately 0.5% to 1.0% of late-adolescent or adult women meet criteria for the diagnosis of anorexia nervosa (AN), and approximately 1% to 2% meet diagnostic criteria for bulimia nervosa (BN). Course and treatment outcomes for AN reveal that approximately one-half will recover, approximately 30% will maintain some symptoms of the disorder, 10% will remain chronically ill, and 10% will die as a consequence of their illness. Regarding women with BN, approximately one-half will recover, 30% will continue to have some symptoms of the disorder or relapse, and approximately 20% will remain chronically ill. The treatment-refractory nature of eating disorders has led some theorists to suggest that there may be some functional value in AN and BN and their associated behaviors. Food restriction and binge-purge behaviors may serve an emotion regulatory function in these individuals. Additionally, disordered eating may result from a preexisting mood disorder and function in terms of repairing negative affect.

Eating Disorders: Anorexia Nervosa and Bulimia Nervosa

AN is characterized by a refusal to maintain a normal body weight and an intense fear of gaining weight even though underweight. The disorder manifests as either a restricting type (AN-R) or a binge-purge type (AN-BP).

The binge-purge subtype is distinguished from the restricting subtype by the presence of binging and purging. BN is characterized by frequent episodes of binge eating and recurring inappropriate compensatory behaviors in order to prevent weight gain. Both disorders place an emphasis on body shape and size as an evaluative measure of the self. AN-BP is distinguished from BN in that individuals with BN are typically within a normal weight range, whereas individuals with AN-BP are typically below an optimally healthy weight. While both AN-BP and BN are characterized by binge-purge episodes, in BN these are the primary symptoms. Conversely, in AN-BP, the chronic and extreme restriction of dietary intake leaves individuals psychologically and physiologically vulnerable to periodic binge-purge cycles.

Recent research has shown that the division between AN and BN may not be the only important diagnostic difference. Studies of temperament and affect among those with eating disorders have determined that restricting anorectics (AN-R) are more overcontrolled, anhedonic, and constricted, whereas those who engage in binging and purging behavior (both BN and AN-BP) appear to be more undercontrolled, volatile, and emotionally labile (e.g., Westen & Harnden-Fischer, 2001). Accordingly, personality profiles may not be as closely related to diagnostic categorization (i.e., AN, BN) as behavioral profiles (i.e., restriction, binging-purging). Consistent with this view, some researchers have reviewed studies reporting taxometric analyses of eating disorders (Williamson, Gleaves, & Stewart, 2005). They reported that disorders involving binge eating (and possibly purging) lie on a separate continuum from restricting anorexia, which was on the same continuum as normalcy and obesity. Therefore, eating disorders may be able to be conceptualized dimensionally and by the underlying taxons of binging and restricting. This type of distinction may have clinical utility and may highlight differences between binge-purge eating disorders versus restricting disorders in terms of depressive symptomatology and affect regulation.

Comorbidity With Depressive Disorders and Suicidality

The lifetime prevalence rate of major depression among individuals with AN is between 46% and 74% (Casper, 1998). Among those with AN-R, 15% to 50% have major depression at some point in their lives, and among those with AN-BP, the lifetime prevalence rate of depression is higher, ranging from 46% to 80% (Casper, 1998). The lifetime prevalence rate of major depression in BN is 50% to 65% (Casper, 1998), and this correlate exceeds the comorbidity of any other Axis I disorder with BN. The rates of depression among those with eating disorders can be compared to the much lower lifetime prevalence rate of major depression in the general population (17%). The high rate of depression among those with AN-BP and BN suggests a relationship between binging and/or purging and depression. Additionally, women with a diagnosis of major depression have higher lifetime prevalence rates of eating disorders. Approximately 1% to 7% of women with major depression will develop AN in their lifetime, and approximately 9% to 21% of these individuals will develop BN in their lifetime (Carter, Joyce, Mulder, Luty, & Sullivan, 1999). Additionally, the presence of depression is associated with higher rates of substance abuse and poorer treatment outcomes in this population.

Individuals with eating disorders have significantly higher rates of suicide attempts and completed suicides than the rest of the population, which may be related to the high comorbidity with depression. AN has the highest mortality rate of any other psychiatric disorder, and among AN patients, suicide is the second leading cause of death (after death from medical complications). Among those with AN, 2.5% die from suicide, and severity of depression has been found to be a predictor of suicide in this population (Franko & Keel, 2006). While *completed* suicide is higher among those with AN, the presence of binging-purging behavior significantly increases the risk of a suicide *attempt*. Suicide attempts occur in up to 20% of patients with

AN and in up to 35% of patients with BN (Franko & Keel, 2006). Higher rates of depression have been found among BN attempters; although, severity of depression did not prospectively predict suicidality in BN.

Sociocultural Etiology of Eating Disorders

There are a number of possible contributing factors to disordered eating behaviors. One commonly accepted theory is the sociocultural model. The sociocultural model of eating pathology hypothesizes that social pressure to be thin fosters an internalization of the thin ideal (see Stice, 2002, for a review). When individuals internalize the thin ideal and place too much value on the importance of appearance, this increases body dissatisfaction, which in turn promotes dieting, negative affect, and eating pathology in general. In other words, societal pressures are related to vulnerability to disordered eating and to the maintenance of these symptoms.

Depression related to the thin ideal and body dissatisfaction is theorized to be an important contributing factor to the development and maintenance of eating disorders. Body dissatisfaction itself, coupled with the belief that weight and/or shape are important may place women at higher risk for depression. Many women turn to dieting as an attempt to reach the thin ideal. However, dieting is not an effective way to manage weight, and these women repeatedly fail to reach an important goal. This profound lack of control over an important aspect of one's life lends itself to the development of lower self-esteem and learned helplessness. As in the learned helplessness theory of depression, the uncontrollability associated with failed attempts (dieting in this case) produces depressive symptoms. The thin ideal and depression model of eating disorders also suggests that these factors could account for the significantly higher incidence of depression in women beginning at puberty and the higher incidence of depression among women in Western societies.

The Neurochemical Connection

Recent research has examined the relationship between eating pathology and depression at the neurochemical level. Dysregulation of the hypothalamic-pituitary-adrenal (HPA) axis is well documented in patients with eating disorders and in patients with depression (Stokes & Sikes, 1991). The HPA axis is responsible for a number of important operations including feeding behaviors and emotional functioning. Tracts of neurons within the HPA axis control a number of neurotransmitters and neuromodulators including those with known relationships to eating disorders and mood, namely serotonin (5-HT). Brain 5-HT systems are known to modulate appetitive behaviors as well as mood.

Kaye and his colleagues (Kaye, Frank, Bailer, & Henry, 2005) have developed a theory about the relationship between eating disorders and serotonin based on 20 years of psychobiological research. Their theory proposes that at baseline, AN patients have higher than normal levels of 5-HT activity, which contributes to the premorbid anxiety and obsessionality frequently observed in these patients. During the acute phase of illness, patients with AN have lower 5-HT activity due to dietary-induced reduction of the amino acid tryptophan (the precursor of 5-HT), thus decreasing their anxiety. This finding is consistent with the clinical observation that many anorectics prefer a vegetarian lifestyle and often have a strong distaste for red meats and dairy (which have high levels tryptophan). Research also shows that during the active phase of illness, anorectics have a significant reduction in cerebrospinal fluid concentrations of 5-HT metabolites (e.g., 5-HIAA); however, after recovery, anorectics had much higher than normal concentrations of these metabolites. So, one possibility is that anorectic individuals are hyperserotonergic compared to non-eating-disordered individuals, which may be associated with their increased levels of anxiety and harm-avoidance.

The 5-HT system has also been found to play an important role in the binge-purge process, albeit in a different way than in AN-R. Acute tryptophan depletion actually increases depressive mood and mood lability in both ill and recovered bulimics (Kaye et al., 2000). Importantly, such disturbances are present when patients with BN are ill and persist after recovery, suggesting that these may be traits that are independent of the state of the illness (Kaye et al., 1998). Further support for this theory are studies showing that purging behaviors (including exercising and vomiting in both BN and AN-BP) release endogenous opioids (Sadock et al., 2005), which facilitates positive affect.

Treatment Implications

Cognitive behavioral therapy (CBT) for BN (CBT-BN) is the most successful treatment yet devised for the treatment of BN, and, based on CBT's success treating BN in randomized controlled trials, it has been designated an empirically supported treatment (Wilson & Pike, 2001). CBT-BN is based on a model that stresses the critical role of cognitive and behavioral factors in the maintenance of BN. Thus, clinicians using CBT-BN target the abnormal attitudes and ideas concerning weight and shape rather than the binging-purging behaviors. Sociocultural pressures on women to be thin and beautiful can lead to an overvaluation of weight and shape, leading to rigid restriction of food intake. This in turn, can leave one susceptible to periodic loss of control and binging behavior, which can then lead to purging behavior to alleviate anxiety about potential weight gain. Given the high rates of comorbidity with depression and the negative affective components of BN, taking a cognitive-behavioral approach may be effective in part because it addresses the negative beliefs and schemas present in depression.

On average, CBT-BN eliminates binge eating and purging in about 50% of all patients and reduces binging and purging in 80% or more. In some studies, CBT-BN has been found to be more advantageous than antidepressants and superior to other psychological treatments such as interpersonal psychotherapy (Wilson & Pike, 2001). However, a recent multidimensional meta-analysis found that there were no substantial differences between specific types of therapies, with the exception that individual treatment is more effective than group therapy (Thompson-Brenner, Glass, & Westen, 2003). While current treatments are particularly efficacious in reducing frequency of binge-purge episodes, they are less effective in treating the vulnerabilities that may give rise to future episodes (Thompson-Brenner et al., 2003). More studies with long-term follow-up are needed in order to determine the effectiveness of CBT-BN at preventing relapse. Furthermore, due to the chronicity and treatment resistance of BN, other treatment modalities are being modified for their application to this disorder. Dialectical behavior therapy has been adapted for use in BN with a specific focus on the emotion dysregulation often present in BN (Safer, Telch, & Agras, 2001). This treatment aims to replace binging and purging with emotion regulation skills, and preliminary studies have shown promising results.

The antidepressant fluoxetine (a selective serotonin-reuptake inhibitor) has been FDA approved for use in BN. In a controlled study examining the effectiveness of fluoxetine for BN, binge-purge episodes decreased by 80% in the fluoxetine group compared to controls. It could be that the 5-HT regulatory function of the SSRI improved the mood of these individuals and decreased depressive symptomatology, thus decreasing disordered eating patterns. These data are again suggestive of important connections between depression and binging behavior.

In stark contrast to the success of clinicians in treating BN, a recent review of randomized controlled trials for treatment of AN determined that there are no pharmacological agents or psychological treatments for adults that have been shown to be effective in large, multicenter randomized controlled trials (Bulik, Berkman, Brownley, Sedway, & Lohr, 2007). For adolescents with AN, the only treatment that has been shown to be effective is family therapy with a focus on parental control of renutrition (e.g., the Maudsley model). For adults with AN, although no psychotherapy has been shown to be effective during the acute stages of the illness, CBT has been shown to reduce the risk for relapse after weight has been restored. Antidepressant drugs targeting depressive symptoms in patients with AN have not been shown to produce significant and consistent improvements in terms of either weight gain or the renunciation of the pursuit of thinness (Krüger & Kennedy, 2000). In clinical practice, antipsychotic medication is widely used, and a few studies have shown promising preliminary results for olanzapine and risperidone, among others. Part of the problem is that pharmacological treatment is not well tolerated among underweight anorectics, which may be related to their abnormally high levels of 5-HT, and to the side effects of starvation, including hypotension, hypothermia, and abnormal EEGs. Clinicians should be aware of the complex relationships between depression and eating disorders when tailoring treatments to their patients.

Conclusions

Although AN and BN appear quite similar in their symptom profile, it is important to differentiate the role that depression plays in the development and maintenance of each disorder. Further complicating the clinical picture is the fact that binging and purging appear closely related to depression whether they occur in the form of AN-BP or BN. Nonetheless, the literature on etiology, neurobiology, and treatment of depression appears to have important implications for our understanding of eating disorders.

DANYALE MCCURDY AND LESLIE KARWOSKI

See also

Comorbidity
Hypothalamic-Pituitary-Adrenal Axis

Suicidal Cognition
Suicide Theories

Wilson, G. T., & Pike, K. M. (2001). Eating disorders. In D. H. Barlow (Ed.), *Clinical Handbook of Psychological Disorders* (3rd ed.) (pp. 332–375). New York: Guilford Press.

References

Bulik, C. M., Berkman, N. D., Brownley, K. A., Sedway, J. A., & Lohr, K. N. (2007). Anorexia nervosa treatment: A systematic review of randomized controlled trials. *International Journal of Eating Disorders, 40,* 310–320.

Carter, J. D., Joyce, P. R., Mulder, R. T., Luty, S. E., & Sullivan, P. F. (1999). Gender differences in the rate of comorbid axis I disorders in depressed outpatients. *Depression and Anxiety, 9,* 49–53.

Casper, R. C. (1998). Depression and eating disorders. *Depression and Anxiety, 8 Suppl. 1,* 96–104.

Franko, D. L., & Keel, P. K. (2006). Suicidality in eating disorders: Occurrence, correlates, and clinical implications. *Clinical Psychology Review, 26,* 769–782.

Kaye, W. H., Frank, G. K., Bailer, U. F., & Henry, S. E. (2005). Neurobiology of anorexia nervosa: Clinical implications of alterations of the function of serotonin and other neuronal systems. *International Journal of Eating Disorders, 37,* S15–S19.

Kaye, W. H., Gendall, K. A., Fernstrom, M. H., Fernstrom, J. D., McConoha, C. W., & Weltzin, T. E. (2000). Effects of acute tryptophan depletion on mood in bulimia nervosa. *Biological Psychiatry, 47,* 151–157.

Kaye, W. H., Greeno, C. G., Moss, H., Fernstrom, J., Fernstrom, M., Lilenfeld, L. R., et al. (1998). Alterations in serotonin activity and psychiatric symptoms after recovery from bulimia nervosa. *Archives of General Psychiatry, 55,* 927–935.

Krüger, S., & Kennedy, S. H. (2000). Psychopharmacotherapy of anorexia nervosa, bulimia nervosa, and binge-eating disorder. *Journal of Psychiatry and Neuroscience, 25,* 497–508.

Sadock, B. J. (2005). Eating disorders and obesity. In H. I. Kaplan & B. J. Sadock (Eds.), *Pocket handbook of clinical psychiatry* (4th ed.) (pp. 225–235). Philadelphia: Lippincott, Williams, and Wilkins.

Safer, D. L., Telch, C. F., & Agras, W. S. (2001). Dialectical behavior therapy adapted for bulimia: A case report. *International Journal of Eating Disorders, 30,* 101–106.

Stice, E. (2002). Risk and maintenance factors for eating pathology: A meta-analytic review. *Psychological Bulletin, 128,* 825–848.

Stokes, P. E., & Sikes, C. R. (1991). Hypothalamic-pituitary-adrenal axis in psychiatric disorders. *Annual Review of Medicine, 42,* 519–531.

Thompson-Brenner, H., Glass, S., & Westen, D. (2003). A multidimensional meta-analysis of psychotherapy for bulimia nervosa. *Clinical Psychology: Science and Practice, 10,* 269–287.

Westen, D., & Harnden-Fischer, J. (2001). Personality profiles in eating disorders: Rethinking the distinction between axis I and axis II. *American Journal of Psychiatry, 158,* 547–562.

Williamson, D. A., Gleaves, D. H., & Stewart, T. M. (2005). Categorical versus dimensional model of eating disorders: An examination of the evidence. *International Journal of Eating Disorders, 37,* 1–10.

Electroconvulsive Therapy

Electroconvulsive therapy (ECT) is a medical treatment used primarily to treat severe depression. In continuous use for over 70 years, procedural refinements and modern anesthesia techniques have made ECT a well-accepted, standard part of contemporary psychiatric practice. The clinical use of ECT has been fully described in the second edition of the guidelines of the American Psychiatric Association's Task Force on Electroconvulsive Therapy (2001) and in the *New England Journal of Medicine* series Clinical Therapeutics (Lisanby, 2007).

Indications for ECT include major depression (in the context of either unipolar or bipolar disorder), mania, and schizophrenia. By far the most common indication is depression. ECT is usually considered when the depressive illness has not responded to one or more trials of an antidepressant medication, or when the clinical situation is so urgent that immediate, definitive intervention is required. Suicide risk, severe psychosis, malnutrition, or catatonia are clinical factors that should be considered in the need for urgent intervention. ECT is also effective as a treatment for acute mania but is much less commonly used for this indication. ECT has a limited role in the treatment of schizophrenia, largely for the relief of acute, positive psychotic symptoms, early in the course of the illness. Finally, ECT may be indicated in the treatment of catatonia of any etiology and in some cases of severe neuroleptic malignant syndrome.

ECT is typically performed in a hospital or ambulatory surgery setting. Prior to ECT, informed consent is obtained, a process in which potential benefits and risks are explained, and alternative treatments are described. The ECT procedure itself consists of the induction of a brain seizure while the patient is under general anesthesia and muscle relaxation.

A short-acting intravenous anesthetic, usually methohexital, is given, followed by a muscle relaxant to block the motor manifestations of the seizure. Oxygen is delivered to the patient via face mask throughout the procedure. The seizure is induced by the passage of a brief electrical stimulus via electrodes applied to the scalp. The type (brief-pulse, square wave) and amount of electrical stimulus have been the subject of extensive study, which has led to clinically accepted guidelines about optimum electrical dosing strategies for each electrode placement. The stimulus must be sufficient to induce a generalized seizure, and optimized to provide maximal antidepressant efficacy, while causing the least cognitive impairment.

Three different placements for the stimulus electrodes are commonly used in contemporary practice: bilateral or bitemporal (electrodes on left and right temples), right unilateral (one electrode on the right temple and one to the right of the vertex of the skull), and bifrontal (both electrodes on either side of the forehead). The three electrode placements differ in their antidepressant efficacy (bilateral is slightly more effective and probably faster acting) and the degree to which they cause cognitive effects (right unilateral causes less memory impairment) (Abrams, 2002).

The side effects of ECT may be divided into medical adverse events, cognitive effects, and common, but not serious, side effects. Serious adverse medical events are rare, and ECT is considered one of the safest procedures performed under general anesthesia. There are no absolute medical contraindications to ECT. Because the seizure causes an increase in heart rate and blood pressure, recent myocardial infarction is a relative contraindication. Because the seizure also causes an increase in intracranial pressure, any neurological condition associated with preexisting increased intracranial pressure (e.g., brain tumor) is a relative contraindication. Because of its safety, ECT may be recommended in the elderly with complex medical problems and in pregnancy. The pre-ECT evaluation includes a full medical and psychiatric history, knowledge of the patient's current medications, and, at a minimum, cardiogram (EKG), complete blood count, and metabolic panel. Additional laboratory studies may be indicated for patients with preexisting medical conditions.

ECT causes predictable cognitive effects, including memory loss. For most patients, these effects are acceptable, in light of the considerable relief from depression that they may expect with ECT. Immediately after ECT there is a period of confusion and disorientation that typically resolves over 10 to 30 minutes. Anterograde amnesia occurs during the course of ECT and typically resolves completely within 1 to 2 weeks. Retrograde amnesia, the cognitive effect of most concern, occurs during and after the course of ECT. It consists of gaps in recent memory, usually extending back weeks or months, and, rarely, years. Recovery of memory often occurs in the weeks or months following ECT but may be incomplete in some patients. The extent of retrograde amnesia is likely correlated with the amount and intensity (a function of several factors, including electrode placement, stimulus dose, and time between treatments) of the ECT administered (Sackeim et al., 1993). The etiology of the cognitive effects of ECT is unknown. Human and animal studies, including MRI studies, have shown that ECT does not cause brain structural anatomic damage. Common, but not serious, side effects of ECT include headache, muscle aches (largely from the muscle relaxant, succinylcholine), and nausea. All usually respond to simple, routine care with analgesics or antinausea agents.

ECT is given as an acute treatment course for the resolution of an episode of psychiatric illness, usually depression. There is no standard number of treatments in a course; rather, the patient should be treated until recovery, or a plateau in improvement occurs. Most patients will require 6 to 12 treatments, but some recover with fewer, and some require more. Treatments are usually given two or three times per week. Depressive symptoms and cognitive status should be monitored during the course of ECT, either by clinical interview or standardized rating scales. The acute antidepressant efficacy of ECT is reported to exceed that of antidepressant medications. Recent data show remission rates of greater than 60% (Kellner et al., 2006), and older studies have reported higher rates. Lower remission rates are reported in highly treatment-resistant samples and when ECT technique is suboptimal. Remission rates are particularly high in psychotic depression, a severe form of major depression.

Maintenance ECT is the term given to the use of a single ECT to prevent symptom recurrence in a remitted patient. This is generally done on an outpatient basis, typically every 2 to 5 weeks. Maintenance ECT is often reserved for those patients with the most severe and refractory forms of depressive illness, and who have not remained well, despite trials of pharmacotherapy.

Despite a wealth of clinical and scientific data to support its efficacy and safety, stigma remains a major impediment to the appropriate use of ECT. Media depictions of ECT continue to show archaic techniques and inhumane treatment. Such misrepresentations, while making for sensational entertainment, may inappropriately frighten and mislead patients. Organized antipsychiatry efforts have often targeted ECT (Shorter & Healy, 2007).

A complete understanding of the mechanism of action of ECT remains elusive. However, a great deal is known about many of the neurobiological effects of ECT on the brain. These include effects on classical neurotransmitter systems (functional increases in dopamine, serotonin, and norepinephrine, as well as GABA), the normalization of the hypothalamic-pituitary-adrenal axis (often dysregulated in mood disorders) and potential anticonvulsant effects. Recent studies also have demonstrated the neurotropic effects of ECT in animal models, including neurogenesis and changes in synaptic plasticity (Perera et al., 2007).

CHARLES KELLNER AND NAMGYAL BHUTIA

See also

Biological Models of Depression
Brain Circuitry

References

Abrams, R. (2002). *Electroconvulsive therapy*. New York: Oxford University Press.

Kellner, C. H., Knapp, R. G., Petrides, G., Rummans, T. A., Husain, M. M., Rasmussen, K., et al. (2006). Continuation electroconvulsive therapy vs. pharmacotherapy for relapse prevention in major depression: A multisite study from the Consortium for Research in Electroconvulsive Therapy (CORE). *Archives of General Psychiatry, 63,* 1337–1344.

Lisanby, S. H. (2007). Electroconvulsive therapy for depression. *New England Journal of Medicine, 357,* 1939–1945.

Perera, T. D., Coplan, J. D., Lisanby, S. H., Lipira, C. M., Arif, M., Carpio, C., et al. (2007). Antidepressant-induced neurogenesis in the hippocampus of adult nonhuman primates. *Journal of Neuroscience, 27,* 4894–4901.

Sackeim, H. A., Prudic, J., Devanand, D. P., Kiersky, J. E., Fitzsimons, L., Moody, B. J., et al. (1993). Effects of stimulus intensity and electrode placement on the efficacy and cognitive effects of electroconvulsive therapy. *New England Journal of Medicine, 328,* 839–846.

Shorter, E., & Healy, D. (2007). *Shock therapy: A history of electroconvulsive treatment in mental illness*. Piscataway, NJ: Rutgers University Press.

Task Force on Electroconvulsive Therapy. (2001). *The practice of electroconvulsive therapy: Recommendations for treatment, training and privileging* (2nd ed.). Washington, DC: American Psychiatric Association.

Endogenous and Reactive Depression

Before the 1920s, a binary view of depression was predominant, with endogenous/psychotic and neurotic/reactive/exogenous depressions representing two conceptually distinct diagnostic categories. This binary paradigm is in contrast to the unitary diagnostic paradigm that currently predominates in which the depressive syndrome is viewed as the common thread among heterogeneous presentations of depression. According to the binary view of depression, several differences exist between an endogenous or psychotic depressive syndrome and a neurotic or reactive syndrome. The endogenous syndrome is thought to be of relatively greater severity, is less likely to result from a recognized life stressor, and represents a marked deviation from an individual's typical psychological functioning. Also, several of the following are often present: acute onset, severe anhedonia, lack of reactivity to positive stimuli, depression experienced as worse in the morning, relatively unvarying mood from day to day, psychomotor retardation, insomnia, and weight loss. The reactive syndrome, by contrast, is thought to be of relatively lesser severity, often triggered by an external event, and including preexisting psychological vulnerability, more responsiveness to positive stimuli, more varied presentation from day to day, and sometimes anxiety (Kendell, 1976).

Some researchers have used the term *psychotic depression* to refer to depressive episodes accompanied by lack of insight, delusions, or hallucinations. Similarly, the term *neurotic* often conveys a relatively circumscribed meaning in contemporary clinical and personality literature. These semantic differences have resulted in some confusion regarding the extent to which endogenous depression and psychotic depression are synonymous and, similarly, the extent to which neurotic depression and reactive depression are synonymous. In the context of the binary view of depression, however, each of these pairs of terms tends to be treated as representing the same type of depressive syndrome (Kendell, 1976).

In the 1920s, British researchers began empirically testing the assumptions of the binary view. Neither the unitary nor binary view emerged as a clear winner in this debate until the 1930s, at which time new multivariate statistical analyses failed to provide conclusive evidence supporting two distinct types of depressive syndromes (see Parker, 2000, for a review). The binary paradigm of depression classification, however, did not disappear after the 1930s. Researchers in the United States began to question the veracity of the unitary view when clinicians observed that patients with endogenous symptoms responded more favorably to treatment with medications than did those with reactive or neurotic features. Empirical research generally supported this observation of differential

response to somatic treatments between individuals with endogenous and reactive depressions as defined by the *Diagnostic and Statistical Manual of Mental Disorders*, second edition (*DSM-II;* American Psychiatric Association [APA], 1968; Klerman, 1971).

The diagnostic criteria for depression changed, however, with the publication of the *DSM-III* (APA, 1980). Instead of making a distinction between endogenous and reactive types of depression, the phrase "with melancholic features" was offered as a diagnostic hook that could added to the major depressive disorder diagnosis to indicate the presence of endogenous sympomatology. This *DSM-III* system for diagnosing depressive disorders was thought to represent the heterogeneity of depressive syndromes while, overall, still adhering to the unitary diagnostic paradigm. As concluded by Zimmerman, Black, & Coryell (1989), however, empirical research examining differential treatment response to medications and electroconvulsive therapy failed to support the *DSM-III*'s melancholic subtyping. The diagnostic criteria for melancholic features were revised in the *DSM-III-R* (APA, 1987) to include favorable treatment response as contributing to a diagnosis of major depressive disorder with melancholic features. With the publication of the *DSM-IV* (APA, 1994), however, this criterion reflecting favorable treatment response was omitted. Therefore, the current diagnostic criteria for the presence of melancholic features in the context of major depressive disorder are largely similar to those outlined the *DSM-III*.

An article published in 1973 by Akiskal and McKinney is often cited as the article that conclusively quashed the dichotomous classification of depression in the United States. In this article, the authors presented a "final common pathway model." With this model, the authors posited that a variety of genetic factors and psychosocial stressors can interact to produce a variety of subsequent neurochemical changes. The primary conclusion of the model is that, although different individuals may exhibit different precipitous neurochemical changes, these changes engender a neurophysiological final common pathway for those who develop depressive disorders. Therefore, all depressive disorders, according to Akiskal and McKinney's model, arise from this common neurophysiological response. This article received an immense amount of attention from researchers interested in the nosology of depression. The resulting movement toward the unitarian view of depression was solidified in North America with the publication of the *DSM-III* (Parker, 2000).

Authors espousing the unitary paradigm or binary paradigm are not alone in their attempts to articulate the proper nosology of depression. Other notable systems for classifying depressive disorders have included dimensional models, hierarchical models, and subtyping systems resulting in greater than two groups. Another way of thinking about the heterogeneity of depression, the so-called kindling hypothesis, has also gotten considerable attention from depression researchers. This approach to depression recognizes that major depression is often characterized by a series of depressive episodes. Furthermore, there seems to be a predictable pattern to accompanying these episodes, such that an individual's first depressive episode is typically reactive, or in response to a recognized life stressor. The likelihood of a precipitous stressor declines, and the likelihood of an endogenous episode increases, however, with each subsequent depressive episode experienced by the individual. This area of depression research is relatively new but may provide insight regarding how the course of depressive illness may influence the presentation of reactive versus endogenous symptomatology over time (e.g., Monroe & Harkness, 2005).

MELINDA A. GADDY

See also

Classification of Depression
Diagnostic and Statistical Manual of Mental Disorders
Melancholia

References

American Psychiatric Association. (1968). *Diagnostic and statistical manual of mental disorders* (2nd ed.). Washington, DC: Author.

American Psychiatric Association. (1980). *Diagnostic and statistical manual of mental disorders* (3rd ed.). Washington, DC: Author.

American Psychiatric Association. (1987). *Diagnostic and statistical manual of mental disorders* (3rd ed., revised). Washington, DC: Author.

American Psychiatric Association. (1994). *Diagnostic and statistical manual of mental disorders* (4th ed.). Washington, DC: Author.

Akiskal, H. S., & McKinney, W. T. (1973). Depressive disorders: Toward a unified hypothesis: Clinical, experimental, genetic, and neurophysiological data are integrated. *Science, 182*, 20–29.

Kendell, R. E. (1976). The classification of depressions: A review of contemporary confusion. *British Journal of Psychiatry, 129*, 15–28.

Klerman, G. L. (1971). Clinical research in depression. *Archives of General Psychiatry, 24*, 305–319.

Monroe, S. M., & Harkness, K. L. (2005). Life stress, the "kindling" hypothesis, and the recurrence of depression: Considerations from a life stress perspective. *Psychological Review, 112*, 417–445.

Parker, G. (2000). Classifying depression: Should paradigms lost be regained? *American Journal of Psychiatry, 157*, 1195–1203.

Zimmerman, M., Black, D. W., & Coryell, W. (1989). Diagnostic criteria for melancholia: The comparative validity of the DSM-III and DSM-III-R. *Archives of General Psychiatry, 46*, 361–368.

Epidemiology

Epidemiology is the study of the occurrence and correlates of disease in the population. Although much epidemiological research is purely descriptive, investigation of disease correlates can provide insights into causes leading to preventive or ameliorative interventions. Epidemiological research is conventionally thought to have three components: descriptive (i.e., estimating incidence prevalence and descriptive correlates), analytical (i.e., searching for causal risk factors), and experimental (i.e., evaluating experimental interventions). Most epidemiological research on depression has been descriptive or analytical, although some experimental studies exist.

Information about the descriptive and analytical epidemiology of depression has proliferated over the past two decades due to development of fully structured research diagnostic interviews that stimulated a number of community epidemiological surveys. The most commonly used instrument of this sort is the World Health Organization's (WHO) Composite International Diagnostic Interview (CIDI; www.hcp.med.harvard.edu/wmhcidi). The WHO coordinates nationally representative CIDI surveys in countries throughout the world through the WHO World Mental Health (WMH) Survey Initiative (2005).

A number of recent literature reviews have presented detailed overviews of the descriptive epidemiological literature on depression (e.g., Somers, Goldner, Waraich, & Hsu, 2006; Waraich, Goldner, Somers, & Hsu, 2004; Wittchen & Jacobi, 2005). Several patterns are consistent in these reviews. One is that major depressive disorder makes up the vast majority (70%–80%) of all lifetime mood disorders, with dysthymic disorder and bipolar disorder much less common than major depressive disorder. The median lifetime prevalence estimate of mood disorders in WHO WMH surveys is approximately 11% with an interquartile range (IQR; 25th–75th percentiles) of 7.6% to 17.9%. Twelve-month prevalence estimates average approximately 5% with an IQR of 3.4% to 6.8%. Prevalence estimates tend to be higher in developed than developing countries, but controversy exists as to whether this is due to genuine differences in prevalence or to more accurate diagnoses in developed than developing countries.

Despite differences in prevalence estimates, retrospectively assessed major depressive disorder age-of-onset (AOO) estimates are remarkably consistent across surveys. AOO distributions based on these estimates show consistently low major depressive disorder prevalence until the early teens, followed by a roughly linear increase through late middle age and a declining increase thereafter. The median AOO of major depressive disorder is in the mid-20s. Caution is needed in interpreting these results, though, as they are based on retrospective lifetime recall and thus are subject to bias. Indeed, somewhat earlier AOO estimates are found in prospective-longitudinal studies than in retrospective studies, although AOO

distributions based on prospective data are generally quite consistent with those based on retrospective data.

Course of illness has been much less well studied in epidemiological surveys than prevalence or AOO. Indeed, few direct questions about course of illness are included in most community epidemiological surveys of depression, and even fewer such surveys were carried out repeatedly in cohorts to allow the course to be studied directly. An indirect assessment of persistence can be obtained by comparing estimates of recent prevalence (variously reported for the year, 6 months, or 1 month before interview) with estimates of lifetime prevalence. The 12-month to lifetime major depressive disorder prevalence ratio is in the range .3 to .5. Although this ratio typically declines with age, the decline is fairly modest, suggesting that depression is often quite persistent throughout the life course. The few long-term longitudinal studies that exist in representative samples of people with major depressive disorder suggest that this persistence is due to a recurrent-intermittent course that often features waxing and waning of episodes.

Comorbidity is a common feature of depression, with up to half those with lifetime depression also meeting criteria for other lifetime mental disorders and even higher proportions of recent cases having comorbidity. Factor analysis of diagnostic comorbidity in community surveys consistently finds that depression is part of an internalizing dimension that has secondary dimensions of fear disorders (panic, phobia) and distress disorders (depression, generalized anxiety disorder, posttraumatic stress disorder; Kendler, Prescott, Myers, & Neale, 2003). Comorbid depression is generally more severe and persistent than noncomorbid depression. As comorbid depression typically has a later AOO than other comorbid disorders, a question has been raised whether early detection and treatment of temporally primary disorders might help either prevent or delay the onset of later depression. No experimental epidemiological studies have been carried out, though, to evaluate this possibility.

Many analytical studies have been carried out on risk and protective factors for the onset and course of major depressive disorder. Commonly found sociodemographic correlates of point prevalence (i.e., the existence of depression at the time of interview) are female gender, young age, and various indicators of disadvantaged social status (low socioeconomic status, separation or divorce, unemployment). Measures of stressors, including retrospective reports about childhood adversities as well as reports about recent stressful life events and difficulties also have been found consistently to be associated with depression, as have a number of protective-vulnerability factors (e.g., social support and various dimensions of personality, cognitive style, and coping disposition) and vulnerability factors. Stressors and protective-vulnerability factors often have been found to have nonadditive associations in predicting depression, a pattern that is typically interpreted as due to stress-buffering effects of the protective factors or stress-exacerbating effects of the vulnerability factors.

Analytical epidemiological studies of depression vary enormously in their sophistication. Most are cross-sectional studies that assess respondents at a single point in time and make no attempt to sort out temporal priorities between the presumed risk factors and depression. In studies of this sort, it is impossible to know if a significant association between, say, low socioeconomic status and depression is due to an effect of socioeconomic status–related stress-vulnerability factors on depression, an effect of depression on socioeconomic status, or some combination of both. Plausible evidence exists for reciprocal effects. A history of depression in early adolescence, for example, is a significant predictor of subsequent truncated educational attainment, although we do not know if this association is causal or due to effects of other variables (e.g., childhood adversities, genes) that are causes of both depression and low educational attainment. At the same time, we know that low educational attainment is associated with elevated risk of the subsequent first onset of depression, although we again

do not know if this association is due to a causal effect of low educational attainment (presumably mediated by more direct effects on life experiences that increase risk of stress exposure) or to effects of other variables that are causes of both depression and low educational attainment.

Longitudinal study designs in which respondents are followed over time can help disentangle complex reciprocal associations. Even long-term longitudinal cohort studies that assess community samples of respondents at numerous points in time over many years are incapable, though, of resolving all uncertainties about causal processes definitively. This is well illustrated by the confusion that continues to exist about the causal mechanisms underlying the widely documented and intriguing time-lagged association between smoking and the subsequent onset of depression and suicide (e.g., Bronisch, Hofler, & Lieb, 2008). One difficulty in establishing a clear causal connection in these studies is that baseline smoking is related to many other variables that are known to predict depression and suicide. Although some of these associated variables can be controlled for statistically in longitudinal studies, failure to explain the predictive effect of smoking with these controls cannot be taken as definitive evidence against common causes being responsible because it is impossible to control perfectly for all common causes. To make matters more complicated, evidence that such controls lead to the disappearance of the predictive association between smoking and later depression cannot be taken as definitive evidence that common causes are responsible because some of the control variables might be mediators (i.e., consequences of smoking that, in turn, caused depression) rather than common causes. More complex statistical methods that help distinguish mediators from common causes address these uncertainties, but these methods require simplifying assumptions that introduce additional sources of uncertainty.

Ongoing uncertainties are a necessary part of nonexperimental research, as robust documentation of causality requires experimentation. The main goals of analytical epidemiology consequently are to generate hypotheses about potential causal processes and to evaluate rival interpretations so as to narrow down the number of such hypotheses to be tested in experimental studies. As noted at the beginning of this entry, though, there have not been many experimental epidemiological studies of risk or protective factors for depression. One major reason for this is that many of the hypothesized causes of depression, such as chronic financial adversity, are difficult to manipulate experimentally. As a result, most important experimental epidemiological studies of these risk factors have been "natural experiments." For example, evidence that financial adversity is a causal risk factor for mental illness comes from natural experiments that compare workers with matched backgrounds in communities that did versus did not experience a recent plant closing (Dew, Bromet, & Schulberg, 1987).

Studies that evaluate the predictive effects of diverse stressful life experiences use the same logic as natural experiments by distinguishing stressors that appear to occur at random (e.g., destruction of a home by a tornado) from those that could have been influenced by prior depression or risk factors for depression (e.g., divorce). The critical design issue here is the selection of an appropriate comparison group, as risk factor exposure can usually be considered random only within some range of comparison. For example, while an adolescent getting into a high-speed car accident driving drunk at 3 a.m. is far from random, the death of one's adolescent child in such an accident might be a random occurrence in the population of parents whose adolescent children had such accidents and either died or survived. Careful consideration of appropriate comparison groups could substantially expand the number and variety of natural experiments carried out to evaluate risk factors for depression (Kessler, 1997).

While most natural experiments focus on risk factors, others study risk-protective factors. One of the most intriguing of these examined the long-term outcomes of adults who were placed in foster homes as children due to extreme abuse or neglect in their childhood family homes (Kessler et al., 2008). All of the study subjects were eligible for placement in a model private foster care program that provided much more intensive services than the public foster care system (e.g., carefully selected and supported foster parents, case workers with low case loads, greater access to psychotherapy and other supportive services, and a guarantee of free college tuition if the foster child is accepted for college admission). Only a random one-fourth of the subjects were actually placed in the model program, though, while the other three-fourths were placed in standard public foster care due to the chance availability of an opening in the model program at the time the subject became eligible for placement. A long-term follow-up study more than a decade after leaving care showed that model foster care alumni had less than half the prevalence of major depressive disorder of public system alumni.

This finding is important because it addresses an uncertainty in the risk factor literature concerning the strong predictive associations found between childhood adversities and adult depression. It is unclear whether these associations are causal or due to genetic determinants of depression, which of course are shared by parents and children, that cause both childhood adversities (i.e., parental depression and the other adversities often associated with it, such as parental violence, divorce, and financial difficulty) and the subsequent onset of depression in the adult offspring of depressed parents. The random assignment in the foster care natural experiment showed that manipulation of exposure to adversity (as well as to other risk-protective factors) can have a dramatic effect in reducing adult major depressive disorder, confirming that an important component of the naturalistic association is, in fact, causal. Based on this result, further nonexperimental analyses of these data are being carried out to help pinpoint the active ingredients in the intervention for future refinement.

Perhaps the largest social policy experiment that manipulated exposure to a variety of childhood risk-protective factors and evaluated effects on depression is the U.S. Department of Housing and Urban Development (HUD) Moving to Opportunity (MTO) experiment (HUD, 2000). MTO was an ongoing research demonstration project that randomly selected experimental samples of very low income single-parent families living in public housing in high-poverty urban neighborhoods in five cities to receive housing vouchers and counseling to help them move into low-poverty areas. Control groups were included to evaluate the effects of the experiment. The 5-year evaluation documented substantial positive effects of the experiment on the mental health of both adults and children (HUD, 2003). A 10-year follow-up study is currently underway to determine if these positive effects persist and to gather more information that can be used in non-experimental analyses aimed at elucidating causal pathways in an effort to guide efforts to improve future iterations of those and other interventions.

A difficulty in interpreting the results of large-scale epidemiological intervention experiments like MTO is that the interventions tend to be multidimensional, making it difficult to determine exactly what it was that had the effect. Even seemingly specific natural interventions, like the accidental death of a spouse, have many components (e.g., financial loss if the deceased was a breadwinner, change in social networks to the extent that the deceased helped maintain networks, change in access to help with practical day-to-day activities to the extent that the deceased was responsible for balancing the checkbook or cooking, etc.), making it difficult to know what was lost or, in some cases gained (e.g., if the deceased was abusive and the surviving spouse felt trapped in the marriage, if the deceased had a large life insurance policy, etc.), by the death. This kind of uncertainty can be addressed in other areas of research by carrying out a large number of small, coordinated, rapid turn around experiments that help refine understanding

by manipulating increasingly more specific components. (For an excellent example of sequential programmatic experimentation of this sort, see Latané & Darley, 1970.) This approach is much more difficult in epidemiological experiments, though, as the latter tend to be very expensive, take quite a few years to carry out, and involve interventions that are very difficult to deliver in such a way as to manipulate only one narrow element. These features have slowed progress in experimental epidemiological research on depression. It is unlikely that this state of affairs will change markedly in the future because of the inherent constraints on mounting a large number of social policy interventions. Increased exploitation of natural experiments is a much more feasible way to move forward the agenda of experimental epidemiological study of depression more rapidly in the future than the past.

One final area of recent epidemiological research on depression that merits discussion is research on the societal consequences of depression. Epidemiologists traditionally have focused on the causes rather than the consequences of the illnesses they study based on the implicit assumption that illness is bad and prevention or cure good. However, in the face of rising health care costs and increasing calls for evidence-based practices that take cost-effectiveness into consideration, epidemiologists increasingly have turned their attention to the investigation of consequences. The most influential work of this sort is the WHO Global Burden of Disease (GBD) project, which attempted to rank-order the societal burden of a wide range of diseases in every country in the world by taking into consideration information about both incidence-prevalence and the adverse effects of specific diseases on role functioning and mortality (WHO, 2004). Perhaps the most striking result of the GBD project was that major depression was found to be the second most burdensome disease in the entire world as well as the single most burdensome disease among people in early adulthood. This result has been disputed based on the fact that the estimates of disease-specific disability burden in the GBD project were expert judgments rather than empirical estimates. However, this controversy has led to a dramatic increase in empirical research on disease-specific burden over the past decade, some of it focused on depression.

Community epidemiological research of the latter sort has shown that the number of days out of role in the entire U.S. population associated with depression is the largest of any health problem other than musculoskeletal disorders, supporting the GBD conclusion that depression is among the most burdensome of all diseases (Merikangas et al., 2007). Epidemiological research has also shown that depression is associated with enormous costs to corporate America in the form of increased sickness absence, decreased on-the-job work performance, and increased job turnover (with associated hiring-training costs and disruptions in workflow). These findings do not document causality, as they are based on naturalistic associations. However, a recent experimental intervention informed by these epidemiological findings showed that screening, outreach, and best-practices treatment of depressed workers is associated with such substantial reductions in adverse workplace outcomes that they have significantly more financial value to employers (in the form of increased work performance and decreased hiring-training costs) than the costs of treatment (Wang et al., 2007). This finding not only indirectly documents that depression has substantial adverse workplace effects, but that an intervention aimed at reversing these effects represents an investment opportunity for employers.

The epidemiological data reviewed here document that depression is commonly occurring in the general population, often has an early AOO and a persistent course, and often is associated with significant adverse societal costs, some of which can be reversed with treatment. Considerable information exists about risk factors for the onset and course of depression. Much less is known about depression subtypes, epidemiological predictors of differential treatment response, and effects of epidemiologically informed interventions in preventing the onset or recurrence of depression, which is why none of these topics was reviewed here. However, all of these topics are the focus of ongoing epidemiological investigation, and there is good reason to believe that progress will be made in addressing these topics in the coming years.

RONALD C. KESSLER

See also

Age of Onset of Depression
Classification of Depression
Course of Depression

References

Bronisch, T., Hofler, M., & Lieb, R. (2008). Smoking predicts suicidality: Findings from a prospective community study. *Journal of Affective Disorders, 108,* 135–145.

Dew, M. A., Bromet, E. J., & Schulberg, H. C. (1987). A comparative analysis of two community stressors' long-term mental health effects. *American Journal of Community Psychology, 15,* 167–184.

Housing and Urban Development. (2003). *Moving to opportunity for fair housing demonstration : interim impacts evaluation.* Retrieved August 12, 2008, from http://www.huduser.org/publications/fairhsg/mtoFinal.html

Housing and Urban Development. (2005). *Moving to opportunity for fair housing.* Retrieved August 12, 2008, from www.hud.gov/progdesc/mto.cfm

Kendler, K. S., Prescott, C. A., Myers, J., & Neale, M. C. (2003). The structure of genetic and environmental risk factors for common psychiatric and substance use disorders in men and women. *Archives of General Psychiatry, 60,* 929–937.

Kessler, R. C. (1997). The effects of stressful life events on depression. *Annual Review of Psychology, 48,* 191–214.

Kessler, R. C., Pecora, P. J., Williams, J., Hiripi, E., O'Brien, K., English, D., et al. (2008). The effects of enhanced foster care on the long-term physical and mental health of foster care alumni. *Archives of General Psychiatry, 65,* 625–633.

Latané, B., & Darley, J. M. (1970). *The unresponsive bystander: Why doesn't he help?* New York: Appleton-Century-Crofts.

Merikangas, K. R., Ames, M., Cui, L., Stang, P. E., Ustun, T. B., Von Korff, M., et al. (2007). The impact of comorbidity of mental and physical conditions on role disability in the US adult household population. *Archives of General Psychiatry, 64,* 1180–1188.

Somers, J. M., Goldner, E. M., Waraich, P., & Hsu, L. (2006). Prevalence and incidence studies of anxiety disorders: A systematic review of the literature. *Canadian Journal of Psychiatry, 51,* 100–113.

Wang, P. S., Simon, G. E., Avorn, J., Azocar, F., Ludman, E. J., McCulloch, J., et al. (2007). Telephone screening, outreach, and care management for depressed workers and impact on clinical and work productivity outcomes: A randomized controlled trial. *Journal of the American Medical Association, 298,* 1401–1411.

Waraich, P., Goldner, E. M., Somers, J. M., & Hsu, L. (2004). Prevalence and incidence studies of mood disorders: A systematic review of the literature. *Canadian Journal of Psychiatry, 49,* 124–138.

Wittchen, H. U., & Jacobi, F. (2005). Size and burden of mental disorders in Europe: A critical review and appraisal of 27 studies. *European Neuropsychopharmacology, 15,* 357–376.

World Health Organization. (2004). *Global burden of disease.* Retrieved August 12, 2008, from http://www.who.int/healthinfo/bodproject/en/index.html

World Mental Health Survey Initiative. (2005). *WMH historical overview.* Retrieved August 12, 2008, from www.hcp.med.harvard.edu/wmh

Evolution

It is now agreed that depression is a mental state that involves a toning down of positive emotion such that the patient is unable to experience pleasure from normally pleasurable activities, nor can he or she anticipate pleasure. In addition there is a disturbance in motivation and drive. These primary symptoms are accompanied by a range of others that link to negative views of the self, world, and future; an accentuation of negative emotion, particularly anxiety and irritability; and sleep and fatigue disturbances. On the face of it these characteristics would seem to put an animal at a severe disadvantage in the struggle for survival and reproduction. Evolutionary psychopathologists are therefore interested in two key questions in relation to depression. First, what might be the adaptive functions of evolving emotional regulation systems that can tone down positive emotions in certain contexts; when might it be useful to be (at least mildly) depressed? Answers to these questions lead on to another: under what conditions and in what way might this natural capacity to tone down positive feelings and increase our threat sensitivity become maladaptive such that the toning down of positive emotion is either too severe or intense, too easily triggered, or lasts too long (Gilbert, 2006)?

Many theories have outlined possible functions for depression. Some of these theories focus on the full syndrome, whereas others focus on the underlying mechanisms of (say) positive and negative emotion regulation. Attachment theorists point out that when young individuals in the wild are separated from their group or caring others (mothers), being able to "hunker down," stop exploring or taking an interest in new things, and hiding, is an advantage. This individual is not wandering about signaling distress, is not attracting the attention of predators, and is conserving energy. What is interesting about linking depression to this regulating system (of being cut off from caring in a potentially hostile environment) is that it mirrors depressed people's subjective experience. They often feel cut off from others, feel emotionally alone, and have a desire to hide away—a kind of "hide at the back of the cave" phenomenon.

Another theory of depression suggests that down regulation of positive emotions occur in the context of serious defeat. This loss of positive emotions goes with loss of confidence, increased submissive behavior, and tendencies to view the self as inferior. This model is interesting because these too are common subjective experiences of depressed people; they can feel defeated and inferior to others and behave submissively. The attachment model and the social defeat or entrapment model are interesting because they indicate how changes in emotion, thinking, attending, self-experience, and social behavior might all be related. Theorists are also suggesting that these two systems can interact, partly because both of them operate on the same affect regulation systems (Gilbert, 2007).

There are many other theories addressing the functional utility of depression. Some theorists point out that depression is more likely when we are confronted by stressors we cannot control and feel trapped in stressful situations. Other theorists believe that changes in positive feelings can be triggered in situations where active behavior and drive are unlikely to pay off; no amount of effort is likely to work. In this context depression helps us to disengage from not-obtainable things that still have high incentive value (Nesse, 2000). Yet other theorists believe that depression can operate as a care-eliciting signal, although depression is often a time that people lose the support of others rather than gain it. So there are a range of theories that look at the functions of emotional regulation in terms of past challenges that animals have had to face. It is suggested that the mechanisms that evolved to cope with those challenges continue to operate as templates for our own emotional regulation systems.

Evolutionary approaches need to be contextualized in biopsychosocial models. Once we have specified the regulating mechanisms for mood variation, the question arises as to the sources of that variation. Just as we can see that anxiety and anger have very useful functions, we can also appreciate that they can become too severe or intense, too easily triggered, or last too long. So the question is why should that occur? Answers to these questions can reside in complex interactions between genes, social environments, developmental history, and current styles of thinking (Gilbert, 2004). Each of these processes individually and in interaction can operate directly on emotional regulation systems. For example, some environments may be very different from our ancestral social environments, may be stressful and offer little means of escape (e.g., poverty and domestic violence, people isolated in homes looking after young children), or be emotionally impoverished. Some individuals may have acquired styles of thinking that focus them on their lack of attachment to others and/or inferiority and submissiveness. Just as our thoughts, fantasies, and images of (say) something sexual can stimulate our pituitary (be physiologically activating), so certain types of negative thoughts may stimulate physiological systems that pattern the brain into a depressive pattern. To put this another way, modern environments and/or our recently evolved human capacities for self-awareness, imagination, and rumination operate as new inputs to the depressive pattern and brain state.

Evolutionary approaches to depression try to understand the challenges that a toned-down positive aspect system and tones threat-sensitive one designed to cope with. Evolutionary approaches to depression try to understand the challenges that a toned-down positive affect system and toned threat-sensitive one are designed to cope with.

PAUL GILBERT

See also

Attachment
Therapeutic Lifestyle Change

References

Gilbert, P. (2004). Depression: A biopsychosocial, integrative and evolutionary approach. In M. Power (Ed.). *Mood disorders: A handbook of science and practice* (pp. 99–142). Chichester, UK: J. Wiley and Sons, Ltd.

Gilbert, P. (2006). Evolution and depression: Issues and implications (invited review). *Psychological Medicine, 36,* 287–297.

Gilbert, P. (2007). Psychotherapy and Counselling for Depression (3rd edition). London: Sage.

Nesse, R. M. (2000). Is depression an adaptation? *Archives of General Psychiatry, 57,* 14–20.

Exercise and Depression

Exercise may have an important role in the prevention and treatment of major depressive disorder. Available research evidence suggests that exercise reduces a person's risk for developing depression, is effective in alleviating depressive symptoms, and can prevent recurrence of depressive symptoms.

Cross-sectional and longitudinal studies have consistently associated high self-reported levels of physical activity with better mental health. For example, cross-sectional analyses have been conducted examining the association among general well-being, levels of anxiety and depressive symptoms, and physical activity (Stephens, 1988). Level of physical activity was found to correlate to levels of depressive symptoms, with scores on a measure of depression lowest for those who engaged in moderate or high amounts of physical activity. Studies like this have consistently found a relationship between physical activity and mental health, but this may be because depression leads to a drop in activity level, rather than because exercise confers some benefit to mood.

Longitudinal studies have also examined the relation between physical activity and depression and provide evidence that exercise habits do predict better mental health outcomes. A large-scale longitudinal study examined physical activity habits and rates of depression in a sample of more than 10,000 men through three successive questionnaires administered over a quarter of a century (Paffenbarger, Lee, & Leung, 1994). Depression was determined based on self-report of physician-diagnosed major depressive disorder. Over the follow-up period, the most active men from the first round of questionnaires were almost a third less likely to have developed major depressive disorder than the men in the least active category. Similar to these results, individuals who initially report exercising for more than an average of a half hour a day had a 50% lower risk of being depressed at follow-up 6 years later than respondents who reported not engaging in physical exercise at baseline (Van Gool et al., 2007). Each minute of reported exercise per day was associated with a 1% decreased risk of depressed mood at follow-up.

Exercise as an Intervention

Although epidemiological studies are an important indicator of a relationship between exercise and depression, they are largely based on correlational data and do not allow for the directionality of the relationship to be determined. Numerous randomized controlled trials (RCTs) have demonstrated that exercise holds promise as an adjunctive or independent treatment for major depressive disorder. During the past several decades, there have been a number of trials comparing exercise with placebo or a well-established treatment for depression (see Brosse, Sheets, Lett, & Blumenthal, 2002, for a thorough review). In a recent meta-analysis, exercise was shown

to significantly reduce scores on a self-report measure of depressive symptoms (Lawlor & Hopker, 2001). The authors concluded that the effect size of exercise is similar to that of cognitive behavioral therapy (CBT).

Most studies have evaluated exercise as an adjunctive treatment, although at least one RCT looked at exercise as a stand-alone treatment for outpatients with mild to moderate depression. Participants who were not receiving any other treatment for depression were assigned to one of five different conditions, four exercise groups that included either high or low energy expenditure and higher or lower frequency of exercise sessions, and one placebo group that did stretching flexibility exercise (Dunn, Trivedi, Kampert, Clark, & Chambliss, 2005). After 12 weeks, those patients in the higher energy expenditure condition showed a 47% reduction in Hamilton Rating Scale for Depression (HRSD) scores, regardless of how many days a week they exercised; this was significantly larger than what was observed in the low-dose and placebo conditions (29% and 30% reductions, respectively). Forty-two percent of the patients in the public health dose group achieved remission, whereas those in the low-dose and placebo group had significantly lower rates of remission.

One study has directly compared the effects of aerobic exercise to antidepressant medication. This study compared aerobic exercise, antidepressant medication, and a combination of the two among depressed older adults (Blumenthal et al., 1996). Those in the aerobic exercise condition walked or jogged at an intensity that would maintain heart rate in an aerobic range three times a week for 30 minutes. Those in the medication condition received a selective serotonin-reuptake inhibitor (sertraline). Both groups received active treatment for 16 weeks, and all three conditions achieved significantly lowered rates of depression (55% for exercise, 59% for medication, and 50% for the combination), and there were no differences between groups. Posttreatment, 60% to 69% of patients had achieved remission according to diagnostic criteria, and again, there were no differences between groups.

Taken together, the controlled trials on exercise indicate that exercise treatment is more effective in treating depression than no treatment or a placebo. Additionally, preliminary studies suggest that exercise may be as effective as psychotherapy and antidepressant medication. However, several authors have pointed out that the majority of studies in this area have important methodological weaknesses, and thus the effectiveness of exercise in treating depression cannot be conclusively determined (Lawlor & Hopker, 2001).

Long-Term Effects of Exercise as a Treatment for Depression

Research has also attempted to determine the effectiveness of exercise in preventing a recurrence of depression. For example, in the medication-exercise prescription study described earlier, researchers advised patients to continue some form of treatment on their own. Ten months after treatment termination, remitted subjects in the exercise group had significantly lower relapse rates than participants in the medication or combination groups (Babyak et al., 2000). Thirty percent of those in the exercise group were depressed at follow-up, compared to 52% of those in the medication group and 55% of those in the combined group.

Patients in another RCT comparing exercise to a control group were followed up for 2 years after the end of the intervention (Singh, Clements, & Singh, 2001). At this point, one-third of those randomly assigned to exercise were still lifting weights regularly, and none of those assigned to the control group (who received health education lectures) were exercising. Regardless of whether they continued to exercise, those in the exercise group showed significantly greater changes in levels of depression at treatment end and were still significantly different from the control group at 2-year follow-up. Additionally, the data from this long follow-up study shows that a substantial portion of depressed individuals introduced to exercise will stick with it, and

that it continues to benefit them long after the study is over.

Among the few follow-up studies of exercise as a long-term treatment for depression, results are promising but inconclusive. These studies indicate that exercise may be a viable treatment for depression over the long-term, and that patients who continue to exercise during the follow-up period will most likely have more favorable results.

Exercise Prescription for Depression

There is now a substantial amount of evidence to suggest that exercise is probably more effective than placebo in reducing depressive symptoms and may even be as effective as existing medications and psychotherapy. However, this preliminary research has not definitively answered the question of *how* to prescribe exercise to depressed populations. In 1995, the American College of Sports Medicine issued guidelines recommending that every U.S. adult accumulate 30 minutes or more of moderate-intensity physical activity on most, preferably all, days of the week (Pate et al., 1995). These recommendations for exercise to promote physical health have influenced many researchers in designing programs for depressed individuals. Some studies have directly investigated what type, duration, and intensity of exercise are most effective for mood elevation. This research can serve as a guide for clinicians on how to most effectively "prescribe" exercise to their clients.

Type of Exercise

There are three basic types of exercise: (a) aerobic (e.g., walking, jogging, biking), in which oxygen is metabolized to produce energy, and thus the heart and lungs must work harder; (b) anaerobic (e.g., weightlifting, resistance training), in which energy is provided without the use of inspired oxygen and thus does not cause increases in respiration and heart rate; and (c) flexibility (e.g., stretching, yoga), which is designed to improve range of motion.

A few studies have directly compared aerobic and anaerobic exercise and found that both types of exercise reduced levels of depression and did not differ significantly from each other. In addition to trials of aerobic versus anaerobic exercise, two meta-analyses have also compared the effect sizes of aerobic and anaerobic exercise on depression across different studies (Lawlor and Hopker, 2001; North, McCullagh, & Tran, 1990). Neither found an association between type of exercise and effect on depressive symptoms. The results of these studies all suggest that aerobic and anaerobic exercise are probably equivalent in their therapeutic effect. Although available evidence suggests that both exercise modalities are equally effective, the majority of RCTs, including the most methodologically sound trials (e.g., Blumenthal, 1996) have used aerobic rather than anaerobic exercise. Thus, at present, aerobic exercise may be considered to have the strongest research support.

Intensity of Exercise

Studies of exercise intensity indicate that nondepressed and depressed participants benefit approximately equally from moderate and high-intensity exercise (e.g., walking may be just as effective for treating depression as running). However, there is some evidence that intensity of exercise does matter. In a controlled trial, patients prescribed a higher dose of exercise per week had significantly greater reductions in depression than those assigned to the placebo or low-dose groups (Dunn et al., 2005). Interestingly, only total energy expenditure was related to depression outcomes, not simply the number of days of exercise. In contrast to earlier studies, this compelling, well-controlled study provides evidence that intensity of exercise does matter. Of course, individuals often have a marked preference for a certain type of physical activity, and thus, a clinician prescribing exercise to clients must balance concerns with adherence with research

indicating low-intensity exercise may be less effective.

Duration of Exercise

A few studies have attempted to determine exactly what number and length of sessions is required to achieve a substantial reduction in depression. A meta-analysis comparing the effect sizes from different studies based on length of exercise program and total number of exercise sessions showed that length of exercise program accounted for more of the total variance in levels of depression than any other variable analyzed (North et al., 1990). The greatest decrease in depression scores took place in programs lasting longer than 4 months. Likewise, a larger number of total sessions was correlated with reduction in depression. However, this meta-analysis did not find a relationship between length of exercise session or number of sessions per week.

Mechanisms of Action

Exercise promotes self-efficacy and enhances social interaction in group activities. It is part of a broader lifestyle intervention that enhances organization, proactivity, and taking ownership of one's life and health, increasing a sense of control, mastery, and engagement in life. There are also compelling lines of research suggesting that exercise may exert its antidepressant effects through physical mechanisms. Candidate mechanisms include effects at the level of neurotransmitter function, neurohormonal function, and other associated physiological processes (reviewed by Brosse et al., 2002).

A growing body of evidence suggests that exercise affects the functions of central monoamines, especially serotonin, dopamine, and norepinephrine, in a manner relevant to major depressive disorder. Exercise is associated with an increase in plasma monoamine levels, and increases the level of basal free fatty acids and free tryptophan levels, which in turn could increase the level of serotonin by increasing the central nervous system level of its amino acid precursor.

Similarly, it is hypothesized that exercise regulates hypothalamic-pituitary-adrenal axis (HPA axis) imbalances. Depression is generally associated with hyperactivity of the HPA axis, an imbalance of which is the neuroendocrine response to stress. Exercise training can lead to a reduction of HPA-axis hyperactivity, which may lead an individual to be more resilient in the face of stress.

Another hypothesized physiological mechanism involves the role of β-endorphin, an endogenous opioid, the release of which has been associated with the calming of the sympathetic nervous system and analgesic pain relief. Research suggests that postexercise mood elevations are associated with increases in basal β-endorphin levels. Although postexercise β-endorphin surges may cause short-term mood improvements, it is less clear that these surges contribute to the relationship between exercise and sustained relief from major depressive disorder. Physical activity may enhance neurotrophic factors and thus augment brain plasticity. This may enhance executive cognitive functions and modulate the effects of stress on neural circuits.

Conclusions and Recommendations

Exercise appears to be a viable treatment option for depression, but there are methodological shortcomings to this literature that limit the conclusions that can be definitively drawn. More research is needed with longer follow-up periods to determine whether exercise can be effective in preventing relapse. Questions still remain about exactly what dose is optimal for treating depression. For example, we still do not know whether accumulated exercise is as beneficial as exercising in a single session. Although a few studies have compared aerobic and anaerobic exercise, a study comparing anaerobic exercise to medication would be essential in demonstrating its effectiveness with depressed populations. Finally, research is needed on how to motivate people with depression to comply with exercise programs. Studies should address the role of personal trainers, exercise groups, and exercise classes in encouraging adherence.

Although clinicians have made a great deal of progress in helping people recover from depression, there remain a significant number of people who do not seek help, do not benefit from acute treatment, do not complete treatment, or relapse later. Thus, clinicians and researchers have increasingly looked to other interventions that can either enhance traditional treatment or have comparable antidepressant effects on their own. Given many patients' dissatisfaction with or inability to access traditional treatments for depression, exercise represents a potentially invaluable alternative means of managing this disorder.

Based on available research, prescribing exercise to patients with major depressive disorder appears to be a beneficial adjunctive, if not stand-alone, treatment. Encouraging patients to get 30 minutes or more of moderate-intensity physical activity 4 to 7 days a week will likely improve mood significantly in this population. This is equivalent to briskly walking 3 to 4 miles per hour for at least a half hour more days than not. Other forms of moderate intensity exercise include cycling, swimming, and racket sports. Both aerobic and anaerobic exercises are likely equivalent in their therapeutic effect; therefore, weight lifting, for example, may be a suitable prescription for patients preferring this form of physical activity. Additionally, research supports the fact that optimal mood benefits occur after at least 4 months of exercise therapy. Patients should be informed that exercise is a cumulative and more time-intensive therapy; however, the benefits are profound. Exercise therapy may be especially attractive to those seeking a more natural treatment for their depression and those wanting to take a more holistic health care approach.

LESLIE KARWOSKI AND DANYALE MCCURDY

See also

Therapeutic Lifestyle Change

References

Babyak, M. A., Blumenthal, J. A., Herman, S., Khatri, P., Doraiswamy, M., Moore, K., et al. (2000). Exercise treatment for major depression: Maintenance of therapeutic benefit at 10 months. *Psychosomatic Medicine, 62,* 633–638.

Blumenthal, J. A., Babyak, M. A., Moore, K. A., Craighead, W. E., Herman, S., Khatri, P., et al. (1996). Effects of exercise training on older patients with major depression. *Archives of Internal Medicine, 159,* 2349–2356.

Brosse, A. L., Sheets, E. S., Lett, H. S., & Blumenthal, J. A. (2002). Exercise and the treatment of clinical depression in adults: Recent findings and future directions. *Sports Medicine, 32,* 741–760.

Dunn, A. L., Trivedi, M. H., Kampert, J. B., Clark, C. G., & Chambliss, H. O. (2005). Exercise treatment for depression: Efficacy and dose response. *American Journal of Preventive Medicine, 28,* 1–8.

Lawlor, D. A., & Hopker, S. W. (2001). The effectiveness of exercise as an intervention in the management of depression: Systematic review and meta-regression analysis of randomized controlled trials. *British Medical Journal, 322,* 763–767.

North, T. C., McCullagh, P., & Tran, V. T. (1990). Effect of exercise on depression. *Exercise and Sport Sciences Reviews, 18,* 379–415.

Paffenbarger, R. S., Lee, I. M., & Leung, R. (1994). Physical activity and personal characteristics associated with depression and suicide in American college men. *Acta Psychiatrica Scandinavica, Suppl. 377,* 16–22.

Pate, R. R., Pratt, M., Blair, S. N., Haskell, W. L., Macera, C. A., Bouchard, C., et al. (1995). Physical activity and public health: A recommendation from the Centers for Disease Control and Prevention and the American College of Sports Medicine. *Journal of the American Medical Association, 273,* 402–407.

Singh, N. A., Clements, K. M., & Singh, M. A. (2001). The efficacy of exercise as a long-term antidepressant in elderly subjects: A randomized, controlled trial. *Journal of Gerontology, 6,* 497–504.

Stephens, T. (1988). Physical activity and mental health in the United States and Canada: Evidence from four population surveys. *Preventive Medicine, 17,* 35–47.

Van Gool, C. H., Kempen, G. I. J. M., Bosma, H., van Boxtel, P. J. M., Jolles, J., & van Eijk, J. T. M. (2007). Associations between lifestyle and depressed mood: Longitudinal results from the Maastricht Aging Study. *American Journal of Public Health, 97,* 887–894.

Expressed Emotion

Expressed emotion (EE) is a relational construct that provides a measure of the family environment. Its origins come from schizophrenia research. However, EE is an important variable for those interested in depression. This is because high levels of EE reliably predict increased risk of relapse and recurrence of illness in depressed patients who have achieved clinical remission.

Measurement

EE is assessed during an interview with the patient's key relative. For most people with depression, this is a spouse. However, the relative could be a parent, sibling, or other caretaker. The relative is interviewed, in the absence of the patient, using a semistructured interview (the Camberwell Family Interview; CFI), that takes 1 to 2 hours to administer. During the interview, the relative is given the opportunity to talk about the patient and his or her symptoms and difficulties and also is asked more generally about how he or she gets along with the patient.

After the interview is completed a trained coder listens to the recorded interview and rates EE. EE is rated based on how much criticism, hostility, or emotional overinvolvement (EOI) the relative shows when talking about the patient. EOI, which reflects a dramatic, overconcerned, or overprotective attitude toward the patient, is rare in the families of depressed patients. It is more commonly found in parents of patients with schizophrenia. In the majority of cases, relatives of depressed patients are classified as high EE because they express an above-threshold number of critical remarks about the patient during the CFI. High levels of EE are far from unusual, being found in around 56% of the relatives of mood-disordered patients.

EE and Relapse in Depression

In the classic EE study, patients are followed for a period of 9 to 12 months after being discharged from a psychiatric hospital in a state of clinical remission. Investigations of this kind have shown that unipolar depressed patients are more likely to relapse or experience a return of symptoms if they return home to live with high-EE versus low-EE relatives. For patients with bipolar disorder, EE predicts the recurrence of depression, but not mania.

In a meta-analysis, Butzlaff and Hooley (1998) reported a weighted mean effect size of $r = .39$ for the association between EE and relapse in mood disorders when a score of 2 critical comments or more was used to define high EE. When 3 critical comments was used to define high EE, the effect size increased to $r = .45$. When data from the single non-replication study (which was published too late to be included in the meta-analysis) are included, the effect size is still an (highly significant) $r = .39$.

In samples of depressed patients and their spouses, high EE is correlated with lower levels of marital satisfaction in both partners. Moreover, supporting the validity of EE, high-EE spouses tend to be more critical during face-to-face interactions with depressed patients than low-EE spouses are. Behavioral observations further reveal that high-EE relationships are characterized by more negativity in other ways, including more verbal disagreements, more negative nonverbal behavior, and a greater tendency toward reciprocated patterns of negative escalation (Hooley, 2007; Miklowitz, 2004). Moreover, the fact that negative behaviors can be found in both partners highlights the transactional nature of EE and suggests that, even though it is measured in a single individual, EE is an indicator of problems in the family system more broadly.

Why patients who live with high-EE relatives are at increased risk for relapse is not fully clear. Family-based interventions (which educate relatives about the illness, and improve problem-solving and communication skills) have proved successful with the relatives of patients with schizophrenia; patients' relapse rates decrease when relatives' levels of EE are reduced. Family-based interventions with depressed or bipolar patients have also been shown to be efficacious. However, improvements in patients are not always mediated by changes in relatives' EE. This suggests that the role of EE in depression might be quite different from the role of EE in schizophrenia.

Bringing EE research into the era of neuroscience, researchers are now using functional neuroimaging approaches (fMRI) to explore how criticism is processed in the brain. In a novel paradigm, Hooley and colleagues have exposed healthy controls and people vulnerable to depression to criticism from their own mothers. The results reveal that, even when they are fully well and symptom free, people who are vulnerable to depression do not process criticism in the same way that healthy (never-depressed) controls do. Relative to controls, formerly depressed participants respond to criticism with greater activation in the amygdala and reduced activation in the dorsolateral prefrontal cortex and anterior cingulate cortex. These are brain areas that have been implicated in depression; they are also involved in emotional responding, attention, conscious control of behavior, working memory, and interpersonal effectiveness. It is also worth noting that the recovered depressed participants and the healthy controls reported no differences with respect to how upset they were after the criticisms or how negative they rated the criticisms as being. In other words, the self-report data of the formerly depressed participants did not indicate that they were experiencing the critical comments in a different way. Nonetheless, at the level of the brain, their processing of criticism was not like that of the controls. Criticism may be involved in the relapse process because it is able to perturb some of the neural circuitry involved in depression. The findings also suggest that people who are vulnerable to depression may be quite unaware of the effect that criticism is having on them.

JILL M. HOOLEY

See also

Recurrence
Relapse

References

Butzlaff, R. L., & Hooley, J. M. (1998). Expressed emotion and psychiatric relapse. *Archives of General Psychiatry, 55,* 547–552.

Hooley, J. M. (2007). Expressed emotion and relapse of psychopathology. *Annual Review of Clinical Psychology, 3,* 329–352.

Miklowitz, D. J. (2004). The role of family systems in severe and recurrent psychiatric disorders: A developmental psychopathology view. *Development and Pychopathology, 16,* 667–688.

Externalizing Disorders

In contrast to internalizing disorders, the other broad category of childhood behavior disorders is externalizing disorders. Although child depression is more commonly linked to internalizing disorders, externalizing disorders can also be comorbid with depression.

Externalizing disorders are manifested in children's outward behavior rather than (or in addition to) internalizing thoughts and feelings. These externalizing disorders include problems of control, such as attention deficit hyperactivity disorder (ADHD), oppositional defiant disorder (ODD), and conduct disorder (CD). In fact, externalizing disorders frequently are comorbid with ADHD, combined type (ADHD-CT), and dysthymic disorder (DD) in primary school–age children. ADHD-CT has sometimes been called a gateway for other forms of externalizing disorders. It is estimated that 60% of children with ADHD will also have some features of ODD, and up to 40% will have some of the features of CD.

ADHD is a neurobehavioral developmental disorder that affects 3% to 5% of the school-age population under 19 years of age. Symptoms of ADHD are often first noted by parents in children by about 4 years of age but are often not formally diagnosed until about age 7 when these children enter primary school. ADHD is characterized by a persistent pattern of inattention and/or hyperactivity. Sometimes the children are forgetful of homework and get into fights due to impulsivity and risk-taking behavior. Distractibility and lack of vigilance make them prone to instructional problems in the classroom. ADHD is a persistent and chronic condition that often continues into adulthood for approximately 60% of children. Approximately 65% of the variance is attributable to heritability on the father's side of the family, although it is clear that children raised in disorganized and chaotic homes are often at increased risk for ADHD. Methods of treatment for ADHD in children usually include a combination of medications, positive behavioral supports, lifestyle changes, counseling, and parent training.

A second externalizing disorder of childhood closely associated with ADHD is oppositional defiant disorder (ODD). All children can be challenges to their parents from time to time, but children with ODD are regularly moody and argumentative. ODD is characterized by a persistent pattern of tantrums, negativity, argumentation, angry outbursts, and other disruptive behaviors toward parents and other authority figures such as teachers. They may be defiant, refuse to comply with teacher requests regarding classroom rules, deliberately annoy other children, blame others for mistakes or misbehavior, act touchy and easily annoyed, harbor anger and resentment, become spiteful and vindictive, become aggressive toward peers at recess, have few friends, and often have associated academic problems.

Differential diagnosis of ODD from a strong-willed child can be difficult, and it is normal for children to seek independence from parents at various points in the developmental course; but when these oppositional behaviors are persistent up to 6 months and are clearly related to the family, home, or classroom environment, then a diagnosis of ODD might be considered.

Treatments for ODD include medications, behavior management, anger control training, social skills training, relaxation training, and remedial education programming.

A third type of externalizing behavior in childhood is conduct disorder (CD). Children with CD often violate the rights and safety of others. These children do not follow the social norms of their environments. The symptoms include verbal and physical aggression, cruelty toward pets and people, lying, cheating, school truancy, vandalism, stealing, setting fires, carrying weapons, and pushing others into sexual activity. Obviously, it is not uncommon for children with CD to have a juvenile record with law enforcement authorities. Bullying is also associated with CD. Once a child reaches 18 years of age, it is not uncommon for mental health practitioners to diagnose these types of externalizing behaviors as antisocial personality disorder. CD is more than just childhood rebelliousness, and contrary to the lore of the rebellious teenager, most children with CD are fully identifiable in middle school or earlier.

Children with the externalizing disorder of CD are often treated with long-term counseling and skills-building programs, but unfortunately many of them will be adjudicated if they run afoul of the law. Research shows that unless intervention is undertaken early, when the child is evidencing some symptoms of ODD perhaps, successful outcome rates for interventions are diminished.

What all three of these externalizing behaviors of childhood have in common is a basis in the coercion model of interaction (Patterson & Yoerger, 2002). If this is the case, then perhaps identifying a child who is in coercion could be a powerful means of deterring the further development of this disruptive behavior. In the coercion model, there is an early pattern of argumentation with authority figures wherein the child feels reinforced for argumentation after regularly "winning" the argument with the parent or teacher (Sharma & Sandhu, 2006). Parents and teachers feel frustrated and the child feels victorious. In the second stage of the coercion model the child will evidence a high rate of covert antisocial behavior during later childhood and early adolescence.

According to the coercion model, practitioners should be aware of the pattern of high rates of overt antisocial behavior during childhood followed by high rates of covert antisocial behavior during early adolescence that constitute the key predictors for early-onset criminal arrest. Snyder has offered the hypothesis that adults will try to apply discipline to the more obvious forms of overt antisocial behavior, sometimes with effect and others times not. What often happens, however, is that the aversive contingencies applied to control behavior often drive the behavior underground to a more covert level. Other hypotheses suggest that the longer a child was engaged in coercion, the greater the increase in frequency of more severe forms of antisocial behavior. It should be noted that during adolescence, availability of deviant peers in the social life of most adolescents indicate enormous increases in contacts during the same intervals found for peak delinquency (Elliott & Menard, 1996). Perhaps early intervention and parent training are key ingredients for the most efficacious outcomes for these children with externalizing disorders.

ROBERT G. HARRINGTON

See also

Adolescent Depression
Attention Deficit Hyperactivity Disorder
Childhood Depression
Internalizing Disorders

References

Elliott, D. S., & Menard, S. (1996). Delinquent friends and delinquent behavior: Temporal and developmental patterns. In D. Hawkins (Ed.), *Delinquency and crime: Current theories* (pp. 28–67). Cambridge, UK: Cambridge University Press.

Patterson, G. R., & Yoerger, K. (2002). A developmental model for early- and late-onset delinquency. In J. B Reid, G. R. Patterson, & J. Snyder (Eds.), *Antisocial behavior in children and adolescents: A developmental analysis and model for Intervention* (pp. 147–172). Washington, DC: American Psychological Association.

Sharma, V., & Sandhu, G. K. (2006). A community study of association between parenting dimensions and externalizing behaviors. *Journal of the Indian Association of Child and Adolescent Mental Health, 2,* 48–58.

F

Family and Parent-Child Therapy

Family and parent-child interventions have become increasingly popular in the treatment and prevention of depression in children and adolescents. This modality emerges from several interpersonal theories that suggest that depression can be precipitated, maintained, or exacerbated by the quality of interpersonal relationships in families.

In addition, extensive developmental and clinical research supports two key assumptions about depression and families. First, the family is the natural and necessary developmental context for healthy child development. Families characterized by strong attachment bonds, good problem-solving and conflict-resolution skills, and an appropriate balance of warmth and demandingness (i.e., structure and guidance) promote positive child development. Contrary to popular belief, research repeatedly suggests that these family characteristics are as important to the development of adolescents as for younger children. Therefore, when the family context functions effectively, children and adolescents develop cognitive and emotional coping skills that help buffer against stressors that may contribute to depression.

The second empirically supported assumption is that negative family environment can be a strong risk factor for child and adolescent depression. Documented family risk factors for depression include parental depression, marital conflict, ineffective parenting practices, loss, negative parent-child interaction, and insecure attachments (Cicchetti & Toth,

1998). Parental psychopathology, especially depression, is one of the strongest risk factors for depression in children and adolescents. Although genetic factors clearly play some role, parental depression is associated with many of the family and parenting factors that increase risk for depression in youths (Goodman & Gotlib, 2002). Given these risk factors, interventions that help resolve family conflict, heal family wounds, or build new strengths can resuscitate or strengthen the attachment environment necessary for promoting normative development.

Given these assumptions, family-based interventions should be particularly effective for preventing and treating child and adolescent depression, and for reducing the effects of parental depression on offspring. In the last decade, there has been a slow but steady increase in family-based interventions for depression. In a comprehensive review of empirically supported treatments for depression in 1998 (Kaslow & Thompson, 1998), only three studies included some form of parental involvement. In a recent update of this review (David-Ferdon & Kaslow, 2008) nearly all the child programs included parents and over half of the adolescent-focused programs include parents. In addition, a recent meta-analysis concluded that family interventions were very promising for treating depression in children and adolescents (Weisz, McCarty, & Valeri, 2006). Parent involvement can range from family therapy focused on resolving interpersonal problems, family psychoeducation teaching communication and problems solving skills, and family education and skills training as an adjunctive to individual or group cognitive behavioral therapy (CBT). Although the field has grown too big for a comprehensive review in this entry, below we highlight some of the important studies and areas for development.

Interventions for Depressed Adolescents

Family Interventions for Depressed Adolescents

Two randomized controlled studies of family therapy have been conducted with depressed adolescents. Brent and colleagues (1997) compared individual CBT, supportive therapy (NST), and a structural-behavioral family treatment (SBFT) as treatments for adolescents with major depression. Major goals of SBFT included engaging the family in therapy, identifying and correcting dysfunctional interaction patterns, and improving communication and problem-solving skills. Adolescents in all three treatment groups improved, and no significant differences were found for suicidality and functional impairment. Both CBT and SBFT reduced suicidal ideation significantly more than NST. CBT did show more rapid improvement than both NST and SBFT and also had a significantly higher percentage of patients who achieved remission at the end of treatment. There were no long-term differences in treatment effects on depression. Further, adolescents reporting more severe depression, parent-child conflict, and/or low family emotional involvement were less likely to improve with therapy, and baseline family conflict was associated with seeking additional services.

Diamond, Reis, Diamond, Siqueland, & Isaac (2002) developed and tested attachment-based family therapy (ABFT) for depressed adolescents. Treatment focuses on helping families identify and resolve core family conflicts that have inhibited the adolescent from trusting his or her parents and utilizing them as a secure base. Treatment uses these unresolved "hot topics" to engage the teen into treatment and as an in vivo context for parents and adolescents to learn more effective problem-solving skills, improve affect regulation, and recalibrate the adolescent's balance of attachment and autonomy. In their study, a 12-week treatment was compared to a 6-week wait list. Remission occurred in 84% of the adolescents treated with ABFT and 36% of the patients in the control group. ABFT also produced more significant reductions in anxiety, hopelessness, and family conflict, and improvement in adolescent attachment to parents. In a more recent study just completed with suicidal youths, ABFT was more effective than enhanced usual care in reducing suicidal ideation and in moving adolescents into a nonclinical range of depression.

Family Interventions as an Adjunct to Treatment for Depressed Adolescents

Parent and family intervention components have been developed for cognitive behavioral, interpersonal, and other treatments for depression in adolescents. A major goal of these components is to educate parents about depression in youth and the skills taught in adolescent sessions. These components aim to increase parents' support and reinforcement of skill acquisition and behavioral change by the adolescents. For example, Clarke and Lewinsohn (Clarke, Rohde, Lewinsohn, Hops, & Seeley, 1999; Lewinsohn, Clarke, Hops, & Andrews, 1990) developed a parent group component to the Coping with Depression Course, a group cognitive behavioral intervention for depressed adolescents. In two randomized controlled trials, the adolescent groups and a combination of adolescent and parent groups reduced diagnoses and symptoms of depression relative to a wait-list control condition. However, neither trial showed a significant added benefit of the parent groups in reducing adolescents' depression. In contrast, Stark (1990) added 11 family sessions to a 26-session, school-based CBT intervention. The combined treatment was significantly more effective in reducing depression than a traditional counseling approach. Recently the Treatment for Adolescents with Depression Study (TADS Team, 2004) was completed as the largest study ever conducted with depressed adolescents. This study randomized 439 clinically depressed adolescents to cognitive behavioral therapy, fluoxetine, combination treatment, or placebo. All CBT treatments were augmented by at least two family education sessions about depression and CBT. Five additional family session modules were developed and used at the discretion of the therapist. These modules focused on family management skills, communication, and family attachment. The authors did not describe this as family therapy but did suggest it was essential for the ultimate engagement and retention of patients in this study.

Interventions for Children of Depressed Parents

Family Interventions for Depressed Parents With School-Age Children

Several family interventions have been developed for families with a currently or recently depressed parent. The structure of these interventions varies considerably. Some are designed for individual families, while others are designed for groups of parents, groups of families, blended parent groups, child groups, and other family components. Despite their different structures, these interventions have many common goals, which include providing social and emotional support to families, educating parents and family members about depression and its effects on parenting, increasing empathy and communication within the family, promoting positive interactions between family members, and helping parents to achieve more positive and consistent discipline. A key component in most interventions is the facilitation of conversations between the parents and children about the ways in which parental depression affects parents and the family, with the goal of reducing children's sense of responsibility and blame for their parents' symptoms and distress.

There is limited research on family interventions for depressed parents, but existing studies suggests that these programs improve family functioning and children's well-being. For example, a randomized controlled study comparing a family intervention and a lecture program for parents found that both interventions improved family functioning (relative to baseline) and these improvements were sustained for 4 years. Compared with the lecture intervention, the family intervention led to greater improvements in communication and in children's understanding of parents' affective disorder, suggesting increased benefits when parents receive more individualized attention and when children are included in the intervention.

A few interventions for families affected by parental depression blend cognitive behavioral and family therapy approaches (e.g., Boyd, Diamond, & Bourjolly, 2006). These interventions focus on improving family functioning and also teach participants cognitive behavioral techniques for challenging pessimistic thinking and coping effectively with stressors in their lives, including stressors related to parental depression. Randomized controlled evaluations of these interventions are underway.

Family Interventions for Depressed Parents With Young Children

Several parent-child interventions have been developed for depressed parents (primarily for mothers) of infants, toddlers, and young children. Programs for parents with infants focus on providing emotional support to parents, increasing parents' understanding of development, and promoting positive parent-child interactions and secure attachments. Programs for parents of toddlers and young children also focus on effective discipline, behavior management, and other parenting skills. Therapy typically includes sessions with the parent and child together and may be administered through home visits or in a clinic setting. Parents receive information and may also receive coaching and feedback as they interact with and try out new parenting approaches with their young children. A recent review of research on interventions for mothers with postpartum depression concluded that interventions that targeted mother and infant were generally effective in reducing negative outcomes in offspring (Nylen, Moran, Franklin, & O'Hara, 2006). Several interventions for currently and recently depressed mothers with young children have been found to improve attachment and/or reduce disruptive behavior in children. For example, adding CBT techniques to parent training reduces mothers' depression and leads to even greater improvements in children's disruptive behavior at follow-up relative to parent training alone. Over all, these programs aim to promote a positive family environment early in life, with the hope that this may prevent the development of depression in latency and beyond.

Prevention

Most programs that aim to prevent depression in youths do not include parent or family components. However, recent work in prevention highlights the importance of targeting family risk and protective factors in prevention efforts. The interventions for depressed parents (described above) are especially promising. In addition, several cognitive behavioral interventions for adolescents have incorporated family or parent components in recent years. For example, the Coping With Stress Course (an adaptation of the Coping With Depression course for adolescents with high but subclinical levels of depression), includes three parent group sessions (Clarke et al., 2001). The major goal of these interventions is to help parents understand and support the cognitive behavioral skills their children are learning through the program. In addition, some interventions aim to teach parents to use skills from CBT in their own lives, with the hope that parents' use of the skills will improve family interactions and

provide ongoing models of adaptive coping for youths (Gillham et al., 2006).

Interventions that support families through traumatic experiences or difficult life transitions may be especially important for preventing depression in children. Examples of these interventions include the Family Bereavement Program, developed for families that have recently experienced the death of a parent (Sandler et al., 2003). This program includes separate and combined group sessions for parents and children. Parent sessions provide parents with emotional and social support and help participants to increase positive activities and positive interactions with their children. In addition, parents learn techniques for effective discipline, challenging their own negative appraisals of situations, and helping their children cope with stressful events more effectively. Parallel groups for children and adolescents provide opportunities for the expression and validation of grief-related experiences through discussions and by encouraging children to discuss these feelings with their parents. In addition, the groups teach problem-solving and coping skills, as well as techniques for challenging negative interpretations of stressful events. In a randomized controlled study, the Family Bereavement Program improved parents' mental health and parenting and reduced parent-reported stressors compared to a comparison group in which families received self-study materials. The program also reduced internalizing symptoms and behavioral problems in girls and in children with high levels of initial symptoms. A similar intervention, developed for families affected by divorce, found positive effects (relative to a self-study control) on parent-child relationships, discipline, and children's behavioral problem.

Conclusions

The above review, although brief, highlights several themes. First, there is an increasing trend, even by traditionally not-family-based treatment researchers, to incorporate parents into the treatment of children and adolescents. Findings from development psychopathology and weak results from early studies of single modality, child-focused interventions have driven investigators to develop multifaceted treatments that better reflect what is practiced in real-world settings. Few child and adolescent therapists would today refuse to meet with, educate, or incorporate into treatment the parents of their patients. With the emergence of manualized family treatments or treatment components, the inclusion of parents into treatment can be structured and guided.

Second, the amount of family-based treatment research still lags far behind that of other modalities, in particular CBTs. This partially results from the relative absence of family-based systems training in psychology and psychiatry departments, which are still dominated by individual psychology and biomedical paradigms. The view that individuals are influenced by the context they live in runs counter to the psychological and medical training that locates risk factors and illnesses within individuals. A more context-driven view of psychopathology also clashes with the more general belief embedded in American individualism.

More family-based treatment research may be one way to counter this mind-set. More studies of family treatments for child and adolescent depression are needed. In addition, more studies of the integration of family and CBT approaches remain needed. Which treatment should come first? How much of each is necessary and for which patient? Do changes in family functioning actually mediate the changes in depressive symptoms, or in contrast, does stress on the family decrease when a child's (or parent's) depressive symptoms diminish? And what about parents? Given the high rates of depression in parents who bring depressed children and adolescents to therapy, should we ignore them, treat them, or refer them? How best can we engage them in this process, when they have come for help for their child? These are the clinical questions that practitioners struggle with daily in practice. Research that helps

to address these kinds of real-world questions will greatly facilitate the adoption of empirically supported treatments for depression.

GUY DIAMOND, JANE GILLHAM,
AND KAREN REIVICH

See also

Adolescent Depression
Childhood Depression
Cognitive Behavioral Couple Therapy
Cognitive Behavioral Therapy
Family Transmission of Depression
Fathers and Depression
Mothers and Depression

References

Boyd, R. C., Diamond, G. S., & Bourjolly, J. (2006). Developing a family-based depression prevention program in urban community mental health clinics: A qualitative investigation. *Family Process, 45,* 187–203.

Brent, D. A., Holder, D., Kolko, D., Birmaher, B., Baugher, M., Roth, C., et al. (1997). A clinical psychotherapy trial for adolescent depression comparing cognitive, family, and supportive therapy. *Archives of General Psychiatry, 54,* 877–885.

Cicchetti, D., & Toth, S. L. (1998). The development of depression in children and adolescents. *American Psychologist, 53,* 221–242.

Clarke, G. N., Hornbrook, M., Lynch, F., Polen, M., Gale, J., Beardslee, W., et al. (2001). A randomized trial of a group cognitive intervention for preventing depression in adolescent offspring of depressed parents. *Archives of General Psychiatry, 58,* 1127–1134.

Clarke, G. N., Rohde, P., Lewinsohn, P. M., Hops, H., & Seeley, J. R. (1999). Cognitive-behavioral treatment of adolescent depression: Efficacy of acute group treatment and booster sessions. *Journal of the American Academy of Child and Adolescent Psychiatry, 38,* 272–279.

David-Ferdon, C., & Kaslow, N. J. (2008). Evidence-based psychosocial treatments for child and adolescent depression. *Journal of Clinical Child and Adolescent Psychology, 37,* 62–104.

Diamond, G. S., Reis, B. F., Diamond, G. M., Siqueland, L., & Isaac, L. (2002). Attachment based family therapy for depressed adolescents: A treatment development study. *Journal of the American Academy of Child and Adolescent Psychiatry, 41,* 1190–1196.

Gillham, J. E., Reivich, K. J., Freres, D. R., Lascher, M., Litzinger, S., Shatté, A., et al. (2006). School-based prevention of depression and anxiety symptoms in early adolescence: A pilot of a parent intervention component. *School Psychology Quarterly, 21,* 323–348.

Goodman, S. H., & Gotlib, I. H. (2002). Transmission of risk to children of depressed parents: Integration and conclusions. In S. H. Goodman & I. H. Gotlib (Eds.),

Children of depressed parents: Mechanisms of risk and implications for treatment (pp. 307–326). Washington, DC: American Psychological Association.

Kaslow, N. J., & Thompson, M. (1998). Applying the criteria for empirically supported treatments to studies of psychosocial interventions for child and adolescent depression. *Journal of Clinical Child Psychology, 27,* 146–155.

Lewinsohn, P. M., Clarke, G. N., Hops, H., & Andrews, J. (1990). Cognitive-behavioral treatment for depressed adolescents. *Behavior Therapy, 21,* 385–401.

Nylen, K. J., Moran, T. E., Franklin, C. L., & O'Hara, M. W. (2006). Maternal depression: A review of relevant treatment approaches for mothers and infants. *Infant Mental Health Journal, 27,* 327–343.

Sandler, I. N., Ayers, T. S., Wolchik, S. A., Tein, J. Y., Kwok, O. M., Haine, R. A., et al. (2003). The family bereavement program: Efficacy evaluation of a theory-based prevention program for parentally bereaved children and adolescents. *Journal of Consulting and Clinical Psychology, 71,* 587–600.

Stark, K. D. (1990). *Childhood depression: School-based intervention.* New York: Guilford Press.

Treatment for Adolescents With Depression Study Team. (2004). Fluoxetine, cognitive-behavioral therapy, and their combination for adolescents with depression. *Journal of the American Medical Association, 292,* 807–820.

Weisz, J. R., McCarty, C. A., & Valeri, S. M. (2006). Effects of psychotherapy for depression in children and adolescents: A meta-analysis. *Psychological Bulletin, 132,* 132–149.

Family Transmission of Depression

Family transmission of depression, or the passage of depression from one generation to the next, has been studied in the context of family, twin, and adoption designs. Strong evidence for family transmission has been found across studies, and results indicate that both genetic and environmental pathways exist for such transmission.

Family studies have consistently demonstrated that offspring of depressed parents are more likely than offspring of nondepressed parents to exhibit depressive symptoms and disorders. A meta-analysis of family, twin, and adoption studies of depression (Sullivan, Neale, & Kendler, 2000) found that family members of depressed individuals are 2.84 times as likely to exhibit depression than families of controls. Evidence from twin and adoption studies suggests that the family transmission of major depression is due to both environmental and genetic influences, with an average heritability rate of 37%. Molecular genetic studies have most recently focused on gene-environment interactions, finding evidence that several genetic polymorphisms interact with family and other environmental factors to increase the risk of major depression.

The majority of the research on the family transmission of depression has focused on children of depressed mothers, with attention toward mechanisms of risk as well as moderators of outcome. One important factor that has been considered in the process of risk is the nature of the maternal depression itself, or more specifically the chronicity, severity, and timing of maternal depression in relation to offspring risk for depression. In the most extensive longitudinal analysis of this question to date, Hammen and Brennan (2003) examined the timing, severity, and chronicity of maternal depression during the first 10 years of a child's life as a predictor of offspring depression diagnoses at age 15. Whereas chronicity of maternal depression predicted nondepressive diagnostic outcomes in these youths, the severity of maternal depression was found to be the strongest predictor of childhood and adolescent depression. Specifically, the presence of severe maternal depression for only 1 or 2 months of the child's life was associated with a significant increase in child depression. Once severity and chronicity of maternal depression were controlled, no independent effects of timing of maternal depression were noted in this study. Maternal depression severity may be a proxy for genetic risk, and/or it may translate into environmental risk factors for children, including increased exposure to parenting problems, stressful life events, and poor role models for social and interpersonal functioning.

The transmission of depression across generations is likely to be a complex process involving several potential avenues of risk. For example, Goodman and Gotlib (1999) describe four potential mechanisms of risk and point out that in most cases, offspring of depressed parents are impacted by not just one, but by several of these risks, in either an additive or an interactive fashion. The first risk mechanism is genetic transmission. As noted above, previous genetic studies have noted substantial heritability rates for depression. Importantly, factors that are often termed *environmental*, such as parenting, stress, or social support, have been found to be in part genetically determined. Genetic risk therefore may be transferred from generation to generation across several levels of functioning.

The second major risk mechanism for depression transmission (outlined by Goodman & Gotlib, 1999) is infant neuroregulatory dysfunction caused by prenatal exposure to maternal depression. Importantly, depressed women have been found to demonstrate higher levels of cortisol, an indicator of stress reactivity, and high stress reactivity has been hypothesized to be a risk for recurrent depressive episodes. Research has demonstrated that maternal and fetal levels of cortisol are correlated with one another, as are maternal and infant cortisol levels. One possible interpretation of these findings is that maternal biological stress processes associated with depression (high cortisol levels) directly impact the developing stress response system of the fetus, thereby "programming" the child to be hyperresponsive to stress later in life. Stress reactivity in turn increases the child's risk for depressive disorders. Other prenatal risks associated with maternal depression are poor prenatal care and increased exposure to maternal smoking and substance use, all of which might impair the offspring's physiological functioning and increase risk for depression.

As described by Goodman and Gotlib (1999), the third mechanism of familial risk for depression is the social transmission of the behavioral, affective, and cognitive components and correlates of depression from parent to child. Decades of research findings focused on several stages of child development provide evidence that the parenting skills of depressed individuals are impaired. Specifically, depressed parents are more likely to be negative, critical, and withdrawn in interactions with their children. Moreover,

depressed individuals are more likely to have and to express negative views of themselves, the world, and others around them. They are less likely to have interpersonal skills that help to forge and maintain successful social relationships. Therefore, through direct impact (e.g., exposure to higher levels of criticism) and/or modeling (e.g., exposure to unsatisfactory social relationship functioning) children of depressed parents are more likely to acquire the behavioral, affective, and cognitive features of depression, and in turn the likelihood of a depressive disorder.

The fourth risk mechanism for depression outlined by Goodman and Gotlib (1999) is exposure to chronic and episodic stressors. Women who are depressed are more likely to have a greater number of stressors in their lives, and by association their children are more likely to be exposed to higher numbers of stressors. Increased stress exposure in children results from several factors. First, maternal depression may occur as a result of exposure to stressful life events. Second, stress and depression may have common causes, such as marital conflict or economic instability, and may co-occur for that reason. Finally, depressed women have been found to actually generate higher levels of stress in their environment, so that the stressors may actually result from the depression itself. Because stressful life events are well-established causal factors for depression, this stress-depression overlap in their family background puts children of depressed mothers at a much-heightened risk for depressive outcomes themselves.

Family transmission of depression has typically been studied in a piecemeal fashion, with a focus on only one risk factor at a time. One exception to this rule is the empirical test of an intergenerational interpersonal stress model of depression presented by Hammen and colleagues (Hammen, Shih, & Brennan, 2004). The sample in this study was a large community cohort of adolescent offspring of both depressed and nondepressed mothers. Youth depressive disorders were assessed at age 15 years. Mediators for the transmission of depression from grandmother to youth and from mother to youth were assessed. Findings indicated that grandmother depression increases the risk for youth depression through its impact on maternal depression and maternal interpersonal stress. Mediators between maternal depression and youth depression included maternal interpersonal stress, poor parent-child relationship quality, and youth social competence deficits. Interpersonal impairment therefore appears to play a critical role in the transmission of risk for depression across generations. Both the depressed mother's inability to interact well with her child and with others, and the youth's inability to perform adequately in social contexts fully explained the family transmission of depression in this study. Although on the surface this sounds like a purely psychosocial explanation for depression transmission, it is important to remember that both stress and interpersonal functioning are likely to have substantial genetic components. Overall, the results of the Hammen and colleagues (2004) study suggest that the process by which depression is passed from generation to generation is complex, interpersonally focused, and both environmentally and genetically determined.

Of course, not all children of depressed parents will succumb to depression themselves. As noted previously, if the parent's depression is less severe, the child is at a lower risk for depression. Additional factors that might protect children with a family background of depression include a positive parent-child relationship, a highly functioning adult role model (potentially the father if the mother is depressed), a temperament that is resistant to stress or facilitates coping, and higher intellectual functioning capabilities. Further study of these and other potential protective factors has direct relevance for the development and implementation of prevention programs aimed at disrupting the family transmission of depression from one generation to the next.

PATRICIA A. BRENNAN

See also

Adolescent Depression
Biological Models of Depression
Childhood Depression
Fathers and Depression
Genetics of Depression
Genetic Transmission of Depression
Mothers and Depression

References

Goodman, S. H., & Gotlib, I. H. (1999). Risk for psychopathology in the children of depressed mothers: A developmental model for understanding mechanisms of transmission. *Psychological Review, 106*, 458–490.

Hammen, C., & Brennan, P. A. (2003). Severity, chronicity, and timing of maternal depression and risk for adolescent offspring diagnoses in a community sample. *Archives of General Psychiatry, 60*, 253–260.

Hammen, C., Shih, J. H., & Brennan, P. A. (2004). Intergenerational transmission of depression: Test of an interpersonal stress model in a community sample. *Journal of Consulting and Clinical Psychology, 72*, 511–522.

Sullivan, P. F., Neale, M. C., & Kendler, K. S. (2000). Genetic epidemiology of major depression: Review and meta-analysis. *American Journal of Psychiatry, 157*, 1552–1562.

Fathers and Depression

As is evident throughout this encyclopedia, major depressive disorder and even subclinical levels of depressive symptoms can be devastating for children, adults, and families. A great deal is known about the role of mothers in the development of depression and the role of family factors in the development of depression, but far less is known about the role of fathers in depression. Before understanding the role of fathers in depression, it is worthwhile to first consider fathers' roles in their children's lives.

Fathers' Involvement With Their Children

Current family demographics in the United States show that 64.2% of children under the age of 18 live with both of their biological parents, 22.7% live with a single mother, 6.7% live within a step family (usually with a biological mother and stepfather), 2.5% live with their single father, and 3.9% do not live with either their biological mother or father. These family constellation patterns vary by race and ethnicity, with 52.5% of African American children, 25.5% of Hispanic-Latino-Latina children, and 15.5% of White children living with their single mother. Even for children who do not live with their biological father, estimates suggest that between 70% and 80% of the children have some type of contact with their father.

Although there has been a great deal of media attention to fathers' increasing involvement in their children's lives, fathers as a group continue to spend less time and to shoulder less ultimate responsibility for their children than do mothers (Lamb, 2004). These findings are evident in two-parent families (regardless of whether both parents are employed full-time) as well as in families where the mother is the primary residential parent.

In terms of how fathers spend time with their children, there are relatively clear patterns across family constellations. In general, fathers tend to spend more time with their sons than their daughters, whereas mothers appear to spend approximately equivalent amounts of time with their sons and daughters. Contrary to the perception that fathers get more involved with children as the children reach their teenage years, both mothers and fathers spend more time with their infants and toddlers, comparatively less time with their school-aged children, and even less time with their teenagers. Across the child's life span, fathers spend a greater proportion of their time with their children in playful or recreational activities than in caretaking activities.

With all of these patterns of time spent with children, there is consistent evidence that for both mothers and fathers who have at least a minimal amount of consistent involvement, the quality of time spent with children is more important than the quantity of time spent with children in relation to the child's well-being. Specifically, mothers and fathers who show warmth and love toward their child along with age-appropriate expectations and structure (known as authoritative

parenting) tend to have children who are well adjusted with few emotional or behavioral problems. These patterns between fathers', mothers', and children's behavior have been seen internationally (Hart, 2007). Given the knowledge of father-child relations within the normative developmental process, it is appropriate to turn now to father-child relations within the context of abnormal development.

Fathers' Involvement in the Development of Depression

A great deal is known about maternal psychopathology in contrast to paternal psychopathology (Phares, Fields, Kamboukos, & Lopez, 2005). In fact, nearly every disorder has been explored in mothers to a much greater extent than in fathers; the one exception to this pattern is alcohol abuse. Thus, fathers are neglected from the bulk of research on most types of mental health problems, whereas mothers are neglected from the research on parental alcohol abuse.

When exploring connections between fathers and the development of psychopathology, there are three research strategies: take samples of troubled children and study their fathers, take samples of troubled fathers and study their children, and take samples of nonclinical groups in the community and study psychological problems in the fathers and children. Across these three designs and across many types of psychological problems, there are more similarities than differences between mothers and fathers in relation to the development of psychopathology. In general, the same can be said for the investigation into the fathers' role in the development of depression. Although there are somewhat stronger associations between fathers' functioning and children's externalizing behavior problems (such as being oppositional, arguing, and fighting) than children's internalizing problems (such as depression and anxiety), fathers appear to play a role in the development of depression in their offspring.

Fathers of Depressed Children

Studies that compare fathers and mothers of depressed children have found greater rates of psychopathology and troubled parenting in mothers than in fathers. In addition, when comparing fathers of depressed children with fathers of children who do not display any problems, few differences emerge. When comparing fathers of depressed children with fathers of children with externalizing problems (e.g., oppositional defiant disorder or conduct disorder), the fathers of children with externalizing problems tend to show higher rates of psychopathology and more problematic parenting behaviors than the fathers of depressed children. Thus, there appears to be a stronger link between depression in children and maladaptive functioning in their mothers as opposed to their fathers (Connell & Goodman, 2002). However, some studies have found increased problems in fathers of depressed children, so this topic remains an important area of study.

Children of Depressed Fathers

A great deal is known about children of depressed mothers, whereas far less is known about children of depressed fathers. Largely due to lower base rates of depression in men and perhaps the perceived stigma by men for seeking treatment for depression, comparatively few studies have explored depression in fathers. There is, however, growing awareness of depression in fathers and even reliable evidence of increased depressive symptoms in fathers after the birth of a child (known as postpartum depression in women as well as in men). Postpartum depression has been documented in fathers in a number of countries, including the United States, Denmark, and Taiwan. Within parental dyads, postpartum depression is strongly associated for mothers and fathers. Thus, infants who have one depressed parent are at greater risk for having both parents experience significant levels of depression.

When studies are conducted on depressed fathers, consistent patterns emerge. Regardless of whether the mother or the father is depressed, infants, children, and adolescents are at increased risk for emotional and behavioral problems. There is evidence that parental depression in the context of interparental conflict (i.e., parents arguing) is associated with externalizing problems in children (such as oppositionality, arguing, and physical fighting), whereas parental depression with little or no interparental conflict is associated with internalizing problems in children (such as depression and anxiety; Franck & Buehler, 2007). Overall, though, paternal depression is associated with greater risk for the development of problems in youths. Depression in fathers is also associated with greater father-child conflict (such as arguing and disagreements). These increased risks are thought to be due to a myriad of factors, such as increased genetic risk, expressions of feelings and cognitions within the family, modeling, and impaired parenting behaviors (Kane & Garber, 2004).

Depression in Nonclinical Samples of Fathers and Children

Like studies of depressed fathers, the associations between depressive symptoms of fathers and their children in nonclinical, community samples are strong. In fact, stronger associations between father and child depressive symptoms are often found in community samples in contrast to samples of children or fathers who are in treatment for depression (Kane & Garber, 2004). Thus, even at subclinical levels, fathers' depressive symptoms appear to be linked to greater risk for children's maladaptive behavior.

Fathers' Involvement in the Treatment of Depression

No discussion of paternal and child depression would be complete without a brief mention of treatment. In contrast to mothers, fathers are rarely included in therapeutic interventions with children (Phares, Fields, & Binitie, 2006). Interestingly, parents (whether mothers or fathers) are included in treatments for children's internalizing problems (such as depression and anxiety) to a much lesser degree than in treatments for children's externalizing problems (such as oppositional and conduct problems). Partly due to the treatments that have been found to be most helpful for different problems, children's externalizing problems tend to be treated with some version of behavioral parent training, whereas internalizing problems in youths tend to be treated within a cognitive-behavioral context in which the parent has only limited involvement in the treatment if any at all. When a parent is involved in treatment for children's depression (even as a collateral contact), then mothers tend to serve in this role to a greater degree than do fathers.

Conclusions

Overall, there are clear connections between fathers' and children's well-being, but those connections are stronger for externalizing versus internalizing problems in children. With that said, it is important to note that there are connections between fathers' functioning and the development of depression in children, so this area of research and treatment remains important for the well-being of all children.

VICKY PHARES

See also

Adolescent Depression
Childhood Depression
Family Transmission of Depression
Mothers and Depression

References

Connell, A. M., & Goodman, S. H. (2002). The association between psychopathology in fathers versus mothers and children's internalizing and externalizing behavior problems: A meta-analysis. *Psychological Bulletin, 128,* 746–773.

Franck, K. L., & Buehler, C. (2007). A family process model of marital hostility, parental depressive affect, and early adolescent problem behavior: The roles of triangulation and parental warmth. *Journal of Family Psychology, 21,* 614–625.

Hart, C. H. (2007). Why are parents important? Linking parenting to childhood social skills in Australia, China, Japan, Russia, and the United States. In A. S. Loveless & T. B. Holman (Eds.), *The family in the new millennium: World voices supporting the "natural" clan* (Vol. 1, pp. 227–247). Westport, CT: Praeger.

Kane, P., & Garber, J. (2004). The relations among depression in fathers, children's psychopathology, and father-child conflict: A meta-analysis. *Clinical Psychology Review, 24,* 339–360.

Lamb, M. E. (Ed.). (2004). *The role of the father in child development* (4th ed.). Hoboken, NJ: Wiley.

Phares, V., Fields, S., & Binitie, I. (2006). Getting fathers' involved in child-related therapy. *Cognitive and Behavioral Practice, 13,* 42–52.

Phares, V., Fields, S., Kamboukos, D., & Lopez, L. (2005). Still looking for Poppa. *American Psychologist, 60,* 735–736.

Functional Neuroimaging

Over the past 15 years, researchers have used functional neuroimaging techniques to study the neural substrates of depression. The results of these investigations have yielded important information about depression-associated abnormalities both in resting-state brain activation and in neural responsivity to emotional stimuli. Researchers are now working to use the results of these studies to gain a more comprehensive understanding of the development and maintenance of depression. Because depression clearly involves difficulties in the regulation of emotion, attempts to understand the neural underpinnings of this disorder have focused primarily on structures implicated in the experience and processing of emotional information. In broad terms, the results of this growing body of research suggest that, in depressed individuals, limbic and paralimbic structures are overactivated, while dorsal cortical structures, which are involved in limbic regulation, are underutilized. Indeed, scientists have postulated that there is a reciprocal relation among these structures in depression that favors limbic over dorsal cortical activity. In this article we describe empirical work examining the association with depression of four key structures in this formulation—the amygdala, the subgenual anterior cingulate cortex (ACC), the hippocampus, and the dorsolateral prefrontal cortex (DLPFC)—and present directions for future research.

Amygdala

The formulation that the amygdala is involved in negative affect and perception of noxious stimuli has been dominant in affective neuroscience. More recently, however, scientists have attributed to the amygdala a more general role in directing attention to stimuli that are particularly salient to an individual. A number of investigators have examined amygdala function in depression. Positron emission tomography (PET) studies of depressed individuals have found elevated baseline amygdala activity in depression (e.g., Drevets, Bogers, & Raichle, 2002) that returns to normal levels following successful pharmacotherapy. Moreover, depressed individuals also show heightened amygdala reactivity to emotional stimuli, most consistently to negative material (e.g., Fales et al., 2008). Two recent studies of memory for emotional information in depression highlight the possible functional significance of this increased amygdala reactivity. Ramel and colleagues (2007) found that amygdala activation in response to negatively valenced self-referent words in remitted depressed individuals predicted recall of words presented after a sad mood induction. Hamilton and Gotlib (2008) found that depressed individuals were characterized by increased amygdala activation during the encoding of negative, but not of neutral or positive, words that were recalled a week after they were encoded. In sum, then, depressed individuals are characterized by heightened resting amygdala activation and by elevated amygdala reactivity to negative emotional stimuli that may function to increase their memory for this negative material.

Subgenual ACC

The subgenual ACC is located in the ventral-most part of the so-called affective cingulate, a region postulated to be involved in monitoring of internal motivational states and in regulation of emotional responses. Although studies of subgenual ACC activity in depression have yielded equivocal results, it appears that when potential depression-related volume loss in the subgenual ACC is taken into account, subgenual ACC activity is increased in major depressive disorder. This conclusion is consistent with a body of work showing that subgenual ACC activity decreases following successful pharmacological treatment of depression. Moreover, complementing work on resting-state activity in the subgenual ACC in depression, functional MRI (fMRI) studies have found that depressed individuals are characterized by increased responsivity of the subgenual ACC. Gotlib and colleagues (2005), for example, found depressed persons to show greater subgenual ACC activity in response to emotional faces than did nondepressed controls. Moreover, Siegle, Carter, and Thase (2006) found that increased subgenual ACC reactivity to affective words in depressed patients predicted poor response to subsequent cognitive behavior therapy.

Hippocampus

Several studies of hippocampal volume indicate both that the hippocampus is smaller in depressed than in nondepressed individuals and that it decreases in volume with recurrence of depression (e.g., Campbell, Marriott, Nahmias, & MacQueen, 2004). This progressive volumetric decrease may be due to the repeated exposure of depressed individuals to stress and the resultant production of glucocorticoids, which serve to reduce hippocampal volume. The functional consequences of this hippocampal atrophy are not well documented. Given that the hippocampus is implicated in negative-feedback control of the hypothalamic-pituitary-adrenal (HPA) axis, which is critically involved in glucocorticoid production, scientists have speculated that decreased hippocampal activity reduces inhibitory regulation of the HPA axis. This formulation is inconsistent, however, with results of PET studies that document *increased* hippocampal activity in depression that decreases following successful pharmacological treatment (Kennedy et al., 2001). It will be important in future investigations to attempt to reconcile these structural and functional findings concerning the hippocampus in depression and their relation to this disorder.

Dorsolateral Prefrontal Cortex

Consistent reports of the expression of context-inappropriate affect in depression, and of an inability to inhibit the processing of negative material, have led investigators to examine executive control processes in major depressive disorder. In this context, scientists have shown that depression is characterized by low levels of activity in brain regions involved in executive control, most consistently, in the DLPFC. Importantly, investigators have found that DLPFC activity decreases when formerly depressed individuals relapse. Studies using fMRI consistently demonstrate that major depressive disorder is associated with attenuated DLPFC response to affective stimuli. For example, Hooley, Gruber, Scott, Hiller, and Yurgelun-Todd (2005), reported that unlike nondepressed controls, depressed individuals failed to activate the DLPFC while listening to taped criticism from their mothers. Schaefer, Putnam, Benca, and Davidson (2006) showed similar findings using positive stimuli; these investigators found diminished DLPFC activity in depression in response to both erotica and positive emotion faces. Thus, DLPFC activity is decreased in depression, both at rest and in response to both negative and positive emotional stimuli.

Conclusions and Future Directions

In this brief review we have documented that depression is associated with structural and functional abnormalities of brain structures that are critically involved in the experience and regulation of emotion. More specifically, limbic structures, such as the amygdala, subgenual ACC, and less consistently, the hippocampus, have been found to be overactive in depression; conversely, the DLPFC has been found to be underactive in

this disorder. Although this research examining individual structures has had a major impact on our understanding of the neural basis of depression, recent attempts to investigate broader, network-level, neural anomalies in depression promise to further increase our knowledge of this disorder. Investigators working from a neural systems perspective have begun to examine the relations among brain structures implicated in depression in painting a more comprehensive picture of neural dysfunction in this disorder. Mayberg and colleagues (2005), for example, investigated brainwide implications of modulating activity in the subgenual ACC in depression by implanting and activating stimulating electrodes near this structure in treatment-refractory depressed patients. These researchers found that, in addition to significantly ameliorating depressive symptoms, stimulation near the subgenual ACC in depressed patients both reduced the previously heightened activity in this structure and increased previously diminished activity in the DLPFC. This pattern of activity is consistent with the general finding in depression of increased limbic and paralimbic activity and decreased dorsal cortical activity, as well as with a network-level neural model of this disorder. According to this model, the normal reciprocal relation between the limbic system and dorsal cortical structures is altered in depression such that limbic overactivity inhibits activation in dorsal structures, reducing their ability to regulate limbic activation.

In future research, it will be important for investigators to delineate the functional relations among the structures implicated in depression. In our laboratory, for example, we recently found that when depressed individuals successfully encode negative information, there is an increased correlation between activity in the amygdala and activation in the caudate-putamen, a structure critical in operant learning and an integral part of the affective division of the cortico-striatal-pallido-thalamic loop, which has also been implicated in depression. Complementing this work on functional connectivity among neural structures in depression, further research is already being conducted using techniques such as diffusion tensor imaging to detect and assess the integrity of pathways that connect brain structures identified by mapping the anatomical foundations of these functional relations.

IAN H. GOTLIB AND J. PAUL HAMILTON

See also

Affective Neuroscience
Behavioral Activation System
Behavioral Inhibition System
Brain Circuitry
Hemispheric Lateralization
Hippocampus
Hypothalamic-Pituitary-Adrenal Axis
Hypothalamic-Pituitary-Thyroid Axis

References

Campbell, S., Marriott, M., Nahmias, C., & MacQueen, G. M. (2004). Lower hippocampal volume in patients suffering from depression: A meta-analysis. *American Journal of Psychiatry, 161,* 598–607.

Drevets, W. C., Bogers, W., & Raichle, M. E. (2002). Functional anatomical correlates of antidepressant drug treatment assessed using PET measures of regional glucose metabolism. *European Neuropsychopharmacology, 12,* 527–544.

Fales, C. L., Barch, D. M., Rundle, M. M., Mintun, M. A., Snyder, A. Z., Cohen, J. D., et al. (2008). Altered emotional interference processing in affective and cognitive-control brain circuitry in major depression. *Biological Psychiatry, 15,* 377–384.

Gotlib, I. H., Sivers, H., Gabrieli, J. D. E., Whitfield-Gabrieli, S., Goldin, P., Minor, K. L., et al. (2005). Subgenual anterior cingulate activation to valenced emotional stimuli in major depression. *Neuroreport, 16,* 1731–1734.

Hamilton, J. P., & Gotlib, I. H. (2008). Neural substrates of increased memory sensitivity for negative stimuli in major depression. *Biological Psychiatry, 63,* 1155–1162.

Hooley, J. M., Gruber, S. A., Scott, L. A., Hiller, J. B., & Yurgelun-Todd, D. A. (2005). Activation in dorsolateral prefrontal cortex in response to maternal criticism and praise in recovered depressed and healthy control participants. *Biological Psychiatry, 57,* 809–812.

Kennedy, S. H., Evans, K. R., Kruger, S., Mayberg, H. S., Meyer, J. H., McCann, S., et al. (2001). Changes in regional brain glucose metabolism measured with positron emission tomography after paroxetine treatment of major depression. *American Journal of Psychiatry, 158,* 899–905.

Mayberg, H. S., Lozano, A. M., Voon, V., McNeely, H. E., Seminowicz, D., Hamani, C., et al. (2005). Deep brain stimulation for treatment-resistant depression. *Neuron, 45,* 651–660.

Ramel, W., Goldin, P. R., Eyler, L. T., Brown, G. G., Gotlib, I. H., & McQuaid, J. R. (2007). Amygdala reactivity and mood-congruent memory in individuals at risk for depressive relapse. *Biological Psychiatry, 61,* 231–239.

Schaefer, H. S., Putnam, K. M., Benca, R. M., & Davidson, R. J. (2006). Event-related functional magnetic resonance imaging measures of neural activity to positive social stimuli in pre- and post-treatment depression. *Biological Psychiatry, 60,* 974–986.

Siegle, G. J., Carter, C. S., & Thase, M. E. (2006). Use of fMRI to predict recovery from unipolar depression with cognitive behavior therapy. *American Journal of Psychiatry, 163,* 735–731.

G

Gender Differences

A well-established fact is that women are diagnosed with depression at twice the rate as men. There are only very small differences from country to country and from ethnic group to ethnic group. Thus, this 2 to 1 ratio generally holds throughout all industrialized countries. This difference also generally holds across ethnic groups within the United States. For example, when income, education, and occupation are controlled, the gender difference persists among Whites, African Americans, and Latinos.

Gender differences first appear in adolescence; up until this point, boys and girls experience depression at low, but roughly the same, rates. At around age 13, however, the rate for girls goes up substantially. In an examination of data from the National Comorbidity Study, Kessler, McGonagle, Swartz, and Blazer (1993) found that women are significantly more likely than men to develop a first episode of depression. After a first episode, however, the rates of recurrence of depressive episodes for men and women are virtually the same.

Is this observed difference real? One early idea about gender differences was that women and men actually experience depression in relatively equal proportions, but that women are more likely to acknowledge their depression and are more likely to be overdiagnosed with depression than men. This artifact hypothesis, however, has not received much empirical support. Hence, gender differences in depression appear to be quite real.

A variety of explanations have been proposed for these differences, although there is little in the way of a satisfactory explanation of the data. Hence, the processes that underlie gender differences are not well understood.

RICK E. INGRAM

See also

Diagnostic and Statistical Manual of
Mental Disorders
Epidemiology

Reference

Kessler, R. C., McGonagle, K. A., Swartz, & Blazer, D. G. (1993). Sex and depression in the National Comorbidity Survey I: Lifetime prevalence, chronicity and recurrence. *Journal of Affective Disorders, 29*, 85–96.

Genetics of Depression

Psychiatric genetics explores to what extent and by what mechanism the information contained in the sequence of bases that make up the DNA influences the causation, course, and outcome of mental disorders. In this entry, we give an overview of four major aspects of the genetics of depression. First, genetic epidemiology estimates the magnitude of genetic contribution from the similarity among relatives in their vulnerability to develop depression. Second, molecular genetics locates the genetic variation and explores the molecular mechanisms that cause the disorder. Third, research on gene-environment interactions and epigenetics studies the interplay between genes and environmental influences. Fourth, pharmacogenetics explores the genetic determinants of response to treatment. Unless specified otherwise, the information here refers to the genetics of unipolar recurrent depressive disorder, the most common form of depression.

Genetic Epidemiology: How Much Do Genes Contribute to the Genesis of Depression?

Depression tends to run in families and first-degree relatives of individuals with depression are about 3 times more likely to fulfill the diagnostic criteria for depression than relatives of healthy controls. Adoption and twin studies indicate that the clustering of depression in families is largely due to genes rather than the environmental factors that are also shared within families. The concordance rate of depression is twice as large between monozygotic twins (who share 100% of their genes) than between dizygotic twins (who, like ordinary siblings, have 50% of their genes in common), approximately 46% and 21%, respectively (McGuffin, Katz, Watkins, & Rutherford, 1996). These findings indicate strong roles for both genetic and nonshared (unique individual) environmental factors. Based on twin data, researchers make estimates of heritability as a proportion of variance in a hypothetical continuous trait of liability to develop depression that is attributable to the additive effect of genes.

The heritability estimates for depression differ across studies and range from .3 to .75 (Sullivan, Neale, & Kendler, 2000). Heritability estimates are crucially dependent on the population prevalence of the disorder under study, as well as a number of assumptions. The latter include (a) equal sharing of environment between monozygotic and dizygotic twin pairs, (b) no interactions between different genes, and (c) no interaction between genetic and shared environmental factors. Less than perfect agreement between

twin and family studies indicates that at least some of these assumptions are violated in the case of depression (Sullivan et al., 2000). Importantly, the heritability of depression increases with reliability and stability of diagnosis over time and is higher in clinically ascertained populations. This suggests that part of the apparent nonshared environment contribution is due to diagnostic error or the inclusion of mild cases. There appears to be a core subtype of depression, characterized by recurrent discrete episodes and typical somatic symptoms, that is more heritable than broadly defined depression.

The genetic predisposition is not entirely specific to unipolar depression and overlaps with genetic vulnerability to bipolar disorder (McGuffin et al., 2003), generalized anxiety disorder (Kendler, Neale, Kessler, Heath, & Eavess, 1992), and alcohol dependence (Kendler, Heath, Neale, Kessler, & Eaves, 1993). While the genetic contribution to the vulnerability to depression is similar in men and women, the individual genetic factors are partially gender specific, as indicated by an imperfect genetic correlation between the genders of approximately .5 (McGuffin et al., 1996).

Molecular Genetics: Finding the Culprit Genes

The specific nature of the genetic predisposition to depression is largely unknown, and great efforts are being extended to identify specific genetic variations and how they contribute to the pathogenesis of depression. It is now clear that there is no single genetic abnormality that causes depression. Rather than a single major gene, it is likely that a large number of genetic variations combine to constitute a genotype of vulnerability to depression. Finding dozens, possibly even hundreds of genetic markers, each with a small effect size, among the millions of known polymorphisms in the human genome is a daunting task, and progress is limited by statistical power and size of available samples. It has been approached in two ways.

First, so-called functional candidate genes, that is, genes that code for proteins relevant to the pathophysiology of depression, have been explored. Influenced by the monoamine deficiency hypothesis of depression (Belmaker & Agam, 2008), numerous candidates have been identified among genes coding for proteins involved in the synthesis and metabolism of the neurotransmitters serotonin, noradrenalin, and dopamine and their receptors. Some of these, especially those related to dopaminergic signaling, including genes for the dopamine transporter and dopamine receptor DRD4, have shown significant associations with depression in a recent meta-analysis (Lopez-Leon et al., 2008). Other genes may be important for specific symptoms of depression: for example, genes for proteins governing the biological rhythm have been implicated in sleep disturbance. However, most reported candidate gene associations have not been replicated, and those that have been only explain a small proportion of the genetic liability to depression.

The second approach consists of a systematic search of the whole human genome. Systematic methods of gene location include linkage and genomewide association studies (GWASs). These methods have the potential to uncover genetic polymorphisms of previously unsuspected functional significance but are hampered by the need for very large samples, and the low power of statistical tests in the context of megavariate data (linkage operates with hundreds and GWASs with hundreds of thousands of genetic markers). Linkage studies use family pedigrees with at least two affected individuals and look for parts of the genome that are shared between affected family members more often than would be expected given the closeness of their biological relatedness. Several large whole-genome linkage studies have recently been completed and have pinpointed genomic regions on the long arms of chromosomes 12 and 15 that tend to be cotransmitted with the disorder (Holmans et al., 2007; McGuffin et al., 2005). As with single candidate genes, the size of association between these genomic regions and depression is modest, and any polymorphisms identified within these regions can potentially explain only a small proportion of genetic risk for depression. Therefore, the most important result of the linkage studies has been the exclusion

of any possibility of major effect genes (i.e., genes contributing more than 10% of the genetic liability to develop the disorder). Any gene that could explain 10% or more of the variance in liability to develop depression would have been identified with a reasonable confidence in the extant linkage studies. Genetic polymorphisms with a much smaller effect size, for example, explaining 1% or less of the genetic liability to depression, will require a fine-grained mapping of the genome in a large sample GWAS. The first two GWAS in depression indicate that there is no genetic marker that would explain even this relatively small proportion of variance consistently across populations. The contrast between these results and the heritability estimates from twin studies may lead to a depreciation of the role of genes as direct causes of depression and point to a complex interplay between various causative factors.

Gene-Environment Interplay

How is it that depression is strongly genetic but depression genes are so difficult to find? One explanation for this apparent discrepancy is that genes do not act in isolation. Most genetic studies so far have aimed to identify "a gene for depression," that is, a polymorphism with a direct, unconditional causative effect. It is now becoming evident that many effects of polymorphic genes may be conditional on other genes (gene-gene interaction, G×G, or epistasis) or on environmental risk factors (gene-environment interaction, or G×E). Indeed, it makes sense that genes directly causing depression would have been pruned out through natural selection during evolution, as depression is associated with reproductive and survival disadvantages. Genes that are advantageous under some (but not other) circumstances, on the other hand, would have been maintained, as their presence fosters adaptability at a group level. In a twin study, an interaction effect between genetic polymorphisms and aspects of the environment that are shared within families would be attributed to heritability. However, finding a gene-disorder association in the presence of G×E depends on the rate of the environmental factor exposure in the population under study, leading to heterogeneity of findings and frequent nonreplications. Thus, conditional effects of genes are consistent with high heritability estimates and may explain inconsistency in gene-disorder association studies between populations.

A specific G×E has been identified between a length polymorphism (i.e., a segment of DNA where a short sequence of bases is repeated 14 or 16 times) in the serotonin transporter gene (SERT) and stressful life events. Individuals carrying two copies or alleles (one from each parent) of the short (i.e., 14 repeats) variant of the gene thrive under favorable circumstances but are more vulnerable to develop depression in the context of stressful experiences (Caspi et al., 2003). Those carrying the long variants (i.e., 16 repeats) appear to be relatively oblivious to negative (and possibly also positive) influences from their surroundings (Uher & McGuffin, 2008). Importantly, there is no significant direct effect of the polymorphism (i.e., the SERT gene is not a gene for depression), but the G×E may explain about 8% of cases of depression in the population. The length polymorphism is in the promoter region of the gene and acts like a dimmer switch to increase or decrease the production of the serotonin transporter in response to changes in the environment. The long allele may be more effective in adjusting this, thereby conferring a better ability to adapt to stress to its carriers (but possibly at a cost) compared to the short allele. In addition, a polymorphism in another gene, the brain-derived neurotrophic factor (BDNF) gene, may further moderate the joint effects of SERT and life stress, thus producing a three-way interaction (Uher & McGuffin, 2008).

The interplay of genes and environment may also take other forms. For example, researchers have identified genetic influences on aspects of life that were until recently considered to be environmental, such as life events or social support (this is called gene-environment correlation). On the other hand, early environment may have lasting effects on the expression of genes that persist throughout the life span and may be even transmitted across generations through epigenetic mechanisms, such as DNA methylation or modification of histones (DNA-supporting proteins). This is a vibrant area of research that is expected to bring more light into the causation of individual differences in emotions and behavior over the years to come. What is clear now is that what may emerge will not be a clean and simple gene-for-depression story.

Genetics of Treatment Response

For a long time, clinicians have noted that a treatment may be more likely to work for a patient if a close relative with similar symptoms had a good response to such treatment. The pharmacogenetic research builds on this observation by trying to identify specific genetic polymorphisms related to individual differences in treatment response. At present, this inquiry is still at the stage of functional candidate genes research. A natural candidate is the SERT gene (same as in the G×E interaction, see previous paragraph), as its product, the serotonin transporter, is the target of the most commonly used group of antidepressants (the serotonin reuptake inhibitors, including fluoxetine, citalopram, and others). Several studies have found that individuals carrying the less-effective short alleles of the length polymorphism in the promoter of this gene are less likely to have a good therapeutic response to serotonin reuptake inhibiting antidepressants (Serretti, Kato, De, & Kinoshita, 2007). Intriguingly, this finding seems to be population specific: it has been replicated in European but not American samples, and findings in the opposite direction have been reported in Asian populations (Kim et al., 2006). These discrepancies may be pointing to another complex conditional effect: population-specific genetic and environmental factors may moderate the relationship between SERT gene and antidepressants.

While pharmacogenetic study of antidepressant response is nowhere near the point where a genetic test could be used clinically to help prescribe decisions, genes may soon become useful in identifying individuals who may be at risk of serious adverse reactions. A small proportion of individuals, especially young men, experience a dangerous reaction to antidepressants, with increase in suicidal thought and risk of suicide. A recent large study indicates that a combination of polymorphisms in the gene for the transcription regulator CREB, involved in the intracellular transduction of the serotonergic and noradrenergic signals, can be used to predict treatment-emergent suicidality in men (Perlis et al., 2007). The usefulness of this promising finding will depend on its robustness in replication.

Conclusions and Future Prospects

Research to date indicates a large genetic contribution especially to the more severe and recurrent forms of depression. However, it is also clear that there is no single depression-causing gene. Instead, a combination of a number of genes may constitute a vulnerability to depression, each having little or even no effect on its own. Such genes may also act indirectly, by interacting with environment. On the other hand, the genetic effects may have multiple facets. For example, the SERT gene appears to be implicated in the etiology of depression when associated with adverse life circumstances, but in addition, the gene also influences the response to antidepressant drugs.

It is likely that depression as currently defined is a heterogeneous group of conditions with varied etiologies. Future research may focus on finding genetic determinants of specific types of depression, such as depression occurring in the context of vascular brain disease, in women around menopause, or in men with a history of anger and antisocial behaviors. Following the realization that there are no genes of large effect, geneticists arm themselves with finer nets to trawl for small-effect genes. Subsequently, any future genetic diagnostic or therapy tools are likely to be multifaceted and give probabilistic rather than definite answers to the old questions: Who gets depressed and why? What treatment will work for whom?

RUDOLF UHER AND ANNE FARMER

See also

Biological Models of Depression
Family Transmission of Depression
Genetic Transmission of Depression
Molecular Genetics

References

Belmaker, R. H., & Agam, G. (2008). Major depressive disorder. *New England Journal of Medicine, 358,* 55–68.

Caspi, A., Sugden, K., Moffitt, T. E., Taylor, A., Craig, I. W., Harrington, H., et al. (2003). Influence of life stress on depression: Moderation by a polymorphism in the 5-HTT gene. *Science, 301,* 386–389.

Holmans, P., Weissman, M. M., Zubenko, G. S., Scheftner, W. A., Crowe, R. R., Depaulo, J. R., Jr., et al. (2007). Genetics of recurrent early-onset major depression (GenRED): Final genome scan report. *American Journal of Psychiatry, 164,* 248–258.

Kendler, K. S., Heath, A. C., Neale, M. C., Kessler, R. C., & Eaves, L. J. (1993). Alcoholism and major depression in women. A twin study of the causes of comorbidity. *Archives of General Psychiatry, 50,* 690–698.

Kendler, K. S., Neale, M. C., Kessler, R. C., Heath, A. C., & Eaves, L. J. (1992). Major depression and generalized anxiety disorder. Same genes, (partly) different environments? *Archives of General Psychiatry, 49,* 716–722.

Kim, H., Lim, S. W., Kim, S., Kim, J. W., Chang, Y. H., Carroll, B. J., et al. (2006). Monoamine transporter gene polymorphisms and antidepressant response in Koreans with late-life depression. *Journal of the American Medical Association, 296,* 1609–1618.

Lopez-Leon, S., Janssens, A. C., Gonzalez-Zuloeta Ladd, A. M., Del Favero, J., Claes, S. J., Oostra, B. A., et al. (2008). Meta-analyses of genetic studies on major depressive disorder. *Molecular Psychiatry, 13,* 772–785.

McGuffin, P., Katz, R., Watkins, S., & Rutherford, J (1996). A hospital-based twin register of the heritability of DSM-IV unipolar depression. *Archives of General Psychiatry, 53,* 129–136.

McGuffin, P., Knight, J., Breen, G., Brewster, S., Boyd, P. R., Craddock, N., et al. (2005). Whole genome linkage scan of recurrent depressive disorder from the depression network study. *Human Molecular Genetics, 14,* 3337–3345.

McGuffin, P., Rijsdijk, F., Andrew, M., Sham, P., Katz, R., & Cardno, A. (2003). The heritability of bipolar affective disorder and the genetic relationship to unipolar depression. *Archives of General Psychiatry, 60,* 497–502.

Perlis, R. H., Beasley, C. M., Jr., Wines, J. D., Jr., Tamura, R. N., Cusin, C., Shear, D., et al. (2007). Treatment-associated suicidal ideation and adverse effects in an open, multicenter trial of fluoxetine for major depressive episodes. *Psychotherapy and Psychosomatics, 76,* 40–46.

Serretti, A., Kato, M., De, R. D., & Kinoshita, T. (2007). Meta-analysis of serotonin transporter gene promoter polymorphism (5-HTTLPR) association with selective serotonin reuptake inhibitor efficacy in depressed patients. *Molecular Psychiatry, 12,* 247–257.

Sullivan, P. F., Neale, M. C., & Kendler, K. S. (2000). Genetic epidemiology of major depression: Review and meta-analysis. *American Journal of Psychiatry, 157,* 1552–1562.

Uher, R., & McGuffin, P. (2008). The moderation by the serotonin transporter gene of environmental adversity in the aetiology of mental illness: Review and methodological analysis. *Molecular Psychiatry, 13,* 131–146.

Genetic Transmission of Depression

Vulnerability to depression reflects the interaction of genetic predispositions with environmental variables, such as life stress. Common variations (polymorphisms) within specific genes may confer individual differences in affective behavior that constitute a vulnerability factor for mood disorders. The most researched example of such a polymorphism is the serotonin (5-HT) transporter gene (5-HTT, SLC6A4), which regulates the availability of the neurotransmitter serotonin. This gene contains a number of polymorphic regions, including a repetitive sequence in the transcriptional control region of the 5-HT transporter gene (the 5-HTT-linked polymorphic region, 5-HTTLPR), which exists in a short and a long variant. Presence of the short variant is associated with reduced transcriptional activity, resulting in lower levels of serotonin transporter.

A population and family-based association study investigated the link between 5-HTTLPR variation and self-reported personality traits. The study focused in particular on the personality trait of neuroticism, which is characterized by a high degree of negative affect and is a risk factor for depression. The investigators reported that carriers of the 5-HTTLPR short variant have significantly higher scores of neuroticism than noncarriers, namely, those who are homozygous for the 5-HTTLPR long variant (Lesch et al., 1996).

Since this initial report, a number of replication studies have been conducted, which have produced mixed results. One reason for nonreplications may be methodological, because many of these studies used smaller sample sizes than the initial report, or heterogeneous subject populations, differing methods of personality assessment, or extreme scorers. However, most meta-analyses concluded that there is a small but significant association between presence of the HTTLPR short variant and trait neuroticism.

Another reason may be that the effect size of 5-HTTLPR genotype on self-reported traits is very small, accounting only for 3% to 4% of the total variance and 7% to 9% of the genetic variance observed in the initial report (Lesch et al., 1996). Recognizing that biological measures of individual differences in emotional processing may constitute a more sensitive endophenotype of 5-HTTLPR action, a number of neuroimaging studies have been conducted. A seminal study by Hariri and colleagues found that presence of the 5-HTTLPR short variant is associated with greater activation in the amygdala, a central brain region involved in the processing of emotional stimuli, when participants matched emotional facial expressions, relative to a neutral matching task (reviewed by Canli & Lesch, 2007). A number of replication studies, using different emotion paradigms, subject populations, and imaging methods, have consistently replicated the basic observation that amygdala activation to emotional, relative to neutral, stimuli is greater in carriers of the 5-HTTLPR short variant than in noncarriers who are homozygous for the long variant (although the interpretation of this observation is currently a matter of debate, see Canli & Lesch, 2007).

In addition to the amygdala, this imaging work has led to the realization that structural and functional network properties also differ between 5-HTTLPR short variant carriers and noncarriers in a manner that may constitute a biological marker for depression vulnerability (reviewed by Canli & Lesch,

2007). In particular, Pezawas and colleagues found that healthy 5-HTTLPR short variant carriers with no history of depression are similar to depressed patients in that they show reduced gray matter volume in the subgenual anterior cingulate cortex (ACC), as well as in the amygdala. Furthermore, the ACC can regulate amygdala activation, but the functional connectivity between these two structures is diminished in 5-HTTLPR short variant carriers compared to noncarriers. These findings lead the authors to propose that vulnerability to depression associated with the 5-HTTLPR short variant may represent both structural and functional deficiencies within a neural circuit that regulates emotional reactivity. In light of gene-by-environment (G×E) studies of depression vulnerability, they further suggested that deficiencies within this circuit could be amplified through negative life experiences.

Clear evidence for an interaction between 5-HTTLPR genotype and life experience was first provided by Caspi and colleagues (2003). These investigators followed a cohort of more than 1,000 individuals over a 23-year period, collecting life history data every few years throughout the period of the study. They genotyped study participants for 5-HTTLPR variation to address the question of whether the association between life stress and depression was moderated by presence of the short variant. Indeed, they found that a high degree of life stress was associated with higher levels of depressive symptoms, diagnosed depression, and suicidality, as a function of the number of short variants: those individuals with no short variants (i.e., homozygous carriers of the long variant) had the least number of symptoms, those individuals who carried one short and one long variant had intermediate numbers of symptoms, and those with two short variants had the highest number of symptoms. In the absence of life stress, individuals did not differ in the number of depressive symptoms as a function of 5-HTTLPR genotype. Thus, depression vulnerability appears to reflect the interaction of genetic vulnerability (presence of the 5-HTTLPR short variant) and life stress history, representing a G×E interaction.

Replication studies have produced somewhat mixed results (reviewed by Canli & Lesch, 2007). For example, some studies have found a G×E interaction only in females, and others failed to replicate the G×E interaction when using older subject samples. There is also evidence that social support can reduce the vulnerability to depression brought about by the presence of the 5-HTTLPR short variant and life stress. It therefore appears that there are likely multiple factors that affect the likelihood of an individual developing depression. Ongoing work is aimed at identifying the relationship between these interacting factors, and at elucidating the underlying molecular mechanisms by which life experience may affect gene expression.

TURHAN CANLI

See also

Biological Models of Depression
Family Transmission of Depression
Genetics of Depression
Molecular Genetics

References

Canli, T., & Lesch, K. P. (2007). Long story short: The serotonin transporter in emotion regulation and social cognition. *Nature Neuroscience, 10,* 1103–1109.

Caspi, A., Sugden, K., Moffitt, T. E., Taylor, A., Craig, I. W., Harrington, H., et al. (2003). Influence of life stress on depression: Moderation by a polymorphism in the 5-HTT gene. *Science, 301,* 386–389.

Lesch, K. P., Bengel, D., Heils, A., Sabol, S. Z., Greenberg, B. D., Petri, S., et al. (1996). Association of anxiety-related traits with a polymorphism in the serotonin transporter gene regulatory region. *Science, 274,* 1527–1531.

Geriatric Depression

Depression in the elderly is an important medical problem. Beyond personal suffering, depression contributes significantly to morbidity and all-cause mortality, increases suicide rates, and causes significant impairment of physical and social functioning. Depression is the leading cause of disability as measured by years lived with the disability, according to the World Health Organization.

Geriatric depression remains underdiagnosed. Challenges that impose greater difficulty to the diagnosis of depression in the elderly include several factors: elders tend to emphasize somatic symptoms and to not report psychological symptoms; depressive symptoms are frequently attributed to the "normal" aging process; and geriatric depression often occurs in the context of medical and neurological diseases, when the overlap of symptoms imposes greater difficulty in the diagnosis.

Applying the categorical diagnostic approach of the *Diagnostic and Statistical Manual of Mental Disorders (DSM;* American Psychiatric Association, 1994) in community surveys showed that, despite the high percentage of elderly reporting significant depressive symptoms (27%), only about 4% meet criteria for depressive disorders (1% for major depression, 2% for dysthymia, and 1.2% for mixed depression and anxiety syndrome in the Epidemiological Catchment Area Study) (Koenig & Blazer, 2004). The *DSM* criteria, not adapted to the depressed elderly, may not apply to all depressive syndromes in late life. Many elderly, with atypical presentations of depression (more somatic and cognitive symptoms, lack of feeling or emotion instead of depressed mood) do not meet criteria for diagnosis. Other epidemiological studies found higher rates of dysthymia in the elderly, from 4% to 7%, suggesting that more severe depressive disorders in the elderly may be replaced by milder forms.

Paired to the low rates of major depression identified by epidemiological studies in elderly in the community, depression is highly prevalent in elderly in clinical settings: up to 21% of hospitalized elderly meet criteria for major depression, and even higher rates were described in elderly in nursing homes.

Depression due to a general medical condition is frequent in the elderly. Medical conditions that can cause depression include: viral infections, endocrinopathies (e.g., hypothyroidism), malignant diseases, cerebrovascular diseases, cardiovascular diseases, metabolic disorders (e.g., B-12 deficiency), neurological disorders (Parkinson's disease), and so forth. Substance-induced depression is also relevant in this age group. Alcohol abuse and dependence often contribute to the onset of depression and worsen its course. Medications that can be related to depression include methyldopa, benzodiazepines, propranolol, reserpine, steroids, antiparkinsonians, beta-blockers, cimetidine, clonidine, hydralazine, estrogens, progesterone, tamoxifen, vinblastine, vincristine, dextropropoxyphene, among others—many of which are frequently used by the elderly. Comorbid anxiety symptoms, cognitive dysfunction, and psychotic symptoms are common in this age group and add complexity to the diagnosis. Psychotic symptoms are more frequent in depressive episodes with onset in late life, and more commonly involve delusions than hallucinations. The most common delusions are of persecution, having an incurable disease, and guilt. Psychotic depression is typically severe, with increased risk of suicide, and responds poorly to antidepressants alone. Electroconvulsive therapy is the treatment of choice.

The etiology of late-life depression is multifactorial. The distribution by gender of 2 women to 1 man persists into late life. However, depression might be underdiagnosed to a greater extent in men, as men report fewer psychological symptoms, leading to increased difficulties in detecting depression.

There is evidence suggesting that depression with onset in later life is distinct from earlier-onset depression. Those with onset earlier in life have clearly had longer histories of depression and many treatments. The length of exposure to depression through life has been associated with reductions in hippocampal volume and deficits in verbal memory, possibly due to hypercortisolemia. Chronic depression may also be associated with medical consequences such as increased risk of ischemic heart disease and osteoporotic bone loss.

Conversely, family histories of depression are less prominent in later-onset depressions, which are more frequently associated with neurological, cerebrovascular, and dementing disorders, and with greater impairment on neuropsychological tests. Many later-onset depressed patients may have enlargement of lateral brain ventricles and white matter hyperintensities. Depression with onset in late life appears also to be more treatment resistant and have a more deteriorating course. Nonetheless, in the absence of collaborative history, it can be difficult to reliably identify early episodes of depression, especially in the context of cognitive impairment (Alexopoulos, 2005).

Depression is frequent in individuals with dementia (it occurs in 17% to 31% of patients with Alzheimer's disease and approximately 25% of those with cerebrovascular disease) and the depressive symptoms can even precede the cognitive decline. Depressed elderly who present with cognitive impairment are at higher risk of developing dementia in a few years than those without cognitive impairment. Lifetime history of depression is associated with increased risk for Alzheimer's disease, and there is suggestion that the risk increases with the number of previous episodes of depression.

Changes in the activity and metabolism of neurotransmitters as part of the aging process may contribute to late-life depression: concentrations of both norepinephrine and serotonine decrease with age, while there is an increase of the enzyme monoaminase oxidase, both leading to an overall decrease of the monoaminergic transmission. Other contributing factors are the dysregulation of the hypothalamic-pituitary-adrenal axis, the thyroid axis, and growth hormone release. Specific structural brain changes have been described in late-life depression. The hypothesis is that the accumulation of vascular lesions can disrupt the prefrontal systems and contribute to depression in some patients. The changes of the sleep cycle with age could also affect the normal physiological circadian rhythms and increase vulnerability to depression.

In addition to the biological factors, psychosocial factors such as inadequate social network, feelings of loneliness, and low educational level can contribute to depression in the elderly as well. Social support refers to the quality of personal relationships, and it is an important protective factor against depression in the elderly. The perceived social support is especially important, for it is associated not only with depression outcomes but with health outcomes in general. Higher levels of social support are linked to less severe depressive symptoms, decreased functional decline, less time to remission, and greater adherence to medications.

Major life events can lead to depression as well. Some depressive symptoms after bereavement are the norm. In the majority of the cases, these symptoms resolve over time; however, studies of widowhood show rates of depression of 16% after the first year. Odds are higher for those with previous history of mood disorder, substance abuse, or poor physical health. Caregiving for a disabled family member is associated with increased risk for depression. Estimates of depression among caregivers of persons with dementia range up to 80%, and the presence of depression may predict general health decline.

Depression is an independent risk factor for suicide in the elderly, being present in most elderly (80%) who commit suicide. Severity of depressive symptoms, in addition to the presence of previous serious attempts, predicts suicidal ideation in elderly. The most common precipitants of suicide in the elderly are physical illness and loss. Suicidal ideation may signal more difficult-to-treat depression (Szanto et al., 2007). Because most elderly who commit suicide have depression, it is critical to be able to identify depression and to offer appropriate care. Elderly with major medical illnesses or a recent loss should be assessed for depressive symptoms and suicide risk.

Geriatric depression is very common in the context of medical disorders and has a negative impact on prognosis and outcome. About 25% of patients with myocardial infarction have major depression, and those with depression are almost 4 times more likely to die within 4 months of the myocardial infarction. Depression is associated with increased cardiovascular events. Different mechanisms seem to be involved, including simpathoadrenal hyperactivity, hypothalamic-pituitary-adrenal hyperactivity, increased cate-cholamine activity, exacerbated platelet aggregation, and decreased compliance with treatment plans (depressed individuals are less likely to exercise regularly, have good diet, etc.). Depression in the elderly is associated with higher rates of all-cause mortality, especially among the medically ill.

Depression is a recurrent disorder, and with age, episodes tend to become more frequent and last longer. Recovery rates of up to 70% to 80% after treatment were reported in physically healthy depressed elderly, however comorbid conditions such as comorbid psychiatric disorders, physical illnesses, and cognitive impairment can complicate the course of depression and have a negative impact on response to treatment (Rabheru, 2004). Factors associated with worse outcomes are psychiatric comorbid diseases (for example, alcohol dependence, or anxiety disorders), more severe symptoms, physical illnesses, disabilities, cognitive impairment, poor access to mental health services, lack of social support, and higher levels of stressors. Factors associated with better outcomes are history of recovery from previous episodes, family history of depression, female gender, extroverted personality, absence of major life events or serious medical illness, and less-severe symptoms.

Assessment and Treatment

The treatment starts with a comprehensive assessment of depressive symptoms, suicidal ideation, medical and neurological comorbidities, medications being used (including over-the-counter and herbal medications), cognitive status, functional impairment, current stressors, and supports available.

Rating scales and structured interviews have been progressively incorporated to the assessment of depression in the elderly. The Center for Epidemiologic Studies Depression Scale is widely used for screening of depression in the community. The Geriatric Depression Scale is a self-report scale that consists of 30 yes-no items, developed specifically for the elderly. To monitor treatment outcomes, in addition to the widely used Hamilton Rating Scale for Depression, another interviewer-rated scale, the Montgomery-Asberg Rating Scale for Depression, has been shown to be sensitive to change during treatment. The Cornell Scale for Depression in Dementia has been validated and can be very useful in nursing homes.

The optimal treatment is a combination of pharmacotherapy and psychotherapy. Either pharmacotherapy alone or psychotherapy alone are acceptable alternatives in mild depression. In addition to pharmacotherapy and/or psychotherapy, interventions for depression in the elderly should also include the following:

- Optimizing control of any comorbid medical conditions (e.g., hypothyroidism, B-12 deficiency)
- Addressing any comorbid psychiatric condition (e.g., anxiety disorder, substance abuse)
- Psychoeducational programs for patients, families, and health providers
- Enhancement of social interactions and social support
- Recreational activities
- Regular exercise, as both aerobic exercise and weight-lifting programs have been shown to decrease depressive symptoms (Singh et al., 2005)

Remission of depression is the goal of treatment. Failure to achieve full remission leads to impaired psychosocial functioning and impaired quality of life, and affects physical health and increases the risk of recurrences.

Psychotherapy

Evidence-based psychotherapies recommended for geriatric depression are behavioral therapy (BT), cognitive behavioral therapy (CBT), interpersonal therapy (IPT), supportive problem-solving therapy, and brief dynamic therapy (Tourigny-Rivard & Buchanan, 2006). Psychotherapy can be very helpful especially when the depression was triggered by a stressor, for those who lack social support or need to develop better coping skills to deal with difficult situations. Despite the efficacy of psychotherapy for depression, it remains underutilized because of availability.

BT focuses primarily on increasing activity levels, in particular increasing pleasant activities. CBT is a short-term intervention (6 to 20 weeks) that incorporates behavioral techniques added to a cognitive approach (changing depressive ways of thinking and interpreting events), with the goals of improving mood management and coping skills. It is the psychotherapeutic intervention that has been more extensively studied in late-life depression. There is evidence of persistence of gains over time in follow-up studies. Most of the trials focused on major depression, and there are limited data on dysthymia and minor depression. BT and CBT delivered via bibliotherapy are also helpful for the depressed elderly.

IPT is another short-term psychotherapy that has been extensively studied in depressed elderly. The focus is on one or more of four common problems in older depressed patients: abnormal grief, role transitions, interpersonal disputes, and interpersonal deficits. It is especially helpful for bereavement-related depression in late life.

Pharmacotherapy

Approximately two-thirds of patients presenting with depression will respond to anti-depressant treatment, and older patients have response rates similar to younger patients. The last two decades have witnessed a great increase in the number of available antidepressants, with different mechanisms of action and different side-effect profiles. Antidepressants used to treat depression in the elderly include selective serotonin-reuptake inhibitors (SSRIs); venlafaxine, bupropion, and mirtazapine; tricyclic antidepressants, and monoamine oxidase inhibitors (MAOIs).

Age-related physiological changes are associated with pharmacokinetic consequences (i.e., on the way the human body processes medications), which result in higher and more variable drug concentrations in the elderly (Table G.1). The fact that elderly with comorbid conditions, and using concurrent medications, are usually not included in pharmacokinetic studies leave us with limited information about most drugs in this age group. In addition to that, homeostatic mechanisms (such as orthostatic circulatory responses and water balance) are less effective in the elderly and may interfere with the ability to adapt physiologically to medications. For example, psychotropics are associated with increased risk of falls in the elderly, and the syndrome of inappropriate antidiuretic hormone secretion has been reported as an age-associated adverse effect of SSRI and venlafaxine (Lotrich & Pollock, 2005).

Table G.1   Physiological Changes in the Elderly Associated With Altered Pharmacokinetics

Organ system	Change	Pharmacokinetic consequence
Gastrointestinal tract	Decreased intestinal and splanchnic blood flow	Decreased rate of drug absorption
Circulatory system	Decreased concentration of plasma albumin and increased concentration of alpha-1-acid glycoprotein	Increased/decreased free concentrations of drugs in plasma
Kidney	Decreased glomerular filtration rate	Decreased renal clearance of active metabolites
Muscle	Decreased lean body mass and increased adipose tissue	Altered volume of distribution of lipid-soluble drugs, leading to increased elimination of half-life
Liver	Decreased liver size; decreased hepatic blood; variable effects on CYP450 isozyme activity	Decreased hepatic clearance

The frequent age-related health problems and the complexity of medication regimens add to the equation, increasing the vulnerability to adverse effects of medications in the elderly. So clinicians face the challenge of trying to avoid side effects associated with high concentrations and at the same time not undertreating elderly patients. The general rule of start low and increase gradually does apply. Most clinicians start antidepressants in elderly at half of the recommended dose for adults. An adequate trial of antidepressants is at least 6 weeks, but after only 4 weeks it is possible to identify those who are more likely to benefit from a change in their treatment (Mulsant et al., 2006).

SSRIs are considered first-line treatment for depression in the elderly, because of their efficacy paired with a safer profile of side effects. Citalopram, escitalopram, and sertraline are good options because of their low anticholinergic properties and low potential for drug interactions. Possible side effects include nausea, sleep changes, agitation, diarrhea, sexual dysfunction, and hyponatremia.

Venlafaxine is the preferred alternative to SSRIs. It may be particularly useful for treatment-resistant depression and for those with comorbid anxiety or chronic pain. Bupropion and mirtazapine are alternatives for those who have not responded to SSRIs and venlafaxine. Bupropion can be especially helpful for patients with significant fatigue or sexual dysfunction, and mirtazapine for those who did not tolerate SSRIs because of sexual dysfunction, tremors, or nausea.

Tricyclics are usually reserved for severe refractory depression. They are avoided in patients with cognitive impairment or cardiac disease because of their potential dangerous side effects that can lead to higher withdrawal rates (Mottram, Wilson & Strobl, 2006) (bradycardia, cardiac conduction abnormalities, orthostatic hypotension, impairment of memory and attention, sedation, convulsions, and coma and death in overdose). Nortriptyline and desipramine—which have fewer anticholinergic properties—are preferred. Blood levels of the antidepressant, ECG, and lying and standing blood pressure should be monitored when using tricyclics.

MAOIs are effective, however the risk of hypertension when combined with foods or drinks containing tyramine, the risk of interactions with other medications, and the dietary restrictions limit their use in the elderly.

The elderly are subject to increasingly complex medication regimens, putting them at particular risk for drug-drug interactions. Antidepressants with lower risk of drug-drug interactions (citalopram, sertraline, venlafaxine, buproprion, and mirtazapine) are preferred.

Electroconvulsive Therapy

Electroconvulsive therapy is a very effective and safe treatment for depression. Electroconvulsive therapy is considered a first-line treatment for psychotic depression. It should also be considered if pharmacotherapy is ineffective or if severe health consequences (e.g., suicide or metabolic derangement) are imminent, because of its rapid onset of action.

Maintenance Treatment

Because rates of recurrence are so high in the elderly—50% to 90% over 2 to 3 years—maintenance treatment in the long term (not only for 6 to 12 months) is essential to maintain recovery and prevent recurrences. It is clear, from controlled studies with nortriptyline, citalopram, and more recently with paroxetine, that maintenance pharmacotherapy is effective in preventing recurrences in the elderly (Reynolds et al., 2006). Patients should be maintained on the same dose of antidepressant that was used to treat the acute episode of depression.

As to the effectiveness of psychotherapeutic interventions in the maintenance phase, there are somewhat conflicting results. The combination of monthly maintenance IPT with nortriptyline was associated with the lowest rate of recurrences in elderly with major depression who had responded to weekly IPT plus nortriptyline. The combination maintenance treatment was especially beneficial for the group 70 years and older and for those who took longer to remit with acute treatment. A more recent study, however, which focused on patients over 70, more than half of them with late-onset depression, failed to show efficacy for monthly IPT in the maintenance treatment. Maintenance treatment with paroxetine, but not with monthly IPT, was effective to prevent recurrences of depression. Older age, more cognitive impairment, more comorbid medical illnesses, and a higher percentage of patients with late-onset depression in the second study may explain the conflicting results. More studies are needed to investigate which psychotherapeutic interventions are effective for which patients in the prevention of recurrences of depression.

Prevention

A preventive approach for depression in the elderly starts with the identification of those at higher risk for developing depression, such as individuals with chronic medical illnesses or recent losses. Relaxation techniques, problem-solving training, cognitive restructuring, improvement of sleep, good nutrition, and regular exercise can reduce symptoms of depression. Public education about depression and initiatives to reduce the stigma associated with depression will facilitate the early diagnosis and early interventions for depression, which are likely to be more effective. Controlling vascular risk factors, such as hypertension, hyperlipidemia, and homocysteine levels, to decrease vascular events also plays a role.

Conclusions and Summary

Depression in the elderly causes significant morbidity and mortality, increases suicide rates, and causes significant impairment of physical and social functioning. It remains underdiagnosed and undertreated despite the fact that treatment can significantly improve quality of life and health. Management of depression in the elderly involves a comprehensive assessment, addressing comorbid conditions and psychosocial interventions. Both pharmacotherapy and psychotherapy are effective interventions. Because of the high rates of recurrences, it is equally important to prevent future episodes with maintenance treatment.

MONICA Z. SCALCO AND BRUCE G. POLLOCK

See also

Medical Conditions and Depression
Suicidal Cognition
Suicide in the Elderly
Suicide Theories

References

American Psychiatric Association. (1994). Diagnostic and statistical manual of mental disorders, 3rd edition, revised. Washington, DC: American Psychiatric Association.

Alexopoulos, G. S. (2005). Depression in the elderly, Lancet, 365, 1961–1970.

DeLuca, A. K., Lenze, E. J., Mulsant, B. H., Butters, M. A., Karp, J. F., Dew. M. A., et al. (2005). International Journal of Geriatric Psychiatry, 20, 848–854.

Dew, M. A., Whyte, E. M., Lenze, E. J., Houck, P. R., Mulsant, B. H., Pollock, B. G., et al. (2007). Recovery from major depression in older adults receiving augmentation antidepressant pharmacotherapy. American Journal of Psychiatry, 164, 892–899.

Johnson, E. M., Whyte, E., Mulsant, B. H., Pollock, B. G., Weber, E., & Begley, A. E. (2006). Cardiovascular changes associated with venlafaxine in the treatment of late-life depression. American Journal of Geriatric Psychiatry, 14, 796–802.

Katz, I. R., & Streim, J. (2004). Treatment of depression in residential settings. In S. P. Roose & H. A. Sackeim (Eds.), Late-life depression. New York: Oxford University Press.

Koenig, H. G., & Blazer, D. G. (2004). Mood disorders. In D. G. Blazer, D. C. Steffens, & E. W. Busse (Eds.), Textbook of geriatric psychiatry (3rd ed., pp. 241–268). Washington, DC: American Psychiatric Publishing.

Lotrich, F. E., & Pollock, B. G. (2005). Aging and clinical pharmacology: Implications for antidepressants. Journal of Clinical Pharmacology, 45, 1106–1122.

Lyketsos, C. G., DelCampo, L., Steinberg M., Miles, Q., Steele, C. D., Munro, C., et al. (2003). Treating depression in Alzheimer disease: Efficacy and safety of sertraline therapy, and the benefits of depression reduction: The DIADS. Archives of General Psychiatry, 60, 737–746.

Mottram, P., Wilson, K., & Strobl, J. (2006). Antidepressants for depressed elderly. Cochrane Database of Systematic Reviews, 1, Art. No. CD003491.

Mulsant, B. H., Houck, P. R., Gildengers, A. G., Andreecu, C., Dew, M. A., Pollock, B. G., et al. (2006). What is the optimal duration of a short-term antidepressant trial when treating geriatric depression? Journal of Clinical Psychopharmacology, 26, 113–120.

Mulsant, B. H., & Pollock, B. G. (2004). Psychopharmacology. In: D. G. Blazer, D. C. Steffens, & Busse, E. W. (Eds.). *Textbook of geriatric psychiatry* (3rd ed., pp. 387–492). Washington, DC: American Psychiatric Publishing.

Pollock, B. G. (2004). Pharmacokinetics and pharmacodynamics in late life. In S. P. Roose & H. A. Sackeim (Eds.). *Late-life depression* (pp. 185–191). New York: Oxford University Press.

Pollock, B. G. (2005a). Psychopharmacology: General principles: Geriatric psychiatry, treatment of psychiatric disorders. In B. J. Sadock & V. A. Sadock (Eds.), *Kaplan and Sadock's comprehensive textbook of psychiatry* (8th ed., pp. 3716–3724). New York: Lippincott Williams and Wilkins.

Pollock, B. G. (2005b). The pharmacokinetic imperative in late-life depression. *Journal of Clinical Psychopharmacology, 25 (4 Suppl. 1),* 19–23.

Rabheru, K. (2004). Special issues in the management of depression in older patients. *Canadian Journal of Psychiatry, 49,* 41–50.

Reynolds III, C. F., Dew, M. A., Pollock, B. G., Mulsant, B. H., Frank, E., Miller, M. D., et al. (2006). Maintenance treatment of major depression in old age. *New England Journal of Medicine, 354,* 1130–1138.

Scalco, M. Z., de Almeida, O. P., Hachul, D. T., Castel, S., Serro-Azul, J., & Weingarten, M. (2000). Comparison of risk of orthostatic hypotension in elderly depressed hypertensive women treated with nortriptyline and thiazides versus depressed normotensive women treated with nortriptyline. *American Journal of Cardiology, 85,* 1156–1158.

Singh, N. A., Stavrinos, T. M., Scarbeck, Y., Galambos, G., Liber, C., Fiatarone Sing, M. A., et al. (2005). A randomized controlled trial of high versus low intensity weight training versus general practitioner care for clinical depression in older adults. *Journal of Gerontology, 60A,* 768–776.

Szanto, K., Mulsant, B. H., Houck, P. R., Dew, M. A., Dombrovsky, A., Pollock, B. G., et al. (2007). Emergence, persistence, and resolution of suicidal ideation during treatment of depression in old age. *Journal of Affective Disorders, 98,* 153–161.

Tourigny-Rivard, M., & Buchanan, D. (2006). *National guidelines for seniors' mental health: The assessment and treatment of depression.* Retrieved January 2, 2009, from www.ccsmh.ca/en/natlGuidelines/depression.cfm

Global Burden of Depression

Until the 1990s, public health priorities were determined primarily by estimating the mortality rates associated with various diseases. This method of determining disease burden, however, failed to account for burden associated with nonfatal psychiatric and medical conditions. In fact, when mortality rates alone were considered, no mental disorder ever made an appearance on the top-10 priority list of public health significance. In their 1990 Global Burden of Disease (GBD) study, however, the World Health Organization (WHO) revolutionized the way global disease burden

was assessed by measuring burden in terms of both death and disability (Murray & Lopez, 1996). This report made clear the immense impact of depressive disorders on individuals worldwide, inspiring new research exploring the economic impact of depression as well as cost-effective methods of reducing the global burden of depression over time (see Ustun, Ayuso-Mateos, Chatterji, Mathers, & Murray, 2004, for a review).

In 2002, the WHO published an updated report based on their 2000 GBD study. In this report, a new standardized metric of disease burden, the Disability Adjusted Life Year (DALY), was introduced to better inform health research, policy, and planning (WHO, 2002). For each disease studied, the DALY metric provided a figure that combined both years lost to premature death and years lived in ill health. The results of this study suggested that, in the year 2000, unipolar depression was the leading cause of nonfatal disease burden, associated with 12% of the total DALYs worldwide. Among fatal and nonfatal diseases, depression ranked fourth in terms of disease burden and accounted for 4.4% of total disease burden. Contributing to the high burden of depression was its high prevalence, early age of onset, and substantial impact on functioning. Although depression was found to be both the leading neuropsychiatric and the leading nonfatal cause of DALYs in both males and females, the burden of depression was found to be 50% higher for females than for males. The WHO calculations of depression burden reflect the combined burden of a range of unipolar depressive syndromes, including dysthymia as well as mild, moderate, and severe depressive disorders as defined by the *International Classification of Disease,* tenth edition (*ICD-10*). In addition, the *Diagnostic and Statistical Manual of Mental Disorders,* third and fourth editions (*DSM-III* and *DSM-IV*; American Psychiatric Association, 1980, 1994) definitions of major depressive episodes were considered alternative definitions, so epidemiological data using either the *ICD* or the *DSM* diagnostic system could inform estimates of the global burden of depression.

The worldwide economic burden of depression is immense in terms of both the cost of treatment (direct cost) and the cost of lost productivity (indirect cost). Individuals with major depression, for example, are at up to fivefold increased risk of dysfunction resulting in disability than are individuals without depressive symptoms. Individuals with minor depressive syndromes are also at increased greater risk of disability than asymptomatic individuals but account for a greater proportion of disability days than those with major depression due to the far greater prevalence of minor depressive syndromes (Broadhead, Blazer, George, & Chiu, 1990). Depression seems to contribute to lost productivity in other ways as well, including decreased motivation and interest in work by employed individuals with depression, the greater number of sick days taken by employed individuals with depression than their nondepressed counterparts, and lower educational attainment among individuals with early-onset depressive illness. With regards to treatment costs, individuals with a diagnosis of depression have annual health care costs that nearly double those of individuals without depression. Depression is associated with higher utilization of services not only in mental health care settings, but also in other medical settings including primary care, laboratory, and medical specialty (Simon, VonKorff, & Barlow, 1995). In many countries, including the United States, the direct cost of treating depression currently exceeds the cost of treating any single medical condition, including hypertension, diabetes, or HIV/AIDS.

Determining the cost-effectiveness of available treatments for depression represents an important piece of current efforts to reduce the global burden of depression. Available evidence suggests that, aside from no treatment, medication-only treatment protocols, using either the newer selective serotonin-reuptake inhibitors or the older trycyclics, currently represent the least cost-effective of the treatment protocols typically employed. In addition, secondary and tertiary preventative care, although targeting greater numbers of individuals for potential treatment, seem more cost-effective in the long term than providing treatment only in response to acute depressive episodes. Therefore, comprehensive care including psychotherapy in conjunction with antidepressant medication may provide the greatest long-term reduction in depression's economic burden, especially when a proactive approach to treatment is employed. Further suggestions for reducing the global burden of depression have included developing strategies for shortening the duration of depressive episodes, integrating cost-effective treatment strategies into primary care services, developing strategies for preventing relapse in previously depressed individuals, and developing and adapting treatments to place greater focus on reducing disability resulting from depression.

MELINDA A. GADDY

See also

Comorbidity
Medical Conditions and Depression

References

American Psychiatric Association. (1980). *Diagnostic and statistical manual of mental disorders* (3rd ed.). Washington, DC: Author.

American Psychiatric Association. (1994). *Diagnostic and statistical manual of mental disorders* (4th ed.). Washington, DC: Author.

Broadhead, W. E., Blazer, D. G., George, L. K., & Chiu, K. T. (1990). Depression, disability days and days lost from work in a prospective epidemiological study. *Journal of the American Medical Association, 264,* 2524–2528.

Murray, C. J. L., & Lopez, A. (1996). *The global burden of disease.* Cambridge, MA: Harvard University Press.

Simon, G. E., VonKorff, M., & Barlow, W. (1995). Health care costs of primary care patients with recognized depression. *Archives of General Psychiatry, 52,* 850–856.

Ustun, T. B., Ayuso-Mateos, J. L., Chatterji, S., Mathers, C., & Murray, C. J. L. (2004). Global burden of depressive disorders in the year 2000. *British Journal of Psychiatry, 184,* 386–392.

World Health Organization. (2002). *World health report 2002: Reducing risks, promoting healthy life.* Geneva, Switzerland: Author.

Guilt

One of a handful of basic human emotions, guilt has been variously classified as one of the "moral," "self-conscious," "social," and "problematic" emotions, underscoring the complexity of this emotion and the many roles it plays in our lives. Systematic theoretical considerations of guilt and depression date back at least to Sigmund Freud, who viewed guilt as a reaction to violations of superego standards. According to Freud, guilt results when unacceptable impulses or behaviors conflict with the moral demands of the superego. Freud saw guilt as part of the normal human experience. But he also viewed unresolved or repressed feelings of guilt as a key component of many psychological symptoms, including depression. For decades, guilt remained largely in the province of psychoanalytic theory. Very little scientific research was conducted on guilt until the mid-1960s and few psychological researchers distinguished between shame and guilt until the so-called affect revolution of the late 1980s.

What Is the Difference Between Shame and Guilt?

People often use the terms *guilt* and *shame* interchangeably, as moral emotions that inhibit socially undesirable behavior or as problematic emotions that play a key role in a range of psychological symptoms. But much recent research indicates that guilt and shame are distinct emotions. Both involve internal attributions (self-directed blame) for negative self-relevant events including failures, transgressions, and social blunders. The crux of the difference between these two emotions centers on the focus of one's negative evaluation. When people feel guilt, they feel badly about a specific behavior—about something they have *done*. When people feel shame, they feel badly about *themselves*. This differential emphasis on self ("*I* did that horrible thing") versus behavior ("I *did* that horrible *thing*") leads to very different emotional experiences and associated action tendencies. Whereas feelings of shame (about the self) involve a sense of shrinking, a sense of worthlessness, and a desire to escape the shame-inducing situation, feelings of guilt (about a specific behavior) involve a sense of tension, remorse, and regret over the "bad thing done." People in the midst of a guilt experience often report a nagging focus or preoccupation with the transgression—thinking of it over and over, wishing they had behaved differently. Rather than motivating a desire to hide, guilt typically motivates reparative behavior—confessing, apologizing, or somehow undoing the harm that was done. Thus, feelings of guilt are more apt to keep people constructively involved in the guilt-inducing situation.

An advantage of guilt is that the scope of blame is less extensive and far-reaching than in shame. In guilt, our primary concern is with a particular behavior, somewhat apart from the self. Because guilt does not threaten one's core identity, it is less likely than shame to trigger defensive denial or retaliation. In effect, guilt poses people with a much more manageable problem than shame. It is much easier to change a bad behavior than it is to change a bad self.

To What Degree Is Guilt Related to Depression?

Notwithstanding the fact that guilt is listed as a key symptom of depression in the *Diagnostic and Statistical Manual of Mental Disorders* of the American Psychiatric Association (1994), several decades of research indicate that shame, not guilt, is the culprit when considering depression and a host of other psychological problems. When measures are used that are sensitive to the distinction between shame (about the self) versus guilt (about a specific behavior), the propensity to experience shame-free guilt is essentially unrelated to depression and other psychological symptoms. In contrast, proneness to shame is consistently related to depression. This pattern of results makes sense from an attributional perspective. To the extent that guilt involves internal but unstable and specific attributions for failures and transgressions, guilt-proneness should be less depressogenic than shame-proneness, which is more closely linked to well-established cognitive vulnerabilities to depression (i.e., the propensity to make internal, stable, and global attributions for negative self-relevant events).

When Does Guilt Become Maladaptive?

Why is guilt frequently cited as a symptom of depression? What is the chronic, ruminative guilt described by so many clinicians? One possibility is that such problematic guilt experiences are actually feelings of guilt *fused with feelings of shame*. When a person begins with a guilt experience ("Oh, look at what a horrible *thing* I have *done*") but then magnifies and generalizes the event to the self ("... and aren't I a horrible *person*"), many of the advantages of guilt are apt to be lost. Not only is a person faced with tension and remorse over a specific behavior that needs to be fixed, he or she is also saddled with feelings of contempt and disgust for a bad, defective self. In effect, shame-fused guilt may be just as problematic as shame itself.

Problems are likely to arise when people develop an exaggerated or distorted sense of responsibility for events beyond their control. Survivor guilt is a prime example of such a problematic emotional reaction that has been consistently linked to posttraumatic stress disorder and other psychological symptoms. It is worth noting that most basic research on guilt and depression utilizes measures that describe situations in which responsibility or culpability is relatively unambiguous. People are asked to imagine events in which they clearly failed or transgressed in some way. The adaptive value of guilt is most likely apparent in cases of actual personal responsibility.

Conclusions

In sum, proneness to shame-free guilt for failures and transgressions does not appear to pose a vulnerability to depression. Shame is the more problematic emotion when considering many aspects of adjustment, including depression. Problems with guilt are more likely to surface in clinical settings when guilt is fused with shame, and when clients are inclined to a distorted sense of responsibility for events beyond their control.

JUNE PRICE TANGNEY

See also

Psychodynamic Model of Depression
Shame

References

American Psychiatric Association. (1994). *Diagnostic and statistical manual of mental disorders* (4th ed.). Washington, DC: Author.

Lewis, H. B. (1971). *Shame and guilt in neurosis*. New York: International Universities Press.

Seligman, M. E. P., Abramson, L. Y., Semmel, A., & von Baeyer, C. (1979). Depressive attributional style. *Journal of Abnormal Psychology, 88,* 242–247.

Tangney, J. P., Stuewig, J., & Mashek, D. J. (2007). Moral emotions and moral behavior. *Annual Review of Psychology, 58,* 345–372.

H

Heart Disease

Depression and heart disease are two of the most common disorders in the Western world. Coronary heart disease (CHD) affects approximately 12 million people in the United States alone. The lifetime prevalence of major depression in the United States is estimated to be about 16%, and at any given time about 7% of the adult population is experiencing an episode of major depression. Heart disease is the most common cause of death in the United States, as well as in most of the industrialized world. The American Heart Association estimates that more than 500,000 people die from heart-disease-related causes in the United States every year, and over 1 million Americans suffer myocardial infarctions (MIs) or other serious but nonfatal cardiac events (American Heart Association, 2002).

Depression and CHD are also highly comorbid. Approximately 15% to 20% of patients with CHD also have major depression, and about 20% have minor depression (Carney & Freedland, 2005). The World Health Organization (WHO) lists depression and heart disease as two of the most disabling and costly illnesses worldwide. Their effects on disability and health care costs are additive.

There have been two kinds of research on the relationship between depression and heart disease. The first addresses the question of whether depression in apparently medically well individuals, or individuals who do not have any clinical manifestations of heart disease, is a risk factor for the development of CHD. The second area of research concerns whether depression is a risk factor for further medical morbidity and mortality in patients with existing CHD. Many studies have also investigated whether depression has negative effects on health care utilization, adherence to medical treatment regimens, psychosocial functioning, and quality of life.

Depression and Incident in Heart Disease

Numerous studies have shown that depression is a risk factor for the development of CHD (Carney & Freedland, 2005). The initial presentation of CHD can take many different forms, ranging from mild exertional angina to acute MI or even sudden cardiac death, and these events occur without warning in many cases. There have been two meta-analyses of this literature. Both reported that the risk of developing CHD is 1.6 times higher in depressed than nondepressed individuals (Rugulies, 2003; Wulsin & Singal, 2003). The first meta-analysis also reported separate findings for clinical depression and for depression defined in terms of elevated scores on depression symptom scales. Clinical depression was associated with a higher relative risk of incident CHD (RR = 2.7) than was depression symptoms (RR = 1.5).

Unfortunately, many of the studies of depression included in these meta-analyses were not originally designed to investigate whether depression is a cardiovascular risk factor. Most were studies of traditional cardiac risk factors such as cholesterol or hypertension in community residents, or in members of large medical care provider organizations or insurance groups. Depression was assessed in many of these studies by study-specific self-report measures with unknown psychometric properties. The relative risk of incident CHD associated with depression tends to be higher in studies based on well-established depression questionnaires or diagnostic interviews than on ad hoc measures. Nevertheless, even when assessed in a less than ideal fashion, most studies have found that having just a few symptoms of depression can increase the risk of developing CHD many years later. A clinical diagnosis of depression seems to confer an even greater risk.

Depression and Established CHD

The point prevalence of major depression may be somewhat higher immediately after major cardiac events than during stable phases of CHD (Carney & Freedland, 2005). In some cases, however, major depressive episodes remit within a few weeks after a major cardiac event. If depressive symptoms are precipitated by an acute MI or other cardiac event, but they start to improve spontaneously within 2 weeks, the patient may be having a transient adjustment reaction rather than a persistent major or minor depressive episode. On the other hand, it is not unusual for the onset of depression to *precede* the onset of major cardiac events, and in fact it does so in about half of cases.

Depression predicts cardiac events throughout the course of CHD, starting when coronary disease is first diagnosed by cardiac catheterization and angiography or by exercise stress testing (Carney & Freedland, 2003). However, the cardiovascular risks associated with depression tend to worsen as CHD progresses. For example, depression is a strong risk factor for morbidity and mortality in patients whose coronary disease is so severe that they require coronary artery bypass graft surgery. A meta-analysis of 20 studies found that having symptoms of depression doubles the risk of mortality in patients with

CHD, and that having clinical depression is associated with an even higher risk (Barth, Schumacher, & Herrmann-Lingen, 2004).

Some of the worst effects of depression are observed in patients who have an acute coronary syndrome, in other words, an acute MI, or unstable angina. In one of the earliest studies, Frasure-Smith and colleagues reported that depression was associated with a more than fourfold increased risk of mortality during the first 6 months following an acute MI, after adjusting for established prognostic variables including left ventricular dysfunction (Frasure-Smith, Lesperance, & Talajic, 1993). Depression was as strongly predictive of mortality as were two major medical risk factors, left ventricular dysfunction and previous MI. Most (but not all) studies of depression after an MI have found it to be a significant risk factor for mortality and medical morbidity. A recent meta-analysis of 22 of the best of these studies found that major depression more than doubles the risk of mortality after an acute MI (van Melle et al., 2004).

Despite strong evidence that depression is a risk factor for cardiac morbidity and mortality, it might not have a direct, causal role in CHD. For example, the relationship between depression and cardiac morbidity and mortality might be due to severe heart disease that contributes to the risk for both. However, most studies have found that depression is a risk factor for cardiac morbidity and mortality after statistical adjustment for a variety of other risk markers and indices of disease severity. Moreover, several plausible biobehavioral pathways through which depression could increase the risk of cardiac morbidity and even mortality have been identified.

Mechanisms

Although the relationship between depression and cardiac events in patients with CHD is well established, the mechanisms underlying this relationship remain unclear. However, there are a number of possibilities (Carney, Freedland, Miller, & Jaffe, 2002; Skala, Freedland, & Carney, 2006). Dysregulation of the autonomic nervous system and the hypothalamic-pituitary-adrenal axis is one of the most plausible possibilities. Reduced parasympathetic and increased sympathetic activity, and elevated levels of glucocorticoids such as cortisol, can lower the threshold for myocardial ischemia and increase the risks of ventricular tachycardia, ventricular fibrillation, and sudden cardiac death. Furthermore, coronary artery disease is a chronic inflammatory process that is triggered by injury to the vascular endothelium. Depression has been associated with elevated markers of inflammation, which may contribute to the inflammatory process that leads to the development of atherosclerosis and to cardiac events. Depression is associated with increased platelet activation and aggregation, which may help to promote procoagulant processes that also contribute to atherosclerosis and thrombotic events. Diabetes and insulin resistance have also been associated with depression. Since they contribute to CHD, these findings may also help to explain the role of depression as a CHD risk factor.

There are also behavioral factors that may help explain how depression increases the risk for cardiac events. Depressed individuals are less likely to exercise and more likely to smoke than their nondepressed counterparts. Furthermore they are less likely to adhere to their medical treatment regimens. This can include nonadherence to diet, exercise, cardiac rehabilitation programs, and medication regimens. Aspirin, beta-blockers, and lipid-lowering drugs have all been shown to greatly reduce mortality and morbidity in patients with heart disease. Patients who do not take these drugs as prescribed will not benefit to the same degree as those who do. Several studies have found that depression is associated with poor adherence to drugs and lifestyle changes in patients with CHD.

Treatment

It is not yet known whether treatment of depression can improve cardiac outcomes in patients with CHD. To date, only one randomized clinical trial has been designed to determine whether treating post-MI depression can improve survival and decrease the rate of recurrent MI. The Enhancing Recovery in Coronary Heart Disease (ENRICHD) trial enrolled patients with major or minor depression and/or low perceived social support after an acute MI (Berkman et al., 2003). The patients were randomly assigned to an intervention or to usual care. The intervention included up to 6 months of cognitive behavior therapy (CBT), augmented with up to 1 year of sertraline for patients who did not respond to CBT or who had severe depression. The depression outcomes were significantly better in the intervention than in the usual care arm, but the between-group difference was relatively small. There were no differences in survival or recurrent MI between the two groups. The relatively small effect of the intervention on depression is often cited as an explanation for lack of an effect on survival, but this is speculative. No one knows whether the survival outcomes would have been better if there had been larger between-group differences in depression outcomes. In short, there is not yet any evidence from clinical trials that treating depression improves medical outcomes in post-MI patients, or in any other subset of the CHD population.

What is known is that depression in patients with CHD can be safely and successfully treated in most cases (Carney & Freedland, 2008; Skala, Freedland, & Carney, 2005). A variety of antidepressants, especially selective serotonin-reuptake inhibitors, have been found to be safe and effective even for patients with a recent MI. Although there have only been few controlled studies of CBT for patients with heart disease, the results have generally been favorable. Interpersonal psychotherapy plus clinical management was not superior to a pill placebo plus clinical management in a study of post–acute coronary syndrome patients, but it has been shown to be an efficacious treatment for depression in other populations. Exercise training has long been thought to have antidepressant effects, and recent controlled studies in patients with heart disease have provided evidence for its effectiveness in treating depression. Exercise also has cardiovascular benefits, making it a particularly attractive intervention for depressed cardiac patients. However, it can be difficult to engage depressed patients in exercise programs and to maintain their involvement long enough to produce either cardiovascular or psychological benefits. Depressed patients are more likely than their nondepressed counterparts to discontinue exercise-based cardiac rehabilitation. Thus, initiation and maintenance of exercise may be particularly important targets of treatment for depressed cardiac patients.

In summary, depression is a risk factor for developing CHD, and for cardiac morbidity and mortality in patients with established CHD. Although there are plausible biobehavioral mechanisms, the pathways through which depression confers these risks are not well understood. Although we do not yet know whether treating depression can decrease the risk of developing CHD, or reduce the risks of cardiac mortality and morbidity once CHD is present, we do know that depression can be safely and effectively treated with certain types of antidepressants, CBT, and structured exercise training. Depression should be identified and treated in patients with CHD in order to improve the quality of their lives, whether or not treatment is eventually shown to improve cardiac prognosis.

ROBERT M. CARNEY AND
KENNETH E. FREEDLAND

See also

Comorbidity
Heart Rate Variability
Medical Conditions and Depression

References

American Heart Association. (2002). Coronary heart disease and angina pectoris. In *Heart and Stroke Facts: 2002 Statistical Supplement*. Dallas, TX: Author.

Barth, J., Schumacher, M., & Herrmann-Lingen, C. (2004). Depression as a risk factor for mortality in patients with coronary heart disease: A meta-analysis. *Psychosomatic Medicine, 66,* 802–813.

Berkman, L. F., Blumenthal, J., Burg, M., Carney, R. M., Catellier, D., Cowan, M. J., et al. (2003). Effects of treating depression and low perceived social support on clinical events after myocardial infarction: The Enhancing Recovery in Coronary Heart Disease Patients (ENRICHD) Randomized Trial. *Journal of the American Medical Association, 289,* 3106–3116.

Carney, R. M., & Freedland, K. E. (2003). Depression, mortality, and medical morbidity in patients with coronary heart disease. *Biological Psychiatry, 54,* 241–247.

Carney, R. M., & Freedland, K. E. (2005). Depression and heart disease. In J. Licinio & M.-L. Wong (Eds.), *Biology of depression: From novel insights to therapeutic strategies, Vol. 2* (pp. 617–631). Weinheim, Germany: Wiley-VCH.

Carney, R. M., & Freedland, K. E. (2008). Depression in patients with coronary heart disease. *American Journal of Medicine, 121,* S20–S27.

Carney, R. M., Freedland, K. E., Miller, G. E., & Jaffe, A. S. (2002). Depression as a risk factor for cardiac mortality and morbidity: A review of potential mechanisms. *Journal of Psychosomatic Research, 53,* 897–902.

Frasure-Smith, N., Lesperance, F., & Talajic, M. (1993). Depression following myocardial infarction: Impact on 6-month survival. *Journal of the American Medical Association, 270,* 1819–1825.

Rugulies, R. (2003). Depression as a predictor for the development of coronary heart disease. A systematic review and meta-analysis of the literature. *American Journal of Preventative Medicine, 23,* 51–61.

Skala, J. A., Freedland, K. E., & Carney, R. M. (2005). *Heart disease.* Cambridge, MA: Hogrefe and Huber Publishers.

Skala, J. A., Freedland, K. E., & Carney, R. M. (2006). Coronary heart disease and depression: A review of recent mechanistic research. *Canadian Journal of Psychiatry, 51,* 738.

van Melle, J. P., de Jonge, P., Spijkerman, T. A., Tijssen, J. G., Ormel, J., van Veldhuisen, D. J., et al. (2004). Prognostic association of depression following myocardial infarction with mortality and cardiovascular events: A meta-analysis. *Psychosomatic Medicine, 66,* 814–822.

Wulsin, L. R., & Singal, B. M. (2003). Do depressive symptoms increase the risk for the onset of coronary disease? A systematic quantitative review. *Psychosomatic Medicine, 65,* 201–210.

Heart Rate Variability

Like many organs in the body, the heart is dually innervated. Although a wide range of physiologic factors determine cardiac functions such as heart rate, the autonomic nervous system is the most prominent. Importantly, when both cardiac vagal (the primary parasympathetic nerve) and sympathetic inputs are blocked pharmacologically (e.g., with atropine plus propranolol, the so-called double blockade), intrinsic heart rate is higher than the normal resting heart rate. This fact supports the idea that the heart is under tonic inhibitory control by parasympathetic influences. Thus, resting cardiac autonomic balance favors energy conservation by way of parasympathetic dominance over sympathetic influences. In addition, the heart rate time series is characterized by beat-to-beat variability over a wide range, which also implicates vagal dominance as the sympathetic influence on the heart is too slow to produce beat-to-beat changes (Figure H.1). There is an increasing interest in the study of this heart rate variability among researchers from diverse fields. Low heart rate variability is associated with increased risk of all-cause mortality, and low heart rate variability has been proposed as a marker for disease. In the following I briefly describe the nature of heart rate variability, the assessment of heart rate variability, and the relationship of heart rate variability to depression.

The basic data for the calculation of all the measures of heart rate variability are

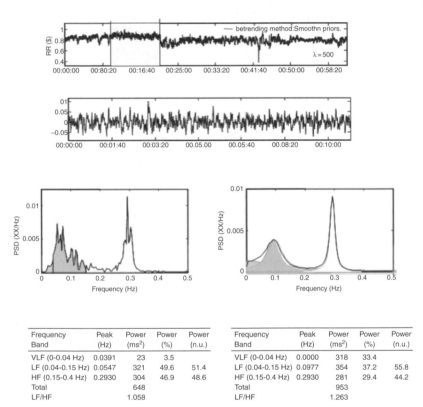

Frequency Band	Peak (Hz)	Power (ms²)	Power (%)	Power (n.u.)
VLF (0-0.04 Hz)	0.0391	23	3.5	
LF (0.04-0.15 Hz)	0.0547	321	49.6	51.4
HF (0.15-0.4 Hz)	0.2930	304	46.9	48.6
Total		648		
LF/HF		1.058		

Frequency Band	Peak (Hz)	Power (ms²)	Power (%)	Power (n.u.)
VLF (0-0.04 Hz)	0.0000	318	33.4	
LF (0.04-0.15 Hz)	0.0977	354	37.2	55.8
HF (0.15-0.4 Hz)	0.2930	281	29.4	44.2
Total		953		
LF/HF		1.263		

Figure H.1   The top trace shows an interbeat interval (IBI) time series. The highlighted portion is shown in more detail in the second tracing. The figure and values at below left are from a fast-Fourier transform analysis, and those at below right are from an autoregressive analysis of the highlighted data. The tables show the frequency band, peak frequency, power, percentage power, and power in normalized units. Whereas the values from the two methods are similar, they are not identical. Figure adapted from the output of free software provided by the Department of Applied Physics, University of Kuopio, Finland. See Niskanen, J. P., Tarvainen, M. P., Ranta-aho, P. O., & Karjalainen, P. A. (2004). Software for advanced HRV analysis. *Computer Methods and Programs in Biomedicine, 76,* 73–81.

based on the sequence of time intervals between heart beats. This interbeat interval time series is used to calculate the variability in the timing of the heart beat. As mentioned earlier the heart is dually innervated by the autonomic nervous system such that relative increases in sympathetic activity are associated with heart rate increases and relative increases in parasympathetic activity are associated with heart rate decreases. Thus relative sympathetic increases cause the time between heart beats (the interbeat interval) to become shorter and relative parasympathetic increases cause the interbeat interval to become longer. The parasympathetic influences are pervasive over the frequency range of the heart rate power spectrum, whereas the sympathetic influences roll off at about 0.15 hertz. Therefore high-frequency heart rate variability represents primarily parasympathetic influences, with lower frequencies (below about 0.15 Hz) having a mixture of sympathetic and parasympathetic autonomic influences. The differential effects of the autonomic nervous system on the sinoatrial node, and thus the timing of the heart beats, are due to the differential effects of the neurotransmitters for the sympathetic (noradrenaline) and parasympathetic (acetylcholine) nervous systems. The sympathetic effects are slow, on the time scale of seconds, whereas the parasympathetic effects are fast, on the time scale of milliseconds. Therefore the parasympathetic influences are the only ones capable of producing rapid changes in the beat-to-beat timing of the heart.

Measures of Heart Rate Variability

A variety of measures have been used to operationalize heart rate variability. Long-term measures such as the standard deviation of all interbeat intervals in 24 hours, short-term measures such as the standard deviation of 5-minute intervals, and beat-to-beat measures such as the root mean square of successive IBI differences (RMSSD) have all been used. Respiratory sinus arrhythmia (RSA) is another measure and is defined as the change in heart period corresponding

with the inspiratory and expiratory phases of the respiratory cycle. In addition, power spectral analysis of interbeat interval time series is frequently used to quantify heart rate variability. The power spectrum of short-term time series contains two major components, a high (0.15–0.40 Hz) and low (0.01–0.15 Hz) frequency component reflecting cardiac vagal influences and a mixture of vagal and sympathetic influences, respectively. RSA, RMSSD, and the high-frequency component of the power spectrum are closely related, and all reflect vagal cardiac influence. More recently, measures derived from nonlinear dynamics have been used to describe aspects of heart rate variability. One such measure is approximate entropy. It quantifies the complexity or irregularity of time series data. This and other chaos-derived parameters have proven valuable in the area of cardiovascular pathology, for example in discriminating cardiac patient groups with respect to the dynamics of their cardiovascular system.

Depression and Heart Rate Variability

Why should those interested in depression need to know anything about heart rate variability? There are several reasons. First, many psychopathological states and dispositions including depression and depressive symptoms have been associated with low heart rate variability. Second, depression is emerging as a risk factor for cardiovascular disease, and one hypothesized link between depression and cardiovascular disease is via low heart rate variability. Third, a core feature of depression, rumination, or more generally perseverative cognition, has been associated with low heart rate variability. Fourth, heart rate variability may be related to the severity of depression, the course of depression, and to treatment outcome. Therefore, heart rate variability may be useful in understanding the etiology, nature, course, severity, and treatment of depression as well as its association with physical health.

The extant literature on the association between depression and heart rate variability has recently been reviewed (Rottenberg, 2007). In both healthy participants and in those with a compromised cardiovascular system the average difference between depressed and nondepressed participants on measures of heart rate variability was approximately one-third of a standard deviation, with the depressed participants showing lower heart rate variability. This is considered a small to medium effect size and would reflect a difference in RMSSD of between 5 and 10 milliseconds approximately. However, there are large individual differences such that some studies have found the differences to be statistically significant, whereas others have found no reliable difference or even a difference in the opposite direction. Thus there is a rather large but mixed literature on the relationship between depression and vagally mediated heart rate variability.

There are several possible explanations for the inconsistency in the extant literature. Rottenberg identified several confounding factors that could contribute to the inconsistent findings in the literature including medication use, psychiatric comorbidities, physical health outcomes, and the heterogeneity of depression itself. Our group has identified gender as a potential confounding factor, with several studies now reporting that depressed females have greater heart rate variability than nondepressed females, whereas the opposite is true for males (Chambers & Allen, 2007).

One idea that has been proposed to help explain the mixed literature is that heart rate variability may be differentially related to various symptoms of depression. For example, some research has suggested that heart rate variability was related to suicidality. We found that reduced serotonin induced by tryptophan depletion was associated with reduced heart rate variability in remitted depressed patients but only in those with a history of suicidal ideation. However, this association between suicidality and heart rate variability has not been consistently found. One salient symptom of depression is rumination or perseverative cognition. Is it possible that depressed individuals differ in their degree of rumination and that heart rate variability is related more strongly to this symptom of depression? Rumination, worry, and perseverative cognition are transdiagnostic features of many psychological disorders. Our group and others have rather consistently found that rumination, worry, and perseverative cognition are associated with low heart rate variability in the laboratory and in ambulatory studies (Brosschot, Gerin, & Thayer, 2006). Thus, the search for associations between depression and heart rate variability may have to transcend the level of diagnostic category and explore the level of specific symptoms or dimensions of dysfunction. This would be consistent with our idea that low heart rate variability may be an endophenotype, or intermediate between phenotype and genotype, that might be associated across various diagnostic boundaries with important functional characteristics of psychopathological disorders.

Recent work has also started to examine more statelike differences in the variability of heart rate variability across situations, or what has been called heart rate variability fluctuations in depressed individuals. This research has found that depressed individuals show decreased heart rate variability across different tasks or situations. Reduced heart rate variability across tasks has also been found in anxiety disorders and is another manifestation of reduced cardiac vagal control.

In summary, heart rate variability, both tonically as reflected in resting levels and phasically as reflected in heart rate variability changes across situations, may serve to illuminate important aspects of depression and depressive symptoms. However, because of the large individual differences and the risk of potential confounding factors such as medication use, physical health and psychiatric comorbidities, the heterogeneity of depression, and possible gender differences, one needs to exercise caution in the interpretation and use of measures of heart rate variability. Despite these limitations, additional studies that use heart rate variability will certainly help to clarify the nature of depression and may guide the search for future treatments.

JULIAN F. THAYER

See also

Comorbidity
Heart Rate Variability
Medical Conditions and Depression

References

Brosschot, J. F., Gerin, W., & Thayer, J. F. (2006). The perseverative cognition hypothesis: A review of worry, prolonged stress-related physiological activation, and health. *Journal of Psychosomatic Research, 60,* 113–124.

Chambers, A. S., & Allen, J. J. B. (2007). Sex differences in cardiac vagal control in a depressed sample: Implications for differential cardiovascular mortality. *Biological Psychology, 75,* 32–36.

Rottenberg, J. (2007). Cardiac vagal control in depression: A critical analysis. *Biological Psychology, 74,* 200–211.

Hemispheric Lateralization

Over the past two decades, understanding the role of the brain in major depressive disorder has become an area of intense research interest. Some of the earliest work in this area focused on the degree to which the two hemispheres of the brain are differentially involved in depression. In particular, a number of researchers have suggested that imbalances in the relative activation of the two hemispheres, in other words, hemispheric lateralization or asymmetry, is linked with both the state of being depressed and trait vulnerability to depression. This asymmetry of activation is thought to reflect the relative importance of each hemisphere for emotional and motivational states relevant for understanding depression. Below, the dominant theories of hemispheric lateralization in emotion and depression are discussed briefly, followed by a review of the data on hemispheric lateralization in depression from lesion, electroencephalography (EEG), and brain imaging studies. This brief review of data will focus primarily on lateralized activation of frontal brain regions, as they have received the most study.

Frontal Asymmetry and Motivation: Implications for Depression

Approach and withdrawal are fundamental affective and motivational states common to all organisms. In humans these motivational states are also associated with experiencing different types of emotions, with approach being linked to more positive emotions and withdrawal linked to unpleasant emotions. Deficits in approach or appetitive behaviors and increases in avoidance behaviors are important aspects of the dysfunction observed in depression. For example, the anhedonia, loss of interest, and lack of motivation often observed in depression are considered deficits in the approach system. Social isolation, also a common feature of depression, represents a form of withdrawal. At the level of the brain, a substantial body of research suggests that approach and avoidance behaviors are differentially represented in the two cerebral hemispheres, with left frontal regions being associated with approach and right frontal regions with avoidance or withdrawal (Davidson, 2003). Accordingly, one would expect to find relatively greater right than left frontal brain activation in depression, reflecting an increase in withdrawal and decrease in approach tendencies. Data examining this hypothesis are reviewed below.

Brain Lesion Studies

The earliest studies in this tradition were conducted in stroke patients who had suffered stroke-induced lesions to one hemisphere. These reports indicated that damage to the left hemisphere tended to be associated with an increase in negative emotions, such as crying, whereas damage to the right hemisphere was more likely to be linked with positive affect, such as joking (Gainotti, 1972). Assuming that lesions lead to a loss of functions previously served by that brain tissue, these data suggest that a loss of left hemisphere cortex resulted in reduced capacity for positive emotion, while leaving the ability to experience negative emotions intact, a state akin to that observed in depression. Using somewhat more precise techniques for localizing such lesions, other researchers replicated these findings and further found that the severity of depression was strongly positively correlated with the proximity of the lesion to the most anterior point of the left frontal lobe (Robinson, Kubos, Starr, Rao, & Price, 1984). These data provided early evidence for the role of deficits in left frontal cortical functioning in depression.

Frontal EEG Asymmetries and Depression

Following the lead of the early lesion work, the bulk of research on hemispheric lateralization and depression has used scalp-recorded EEG to assess asymmetries in activation of the two hemispheres, particularly the two frontal lobes. Using a measure of activity in the alpha frequency band (8–13 Hz synchronized waveforms) while individuals are sitting at rest and not engaged in any specific cognitive task, numerous studies have demonstrated that currently depressed individuals exhibit relatively less left than right frontal brain activation (Henriques & Davidson, 1991). Similarly, examinations of individuals who are not currently diagnosed with a clinically significant depression, but who report relatively high levels of depression on questionnaire measures, also exhibit this pattern of asymmetry. Other investigations have linked relative decreases in left compared to right frontal activation to other forms of depression such as seasonal affective disorder. Furthermore, treatment response has also been linked to resting frontal EEG

asymmetry, with nonresponders to pharmacological intervention exhibiting less left compared to right frontal activation prior to treatment, and treatment responders showing an absence of this pretreatment laterality (Bruder et al., 2001).

Thus, it seems that frontal asymmetry of resting brain activation is linked with a current state of depression. Other researchers have begun to address the extent to which this relative left frontal hypoactivation is state dependent, that is present only during depressive episodes, or is a traitlike marker of vulnerability to depression that is present even in the absence of actual symptoms of the disorder. For example, previously depressed patients who are currently not experiencing symptoms of depression have also been shown to exhibit relatively less left than right frontal activation (Henriques & Davidson, 1990). While these data cannot elucidate whether the frontal asymmetry preceded the initial depressive episode, or was precipitated by the depression, it is apparent that decreases in left frontal activation are not limited to an active state of depression. While one prospective longitudinal study found that relatively greater right frontal brain activation predicted symptoms of anxiety a year later, such data for depression is still lacking.

These hemispheric asymmetry effects appear to be more evident in women with depression. Many of the studies conducted to date have used only or predominantly female participants, and those that have directly compared men to women have found a lack of frontal asymmetry or even the opposite pattern of asymmetry in male depressed participants. Of note, two twin studies also found that frontal asymmetry was heritable only for young adult females, not males. Furthermore, the correlation between frontal asymmetry and risk for depression in these young women was accounted for by shared genetic influence common to both frontal asymmetry and risk for mood disorder (Smit, Posthuma, Boomsma, & De Geus, 2007). Interestingly, in a number of studies, infants of depressed mothers also have been found to exhibit relative left frontal hypoactivity

(Field, Fox, Pickens, & Nawrocki, 1995). This may be a result of an inherited vulnerability for depression and the associated decreases in left frontal brain activation, or the result of the environmental influences of living with a depressed caregiver.

Comparatively fewer studies have examined asymmetry of activation of the two hemispheres during a task. However, the data that do exist are consistent with the resting EEG data. For example, early-onset depression appears to be associated with relative left frontal hypoactivation when anticipating the possibility of winning a monetary reward (Shankman, Klein, Tenke, & Bruder, 2007).

Brain Imaging Studies

While the bulk of the data supporting lateralization of hemispheric activation in depression stems from EEG studies, brain imaging techniques measuring cerebral blood flow or glucose metabolism have also been used to examine these resting frontal asymmetries. Hypoactivation of the left dorsolateral prefrontal cortex among depressed individuals has been observed using both positron emission tomography (PET) and single-photon emission computed tomography (SPECT) (Drevets et al., 1992). These techniques have also revealed increased right frontal blood flow and glucose metabolism in depression. In addition, PET studies of neurotransmitter function have found increased uptake of serotonin in right frontal regions in depression. Notably, one investigation found that treatment with paroxetine resulted in normalization, or decreases, in right inferior frontal activation.

While there is evidence from PET and SPECT studies to support the pattern observed in lesion and EEG studies, the neuroimaging data are more equivocal, with a larger number of studies failing to replicate, or even showing the opposite pattern of results. One possible reason that the neuroimaging findings may show a less consistent picture lies in the increased spatial precision of these tools. Whereas scalp-based EEG recordings have quite crude spatial resolution,

resulting in aggregation of activity across large regions of brain tissue, the increased precision of neuroimaging procedures allows for localization to more specific brain regions, and thus more specific localization of psychological functions. While at a very general level the two frontal hemispheres may reflect approach and withdrawal behaviors, specific regions within each hemisphere may not exhibit these same asymmetric patterns, thus yielding inconsistencies between the EEG and brain imaging literature. The advent of widespread use of neuroimaging techniques will undoubtedly assist in refining understanding of frontal hemispheric asymmetries in depression in the years to come.

Beyond Frontal Asymmetries: Arousal and Posterior Asymmetries

While a number of theorists have linked frontal asymmetries to approach and avoidance tendencies, and in turn with positive and negative emotions, less attention has been paid to asymmetries of posterior brain regions. However, several researchers have suggested that, while frontal regions are associated with affective valence, right posterior regions, particularly parietal cortex, are implicated in arousal, including behavioral and autonomic nervous system arousal (Heller, 1993). Some depressed individuals exhibit symptoms consistent with low arousal, such as fatigue and loss of energy. Thus, according to the arousal asymmetry model, these individuals would be expected to show right posterior hypoactivation. Indeed, a number of EEG and brain imaging studies have found decreased activation in right posterior regions in depression. For example, one group showed that depressed individuals had reduced right parietal EEG activation in response to unpleasant pictures. However, there are also numerous studies in which the opposite pattern, increased right posterior activation, was found. In the context of the arousal hypothesis, these data have typically been interpreted as reflecting the likely presence of comorbid anxiety symptoms. Depression and anxiety commonly co-occur, and anxiety is often associated with increased behavioral and autonomic arousal. Thus, greater right posterior activation may reflect a more anxious depression. While these posterior lateralization effects have received less attention, there is sufficient evidence to warrant consideration of these asymmetries for theories of the role of the brain in depression, and particularly in understanding comorbidity of anxiety and depression.

Conclusions

The aforementioned data show broad support for the notion that the two hemispheres of the brain show different levels of activation in depression, and perhaps even in individuals at increased risk for depression. Indeed, given the data indicating heritability of frontal EEG asymmetry and the presence of left frontal hypoactivation in infants of depressed mothers, it is possible that these laterality effects are present very early in development among those vulnerable to becoming depressed. These laterality effects are linked not to depression per se, but rather to dysregulation of major motivational and affective processes associated with the disorder. Thus, the degree to which these asymmetries are present in a given individual is likely a function of specific deficits or dysregulation of approach and avoidance behaviors.

CHRISTINE L. LARSON

See also

Affective Neuroscience
Brain Circuitry
Brain Function in Depressed Children and Adolescents
Brain Function in Midlife Unipolar Depression
Functional Neuroimaging

References

Bruder, G. E., Stewart, J. W., Tenke, C. E., McGrath, P. J., Leite, P., Bhattacharya, et al. (2001). Electroencephalographic and perceptual asymmetry differences between responders and nonresponders to an SSRI antidepressant. *Biological Psychiatry, 49*, 416–425.

Davidson, R. J. (2003). Affective neuroscience and psychophysiology: Toward a synthesis. *Psychophysiology, 40*, 655–665.

Drevets, W. C., Videen, T. O., Price, J. L., Preskorn, S. H., Carmichael, S. T., & Raichle, M. E. (1992). A functional anatomical study of unipolar depression. *Journal of Neuroscience, 12*, 3628–3641.

Field, T., Fox, N. A., Pickens, J., & Nawrocki, T. (1995). Relative right frontal EEG activation in 3- to 6-month old infants of depressed mothers. *Developmental Psychology, 31*, 358–363.

Gainotti, G. (1972). Emotional behavior and hemispheric side of lesion. *Cortex, 8*, 41–55.

Heller, W. (1993). Neuropsychological mechanisms of individual differences in emotion, personality, and arousal. *Neuropsychology, 7*, 476–489.

Henriques, J. B., & Davidson, R. J. (1990). Regional brain electrical asymmetries discriminate between previously depressed and healthy control subjects. *Journal of Abnormal Psychology, 99*, 22–31.

Henriques, J. B., & Davidson, R. J. (1991). Left frontal hypoactivation in depression. *Journal of Abnormal Psychology, 100*, 535–545.

Robinson, R. G., Kubos, K. L., Starr, L. B., Rao, K., & Price, T. R. (1984). Mood disorders in stroke patients: Importance of location of lesion. *Brain, 107*, 81–93.

Shankman, S. A., Klein, D. N., Tenke, C. E., & Bruder, G. E. (2007). Reward sensitivity in depression: A biobehavioral study. *Journal of Abnormal Psychology, 116*, 95–104.

Smit, D. J., Posthuma, D., Boomsma, D. I., and De Geus, E. J. (2007). The relation between frontal EEG asymmetry and the risk for anxiety and depression. *Biological Psychology, 74*, 26–33.

High-Risk Research Paradigm

The high-risk research paradigm provides an important research strategy for generating information on causal processes in depression. In high-risk research paradigms, individuals are assessed on the basis of some theoretically defined high-risk factors to determine whether a particular risk factor predicts depression. Such paradigms are typically longitudinal, that is, they follow individuals over some period of time, and in the case of these paradigms, see if depression develops and whether the studied variable is related to the occurrence of depression.

Definitions of Risk Guided by Theory

Risk can be defined in a variety of ways. One common definition is theoretically based, that is, a theory of depression will typically suggest one or more variables that should be related to the onset of depression. The Temple-Wisconsin Cognitive Vulnerability to Depression Project, initiated by Lauren Alloy at Temple University and Lynn Abramson at the University of Wisconsin, represents a prototype of the translation of a theory-driven variable into an operational definition of vulnerability. In this project, risk was defined in large part by attributional models of depression, which suggest certain patterns of attributions made by people reflect vulnerability to depression. Hence, in this project, the Cognitive Style Questionnaire was used to measure these attributional tendencies in a pool of over 5,000 students who attended the University of Wisconsin or Temple University, and who were followed over a period of several years. Results of this project have been reported in a number of publications, but reports by Alloy, Abramson, Whitehouse, and colleagues (2006) and Alloy, Abramson, Safford, and Gibb (2006) provide nice summaries of the major findings; these findings suggest that inferential style is indeed related to the development of depression.

Other examples of theoretically defined risk factors are available. For instance, variables such as attachment, dependency and self-criticism, parental bonding patterns, and sociotropy or autonomy can be considered as theoretically defined vulnerability factors for depression. Any theory that specifies a risk factor could employ a high-risk research paradigm to test whether the proposed risk factor does in fact predict depression.

Empirically Guided Definitions of Risk

Definitions do not have to be theory guided; research has identified variables that are associated with risk but that are not necessarily linked to a theory. A common way of defining risk in this context is to examine history of depression. The chances of experiencing a subsequent episode of depression after a first onset are high for many people, and so previously depressed individuals would be appropriate participants in a high-risk paradigm. Not all of these individuals will experience another episode, but as a group, they are at risk. Other risk factors that are empirically guided that have been reported include developmental history of abuse and a family history of depression. The important point is that any variable that has been empirically identified to be associated with risk for depression, whether or not it is tied to a theory, can serve as a factor in the high-risk research paradigm.

RICK E. INGRAM

See also

Cognitive Vulnerability
Risk
Vulnerability

References

Alloy, L. B., Abramson, L. Y., Safford, S. M., & Gibb, B. (2006). The Cognitive Vulnerability to Depression (CVD) Project: Current findings and future directions. In L. B. Alloy & J. Hiskind (Eds.), *Cognitive vulnerability to emotional disorders* (pp. 33–61). Mahwah, NJ: Lawrence Erlbaum Associates.

Alloy, L. B., Abramson, L. Y., Whitehouse, W. G., Hogan, M. E., Panzarella, C., & Rose, D. T. (2006). Prospective incidence of first onsets and recurrences of depression in individuals with high and low cognitive risk for depression. *Journal of Abnormal Psychology, 115,* 145–156.

Hippocampus

The enigmatic beauty of the hippocampus has captivated anatomists since the first dissections took place in ancient Egypt. *Hippocampus* means "seahorse" (derived from the Greek words *hippos* meaning "horse" and *kampos* meaning "sea monster"), and was so named because of its supposed gross anatomical resemblance to this sea creature. The hippocampus was named toward the end of the 16th century by the medieval anatomist, Arantius. At the beginning of the 19th century, the German comparative neuroanatomist Gottfried Reinhold Treviranus noted the multiple connections the hippocampus had with other brain structures, and toward the end of the 19th century, many significant contributions were made on the fine structure of the hippocampus by Ramón y Cajal, Camillo Golgi, and Theodor Meynert. Despite this progress on the structural front, the functions of the hippocampus remained a matter of speculation. Surprisingly, the hippocampus had been little studied by neurologists and behavioral scientists before the second half of the 20th century. This changed completely after the famous case of H.M., who showed striking memory loss after bilateral resection of the medial temporal lobe. This clinical finding stimulated many researchers to conduct lesion experiments and electrophysiological recording studies on experimental animals, and today, the hippocampus is one of the most thoroughly investigated brain structures in neuroscience, as well as in research on the neurobiology of depressive illness. Despite this, as we shall see, there remains much to learn about this brain structure.

Anatomy of the Human Hippocampus

In the human brain, the hippocampus is situated deep within the left and right medial temporal lobes. Although it lies beneath the cerebral cortex, the hippocampus is not regarded as a subcortical structure. The hippocampus is a cortical infolding, although it is much more primitive in structure than the surrounding neocortex; hence, it is also referred to as the archipallium. In proper neuroanatomical terms, the hippocampus is called the *hippocampal formation*, representing a group of brain areas consisting of the dentate gyrus, the hippocampus proper or cornu ammonis (CA), the subiculum, presubiculum,

parasubiculum, and entorhinal cortex. In the following text, and for reasons of simplicity, we call this group of brain structures the hippocampus.

The hippocampus receives highly processed information about the external world from various neocortical areas via the entorhinal cortex, whereas information about the internal world is conveyed by its subcortical inputs. Information flow within the hippocampus is largely unidirectional from the entorhinal cortex → dentate gyrus → CA3 → CA1 → subiculum and back to the entorhinal cortex. Thus, the entorhinal cortex is bidirectionally connected to nearly all areas of the neocortical mantle, and it conveys information into the hippocampus and returns the results of hippocampal processing back to the neocortical targets.

Based on studies by Paul Broca, James Papez, and Paul McLean, the hippocampus is often regarded as part of the so-called limbic system, which is an assembly of rather diverse brain areas that includes the cingulate cortex, hippocampus, hypothalamus, fornix, amygdala, and thalamus, among others. The major role of the limbic system is to regulate bodily stress responses and emotional experiences by coordinating the proper functioning of the endocrine system and the autonomic nervous system. Here, we would like to emphasize that most of our current knowledge on the hippocampus originates from studies in rodents. Not surprisingly, results from human and nonhuman primate studies repeatedly point out that the human brain has unique characteristics compared with the rodent and nonhuman primate brain (Amaral & Lavenex, 2007). Therefore, one should keep in mind that preclinical findings in animals do not necessarily mirror situations in humans.

Function

The belief that damage to the hippocampus may affect memory can be traced back to 1887 when Sanger Brown and Edward Albert Schäfer demonstrated that temporal lobe lesions in rhesus monkeys resulted in clear memory impairments. Nearly 80 years after these initial findings, a new era of studies on the neuropsychology of learning and memory was initiated by the famous case of the young patient H.M., who underwent brain surgery in 1953 to treat his severe epilepsy, demonstrating that bilateral resection of the medial temporal lobe (including the hippocampus and surrounding structures) caused profound anterograde amnesia.

Today we know that the hippocampus plays an essential role in fundamental cognitive functions such as learning and memory, as well as in the regulation of emotional and stress responses. In humans, the hippocampus mediates the formation of spatial, episodic, and semantic memories; however, it is also involved in other functions such as sensorimotor processing or detection of novelty (Morris, 2007). This does not mean that the hippocampus is the library (or "hard disc") of all our memories, because memory traces are gradually reorganized over time, and after consolidation, long-term memory traces are stored in the neocortex. Importantly, the hippocampus does not carry out these vital tasks single-handedly; instead, it functions as part of a larger network system. A further significant role of the hippocampus is in modulating endocrine responses to challenging situations (stressors), providing a negative feedback control of the hypothalamic-pituitary-adrenocortical (HPA) system. It is assumed that higher limbic structures, which are rich in glucocorticoid and mineralocorticoid receptors, such as the hippocampus and the prefrontal cortex, provide a tonic inhibition to the activity of the HPA system. In response to stressors, these limbic structures appear to reduce their activity, which in turn disinhibits the HPA system and initiates, via adrenocorticotropic hormone, the release of the stress hormone cortisol from the adrenal cortex.

Hippocampal Volume and Depression

High-resolution in vivo MRI studies document a small (~10%) but significant reduction in hippocampal volume in depressed patients (Campbell, Marriott, Nahmias, & MacQueen, 2004; Videbech & Ravnkilde, 2004). The significance and etiology of this volume loss is unclear. Meta-analysis studies have revealed that in patients with unipolar major depression, both hemispheres are affected, and the total number of depressive episodes seems to correlate with hippocampal volume reduction in the right hemisphere. It has been hypothesized that hippocampal volume reduction might be the consequence of repeated periods of major depressive disorder. Bipolar patients do not seem to show a reduction in hippocampal volume; however, this has been less investigated. Traumatic experiences, especially chronic stress, seem to play a key role in this volume change, because experiencing more chronic life stress has been linked to decreases in gray matter volume in the right hippocampus of healthy elderly women (Gianaros et al., 2007).

The exact underlying cellular mechanisms behind this volume decrease are unclear. Because numerous clinical observations indicate that the HPA system is hyperactive in at least a subpopulation of depressed individuals, the traditional explanation for this volume decrease was that elevated glucocorticoids have neurotoxic effects on the hippocampus. However, postmortem histopathological analyses did not substantiate neuronal cell loss or any obvious signs of neuropathology in the hippocampi of depressed patients (Lucassen et al., 2001; Stockmeier et al., 2004).

Because stressful life events are associated with an increased risk of developing depression, preclinical studies in which animals are exposed to chronic stress have been used to understand the cellular mechanisms underlying hippocampal shrinkage in depressed patients. Based on morphometrical studies, parameters such as alterations in somato-dendritic, axonal, and synaptic components, suppressed adult neurogenesis, and changes in glial cell numbers have been suggested as major causative factors in hippocampal shrinkage (Czéh & Lucassen, 2007). Other factors such as shifts in fluid balance or changes in the extracellular space cannot be excluded. In summary, more recent studies suggest that hippocampal volume decrease in depressed patients is because of impaired neuroplasticity and cellular resilience; thus, most of this is probably reversible and not a result of neurodegenerative processes.

However, there is another route of explanation. Smaller hippocampal volume might be a preexisting, specific, neuroanatomical vulnerability factor related to the development of depression, rather than a consequence of depressive episodes. There is evidence that first-episode depressed patients have smaller hippocampal volume, and such findings challenge the notion of the neurotoxic effect of depressive episodes (Frodl et al., 2002). However, another study found the opposite. That is, the study revealed a significant association between illness duration and hippocampal volume decrease and found that such morphological changes were not detectable in patients with a first episode of depression (MacQueen et al., 2003).

Notably, hippocampal volume shows high individual variability. The minimum and maximum size of the hippocampus varies between 3.31 and 5.13 cubic centimeters in healthy young adults aged 18 to 40 years, and about 25% of healthy young adults have relatively small hippocampal volumes (Lupien et al., 2007). These data raise the possibility that preexisting interindividual differences in hippocampal volume may determine the vulnerability for psychopathology. It is also possible that reduced hippocampal volume is the cumulative result of multiple major depressive episodes, and, at the same time, a smaller-sized hippocampus represents a trait marker of vulnerability for the disease. Longitudinal studies could resolve this issue by examining whether hippocampal volume is stable or progressively shrinks during the course of the illness. There is, however, one problematic factor with such an approach, namely, that recent animal studies indicate that antidepressant treatment may counteract those cellular processes that contribute to the volume decrease. A few clinical studies also suggest that antidepressant treatment may have a neuroprotective effect in patients with depression or posttraumatic stress disorder

(Sheline, Gado, & Kraemer, 2003; Vermetten, Vythilingam, Southwick, Charney, & Bremner, 2003). This highlights another difficulty in depression research, namely, that it would be ideal to investigate the pathophysiology of depression in nonmedicated subjects; however, such patients are rare nowadays, and this approach is ethically questionable.

Finally, it should be noted that reduced volume has been reported in other brain areas of depressed patients and that hippocampal shrinkage is not specific to depressive disorders. Hippocampal volume reduction has been reported in individuals who have experienced traumatic stress, such as patients with posttraumatic stress disorder or in survivors of severe sexual or physical childhood abuse. Hippocampal shrinkage is a common finding in a large number of neuropsychiatric disorders such as schizophrenia, dementia, Alzheimer's, Parkinson's, and Huntington's diseases, epilepsy, chronic alcoholism, herpes simplex, encephalitis, and traumatic brain injury.

There are a number of other noninvasive in vivo diagnostic methods currently in use, for example, localized proton magnetic resonance spectroscopy, which enables the investigation of cerebral metabolites in a large variety of pathologies, including neuropsychiatric disorders. This technique allows the in vivo quantification of concentrations of major brain metabolites and certain neurotransmitters in specific areas of the brain. The aim of this approach is to reveal specific biological trait markers of distinct psychiatric disorders; however, so far results are inconclusive.

Hippocampal Function in Depressed Patients

To date, in vivo imaging studies have focused more on structure (volume) and less on function, mainly because the spatial resolution of the functional imaging techniques, such as positron emission tomography (PET) and single-photon emission computed tomography, is rather low and not suitable for the examination of small structures such as the hippocampus. Functional MRI studies produce better resolution; however, convincing demonstration of hippocampal dysfunction in depressed patients is lacking. Instead, altered hippocampal function is indicated by cognitive impairment, which is one of the core symptoms of major depression. Patients exhibit deficits in explicit memory and deficiencies in a certain spatial memory navigation task that requires cognitive capacities dependent on the intact functioning of the hippocampal formation. Altered hippocampal function is likely to influence the activity of other brain structures, in particular the prefrontal cortex, a structure that conveys several higher-order cognitive functions and plays a vital role in emotional processing. A number of other structures that are associated with emotion, such as the amygdala and nucleus accumbens, receive inputs from the hippocampus; hence, their functioning also depends on the hippocampus. Moreover, distorted function of the hippocampus may contribute to the dysregulation of the HPA system, which occurs in almost half of depressed patients.

Adult Neurogenesis in the Hippocampus

The hippocampus has a remarkable capacity for plasticity, even in the adult differentiated brain. Adult neurogenesis, the formation and incorporation of new neurons into the preexisting circuitry, is a prominent example of hippocampal structural plasticity. A central hypothesis of neuroscience has been that the production of neurons in the mammalian brain occurs only during development and that neurons die but are not generated in the adult brain. However, recent evidence demonstrates that in mammals, including nonhuman primates and humans, certain brain areas retain the capability to generate new neurons throughout the entire life span (Eriksson et al., 1998). Spontaneous neurogenesis takes place in selected regions of the adult brain, such as the subgranular zone of the hippocampal dentate gyrus and the subventricular zone of the lateral ventricle. In the dentate gyrus, newly generated granule cells become incorporated into the granule cell layer and attain the morphological and biochemical characteristics of neurons. The neuronal nature of these cells documents itself by the formation of synapses on the cell bodies and dendrites, extension of axons into the CA3 region, and the generation of action potentials. However, the newborn cells have distinct morphological and electrophysiological properties compared with mature granule cells; for example, they present a lower threshold for induction of long-term potentiation (LTP) and display robust LTP. Because the hippocampus plays a central role in the acquisition and consolidation of episodic-declarative memories, the fact that continuous neurogenesis occurs in a substructure of the hippocampal formation may indicate that newborn neurons could participate in learning and memory processes. Indeed, a continually rejuvenating population of new neurons seems well suited for the proposed transient role of the hippocampus in information storage. An increasing number of preclinical studies indicate that adult hippocampal neurogenesis is involved in learning and memory processes. However, the exact functional role of the newborn granular neurons remains to be determined.

Recently, a new hypothesis, the neurogenic theory of depression, has been put forward, linking impaired neuroplasticity and a suppressed rate of adult hippocampal neurogenesis to a depressed mood. This idea has become one of the most heavily investigated and debated topics in current neuroscience. The most important building blocks of this theory are findings in experimental animals that stress inhibits adult hippocampal neurogenesis, whereas antidepressant treatment has an opposite effect, and that patients with mood disorders often have smaller hippocampal volumes. This theory proposes adult hippocampal neurogenesis as a candidate for the etiology and treatment of major depressive disorders (Duman, 2004). This view has since been refined and the current view of some scientists is that newborn hippocampal granule cells may not be critical contributors to the development of depression; however, they may be required for certain behavioral antidepressant effects (Sahay & Hen, 2007). In contrast, others vigorously dispute the functional significance of newly generated neurons in the pathophysiology of mood disorders.

To obtain convincing evidence for the central role of reduced neurogenesis in depression requires the direct examination of this process in the hippocampi of depressed patients. To date, the only study that addresses this question has been published recently by Reif and colleagues (2006). In this study, the authors compared the level of neural stem cell proliferation in postmortem brain samples from patients with major depression, bipolar affective disorder, schizophrenia, and control subjects. They could not find any evidence of reduced neurogenesis in the hippocampi of depressed patients. Furthermore, antidepressant treatment did not increase neural stem cell proliferation. Unexpectedly, significantly reduced numbers of newly formed cells were found only in schizophrenic patients. However, this study was based on a relatively small sample size, and further studies are warranted. Future studies in which adult neurogenesis can be visualized in live subjects using advanced PET or MRI techniques, for example, might address this issue more precisely; however, to date there is no clinical evidence that an altered rate of adult dentate neurogenesis is critical to the etiopathology of major depression. In this context, it is important to mention that new theories have linked a number of various psychiatric disorders, such as depression and schizophrenia, as well as dementia and drug addiction, to a failure of neurogenesis in the adult dentate gyrus.

BOLDIZSÁR CZÉH AND EBERHARD FUCHS

See also

Amygdala
Brain Circuitry
Hypothalamic-Pituitary-Adrenal Axis
Hypothalamic-Pituitary-Thyroid Axis

References

Amaral, D., & Lavenex, P. (2007). Hippocampal neuroanatomy. In P. Andersen, R. Morris, D. Amaral, T. Bliss, & J. O'Keefe (Eds.), *The hippocampus* (pp. 37–114). New York: Oxford University Press.

Campbell, S., Marriott, M., Nahmias, C., & MacQueen, G. M. (2004). Lower hippocampal volume in patients suffering from depression: A meta-analysis. *American Journal of Psychiatry, 161,* 598–607.

Czéh, B., & Lucassen, P. J. (2007). What causes the hippocampal volume decrease in depression? Are neurogenesis, glial changes, and apoptosis implicated? *European Archives of Psychiatry and Clinical Neuroscience, 257,* 250–260.

Duman, R. S. (2004). Depression: A case of neuronal life and death? *Biological Psychiatry, 56,* 140–145.

Eriksson, P. S., Perfilieva, E., Björk-Eriksson, T., Alborn, A. M., Nordborg, C., Peterson, D. A., et al. (1998). Neurogenesis in the adult human hippocampus. *Nature Medicine, 4,* 1313–1317.

Frodl, T., Meisenzahl, E. M., Zetzsche, T., Born, C., Groll, C., Jäger, M., et al. (2002). Hippocampal changes in patients with a first episode of major depression. *American Journal of Psychiatry, 159,* 1112–1118.

Gianaros, P. J., Jennings, J. R., Sheu, L. K., Greer, P. J., Kuller, L. H., & Matthews, K. A. (2007). Prospective reports of chronic life stress predict decreased grey matter volume in the hippocampus. *Neuroimage, 35,* 795–803.

Lucassen, P. J., Müller, M. B., Holsboer, F., Bauer, J., Holtrop, A., Wouda, J., et al. (2001). Hippocampal apoptosis in major depression is a minor event and absent from subareas at risk for glucocorticoid overexposure. *American Journal of Pathology, 158,* 453–468.

Lupien, S. J., Evans, A., Lord, C., Miles, J., Pruessner, M., Pike, B., et al. (2007). Hippocampal volume is as variable in young as in older adults: Implications for the notion of hippocampal atrophy in humans. *Neuroimage, 34,* 479–485.

MacQueen, G. M., Campbell, S., McEwen, B. S., Macdonald, K., Amano, S., et al. (2003). Course of illness, hippocampal function, and hippocampal volume in major depression. *Proceedings of the National Academy of Sciences of the U. S. A., 100,* 1387–1392.

Morris, R. (2007). Theories of hippocampal function. In P. Andersen, R. Morris, D. Amaral, T. Bliss, & J. O'Keefe (Eds.), *The hippocampus* (pp. 581–714). New York: Oxford University Press.

Reif, A., Fritzen, S., Finger, M., Strobel, A., Lauer, M., Schmitt, A., et al. (2006). Neural stem cell proliferation is decreased in schizophrenia, but not in depression. *Molecular Psychiatry, 11,* 514–522.

Sahay, A., & Hen, R. (2007). Adult hippocampal neurogenesis in depression. *Nature Neuroscience, 10,* 1110–1115.

Sheline, Y. I., Gado, M. H., & Kraemer, H. C. (2003). Untreated depression and hippocampal volume loss. *American Journal of Psychiatry, 160,* 1516–1518.

Stockmeier, C. A., Mahajan, G. J., Konick, L. C., Overholser, J. C., Jurjus, G. J., Meltzer, H. Y., et al. (2004). Cellular changes in the postmortem hippocampus in major depression. *Biological Psychiatry, 56,* 640–650.

Vermetten, E., Vythilingam, M., Southwick, S. M., Charney, D. S., & Bremner, J. D. (2003). Long-term treatment with paroxetine increases verbal declarative memory and hippocampal volume in posttraumatic stress disorder. *Biological Psychiatry, 54,* 693–702.

Videbech, P., & Ravnkilde, B. (2004). Hippocampal volume and depression: A meta-analysis of MRI studies. *American Journal of Psychiatry, 161*, 1957–1966.

History of Depression

A history of any mental affliction can be meaningfully written about only if the specific histories of its name, referent behaviors, and explanatory concepts are differentiated. For example, and given that names are usually the only continuous element of such a triad, a book entitled *The History of Melancholia From the Greek to the Present Day* can but be a history of the word. By the same token, *history of depression* can variously refer to the usages of the word *depression* in psychiatry—in which case it can only start during the 19th century—or to the history of the mood forms that *depression* is believed to name, or to the set of concepts that since the 19th century have been marshalled to explain the age-old observation that human beings can get despondent, anhedonic, apathetic, and so on.

The term *depression* can name a mood state (symptom), a set of symptoms (syndrome), and a putative disease (e.g., *DSM-IV* major depressive disorder [American Psychiatric Association, 1994]). All this has resulted from the analogical application to a psychiatric complaint of a term that first appeared in 19th-century physiology. Those writing on the history of depression often make an assumption that depression refers to an immutable object (a natural kind) that has been only incompletely noticed, captured, or explained by the medics of yesteryear. These early efforts are then unfavorably contrasted with views held in the present. Such accounts leave out the most important part of the story, to wit, that psychiatrists and psychologists and their language actively participate in the construction of the objects that they purport to describe, research, and understand (including depression).

This is not to negate the obvious fact that throughout the ages, with or without motive, people have felt sad, despondent, "down in the dumps," "under the weather," "out of sorts," or as it is said nowadays, "depressed." Before deciding that these mood changes result from some brain abnormality, it is the obligation of those involved to undertake a hermeneutic analysis of sadness and its accoutrements. Without the help of the historian and the epistemologist, this task is well beyond the reach of the clinician. In order to be of help, the historian must refrain from joining the bandwagon of the hasty medicalizers.

Although the history of the word itself is of limited explanatory value, it still can be used to show how ramifications of its metaphorical core (which conveys the action of flattening, pressing down, lowering, reducing, etc.) have shaped biological explanations; specifically, in depressive illness it is believed that something in the brain must be lacking or reduced, while in mania something must be in excess.

Be that as it may, an adequate contextualization of depression and its referents confirms the view that their history is entangled with that of human sadness. However, one must resist the temptation of using "sadness" as the next organizing invariant, as the object that remains the same throughout the centuries. This would be tantamount to assuming that there is a stereotyped panoply of emotions that, at least since the time of Darwin, are believed to be inscribed in the biology of evolution. The historian would assume this at his or her peril.

The issue is not whether, since history began, people have felt or been reported as feeling despondent; the question is whether that experience has anything to do with the feelings that are currently attributed to despondency. In fact, there is evidence that it was only during the 18th century that the passions of old were reshaped into the emotions of today, and that such reshaping entailed a major semantic reformulation. In this sense, the emotions can be said to be social constructs. The fact that since their construction they have remained more or less unchanged should not for a moment be taken as evidence of some biological invariance, as it could simply reflect the presence of social stabilizers.

This caveat notwithstanding, it is clear that the interaction of the history of sadness with that of successive concepts such as melancholia, monomania, lypemania, partial insanity, and so on is worth exploring, as it informs the clinician of their kaleidoscopic and transient nature.

The History of Depression

The story that best saves the historical facts goes more or less like this: in 1800, mania, melancholia, dementia, and *phrensy* referred to forms of mental affliction that had nothing to do with the afflictions that the same terms are found naming in 1900. In 1800, *mania* referred to furious madness; *melancholia* to partial madness; *dementia* to a ragbag of states of weakened psychological resources and behavioral incapacities, whether acquired or congenital; and *phrensy* to forms of acute mental disorganization seen in the wake of severe and acute disease of the brain.

During the first half of the 19th century, these monolithic categories became fragmented under the analytical surgical knife of associationism. The resulting fragments constitute the mental symptoms of today. A process of reclustering of these fragments or symptoms followed under the conceptual governance of faculty psychology. The question that alienists tried to respond to then was, Are there mental afflictions that are a primary disorder of the intellectual, emotional, or volitional functions? In relation to his *monomanias*, Esquirol replied positively and constructed *lypemania*, a condition that the French nosologist considered to be due to a primary disorder of mood.

By the middle of the same century the word *depression* gradually replaced *lypemania*, a term that was soon to disappear together with the other monomanias. At the beginning called *mental depression* (as opposed to *cardiac depression*), it became plain *depression* by the 1880s, when the term ceased to be used in heart physiology. During this period the terms *depression* and *melancholia* were used in tandem, with the latter referring to the more severe forms of the disorder. In the hands of Kraepelin, depression became firmly associated with mania (which, by the way, had undergone a similar metamorphosis). Indeed, the German psychiatrist created a large category of disorders whose common feature was a primary abnormality of mood.

Carl Wernicke also developed a nosological program that many consider to have been more original and heuristic than Kraepelin's. His premature death, however, allowed the latter to reign unopposed and has encouraged historians to wonder what would it have been like for psychiatry to live in a Wernickian world. For Wernicke, melancholia was an akinesia of the mind, and hence the disease was not a primary manifestation of a mood disorder.

The early 20th century inherited the view that depression was a psychosis, in other words, a form of madness. Clinical experience suggested, however, that many a depressed patient was not mad. A new category was required to place the latter. Influenced by Freud, Gillespie and McCurdy constructed in the Cambridge (UK) of the 1920s the interesting concept of minor, neurotic, or reactive depression. A decade later, a debate started between the defenders of the unimodal and bimodal views of depression. In the event, the debate was not resolved, as the unimodal view was shown to be more convenient for the so-called continuity view sponsored by the defenders of the biological model of depression.

The development during the 1970s of successful psychological treatments (e.g., cognitive behavioral therapy, CBT) once again challenged the foundations on which the concept of depression had been constructed. While the fashionable approach in depression remains to search for brain inscriptions in areas primarily related to mood, clinical psychologists are proposing little less than a Copernican revolution. By claiming that negative cognitions (the target of CBT) are primary and mood changes secondary to the etiology of depression, they are in fact returning to the cognitive conceptions of melancholia upheld during the 1840s. This brings the history of depression back full circle. Indeed, it seems to confirm the view that a circular model (à la Vico) may be more useful to the history of psychiatry and psychology than the progressist, linear, presentistic, and misleading historiography that afflicts psychiatry and psychology today.

GERMAN E. BERRIOS

See also

Classification of Depression
Diagnostic and Statistical Manual of Mental Disorders

References

American Psychiatric Association. (1994). *Diagnostic and statistical manual of mental disorders* (4th ed.). Washington, DC: Author.

Berrios, G. E. (1996). *History of mental symptoms.* Cambridge, UK: Cambridge University Press.

Callahan, C., & Berrios, G. E. (2005). *Reinventing depression. A history of the treatment of depression in primary care 1940–2004.* Oxford, UK: Oxford University Press.

Jackson, S. W. (1986). *Melancholia and depression.* New Haven, CT: Yale University Press.

Hopelessness

From Timothy Bright (1586) to Emil Kraepelin (1921) to contemporary scholars of depression, hopelessness has long been considered a hallmark symptom of depression. Surprisingly, however, during the past 422 years, hopelessness has not been researched nearly as much as one would expect given the central role it is considered to play in depression and suicide. The purposes of the current entry are to identify the defining elements of hopelessness and to discuss the ways in which it is related to depression.

Hopelessness Theory of Depression

Abramson, Metalsky, and Alloy's (1989) hopelessness theory of depression was the first to explicitly focus on hopelessness in depression as the centerpiece of their theory, the hopelessness theory of depression. Abramson and colleagues provided a conceptualization of hopelessness as comprising two expectations about the future. The negative outcome expectancy comprises a belief that highly aversive outcomes (e.g., going bankrupt) will occur *or* that highly desired outcomes (e.g., being successful in one's career) will not occur. Although this negative outcome expectancy may appear to capture the concept of hopelessness, taken alone it is not sufficient to delineate hopelessness, because if a person also expects circumstances to change for the better, he or she will retain hope. Thus, Abramson and colleagues also postulated that in conceptualizing hopelessness, the negative outcome expectancy needs to be coupled with an expectation that there is no response in one's repertoire that will change the likelihood of occurrence of these outcomes. They refer to the latter expectation as the helplessness expectancy. The common-language term *hopelessness* captures the two core elements—negative outcome expectancy and helplessness expectancy. When someone has both the negative outcome expectancy and helplessness expectancy, that person will be hopeless as conceptualized by Abramson and colleagues. Finally, Abramson and colleagues used the phrase *generalized hopelessness* when people exhibit negative outcome and helplessness expectancy about many areas of life. In contrast, *circumscribed pessimism* occurs when people exhibit negative outcome and helplessness expectancy about only a limited domain. Cases of generalized hopelessness should produce severe symptoms of depression, whereas circumscribed pessimism is likely to be associated with fewer or less severe symptoms, or both.

Hopelessness as a Cause, Symptom, or Both?

Although hopelessness traditionally has been viewed as a symptom of depression, Abramson and colleagues (1989) proposed that hopelessness be elevated from symptom status to causal status. That is, in the hopelessness theory of depression, hopelessness is viewed as a proximal sufficient cause of a proposed subtype of depression, hopelessness depression. Proximal causes occur late in a chain of causal events, close to the occurrence of symptoms. *Sufficient* refers to a cause that guarantees the occurrence of symptoms (i.e., probability of hopelessness depression occurring when hopelessness is present = 1.0). Hopelessness depression does not include hopelessness as a symptom. Instead, hopelessness is a proximal sufficient cause of hopelessness depression, which comprises the following symptoms: (a) retarded initiation of voluntary responses (motivational deficit), (b) sad affect, (c) apathy, (d) lack of energy, (e) suicidality, (f) psychomotor retardation, (g) sleep disturbance, (h) difficulty in concentration, and (i) mood-exacerbated negative cognitions. If hopelessness is accompanied by a negative causal attribution concerning why the event occurred or by negative thoughts about oneself given the occurrence of the event, then hopelessness depression also will include symptoms of lowered self-esteem and interpersonal dependency.

As can be seen, Abramson and colleagues raised hopelessness from symptom status to etiological status in the theoretically based subtype of depression, hopelessness depression. This does not mean that hopelessness is a causal agent in all depressions. Instead, hopelessness is viewed as a proximal sufficient cause of this particular subtype of depression, hopelessness depression. Other subtypes of depression may very well include hopelessness as a symptom. However, from the perspective of the hopelessness theory, if hopelessness develops as a symptom, once present, it also will serve as a proximal sufficient cause of hopelessness depression.

Thus, even when hopelessness develops as a symptom in another subtype of depression, it will lead to the development of hopelessness depression as a superimposed disorder. In this case, hopelessness serves as both a symptom of another subtype of depression and subsequently as a cause of hopelessness depression.

Causes of Hopelessness

Why is it that in the face of highly aversive negative life events, some people maintain hope and continue to make every effort to continue on, whereas others develop hopelessness and subsequently hopelessness depression? Insofar as there are numerous proposed causes of hopelessness, a comprehensive review of this body of work is beyond the scope of this entry. On the other hand, it is worthwhile to provide a brief synopsis of the causes of hopelessness that are proposed in the hopelessness theory of depression. As a cognitive theory of depression, the hopelessness theory delineates three types of inferences that contribute to the development of hopelessness and, in turn, hopelessness depression: (a) negative inferences about why the event occurred (i.e., inferred cause), (b) negative inferences about the consequences that will arise as a result of the occurrence of the event (i.e., inferred consequences), and (c) negative inferences about oneself given the occurrence of the event (i.e., inferred characteristics about the self). For example, consider a hypothetical person, Johnny U. R. Hopeless, who has the most negative thoughts imaginable, including negative inferences about cause, consequences, and self. When Johnny woke up this morning, he accidentally knocked his head against a door. He inferred that he is a "clumsy idiot" in that he cannot even wake up without giving himself a headache (internal, stable, global inferred cause). Johnny also inferred that he will wind up with brain damage from repeatedly hitting his head (negative inferred consequence), and finally that he is the type of person who is a complete and utter failure (i.e., negative inferences about self). Thus, Johnny goes from the event (accidentally knocking his head) to inferring that he is a clumsy idiot who will develop brain damage and who, in the end, is a complete and utter failure. In addition to the inferences made when life events occur, some people have cognitive risk factors (cognitive diatheses) that leave them at risk for developing hopelessness and, in turn, hopelessness depression. Three cognitive diatheses (risk factors) coincide with the three cognitive inferences discussed earlier: depressogenic inferential styles about cause, consequence, and self. In contrast to inferences made for a specific life event, inferential styles are generalized tendencies to think in a particular way, such as a tendency to make depressogenic causal attributions (depressogenic attributional style) when negative life events occur. Although I have focused on cognitive-based causes of hopelessness and hopelessness depression, interpersonal-based causes (e.g., reassurance-seeking) also are being investigated.

skills after completing treatment, thereby reducing relapses and recurrences. Ultimately, it is important to shift from treatment to primary prevention. Insofar as the depressogenic inferential styles develop during childhood, it is possible to target children who are at high risk but who are not yet depressed, by identifying those who have one or more of the depressogenic inferential styles. These at-risk children would then be given a cognitive-behavioral-based prevention protocol in order to test the rates of depression later in life for those who were and were not given the prevention protocol. If effective, these cognitive risk factors and the prevention protocol would allow mental health professionals to identify children who would have developed hopelessness and, in turn, hopelessness depression but who were spared going through such emotional hardship.

GERALD I. METALSKY

Treatment of Hopelessness and Depression

In addition to this work on conceptualizing hopelessness and researching its theoretically proposed causes, it is important to examine treatments that are especially helpful in combating hopelessness and hopelessness depression. Although the empirical literature on the treatment of depression is robust, there is very little research that focuses specifically on the treatment of hopelessness and hopelessness depression. Therefore, this section requires some speculation as to effective treatments. As one might expect, cognitive behavioral therapy (CBT) may be the treatment of choice in this context given its focus on helping clients to examine their negative thoughts, become skillful at identifying these thoughts when they occur, and to test these thoughts by objectively examining the evidence for and against these inferences. Among the many benefits of CBT, clients become proficient in using these skills between sessions and continue to use these

See also

Attributional Style
Attributional Theories of Depression
Cognitive Theories of Depression

References

Abramson, L., Metalsky, G., & Alloy, L. (1989). Hopelessness depression: A theory-based subtype of depression. *Psychological Review, 2,* 358–372.
Bright, T. (1586). *A treatise of melancholie.* New York: Facsimile Text Society.
Kraepelin, E. (1921). Manic-depressive insanity and paranoia. In *Textbook of psychiatry* (R. M. Barclay, Trans.). Edinburgh, Scotland: E. S. Livingstone.

Hormones

The healthy regulation of affective behavior is vital to our social milieu. Dysregulation of such affective systems can alter mood and as such cultivate the development of depression. The etiology of depression is thought to involve neuroendocrine dysfunction and in particular highlights a role for hormones and the hypothalamic-pituitary-adrenal (HPA) and hypothalamic-pituitary-gonadal (HPG) systems in the disorder.

HPA Axis

The HPA axis balances the release of stress hormones to create homeostasis in both peripheral and central nervous systems. In response to stress, corticotropin-releasing hormone is released from the hypothalamus, activating adrenocorticotropin from the anterior pituitary and finally cortisol from the adrenal gland. An often-reported abnormality of the HPA system in depression is hypercortisolemia. This dysregulation of the HPA axis is associated with phase of illness rather than trait, as hyperactivity of the HPA axis is ameliorated once treated with antidepressants. A by-product of this hypersecretion of cortisol is the general adaptation syndrome. This syndrome, as coined by Selye (1949), describes persistent exposure to stress as a contributing factor to pathology and in particular withdrawal behaviors. This is in agreement with reports of a relation between hypercortisolemia and behaviors such as decreased sexual drive, altered eating habits, and restricted activity or lethargy. A recent study suggests that social support may sublimate an increased neuroendocrine response to stressors, especially in brain regions such as the dorsal anterior cingulate and Brodmann area 8 of the prefrontal cortex (Eisenberger, Taylor, Gable, Hilmert, & Lieberman, 2007). However, it has yet to be found if social support is effective in treating the overactive HPA axis seen in depression and brain regions associated with the disorder.

HPG Axis

Closely intertwined with the HPA axis is the HPG or reproductive system. The release of gonadotropin-releasing hormone is signaled by the hypothalamus in a pulsatile fashion.

The pituitary responds by releasing luteinizing and follicular stimulating hormones that cause the release of estrogen and testosterone by the gonads. Lifetime prevalence rates of depression are approximately twice that in women after puberty as compared to men. Disruptions in sex steroid hormones stimulated by the gonadotropins at the onset of puberty may precipitate this sex difference and alter mood regulation in girls. For example, rapid increases in estradiol secretion that occur during puberty are associated with depressive affect in girls. Links between depressive affect, early puberty timing, and increased estrogen and testosterone production have also been reported and further suggest a role for reproductive hormones in the gender differences reported in depression.

The interaction between HPA and HPG systems ultimately lead to the two systems influencing one another. Increases in HPA responses inhibit the gonadotropins, including ovarian estrogen and progesterone secretion. Reciprocally, estrogen stimulates the HPA axis. However, this relationship is not well characterized and warrants further studies of the interplay between HPA and HPG systems in depression, as multiple variables must be considered.

REBECCA E. BLANTON

See also

Biological Models of Depression
Cortisol
Hypothalamic-Pituitary-Adrenal Axis
Hypothalamic-Pituitary-Thyroid Axis

References

Eisenberger, N. I., Taylor S. E., Gable, S. L., Hilmert, C. J., & Lieberman, M. D. (2007). Neural pathways link social support to attenuated neuroendocrine stress responses *Neuroimage, 35*, 1601–1612.

Selye, H. (1949). The general adaptation syndrome and the diseases of adaptation. *Practitioner, 163*, 393–405.

Human Immunodeficiency Virus

Depression is a highly prevalent, chronic, and impairing illness in people living with human immunodeficiency virus (HIV; Evans et al., 2005). Nevertheless, confounding somatic symptoms common to depression and HIV illness itself (including fatigue, appetite loss, and sleep disturbance) and the overlooking of certain cognitive symptoms of depression (as poor attention, impaired decision making, and loss of interest), which occur in advanced stages of the disease, may lead to underdiagnosis and undertreatment. However, in the presence of persistent depressed mood and/or loss of interest required by the *Diagnostic and Statistical Manual of Mental Disorders* (*DSM-IV-TR;* American Psychiatric Association, 2000) for diagnosing depressive disorders, an inclusive approach toward somatic symptoms should be employed (Ferrando & Freyberg, 2008).

Depressive symptoms may be associated with an increase in risk-taking behaviors, including needle sharing and unprotected sex (Berger Greenstein, Cueva, Brady, Trezza, & Rich, 2007). This is not only of concern to transmitting the virus to noninfected individuals but also to reinfecting seropositive individuals with other viral strains. This may increase the likelihood of resistance to treatment.

Depression is important not only because of its psychological impact, but because it also has impacts on the course of HIV. Studies have shown that depressive symptoms are associated with more rapid progression to AIDS, mortality, and other indicators of immune compromise (Lesserman et al., 2003).

Prevalence

Lifetime rates of major depression in at-risk HIV cohorts are as high as 50%. Reported prevalence rates of depression within the HIV population vary markedly from 5% to almost 50%. These variations have been attributed to a number of factors, namely, different assessment strategies, varying recruitment approaches, disease stage, and treatment status (Berger Greenstein, et al., 2007). Rates of current depression among HIV-infected patients are at least twice that of the general population (Ciesla & Roberts, 2001). Overall, prevalence studies suggest that HIV-positive women are at significantly greater risk of major depressive disorder compared with demographically similar groups of HIV-negative women (Cruess, Evans, Repetto, Douglas, & Petitto, 2003).

Risk Factors

In a 2-year prospective cohort study of HIV-infected individuals, those at highest risk of a depressive disorder had a prior history of depressive disorders, suicide attempts, alcohol and substance abuse, and anxiety disorders (especially multiple comorbidity), more advanced HIV disease, symptomatic disease, and marked life adversity (Atkinson et al., 2008). People with HIV may be at higher risk of suicide throughout their illness, but perhaps more so early in the course of the disease when they are adjusting to the diagnosis, and then late in the disease when the physical burden of AIDS becomes severe.

Psychobiology

Depression in HIV may be a consequence of a primary depressive disorder or secondary to the effects of the virus on the brain, other infections or tumors, and antiretrovirals and other treatments.

Primary Depression

Factors that may contribute to depression in HIV-infected individuals include stigmatization, lack of social support, and the death of a loved one from HIV or AIDS. HIV-infected individuals who are at greatest risk for developing depression are those with a prior history of depression, homosexual men, and intravenous drug users (Maj, Satz, Janssen, & Zaudig, 1994).

Effects of the Virus on the Brain

Neurological impairment is found in 60% of HIV-infected patients (Ghafouri, Amini, Khalili, & Sawaya, 2006). HIV 1 enters the central nervous system at an early phase of infection, probably at the time of sero-conversion, and persists in that system for decades. Although the mechanism of this invasion through the blood-brain barrier is unclear, indications are that it occurs through HIV infection of macrophages, and microglia HIV is most likely to affect the subcortical areas and frontostriatal circuits (Brew, 2001). Disruption of these circuits may result in depressive symptoms. A number of mechanisms of HIV neurotoxicity have been postulated. These include damage induced by viral proteins (gp120 or tat), cytokine disturbance (tumor necrosis factor and interleukins), and neurotransmitter-mediated toxicity (glutamate and calcium). In the absence of opportunistic infections, the major clinical symptoms include impaired short-term memory, reduced concentration, slowness of movement and gait, and as depression (Ghafouri et al., 2006).

Other Infections or Tumors

Opportunistic infections of the central nervous system may also lead to depression. These secondary mood disorders become more likely as the disease progresses. Systemic manifestations of HIV disease may also cause or precipitate depression. Hypogonadism is not uncommon in advanced HIV infection and may be associated with depressive symptoms. Nutritional deficiencies associated with long-standing substance abuse, for example, vitamin B-12 or folate, are associated with the development of depressive symptoms in some patients.

Antiretrovirals

Depression has been documented with the use of efavirenz, ritonavir, abacavir, and nevirapine. Neuropsychiatric adverse effects related to potent antiretroviral therapy can lead to poor adherence, treatment interruptions, or change of therapy regimens. Symptoms usually occur within the first few weeks of initiation and then resolve. In the majority of cases, symptoms abate when the offending agent is discontinued. Efavirenz has been found to cause depression, insomnia, disorientation, and vivid dreams in 40% to 70% of patients (Cespedes, 2006).

Diagnosis

Fewer than half of HIV-positive patients with major depressive disorder are correctly diagnosed by their primary care providers (Asch et al., 2003). The reasons for underdiagnosis are varied. It may be difficult for the clinician to differentiate between somatic symptoms of HIV disease and symptoms arising from major depressive disorder (Perkins et al., 1995), as there is significant overlap between the neurovegetative symptoms of depression and symptoms associated with HIV, opportunistic infections, or common comorbidities such as hepatitis C.

Patients who are in the asymptomatic stage of HIV infection are less likely than those with more advanced disease to experience opportunistic infections, neurological diseases, or cognitive impairments such as dementia, all of which may present as depression (Cabaj et al., 1992).

Assessment

The most commonly used instruments for assessment of the severity of depression in HIV-infected individuals include the Beck Depression Inventory and the Centre for Epidemiological Studies Depression Scale. Such simple screening measures should be incorporated into the routine assessment of patients in the primary care setting so as to better identify patients in need of treatment. If screening and examination reveal that the HIV-infected patient likely has symptoms of depression, the clinician should also ask directly about suicidal ideation. Clinicians who suspect major depressive disorder should always screen for manic or hypomanic symptoms to determine whether a depressive episode may be a manifestation of a bipolar disorder.

Depression and cognitive disorders in late HIV are commonly comorbid. An assessment of cognition using brief bedside tests, such as the Folstein Mini-Mental State Examination and the HIV Dementia Scale, is recommended. HIV-infected persons may be affected by HIV-associated neurocognitive disorders (HAND). HAND includes mild neurocognitive disorder and HIV-associated dementia (Cherner et al., 2007). These disorders present with apathy and withdrawal, have an insidious onset, and include motor problems such as weakness and clumsiness.

Course

Depressive symptoms have been associated with a variety of problems for people with HIV or AIDS. Perhaps the most worrisome is faster progression to AIDS and higher mortality rates for those with depressive symptoms (Mayne et al., 1996). Faster progression to AIDS in depressed patients remained significant after controlling for CD4 cell count, viral load, age, employment, HIV symptoms, and use of HAART (Elliot, Russo, & Roy-Byrne, 2002). Reducing depressive symptoms in HIV individuals has a positive impact on health-related quality of life and also further enhances adherence.

The mechanisms mediating these relationships are less clear. Although it is possible that poor health habits such as smoking, substance abuse, risky sexual behavior, and medication use related to stress and depression might account for these findings, studies have not found that these habits entirely explain the effect of depression on HIV progression (Leserman et al., 2002). There is also the possible mediating role of HIV medication on nonadherence.

It has also been suggested that an increased risk of AIDS is associated with higher cumulative depressive symptoms after 5 years of follow-up. Depressive symptoms, especially in the presence of severe stress, were related to declines in several lymphocyte subsets (e.g., CD16+ and CD56+ natural killer cells, and CD8+ cytotoxic-suppressor cells) over a 2-year period (Leserman et al., 1997). There is some evidence that natural killer cells might have a role in suppressing HIV and thus have clinical significance.

In terms of biological mediators, most published data to date has focused on the HPA axis and sympathetic nervous system as possible mediators. Because disturbances of hypothalamic-pituitary-adrenal axis function (e.g., increases in adrenocorticotrophin-releasing hormone and cortisol) have been associated with stress and depression in humans, and such dysregulation can negatively impact the immune response, glucocorticoids may be a mediating mechanism explaining the negative immune effects of depression and stress in HIV infection. There is some evidence to suggest that cortisol is positively related to stress and depression in HIV (Gorman et al., 1991). Glucocorticoids may affect HIV pathogenesis directly through increased viral replication, or more indirectly by inhibiting the immune response to other pathogens (Leserman et al., 2003). Chronic elevations of sympathetic nervous system activity (e.g., norepinephrine) among those infected with HIV may adversely affect immune system functioning (e.g., reduced lymphocyte proliferation, alteration in cytokine production). It has been suggested that norepinephrine may suppress Th-1 type cytokines and increase Th-2 type changes associated with increased risk of HIV viral replication and increased vulnerability to opportunistic infections (Cole, 1997).

Treatment

Depression in HIV has been associated with poor adherence to antiretroviral treatment regimes and faster progression of the disease. A recent study found that after controlling for a number of factors, patients with depression and/or anxiety were significantly less likely to initiate HAART compared with patients without mental illness. However if patients with depression and or anxiety were treated with antidepressants, they were equally likely to initiate HAART as those without mental illness (Tegger et al., 2008).

In choosing a treatment modality, clinicians should be aware of individual patient needs, in particular the staging of the disease and the presence of comorbidity (e.g., substance abuse, suicidality). As psychotropic medications used to treat depression are metabolized by the same cytochrome P450 hepatic enzymes as the protease inhibitors and the nonnucleoside reverse transcriptase inhibitors, and are highly protein bound, clinically significant drug-drug interactions may result when these drugs are combined. If treatment is required, it should be noted that HIV-positive patients are more susceptible to the sedative properties of antidepressant medications (Price et al., 2002).

Pharmacotherapy

Selective Serotonin-Reuptake Inhibitors and Tricyclics

A qualitative review of the literature suggests that selective serotonin-reuptake inhibitors (SSRIs), tricyclic antidepressants (TCAs), and psychostimulants appear to be effective in the treatment of depression in HIV-positive individuals (Olatunji, Mimiaga, Cleirigh, & Safren, 2006). Overall, the various pharmacological agents appear to be superior to placebo (Table H.1). However there is no definitive evidence suggesting that any one pharmacologic agent is more effective than another. Himelhoch and colleagues (2005) performed a systematic review and meta-analysis of double-blinded, randomized controlled trials to examine efficacy of antidepressant treatment among HIV-positive depressed individuals. This study suggests that antidepressant medication is efficacious in treating depression among depressed, outpatient, HIV-positive men. However, the underrepresentation of women and minorities limits the generalizability of these findings.

High attrition rates are common, with dropout rates at approximately 27%. One of the most frequent reasons cited for drop out was side effects. Half of the patients taking fluoxetine reported at least one side effect in a study by Rabkin, Wagner, and Rabkin (1999); the most frequently reported side effects reported were gastrointestinal symptoms including stomach upset and diarrhea, nervousness, sleepiness, appetite and weight loss, dry mouth, and sexual dysfunction.

Relative to the TCAs, with their marked anticholinergic side effects, SSRIs are safer and better tolerated in treating depression in HIV-positive patients, although there is no definitive evidence that they are more efficacious than the TCAs (Olatunji et al., 2006).

To date, the majority of studies examining SSRI-based treatment of depression in the context of HIV disease have employed fluoxetine, which may potentially interact with antiretroviral drugs used in the HAART regimen, primarily through the cytochrome P450 3A4 and 2D6 isozymes. In comparison to the other SSRIs, citalopram is largely metabolized by the 2C19 isozyme, making interactions with HIV drugs less likely, thereby lowering the possibility of altered serum levels of either type of medication. HIV-positive individuals with depression treated with 10 to 40 mg daily of citalopram had response rates that were comparable to other studies of fluoxetine (Rabkin et al., 1999). There is some evidence that HIV patients receiving antiretroviral and SSRI therapy may be at heightened risk of developing serotonin syndrome (DeSilva, Le Flore, Marston, & Rimland, 2001); therefore, starting at a low dose and increasing slowly is recommended.

Other Newer-Generation Antidepressants

Other newer antidepressant medications represent a potential alternative to treating depression, although there is a paucity of controlled studies in the context of HIV disease. Nefazodone was found to be efficacious in a 12-week, open trial of 15 HIV outpatients (Elliot et al., 1999); however, there is a potential for drug interactions between nefazodone and

Table H.1   Depression Treatments Studied in HIV-Infected Patients

Psychopharmacological treatments

Tricyclic antidepressants

Despiramine

Imipramine[a]

SSRIs

Citalopram

Fluoxetine[a]

Paroxetine[a]

Sertraline

Psychostimulants

Dextroamphetamine[a]

Methylphenidate

Pemoline

Other antidepressants

Bupropion

Mirtazapine

Modafinil

Nefazodone

Venafaxine

Nonconventional agents with antidepressant activity

Dehydroepiandrosterone (DHEA)[a]

S-adenosyl-methionine (SAM-e)

Testosterone[a]

Psychotherapeutic treatments

Brief supportive psychotherapy (individual)

Cognitive behavioral psychotherapy (group and individual)

Cognitive behavioral stress management (group[a])

Interpersonal psychotherapy (individual[a])

[a]*Treatment for which there is randomized placebo-controlled trial evidence of efficacy for depression in HIV-infected patients (Ferrando & Freyberg, 2008).*

protease inhibitors, such as efavirenz. Moreover, several cases of nefazodone-induced hepatitis have also been reported. This is of relevance to HIV patients because of the frequent comorbidity of HIV and viral hepatitis. This drug has now been withdrawn.

One study reported that mirtazapine is an efficacious antidepressant with a profile that can benefit HIV patients by promoting weight gain and also decreasing nausea (Elliot, 2000), although its sedating properties may complicate existing complaints of fatigue.

Venlafaxine has limited drug interaction effects at the level of the CYP450 enzymes, perhaps decreasing the potential interaction with antiretrovirals (Ereshefsky, 2000); however, doses should be reduced when it is used concurrently with ritonavir. Bupropion may be an alternative for anergic HIV patients because of its potential activating effects; however, HIV medications such as ritonavir, efavirenz, and nelfinavir significantly interfere with the metabolism of bupropion by inhibiting CYP450 2B6 (Hesse, von Moltke, Shader, & Greenblatt, 2001).

Overall, controlled studies are needed to further examine the effects and potential drug interactions of these new-generation antidepressants among HIV-infected individuals.

Nonconventional Agents With Antidepressant Activity

Although treatment with psychostimulants and hormonal therapies are currently still experimental, methylphenidate and dexamphetamine have shown significant reductions in depressed mood, increases in energy levels, and improved cognition (Wagner & Rabkin, 2000).

Because HIV-related reductions in testosterone are related to changes in mood, appetite, energy, and sexual dysfunction, hormonal therapies have also been employed to treat depression. Rabkin, Wagner, and Rabkin (2000) found that testosterone injections were effective in improving mood as well as libido, energy, and body muscle mass among 70 HIV hypogonadal men.

St. Johns wort should be avoided as it induces the CYP450 system and may reduce the level of antiretrovirals, with potentially serious consequences (i.e., an increase in viral load). A recent critical review on treatment of depression in HIV concluded that there is substantial literature documenting the efficacy of conventional antidepressants, particularly SSRIs, novel agents such as dehydroepiandrosterone, psychostimulants, and some psychotherapies (particularly interpersonal and group psychotherapy) for the treatment of depression in HIV. However, lack of comparative studies makes it difficult to draw a firm consensus regarding the best course of treatment. In devising a treatment plan, clinicians should take into account stage of HIV illness, comorbid illnesses such as hepatitis B and C, the potential for drug interactions with antiretroviral and other medications used to treat HIV, and patient preference (Ferrando & Freyberg, 2008).

The following general principles should be adhered to when initiating antidepressant treatment:

1. Start with a low dose and titrate according to tolerability and response.
2. Select the simplest possible dosing regime, as these patients are likely to already be on a complicated medication schedule.
3. Select an agent with the lowest risk of side effects and the fewest possible drug-drug interactions.
4. Ensure that treatment is multimodal and conducted in close consultation with the patient's primary HIV physician and the rest of the multidisciplinary team (Ayuso, 1994).

Psychotherapy

A review of treatment studies of depression in HIV by Olatunji and colleagues (2006) found that psychosocial treatment of depression in HIV appears to be effective. The review suggests that psychosocial interventions derived from a wide variety of theoretical origins are effective in treating depression among HIV-positive individuals. Social support interventions have incremental efficacy for the treatment of depression in HIV-infected individuals, as does interpersonal psychotherapy. Very few studies have compared cognitive behavioral therapy–based treatments of depression in HIV-infected individuals with other interventions in the treatment of depression in HIV-infected individuals. A systematic review and meta-analysis of double-blinded, randomized controlled trials of group psychotherapy treatment among HIV-infected with depressive symptoms suggests that group psychotherapy is efficacious in reducing depressive symptoms (Himelhoch, Medoff, & Oyeniyi, 2007).

Conclusions

Depression in HIV-positive individuals is highly prevalent and often underdiagnosed due to overlapping symptoms. Depression has a significant impact on quality of life, adherence to drug therapies, and progression of disease. A variety of psychopharmalogical and psychosocial treatments have proven efficacy in treating depression in HIV-positive individuals. Thus, early detection through routine screening for depression in HIV-positive individuals in consultation with mental health professionals is warranted.

JACQUELINE HOARE, JOHN A. JOSKA, SORAYA
SEEDAT, PAUL CAREY, AND DAN J. STEIN

See also

Comorbidity
Medical Conditions and Depression

References

American Psychiatric Association. (2000). *Diagnostic and statistical manual of mental disorders* (4th ed., text revision). Washington, DC: Author.

Atkinson J. H., Heaton, R. K., Patterson, T. L., Wolfson, T., Deutsch R., Brown, S. J., et al. (2008). Two year prospective study of major depressive disorder in HIV-infected men. *Journal of Affective Disorders, 108,* 225–234.

Ayuso, J. L., (1994). Use of psychotropic drugs in patients with HIV infection. *Drugs, 47,* 599–610.

Berger Greenstein, J. A., Cueva, C. A., Brady, S. M., Trezza, G., & Rich, M. A. (2007). Major depression in patients with HIV/AIDS and substance abuse. *AIDS Patient Care and STDs, 21,* 942–955.

Brew B. (2001). *AIDS dementia complex in HIV Neurology.* New York: Oxford University Press.

Cabaj, R. P. (1996). Management of anxiety and depression in HIV-infected patients. *Journal of the International Association of Physicians in AIDS Care, 2,* 11–16.

Cespedes, M. S., & Berg, J. A. (2006). Neuropsychiatric complications of antiretroviral therapy. *Drug Safety, 29,* 865–874.

Cherner, M., Cysique, L., Meaton, R. K., Marcotte, T. D., Ellis, R. J., Masliah, E., et al. (2007). Neuropathologic confirmation of definitional criteria for HIV associated cognitive disorders. *Journal of Neurology, 13,* 22–28.

Ciesla, J. A., & Roberts, J. E. (2001). Meta-analysis of the relationship between HIV infection and risk for depressive disorders. *American Journal of Psychiatry, 158,* 725–730.

Cole, S. W., & Kemeny, M. E. (1997). Psychobiology of HIV infection. *Critical Reviews in Neurobiology, 11,* 289–321.

Cruess, D. L., Evans, M. J., Repetto, D. G., Douglas, S. D., & Petitto, J. M. (2003). Prevalence, diagnosis, and pharmacological treatment of mood disorders in HIV disease. *Biological Psychiatry, 54,* 307–316.

DeSilva, K. E., Le Flore, D. B., Marston, B. J., & Rimland, D. (2001). Serotonin syndrome in HIV-infected individuals receiving antiretroviral therapy and fluoxetine. *AIDS, 15,* 1281–1285.

Elliot, A. J., Karina, K. K., Bergam, K., Russo, J., Claypoole, K., Uldall, K. K., et al. (1999). Antidepressant efficacy in HIV-seropositive outpatients with major depressive disorder: An open trial of nefazodone. *Journal of Clinical Psychiatry, 60,* 226–231.

Elliott, A. J., & Roy-Byrne, P. P. (2000). Mirtazapine for depression in patients with human immunodeficiency virus. *Journal of Clinical Psychopharmacology, 20,* 265–267.

Elliott, A. J., Russo, J., & Roy-Byrne, P. P. (2002). The effect of changes in depression on health related quality of life (HRQoL) in HIV infection. *General Hospital Psychiatry, 24,* 43–47.

Ereshefsky, L., & Dugan, D. (2000). Review of the pharmacokinetics, pharmacogenetics, and drug interaction potential of antidepressants: Focus on venlafaxine. *Depression and Anxiety, 12,* 30–44.

Evans, D. L., Charney, D. S., Lewis, L., Golden, R. N., Gorman, J. M., Krishnan, K. R., et al. (1997). Selective serotonin reuptake inhibitor treatment of depression in symptomatic HIV infection and AIDS. *General Hospital Psychiatry, 19,* 89–97.

Ferrando, W. S. J., & Freyberg, Z. (2008). Treatment of depression in HIV positive individuals: A critical review. *International Reviews in Psychiatry, 20,* 61–71.

Ghafouri, M., Amini S., Khalili, K., & Sawaya, B. (2006). HIV-1 associated dementia: Symptoms and causes. *Retrovirology, 3,* 1–11.

Gorman, J. M., Kertzner, R., Cooper, T., Goetz, R. R., Lagomasino, I., & Novacenko, H. (1991). Glucocorticoid level and neuropsychiatric symptoms in homosexual men with HIV infection. *American Journal of Psychiatry, 148,* 41–45.

Hesse, L. M., von Moltke, L. L., Shader, R. I., & Greenblatt, D. J. (2001). Ritonavir, efavirenz, and nelfinavir inhibit CYP2B6 activity in vitro: Potential drug interactions with bupropion. *Drug Metabolism and Disposition, 29,* 100–102.

Himelhoch, S., & Medoff, D. R. (2005). Efficacy of antidepressant medication among HIV-positive individuals with depression: A systematic review and meta-analysis. *AIDS Patient Care and STDs, 19,* 813–822.

Himelhoch, S., Medoff, D. R., & Oyeniyi, G. (2007). Efficacy of group psychotherapy to reduce depressive symptoms among HIV-infected individuals: A systematic review and meta-analysis. *AIDS Patient Care and STDs, 21,* 732–739.

Leserman, J. (2003). HIV disease progression, stress and possible mechanisms. *Biological Psychiatry, 54,* 295–306.

Leserman, J., Petitto, J. M., Gu, H., Gaynes, B. N., Barroso, J., & Golden, R. N. (2002). Progression to AIDS, a clinical AIDS condition, and mortality: Psychosocial and physiological predictors. *Psychological Medicine, 32,* 1059–1073.

Leserman, J., Petitto, J. M., Perkins, D. O., Folds, J. D., Golden, R. N., &. Evans, D. L. (1997). Severe stress, depressive symptoms, and changes in lymphocyte subsets in human immunodeficiency virus-infected men. *Archives of General Psychiatry 54*, 279–285.

Maj, M., Satz, P., Janssen, R., & Zaudig, M. (1994). WHO neuropsychiatric AIDS study, cross sectional phase 2: Neuropsychological and neurological findings. *Archives of General Psychiatry, 51*, 51–61.

Mayne, T. J., Vittinghoff, E., Chesney, M. A., Barrett, D., & Coates, T. J. (1994). Depressive affect and survival among gay and bisexual men infected with HIV. *Archives of Internal Medicine, 156*, 2223–2238.

Olatunji, B. O., Mimiaga, M. J., Cleirigh, C. O., & Safren, S. A. (2006). A review of treatment studies of depression in HIV. *Topics in HIV Medicine, 14*, 112–124.

Perkins, D. O., Leserman, J., Stern, R. A., Baum, S. F., Liao, D., & Golden, R. N. (1995). Somatic symptoms and HIV infection: Relationship to depressive symptoms and indicators of HIV disease. *American Journal of Psychiatry, 152*, 1776–1781.

Rabkin, J. G., Wagner, G., & Rabkin, R. (1999). Fluoxetine treatment for depression in patients with HIV and AIDS: A randomized, placebo-controlled trial. *American Journal of Psychiatry, 156*, 101–107.

Rabkin, J. G., Wagner, G. J., Rabkin, R. (2000). A double-blind, placebo-controlled trial of testosterone therapy for HIV-positive men with hypogonadal symptoms. *Archive of General Psychiatry, 57*, 141–147.

Tegger, M. K., Crane, H. M., Tapia, K. A., Uldall, K. K., Holte, S. E., & Kitahata, M. M. (2008). The effect of mental illness, substance use and treatment for depression on the initiation of highly active antiretroviral therapy among HIV-infected individuals. *AIDS Patient Care and STDs, 22*, 233–243.

Wagner, G. J., & Rabkin, R. (2000). Effects of dextroamphetamine on depression and fatigue in men with HIV: A double-blind, placebo-controlled trial. *Journal of Clinical Psychiatry, 61*, 436–440.

Zinkernagel, C., Taffe, P., Rickenbach, M., Amiet, R., Ledergerber, B., & Volkart, A. C. (2001).

Hypothalamic-Pituitary-Adrenal Axis

Elevated cortisol levels and hypothalamic-pituitary-adrenal (HPA) hyperactivity are found in depressed individuals at a higher rate than in the general population. Cortisol hyperactivity in depression was first identified in the 1950s and 1960s. Research over the last half century has provided much specific information with regard to the HPA abnormalities in depression. However, knowledge pinpointing the primary cause or locus of HPA alterations in depression remains elusive. Recent research identifies alterations in the glucocorticoid receptor (GR; one the two types of receptors for cortisol). However, the ultimate causes of HPA dysregulation and GR alterations in depression are likely to be multifaceted. Presented here is a brief review

of HPA axis function and recent findings on HPA alterations in depression.

Overview of HPA Axis Physiology and Cortisol Negative Feedback

Secretion of glucocorticoids from the adrenal gland is under the control of several upstream hormonal regulators, namely, corticotropin-releasing hormone (CRH) and arginine vasopressin (AVP), released from the hypothalamus, and adrenocorticotropin hormone (ACTH), released from the pituitary gland. Cortisol is the primary endogenous glucocorticoid in primates, and corticosterone is primary in rodents. Variation in glucocorticoid levels occurs as a function of many factors, including circadian variation (glucocorticoids are high in the morning and low in the evening), and in response to food intake, physical activity, and psychological stress (e.g., psychosocial threat).

One of cortisol's most important functions is in shutting down or "containing" a stress response. For instance, cortisol plays a negative feedback role in reducing its own further release. In other words, when cortisol is released into the bloodstream from the adrenal gland, the elevated blood levels of cortisol impinge upon the pituitary gland and the brain, causing a reduction in HPA-axis activity, and thus a reduction in cortisol secretion. In addition, cortisol elevations regulate sympathetic nervous system and immune activation (e.g., inflammation) during recovery from a stress response.

Cortisol is considered a stress hormone because adrenal production and secretion of cortisol occur during situations that are considered stressful. *Stress* is alternatively conceived as a pathophysiological process related to real or perceived inability to cope with environmental demands, or as an adaptation to environmental demands that promotes homeostasis. Research has associated cortisol with stress-related disease and pathology, and in popular culture, cortisol elevations are commonly thought of as harmful. Indeed, chronic cortisol elevations due to a failure to adequately regulate the HPA axis can eventually damage target tissues. However, cortisol is a life-sustaining hormone and has many essential functions that allow coping and adaptation to stressors. For instance, cortisol plays a role in metabolism by increasing availability of energy stores. Equally important are cortisol's effects on psychological functioning. Acute elevations facilitate memory formation. Chronic elevations impair many cognitive processes. The effects of glucocorticoids on many target tissues and behavioral processes follow an inverted U-shaped function in which moderate elevation of cortisol enhances functioning, while extreme or prolonged glucocorticoid elevation impairs functioning. Thus, the problem occurs when cortisol fails to restrain aspects of a stress response, including failure to contain its own activity through negative feedback.

The Nature of Glucocorticoid Alterations in Depression

Most depressed individuals are not hypercortisolemic on a daily basis. However, when examined longitudinally, depressed individuals are more likely to show elevated cortisol levels (especially in the evening) than healthy individuals. Research has established the existence of an enhanced CRH drive, and a related cortisol negative feedback deficit in a subset of individuals with major depressive disorder. In other words, research has shown both enhancement of excitatory control as well as reduced negative feedback inhibition of the HPA.

The dexamethasone suppression test (DST) was the first test used to study the negative feedback effects of cortisol. Dexamethaone (DEX) is a synthetic glucocorticoid that, acting as a negative feedback signal, suppresses ACTH secretion and thus suppresses cortisol release. The classic DST entails administration of DEX at 11:00 p.m. and measurement of cortisol levels the next day at one or more time points. Depressed individuals show an escape from the suppressive effects of DEX (i.e., fail to show suppressed cortisol levels on the day following DEX administration) at a higher rate than healthy controls.

However, the DST is a crude measure of HPA negative feedback with low sensitivity, detecting only 20% to 30% of depressed individuals (Holsboer, 2001). More sophisticated assessments have confirmed the existence of the negative feedback deficit in a larger percentage of patients with major depressive disorder. For instance, Holsboer and colleagues developed the combined DEX-CRH test, in which they measured ACTH response to CRH infusion in patients pretreated with DEX (Holsboer, 2001). On this test, pretreatment with DEX fails to restrain ACTH response to CRH administration in up to 80% of depressed patients. This test provides further evidence for a negative feedback deficit in depression (Holsboer, 2001).

HPA alteration is most prevalent in depressed individuals who have a history of childhood trauma (Heim & Nemeroff, 2001), are older, or show severe symptoms. In addition, research conducted by Schatzberg and colleagues (Belanoff, Kalehzan, Sund, Fleming Ficek, & Schatzberg, 2001) suggests that cortisol elevation is more likely to occur in depressed individuals who are psychotic, and is hypothesized to be causally related to psychotic symptoms in psychotic depression. It is also important to note that hypocortisolism (i.e., low cortisol) is sometimes found in depression, particularly in atypical depressives (Murck, 2003). The mapping between HPA alteration and depressive subtype is far from one-to-one. HPA alteration has also been found in other forms of psychopathology and stress-related pathology, including schizophrenia and posttraumatic stress disorder.

Glucocorticoid Signaling in the Brain

Cortisol crosses the blood-brain barrier and modulates activity in brain structures primarily via two types of corticosteroid receptors: mineralocorticoid receptors (MRs) and glucocorticoid receptors (GRs). Negative feedback regulation of the HPA axis is mediated both by MRs and GRs. GRs have low affinity for cortisol and are occupied only when circulating cortisol levels are high.

Therefore, the role of GRs in inhibition of the HPA axis is specific to times when circulating glucocorticoids are high. Conversely, because of MRs' high affinity for glucocorticoids, MRs are occupied when circulating levels of cortisol are low. To use an automobile analogy, MR can be thought of as keeping the system in "first gear," whereas GR put on the "brakes" when the system runs fast. Thus, MRs are important in tonic inhibition of the HPA axis.

A GR deficit has long been hypothesized to underlie the HPA negative feedback deficit in depression (Sapolsky & Plotsky, 1990). Such a GR deficit would cause inefficient return to baseline cortisol elevation following the cessation of a stressor (i.e., to use the above analogy: "faulty breaks"). An accumulation of research provides circumstantial evidence for such a GR deficit. For instance, peripheral immune cell activity is not as sensitive to the immunosuppressive effects of glucocorticoids (which are mediated by GRs) in depressed compared to healthy individuals (Pariante & Miller, 2001, for review). In fact, individuals who show escape from the suppressive effects of DEX exhibit less GR-mediated inhibition of immune activity by glucocorticoids. Furthermore, antidepressants increase GR function through a variety of mechanisms, which is associated with enhancement of HPA feedback inhibition in animals (Holsboer & Barden, 1996; Pariante, Thomas, Lovestone, Makoff, & Kerwin, 2004).

Consequently, several investigators have hypothesized that "insufficient glucocorticoid signaling" (i.e., insensitivity of target tissues to the effects of glucocorticoids) is an important aspect of major depressive disorder (Holsboer, 2001; Pariante et al., 2004). It is important to note that numerous pathways could account for reduced capacity of glucocorticoids to modulate activity in target tissues. In addition to reduced number or sensitivity of corticosteroid receptors, insufficient glucocorticoid elevation (i.e., hypocortisolism) or reduced access of glucocorticoid to its receptor (i.e., reduced bioavailability of cortisol) may also play a role in insufficient glucocorticoid signaling (Pariante et al., 2004). As mentioned

above, hypocortisolism has at times been found in depression (Murck, 2003). In addition, new evidence suggests that alterations in the blood-brain barrier reduce the bioavailability of cortisol (Pariante et al., 2004). Cortisol's access to the brain is limited by steroid transporters at the blood-brain barrier that regulate intracellular concentration of glucocorticoids by expelling the hormone back into the plasma. Variation in steroid transporter functioning has been shown to modulate activity of the HPA axis. Thus, even within the context of cortisol excess in the periphery, overactivation of steroid transporters could cause inadequate access of cortisol to the brain. This mechanism may have importance for depression. Antidepressant medications regulate cellular levels of cortisol by inhibiting steroid transporters (Pariante et al., 2004). In summary, several mechanisms in addition to reduced sensitivity or number of GRs could account for altered glucocorticoid signaling in the brain in depression.

The ramifications of data regarding glucocorticoid signaling are currently unknown. It may be the case that cortisol elevation in the periphery bathes the brain in too much cortisol, causing a "vicious cycle" with down regulation of GRs, which causes negative feedback deficits, further cortisol elevation, further down regulation of GRs and so on. This scenario is at times observed during chronic stress in animals and has been described with the glucocorticoid cascade hypothesis (Sapolsky, Krey, & McEwen, 1986). Another possible scenario entails reduced bioavailability of cortisol and reduced access of cortisol to the brain. This situation would entail elevated cortisol in the periphery paired with too little cortisol or ineffective activity of cortisol in the brain. Thus, it is currently unknown whether depression entails too much or too little cortisol "bathing" the brain. Either way, evidence suggests that insufficient glucocorticoid signaling in the brain (due either to GR down regulation or other factors) is an important aspect of depression. In sum, alterations in glucocorticoid signaling at GRs are hypothesized to underlie HPA negative feedback deficits observed in depression. Consistent with these findings, pharmacological treatments that target GRs have shown some success in the treatment of depressive symptoms. Various research groups are investigating the use of drugs that alter corticosteroid signaling as an adjunct to traditional antidepressant medication (e.g., Belanoff et al., 2002).

It should also be noted that in addition to negative feedback pathways, positive feedback loops exist through the amygdala and other brain regions, in which cortisol elevations serve to increase brain CRH and HPA activation. Thus, not all glucocorticoid effects on the brain dampen HPA activity. Positive and negative feedback circuitry operate in parallel. In addition to the deficits in HPA negative feedback described above, evidence suggests that positive feedback loops in depression may be overactive (Reul & Holsboer, 2002). Thus, positive feedback loops through the amygdala and other brain regions, which mediate enhancement of brain CRH by peripheral cortisol elevations, are hypothesized to play a role in the etiology of depression.

Lifelong Alterations in GR Gene Expression

HPA dysregulation in depression is primarily state dependent. However, it is unknown whether the hypothesized deficits in glucocorticoid signaling are state dependent or represent lifelong individual differences. Research in animals has established the existence of lifelong individual differences in GR functioning in the brain, which are a result of either inherited species differences or early environmental manipulation (Meaney et al., 1996). In rodents, early life experiences, such as maternal separation and "handling," cause lifelong effects on HPA regulation and GR function. Maternally separated rodents are taken from their mothers daily for relatively long intervals (e.g., 3 hours a day). Handling is a manipulation in which young rodents are taken away from their mothers for a short time (approximately 15 minutes a day). When compared to control rodent pups, these manipulations

cause changes in stress sensitivity and HPA-axis regulation that last through adulthood. Maternal separation causes elevated corticosteroid responses to stress and reduced tone in HPA negative feedback functioning, whereas handling has the opposite effects on HPA responses, causing salubrious effects which last into the rodents' adult life.

Michael Meaney and colleagues have performed a series of elegant studies, which have shown that the effects of handling are mediated by lifelong effects on GR gene expression (Weaver, Diorio, Seckl, Szyf, & Meaney, 2004). They have found that handled rat pups receive more attention (i.e., licking and grooming) from their mothers. This enhanced maternal care in early life permanently alters the development of GR gene expression in the hippocampus and causes reduced HPA responses to acute or chronic stress. While these early environmental conditions do not alter the DNA sequence itself, they cause epigenetic changes in the expression of transcription factors that drive GR expression. These data provide a very important example in mammals of how early life experiences can cause changes in gene expression that alter stress sensitivity into adulthood. As described above, GR functioning appears to have important ramifications for HPA dysregulation in depression. It is thus very compelling that maternal separation and handling have opposite lifelong effects on GR functioning. This animal model provides an important demonstration of how early life experiences may cause lifelong biological changes that act as a diathesis for depression.

Conclusions

Presented herein is a biologically oriented perspective arguing that alterations in GR and cortisol signaling in the brain may represent a primary causal factor in depression. However, it should be noted that psychological factors are of utmost importance with regard to HPA regulation. The HPA axis is extraordinarily sensitive to environmental factors. Psychological factors (such as perception of negative social evaluation of oneself) determine the magnitude of a stress-related cortisol response. Clinicians and investigators have long wondered whether cortisol alterations in depression are a neuroendocrine response to psychological suffering (i.e., depression causes HPA disturbance), or whether HPA hyperactivity triggers depressive symptoms (i.e., HPA disturbance causes depression). In fact, chronically elevated cortisol levels (e.g., due to a pituitary tumor as in Cushing's syndrome) can bring on aspects of depression. However, these polarized causal views are oversimplified. In general, neither cortisol alterations nor distress should be conceptualized as the primary causal factor in depression. Instead, the neural mechanisms associated with HPA dysregulation are intimately intertwined with the mechanisms that underlie psychological processes involved in major depressive disorder. Further research is needed to show how the dynamics of the HPA in depression are not merely a cause, or an effect, or an underlying feature of depression, but how they are intimately connected to the psychological features, self-disparagement, and suffering that characterize the phenomenological and behavioral aspects of depression.

HEATHER C. ABERCROMBIE

See also

Biological Models of Depression
Brain Circuitry
Cortisol
Hormones
Hypothalamic-Pituitary-Thyroid Axis

References

Belanoff, J. K., Kalehzan, M., Sund, B., Fleming Ficek, S. K., & Schatzberg, A. F. (2001). Cortisol activity and cognitive changes in psychotic major depression. *American Journal of Psychiatry, 158,* 1612–1616.

Belanoff, J. K., Rothschild, A. J., Cassidy, F., DeBattista, C., Baulieu, E. E., Schold, C., et al. (2002). An open label trial of C-1073 (mifepristone) for psychotic major depression. *Biological Psychiatry, 52,* 386–392.

Heim, C., & Nemeroff, C. B. (2001). The role of childhood trauma in the neurobiology of mood and anxiety disorders: Preclinical and clinical studies. *Biological Psychiatry, 49,* 1023–1039.

Holsboer, F. (2001). Stress, hypercortisolism and corticosteroid receptors in depression: Implications for therapy. *Journal of Affective Disorders, 62,* 77–91.

Holsboer, F., & Barden, N. (1996). Antidepressants and hypothalamic-pituitary-adrenocortical regulation. *Endocrine Reviews, 17,* 187–205.

Meaney, M. J., Diorio, J., Francis, D., Widdowson, J., LaPlante, P., Caldji, C., et al. (1996). Early environmental regulation of forebrain glucocorticoid receptor gene expression: Implications for adrenocortical responses to stress. *Developmental Neuroscience, 18,* 49–72.

Murck, H. (2003). Atypical depression spectrum disorder: Neurobiology and treatment. *Acta Neuropsychiatrica, 15,* 227–244.

Pariante, C. M., & Miller, A. H. (2001). Glucocorticoid receptors in major depression: Relevance to pathophysiology and treatment. *Biological Psychiatry, 49,* 391–404.

Pariante, C. M., Thomas, S. A., Lovestone, S., Makoff, A., & Kerwin, R. W. (2004). Do antidepressants regulate how cortisol affects the brain? *Psychoneuroendocrinology, 29,* 423–447.

Reul, J., & Holsboer, F. (2002). Corticotropin-releasing factor receptors 1 and 2 anxiety and depression. *Current Opinion in Pharmacology, 2,* 23–33.

Sapolsky, R. M., Krey, L. C., & McEwen, B. S. (1986). The neuroendocrinology of stress and aging: The glucocorticoid cascade hypothesis. *Endocrine Reviews, 7,* 284–301.

Sapolsky, R. M., & Plotsky, P. M. (1990). Hypercortisolism and its possible neural bases. *Biological Psychiatry, 27,* 937–952.

Weaver, I. C. G., Diorio, J., Seckl, J. R., Szyf, M., & Meaney, M. J. (2004). Early environmental regulation of hippocampal glucocorticoid receptor gene expression: Characterization of intracellular mediators and potential genomic target sites. *Annals of the New York Academy of Sciences, 1024,* 182–212.

Hypothalamic-Pituitary-Thyroid Axis

As early as the late 19th century, clinicians recognized that disruptions of the hypothalamic-pituitary-thyroid (HPT) axis were associated with mood disorders. The relationship between HPT-axis disruption and psychiatric morbidity has been among the most scrutinized of the endocrine axes, second only to the hypothalamic-pituitary-adrenal (HPA) axis. As HPT-axis disturbances are corrected, psychiatric symptoms also tend to abate.

The HPT axis consists of the hypothalamus, the anterior pituitary gland (adenohypophysis), and the thyroid gland. The hypothalamus, located at the base of the diencephalon, is connected with the anterior pituitary gland via the hypothalamo-hypophyseal portal vessels allowing the hypothalamic release and releasing inhibitory hormones manufactured in hypothalamic neurons to be transported vascularly in this unique venous system connecting with capillary beds that supply the anterior pituitary cells. The anterior pituitary trophic hormones in turn act upon endocrine target glands such as the thyroid gland, located anterior to the trachea and just below the larynx.

Thyrotropin-releasing hormone (TRH) is a tripeptide, discovered in 1970, secreted from nerve terminals in the median eminence of the hypothalamus that stimulates the thyrotrophs in the anterior pituitary gland to release thyroid-stimulating hormone (TSH), also known as thyrotropin. TSH, a large peptide hormone, travels via the general circulation to the thyroid gland, causing increased iodine uptake and increased synthesis and release of tri-iodothyronine (T_3) and thyroxine (T_4), the two active thyroid hormones. Once in the general circulation, T_3 and T_4 are largely bound to plasma proteins including thyroxine-binding globulin (TBG) and transthyretin. Free T_3 and T_4 are major regulators of cellular metabolism in every cell in the body. Circulating T_3 and T_4 act directly on the hypothalamus and anterior pituitary as part of a negative feedback loop to inhibit the synthesis and release of TRH and TSH, respectively, decreasing HPT-axis activity.

Reduction in the HPT axis secondary to a reduction in activity of any one of its three major components (TRH, TSH, or thyroid hormones) can lead to hypothyroidism, the decreased availability of thyroid hormone. In contrast, hyperthyroidism is defined as an increased availability of thyroid hormone. These altered thyroid states have considerable psychiatric consequences. In the general population, hypothyroidism is more prevalent than hyperthyroidism, and the first clinical symptoms are frequently psychiatric. Cognitive disturbances (such as slowed mentation and difficulty concentrating) are the most common presenting psychiatric symptoms, followed by depression. The majority of patients with hypothyroidism will exhibit some symptoms of depression, and nearly 50% will fulfill criteria for major depressive disorder.

Although hyperthyroidism is not as common as hypothyroidism, it also often presents with prominent psychiatric symptoms. Psychosis is mistakenly often cited as the most common psychiatric symptom of hyperthyroidism due largely to the outdated term *myxedema madness*. In fact, depression is the most commonly seen psychiatric symptom in hyperthyroidism, though the percentage of patients meeting criteria for a syndromal depressive disorder is not as high as in patients with hypothyroidism. Because of the historical association of hyperthyroidism and psychosis, depression is often overlooked in these patients.

As can be seen in Table H.2, primary hypothyroidism is classified in grades from grades 1 to 4, with grade 1 patients demonstrating the most severe hypothyroidism and psychiatric symptoms and grade 4 the least.

Table H.2   Classification of Primary Hypothyroidisms

Grade	T3, T4	TSH	TRH stimulation test	Antithyroid antibodies
1	$\Downarrow$	$\Uparrow$	$\Uparrow$	+
2	Normal	$\Uparrow$	$\Uparrow$	+
3	Normal	Normal	$\Uparrow$	+
4	Normal	Normal	Normal	+

- Grade 1: (classic primary hypothyroidism) increased basal serum TSH, decreased basal serum thyroid hormone concentrations, and an increased TSH response to TRH in the TRH stimulation test
- Grade 2: basal serum thyroid hormone concentrations are normal, increased basal serum TSH concentrations, and an increased TSH response to TRH in the TRH stimulation test
- Grade 3: detectable only by an increased TSH response to TRH in the TRH stimulation test; basal serum thyroid hormone and TSH concentrations normal
- Grade 4: (symptomless autoimmune thyroiditis) all measures of HPT axis function normal, but antithyroglobulin and/or antimicrosomal thyroid antibodies present

TRH stimulation test abnormalities have also been repeatedly observed in patients with major depression. Nearly 25% of euthyroid patients with major depression exhibit a blunted TSH response to TRH. One proposed explanation for this blunting is chronic hypersecretion of TRH from the median eminence of the hypothalamus leading to a down regulation of anterior pituitary TRH receptors and a reduced thyrotroph response to exogenous TRH. In support of this hypothesis are reports that cerebrospinal fluid (CSF) concentrations of TRH are elevated in patients with major depression. There is some specificity in these observations in that elevated CSF TRH concentrations have *not* been observed in patients with Alzheimer's disease, anxiety disorders, anorexia nervosa, or alcohol dependence. In contrast to the blunted TSH response to TRH noted above, 15% of depressed patients exhibited an exaggerated TSH response to TRH stimulation, and these patients were found to have grades II to IV hypothyroidism. Indeed, depressed patients as a group show higher rates of autoimmune thyroiditis than the general population.

Grade 2 hypothyroidism has been linked to an increased susceptibility to major depressive disorder. Furthermore, subclinical hypothyroidism in the elderly seems to increase the risk for depression substantially.

Patients with hypothyroidism also demonstrate alterations in regional cerebral blood flow (rCBF), a proxy for changes in regional neural activity. One study demonstrated correlations of thyroid state with changes in rCBF using positron emission tomography (PET). In this study, [O15] water was used to measure rCBF and [F18] 2-deoxy-2-fluoro-D-glucose was used to measure glucose uptake, another proxy of neural activity. Ten patients with thyroid carcinoma scheduled for thyroidectomy were studied prior to surgery when euthyroid, and again postoperatively when hypothyroid. These second scans revealed a profound depression in brain activity as compared to the initial scans. Regions where this reduction was seen included the right primary motor cortex, posterior cingulate, fusiform gyri, insula, and right parietooccipital cortex. Interestingly, postthyroidectomy patients also demonstrated significant depression, anxiety, and psychomotor slowing. It is important, however, to consider this as a pilot study, and the results may have been influenced by a myriad of factors including severity of intentionally untreated hypothyroidism and preexisting depression, and the presence of neoplastic disease.

A 2004 study obtained MRI and single photon emission computed tomography (SPECT) imaging in 10 mildly hypothyroid patients and 10 healthy controls. SPECT scans were obtained in hypothyroid patients in both the hypothyroid and euthyroid state (within 4–43 days, as evidenced by normalized plasma TSH concentrations). A persistent and significant reduction in rCBF was observed in the hypothyroid patients even when euthyroid. Areas in the brain demonstrating decreased rCBF included posterior cingulate, right primary motor cortex, fusiform gyri, right parietooccipital cortex, and insula. The observed alterations in regional brain activity may contribute to the emotional and/or cognitive alterations noted in mildly hypothyroid patients.

Genetic links between depression and hypothyroidism have been postulated as well.

A cohort study of adoptees noted a possible association between increased susceptibility for major depressive disorder and genetic polymorphisms in the Xq13 thyroid receptor coactivator HOPA. Thyroid hormone signal transduction is partially regulated by this gene.

The most obvious line of treatment to emerge from the link between the HPT axis and depression is the use of thyroid hormone to augment antidepressant treatment. Indeed, early studies appeared quite promising. In 1969, a seminal study demonstrated that thyroid hormone supplementation increased the rapidity of onset of tricyclic antidepressants (TCAs). Later research found T_3 augmentation as effective as lithium in converting TCA nonresponders to responders. Of note, T_3 is appreciably superior to T_4 in this regard.

The selective serotonin reuptake inhibitors (SSRIs) have largely supplanted the TCAs as the most widely prescribed class of antidepressants. Augmentation of SSRIs with thyroid hormone (T_3) has been studied. In the large multicenter STAR*D trial of antidepressant effectiveness, 142 patients who failed citalopram treatment and subsequently failed a medication switch or augmentation were randomized to receive lithium (900 mg/day) or T_3 (50 µg/day). T_3 was superior to lithium in augmentation; 24.7% of patients in the T_3 arm attained clinical remission, whereas only 11.8% of patients in the lithium arm attained remission, though most investigators consider the lithium dose used in this study suboptimal. Other studies support these findings. In contrast, a double-blind, placebo-controlled trial showed no distinct advantage of 25 or 50 µg/day of T_3 augmentation with the SSRI paroxetine. Although efficacy of T_3 augmentation was subsequently demonstrated in a multisite, double-blind, placebo-controlled trial with sertraline, our group failed to demonstrate any such advantage. Of note, the mean dose of sertraline administered in our study was 153 mg/day, considerably higher than that of the first study in which the mean dose was 100 mg/day.

Finally, augmentation of antidepressants with both T_3 and T_4 has also been studied. This combination of the two thyroid hormones appeared to improve results on both neuropsychological and mood scales. When T_4 dose was reduced in all patients and T_3 added, 78% (seven of the nine) patients showed significant improvement. A follow-up randomized study of 33 patients also showed improvement in both cognitive function and mood scales when T_4 was augmented with T_3. However, recent placebo-controlled studies have failed to show clinically significant improvement of T_3 augmentation in patients treated with T_4.

TRH has also been studied as an antidepressant. However, research has been relatively limited, and the majority of the trials (conducted in the 1970s and 1980s) yielded few encouraging results.

There is sufficient evidence of both HPT-axis dysfunction in depression and therapeutic utility of thyroid hormone augmentation to merit continued investigation of the role of this important system in depressive disorders. Undiagnosed hypothyroidism remains one of the leading causes of treatment-refractory depression. Future research efforts should focus on better identification of those patients who would clearly benefit from a thyroid-hormone augmentation strategy. Second-generation antipsychotics are gaining recognition for their utility in converting antidepressant nonresponders to responders. The role of thyroid-hormone augmentation in combination with these medications remains unexplored. As our knowledge of the HPT axis and its role in depression continues to increase, much promise exists for further diagnostic and therapeutic development.

ELIZABETH DEOREO AND
CHARLES B. NEMEROFF

See also

Biological Models of Depression
Brain Circuitry

Hypothalamic-Pituitary-Thyroid Axis Thyroid Function

References

Gillespie, C. F., Garlow, S. J., Schatzberg, A. F., & Nemeroff, C. B. (in press) Biology of mood disorders. In A. F. Schatzberg and C. B. Nemeroff (Eds.), *Textbook of psychopharmacology* (4th Ed.). Washington: American Psychiatric Press, Inc.

Musselman, D. L., & Nemeroff, C. B. (1996). Depression and endocrine disorders: Focus on the thyroid and adrenal system. *British Journal of Psychiatry, 168,* 123–128.

Prange, A. J., Lara, P. P., Wilson, I. C., Alltop, L. B., & Breese, G. R. (1972). Effects of thyrotropin-releasing hormone in depression. *Lancet, ii,* 999–1002.

I

Immune System

Depression has been linked to a variety of chronic medical conditions, including heart disease, stroke, Alzheimer's disease, diabetes, some cancers, obesity, arthritis, and osteoporosis. The prevalence of depression among patients with these conditions is generally higher than the prevalence of depression in the general population (10.3%; Kessler et al., 1994). Furthermore, depression has been shown to exacerbate and increase mortality from many of these conditions. For example, depression has been shown to hasten the onset of heart disease as well as to increase the risk of dying following a heart attack. Given its emerging prominence as a risk factor, researchers have begun to explore the underlying pathophysiological processes that depression may share with these conditions. Immune system dysregulation is one important link that connects depression to poor medical outcomes.

The immune system, once thought to operate relatively autonomously within the body, is now known to communicate closely with the central nervous system via both hormonal pathways and direct connections between nerves and immune organs. Thus, it is plausible that affective states, such as depression, could influence immune system function. Further, there is increasing evidence that the paths of communication are bidirectional; the immune system can convey information to the central nervous system just as the central nervous system can signal the immune system (Maier & Watkins, 1998).

The immune system's primary means of communication is via the release of cytokines, a group of molecules that regulate immune function and also act as messengers between the immune system and the brain. The immune system can be divided into two arms: innate or nonspecific immunity, and adaptive or specific immunity. The innate arm of the immune system responds to all invaders in a similar way and does not need prior exposure to a pathogen in order to be effective. This is often thought of as the body's first line of defense. Part of this innate system of defense is inflammation. Inflammation is a set of specific changes initiated in response to infection or tissue damage and can occur anywhere in the body. Inflammation is regulated by pro-inflammatory cytokines (e.g., IL-1β, IL-6, and TNF-α). These molecules attract immune cells toward the infection, induce them to divide, and activate proper function. Researchers can assess the amount of inflammation in the body by measuring levels of one or more of these cytokines. In addition, inflammation is supported by the release of acute-phase proteins, such as C-reactive protein, from the liver. Since this protein is produced in response to IL-6, its levels can be used as a marker of inflammation. Although it is possible to measure the degree of inflammation taking place, these molecules do not indicate *where* in the body the inflammation is occurring.

Inflammation has been identified as the underlying pathogenic process involved in several diseases, such as heart disease, stroke, Alzheimer's, obesity, diabetes, and arthritis.

These diverse conditions arise due to the body's inability to regulate inflammation in a variety of contexts. Although inflammation is important for fighting infections and repairing damaged tissue, it can become harmful when it is directed against the body's own tissues, when these tissues become "collateral damage" in the immune system's fight against invading organisms, or when the inflammatory response is not turned off once the infection or injury is under control. For example, heart disease is a result of the buildup of atherosclerotic plaque in the coronary arteries. Recent insights have shown these atherosclerotic plaques to be sites of active, ongoing inflammation within the artery walls, rather than a passive accumulation of excess cholesterol. The role of inflammation is highlighted by the fact that levels of a marker of inflammation, C-reactive protein, can predict heart attack risk as well if not better than cholesterol levels (Libby, 2002). So although inflammation was once associated primarily with infectious diseases like pneumonia or influenza, it is now believed to contribute to many of the leading causes of death and disability, even though a specific infectious agent may not be involved.

Persistent, unregulated inflammation has also been associated with depression. Among medically healthy adults suffering from clinical depression, levels of pro-inflammatory cytokines and C-reactive protein were increased by 40% to 50% compared to matched adults not suffering from depression (Miller, Stetler, Carney, Freedland, & Banks, 2002). A recent meta-analysis also showed that IL-6 concentrations were reliably higher among depressed individuals (Zorilla et al., 2001). Another synthesis of the published literature showed that depression was associated with higher levels of white blood cells involved in inflammation: neutrophils and monocytes (Herbert & Cohen, 1993). Together, these two reviews suggest that while inflammation is increased during depression, the other arm of the immune system, adaptive (specific) immunity, is deceased during depression. For example, immune cells that need to be triggered by specific pathogens, such as natural killer cells and T lymphocytes, are reduced in number and are weaker in function during depression. Thus, the excess inflammation seen during depression is not just a result of an overall immune activation but is an increase in one division of the immune system at the expense of the other.

The path between depression and immune changes may be bidirectional in nature. An emerging body of evidence suggests that at least some forms of depression are due to immune system activation (namely, increases in proinflammatory cytokines), although causality has not been demonstrated definitively in humans. In animal models, administration of immune stimulants has been shown to elicit the behavioral signs of depression, such as reduced food intake and weight loss, reduced motor activity and social exploration, and altered sleep patterns. The same symptoms arise in roughly 50% of cancer patients who are treated with cytokines in an attempt to stimulate their immune systems, and this depressogenic effect can be reversed if these patients take antidepressants prophylactically. Thus, it cannot be concluded with certainty that any observed changes in immunity are a *result* of depression, given the predominance of cross-sectional studies in the literature and the evidence cited above. Even if future research finds that changes in immunity do not precede most episodes of depression, they may kick off a vicious cycle during which the symptoms of depression are perpetuated due to immune activation.

Depression is more prevalent during a variety of serious medical conditions, including heart disease—the leading cause of death in the United States. Well-controlled studies have shown that this is not merely a function of the stress associated with a life-threatening illness. Dysregulation of inflammatory processes appears to underlie many of these diseases, including depression. Although it is currently unclear which comes first, the depression or the inflammation, this issue may be less critical than understanding how affective states are linked to immune processes occurring elsewhere in the body. Answers to these questions may produce innovative treatments for some of the leading causes of death facing society.

CINNAMON STETLER

See also

Human Immunodeficiency Virus
Medical Conditions and Depression

References

Herbert, T. B., & Cohen, S. (1993). Depression and immunity: A meta-analytic review. *Psychological Bulletin, 113*, 472–486.

Kessler, R. C., McGonagle, K. A., Zhao, S., Nelson, C. B., Hughes, M., Eshleman, S., et al. (1994). Lifetime and 12-month prevalence of DSM-III-R psychiatric disorders in the United States. Results from the National Comorbidity Survey. *Archives of General Psychiatry, 51*, 8–19.

Libby, P. (2002). Atherosclerosis: The new view. *Scientific American, 286*, 46–55.

Maier, S. F., & Watkins, L. R. (1998). Cytokines for psychologists: Implications of bidirectional immune-to-brain communication for understanding behavior, mood, and cognition. *Psychological Review, 105*, 83–107.

Miller, G. E., Stetler, C. A., Carney, R. M., Freedland, K. E., & Banks, W. A. (2002). Clinical depression and inflammatory risk markers for coronary heart disease. *American Journal of Cardiology, 90*, 1279–1283.

Zorilla, E. P., Luborsky, L., McKay, J. R., Rosenthal, R., Houldin, A., Tax, A., et al. (2001). The relationship of depression and stressors to immunological assays: A meta-analytic review. *Brain, Behavior, and Immunity, 15*, 199–226.

Insomnia

Occasional bouts of insomnia are of little consequence to a healthy adult; however, insomnia appears to be particularly problematic for those who are vulnerable to psychological problems or who have a comorbid psychological disorder such as clinical depression. In the following sections we review what is known about the relationship between depression and insomnia, focusing specifically on the role of insomnia in the etiology and course of depression, issues related to treatment of depressed individuals with sleep problems, and possible implications of insomnia for relapse.

Epidemiology

Although occasional nights of insomnia are common, clinically significant insomnia is less common. Epidemiological studies show that in the general population approximately 6% to 12% report chronic problems initiating or maintaining sleep (Ford & Kamrerow, 1989). The prevalence of insomnia in those with major depressive disorder is estimated to be 90% (Mendelson, Gillin, & Wyatt, 1977) and is also likely to be high in other mood disorders such as dysthymia. The prevalence of comorbid insomnia also appears to change across the life span and is even higher in older adults. These epidemiological data indicate that insomnia is nearly always present in individuals with depression. Thus, it is important to carefully assess insomnia symptoms in patients with depression.

Diagnostic Criteria for Insomnia

Systems for classifying sleep disorders are presented in the *Diagnostic and Statistical Manual of Mental Disorders* (*DSM-IV*; American Psychiatric Association, 1994), in the *International Classification of Sleep Disorders Revised* (*ICSD-R*; American Academy of Sleep Medicine, 2001), and by the American Academy of Sleep Medicine (AASM). Each of these nosological systems classifies insomnia as a form of dyssomnia, or a disorder associated with getting too much or too little sleep. Insomnia is the most common dyssomnia and can be characterized as difficulty initiating sleep (early insomnia), difficulty maintaining sleep (middle insomnia), waking too early (terminal insomnia), or nonrestorative sleep despite adequate opportunity for sleep. In addition to a sleep-complaint these classification systems specify that clinically significant insomnia is also characterized by impairment in one or more area of daily living, and the common consensus is that symptoms must be present for at least 1 month. In recent years, there has been growing interest in further classifying the nature of sleep-related complaints. The AASM Work Group (Edinger et al., 2004) has proposed nine standard subtypes of insomnia to build on current definitions and has proposed that insomnia be further specified according to duration (acute or chronic), severity (mild, moderate, or severe), and presentation (sleep onset or sleep maintenance).

Objective sleep data are not necessary to diagnose insomnia, and the discrepancy between objective and subjective sleep may be high. Overall, individuals with insomnia tend to underestimate their total sleep time (Means, Edinger, Glenn, & Fins, 2003). Individuals who consistently report poor or little sleep despite normal polysomnography (PSG) findings have been described as having sleep-state misperception or paradoxical insomnia, and the nature of these sleep-related complaints is not entirely understood. Current measures of sleep may be inadequate in quantifying these individual's problems, or their symptoms may reflect other factors.

Assessment of Insomnia

Assessment of insomnia may be made by clinical interview. Diagnostic interviews should include all of the following information: symptoms, duration, frequency, and severity, other contributing factors (e.g., medication, substance use, psychological or medical disorders, environmental factors), and the presence of other sleep disorders should also be ruled out (see for best-practice assessment, Buysee, Ancoli-Israel, Edinger, Lichstein, & Morin, 2006). Insomnia symptoms can be assessed using a variety of assessment devices including structured interviews, self-report questionnaires, and sleep diaries. Sleep diaries are useful in assessing sleep hygiene and are often used in conjunction with treatment. Objective measures of sleep include actigraphy and PSG. An actigraph is a small wrist-worn device used to detect movement during sleep. Actigraphy has been validated against PSG with normal sleepers but may be less reliable in distinguishing between quiet wake and sleep. Nevertheless, actigraphy remains a useful and cost-effective adjunct to subjective measures. PSG is not routinely used in the assessment of insomnia but may be useful in

research settings to characterize specific sleep parameters (sleep onset latency or number of arousals) and should be used when the presence of other sleep disorders (e.g., sleep apnea or restless leg syndrome) are suspected.

The Role of Insomnia in the Etiology of Depression

The high comorbidity of depression and insomnia have led some to theorize that insomnia may have a causal role in the onset of depression. Insomnia symptoms often precede the onset of a depressive episode. Large, prospective epidemiological studies that control for a wide variety of demographic and health-related confounds have shown that chronic insomnia increases the risk of developing psychiatric disorders including major clinical depression. In fact, a recent meta-analysis documented that a person with insomnia is at 3.95 to 39.8 times higher risk of developing a mood disorder than someone without chronic sleep difficulties (Taylor, Lichstein, & Durrence, 2003).

Insomnia and Depression: Linked Processes

The high comorbidity of depression and insomnia has led to theories that insomnia is related to depression in the following ways: as a causal agent, a diathesis, or that depression and insomnia share a common cognitive antecedent.

Insomnia and Mood

One obvious pathway between insomnia and depression is through changes in mood. Insomnia has been found to be related to higher daily negative affect, sleepiness and fatigue, and lower positive affect and feelings of alertness (Buysee et al., 2007). Reduced sleep has been linked to more dysphoric affect, and chronic sleep deprivation is likely to be more troubling than acute sleep problems (Hamilton et al., 2008). Hamilton showed that multiple nights of experimental partial sleep deprivation produce a progressively worsened mood. Thus, across populations and research methodologies, sleep appears to have a direct prospective relationship with mood and emotional health.

Sleep and Stress

Sleep also appears to interact with the stress process and may serve as a cognitive resource. Adequate sleep serves as a biobehavioral resource that facilitates adaptive responses to stress and limits alostatic load. Consistent with these formulations, medical residents who were not able to obtain adequate sleep were found to have a heightened stress-response as well as reduced enjoyment of intellectually challenging tasks (Zohar, Tzischinsky, Epstein, & Lavie, 2005). Chronic pain patients with disrupted or inadequate sleep were more vulnerable to pain-related changes in mood (Hamilton et al., 2008). Furthermore, among patients with chronic pain, shorter sleep times inhibited full affective recovery from stress. Thus, insomnia may not have a direct effect on mood. Instead, insomnia may limit enjoyment of cognitively stimulating events while enhancing the emotional salience of, and preventing recovery from, negative events or unpleasant physical symptoms such as pain.

Cognitive Arousal, the Third Variable

In contrast with the previous models that postulate either a direct or indirect causal role for insomnia in the onset of depression, cognitive models of insomnia suggest that insomnia and depression are activated and maintained by similar cognitive processes. Cognitive arousal in the form of worry and excessive rumination about sleep, fear of the consequences of inadequate sleep, and unrealistic expectations about sleep are proposed to play a causal role in insomnia (Morin, Rodrigue, & Ivers, 2003). Excessive negatively oriented cognitive activity triggers both autonomic arousal and emotional distress.

The resulting anxious state is thought to trigger selective attention toward, and monitoring of, internal and external sleep-related threat cues. The combination of the anxious state and the attentional processes that are triggered by this state cause the individual to overestimate the extent of the perceived deficit in sleep and daytime performance. This process may explain why insomnia patients cannot always be differentiated from healthy sleepers using polysomnography. The unfortunate consequence of this process is that the excessive and escalating anxiety may cause a real deficit in sleep and daytime functioning.

Many of the cognitive processes involved in insomnia are also associated with depression and suggest a common cause. A number of studies have found that poor sleepers tend to engage in rumination about their sleep-related problems (Carney, Edinger, Meyer, Lindman, & Istre, 2006). Rumination is also a major cognitive risk factor for depression. It is thought that people with a high ruminative tendency may be especially vulnerable to depression when experiencing sleep disturbance because the mood symptoms associated with poor sleep could activate the ruminative process. Further, people with chronic insomnia tend to focus on their somatic symptoms as well as the consequences and daytime symptoms of their chronic sleep difficulties.

The causal association between cognitive processes in insomnia and risk for depression, however, is unclear. It is possible that cognitive arousal that results from sleepiness is itself a stressor that might trigger depressive episodes. Or, lack of restful sleep might magnify the appraisal of negative events, and fatigue might increase feelings of loss and helplessness that result in depression. Cognitive arousal, however, can also be a consequence of the depressive state. Careful longitudinal research would be needed to fully untangle causes from effects.

Although different in terms of the causal precedence assigned to cognition, emotion, sleep disturbance, and depression, these models illustrate the importance of attending to insomnia symptoms as a possible method to prevent the onset of a depressive episode. The next section focuses on the importance of attending to both insomnia and depression in the course of treatment.

Depression, Insomnia, and Intervention

The presence of insomnia may place a depressed patient at greater risk for negative outcomes. For instance, depressed patients with insomnia symptoms appear to be more impaired than those without insomnia. When depressed primary care patients with insomnia symptoms were compared to depressed patients without insomnia, patients with depression and insomnia reported more than twice the number of days in which social and occupational activities were limited because of illness (Simon & Von Korff, 1997). Insomnia may also indicate an increased risk for suicidality (Arargun et al., 2007). Clinicians should carefully assess insomnia symptoms in patients with depression. The presence of insomnia also presents an added risk factor for patients with depression. Thus, it is important to evaluate treatment modalities as they relate to the course of both insomnia symptoms and depression.

Cognitive behavioral therapy (CBT) has been repeatedly validated as an effective treatment for both unipolar depressive disorders and insomnia. In fact, in randomized controlled trials, CBT produces either similar or larger effect sizes than most antidepressants for both the treatment of depression and insomnia and has more stable long-term results.

Similar to CBT for depression, CBT for insomnia (CBT-I) has been used effectively with a variety of populations with insomnia, including those in which insomnia is comorbid with various medical and psychiatric conditions. CBT-I has repeatedly been found to be more effective than pharmacological treatment of insomnia (e.g., Edinger, Wohlgemuth, Radtke, Marsh, & Quillian, 2001). CBT-I is a modification of CBT for depression and therefore has similar therapeutic content and focus, although specific treatment is tailored to sleep disturbance (Perlis, Jungquist, Smith, & Posner, 2005). For example, both CBT for depression and CBT-I target cognitive distortions and false beliefs. Additionally, both treatments include relaxation training and behavioral therapy that focuses on the areas of deficit. CBT-I differs from CBT in that it also includes behavioral interventions such as sleep-restriction and sleep hygiene that are specific to insomnia.

Given the observed comorbidity of depression and insomnia, and similarity in recommended treatment course, it may not be surprising that treating one disorder will often lead to improvements in the other. For instance, treatment of insomnia has been found to improve treatment outcomes for depression (Smith, Huang, & Manber, 2005).

Although insomnia often disappears when depression is treated, sleep is physiologically abnormal in persons at risk for depression, and sleep disturbances frequently persist after remission of other depressive symptoms. In fact, insomnia is the most persistent residual symptom following treatment of depression and is present in approximately 44% of treatment completers (Nierenberg et al., 1999). The persistence of insomnia after a depressive episode may indicate a continued vulnerability to depression, with patients being at risk for poorer clinical outcomes and higher rates of relapse. Thus, clinicians should be vigilant in treating both depression and insomnia.

Despite empirical findings that CBT-I is the most effective long-term treatment for insomnia, medication usage is extremely common, with the most commonly prescribed medications being sedatives, hypnotics, and antidepressants. Historically, sedatives (barbiturates and benzodiazepines) and hypnotics (benzodiazepinelike agents and ethanol) have been the most commonly prescribed; however, these medications often cause daytime sleepiness, tolerance, and dependence. Thus, the number of sedatives and hypnotics prescribed for insomnia has decreased over the past 30 years.

The effects of antidepressant medications on sleep vary according to medication class. Tricyclic antidepressants (TCAs) are well known to produce side effects such as sedation and thus are often used as treatments for insomnia. However, TCAs are not uniform in how they affect sleep (see for a review of antidepressant medications on sleep physiology, Winokur et al., 2001). Amitriptyline, doxepin, and nortriptyline, have been shown to reduce sleep-onset latency, improve the ability to remain asleep (sleep continuity), increase deep restorative sleep, and reduce REM sleep. Impirimine, desipramine, and clomipramine increase sleep-onset latency, may reduce continuity, but appear to increase the amount of deep restorative sleep and reduce REM sleep. In contrast, commonly used selective seratonin-reuptake inhibitors (SSRIs) such as fluoxetine, paroxetine, and sertraline appear to increase nighttime awakenings and also suppress REM sleep. Monoamine oxidase inhibitors, seratonin receptor modulators, and other classes of antidepressants also have been documented to affect the ability to fall asleep, stay asleep, and feel refreshed the next day. Given the documented effects of insomnia on treatment response and relapse rates, it is imperative for clinicians working with depressed patients to investigate whether patients' medication regimens are improving or worsening insomnia symptoms.

Paradoxical Effects of Sleep Restriction

The link between insomnia and depression has been clearly established. Sleep disruption increases vulnerability to depression, and treatment of insomnia often improves depressive symptoms. Paradoxically, total sleep deprivation produces temporary but significant improvements in approximately 60% of all patients with affective disorders (Wu & Bunney, 1990). Even higher rates of improvement are observed among patients with melancholic unipolar depression, among those with diurnal mood variability, and among those who have experienced only a single episode of depression. Unfortunately, the observed improvement in mood is transient and usually dissipates after a night of recovery sleep. In terms of treatment, however, there are some indications that even a single night of sleep deprivation may speed the therapeutic response to antidepressant medications for individuals with depression.

Although the effects of sleep deprivation are well documented and reliable, the phenomenon of mood improvement is not well understood. It has been theorized that the effects of sleep deprivation on improved mood are mediated by changes to the hypothalamic-pituitary-adrenal axis (Wu & Bunney, 1990). Specifically, sleep restriction may increase secretion of growth hormone (hGh) and decrease secretion of cortisol. More recently, this theory was substantiated by laboratory studies showing that total sleep deprivation produces a significant decrease in circadian cortisol levels, increases in hGH during the recovery night, and also changes variability in both cortisol and hGH. Thus, total sleep deprivation may ameliorate depressive symptoms via the effects on the stress response.

Other theories focus on the effects of the serotonin system. Using nonhuman animal models, it has been documented that chronic partial sleep deprivation gradually reduces the sensitivity of the serotonin-1A autoreceptors (Roman, Hagewoud, Luiten, & Meerlo, 2006). However, a single night of total sleep deprivation appears to decrease the sensitivity of presynaptic serotonin-1A autoreceptors, which ultimately increases the availability of serotonin within the synapse.

It is well documented that temporary sleep restriction immediately, albeit temporarily, relieves depression. Although sleep-restriction cannot be used for prolonged periods of time, clinical applications of sleep restriction warrant further study. Investigation of this phenomenon may lead to further understanding of the neurochemical profiles associated with both depression and insomnia.

Summary and Conclusions

The exact mechanism linking insomnia to depression is unknown. Although epidemiological data clearly show that insomnia often precedes onset of major depression, it is not known whether insomnia is part of the causal chain or whether it is a prodromal symptom or early warning sign. Nevertheless, it is possible that early intervention with insomnia could prevent onset of depression. More clear is the role of insomnia in the course of major depression. The data clearly indicate that successful treatment of depression does not always lead to remission of insomnia symptoms. Addition of CBT-I or referral of a patient to therapist that specializes in CBT-I may be an important aspect of relapse prevention that has not been fully appreciated by many depression researchers.

NANCY A. HAMILTON, CYNTHIA KARLSON,
DAVID D. LUXTON, CHRISTY NELSON,
AND NATALIE R. STEVENS

See also

Circadian Rhythms
Stressful Life Events

References

American Academy of Sleep Medicine. (2001). *International classification of sleep disorders, revised: Diagnostic and coding manual*. Rochester, Minnesota: Author.

American Psychiatric Association. (1994). *Diagnostic and statistical manual of mental disorders* (4th ed.). Washington, DC: Author.

Arargun, M. Y., Besiroglu, L., Cilli, A. S., Gulec, M., Aydin, A., Inci, R., et al. (2007). Nightmares, suicide attempts, and melancholic features in patients with unipolar major depression. *Journal of Affective Disorders, 98,* 267–270.

Buysee, D. J., Ancoli-Israel, S., Edinger, J. D., Lichstein, D. L., & Morin, C. M. (2006). Recommendations for a standard research assessment of insomnia. *Sleep, 29,* 1155–1173.

Buysee, D. J., Thompson, W., Scott, J., Franzen, P. L., Germain, A., Hall, M., et al. (2007). Daytime symptoms in primary insomnia: A prospective analysis using ecological momentary assessment. *Sleep Medicine, 8,* 198–208.

Carney, C. E., Edinger, J. D., Meyer, B., Lindman, L., & Istre, T. (2006). Symptom focused rumination and sleep disturbance. *Behavioral Sleep Medicine, 4,* 228–241.

Edinger, J. D., Bonnet, M. H., Bootzin, R. R., Doghramji, K., Dorsey, C. M., Espie, C. A., et al. (2004). Derivation of research diagnostic criteria for insomnia: Report of an American Academy of Sleep Medicine Work Group. *Sleep, 27,* 1567–1596.

Edinger, J. D., Wohlgemuth, W. K., Radtke, R. A., Marsh, G. R., & Quillian, R. E. (2001). Cognitive behavioral therapy for treatment of chronic primary insomnia. *Journal of the American Medical Association, 285,* 1856–1864.

Ford, D. E., & Kamrerow, D. B. (1989). Epidemiological study of sleep disturbances and psychiatric disorders. *Journal of the American Medical Association, 262,* 1479–1484.

Hamilton, N., Affleck, G., Tennen, H., Karlson, C., Luxton, D., Preacher, K. J., et al. (2008). Fibromyalgia: The role of sleep in affect and in negative event reactivity and recovery. *Health Psychology, 27,* 490–497.

Means, M. K., Edinger, J. D., Glenn, D. M., & Fins, A. I. (2003). Accuracy of sleep perceptions among insomnia sufferers and normal sleepers. *Sleep Medicine, 4,* 285–296.

Mendelson, W. B., Gillin, J. C., & Wyatt, R. D. (1977). *Human sleep and its disorders*. New York: Plenum Press.

Morin, C. M., Rodrigue, S., & Ivers, H. (2003). Role of stress, arousal, and coping skills in primary insomnia. *Psychosomatic Medicine, 65,* 259–267.

Nierenberg, A. A., Keefe, B. R., Leslie, V. C., Aplert, J. E., Pava, J. A., Worthington, J. J., et al. (1999). Residual symptoms in depressed patients who respond acutely to fluoxetine. *Journal of Clinical Psychiatry, 60,* 221–225.

Perlis, M. L., Jungquist, C., Smith, M. T., & Posner, D. (2005). *Cognitive behavior treatment of insomnia: A session-by-session guide*. New York: Springer.

Roman, V., Hagewoud, R., Luiten, P. G., & Meerlo, P. (2006). Differential effects of chronic partial sleep deprivation and stress on serotonin-1A and muscarinic acetylcholine receptor sensitivity. *Journal of Sleep Research, 15,* 386–394.

Simon, G. E., & Von Korff, M. (1997). Prevalence, burden, and treatment of insomnia in primary care. *American Journal of Psychiatry, 154,* 1417–1423.

Smith, M. T., Huang, M. T., & Manber, R. (2005). Cognitive behavior therapy for chronic insomnia occurring within the context of medical and psychiatric disorders. *Clinical Psychology Review, 25,* 559–592.

Taylor, D. J., Lichstein, K. L., & Durrence, H. H. (2003). Insomnia as a health risk factor. *Behavioral Sleep Medicine, 1,* 227–247.

Winokur, A., Gary, K. A., Rodner, S., Rae-Red, C., Fernando, A. T., & Szuba, M. P. (2001). Depression, sleep physiology, and antidepressant drugs. *Depression and Anxiety, 14,* 19–28.

Wu, J. C., & Bunney, W. E. (1990). The biological basis of an antidepressant response to sleep deprivation and relapse: Review and hypothesis. *American Journal of Psychiatry, 147,* 14–21.

Zohar, D., Tzischinsky, O., Epstein, R., & Lavie, P. (2005). The effects of sleep loss on medical residents' emotional reactions to work events: A cognitive-energy model. *Sleep, 28,* 47–54.

Internal Working Models

The idea of an internal working model was proposed by Bowlby (1980). Internal working models are seen as so-called cognitive-interpersonal blueprints that form the basis of how interpersonal interactions are to be processed and interpreted. These blueprints encompass implicit beliefs about the self and others, along with procedural rules and knowledge for processing information and determining behavioral, emotional, and verbal responses to interpersonal situations. This knowledge also includes internal representations of the self and others, expectations for self and others in interactions, rules for assigning meaning to the behavior of self and others, and tendencies for the selection of information and how information is encoded, stored, and retrieved. In theory, such blueprints are developed through generalizations that are abstracted from real or perceived regularities in past experience, frequently from past experience with important attachment figures (Bowlby, 1969). Internal working models thus form a link between past interpersonal experiences and current interactional patterns.

Westen (1991) points out that these internal working models function outside conscious awareness and constitute a powerful basis for determining numerous facets of interactional patterns. These models shape how, and with who, new relationships are formed, as well as how one interprets information and interacts within these relationships. For example, the woman who as a child experienced a sexually inappropriate stepfather will have certain expectations for how men will behave when she is an adult and will behave accordingly. Conversely, the woman with a caring and appropriate father will interpret interactions with men in a very different fashion.

These models lead to reciprocal interpersonal interactions and create self-fulfilling prophecies in the case of unhealthy models. Hence, the person with an internal working model that leads to the perception and prediction of hostility from others will not only perceive hostility in messages where there is none, but will respond accordingly with anger and hostility. Repeated interactions with such a person might ultimately elicit hostility from others, which reinforces and strengthens the working model and leads to a dysfunctional and reciprocal interpersonal cycle of perceived and actual hostility. Because there are blueprints for interactions, these cogni-

tive and interpersonal cycles will be repeated with many people who enter the person's life, regardless of the context of the interaction (academic, business, interpersonal). The internal working models idea suggests that these cycles are due to powerful cognitive maps that operate beyond ordinary awareness and, as such, are very difficult to modify in the event that they are dysfunctional.

RICK E. INGRAM

See also

Attachment
Schemas

References

Bowlby, J. (1969). *Attachment and loss, Vol. 1: Attachment.* New York: Basic Books.
Bowlby, J. (1980). *Attachment and loss, Vol. 3: Loss: Sadness and depression.* New York: Basic Books.
Westen, D. (1991). Social cognition and object relations. *Psychological Bulletin, 109,* 429–455.

Internalizing Disorders

Reynolds (1992) described internalizing disorders in children and adolescents as "a class of disorders that are considered to be inner-directed, in which core symptoms are associated with overcontrolled behaviors" (p. 1). The term *internalizing*, ironically, was not born out of a disorder-based classification scheme, but rather from an empirical approach to understanding the organization of children's emotional and behavioral symptoms. Over time, those disorders whose symptoms were related to these dimensions became referred to as *internalizing disorders*. Internalizing disorders are generally conceptualized as emotional disorders that cause distress for the youth, as opposed to externalizing disorders, which are often described as behavioral disorders that result in distress for others. Internalizing disorders have been said to include anxiety, mood, psychosomatic, eating, gender identity, and psychotic disorders, the most prevalent of which are anxiety and mood disorders in child and adolescent populations. Internalizing problems not specific to particular disorders include suicidal behavior and social problems. Internalizing problems, including subclinical problems, can impede development across multiple domains and may negatively impact family relationships, academic achievement, and social functioning (Reynolds, 1992).

Epidemiology

Rates of internalizing disorders vary by disorder and developmental stage. Epidemiological studies estimate anxiety disorder prevalence rates to be 7% to 21% in school-aged child and adolescent community populations. Separation anxiety disorder, generalized anxiety disorder, specific phobias, and social phobia are the most common anxiety disorders in youths. Rates of depressive disorders in school-age children and adolescents range from 1.8% to 18%. Age differences account for much of the observed variability in prevalence rates; younger child populations tend to exhibit lower rates of internalizing disorders than older adolescent populations (Albano, Chorpita, & Barlow, 2003; Hammen & Rudolph, 2003; Kovacs & Devlin, 1998).

Internalizing disorders, particularly anxiety and depressive disorders, are frequently comorbid in clinical samples, although internalizing disorders, to a lesser extent, may co-occur with externalizing disorders as well. The commonly observed comorbidity may be an artifact of current diagnostic categories and symptom overlap or developmental level, rather than representative of discrete problem areas within the individual. In other words, children with multiple disorders may suffer from a common underlying psychopathology that expresses itself in a number of different symptom patterns. Some evidence suggests that youths with comorbid conditions display greater symptom severity and functional impairment.

Anxiety disorders onset in early childhood more frequently than depressive disorders, while depressive disorders typically onset during adolescence. Onset of anxiety precedes the onset of depressive disorders in the large majority of youths with comorbid anxiety and depression. Factors hypothesized to explain the observed difference in age of onset between anxiety and depressive disorders include biological constraints, cognitive development, social feedback, and learning history.

Gender differences exist in rates of internalizing disorders, with females displaying higher rates of internalizing disorders and males exhibiting higher rates of externalizing disorders. The pattern of gender differences, however, varies by specific disorder and, in those where differences emerge, tends to become more pronounced as children reach adolescence. The greatest differences have been observed for the rates of depressive disorders in adolescents, with girls being more likely to be depressed than boys. Explanations of gender differences include hormonal differences, biological sex, differences in affiliative needs and socialization experiences, higher rates of sexual assault experienced by females, and the tendency for females to utilize rumination and passive coping skills more frequently than males (Hammen & Rudolph, 2003).

Common Factors

Research suggests that personality traits and temperaments characterized by high levels of negative affectivity, neuroticism, negative emotionality, or behavioral inhibition may underlie both anxiety and depressive disorders. Individuals with high levels of negative affect may have temperamental difficulty regulating negative mood states and thus respond sensitively to stress and negative life events.

The tripartite model of emotion serves as a theory to explain the relationship between anxiety and depression. The model posits three main factors: negative affect (i.e., general distress), positive affect (i.e., enthusiasm and energy), and physiological hyperarousal (i.e., activity of the autonomic nervous system).

According to the model, lack of positive affect is specific to depressive disorders, high levels of physiological arousal are specific to most anxiety disorders, and high levels of negative affect are common to both anxiety and depressive disorders. The tendency for the onset of anxiety disorders to precede the onset of depressive disorders and the tendency for youths with depressive disorders to also have an anxiety disorder, but for anxiety disorders to occur without depressive disorders is consistent with some of the fundamental assumptions of the tripartite model. Specifically, negative affectivity can be construed as a developmentally constant trait, which expresses itself more often as anxiety early in development and later can manifest as depression.

Etiology

Present theories regarding the etiology of internalizing disorders consider complex and dynamic interplays between biological or genetic vulnerability, psychological vulnerability, and environmental factors (e.g., early learning experiences). Genetic vulnerability may produce neurobiological deficits in stress regulation, and negative life events coupled with chronically elevated levels of stress may serve to further elevate risk for internalizing disorders. General psychological vulnerabilities, such as the perception of events as outside one's control, can interact with early learning experiences to shape or color subsequent experience, thus perpetuating a pathogenic cycle for internalizing disorders (Barlow, 2000; Chorpita, 2001).

Caregivers provide a salient source of early learning experiences for children, and certain parenting styles are associated with higher rates of internalizing disorders in children and adolescents. Inconsistent and overprotective parenting styles, particularly in combination with low caregiver sensitivity and warmth, are correlated with an external locus of control and increased rates of anxiety and depression. Overprotective parenting may reduce opportunity for the child to develop skills and a sense of control over the environment, while inconsistency and lack of caregiver warmth may diminish a sense of control over parental reinforcement.

Future Directions

Identification of internalizing disorders in youths can be particularly challenging because many of the symptoms may not be directly observable to external sources and may, therefore, remain unrecognized for long durations. Failure to recognize internalizing disorders and to intervene early may contribute to the persistence of internalizing problems and impairment throughout the lifespan. Given the subjective and covert nature of internalizing problems, children are often considered the preferred informants of symptoms, whereas parents and teachers are often more reliable sources of information regarding externalizing disorders (Reynolds, 1992).

More research, particularly longitudinal study of the development and course of internalizing disorders in nonclinical samples, is needed to develop, support, and enhance integrated models of etiology. A clearer and more thorough knowledge of the early stages, signs, and predictors of internalizing disorders may enhance early identification, treatment, and prevention of internalizing disorders in children and adolescents.

NICOLE K. STARACE AND
BRUCE F. CHORPITA

See also

Externalizing Disorders

References

Albano, A. M., Chorpita, B. F., & Barlow, D. H. (2003). Childhood anxiety disorders. In E. Mash & R. Barkley (Eds.), *Child psychopathology* (pp. 279–329). New York: Guilford Press.

Barlow, D. H. (2000). Unraveling the mysteries of anxiety and its disorders from the perspective of emotion theory. *American Psychologist, 55,* 1247–1263.

Chorpita, B. F. (2001). Control and the development of negative emotion. In M. Vasey & M. Dadds (Eds.), *The developmental psychopathology of anxiety* (pp. 112–142). New York: Oxford University Press.

Hammen, C., & Rudolph, K. D. (2003). Childhood mood disorders. In E. Mash & R. Barkley (Eds.), *Child psychopathology* (pp. 233–278). New York: Guilford Press.

Kovacs, M., & Devlin, B. (1998). Internalizing disorders in childhood. *Journal of Child Psychology and Psychiatry, 39*, 47–63.

Reynolds, W. M. (1992). The study of internalizing disorders in children and adolescents. In W. Reynolds (Ed.), *Internalizing disorders in children and adolescents* (pp. 1–18). New York: Wiley.

Interpersonal Model of Depression

The interpersonal approach to depression focus on interactional patterns as a primary source of the onset and maintenance of depression. The interpersonal approach to depression also serves as the theoretical foundation of an approach to the treatment of depression (see Interpersonal Psychotherapy in this encyclopedia).

The interpersonal model stems from two historical foundations. As Gotlib and Schraedley (2000) have noted, the first can be found in the work of the Harry Stack Sullivan and Adolph Meyer in the 1950s. Unlike the predominant psychoanalytic models of the day, which located the causes of psychopathology in interpersonal factors such as psychic conflicts and unacceptable impulses, interpersonal models suggested that psychopathology was caused in large part from problematic interpersonal interactions.

The second historical foundation of the interpersonal model can be seen in the evolution of the behavioral approach to psychology, which in the case of application to depression, also evolved to some degree in opposition to cognitive models of depression (Hammen, 1999). Unlike the cognitive model, which also locates the primary source of depression in internal factors such as cognitive models, the interactional approach suggests that behaviors within an interpersonal context are important in the genesis of depression. Whereas the work of the interpersonal theorists of the 1950s introduced the idea of an interpersonal context in psychopathology, the behavioral roots of this approach

as seen in a paper by Coyne (1976) applied similar ideas to the more specific area of psychopathology as seen in depression.

Cause of Depression

The initial formulation of the interpersonal model seen in Coyne's (1976) work focused more on factors that maintain than cause the depressed state. Subsequently, however, a number of researchers have suggest possible causal mechanisms that are rooted in an interpersonal perspective. For example, Sacco (1999) suggested that a negative view of oneself is caused by others viewing the person in a negative fashion. Such a view is reminiscent of Mead's (1934) "looking glass" hypothesis, which suggests that self-views are formed in response to feedback from, and the perception of, other people.

In a similar fashion, Hammen (1999) has argued for the relevance of attachment style in setting the stage for depression. Attachment theory argues that a fundamentally and biologically motivated need for individuals is the connection with others. When these connections are problematic in childhood or adolescence, they may create a vulnerability for later depression. In particular, they form the basis of a template for how interactions are conceptualized, which can lead to the misinterpretations of interactions and provide a heightened sensitivity to criticism. In the case of depression, these negative self-views prime the person to experience depression when interpersonal problems arise. Most notably, it may be that interpersonal criticism is a key event in this causal process. The causes of depression thus arise by a self-view that misinterprets interactions with others as critical of the self, and/or the very real criticism that the person encounters.

Maintenance of Depression

Perhaps the greatest strength of the interpersonal model is its description of the processes that maintain depression. The model argues that once depressed, the person seeks out reassurance from significant others. Although they may initially be supportive, the positive effects are either short-lived or the depressed person doubts the authenticity of the support. In either event the depressed person then seeks out more support, with similar effects. At some point, significant others begin to withdraw or become critical, which leads to an intensification of reassurance-seeking from the depressed person. Hence a dysfunctional cycle becomes engaged, consisting of support-seeking, withdrawal, and more support-seeking and withdrawal.

Summary

Arising from interpersonal psychiatry in the 1950s and the evolution of the behavioral approach to psychology, interpersonal theories place the emphasis for depression on the interpersonal context—the interactional patterns and pitfalls of the depressed person. Although the initial formulations of an interpersonal perspective did not emphasize causal processes, subsequent examinations of the perspective have suggested that interpersonal processes may create vulnerability wherein the individual is particularly sensitive to criticism, either misperceived or real. The maintenance of depression is embodied in a dysfunctional cycle of support-seeking and, eventually, rejection. Although the origins of this approach are over 50 years old, in its contemporary incarnation, the interpersonal model represents a major and important psychosocial perspective on depression.

RICK E. INGRAM

See also

Interpersonal Psychotherapy

References

Coyne, J. (1976). Toward and interactional description of depression. *Psychiatry, 39,* 28–40.

Gotlib, I. H., & Schraedley, P. K. (2000). Interpersonal psychotherapy. In C. R. Snyder & R. E. Ingram (Eds.), *Handbook of psychological change: Psychotherapy processes and practice for the 21st century* (pp. 258–279). New York: Wiley.

Hammen, C. (1999). The emergence of an interpersonal approach to depression. In T. Joiner & J. C. Coyne (Eds.), *The interactional nature of depression* (pp. 21–35). Washington, DC: American Psychological Association.

Mead, G. H. (1934). *Mind, self, and society.* Chicago: University of Chicago Press.

Sacco, W. P. (1999). A social-cognitive model of interpersonal processes in depression. In T. Joiner & J. C. Coyne (Eds.), *The interactional nature of depression* (pp. 329–362). Washington, DC: American Psychological Association.

Interpersonal Psychotherapy

Interpersonal Psychotherapy (IPT) is a time-limited psychotherapy specified in a manual (Weissman et al., 2000, 2007) and tested in numerous clinical trials that have established its efficacy. Initially developed for adult patients with depression, it has been adapted for adolescents and the elderly with depression, medical patients, and pregnant and postpartum depressed women, and for dysthymia and bipolar depression. It has been tested as acute and as maintenance treatment for depression. The most exciting recent work has been the successful adaptation and testing in Uganda for adults and adolescents with depression (Bolton et al., 2003). IPT has been translated into French, German, Italian, and Spanish. International training and studies are ongoing in China, Japan, Goa, Thailand, United Kingdom, Spain, Sweden, Ethiopia, and numerous other countries. There is an International Society of Interpersonal Psychotherapy (http://www.inter personalpsychotherapy.org/). Designed for administration by experienced and trained mental health professionals including physicians, psychologists, social workers, and nurses, it can also be taught to less-trained persons. IPT has been used with and without medication. The primary example of IPT presented here illustrates the treatment of patients with major depressive disorder because that is its best-established and most widely employed use.

IPT is built on the idea that the symptoms of depression have multiple causes, genetic and environmental, but the symptoms do not arise in a vacuum. Depressive symptoms are usually associated with something going on in the patient's current personal life, usually in association with people they feel close to.

Some common events include the following:

- A marriage breaks up.
- A dispute threatens an important relationship.
- A spouse has an affair.
- A job is lost or in jeopardy.
- A move to a new neighborhood is made.
- A loved one dies.
- A promotion or demotion occurs.
- A person retires.
- A medical illness is diagnosed.

Understanding the social and interpersonal context of the development of the depression may help to unravel the immediate reasons for the symptoms. This can be the first step in helping the patient to understand depression as an illness and to develop new ways of dealing with people and situations. Developing these new social skills may help treat the current episode and reduce future vulnerability.

The IPT therapist views depression as having three parts:

1. *Symptoms.* The emotional, cognitive, and physical symptoms of depression include depressed and anxious mood, difficulty concentrating, indecisiveness, pessimistic outlook, guilt, sleeping and eating disturbances, loss of interest and pleasure in life, fatigue, and suicidality.
2. *Social and Interpersonal Life.* The ability to get along with other important people in the patient's life (e.g., family, friends, work associates). Social supports protect against depression, whereas social stressors increase vulnerability for depression.
3. *Personality.* There are enduring patterns with which people deal with life: how they

assert themselves, express their angers, maintain their self-esteem, and whether they are shy, aggressive, inhibited, or suspicious. These interpersonal patterns may contribute to developing or maintaining depression.

Some therapists begin by trying to treat a person's personality difficulties and see personality as the underlying cause of depression. The IPT therapist does not try to treat personality and, in fact, recognizes that many behaviors that appear enduring and lifelong may be a reflection of the depression itself. Patients may seem dependent, self-preoccupied, and irritable while depressed, yet when the depression lifts, these supposedly lasting traits also disappear or recede.

The thrust of IPT is to try to understand the interpersonal context in which depressive symptoms arose and how the symptoms relate to the current social and personal context. The IPT therapist looks for what is currently happening in the patient's life ("here and now" problems) rather than problems in childhood or the past.

Progress in genetics and the neurosciences has made psychotherapy an even more important therapeutic tool in psychiatry. Psychiatric disorders are genetically complex syndromes, comparable to diabetes and hypertension, in which genes and environment are both important and interact. The genotype, influenced by the environment, is expressed in the phenotype (the clinical picture).

For psychiatric disorders, the most important environment consists of close personal attachments. These connections, their availability, and their disruption (or threat of disruption) can powerfully influence the emergence of symptoms (phenotype expression), especially in genetically vulnerable individuals. Situations in which these disruptions can be found and where symptoms may erupt have been defined as the focal problem areas in IPT:

- Grief (complicated bereavement)
- Interpersonal role disputes

- Interpersonal role transitions
- Interpersonal deficits (paucity of attachments)

IPT is used with patients who develop symptoms in association with these situations. Genetic vulnerability cannot be readily altered, but the environment can. Symptoms can improve with the clarification, understanding, and—especially—handling of these interpersonal situations associated with symptom onset. Psychotherapy can be crucial to this change. Evidence has shown that this paradigm works for major depression in patients of all ages.

A Brief Outline of IPT

Initial Sessions

Throughout these sessions, the therapist simultaneously works to establish a positive treatment alliance: listening carefully, eliciting affect, helping the patient to feel understood by identifying and normalizing feelings, and providing support, encouragement, and psychoeducation about depression.

Diagnosing Depression

Review the depressive symptoms or syndrome. Assist the patient's symptoms and their severity. Use the *Diagnostic and Statistical Manual of Mental Disorders,* fourth edition (*DSM-IV;* American Psychiatric Association, 1994) to help the patient understand the diagnosis. Use a scale such as the Hamilton Depression Rating Scale or the Beck Depression Inventory to help the patient understand the severity and the nature of his or her symptoms. Explain what the score means, and alert the patient that you will be using the scale regularly to see how treatment is progressing.

Give the syndrome a name: "You are suffering from major depression."

Explain depression as a medical illness, and explain its treatment. Depression is a treatable illness, and not the patient's fault. Despite its symptom of hopelessness, depression has a good prognosis.

IPT is a time-limited treatment that focuses on the relationship between interactions with other people and how the patient is feeling. The patient will be meeting for X weekly sessions (define the number), and the patient has a good chance of feeling better soon.

Give the patient the "sick role": "If there are things you can't do because you're feeling depressed, that's not your fault: You're ill." However, the patient has a responsibility to work *as* a patient to get better.

Evaluate the Patient's Need for Medication

Relate depression to an interpersonal context by reviewing with the patient his or her current and past interpersonal relationships. Explain their connection to the current depressive symptoms. Determine with the patient the "interpersonal inventory," which includes the following:

- Nature of interaction with significant persons
- Expectations of the patient and significant persons (differentiate them from one another and discuss whether these were fulfilled)
- Satisfying and unsatisfying aspects of the relationships
- Changes the patient wants in the relationships

Identify a focal problem area: grief, role disputes, role transitions, or interpersonal deficits.

- Determine the problem area related to current depression, and set the treatment goals.
- Determine which relationship or aspect of a relationship is related to the depression and what might change in it.

Explain the IPT concepts and contract. Outline your understanding of the problem, linking illness to a life situation in a formulation: "You're suffering from depression, and that seems to have something to do with what's going on in your life. We call that (complicated bereavement, a role dispute, etc.). I suggest that we spend the next X weeks working on solving that difficult life crisis. If you can solve that problem, your depression is likely to lift as well."

Agree on treatment goals and determine which problem area will be the focus. Obtain the patient's explicit agreement on the focus.

Describe the procedures of IPT. Focus on current issues and the need for the patient to discuss important concerns, review the patient's current interpersonal relations, discuss the practical aspects of the treatment (length, frequency, times, fees, policy for missed appointments).

Intermediate Sessions: The Problem Areas

With the patient's agreement to your formulation, you will enter the middle phase of treatment and spend all but the final few sessions working on one of the four IPT problem areas: grief, role dispute, transitions, or deficits. During this time do the following:

- Maintain a supportive treatment alliance: listen and sympathize.
- Keep the treatment centered on the focus, as your treatment contract specified you would.
- Provide psychoeducation about depression, where appropriate, to excuse the patient for low energy, guilt, and so on.
- Explore for affect.
- Focus on interpersonal encounters and how the patient handled them:
  - What the patient felt.
  - What the patient said.
  - If things went well, congratulate the patient, and reinforce adaptive social functioning.
  - If things went badly, sympathize and explore other options.
  - In either case, link the patient's mood to the interpersonal outcome.
- Role play interpersonal options.

- Summarize the sessions at their end.
- Regularly (e.g., every 3–4 weeks) repeat the depression measure to assess symptom severity.

Termination

The third phase of IPT is the termination phase, in which the progress of the previous sessions is reviewed. Discuss with the patient what has been accomplished and what remains to be considered. Address termination several weeks before it is actually scheduled. If the patient remains symptomatic, consider another course of treatment, such as maintenance IPT, the addition of medication, a different medication, or a different kind of psychotherapy.

For further description of this adaptation for different populations, disorders, and format, see Weissman and colleagues (2000, 2007). For training opportunities, consult the International Society of IPT Web site.

Myrna Weissman

See also

Bereavement
Cognitive Behavioral Therapy
Interpersonal Model of Depression

References

American Psychiatric Association. (1994). *Diagnostic and statistical manual of mental disorders* (4th ed.). Washington, DC: Author.

Bolton, P., Bass, J., Neugebauer, R., Clougherty, K. F., Verdeli, H., Wickramaratne, P. J., et al. (2003). Group interpersonal psychotherapy for depression in rural Uganda. A randomized controlled trial. *Journal of the American Medical Association, 289,* 3117–3124.

Weissman, M. M., Markowitz, J. C., & Klerman, G. L. (2000). *Comprehensive guide to interpersonal psychotherapy.* New York: Basic Books.

Weissman, M. M., Markowitz, J. C., & Klerman, G. L. (2007). *A clinician's quick guide to interpersonal psychotherapy.* New York: Oxford University Press.

Intrusive Memory

Many patients with depression, like those with posttraumatic stress disorder (PTSD), experience unwanted memories of one or more significant events in their lives that intrude frequently into their minds. These memories are vivid, distressing, absorbing, and associated with intense negative emotions. Most research has concerned unipolar depression, but recent research suggests intrusive memories are also a feature of bipolar disorder (Tzemou & Birchwood, 2007). In studies to date, the proportion of depressed unipolar patients reporting intrusive memories has varied from 44% to 87%. Typically, frequency of intrusions (and the amount of effort put into blocking them out) is related to depression severity, so that intrusions are more likely to be a feature of severe depression.

The first systematic study of intrusive memories focused on memories of child abuse in depressed female patients (Kuyken & Brewin, 1994). Intrusions were more likely when the abuse had been more severe. Typical features of depressive cognition such as lower self-esteem, a more negative attributional style, and the use of avoidant coping were strongly related to the amount memories of this abuse intruded. In contrast they were much less strongly related to the simple fact of whether or not abuse had occurred. This suggests that a lot of depressive thinking may be fuelled by the presence in the consciousness of repeated reminders of sad, frustrating, or humiliating events, rather than by depressed mood itself. Consistent with this idea, high levels of intrusive memories were found to be associated with low self-esteem regardless of how depressed patients were (Kuyken & Brewin, 1999).

Kuyken and Brewin (1995) also found that greater attempts to avoid intrusive memories of abuse were related to overgeneral memory recall on the Autobiographical Memory Test (AMT). Overgeneral memory is another well-established feature of depressive thinking whereby the depressed struggle to recall specific autobiographical events in response to cue words such as *happy* or *lonely*. This finding of a link between intrusive memories and overgeneral recall has since been replicated a number of times. One possible explanation is that the effort involved in avoiding intrusions reduces the available capacity to perform the AMT. Another is that overgeneral memory recall is a defensive strategy designed to prevent the retrieval of upsetting personal memories. Both these explanations have been discussed in detail by Williams and colleagues (2007).

Subsequent research has investigated whether intrusive memories are really a product of depression or simply of being exposed to a large number of upsetting events. It has been shown that intrusive memories are much more frequent in people who are depressed than in individuals exposed to a similar number or type of stressors. Further, the intrusions are not a permanent feature of vulnerable individuals but begin with or are exacerbated by an episode of depression (Brewin, Watson, McCarthy, Hyman, & Dayson, 1998). Critically, the presence of frequent intrusive memories has been found to predict the course of the disorder even when initial symptoms are controlled for. These findings suggest not just that intrusive memories are centrally involved in the experience of depression, but that they can be an important maintaining factor (Brewin, Reynolds, & Tata, 1999).

Since then we have learned that whereas intrusive memories of personal illness, injury, or assault are somewhat more common in PTSD, memories of death, illness, or injury to family members, and memories of interpersonal problems, are more common in depression (Birrer, Michael, & Munsch, 2007; Reynolds & Brewin, 1999). Although intrusive memories tend to be somewhat less common and less intense in depression than in PTSD, when they do occur they are equally distressing, and there are few qualitative differences between them. For example, both groups tend to report some degree of reliving past experiences, as well as accompanying physical sensations. Whereas intrusions in depression are usually experienced as ordinary autobiographical memories that belong in the past, in PTSD they are more likely to have a "here and now" quality ("flashbacks") and be linked to an out-of-body experience

(Birrer et al., 2007; Reynolds & Brewin, 1999). These differences are probably due to the fact that, compared with depressed patients, PTSD patients experience higher levels of dissociation (Patel et al., 2007), resulting in distortions of time and place that are reflected in their intrusive memories.

Recent evidence suggests that intrusive memories in depression are often part of a network of related representations. In Patel and colleagues' (2007) study, just over half the patients in the sample who received psychological treatment reported experiencing additional intrusive memories, as their original, main intrusion began to subside. The number of new memories ranged between two and three, with the thematic component being similar to the dominant intrusion. For example, two patients reported childhood sexual abuse as their main intrusion. During treatment both patients reported experiencing additional intrusive memories of incidents of teenage and/or adult sexual abuse, intrusions that had not been present during the original assessment. This emphasizes that single assessments may not capture all aspects of a memory network associated with a depressive episode.

The observations concerning intrusive memories in depression are consistent with the claims of many social psychologists that knowledge about the self does not just exist in a generalized, semantic form (cf., trait knowledge about the worthlessness of the self), but in the form of episodic memories of specific autobiographical events. Such events (e.g., a child being told by a parent that he or she was not wanted) may form "turning points" that help to define or provide evidence for the conclusions about the self at which depressed patients may have arrived. Thus, asking about intrusive memories can furnish important clues about how the person's history is related to current depressive symptoms and negative styles of thinking.

Apart from their theoretical importance in understanding the nature of negative self-representations in depression, the presence of intrusive memories suggests that novel forms of therapy such as imagery rescripting may be relevant to a subset of depressed patients. Imagery rescripting involves having patients focus on the contents of their intrusive memory and imagine an alternative, more positive outcome that they have previously generated and rehearsed with their therapist. Typically this involves a strong sense of mastery or compassion that replaces feelings of helplessness or shame associated with the memories. In contrast to standard cognitive-behavioral methods, rescripting can be implemented purely through imagery and without any cognitive challenging of negative beliefs or behavioral experiments. A recent article describes two patients with major depressive disorder who were successfully treated with a short course of imagery rescripting and remained well at 1 year follow-up (Wheatley et al., 2007). Rescripting produced a rapid and powerful experience of increased positive affect that arguably would have been difficult to achieve using traditional methods.

CHRIS R. BREWIN

See also

Memory Processes
Posttraumatic Stress Disorder

References

Birrer, E., Michael, T., & Munsch, S. (2007). Intrusive images in PTSD and in traumatised and non-traumatised depressed patients: A cross-sectional clinical study. *Behaviour Research and Therapy, 45,* 2053–2065.

Brewin, C. R., Reynolds, M., & Tata, P. (1999). Autobiographical memory processes and the course of depression. *Journal of Abnormal Psychology, 108,* 511–517.

Brewin, C. R., Watson, M., McCarthy, S., Hyman, P., & Dayson, D. (1998). Intrusive memories and depression in cancer patients. *Behaviour Research and Therapy, 36,* 1131–1142.

Kuyken, W., & Brewin, C. R. (1994). Intrusive memories of childhood abuse during depressive episodes. *Behaviour Research and Therapy, 32,* 525–528.

Kuyken, W., & Brewin, C. R. (1995). Autobiographical memory functioning in depression and reports of early abuse. *Journal of Abnormal Psychology, 104,* 585–591.

Kuyken, W., & Brewin, C. R. (1999). The relation of early abuse to cognition and coping in depression. *Cognitive Therapy and Research, 23,* 665–677.

Patel, T., Brewin, C. R., Wheatley, J., Wells, A., Fisher, P., & Myers, S. (2007). Intrusive images and memories in major depression. *Behaviour Research and Therapy, 45,* 2573–2580.

Reynolds, M., & Brewin, C. R. (1999). Intrusive memories in depression and post-traumatic stress disorder. *Behaviour Research and Therapy, 37,* 201–215.

Tzemou, E., & Birchwood, M. (2007). A prospective study of dysfunctional thinking and the regulation of negative intrusive memories in bipolar 1 disorder: Implications for affect regulation theory. *Psychological Medicine, 37,* 689–698.

Wheatley, J., Brewin, C. R., Patel, T., Hackmann, E. A., Wells, A., Fisher, P., et al. (2007). "I'll believe it when I can see it": Imagery re-scripting of intrusive sensory memories in depression. *Journal of Behavior Therapy and Experimental Psychiatry, 38,* 371–385.

Williams, J. M. G., Barnhofer, T., Crane, C., Hermans, D., Raes, F., Watkins, E., et al. (2007). Autobiographical memory specificity and emotional disorder. *Psychological Bulletin, 133,* 122–148.

K

Kindling

Kindling is the increased behavioral and electrophysiological responsivity to repeated intermittent stimulation of the brain with initially subthreshold and subconvulsant stimulation, usually of the amygdala, that comes to evoke full-blown major motor seizures (Goddard & Douglas, 1975). It forms a useful nonhomologous animal model for several components of the course of recurrent affective disorders (Post, 2007a, 2007b). Instead of electrical stimulation of the brain inducing major motor seizures in classical kindling, the parallel processes in the affective disorders are recurrent stressors eventually evoking full-blown affective episodes.

A number of components of the longitudinal evolution of the kindling process make it a very interesting analogy for affective illness evolution.

1. Initial stimulations may not evoke a notable electrophysiological or behavioral response.
2. With repetition, the threshold for electrical responsivity in the amygdala, for example, decreases, and local spiking on the EEG (afterdischarges) become manifest.
3. With further repetitions, the after-discharges spread first unilaterally and then bilaterally throughout the brain and are accompanied by a progression of seizurelike phenomena from head-nodding and behavioral arrest to unilateral and then bilateral forepaw-twitching, and ultimately major motor seizures with rearing and falling.

4. Following sufficient numbers of stimulations evoking full-blown seizures, seizures can begin to emerge spontaneously without an exogenous electrophysiological trigger.
5. The kindling process involves the induction of immediate early- and late-effector genes, with alterations in peptides and neurotrophic factors leading to a state of permanent increased excitability, such that the occurrence of a previous subconvulsant stimulation will evoke a full-blown seizure even a year after the initial kindling process.
6. Pharmacological interventions for preventing kindling development versus full-blown seizures versus spontaneous seizures are differential, with some agents being effective in one phase of kindling evolution, but not another.
7. Interestingly, activation of the brain-derived neurotrophic factor (BDNF) pathway via stimulation of its Trk B receptors is essential to the kindling process; if Trk B receptors are knocked out, the animals do not kindle (He et al., 2004).

These elements of kindling evolution mirror many aspects of affective evolution in which initial episodes of both unipolar and bipolar depression are often associated with psychosocial stressors, but with sufficient numbers of repetitions, these can also begin to emerge spontaneously. Data reported by Kessing, Andersen, Mortensen, and Bolwig (1998) also demonstrate a progressive increased vulnerability to episode occurrence and a shorter latency as a function of number of prior hospitalizations for either unipolar or bipolar depression. Moreover, they have seen that increased numbers of depressions (four or more) are associated with an increased risk of cognitive decline and dementia occurring in late life.

Thus, the kindling model provides a framework for considering how stresses may leave behind long-lasting memory traces (Goddard & Douglas, 1975; Post, 1992), such that their recurrence could evoke increasing behavioral and neurobiological responsivity, and, as well, how affective episodes might progress from the triggered variety to more spontaneous occurrences even in the absence of stressors. Kraepelin (1921) originally noted that many episodes of unipolar and bipolar illnesses were associated with psychosocial stress, but with enough recurrences, began to occur in their absence. These phenomena have now been generally replicated in the clinical literature (Kendler, Thornton, & Gardner, 2000, 2001), and the parallel occurrence in the kindled seizure model provides a readily reproducible paradigm for exploring some of the potential molecular mechanisms involved.

However, the caveat must be emphasized that the progressive emergence of minor to major seizures, and then their conversion from triggered to spontaneous, may be occurring in very different neurochemical substrates from those involved in the affective disorders, which obviously have completely different characteristics (Weiss & Post, 1994). While seizures occur over a period of seconds to minutes, affective episodes occur over a period of weeks to months and do not involve a convulsive process. Nonetheless, some of the principles of kindling evolution may also be pertinent to affective disorder evolution, including that the pharmacology may differ as a function phase of kindling evolution, and what may prevent the early development of affective episodes may not be the same as what prevents full-blown episodes or even those that occur more spontaneously. It should also be noted that the kindling model does not posit that affective episode progression is irrevocable and relentless, as it refers only to the course of illness in a subgroup of patients with no or inadequate treatment. At any juncture in illness progression, episodes can be stopped with appropriate maneuvers.

We have also seen tolerance develop to repeated administration of effective anticonvulsants in full-blown kindled seizures, and this is of interest in relationship to recent observations of a proportion of patients with recurrent affective episodes who show initial excellent and sustained periods of complete pharmacoprophylaxis of their affective disorders but then begin to experience the eventual reemergence of episodes in a tolerancelike process. The kindling model provides a number of hints about factors that may be relevant, because tolerance in the kindling model is slowed by use of higher rather than minimal doses of the drug, by treatment earlier in the course of full-blown seizures rather than after a great many have occurred, and combination treatment is more effective in slowing tolerance than monotherapy.

Interestingly, once tolerance has occurred, a period of amygdala-stimulation evoking seizures in the absence of the drug is sufficient to reverse the tolerance process, and animals again become responsive to the initial treatment (Post, 2007b; Weiss, Clark, Rosen, Smith, & Post, 1995). A few case vignettes suggest that this may also occur in clinical epilepsy and in the affective disorders once tolerance has occurred. However, the kindling model makes a clear set of predictions that discontinuing ongoing effective treatment would have very different consequences from discontinuing a treatment to which an individual has already become tolerant. In the former case we have observed that about 10% to 15% of highly treatment-refractory patients referred to the NIMH for lithium-nonresponsiveness appeared to acquire this problem after long periods of wellness with continuous lithium treatment, but discontinued treatment, experienced new episodes, and then failed to rerespond to lithium once it was reinstituted (Post, Leverich, Altshuler, & Mikalauskas, 1992). This process could be understood from the perspective that not only are new episodes engendering additional pathological processes in a kindlinglike process, but also that lithium discontinuation is associated with loss of a variety of neurotrophic and neuroprotective effects (Chuang et al., 2002) that could render an episode recurrence more pernicious in terms of its neurochemical consequences (Post, Speer, Hough, & Xing, 2003).

The term *kindling* generally encompasses another behavioral and/or pharmacological phenomenon, that of behavioral sensitization to psychomotor stimulants. In this instance, animals show increased behavioral reactivity (hyperactivity and stereotypy) in response to the same dose of stimulant over time, particularly when administered in the same environmental context (Post, Weiss, Pert, & Uhde, 1987). Thus, there appears to be a conditioned component to this increased behavioral reactivity linked to the specific environment in which the behavior was originally manifest.

Stimulant-induced behavioral sensitization with cocaine not only shows cross-sensitization to other stimulants, but also to glutamate antagonists such as MK-801 or phencyclidine and, as well, to a variety of stresses. Thus, if an animal has repeated exposure to some stressors, it not only shows a phenomenon of stress sensitization, but it is more responsive to a challenge with cocaine or a related agent (Kalivas & Stewart, 1991). Similarly, cocaine-sensitized animals are more sensitive to stressors (Post & Post, 2004). Stress sensitization involves a different neurochemistry from kindled seizure evolution and is a more behaviorally homologous model for increased reactivity to psychosocial stresses typically seen in the recurrent affective disorders.

This is particularly evident in the defeat stress model, in which an intruder rodent is subjected to aggressive attack by a home-caged animal defending its own territory. Repeated defeat-stress experiences lead to a behavioral state manifesting many of the characteristics of clinical depression (Berton et al., 2006; Tsankova et al., 2006).

While a variety of chronic stressors in animals result in decreases in BDNF in the hippocampus and prefrontal cortex (Post, 2007c), defeat stress, conversely, also results in increases in BDNF in the dopaminergic pathway, from the midbrain ventral-tegmental area to the nucleus accumbens, an area of the brain intimately involved with motor activity, motivation, and reward. Learned helplessness behavior does not occur if the decreases in BDNF in hippocampus are prevented by antidepressant cotreatment, and the defeat-stress behaviors do not occur if the BDNF increases in the dopaminergic pathway are prevented by antidepressants or direct molecular manipulations. Consistent with the phenomenon of cross-sensitization between stressors and cocaine, repeated cocaine-induced behavioral sensitization is associated with increases in BDNF in the ventral-tegmental area nucleus accumbens pathway as well, and if this is blocked, behavioral sensitization does not occur.

If stresses occur early enough in life and are severe enough, an animal will show decreases in BDNF and neurogenesis, and increases in cortisol and anxiety-related behavior for the rest of its life (Post, 2007c). Most of these BDNF-related phenomena in animal models of behavioral sensitization to stimulants and stress sensitization appear highly parallel to observations in humans with affective disorders. In bipolar patients with early life adversity (physical or sexual abuse in childhood), serum BDNF levels are lower than in those without these stressful life events (Kauer-Sant'Anna et al., 2007). Moreover, there are now robust data that each episode of mania and depression is associated with decrements in BDNF in the serum, which occurs in proportion to the severity of the episode. In addition to episode-related decreases in BDNF, there also appears to be evidence of episode-related increases in inflammatory processes, cytokine secretion, and increases in oxidative stress (Kapczinski et al., 2008).

Thus, to the extent that BDNF is important for synaptic plasticity, long-term memory, and cell survival, episode-related decrements in BDNF and increases in oxidative stress could provide one of the mechanisms for kindlinglike episode sensitization and its consequences of increasing cognitive dysfunction, which occurs in many patients with even euthymic bipolar illness, and as a function of the number of prior episodes.

The clinical data about episode sensitization and conversion of triggered episodes to those that can occur more spontaneously is now well documented in the clinical literature. The kindling and sensitization models thus make very explicit predictions about therapeutic principles and maneuvers that may be effective in warding off affective illness progression. It is noteworthy that many are also highly convergent with the known empirical data on clinical therapeutics of the affective disorders. Early intervention before multiple episodes accumulate should help prevent aggressive episode sensitization and kindlinglike processes from developing, and the earlier that this is instituted, the more likely it is to be successful. Each episode carries with it the risk for increasing pathological processes in kindling evolution and now, in the findings of BDNF decreases and oxidative stress increases that occur with each clinical episode of affective disorder as noted above, we have at least initial candidate mechanisms for how episodes could engender progressively more severe consequences, not only to the organism's psychosocial behaviors, but to neuropathological alterations in the brain as well.

The increased incidence of substance use in those with the affective disorders is also convergent with the notions of cross-sensitization among stressors, affective episodes, and substances of abuse observed clinically. It would appear that several of these processes share neurobiological alterations in common, and BDNF at least provides one candidate mechanism for such cross-sensitization.

Taken together, the kindling and sensitization formulations suggest that the recurrent affective disorders are potentially progressive disorders involving increases in dysfunction and even the microstructure of the brain, and treatment should be reconceptualized as not only helping prevent episode recurrence, but, potentially, either reversing or preventing the progression of such neurobiological abnormalities. Earlier, more effective, and sustained pharmacoprophylaxis may help ward off the now all-too-common consequences of the recurrent affective disorders of substantial morbidity, disability, substance abuse comorbidity, cognitive dysfunction, and early demise either from suicide or the associated increases in medical mortality from heart attacks and strokes, which are both more highly likely to occur and more lethal in those who are depressed than in those not so.

While the empirical data on their own strongly support this notion of importance of early and sustained pharmacoprophylaxis of the affective disorders, the kindling and sensitization perspective provides an additional theoretical rationale and heuristically important predictions for direct hypothesis testing. The BDNF link also helps solidify the kindling and sensitization notions with clinical phenomena observed in the affective disorders and should help in the notion that preventive treatment is of great neurobiological as well as clinical importance.

This is all the more the case given the fact that lithium, carbamazepine, and valproate, all of the antidepressants, and some of the atypicals either directly increase BDNF or prevent stress from decreasing hippocampal BDNF. There is no longer any doubt that the recurrent affective disorders represent serious medical diseases of the brain and body with potentially catastrophic consequences, but at the same time, ones that can be highly manageable with a variety of therapeutic modalities that not only are clinically effective, but may help protect the brain.

ROBERT M. POST

See also

Amygdala
Biological Models of Depression
Brain Circuitry

References

Berton, O., McClung, C. A., DiLeone, R. J., Krishnan, V., Renthal, W., Russo, S. J., et al. (2006). Essential role of BDNF in the mesolimbic dopamine pathway in social defeat stress. *Science, 311,* 864–868.

Chuang, D. M., Chen, R. W., Chalecka-Franaszek, E., Ren, M., Hashimoto, R., Senatorov, V., et al. (2002).

Neuroprotective effects of lithium in cultured cells and animal models of diseases. *Bipolar Disorders, 4,* 129–136.

Goddard, G. V., & Douglas, K. M. (1975). Does the engram model of kindling model the engram of normal long-term memory? *Canadian Journal of Neurological Sciences, 2,* 385–394.

He, X. P., Kotloski, R., Nef, S., Luikart, B. W., Prada, L. F., & McNamara, J. O. (2004). Conditional deletion of TrkB but not BDNF prevents epileptogenesis in the kindling model. *Neuron, 43,* 31–42.

Kalivas, P. W., & Stewart, J. (1991). Dopamine transmission in the initiation and expression of drug- and stress-induced sensitization of motor activity. *Brain Research Reviews, 16,* 223–244.

Kapczinski, F., Frey, B. N., Andreazza, A. C., Kauer-Sant'Anna, M., Cunha, A. B., & Post, R. M. (2008). Increased oxidative stress as a mechanism for decreased BDNF levels in acute manic episodes. *Rev Bras Psiquiatr. 30*(3), 243–245.

Kauer-Sant' A. M., Tramontina, J., Andreazza, A. C., Cereser, K., deCosta, S., Santin, A., et al. (2007). Traumatic life events in bipolar disorder: Impact on BDNF levels and psychopathology. *Bipolar Disorder, 9,* 128–135.

Kendler, K. S., Thornton, L. M., & Gardner, C. O. (2000). Stressful life events and previous episodes in the etiology of major depression in women: An evaluation of the "kindling" hypothesis. *American Journal of Psychiatry, 157,* 1243–1251.

Kendler, K. S., Thornton, L. M., & Gardner, C. O. (2001). Genetic risk, number of previous depressive episodes, and stressful life events in predicting onset of major depression. *American Journal of Psychiatry, 158,* 582–586.

Kessing, L. V., Andersen, P. K., Mortensen, P. B., & Bolwig, T. G. (1998). Recurrence in affective disorder, I: Case register study. *British Journal of Psychiatry, 172,* 23–28.

Kraepelin, E. (1921). *Manic-depressive insanity and paranoia.* Edinburgh, Scotland: E. S. Livingstone.

Post, R. M. (1992). Transduction of psychosocial stress into the neurobiology of recurrent affective disorder. *American Journal of Psychiatry, 149,* 999–1010.

Post, R. M. (2007a). Kindling and sensitization as models for affective episode recurrence, cyclicity, and tolerance phenomena. *Neuroscience and Biobehavioral Reviews, 31,* 851–873.

Post, R. M. (2007b). Animal models of mood disorders: Kindling as a model of affective illness progression. In S. Schacter, G. Holmes, & D. Kastelijn-Nolst Trenite (Eds.), *Behavioral aspects of epilepsy: Principles and practice.* New York: Demos Medical Publishing.

Post, R. M. (2007c). Role of BDNF in bipolar and unipolar disorder: Clinical and theoretical implications. *Journal of Psychiatric Research, 41,* 979–990.

Post, R. M., Leverich, G. S., Altshuler, L., & Mikalauskas, K. (1992). Lithium-discontinuation-induced refractoriness: Preliminary observations. *American Journal of Psychiatry, 149,* 1727–1729.

Post, R. M., & Post, S. L. W. (2004). Molecular and cellular developmental vulnerabilities to the onset of affective disorders in children and adolescents: Some implications for therapeutics. In H. Steiner (Ed.), *Handbook of mental health interventions in children and adolescents* (pp. 140–192). San Francisco: Jossey-Bass.

Post, R. M., Speer, A. M., Hough, C. J., & Xing, G. (2003). Neurobiology of bipolar illness: Implications for future study and therapeutics. *Annals of Clinical Psychiatry, 15,* 85–94.

Post, R. M., Weiss, S. R. B., Pert, A., & Uhde, T. W. (1987). Chronic cocaine administration: Sensitization and kindling effects. In A. Raskin & S. Fisher (Eds.), *Cocaine: Clinical and biobehavioral aspects* (pp. 109–173). New York: Oxford University Press.

Tsankova, N. M., Berton, O., Renthal, W., Kumar, A., Neve, R. L., & Nestler, E. J. (2006). Sustained hippocampal chromatin regulation in a mouse model of depression and antidepressant action. *Nature Neuroscience, 9,* 519–525.

Weiss, S. R., Clark, M., Rosen, J. B., Smith, M. A., & Post, R. M. (1995). Contingent tolerance to the anticonvulsant effects of carbamazepine: Relationship to loss of endogenous adaptive mechanisms. *Brain Research Reviews, 20,* 305–325.

Weiss, S. R., & Post, R. M. (1994). Caveats in the use of the kindling model of affective disorders. *Toxicology and Industrial Health, 10,* 421–447.

L

Loss

The notion that painful life experience is critically linked with depressive illness is in no way new. On the one hand within orthodox psychiatry, well before World War II, despite acknowledgment that many depressions were endogenous (and thus presumed biological), there was also the accepted notion that just as many were reactive to circumstances. On the other hand, Freud's insights in his "Mourning and Melancholia" (1971) show how the experience of loss as a candidate to explain depression was also already current on the other side of the ideological divide, in psychoanalytic circles. By the 1960s the notion of hopelessness and/or helplessness as central to the depressive experience had gained prominence in many schools of thought. The founder of cognitive behavioral therapy had embodied it in his famous cognitive triad—that the self seems worthless, the world seems pointless, and the future hopeless (Beck 1967); animal research had charted the process of "learning helplessness" through entrapping experiences (Seligman, 1975); and it was but a step for those with a psychoanalytic background to highlight the link between these feelings and loss (Melges & Bowlby, 1969).

Around this time Brown and Harris were developing an approach to the measurement of stressful life events that aimed to capture the "meaning" of these experiences. Following the insights of Schutz about *verstehen* (Schutz, 1954), they elaborated rules for greater understanding of each event by taking account of its context. Thus the meaning of discovering a pregnancy will vary according to whether the woman has planned it, whether she already has children, whether her financial and housing circumstances are adequate, whether she will have good marital and other family support, and whether she has a health history of difficult pregnancies. In a study in Camberwell, South London, Brown and Harris compared depressed psychiatric patients at the local hospital with a representative sample of the general population (published later in 1978). Seventeen percent of this community was found to be suffering depression at a severity comparable to outpatients (a threshold later verified as close to the major depression of the American *Diagnostic and Statistical Manual of Mental Disorders* [American Psychiatric Association, 1994]). Those with depressive onset reported significantly more severe events or events judged likely to be experienced as highly distressing by others in similar biographical circumstances. Over ensuing decades these probabilistic standards of severity have been embodied in detailed manuals of anchoring examples collected from over 100 studies in varying cultures, with consequent high interrater reliability. But it was this early study that already revealed that the events preceding depression particularly involved loss, either of person, role, object, or cherished idea, such as the idea of one's child's honesty or spouse's fidelity. While it is easy to appreciate that a loss of income consequent upon unemployment may be as devastating as a bereavement, particularly if the respondent also loses his key role as provider for the family, the notion of lost cherished ideas gave a new slant on the meaning of *depressogenic events*. Other examples have involved a respondent discovering he was adopted and that his parents had thus lied about his birth origins, discovering a brother had sexually abused a sister, finding a son was a transvestite. The exploration of these narratives revealed types of loss that differed from the context of simple bereavement and mourning, or loss of role, because of the overtone of secrets and lies, that the self was not only left behind or abandoned, but somehow devalued, if not positively rejected. It was, however, only after another decade of work on prior vulnerability to depressogenic events, and in particular on low self-esteem (Brown, Andrews, Harris, Adler, & Bridge, 1986), that Brown and Harris introduced ratings of humiliation as a refinement to the concept of loss.

Humiliation or Entrapment and Depressive Onset

Reworking qualitative data on individuals' experiences of stress in the light of the three-fold greater vulnerability to depression of those with initial negative self-evaluation brought new insights. First it emerged that after losses of close relationships due to separation, onset of depression was more than 4 times more common if the separation was initiated by the other person than if the respondent had been the source of the breakup. It became clear that the loss of the other person was not per se the crucial element: rather some implication about the acceptability of the self implied by whether or not one had the separation forced upon oneself. Later refinement identified experiences of humiliation or entrapment as particularly prominent before depressive onset among the losses of cherished idea (Brown, Harris, & Hepworth, 1995). Apart from deaths, those losses that did not involve humiliation—for example redundancy and temporary unemployment as a result of a large firm going bankrupt, a loss for which

the interviewee would therefore not be held to blame—were followed by a much lower rate of depressive onset (13% as compared with 31%; Brown et al., 1995). The match between the shamefulness of such events and the shame felt by people with low self-esteem, whose vulnerability to depression was already acknowledged, encouraged a perspective akin to that of Gilbert's insights about shame and depression (Gilbert & Andrews, 1998) and akin to evolutionary theory, with its challenging notions that depression has proved a condition of great functional benefit for the survival of the human species (Price, Sloman, Gardner, Gilbert, & Rohde, 1994).

Regaining Lost Hope: Fresh Start Experiences and Remission From Depression

A final insight about loss comes from the investigation of the meaning of those fresh start experiences that, more often than not, preceded depressive remission (Brown et al., 1988). Although all this data was collected retrospectively, the time order between these and remission, and the high proportion of such events that were independent of the subject's agency, lent plausibility to this being the effect of the environment on pathology. It seemed fresh starts were the mirror image of those producing the generalized hopelessness of Beck's depressive cognitive triad. They either involved events such as starting a new job after months unemployed, starting a course after years as a housewife, establishing a regular relationship with a new boyfriend or girlfriend after many months single, or the reduction of a severe difficulty, usually with interpersonal relationships, housing, or finance. They seemed to embody the promise of new hope against a background of deprivation. It was notable that even for women who continued to experience difficulties of a depressogenic severity in one life domain such as marriage, a fresh start in another life domain—starting an access course—often seemed to tip the balance and set them on course for remission (Brown et al., 1992; Leenstra et al., 1995).

Conclusions

It is important to emphasize that this work on the losses preceding depression has been done in parallel with explorations of people's vulnerability to their impact. Low self-esteem has already been mentioned in this connection, but work on the protective effect of emotional support from a close other in coping with the loss (Brown et al., 1986; Paykel et al., 1994), and on increased vulnerability stemming from childhood experiences of abuse and neglect—themselves prime examples of loss and humiliation (Brown, Craig, & Harris, 2008)—substantiate the perspective that central to depression is the sense of a depleted self.

TIRRIL HARRIS

See also

Bereavement
Interpersonal Model of Depression
Interpersonal Psychotherapy

References

Beck, A. T. (1967). *Depression: Clinical experimental and theoretical aspects*. London: Staples Press.

Brown, G. W., Adler, Z., & Bifulco, A. (1988). Life events difficulties and recovery from chronic depression. *British Journal of Psychiatry, 152*, 487–498.

Brown, G. W., Andrews, B., Harris, T. O., Adler, Z., & Bridge, L. (1986). Social support, self-esteem, and depression. *Psychological Medicine, 16*, 813–831.

Brown, G. W., Craig, T. K. J., & Harris, T. O. (2008). Early maltreatment and proximal risk factors using the Childhood Experience of Care and Abuse (CECA) instrument: A life-course study of adult chronic depression, 5. *Journal of Affective Disorders, 110*, 222–233.

Brown, G. W., & Harris, T. O. (1978). *Social origins of depression: A study of psychiatric disorder in women*. London: Tavistock.

Brown G. W., Harris, T. O., & Hepworth, C. (1995). Loss, humiliation, and entrapment among women developing depression: A patient and non-patient comparison. *Psychological Medicine, 25*, 7–21.

Brown, G. W., Lemyre, L., & Bifulco, A. (1992). Social factors and recovery from anxiety and depressive disorders: A test of the specificity hypothesis. *British Journal of Psychiatry, 161*, 44–54.

Freud, S. (1971). Mourning and melancholia. In *Collected papers* (Vol. 4). London: Hogarth Press. (Originally published 1917)

Gilbert, P., & Andrews, B. (1998). *Shame: Interpersonal behavior, psychopathology, and Culture*. Oxford, UK: Oxford University Press.

Leenstra, A. S., Ormel, J., & Giel, R. (1995). Positive life change and recovery from anxiety and depression. *British Journal of Psychiatry, 166*, 333–343.

Melges, F. T., & Bowlby, J. (1969). Types of hopelessness in psychopathological process. *Archives of General Psychiatry, 20*, 690–699.

Paykel, E. S. (1994). Life events, social support, and depression. *Acta Psychiatrica Scandinavica Suppl., 377*, 50–58.

Price, J., Sloman, L., Gardner, R., Jr., Gilbert, P., & Rohde, P. (1994). The social competition hypothesis of depression. *British Journal Psychiatry, 164*, 309–315.

Schutz, A. (1954). Concept and theory formation in the social sciences. *Journal of Philosophy, 51*, 257–273.

Seligmann, M. E. P. (1975). *Helplessness: On depression, development, and death*. San Francisco: W. H. Freeman.

M

Maltreatment and Depression

Childhood maltreatment, including physical abuse, emotional maltreatment, sexual abuse, and neglect, has long been implicated in the development of depression in children, adolescents, and adults. Child maltreatment places individuals at markedly elevated risk for the development of major depressive disorder, depressive symptomatology, and dysthymia (Cicchetti, Rogosch, & Sturge-Apple, 2007). Child maltreatment has also been related to higher likelihood of a relapse after an initial remission of depression. Studies have consistently found high prevalence rates of depression among individuals with histories of child maltreatment. For instance, one study found that, among non–clinically referred samples of protective services cases, 18% of preadolescents and 40% of adolescents with histories of child maltreatment met the diagnostic criteria for major depressive disorder (Kaufman & Charney, 2001). In general, compared to their nonmaltreated counterparts, individuals with histories of childhood sexual abuse or physical abuse exhibit more symptoms of depression and anxiety, higher attempted suicide rates, and earlier onset and more chronic levels of depression.

Various mechanisms have been proposed to explain the association between maltreatment and depression, including the following: (a) quality of the mother-child attachment relationship, (b) low social support in the context of highly stressful life events, (c) attributional styles, (d) social competence, (e) self-esteem, and (f) neuroendocrine and neurotransmitter dysregulation (Cicchetti et al., 2007). These factors can be broadly categorized as psychosocial and neurobiological mechanisms by which childhood maltreatment leads to depression. One of the predominant perspectives in describing the psychosocial mechanism is that children who experienced maltreatment are likely to develop negative representational models of attachment figures, self, and self in relationship to significant others (Toth & Cicchetti, 1996). Maltreated children often show insecure attachment relationships and negative self-images, which lead to the emergence of depressive symptoms. The effects of maltreatment on depression also appear to be mediated through social support and stress (Vranceanu, Hobfoll, & Johnson, 2007). Individuals with maltreatment histories tend to have smaller support networks, to be less satisfied with their supportive networks, and/or to perceive their relationships as less supportive. Perhaps this is because maltreatment affects children's cognition regarding themselves and others. It may also be the case that maltreated children have smaller actual support networks due to dysfunctional family environments. Besides having impaired social support, individuals with maltreatment histories are more susceptible to daily stressors and report more stress compared to their nonmaltreated counterparts. They may perceive life events as more stressful because of a predisposition to a sense of helplessness. A lack of coping skills may also contribute to this process.

The growing interest in the neurobiological effects of childhood maltreatment on later adjustment adds significant insight into the neurobiological processes in the association between maltreatment and the development of depression (Heim, Plotsky, & Nemeroff, 2004). Currently, the effects of maltreatment on depression are believed to be mediated by the central nervous system. Childhood maltreatment experiences may cause long-term changes in the brain regions that mediate stress and emotion regulation, leading to altered emotional processing and heightened responsiveness to stress, which may be associated with psychiatric disorders such as depression (Heim et al., 2004). Recent research has shown evidence that the higher vulnerability for depression among maltreated children may be closely related to stress-responsive neurobiological systems. One major stress-response system that has been closely examined in depression is the hypothalamic-pituitary-adrenal (HPA) axis. Several brain pathways modulate HPA-axis activity, and disruptions in these neural circuits stemming from maltreatment may lead to altered stress reactivity and to the emotional, cognitive, and vegetative changes often found in depression (Heim et al., 2004; Kaufman, & Charney, 2001).

Additional factors have been proposed to moderate the effects of maltreatment on depression. Differential effects of specific subtypes of maltreatment on depression have been observed. Some researchers have argued that childhood emotional abuse, compared to physical or sexual abuse, has a stronger association with hopelessness depression among young adults (Gibb, Wheeler, Alloy, & Abramson, 2001). Other researchers have argued that psychological abuse, compared to physical abuse, sexual abuse, physical neglect, and exposure to family violence, is the most prominent predictor of adolescents' internalizing problems (McGee, Wolfe, & Wilson, 1997). However, it is important to note that most maltreated children experience more than one form of abuse and neglect (Pears, Kim, & Fisher, 2008), though the effects of such multitype maltreatment on depression have not been well studied.

Another important factor in the association between maltreatment and depression is gender. Some researchers have suggested that, compared to their male counterparts, women with maltreatment histories are more vulnerable to the development of depression. However, little is known about gender differences in the mechanisms of risk and protection. Besides gender, factors such as genetic variations, family environment, and ongoing stress have all been shown to influence the effects of maltreatment on the development of depression.

The high frequency of depression in maltreated individuals suggests that depression screening should be part of any standardized assessment protocol in this population, with follow-up treatment and monitoring for those who appear to be manifesting depressive symptoms. Similarly, individuals being treated for depression should be evaluated for prior maltreatment as a possible etiological factor, with maltreatment being addressed in the context of psychotherapy as needed.

HYOUN K. KIM AND PHILIP A. FISHER

See also

Early Adversity
Parenting
Stressful Life Events

References

Cicchetti, D., Rogosch, F. A., & Sturge-Apple, M. L. (2007). Interactions of child maltreatment and serotonin transporter and monoamine oxidase A polymorphisms: Depressive symptomatology among adolescents from low socioeconomic status backgrounds. *Development and Psychopathology, 19,* 1161–1180.

Gibb, B. E., Wheeler, R., Alloy, L. B., & Abramson, L. Y. (2001). Emotional, physical, and sexual maltreatment in childhood versus adolescence and personality dysfunction in young adulthood. *Journal of Personality Disorder, 15,* 505–511.

Heim, C., Plotsky, P. M., & Nemeroff, C. B. (2004). Importance of studying the contributions of early adverse experience to neurobiological findings in depression. *Neuropsychopharmacology, 29,* 641–648.

Kaufman, J., & Charney, D. (2001). Effects of early stress on brain structure and function: Implications for understanding the relationship between child maltreatment and depression. *Development and Psychopathology, 13,* 451–471.

McGee, R. A., Wolfe, D. A., & Wilson, S. K. (1997). Multiple maltreatment experiences and adolescent behavior problems: Adolescents' perspectives. *Development and Psychopathology, 9,* 131–149.

Pears, K. C., Kim, H. K., & Fisher, P. A. (2008). Psychosocial and cognitive functioning of children with specific profiles of maltreatment. *Child Abuse and Neglect.*

Toth, S., & Cicchetti, D. (1996). Patterns of relatedness, depressive symptomatology, and perceived competence in maltreated children. *Journal of Consulting and Clinical Psychology, 64,* 32–41.

Vranceanu, A.-M., Hobfoll, S. E., & Johnson, R. J. (2007). Child multi-type maltreatment and associated depression and PTSD symptoms: The role of social support and stress. *Child Abuse and Neglect, 31,* 71–84.

Marital Functioning and Depression

Researchers have focused specifically on the quality of the marital and romantic relationships of depressed individuals to better understand the role of interpersonal factors in the onset, maintenance, and recurrence of depressive symptoms. This focus is warranted for several reasons. First, there is converging evidence for a robust cross-sectional association of marital distress and depression across different populations (e.g., clinical and subthreshold depression) and different assessment methods (e.g., self-report vs. interview) (for a review, see Whisman, 2001). There is also evidence suggesting that depressed individuals' interpersonal problems and difficulties are most likely to manifest in their interactions with significant others (Marcus & Nardone, 1992). Furthermore, living with a depressed spouse has been associated with negative outcomes for the nondepressed spouse (Coyne et al., 1987).

The strong association between depression and marital distress has prompted researchers to investigate whether the two variables are causally related. Efforts to elucidate the longitudinal association between depression and marital dysfunction should be informed by epidemiological data on the prevalence and course of depression and marital dysfunction (Coyne & Benazon, 2001). Notably,

epidemiological findings suggest that age of onset of depression is decreasing, whereas the age of first marriage is increasing (Coyne & Benazon, 2001). Thus, for most depressed individuals, their first episode of depression will precede their marriage, suggesting that most of the research on the longitudinal association between depression and marital distress is appropriately conceptualized in terms of the link between marital dysfunction and depression maintenance and recurrence, rather than incident (first episode) depression. With respect to understanding how marital variables influence the course of clinical depression, evidence suggests that depressed individuals in unhappy marriages recover less quickly from a depressive episode and are more likely to experience a relapse in their depressive symptoms. Thus, overall, disruptions in the marital relationship appear to maintain, exacerbate, and lead to a recurrence of depressive symptoms (see Joiner, 2001).

Although there is empirical support for the position that marital distress adversely effects the course of a depressive episode, there is also evidence that depression temporally precedes declines in marital quality (see Whisman, 2001). Thus, studies examining the prospective, longitudinal association between depression and marital distress have produced inconclusive results. One potential reason for the discrepant findings is the methodological difference across the studies. However, other theorists have argued that determining the temporal primacy of depression or marital dysfunction is not the most relevant or fruitful line of inquiry. Rather, it is possible that marital dysfunction and depression exert bidirectional, reciprocal influences with changes in one variable both preceding and following changes in the other variable. To explore this possibility, more recent longitudinal studies have used multiwave designs, as opposed to a two-wave design, and have employed statistical tools that are designed to measure within-couple changes over time. These studies have found support for such a doubly developmental perspective (see review by Rehman, Gollan, & Mortimer, 2008).

The association between marital distress and depression does not inform us about the mechanisms by which marital dysfunction leads to depression, and vice versa. To answer this question, an important line of research has compared the interpersonal behaviors of couples with a depressed partner to couples where neither partner is depressed. Across numerous studies, the evidence suggests that marital interactions of couples with a depressed partner are reliably more negative than the marital interactions of nondepressed couples (see a review by Rehman et al., 2008). However, it is unclear whether these findings are specific to depression or whether the observed behaviors are nonspecific markers of a troubled interpersonal milieu. More promising results have emerged from research that has used interpersonal theories of depression to focus on theoretically derived, depression-relevant behaviors. For example, consistent with Coyne's (1976) interactional theory of depression, Joiner and colleagues found evidence that a dependent interpersonal style, characterized by excessive reassurance-seeking from others in the social environment about one's value and worth, represents a specific vulnerability factor for future depressive symptoms (see Joiner, 2001). Joiner and colleagues have further integrated Coyne's interactional model with Swan's self-verification model, which posits that individuals seek to maintain their self-concepts and, to do so, solicit feedback that is consistent with their self-views, even if their self-views are negative (Swann, Wenzlaff, Krull, & Pelham, 1992). By using an integrative framework that combined key elements from both of these perspectives, Joiner and colleagues have found that depressed individuals simultaneously solicit reassurance from others about their worth, while engaging in behaviors that confirm their negative self-views, thereby generating interpersonal processes that frustrate others and contribute to their own ongoing distress (see Joiner, 2001). In a similar vein, empirical tests of Hammen's (1991) stress generation model of depression demonstrate that depressed individuals can unwittingly play an active role

in the chronicity of their symptoms through their interpersonal interactions.

Increasingly, theorists are developing models that integrate different interpersonal perspectives on depression as well as models that integrate interpersonal and cognitive perspectives. This focus acknowledges the complexity and heterogeneity of depressive disorders by recognizing that it is unlikely that one level of analysis—be it intrapersonal or interpersonal—is sufficient to explain the progression of depressive illness. Furthermore, within the interpersonal level of analysis, marital dysfunction is only one, though a vital, pathway to consider.

As knowledge of the marital context of depression has evolved, the clinical implications of the high comorbidity between depression and marital dysfunction have also been investigated. A number of well-controlled clinical trials have compared the efficacy of marital therapy versus individual therapy when both depression and marital distress are present. Based on their review of all relevant outcome studies, Beach, Fincham, and Katz (1998) conclude that the current evidence suggests that when depression occurs in the context of marital dysfunction, marital therapy may be preferred over individual treatment, as it has been demonstrated both to improve symptoms of depression and to improve marital quality, whereas individual depression treatment has been found only to improve symptoms of depression. The authors caution, however, that marital therapy may be most appropriate for those couples who view marital problem as preceding the onset of depression and who report significant marital difficulties.

Conclusions

Depression occurs within an interpersonal context, substantially alters that context, and is, in turn, altered by it. There has been a burgeoning of research examining marriage and depression, beginning with seminal studies demonstrating that depression and marital dysfunction are strongly associated. More recent work sheds light on the nature of this link. The quality of depressed individuals' romantic relationships influence the course of their depressive symptoms, with individuals in distressed relationships recovering less quickly from an episode of depression and more likely to relapse than those in nondistressed relationships.

UZMA S. REHMAN AND JAMES C. COYNE

See also

Interpersonal Model of Depression
Marital Therapy
Stress Generation

References

Beach, S. R. H., Fincham, F. D., & Katz, J. (1998). Marital therapy in the treatment of depression: Toward a third generation of therapy and research. *Clinical Psychology Review, 18*, 635–661.

Coyne, J. C. (1976). Toward an interactional description of depression. *Psychiatry, 39*, 28–40.

Coyne, J. C., & Benazon, N. R. (2002). Not agent blue: Effects of marital functioning on depression and implications for treatment. In S. Beach (Ed.), *Marital and family processes in depression: A scientific approach* (pp. 25–43). Washington, DC: American Psychological Association.

Coyne, J. C., Kessler, R. C., Tal, M., Turnbull, J., Wortman, C. B., & Greden, J. F. (1987). Living with a depressed person. *Journal of Consulting and Clinical Psychology, 55*, 347?352.

Hammen, C. (1991). The generation of stress in the course of unipolar depression. *Journal of Abnormal Psychology, 100*, 555–561.

Joiner, T. E. (2001). Node of consilience between interpersonal-psychological theories of depression. In S. R. H. Beach (Ed.), *Marital and family processes in depression: A scientific foundation for clinical practice* (pp. 129–138). Washington, DC: American Psychological Association.

Marcus, D. K., & Nardone, M. E. (1992). Depression and interpersonal rejection. *Clinical Psychology Review, 12*, 433–449.

Rehman, U. S., Gollan, J., & Mortimer, A. (2008). The marital context of depression: Research, limitations, and new directions. *Clinical Psychology Review, 28*, 179–198.

Swann, W. B., Wenzlaff, R. M., Krull, D. S., & Pelham B. W. (1992). Allure of negative feedback: Self-verification strivings among depressed persons. *Journal of Abnormal Psychology, 101*, 293–306.

Whisman, M. A. (2001). The association between depression and marital dissatisfaction. In S. R. H. Beach (Ed.), *Marital and family processes in depression: A scientific foundation for clinical practice* (pp. 3–24). Washington, DC: American Psychological Association.

Marital Therapy

Given its incidence and prevalence across the life span, depression has considerable potential to disrupt the lives of both sufferers and family members, with tremendous social and familial costs, along with economic costs estimated at $83 billion annually in the United States alone. It is not surprising, therefore, that depressed individuals often report problems with family relationships, and that concerns about family relationships are prominent for many depressed persons (Whisman, 2006). This has led to suggestions that depressed persons may often benefit from marital therapy and has created interest in marital approaches to intervention with depressed patients.

Historical Roots

Marital therapy for depression began as an adjunctive treatment for depressed patients (Beach, Sandeen, & O'Leary, 1990), and as an adjunctive treatment it has steadily gained adherents over the past 20 years. Its popularity is driven by the need for, and potential benefits of, enhanced social functioning for depressed patients, particularly in the context of their closest relationships. Initially, the conceptual foundation for marital therapy for depression was provided by the empirical literature on stress and social support in depression, which suggested that addressing social difficulties in depression would be palliative for most depressed individuals and in some cases might be curative. Marital therapy for depression was also offered as a treatment for depressed persons with marital role disputes, highlighting its similarity to interpersonally oriented psychotherapy (IPT), which has also gained adherents over the past 20 years. For this reason, marital therapy for depression is typically presented as having a more focused target population and more modest claims for its range of applicability than are individual treatments for depression.

Marital Distress and Depression

How strong is the link between marital distress and depression? There is a moderate, negative association between marital quality and depressive symptomatology for both women ($r = -.42$) and men ($r = -.37$), indicating a significant relationship overall, and a significant, albeit small, gender difference. It is also reliably found that the average depressed individual scores in the maritally distressed range of widely used inventories of marital quality. For instance, on the Dyadic Adjustment Scale the mean score for the diagnosed population is 93.7 ($SD = 25.2$), which falls below the cutoff for marital distress (97). Thus, the marital relationships of depressed men and women are often (but not always) distressed. This finding is consistent with work indicating that marital satisfaction is the strongest predictor of life satisfaction across many specific domains of life satisfaction, and that marital dissolution is strongly associated with increases in depression and depressive symptoms for both men and women. In addition, marital dissolution by the death of a partner is associated with a ninefold increase in major depression and a fourfold increase in depressive symptoms among recently bereaved older adults. Underscoring the importance of the broader interpersonal realm, the effect of bereavement is especially pronounced for those lacking alternative sources of social support.

Marital Events and Etiology of Depression

Events in the marital relationship can precipitate or exacerbate depressive symptoms among the vulnerable and so initiate a stress-generation process the results in depression. For example, several researchers have reported that an index of humiliating marital events such as partner infidelity and threats of marital dissolution resulted in a significant increase in depression. In one study these events resulted in a sixfold increase in diagnosis of depression, and that this increased risk remained after controlling for family and personal history of depression. Further, marital dissatisfaction has been found to increase risk of subsequent diagnosis of depression by 270% in a large, representative community sample, and the increased risk remained significant after controlling for demographic variables and personal history of depression. Similarly, marital conflict that includes physical abuse predicted increased depressive symptoms over time, controlling for earlier symptoms. As these findings suggest, marital distress and specific types of marital events may be sufficiently potent to precipitate a depressive episode. In keeping with this growing literature, the targets of marital therapy for depression have been broadened, and the goal of marital therapy for depression has been conceptualized as both increases in positive marital behavior as well as interruption of patterns that may be stressful and humiliating.

Interestingly, recent work in behavioral genetics, using genetically informed designs, suggests that some interpersonal environments, such as the marital environment, are best represented as nonshared environmental effects. That is, they are not well modeled as resulting from the same genetic factors that produce general vulnerability for depressive symptoms. This means that the genetic diathesis that produces depression is not one that also produces conflicted marital relationships. One implication is that the marital environment is a causally significant, nonredundant point of intervention that may yield therapeutic results. It also suggests the potential for marital therapy to exert its therapeutic effects through different mechanisms than do individual or pharmacological interventions.

Treatment Efficacy

Several studies have examined the efficacy of well-specified marital therapy approaches in both reducing symptoms of depression and in enhancing marital satisfaction. Three trials compared a standard couple therapy, behavioral marital therapy, to individual therapy (see Beach, Franklin, Dreifus, Kamen, & Gabriel, 2008). Two further clinical trials have involved adaptation of individual therapies for depression to a couple format. There has been one trial of cognitive couple therapy and one trial comparing marital therapy to antidepressant medication, but these did not examine change in marital satisfaction. In addition, there has been a published pilot test of emotion-focused marital therapy for depression that indicated the likelihood of positive effects using this approach, but its very small sample size precluded reliable statistical analyses. Finally, there is also a large, interesting study of marital therapy for depression that has not yet been published, but that offers some new ideas for the marital treatment of depression focused on support provision.

The three studies comparing behavioral marital therapy to individual therapy all produced similar results. Across the three studies, behavioral marital therapy and individual therapy yielded equivalent outcomes when the dependent variable was depressive symptoms, and a better outcome in marital therapy than in individual therapy when the dependent variable was marital functioning. In addition, in one of the studies, marital therapy was found to be significantly better than a wait-list control group.

However, it does not appear that the potentially positive effects of marital therapy for depression are confined to behavioral approaches. A conjoint marital (CM) format for interpersonal psychotherapy (IPT-CM) examined outcome for 18 depressed outpatients who were randomly assigned to either individual IPT or a newly developed, couple-format version of IPT. Consistent with the findings of the studies comparing behavioral marital therapy with an individual approach, participants in both treatments exhibited a significant reduction in depressive symptoms, but there were no significant differences between treatment groups in reduction of depressive symptoms. Consistent with observations in behavioral marital therapy, participants receiving couple IPT-CM reported marginally higher marital satisfaction scores on one measure of marital quality, the Locke-Wallace Short Marital Adjustment Test, and scored significantly higher on one

subscale of the Dyadic Adjustment Scale at session 16 than those receiving IPT with no marital component. Similarly, the investigation of emotionally focused therapy in the treatment of depression provided suggestive evidence that emotionally focused therapy would provide a useful framework for intervention with depressed couples as well.

Because we suspect that enhancement of relationship quality and interruption of vicious cycles maintaining depression are key to any successful approach to marital therapy for depression, it follows that any marital therapy approach that can be shown to be efficacious has the potential to be efficacious in the treatment of depression as well. Accordingly, marital therapy for depression is open to the potential for alternative formats and innovative developments that may be useful depending on particular couple characteristics.

Should we expect marital interventions to be useful for all depressed persons who are married? Predictors of response to marital therapy suggest that there are decision rules that may help guide the application of marital therapy for depression. Behavioral marital therapy, and perhaps other forms of marital intervention, appear to work best when the marital problems are salient to the depressed spouses or when the depressed persons believe that their marital difficulties have caused their current episode of depression. Likewise, although severity of depressive symptoms may influence the ease of treatment, moderate to severe depression does not appear to preclude the use of marital therapy as an adjunctive intervention strategy. It seems, therefore, that behavioral marital therapy can be a safe and effective alternative to individual therapy for depression. Although it is in need of additional direct examination, it also seems likely that marital therapy could prove a useful adjunctive treatment to medication. Similar conclusions are likely to hold for IPT provided in a couples format (e.g., IPT-CM). Although predictors of response to treatment have not been examined empirically for IPT-CM, it is consistent with IPT to choose as targets those problem areas that are salient to the patient and that may be related to the maintenance of the current depressive episode. Given the loss of positive interactions that is common in depression, it may be that marital approaches focused on the enhancement of positive interactions would be more universally applicable to depressed patients, suggesting the potential to develop marital approaches that interrupt stress-generating processes and are more universally applicable than are current approaches.

Conclusions

We have come a long way in the study of effective ways to intervene with the families of depressed patients. Although the current level of success should not be oversold, a solid conceptual foundation grounded in a stress-generation framework is emerging to guide and support marital and family interventions with depressed patients. A large and robust literature indicates that marital and parenting relationships are often problematic for depressed persons. From the perspective of the stress-generation framework, difficulties in the area of marital and parenting relationships, and the likelihood that these processes will continue even after successful individual treatment, are troubling. At the same time, there is good evidence that these problematic relationships can be repaired, and it seems appropriate to recommend an efficacious, targeted intervention to effect that repair.

FRANK D. FINCHAM AND STEVEN R. H. BEACH

See also

Cognitive Behavioral Couples Therapy
Interpersonal Psychotherapy
Marital Functioning and Depression

References

Beach, S. R. H., Franklin, K., Dreifus, J., Kamen, C., & Gabriel, B. (2008). Couple therapy and the treatment of depression. In A. S. Gurman (Ed.), *Clinical handbook of couple therapy* (4th ed.). New York: Guilford Press.

Beach, S. R. H., Sandeen, E. E., & O'Leary, K. D. (1990). *Depression in marriage: A model for etiology and treatment*. New York: Guilford Press.

Whisman, M. A. (2006). Role of couples relationships in understanding and treating mental disorder. In S. R. H. Beach, M. Z. Wamboldt, N. J. Kaslow, R. E. Heyman, M. B. First, L. G. Underwood, & D. Reiss (Eds.), *Relational processes and DSM-V: Neuroscience, assessment, prevention, and treatment* (pp. 3–24). Washington, DC: American Psychiatric Publishing.

Medical Conditions and Depression

Medical conditions and depression go hand in hand. Many studies show that patients with conditions as diverse as arthritis, cancer, diabetes, heart disease, kidney disease, lung disease, and neurological disorders are more likely also to experience depression than are individuals without such medical conditions (Dew, 1998). Beyond cross-sectional associations, medical conditions both predict and are themselves predicted by depression. Although most studies cannot ascertain whether these are truly cause-and-effect linkages, a growing literature provides convincing evidence of risk-factor effects in both directions. For example, during the first 2 years after an initial diagnosis of cancer, individuals' risk of developing clinically significant depressive symptoms was found to be 3 times greater than for individuals without a cancer diagnosis (Polsky et al., 2005). The risk of significant depressive symptoms was 2 times greater for individuals diagnosed with lung disease, and almost 1.5 times greater for individuals diagnosed with heart disease (Polsky et al., 2005). Conversely, across a 13-year period, individuals with diagnosable depressive disorder at baseline were 4 times more likely than nondepressed individuals to experience a myocardial infarction, almost 3 times more likely to have a stroke, over twice as likely to develop diabetes, and 1.3 times more likely to develop arthritis (Eaton et al., 2006). Moreover, among persons with ongoing, chronic disease, co-occurring depression predicts greater physical health decline, disability, medical costs of the chronic disease, and mortality (Katon, 2003).

What could account for these effects? At a conceptual or theoretical level, they argue strongly argue against any position of mind-body dualism in which physical and mental processes occur independently or co-occur only spuriously (due solely to other factors that cause both). Indeed, the mutually predictive relationships frequently observed between medical conditions and depression are prime examples of the types of effects that have driven much of the clinical and research activity in the overlapping fields of health psychology, psychosomatic medicine, and behavioral medicine.

Researchers in these fields face numerous challenges in studying linkages between medical conditions and depression. One challenge pertains to the application of diagnostic criteria, particularly with respect to ascertainment of depression in medically ill populations. Symptoms cardinal for depressive illness, including lack of energy, sleep problems, and weight change, can be produced by other medical conditions as well. Thus, their attribution to one underlying illness versus another is often difficult. Another challenge concerns the difficulty of examining—and consequent dearth of data about—the pathways or intervening sequence of events that may explain *how* medical conditions affect risk for depression and vice versa. The development of a given medical condition may predict, for example, other biological or psychological changes in the individual that may, in turn, predict the development of depression. Alternatively, depressed individuals may show neurobiological or behavioral changes that are associated with the subsequent development of one or more medical conditions. Work delineating such pathways remains in early stages and, at present, is based primarily on correlational rather than longitudinal or experimental data.

A third challenge concerns the identification of patient characteristics or environmental circumstances that moderate or affect the strength of the associations between medical conditions and depression. In other words, specific medical conditions may increase risk for depression primarily among individuals with certain attributes (e.g., male gender, older age) or in certain psychosocial circumstances (e.g., in the context of low social supports). Similarly, depression may be a particularly potent risk factor for medical conditions in certain patient subgroups or circumstances. If research in this field more fully identified subgroup differences or variability due to other circumstances in the patient's environment, clinical interventions seeking to mitigate the links between medical conditions and depression might be more carefully targeted to maximize positive outcomes.

In the sections below, we first summarize key diagnostic and measurement issues involved in understanding the associations between medical conditions and depression. Then we describe mechanisms or pathways by which medical conditions may affect risk for depression and vice versa. Last, we consider evidence on factors that appear to affect the strength of the linkages between medical conditions and depression.

Diagnosing and Measuring Depression Versus Other Medical Conditions

For many medical conditions, diagnostic tests and procedures are available that, when used in conjunction with a patient history and physical examination, yield accurate determinations of the presence of specific disease. There are no such definitive tests and procedures for most psychiatric illnesses, including the spectrum of depressive disorders. Instead, the assessment of depressive disorders (e.g., major depression, dysthymia) is based primarily on taking a patient history and querying the individual on the severity and duration of symptoms cardinal for these disorders, including mood, cognitive functioning, and somatic complaints. Attribution of the symptoms to an underlying depression versus another medical condition can be very difficult. Indeed some symptoms, somatic complaints in particular, may be products of both depression and other comorbid medical conditions.

In both clinical practice and research studies, evaluators attempt to distinguish depressive disorders from other medical conditions by careful questioning, followed by the application of one or more strategies to assign a diagnosis (Boland, 2006; Dew, 1998). One such strategy is to assign a diagnosis of depression based on only those symptoms that remain after excluding others (e.g., somatic symptoms) that could be due to other medical conditions. Another approach is to consider all symptoms, even if they may be due in part to another medical condition, but to count them as contributing to a diagnosis of depression only if they are clinically severe, disproportionate to any coexisting medical condition, and temporally coincide with the onset of the primary mood disorder symptoms. The development of standardized assessment interviews to assign diagnoses of depression and other psychiatric disorders has helped to ensure that questioning about possible causes of symptoms is done in a systematic manner (Dew et al., 2005).

Evaluation of depression also differs from the diagnosis of many medical conditions in that depression has frequently been conceptualized as a dimension, ranging from none to very high degrees of severity, rather than as a condition that is present or absent. This is a departure from the biomedical model in which even continuous measures such as blood pressure are dichotomized to indicate the presence versus absence of clinically significant conditions. Proponents of the dimensional approach to depression argue that it is more accurately viewed as a continuum on which diagnostic cut points or thresholds would serve only as artificial boundaries that attenuate reliability of measurement and obscure relationships to other variables (Dew et al., 2005). Depression, under this approach, is typically measured with multi-item symptom scales. These scales are often completed by the patient and use closed-ended checklists and ratings. Because these measures do not incorporate additional probes to determine the attribution of individual symptoms, the resulting symptom scores may be influenced not only by depression but also by comorbid medical conditions.

Confounding of the measurement of depression and other medical conditions—particularly when depression symptom scales are used—constitutes a major limitation in studies attempting to examine the relationships between mental and physical illnesses. This problem may be remedied in the future through the Patient Reported Outcomes Measurement Information System (PROMIS; Cella et al., 2007), under development through the "roadmap initiative" of the National Institutes of Health. PROMIS is supporting the development of item banks (sets of items calibrated based on item response theory models) to measure many areas of patient well-being, including depression, anxiety, anger, physical functioning, fatigue, pain, and social functioning. The items will be calibrated across various medical, psychiatric, and community-based samples. The result will be that future investigators wishing to study depression in a given medical population will be able to select those depression items best able to identify depressive symptomatology—as opposed to symptoms reflecting other disease processes—in their samples.

Medical Conditions as Risk Factors for Depression

There are multiple mechanisms by which medical conditions may lead directly or indirectly to increased risk for depressive disorders and elevated depressive symptom levels. Among the most common of these postulated pathways are the direct biologic effects of medical illness or its treatments on components of the central nervous system that affect mood; the impact of such medical symptoms as fatigue, insomnia, and pain on mood; and the impact of psychosocial stressors stemming from the medical illness.

Direct Biologic Effects of Medical Conditions and Their Treatment

Certain conditions, including neurological diseases, may have a direct effect on brain areas associated with emotion regulation. Although findings have been somewhat mixed, some studies of glucose metabolism and cerebral blood flow among patients with neurologic disorders such as stroke, Parkinson's disease, Huntington's disease, and multiple sclerosis support an association between depressive symptoms and decreased activity or brain lesions in the orbital frontal cortex and basal ganglia (Boland, 2006). Other conditions, including heart disease, diabetes, lung disease, nutritional or electrolyte abnormalities, and viral disorders, may also have repercussions on central nervous system function related to mood (Dew, 1998; Lustman et al., 2005; Norwood, 2006). Moreover, certain medical treatments may have unintended physiologic effects that impact mood and related depressive symptoms. For example, cytokine therapies for infectious diseases or cancer trigger or exacerbate depression in many patients (Capuron et al., 2003).

Impact of Medical Symptoms

Common somatic symptoms of medical illness, such as fatigue, sleep disruption, and pain, may significantly increase risk for depression. Because these symptoms are themselves associated with depression, it can be difficult to establish their medical versus psychiatric etiology, as discussed earlier. Nonetheless, these somatic symptoms may increase patients' risk of developing a full-blown major depressive disorder. For example, current insomnia increases the likelihood of the subsequent development of depression (Buysse, 2004). Similarly, pain appears to leave medical patients vulnerable to the subsequent development of comorbid depressive symptoms or syndromes.

Medical Conditions as Psychosocial Stressors

The onset, worsening, or functional disability associated with medical illness and its treatment may lead to changes in body image, self-esteem, and capacity to perform work-related, social, and familial roles. These changes, in turn, may precipitate or exacerbate depressive symptoms (Boland, 2006; Dew, 1998). For example, one of the strongest risk factors for depression among end-stage organ disease patients undergoing transplantation is poor perceived physical functioning after surgery. In patients with diabetes, perceived illness status and the extent to which it interferes with daily life increase depression risk (Talbot & Nouwen, 2000). Even in neurologic conditions such as stroke, for which there are clear biologic pathways to depression, research indicates that the degree of functional disability post-stroke is a critical risk factor for subsequent depression, independent of the neurological damage involved (Starkstein & Robinson, 1989).

Depression as a Risk Factor for Medical Conditions

An area of growing clinical and research interest concerns the delineation of mechanisms that may explain why depression increases one's risk for many medical conditions; evidence points to the potential impact of depressive symptoms or syndromes on markers of physiologic dysregulation, behavioral indicators of health risk, and patterns of poor medical adherence.

Depression-Related Markers of Physiologic Dysregulation

Depression has been associated with dysregulation across a variety of neuroendocrine, autonomic, and immune or inflammatory systems that may promote the development of various medical conditions. For example, correlational data suggest that depression may promote cardiovascular disease via hypothalamic-pituitary-adrenal (HPA) axis dysregulation, decreased heart rate variability, dysregulation of inflammatory and immune function, and increased platelet and endothelial aggregation (Fenton & Stover, 2006). Diabetes may be more likely to develop in the context of depression because depression disrupts physiological functions that influence normal glucose-insulin homeostatis. These include, for example, HPA-axis dysregulation, abnormal sleep physiology, and inflammatory cytokine activation (Fenton & Stover, 2006; Lustman et al., 2005).

Depression and Behavioral Health Risk Factors

Individuals who are depressed are more likely to display poor health behaviors, such as smoking, drug and alcohol abuse, and physical inactivity (Eaton et al., 2006; Norwood, 2006). In addition, depression has been linked to elevated rates of metabolic syndrome. Metabolic syndrome is defined as a cluster of risk variables including visceral obesity, dyslipidemia, hyperglycemia, and hypertension. These variables, as a set, increase risk for cardiovascular disease, type II diabetes, all-cause mortality, and perhaps even cancer (Gans, 2006). The presence of the metabolic syndrome has been associated with a lifetime history of major depressive disorder, and self-reported depressive symptoms have been shown to predict subsequent onset of the metabolic syndrome (Gans, 2006).

Depression and Medical Nonadherence

Nonadherence with medical regimens (including failure to take medications as prescribed, monitor symptoms, attend medical appointments, and/or adhere to medically prescribed behavioral regimens associated with diet, exercise, and smoking cessation) can have profound effects on chronic disease management and medical outcomes. The experience of comorbid depression has

been associated with decreases in medical adherence across many medical populations. In a recent meta-analysis, DiMatteo, Lepper, and Croghan (2000) found that, among patients receiving treatment for a variety of medical conditions, those who were depressed were over 3 times more likely than nondepressed patients to fail to adhere to medical treatment recommendations.

Moderators of the Associations Between Medical Conditions and Depression

Although medical conditions and depression have been found to serve as risk factors for each other, the degree of risk conferred is much less than 100%. This may be due in part to random noise, including measurement error, in the data. However, it is probably also explained by other characteristics of individuals and their environments. These other characteristics may moderate, or alter the strength of, the risk factor–outcome relationship. Identification of potential moderating variables is an important but relatively neglected area of work, with relevant findings appearing only sporadically in the literature. Virtually all of the evidence pertains to factors that increase individuals' risk for depression in the face of medical illness (see Dew, 1998, for a review). Past history of depression appears to be one of the strongest moderating variables: the link between medical conditions and risk for depression is stronger among individuals with histories of depression than in those with no such history. Evidence for the moderating effects of demographic characteristics such as age, gender, and ethnicity is mixed and inconsistent. For example, some studies show that medical conditions confer greater risk for depression in men than women, and in younger persons than older persons. However, other studies find no differential effects. With respect to environmental moderators, some studies suggest that the impact of medical conditions on depression is stronger in individuals with poor social supports.

Conclusions

Considerable evidence shows that medical conditions and depression are strongly linked. Although it can be difficult to differentially diagnose depression in the context of medical illness, a growing body of research indicates that medical conditions increase risk for depression, and that depression is also a potent risk factor for the development of medical conditions and their sequelae. A rich literature elaborates hypotheses about the pathways by which these effects unfold. Data relevant to those hypotheses suggest that both biologic and psychosocial mechanisms are likely to be involved. Less evidence is available concerning factors that magnify the strength of the ties between medical conditions and depression; virtually all such evidence considers risk flowing from medical illness to depression rather than the reverse. Work to intervene to break the linkages between medical conditions and depression will depend on better delineation of both the pathways by which these conditions are linked and the factors that moderate the strength of these linkages.

MARY AMANDA DEW, JILL M. CYRANOWSKI,
AND PAUL A. PILKONIS

See also

Cancer
Chronic Pain
Heart Disease
Heart Rate Variability
Human Immunodeficiency Virus
Hypothalamic-Pituitary-Thyroid Axis
Immune System
Parkinson's Disease

References

Buysse, D. J. (2004). Insomnia, depression and aging: Assessing sleep and mood interactions in older adults. *Geriatrics, 59,* 47–51.

Capuron, L., Neurauter, G., Musselman, D. L., Lawson, D. H., Nemeroff, C. B., Fuchs, D., et al. (2003). Interferon-alpha-induced changes in tryptophan metabolism: Relationship to depression and paroxetine treatment. *Biological Psychiatry, 54,* 906–914.

Cella, D., Yount, S., Rothrock, N., Gershon, R., Cook, K., Reeve, B., et al. (2007). The Patient-Reported Outcomes Measurement Information System (PROMIS): Progress of an NIH Roadmap Cooperative Group during its first two years. *Medical Care, 45 (5 Suppl. 1),* S3–S11.

Dew, M. A. (1998). Psychiatric disorder in the context of physical illness. In B. P. Dohrenwend (Ed.), *Adversity, stress, and psychopathology* (pp. 177–218). New York: Oxford University Press.

Dew, M. A., Switzer, G. E., Myaskovsky, L., DiMartini, A. F., & Tovt-Korshynska, M. I. (2005). Rating scales for mood disorders. In D. Stein, D. J. Kupfer, & A. F. Schatzberg (Eds.), *The American Psychiatric Publishing textbook of mood disorders* (pp. 69–97). Washington, DC: American Psychiatric Publishing.

DiMatteo, M. R., Lepper, H. S., & Croghan, T. W. (2000). Depression is a risk factor for noncompliance with medical treatment: Meta-analysis of the effects of anxiety and depression on patient adherence. *Archives of Internal Medicine, 160,* 2101–2107.

Eaton, W. W., Fogel, J., & Armenian, H. K. (2006). The consequences of psychopathology in the Baltimore Epidemiologic Catchment Area follow-up. In W. W. Eaton (Ed.), *Medical and psychiatric comorbidity over the course of life* (pp. 21–36). Washington, DC: American Psychiatric Publishing.

Fenton, W. S., & Stover, E. S. (2006). Mood disorders: Cardiovascular and diabetes comorbidity. *Current Opinion in Psychiatry, 19,* 421–427.

Gans, R. O. (2006). The metabolic syndrome, depression, and cardiovascular disease: Interrelated conditions that share pathophysiologic mechanisms. *Medical Clinics of North America, 90,* 573–591.

Katon, W. J. (2003). Clinical and health services relationships between major depression, depressive symptoms, and general medical illness. *Biological Psychiatry, 54,* 216–226.

Norwood, R. (2006). Prevalence and impact of depression in chronic obstructive pulmonary disease patients. *Current Opinion in Pulmonary Medicine, 12,* 113–117.

Polsky, D., Doshi, J. A., Marcus, S., Oslin, D., Rothbard, A., Thomas, N., et al. (2005). Long-term risk for depressive symptoms after a medical diagnosis. *Archives of Internal Medicine, 165,* 1260–1266.

Starkstein, S. E., & Robinson, R. G. (1989). Affective disorders and cerebral vascular disease. *British Journal of Psychiatry, 154,* 170–182.

Talbot, F., & Nouwen, A. (2000). A review of the relationship between depression and diabetes in adults: Is there a link? *Diabetes Care, 23,* 1556–1562.

Melancholia

The term *melancholia* has origins in the humoral theory, which imputed disease as reflecting an imbalance in one or more of the bodily humors—blood, black bile, yellow bile, and phlegm. Melancholia was considered to reflect an excess of black bile, with the two Greek words *melas* for "black" and *kholè* for "bile" giving the word its origins.

Melancholia was identified by Hippocrates in the 5th century B.C. as describing a mental condition involving prolonged fear and depression. Jackson (1986) stated that it was then translated into Latin as *atra bilis* and into English as *black bile*, although *black bile* was more thought to determine the melancholic temperament. Thus, we can observe two differing interpretations of *melancholia*—a psychiatric disease state and a temperament style. Taylor and Fink (2006, p. 2) note that, except for two periods in Western history, "the Middle Ages, when church teaching dominated western thought, and again in the Twentieth Century . . . when psychoanalytic notions dominated psychiatric thinking—melancholia was identified as a disorder in brain function."

When it was alternatively used to describe a melancholic temperament, adjectival descriptors weighted insular, serious, pensive, and reflective characteristics, and with that temperament viewed as overrepresented in creative writers. As mood disorders also appear overrepresented in writers and as the temperament descriptors captured some aspects of melancholic depression, a link between melancholia and creative achievement emerged in the Renaissance and again in the 19th century—and was commonly romanticized.

As a descriptor of depression as a disease, melancholia again lost favor in the early 20th century when Freud wrote a seminal paper in 1917 focusing on intrapsychic mechanisms involved in depression (Freud, 1967). That metaphor-rich paper (for example, describing the shadow of the superego falling on the ego) caused psychiatrists to focus on intrapsychic symptoms of depression and move away from a previous focus on melancholia as primarily a behavioral disturbance associated with pathological mood changes. For example, Berrios (1988, p. 298) stated that in classical antiquity "melancholia was defined in terms of overt behavioural features [. . . or] . . . reduced behavioural output . . . [and] that symptoms reflecting pathological affect . . . were not part of the concept."

Unsurprisingly, historical observation tended to impute etiological theories of the day to explain such behavioral changes (rather than the mood state). Initially, humoral theories were invoked but were followed by a range of alternative theories. Jackson (1986) describes Pitcairn's explanation of the blood being thicker than usual, accumulating in the brain, and so causing a sluggish circulation; Hoffman suggesting that body fluids turned acidic and fixed, causing the person to be slow; Mead's "neurocentric explanation," which positioned "aetherial nerve fluids" having irregular motions; and Cullen's proposition that there was too little nervous fluid, with depleted state explaining the observable low energy in melancholia.

Such behavioral changes are now referred to as psychomotor disturbance (PMD). In essence, during a melancholic depressive episode, individuals may show motor retardation (losing the light in their eyes, being slow in action and in response to questions, losing voice resonance, and having poverty of thought), motor agitation (appearing apprehensive, pacing up and down, wringing their hands, and importuning with a characteristic coda of "What's going to become of me"), and report or demonstrate impaired concentration.

In the 20th century, this disease type was termed *endogenous depression*, with depression viewed as emerging from within rather than following social stressors, and therefore presumably reflecting underlying biological mechanisms. This led to a binary view of the depressive disorders whereby endogenous depression (or melancholia, autonomous depression, or endogenomorphic depression) was contrasted with exogenous or reactive depressions (with the latter viewed as reflecting neurotic predispositions and stress vulnerability).

The binarians held that melancholia had a number of ascriptions. It was more severe, possessed a distinctive pattern of symptoms and signs, had stronger genetic and other biological determinants, and was preferentially responsive to physical treatments (e.g., drugs and electroconvulsive therapy) rather than to the psychotherapies.

The binary view lost favor when it was demonstrated that those experiencing endogenous depression were almost as likely to

report antecedent stresses as those with exogenous depression, and when Aubrey Lewis
(1931) undertook a longitudinal evaluation
of those with depressive disorders and found
that the binary distinction did not inform
about cause, natural history, or treatment
response.

Lewis's thesis led to 20 years of research
seeking to find support for the binary or unitary view, with multivariate analyses failing
to find clear-cut support for the binary view.
In 1980, when a new criteria-based *DSM*
system (*Diagnostic and Statistical Manual of
Mental Disorders*, third edition [*DSM-III*];
American Psychiatric Association [APA],
1980) was introduced to classify psychiatric
conditions, the unitary view dominated, and
the depressive disorders were largely modeled dimensionally—varying principally by
severity and also by persistence and recurrence. Nevertheless, *DSM-III* did allow for
a melancholic subtype, if criteria for major
depression were met.

In terms of any distinctive signs, a lengthy
set of so-called endogeneity symptoms has
been held as distinctive to or overrepresented in melancholia, in addition to PMD
signs. They include a severe depressive mood
state (e.g., feelings of complete unworthiness, hopelessness and despair, mixed with
remorse and marked self-reproach), an anhedonic mood (where the individual is unable
to anticipate or receive pleasure in any activity), a nonreactive mood (where the individual cannot be cheered up), a loss of interest in
activities, appetite and weight loss, insomnia
(particularly early-morning wakening), and
diurnal variation (where mood and energy
are worse in the morning). It is likely, however, that many of these features are either
nondifferentiating or minimally differentiating. More recent analyses have refined the
set of overrepresented features to a small set
of melancholic signals (i.e., observable—not
merely reported—PMD, an anhedonic and
nonreactive mood, a distinct reduction in
energy levels, and diurnal variation of mood
and energy).

If melancholia is a physical disease, what
is its pathogenesis? A neural network model

(Parker & Hadzi-Pavlovic, 1996) positions
melancholia as a disruption of brain neurocircuits linking the prefrontal cortex and the
basal ganglia. If disrupted (functionally and/
or structurally), then a triad of symptoms is
generated—depression, concentration impairment, and PMD. What might cause the
disruption? In those who carry a family history of melancholia, a genetic predisposition
is assumed, and with the initial episode likely
triggered by a stressful event that dysregu-
lates the relevant circuits. Structural brain
imaging in such individuals generally shows
a normal brain. In those who develop melancholia in later life, there may be no family
history of mood disorders but one of cerebrovascular and cardiovascular diseases, and
here a differing pathogenesis is proposed. In
essence, brain imaging studies tend to show
evidence of microvascular brain damage,
and it is believed that such individuals develop melancholic depressive symptoms as
a consequence of those structural factors,
often with the melancholic picture presaging
a later subcortical dementia.

Prior to effective physical treatments
emerging in the 1950s, the natural history of
melancholia indicated a pessimistic life trajectory. Individuals getting psychiatric attention
(usually by requiring hospitalization) might
require admission for months to decades before seemingly having a spontaneous remission and being able to leave the hospital.

In the 1950s, randomized controlled trials
of broad-spectrum antidepressants (tricyclic
and monoamine oxidase inhibitor drugs) indicated their clear-cut efficacy in randomized
placebo-controlled trials. Similarly, electroconvulsive therapy was shown to be distinctly efficacious, although less commonly
required. Over the last 20 years, a number of
newer and more-refined antidepressant drugs
have been introduced to the market, including selective serotonin-reuptake inhibitors
(SSRIs), which act principally on the serotonergic system, and dual-action drugs, which
act on both the noradrenergic and serotonergic systems. There is increasing evidence
to suggest that the narrower-action drugs
are less effective for those with melancholic

depression, indirectly suggesting that there is a noradrenergic and possible dopaminergic neurochemical contribution to melancholic depression.

Over the last three decades, melancholia was somewhat marginalized in the eyes of most psychiatrists. This largely reflected two causes: the dominance of the severity-based unitary model of depression, and poor clinical delineation of melancholia. Current *DSM-IV* (APA, 1994) clinical descriptors of melancholia tend to overlap with descriptors of the higher-order generic major depression category, with such minimal differentiation leading to queries as to whether melancholia is a distinct type and worthy of preservation.

Over the centuries, clinical depression and the "black dog" of depression (Eyers, 2006) largely described melancholia and quantified a low lifetime risk. In the last few decades, definition of *depression* has broadened considerably to include many minor and transient states, so that the lifetime risk of depression has increased to be almost a ubiquitous lifetime experience. As this merging of melancholia and less substantive states has occurred—often with the two equated or poorly differentiated—much confusion has emerged, with accusations that depression is at risk of being overdiagnosed. More importantly, treatments proven as effective for melancholia have shown to be either ineffective or of minimal utility for many nonmelancholic depressive conditions. This has then led to many with melancholia receiving less than satisfactory treatment.

As a consequence, there is a resurgence of interest in melancholia as a depressive disease, albeit requiring more precise definition. That movement was advanced by the three-day Copenhagen Melancholia Conference in May 2006, with the proceedings extensively reported (Bolwig & Shorter, 2007), and with substantive background information overviewed in two monographs (Parker & Hadzi-Pavlovic, 1996; Taylor & Fink, 2006).

GORDON PARKER

See also

Endogenous and Reactive Depression
History of Depression

References

American Psychiatric Association. (1980). *Diagnostic and statistical manual of mental disorders* (3rd ed.). Washington, DC: Author.

American Psychiatric Association. (1994). *Diagnostic and statistical manual of mental disorders* (4th ed.). Washington, DC: Author.

Berrios, G. E. (1988). Melancholia and depression during the 19th century. *British Journal of Psychiatry, 145,* 372–382.

Bolwig, T. G., & Shorter, E. (2007). Melancholia: Beyond DSM, beyond neurotransmitters. *Acta Psychiatrica Scandinavica, Suppl. 433,* 1–183.

Eyers, K. (Ed.). (2006). *Tracking the black dog.* Sydney: University of New South Wales Press.

Freud, S. (1967). Mourning and melancholia. In *Collected papers* (Vol. 4). London: Hogarth Press. (Originally published 1917)

Jackson, S. W. (1986). *Melancholia and depression: From Hippocrates to modern times.* New Haven, CT: Yale University Press.

Lewis, A. J. (1931). *A clinical and historical survey of depressive states based on the study of 61 cases.* PhD thesis, University of Adelaide.

Parker, G., & Hadzi-Pavlovic, D. (Eds.). (1996). *Melancholia: A disorder of movement and mood. A phenomenological and neurobiological review.* New York: Cambridge University Press.

Taylor, M. A., & Fink, M. (2006). *Melancholia: The diagnosis, pathophysiology, and treatment of depressive illness.* New York: Cambridge University Press.

Memory Processes

In everyday discourse, questions about memory sometimes concern the qualities of memory, and other times they address issues of overall skill in remembering. This distinction turns out to be particularly useful in describing depression-related differences in memory. Compared to others, depressed individuals remember experiences that are more emotionally negative and less specific in detail. And, compared to others, they remember emotionally neutral events less well. These general truths are closely related to poor self-control of attention and mental activity in depression. Fortunately, external procedures sometimes ameliorate such difficulties with cognitive self-control.

Cognitive Control and Depression

Three separate lines of research, coincidentally published in 1991, serve to illustrate and implicate deficient cognitive control in depression. Among others, Nolen-Hoeksema (1991) documented self-reported repetitive thinking about personal concerns—rumination—in depressed states. Mood states become more negative after depressed participants engage in ruminative thinking and less negative when such thoughts are prevented. Clearly, depressed individuals are capable of thinking about matters other than their own concerns, but the development of ruminative habits suggests that cognitive control is impaired. Second, in the realm of memory research, Hertel and Rude (1991) showed that unanticipated recall of words encountered in an earlier task was impaired in a depressed sample, but only if the requirements of the earlier task did not control the focus of attention. When attention was experimentally controlled, depressed participants subsequently recalled as well as others. Third, Henriques and Davidson (1991) reported the first results concerning diminished activation in the left prefrontal cortex in depression. Such neural activity is associated with approach (or with initiation in terms of a cognitive level of analysis). Since these early studies, we have learned a lot more about depression-related differences in neural correlates of cognitive control (see Joormann, Yoon, & Zetsche, 2007) and about the memory phenomena that reflect control deficits.

Working Memory Deficits

The term *working memory* is used to represent that portion of memory content that is active or attended at a particular time. For example, ruminative thoughts about matters related to one's personal concerns can be said to occupy working memory while they are being entertained. In depression, rumination can interfere with other cognitive acts requiring working memory, and difficulties in disengaging attention from such concerns is an example of impaired cognitive control.

A variety of tasks have been used to investigate depression-related differences on working memory tasks, as illustrated by two examples from Joormann's research (see the review by Joormann, Yoon, & Zetsche, 2007). In the first example—negative affective priming—each trial began with the simultaneous presentation of two trait words of opposite emotional valence; the task was to evaluate the self-relevance of one of the traits and ignore the other. On some trials the emotional valence of the trait to be evaluated was the same as the valence of the trait ignored on the previous trial. In these cases, nondepressed participants took longer to judge negative traits, indicating that they had dutifully ignored the negative trait on the previous trial and therefore required slightly more time to bring such qualities to mind (negative priming). In contrast, subclinically and previously depressed participants responded more *quickly* under similar circumstances, as if in fact they did not successfully ignore the previous negative trait. In a later study, a modified Sternberg paradigm was used to address the specific locus of such an effect. Each trial began with the simultaneous presentation of two short lists of words, one positive and one negative. Then when the lists disappeared, a signal indicated which list was relevant for judging a test item (a new word or a word from the relevant or irrelevant list). Depressed participants took longer to respond to negative words from irrelevant lists, particularly if they scored higher on a scale for self-reported rumination (Joormann & Gotlib, 2008). These results very clearly demonstrated a depression-related deficit in turning attention away from negative thoughts in working memory.

Memory Biases and Deficits in Experimental Tasks

Impaired ability to disengage from negative thoughts or to maintain attention to other matters has consequences for memory in the long term, beyond the immediacy of working memory tasks. The ability to concentrate on the task at hand is essential for the sort of elaborative processing that facilitates subsequent deliberate recall. If the task at hand happens to involve emotionally negative concepts, no cost is experienced because such concepts receive adequate attention. A meta-analysis conducted by Matt, Vasquez, and Campbell (1992) revealed that research participants with major depression recall negative words more frequently than positive, unlike nondepressed controls, who show the opposite pattern. This pattern of mood-congruent memory tends to occur to the extent that the cognitive procedures at the test recapitulate the procedures at work during initial exposure, even when memory is used nondeliberately, as on implicit tests (see Hertel, 2004). In this way, events related to one's ruminative concerns more easily come to mind later, partly because those concerns prevail.

In neurophysical terms, emotion-related biases in memory are enacted through the involvement of the amygdala with hippocampal and prefrontal functions, both during initial experience of the event to be remembered and at the time of remembering, which can be seen as reexperiencing. Recently, functional MRI scans have revealed that activation of the amygdala during self-referential judgments about negative words predict their superior recall by formerly depressed participants placed in a negative mood state, but not by similar controls (Ramel et al., 2007). This finding and other behavioral data suggest that memory biases characterize vulnerability to depression.

If the task at hand does not involve negative emotional concepts, cognitive control is required to put aside other thoughts and focus appropriately. Deficient control is therefore a likely explanation for depression-related impairments in the deliberate remembering of emotionally neutral events. Deficient control can occur during the event to be remembered or during the attempt to remember it. By using techniques to distinguish between controlled and more habitual or automatic uses of memory, experiments have located depression-related deficits in the controlled

components. Yet if immediately before the memory test the attention of research participants is focused experimentally on emotionally neutral, distracting tasks instead of on personal concerns, the controlled component of remembering is not impaired, at least in a subclinical sample (for review, see Hertel, 2004). This type of evidence is important, because it suggests that depressed persons are capable of normal memory functions when opportunities for habitual thinking are prevented. The same might be said for another important function of memory: forgetting.

In some ways forgetting is a particularly important cognitive outcome when one is depressed. Everyday acts should be more easily achieved if cues previously associated with ruminative thoughts did not so automatically invoke them. But because cognitive control is required for the deliberate suppression of memories, depressed individuals should have trouble when left to their own devices for suppression. Initial laboratory experiments performed on the topic of forgetting emotional materials provide mixed support for that claim, although findings are sometimes confounded by differences in initial learning. In an early set of experiments on depression and forgetting, instruction to forget all words in a prior list was less effective for depressed participants for that portion of the list that was negatively emotional (Power, Dalgleish, Claudio, Tata, & Kentish, 2000). Later studies have used the think/no-think paradigm to investigate forgetting. In this paradigm multiple trials of practicing suppression follow a learning phase and precede a final test that requests recall for all material, including suppressed items. On each suppression trial, research participants attempt to not think about a target word when the previously associated cue is presented. On the final test, subclinically depressed students recalled more targets that had been targeted for suppression practice (Hertel & Gerstle, 2003). However, the provision of thought substitutes to use in place of the thoughts to be suppressed establish levels of forgetting that are similar to those of nondepressed controls (e.g., Joormann, Hertel, LeMoult, & Gotlib, in press). Once again, the provision of external support appears to overcome problems arising from deficient cognitive control.

Memory for the Personal Past

Depression is associated with the tendency to remember more negative events from one's personal past. Even efforts to repair sad moods by recalling happy events—a strategy sometimes used by nondepressed individuals—are not effective in depressed and formerly depressed samples (Joorman, Siemer, & Gotlib, 2007). Moreover, the tendency to recall negative events is exaggerated by rumination and reduced or eliminated by distraction. Following a period of negative self-focus, it is difficult for depressed people to exert the control necessary for recalling positive events from their past. Distraction puts everyone on similar footing.

Impaired ability to exert cognitive control, at least in dysphoric samples, has been related experimentally to overly general autobiographical memory (Dalgleish et al., 2007). When depressed and particularly suicidal people are cued to recall specific events from their past—events that last less than one day—their responses often refer to a general category of such events or to longer-lasting events instead. A review of this literature by Williams and colleagues (2007) revealed reduced specificity in a variety of depression-related samples. Specificity in autobiographical memory is directly related to success in control-reliant aspects of laboratory memory tasks and inversely related to self-reported ruminative habits. Yet, as has been the case in laboratory memory experiments, procedures that prevent or change the nature of rumination can increase specificity in depressed samples (e.g., experiential in place of abstract thinking). Included among these procedures was a course in mindfulness-based cognitive behavioral therapy for formerly depressed individuals (see Williams et al., 2007).

Williams and colleagues (2007) accounted for reduced specificity in depressed persons' autobiographical memory by suggesting that it functions in part to avoid the possibly negative emotional consequences of remembering specific events. One basis for positing this function is the relation between reduced specificity and avoidance of intrusive memories (see Intrusive Memory, this volume). Such a strategy might operate habitually, without cognitive control, and without regard to the emotional valence of the cue. In effect, overly general memory is a method to ensure forgetting of specific autobiographical events, without the need to exert the sort of deliberate control that is required for thought suppression. Also, to the extent that cues for remembering match up to abstract themes of personal concerns, they reflect and reinforce ruminative habits that operate on a thematic level. Thus, rumination is perpetuated while remembering becomes less specific.

Conclusions

The ruminative habits of depressed individuals possibly derive from attempts to "think" oneself out of depression but, ironically, they increase the state from which escape is sought. And clearly memory is the oil for this vicious cycle. Ruminative habits encourage memories of depression-related episodes. They interfere with attempts to suppress memories and to control the focus of attention on more productive thoughts that, were they entertained, would provide more adaptive memories in the future and possibly override schematic forms of remembering. Cognitive habits, like any other sort of habit, are difficult to break. However, in most domains of memory research, there are examples of ways in which environmental aids can focus attention appropriately to reduce depression-related memory impairments. Ultimately, attempts to train cognitive control offer the best hope for breaking the cycle.

PAULA T. HERTEL

See also

Attention
Intrusive Memory
Metacognition
Rumination

References

Dalgleish, T., Williams, J. M. G., Golden, A. J., Perkins, N., Barrett, L. F., Barnard, P. J., et al. (2007). Reduced specificity of autobiographical memory and depression: The role of executive control. *Journal of Experimental Psychology: General, 136,* 23–42.

Depue, B. E., Curran, T., & Banich, M. T. (2007). Prefrontal regions orchestrate suppression of emotional memories via a two-phase process. *Science, 317,* 215–219.

Henriques, J. B., & Davidson, R. J. (1991). Left frontal hypoactivation in depression. *Journal of Abnormal Psychology, 100,* 535–545.

Hertel, P. T. (2004). Memory for emotional and nonemotional events in depression: A question of habit? In D. Reisberg & P. Hertel (Eds.), *Memory and emotion* (pp. 186–216). New York: Oxford University Press.

Hertel, P. T., & Gerstle, M. (2003). Depressive deficits in forgetting. *Psychological Science, 14,* 573–578.

Hertel, P. T., & Rude, S. S. (1991). Depressive deficits in memory: Focusing attention improves subsequent recall. *Journal of Experimental Psychology: General, 120,* 301–309.

Joormann, J., & Gotlib, I. H. (2008). Updating the contents of working memory in depression: Interference from irrelevant negative material. *Journal of Abnormal Psychology, 117,* 182–192.

Joormann, J., Hertel, P. T., LeMoult, J., & Gotlib, I. H. (in press). Training forgetting of negative material in depression. *Journal of Abnormal Psychology.*

Joormann, J., Siemer, M., & Gotlib, I. H. (2007). Mood regulation in depression: Differential effects of distraction and recall of happy memories on sad mood. *Journal of Abnormal Psychology, 116,* 484–490.

Joormann, J., Yoon, K. L., & Zetsche, U. (2007). Cognitive inhibition in depression. *Applied and Preventive Psychology, 12,* 97–98.

Matt, G. E., Vazquez, C., & Campbell, W. K. (1992). Mood-congruent recall of affectively toned stimuli: A meta-analytic review. *Clinical Psychology Review, 12,* 227–255.

Nolen-Hoeksema, S. (1991). Responses to depression and their effects on the duration of depressive episodes. *Journal of Abnormal Psychology, 100,* 569–582.

Power, M. J., Dalgleish, T., Claudio, V., Tata, P., & Kentish, J. (2000). The directed forgetting task: Application to emotionally valent material. *Journal of Affective Disorders, 57,* 147–157.

Ramel, W., Goldin, P. R., Eyler, L. T., Brown, G. G., Gotlib, I. H., & McQuaid, J. R. (2007). Amygdala reactivity and mood-congruent memory in individuals at risk for depressive relapse. *Biological Psychiatry, 61,* 231–239.

Williams, J. M. G., Barnhofer, T., Crane, C., Hermans, D., Raes, F., Watkins, E., et al. (2007). Autobiographical memory specificity and emotional disorder. *Psychological Bulletin, 133,* 122–148.

Metacognition

Metacognition refers to the aspect of cognition that is responsible for monitoring, appraising, and controlling thinking. Metacognition is essentially cognition applied to cognition. If psychological disturbance such as depression is causally linked to biases or disturbances in thinking, it is likely that the source of disorder is the metacognition that regulates thinking.

The distinction between cognition and metacognition is based on the idea that the metacognitive level constantly monitors and controls the activities of the cognitive level. Monitoring and control are therefore identified as important processes of metacognition. Metacognition has also been divided into aspects of beliefs or knowledge, conscious experiences such as feeling states (e.g., "tip of the tongue") and appraisals, and strategies such as the way an individual alters the status of his or her thinking, for example, by suppressing intrusive thoughts.

We tend to become aware of monitoring and control processes when things go wrong. For example, a busy person might suddenly and unexpectedly remember that he has forgotten to do something that he had intended to do. Thus, monitoring of goals and intentions occurs in the background and failure to achieve them leads to the generation of intrusions that interrupt ongoing awareness.

The study of metacognition began in the field of developmental psychology and learning as crystallized in the seminal article of Flavell (1979); it then became linked to experimental psychology of human memory. Recently, Wells and colleagues have developed metacognition as the basis of a comprehensive theory and treatment of psychological disorder.

Wells and Matthews (1994) proposed that all psychological disorder is linked to a pattern of persistent thinking or brooding that is difficult to bring under control. They called this style the cognitive attentional syndrome (CAS). It comprises worry and rumination, attentional fixation on threat and coping behaviors that backfire because they interfere with self-regulation and adaptive learning. The CAS emerges from the individual's metacognitive beliefs, and two broad types of erroneous belief were delineated: positive beliefs and negative beliefs. Positive beliefs consist of knowledge that supports elements of the CAS and examples include "I must worry in order to avoid threats in the future," "If I analyze why I'm a failure I'll be able to find an answer," and "Focusing on potentially dangerous symptoms will keep me safe." Negative beliefs concern the uncontrollability and importance of thoughts and include examples such as "I have no control over my depressive thoughts," "Some thoughts mean I'm a bad person," and "Depression is a sign of illness in my brain."

According to Wells and Matthews (1994), for most people periods of anxiety, sadness or negative self-belief is transient. However, if the CAS is activated, this leads to a prolongation and strengthening of these negative inner experiences and ultimately to psychological disorder. The CAS is problematic because processes such as worry and rumination focus thinking onto negative information that does not modify erroneous appraisals. Threat monitoring increases awareness of potential danger, leading to greater activation of an anxiety response. Worry, rumination, and threat monitoring can interfere with cognition returning to a more usual pattern of processing following trauma. Instead the individual becomes a more sensitive detector of potential threats, leading to activation of the anxiety program even in present-moment benign circumstances. Some coping behaviors such as trying to avoid certain thoughts leads to a greater preoccupation with mental events such that unwanted thoughts are more likely to occur. Successful avoidance maintains the sense of threat, as the person can attribute the nonoccurrence of catastrophe to use of her behavior rather than to her belief about threat being mistaken.

The generic metacognitive model has been developed into disorder-specific conceptualizations aimed at capturing the predominance of particular mechanisms and the more specific content of metacognitive beliefs in individual disorders.

Metacognitive Model of Depression

In the model of depression (Wells, 2009), negative thoughts and sadness are usually transient experiences as the individual engages in cognitive and behavioral strategies that shift to task-focused processing such as diverting attention away from emotion and onto activities. However, depression occurs when sadness is prolonged and intensified by the activation of the CAS. Typically, a negative thought or emotion acts as a trigger for positive metacognitive beliefs that guide the depression-prone individual to select sustained thinking (rumination) as a means of dealing with the thought or emotion. An example of a positive metacognitive belief, expressed in a verbal form is "If I analyze my reasons for sadness, I'll find a solution to depression." Such a belief leads to prolonged thinking in the form of rumination that has a direct effect of prolonging sadness. But this is not the only type of metacognitive belief that can play a role. Negative metacognitive beliefs also contribute to prolongation of dysfunctional thinking and coping. In particular, there are negative beliefs about the uncontrollability and meaning of depressive thoughts and symptoms (e.g., "I have no control over my thoughts and feelings"), which contribute further to depression through mechanisms such as behavioral disengagement and a sense of hopelessness. In many instances patients lack awareness of rumination and do not have insight into its deleterious nature. Instead they believe that it is a useful coping or self-regulatory strategy.

Other aspects of the CAS contribute to the persistence of depression. After one or more episodes of depression the individual becomes more vigilant for signs and symptoms of possible depressive relapse. This leads to excessive monitoring of changes in variables such as fatigue, mood, and energy levels. In some cases patients monitor their feeling state as a means of trying to detect when they might be beginning to recover so that they may return to usual functioning. In each case these threat-monitoring tendencies increase awareness of the variability and instability of internal states that act as potential triggers for worry about relapse and future rumination as a means of trying to deal with it when it does occur.

Behavioral changes also occur that are features of the CAS. In particular, depressed individuals often reduce their activity levels in order to give more time to ruminate as a means of finding solutions to their problem. These responses prevent the person discovering that he or she is still able to function and lead to interpersonal and social difficulties that contribute further stress.

Treatment of Depression

Unlike cognitive behavior therapy (CBT), which aims to challenge the validity of negative automatic thoughts and beliefs about the self and world, metacognitive therapy (MCT) does not focus on testing thoughts or beliefs of this kind. Instead, it focuses on removing the CAS and modifying the metacognitive beliefs behind it. It shares with CBT a focus on changing behaviors, such as increasing activity levels, but this is not with the goal of increasing mastery and pleasure but simply as a means of limiting the CAS and introducing alternative ways of responding to sadness and negative thoughts.

Treatment incorporates a technique called attention training to increase flexible control over thinking, which acts as a useful resource in interrupting strongly established emotion-linked ruminative responses. The technique strengthens flexible metacognitive control processes that are depleted by chronic exposure to the CAS and low mood. It uses rumination postponement experiments to both limit rumination and challenge metacognitive beliefs about its uncontrollability. Treatment focuses on identifying and challenging positive beliefs about the need to ruminate as a means of coping with sadness and depression. The therapist explores with the patient alternative plans and strategies for dealing with symptoms such as maintaining normal activity levels and task focus, banning self-monitoring, and disengaging rumination. As part of treatment, therapist and patient explore alternative ways of relating to and experiencing negative inner events such as thoughts and feelings; this often consists of developing the skill of detaching from them, not engaging with them by sustained thinking or coping, and seeing them as separate from awareness of self.

Empirical Status

Data on rumination, worry, and attention bias support the idea that these factors play a significant role in depression. Furthermore, the metacognitive model has been directly tested in several studies (for reviews, see Wells, 2009; Wells & Matthews, 1994).

Metacognitive treatment and individual strategies such as attention training have been evaluated in preliminary studies with promising results. The treatment appears to be associated with large and rapid improvements in depression and changes in metacognitive beliefs. There is also some initial evidence that attention modification is associated with neuropsychological changes in subcortical processing in depressed patients (for a review of evidence, see Wells, 2009).

ADRIAN WELLS

See also

Attention
Cognitive Behavioral Therapy
Mindfulness-Based Cognitive Therapy
Rumination

References

Flavell, J. H. (1979). Metacognition and metacognitive monitoring: A new area of cognitive-developmental inquiry. *American Psychologist, 34,* 906–911.
Wells, A. (2009). *Metacognitive therapy for anxiety and depression.* New York: Guilford Press.
Wells, A., & Matthews, G. (1994). *Attention and emotion: A clinical perspective.* Hove, UK: Erlbaum.

Mindfulness-Based Cognitive Therapy

Mindfulness-based cognitive therapy (MBCT) is a manualized, group skills-training program

(Segal, Williams, & Teasdale, 2002; Williams, Teasdale, Segal, & Kabat-Zinn, 2007) that is based on an integration of aspects of cognitive therapy (CT) for depression (Beck, Rush, Shaw, & Emery, 1979), with components of the mindfulness-based stress reduction program (MBSR) developed by Kabat-Zinn (1990). It is designed to teach patients in remission from recurrent major depression to become more aware of, and to relate differently to, their thoughts, feelings, and bodily sensations, for example, relating to thoughts and feelings as passing events in the mind, rather than identifying with them or treating them as necessarily accurate readouts on reality. The program teaches skills that allow individuals to disengage from habitual (automatic) dysfunctional cognitive routines, in particular depression-related ruminative thought patterns, as a way to reduce future risk of relapse and recurrence of depression.

After an initial individual orientation session, the MBCT program is delivered by an instructor in eight weekly 2-hour group training sessions involving 10 to 12 remitted depressed patients. The program includes daily homework exercises. Homework typically refers to some form of guided (taped) or unguided awareness exercises, directed at increasing moment-by-moment nonjudgmental awareness of bodily sensations, thoughts, and feelings, together with exercises designed to integrate application of awareness skills into daily life. Key themes of the program include empowerment of participants and a focus on awareness of present moment experience. With practice, participants are helped to develop an open and acceptant mode of response, in which they intentionally face and move into difficulties and discomfort. Evidence suggests that this decentered or metacognitive perspective can reduce relapse risk in recovered depressed patients (Teasdale et al., 2002).

Theoretical Model Underlying the Development of MBCT

The impetus for developing MBCT came from the growing literature depicting depression as a chronic, recurrent disorder with a high risk for relapse and/or recurrence (Judd, 1997). For example, those who recover from an initial episode of depression have a 50% chance of a second episode, and for those with a history of two or more episodes, the relapse or recurrence risk increases to 70% to 80%. Such data point to effective prevention of relapse and recurrence as a central challenge in the overall management of major depressive disorder. While maintenance pharmacotherapy is the best-validated and most widely used approach to prophylaxis in depression (e.g., Kupfer et al., 1992), the protection from maintenance pharmacotherapy lasts only as long as patients continue to take their medication. Segal and colleagues (2002) investigated the possibility that a treatment designed to address cognitive risk factors for relapse might offer patients who were in recovery a psychosocial alternative or adjunct to pharmacotherapy.

A Model of Cognitive Vulnerability to Relapse

According to Teasdale's (1988) differential activation hypothesis, repeated associations between depressed mood and patterns of negative thinking during episodes of depression increase the accessibility for this material during transient, everyday sadness. When patients, especially those who have had multiple depressive episodes, are faced with an emotional trigger, the reinstatement of depressive thinking styles can occur automatically, interfering with effective problem solving and perpetuating emotional distress. In fact, Segal and colleagues (2006) found that increased depressive thinking during a brief sad mood induction significantly predicted whether recovered depressed patients relapsed over an 18-month follow-up.

The therapeutic implications of this view are that relapse risk might be reduced first by increasing patients' awareness of negative thinking at times of potential relapse and, second, by responding in ways that would allow them to uncouple from the reactivated negative thought streams. It is not essential, or even desirable, that the treatment should eliminate the experience of sadness. Rather, the aim should be to normalize the pattern of thinking in states of mild sadness so that these moods remain mild and do not escalate to more severe affective states.

Core Elements of MBCT

MBCT consists primarily of training in mindfulness meditation combined with standard CT techniques. Patients are taught formal mindfulness meditation practices such as the body scan mindful stretching; mindfulness of breath, body, sounds, and thoughts; as well as informal practices that encourage the application of mindfulness skills in everyday life (e.g., eating a meal mindfully; monitoring physical sensations, thoughts, and feelings during pleasant and unpleasant experiences). The CT techniques include psychoeducation about the range of depressive symptomatology and automatic thoughts, exercises designed to demonstrate the cognitive model and how the nature of one's thoughts can change depending on the situation, questioning of automatic thoughts, identifying activities that provide feelings of mastery and/or pleasure, as well as creating a specific relapse prevention plan. In addition, MBCT includes the introduction of the 3-minute breathing space to facilitate present moment awareness in everyday upsetting situations (Segal et al., 2002).

Participants in the MBCT program are asked to engage in daily meditation practice and homework exercises directed at integrating the application of awareness skills into daily life. Taken together, the skills taught in MBCT can facilitate awareness of negative thinking patterns with an accepting attitude in order to help the individual respond in a flexible and deliberate way to these thinking patterns at times of potential relapse. There are a number of common themes in the program that are emphasized across the 8 weeks.

Awareness of Present Experience With Acceptance

The first four MBCT sessions are devoted, in large part, to facilitating nonjudgmental awareness of present experience. This is accomplished via the formal meditation practices that help participants to learn a number of important skills, including concentration, awareness of thoughts, feelings, and bodily sensations, and being in the present moment. Together, these skills facilitate the participants' ability to deconstruct their experience into the component elements of physical sensations and the accompanying thoughts and emotions. This awareness is enhanced and made more specific to depression using a CT exercise that teaches that one's reactions to situations are influenced by one's thoughts or interpretations of events. Furthermore, the implicit message of this exercise is that thoughts are not facts, a point that is returned to more fully in session 6.

Awareness of Depression-Related Experience

Participants review the diagnostic criteria for major depression along with the types of negative thinking that often occur during an episode. The aim here is to show how when depression arrives it is often as a package that includes both physical and cognitive changes. Very often, patients will only recognize, or consider as legitimate, the vegetative changes and disregard the onset of self-critical or judgmental views. Greater familiarity with the whole package can facilitate one's ability to detect experiences indicative of potential relapse.

Developing More Flexible and Deliberate Responses at Times of Potential Relapse

The second half of the program is directed toward developing more flexible, deliberate responses at times of potential relapse. In session 5, acceptance is presented as a skillful first step in taking action. Up to this time, participants have been implicitly practicing acceptance in their meditations by being encouraged to bring awareness to their experience with an attitude of nonjudgment. Acceptance is made explicit as a first step in dealing with difficulties, for example, by introducing specific instructions that encourage acceptance near the end of the 3-minute breathing space. The emphasis now moves to the action step, a way of informing behavioral choices and problem solving based on a clearer view of the challenge at hand. In session 6, the theme is "thoughts are not facts." This theme is made explicit, in part, via a CT exercise that involves describing one's thoughts after a coworker rushes off without stopping to talk, depending on whether one was in a good mood or already upset when this happened. This exercise is designed to illustrate that one's interpretations can depend on one's mood and may not necessarily represent reality. Thus, the suggestion is to take a step back and question the veracity of one's thoughts. In session 7, participants engage in specific CT relapse prevention strategies geared toward creating a deliberate action plan that can be utilized at the time of potential relapse (such as involving family members in an "early warning" system, keeping written suggestions to engage in activities that are helpful in interrupting relapse-engendering processes, or to look out for habitual negative thoughts).

Clinical Efficacy of MBCT

Three randomized controlled clinical trials (Kuyken et al., 2008; Ma & Teasdale, 2004; Teasdale et al., 2000) support the efficacy of MBCT in preventing depressive relapse. The first multicenter trial (N = 145) was conducted at three sites (Toronto, Canada; Cambridge, England; Bangor, Wales), while the second trial (N = 75) was a single-site replication (Cambridge, England). In both trials, individuals who had recovered from at least two episodes of depression and were symptom free and off medication for at least 3 months before the study were randomized

to receive either MBCT or to continue with treatment as usual (TAU). In the MBCT group, individuals participated in eight weekly group sessions plus four follow-up sessions scheduled at 1-, 2-, 3-, and 4-month intervals. Individuals in both groups were followed for a total of 60 weeks from the time of enrollment, with the primary outcome being total relapse-free time in follow up. In both trials, the samples were stratified according to the number of previous episodes (two vs. three or more). The first study revealed a significantly different pattern of results for individuals with two versus three or more episodes. For those individuals with only two previous episodes (23% of the sample), the relapse rates between the MBCT and TAU groups were not statistically different. On the other hand, for the group with three or more episodes (77% of the sample), there was a statistically significant difference in relapse rates between those who received a "minimum effective dose" (at least four of the eight weekly MBCT sessions) of MBCT (37%) and TAU (66%) groups over the 60-week study period. The difference in relapse rates between TAU and MBCT remained statistically significant when all those allocated to the MBCT condition were considered (irrespective of whether they received a "minimally adequate dose" of MBCT). For this sample, the relapse rate following MBCT was 40%. The benefits of MBCT could not be accounted for by a greater use of antidepressant medication, as those in the MBCT group actually used less medication than those in the TAU group. Similarly, Ma and Teasdale (2004) reported relapse rates for individuals with three or more depressive episodes (73% of the sample) of 36% for MBCT versus 78% for TAU, whereas there was no prophylactic advantage of MBCT for individuals with a history of only two depressive episodes.

More recently, Kuyken and colleagues (2008) reported on the first controlled trial of MBCT versus antidepressant medication (ADM). Patients who were previously treated to full or partial remission with an ADM and were randomized to maintenance ADM or

MBCT plus support to discontinue ADM. There was no difference in relapse rates between the groups (47% MBCT vs. 60% ADM), and MBCT was found to be more effective in reducing residual symptoms and enhancing quality of life. This suggests that MBCT may be an efficacious alternative to maintenance ADM, the current standard for depression prophylaxis.

Studies of MBCT have also been undertaken to examine its utility for the treatment of more acute depression. While much of this work is in its preliminary stages and the evidence gathered is based largely on case series reports, there are indications that depressed patients may benefit from certain aspects of the program (Kenny & Williams, 2007; Kingston, Dooley, Bates, Lawlor, & Malone, 2007). Finally, extensions of the MBCT model to related disorders such as suicidal ideation (Williams, Duggan, Crane, & Fennell, 2006) and bipolar (Williams et al., 2008) or anxiety disorders (Evans et al., 2008) have also reported positive outcomes.

In conclusion, there is a growing evidentiary base for MBCT in its initial focus on prevention of recurrence in unipolar affective disorder. Future research will need to evaluate the application of this model to divergent disorders, with the likelihood that modifications to some program content will be required to maximize its impact on patient presentations. Finally, the next decade should witness a shift from studies of clinical efficacy to those in which the mechanisms underlying MBCT's effectiveness are evaluated. Especially clarifying would be studies comparing the generic therapeutic benefits associated with group membership, such as affiliation, destigmatization, and information provision, with the putatively specific contributions of training in mindfulness meditation for both the patient and instructor.

ZINDEL V. SEGAL

See also

Attention
Cognitive Behavioral Therapy
Cognitive Vulnerability
Metacognition
Recurrence
Relapse

References

Beck, A. T., Rush, A. J., Shaw, B. F., & Emery, G. (1979). *Cognitive therapy of depression.* New York: Guilford Press.

Evans, S., Ferrando, S., Findler, M., Stowell, C, Smart, C., & Haglin, D. (2008). Mindfulness-based cognitive therapy for generalized anxiety disorder. *Journal of Anxiety Disorders, 22,* 716–721.

Judd, L. L. (1997). The clinical course of unipolar major depressive disorders. *Archives of General Psychiatry, 54,* 989–991.

Kabat-Zinn, J. (1990). *Full catastrophe living: Using the wisdom of your mind to face stress, pain and illness.* New York: Dell Publishing.

Kenny, M. A., & Williams, J. M. G. (2007). Treatment-resistant depressed patients show a good response to mindfulness-based cognitive therapy. *Behaviour Research and Therapy, 45,* 617–625.

Kingston, T., Dooley, B., Bates, A., Lawlor, E., & Malone, K. (2007). Mindfulness-based cognitive therapy for residual depressive symptoms. *Psychology and Psychotherapy: Theory, Research, and Practice, 80,* 193–203.

Kupfer, D. J., Frank, E. F., Perel, J. M., Cornes, C., Mallinger, A. G., Thase, M. E., et al. (1992). Five year outcome for maintenance therapies in recurrent depression. *Archives of General Psychiatry, 49,* 769–773.

Kuyken, W., Byford, S., Taylor, R. S., Watkins, E., Holden, E., White, K., Barrett, B., Byng, R., Evans, A., Mullan, E., & Teasdale, J. D. (2008). Mindfulness-based cognitive therapy to prevent relapse in recurrent depression. *Journal of Consulting and Clinical Psychology, 76,* 966–978.

Ma, H., & Teasdale, J. D. (2004). Mindfulness-based cognitive therapy for depression: Replication and exploration of differential relapse prevention effects. *Journal of Consulting and Clinical Psychology, 72,* 31–40.

Segal, Z. V., Kennedy, S., Gemar M., Hood, K., Pedersen, R., & Buis, T. (2006). Cognitive reactivity to sad mood provocation and the prediction of depressive relapse. *Archives of General Psychiatry, 63,* 749–755.

Segal, Z. V., Williams, J. M. G., & Teasdale, J. D. (2002). *Mindfulness-based cognitive therapy for depression: A new approach for preventing relapse.* New York: Guilford Press.

Teasdale, J. D. (1988). Cognitive vulnerability to persistent depression. *Cognition and Emotion, 2,* 247–274.

Teasdale, J. D., Moore, R. G., Hayhurst, H., Pope, M., Williams, S., & Segal, Z. V. (2002). Metacognitive awareness and prevention of relapse in depression: Empirical evidence. *Journal of Consulting and Clinical Psychology, 70,* 275–287.

Teasdale, J. D., Segal, Z. V., Williams, J. M. G., Ridgeway, V. A., Soulsby, J. M., & Lau, M. A. (2000). Prevention of relapse/recurrence in major depression by mindfulness-based cognitive therapy. *Journal of Consulting and Clinical Psychology, 68,* 615–623.

Williams, J. M. G., Alatiq, Y., Crane, C., Barnhofer, T., Fennell, M. J., Duggan, D. S., et al. (2008). Mindfulness-based cognitive therapy (MBCT) in bipolar disorder: Preliminary evaluation of immediate effects on between-episode functioning. *Journal of Affective Disorders, 107,* 275–279.

Williams, J. M. G., Duggan, D. S., Crane, C., & Fennell, M. J. (2006). Mindfulness-based cognitive therapy for prevention of recurrence of suicidal behavior. *Journal of Clinical Psychology, 62,* 201–210.

Williams, J. M. G., Teasdale, J., Segal, Z. V., & Kabat-Zinn, J. (2007). *The mindful way through depression: Freeing yourself from chronic unhappiness.* New York: Guilford Press.

Minor Depression

Minor depression is described as a stable affective syndrome (or possibly a set of syndromes) characterized by at least two but no more than four depressive symptoms that persist for at least 2 weeks but not longer than 2 years. Minor depression was first included in the *Diagnostic and Statistical Manual of Mental Disorders*, fourth edition (*DSM-IV;* American Psychiatric Association, 1994) not as a formal diagnosis, but as a clinical syndrome to be researched. Prior to this, minor depression lacked a uniform set of criteria and was at times used as a catchall term for any depressive syndrome that did not meet major depression criteria. Although its parameters have narrowed and solidified, minor depression is at times referred to as *subclinical* or *subthreshold* depression in contemporary research. In clinical settings where diagnosis is typically required, clinicians currently diagnose minor depression as *adjustment disorder with depressive mood* or *depressive disorder not otherwise specified.*

According to the *DSM-IV*, minor depression is characterized by depressed mood and/or anhedonia, with other possible symptoms including loss of energy, significant changes in weight or sleep patterns, difficulty concentrating or making decisions, excessive guilt or feelings of worthlessness, psychomotor retardation or agitation, or suicidal ideation. In general, minor depression is characterized by mood and cognitive symptoms, and not the neurovegetative symptoms more commonly associated with major depression.

Prevalence and Assessment

Minor depression tends to be more common than major depression, with reported point and lifetime prevalence rates ranging from 2% to 5% and 10% to 23%, respectively (Kessler, Zhao, Blazer, & Swartz, 1997; Rapaport et al., 1997). In terms of sociodemographic variables, lifetime prevalence of minor depression has been reported to be elevated in women, non-Hispanic Whites, and unemployed individuals, and is positively correlated with education.

Being that current criteria for minor depression are derived from the *DSM-IV*, the Structured Clinical Interview for DSM-IV is the primary instrument utilized to assess minor depression; however, the Composite International Diagnostic Interview has also been used. The Center for Epidemiological Studies Depression scale is a self-report instrument that has often been utilized to classify minor depression.

Clinical Presentation and Correlates

Similar to major depression, minor depression has been associated with a range of deleterious outcomes, including decreased physical, social, and role functioning; high health care utilization; separation and divorce; and poor quality of life. In older adults, minor depression has been found to be associated with increased risk of mortality, even after accounting for sociodemographics, health status, and health behaviors. At a societal level, minor depression accounts for greater employment absenteeism than major depression and accounts for 9% to 16% of total disability days in community samples (Beck & Koenig, 1996).

Annual economic costs related to minor depression are comparable in magnitude to those associated with major depression. Because individuals are typically show less impairment in minor depression than in major depression, they may be more likely to present to primary care physicians than to mental health professionals, if they seek help at all. Help-seeking behavior is particularly important given evidence that interventions can effectively treat minor depression and reduce the risk of developing major depression.

First, a history of minor depression represents a strong risk factor for the future development of major depressive disorder over the long term. Second, evidence suggests that treating cases of minor depression will ultimately decrease the number of new cases of major depressive disorder over time.

Conceptualization, Etiology, and Treatment

A dimensional approach to depression might suggest that minor depression represents a lower point along a depressive severity continuum with major depression. This approach is supported by evidence that minor depression is associated with parallel though less severe impairments and adverse outcomes than major depressive disorder. In contrast, a categorical approach, upon which diagnostic systems are built, conceptualizes mental disorders as qualitatively different than normal functioning, suggesting that major depression, minor depression, and normal nondepressed functioning are discrete phenomena. This debate is yet unresolved in the research literature, however it is already relevant to conceptualizing etiology and strategizing treatment of minor depression.

Research focusing specifically on the etiology of minor depression has been very limited, with an implicit assumption that empirically supported theories of major depression can aptly explain minor depression as well. Therefore, minor depression is commonly explained in diathesis-stress terms. With regard to an apparent diathesis, minor depression has been associated with increased rates of familial unipolar depression, suggesting a common genetic predisposition. Similarly, dysregulated serotonergic functioning has been implicated in minor depression. In addition, neurological dysfunction (e.g., stroke) can lead to minor depression or major depression. From the stress angle, research suggests that life stressors interact with a predisposition to bring about the syndrome identified as minor depression. In some cases, however, minor depression is described as an endogenous phenomenon, seemingly without preceding stressors.

Given the assumption that minor depression and major depression are related, it follows that effective treatments for major depressive disorder would be utilized with minor depression, with similarly favorable results. A preliminary collection of findings suggests that minor depression can be effectively treated with psychotherapy, antidepressant pharmacotherapy, or other nontraditional interventions. Cognitive behavior therapy, problem-solving therapy, and selective serotonin-reuptake inhibitor medications (e.g., paroxetine) are the treatment options with the most empirical support. Nontraditional interventions such as exercise or acupuncture may also have mood enhancement or stress reduction effects on individuals with minor depression. Minor depression should be considered a target for prevention and treatment interventions; however, the body of directly applicable research remains underdeveloped.

STEVEN L. BISTRICKY AND JASON KLEIN

See also

Classification of Depression
Diagnostic and Statistical Manual of Mental Disorders

References

American Psychiatric Association. (1994). *Diagnostic and statistical manual of mental disorders* (4th ed.). Washington, DC: Author.

Beck, D. A., & Koenig, H. G. (1996). Minor depression: A review of the literature. *International Journal of Psychiatry in Medicine, 26,* 177–209.

Kessler, R. C., Zhao, S., Blazer, D. G., & Swartz, M. (1997). Prevalence, correlates, and course of minor depression and major depression in the National Comorbidity Survey. *Journal of Affective Disorders, 45,* 19–30.

Rapaport, M. H., Judd, L. L., Schettler, P. J., Yonkers, K. A., Thase, M. E., Kupfer, D. J., et al. (2002). A descriptive analysis of minor depression. *American Journal of Psychiatry, 159,* 637–643.

Molecular Genetics

Extensive research efforts over the last decade have begun to reveal clues about the genetic mechanisms of depression and related psychiatric conditions. Depression is a common and disabling condition affecting human beings throughout the world, and the identification of genetic susceptibility mechanisms has potentially enormous public health implications related to diagnostics and drug development. Recently, applications of genomewide association (GWA) studies (Baum et al., 2008; Wellcome Trust Case Control Consortium, 2007) have become possible because of the availability of appropriately powered sample sizes; because of genetic variation information from the International HapMap Project, which provides patterns of genomewide variation and linkage disequilibrium; and the availability of dense genotyping chips, containing most of the single-nucleotide polymorphisms of the human genome. These studies have implicated several genes, based on statistical thresholds, but replication across studies is not clear, and statistical evidence of association is not the same as evidence of a susceptibility mechanism. In this review, we highlight two genes implicated in depression, based on evidence of a mechanism for statistical association. We spotlight these two genes because the strategy for characterizing mechanisms underlying psychiatric susceptibility genes illustrates principles that will have broader application in the future with other genes.

Serotonin System

The importance of the serotonin (5-HT) system for the pathogenesis of depression is clinically suggested by the efficacy of selective serotonin-reuptake inhibitors (SSRIs), the first-line treatment of depression, and by the induction of depressive mood states by tryptophan depletion in susceptible individuals. Postmortem and in vivo studies of the serotonin transporter (5-HTT) and postsynaptic 5-HT receptors such as 5-HT1A further support its role in depression. It is noteworthy that 5-HT appears to be critical for the development of emotional circuitry in the brain, and even transient alterations in 5-HT homeostasis during early developmental stages in animals have been shown to modify neural connections implicated in depression, causing a permanent increase in anxiety-related behavior during adulthood (Gaspar, Cases, & Maroteaux, 2003). Serotonergic neurons are among the first neurons to be generated, and even nonserotonergic neurons such as glutamatergic projection neurons may transiently express 5-HTT within the anterior cingulate cortex in animals. This pattern of expression in nonserotonergic neurons within a specific temporal window has been hypothesized to underlie the formation and fine-tuning of specific connectivity patterns, possibly through regulation of synaptogenesis and growth cone motility.

Due to the well-established heritability of depression and the implication of the 5-HT system in depression, research has focused on candidate genes related to serotonergic neurotransmission and depression-related phenotypes. A variable number of tandem repeats in the 5' promoter region (5-HTTLPR) of the human serotonin transporter gene (SLC6A4) has been shown in both in vitro and in vivo studies to influence transcriptional activity and subsequent availability of the 5-HTT. Specifically, the 5-HTTLPR short (S) allele has reduced transcriptional efficiency in comparison to the long (L) allele, and individuals carrying the S allele tend to have increased anxiety-related temperamental traits (Lesch et al., 1996) and a risk factor for depression, and in patients it adversely affects the clinical outcome of SSRI treatment. It has further been pointed out that S allele translates only into the clinical phenotype of depression in the context of environmental adversity, representing a clinically observable gene-environment interaction (Caspi et al., 2003).

Over the last decade neuroimaging techniques have made large strides forward, and recently it has become possible to detect subtle changes introduced by 5-HTTLPR. Using functional MRI (fMRI) a pioneering study found that healthy, nondepressed S allele carriers showed an exaggerated amygdala response to threatening visual stimuli in comparison to individuals with the LL genotype, suggesting a possible link between variation in the gene and a basic-brain mechanism involved in the regulation of negative emotion (Hariri et al., 2002). This finding was subsequently confirmed in several independent studies, confirming that S allele carriers show exaggerated amygdala responses to potentially threatening stimuli. It is noteworthy that this neurobiological association did not explain the mechanism of amygdala hyperreactivity in S allele carriers, or whether this might be related to clinical endpoints, and if so, to whom, since variation in amygdala response did not account for individual differences in behavioral measures of emotional reactivity.

A broader mechanistic perspective emerged when anatomical and functional neuroimaging techniques investigated 5-HTTLPR effects on both a local and brain-systems level (Pezawas et al., 2005). As predicted from preclinical work, anatomical human imaging data in healthy controls were able to demonstrate that the S allele leads to a significant decrease of gray matter volume in the amygdala and specifically in the rostral subgenual portion of the anterior cingulate (rACC). This finding was in accordance with evidence from other neuroimaging and neuropathological studies suggesting a key regulatory role of the rACC in depression, induced sadness, antidepressant response, efficacy of therapeutic sleep deprivation, and even anecdotal reports of therapeutic response in therapy-refractory depression by cingulotomy and more recently deep brain stimulation. Remarkably, the region showing the greatest effect of 5-HTTLPR genotype is located within the phylogenetically older archicortical portion of the cingulate cortex, a region that displays the highest density of 5-HTT terminals and 5-HT1A receptors within the human cortex and is a target zone of dense projections from the amygdala via the uncinate bundle. Studies on a brain-systems level revealed in both functional and anatomical data that the S allele of 5-HTTLPR leads to a decrease in coupling between the amygdala and the rACC, resulting in increased amygdala reactivity, and that the measure of coupling predicted normal variation in temperamental measures of harm avoidance, a temperamental dimension that is linked to risk for depression. These genotype-related alterations in anatomy and function of an amygdala-cingulate feedback circuitry critical for emotional regulation have been implicated in a developmental, systems-level mechanism underlying emotional reactivity and genetic susceptibility for anxiety and depression.

Brain-Derived Neurotrophic Factor

A large amount of human and animal evidence supports the idea that brain-derived neurotrophic factor (BDNF) modulates hippocampal plasticity and hippocampal-dependent learning and memory. This specific role of BDNF in learning and memory has been related to the modulation of synaptic transmission and plasticity, particularly long-term potentiation (LTP), but also to its importance in mediating long-term developmental effects such as neuronal survival, migration, and differentiation, as well as activity-dependent refinement of synaptic architecture. BDNF also has been implicated in mediating the trophic effects of serotonin signaling in development and also in the effects of antidepressant drugs.

A common polymorphism in the BDNF gene (val66met) in the 5' signal domain has been shown to affect intracellular packaging and regulated secretion of BDNF, and also human hippocampal function and episodic memory (Egan et al., 2003; Hariri et al., 2003). Cultured hippocampal neurons transfected with met BDNF show reduced depolarization-induced secretion and fail to localize BDNF to secretory granules and dendritic processes. In accordance with preclinical studies, normal met allele carriers have been shown to exhibit poorer episodic memory performance (Egan et al., 2003) and reduced hippocampal physiologic engagement during memory tasks studied with fMRI (Hariri et al., 2003). Similarly, anatomical imaging studies (Pezawas et al., 2004), which found bilateral hippocampus and dorsolateral prefrontal cortical volume reductions in met BDNF carriers, suggest that effects of this polymorphism may not only reflect rapid, context-dependent plasticity in the hippocampal formation, but also a trait characteristic related to hippocampal and prefrontal development and morphology. It is noteworthy that none of the human imaging studies revealed effects of BNDF on the amygdala-rACC circuitry, which has been shown to be modulated by 5-HTTLPR.

Studies of genetic association of BDNF with depression have produced mixed results. Interestingly, positive genetic associations of BDNF with mood disorders have usually, but not consistently, found the val allele of val66met BDNF to be the risk allele, which is counterintuitive given the fact that the met allele is associated with abnormal intracellular sorting and regulated secretion of BDNF and abnormal hippocampal structure and function, which has been related to depression in animal stress-models. Further evidence for the complex role of BDNF in depression comes from preclinical studies suggesting that BDNF mediates biological consequences of social defeat stress as well as antidepressive effects including most treatment modalities such as electroconvulsive therapy, drug treatment with SSRIs and enhancers, as well as mood stabilizers such as lithium and valproate.

5-HT-by-BDNF Interaction

Molecular mechanisms of serotonergic neurotransmission during development are poorly understood, but recent studies indicate that BNDF mediation of neuroplastic changes in response to 5-HT signaling may be involved. Many studies highlight the molecular relationship between 5-HT and BDNF, whose expression is partly mediated via the transcription factor cAMP response element-binding protein (CREB), which is responsive to 5-HT-induced intracellular signaling. Further evidence suggests that BDNF

promotes the development and function of 5-HT neurons, resulting in the formulation of an alternative hypothesis of depression called the neuroplasticity hypothesis. Recent support for this hypothesis stems from an animal study demonstrating that fluoxetine treatment restores activity-dependent neuroplasticity in the visual cortex, whereas diazepam cotreatment blocks its effects (Maya Vetencourt et al., 2008).

This biological interaction of BDNF and 5-HT signaling also supports the idea of epistasis (gene-by-gene interaction) between 5-HTTLPR and val66met BDNF in biasing brain development toward susceptibility for depression, which has been explored to a limited degree in animals genetically engineered to be hypomorphic at both genes (Murphy et al., 2003). Results suggest that a loss of BDNF exacerbates brain 5-HT deficiencies and increases stress abnormalities in SLC6A4 knock-out mice. More compelling are data from a genetically engineered mouse model containing humanized BDNF variants demonstrating that anxiety behavior in animals carrying met BDNF alleles is unresponsive to SSRIs, which can be viewed as pharmacological analogs of 5-HTTLPR S alleles (Krishnan et al., 2007). Clinical data are limited and contradictory. However, most studies also suggested a protective effect of the BDNF met allele for anxiety, depression, and bipolar disorder. Similarly, a study reported enhanced response to lithium in 5-HTTLPR S and BDNF met allele carriers. In this context, a recent anatomical imaging study expands on previously reported evidence that development of the amygdala-rACC mood circuitry is genetically modulated by 5-HTTLPR (Pezawas et al., 2008). This study demonstrated that val66met BDNF interacts epistatically with 5-HTTLPR, presumably affecting the development and integrity of this neural system, which is consistent with polygenetic concepts of depression as well as animal models of social defeat stress–related plasticity. Specifically, this study found that the met BDNF allele protects against the adverse effects of 5-HTTLPR S alleles, which the ancestral val BDNF allele potentiates. Therefore, it has been suggested that the met BDNF allele reduces effects of HTTLPR S alleles on the amygdala-rACC circuitry, resulting in increased resilience to environmental adversity and consequently reduced vulnerability to depression, which represents a unique genetic model of depression that takes genetic complexity of depression into account.

Conclusions

Several risk genes for depression have suggested by genetic association studies and provide a preliminary basis for molecular genetic studies on animals and for neuroimaging studies on humans. However, only a few single-nucleotide polymorphisms such as 5-HTTLPR and val66met BDNF have been shown so far to have in vivo effects in the human brain. The evidence for such effects has emerged using a strategy called imaging genetics, and the results are in line with many other levels of evidence. We have highlighted the importance of the genetic make-up of the serotonin transporter as well as the BDNF gene in the context of depression, which illustrate this approach to mechanistic validation but also reflect the genetic complexity of depression by showing epistatic effects and the potential importance of neuroplasticity during development for susceptibility for depression. Studies utilizing such an approach will further facilitate the understanding of brain effects of depression risk genes within the next decade of brain research.

LUKAS PEZAWAS AND DANIEL R. WEINBERGER

See also

Family Transmission of Depression
Genetics of Depression
Genetic Transmission of Depression
Serotonin

References

Baum, A. E., Hamshere, M., Green, E., Cichon, S., Rietschel, M., Noethen, M. M., et al. (2008). Meta-analysis of two genome-wide association studies of bipolar disorder reveals important points of agreement. *Molecular Psychiatry, 13*, 466–467.

Caspi, A., Sugden, K., Moffitt, T. E., Taylor, A., Craig, I. W., Harrington, H., et al. (2003). Influence of life stress on depression: Moderation by a polymorphism in the 5-HTT gene. *Science, 301*, 386–389.

Egan, M. F., Kojima, M., Callicott, J. H., Goldberg, T. E., Kolachana, B. S., Bertolino, A., et al. (2003). The BDNF val66met polymorphism affects activity-dependent secretion of BDNF and human memory and hippocampal function. *Cell, 112*, 257–269.

Gaspar, P., Cases, O., & Maroteaux, L. (2003). The developmental role of serotonin: News from mouse molecular genetics. *Nature Reviews Neuroscience, 4*, 1002–1012.

Hariri, A. R., Goldberg, T. E., Mattay, V. S., Kolachana, B. S., Callicott, J. H., Egan, M. F., et al. (2003). Brain-derived neurotrophic factor val66met polymorphism affects human memory-related hippocampal activity and predicts memory performance. *Journal of Neuroscience, 23*, 6690–6694.

Hariri, A. R., Mattay, V. S., Tessitore, A., Kolachana, B., Fera, F., Goldman, D., et al. (2002). Serotonin transporter genetic variation and the response of the human amygdala. *Science, 297*, 400–403.

Krishnan, V., Han, M.-H., Graham, D. L., Berton, O., Renthal, W., Russo, S. J., et al. (2007). Molecular adaptations underlying susceptibility and resistance to social defeat in brain reward regions. *Cell, 131*, 391–404.

Lesch, K. P., Bengel, D., Heils, A., Sabol, S. Z., Greenberg, B. D., Petri, S., et al. (1996). Association of anxiety-related traits with a polymorphism in the serotonin transporter gene regulatory region. *Science, 274*, 1527–1531.

Maya Vetencourt, J. F., Sale, A., Viegi, A., Baroncelli, L., De Pasquale, R., O'Leary, O. F., et al. (2008). The antidepressant fluoxetine restores plasticity in the adult visual cortex. *Science, 320*, 385–388.

Murphy, D. L., Uhl, G. R., Holmes, A., Ren-Patterson, R., Hall, F. S., Sora, I., et al. (2003). Experimental gene interaction studies with SERT mutant mice as models for human polygenic and epistatic traits and disorders. *Genes, Brain, and Behavior, 2*, 350–364.

Pezawas, L., Meyer-Lindenberg, A., Drabant, E. M., Verchinski, B. A., Munoz, K. E., Kolachana, B. S., et al. (2005). 5-HTTLPR polymorphism impacts human cingulate-amygdala interactions: A genetic susceptibility mechanism for depression. *Nature Neuroscience, 8*, 828–834.

Pezawas, L., Meyer-Lindenberg, A., Goldman, A. L., Verchinski, B. A., Chen, G., Kolachana, B. S., et al. (2008). Evidence of biologic epistasis between BDNF and SLC6A4 and implications for depression. *Mol Psychiatry, 13*, 709–716.

Pezawas, L., Verchinski, B. A., Mattay, V. S., Callicott, J. H., Kolachana, B. S., Straub, R. E., et al. (2004). The brain-derived neurotrophic factor val66met polymorphism and variation in human cortical morphology. *Journal of Neuroscience, 24*, 10099–10102.

Wellcome Trust Case Control Consortium. (2007). Genome-wide association study of 14,000 cases of seven common diseases and 3,000 shared controls. *Nature, 447*, 661–678.

Monoamine Oxidase Inhibitors

Monoamine oxidase (MAO) inhibitors are one of the two oldest classes of antidepressants, having been discovered to have antidepressant properties in the early 1950s. After the development of agents that were less toxic than the first MAO inhibitor (iproniazid), they were second-line agents after the tricyclics. However, over the last 20 years, with the advent and now dominance of the newer antidepressants such as the selective serotonin-reuptake inhibitors (SSRIs), MAO inhibitors are currently third-line agents, rarely prescribed for other than treatment-resistant depression (i.e., depression that has failed to respond to multiple other antidepressants). This is mostly due to the MAO inhibitors' side-effect profile and the required dietary restrictions (see below) inherent with their use. Nonetheless, they are still valuable and effective for a small subgroup of patients.

Clinical Uses

The predominant use of MAO inhibitors is for depression. Initial efficacy studies seemed to show that MAO inhibitors were less effective than tricyclics. In retrospect, these early findings were almost assuredly due to inadequate dosing. More recent studies, using higher and more appropriate doses, find equal efficacy between the MAO inhibitors and other antidepressants. In general, then, MAO inhibitors should be considered equivalently effective compared to other antidepressants (Davis, Wang, & Janicak, 1993).

MAO inhibitors may have selective efficacy in treating atypical depression as defined in the *Diagnostic and Statistical Manual of Mental Disorders*, fourth edition (*DSM-IV*; American Psychiatric Association, 1994; Liebowitz et al., 1988). These patients have so-called reverse vegetative features such as hypersomnia and hyperphagia (excessive sleeping and eating) in contrast to the more typical symptoms of insomnia and anorexia. Atypical depression is also characterized by

mood reactivity (the ability to be cheered up, albeit temporarily, in response to positive events), marked interpersonal rejection sensitivity, and leaden fatigue (a concept of dubious clinical helpfulness). Atypically depressed patients clearly respond better to MAO inhibitors than to tricyclics. Although the database in support of SSRIs for atypical depression is mixed, most clinicians prescribe them before MAO inhibitors because of their relative ease of use.

A secondary use of MAO inhibitors is in treating some anxiety disorders, such as panic disorder and social anxiety disorder. Here, too, given the difference in side-effect profiles, the vast majority of patients with these anxiety disorders are appropriately treated with other agents, such as SSRIs, first. As in treating depression, MAO inhibitors, however, should be considered as viable treatments for those patients who have failed to respond to other agents.

Even less commonly, MAO inhibitors may be prescribed for some patients with borderline personality disorder or posttraumatic stress disorder.

Biologic Effects

As evidenced by their class name, all MAO inhibitors inhibit the enzyme monoamine oxidase. Since this enzyme metabolizes neurotransmitters such as norepinephrine and serotonin (thereby decreasing the amounts available), MAO inhibitors increase the amount or function of these neurotransmitters (as do other antidepressant classes such as tricyclics and SSRIs, but by a different mechanism). MAO exists in two forms, MAO-A and MAO-B. All available MAO inhibitors available in the United States inhibit both forms of MAO. It is likely that MAO-A, which inhibits norepinephrine and serotonin, is the more important subenzyme for both the efficacy of MAO inhibitors and explaining the dietary restrictions required with their use (see below). All MAO inhibitors in the United States are irreversible, that is, they bind to the MAO molecule permanently, requiring the synthesis of new enzymes to reverse their effect. A class of MAO inhibitors called reversible inhibitors of MAO-A (RIMAs) can be displaced from the MAO enzyme and do not require dietary restrictions, but none are available in this country.

Choice of Agents

Table M.1 shows the four MAO inhibitors available in the United States. They should be considered equivalently effective. The four oral agents differ somewhat in side-effect profiles (although not in the required dietary restrictions). Tranylcypromine is the least sedating and least weight gaining, phenelzine and isocarboxazid (which are very rarely prescribed) are the most sedating and weight gaining, while selegiline probably has the fewest overall side effects.

In 2006, transdermal selegiline (Emsam) was released. The transdermal preparation is administered as a daily patch. Because a transdermal preparation bypasses both the gut and the liver, the hypertensive effect of dietary tyramine is markedly diminished. Therefore, in low but still effective doses (6 mg per patch), transdermal selegiline does not require any dietary restrictions and is the only MAO inhibitor preparation available in the United States without these requirements. At 9- and 12-mg patch doses, dietary restrictions are required, although the risk of hypertensive reactions is still less than with oral MAO inhibitors. Additionally, the nondangerous MAO inhibitor side effects noted above are, in general, less common with transdermal selegiline compared to the oral MAO inhibitors. The major concerns about transdermal selegiline are whether it is as effective as the oral MAO inhibitors and its high cost.

Food and Drug Interactions

MAO inhibitors are the only class of psychopharmacological agents that require dietary restrictions. The dietary restrictions are predicated on the need to avoid certain amines in foods, especially tyramine, which can raise blood pressure to dangerous levels in the presence of an MAO inhibitor. The mechanisms by which MAO inhibitors cause hypertension in association with certain foods are well understood. In the absence of MAO inhibitors, ingested tyramine is metabolized by the enzyme MAO, which exists in both the lining of the intestinal tract and in the liver. Additionally, tyramine releases norepinephrine intracellularly. Therefore, the amount of norepinephrine available is increased in the presence of an MAO inhibitor. Both of these mechanisms independently contribute to the food-related hypertension. By far, aged cheeses, which contain a great deal of tyramine, are the most dangerous foods for patients taking MAO inhibitors and should be strictly forbidden. Other foods that are of some concern are some aged meats (such as summer sausage), sauerkraut, and some soy products. All competent psychopharmacologists will have a written list of proscribed foods to be given to any patient taking an MAO inhibitor (Gardner, Shulman, Walker,

Table M.1   Monoamine Oxidase Inhibitors

Name (trade name)	Dosage range (mg/day)	Comments
Isocarboxazid (Marplan)	30–60	Rarely prescribed
Phenelzine (Nardil)	45–90	Most weight gain
Selegiline (Eldepryl)	30–60	Few side effects
Selegiline (Emsam patch)	6–12	Few side effects; no dietary restrictions at low dose
Tranylcypromine (Parnate)	30–60	Most stimulating, highest risk for hypertensive episodes

& Tailor, 1996). Any patient incapable of following the dietary rules should not be treated with an MAO inhibitor.

By somewhat different mechanisms, certain medications are also contraindicated for use with an MAO inhibitor. Medications can cause either a hypertensive episode, similar to the food reactions, or a serotonin syndrome, characterized by excessive serotonin activity in the central nervous system. Serotonin syndrome when severe is potentially fatal and is characterized by fever, muscle rigidity, low blood pressure, and mental status changes.

Medications that increase norepinephrine or dopamine will cause hypertensive reactions, while those increasing serotonin will cause (not surprisingly) serotonin syndrome. Most important among the hypertension-producing medications are over-the-counter cold preparations containing pseudoephedrine, cocaine, or amphetamines (although the latter may be prescribed with caution with MAO inhibitors). Medications most likely to cause serotonin syndrome are a few opiates, including meperidine (Demerol) and dextromethorphan (which is commonly used as an over-the-counter cough suppressant), and all strongly serotonergic antidepressants, such as the SSRIs, venlafaxine, and duloxetine.

MAO inhibitors are also characterized by nondangerous but problematic side effects that further limit their acceptance by patients and that severely decrease compliance with their use. These include postural dizziness, weight gain (especially with phenelzine and isocaroxazid), insomnia, daytime fatigue, and sexual dysfunction.

Summary

MAO inhibitors are not currently primary agents in the treatment of psychiatric disorders. Their problematic everyday side effects, dietary and medication restrictions, and the potential consequences of violating these restrictions make these medications unpopular with prescribing physicians and patients alike. Nonetheless, for a small subgroup of patients, they can be dramatically effective and should therefore still be considered in the treatment of refractory patients.

MICHAEL J. GITLIN

See also

Biological Models of Depression

References

American Psychiatric Association. (1994). *Diagnostic and statistical manual of mental disorders* (4th ed.). Washington, DC: Author.

Davis, J. M., Wang, Z., & Janicak, P. G. (1993). A quantitative analysis of clinical drug trials for the treatment of affective disorders. *Psychopharmacological Bulletin, 29,* 175–181.

Gardner, D. M., Shulman, K. I., Walker, S. E., & Tailor, S. A. N. (1996). The making of a user friendly MAOI diet. *Journal of Clinical Psychiatry, 57,* 99–104.

Liebowitz, M. R., Quitkin, F. M., Stewart, J. W., McGrath, P. J., Harrison, W. M., Markowitz, J. S., et al. (1988). Antidepressant specificity in atypical depression. *Archives of General Psychiatry, 45,* 129–137.

Mothers and Depression

Several models of risk for the development of psychopathology suggest reasons to be concerned about children born to and raised by women who suffer from depression. Concern also stems from depression in women being highly prevalent, even if the definition is restricted to a diagnosis of depression as defined by the *Diagnostic and Statistical Manual of Mental Disorders*, fourth edition (*DSM-IV*; American Psychiatric Association, 1994), and especially for depression that might just miss meeting diagnostic criteria but is reflected in depression symptom scales. Depression is also a highly recurrent disorder, with most depressed individuals having more than one episode, and women being particularly likely to have recurring short depressive episodes (Kessler, 2006). Although depression in both mothers and fathers is problematic for children, a meta-analysis of 134 samples, with a total of more than 60,000 parent-child dyads, showed that both internalizing and externalizing problems in children are more strongly associated with depression in mothers relative to depression in fathers (Connell & Goodman, 2002).

Associations With Psychopathology and Other Problems in Children

Multiple studies over the last few decades reveal a broad range of outcomes in children, from newborns (and even fetuses) to adolescents, that have been found to be associated with depression in mothers. Of particular interest has been depression in these children. A strong consensus from this literature is that from the earliest ages when depression can reliably be measured, rates of depression are significantly higher in children whose mothers suffer from depression relative to several groups to whom they have been compared. Rates of depression in the school-aged and adolescent children of depressed mothers range from 20% to 41%, with the variability within that range explained by the severity or impairment of the parent's depression, whether the father is also depressed, and a number of other sociodemographic variables. Only at adolescence are those rates higher in daughters relative to sons of depressed mothers. And compared to depression in same-age children of nondepressed parents, depression in children of depressed mothers has an earlier age of onset, has longer duration, and is associated with greater functional impairment and a higher likelihood of recurrence. Further, depression in mothers is also associated with children's higher rates of anxiety and with more externalizing behavior problems, even in very young children.

Other studies on children of depressed mothers, from infancy through adolescence, show problems in affective, cognitive, interpersonal, neuroendocrine, and brain functioning. These include more negative affect, early signs of cognitive vulnerability to depression (e.g., being more likely than controls to blame themselves for negative outcomes, being less likely to recall positive self-descriptive adjectives, and having lower self-concept), and scoring lower on measures of intelligence and having poorer academic performance overall. In terms of interpersonal functioning, compared to controls, infants of depressed mothers show less-secure attachment relationships, and, over the course of development, children of depressed mothers show problems in their interactions with their mothers (e.g., excessive compliance seen in preschool-aged children) and with peers (e.g., kindergarten-aged children of depressed mothers more often being excluded by peers). In studies of neurobiological or neuroendocrine functioning, researchers have found significant associations between maternal depression and two psychobiological systems in children that have been found to play a role in emotion regulation and expression: (a) stress responses measured in either autonomic activity (higher heart rate and lower vagal tone) or in stress hormonal levels (higher cortisol as an index of hypothalamic-pituitary-adrenal axis activity) and (b) cortical activity in the prefrontal cortex (greater relative right frontal EEG asymmetries). In sum, maternal depression is associated with higher rates of psychopathology in children and also with other problems that may be early signs of (or markers for) depression or other disorders or may represent vulnerabilities to the later development of psychopathology.

Mechansims for Transmission of Risk for Psychopathology From Depression in Mothers

The integrative model for the transmission of risk to children of depressed mothers (Goodman & Gotlib, 1999) proposed four mechanisms, individual and interacting, to explain associations between maternal depression and the development of psychopathology and other disorders in children: heritability; innate dysfunctional neuroregulatory mechanisms; exposure to mother's negative and/or maladaptive cognitions, behaviors, and affect; and exposure to stressful environments. The term *mechanism* refers to the statistical concept of mediation, meaning intervening or causal variables or processes by which maternal depression has its effects on the development of psychopathology in the children.

With regard to genetic mechanisms, heritability likely plays several roles. First, heritability explains significant amounts of the variance in depression and other disorders found in children of depressed mothers. Although some recent findings have been promising, no particular genes have been definitively tied to these associations. Identifying such genes promises to reveal the biological mechanisms regulated by these genes, which may increase vulnerability to the development of psychopathology in children who inherit these gene variations. Second, heritability also contributes significantly to vulnerabilities to depression and other disorders. That is, high levels of heritability are found for individual differences in behavioral inhibition and shyness, low self-esteem, neuroticism, sociability, subjective well-being, expression of negative emotion, and frontal EEG asymmetry.

The second proposed mechanism of the Goodman and Gotlib (1999) model is that, whether through genetics or adverse prenatal experiences, children of depressed mothers may be born with dysfunctional neuroendocrine systems (especially cortisol basal levels and reactivity) or abnormal brain development (e.g., frontal lobe activity). Such systems are known to play important roles in emotional regulation processes and, thus, likely increase vulnerability to the later development of psychopathology. The 10% to 15% of women who experience prenatal depression may expose their fetuses to conditions that impair their psychobiological systems, although knowledge of what those conditions might be is just beginning to be revealed. Possibilities being studied include neuroendocrine alterations associated with depression or stress, constricted blood flow, poor health behaviors (e.g., smoking, drinking, inadequate nutrition), and exposure to antidepressant medications. Even without yet understanding how it might happen, evidence is already beginning to suggest that antenatal maternal mood can have lasting effects on the psychological development of a child.

The third proposed mechanism concerns depression in mothers being associated with children's exposure to problematic qualities of parenting, which are understood to be a reflection of the interpersonal deficits associated with depression in women. These interpersonal deficits serve both as models of maladaptive social functioning and also as stressors to the children. Decades of research, summarized in a meta-analytic review (Lovejoy, Graczyk, O'Hare, & Neuman, 2000), reveal that maternal depression is strongly associated with negative (hostile or coercive) parenting behavior, moderately associated with parenting characterized as disengagement, and slightly associated with lower levels of positive behavior. At least some of these parenting qualities have also been shown to mediate associations between depression in mothers and children's development of psychopathology. In addition, researchers are finding that living with a parent with depression is stressful both in relation to and beyond the problems with parenting (Hammen, 2002), and children struggle to cope with these stressors (Compas, Langrock, Keller, Merchant, & Copeland, 2002). In particular, depressed mothers' less responsive, harsh, or inconsistent parenting of infants and young children may serve as an early life stressor.

The fourth mechanism in the Goodman and Gotlib (1999) model concerns maternal depression increasing children's exposure to stress. Depression in mothers may be stressful for children because of the inadequate parenting, as reviewed above, the symptoms and episodic course of the mothers' depression, the chronic and episodic stressors that are often the context for depression, and the stress generation (e.g., marital conflict) found to be associated with depression. Among findings consistent with these ideas are that (a) infants' interaction with an insensitive depressed mother was associated with the development of the infants' pattern of brain activity characterized by reduced activity in the left frontal region (Dawson et al., 2003),

(b) depression in adolescent offspring of depressed parents was more strongly associated with chronic and episodic social stressors than depression in adolescents of parents who had not suffered from depression (Grant et al., 2003), (c) social disadvantage (e.g., poverty), which is often found to be associated with depression, mediated associations between maternal depression and children's depression or other behavioral problems (Cicchetti, Rogosch, & Toth, 1998), although not for the association between postnatal depression and 11-year-old children's IQ scores (Hay & Pawlby, 2001), (d) marital distress mediated the association between maternal depressive symptoms and adolescents' externalizing symptoms, although a pathway from marital distress through maternal depression predicted adolescents' depression (Davies & Dumenci, 1999), and (e) maternal depression symptoms mediated the relation between parents' problematic drinking and 6- to 12-year-old children's internalizing problems (El-Sheikh & Flanagan, 2001).

In addition to the support for each of the four mechanisms of risk, researchers are increasingly addressing the complex ways that the individual mechanisms of risk may interact to create diverse pathways to disorder, even if the outcome (e.g., depression), is the same. This concept is termed *equifinality* (Cicchetti & Rogosch, 1996). Transactional models are particularly helpful for understanding these individual, complex pathways, emphasizing how the mutual exchanges between characteristics of the child and the environment, as they unfold over time, result in the development of psychopathology (Cicchetti & Toth, 1995). Examples of theoretical models of the interface between two or more mechanisms include passive, reactive, and active gene-environment correlation or covariation, gene-environment interactions such as stress-diathesis models, genetic vulnerabilities interacting with other biological vulnerabilities or cognitive vulnerabilities, genes interacting with other genes, stress-diathesis models with diatheses other than genetics (such as temperament), and child qualities evoking environmental qualities.

Moderators of Risk for the Transmission of Psychopathology From Depression in Mothers

Equally important as understanding *how* depression in mothers negatively impacts children is determining which children may be more at risk (i.e., moderators of risk), given that not all children of depressed mothers develop psychopathology. Although most studies did not include tests of moderators, several important findings have emerged. First, maternal characteristics are important. For example, the pattern of mothers' depression symptoms (mean, maximum, minimum, and variability in numbers of symptoms per month) over children's ages from 14 to 30 months predicted observed children's functioning even after controlling for diagnostic status (Seifer, Dickstein, Sameroff, Magee, & Hayden, 2001). Similarly, postnatal depression that remits by 6 months, although characterizing only about 25% of women with postpartum depression, is not associated with mothers' qualities of interaction with their 6-month-old infants (Field, 1992) or with Bayley mental and motor scale scores at 1 year of age (Field, 1992), in contrast to babies of women whose postpartum depression persists.

In another prospective study of infants followed through age 5, exposure as infants predicted higher levels of co-occurring internalizing and externalizing symptoms relative to children who were not first exposed to their mothers depression until they were toddlers or preschool-aged; later initial exposure was associated with increased risk of externalizing symptoms not co-occurring with internalizing symptoms, especially among girls (Essex, Klein, Miech, & Smider, 2001). Severity and chronicity of maternal depression symptoms from pregnancy through child age 5 years, as well as their statistical interaction, also predicted 5-year-olds' higher levels of behavior problems, as did timing (more recent timing was associated with more behavior problems), although when that sample of children reached age 15, severity was a stronger predictor of children's depression than was chronicity, but chronicity was the stronger predictor of psychopathology other than depression. Finally, Hammen and colleagues (1991) reported a synchrony between maternal and child depression in that children of depressed mothers tended to have their depressive episodes in close proximity in time following their mothers' episodes. Another suspected moderating characteristic of depression is comorbidity. Although studies are limited, they are suggestive of the additive, if not interacting, role of panic disorder, and personality disorders among women with depression.

Second, in addition to maternal characteristics as moderators, several theoretical models suggest that fathers will play at least a moderating role in the association between maternal depression and children's development, if not an independent role. At minimum, through their genes, fathers contribute to children's risk for depression as much as mothers, albeit potentially through different mechanisms. As a function of assortative mating, children whose mothers are depressed have a higher-than-average likelihood of having a father who has depression **or another** disorder. Researchers found that fathers' depression contributes to the prediction of child psychopathology beyond that explained by maternal depression, although some find that results differ for male and female offspring and for the specific child outcome.

Third, child characteristics such as temperament, gender, and intellectual and social-cognitive skills also might moderate associations between maternal depression and the development of psychopathology. Although each of these child characteristics other than gender are also potential outcomes, they also may enhance positive adaptation or, alternatively, exacerbate risk in the context of adversities associated with depression in mothers. For example, temperament is sometimes found to be directly associated with maternal depression and also to be a moderator: the temperament construct of impulsivity (being low) was found to be associated with increases in externalizing behavior from ages 5 to 17 among sons, but not daughters of depressed mothers (Leve, Kim, & Pears, 2005). Coping styles also were found to play a moderating role in that children who report using volitional coping responses to the stressors associated with having a depressed mother have fewer emotional and behavior problems (Compas et al., 2002). Similarly, among adolescents whose parents were depressed, having more advanced social-cognitive skills was associated with better adaptation (Beardslee, Schultz, & Selman, 1987). In fact, Gladstone and Beardslee (2002) have had success with interventions including a component of enhancing adolescent offspring's perspective-taking and other skills to prevent their development of psychopathology.

Conclusions

The strongest conclusion to be drawn from this field of study is that there are multiple alternative pathways that the children of depressed mothers may follow, and transactional models are essential to these understandings. Understanding the complexities of the nature of the risk (having a mother with depression), mechanisms, moderators, and transactional processes provides a daunting challenge to clinicians and clinical researchers who feel compelled to intervene, driven by the needs of these children. Gladstone and Beardslee (2002) provided a helpful review of this limited literature from a developmental perspective and empirically based suggestions for interventions targeted to particular ages of children. Although there are limits in applying knowledge of risk factors to the design of preventive interventions (Silberg & Rutter, 2002), the literature reviewed here ideally will serve as beginning for considerations of the development of guidelines for preventive interventions or treatments for children whose mothers have suffered from depression.

SHERRYL H. GOODMAN

See also

Childhood Depression: Family Context
Family Transmission of Depression

Fathers and Depression Parenting

References

American Psychiatric Association. (1994). *Diagnostic and statistical manual of mental disorders* (4th ed.). Washington, DC: Author.

Beardslee, W. R., Schultz, L. H., & Selman, R. L. (1987). Level of social-cognitive development, adaptive functioning, and DSM-III diagnoses in adolescent offspring of parents with affective disorders: Implications for the development of the capacity for mutuality. *Developmental Psychology, 23,* 807–815.

Cicchetti, D., & Rogosch, F. A. (1996). Equifinality and multifinality in developmental psychopathology. *Development and Psychopathology, 8,* 597–600.

Cicchetti, D., Rogosch, F. A., & Toth, S. L. (1998). Maternal depressive disorder and contextual risk: Contributions to the development of attachment insecurity and behavior problems in toddlerhood. *Development and Psychopathology, 10,* 283–300.

Cicchetti, D., & Toth, S. L. (1995). Developmental psychopathology and disorders of affect. In D. Cicchetti & D. J. Cohen (Eds.), *Developmental psychopathology, Vol. 2: Risk, disorder, and adaptation* (pp. 369–420). Oxford, UK: Wiley.

Compas, B. E., Langrock, A. M., Keller, G., Merchant, M. J., & Copeland, M. E. (2002). Children coping with parental depression: Processes of adaptation to family stress. In S. H. Goodman & I. H. Gotlib (Eds.), *Children of depressed parents: Mechanisms of risk and implications for treatment* (pp. 227–252). Washington, DC: American Psychological Association.

Connell, A. M., & Goodman, S. H. (2002). The association between psychopathology in fathers versus mothers and children's internalizing and externalizing behavior problems: A meta-analysis. *Psychological Bulletin, 128,* 746–773.

Davies, P. T., & Dumenci, L. (1999). The interplay between maternal depressive symptoms and marital distress in the prediction of adolescent adjustment. *Journal of Marriage and the Family, 61,* 238–254.

Dawson, G., Ashman, S. B., Panagiotides, H., Hessl, D., Self, J., Yamada, E., et al. (2003). Preschool outcomes of children of depressed others: Role of maternal behavior, contextual risk, and children's brain activity. *Child Development, 74,* 1158–1175.

El-Sheikh, M., & Flanagan, E. (2001). Parental problem drinking and children's adjustment: Family conflict and parental depression as mediators and moderators of risk. *Journal of Abnormal Child Psychology, 29,* 417–432.

Essex, M. J., Klein, M. H., Miech, R., & Smider, N. A. (2001). Timing of initial exposure to maternal major depression and children's mental health symptoms in kindergarten. *British Journal of Psychiatry, 179,* 151–156.

Field, T. (1992). Infants of depressed mothers. *Development and Psychopathology, 4,* 49–66.

Gladstone, T. R. G., & Beardslee, W. R. (2002). Treatment, intervention, and prevention with children of depressed parents: A developmental perspective. In S. H. Goodman & I. H. Gotlib (Eds.), *Children of depressed parents: Mechanisms of risk and implications for treatment* (pp. 277–305). Washington, DC: American Psychological Association.

Goodman, S. H., & Gotlib, I. H. (1999). Risk for psychopathology in the children of depressed mothers: A developmental model for understanding mechanisms of transmission. *Psychological Review, 106,* 458–490.

Grant, K. E., Compas, B. E., Stuhlmacher, A. F., Thurm, A. E., McMahon, S. D., & Halpert, J. A. (2003). Stressors and child and adolescent psychopathology: Moving from markers to mechanisms of risk. *Psychological Bulletin, 129,* 447–466.

Hammen, C. (1991). Generation of stress in the course of unipolar depression. *Journal of Abnormal Psychology, 100,* 555–561.

Hammen, C. (2002). Context of stress in families of children with depressed parents. In S. H. Goodman & I. H. Gotlib (Eds.), *Children of depressed parents: Mechanisms of risk and implications for treatment* (pp. 175–202). Washington, DC: American Psychological Association.

Hammen, C., Burge, D., & Adrian, C. (1991). Timing of mother and child depression in a longitudinal study of children at risk. *Journal of Consulting & Clinical Psychology, 59*(2), 341–345.

Hay, D. F., & Pawlby, S. (2001). Intellectual problems shown by 11-year-old children whose mothers had postnatal depression. *Journal of Child Psychology and Psychiatry and Allied Disciplines, 42,* 871–889.

Kessler, R. C. (2006). The epidemiology of depression among women. In C. L. M. Keyes & S. H. Goodman (Eds.), *Women and depression: A handbook for the social, behavior, and biomedical sciences* (pp. 22–40). New York: Cambridge University Press.

Leve, L. D., Kim, H. K., & Pears, K. C. (2005). Childhood temperament and family environment as predictors of internalizing and externalizing trajectories from ages 5 to 17. *Journal of Abnormal Child Psychology, 33,* 505–520.

Lovejoy, M. C., Graczyk, P. A., O'Hare, E., & Neuman, G. (2000). Maternal depression and parenting behavior: A meta-analytic review. *Clinical Psychology Review, 20,* 561–592.

Rutter, M., Dunn, J., Plomin, R., Simonoff, E., Pickles, A., Maughan, B., et al. (1997). Integrating nature and nurture: Implications of person-environment correlations and interactions for developmental psychopathology *Development and Psychopathology, 9,* 335–364.

Seifer, R., Dickstein, S., Sameroff, A. J., Magee, K. D., & Hayden, L. C. (2001). Infant mental health and variability of parental depression symptoms. *Journal of the American Academy of Child and Adolescent Psychiatry, 40,* 1375–1382.

Silberg, J., & Rutter, M. (2002). Nature-nurture interplay in the risks associated with parental depression. In S. H. Goodman & I. H. Gotlib (Eds.), *Children of depressed parents: Mechanisms of risk and implications for treatment* (pp. 13–36). Washington, DC: American Psychological Association.

N

Neural Systems of Reward

Depression has been conceptualized as a disorder of dysregulated positive affect and unusual reward processing. And although much research on the affective features of the disorder has focused on topics related to negative affect, several theoretical perspectives lead to the assertion that depression involves difficulties with positive affect. These difficulties can include dampened subjective experience of emotions such as joy, reduced motivation to experience pleasant events, and infrequent engagement in behavior likely to lead to reinforcement or subjective positive affect. From an affective neuroscience perspective in particular, the neural substrates of these subjective and behavioral alterations in positive affect lie in the brain's reward processing systems (Forbes & Dahl, 2005).

To illustrate this assertion, consider the example of a young woman experiencing a major depressive episode. She may feel less happiness during activities she typically enjoys. When she is spending time with friends, pursuing hobbies, interacting with her romantic partner, or dealing with a challenging project at work, she might find that her pleasant mood is less intense or more fleeting than usual. She might lose interest in pursuing these formerly pleasant activities, and as a result she might pursue them less often. If she does not have fun while spending time with close friends, for instance, she might be less likely to initiate social plans or join in when invited. When she thus withdraws from social contact, she reduces her chances of experiencing the rewards of pleasant emotions, affiliation, or social support. This reduced experience of reward could lead her motivation and mood to decline further, maintaining her depression.

In this example, rewards—or appealing stimuli that inspire behavior and reinforce it once it occurs—play a pivotal role in the affect, motivation, and behavior associated with a depressive episode. This young woman does not respond to social rewards in her depressed state, she experiences changes in her motivation to obtain reward, and through her subsequent social withdrawal, she misses opportunities to experience rewards. Presumably, the neural systems that respond to rewarding stimuli, initiate behaviors that result in rewards, form expectations of rewarding outcomes for behavior, and maintain associations between circumstances and rewards are operating differently for her. Unlike someone without depression, and unlike herself in a nondepressed state, she responds weakly to rewarding circumstances and even fails to put herself in those circumstances.

Reward Neuroanatomy

The neural systems important to reward include brain areas such as the ventral and dorsal striatum, the orbitofrontal cortex, and the amygdala. The ventral striatum contains the nucleus accumbens, which is well established as critical to the experience of pleasure and the initial neural response to a wide variety of rewards. The dorsal striatum, including the caudate and putamen, has proposed functions related to decision-making and reward-motivated behaviors. The orbitofrontal cortex processes the affective and motivational aspects of stimuli and serves in part to regulate striatal reactivity to reward. The amygdala responds to the presence of reward and contributes to affective and behavioral responses to reward. Finally, the dopamine neuromodulatory system plays an important role in the functioning of reward systems through projections of dopamine neurons in the midbrain to the ventral striatum, dorsal striatum, and prefrontal cortex.

Theoretical Role of Reward Systems in Depression

The development of neural systems of reward during adolescence has also been identified as important to the striking rates of onset of depression during this period. In a recently proposed model, the development of the dopamine system and the prefrontal cortex during adolescence are claimed both to support social and affective changes and to create vulnerability to the development of depression during this period (Davey, Yucel, & Allen, 2008). Because of development in these neural systems, adolescents engage in more sensation-seeking behaviors, find romantic experiences especially exciting and meaningful, and are able to set long-term, abstract goals such as starting a new romantic relationship. However, the increased self-awareness and improved social cognition of this developmental period can make failures in achieving goals particularly devastating to adolescents' mood and can lead to dysregulation of dopamine signaling. In vulnerable adolescents, this process is postulated to trigger the onset of a depressive episode.

Dopamine signaling has been proposed to be disrupted in depression. Specifically, animal models of depression, studies of response to psychostimulants in adults with severe depression, and imaging studies of dopamine receptor binding all point to the possibility

of reduced dopamine transmission in at least a subset of people with depression (Dunlop & Nemeroff, 2007). Similarly, manipulation of brain-derived neurotrophic factor, a protein that promotes the growth and survival of neurons, in dopamine pathways from the ventral tegmental area to the nucleus accumbens of rodents further implicates the dopamine system in depression-related behaviors (Nestler & Carlezon, 2006).

Findings on Reward-Related Brain Function in Depression

People with depression exhibit reduced brain reactivity to rewarding stimuli. To date, functional neuroimaging studies have reported that relative to their healthy peers, adults with depression experience less reward-related—especially striatal—activation when processing reward stimuli. The procedures employed in these studies have included responding to affective stimuli such as positive-valence words and undergoing induction of positive mood, such as through recall of positive autobiographical events. Studies of depression in young people have reported a similar pattern, with reduced activation in reward-related areas such as the striatum and the orbitofrontal cortex during reward tasks such as making guesses or decisions that could result in monetary reward. Assessment of reward-related brain function in people with depression has indicated that both the anticipation of reward and the receipt of reward seem to elicit reduced function in reward circuits.

Treatments Targeting Neural Systems of Reward

Current mainstream treatments for depression have begun to explicitly target positive affect in general and neural reward systems in particular. While traditional cognitive psychotherapy for depression often emphasizes reducing negative affect rather than enhancing positive affect, a new generation of psychotherapy is incorporating activities such as savoring positive experiences into treatment. Also, more behavioral approaches generally strive to encourage behavioral activation, which is likely to increase exposure to rewarding stimuli and to enhance motivation to obtain reward.

Pharmacologic approaches to treating depression now include several that enhance dopamine signaling, either by blocking dopamine removal or reuptake from the synapse or by preventing degradation of dopamine. In addition, antidepressant medications that inhibit norepinephrine reuptake also serve to increase prefrontal dopamine levels. These pharmacologic approaches are thus likely to improve reactivity in reward-related brain areas.

Very recently, a neurosurgical technique called deep-brain stimulation has been applied to the functioning of neural systems of reward in adults with treatment-resistant depression (Schlaepfer et al., 2008). In this technique, electrodes are surgically implanted in the ventral striatum bilaterally and automatically activated in pulses. Preliminary findings suggest that deep-brain stimulation of this important reward-related region can produce long-term improvement of symptoms and changes in resting brain function.

Conclusion

Neural systems of reward appear to play an important role in depression. These systems have been relatively ignored in research to date, but they provide a potentially fruitful topic for understanding both the pathophysiology and the treatment of depression.

ERIKA E. FORBES

See also

Amygdala
Brain Circuitry
Neuroimaging and Psychosocial Treatments for Depression

References

Davey, C. G., Yucel, M., & Allen, N. B. (2008). The emergence of depression in adolescence: Development of the prefrontal cortex and the representation of reward. *Neuroscience and Biobehavioral Reviews, 32*, 1–19.

Dunlop, B. W., & Nemeroff, C. B. (2007). The role of dopamine in the pathophysiology of depression. *Archives of General Psychiatry, 64*, 327–337.

Forbes, E. E., & Dahl, R. E. (2005). Neural systems of positive affect: Relevance to understanding child and adolescent depression? *Development and Psychopathology, 17*, 827–850.

Nestler, E. J., & Carlezon, W. A., Jr. (2006). The mesolimbic dopamine reward circuit in depression. *Biological Psychiatry, 59*, 1151–1159.

Schlaepfer, T. E., Cohen, M. X., Frick, C., Kosel, M., Brodesser, D., Axmacher, N., et al. (2008). Deep brain stimulation to reward circuitry alleviates anhedonia in refractory major depression. *Neuropsychopharmacology, 33*, 368–377.

Neuroimaging and Psychosocial Treatments for Depression

The availability of neuroimaging techniques such as positron emission tomography (PET) and functional MRI (fMRI) have stimulated interest in examining the brain changes that occur with psychotherapy. These techniques enable researchers not only to identify the neural substrates of cognitive and emotional processes that characterize depressive disorders, but also to examine, by observation of localized changes in blood flow or glucose metabolism, how those processes are affected by treatment. Imaging methods provide a complementary approach to behavioral measures of affect and cognition for generating and testing hypotheses about the processes involved in recovery from depression.

Although interest in brain mechanisms that mediate the response to psychotherapy is not new, the application of neuroimaging techniques in psychotherapy research is a relatively recent development. While a growing number of studies have examined treatment-related neural changes in depression, most have focused on changes associated with antidepressant medications. Pharmacological studies converge on the idea that antidepressants target primarily subcortical and limbic brain areas. Does psychotherapy act via the same, overlapping, or entirely different pathways in the brain?

An influential model describing the neural substrates of depressed mood has been proposed by Mayberg (Mayberg, 1997). This limbic-cortical systems model proposes the involvement of two compartments within the brain. The dorsal compartment includes the dorsolateral prefrontal cortex, inferior parietal, dorsal anterior cingulate, and medial frontal. Dysfunctions in these areas are thought to play a role in the cognitive aspects of depression, such as impaired attentional control and executive functioning. The ventral component includes the hypothalamic-pituitary-adrenal axis and limbic-paralimbic areas (e.g., the hippocampus, subgenual anterior cingulate, and insula). Dysfunctions in these areas are thought to underlie vegetative aspects of depression, such as sleep disturbances, diminished libido, and loss of appetite. Affect regulation involves the reciprocal interaction between the ventral and dorsal compartments.

Skill-based psychosocial treatments for depression such as cognitive behavior therapy (CBT) teach patients strategies to cope with the maladaptive cognitive, affective, and behavioral changes that characterize depressive episodes. These strategies include, for example, restructuring negative interpretations of daily life events and learning to redirect attention toward more positive pursuits. These strategies are thought to recruit higher-order executive areas of the brain, such as the prefrontal cortex, represented by the dorsal compartment of Mayberg's model. Thus, it would be expected that changes in these top-down areas may be more likely seen in psychosocial treatments compared to pharmacological interventions.

PET and fMRI studies have demonstrated that recovery from an acute episode of depression is associated with discernible patterns of cortical and subcortical changes. Although there are inconsistencies among these studies, there have been a handful of replicated findings. For example, perhaps the most consistent finding is the normalization of activation patterns in the frontal lobes, which has been observed across a variety of different treatments (including placebo).

The next question, then, is whether there are changes in neural function that can *discriminate* among treatment modalities. In other words, are there patterns of brain changes that are *specific to* psychotherapy compared to antidepressant medications or unassisted recovery?

Only a handful of studies to date have examined the neural correlates of recovery from depression specific to some form of psychotherapy (either interpersonal therapy, IPT, or CBT). A study comparing IPT to paroxetine found no specific neural changes that differentiated the two treatments (Brody et al., 2001). However, treatment-specific patterns of change have been reported with CBT. For example, changes in resting glucose metabolism in the anterior cingulate cortex (ACC) and areas of prefrontal cortex (including dorsolateral and ventromedial) have been observed in CBT but not in pharmacotherapy (Goldapple et al., 2004; Kennedy et al., 2007), suggesting that distinct neural changes may mediate the response to different modes of treatment.

The pattern of brain changes that correlate with symptom remission in CBT appears to occur early in treatment and supports the notion that CBT may operate primarily through top-down mechanisms of action (Mayberg, 2006). For example, the ACC is thought to be involved in cognitive control and allocation of attentional resources. Thus, CBT may act, at least in part, by correcting information processing dysfunctions that underlie depressive cognitions. This pattern differs from that seen with pharmacotherapy-induced changes, which typically involve bottom-up limbic and subcortical changes.

The use of neuroimaging methods to examine the neural mediators of change in psychotherapy is clearly in its infancy, but there is empirical evidence to suggest that CBT is associated with changes in brain areas that subserve cognitive functions logically connected to the strategies used in CBT. It should be noted, however, that the experimental designs used in the treatment studies discussed here have only examined changes in brain function assessed during a resting state (i.e., participants undergo brain imaging while resting quietly). An alternative design, which has been less widely used in psychotherapy research, correlates changes in brain blood flow with performance on some behavioral measure. In this type of study, participants undergo neuroimaging while completing a cognitive task intended to activate certain areas of the brain. This latter design may be particularly promising for examining questions about mechanisms of action associated with treatment and may yield new information about how different treatment modalities affect the brain.

KARI M. EDDINGTON AND TIMOTHY J. STRAUMAN

See also

Cognitive Behavioral Therapy
Functional Neuroimaging

Interpersonal Psychotherapy
Neural Systems of Reward

References

Brody, A. L., Saxena, S., Stoessel, P., Gillies, L. A., Fairbanks, L. A., Alborzian, S., et al. (2001). Regional brain metabolic changes in patients with major depression treated with either paroxetine or interpersonal therapy: Preliminary findings. *Archives of General Psychiatry, 58,* 631–640.

Goldapple, K., Segal, Z. V., Garson, C., Lau, M., Bieling, P., Kennedy, S., et al. (2004). Modulation of cortical-limbic pathways in major depression: Treatment-specific effects of cognitive behavior therapy. *Archives of General Psychiatry, 61,* 34–41.

Kennedy, S. H., Konarski, J. Z., Segal, Z. V., Lau, M. A., Bieling, P. J., McIntyre, R. S., et al. (2007). Differences in brain glucose metabolism between responders to CBT and venlafaxine in a 16-week randomized controlled trial. *American Journal of Psychiatry, 164,* 778–788.

Mayberg, H. S. (1997). Limbic-cortical dysregulation: A proposed model of depression. *Journal of Neuropsychiatry and Clinical Neuroscience, 9,* 471–481.

Mayberg, H. S. (2006). Defining neurocircuits in depression: Strategies toward treatment selection based on neuroimaging phenotypes. *Psychiatric Annals, 36,* 259–268.

O
_____

Omega-3 Fatty Acids

Reduced dietary consumption of omega-3 fatty acids, one class of the polyunsaturated fatty acids (PUFAs), has been proposed to account for at least some of the increase in the prevalence of depression observed over the last 50 to 100 years. Theoretical arguments tend to center around evidence that sources of omega-3, predominantly found in cold-water fish and some botanical seeds in the modern diet but which included grass-fed livestock and intertidal shellfish in the Pleistocene human diet, have been supplanted disproportionately by foods with predominantly omega-6 fatty acid. This trend highlights a number of historical changes in human dietary and agricultural practices (e.g., movement from aquatic to terrestrial meat sources, and reliance on grain-based feeds for cattle) occurring principally as a result of a movement from a hunter-gather lifestyle to agrarian and industrial lifestyles dating from the Neolithic revolution. Various epidemiological, observational, and clinical trial data support the notion that the activity or metabolism of omega-3—particularly two long-chain forms, eicosapentaenoic acid (EPA) and docosahexaenoic acid (DHA)—may be implicated in antidepressant physiological pathways.

Possible Mechanisms of Antidepressant Action

DHA is an important component in the development and action of numerous neurological structures. In particular, its actions in promoting flexible cell membranes and receptor activity play a key role in healthy neurological development. Many of these processes are not merely attributed to DHA independently but instead to the proportion of DHA to arachidonic acid (an omega-6 form) in the brain. This attribution has tended to focus research on both types of fatty acid chains when developing fatty-acid-based interventions.

Conversely, EPA has not been implicated in neurological development to the same extent as DHA. Nevertheless, EPA has been suggested to contribute to omega-3 antidepressant activities by inhibiting the production of proinflammatory molecules, which are often found to be elevated in individuals suffering from depression. Several converging lines of evidence, therefore, suggest that omega-3 metabolism may result in multiple routes of antidepressant action demanding both balanced proportions of omega-3 to omega-6 (with 3:1 to 1:1 ratios often being cited) and balanced proportions of EPA to DHA (with a 2:1 ratio being most commonly cited).

A shorter form of omega-3, α-linolenic acid (ALA), rarely has been researched in connection to the physiology of depression due to the relatively inefficient metabolism of ALA to longer-chain omega-3 in the human body.

Epidemiological and Observational Data

Inverse relationships between fish consumption and depression were first identified by

Hibbeln (1998). Since that time, several studies have identified omega-3 depletion in human tissues among individuals suffering from depression, and inverse correlations also have been found between durations of fish oil supplementation and depressive symptomatology in cross-sectional surveys. Such studies, however, are confounded by abundant evidence suggesting that increased omega-3 intake also tends to be associated with other lifestyle-based activities negatively linked to depression. Subsequent findings positively linking omega-3 consumption to increased brain volume of several structures, including areas involved in mood regulation, are more authoritative, especially given that significant differences have been found both through neuroimaging of live participants and postmortem studies. Additionally, several studies on rats have confirmed a link between omega-3 fatty acids and depression-like behaviors, with controlled supplementation being associated with a decrease and depletion being associated with an increase in analog behaviors.

Clinical Trials

Opportunities to perform clinical trials on the efficacy of omega-3 supplementation have been complicated by several factors, including the difficulty of effectively blinding participants to treatment levels, finding appropriate placebos, and determining the appropriateness of using omega-3 supplementation as a monotherapy rather than an adjunctive treatment. Additionally, conclusions about omega-3 antidepressant efficacy often have been extrapolated from findings in the treatment of depressive episodes of participants diagnosed with bipolar disorder, as opposed to those suffering from major depression. Overall, data from randomized controlled trials (RCTs) and other clinical trials have tended to support omega-3 supplementation as an adjuvant treatment for depressive symptoms (Owen, Rees, & Parker, 2008).

A double-blind, placebo-controlled study by Stoll and colleagues (1999) suggested that a 6.2-g to 3.4-g ratio of EPA to DHA as adjuvant treatment to medication was effective in preventing depressive relapse in bipolar patients when compared to placebo over a 4-month treatment period. Subsequent acute-treatment RCTs for bipolar disorder using EPA alone, however, have yielded mixed results. Of note, better antidepressant response has been linked to relatively low doses of EPA (1–3 g) when administered in the absence of DHA. In almost all cases, however, any evidence supporting the efficacy of omega-3 in the treatment of bipolar disorder has been limited to depressive, rather than manic, episodes.

Studies on unipolar depression have yielded more uniform results. At least one small-scale RCT has suggested that omega-3 supplementation (approximately 0.4-g EPA and 0.2-g DHA) in children may be effective (Nemets, Nemets, Apter, Bracha, & Belmaker, 2006); unfortunately, this and other studies have been markedly compromised by methodology problems and poor choice of placebo. Several RCTs have shown significant contributions of omega-3 supplementation (including both EPA-alone and EPA-DHA combination treatments) in ameliorating unipolar depression in adults; conversely, DHA-alone treatments have not yielded significant effect sizes. Dosages found effective are similar to those found to be effective in treating bipolar depression. Lack of significant effects of omega-3 fatty acid supplementation in some RCTs often are attributed to ineffective dosing or selection of samples in which patients do not have depleted omega-3 levels prior to treatment. Clinical findings, while preliminarily supporting the use of EPA and EPA-DHA combinations as adjuvant treatments for depression, in both unipolar and bipolar types, have not adequately investigated the use of omega-3 as monotherapy for depression.

K. A. Lehman

See also

Exercise and Depression
Therapeutic Lifestyle Change

References

Hibbeln, J. R. (1998). Fish consumption and major depression. *Lancet, 351,* 1213.

Nemets, H., Nemets, B., Apter, A., Bracha, Z., & Belmaker, R. H. (2006). Omega-3 treatment of childhood depression: A controlled, double-blind pilot study. *American Journal of Psychiatry, 163,* 1098–1100.

Owen, C., Rees, A.-M., & Parker, G. (2008). The role of fatty acids in the development and treatment of mood disorders. *Current Opinion in Psychiatry, 21,* 19–24.

Stoll, A. L., Severus, W. E., Freeman, M. P., Rueter, S., Zboyan, H. A., Diamond, E., et al. (1999). Omega 3 fatty acids in bipolar disorder: A preliminary double-blind, placebo-controlled trial. *Archives of General Psychiatry, 56,* 407–412.

P

Parenting

As part of the ongoing search for information on the etiology and maintenance of depression, researchers are increasingly examining potential developmental factors. One such developmental factor is parenting. Parenting is hypothesized to contribute to depression in numerous ways, including conferral of information processing biases and self and world views that may both cause and maintain depression. Thus, empirical identification of parenting behaviors that are linked to offspring depression can both increase knowledge regarding the development and maintenance of depression and suggest targets for preventive intervention. What follows is a brief, selective review of relationships between received parenting and depression, with a focus on determinants of adult depression. Several specific topics are addressed: (a) major theories that gave rise to empirical research on parenting received by depressed individuals, (b) empirical research on parenting received by depressed individuals, and (c) possible mechanisms through which parenting might exert its effects on depression, including empirical support for such mechanisms.

Theories on the Relationship of Parenting to Offspring Depression

Bowlby's Attachment Theory

Among the most prominent theories guiding investigations of parenting and depression is Bowlby's attachment theory. Bowlby (1982) suggested that an attachment relationship consisting of proximity-maintaining behaviors by the human infant and caregiving behaviors of his or her primary caregivers typically forms during the first year of an infant's life. The purpose of this attachment is security and protection of the infant. These attachment relationships differ from many other types of social relationships in significant ways. First, attachment relationships are thought to be enduring. Attachment relationships formed during childhood appear to persist throughout the life span. Second, although a child may form more than one early attachment relationship, attachment figures are not interchangeable. For example, an attachment relationship with a deceased parent cannot be replaced by an attachment relationship with a surviving parent. Third, a child desires physical and emotional closeness with his or her attachment figure(s), and may become distressed upon uncontrollable separation. Finally, a child seeks security and comfort in attachment relationships; this latter component distinguishes attachment relationships from other social relationships. In sum, attachment relationships are unique and, according to attachment theorists, long-lasting parts of most people's lives.

During the course of a healthy, or secure, early attachment relationship, a child experiences consistently accessible and responsive caregiving on the part of the attachment figure. Through such experiences, a child may surmise that he or she is loved and valued. During the course of an unhealthy, or

416

insecure, attachment relationship, however, a child finds his or her caregivers to be inaccessible or unresponsive. Bowlby (1980) hypothesized that the childhood attachment relationships of depressed individuals are characterized by hostility and rejection by attachment figures, including active rebuffs of children's bids for responsive behavior and being told that one is inadequate and incompetent. Such messages of personal inadequacy and incompetency may be especially meaningful in that they are coming from someone who is uniquely valued by the child and who functions as one of only a few sources of security and comfort. Thus, the messages are likely to be quite well established in a child's developing belief system. These beliefs, in turn, may lead to depression.

Parental Bonding Theory

Parker's parental bonding theory (Parker, 1994; Parker, Tupling, & Brown, 1979) draws upon and complements the perspective of Bowlby by focusing on the concept of a caregiver- child bond. This bond may be either healthy or unhealthy and may contribute to depression and other forms of psychopathology in some circumstances. Parker suggests that the caregiver contribution to a bond can be defined along two dimensions: care and overprotection. Care is characterized as the degree of warmth and affection versus rejection or indifference demonstrated by a caregiver toward a child. Overprotection is characterized as the degree of control, intrusiveness, and discouragement of autonomy versus encouragement of developmentally appropriate independence and autonomy demonstrated by a caregiver toward a child. Optimal bonding is characterized by high levels of care coupled with low levels of overprotection, while distorted bonding may be characterized by high care and high overprotection (i.e., affectionate constraint), low care and low overprotection (i.e., absent or weak bonding), or low care and high overprotection (i.e., affectionless control).

According to the theory, parenting characterized by affectionless control may put individuals at particularly strong risk for depression. Parker focuses on the concept of self-esteem as the mechanism through which affectionless control creates risk for depression. He posits that low levels of care lead to low global self-esteem or, perhaps, gaps in self-esteem that leave individuals overly sensitized to negative interpersonal interactions and to perceive interpersonal interactions negatively. He further suggests that overprotective caregivers impede the development of social competence and increase the likelihood of children having low self-esteem in interpersonal interactions. Such low self-worth and poor social competence in turn confer risk for depression.

Empirical Research Examining the Parenting-Depression Link

Most of the research examining relationships between parenting and adult depression has been cross-sectional in nature, with retrospective assessment of parenting. In a typical study examining the roles of parental care and overprotection, adults with and adults without depression histories are compared on parenting variables. For example, Oakley-Browne and colleagues (Oakley-Browne, Joyce, Wells, Bushnell, & Hornblow, 1995) compared never-depressed and recently depressed adult women on levels of care and overprotection received by both parents. The recently depressed group reported lower levels of parental care and higher levels of parental overprotection compared to the never depressed group. Moreover, maternal care bore the strongest relationship to depression status, and this relationship persisted even after accounting for several other potential risk factors. Findings of this and other studies generally support the idea that low levels of care and high levels of overprotection confer risk for adult depression, with a somewhat greater impact of care in determining depression status (Parker, 1994).

Among the most relevant studies examining links between insecure childhood attachment and adult depression are those studies that explore the effects of childhood emotional abuse; such abuse typically includes the types of hostile, rejecting behaviors Bowlby suggested can be characteristic of insecure attachment relationships. In one recent effort, Hankin (2005) conducted two studies that examined whether childhood maltreatment was related to changes in adult depressive symptoms. Emotional abuse was related to depressive symptoms in the student samples of both studies. In a second recent effort, Maciejewski and Mazure (2006) found emotional abuse differentiated between individuals with and individuals without a history of major depression. Similar findings have been reported in a national sample (Sachs-Ericsson, Verona, Joiner, & Preacher, 2006). Such studies support a link between insecure childhood attachment and adult depression, although more studies conducting a direct assessment of childhood attachment would be useful.

Mechanisms Through Which Parenting Might Exert Its Effects on Depression

Along with studies linking various types of received parenting to adult depression, researchers have examined the mechanisms through which parenting might exert its effects. Such work may be particularly relevant to preventing and treating adult depression. Indeed, although the childhood experiences of depressed adults cannot be altered, the mechanisms through which such experiences still exert their effects often *can* be changed. Altering such mechanisms through mental health treatment has the potential to change the course of the disorder as well as prevent recurrences. Both attachment and parental bonding theories, as well as those of other depression theorists such as Beck (1967), provide direction for investigations of mediating mechanisms. Prominent among potential mediators suggested by these theories are dysfunctional beliefs about oneself and others and information-processing biases such as enhanced attention and memory for negative information.

Consistent with the direction of these theorists, a body of evidence is emerging that supports dysfunctional beliefs and biased information processing as mediators of relationships between maladaptive parenting and adult depression. For example, researchers have demonstrated that both maladaptive attachment-related beliefs and self-critical beliefs mediate between childhood emotional abuse and internalizing symptoms (Hankin, 2005; Sachs-Ericsson et al., 2006). Low levels of maternal care have also been linked to increased attention toward negative information among adults at risk for depression (Ingram & Ritter, 2000). Such studies have strong potential to inform the prevention and treatment of depression, as beliefs and information-processing biases are both modifiable through mental health interventions such as cognitive therapy and attention retraining.

Conclusions

Both theory and research suggest that parenting experiences of low care, high overprotection, hostility, and rejection may all contribute risk for depression in adulthood. Perhaps the next best step for investigating parenting-depression links is to continue evaluating potential mediating mechanisms of this risk. By identifying modifiable mediators of relationships between parenting and depression, including specific types of dysfunctional beliefs and information processing biases, mental health professionals may be better positioned to intervene with at-risk individuals through treatment of current depressive episodes and prevention of future episodes.

CHRISTINE D. SCHER

See also

Attachment
Early Adversity

Childhood Depression: Family
Context
Family Transmission of Depression
Fathers and Depression
Maltreatment
Mothers and Depression

References

Beck, A. T. (1967). *Depression: Causes and treatment.* Philadelphia: University of Pennsylvania Press.

Bowlby, J. (1980). *Attachment and loss: Loss.* London: Hogarth Press.

Bowlby, J. (1982). *Attachment and loss: Attachment.* New York: Basic Books. (Originally published in 1969)

Hankin, B. L. (2005). Childhood maltreatment and psychopathology: Prospective tests of attachment, cognitive vulnerability, and stress as mediating processes. *Cognitive Therapy and Research, 29,* 645–671.

Ingram, R. E., & Ritter, J. (2000). Vulnerability to depression: Cognitive reactivity and parental bonding in high-risk individuals. *Journal of Abnormal Psychology, 109,* 588–596.

Maciejewski, P. K., & Mazure, C. M. (2006). Fear of criticism and rejection mediates an association between childhood emotional abuse and adult onset of major depression. *Cognitive Therapy and Research, 30,* 105–122.

Oakley-Browne, M. A., Joyce, P. R., Wells, J. E., Bushnell, J. A., & Hornblow, A. R. (1995). Adverse parenting and other childhood experience as risk factors for depression in women aged 18–44 years. *Journal of Affective Disorders, 34,* 13–23.

Parker, G. (1994). Parental bonding and depressive disorders. In M. B. Sperling & W. H. Berman (Eds.), *Attachment in adults* (pp. 299–312). New York: Guilford Press.

Parker, G., Tupling, H., & Brown, L. B. (1979). A parental bonding instrument. *British Journal of Medical Psychology, 52,* 1–10.

Sachs-Ericsson, N., Verona, E., Joiner, T., & Preacher, K. J. (2006). Parental verbal abuse and the mediating role of self-criticism in adult internalizing disorders. *Journal of Affective Disorders, 93,* 71–78.

Parkinson's Disease

Parkinson's disease (PD) is a neurodegenerative movement disorder that affects approximately 1% to 2% of the population over the age of 65 years. Neuropsychiatric symptoms are commonly reported in PD patients, especially in those with concurrent dementia, known as PD dementia (Aarsland et al., 2007).

As seen in Table P.1, reports of a higher prevalence of depression in PD compared to the general population have come from early case-only observational studies, case-control studies, and several retrospective and prospective cohort studies. Prevalence estimates of depression in PD have a large range, from 3% to 90%, but the majority of estimates are between 30% and 50%. The prevalence of anxiety in PD is estimated to be 25% to 40%, and anxiety and depression co-occur in PD, although the prevalence of co-occurrence is not well reported. A meta-analysis of 36 studies reported the weighted prevalence of major depressive disorder was 17% of PD patients, that of minor depression 22%, and dysthymia 13% (Reijnders, Ehrt, Weber, Aarsland, & Leentjens, 2007). Clinically significant depressive symptoms, regardless of a *DSM*-defined depressive disorder were present in 35% of PD patients. This is double the prevalence (16%) estimated in the general population. The reported prevalence of major depression in PD ranges from 8% to 64%. The variation between studies could be due to the instruments used to diagnose PD and depression in PD. PD is often underdiagnosed because of insidious onset and signs and symptoms that are not specific to PD (e.g., tremor). Depression is underdiagnosed in PD, partially because some of the symptoms of depression overlap with symptoms of PD and may not be recognized as depression.

The NINDS-NIMH working group published recommendations for adaptation of the *Diagnostic and Statistical Manual of Mental Disorders* (*DSM*; American Psychiatric Association, 2000) criteria for depression and dysthymia for use in PD. The overlap of symptoms in depression and PD was addressed. Other subtypes of depression may be present in PD and contribute to morbidity, therefore it was recommended that other types of depression should be included in studies of depression in PD, rather than restricting to major depression.

Depression scales have also been used as diagnostic tools but are indicators of depression severity and should not be used to substitute for a diagnostic interview. There has been much discussion about whether all depression scales are valid in PD, and whether

Table P.1   Prevalence of Depression in Parkinson's Disease

Reference	Exposure	RR (95% CI)	Cases/controls or cohort size
Case-control studies			
Hubble et al., 1993	History of depression	2.95 (1.08–8.01)	63/86
McCann et al., 1998	History of treated depression	1.20 (0.70–2.20)	224/310
Taylor et al., 1999	Depression	2.46 (1.25–4.85)	140/147
Shiba et al., 2000	Depressive disorders	1.90 (1.10–3.20)	202/202
Van den Eeden et al., 2000	Ever depressed	1.50 (1.10–2.00)[a]	496/541
Van den Eeden et al., 2000	Ever used anti-depressants or seen a physician for depression	1.80 (1.10–2.70)[a]	496/541
Behari et al., 2001	Prior depression ≤10 years	1.54 (1.06–2.23)	377/377
Behari et al., 2001	Prior depression >10 years	1.51 (0.54–2.50)	377/377
Nuti et al., 2004	Diagnosis of depression	$p < 0.01$ more common in PD[a]	90/90
Cohort studies			
Nilsson et al., 2001	Depression vs. diabetes cohort	2.20 (1.70–2.84)	72/11741; 111/69149
Nilsson et al., 2001	Depression vs. osteoar-thritis cohort	2.24 (1.72–2.93)	72/11741; 111/69149
Schuurman et al., 2002	History of depression	3.13 (1.95–5.01)	278/68928
Leentjens et al., 2003	History of depression	2.40 (2.10–2.70)	338/32077

RR = Relative Risk and refers to odds ratios in case-control studies; CI = Confidence Interval.
[a]*Unadjusted estimates.*

a PD-specific cutoff score can be specified to identify a probable diagnosis of depression. The American Academy of Neurology recommended that the Beck Depression Inventory and Hamilton Depression Rating Scale be used to screen for depression in PD. The Hamilton Depression Scale, the Montgomery Asberg Depression Rating Scale, Beck Depression Inventory, and Lieberman Lyons Scale have been validated for assessing the presence of depression in PD. The Hamilton Depression Inventory, Hospital Anxiety and Depression Scale, and Geriatric Depression Scale also appear to show utility for screening for depression in PD. The Unified Parkinson's Disease Rating Scale Section 1 was shown to have limited utility in identifying depression in PD compared to the Hamilton Depression Rating Scale and Beck Depression Inventory II. Many of the depression rating scales assess affective and somatic symptoms, but somatic symptoms of depression may also be symptoms of PD, therefore an adjustment of the cutoff scores is necessary. For example, tiredness, sleep disorders, weight loss, and movement slowness are symptoms of both depression and PD. The Zung Self-Rating Depression Scale has been recommended for the assessment of the severity of depressive symptoms in PD. Many of the PD patients with depressive symptoms do not meet *DSM-IV* criteria for major depression.

It is important to distinguish between apathy and depression in PD. Apathy is common in PD, although it does not overlap completely with depression. In a case-control study of PD patients, 32% of PD patients were classified as apathetic using the Lille Apathy Rating Scale (Dujardin et al., 2007). The study found that apathy was mainly determined by cognitive impairment, was not associated with motor symptom severity, and was only associated with the apathy subcomponent of the Montgomery and Asberg Depression Rating Scale.

Studies indicate that patients with PD have a higher risk of depression than patients with other chronic diseases experiencing similar levels of disability. It is unlikely that depression in PD is due only to progressive motor disabilities, as prospective studies have shown that depression is often present early in PD. There is conflicting evidence for a correlation between depression and increased PD severity. Depression has been associated with decreased quality of life, and with increased disability, psychiatric and medical comorbidity, health care utilization, and mortality in PD patients. It is possible that the increased disability is due to perception, and that the depressed PD patients perceive themselves to be more disabled than the nondepressed PD patients.

A Norwegian study of depression in patients with and without PD showed that the symptom profiles differed between these two groups (Ehrt, Bronnick, Leentjens, Larsen, & Aarsland, 2006). Depression in PD was characterized by less severe sadness, less feelings of guilt, and slightly less loss of energy, but more severe concentration difficulties compared to the group without PD. The use of antidepressants was much more common in depressed individuals without PD, but symptom profiles within PD and non-PD groups were similar despite antidepressant status. Other studies have also found that depression in PD differs from depression in non-PD populations, in aspects such as decreased feelings of guilt, self-blame, and suicidal ideation compared to those with primary major depression.

The cause-effect relationship between PD and depression is unknown. Some studies suggest that depression may be related to the general changes occurring in the dopaminergic, serotonergic, and noradrenergic neurotransmitters in the brain. Lower serotonin (5-HT) levels have been observed in the brain and cerebrospinal fluid of PD patients, which led to the proposal of a serotonergic hypothesis for depression in PD. This suggests that the reduced cerebral serotonergic activity that occurs in PD constitutes a biological risk factor for depression. Serotonin levels are known to be lower in depression; however, it is not known if this is directly related to PD. Both PD and depression have been associated with decreased activity or brain lesions in the orbital frontal cortex and basal ganglia. PD has an insidious onset, and the length of the presymptomatic period is unknown, therefore it is not possible to determine if depression precedes PD onset or is related to the disease process of PD.

Clinical trials of antidepressants for depression in PD have equivocally shown improvement in managing depressive symptoms; however, there is concern that selective serotonin-reuptake inhibitors (SSRIs) may worsen motor functioning in some PD patients, and tricyclic antidepressants may increase cognitive impairment and orthostatic hypotension. SSRIs are the most commonly used first-line treatment for depression in PD. A meta-analysis of depression treatment studies in PD showed that there was less benefit from typical antidepressants, especially SSRIs, than in elderly individuals without PD (Chung, Deane, Ghazi-Noori, Rickards, & Clarke, 2003; Weintraub et al., 2005). Selegiline, a monoamine oxidase inhibitor, was previously approved for the treatment of PD and has recently been approved by the U.S. Food and Drug Administration for the treatment of major depressive disorder. The dopamine agonist pramipexole also has potentially antidepressive properties. A small trial suggested that citalopram improves depression, disability, and comorbid anxiety. As with medications for PD, the medications for depression in PD need to be optimized to the patient, may change in effectiveness over time, and should be considered for benefits compared to side effects.

Nonpharmacological treatments such as cognitive behavioral therapy are currently being investigated for depression in PD. Deep brain stimulation (DBS), transcranial magnetic stimulation, and electroconvulsive therapy are sometimes used to treat the motor symptoms of PD. DBS of the subthalamic nucleus can affect movement and mood. A meta-analysis of DBS found that there may be a slight increase in the incidence of neuropsychiatric events, including depressive episodes, following DBS (Appleby, Duggan, Regenberg, & Rabins, 2007). The most serious concern is the possible increase in suicidal behavior in patients receiving DBS.

Conclusions

Depression commonly occurs in PD, although the depressive symptoms differ from those of major depressive disorder, especially the lack of feelings of guilt. Depression is underrecognized and underdiagnosed in PD, possibly because of the overlap in somatic symptoms between the two conditions. However it negatively impacts quality of life and is a significant problem that is unlikely to be due only to progressive disability. Depressive symptoms have been reported early in PD, before occurrence of severe motor disabilities. Further specific research is needed to determine whether antidepressant or nonpharmacological treatments significantly improve depression in PD.

LIANNA S. ISHIHARA-PAUL AND CAROL BRAYNE

See also

Medical Conditions and Depression

References

Aarsland, D., Bronnick, K., Ehrt, U., De Deyn, P. P., Tekin, S., Emre, M., et al. (2007). Neuropsychiatric symptoms in patients with Parkinson's disease and dementia: Fre-

quency, profile and associated care giver stress. *Journal of Neurology, Neurosurgery, and Psychiatry, 78,* 36–42.

American Psychiatric Association. (2000). *Diagnostic and statistical manual of mental disorders* (4th ed., text revision). Washington, DC: Author.

Appleby, B. S., Duggan, P. S., Regenberg, A., & Rabins, P. V. (2007). Psychiatric and neuropsychiatric adverse events associated with deep brain stimulation: A meta-analysis of ten years' experience. *Movement Disorders, 22,* 1722–1728.

Chung, T. H., Deane, K. H. O., Ghazi-Noori, S., Rickards, H., & Clarke, C. E. (2003). Systematic review of antidepressant therapies in Parkinson's disease. *Parkinsonism and Related Disorders, 10,* 59–65.

Dujardin, K., Sockeel, P., Devos, D., Delliaux, M., Krystkowiak, P., Destee, A., et al. (2007). Characteristics of apathy in Parkinson's disease. *Movement Disorders, 22,* 778–784.

Ehrt, U., Bronnick, K., Leentjens, A. F., Larsen, J. P., & Aarsland, D. (2006). Depressive symptom profile in Parkinson's disease: A comparison with depression in elderly patients without Parkinson's disease. *International Journal of Geriatric Psychiatry, 21,* 252–258.

Reijnders, J. S., Ehrt, U., Weber, W. E., Aarsland, D., & Leentjens, A. F. (2008). A systematic review of prevalence studies of depression in Parkinson's disease. *Movement Disorders, 23,* 183–189.

Weintraub, D., Morales, K. H., Moberg, P. J., Bilker, W. B., Balderston, C., Duda, J. E., et al. (2005). Antidepressant studies in Parkinson's disease: A review and meta-analysis. *Movement Disorders, 20,* 1161–1169.

Peer Relations

Peer relationships are associated with a wide range of psychological outcomes. Several symptoms of psychopathology, including depressive symptoms, are associated with changes in youths' peer relations. Inversely, negative experiences among peers are associated with increased risks for depression. Each of these associations is described briefly.

Within the first few years of life, children begin to spend a remarkable amount of their time in the company of peers. Research has suggested that many distinct aspects of peer relationships are relevant for psychological adjustment. Three specific aspects are discussed here, including (a) youths' overall likability among peers (i.e., peer acceptance and rejection), including behaviors that correlate with overall peer status (e.g., victimization from peers); (b) youths' participation in a mutual, close dyadic friendship, including the quality of this relationship; and (c) the types of friends with whom youths' affiliate, and potential peer influence within this relationship.

Depressive Symptoms as a Risk Factor for Peer Relationship Difficulties

It is probably not surprising that children and adolescents experiencing depressive symptoms have difficulties interacting with their peers. Findings suggest that these difficulties include children's overall reputations, or status, within the peer group. Some results suggest that depressed children are more likely than their peers to be rejected, defined as many nominations by peers as someone who is disliked. However, it should be noted that the effects of peer rejection on later depression are somewhat mild. Children's aggressive behavior is a far stronger predictor of rejected peer status. In contrast, some work has suggested that children with specific depressive symptoms, such as social withdrawal and flat affect, also may be likely to be neglected by peers, receiving few nominations as a classmate who is liked or disliked by others.

Research on antecedents of peer victimization routinely suggest that several behaviors concomitant to depression strongly increase a child's risk for being a target by bullies. Children who exhibit passive problem-solving strategies and sad affect are especially likely to be victimized both physically (hitting, kicking, etc.) and relationally (e.g., excluded by peers, the subject of gossip, withdrawal of emotional support).

Although findings regarding the effects of depressive symptoms on peer reputations and behaviors within the overall peer group are somewhat equivocal, a substantial body of evidence suggests that youths reporting depressive symptoms are likely to experience difficulties within close dyadic friendships. Although initial evidence suggested that depressed youths may be unsuccessful in forming friendships, or establishing friendships characterized by mutual liking, more recent evidence has suggested that depressed youths do establish and maintain reciprocal dyadic relationships. However, these relationships are characterized by behaviors that may substantially reduce friendship quality. Observational studies suggest that depressed youths'

interactions with a best friend are characterized by fewer expressions of positive affect and less validation of one another's feelings. As compared to individuals in friendship dyads with a nondepressed child, individuals interacting with a depressed child also are more likely to report lower satisfaction with their friendship, and a less pleasurable social interaction. It may be for this reason that adolescents' depression appears to be associated with increases in interpersonal stressors—a concept that is discussed in stress-generation theories of depression (Hammen, 1991).

Recent work has articulated several depression-related social behaviors that may be associated with interpersonal difficulties within adolescents' friendships (Prinstein, Borelli, Cheah, Simon, & Aikins, 2005). For instance, recent work has suggested that dysphoric adolescents may engage in repeated requests for reassurance from close friends to help bolster their sense of self-worth and relationship security. Although these requests are often met with the reassurance requested, continued doubt and insecurity prompt continued and excessive requests for reassurance. Ironically, these requests in themselves have the unintended consequence of alienating best friends and may contribute to a process that leads to friendship dissolution. This process is especially unfortunate since it ultimately reifies and reinforces adolescents' initial concerns regarding relationship security, rather than providing feedback regarding the alienating nature of excessive reassurance seeking.

Other work has suggested that some adolescents with a low sense of self-worth request feedback from close friends in a manner that is likely to elicit negative feedback. Self-verification theory suggests that such behavior might be motivated by an attempt to seek experiences that will confirm a low sense of self-worth. However, the consequences of negative feedback-seeking instead include an exacerbation of depressive symptoms, as well as an increasing sense of negative friendship quality within the friendship dyad.

Maladaptive social behaviors also are apparent in dyads that include two youths with depressive symptoms. In some of these dyads, adolescents may be especially likely to discuss stressors in a manner that emphasizes negative emotional responses but does not include adaptive problem-solving or coping strategies. This process, known as *corumination* appears to be reinforced within the friendship dyad. Corumination is associated with high levels of friendship quality, but also increasing levels of depressive symptoms over time.

Much recent research has examined whether the consequences of depressive symptoms on peer relationship difficulties may vary by gender. Findings suggest that before the adolescent transition, both boys and girls experience comparable levels of interpersonal stressors. However, after the transition to adolescence, girls report a substantial increase in interpersonal stressors, particularly among peers. This may be associated with adolescents' increased reliance on peers as primary sources of social support, the use of peer feedback as a reflected appraisal of self-worth, and the substantial attention placed on females' success within interpersonal relationships as an expected area of competency in adolescence. Interestingly, the increase in girls' interpersonal stressors at the adolescent transition closely parallels the increase in depressive prevalence among girls also observed at this developmental stage.

Peer Relationship Difficulties as a Risk Factor for Depressive Symptoms

Developmental psychopathology theory suggests that individuals reciprocally transact within their environment over time; individuals' specific behaviors lead to changes in social opportunities, and these altered social experiences ultimately reinforce or exacerbate the development of maladaptive behaviors. In addition to the association between depressive symptoms and subsequent experiences among peers, much research has examined whether negative peer experiences may confer a risk for later depressive symptoms.

Findings have been mixed. Some work has suggested that rejected peer status is associated longitudinally with increasing levels of depressive symptoms, or that the combination of peer rejection and aggression is associated with depression. However, several studies also have failed to find an association between peer rejection and depressive symptoms. More recent research suggests that the link between peer rejection and depressive symptoms may be best understood through the integration of work on cognitive theories of depression. Several discrete cognitions appear to mediate or moderate the effects of peer rejection. For instance, consistent with a social information-processing model, youths' encoding of peer rejection experiences may be critical to internalizing outcomes. Several studies have suggested that youths' perceptions of rejection by peers are more proximal longitudinal predictors of depression and may mediate the association between actual peer rejection and later depressive symptoms. Research invoking a cognitive vulnerability model of depression suggests that peer rejection is a relevant stressor that interacts with a depressogenic attributional style predicting depression. This effect appears to be particularly significant for girls.

Prior work on friendship qualities or behaviors that may be associated with later depressive symptoms also have yielded somewhat mixed findings. Recent work has suggested bidirectional associations between excessive reassurance-seeking and depressive symptoms. Depression seems to be both an antecedent and a consequence of depressive symptoms. A similar pattern is evident for negative feedback-seeking and corumination.

Perhaps most consistently, findings have suggested a peer influence effect for depressive symptoms within a close friendship (e.g., Prinstein, 2007). Peer influence is a quite common and potent phenomenon for a variety of psychological symptoms that is often explained by two related processes. Selection processes suggest that individuals are likely to befriend individuals who already share similar attitudes and social-psychological characteristics. Socialization processes suggest that affiliation with specific peers may lead to increases in maladaptive behaviors over time. Several studies have demonstrated that within adolescent best friendships, higher levels of their friend's depressive symptoms are associated with increases in adolescents' own depressive symptoms over time. This effect appears to also be evidenced when examining the average level of depressive symptoms within an adolescents' peer clique, or broader friendship network. Ongoing work has begun to examine possible mechanisms by which such peer influence processes may occur.

Overall, substantial research has suggested bidirectional associations between depressive symptoms and many dimensions of youths' peer experiences. A thorough assessment of multiple aspects of peer relationships is needed when identifying youths at risk for depression, and when considering the effectiveness of treatments that are designed to ameliorate depressive symptoms.

MITCHELL J. PRINSTEIN, NICOLE HEILBRON, CAROLINE B. BROWNE, JOHN D. GUERRY, AND JOSEPH C. FRANKLIN

See also

Adolescent Depression
Childhood Depression
Risk

References

Hammen, C. (1991). Generation of stress in the course of unipolar depression. *Journal of Abnormal Psychology, 100*, 555–561.

Prinstein, M. J. (2007). Moderators of peer contagion: A longitudinal examination of depression socialization between adolescents and their best friends. *Journal of Clinical Child and Adolescent Psychology, 36*, 159–170.

Prinstein, M. J., Borelli, J. L., Cheah, C. S. L., Simon, V. A., & Aikins, J. W. (2005). Adolescent girls' interpersonal vulnerability to depressive symptoms: A longitudinal examination of reassurance-seeking and peer relationships. *Journal of Abnormal Psychology, 114*, 676–688.

Perfectionism

Perfectionism has long been recognized as a risk factor for depression. Clinical case studies of depressed perfectionists tend to highlight the harsh self-scrutiny and punitive self-evaluative criteria of perfectionists, as well as the chronic stress associated with the relentless pursuit of unrealistic standards. These accounts are very much in keeping with initial conceptualizations that portrayed the perfectionist as someone who compensates for feelings of inferiority and insignificance by striving for exceedingly high standards and then reacting poorly when perfection is not attained.

Perfectionism Is Multidimensional

Initial attempts to conceptualize perfectionism focused on perfectionism as a unidimensional construct with an emphasis on personal standards. Measures such as the Burns Perfectionism Scale and the perfectionism subscale of the Eating Disorder Inventory assessed perfectionism in terms of an overall score. In contrast, subsequent conceptualizations emphasized the multidimensionality of the perfectionism construct. Frost, Marten, Lahart, and Rosenblate (1990) postulated that perfectionism consists of six dimensions. They created the 35-item Frost Multidimensional Perfectionism Scale to assess personal standards, concern over mistakes, doubts about actions, organization, parental expectations, and parental criticism.

Hewitt and Flett (1991) created their Multidimensional Perfectionism Scale to assess three trait dimensions. First, self-oriented perfectionism was conceptualized as a dimension that not only included the exacting personal standards of perfectionistic people, it also incorporated the goal-directed and tenacious striving to attain these standards. Second, other-oriented perfectionism was conceptualized to reflect the tendency to evaluate other people by exacting criteria. Finally, socially prescribed perfectionism was envisioned as the tendency to perceive that perfectionistic demands are being imposed on the self. Socially prescribed perfectionism can be linked with depression via several associated processes and factors. It has been suggested that extreme forms of socially prescribed perfectionism include elements of helplessness and hopelessness because approximations of success only result in expectations being raised even higher. Feelings of dejection and resentment could also stem from a sense of being targeted unfairly by demanding significant others.

The various perfectionism dimensions have been investigated in numerous studies over the past two decades. Which dimensions are linked most consistently with depression? No meta-analyses have been conducted thus far, but some clear patterns have emerged. Empirical research with the Frost and colleagues (1990) measure has found repeatedly that the concern over mistakes and doubts about action dimensions are associated with depression, while research with the Hewitt and Flett measure has found time and again that socially prescribed perfectionism is associated with depression. Depressed perfectionists characterized jointly by an excessive concern over mistakes and socially prescribed perfectionism would be dejected about past mistakes and their inability to meet excessive standards imposed on the self. This could foster a deeply rooted sense of shame about inadequate aspects of the self.

Perfectionism Cognitions in Depression

Research and theory on automatic, perfectionistic thoughts is a viable alternative to the primary focus thus far in the literature on trait perfectionism and depression. The despair that characterizes certain perfectionists stems from a tendency to engage in cognitive rumination over mistakes and shortcomings. Flett, Hewitt, Blankstein, and Gray (1998) hypothesized that a perfectionistic self-schema exists such that perfectionists who sense a discrepancy between the actual self and the ideal self, or their actual level of attainment and their perfectionistic standards and ideals, will tend to experience automatic thoughts that reflect their need to be perfect. They developed the Perfectionism Cognitions Inventory (PCI) to assess the frequency of such thoughts as "I should be perfect" and "I should never make the same mistake twice." It has been confirmed empirically that perfectionistic automatic thoughts predict levels of depression, over and above the variance attributable to trait dimensions such as socially prescribed perfectionism (see Flett et al., 1998; Flett, Hewitt, Whelan, & Martin, 2007). Also, elevated PCI scores are associated with deficits in self-reinforcement and higher levels of self-blame (Flett et al., 2007).

Conceptualizations of Perfectionism and Depression

While most current research stems from these multidimensional conceptualizations, it is important to acknowledge the work of several influential theorists who have sought to account for the link between perfectionism and depression. These theorists include luminaries such as Aaron Beck, Albert Ellis, and Sidney Blatt, among others. Their work and views on perfectionism and depression can be found in a 2002 edited volume by Flett and Hewitt.

Consistent with the general tenets of Beck's cognitive model, Beck and associates conceptualize perfectionism as a maladaptive, rigid form of thinking (see Brown & Beck, 2002). Perfectionism is best conceptualized as a set of dysfunctional attitudes in the form of an if-then rule or condition (e.g., "If I am perfect all of the time, then people will love me"). Depression ensues because the depression-prone individual lives his or her life according to extreme and unrealistic contingencies and imperatives (e.g., "I should always have control over my feelings"), but the reality is that life setbacks and environmental conditions make it impossible for the perfectionist to live up to these contingencies. Thus, the perfectionist has a specific cognitive vulnerability to depression. Brown and Beck (2002) also advanced the argument that the inventory used to assess dysfunctional attitudes, the Dysfunctional

Attitude Scale, is "to a substantial degree a measure of perfectionism, if perfectionism is construed in broad terms" (p. 236), because the Dysfunctional Attitude Scale reflects imperatives that are rigid, extreme, and unconditional.

Ellis (2002) also focused on perfectionism as a cognitive vulnerability by conceptualizing perfectionism as a specific irrational belief. Ellis maintained that perfectionism results in depression when irrational importance has been attached to the need to be perfect. In this formulation, it is important to distinguish between the person who merely wishes to be perfect versus the person who feels that he or she absolutely must be perfect. According to Ellis, this irrational need to be perfect is fuelled by a sense of hypercompetitiveness and associated thinking styles that escalate small failures and setbacks into profound catastrophes. Ellis (2002) also suggested that perfectionists are influenced unduly by stressful circumstances, and when stress occurs, perfectionistic standards are applied to the coping process; that is, perfectionists demand that perfect solutions be found for life problems, and depression results from the inevitable sense of powerlessness that results when these perfect solutions are not found.

Blatt (1995) emphasized perfectionism as an outgrowth of the introjective personality orientation and "feelings of unworthiness, inferiority, failure, and guilt" (p. 1009). This orientation is fuelled by chronic fears of disapproval, criticism, and rejection. It can be traced developmentally to harsh parental expectations along with a Rogerian sense that approval is contingent on meeting perfectionistic expectations. In his seminal paper, Blatt (1995) not only detailed the link between perfectionism and profound self-criticism, he also implicated self-critical perfectionism in the suicides of three well-known, highly accomplished people. These case examples illustrate that personal accomplishments are not enough to outweigh the sense of self-dissatisfaction, depression, and shame that is experienced acutely by some perfectionists.

Perfectionism and the Treatment of Depression

Unfortunately, when a perfectionistic person suffers depression and treatment is warranted, several factors associated with perfectionism can undermine treatment success. Blatt and Zuroff (2002) summarized the results of several investigations conducted on the data from the National Institute of Mental Health Collaborative Treatment of Depression Collaborative Research Program. Collectively, these studies indicate that perfectionism is relatively treatment resistant, and longer-term interventions are favored over brief short-term interventions. This conclusion accords with descriptions of perfectionism as a deeply ingrained personality characteristic that has been reinforced since early childhood. Blatt and his associates have also found that perfectionists tend to have relatively poor alliances with their therapists.

Recent work in our laboratories is attempting to help identify how perfectionism undermines treatment success by focusing on the significance of individual differences in perfectionistic self-presentation. Certain perfectionists are highly invested in the image that they portray or express in public; these people are highly focused on seeming perfect to others (i.e., perfectionistic self-promotion), and they go to great lengths to avoid putting their mistakes and shortcomings on display where they can be detected by other people. That is, they seek to portray and live their lives according to a highly false sense of the perfect self. Not surprisingly, these individuals are also hesitant to verbally disclose mistakes and shortcomings that promote an image of imperfection (see Hewitt et al., 2003). This form of perfectionistic self-presentation can substantially undermine treatment progress for highly depressed people. Core themes and issues will be avoided by the perfectionist, who tends to be overly concerned with not seeming imperfect to his or her counselor or clinician. Ongoing research in our laboratories is investigating perfectionistic self-presentation and unresponsiveness in the form of emotional inexpressiveness. We are also exploring the role of perfectionistic self-presentation in negative help-seeking orientations. It seems that the act of seeking help is very threatening for certain perfectionists because they are averse to openly acknowledge their imperfection.

Moderators and Mediators of the Perfectionism-Depression Association

Given that it is well established that perfectionism is linked with depression, contemporary research has shifted the focus to the search for conceptually meaningful factors that may moderate or mediate the association between perfectionism and depression. Initial research in this area focused on diathesis-stress models and the notion that perfectionism is a vulnerability to depression that is activated following the experience of negative life events that represent personal failures. Certain findings are not in accordance with this model, but overall, there is general empirical support for diathesis-stress models of perfectionism and depression in patient samples and student samples (see Hewitt & Flett, 2002).

Several other factors have been tested and found to be important mediators of the link between perfectionism and depression. These factors include maladaptive coping styles (including emotion-focused coping and rumination), poor coping resources (i.e., low social support), and negative self-representations (i.e., low self-esteem and a conditional sense of self-regard). Collectively, these investigations highlight the fact that the perfectionists who are most vulnerable to depression are those who are perfectionistic but also have other negative characteristics and attributes that are known to confer risk for depression. Indeed, it seems that perfectionism is particularly maladaptive in terms of personal well-being when it is combined with other factors linked with psychopathology.

GORDON L. FLETT AND PAUL L. HEWITT

See also

Anaclitic and Introjective Depression
Cognitive Theories of Depression
Risk
Vulnerability

References

Blatt, S. J. (1995). The destructiveness of perfectionism: Implications for the treatment of depression. *American Psychologist, 50*, 1003–1020.

Blatt, S. J., & Zuroff, D. C. (2002). Perfectionism in the therapeutic process. In G. L. Flett & P. L. Hewitt (Eds.), *Perfectionism: Theory, research, and treatment* (pp. 393–406). Washington, DC: American Psychological Association.

Brown, G. P., and Beck, A. T. (2002). Dysfunctional attitudes, perfectionism, and models of vulnerability to depression. In G. L. Flett & P. L. Hewitt (Eds.), *Perfectionism: Theory, research, and treatment* (pp. 231–251). Washington, DC: American Psychological Association.

Ellis, A. (2002). The role of irrational beliefs in perfectionism. In G. L. Flett & P. L. Hewitt (Eds.), *Perfectionism: Theory, research, and treatment* (pp. 217–229). Washington, DC: American Psychological Association.

Flett, G. L., Hewitt, P. L., Blankstein, K. R., & Gray, L. (1998). Psychological distress and the frequency of perfectionistic thinking. *Journal of Personality and Social Psychology, 75*, 1363–1381.

Flett, G. L., Hewitt, P. L., Whelan, T., & Martin, T. R. (2007). The Perfectionism Cognitions Inventory: Psychometric properties and associations with distress and deficits in cognitive self-management. *Journal of Rational-Emotive and Cognitive-Behavior Therapy, 25*, 255–277.

Frost, R. O., Marten, P. A., Lahart, C., & Rosenblate, R. (1990). The dimensions of perfectionism. *Cognitive Therapy and Research, 14*, 449–468.

Hewitt, P. L., & Flett, G. L. (1991). Perfectionism in the self and social contexts: Conceptualization, assessment, and association with psychopathology. *Journal of Personality and Social Psychology, 60*, 456–470.

Hewitt, P. L., & Flett, G. L. (2002). Perfectionism and stress processes in psychopathology. In G. L. Flett & P. L. Hewitt (Eds.), *Perfectionism: Theory, research, and treatment* (pp. 255–284). Washington, DC: American Psychological Association.

Hewitt, P. L., Flett, G. L., Sherry, S. B., Habke, M., Parkin, M., Lam, R. W., et al. (2003). The interpersonal expression of perfection: Perfectionistic self-presentation and psychological distress. *Journal of Personality and Social Psychology, 84*, 1303–1325.

Personality Disorders and Depression

Personality disorders are defined by the *Diagnostic and Statistical Manual of Mental Disorders* (*DSM-IV-TR*; American Psychiatric

Association, 2000, p. 689) as an "enduring pattern of inner experience and behavior that deviates markedly from the expectations of an individual's culture" in two of the following domains: cognition, affectivity, interpersonal functioning, and impulse control. The symptoms associated with personality disorders must be "inflexible and pervasive," "lead to clinically significant distress or impairment" in various domains of functioning (e.g., occupational), and be "stable and of long duration" (i.e., present since adolescence or young adulthood). In this entry we focus primarily on three questions: (a) are *DSM-IV* personality disorders comorbid with unipolar depression, (b) if there is comorbidity, is it clinically significant, and (c) what factors might explain this comorbidity?

Are DSM-IV Personality Disorders Comorbid With Unipolar Depression?

The comorbidity between unipolar depression and personality disorders is quite substantial. In their review of the literature, Corruble, Ginestet, and Guelfi (1996) state that "among patients with current major depressive disorder, it may be estimated that 20% to 50% of inpatients and 50% to 85% of outpatients have an associated personality disorder" (p. 164). This review found that Cluster B personality disorders (i.e., antisocial, borderline, histrionic; not narcissistic personality disorder, however) are quite prevalent in individuals with depression. Although there was greater variability across studies, Cluster C personality disorders (i.e., avoidant, dependent, and, to a lesser degree, obsessive-compulsive) are also common in these patient populations. There is some evidence of significant comorbidity for certain Cluster A personality disorders (i.e., schizotypal) with depression, although the results were inconsistent for others (i.e., paranoid; schizoid). While lower than the prevalence in patient populations, the prevalence of personality disorders in community samples of depressed individuals is also quite high (i.e.,

22%; Cluster C personality disorders being the most common). Finally, some research has found that personality disorders may be even more comorbid with dysthymia than major depression. It is important to note that assessment methodology may influence the degree of comorbidity found between depression and personality disorders, as depressed individuals may endorse personality disorder symptoms because of their current state rather than the existence of a longstanding trait. Given this bias, it is important to use semistructured interviews to assess for personality disorder symptoms, as they allow the interviewer more input as to whether the personality disorder symptoms are "stable and of long duration." Informant reports (e.g., significant others, friends) may also be used in an attempt to parse these state-trait questions.

Is the Comorbidity That Exists Between Depression and Personality Disorders Clinically Meaningful?

At this time, the best answer may be a tentative "yes." For instance, Brieger, Ehrt, Bloeink, and Marneros (2002) found that depressed individuals with two or more personality disorders had a substantially earlier age of onset of depression and lower quality of life rating at discharge than individuals with one or zero personality disorders; they did not find differences in other key variables such as number of depressive episodes, duration of hospital stay, and ratings of overall functioning. Although this study found no effect of depression–personality disorder comorbidity on suicidality, this finding is contradicted by several studies that have found that the presence of one or more personality disorders with depression increases the likelihood of suicide and suicidal behavior. Other studies have supported the notion that individuals with both depression and personality disorder are more likely to experience an earlier onset of depression as well as a greater severity of symptoms.

The clinical significance of depression–personality disorder comorbidity is particularly unclear with regard to whether it has a significant, negative impact on treatment efficacy for depressive symptoms and likelihood of relapse. The most recent and inclusive review of the literature on the effect of personality disorder comorbidity on the treatment of depression found that it results in a poorer outcome with regard to depressive symptomatology (Newton-Howes, Tyrer, & Johnson, 2006); this result held across treatment modalities for which there were sufficient number of studies (e.g., medication, psychotherapy, medication, and/or psychotherapy). It must be noted that this finding is quite controversial, as two other reviews have shown that the negative effect of personality disorders on treatment of depression is not found in more rigorously designed studies (e.g., randomized controlled trials; Kool et al., 2005; Mulder, 2002). Similar debate surrounds the question of whether the presence of a personality disorder co-occurring with depression makes relapse more likely, with some studies finding that the presence of a personality disorder decreases the time to relapse, while others have found no evidence of this effect. Clearly, further work is necessary on this important topic. Given the heterogeneity of findings across many studies, it is important that future research work to identify other potential moderators (i.e., variables that affect the size or direction of a relation; methodological issues appear to be one such moderator) of the personality disorder and depression outcome relation. Another meaningful moderator may be the type of treatment used, as some research has found that the presence of a comorbid personality disorder (particularly those in Clusters A and C) does not have a negative effect on the treatment of depression when treated with certain types of psychotherapy (i.e., cognitive-behavioral) but does when treated with other types (i.e., interpersonal psychotherapy).

A parallel question to ask might be what effect does treatment for depression have on the nature or severity of the comorbid personality disorders? Evidence suggests that treatment for depression (or treatments typically used for depression, e.g., fluoxetine) may have a beneficial effect on the severity of personality disorders. For instance, in a large sample of patients with depression, Fava and colleagues (2002) found that an 8-week trial of the antidepressant medication fluoxetine resulted in significant reductions in the mean number of symptoms for the following personality disorders: paranoid, schizotypal, narcissistic, borderline, avoidant, dependent, and obsessive-compulsive (on average, the personality disorder symptoms decreased by approximately 20% of one standard deviation).

What Is the Nature of the Relations Between Depression and Personality Disorders?

What explains the high degree of comorbidity, and is there a distinct temporal pattern of onset? First, a small number of specific personality disorder symptoms appear to overlap either directly or indirectly with symptoms of depression. For instance, major depression and borderline personality disorder share symptoms related to suicidal ideation or behavior. However, the extent of actual symptom overlap is quite limited. The one area where there is a great deal of explicit overlap is for depressive personality disorder, which combines the two constructs—depression and personality disorder. Depressive personality disorder, which is listed in Appendix B ("criteria sets and axes provided for further study") of the *DSM-IV*, assesses an enduring personality disorder characterized by cognitions (e.g., viewing self as inadequate, worthless; pessimism; thinking of others in a critical, judgmental manner), emotions ("mood is dominated by dejection, gloominess . . . unhappiness"), and behaviors (e.g., "brooding," "prone to feeling guilty or remorseful") associated with depression. This disorder reflects an early-occurring and chronic form of depressive traits.

There are a number of different theoretical models that explain the ways in which depression and personality disorders may be related. The extant research suggests that no single model is sufficient to describe the high degree of comorbidity between depression and personality disorders. Akiskal and colleagues (Akiskal, Hirschfeld, & Yerevanian, 1983) articulated a number of these models; for the sake of brevity we review only a few here. One model is titled "the characterologic predisposition to affective episodes" (also known as the vulnerability model), which argues that certain personality traits and/or disorders may predispose individuals to the development of a depressive disorder. For instance, an individual with avoidant personality disorder may become depressed due to the social isolation that often accompanies the disorder. Alternatively, antisocial personality disorder may lead to depression as serious negative consequences are accrued (e.g., imprisonment) because of the personality disorder symptoms (e.g., impulsivity, aggression). There is evidence to support this model, as several studies have shown that personality disorder symptoms (e.g., schizotypal, Cluster B personality disorders, dependent) are a risk factor for the later development of depression; this finding has held over short periods of time (e.g., 6 months) as well as much longer periods (e.g., 11–19 years). In fact, there is some evidence that Cluster C personality disorders are a significant risk factor for the later development of postpartum major depression.

We have already reviewed the controversial evidence for the second model titled "personality as a modifier of affective episodes" (also known as the pathoplasty model). This model focuses on whether the presence of a personality disorder or personality disorder symptoms impact the presentation, course, or treatment of depression. As noted earlier, there is some evidence, albeit mixed, that personality disorders do negatively impact various issues related to treatment of personality disorders, such as time to remission, degree of change, and likelihood of relapse.

The next model states that personality disorders can arise as a "complication of affective illness" (also known as the scar model). For instance, an individual suffering from depression may begin to manifest symptoms of dependent personality disorder as the individual feels the need to rely on others for support of an emotional and pragmatic nature. A number of studies have documented a link between depression in childhood or adolescence and personality disorders in adulthood such as borderline and dependent. In this case the personality disorder can be thought of as a "scar" or "complication" of the depressive disorder.

Finally, another way to examine this comorbidity is to question whether *comorbidity* is the appropriate term for this phenomenon, as it implies the presence of two independent diagnoses. Alternatively, one could argue that depression and certain personality disorders "co-occur" at high rates because they involve the same underlying personality traits. A number of researchers have noted that depression appears to be a combination primarily of two personality dimensions: high negative affectivity (also known as neuroticism) and low positive affectivity (also known as extraversion). It is noteworthy that these two personality dimensions are thought to be central to a number of personality disorders as well. For example, a meta-analytic review of the relations between *DSM-IV* personality disorders and the five-factor model of personality (Saulsman & Page, 2004) demonstrated that the personality domain of neuroticism is positively related with 8 of the 10 *DSM-IV* personality disorders, whereas extraversion is negatively related to 5 of the 10 personality disorders. Five *DSM-IV* personality disorders demonstrated the pattern of personality correlates that one would expect to be associated with depression (high neuroticism, low extraversion): paranoid, borderline, avoidant, dependent, and obsessive-compulsive. There is some empirical evidence documenting a significant rate of co-occurrence between depression and all of these personality disorders. These findings suggest that certain personality disorders may co-occur at high rates with depression because they share many of the same central features. This framework may be most consistent with the common cause model that there are shared etiological factors (e.g., serotonergic functioning) that contribute to both personality disorders and depression.

In sum, depression and personality disorders tend to co-occur at substantial rates, especially in individuals seeking treatment. There is some evidence that these rates are even higher if one focuses on early-onset depression and/or dysthymia. The evidence is mixed as to whether the presence of a comorbid personality disorder has a negative effect on treatment of depressive disorders. Future work is needed to identify factors that might explain the lack of consistency among the empirical findings on this topic. Finally, multiple models exist that explain how depression and personality disorders may be linked. Given the heterogeneity of both depression and personality disorders, it is not surprising that there is empirical support for several of these models (e.g., depression → personality disorder; personality disorder → depression; depression = personality disorder).

JOSHUA D. MILLER AND R. MICHAEL BAGBY

See also

Comorbidity
Diagnostic and Statistical Manual of
Mental Disorders
Scar Hypothesis

References

Akiskal, H. S., Hirschfeld, R. M. A., & Yerevanian, B. I. (1983). The relationship of personality to affective disorders. *Archives of General Psychiatry, 40,* 801–810.

American Psychiatric Association. (2000). *Diagnostic and statistical manual of mental disorders* (4th ed., text revision). Washington, DC: Author.

Brieger, P., Ehrt, U., Bloeink, R., & Marneros, A. (2002). Consequences of comorbid personality disorders in major depression. *Journal of Nervous and Mental Disease, 190,* 304–309.

Corruble, E., Ginestet, D., & Guelfi, J. D. (1996). Comorbidity of personality disorders and unipolar major depression: A review. *Journal of Affective Disorders, 37,* 157–170.

Fava, M., Farabaugh, A. H., Sickinger, A. H., Wright, E., Alpert, J. E., Sonwalla, S., et al. (2002). Personality disorders and depression. *Psychological Medicine, 32,* 1049–1057.

Kool, S., Schoevers, R., De Maat, S., Van, R., Molenaar, P., Vink, A., et al. (2005). Efficacy of pharmacotherapy in depressed patients with and without personality disorders: A systematic review and meta-analysis. *Journal of Affective Disorders, 88,* 269–278.

Mulder, R. T. (2002). Personality pathology and treatment outcome in major depression: A review. *American Journal of Psychiatry, 159,* 359–371.

Newton-Howes, G., Tyrer, P., & Johnson, T. (2006). Personality disorder and the outcome of depression: Meta-analysis of published studies. *British Journal of Psychiatry, 188,* 13–20.

Saulsman, L. M., & Page, A. C. (2004). The five-factor model and personality disorder empirical literature: A meta-analytic review. *Clinical Psychology Review, 23,* 1055–1085.

Positive and Negative Affect Schedule

Arising from the seminal influence of Charles Darwin, research on mood and emotion was dominated for more than a century by theories emphasizing the importance of discrete, fundamental emotions (see Watson, 2000). All of these theories argued for a relatively small number (typically, 7 to 11) of basic emotions, including a core set—joy, interest, surprise, fear, anger, sadness, and disgust—that is common to nearly all of them. Each basic emotion is thought to reflect a different set of precipitating circumstances and to initiate a specific range of adaptive behavior. For example, fear motivates escape from situations of physical harm, whereas interest generates novel, goal-directed behavior, thereby promoting exploration and mastery of the environment. In addition, each of the fundamental emotions is thought to have its own unique physiological substrate, as well as a distinctive form of expression (with the greatest attention being paid to prototypic facial expressions).

Starting in the 1970s, however, extensive evidence began to accumulate that established the existence of two dominant, general dimensions of emotional experience: negative affect (or negative activation) and positive affect (or positive activation) (Watson, 2000). These general dimensions reflect the empirical overlap and/or co-occurrence of the basic emotions posited in the older models. That is, negative affect is a general dimension of subjective distress and dissatisfaction. It represents a broad range of negative emotional states, including fear, anger, sadness, guilt, and disgust. As noted, its existence reflects the fact that these various negative emotions actually co-occur to a considerable extent, both within and across individuals. For example, someone who is feeling sad at a given moment also is likely to report feeling fearful, angry, and guilty; similarly, individuals who typically experience frequent, intense episodes of sadness also tend to report generally elevated levels of anxiety, anger, guilt, and shame. In a parallel manner, the general positive affect dimension reflects important co-occurrences among different types of positive mood; for instance, someone who reports feeling happy and joyful also will report feeling interested, excited, proud, confident, and alert.

The Positive and Negative Affect Schedule (PANAS; Watson, Clark, & Tellegen, 1988) is a simple, easy-to-use instrument that was designed to measure these two general mood dimensions. It consists of two 10-item scales. The PANAS Negative Affect scale contains the following mood terms: afraid, ashamed, distressed, guilty, hostile, irritable, jittery, nervous, scared, and upset. The PANAS Positive Affect scale includes these terms: active, alert, attentive, determined, enthusiastic, excited, inspired, interested, proud, and strong. Respondents rate the extent to which they feel each of these affects on a 5-point scale ranging from very slightly or not at all to extremely.

The PANAS items can be used with different instructions and with different time frames, which means that they can be adapted to measure anything from transient short-term mood states to stable long-term traits; for example, respondents can rate how they feel "right now" (that is, at the present moment), or how they have felt "today," "during the past few days," "during the past week," "during the past few weeks," "during the past month," "during the past year," or even how they feel "in general, that is, on the average." The instructions also can be modified to yield other types of ratings; for instance, the PANAS can be used to rate feelings and emotions in friends, dating partners, and spouses (see Watson, 2000).

It is important to emphasize that scores on the PANAS Negative and Positive Affect scales are only weakly related to one another (Watson, 2000; Watson et al., 1988). The scales now have been used in thousands of studies; the resulting data clearly establish that they have very distinctive qualities and tend to be associated with different types of variables (see Watson, 2000). For example, positive affect shows a strong, consistent circadian rhythm (i.e., levels of positive affect tend to rise throughout the morning and then remain elevated throughout the rest of day, before declining substantially during the evening), whereas negative affect does not. Furthermore, negative affect is highly related to the general trait of neuroticism, whereas positive affect is more strongly linked to the broad trait of extraversion (Watson, 2000; Watson, Gamez, & Simms, 2005).

The scales have been heavily used in psychopathology research, and they show a particularly interesting pattern in relation to major depression and the anxiety disorders. Negative affect has been shown to be a nonspecific factor that is strongly related to both depression and anxiety. That is, elevated levels of negative affect have been identified in individuals diagnosed with major depression and various anxiety disorders. Within the anxiety disorders, negative affect is particularly strongly related to generalized anxiety disorder; it is more moderately associated with panic disorder, social phobia, and obsessive-compulsive disorder, and only weakly related to specific phobia (Watson et al., 2005).

In contrast, low levels of positive affect are more strongly linked to depression than to anxiety. That is, measures of positive affect (including the PANAS scale) show stronger and more consistent (negative) associations with symptoms and diagnoses of depression than with anxiety (although they also are consistently related to social phobia; see Watson et al., 2005). Thus, taken together, the evidence essentially shows that negative affect is nonspecifically related to depression and anxiety, whereas low positive affect is a specific factor that is related primarily to depression.

DAVID WATSON

See also

Assessment of Depression
Positive Emotion Dysregulation

References

Watson, D. (2000). *Mood and temperament.* New York: Guilford Press.

Watson, D., Clark, L. A., & Tellegen, A. (1988). Development and validation of brief measures of positive and negative affect: The PANAS scales. *Journal of Personality and Social Psychology, 54,* 1063–1070.

Watson, D., Gamez, W., & Simms, L. J. (2005). Basic dimensions of temperament and their relation to anxiety and depression: A symptom-based perspective. *Journal of Research in Personality, 39,* 46–66.

Positive Emotion Dysregulation

Depression is a disorder of positive, as well as negative, emotion. In recognition of this fact, the *Diagnostic and Statistical Manual of Mental Disorders,* fourth edition revised (American Psychiatric Press, 2000), specifies that either depressed mood *or* loss of interest and pleasure must be present to diagnose a major depressive episode. This diagnostic criterion elevates the dysregulation of positive emotion from one of several possible symptoms of depression to a primary hallmark of the disorder. Depressed individuals experience not only more negative emotions, such as sadness and irritability; they also experience fewer positive emotions, such as interest, appreciation, and contentment.

A rich history of theoretical and empirical work supports this clinically observable fact. Although negative emotions are inevitable and at times useful, if a person's negative emotions are not offset by a healthy dose of positive emotions, mental health is compromised. In support of this hypothesis, Fredrickson and Losada (2005) found that

optimal mental health is associated with a ratio of positive-to-negative emotions of at least three-to-one. Similarly, Schwartz and colleagues (2002) found that, before treatment, depressed clients reported ratios of positive-to-negative emotions of less than one-to-one. Following successful treatment, however, their ratios rose above four-to-one.

Mechanisms of Action

Fredrickson's (2001) broaden-and-build theory of positive emotions offers an explanation for the importance of positive emotions in depression. The theory postulates that positive emotions briefly alter one's cognitive functioning by expanding the scope of attention and increasing access to flexible thinking and diverse behavioral repertoires. These cognitive changes facilitate the individual's ability to build a variety of enduring personal resources. Personal resources can be cognitive (e.g., expert knowledge, mindfulness), psychological (e.g., feeling competent to meet the demands of one's environment), social (e.g., friendships, social support networks), or physical (e.g., physical skills, health, vitality). Although the experience of any positive emotion, with its concomitant cognitive broadening, is fleeting, the resources one builds during these pleasant moments accrue over time. These resources can then serve as protective factors in times of stress and, more generally, influence overall life satisfaction.

The broaden-and-build theory suggests two reasons why people who experience positive emotions infrequently are more likely to become depressed. The first is that with infrequent positive emotions, a person is deprived of a naturally occurring antidote to negative emotions. Negative emotional states, including depression, are associated with narrowed attention and limited thought-action repertoires. These cognitive and behavioral changes implement a form of tunnel vision, whereby the afflicted individual has difficulty viewing his or her situation from different perspectives and devising a variety of behavioral responses.

This tunnel vision then serves to perpetuate negative emotional states. In recognition of this painful reality, cognitive-behavioral treatment approaches—such as identifying, evaluating, and reframing depressogenic thoughts, or encouraging nondepressive behavior, such as socializing—are intended to counteract the tunnel vision that depression creates. Positive emotions broaden the very cognitive and behavioral processes that become restricted in depression, and that cognitive-behavioral treatments seek to change in a more deliberate way. Thus, by loosening the self-perpetuating grip that negative emotions exert on cognitive and behavioral processes, positive emotions may accomplish the same thing as do cognitive-behavioral treatment approaches for depression.

Relatedly, positive emotions counteract the effects of negative emotions at the physiological level as well. Fredrickson, Mancuso, Branigan, and Tugade (2000) induced anxiety in participants, then showed them one of four films, in a between-groups design. Two films were designed to elicit positive emotions (contentment and joy), one served as a neutral control, and a fourth elicited sadness. Participants who viewed one of the two positive-emotion films exhibited the fastest cardiovascular recovery time to baseline. Those who viewed the sad film exhibited the slowest. Thus, positive emotions induce both cognitive and physiological changes that serve as antidotes for negative emotional states, decreasing the likelihood that someone who frequently experiences positive emotions will become inextricably stuck in negative emotional states.

The broaden-and-build theory suggests that people who infrequently experience positive emotions are more likely to become depressed for a second reason as well. People who experience fewer positive emotions also build fewer enduring resources with which to confront the inevitable bumps and bruises in life. Having fewer resources can in turn place a person low in positive emotions at increased risk for depression. Fredrickson, Tugade, Waugh, and Larkin (2003) examined differences in depressive symptomatology in a sample of college undergraduates following the September 11, 2001, terrorist attacks. They found that differences in positive emotions following the attacks predicted differences in resources and depressive symptomatology. Participants who reported more positive emotions reported more resources and less depressive symptomatology. Of particular interest, individuals who had reported greater levels of resilience before the attacks reported higher levels of positive emotions following the attacks, suggesting that resilient people cope more effectively with stressors by cultivating positive emotions during trying times.

Treatment Implications

Conceptualizing depression as a dysregulation of positive emotions points to several treatment implications. The broaden-and-build theory suggests that a depressed individual who begins to experience more positive emotions will show broader and more flexible thinking and build more personal resources, increasing his or her ability to recover from depression and reducing risk of future relapse. Fredrickson, Cohn, Coffey, Pek, and Finkel (2008) used loving-kindness meditation, a form of meditation that focuses on loving and compassionate feelings, as an intervention to regularly activate positive emotions and build resources over time. The researchers found that loving-kindness meditation increased positive emotions over an 8-week period. Increases in positive emotions predicted increases in personal resources over the same period, which in turn predicted decreases in depressive symptomatology. Similarly, Seligman, Rashid, and Parks (2006) tested a treatment for depression known as positive psychotherapy, which strives to increase positive emotions, sense of engagement with life, and sense of meaning in life. The researchers found that positive psychotherapy produced significant improvement in depressive symptoms. Furthermore, despite the absence of booster sessions, these improvements were maintained at 1-year follow-up. This suggests that the treatment activated enduring processes, which persisted beyond the intervention period.

The broaden-and-build theory also suggests that placebo responding for depression may be more complex than the mere expectation of improvement leading to some degree of improvement. Snyder, Michael, and Cheavens (1999) proposed that hope is an important component in psychotherapy. They argue that effective psychotherapy inspires in clients both a sense that there are ways to help themselves feel better and that they are empowered to implement these strategies, resulting in positive, hopeful feelings that facilitate improvement. The mechanism by which these feelings facilitate improvement has previously been unclear. According to the broaden-and-build theory, one possibility is that, to the extent that placebo treatment inspires hopeful positive emotions, it instantiates the upward spirals in well-being associated with positive emotions. For instance, the positive emotion of hope may result in cognitive broadening, causing the individual to engage with his or her world in a slightly different way by interacting more with others. These changes might in turn begin to build resources, such as social relationships, which further improve well-being and decrease depression. Unfortunately, not all depressed patients would be expected to experience the benefits associated with placebo responding. A subset of depressed patients is unable to experience positive emotions or pleasure, a symptom known as anhedonia. If placebo responding reflects in part the benefits of cognitive broadening and resource building, these patients' inability to experience the positive emotions associated with expectation of improvement would prevent them from implementing the escalating cycles of well-being associated with broadening and building. Analysis of placebo responders for depression is a promising avenue of future inquiry to better understand the role of positive emotions in depression.

KIMBERLY A. COFFEY AND BARBARA L. FREDRICKSON

See also

Positive and Negative Affect Schedule

References

American Psychiatric Press. (2000). *Diagnostic and statistical manual of mental disorders* (4th ed.-revised). Washington, DC: Author

Fredrickson, B. L. (2001). The role of positive emotions in positive psychology: The broaden-and-build theory of positive emotions. *American Psychologist, 56,* 218–226.

Fredrickson, B. L., Cohn, M. A., Coffey, K. A., Pek, J., & Finkel, S. M. (2008). Open hearts build lives: Positive emotions, induced through meditation, build consequential personal resources. *Journal of Personality and Social Psychology, 95,* 1045–1062.

Fredrickson, B. L., & Losada, M. F. (2005). Positive affect and the complex dynamics of human flourishing. *American Psychologist, 60,* 678–686.

Fredrickson, B. L., Mancuso, R. A., Branigan, C., & Tugade, M. M. (2000). The undoing effect of positive emotions. *Motivation and Emotion, 24,* 237–258.

Fredrickson, B. L., Tugade, M. M., Waugh, C. E., & Larkin, G. R. (2003). What good are positive emotions in crises? A prospective study of resilience and emotions following the terrorist attacks on the United States on September 11th, 2001. *Journal of Personality and Social Psychology, 84,* 365–376.

Schwartz, R. M., Reynolds, C. F., Thase, M. E., Frank, E., Fasiczka, A. L., & Haaga, D. A. F. (2002). Optimal and normal affect balance in psychotherapy of major depression: Evaluation of the balanced states of mind model. *Behavioural and Cognitive Psychotherapy, 30,* 439–450.

Seligman, M. E. P., Rashid, T., & Parks, A. C. (2006). Positive psychotherapy. *American Psychologist, 61,* 774–788.

Snyder, C. R., Michael, S. T., and Cheavens, J. S. (1999). Hope as a psychotherapeutic foundation of common factors, placebos, and expectancies. In M. A. Hubble, B. L. Duncan, & S. D. Miller (Eds.), *The heart and soul of change: What works in therapy* (pp. 179–200). Washington, DC: American Psychological Association.

Postmenopausal Depression

Menopause is defined as the absence of menses for 12 consecutive months. Early postmenopause is defined as the first 4 years after the menopause (Soules et al., 2001). When depression occurs during this time, some have referred to it as postmenopausal depression. Major depressive disorder is defined in the *Diagnostic and Statistical Manual of Mental Disorders* (*DSM-IV-TR;* American Psychiatric Association [APA], 2000) by a cluster of symptoms, specifically, when sadness and/or loss of interest are present most days, most of the day, persisting for at least 2 weeks, and associated with neurovegetative features (e.g., poor sleep, poor concentration, appetite changes, low interest, low energy, and/or suicide thoughts). Yet *DSM-IV-TR* does not recognize a specific category of postmenopausal depression, nor emphasizes an increased risk of depression following menopause. Therefore, several questions have been raised about the validity of the diagnosis of postmenopausal depression. Specifically, is depression occurring during this time distinct from that occurring at other times in a woman's life? If depression is associated with postmenopause, what might the cause be, and how might it be treated?

The evidence as to whether there is postmenopausal depression, distinct from depression occurring at other times in a woman's life, is not clear. There is evidence both for and against the diagnosis. Moreover, menopause occurs against a background of aging, and thus it is difficult to make definitive attributions as to the cause of a depression when it occurs postmenopause (National Institute on Aging [NIA], 2004).

Epidemiological studies have been conducted comparing rates of depression among postmenopausal women to rates of depression in other stages of women's lives. The cumulative literature suggests that there may be an increase in depressive symptoms during the transition to menopause; however, evidence so far suggests that there is no increase in depressive symptoms or depression postmenopause. In fact there is even some evidence that there may be decreases in depressive symptoms after menopause (Freeman et al., 2004). Nonetheless, some women's experience with menopause places them at an increased risk for depression.

Theories relating postmenopause to depression include psychological, social, biological, and hormonal explanations. A traditional psychological explanation is so-called empty-nest syndrome and other variables associated with being a middle-aged woman in a society that places a high value on youth. Another theory is that there are hormonal fluctuations occurring during and following menopause that may increase the risk of depression. Specifically, withdrawal or variability in the levels of estradiol may lead to major depressive disorder in some women through changes in neurotransmitters involved in mood regulation (Schmidt, 2005). However these changes are more likely to occur during the transition to menopause and in the very early stage of postmenopause.

There are other variables associated with menopause that may increase the risk of depression. These include weight gain, memory decline, sleep disturbance, vasomotor symptoms (e.g., hot flashes, night sweats), and a longer duration of the transition to menopause (Freeman et al., 2004).

The diathesis-stress (Monroe & Simons, 1991) conceptualization of postmenopausal depression suggest that menopause is associated with an increased susceptibility to depression in combination with other risk factors. For example, an individual may have a genetic predisposition for depression that may be triggered by hormonal changes. There are other risk factors associated with postmenopausal depression, but these risk factors are not specific to postmenopausal depression and apply to major depressive disorder during other stages of life as well. The risk factors include a prior history of depression, history of premenstrual syndrome or postpartum depression, stressful life events, poor health, and low social support (Freeman et al., 2004). Finally, a cascade model has been suggested, in which an initiating symptom highly specific to the menopausal transition, such as vasomotor symptoms, disrupts sleep, which leads to adverse mood, and the subsequent chain reaction leads to a significant loss of quality of life (NIA, 2006b).

Postmenopausal women presenting with depressive symptoms should be carefully evaluated, and several treatment options should be considered. The severity of depressive symptoms is important to assess and are typically characterized as mild, moderate, or severe. Mild depressive symptoms may not necessarily represent a clinical problem requiring treatment unless they are persistent and interfere with social or occupational functioning (NIA, 2006a).

Physical exam should be performed to assess if other health problems (such as thyroid disease) may contribute to the depression. Treatment with estrogen alone may improve mood in women with mild depressive symptoms. Estrogen may potentate the effects of some antidepressants in menopausal women. However, the effectiveness of estradiol appears to be limited to the menopausal transition and to very early postmenopause (Richardson & Robinson, 2000). Women who have moderate to severe depression should be considered for antidepressant medication (Dell & Stewart, 2000) and/or psychotherapy. The combination of both has been found to be most efficacious for depression in general (Rubin et al., 2000). The antidepressant medications most frequently prescribed for postmenopausal depressed women are the selective serotonin-reuptake inhibitors (SSRIs). The two types of psychotherapy that are most effective are interpersonal psychotherapy, which would most typically focus on the role transitions that the postmenopausal woman is experiencing (Miller et al., 1998), and cognitive behavioral therapy, which seeks to identify and change distorted or unrealistic ways of thinking (Beck, 1987).

Whether postmenopausal depression is a separate entity or a variant of major depression that can occur across the life cycle, accurate diagnosis of depression, including its unique symptoms, severity, and comorbidity with other disorders is essential in assuring the health of the woman experiencing the symptoms. Despite the controversy regarding the etiology and whether the entity is truly unique, the guidelines for appropriate therapy are relatively straightforward.

NATALIE SACHS-ERICSSON AND DAN G. BLAZER

See also

Diathesis-Stress Models of Depression Risk

References

American Psychiatric Association. (2000). *Diagnostic and statistical manual of mental disorders* (4th ed., text revision). Washington, DC: Author.

Beck, A. (1987). Cognitive model of depression. *Journal of Cognitive Psychotherapy, 1*, 2–27.

Dell, D. L., & Stewart, D. E. (2000). Menopause and mood: Is depression linked with hormone changes? *Postgraduate Medicine, 108*, 34–36, 39–43.

Freeman, E. W., Sammel, M. D., Liu, L., Gracia, C. R., Nelson, D. B., & Hollander, L. (2004). Hormones and menopausal status as predictors of depression in women in transition to menopause. *Archives of General Psychiatry, 61*, 62–70.

Miller, M. D., Wolfson, L., Frank, E., Cornes, C., Silberman, R., Ehrenpreis, L., et al. (1998). Using interpersonal psychotherapy (IPT) in a combined psychotherapy/medication research protocol with depressed elders: A descriptive report with case vignettes. *Journal of Psychotherapy Practice and Research, 7*, 47–55.

Monroe, S., & Simons, A. (1991). Diathesis-stress research: Implications for the depressive disorders. *Psychological Bulletin, 110*, 406–425.

National Institute on Aging. (2004). *Biology of the perimenopause: Impact on health and aging, Vol. 9–10.* Bethesda, MD: National Institutes of Health.

National Institute on Aging. (2006a). Mood disturbance. In N. Santoro & S. Sherman (Eds.), *New interventions for menopausal symptoms* (pp. 12–14). Bethesda, MD: Department of Health and Human Services.

National Institute on Aging. (2006b). Quality of life. In N. Santoro & S. Sherman (Eds.), *New interventions for menopausal symptoms* (pp. 18–19). Bethesda, MD: Department of Health and Human Services.

Richardson, T., & Robinson, R. (2000). Menopause and depression: A review of psychological function and sex steroid neurobiology during the menopause. *Primary Care Update for OB/GYNs, 7*, 215–223.

Rubin, R. T., Umanoff, D. F., Veijola, J. M., Duncan, B. L., Miller, S. D., Keller, M. B., et al. (2000). Nefazodone, psychotherapy, and their combination for chronic depression. *New England Journal of Medicine, 343*, 1041—1043.

Schmidt, P. (2005). Mood, depression, and reproductive hormones in the menopausal transition. *American Journal of Medicine, 118 Suppl. 12B*, 54–58.

Soules, M. R., Sherman, S., Parrott, E., Rebar, R., Santoro, N., Utian, W., et al. (2001). Executive summary: Stages of reproductive aging workshop (STRAW). *Fertility and Sterility, 76*, 874.

Postpartum Depression

Shortly after the birth of a child, many women experience a period of dysphoria known as postpartum blues. It has been estimated that up to 80% of postpartum women experience symptoms of negative mood and affect that sharply contrast with expectations of feeling happy and a sense of accomplishment. These feelings usually remit without intervention.

Postpartum depression, however, is a more serious and less common condition that threatens a mother's emotional and physical health, and the health of her infant.

Diagnosis and Definitions

Postpartum mood disorders encompass a range of clinical symptoms. Interpretation of epidemiological data requires understanding how these disorders are defined diagnostically and in clinical research. First, postpartum depression is not distinguished from major depression except in terms of its timing. A diagnosis of postpartum depression requires onset of a major depressive episode within 4 weeks of delivery. However, most researchers apply the term more liberally and generally consider a major or minor depressive episode occurring up to 12 months postdelivery to fall within the scope of postpartum depression. Minor depression, also called subclinical depression, has no formal diagnosis but is used to label mood disorders presenting with fewer symptoms than required for a diagnosis of major depression. Postpartum minor depression is not to be confused with postpartum blues. Postpartum blues is a milder constellation of symptoms, including depressed mood, emotional lability, insomnia, tearfulness, irritability, and anxiety, usually beginning within the first few days after delivery, and is relatively transient. Despite the somewhat fluid nature of these definitions, postpartum blues is viewed as categorically distinct from postpartum depression. Typically, blues symptoms resolve within a few days and do not require intervention.

Although there are nosological distinctions between postpartum depression and subclinical postpartum depression, the body of postpartum depression research encompasses both clinically significant and subclinical depression and has produced valuable knowledge of epidemiology, risk factors, screening tools, and successful treatments. Therefore, the reader should note that in this entry, postpartum depression refers to both minor and major depression.

Epidemiological Data

Although the prevalence of postpartum depression has been estimated to be 10% to 15%, a more recent study suggests that it is really much lower. In an effort to more accurately quantify the disease burden of depression in new mothers, the Agency for Healthcare Research and Quality and the Safe Motherhood Group conducted a systematic review of postpartum depression literature with the aim of generalizing prevalence to the U.S. population (Gaynes et al., 2005). Included studies were those carried out in developed countries and that used clinical interviews to confirm episodes of major or minor depression from 1 week after delivery to 12 months postpartum. Prevalence estimates ranged from 1.0% to 5.9% for major depression alone, and from 6.5% to 12.9% for major and minor depression. Although prevalence estimates for postpartum depression are similar to the prevalence of depression in women across the life span, much evidence supports the argument that the birth of a child is an especially vulnerable time, and certain factors may lead to a depressive disorder. Physiologic underpinnings and biopsychosocial risk factors are reviewed in the following sections.

Neuroendocrine Basis of Postpartum Depression

Empirical data provide generally limited support for a neurological or endocrinological basis of postpartum depression. Nonetheless, the postpartum period is marked by distinct physiological changes that do not occur with the onset of nonpuerperal mood disorders. Normal pregnancy is characterized by marked elevations in estradiol, progesterone, and cortisol. Following childbirth, these hormones rapidly return to prepregnancy levels. The onset and maintenance of lactation during the postpartum period is associated with rapid increases in prolactin. Despite these changes, the data do not support the hypothesis that the rapid decline in hormone levels is responsible for depression onset (Zonana &

Gorman, 2005). With few exceptions, most research has found no relationship between estrogen or magnitude of change in estrogen levels in depressed versus nondepressed postpartum women, and evidence for the relationship between the decline in progesterone and postpartum depression remains contradictory. Change in cortisol levels has also shown an inconsistent relationship to postpartum mood. There is little evidence that lower levels of prolactin are associated with depressive symptomatology. However, studies of breast-feeding and negative mood indicate a potential buffering effect, possibly mediated by the elevations of prolactin and oxytocin in mothers who breast-feed.

Despite these inconsistent data, research continues to examine the possible neuroendocrine underpinnings of postpartum depression. For instance, recent research shows depressed postpartum women to have significantly reduced bioavailability of serotonin compared to nondepressed postpartum women (Newport et al., 2004). Serotonin has a well-established role in the etiology and treatment of depression. It is possible that the precipitous decline in estrogen and cholesterol during the postpartum period, both of which are associated with the synthesis and metabolism of serotonin, may explain these findings. Taken together, these data indicate that further investigation into biological factors is warranted.

Biopsychosocial Risk Factors

Although the proximal cause is not well understood, researchers have identified a number of biopsychosocial risk factors of postpartum depression. Significant postpartum fatigue, postpartum pain, depression history, depression during pregnancy, poor social support, negative events, and stress are all predictors of postpartum depression (Kendall-Tackett, 2005).

Fatigue and Pain

Fatigue is a prominent clinical feature of depression. Maternal fatigue during the first postpartum week has been found to predict depressive symptomatology at 1 month. Although other factors contribute to fatigue, inadequate sleep may play an etiological role in the development of postpartum depression. Mothers with no immediate symptoms of postpartum depression who report poor infant sleep patterns are more likely to report significant symptoms of depression weeks later (Dennis & Ross, 2005). Disturbed sleep patterns are often expected with a new infant. The normalcy of reduced sleep throughout the early postpartum period does not, however, invalidate the role it may play in the development of postpartum depression. Objective sleep data is extremely limited in this population because polysomnographic procedures are highly invasive for new mothers. Still, research would benefit from further examining characteristics of sleep patterns in postpartum women (e.g., reduced rapid eye movement latency).

Major depression is also highly comorbid with chronic pain. Although the physical pain women experience during the postpartum period is transient, it is often constant and severe. Types of postpartum pain can arise from a variety of sources including abdominal pain from surgical delivery, breast pain from feeding difficulties, uterine contractions, perineal pain from tears or episiotomies, or lumbar-pelvic pain. Postpartum low-back pain is relatively common. Healthy women with postpartum lumbar-pelvic pain have been found to experience more significant depressive symptomatology than those without pain (Gutke, Josefsson, & Oberg, 2007). Women whose deliveries require instrumental assistance (i.e., forceps or vacuum extractor) or cesarean section tend to report more depression and negative mood symptoms several months postpartum compared to women who deliver normally.

Similar to fatigue, a certain amount of discomfort may be an expected part of postpartum adjustment. But effective postpartum pain management is not impossible. Thorough screening for pain in primary care (using subjective history and objective assessment) would be extremely useful to identify women who are at risk and to develop strategies that target a mother's specific type of pain.

Depression History

Evidence from nonpuerperal depression literature strongly indicates that having a history of major depression significantly increases one's likelihood of developing a subsequent episode. The same risk applies to postpartum women. Among the strongest risk factors for developing postpartum depression is previous experience of depression at any time, not just in relation to a previous childbirth (Robertson, Grace, Wallington, & Stewart, 2004). Consistent evidence also demonstrates that experiencing depressed mood and anxiety during pregnancy significantly predicts postpartum depression. Although postpartum blues is usually expected to remit without intervention, blues symptoms have been found to increase vulnerability to postpartum depression, though effect sizes are small. This relationship may indicate that in some women, blues symptoms persist, become more severe, and develop into depression.

Social Support and Marital Relations

Whether it is a mother's first or subsequent child, the addition of a new infant creates a substantial shift in roles and responsibilities. The perinatal period is demanding both physically and emotionally. Experiencing inadequate social support during the postpartum period increases risk of depressive symptoms. The most important support often comes from women's partners, who, in most Western cultures, are expected to share in the responsibility of infant care. It is not surprising that another predictor of postpartum depressed mood is distress within the marital relationship. When social support is not available, particularly during times of stress, depression is also more likely to result.

Negative Events and Stress

Experiencing negative life events during the postpartum period increases risk of postpartum depression. Psychological models of depression are often presented within a vulnerability-stress paradigm. O'Hara, Schlechte, Lewis, and Varner (1991) found support for a vulnerability-stress model of postpartum depression; in their study, depression history and measures of social and cognitive vulnerability interacted with life stress, accounting for 19% of the variance in postpartum depression diagnoses. The postpartum period is a time when women are particularly vulnerable to the effects of negative life events and stress, even if stress is brought on by chronic or ongoing situations that were present before the pregnancy. For instance, lower socioeconomic status and economic hardship are chronic stressors that are predictive of postpartum depression, albeit with small effect sizes.

The childbirth experience itself has been found to affect risk of postpartum depression. Childbirth can be an extremely stressful and even traumatic experience for some women. Characteristics of negative birth experiences include lack of control and inadequate support, both positively correlated with postpartum depressive symptomatology. Incidence of adverse birth outcomes, including prematurity, also contributes to postpartum depressive symptoms. Research has suggested that underlying hormonal processes of stress-related depression and preterm delivery are largely overlapping, in turn suggesting that a preterm delivery may be predictive of postpartum depressive symptomatology (Halbreich, 2005). While ensuring the health and normal development of the infant is paramount, the impact of preterm delivery on a mother's mental health should not be overlooked.

Although the temporal precedence differs among physiologic and psychosocial variables and postpartum depression, research clearly illustrates the importance of identifying and addressing risk factors to prevent the onset of a major depressive episode.

Cultural Issues

In early research, postpartum depression was described as a culture-bound illness, largely absent from non-Western countries because of protective features such as postpartum social structure, recognition of a new mother's vulnerability, required rest, recognized social status, and practical support from family, friends, and other caregivers (Posmontier & Horowitz, 2004). However, the so-called absence of postpartum depression in non-Western cultures may be largely a myth, driven by culture-specific presentations of depression. In non-Western cultures, depression may be more commonly expressed via physical complaints. Moreover, certain social support or traditional customs, such as family members moving in, can be intrusive and may not necessarily protect against postpartum depression.

A growing body of cross-cultural research provides substantial evidence that postpartum depression occurs in numerous non-Western cultures at rates that are similar to or higher than in Western countries, including, Korea, Japan, India, Costa Rica, Taiwan, Chile, South Africa, Nigeria, and the United Arab Emirates (see for a review, Halbreich & Karkun, 2006; Ponsmontier & Horowitz, 2004). Research also shows that risk factors are largely similar cross-culturally, with the exception that the impact of infant gender on postpartum depression was more significant in countries that place higher value on male children (e.g., China, Turkey, and India). Rates of postpartum depression among ethnic minority women do not appear to differ from general prevalence estimates, with factors such as history of psychiatric illness, stress, and impaired support contributing to overall risk. In general, findings conclude that there is universality to postpartum depression, although not all cultures share the same label for it, if it is labeled at all.

Future research should further explore cross-cultural aspects of postpartum depression, particularly as it applies to ethnic minority populations in Western countries and the process of acculturation. The relationship between acculturation and postpartum depression in U.S. populations has not been clearly identified, mostly because this research is limited in its assessment of acculturation, focusing only on language proficiency and childhood exposure to U.S. culture. Future research should benefit from the work of the Transcultural Study of Postnatal Depression (TCS-PND), which has developed reliable and culturally valid measures that will enhance research of postpartum depression across different health care systems and countries (Asten, Marks, Oates, & the TCS-PND Group, 2004).

Screening of Postpartum Depression

Accurate screening is an essential first step to identifying women who are at risk of having postpartum depression. Most of the research described in this entry utilized screening tools to assess depressive symptomatology. Screening instruments vary in their ability to detect major and minor depression, both in terms of sensitivity (proportion of true positives) and specificity (proportion of true negatives). Two instruments specific to the postpartum period are the Postpartum Depression Screening Scale (PDSS) and the most commonly used Edinburgh Postnatal Depression Scale (EPDS), which include fewer somatic symptoms than the Beck Depression Inventory (BDI). In general, the PDSS and EPDS seem to be more sensitive than the BDI and the Center for Epidemiological Studies Depression Scale (though estimates of sensitivity are variable for each measure), and all four instruments provide high degrees of specificity for detecting both major and minor depression (Gaynes et al., 2005).

Two logical opportunities for routine depression screening are the standard 4- to 6-week postpartum check-up and the infant's first pediatric visit. Despite these opportunities and the availability of validated screening tools, screening for postpartum depression in primary care settings occurs for fewer than half of new mothers. Even when women are screened positively for postpartum depression, appropriate follow-up is not always incorporated into clinical practice. Screening and appropriate clinical follow-up are key components of regular postpartum care that may prevent postpartum depression onset, or identify women who may benefit from treatment. The next section focuses on current available treatment modalities for postpartum depression.

Treatment Approaches

Similar to nonpuerperal depressive disorders, approaches to treating postpartum depression can consist of a range of methods, including dietary modifications, supplements, exercise, and community interventions (e.g., support groups), as well as traditional pharmacotherapies and psychotherapies. What follows are recent developments in pharmacologic and psychotherapeutic treatment of postpartum depression.

Pharmacologic Treatment

Women make countless lifestyle adjustments during pregnancy in order to prevent adverse outcomes. Many mothers are cautious about what can safely be consumed, and for those who choose to breast-feed, concerns persist after the baby is born. These concerns can lead to hesitation when it comes to pharmacologic treatments that have demonstrated efficacy in the treatment of depression. Depressed postpartum women are more likely than nondepressed women to stop breast-feeding earlier, and some do so in part because of concerns surrounding the effects of antidepressants on infants. Antidepressants can be an effective method of depression treatment and do not necessarily require termination of breastfeeding. These treatments may be especially indicated for cases of severe major postpartum depression but also in cases of minor postpartum depression.

Most drugs enter human breast milk by passive diffusion, with concentration levels rising in maternal milk as they rise in the mother's plasma, but most antidepressants have been found to pose minimal risk of adverse outcomes in neonates. Both tricyclics and selective serotonin-reuptake inhibitors including amytriptyline (Elavil), nortriptyline (Pamelor), imipramine (Tofranil), sertraline (Zoloft), and paroxetine (Paxil) are not found in quantifiable amounts in breast-fed infants, and risk of adverse effects is extremely small (Wisner, Perel, & Findling, 1996). Fluoxetine (Prozac), citalopram (Celexa), and buproprion (Wellbutrin) are typically recommended only when the potential benefit to the mother outweighs a moderate risk to younger infants. Despite the availability of relatively safe pharmacologic options, some mothers may wish to avoid medications. For these women, psychological treatments are another option.

Psychological Treatments

Psychotherapeutic treatments are an efficacious approach to postpartum depression for women who do not wish to take medications or as an adjuvant therapy. Cognitive behavioral therapy (CBT) and interpersonal psychotherapy (IPT) have both been shown to be just as effective as medication in treating postpartum depression (see for a review, Chabrol & Callahan, 2007). Similar to CBT, IPT is a time-limited treatment in which individuals are asked to focus on problem areas particularly significant to postpartum women, including role transitions and interpersonal disputes. The goal of most postpartum depression treatments is to reduce depressive symptomatology and enhance the mother's adjustment to her new role. However, researchers have recently argued that effectively treating depression is not adequate to improve the maternal-infant relationship.

Effects of postpartum depression on new mothers pose a threat to their psychological, emotional, and physical health. Research also shows a range of deficits in infants of depressed mothers that are attributable to impaired mother-infant interactions. Evidence that treatments targeting maternal symptoms also extend benefits to infants is extremely limited. Infant attachment security, behavior problems, and temperament have been found to be unaffected by symptom-relieving treatment such as IPT. In contrast, psychotherapies that focus on the mother-infant interaction, promote maternal sensitivity, responsivity, and nonintrusiveness, and seek to improve maternal self-efficacy have been found to reduce levels of depression while also increasing infant cognitive ability, emotion regulation, and attachment security (Nylen, Moran, Franklin, & O'Hara, 2006). Some of these therapies add a home-based component, likely to be helpful for depressed mothers who lack energy and motivation to attend regular therapy sessions.

Conclusions

Postpartum depression poses a significant risk to a new mother's physical and emotional health, as well as her ability to care for herself and her infant. Recent epidemiological data for both major and minor depression suggest that postpartum depression afflicts 6% to 13% of new mothers at various times during the first postpartum year. Biopsychosocial risk factors for developing postpartum depression include fatigue, pain, history of postpartum depression, depression or anxiety during pregnancy, stress, inadequate support, and marital dissatisfaction. Although a clear neuroendocrine basis of postpartum depression remains uncertain, extreme physiological changes that take place in the immediate postpartum may have an etiological role. Recent research has indicated that women across nearly all cultures experience postpartum depression. Finally, availability of screening measures and therapies provide multiple options for treating depression while accounting for the specific needs of new mothers and their infants. The addition of a mother-infant interaction focus to treatment may enhance outcomes beyond the remission of symptoms that most effective treatments provide.

NATALIE R. STEVENS

See also

Chronic Pain
Cognitive Behavioral Therapy
Hormones

References

Asten, P., Marks, M. N., Oates, M. R., & the TCS-PND Group. (2004). Aims, measures, study sites and participant samples of the Transcultural Study of Postnatal Depression. *British Journal of Psychiatry, 184 Suppl. 46,* S3–S9.

Chabrol, H., & Callahan, S. (2007). Prevention and treatment of postnatal depression. *Expert Review of Neurotherapeutics, 7,* 557–576.

Dennis, C., & Ross, L. (2005). Relationships among infant sleep patterns, maternal fatigue, and development of depressive symptomatology. *Birth: Issues in Perinatal Care, 32,* 187–193.

Gaynes B. N., Gavin, N., Meltzer-Brody, S., Lohr, K. N., Swinson, T., Gartlehner, et al. (2005). *Perinatal depression: Prevalence, screening accuracy, and screening outcomes.* Evidence Report/Technology Assessment No. 119. AHRQ Publication No. 05-E006-2. Rockville, MD: Agency for Healthcare Research and Quality.

Gutke, A., Josefsson, A., & Oberg, B. (2007). Pelvic girdle pain and lumbar pain in relation to postpartum depressive symptoms. *Spine, 32,* 1430–1436.

Halbreich, U. (2005). The association between pregnancy processes, preterm delivery, low birth weight, and postpartum depressions: The need for interdisciplinary integration. *American Journal of Obstetrics and Gynecology, 193,* 1312–1322.

Halbreich, U., & Karkun, S. (2006). Cross-cultural and social diversity of prevalence of postpartum depression and depressive symptoms. *Journal of Affective Disorders, 91,* 97–111.

Kendall-Tackett, K. A. (2005). *Depression in new mothers: Causes, consequences, and treatment alternatives.* Binghamton, NY: Haworth Press.

Newport, J. D., Owens, M. J., Knight, D. L., Ragan, K., Morgan, N., Nemeroff, C. B., et al. (2004). Alterations in platelet serotonin transporter binding in women with postpartum onset major depression. *Journal of Psychiatric Research, 38,* 467–473.

Nylen, K. J., Moran, T. E., Franklin, C. L., & O'Hara, M. W. (2006). Maternal depression: A review of relevant treatment approaches for mothers and infants. *Infant Mental Health Journal, 27,* 327–343.

O'Hara, M. W., Schlechte, J. A., Lewis, D. A., & Varner, M. W. (1991). Controlled prospective study of postpartum mood disorders: Psychological, environmental, and hormonal variables. *Journal of Abnormal Psychology, 100,* 63–73.

Posmontier, B., & Horowitz, J. A. (2004). Postpartum practices and depression prevalences: Technocentric and ethnokinship cultural perspectives. *Journal of Transcultural Nursing, 15,* 34–43.

Robertson, E., Grace, S., Wallington, T., & Stewart, D. E. (2004). Antenatal risk factors for postpartum depression: A synthesis of recent literature. *General Hospital Psychiatry, 26,* 289–295.

Wisner, K. L., Perel, J. M., & Findling, R. L. (1996). Antidepressant treatment during breastfeeding. *American Journal of Psychiatry, 153,* 1132–1137.

Zonana, J., & Gorman, J. M. (2005). The neurobiology of postpartum depression. *CNS Spectrums, 10,* 792–799.

Posttraumatic Stress Disorder

Posttraumatic stress disorder (PTSD) is an anxiety disorder that develops after exposure to a traumatic event and is frequently comorbid with depression. Examples of traumatic events that might lead to PTSD include but are not limited to military combat, motor vehicle accidents, sexual or violent physical assaults, and natural or human-caused disasters. In order to meet initial *Diagnostic and Statistical Manual of Mental Disorders (DSM-IV;* American Psychiatric Association, 1994) diagnostic criteria for PTSD, a person must have experienced or witnessed an event or events that involved actual or threatened death or serious injury, or a threat to the physical integrity of self or others. Further, the person's response must have involved intense fear, helplessness, or horror. Although other disorders (e.g., major depressive disorder) can be precipitated by external events, these disorders can occur independent of stressors and do not require a link between symptoms and an identifiable traumatic event in their diagnostic criteria.

PTSD is characterized by three primary symptom areas: (a) persistent reexperiencing of the traumatic event, (b) persistent avoidance of stimuli associated with the trauma and emotional numbing, and (c) increased arousal (sleep disturbance, hypervigilance, etc.). The specific symptoms must not have been present before the experience of the traumatic event. Examples of reexperiencing the traumatic event include recurrent and intrusive recollections of the event, nightmares, or acting or feeling as if the event were recurring. Reexperiencing can also be characterized by intense psychological distress and/or physiological reactivity triggered by reminders of the trauma. In some instances, a person with PTSD might experience intense dissociative states during which aspects of the event are relived and acted out as if experiencing the event in the present moment. These dissociative states can last from a few seconds to several hours, or even days in some cases. Persistent avoidance of stimuli associated with the trauma and numbing symptoms include efforts to avoid thoughts, feelings, or conversations associated with the trauma, as well as efforts to avoid activities, places, or people that arouse memories of the trauma. Further, a person with PTSD might experience an inability to recall important aspects of the trauma. Other examples of avoidance and numbing include diminished interest or participation in activities, feelings of detachment or estrangement from others, and restricted range of emotions. Furthermore, some persons with PTSD might exhibit a sense of a foreshortened future characterized by lack of an expectation to have a career, marriage, children, or a normal life span. Persistent symptoms of increased arousal might include difficulty falling or staying asleep, increased irritability or expressions of anger, concentration difficulties, hypervigilance of the environment, and an exaggerated startle response.

PTSD is diagnosed after a person has been experiencing symptoms for at least 1 month following a traumatic event. Acute stress disorder is distinguished from PTSD because the set of symptoms in acute stress disorder must occur within 4 weeks of the traumatic event and are resolved within the initial 4-week period. If the symptoms persist for more than 1 month and all the criteria for PTSD are met, then the diagnosis is changed from acute stress disorder to PTSD. Also, in order to be classified as PTSD, the symptoms must cause clinically significant distress or impairment in social, occupational, or other important areas of functioning.

PTSD can develop at any age during the life span, including childhood. It is important to note that some symptoms of PTSD might present differently in children compared to adults. For example, an adult's response of intense fear, helplessness, or horror might be expressed as disorganized or agitated behavior among children.

PTSD symptoms usually begin within the first 3 months after the trauma; however, delays of months or even years are possible before symptoms appear. The expression, duration, and the relative severity of PTSD symptoms might vary over time. Data have indicated that complete recovery occurs within 3 months in approximately 50% of PTSD cases, whereas many others experience symptoms that persist for more than 12 months after the trauma (Kessler, Sonnega, Bromet, Hughes, & Nelson, 1995).

According to data from the National Comorbidity Study, the lifetime prevalence of PTSD among persons exposed to traumatic events is 8% in men and 20% in women. The prevalence of PTSD is higher among at-risk populations to include combat veterans, citizens and refugees of war-torn countries, inner-city children, and survivors of crimes, disasters, and terrorist attacks. The severity, duration, and proximity of a person's exposure to a traumatic event are the most important factors that affect the likelihood of developing PTSD. Studies have indicated that a number of variables to include social supports, family history of psychopathology, history of prior trauma, personality variables, and preexisting mental disorders may influence the development of PTSD (Ozer, Best, Lipsey, & Weiss, 2003). The disorder can develop in persons without any predisposing factors, especially when the severity of the stressor is extreme.

PTSD has a high commorbidity with other psychiatric disorders, with up to 80% of persons with PTSD meeting the criteria for at least one other psychiatric disorder (see Brady, Killeen, Brewerton, & Lucerini, 2000, for review). Common co-occurring disorders include depression, substance abuse, somatic disorders, and other anxiety disorders. Rates of major depression among persons with PTSD range up to 56% (Shalev, 2001). The presence of co-occurring disorders, such as depression, can influence and complicate the presentation and clinical course of PTSD.

There are a number of brain regions that have been identified as involved in PTSD to include the prefrontal cortex, amygdala, hippocampus, dorsal raphe nucleus, and locus coeruleus. Neuroimaging studies have indicated enhanced activity in the amygdala among people with PTSD—a key brain structure that is involved in emotional processing. Further, studies indicate reduced volume of the hippocampus, a brain structure that is associated with learning and memory. PTSD is also associated with the dysregulation of neurotransmitters (i.e., serotonergic system) and stress hormones that are responsible for the flight-or-flight response to stress (i.e., noradrenic system and hypothalamic-pituitary-adrenal axis). Studies have indicated that persons with PTSD have lower levels of cortisol than those who do not have PTSD, and higher than average levels of epinephrine and norepinephrine (see Vasterling & Brewin, 2005, for reviews).

Many treatments for PTSD are available today. The psychotherapy programs that have demonstrated the strongest efficacy are cognitive behavioral programs to include prolonged exposure therapy, stress inoculation training, cognitive-processing therapy, eye movement desensitization and reprocessing, and various combinations of these treatments (Foa, Keane, & Friedman, 2000). Psychotherapy, conducted individually or in groups, may also include techniques such as deep-breathing exercises, muscle-relaxation techniques, mindfulness meditation, and biofeedback procedures.

Selective serotonin reuptake inhibitors such as paroxetine (Paxil) and sertraline (Zoloft) are first-line pharmacotherapy for PTSD. There is also evidence that serotonin-norepinephrine reuptake inhibitors, mirtazapine, and nefazodone are also useful for treating the symptoms of PTSD. Further, atypical antipsychotics, such as olanzapine, risperidone, and quetiapine, are sometimes used adjunctively to treat intrusive thoughts and hyperarousal symptoms associated with PTSD. Anxiolytics such as buspirone (BuSpar) and benzodiazepines (e.g., Valium, Xanax) are also used to reduce acute anxiety symptoms. The majority of persons with PTSD benefit from the combination of psychotherapy and medications.

PTSD is often a chronic disorder that can cause profound impairment of functioning in many areas of a person's life. The symptoms of PTSD can lead to family and marital problems as well as occupational instability. Further, the disorder is frequently complicated and made more distressing by co-occurring disorders, sleep disturbance, memory and concentration deficits, and problems with physical health (e.g., cardiovascular disease). PTSD is thus associated with a very high rate of medical and other service use and is therefore a very costly disorder. The psychiatric, physical, and functional impairments associated with the disorder can be detrimental not only to the person afflicted, but to the person's family, as well as society as a whole.

DAVID D. LUXTON

See also

Anxiety
Comorbidity

References

American Psychiatric Association. (1994). *Diagnostic and statistical manual of mental disorders* (4th ed.). Washington, DC: Author.

Brady, K. T., Killeen, T. K., Brewerton, T., & Lucerini, S. (2000). Comorbididty of psychiatric disorders and posttraumatic stress disorder. *Journal of Clinical Psychiatry, 6*(Suppl. 7), 22–32.

Foa, E. B., Keane, T. M., & Friedman, M. J. (2000). *Effective treatments for PTSD: Practice guidelines from the International Society for Traumatic Stress studies.* New York: Guilford Press.

Kessler, R. C., Sonnega, A., Bromet, E., Hughes, M., & Nelson, C. B. (1995). Posttraumatic stress disorder in the National Comorbidity Survey. *Archives of General Psychiatry, 52,* 1048–1060.

Ozer, E. J., Best, S. R., Lipsey, T. L., & Weiss, D. S. (2003). Predictors of posttraumatic stress disorder and symptoms in adults: A meta-analysis. *Psychological Bulletin, 129,* 52–73.

Shalev, A. Y., (2001). What is posttraumatic stress disorder? *Journal of Clinical Psychiatry, 62*(Suppl. 17), 4–10.

Vasterling, J. J., & Brewin, C. R. (2005). *Neuropsychology of PTSD: Biological, cognitive, and clinical perspectives.* New York: Guilford Press.

Prevention

As the 21st century begins, the World Health Organization estimates that 121 million people in the world suffer from clinical depression. Treatment resources to address this massive need are currently insufficient and likely to remain so in the foreseeable future. Moreover, depression is estimated to become the second-greatest burden of disease in the world by the year 2020. Therefore, we must develop practical approaches to reduce its impact on humanity. Preventing the onset of clinical depression would provide one more method to address this massive health problem.

The Institute of Medicine (IOM) of the United States, in a 1994 report (Mrazek & Haggerty, 1994) on the prevention of mental disorders, defined prevention efforts as those that occur prior to the onset of the disorder to be prevented. Treatment was defined as interventions occurring during the acute phase of the disorder, and maintenance as interventions occurring after the acute phase, in order to reduce likelihood of relapse or recurrence, or to reduce disability resulting from the disorder. Prevention services were themselves divided into universal, selective, and indicated interventions. Universal interventions were focused on entire populations; selective interventions on subgroups of the population deemed to be at greater risk due to characteristics such as family history, gender, age, or socioeconomic status; and indicated interventions on individuals who were showing early signs or symptoms of the disorder but had not yet met diagnostic criteria for the full-blown disorder (Mrazek & Haggerty, 1994). The IOM report strongly advocated the need to increase research on the prevention of mental disorders in order to reduce the incidence (that is, the number of new cases) as a way to reduce the prevalence (that is, the total number of cases) in the population. Prevention research requires at least five steps: a clear definition of the target to be prevented, a theory specifying the mechanisms involved in the development of the disorder, identification of groups at high imminent risk for the disorder, interventions designed to counteract the mechanisms involved in the development of the disorder, and a research design to test whether the intervention modifies the theorized mechanisms as intended and whether these changes result in a significantly lower proportion of new cases.

One of the major obstacles in early prevention trials was identifying groups at high imminent risk for depression. If the control group has a relatively low proportion of new cases within the study period, it is difficult to obtain significantly lower proportions of new cases in the group receiving the preventive intervention. Recent studies are finding reliable ways to identify groups at high imminent risk. For example, adolescent children of patients being treated for depression who score high in depression symptom scales are at higher risk of developing a clinical depression within the following year. Similarly, women who are pregnant and have high symptom levels are at high risk of developing pre- or postpartum depression. Individuals with one or two short alleles of the serotonin transporter gene are more likely to develop a clinical depression when they are faced with stressful life events.

Because high-risk groups are now being identified more reliably, the number of randomized control trials designed to test whether depression can be prevented has increased. There are now several studies that have documented a significant reduction in the proportion of new cases of clinical depression in groups receiving preventive interventions compared to control groups. The preventive interventions often utilize methods that have been found helpful in the treatment of depression. For example, cognitive-behavioral approaches in which depressed individuals are taught methods to change thoughts and behaviors that are associated with depressed mood have been found to be very effective in the treatment of major depression. If these methods can help individuals already clinically depressed to improve their mood, the logical question

was why wait until people were seriously depressed to teach them these mood management skills. Several studies have now shown that, indeed, using these methods can reduce onset of clinical depression in persons at risk. Similarly, interpersonal therapy approaches for the treatment of depression have been adapted for prevention interventions with documented success.

In addition to the need to prevent first onset of major depressive episodes, there is a strong need to develop methods to prevent relapse and recurrence of depressive episodes in individuals who have already experienced one or more major depressive episodes. Once a person develops a major depressive episode, the risk of developing another in the future increases significantly. In addition, high levels of depressive symptoms, even if they do not reach the level of a diagnosable clinical depression, can have a disruptive impact on one's daily life. Therefore, methods to maintain mood levels within normal limits are an important area of research. We now describe studies designed to prevent first onset and recurrence.

Prevention of First Onset of Major Depressive Episodes

The initial step in prevention of first onset of depression has been to specify new episodes of major depression in participants without a history of depression as the target of prevention. The second step, that is, choosing a theoretical approach to prevention, has generally borrowed from the treatment literature, such as cognitive behavioral or interpersonal psychotherapy conceptualizations of the depressive process. The third step, the identification of groups at high imminent risk for depressive episodes, has been harder to accomplish, but there has been substantial progress, as mentioned below. The fourth step, development of interventions, has focused on creating intervention manuals adapted to the populations studied, such as Spanish- and English-speaking individuals, adolescents, and so on. The fifth step, the research design, has focused on randomized control trial methodology (Muñoz & Ying, 1993).

The importance of identifying groups at high imminent risk can be illustrated by contrasting early and more recent depression prevention studies (Muñoz, Le, Clarke, Barrera, & Torres, 2008; Muñoz & Ying, 1993). The first randomized control trial to study the prevention of major depressive episodes was conducted in 1983 by Ricardo F. Muñoz and colleagues at San Francisco General Hospital in San Francisco, California. This study serves as a useful example of the fundamental challenges of conducting prevention research. In this community investigation, the selective sample comprised ethnic-minority, low-income, English- and Spanish-speaking primary care patients attending a public sector hospital. None of the participants met diagnostic criteria for depression or any other psychiatric disorder at study entry. At the 1-year follow-up, 4 out of 72 participants (5.6%) randomly assigned to the treatment-as-usual control condition and 2 out of 67 participants (3%) randomly assigned to the 8-session cognitive-behavioral experimental condition met criteria for major depressive episode. Although incidence rates in this study were higher than previously reported (0.23% to 1.6%) in epidemiological studies, and despite the reduction in incidence by approximately half in a straight comparison of the two conditions, the rates of new episodes were insufficient to detect statistically significant differences in major depressive episode incidence.

More recent studies by Gregory Clarke and his colleagues at the Kaiser Permanente Center for Health Research in Portland, Oregon, have successfully addressed these limitations. Two randomized control trials have found significant reductions in incidence of major depressive episodes by targeting adolescents with elevated levels of depressive symptoms. In the first, youths scoring above the 75th percentile on a self-report depression symptom measure, but not meeting criteria for clinical depression, were randomly assigned to either a 15-session cognitive group intervention or to a "usual care" control condition. The control group had a 25.7% incidence rate over the follow-up period, compared to 14.5% for the experimental group. In a second study, adolescent offspring of depressed parents receiving treatment at a health maintenance organization were screened, and those who scored high on depressive symptom scales but were not currently clinically depressed were randomly assigned to either usual care or usual care plus a 15-session group cognitive prevention program. The usual care control condition had a 28.8% incidence rate through the follow-up period, compared to 9.3% for the experimental condition. The results of both of these studies reached statistical significance, supporting the contention that new episodes of major depression had in fact been prevented by the cognitive intervention.

Studies focusing on other age groups throughout the life cycle are starting to be carried out. Among infants and young children, assessing for mood is challenging and often requires a parent report the child's symptoms and behaviors. Of the prevention studies that have been conducted, many target externalizing more than internalizing symptoms and focus on teaching depressed parents parenting skills and about the impact of their relationship on their child. A number of studies implementing family-based interventions to reduce internalizing symptoms among children of depressed parents have been successful in reducing depressive symptoms among children.

In spite of the growth in the literature on prevention of late-life depression, the focus on preventive interventions with older adults remains limited. Much of the prevention research with older adults has focused on preventing depression in late life among individuals with health-related illnesses that increase the risk of depression. Emerging reports in the literature have suggested that selective and indicated interventions may be effective in reducing the incidence of major depressive episode among older adults.

One area that is showing greater activity is the prevention of depression during pregnancy and postpartum. Previous studies have shown that if the mother is depressed during pregnancy and postpartum, both the mother and the child can experience negative consequences in terms of emotional and behavioral sequelae. Prevention efforts to reduce the incidence of depression among women during the childbearing period have been promising, but few have reported significant, long-lasting intervention effects. A psychoeducation group intervention by Elliott and colleagues yielded lower rates of postpartum depression among first-time mothers in the intervention when compared to women not invited to participate (19% vs. 39%). An intervention based on interpersonal psychotherapy principles tested by Zlotnick and colleagues reduced the occurrence of postpartum depression among pregnant women receiving public assistance who had at least one depression risk factor; none of the women assigned to the intervention developed postpartum depression within the 3-month follow-up period, whereas 33% of those in the treatment-as-usual condition developed postpartum depression.

Thus, there is evidence to suggest that targeting at-risk pregnant women is a viable means of reducing the incidence of postpartum depression and may have benefits for both the mother and the infant. If these studies eventually show a consistent preventive effect and demonstrate benefits to the child, they may help to reduce the generational transmission of depression from parent to child.

In sum, the prevention of first onset of major depressive episodes appears to be a feasible goal because of two major advances. The first advance is the development of consistently successful means to identify groups at imminent risk for major depressive episodes. These methods, primarily focusing on individuals who are not clinically depressed but scoring high on depression symptom scales, are yielding incidence rates of 25% or higher in the control groups. The second advance is the reduction in incidence reported in several randomized control trials from the 25% found in control groups to rates of 9% to 14% or lower in the experimental conditions, which works out to a reduction of 40% or better in new episodes of major depression. If we are able to consistently reduce 40% of new episodes of major depression, widespread availability of such preventive services could substantially reduce the burden of depression on our society.

Prevention of Recurrence of Major Depressive Episodes

Most acute episodes of major depression eventually subside but leave behind a heightened risk for further episodes. Given the distinction between relapse and recurrence, targeting recurrence should be the first step in prevention following recovery from an episode of depression. Recurrence represents a new episode following recovery, while relapse represents a continuation of the previous episode following temporary symptom reduction without recovery. Theoretically, the vulnerability to depression appears to be heightened by the experience of a major depressive episode, so choosing a theoretical approach that addresses this vulnerability is the second step. Further specifying those groups at high risk for recurrence is the third step. The fourth step is the development of interventions for preventing recurrence, which may be continuous or time-limited maintenance interventions. Finally, the fifth step is designing adequate tests of these interventions.

According to kindling theory, individuals become more vulnerable to depression over successive episodes. This increased vulnerability may be kindled biological or psychological processes that render individuals so sensitive to depressive precipitants that episodes are essentially triggered autonomously or by nearly ubiquitous precipitants that were previously incapable of bringing about depression. This increasing susceptibility to depression is reflected in the widely acknowledged observation that the risk of a major depressive episode increases with successive episodes such that over 80% of individuals who have had three episodes will go on to a fourth. Kindling theory underscores the need to avert this worsening course of depression by preventing recurrence as early as possible after an individual has experienced a major depressive episode.

By definition, individuals who have recovered from an episode of depression are at risk for recurrence. This risk appears particularly heightened for individuals with three or more previous episodes. In addition, individuals with a family history of depression, particularly early-onset recurrent depression, are at increased risk. Individuals with comorbidities such as anxiety or substance-use disorders are also at increased risk of recurrence, as are those individuals with current dysthymia, minor depression, or residual depressive symptoms. Other reliable indicators of high risk for recurrence, such as genetic markers or psychosocial factors, await specification by further research.

The prevention of recurrence may occur through continuous or time-limited maintenance interventions. Maintenance medication, the continuation of antidepressant medication after recovery, is the best example of the former, exemplified by the landmark imipramine maintenance treatment trial at Western Psychiatric Institute and Clinics. Subsequent studies have demonstrated that maintenance medication is very effective while it is continued, reducing the likelihood of recurrence by as much as 70%. Other studies have shown that interpersonal psychotherapy and cognitive behavioral therapy can also function as continuous maintenance interventions (Muñoz et al., 2008).

While no time-limited interventions have demonstrated preventive effects specifically against recurrence, some studies provide suggestive results. Investigations testing relapse prevention have found reductions in subsequent episodes for follow-up periods of 1 year and more, suggesting that recurrence as well as relapse can be prevented. Indeed, in the treatment approach used by Fava and colleagues, only 40% of those who received the intervention had a subsequent episode of depression by the end of a 6-year follow-up period, compared to 90% of individuals receiving only clinical management. Similarly, mindfulness based cognitive therapy has been found to be effective for individuals whose previous episode was both less than and more than 1 year prior to entering treatment. Con-

servative definitions of recovery require at most 6 months of remission, so if the preventive effects of these relapse prevention studies are not limited to the first 6 months of follow-up, then it is likely that recurrence was also prevented (Muñoz et al., 2008).

Research designs testing the prevention of recurrence of major depression hinge on recovery. Recovery must be defined, assessed, and achieved. Ideally, randomization to the intervention or control condition must occur after individuals have achieved recovery. While the prevention of recurrence with continuous maintenance interventions has been tested with these designs, time-limited maintenance interventions have not yet been. Future studies must be conducted to follow-up on the promising suggestions from time-limited relapse prevention efforts. In addition, refinements in the definition of recovery, particularly the duration and level of symptom improvement required to declare recovery, are needed. It is thought that current definitions of recovery may be too permissive, contaminating the category of recovered individuals with individuals who may still be unwell, despite reduced symptom levels. As the definition of recovery and thus recurrence is improved, so will maintenance strategies designed to prevent the recurrence of depression and improve the long-term health of affected individuals.

Making Prevention Interventions Widely Available

In order to make depression prevention interventions widely available, we will need to address many of the same limitations inherent in treatment interventions. For example, face-to-face interventions or pharmacological interventions are consumable. Once a therapy hour ends, no other patient can ever benefit from it. Once an antidepressant has been used, it cannot be used again. We need to develop intervention methods that can be used again and again, without losing their preventive or therapeutic ability. For example, the development of evidence-based Internet interventions may allow tested methods to be provided worldwide and in many languages, while allowing ongoing evaluation of these methods as people from different countries and cultures begin to use them. The use of other mass media to reach large numbers of people also needs to be investigated. The marginal cost of administering an intervention using the Internet, radio, or television, that is, the cost of having one more person benefit from such an intervention, eventually approaches zero. Advances in these nontraditional methods to provide services may make worldwide preventive and treatment approaches economically feasible.

Depression is one of the most painful of human conditions. Helplessness and hopelessness are often excruciatingly present during a major depressive episode. It is not surprising, then, that most cases of suicide are the result of severe depressive states. Even moderate depression erodes one's ability to handle everyday responsibilities, to enjoy life, to express affection and caring for one's loved ones, and to consider oneself worthwhile. The impact of depression on society includes a reduction in our ability to be effective and loving parents, spouses, friends, and productive contributors to our jobs and communities. If we develop and implement methods to prevent a substantial proportion of cases of clinical depression, we will significantly reduce the global burden of disease, and increase the level of well-being and satisfaction in our societies. The prevention of depression is an achievable challenge for the 21st century.

RICARDO F. MUÑOZ, ALINNE Z. BARRERA,
AND LEANDRO TORRES

See also

Kindling
Mindfulness-Based Cognitive Therapy
Postpartum Depression
Recurrence

References

Mrazek, P., & Haggerty, R. (1994). *Reducing risks for mental disorders: Frontiers for preventive intervention research.* Washington, DC: National Academy Press.

Muñoz, R. F., Le, H. N., Clarke, G. N., Barrera, A. Z., & Torres, L. D. (2008). Preventing the onset of major depression. In I. H. Gotlib and C. L. Hammen (Eds.). *Handbook of depression* (2nd ed., pp. 533–553). New York: Guilford Press.

Muñoz, R. F., & Ying, Y. W. (1993). *The prevention of depression: Research and practice.* Baltimore, MD: Johns Hopkins University Press.

Problem-Solving Therapy

Problem-solving therapy (PST) is an evidenced-based, cognitive-behavioral intervention, based on research identifying social problem-solving deficits to serve as an important vulnerability factor for psychopathology and emotional distress. The overarching treatment goal of PST is to foster adoption and effective implementation of adaptive problem-solving attitudes and behaviors as a means of decreasing emotional distress and improving one's overall quality of life. Originally developed by D'Zurilla and Goldfried (1971), Nezu and his colleagues (e.g., Nezu, 1987; Nezu, Nezu, & Perri, 1989) specifically adapted the general PST model for the treatment of major depressive disorder.

Social Problem Solving

Social problem solving is the cognitive-affective-behavioral process by which individuals attempt to identify or discover adaptive means of coping with the wide variety and range of stressful problems, both acute and chronic, encountered during the course of everyday living. More specifically, problem solving reflects the process whereby people direct their coping efforts at altering the problematic nature of the situation itself and/or their reactions to such problems. Rather than describing a singular type of coping behavior or activity, real-life problem solving represents the multidimensional meta-process of idiographically identifying and selecting various coping responses to implement in order to adequately address the unique features of a given stressful situation at a given time.

According to contemporary theory, problem-solving outcomes are conceptualized as being largely determined by two general, but partially independent, dimensions: (a) problem orientation, and (b) problem-solving style (D'Zurilla & Nezu, 2007). Problem orientation is the set of relatively stable cognitive-affective schemas that represents a person's generalized beliefs, attitudes, and emotional reactions about problems in living and one's ability to successfully cope with such problems. Problem orientation can be either positive or negative. A positive problem orientation involves the tendency to appraise problems as challenges, be optimistic in believing that problems are solvable, perceive one's own ability to solve problems as strong, believe that successful problem solving involves time and effort, and be willing to attempt to cope with the problem rather than avoid it. Conversely, a negative problem orientation is one that involves the tendency to view problems as threats, expect problems to be unsolvable, doubt one's own ability to solve problems successfully, and become particularly frustrated and upset when faced with problems or confronted with negative emotions. As implied by its description, problem orientation serves a motivational function, that is, a positive orientation can facilitate later adaptive problem-solving efforts, whereas a negative orientation can serve to inhibit or disrupt subsequent problem-solving attempts.

Problem-solving style refers to the core cognitive-behavioral activities that people engage in when attempting to cope with problems in living. There are three differing styles that have been identified: one is adaptive in nature, whereas the remaining two reflect maladaptive ways of coping. Rational problem solving is the constructive problem-solving style that involves the systematic and planful application of specific skills, each of which makes a distinct contribution toward the discovery of an adaptive solution or coping response. This style encompasses four specific rational problem-solving skills: (a) defining a problem (i.e., delineating a realistic problem-solving goal and identifying those obstacles that prevent one from reaching such goals),

(b) generating alternative solution ideas (i.e., producing a wide range of possible solution strategies using various brainstorming principles), (c) decision making (i.e., predicting the likely consequences of the differing solution ideas in order to conduct a cost-benefit analysis that informs the decision-making process), and (d) implementing and evaluating the solution plan (i.e., monitoring and evaluating the consequences after a solution is carried out and determining whether one's problem-solving efforts have been successful or needs to continue).

The two dysfunctional problem-solving styles include (a) impulsivity/carelessness, which is characterized by impulsive, hurried, and careless attempts at problem resolution, and (b) avoidance, which is represented by procrastination, passivity, and overdependence on others to provide solutions. In general, both styles can lead to ineffective or unsuccessful problem resolution. In fact, they are likely to worsen existing problems or even create new ones.

With regard to the treatment of depression, the goals of PST are to foster one's positive orientation, decrease one's negative orientation, promote the effective implementation of a rational problem-solving style when coping with stressful problems, and decrease the tendency to be either impulsive or avoidant when confronted with such life difficulties.

Problem-Solving Model of Depression

In essence, PST is based on a diathesis-stress model of depression, whereby various social problem-solving vulnerabilities (either actual problem-solving deficits or difficulties in utilizing such skills under stress) are posited to serve as risk factors for the experience of depression (Nezu, Nezu, & Clark, 2008). More specifically, the experience of both major negative life events and persistent negative daily problems require an individual to adequately cope in order to adapt well and prevent continued negative affect. If one's problem-solving abilities are effective, then the likelihood that stress leads to a depressive disorder is attenuated. Conversely, poor or ineffective problem-solving abilities, in combination with stress, is hypothesized to lead to major depressive disorder, particularly if one engages in excessive rumination about one's problems rather than actively attempting to solve them.

Initial support for this model emanates from research that has provided strong evidence documenting the basic association between depression and social problem-solving deficits. These types of investigations cut across differing age groups, ethnic and cultural backgrounds, clinical populations, and modes of problem-solving assessment (i.e., both self-report and behavioral outcome measures). In addition, both cross-sectional and prospective investigations indicate that social problem solving serves as both a mediator (i.e., a major mechanism of action) and moderator of the stress-depression link.

Clinical Guidelines

Although PST involves teaching individuals specific coping skills, it should be conducted within a therapeutic context. As such, it is important for the problem-solving therapist to be careful not to (a) conduct PST in a mechanistic manner, (b) focus only on skills training and not on the patient's emotional experiences, (c) deliver a "canned" treatment that does not address the unique strengths, weaknesses, and experiences of a given patient, and (d) assume that PST only focuses on superficial problems, rather than on more complex interpersonal, psychological, and existential issues (when and if warranted). Thus, in addition to teaching the depressed individual certain techniques to cope better with stress, effective PST requires the therapist to be competent in a variety of other assessment and intervention strategies, such as fostering a positive therapeutic relationship, assessing for complex clinical problems, modeling, behavioral rehearsal, assigning homework tasks, and appropriately providing corrective feedback.

Structurally, PST training can be broken into three major foci: (a) training in problem orientation; (b) training in the four specific rational problem-solving skills (i.e., problem definition and formulation, generation of alternatives, decision making, solution verification), and (c) practice of these skills across a variety of real-life problems.

Training in Problem Orientation

The goal of training in this problem-solving component is to foster adoption and facilitation of a positive problem orientation. Obstacles to adopting such a perspective include (a) poor self-efficacy beliefs, (b) negative thinking, and (c) negative emotions (i.e., a strong negative problem orientation).

A clinical strategy included in our model of PST for depression to help enhance patients' optimism or sense of self-efficacy is visualization. This is used to help depressed individuals create the experience of successful problem resolution in their "mind's eye" in order to vicariously experience the potential reinforcement to be gained. Visualization in this context requests people to close their eyes and imagine that they have successfully solved a current problem. The focus is on the end point, that is, not on how one got to the goal, but rather focusing on the feelings of having reached the goal. The central aim of this strategy is to have patients create and "experience" their own positive consequences related to solving a problem as a motivational step toward enhanced self-efficacy. In essence, this technique helps create a visual image of "the light at the end of the tunnel."

To help overcome negative thinking, various cognitive restructuring and reframing strategies can be used, including those advocated in more formal cognitive therapy. One technique focuses on the ABC method of constructive thinking. With this approach, patients are taught to view depressive reactions from the ABC perspective, where A = the activating event (such as a problem), B = one's beliefs about the event (including what one says to oneself), and C = emotional and behavioral consequences. In other words, how individuals feel and act often are products of how they think. Using a current problem, the PST therapist can use this procedure to diagnose negative self-talk and thoughts that are likely to lead to distressing emotions for a given patient. The depressed patient can then be given a list of positive self-statements that can be used to substitute for or help dispute the negative self-talk.

Another clinical strategy to help overcome negative thinking is the reverse advocacy role-play strategy. In this technique, the PST therapist pretends to adopt a particular belief about problems (e.g., "problems are not common to everyone, if I have a problem, that means I'm crazy") and asks the patient to provide several reasons why that belief is irrational, illogical, incorrect, or maladaptive. If the patient initially has difficulty generating arguments against the therapist's position, the counselor then adopts a more extreme form of the belief. This procedure is intended to help depressed individuals identify alternative ways of thinking and then to dispute or contradict previously held negative beliefs with more adaptive perspectives.

To help overcome immediate negative emotions that occur in reaction to a problem, the depressed patient is taught to better manage such affect by interpreting such negative feelings as cues that a problem exists. In other words, rather than labeling one's negative emotions as "the problem" (i.e., "My problem is that I'm depressed"), individuals are taught to conceptualize such emotions as a signal or cue that "certain problems exist that need to be solved" and then to observe what is occurring in their environment in order to recognize the "real problem" that is causing the depressive reaction. Once such feelings of depression (or anger, muscle tension, nausea, or anxiety) arise, the depressed patient is then instructed to use the mnemonic *STOP and THINK* as a means of inhibiting avoidance or impulsive problem-solving behavior. The *think* aspect of this phrase refers to the use of the various rational problem-solving skills. In addition,

PST emphasizes that combining emotions and rational thinking (rather than relying solely on only one of these areas) leads to wisdom, which represents effective real-life problem solving.

Training in Rational Problem Solving

Problem definition. The major focus of this task is to better understand the nature of the problem and to set clearly defined and reasonable goals. Training in problem definition focuses on the following tasks—gathering necessary additional information about a problem, using clear language, separating facts from assumptions, setting realistic problem-solving goals, and identifying those factors that exist that prevent one from reaching such goals.

Generating alternatives. When generating alternative solutions to a problem, PST encourages broad-based, creative, and flexible thinking. In essence, depressed individuals are taught various brainstorming strategies (e.g., "the more the better," "defer judgment of ideas until a comprehensive list is created," "think of a *variety* of ideas"). Using such guides helps to increase the likelihood that the most effective solution ideas will be ultimately identified or discovered. Moreover, it provides a concrete means by which one can creatively identify additional ways of coping, rather than narrowly believing that there is only one solution (e.g., suicide) that exists.

Decision making. Once a list of alternative options has been generated, the depressed individual is taught to evaluate the likelihood that a given solution will meet the previously defined goal(s). Individuals are taught to use the following criteria to rate the various alternatives: (a) the likelihood that the solution will meet the defined goal, (b) the likelihood that the person responsible for solving the problem can actually carry out the solution plan optimally, and (c) both the short-term and long-term value associated with various personal (e.g., emotional cost versus gain, physical well-being) and social (e.g., effects on spouse or partner, effects on family) consequences associated with each alternative.

Solution verification. This last rational problem-solving task involves monitoring and evaluating the consequences of the actual outcome after a solution plan is carried out. In addition, PST encourages the depressed person to practice carrying out the solution as a means of enhancing the probability that it will be carried out in its optimal form. At times, it may be advisable for the PST counselor to include training in various other skills where appropriate (e.g., communication skills, assertiveness skills, interpersonal skills). Once the plan is underway, the patient is encouraged to monitor the actual results. Using this information allows individuals to evaluate the results by comparing the actual outcome with their expectations or predictions about the outcome. Depending on the results, individuals are then guided to either troubleshoot where in the problem-solving process they need to extend additional effort if the problem is not adequately resolved, or to engage in self-reinforcement if the problem is solved.

Supervised practice. After the majority of training has occurred, the remainder of PST should be devoted to practicing the newly acquired skills and applying them to a variety of stressful problems. Beyond actually solving such problems, continuous in-session practice serves three additional purposes: (a) the patient can receive professional feedback from the therapist, (b) increased facility with the overall PST model can decrease the amount of time and effort necessary to apply the various problem-solving tasks with each new problem, and (c) practice fosters relapse prevention.

In addition to focusing on resolving and coping with current problems, these practice sessions should also allow for future forecasting, whereby individuals are encouraged to look to the future and anticipate where potential stressful situations might arise in order to apply such skills in a preventive manner (e.g., anticipated geographic move, request for promotion, contemplating raising a family).

Efficacy of Problem-Solving Therapy for Depression

Studies evaluating the efficacy of PST to treat adults with major depressive disorder, older adults with major depressive disorder, and adult cancer patients experiencing clinically high levels of depression have found it to be particularly effective. For example, a recent meta-analysis that included 13 randomized controlled trials evaluating PST for depression led to the conclusion that, although somewhat variable in its impact, "there is no doubt that PST can be an effective treatment for depression" (Cuijpers, van Straten, & Warmerdam, 2007, p. 9). Of conceptual importance is an investigation by Nezu and Perri (1989) that involved a dismantling study whereby adults with major depressive disorder were randomly assigned to one of three conditions: PST, PST minus training in the problem-orientation component, and a waiting-list control. The results of this investigation underscore the importance of training in the full model, in that although patients who received training in rational problem-solving skills but without problem orientation training fared significantly better that wait-list control participants, patients who received the full PST package experienced the greatest reduction in depression among the three experimental conditions.

PST has also been evaluated as a treatment for minor depression and dysthymia among primary care patients, although the findings supporting its efficacy for these disorders are not as strong as for patients with major depressive disorder. However, this may be due to the fact that such treatment protocols did *not* include problem-orientation training, as would be suggested by the Nezu and Perri (1989) results. Consistent with this view is a finding of another meta-analysis, one that looked at a larger pool of PST studies addressing a variety of mental and physical health problems (Malouff, Thorsteinsson, & Schutte, 2007). Specifically, these authors found that a significant moderator of outcome across studies was the inclusion or exclusion of training in the problem-orientation component.

ARTHUR M. NEZU AND CHRISTINE MAGUTH NEZU

See also

Cognitive Behavioral Therapy

References

Cuijpers, P., van Straten, A., & Warmerdam, L. (2007). Problem solving therapies for depression: A meta-analysis. *European Psychiatry, 22,* 9–15.

D'Zurilla, T. J., & Goldfried, M. R. (1971). Problem solving and behavior modification. *Journal of Abnormal Psychology, 78,* 107–126.

D'Zurilla, T. J., & Nezu, A. M. (2007). *Problem-solving therapy: A positive approach to clinical intervention* (3rd ed.). New York: Springer Publishing.

Malouff, J. M., Thorsteinsson, E. B., & Schutte, N. S. (2007). The efficacy of problem solving therapy in reducing mental and physical health problems: A meta-analysis. *Clinical Psychology Review, 27,* 46–57.

Nezu, A. M. (1987). A problem-solving formulation of depression: A literature review and proposal of a pluralistic model. *Clinical Psychology Review, 7,* 122–144.

Nezu, A. M., Nezu, C. M., & Clark, M. A. (2008). Social problem solving as a risk factor for depression. In K. S. Dobson & D. Dozois (Eds.), *Risk factors for depression* (pp. 263–286). New York: Elsevier Science.

Nezu, A. M., Nezu, C. M., & Perri, M. G. (1989). *Problem-solving therapy for depression: Therapy, research, and clinical guidelines.* New York: Wiley.

Nezu, A. M., & Perri, M. G. (1989). Social problem solving therapy for unipolar depression: An initial dismantling investigation. *Journal of Consulting and Clinical Psychology, 57,* 408–413.

Psychodynamic Model of Depression

Writing about a psychodynamic model of depression is difficult because psychodynamic theory is not a unified approach. In fact, it is often said that the term *psychodynamic*, although frequently used singularly, is in actuality a plural noun representing an array of theoretical ideas and technical applications. There is enormous diversity among the many schools of psychodynamic thought. These schools include, but are not limited to, ego psychology, object relations theory, self-psychology, and attachment theory. Compounding this issue is that the term *depression* can be conceptualized at multiple levels. Depression is an affect state that can range in intensity form mild, transient, intermittent, and even appropriate dysphoria to severe, sustained, and disabling clinical disorders that involve profound dysphoric affect, distorted cognition, and neuron-vegetative disturbances such as difficulty sleeping, loss of appetite and weight, psychomotor retardation and/or agitation, and physical and social anhedonia.

Thus, when discussing a psychodynamic theory of depression, one needs to ask, which psychodynamic theory for what experience of depression? This entry does not attempt to represent the breadth of these ideas, but rather describe central principles about which most psychodynamic theorists could agree. Several themes run throughout the various psychodynamic formulations. First, almost all psychoanalytic formulations stress the development of poor self-esteem. Most psychoanalytic theories note anger and aggression, albeit in different ways, particularly in producing guilt and self-denigration. Many of the theories acknowledge the role of both the overly dependent longings toward others and demanding and/or perfectionist attitude toward the self. In order to be psychodynamic, mental processes are conceived as in interaction with each other. For example, an interaction may develop between dependent longings, feelings of disappointment or even anger regarding unmet longings, and the guilt or self-condemnation that these feelings engender.

The initial psychodynamic formulation of depression was presented in Sigmund Freud's "Mourning and Melancholia" (1953). This paper was a monumental contribution to psychology's conceptualization and understanding of depression. In it, Freud presents a developmental model of depression suggesting that early loss in childhood leads to increased vulnerability to depression in adulthood—a view that has been generally confirmed by both animal and human research (Nemeroff,

1999). In this paper, Freud was also beginning to elaborate a universal model of the mind in which a psychopathological state was linked to a normal one. Freud carefully compared and contrasted mourning and melancholy. In distinguishing mourning from melancholia, Freud proposed that while mourning occurs with a real loss, depression can sometimes occur without an actual loss, and most importantly that depression is characterized by a loss in self-esteem, while in mourning self-esteem is maintained. He hypothesized that the marked self-deprecation so common in depressed patients was the result of anger turned inward. Freud felt this was likely when there were unresolved ambivalences toward the lost person. He proposed that the unacknowledged anger is directed at the self through the patient's identification with aspects of the lost person. He further postulated that those with a particularly strong sense of right and wrong might be prone toward depression because of guilt over having experienced aggression toward lost loved ones. Consistent with Freud's hypothesis regarding the role of anger and hostility in depression, recent research in a large sample by John Mann found that hostility more than hopelessness predicted suicidality across age groups.

Following Freud, Karl Abraham suggested that those who suffered from low self-esteem in childhood were more likely to become depressed as adults when triggered by a new loss or disappointment. Elaborating on Freud's writings, Melanie Klein increasingly emphasized the role of the internal mental processes as influenced by the process of internalization (representing in one's own mind experiences of people or events) and the defensive need to project onto other people intolerable mental states. The interplay between these two processes of internalization and projection leads to increased levels of integration of previously unintegrated or "part" representations of others. Integration of these part representation leads to a greater awareness or realization of ambivalences toward loved ones. Klein called this developmental achievement the *depressive position*, a concept that is similar to the social psychological concept of depressive realism.

In the 1950s, Edward Bibring (1953) saw depression as arising from the tension between ideals and reality and as not necessarily related to loss or dependence. Predating, Martin Seligman's learned helplessness theory of depression, both Bibring and Sandler (Sandler & Joffe, 1965) stressed that depression developed from feelings of helplessness in the face of loss or other uncontrollable events and traumas. The British psychiatrist and psychoanalyst John Bowlby developed a variant of object relations theory called attachment theory in which he posited that children who experience neglectful or inconsistent care come to view caregivers as undependable and rejecting and develop a complementary view of the self as unlovable and unworthy of dependable care, and hence are vulnerable to depression.

Focusing on the phenomenological aspects of depression, Sidney Blatt distinguished between relational and self-definitional forms of depression (Blatt, 1974) as a function of personality development. Blatt posited that psychological development involves two primary maturational tasks: (a) the establishment of stable, enduring, mutually satisfying interpersonal relationships and (b) the achievement of a differentiated, stable, and cohesive identity. Normal maturation involves a complex reciprocal transaction between these two developmental lines throughout the life cycle. For instance, meaningful and satisfying relationships contribute to the evolving concept of the self, and a new sense of self leads, in turn, to more mature levels of interpersonal relatedness. Blatt proposed that disruptions in interpersonal relations and feelings of self-worth as corresponding to two types of depression: (a) dependent and (b) self-critical. The dependent type (anaclitic) is an interpersonally oriented depression characterized by dependency, fears of abandonment, feelings of helplessness, concerns with loss, separation, and abandonment, and the need for emotional contact. The self-critical type (introjective) is a self-evaluative depression characterized by self-criticism, guilt, failure, the need for achievement, and feelings of unworthiness. This distinction was made years before the cognitive-behavioral theorist Aaron Beck (1983) proposed the similar distinction of sociotropic versus autonomous depressions.

Otto Kernberg (1992) described characterological depression or a depressive personality as having an extremely punitive set of internal values, which leads to self-defeating behavior that is unconsciously motivated to result in suffering in order to relieve feelings of guilt. In addition to excessive guilt, he describes these individuals as being characterized by having excessive dependency and difficulties expressing anger. These individuals are likely to feel depressed in response to feeling or behaving in an angry manner because of intense guilt about expressing anger. In fact, Kernberg has noted that one often sees a vicious cycle develop between extreme dependent longings and the inevitable feelings of disappointment and anger that arise from idealizing significant others, and the guilt that the anger engenders. The guilt combined with overdependency often leads to an inability to express appropriate disappointment. Over time these disappointments build up and may eventually be expressed in an angry outburst, leading to guilt, depression, and inhibition. Overdependency leaves these individuals inhibited about expressing their needs for fear that the other will be upset with them or even abandon them. As a result, a typically excessively aggressive response to the frustration of dependency needs may rapidly turn into a renewed depressive response, as a consequence of excessive guilt feelings over aggression.

A common misperception of the psychodynamic model of depression is that it fails to recognize the importance of biological contributions to development—while stressing the intrapsychic and interpersonal contributions, it is recognized there are certainly biological and temperamental underpinnings that either facilitate or complicate one's experience and ultimate vulnerability to depression. It is also worth noting that psychoanalytic theory does not make a linear relationship between early experience and later development. Consistent with a developmental psychopathology perspective, the influence of early experiences is thought to be probabilistic rather than deterministic and dependent on later experiences. In a psychodynamic perspective, it is not just the occurrence of a negative life event, but rather the person's interpretation of the meaning of the event and its significance in the context of its occurrence.

There are a number of contemporary psychodynamic and nonpsychodynamic treatments for depression that have evolved out of the psychodynamic model of depression. Lester Luborsky's supportive-expressive psychotherapy is an explicitly psychodynamic model. Although not necessarily psychodynamic in terms of technique, both Robert Klerman's interpersonal psychotherapy—based on the psychoanalytic writings of Harry Stack Sullivan's interpersonal theory and Bowlby's attachment theory—and Beck's cognitive behavioral therapy were derived out of psychodynamic models.

Conclusions

The psychodynamic model of depression represents a diverse set of models and has evolved over time to incorporate the multiplicity of influences on the experience of both normal and pathological depressive affect. Contemporary psychodynamic models acknowledge the enormous advances in our knowledge about genetic influences on certain neurotransmitters such as dopamine, neuroephinephrine, and serotonin that play a role in the activation of the limbic system and the frontal cerebral cortex involved in generating depressive affect. However, the focus across these diverse models is on the role of personality and psychological processes, their interaction with one another, and the resulting phenomenological experience of depression. Central to a psychodynamic theory of depression are the experience of a real or imagined loss, changes in self-worth or self-esteem consequent of an internal experience of ambivalence, and the absence of certain aspects of this core conflict from awareness (likely due to the fact that it is incongruent with conscious ideas about the self and would therefore be seen as unacceptable). Similar to other contemporary approaches to depression, a psychodynamic theory views depression as an interpersonally oriented problem and as resulting largely from cognitive-affective representations formed in the very earliest years of childhood and elaborated over a multitude of subsequent experiences. What is unique about a psychodynamic approach is that key aspects of these representations are believed to be out of one's immediate awareness and not easily accessible for consideration or introspection. Moreover, ambivalent feelings lead to an unconscious defensive push of thoughts or feelings from awareness. These out-of-awareness experiences, thoughts, and feelings are seen as important not only in the generation of pathological depressive affect, but also in its treatment.

KENNETH N. LEVY AND RACHEL H. WASSERMAN

See also

Anaclitic and Introjective Depression
Psychodynamic Therapy

References

Beck, A. T. (1983). Cognitive therapy of depression: New perspectives. In P. Clayton & J. Barnett (Eds.), *Treatment of depression: Old controversies and new approaches* (pp. 265–290). New York: Raven Press.

Bibring, E. (1953). The mechanism of depression. In P. Greenacre (Ed.), *Affective disorders* (pp. 13–48). New York: International Universities Press.

Blatt, S. J. (1974). Levels of object representation in anaclitic and introjective depression. *Psychoanalytic Study of the Child, 29,* 7–157.

Freud, S. (1953). Mourning and melancholia. In J. E. Strachey (Ed. and Trans.), *The standard edition of the complete psychological works of Sigmund Freud* (Vol. 14, pp. 237–258). London: Hogarth Press. (Original work published 1917)

Kernberg, O. F. (1992). Psychopathic, paranoid, and depressive transferences. *International Journal of Psychoanalysis, 73,* 13–28.

Nemeroff, C. B. (1999). The pre-eminent role of early untoward experience on vulnerability to major psychiatry disorders: The nature-nurture controversy revisited and soon to be resolved. *Molecular Psychiatry, 4,* 106–108.

Sandler, J., and Joffe, W. G. (1965). Notes on childhood depression. *International Journal of Psychoanalysis, 45,* 66–96.

Psychodynamic Therapy

Whereas systematic reflection on the treatment of depression dates back at least to the time of Hippocrates and Galen, psychodynamic approaches could be considered a watershed of modern psychological thought. The family of treatments known as the psychodynamic (also termed dynamic or psychoanalytic) therapies all share a common lineage, with Sigmund Freud (1856–1939) as their intellectual forebear.

Psychoanalysis, as both a psychological system and treatment approach, is remarkable for its scope, originality, ability to generate controversy, and also for the sheer number of its ideas that have become popular parlance (e.g., defense mechanisms, "slips" of the tongue). Most important for contemporary psychological thought, however, were Freud's discussions of the unconscious and, specifically, his insistence that unconscious motivations were ubiquitous in normal and pathological human life. Although systematic thinking about the unconscious certainly predates Freud (e.g., Schopenhauer and Nietzsche), his major contribution to the history of ideas was to systematize its study, thus making seemingly random events (e.g., dreams and forgetting) both meaningful and potentially comprehensible. Since their genesis, Freud's methods and ideas have been widely utilized, applied to other disciplines (e.g., philosophy and literary theory), and migrated far beyond their Viennese origins to take root in many parts of North America, Latin America, and Europe.

In spite of the fact that Freud's conception of human nature involved strong hedonistic elements (namely, it was based on the so-called pleasure principle), a large portion of his voluminous body of work was devoted to charting human misery in all of its many shades and variations. Not surprisingly, the seemingly common human vicissitude of depression was an object of great interest to him and those who followed. Freud's (1953) major work on the subject, "Mourning and Melancholia," emphasized the similarities and differences between bereavement and depression. He saw the predisposition for depression as resulting from the real or imagined loss of loved ones in childhood. The image of the lost "object," whom the child has ambivalent (namely, both loving and hateful) feelings for, is then internally reconstructed and taken into the child's psyche by a process known as introjection. The lost object then becomes part of the child's ego, and the ambivalent feelings are directed inward. A steady stream of anger, self-criticism, and reproach are thus directed at the self (instead of the lost object), and this is thought to result in depression.

In general, dynamic understandings of depression have followed the development and evolution of psychodynamic thought itself, and theorists subsequent to Freud have amplified, subtly shifted focus on, or departed from his earlier ideas. This is perhaps reflective of variations in the causes or specific manifestations of depression across time or societies. For instance, Karl Abraham and Sandor Rado focused on the depressive consequences of early injuries to a child's self-esteem. Edward Bibring saw the origin of depression in a self-perceived gulf between who one is or what one has accomplished (i.e., the actual ego) and who one wished to be or what one hoped to achieve (i.e., the ego ideal). Marked discrepancies between the actual and the ideal were thought to lead to the incessant self-criticism and debasement so characteristic of depression. More recently, object relations theorists and self psychologists have sought the origins of depression in what could be termed a deficiency disease during the first few years of life wherein children either do not receive enough caregiving or do not receive it in an empathic and comfortable manner. Summarizing across these and other models (which is a precarious, if not impossible task), psychodynamic conceptions of depression tend to focus on such themes as real or perceived loss, narcissistic vulnerability, conflicted anger (often directed toward the self), disturbances in the self, early parental failures, guilt, shame, and interpersonal struggles.

One way to introduce psychodynamic therapies for depression is to discuss what has been termed the psychoanalytic *attitude* or *sensibility* (e.g., McWilliams, 2004). In general, psychodynamic therapists value a particular type of honesty over the entire course of therapy. Self-examination and introspection are highly valued for both patients and therapists, and this includes a sustained investigation into aspects of oneself that may be disavowed or unknown, yet nonetheless highly influential. These aspects may include wishes, desires, dreams, and fantasies that serve as personal motivations. There is also an overriding respect for the complexity of the mind and the many layers and levels (e.g., conscious, unconscious) of thought, emotion, and behavior. This is epitomized in what have been termed the principles of *overdetermination* and *multiple function* (Wäelder, 1936). Overdetermination refers to the belief that every significant mental event is preceded by multiple causes (i.e., depression is not due to just one discrete cause). Similarly, the principle of multiple function holds that every action intended to solve one problem is simultaneously an attempt to solve other problems (e.g., depression may serve to punish oneself for perceived misdeeds, express hostility toward a partner, and emotionally connect with a depressed parent). Dynamic therapies attempt to clarify these causes and motivations. Similarly, all symptoms are understood not just as symptoms per se, but within the overarching context of the entire person and their historical development. Some specific approaches (especially time-limited therapies) spend relatively less time on past events, but all express unanimity on the contextual nature of psychopathology. Finally, psychodynamic therapists believe that pathology is linked to fundamental human processes and adaptations. Thus, given similar biological predispositions and environmental circumstances, anyone could fall victim to depression or other psychological disturbances, as there is clearly a continuum between normal and pathological states. No one is immune to pathology, and psychodynamic therapists must be aware of and empathically utilize their own personal struggles in order to effectively help their patients. These various aspects of the psychodynamic sensibility may explain the tendency for most dynamic therapists to supplement standard symptom-based definitions of depression (e.g., the *Diagnostic and Statistical Manual of Mental Disorders* [*DSM-IV*; American Psychiatric Association, 1994] and *International Classification of Disease*, tenth edition [*ICD-10*, World Health Organization, 1992]) with more holistic models (e.g., Kernberg's [1975] structural diagnosis or the recent *Psychodynamic Diagnostic Manual* [PDM Task Force, 2006]).

There is a great deal of heterogeneity in the concept of psychodynamic psychotherapy. This plurality represents a strength of the dynamic approach, as it allows for responsiveness to a broad range of disorders (including depression), as well as different levels of disorder severity. When structuring a psychodynamic treatment, we have found it helpful to consider three different dimensions or continua. Using variations of these three dimensions, it is possible to meet the needs of patients with different treatment goals, degrees of suffering, and resources. The first dimension or continuum would be session frequency. At one pole of this dimension would be psychoanalysis proper, with a session frequency of four to five times per week. At the other end would be a purely supportive dynamic therapy (described below) in which sessions may occur on a twice-monthly basis. Between these two extremes would be so-called standard psychodynamic therapies with weekly or twice-weekly sessions.

The second dimension would be length of treatment. A complete psychoanalysis, with its open-ended and exploratory nature, likely spans 4 years or more. At the other extreme are the time-limited or brief psychodynamic therapies. In these approaches (which are those most studied in treatment outcome research), patients typically receive a total of 12 to 40 weekly or twice-weekly sessions.

The third dimension could be described as the expressive versus supportive continuum of techniques. In general, expressive or interpretative techniques are intended to uncover, understand, process, and emotionally attune patients to the origins of their problems and repetitive patterns. Therapist interpretations (in which observed thoughts, feelings, or behaviors are directly tied to the dynamic content that gives rise to them) would epitomize a more expressive approach, and they are also the primary tools used in psychoanalysis and intensive long-term psychodynamic therapies. In contrast, supportive techniques are utilized to make the patient feel more comfortable. The more supportive therapies often remain focused on the surface of a patient's life, spending less time on past events, and are intended to combat immediate distress as well as return the patient to his or her typical baseline level of functioning. Regression to earlier and distressing events is not encouraged, and supportive therapies instead rely upon the shoring up of adaptive defenses. These techniques are sometimes described as creating a holding environment for patients.

One may wonder in what circumstances a depressed person would benefit from these different variations of dynamic therapy. There are many factors to consider, obviously, but we attempt here to provide some generalizations. Whereas some theorists have suggested in the past that all psychodynamic psychotherapies are inferior or baser alloys of the pure "gold" of psychoanalysis, most current therapists would disagree. They realize that not all people are appropriate for psychoanalysis and its many requirements. Most also believe that the approach taken must be adapted to the particular needs of the individual. Thus, in contrast to the early days of psychoanalysis when many patients were recommended for analysis, there is no longer a one-size-fits-all psychodynamic approach. However, there certainly are better and worse approaches, depending upon the idiosyncratic needs of a depressed patient.

Patients' needs can be grouped into goals, the degree of suffering, and resources. With regard to goals, dynamic therapists take patient goals seriously and spend time revisiting them throughout the course of treatment. These goals can range widely. Some patients desire reduction of their depressive symptoms, while others hope to change their maladaptive interpersonal patterns and make significant modifications to their personality. Sometimes patients and therapists may disagree on goals, or even on what is driving the depression, and such a state of affairs requires continued clarification and discussion.

Degree of suffering can range from a relatively mild first episode of depression, just barely interfering with a person's life, to a recurrent and severe major depression that causes widespread and global functional impairment. In some cases, patients in the darkest depths of depression may also experience problems with reality testing.

Resources of the patient must be realistically considered as well. Whereas this includes such factors as money and time (both legitimate concerns), it also includes the patient's appropriateness for the demands of psychodynamic psychotherapy (i.e., his or her psychological resources). Over the course of the past 100 years, a great deal of speculation on these potential factors has taken place. In general, the closer that depressed patients approximate the prototypical "good" patient for psychoanalysis, the more appropriate they are for more expressive approaches. The further patients deviate from this template, the more likely they are to benefit from more supportive approaches. Unfortunately, the empirical validation of these concepts remains at the beginning stages.

The prototypical patient should be suffering, curious about his or her problems, motivated to change, willing and able to think psychologically, capable of understanding metaphor, and able to acknowledge his or her emotional experiences. Sans these attributes, expressive techniques may be less effective (however, the empirical findings on this are mixed). Further, given the interpersonal focus of psychodynamic therapy and the importance of the therapeutic relationship, it is helpful if the patient has had at least one good relationship in the past (or present). Anecdotal evidence would also suggest that people with antisocial personalities tend to do poorly in psychodynamic therapy, but this may not be the case if they are concurrently depressed (Woody, McLellan, Luborsky, & O'Brien, 1985). Presumably, profound interpersonal deficits would impede the formation of a good and authentic therapeutic alliance. Adequate reality testing is also a requirement of expressive work, and patients suffering from psychotic depressions are more likely to benefit from supportive treatments. Again, these are broad generalizations, but we have found them to be useful heuristics nonetheless.

Psychodynamic authors (e.g., Busch, Rudden, & Shapiro, 2004) often describe hypothetical stages of therapy for depression. In the beginning stage, an extensive history of the patient's depression, overall development, and general functioning (e.g., work history, interpersonal life) is taken. This is important, as it reveals the dominant depression themes and yields insight into the development and maintenance of these problems. A history also consists of exploratory work to uncover the hidden or suppressed wishes, fears, impulses, and desires in the patient's inner life and also to understand the characteristic ways in which the patient deals with them. This work eventuates in the therapist forming a dynamic conceptualization of the patient's depression. For example, a depressed male patient may be understood as continually seeking out depressed women with unconscious wishes that he can "save them" from their depression (perhaps in a way that he could not save his mother) and also be recognized as "good" and "masculine" by them. These attempts ultimately fail due to his inability to connect with them beyond a superficial level, and these repeated failures leave him feeling inadequate and isolated. This conceptualization will then be used to help determine treatment goals and the general plan to reach these goals. However, the formation of a good therapeutic alliance, an essential achievement of this stage, is likely a precondition for treatment progress.

The middle phase of treatment is characterized by helping the patient thoroughly understand his or her depressive dynamics and the many ways in which these dynamics affect the patient's life and interpersonal relationships. Therapeutic work may involve the exploration of repetitive patterns of behavior as well as the patient's relationship with the therapist (e.g., in the transference). Using the example above, the patient at this stage begins to recognize and understand the emotional pull that depressed women seem to possess for him. He also begins to understand the problematic ways in which his neediness emerges in relationships with others, as it is simultaneously arising in the therapeutic relationship.

It is important to note, however, that gaining insight is not held to be merely an intellectual process, but is an emotional one as well, and therapists work to link patients' feelings to their experiences in a safe and moderated fashion. Distinctions are also made between feeling and acting, as some depressed patients may have difficulties with impulsive behavior (especially suicidal patients). Insight into the patient's depression and the "working through" of these insights into different areas of the patient's life often results in increased freedom from maladaptive patterns. Another primary goal at this stage is to "inoculate" the person from future depressions through eliminating vulnerabilities that would make this likely (e.g., by reducing unrealistic guilt, increasing understanding of underlying dynamics, or working toward a more realistic self-concept).

The final phase of therapy includes the actual termination of the treatment and therapeutic relationship. Termination is often experienced as a recapitulation of earlier losses that may have served to elicit the patient's depression. This being the case, substantial time is devoted to exploring the patient's experiences of impending loss. Such time is necessary, as these feelings may be very confusing and conflicted for the patient (e.g., sadness over the loss combined with anger over abandonment). In general, exploration and discussion of the end of therapy is intended to ultimately provide a new experience or provide the possibility for separating in a manner different from the past. Successfully weathering a separation with a well-intended and responsive person may serve as both a model for other nondisruptive separations and as a preventative for future episodes of depression. Using our previous example, the patient at this stage has made progress in both his depressive symptoms and in the quality of his relationships. As termination nears, he begins to feel increasingly angry and fearful. In response, a great deal of time is spent resolving his ambivalent feelings toward the separation, and he is eventually able to move on and interact with people in a new and more flexible manner.

We end by briefly reviewing empirical evidence for the efficacy of psychodynamic therapies for depression. When compared to other treatments for depression (e.g., cognitive therapy), there have been relatively few large trials of psychodynamic therapy. This paucity of research is likely due to several factors. First, the research tradition of psychodynamic therapists historically relied upon in-depth descriptions of individual case studies as opposed to large-scale controlled clinical trials. Second, some prominent scholars have expressed skepticism that dynamic therapy could be adequately operationalized into specific and detailed therapy manuals (a major requirement for randomized controlled trials) while simultaneously maintaining an individualistic approach to patient treatment. However, not everyone agrees with these assessments, and clinical research into brief psychodynamic therapy for depression has taken place. Comparisons of brief dynamic therapy to either cognitive therapy or behavior therapy indicate essentially equivalent effectiveness in treating depression (e.g., Leichsenring, Rabung, & Leibing, 2004). Similarly, two studies to date have compared brief dynamic therapy to antidepressant medication. Results did not indicate superiority for either approach. Unfortunately, no long-term follow-up studies were conducted for these medication trials, and it remains to be seen whether dynamic therapy, like cognitive therapy, will demonstrate lower relapse rates than medication. In addition to these findings derived from clinical trials, research into the process of therapeutic change has been conducted. Specifically, investigations into nonspecific therapy factors (e.g., the therapeutic alliance) as well as psychodynamic-specific factors (accurate interpretations of patient's core dynamic difficulties and the competent delivery of interpretative techniques) have consistently been associated with positive treatment outcome. In summary, although psychodynamic therapy in existing trials appears to be as effective as other treatment approaches and possesses some level of empirical support for several mechanisms of change, more therapy process and outcome research is warranted. This is particularly the case for more intensive forms of psychodynamic therapy.

BRIAN A. SHARPLESS AND JACQUES P. BARBER

See also

Bereavement
Psychodynamic Model of Depression

References

American Psychiatric Association. (1994). *Diagnostic and statistical manual of mental disorders* (4th ed.). Washington, DC: Author.

Busch, F. N., Rudden, M., & Shapiro, T. (2004). *Psychodynamic treatment of depression*. Washington, DC: American Psychiatric Publishing.

Freud, S. (1953). Mourning and melancholia. In J. E. Strachey (Ed. and Trans.), *The standard edition of the complete psychological works of Sigmund Freud* (Vol. 14, pp. 237–258). London: Hogarth Press. (Originally published 1917)

Kernberg, O. F. (1975). *Borderline conditions and pathological narcissisim*. New York: Jason Aronson.

Leichsenring, F., Rabung, S., & Leibing, R. (2004). The efficacy of short-term psychodynamic psychotherapy in specific psychiatric disorders: A meta-analysis. *Archives of General Psychiatry, 61,* 1208–1216.

McWilliams, N. (2004). *Psychoanalytic psychotherapy: A practitioner's guide*. New York: Guilford Press.

PDM Task Force. (2006). *Psychodynamic diagnostic manual*. Silver Spring, MD: Alliance of Psychoanalytic Organizations.

Wäelder, R. (1936). The principle of multiple function: Observations on over-determination. *Psychoanalytic Quarterly, 5,* 45–62.

Woody, G. E., McLellan, A. T., Luborsky, L., & O'Brien, C. P. (1985). Sociopathy and psychotherapy outcome. *Archives of General Psychiatry, 42,* 188–193.

Psychophysiology of Depression

As its name implies, psychophysiology is the study of mind-body relations. In particular, it examines relations between physiological and psychological variables, and especially how psychological constructs are reflected in patterns of physiological activity. Psychophysiological techniques are useful for the understanding of emotion, cognition, personality organization, and mental illness. Sweat gland activity, heart rate, blood pressure, muscle tension, brain activity, and other electrophysiological responses are commonly measured, as are stomach activity, breathing patterns, stress hormones, and immune system functioning. Emotional states tend to be reflected in such physiological activity, which makes physiological measurement an invaluable research and assessment tool.

The literature in the area of relations of physiological response systems to emotional disorders is vast and diverse, and the study of each of these response systems is complex and technical. As such, this entry briefly discusses two common examples and their interpretation. The interested reader is referred to Santerre and Allen (2007) for a broader overview of the application of psychophysiological methods to psychopathology.

Distinguishing Psychophysiology From Biological Psychiatry

The predominant viewpoint in biological psychiatry tends to conceptualize mental illnesses as manifestations of various brain disorders. Researchers of this mind-set tend to interpret the results of their studies from the standpoint of general "abnormalities" in physiology and functional neuroanatomy, which are conceptualized as causing or contributing to psychopathology (Insel, 2007). These models can be quite intricate, focusing on subtypes of neurotransmitter receptors, complex brain circuitry, and feedback mechanisms between the brain and the endocrine system, for example.

In contrast, psychophysiological perspectives take into account complex interconnections between the mind and the body. In addition to an interest in abnormal activity in neural circuitry on emotional dysfunction, psychophysiology also considers the effects of cognitive, motivational, and affective processes on patterns of physiological activity. Like biological psychiatry, the psychophysiological perspective assumes that the mind is instantiated in the brain-body. Unlike biological psychiatry, psychophysiology does not typically make the additional assumption that the mind is reducible to brain function. Instead, psychology and physiology are conceptualized as separate, complimentary levels of analysis (Kline, LaRowe, Donohue, Minnix, & Blackhart, 2003).

Cortisol and the Hypothalamic-Pituitary-Adrenal Axis

Some patients with mood disorders show an abnormality in the hypothalamic-pituitary-adrenal (HPA) axis, which is a neural-endocrine system that is involved in stress responses. The HPA axis is normally a negative feedback system: as blood levels of cortisol rise, they signal the hypothalamus to shut down its signals to the pituitary gland, which in turn signals the adrenals to cease cortisol production. Some depressed individuals evince chronically elevated cortisol levels, presumably because this normal negative feedback mechanism is somehow disrupted. The disruption of this feedback mechanism is determined by the dexamethasone suppression test (DST). Because dexamethasone binds to the same receptors in the hypothalamus as cortisol, yet is chemically distinct from it, dexamethasone administration normally leads to a decrease in plasma cortisol levels. If the normal negative feedback mechanism of the HPA axis is disrupted, then dexamethasone does not suppress cortisol production (Stewart, Quitkin, McGrath, & Klein, 2005).

Being influenced heavily by the biological psychiatry perspective, the interpretation of DST results often occurs in isolation, that is, the dysfunction is considered to be a marker of some forms of depression. However, the mechanisms by which these processes relate, and the circumstances under which they might be expected to do so, have not been fully explained. This leaves open the possibility of intervening psychological variables: the explanation of relationships between physiological systems and psychological dysfunction must take into account that behavior patterns can affect physiology.

For example, cortisol tends to increase metabolic activity and psychological vigilance, which are important aspects of the well-known fight-or-flight response. The breakdown of the negative feedback mechanism of the HPA axis could occur as a sedentary person engages in futile attempts to maintain vigilance and prepare for increases in metabolic activity. Since physical inactivity is common in depression, impaired negative feedback in the HPA axis may persist until the individual corrects the feedback loop by once again becoming more active physically.

Proponents of a biological psychiatry formulation of the DST could argue that this example is not parsimonious, stating that it is more complicated than it needs to be. Advocates of a psychophysiological framework can counter this criticism by pointing to the fact that *parsimony* and *simplicity* are not synonymous: the former implies that explanations should not make unnecessary assumptions, including the implicit assumption that so-called abnormal DST results can be explained solely by the physiological level of analysis, even if doing so seems simpler than recourse to psychological constructs.

Frontal Encephalographic Asymmetry

Asymmetrical activity in the frontal lobes provides another example of a physiological correlate of depression. Lower levels of left frontal activity as measured by EEG have been associated with some forms of depression and anxiety. This literature is typically interpreted from the standpoint of a left frontal advantage for processing appetitive, approach-related motivation and emotion, and a similar right frontal advantage for processing aversive, withdrawal-related motivation and emotion. A relation between less left frontal activity and emotional distress has been reported in many studies, and although there is a reliable effect, it generalizes only to right-handed individuals and is not always replicated (Thibodeau, Jorgensen, & Kim, 2006).

Although both biological psychiatry and psychophysiology show interest in cortisol and EEG parameters, the latter tends to consider the patterning of physiological responses according to psychological factors, whereas the former searches for causes of mental suffering and abnormal behavior in structural and functional brain abnormalities.

From the psychophysiological perspective, physiological systems can be patterned by psychological processes. For example, sadness involves its own characteristic pattern of physiological activity states, resulting in changes in body postures, facial expressions, tear duct activity, endocrine responses, and cardiovascular activation patterns. Anxiety, anger, and fear are also associated with distinct behavioral manifestations of patterns of autonomic, motor, endocrine, and somatovisceral activity (Santerre & Allen, 2007). It stands to reason, then, that disordered emotion would be reflected not only in neurobiological anomalies, but in complex response patterns, including central, autonomic, neuroendocrine, somatovisceral, and muscular parameters (Schwartz, 1982).

The conceptualization of a simple relation between relative right frontal activity and decreased positive emotion and/or decreased approach motivation leaves much to be explained. Again, *simple* and *parsimonious* are not synonymous, and simplistic explanations can make unnecessary assumptions that are not immediately obvious. Indeed, cognitive processes instantiated in the frontal lobes also appear to show relative lateralities. Because these processes have been demonstrated to predispose a person to more or less distress, they should not be assumed to be irrelevant. Worry and rumination, for example, have been found to relate to relative left frontal activity and are also associated with vulnerability to anxiety and depression (Borkovec, Ray, & Stober, 1998). Furthermore, although left frontal activity predicts fewer social deficits in high-functioning autistic children, it also predicts increased emotional distress, including anxiety and depression (Sutton et al., 2005). Since anger and irritability can also be present during depressive episodes, the well-established link between anger and relative left frontal activity adds yet another layer of complexity to the depression–frontal asymmetry connection (Harmon-Jones, 2004).

Conclusions

Psychophysiology not only reflects a distinct discipline studying mind-body relations, but also suggests an explanatory framework that distinguishes it from related disciplines. Given the same data, biological psychiatry and psychophysiology may offer vastly different explanations.

It also bears mentioning that cognitive and affective neurosciences are related disciplines that endeavor to map out the neural circuits that instantiate various psychological functions. These areas of inquiry have proliferated since functional neuroimaging techniques have become available. As inquiry into the mind-body connections in healthy and disordered emotion move forward, the interpretation of neural activity patterns poses similar challenges to those encountered by psychophysiological researchers. Again, psychological and physiological variables constitute separate levels of analysis. Furthermore, the brain is part of the body, and not only affects the rest of the body, but is also affected by it. These are especially important considerations for the psychophysiological and affective neuroscience research that delves into depression and other forms of disordered emotion.

JOHN P. KLINE

See also

Cortisol
Dexamethasone Suppression Test
Hypothalamic-Pituitary-Adrenal Axis

References

Borkovec, T. D., Ray, W. J., & Stober, J. (1998). Worry: A cognitive phenomenon intimately linked to affective, physiological, and interpersonal behavioral processes. *Cognitive Therapy and Research, 22*, 561–576.

Harmon-Jones, E. (2004). Contributions from research on anger and cognitive dissonance to understanding the motivational functions of asymmetrical frontal brain activity. *Biological Psychology, 67*, 51–76.

Insel, T. R. (2007). Shining light on depression. *Science, 317*, 757–758.

Kline, J. P., LaRowe, S. D., Donohue, K. F., Minnix, J., & Blackhart, G. C. (2003). Adult experimental psychopathology. In M. C. Roberts & S. S. Ilardi (Eds.), *Methods of research in clinical psychology: A handbook* (pp. 234–259). Malden, MA: Blackwell.

Santerre, C., & Allen, J. J. B. (2007). Methods for studying the psychophysiology of emotion. In J. Rottenberg & S. L. Johnson (Eds.), *Emotion and psychopathology: Bridging affective and clinical science* (pp. 53–79). Washington, DC: American Psychological Association.

Schwartz, G. E. (1982). Psychophysiological patterning and emotion from a systems perspective. *Social Science Information/sur les sciences sociales, 21*, 781–817.

Stewart, J. W., Quitkin, F. M., McGrath, P. J., & Klein, D. F. (2005). Defining the boundaries of atypical depression: Evidence from the HPA axis supports course of illness distinctions. *Journal of Affective Disorders, 86*, 161–167.

Sutton, S. K., Burnette, C., Mundy, P. C., Meyer, J., Vaughan, A., Sanders, C., et al. (2005). Resting cortical brain activity and social behavior in higher functioning children with autism. *Journal of Child Psychology and Psychiatry, 46*, 211–222.

Thibodeau, R., Jorgensen, R. S., & Kim, S. (2006). Depression, anxiety, and resting frontal EEG asymmetry: A meta-analytic review. *Journal of Abnormal Psychology, 115*, 715–729.

Psychosocial Functioning

Recent estimates suggest 1 out of 6 Americans will suffer from depression during their lifetime. Since the 1960s, researchers have consistently shown that individuals diagnosed with depression have greater impairment in all areas of psychosocial functioning than people who are not depressed. In fact, to be diagnosed with major depressive disorder or dysthymia, the persistent, associated depressive symptoms listed in the criteria must cause "significant distress or impairment in social, occupational, or other important areas of functioning" (American Psychiatric Association, 2000, p. 356). In other words, impairment in psychosocial functioning is built into the diagnosis of depression. The severity of this psychosocial impairment rivals that found in such chronic diseases as cardiovascular disease, cancer, and arthritis (Hays, Wells, Sherbourne, Rogers, & Spritzer, 1995) and represents the "leading cause of disease-related disability among women in the world today" (Kessler, 2003, p. 5).

As suggested above, impairment in psychosocial functioning is linked to changes in the course of illness, such as onset and persistence of depressive symptoms, poor treatment response, and higher rates of relapse and recurrence. In addition, researchers have shown that the impairment in psychosocial functioning associated with depression can be stable over time, especially in patients with depression who suffer treatment resistance or psychosis. Estimates of this impairment increase further in patients with depression who also have nonpsychiatric medical disorders.

Definition of Psychosocial Functioning

Given the prominence of psychosocial functioning in the experience and diagnosis of depression, it is surprising that the role and measurement of psychosocial functioning is not more frequently studied. At present, psychosocial functioning can be thought of as a person's performance in and satisfaction with his or her occupational, social-interpersonal, and recreational roles (Hirschfeld et al., 2000). In other words, psychosocial functioning is based on both objective and subjective assessments of role performance. Objective estimates of role performance involve someone besides the person who is depressed describing or quantifying the behaviors that fulfill the depressed person's social obligations. Subjective estimates of satisfaction involve the depressed person quantifying the extent to which fulfilling these roles meets personally relevant standards, which include both satisfaction with the role itself and the person's performance within the role.

Table P.2 provides a heuristic for conceptualizing psychosocial functioning. Social-interpersonal functioning can be viewed as fulfilling or performing within social roles such as a partner, lover, significant other, parent, family member, extended relative, friend, or neighbor. Within these roles, consideration is given to the frequency, quality, and content of relationships, including sexual functioning. With occupational functioning, a person rates his or her performance at work, school, and/or home in such terms as investment, workload, or productivity. Finally, to rate their recreational functioning, people report on the quantity and quality of leisure activities and hobbies (e.g., sports, gardening, reading, watching TV, going to movies, church).

Social roles and evaluation of functioning within each role can overlap and may conflict. For example, a father who plays with his children after work can be functioning in both the recreational and social-interpersonal domains. Likewise, an employee who aggressively (but rudely) promotes her own agenda items in a business conference may perceive herself as functioning well within the occupational domain, while her colleagues perceive her as having poor social and interpersonal skills.

Social-Interpersonal Functioning

Depressed people have more difficulty in their relationships with spouses, coworkers, family, and friends than people who are not depressed. Bothwell and Weissman (1977) reported that this impairment in intimate relationships can persist for over 4 years, even after the complete remission of depressive symptoms. Interestingly, family members of depressed patients also endorse greater impairment in psychosocial functioning than normative samples, suggesting that the family members might also be depressed or have suffered a loss in psychosocial functioning due to some yet to be identified mechanism.

Occupational Functioning

When considering occupational impairment, depression costs employers more than any other psychiatric disorder and accounts for more days missed at work than chronic medical conditions such as diabetes, heart disease, hypertension, and lower back pain. In fact, epidemiologists estimate 172 million days of work are lost each year in the United States due to depression. Researchers also estimate that the United States loses $51.5 billion each year due to absenteeism and reduced productivity related to depression.

Table P.2 Measuring Psychosocial Functioning Using Both Objective and Subjective Perspectives

	Measurement of Psychosocial Functioning		
	Social-interpersonal functioning with:	Occupational functioning at:	Recreational functioning in:
Objective assessment of performance in each role	Spouse/Partner	Work	Hobbies
	Parents	School	Exercise
	Children	Home	Religious service
	Siblings		Community service
	Extended family		Other recreational
	Neighbors		activities
	Friends		
	Satisfaction with contents and performance in each role		

In addition, when depressed workers lose their employment, they have difficulty accessing health care services, as many receive health care benefits only through work. Of these individuals, only 33% go on to receive treatment, compared to 40% or 54% of individuals with depression who stay employed or are otherwise out of the work force, respectively (Greenberg et al., 2003). Even when treatment is obtained, however, improvements in occupational functioning take time and are undone with each recurrence of depressive symptoms (Mintz, Mintz, Arruda, & Hwang, 1992).

Recreational Functioning

Compared to social-interpersonal or occupational functioning, recreational functioning has received the least attention in the depression literature. Despite this, researchers show individuals with depression report greater impairment in recreational functioning than those without depression. This impairment is most prevalent in individuals over the age of 60. Like social-interpersonal and occupation functioning, impairment in recreational functioning is relatively stable and may persist even after individuals experience remission of depressive symptoms.

Treatment Effects on Psychosocial Functioning

Researchers have shown that both pharmacological and psychosocial interventions significantly reduce impairment in psychosocial functioning in depressed populations. The data suggest that exposure to pharmacotherapy, interpersonal psychotherapy, and cognitive behavioral therapy (CBT), is associated with improvements in social-interpersonal, occupational, and recreational functioning (e.g., Papakostas et al., 2004). These findings have been replicated with those receiving inpatient or outpatient treatment for acute or chronic depression, and with primary care, elderly, low-income, and minority women populations. Of note, researchers suggest that psychosocial interventions involving both partners (e.g., marital behavioral therapy) are most effective at reducing impairment in marital or sexual functioning.

Despite these encouraging results, however, the data are inconclusive regarding the extent to which depression-specific treatment restores or creates psychosocial functioning that falls within so-called normal ranges. In a 12-week trial of antidepressant medication, Miller and colleagues (1998) showed that chronically depressed outpatients had significantly more impairment in psychosocial functioning after treatment than normative samples. In contrast, Vittengl, Clark, and Jarrett (2004) reported that over 60% of outpatients with recurrent major depressive disorder returned to normative, healthy levels of psychosocial functioning after 12 to 14 weeks of CBT. Researchers have yet to determine the extent to which these disparate findings reflect the influence of different treatment modalities, measurement intervals, and/or effects or special characteristics of setting criteria for normality, distinct patient populations, or disease processes.

Researchers also remain uncertain about the timing and mechanisms of change in psychosocial functioning during treatment and across the course of illness. This may be due to the high correlation between psychosocial functioning and depressive symptom severity before, during, and after treatment. On one hand, improvements in psychosocial functioning may precede and facilitate reductions in depressive symptoms. If this hypothesis is substantiated, depression-specific interventions may more effectively reduce depressive symptoms by initially targeting and improving functional impairment. Alternatively, reductions in depressive symptoms may also account for improvements in psychosocial functioning, as shown by Vittengl and colleagues (2004). If research continues to support this second hypothesis, efforts to treat impairment in psychosocial functioning in individuals with major depressive disorder may first focus on reducing depressive symptomatology. With either pathway, a better understanding of the timing and process of change in psychosocial functioning during treatment will facilitate researchers' and clinicians' efforts to optimize targeted interventions and better understand illness course.

Conclusions and Recommendations

Depression is a highly prevalent disease that impairs all aspects of life, including an individual's ability to work, relate to others, and engage in leisure activities. Surprisingly, researchers have not developed a consensus or standard technology to define this impairment. Furthermore, while depression-specific treatments effectively reduce impairment in psychosocial functioning, it is unclear what processes drive this change or when this change occurs in relation to improvements in depressive symptomatology across the course of illness.

We recommend that researchers and clinicians work to clarify these issues. By developing a consensus definition and measurement of psychosocial functioning, researchers and clinicians can validly and reliably assess functional impairment, improve diagnostic practices, and better quantify treatment effects. Such advances foster the field's understanding of how psychosocial functioning relates to the course and treatment of depression and will increase the relevance of research findings to public health, policy decisions, and the everyday lives of individual patients.

TODD W. DUNN AND ROBIN B. JARRETT

See also

Cognitive Behavioral Therapy
Interpersonal Psychotherapy
Marital Functioning and Depression

References

American Psychiatric Association. (2000). *Diagnostic and statistical manual of mental disorders* (4th ed., text revision). Washington, DC: Author.

Bothwell, S., & Weissman, M. M. (1977). Social impairments four years after an acute depressive episode. *American Journal of Orthopsychiatry, 47,* 231–237.

Greenberg, P. E., Kessler, R. C., Birnbaum, H. G., Leong, S. A., Lowe, S. W., Berglund, P. A., et al. (2003). The economic burden of depression in the United States: How did it change between 1990 and 2000? *Journal of Clinical Psychiatry, 64,* 1465–1475.

Hays, R. D., Wells, K. B., Sherbourne, C. D., Rogers, W., & Spritzer, K. (1995). Functioning and well-being outcomes of patients with depression compared with chronic general medical illnesses. *Archives of General Psychiatry, 52,* 11–19.

Hirschfeld, R. M., Montgomery, S. A., Keller, M. B., Kasper, S., Schatzberg, A. F., Möller, H. J., et al. (2000). Social functioning in depression: A review. *Journal of Clinical Psychiatry, 61,* 268–275.

Kessler, R. C. (2003). Epidemiology of women and depression. *Journal of Affective Disorders, 74,* 5–13.

Miller, I. W., Keitner, G. I., Schatzberg, A. F., Klein, D. N., Thase, M. E., Rush, A. J., et al. (1998). The treatment of chronic depression, Part 3: Psychosocial functioning before and after treatment with sertraline or imipramine. *Journal of Clinical Psychiatry, 59,* 608–619.

Mintz, J., Mintz, L. I., Arruda, M. J., & Hwang, S. S. (1992). Treatments of depression and the functional capacity to work. *Archives of General Psychiatry, 49,* 761–768.

Papakostas, G. I., Petersen, T., Mahal, Y., Mischoulon, D., Nierenberg, A. A., & Fava, M. (2004). Quality of life assessments in major depressive disorder: A review of the literature. *General Hospital Psychiatry, 26,* 13–17.

Vittengl, J. R., Clark, L. A., & Jarrett, R. B. (2004). Improvement in social-interpersonal functioning after cognitive therapy for recurrent depression. *Psychological Medicine, 34,* 643–658.

R

Reassurance-Seeking

Reassurance-seeking, first discussed as part of Coyne's (1976) interpersonal theory of depression, is an interpersonal process in which depressed individuals persistently seek support and validation from other people. While these other people in the depressed person's life may initially provide the reassurance and support sought by the depressed person, over time, they become frustrated by their inability to satisfy the depressed person's mounting needs for reassurance. Ultimately, they choose to avoid or reject the depressed person. This process becomes cyclical and serves to maintain and exacerbate the person's depression—as the depressed person seeks reassurance from others, he or she is rejected by others and intensifies the process of seeking support, which in turn, leads to him or her continually being rejected. In this model, depressed people's demands for reassurance is an important pathway through which they unknowingly alienate those around them and maintain their feelings of depression.

Excessive Reassurance-Seeking

A central component of this theory is that reassurance-seeking becomes excessive. Joiner, Metalsky, Katz, and Beach (1999) described excessive reassurance-seeking as "the relatively stable tendency to excessively and persistently seek assurances from others that one is loveable and worthy, regardless of whether such assurance has already been provided"

(p. 270). Thus, despite whether reassurance has been obtained, the person continues to seek reassurance and validation repeatedly. In a number of psychological studies, excessive reassurance-seeking has been correlated with depression and also has been found to predict subsequent depression, suggesting that reassurance-seeking is closely tied to the experience of depression and may be a vulnerability factor for depression.

Measurement

One instrument developed to measure reassurance-seeking is the Depressive Interpersonal Relationships Inventory: Reassurance-Seeking Subscale (DIRI-RS; Joiner & Metalsky, 2001). The DIRI-RS is a self-report measure of reassurance-seeking, with four items rated on a 1 to 7 scale. Higher scores on the DIRI-RS indicate higher levels of reassurance-seeking. The DIRI-RS has been found to be both a reliable and a valid instrument (Joiner & Metalsky, 2001).

Specificity to Depression

Research also indicates that the tendency to seek reassurance excessively is unique to depression, as opposed to other psychological disorders, such as anxiety, schizophrenia, substance abuse, and externalizing disorders. In one study, researchers found that both depressed adults and children exhibited significantly more reassurance-seeking than individuals with other diagnoses (Joiner,

Metalsky, Gencoz, & Gencoz, 2001). In another study, researchers found that depressed people scored significantly higher on measures of reassurance-seeking than individuals diagnosed with anxiety or substance disorders (Joiner & Metalsky, 2001).

Consequences of Reassurance-Seeking

A major consequence of excessively seeking reassurance is the increased risk of being rejected by other people. A large body of evidence suggests that individuals with symptoms of depression who seek reassurance excessively are much more likely to be rejected or evaluated negatively than nondepressed individuals (e.g., Joiner & Metalsky, 1995). Taken together, these findings suggest that reassurance-seeking acts as the link between depression and rejection by others. Thus, depressed individuals' persistent attempts to elicit reassurance and support from close others negatively influences their relationships and increases the likelihood they will be rejected by those from whom they seek support.

In summary, a large body of evidence supports the idea that depressed individuals experience interpersonal difficulties that maintain and intensify their depressive symptoms. Specifically, individuals' persistent attempts to gain positive reassurance from close others negatively influences their relationships and increases the likelihood they will be rejected.

BRENDA SAMPAT

See also

Interpersonal Model of Depression

References

Coyne, J. (1976). Depression and the response of others. *Journal of Abnormal Psychology, 85,* 186–193.

Joiner, T. E., & Metalsky, G. I. (1995). A prospective test of an integrative interpersonal theory of depression: A naturalistic study of college roommates. *Journal of Personality and Social Psychology, 69,* 778–788.

Joiner, T. E., & Metalsky, G. I. (2001). Excessive reassurance-seeking: Delineating a risk factor involved in the development of depressive symptoms. *Psychological Science, 12,* 371–378.

Joiner, T. E., Metalsky, G. I., Gencoz, F., & Gencoz, T. (2001). The relative specificity of excessive reassurance-seeking to depressive symptoms and diagnoses among clinical samples of adults and youth. *Journal of Psychopathology and Behavioral Assessment, 23,* 35–41.

Joiner, T. E., Metalsky, G. I., Katz, J., & Beach, S. R. H. (1999). Depression and excessive reassurance-seeking. *Psychological Inquiry, 10,* 269–278.

Recurrence

Defined as the presence of a new episode of major depressive disorder, recurrence occurs following a period of recovery from a prior episode of major depressive disorder (Frank et al., 1991). In contrast with relapse, which is defined as the development of clinically significant symptoms within 8 weeks of the resolution of the index episode, recurrence is considered to be a separate episode from the original one, occurring at least 8 weeks from the resolution of the prior episode, with no diagnosis of major depressive disorder made during the intervening period. Of those individuals who experience an episode of major depressive disorder, 60% will experience a second episode (American Psychological Association [APA], 2000), with the majority experiencing recurrence within 5 years of the original episode. With each additional episode experienced by an individual, the likelihood of future recurrence increases, with individuals with two and three prior episodes having a 70% and 90% chance of experiencing another episode, respectively (APA, 2000).

Risk factors for recurrence have been extensively studied (see Burcusa & Iacono, 2007, for a review). Consistently, the number of prior depressive episodes has predicted the likelihood of recurrence, with decreased time to recurrence associated with increased number of prior episodes (Conradi, de Jonge, & Ormel, 2008). Furthermore, residual symptomatology following treatment is predictive of recurrence, as are high levels of self-criticism. Individuals with suicidal ideation during the index episode or more severe symptomatology are at increased risk of recurrence within 12 months. Additionally, increases in dysfunctional attitudes following a sad mood induction have been found to be predictive of recurrence 18 months later (Segal, Gemar, & Williams, 1999). The presence of dysthymia, as well as comorbid Axis I disorders, appears to increase the risk of recurrence. Although findings are somewhat inconclusive, research has typically found that earlier age of onset is associated with greater risk of recurrence. Stressful life events also increased risk for recurrence; individuals high or low on both cortisol levels and fear perception appear to be at heightened risk for developing another episode of depression (Burcusa & Iacono, 2007). However, neither gender nor socioeconomic status seems to be associated with the likelihood of recurrence.

Various treatments have been studied in regards to reducing the likelihood of recurrence. Treatment with selective serotonin-reuptake inhibitors (SSRIs), particularly extended and maintenance-type treatments, is associated with decreased risk of and increased time to recurrence compared to placebo. Cognitive therapy also reduced likelihood of recurrence. Moreover, cognitive therapy appears to have more of a protective effect than pharmacotherapy (Segal et al., 1999), with up to a 22% decreased likelihood of recurrence compared to pharmacotherapy (Vittengl, Clark, Dunn, & Jarrett, 2007). While acute cognitive therapy produced similar rates of decreased recurrence as other psychotherapies (e.g., interpersonal therapy), maintenance cognitive therapy reduced recurrence rates similarly to those attained by maintenance pharmacotherapy (Vittengl et al., 2007). Despite these reductions in recurrence rates, many formerly depressed individuals will experience at least one additional episode of major depression.

TIFFANY MEITES

See also

Prevention
Relapse

References

American Psychiatric Association. (2000). *Diagnostic and statistical manual of mental disorders* (4th ed., text revision). Washington, DC: Author.

Burcusa, S. L., & Iacono, W. J. (2007). Risk for recurrence in depression. *Clinical Psychology Review, 27,* 959–985.

Conradi, H. J., de Jonge, P., & Ormel, J. (2008). Prediction of the three-year course of recurrent depression in primary care patients: Different risk factors for different outcomes. *Journal of Affective Disorders, 105,* 267–271.

Frank, E., Prien, R. F., Jarrett, R. B., Keller, M. B., Kupfer, D. J., Lavori, P. W., et al. (1991). Conceptualization and rationale for consensus definitions of terms in major depressive disorder. *Archives of General Psychiatry, 48,* 851–855.

Klein, D. N., Schatzberg, A. F., McCullough, M. E., Dowling, F., Goodman, D., Howland, R. H., et al. (1999). Age of onset in chronic major depression: Relations to demographic and clinical variables, family history, and treatment response. *Journal of Affective Disorders, 55,* 149–157.

Segal, Z. V., Gemar, M., & Williams, S. (1999). Differential cognitive response to a mood challenge following successful cognitive therapy or pharmacotherapy for unipolar depression. *Journal of Abnormal Psychology, 108,* 3–10.

Vittengl, J. R., Clark, L. A., Dunn, T. W., & Jarrett, R. B. (2007). Reducing relapse and recurrence in unipolar depression: A comparative meta-analysis of cognitive-behavioral therapy's effects. *Journal of Counseling and Clinical Psychology, 75,* 475–488.

Relapse

Symptoms of depression tend to occur during distinct periods of time called major depressive episodes. However, at times, symptoms of depression may largely or completely disappear. Relapse refers to an increase in depressive symptoms after a period in which symptoms of a major depressive episode have been noticeably decreased or absent; the length of the improved period preceding the worsening of symptoms must have been less than 2 months (Frank et al., 1991). This pattern of lessening and subsequent reemergence of symptoms is not uncommon, and thus depression is referred to as a relapsing/remitting disorder. Fatigue, anxiety, sleep disturbance, and difficulty focusing are some common lingering symptoms (Fava, 2006).

The term *relapse* is often incorrectly used interchangeably with recurrence. However, whereas relapse is conceptualized as a reemergence of the prior depressive episode, recurrence refers to an additional depressive episode that occurs after symptoms of a prior episode have been absent for more than 2 months (Frank et al., 1991; see Recurrence entry). Although a distinction is made between relapse and recurrence, in practice it is often difficult to identify whether symptoms have been fully remitted and for what period of time. It is especially complicated in cases in which additional mood disturbance such as dysthymia is present. Thus, it is not unusual for the terms to be used together (i.e., "relapse/recurrence") in published research. Nevertheless, researchers have suggested that it is important to distinguish between the two terms, as they may be associated with distinct risk factors and long-term outcomes (Frank et al., 1991).

Researchers have found that depression relapse/recurrence rates are as high as 60% to 90% or more (Kessler & Walters, 1998). Thus, relapse/recurrence prevention strategies have become a large focus of research. Most research has focused on risk factors for recurrence. However, several factors have been identified as predictive of a longer course of depression and, presumably, relatively higher relapse including greater initial severity of episode and longer length of treatment (Joffe et al., 1999), negative cognitive style (Iacoviello, Alloy, Abramson, Whitehouse, & Hogan, 2006), and poor social support (Wildes, Harkness, & Simons, 2002).

DANA STEIDTMANN

See also

Prevention
Recurrence

References

American Psychiatric Association. (2000). *Diagnostic and statistical manual of mental disorders* (4th ed., text revision). Washington, DC: Author.

Fava, M. (2006). Pharmacological approaches to the treatment of residual symptoms. *Journal of Psychopharmacology, 20,* 29–34.

Frank, E., Prien, R. F., Jarrett, R. B., Keller, M. B., Kupfer, D. J., Lavori, P. W., et al. (1991). Conceptualization and rationale for consensus definitions of terms in major depressive disorder. *Archives of General Psychiatry, 48,* 851–855.

Iacoviello, B. M., Alloy, L. B., Abramson, L. Y., Whitehouse, W. G., & Hogan, M. E. (2006). The course of depression in individuals at high and low cognitive risk for depression. *Journal of Affective Disorders, 93,* 61–69.

Kessler, R. C., & Walters, E. E. (1998). Epidemiology of DSM-III-R major depression and minor depression among adolescents and young adults in the National Comorbidity Study. *Depression and Anxiety, 7,* 3–14.

Wildes, J. E., Harkness, K. L., & Simons, A. D. (2002). Life events, number of social relationships, and twelve-month naturalistic course of major depression in a community sample of women. *Depression and Anxiety, 16,* 104–113.

Risk

Risk and *vulnerability* are terms that are often used interchangeably and, indeed, share substantial characteristics. Nonetheless, vulnerability and risk are not the same. Risk describes any factor that is associated with an increased likelihood of experiencing depression; the concept of risk is frequently used to predict onset. However, the presence of a risk factor only suggests an increased probability of depression onset but *not* what causes the disorder. Hence, risk refers to a statistical or descriptive analysis rather than to a causal analysis. Vulnerability factors, on the other hand, are seen as factors that tell us something about the mechanisms of depression and, hence, are relevant to the causes of depression.

Because data show that risk variables can predict the onset of psychopathology, it may be tempting to suggest that risk factors are causal. In an important analysis of this possibility, however, Rutter (1988), cautions against drawing casual conclusions solely from risk variables that appear linked to a disorder. He argues that risk and vulnerability are correlated because they frequently interact to produce psychopathology. To illustrate this point, Rutter (1988) points to findings from his research that showed that test results on a national examination were superior for schools where children's work was exhibited on the wall. This can easily be seen as a predictor of better test performance, but no one would argue that putting children's work on the wall caused their better grades. More likely, such behavior was indicative of an enhanced school atmosphere that was associated with better performance. In a similar fashion, the fact that a given risk variable predicts depression (e.g., being unmarried) does not suggest that it caused the depression; it may be associated with depression for a number of reasons. For instance, being unmarried may reflect the state of affairs for a man whose self-esteem is so deficient that he is unable to initiate or maintain a romantic relationship. If deficient self-esteem is a causal (i.e., vulnerability) factor, then being not married may be associated with depression but is only a correlate of depression rather than a cause.

This is not to suggest that "mere" risk factors are unimportant. To the degree that a variable can be shown to be related to an increased probability of onset, that variable can be considered to be a risk factor, and in fact a number of risk factors have been identified. Kaelber, Moul, and Farmer (1995) have summarized a multitude of potential risk factors for the occurrence of depression, and distinguish between risk factors that are (a) highly plausible, (b) plausible, and (c) possible. In the *highly plausible* category are factors such as experiencing depression in the past, being female, being divorced or separated, living in low socioeconomic circumstances, and having smoked. In the *plausible* category, factors include having a family history of depression, being never married, losing a mother before age 11, and having small children at home. In the *possible* category, they cite examples such as living in a city, doing housework, being infertile, or being Protestant. Some factors on this list may provide clues about causes of depression, but others provide no such clues. Hence, what ties together these factors is that each is linked to an enhanced possibility of becoming depressed.

As noted, although the experience of risk factors suggest an enhanced probability of disorder, the risk factors are relatively uninformative about an individual's vulnerability; they do not tell us much about the actual mechanisms that bring about depression. Hence, they suggest that a given person is at risk but say little in and of themselves about the psychological or biological processes that bring about depression. Moreover, knowledge of risk indicators is not necessarily helpful for informing intervention strategies. For example, changing religions (and even gender) is possible but unlikely to directly influence vulnerability to depression. Thus, there is nothing inherent in a risk factor that causes depression.

Vulnerability factors, on the other hand, are those that say something about the mechanisms of depression. For example, a propensity to dysregulate a given neurotransmitter that leads to depression would constitute a mechanism of depression onset and would thus serve as a vulnerability factor. Similarly, if depression is linked to the activation of schemas that influence how information is processed, this too would comprise a vulnerability factor.

Vulnerability as a Risk Factor

It is also important to acknowledge that, given the above definition of risk, vulnerability factors must also be risk factors. That is, possession of a vulnerability factor also places the individual at risk. Vulnerability is thus most properly seen as a category of risk. Risk, therefore, comprises a broader network of factors than does vulnerability. It should also be noted that a conceptual separation of risk and vulnerability does not imply that these variables are unrelated. Rutter (1988) and Luthar and Zigler (1991) each pointed out a similar distinction and argued in at least some cases these variables interact with each other to produce the onset of a disorder. For example, the woman who is at risk because she lives in a particularly stressful environment will see this risk realized in depression if she also possesses vulnerability mechanisms.

RICK E. INGRAM

See also

Vulnerability

References

Kaelber, C. T., Moul, D. E., & Farmer, M. E. (1995). Epidemiology of depression. In E. E. Beckham & W. R. Leber (Eds.), *Handbook of depression* (2nd ed.) (pp. 3–35). New York: Guilford Press.

Luthar, S. S., & Zigler, E. (1991). Vulnerability and competence: A review of research on resilience in childhood. *American Journal of Orthopsychiatry, 61,* 6–22.

Rutter, M. (1988). Longitudinal data in the study of casual processes: Some uses and some pitfalls. In M. Rutter (Ed.), *Studies of psychosocial risk: The power of longitudinal data* (pp. 1–28). Cambridge, UK: Cambridge University Press.

Romantic Relationships

A central feature of social development in adolescence is the emergence of romantic relationships. Motivated by the onset of sexual maturation, adolescents begin to seek relationships with opposite-sex peers, to whom they are romantically attracted. Over the course of adolescence, involvement in romantic relationships becomes increasingly common; by age 18 over 85% of teens report having had a boyfriend or girlfriend. These relationships are highly desirable to young people, and their involvement satisfies both emotional and developmental needs. In spite of these positive features, romantic relationships are also challenging for adolescents because of the unfamiliarity of establishing an intimate relationship with an opposite-sex peer. Immature romantic skills are compounded by the heightened emotions that these relationships engender. Managing romantic involvements may be especially challenging for adolescents whose previous experiences may have fostered insecure or maladaptive schemas about relationships (Connolly & McIsaac, 2009).

The challenge of initiating romantic relationships may have implications for adjustment. Indeed their emergence in adolescence occurs at the same time as the rapid increase in the prevalence of depression. Researchers have been struck by these co-occurring

trajectories and have postulated that romantic relationships are among the life events of adolescence that contribute to depression. Consistent with this perspective, a population-based study of American adolescents revealed that youths who became involved in romantic relationships over an 18-month period reported more depressive symptoms than did adolescents who were not involved in any romantic relationships during the same interval of time (Joyner & Udry, 2000). These findings have motivated the search for possible underlying mechanisms that might account for individual differences in maladaptive responses to romantic relationships. These include developmental readiness, negative patterns of interaction between romantic partners, attachment style, and negative cognitive schemas.

Developmental Readiness

In adulthood, romantic relationships are typically characterized as an exclusive, committed, and dyadic bond. While adolescents may progress toward this form of romantic involvement, they lack the developmental readiness to engage in these relationships before acquiring formative intimacy skills with opposite-sex peers. Instead, it is normative for romantic experiences to unfold through a series of developmental stages that move from peer-based affiliative connections, to dating in groups, to casual dyadic relationships, and finally to the serious commitments typical of late adolescents or young adults. This progression has protective functions when peers are at a similar age and stage, because there is collective discouragement of overly advanced romantic involvements outside of the peer group. Parents may also play a role in safeguarding against inappropriate involvements by careful monitoring of their adolescents' romantic activities. When adolescents are off track from this normative progression, they are at risk for negative outcomes. For example, having a boyfriend or girlfriend by the age of 13 years is linked to depressive symptoms. If by mid-adolescence, there have been repeated involvements in dating relationships, depression has also been noted. It is likely that stress is engendered by these off-time or atypical experiences, and this may translate into feelings of depression (Connolly & McIsaac, 2009).

Negative Romantic Interactions

Managing dynamic of romantic relationships, whether they are on- or off-time, is a challenge for many young people. These struggles come to the fore when adolescents begin dyadic relationships as these contexts necessitate an increasing reliance on their own judgments about what to do in different situations, rather than a sole dependence on group norms. When adolescents do not have positive experiences in their dyadic romantic relationships and instead experience conflict, criticism, and low support, depression is often reported (La Greca & Harrison, 2005). Negative interactions can also be characterized by an imbalance in how adolescents perceive their own contributions to the emotional well-being of the relationship, relative to their partner (Bentley, Galliher, & Fergusen, 2007). Boys and girls are sensitive to different aspects of the power imbalance. Boys feel more depressed when they believe that they are contributing less than their partner, while girls feel more depressed when they detect inequitable contributions from either themselves or their partner. Finally, adolescents may experience their romantic relationships negatively when they engage in self-silencing behaviors for the sake of avoiding conflict or preserving harmony. Teenage boys and girls who inhibit the expression of their true feelings and opinions with a romantic partner are also at risk for depression (Harper & Welsh, 2007).

When negative experiences accumulate, the continuation of the relationship is threatened and dissolution is often the outcome. The dissolution of a romantic relationship is considered to be a highly stressful episode in adolescents' lives, and exposure to interpersonal stressors is a known risk factor for depression. In a prospective study of the prevalence of depressive disorders in adolescence, romantic breakups emerged as a major predictor of first onset major depressive disorder for both boys and girls (Monroe, Rhode, Seeley, & Lewinsohn, 1999). Other studies have suggested that experiencing multiple romantic terminations is associated with depressive symptoms, further substantiating the stress of romantic loss for mental health.

Individual Attachment Style

Adolescents' internal representations of themselves in romantic relationships may predispose them to feelings of depression when they are romantically involved. Attachment theory suggests that styles of relating in a romantic relationship develop out of children's earlier experiences with their caregivers. These styles may be characterized as secure or insecure. Secure adolescents view themselves as deserving of love, and trust that their partners will meet their needs. Insecurely attached adolescents, on the other hand, are unsure of their worth as a romantic partner. When insecure romantic attachment takes the form of a worried preoccupation with the partner's unavailability, the risk of depression is increased. In a series of studies of early and late adolescents who were in a romantic relationship, depressive symptoms were noted both concurrently and over time only for those youths who had a preoccupied attachment style (Davila, Steinberg, Kachadourian, Cobb, & Fincham, 2004).

Negative Cognitive Schemas

Vulnerability-stress models of depression suggest that interpersonal stressors may make some adolescents more depressed than others, depending on their preexisting cognitions about relationships. An example of a cognitive vulnerability that has been linked to depression is the tendency to react to feelings of sadness with an increase in negative thoughts about the self. This cognitive reactivity has been identified among adolescent girls whose romantic interactions lack intimacy (Williams, Connolly, & Segal, 2001). Another cognitive vulnerability is rejection sensitivity, defined as the tendency to anxiously expect, readily perceive, and intensely react to rejection. When adolescents who are high in rejection sensitivity become involved in romantic relationships, they are prone to feelings of depression (Harper & Welsh, 2007). Interpersonal sensitivity, defined more broadly as an excessive awareness of and reactivity to the behaviors and feelings of others, has been shown by Rizzo, Daley, and Gunderson (2006) to moderate the relationship between romantic stressors and later depressive symptoms in girls. This study extends the stress-vulnerability model to the romantic domain and highlights the complex interactions between developmental, individual, and contextual variables in the etiology of depression in adolescence.

Conclusions

It is well documented in the adult literature that problems in intimate relationships can engender feelings of depression. There is now an emerging body of research on adolescent romantic relationships that provides evidence of continuity across the life span in the types of romantic problems that lead to depression. This continuity highlights the significance of studying adolescents' emotional responses to romantic relationships as they provide a window on emergent patterns of maladaptive relating that may set the stage for more engrained patterns in adulthood. Yet the fluid nature of adolescents' romantic relationships implies that there may be discontinuity in depressive reactions to dating stressors. As such, adolescent romantic relationships provide a valuable context for mapping the individual and interactional dynamics that precipitate depression or, conversely, promote healthy relationships.

JENNIFER CONNOLLY AND CAROLINE MCISAAC

See also

Attachment
Parenting
Schemas

References

Bentley, C. C., Galliher, R. V., & Fergusen, T. (2007). Association among aspects of interpersonal power and relationship functioning in adolescent romantic couples. *Sex Roles, 57,* 483–495.

Connolly, J. A., & McIsaac, C. (2009). Romantic relationships and intimacy in adolescence. In R. Lerner & L. Steinberg (Eds.), *Handbook of adolescent psychology* (3rd ed., pp. 104–151). Hoboken, NJ: Wiley.

Davila, J., Steinberg, S. J., Kachadourian, L., Cobb, R., & Fincham, F. (2004). Romantic involvement and depressive symptoms in early and late adolescence: The role of a preoccupied relational style. *Personal Relationships, 11,* 161–178.

Harper, M. S., & Welsh, D. P. (2007). Keeping quiet: Self-silencing and its association with relational and individual functioning among adolescent romantic couples. *Journal of Social and Personal Relationships, 24,* 99–116.

Joyner, K., & Udry, J. R. (2000). You don't bring me anything but down: Adolescent romance and depression. *Journal of Health and Social Behavior, 41,* 369–391.

La Greca, A. M., & Harrison, H. M. (2005). Adolescent peer relations, friendships, and romantic relationships: Do they predict social anxiety and depression? *Journal of Clinical Child and Adolescent Psychology, 34,* 49–61.

Monroe, S., Rohde, P., Seeley, J., & Lewinsohn, P. (1999). Life events and depression in adolescence: Relationship loss as a prospective risk factor for first onset of major depressive disorder. *Journal of Abnormal Psychology, 108,* 606–614.

Rizzo, C. J., Daley, S. E., & Gunderson, B. H. (2006). Interpersonal sensitivity, romantic stress, and the prediction of depression: A study of inner-city, minority adolescent girls. *Journal of Youth and Adolescence, 35,* 469–478.

Williams, S., Connolly, J., & Segal, Z. V. (2001). Intimacy in relationships and cognitive vulnerability to depression in adolescent girls. *Cognitive Therapy and Research, 25,* 477–496.

Rumination

Rumination is a mode of responding to distress that involves repetitively and passively focusing on symptoms of distress and the possible causes and consequences of these symptoms (Nolen-Hoeksema, 1991). When distressed people are ruminating, they tend to rehash events from the past (e.g., "How could my sister have been so mean to me?"), analyze current problems (e.g., "My spouse doesn't seem interested in me any longer"), worry about the future (e.g., "What happens if I lose my job?"), and think about their symptoms of distress (e.g., "I'm just so tired and unmotivated"). Rumination does not lead to active problem solving to change circumstances surrounding symptoms. Instead, people who are ruminating remain fixated on the problems and their feelings about them without taking action. Rumination is related to a variety of negative styles of thinking, such as pessimism, self-criticism, dependency, and low mastery. Rumination is conceptualized as a process of thinking perseveratively about one's symptoms and problems, however, rather than in terms of the specific content of thought.

The most commonly used self-report measure of rumination is the Ruminative Responses Scale from the Response Styles Questionnaire (Nolen-Hoeksema & Morrow, 1991). Respondents are asked to indicate how often they engage in each of 22 ruminative thoughts or behaviors when they feel sad, blue, or depressed. These 22 items describe responses to depressed mood that are self-focused (e.g., "I think 'Why do I react this way?'"), symptom focused (e.g., "I think about how hard it is to concentrate"), and focused on the possible consequences and causes of one's mood (e.g., "I think 'I won't be able to do my job if I don't snap out of this'"). This scale has high internal consistency and acceptable convergent validity, and tendency to ruminate is relatively stable even in individuals who experience significant change in their levels of depression.

Prospective longitudinal studies using this scale have shown that people who engage in rumination when distressed have more prolonged periods of depression and are more likely to develop depressive disorders (see Nolen-Hoeksema, Wisco, & Lyubomirsky, 2008). Other measures of rumination—in particular, those assessing a perseverative focus on the self and one's problems—relate to depression in a similar way as the Ruminative Responses Scale.

Factor analyses of the Ruminative Responses Scale suggest that, once items that may overlap with depression are removed, the remaining 10 items comprise two factors: brooding and pondering (Treynor, Gonzalez, & Nolen-Hoeksema, 2003). Brooding taps negative aspects of self-reflection, including a focus on abstract "why me?" issues (e.g., "I think, 'What am I doing to deserve this?'") and a focus on obstacles to overcoming problems (e.g., "I think, 'Why can't I handle problems better?'"). The brooding factor has been positively correlated with depression scores both concurrently and longitudinally over 1 year (Treynor et al., 2003). The pondering scale includes items that suggest a more general self-reflective tendency (e.g., "I go someplace alone to think about my feelings") and other items suggesting a problem-solving orientation to problems (e.g., "I analyze recent events to try to understand why I am depressed"). It has been inconsistently related to depression concurrently and longitudinally.

Experimental studies testing the effects of rumination have generally used a rumination induction in which participants are asked to focus on the meanings, causes, and consequences of their current feelings for 8 minutes (e.g., "Think about the level of motivation you feel right now," "Think about the long-term goals you have set"). Because these are emotionally neutral prompts, they are expected to have no effect on the moods of nondysphoric people. But because dysphoric or depressed people have more negative feelings and cognitions, this ruminative self-focus is expected to lead them to become significantly more dysphoric. The contrasting distraction induction is meant to take participants' minds off themselves and their problems temporarily. In this condition, participants' attention is focused on non-self-relevant images (e.g., "Think about a fan slowly rotating back and forth," "Think about the layout of your local shopping center"). These distracting prompts are expected to have no effect on the moods of nondysphoric people, but to lead dysphoric people to become significantly less depressed for a short time.

Dozens of studies using these rumination and distraction manipulations have found that the rumination induction reliably and significantly increases dysphoric mood in dysphoric but not in nondysphoric participants. The distraction induction decreases dysphoric mood in dysphoric participants but has no effect on mood in nondysphoric participants (see Nolen-Hoeksema et al., 2008). Similar effects of these rumination and distraction inductions have been found in clinically depressed participants.

Rumination appears to maintain and exacerbate depression through several mechanisms (see Nolen-Hoeksema et al., 2008). First, experimental studies show that dysphoric or clinically depressed individuals induced to ruminate generate more negative thoughts about the past, the present, and the future, compared to distressed individuals who are distracted or nondistressed comparison groups. Second, both experimental and correlational studies show that rumination leads distressed people to generate suboptimal solutions to problems and to be more uncertain in implementing solutions to problems. Third, experiments in which distressed people are induced to ruminate find that rumination makes them less willing to engage in instrumental behaviors that could lift their moods. Fourth, longitudinal and experimental studies show that people who ruminate may lose social support because others become frustrated with their chronic rumination, and because ruminators appear to be needy on the one hand and prone to hostility on the other.

Although most research has been concerned with the relationship between rumination and depression, rumination has also been found to predict increases in anxiety, binge-drinking and substance abuse symptoms, binge-eating and bulimia nervosa symptoms, and suicidality (see Nolen-Hoeksema et al., 2008). In addition, rumination is related to nonsuicidal self-injury (e.g., self-cutting) in adolescent girls. It may be that distressed ruminators turn to maladaptive behaviors such as binge-drinking, binge-eating, or self-injury as a way to escape their aversive self-focus. As such, rumination may help to explain the comorbidity between these symptoms and syndromes, and depression.

Interventions specifically focused on helping depressed patients overcome rumination have integrated cognitive behavioral therapy techniques with mindfulness meditation techniques (Watkins et al., 2007). The goal of these interventions is to give depressed ruminators tools for interrupting their episodes of rumination and engaging in more adaptive emotion-regulation strategies. Preliminary studies have indicated that these integrative interventions may be effective.

SUSAN NOLEN-HOEKSEMA

See also

Automatic Thoughts
Cognitive Theories of Depression
Mindfulness-Based Cognitive Therapy
Self-Focused Attention

References

Nolen-Hoeksema, S. (1991). Responses to depression and their effects on the duration of depressive episodes. *Journal of Abnormal Psychology, 100*, 569–582.

Nolen-Hoeksema, S., & Morrow, J. (1991). A prospective study of depression and posttraumatic stress symptoms after a natural disaster: The 1989 Loma Prieta earthquake. *Journal of Personality and Social Psychology, 61*, 115–121.

Nolen-Hoeksema, S., Wisco, B., & Lyubomirsky, S. (2008). Rethinking rumination. *Perspectives on Psychological Science, 3*, 400–424.

Treynor, W., Gonzalez, R., & Nolen-Hoeksema, S. (2003). Rumination reconsidered: A psychometric analysis. *Cognitive Therapy and Research, 27*, 247–259.

Watkins, E., Scott, J., Wingrove, J., Rimes, K., Bathurst, N., Steiner, H., et al. (2007). Rumination-focused cognitive behaviour therapy for residual depression: A case series. *Behaviour Research and Therapy, 45*, 2144–2154.

S

Scar Hypothesis

The scar hypothesis has been discussed largely in the consideration of cognitive research, and what this research suggests for the causal aspects of cognitive models; that is, does this research support models that specify a given cognitive cause of depression? However, although usually confined to discussion of cognitive approaches to depression, the implications of the scar hypothesis are relevant to all models, cognitive or not, that have something to say about what causes depression. Because discussion of this hypothesis is generally limited to cognitive approaches, however, it will be illustrated here within a cognitive context.

A variety of studies have demonstrated cognitive deficits in depression (see Ingram, Miranda, & Segal, 1998). For example, depressed individuals have been found to make inaccurate attributions as to the cause of the events, engage in a number of cognitive errors, and show distorted information processing. In the early days of this research, investigators suggested that the observation of such deficits helped to confirm models of depression that had proposed that such deficits play at least some role in the onset of the disorder. The scar hypothesis, however, posed a serious challenge to these conclusions. The hypothesis was first proposed by Lewinsohn, Steinmetz, Larson, and Franklin (1981) to suggest that observed cognitive deficits in depression may represent an effect, or a scar, of the disorder rather than a cause. The idea is that the processes involved in the experience of a depressive episode may alter people's cognitions. If so, then what had been thought to have been a cause of depression was instead a result of the depression.

Studies have tended to not find evidence of depressive scars. Such studies, however, are inconclusive because of cognitive reactivity ideas and research paradigms. Cognitive reactivity suggests that depression-prone individuals may not display negative cognitive patterns during the nondepressed state, but that these cognitive patterns are nevertheless present and can be brought to the forefront by negative events. If scars exist, but are latent, then they need to be activated to be detected.

Data have begun to accumulate that appear to support the major propositions of cognitive models (Scher, Ingram, & Segal, 2005). By far, however, the most difficult aspect of cognitive models to validate is the argument that certain cognitive variables play an important role in the causes of the disorder. It has been within this context that it has been difficult to disconfirm the scar hypothesis.

Even though failure to find empirical evidence of scars does not negate cognitive vulnerability models, the scar hypothesis does present a serious challenge and cannot, as yet, be ruled out. Hence, although studies have found evidence of depressotypic processing in previously depressed individuals, researchers cannot rule out that this processing represents scars that are now detectable. If this is the case, such variables arose as consequences of having experienced depression rather than serving as vulnerability processes for past and, presumably, future depression.

RICK E. INGRAM

See also

Causality
Cognitive Reactivity
Cognitive Theories of Depression
Diatheses-Stress Models of
Depression

References

Ingram, R. E., Miranda, J., & Segal, Z. V. (1998). *Cognitive vulnerability to depression.* New York: Guilford Press.
Lewinsohn, P. M., Steinmetz, L., Larson, D. W., & Franklin, J. (1981). Depression-related cognitions: Antecedent or consequence? *Journal of Abnormal Psychology, 90,* 213–219.
Scher, C. D., Ingram, R. E., & Segal, Z. V. (2005). Cognitive reactivity and vulnerability: Empirical evaluation of construct activation and cognitive diathesis in unipolar depression. *Clinical Psychology Review, 25,* 487–510.

Schemas

The schema is the central organizing concept in the majority of cognitive theories of depression. In the context of depression, Beck (1967) was the first to propose the idea that schemas play a causal role in depression. The schema is seen as a cognitive processing structure that allows the individual to organize the world in a meaningful way. Building on similar ideas, Beck (1967) defined the schema as "a structure for screening, coding, and evaluating the stimuli that impinge on the organism. It is the mode by which the environment is broken down and organized into its many psychologically relevant facets. On the basis of the matrix of schemas, the individual is able to orient himself in relation to time and space and to categorize and interpret his experiences in a meaningful way" (p. 283).

Schemas are developed from experience and, in some sense, can be thought of as a stored body of knowledge that interacts with the environment to influence memory search, selective attention, and based on memory and attention, decision making. Schemas are also proposed to be self-perpetuating since available information is screened though the filter of the schema. As a result, information that disconfirms or contradicts the individual's beliefs systems is not attended to or processed with much depth. Moreover, schemas can create self-fulfilling prophecies. The person with a "hostility schema" will not only perceive hostility in situations where there is none, but is more likely to verbally and behaviorally respond with anger and hostility. Interactions with a person with such a schema ultimately provoke hostility from others, which then reinforces and perpetuates the schema.

The Schema in Depression

Cognitive models of depression, for example, suggest that depressed persons have schemas of the self that are negatively biased, filter out positive information and self-knowledge, and exaggerate negative aspects of the environment and negative self-referent information. For individuals who possess such schemas, negative events trigger their activation that then leads to information being more negatively processed than is warranted by the reality of the situation. Of course, this is not to suggest that depressed people do not experience genuinely and severely negative events, but that these events are interpreted in a way that is out of proportion to the event, and that also interferes with problem solving.

Beck also elaborated on the causal aspects of schemas that go beyond distorted information processing to propose several layers of cognitions that are involved in causing depression. First, negative automatic thoughts regularly occur in depressed individuals, and they are a function of the schema. Underlying these automatic thoughts are irrational beliefs that are a product of deeper depressive schemas.

As is evident from this description of schemas, these structures are conceptualized in a diathesis-stress context; schemas represent this diathesis, or vulnerability. While not influencing information processing when dormant, negative events will trigger their activation, at which point they become the predominant mechanism through which information is filtered and processed. Beck also argued that at least initially, the stress that is most potent for activating schemas is the stress to which the individual has been previously sensitized. Thus, the person who has become sensitized to interpersonal difficulties is more likely to have depressive schemas activated by later interpersonal difficulties. Beck also argues, however, that as depression persists, less-specific stress is needed to perpetuate schemas: "As these schemas become more active they are capable of being evoked by stimuli less congruent with them . . . only those details of the stimulus situation compatible with the schema are abstracted, and these are reorganized in such a way as to make them congruent with the schema. In other words, instead of a schema being selected to fit the external details, the details are selectively extracted and molded to fit the schema" (p. 286).

Schema definitions among cognitive models of depression can vary somewhat, but all share the fundamental assumption that the schema is an information-processing structure that is an important part of the cause of depression. Given the popularity of cognitive models to depression and other disorders, and widespread empirical investigation of these models, the schema is perhaps the single most predominant concept among psychosocial models of depression. It provides a very powerful construction for understanding a variety of phenomena in both the depressed state and the vulnerable to depression state.

RICK E. INGRAM

See also

Aaron Beck
Automatic Thoughts

Cognitive Behavioral Therapy
Cognitive Distortion
Cognitive Mediation
Cognitive Reactivity
Cognitive Theories of Depression
Cognitive Vulnerability
Diatheses-Stress Models of Depression

Reference

Beck, A. T. (1967). *Depression*. New York: Harper and Row.

Seasonal Affective Disorder

Seasonal affective disorder (SAD) is a subtype of recurrent depression that involves a regular temporal pattern in the onset and remission of major depressive episodes at characteristic times of year (Rosenthal et al., 1984). The substantial majority of cases are winter-type SAD,[1] major depressive episodes that begin in the fall or winter and remit in the spring. A small minority of cases are summer-type SAD, regular major depressive episode recurrence in the summer. (The term *SAD* will be used to refer to *winter-type SAD* for the rest of the entry.) In *Diagnostic and Statistical Manual of Mental Disorders* (*DSM-IV-TR*) nomenclature, SAD is subsumed under the seasonal pattern specifier, which can be applied to a diagnosis of major depressive disorder or bipolar I or II disorder when a predictable seasonal pattern of major depression recurrence has been observed over the past 2 years and predominates the lifetime course of the disorder (American Psychiatric Association, 2000). The diagnosis is not given when an obvious seasonally linked psychosocial stressor is responsible for the seasonal pattern. The diagnostic criteria for major depressive disorder, recurrent with seasonal pattern require that the major depressive episodes fully remit at a characteristic time of year. For bipolar I or II disorder with a seasonal pattern, the criteria allow for a change from major depression to mania or hypomania at a characteristic time of year.

Seasonality, the tendency to vary across the seasons in mood and behavior, differs in degree across individuals. Seasonality scores are relatively normally distributed in the general population, and the vast majority of people experience some degree of seasonality (Kasper, Wehr, Bartko, Gaist, & Rosenthal, 1989; Rosen et al., 1990). Full-blown clinical SAD symptoms appear to represent an extreme along a continuum of human seasonality, with no seasonality at the other extreme. Mild to moderate seasonal changes that cause some difficulties but do not meet criteria for major depression have been termed subsyndromal SAD (S-SAD; Kasper, Rogers, et al., 1989).

Symptom Profile

Given that seasonally recurrent major depressive episodes define SAD, *DSM-IV-TR* criteria for a major depressive episode represent the spectrum of possible SAD symptoms. The majority of SAD patients endorse depressed mood, loss of interest or pleasure in activities, and persistent fatigue (Magnusson & Partonen, 2005). In contrast to nonseasonal major depression, the *DSM-IV-TR* symptom related to a significant change in appetite or weight more frequently manifests as increased appetite, excessive carbohydrate craving, or weight gain, than as decreased appetite or weight loss in SAD (Magnusson & Partonen, 2005). Similarly, hypersomnia is a more frequent sleep disturbance than insomnia in SAD (Magnusson & Partonen, 2005). Suicidal ideation is relatively infrequent in SAD as compared to nonseasonal major depression but is endorsed by about one-third of SAD patients (Magnusson & Partonen, 2005).

The most common psychiatric diagnosis among SAD patients is major depression, recurrent with seasonal pattern. Bipolar II–type SAD is relatively common, whereas bipolar I–type SAD is rare. Of 662 SAD patients in the National Institute of Mental Health (NIMH) Seasonal Studies Program between 1981 and 2001, 61% were diagnosed with major depressive disorder, 34% with bipolar II disorder, and only 5% with bipolar I disorder (Rosenthal, 2005).

Course

The typical age of onset for SAD is between 20 and 30 years. In a multisite study including over a thousand SAD patients, participants reported a mean age for onset of 27.2 years and, on average, 13.4 past fall and/or winter major depressive episodes (Modell et al., 2005). The mean age of onset was 23.3 years in data collected from patients in the NIMH Seasonal Studies Program, described above (Rosenthal, 2005). Standard deviations around these means in the range of 10.5 to 12 indicate individual differences in mean age of onset. The few available population surveys of children and adolescents suggest that SAD can occur in youths, and that SAD prevalence rates in children and adolescents are slightly lower than those reported for adult samples at nearby latitudes and increase with age, especially after puberty (Magnusson & Partonen, 2005).

When the initial diagnosis is SAD, there is heterogeneity in the course of the expression of depression over time. In a review of four longitudinal follow-up studies of SAD patients, Lam, Tam, Yatham, Shiah, and Zis (2001) concluded that 28% to 44% of these SAD patients later developed a nonseasonal pattern of depression recurrence or incomplete summer remission, 14% to 38% went from having SAD to S-SAD or into remission, and 22% to 42% continued to have pure SAD (i.e., winter depressive episodes and complete summer remission). There are no published studies on the natural course of untreated SAD cases over time. Therefore, some of the heterogencity in the course of SAD may be attributable to factors in the interim (e.g., retreatment, changing treatments).

Epidemiology

Population surveys using prospective assessment of *DSM-IV-TR* criteria for the seasonal pattern specifier are needed. Population surveys to date have relied largely on retrospective questionnaire measures to estimate SAD prevalence. In U.S. adults, SAD prevalence, in general, increases with latitude and ranges from 1.4% in Sarasota, Florida, to over 9% in Nashua, New Hampshire, and Fairbanks, Alaska (Booker & Hellekson, 1992; Rosen et al., 1990). Reported SAD prevalence rates are about 2 times higher in North America than in Europe (Mersch, Middendorp, Bouhuys, Beersma, & van den Hoofdakker, 1999). In addition, the positive correlation between SAD prevalence and latitude is statistically significant in North America but not in Europe (Mersch et al., 1999). Reasons for these continental differences are currently not known.

Epidemiological surveys consistently report a gender difference in SAD prevalence, favoring females over males. The magnitude of the gender difference varies across studies but appears to be at least as high as the widely documented 2:1 gender difference in nonseasonal major depression prevalence. Mechanisms underlying the gender difference in SAD are currently understudied and, therefore, not known.

Etiology

Major biological theories of SAD etiology focus on circadian rhythms, seasonal changes in the duration of melatonin release at night, neurotransmitters, retinal subsensitivity to light, and molecular genetics. Recent theories integrate a role for psychological factors (i.e., maladaptive cognitions and behaviors) in explaining SAD onset and maintenance. No one theory has been uniformly supported. The following etiological theories may be interactive with, rather than independent of, each other in explaining SAD. Alternatively, SAD may represent a final common pathway that results from multiple etiologies for subgroups of patients (Sohn & Lam, 2005).

Circadian Rhythms

In humans, the master biological clock in the suprachiasmatic nucleus (SCN) of the hypothalamus entrains circadian rhythms to external time cues such as the light-dark cycle. The phase-shift hypothesis suggests that SAD results from a phase-delay in circadian rhythms (i.e., the timing of a physiological function occurs later than expected) relative to objective time or to other rhythms such as the sleep-wake rhythm (Lewy, Sack, Singer, & White, 1987). This is the most popular and the most frequently tested theory of SAD but remains controversial because it has produced inconsistent and sometimes conflicting findings (Sohn & Lam, 2005).

Photoperiod (Melatonin)

The central circadian clock underlies seasonal changes in photoperiodic mammals (i.e., those with seasonal breeding and hibernation patterns). In photoperiodic mammals, duration of nocturnal melatonin release is directly related to photoperiod (i.e., day length from dawn to dusk), and a change in nocturnal melatonin release is the main signal to initiate seasonal changes in behavior. Wehr and colleagues (2001) reported that men with SAD had a longer duration of nocturnal melatonin release in winter than in summer (by about 38 minutes), whereas men without SAD did not differ from winter to summer in duration of nocturnal melatonin release. Wehr and colleagues (2001) proposed that individuals with SAD are similar to photoperiodic mammals in that they may have retained a primitive biological mechanism for tracking changes in day length, a "circadian signal of change of season" (p. 1108) that distinguishes them from individuals without SAD. In pre-industrial times, wintertime energy-conserving, hibernationlike behaviors in SAD (i.e., hypersomnia, carbohydrate craving, lethargy) were likely more adaptive for an agrarian lifestyle, but in modern times, they are less adaptive and interfere with social and occupational roles.

Serotonin

Similar to nonseasonal depression, serotonin has been implicated in SAD to explain changes in behaviors such as sleep and appetite that are known to be mediated by serotonergic pathways in the brain. In a study that sampled blood from the human brain via a catheter to the internal jugular vein, levels of serotonin turnover in the brain were highest in summer and lowest in winter; and, regardless of season, serotonin production correlated positively with total hours of bright sunlight per day (Lambert, Reid, Kaye, Jennings, & Esler, 2002). Although not yet tested, SAD-prone individuals may be especially sensitive to these seasonal and/or luminosity-related changes in serotonin function or may show an even larger wintertime decrease in serotonin activity than people without SAD.

Retinal Subsensitivity to Light

Normally, under low-light conditions, the retina increases its sensitivity to light in order to maintain proper functioning. The retinal subsensitivity hypothesis proposes that the retina, as a whole, is less sensitive to environmental light cues in SAD due to abnormalities in rods, cones, or other retinal photoreceptors, such that low winter light levels lead to subthreshold levels of light input to the brain (Hebert, Dumont, & Lachapelle, 2002). Studies using different methods of measuring retinal sensitivity in SAD and studies assessing different specific photoreceptors have yielded conflicting results (Hebert, Beattie, Tam, Yatham, & Lam, 2004). Future studies should control for factors that may impact retinal sensitivity such as season and time of day assessed, so firmer conclusions can be drawn.

Genetics

In twin studies, an estimated 29% to 69% of the variance in seasonality is believed to be heritable (Jang, Lam, Livesley, & Vernon, 1997; Madden, Heath, Rosenthal, & Martin, 1996). The heritability of SAD has not yet been estimated; however, family studies estimate a 13% to 17% risk of SAD in first-degree relatives of SAD probands (Sohn & Lam, 2005), which is higher than the general population prevalence. Several candidate gene association studies focusing on serotonin, dopamine, G-protein, and clock-related genes have yielded some positive and some negative findings (Sohn & Lam, 2005).

Cognitive and Behavioral Factors

Psychological factors may interact with biological factors in SAD episode maintenance, severity, and recurrence. SAD is associated with negative cognitions (e.g., dysfunctional attitudes, negative automatic thoughts, rumination, and a negative attributional style), a low rate of response-contingent positive reinforcement in the wintertime, and emotional and psychophysiological reactivity to environmental stimuli signaling low-light availability and the winter season (Rohan & Nillni, 2008). These factors are correlated with SAD, but whether they constitute a psychological vulnerability to develop SAD is not yet known.

Treatment Options

Available treatment options for SAD include light therapy and antidepressant medications, both of which are supported by evidence from several studies, and newer treatments that show promise such as cognitive behavioral therapy, dawn simulation, negative ions, and exercise. Except for possibly cognitive behavioral therapy, which may have benefits that endure beyond the cessation of acute treatment, the majority of currently available SAD treatments are palliative treatments that presumably work by suppressing symptoms so long as treatment is ongoing. For a recurrent form of depression such as SAD, noncompliance with palliative treatments places patients at considerable risk for depression recurrence over subsequent fall or winter seasons. Therefore, patient preferences and the likelihood of adhering to a daily treatment regimen during the symptomatic months each year warrant careful consideration in selecting a treatment plan.

Light Therapy

Light therapy, a minimum of 30 minutes of daily scheduled exposure to 10,000-lux of cool-white or full-spectrum fluorescent light, with ultraviolet rays filtered out, is recommended as the first-line treatment for SAD (Lam & Levitt, 1999). Proper positioning of and distance from the device are necessary to ensure that the retina receives the intended 10,000-lux of luminosity. Available clinical practice guidelines for SAD recommend daily use of light therapy from onset of first symptom through spontaneous springtime remission during every fall or winter season, generally spanning 3 to 5 months of the year (Lam & Levitt, 1999). The starting dose of light therapy, and the one that is most commonly adopted in recent randomized clinical trials, is typically 30 minutes first thing the morning upon waking. However, the optimal dose of light therapy for SAD (i.e., daily duration and scheduled time of day in the morning, evening, or both) is not a one-size-fits-all prescription. Although light-therapy devices are commercially available without prescription, unsupervised treatment is not advisable because of the need to carefully monitor the effect of adjustments to these dosing dimensions on mood and on the sleep-wake cycle to determine the optimal light-therapy prescription for a given individual, and because of the possibility of side effects that must be managed, including headaches, eye strain, insomnia, agitation, and mania or hypomania.

Light therapy is the established and best available acute SAD treatment. A quantitative analysis of eight trials comparing light therapy to credible controls concluded that light therapy is associated with significant reductions in depression severity for SAD in the initial winter months (Golden et al., 2005). A pooled analysis of light-therapy studies (Terman et al., 1989) concluded that 53% of individuals with SAD overall and 43% of moderate to severe SAD cases meet remission criteria by the end of a supervised light-therapy trial. Long-term compliance with light therapy over subsequent winter seasons has not been thoroughly evaluated but appears to be lower than hoped. A retrospective follow-up survey of SAD patients treated at the NIMH between 1981 and 1985 revealed that only 41% of patients continued regular use of light therapy (Schwartz, Brown, Wehr, & Rosenthal, 1996).

Medications

After light therapy, antidepressant medications are widely regarded as the second line of treatment for SAD (Lam & Levitt, 1999). Bupropion XL is the first and only FDA-approved drug for SAD, approved specifically for the prevention of winter depression in 2006. Three double-blind, placebo-controlled trials using a total of 1,042 adults with a history of SAD initiated bupropion XL (300 mg/day) or pill placebo prior to the onset of clinically significant SAD symptoms in the fall and followed participants until treatment was discontinued following a 2-week taper that began the fourth week of March (Modell et al., 2005). For all three studies combined, the overall proportion of depression recurrences at the end of treatment was statistically lower for buproprion (16%) than for placebo (28%). However, these recurrence rates are surprisingly low overall, even in the placebo group.

Other antidepressants have shown efficacy in treating acute SAD, particularly fluoxetine (20 mg/day) and sertraline (50–200 mg/day), although other medications such as citalopram (20–40 mg/day), reboxetine, moclobemide, and modafinil may be effective and warrant further study (Westrin & Lam, 2007). No study to date has assessed compliance with or clinical outcomes for medication treatments for SAD over subsequent winters. Anecdotal evidence suggests that many patients use both light and antidepressants, indicating that future work on the possible efficacy, safety, and cost-benefit ratio of combined treatments is warranted. Ongoing studies are focusing on maintenance of an initial response to light therapy with antidepressant medications to lessen the burden of continuing daily light therapy for the rest of that winter (Westrin & Lam, 2007).

Cognitive Behavioral Therapy

Preliminary studies show promise for a SAD-tailored version of Beck's cognitive therapy for depression that uses behavioral activation and cognitive restructuring to improve coping with winter. The results of two pilot studies found that cognitive behavioral therapy (CBT) for SAD, either administered alone or in combination with light therapy, was efficacious as an acute SAD treatment over a 6-week trial in the winter; that solo CBT and solo light therapy were comparably efficacious from pre- to posttreatment; that all active treatments improved depression relative to a wait-list control; and that initial treatment with CBT, with or without adjunct light therapy, was associated with lower depression recurrence (6% vs. 39%) and less severe depressive symptoms in the subsequent winter season compared to initial treatment with solo light therapy (Rohan & Nillni, 2008). These results require replication.

Dawn Simulation

Dawn simulation devices simulate a naturalistic summer dawn in the winter by gradually increasing ambient light intensity up to 250-lux while the user is asleep. These devices vary in sophistication, but can generally be programmed by the user to begin the dawn transition at a specific time and to reach full irradiance around the desired wake time. Most direct comparisons found that standard light therapy is more effective than dawn simulation as a stand-alone SAD treatment; however, the most recent trial found that light therapy and dawn simulation yielded similar improvements (Terman & Terman, 2006). The body of evidence for dawn simulation is currently inconclusive;

but patients with difficulty waking in the morning may find it helpful.

Negative Ions

A negative ion generator produces negatively charged ions (i.e., air particles) at a high flow rate to maintain an overall high density of negative relative to positive ions in the immediate vicinity. A few studies have compared standard light therapy, a high-density negative ion generator, and a placebo control device calibrated to generate a low-density flow of negative ions with the ion conditions administered for at least 30 minutes either first thing in the morning or during the end of sleep using a grounded conductive bed sheet. These studies report that high-density negative ions are comparably effective to light therapy in treating SAD, and that both active treatments are more effective than low-density negative ions (Terman & Terman, 2006). It is not known how or why negative ions would have antidepressant effects.

Exercise

Pinchasov, Shurgaja, Grischin, and Putilov (2000) found that aerobic exercise on a stationary bike (i.e., 5-minute warm-up following by 10 minutes of basic pedaling and 10 minutes of pedaling at 75% maximal heart rate, a 5-minute rest, and then repetition) and light therapy were similarly effective in a sample of women with SAD. However, both exercise and light were administered in the afternoon in this study in contrast to the more typical morning dose of light therapy. It is possible that exercise has direct physiological effects on mood or functions in a way analogous to behavioral activation in CBT for SAD. Exercise interventions for SAD deserve further study.

Conclusion

Clinicians should be vigilant in recognizing seasonality in their patients because it takes most individuals with SAD several years to recognize their own seasonal pattern. Once properly diagnosed, evidence-based treatments are available for SAD, and several novel treatments under investigation show promise. For researchers, given its predictable annual pattern of major depressive episodes during the fall and/or winter months that remit in the spring, SAD represents a unique natural laboratory for studying (a) factors relevant to depression onset, remission, and recurrence toward a better understanding of SAD etiology and these processes as they pertain to depression, in general; (b) short-term treatment efficacy in a given winter; and (c) more importantly, the longer-term durability of acute treatment effects, particularly with regard to prevention of winter depressive episode recurrence over subsequent years.

KELLY J. ROHAN AND KATHRYN A. ROECKLEIN

See also

Circadian Rhythms
Classification of Depression
Diagnostic and Statistical Manual of Mental Disorders
Seasonal Affective Disorder
Seasonal Affective Disorder: Light Treatment

References

American Psychiatric Association. (2000). *Diagnostic and statistical manual of mental disorders* (4th ed., text revision). Washington, DC: Author.

Booker, J. M., & Hellekson, C. J. (1992). Prevalence of seasonal affective disorder in Alaska. *American Journal of Psychiatry, 149,* 1176–1182.

Golden, R. N., Gaynes, B. N., Ekstrom, R. D., Hamer, R. M., Jacobsen, F. M., Suppes, P., et al. (2005). The efficacy of light therapy in the treatment of mood disorders: A meta-analysis of the evidence. *American Journal of Psychiatry, 162,* 656–662.

Hebert, M., Beattie, C. W., Tam, E. M., Yatham, L. N., & Lam, R. W. (2004). Electroretinography in patients with winter seasonal affective disorder. *Psychiatry Research, 127,* 27–34.

Hebert, M., Dumont, M., & Lachapelle, P. (2002). Electrophysiological evidence suggesting a seasonal modulation of retinal sensitivity in subsyndromal winter depression. *Journal of Affective Disorders, 68,* 191–202.

Jang, K. L., Lam, R. W., Livesley, W. J., & Vernon, P. A. (1997). Gender differences in the heritability of seasonal mood change. *Psychiatry Research, 70,* 145–154.

Kasper, S., Rogers, S. L. B., Yancey, A., Schultz, P. M., Skwerer, R. G., & Rosenthal, N. E. (1989). Phototherapy in individuals with and without subsyndromal seasonal affective disorder. *Archives of General Psychiatry, 46,* 837–844.

Kasper, S., Wehr, T. A., Bartko, J. J., Gaist, P. A., & Rosenthal, N. E. (1989). Epidemiological findings of seasonal changes in mood and behavior: A telephone survey of Montgomery County, Maryland. *Archives of General Psychiatry, 46,* 823–833.

Lam, R. W., & Levitt, A. J. (1999). *Clinical guidelines for the treatment of seasonal affective disorder.* Vancouver, BC: Clinical and Academic Publishing.

Lam, R. W., Tam, E. M., Yatham, L. N., Shiah, I.-S., & Zis, A. P. (2001). Seasonal depression: The dual vulnerability hypothesis revisited. *Journal of Affective Disorders, 63,* 123–132.

Lambert, G. W., Reid, C., Kaye, D. M., Jennings, G. L., & Esler, M. D. (2002). Effect of sunlight and season on serotonin turnover in the brain. *Lancet, 360,* 1840–1842.

Lewy, A. J., Sack, R. L., Singer, C. M., & White, D. M. (1987). The phase shift hypothesis for bright light's therapeutic mechanism of action: Theoretical considerations and experimental evidence. *Psychopharmacology Bulletin, 23,* 349–353.

Madden, P. A., Heath, A. C., Rosenthal, N. E., & Martin, N. G. (1996). Seasonal changes in mood and behavior: The role of genetic factors. *Archives of General Psychiatry, 53,* 47–55.

Magnusson, A., & Partonen, T. (2005). The diagnosis, symptomatology, and epidemiology of seasonal affective disorder. *CNS Spectrums, 10,* 625–634.

Mersch, P. P., Middendorp, H. M., Bouhuys, A. L., Beersma, D. G. M., & van den Hoofdakker, R. H. (1999). Seasonal affective disorder and latitude: A review of the literature. *Journal of Affective Disorders, 53,* 35–48.

Modell, J. G., Rosenthal, N. E. Harriett, A. E., Krishen, A., Asgharian, A., Foster, V. J., et al. (2005). Seasonal affective disorder and its prevention by anticipatory treatment with Buprorion XL. *Biological Psychiatry, 58,* 658–667.

Pinchasov, B. B., Shurgaja, A. M., Grischin, O. V., & Putilov, A. A. (2000). Mood and energy regulation in seasonal and non-seasonal depression before and after midday treatment with physical exercise or bright light. *Psychiatry Research, 94,* 29–42.

Rohan, K. J., & Nillni, Y. I. (2008). Thinking outside of the light box: Applications of cognitive-behavioral theory and therapy to seasonal affective disorder. *International Journal of Child Health and Human Development, 1,* 155–164.

Rosen, L. N., Targum, S. D., Terman, M., Bryant, M. J., Hoffman, H., Kasper, S. F., et al. (1990). Prevalence of seasonal affective disorder at four latitudes. *Psychiatry Research, 31,* 131–144.

Rosenthal, N. E. (2005). Clinical picture and epidemiology of seasonal affective disorder. In N. E. Rosenthal (Chair), *Seasonal affective disorder: New concepts, practical strategies.* Industry-Sponsored Continuing Medical Education Dinner Symposium presented at the annual meeting of the American Psychiatric Association, Atlanta.

Rosenthal, N. E., Sack, D. A., Gillin, C., Lewy, A. J., Goodwin, F. K., Davenport, Y., et al. (1984). Seasonal affective disorder: A description of the syndrome and preliminary findings with light therapy. *Archives of General Psychiatry, 41,* 72–80.

Schwartz, P. J., Brown, C., Wehr, T. A., & Rosenthal, N. E. (1996). Winter seasonal affective disorder: A follow-up study of the first 59 patients of the National Institute of Mental Health Seasonal Studies Program. *American Journal of Psychiatry, 153,* 1028–1036.

Sohn, C.-H., & Lam, R. W. (2005). Update on the biology of seasonal affective disorder. *CNS Spectrums, 10,* 635–646.

Terman, M., & Terman, J. S. (2006). Controlled trial of naturalistic dawn simulation and negative air ionization for seasonal affective disorder. *American Journal of Psychiatry, 163,* 2126–2133.

Terman, M., Terman, J. S., Quitkin, F., McGrath, P., Stewart, J., & Rafferty, B. (1989). Light therapy for seasonal affective disorder: A review of efficacy. *Neuropsychopharmacology, 2,* 1–22.

Wehr, T. A., Duncan, W. C., Jr., Sher, L., Aeschbach, D., Schwartz, P. J., Turner, E. H., et al. (2001). A circadian signal of change of season in patients with seasonal affective disorder. *Archives of General Psychiatry, 58,* 1108–1114.

Westrin, A., & Lam, R. W. (2007). Seasonal affective disorder: A clinical update. *Annals of Clinical Psychiatry, 19,* 239–246.

Seasonal Affective Disorder: Light Therapy

Seasonal affective disorder (SAD) is a subtype of recurrent major depressive or bipolar disorder in which the individual regularly experiences depressive episodes annually (usually late fall and winter) with symptom remission in the opposite season (usually in late spring, with risk of hypomania or mania in bipolar disorder). In addition to depressed mood, most patients experience atypical neurovegetative symptoms (extreme fatigue, longer sleep with difficulty awakening, and craving and eating carbohydrate-rich foods with weight gain), which are often noticeable weeks before the depressive relapse. These symptoms are labeled *atypical* by contrast with the agitation, insomnia, and poor appetite characteristic of melancholic depression. The standard diagnosis in the *Diagnostic and Statistical Manual of Mental Disorders* (American Psychiatric Association, 2000, however, does not include the atypical features specifier. Rather, SAD is defined as major depressive disorder (recurrent) or bipolar I or II disorder, with seasonal pattern. Indeed, an individual may suffer melancholic depressions seasonally.

Variants of SAD

The population prevalence of SAD is approximately 3% to 5% in the temperate zones of the United States and Europe. Far more people, however, experience significant winter worsening short of major depression, with relief in spring. Approximately 4 times as many people experience subsyndromal SAD (also called the winter doldrums or winter blues), which seriously compromises their quality of life and work productivity. Although the depression is not severe, the atypical neurovegetative symptoms can be as disabling as they are in SAD. Indeed, another group experiences seasonal atypical neurovegetative syndrome, in which atypical symptoms are prominent but depressive symptoms are completely absent. Another common variant is seasonally modulated depression with distinct winter exacerbation that overlays chronic dysthymia or intermittent nonseasonal depression.

In summer SAD, patients find winters invigorating rather than depressing. Its prevalence and etiology are not well understood, but it is likely associated with high heat and humidity rather than excessive light availability. Patients report low appetite and insomnia, in contrast with the atypical pattern of winter depression. In a random sample population survey in New York City (41°N latitude), 12.3% of respondents reported distinct mood worsening in summer, while 49.8% reported winter worsening. An unlucky 6.6% reported worsening in both seasons, feeling well only around the equinoxes.

All told, approximately half the population experiences noticeable seasonal cycles throughout the range of mild to severe (Terman, 1988). In general, the problem is increasingly prevalent at more northerly latitudes. In the United States, it rises rapidly from 25°N at the southern extreme to 38°N at midcountry, and then levels off up to 50°N. Some patients with SAD have solved their problem by moving south, but others continue to experience symptoms after such a move.

Winter Daylight Availability as a Causal Factor

When a random population sample rated the months of the year they experienced best and worst moods, the worst period lay clearly between the autumnal equinox (late September) and the vernal equinox (late March), the period when day length is the shortest of the year. The critical factor is the delayed sunrise in winter relative to spring and summer. Many investigations have homed in on early sunrise time (or the dawn interval) as essential for preventing internal clockwork from drifting late. On average, the human circadian timing system operates on a cycle slightly longer than 24 hours. Barring daily corrections to match the day-night cycle, the system tends to drift later, causing difficulty awakening. Early morning light exposure selectively pushes back the internal clock every day, allowing brain function and sleep propensity to stay synchronized with local time. It is theorized that when circadian rhythms drift late, but we remain under pressure to maintain an earlier work and sleep schedule, depressive symptoms emerge.

Clinical Alleviation of Winter Depression With Light

It is not surprising, then, that artificial light supplementation on winter mornings can resolve the symptoms of SAD. Bright light therapy was initially designed to extend the winter day length at both ends, morning and evening. Clinical trials then compared morning plus evening light with morning light alone (Terman et al., 1989) and found that the morning signal was sufficient. In dosing the light, the more intense signal of 10,000 lux (similar to outdoor skylight 40 minutes after sunrise) provided positive response in 30-minute daily exposure sessions, by comparison with 2 hours needed at 2,500-lux (Figure S.1). The effective dose—intensity × duration—may require individual adjustment to maximize response and minimize side effects such as nausea, agitation, and headache.

Figure S.1   Light therapy apparatus for 10,000-lux dosing. Features include complete ultraviolet filtering, diffuse white fluorescent illumination at moderate color temperature (4,100 K), and screen tilt downward toward the head. (Photo courtesy of Center for Light Treatment and Biological Rhythms, Columbia University.)

The circadian timing system is exquisitely sensitive to the precise timing of light presentation. Given too early in the morning, the clock will shift later rather than earlier as desired. Given too late in the morning, the amount of shifting earlier is reduced. The antidepressant response is thus influenced by timing considerations. In the laboratory, circadian clock time can be measured by testing for the evening onset of melatonin secretion by the pineal gland, as measured in the blood or saliva; during the day, circulating melatonin is largely absent. Melatonin onsets vary widely across individuals, from about 7:00 p.m. to 1:00 a.m. To achieve the desired corrective effect of morning light, it should be presented approximately 7.5 to 9.5 hours after melatonin onset, following the night's sleep. Users of light therapy can estimate their circadian clock time without melatonin sampling by using an online questionnaire that scores preferred times of day for sleep, exercise, work, and so on. (Terman, White, & Jacobs, 2002).

The program feeds back the recommended time for initiating light therapy.

When light therapy is taken later than at the recommended hour, it can still provide some benefit. It is theorized that three factors determine the efficacy of light therapy: (a) the circadian factor, (b) a direct energizing factor, and (c) a direct antidepressant factor. Bright-light supplementation later in the day can serve to increase concentration ability and fight slumping, perhaps by stimulating adrenal corticosteroid production (e.g., cortisol). Light exposure may also excite serotonergic and noradrenergic neurotransmitter activity, much like antidepressant drugs (which also can be used therapeutically in SAD).

Investigational Treatments for SAD

Bright-light therapy is widely acknowledged as the first-line intervention for SAD (Golden et al., 2005). A derivative method that holds promise is dawn simulation, in which a microprocessor drives a diffuse light source in the bedroom to provide gradual, incremental illumination during the final hours of sleep. The patient wakes up at simulated sunrise time, while it is still dark outdoors in winter. A clinical trial showed dawn simulation similar in efficacy to postawakening bright light therapy (Terman and Terman, 2006). Illumination level is markedly lower for dawn simulation (which rises to about 300-lux) than for bright light therapy (at 10,000-lux), and there is the procedural advantage of time saved by taking treatment while still in bed.

A novel, nonphotic antidepressant modality, negative air ionization, has also shown efficacy in placebo-controlled clinical trials for SAD (Terman and Terman, 2006). In nature, high concentrations of negatively charged superoxide particles embedded in microdroplets of water are found at the seashore, by waterfalls, after springtime thunderstorms, and in the rain forest. Indoors—especially in dry, heated, or air conditioned living and working spaces—negative ion concentration is far lower. A simple electronic device can flood a room with negative air ions to counteract this deficiency. It is interesting and important to note that air ions are imperceptible; we cannot directly sense the level in circulation. In clinical trials, some patients were exposed to high concentrations of negative ions, while others received a low-level placebo. The antidepressant response to high, but not low, concentrations approximately matched the results for light therapy. That said, discovery of the physiological mechanism of action of negative air ionization awaits new research.

Conclusions

SAD is notable as a "new" syndrome, first formally identified in the 1980s. The ensuing international research effort was founded—for the first time among depressive disorders—on established biological principles (photoperiodism, seasonality, and the circadian timing system). For many years, it was suspected that light therapy would prove to be SAD-specific and not useful for treatment of nonseasonal depression. As the field evolves, however, the therapeutic application of light is stretching beyond SAD, with important initiatives in chronic and nonseasonal recurrent depression; nonseasonal bipolar disorder; delayed sleep-phase disorder; and, importantly, adult attention deficit hyperactivity disorder, where the circadian timing system may also drift out of phase with external day and night (Terman, 2007).

MICHAEL TERMAN

See also

Circadian Rhythms
Classification of Depression
Diagnostic and Statistical Manual of Mental Disorders
Seasonal Affective Disorder

References

American Psychiatric Association. (2000). *Diagnostic and statistical manual of mental disorders* (4th ed., text revision). Washington, DC: Author.

Golden, R. N., Gaynes, B. N., Ekstrom, R. D., Hamer, R. M., Jacobsen, F. M., Suppes, T., et al. (2005). The efficacy of light therapy in the treatment of mood disorders: A review and meta-analysis of the evidence. *American Journal of Psychiatry, 162,* 656–662.

Terman, M. (1988). On the question of mechanism in phototherapy for seasonal affective disorder: Considerations of clinical efficacy and epidemiology. *Journal of Biological Rhythms, 3,* 155–172.

Terman, M. (2007). Evolving applications of light therapy. *Sleep Medicine Reviews, 11,* 497–507.

Terman, M., & Terman, J. S. (2006). Controlled trial of naturalistic dawn simulation and negative air ionization for seasonal affective disorder. *American Journal of Psychiatry, 163,* 2126–2133.

Terman, M., Terman, J. S., Quitkin, F. M., McGrath, P. J., Stewart, J. W., & Rafferty, B. (1989). Light therapy for seasonal affective disorder: A review of efficacy. *Neuropsychopharmacology, 2,* 1–22.

Terman, M., White, T. M., & Jacobs, J. (2002). *Automated Morningness-Eveningness Questionnaire.* New York: New York State Psychiatric Institute.

Self-Efficacy

After several years of research on the manner in which children learn to regulate their own behavior, Bandura (1977) published a book titled *Social Learning Theory.* This highly cited text was seminal, in part, because it highlighted the role of observation and thought in human learning and behavior. The foundations of this theory are rooted in the belief that people are actively involved in making sense of their experiences and planning for the future. It is assumed that we do not passively react to the environment, but rather reflect on past and present experiences, set goals for ourselves, and respond and adapt to challenges accordingly. Bandura (1986) later referred to his approach as *social cognitive theory,* further highlighting the importance of the social context and cognition on behavior.

Definition

In this approach to understanding behavior, there are two important terms. *Self-efficacy* refers to the strength of belief in one's ability to perform a given behavior. An *outcome expectancy* refers to a belief in the extent to which engaging in a given behavior will lead to positive outcomes. No matter the level of self-efficacy, an individual is unlikely to engage in a behavior that will not lead to valued outcomes. Even when highly valued outcomes are believed to be probable, if there is no confidence in one's ability to perform the necessary behavior, again it will not be performed. Thus, the combination of these expectancies determines whether a behavior is performed, the amount of effort expended, and persistence in the face of difficulties.

Efficacy beliefs are relevant to any form of behavior. In this context, *behavior* is used as a generic term that not only refers to observable movement, but also applies to cognitive behavior, including the ability to learn, solve problems, make decisions, regulate emotions, and cope with stressful circumstances. It should also be noted that efficacy beliefs are often thought of in terms of behavior-specific and situation-specific constraints. However, some have also suggested that beliefs that have been formed by experience in some circumstances may be applied more broadly to related circumstances. These generalized expectancies can be applied to classes of behavior like social skill, athletic skill, or coping with pain, for example.

Relation to Depression

As a disorder, depression is associated with loss and a sense of hopelessness about the likelihood that things might be better in the future. In other words, valued outcomes have been removed and are not expected to be forthcoming. When one comes to the conclusion that there is little that can be done to influence the important events in life, despondency and low motivation are natural consequences. Feelings of worthlessness, guilt over failures or lack of accomplishment, hopelessness, self-devaluation, and ineffectualness are corollaries of generalized low efficacy expectancies.

Low self-efficacy for performing a behavior (or class of behaviors) that is seen as necessary for highly valued outcomes is at the crux of depression. Bandura (1997) has suggested that vulnerability to depression arises from life experiences that weaken a sense of competency and belief in one's ability to regulate personal functioning. In particular, low self-efficacy associated with unachieved goals, limitations in meaningful social relationships, and difficulties in controlling ones thoughts and emotions provide alternative and complementary routes to the development of depression. Developmental research has supported the view that self-efficacy (and perceived competence) in academic and social endeavors is predictive of the later onset of depression in children (Bandura, Pastorelli, Barbaranelli, & Caprara, 1999). In addition, it has been suggested that low self-efficacy may be related to depressive symptoms among the elderly (Blazer, 2002) and those with chronic medical problems (Turner, Ersek, & Kemp, 2005).

It should be noted, that while self-efficacy has clearly been related to depression symptoms and vulnerability, the concept is about human agency more broadly and is not specifically a theory of depression. Low self-efficacy beliefs are consistent with other theories of depression including cognitive theory, in which negative views of the self play an important role; hopelessness theory, in which attributions about the causes of negative events and the belief in one's inability to affect positive outcomes are central; and self-management theory, in which high and unmet standards for achievement are associated with negative self-evaluation. In each of these cases, the concept of low self-efficacy can be associated with a critical mechanism postulated to influence depressive phenomena.

Self-Efficacy and Interventions for Depression

Bandura proposed that when psychological interventions are successful, they are successful precisely because they restore confidence in one's ability to manage important life events, i.e., they increase self-efficacy. Indeed, many of the empirically supported interventions focus on the development of skills that lead to an improvement in one's sense of control in stressful situations. In one study of cognitive therapy for depression it was found that improvements in self-efficacy for controlling negative thoughts were associated with improvements in depression and, as importantly, were predictive of successful outcomes over the next year (Kavanagh & Wilson, 1989). Though there are few treatments where the specific goal is to increase self-efficacy, it is plausible that changes in self-efficacy are an important part of their effectiveness.

DANIEL M. STOUT AND PAUL D. ROKKE

See also

Vulnerability

References

Bandura, A. (1977). *Social learning theory*. Oxford, England: Prentice-Hall.

Bandura, A. (1986). *Social foundations of thought and action: A social cognitive theory*. Englewood Cliffs, NJ: Prentice-Hall.

Bandura, A. (1997). *Self-efficacy: The exercise of control*. New York: W. H. Freeman/Times Books/ Henry Holt and Co.

Bandura, A., Pastorelli, C., Barbaranelli, C., & Caprara, G. V. (1999). Self-efficacy pathways to childhood depression. *Journal of Personality and Social Psychology, 76*, 258–269.

Blazer, D. G. (2002). Self-efficacy and depression in late life: A primary prevention proposal. *Aging and Mental Health, 6*, 315–324.

Kavanagh, D. J., & Wilson, P. H. (1989). Prediction of outcome with group cognitive therapy for depression. *Behaviour Research and Therapy, 27*, 333–343.

Turner, J. A., Ersek, M., & Kemp, C. (2005). Self-efficacy for managing pain is associated with disability, depression, and pain coping among retirement community residents with chronic pain. *Journal of Pain, 6*, 471–479.

Self-Esteem

Clinical theorists have long assumed that self-esteem plays a key role in depression. Such ideas date back to early psychodynamic models of vulnerability to depression. More recently, cognitive accounts of depression have posited that schemas involving negative memories and beliefs about the self contribute to the onset and maintenance of depression. Clearly there is a close conceptual affinity between cognitive concepts such as negative schemas and low self-esteem. In turn, these clinical perspectives have led to the development of treatment approaches that attempt to ameliorate depression in part by increasing the individual's self-esteem. Indeed clinical experience and research clearly demonstrate that negative views of the self predominate the mind-set of currently depressed individuals; depression is associated with a deflated sense of self. However, such observations could merely point to the fact that worthlessness is a symptom of depression rather than providing evidence of a causal influence of self-esteem on depression.

If self-esteem plays a causal role in the pathogenesis of depression, vulnerable self-esteem should be present in individuals at risk for depression. More specifically, vulnerable self-esteem should prospectively predict the onset and/or maintenance of depression. Likewise, it should be apparent in previously depressed compared to never depressed individuals.

In addition, if self-esteem plays a causal role in depression, it will be important to define what aspects of it are crucially involved. As a matter of fact, in contrast to the view that vulnerable self-esteem simply refers to how badly persons feel about themselves, more basic research has demonstrated that self-esteem is a complex and multifaceted construct that is only partially captured by self-report measures asking persons how highly or poorly they think of themselves. In addition to level of self-esteem (i.e., the degree to which self-esteem is high vs. low), stability of self-esteem (i.e., the degree to which self-esteem fluctuates over time), implicit self-esteem (i.e., self-esteem that may operate outside of conscious awareness), and the pursuit of self-esteem may each be important to consider in vulnerability to depression. In addition, some theorists have proposed a componential view of self-esteem, differentiating, for instance, self-liking and self-competence as two separate dimensions within self-esteem.

Level and Stability of Self-Esteem

A number of studies have tested whether low self-esteem predicts future depressive symptoms or episodes. For the most part, these studies fail to find evidence that individuals who report relatively lower self-esteem on self-report measures are more prone to developing future depression than those with higher self-esteem. Furthermore, once differences in subclinical depressive symptoms are adjusted for, previously depressed individuals do not report lower self-esteem than never depressed persons (see Roberts & Monroe, 1999, for a review). Apparently, low self-esteem does not act as a risk factor for depression, though there is evidence that it increases the potency of negative attributional styles to act as cognitive diatheses for depressive symptoms. In contrast, other theoretical models suggest that temporally unstable or labile SE would pose vulnerability to depression (Roberts & Monroe, 1994). Labile self-esteem is characterized by short-term fluctuations in self-esteem over time in response to internal and external circumstances. For example, one person's self-esteem might be drastically impacted by positive and negative social events (raising and deflating self-esteem, respectively), while these have little or no impact on self-esteem for another person. A number of studies have shown that labile self-esteem prospectively predicts the onset of depressive symptoms (Franck & De Raedt, 2007), particularly following life stress. Furthermore, previously depressed individuals exhibit greater labile self-esteem compared to never depressed individuals (Franck & De Raedt, 2007). In summary, labile self-esteem appears to act as a risk factor for depression.

Implicit Self-Esteem

More recently, distinctions have been made between explicit self-esteem, which is consciously accessible and measured by self-report, and implicit self-esteem, which potentially is not consciously accessible, is overlearned and automatic, and is measured indirectly. Presumably, explicit self-esteem is prone to presentation style biases, whereas implicit self-esteem is immune to such biases, making it particularly well suited to testing the role of self-esteem in vulnerability to depression. Measures of implicit self-esteem are only weakly correlated with explicit measures, have different correlates, and potentially assess different facets of self-esteem (see Bosson, Swann, & Pennebaker, 2000). Although there are a number of different measures of implicit self-esteem, such as the name letter preference task (higher self-esteem being inferred by the degree to which a person prefers the letters of his or her own name) and priming tasks that attempt to identify the degree to which self-related information speeds the response to positive versus negative stimuli (increased ease in identifying positive stimuli would reflect higher self-esteem), the Implicit Associate Test (IAT) is the approach that has been applied to depression most frequently. The IAT is a categorization task in which self-esteem is inferred based on the strength of association between self-related stimuli and positive stimuli. Although there has only been preliminary research, there are some data showing that low implicit self-esteem as measured by the name letter preference task prospectively predicts depressive symptoms (Franck, De Raedt, & De Houwer, 2007). In addition, a study by Steinberg, Karpinski, and Alloy (2007) showed that a self-esteem IAT predicted level of depression at follow-up. More specifically, these authors demonstrated that in participants at high cognitive risk for depression, the effects of life stress on depressive symptoms were especially pernicious for those demonstrating low self-esteem as measured by the IAT. Furthermore, there is evidence that negative mood inductions have a greater impact on implicit self-esteem among individuals with previous depression compared to never depressed persons (Gemar et al., 2001), though implicit self-esteem might be relatively high under normal moods in previously depressed persons (see De Raedt, Schacht, Franck,

& De Houwer, 2006). Relatedly, there is evidence that negative self-evaluation assessed through an interview predicts onset of depression following life stress (Brown, Bifulco, & Andrews, 1990). Negative self-evaluation was inferred on the basis of how individuals described themselves, including spontaneous negative comments, rather than solely on responses to direct questions about feelings of self-worth. This interview-based approach likely tapped into the nonconscious, overlearned, and automatic self-attitudes that reflect implicit self-esteem.

Synthesis of Self-Esteem

This discussion raises the thorny question of what exactly self-esteem is. Is it something durable that is retrieved when persons reflect on themselves? From a network model, self-esteem would be represented by its own unique node or nodes (e.g., worthless, incompetent, unlovable). In contrast, is it something that is synthesized in the moment during the process of self-reflection? From a network model, self-esteem would be represented by the resulting valence that arises from the activation of mental nodes related to the self that involve traits (e.g., weak, dull, insensitive) or autobiographical memories (e.g., being rejected). Although this latter view contrasts with traditional views of attitudes, more recently attitude construal models have been advocated (e.g., Schwarz, 2007). If self-esteem is something that is actively synthesized, it may make sense to consider the possibility that it operates and has effects on behavior at times when self-evaluative thinking is taking place, but perhaps not at other times. In this sense self-esteem would exist only when the person is engaged in reflective thinking. It may be a different construct when it is measured in states of high self-awareness, such as depression, than when it is measured in states of low awareness. This perspective suggests that the frequency with which self-esteem is "online" and in awareness would be a key variable. If it is synthesized in the process of self-reflection, people would likely vary in terms of the degree and situations in which it would be active and operative. Given that explicit self-esteem involves conscious deliberate judgments about the self, it would appear that this form would be more likely to be synthesized, whereas implicit self-esteem, which is overlearned and automatic, would likely be ever present, operating in the background.

Maladaptive Pursuit of Self-Esteem

William James suggested that self-esteem might be defined as the ratio of a person's accomplishments to his or her aspirations. Interestingly this perspective falls in line with recent third wave approaches such as behavioral activation (e.g., Jacobson, Martell, & Dimidjian, 2001). These approaches suggest that directly attempting to modify the content of self-evaluative thinking will be less successful than targeting behavior: here the motto would be "improve self-esteem by living a worthy and valued life." Self-esteem would be seen as important to the extent to which it interferes with goal-directed behavior and the living of a full life. Third wave behavioral approaches suggest that problematic goal directed is best addressed by redirecting the individual away from the pursuit of positive goal directed and toward the living of a valued life. Particularly, engaging in activities that bring a sense of pleasure and/or accomplishment would be helpful in changing self-esteem. Interesting similar arguments have come from self-esteem theorists who have posited that optimal self-esteem involves a lack of concern with self-esteem and instead an emphasis on striving toward valued goals (Ryan, 2007). "Gaining optimal self-esteem comes about not by seeking self-esteem, but by actually leading a life that satisfies basic psychological needs. . . . The less salient self-esteem is, the more optimal is one's self-esteem" (Ryan & Brown, 2006, p. 129). In contrast, self-esteem is problematic to the extent that persons buy into the idea that it must be somehow repaired before moving forward with their lives.

Likewise, from a behavioral perspective, it may prove valuable to take a functional analytic approach with client who presents with low self-esteem as a primary concern. A functional analysis would examine the behavior involved on occasions of experiencing low self-esteem (e.g., avoidance, verbalized negative self statements, negative self-disclosures, rumination, body posture, vocal tone) and identify the antecedent triggers and consequences of these self-esteem-relevant behaviors. Treatment would involve modification of the antecedent triggers, as well as any maladaptive behavioral responses. Changing self-worth by altering the behavioral base for these self-attitudes might prove more fruitful than a top-down approach that is directed at altering the explicit construals (e.g., "I am worth nothing as a person"). As a matter of fact, interventions aimed at cognitively challenging inappropriately low self-esteem might paradoxically render the very dimension of self-worth more important than it actually is. In a sense, self-worth is a strange construct that completely lacks objective measurement. As compared to one's height, weight, IQ, or even more subjective qualities such as extraversion, there are no criteria or standards to assess someone's personal worth. In this sense, treatment might benefit from coaching the client to abolish the use of this construct as a force that drives emotions, motivation, or behavior. Changing the behavioral base for feelings of self-liking (pleasantness) and self-competence (mastery) would be a more preferred option from this perspective.

Future Directions

Future advances require increased understanding of the nature of self-esteem, particularly the extent to which it is a product of reflective cognitive processes and what that implies concerning the ebbs and flows of such processing. In a way, self-esteem appears problematic to the extent that individuals are hooked into the idea that they need self-esteem, raising the possibility that individual differences in the salience of self-esteem concerns would be a key vulnerability characteristic. Another largely ignored issue involves the mechanisms by which self-esteem would be involved in the pathogenesis of depression. Although cognitive theory tends to focus on how beliefs about the self, such as self-esteem, influence more immediate forms of negative thinking (automatic thoughts) that in turn directly influence mood, another possibility is that self-esteem influences goal setting, planning, and the initiation of behavior in a manner that contributes to the onset and maintenance of depression. In other words, vulnerable self-esteem may lead individuals to live their lives in a manner that is less fulfilling, decreasing positive reinforcement and thereby generating depression.

JOHN E. ROBERTS AND DIRK HERMANS

See also

Cognitive Theories of Depression Vulnerability

References

Bosson, J. K., Swann, W. B., Jr., & Pennebaker, J. W. (2000). Stalking the perfect measure of implicit self-esteem: The blind men and the elephant revisited? *Journal of Personality and Social Psychology, 79,* 631–643.

Brown, G. W., Bifulco, A., & Andrews, B. (1990). Self-esteem and depression, 3: Aetiological issues. *Social Psychiatry Psychiatric Epidemiology, 25,* 235–243.

De Raedt, R., Schacht, R., Franck, E., & De Houwer, J. (2006). Self-esteem and depression revisited: Implicit positive self-esteem in depressed patients? *Behavior Research and Therapy, 44,* 1017–1028.

Franck, E., & De Raedt, R. (2007). Self-esteem reconsidered: Unstable self-esteem outperforms level of self-esteem as vulnerability marker for depression. *Behavior Research and Therapy, 45,* 1531–1541.

Franck, E., De Raedt, R., & De Houwer, J. (2007). Implicit but not explicit self-esteem predicts future depressive symptomatology. *Behavior Research and Therapy, 45,* 2448–2455.

Gemar, M. C., Segal, Z. V., Sagrati, S., & Kennedy, S. J. (2001). Mood-induced changes on the Implicit Association Test in recovered depressed patients. *Journal of Abnormal Psychology, 110,* 282–289.

Jacobson, N. S., Martell, C. R., & Dimidjian, S. (2001). Behavioral activation therapy for depression: Returning to contextual roots. *Clinical Psychology: Science and Practice, 8,* 255–270.

Roberts, J. E., & Monroe, S. M. (1994). A multidimensional model of self-esteem in depression. *Clinical Psychology Review, 14,* 161–181.

Roberts, J. E., & Monroe, S. M. (1999). Vulnerable self-esteem and social processes in depression: Toward an interpersonal model of self-esteem regulation. In T. Joiner & J. Coyne (Eds.), *The interactional nature of depression: Advances in interpersonal approaches* (pp. 149–187). Washington, D.C.: American Psychological Association.

Ryan, R., & Brown, K. (2006). *What is optimal self-esteem? The cultivation and consequences of contingent vs. true self-esteem as viewed from the self-determination theory perspective. Self-esteem issues and answers: A sourcebook of current perspectives* (pp. 125–131). New York: Psychology Press.

Schwarz, N. (2007). Attitude construction: Evaluation in context. *Social Cognition, 25,* 638–656.

Steinberg, J. A., Karpinski, A., & Alloy, L. B. (2007). The exploration of implicit aspects of self-esteem in vulnerability-stress models of depression. *Self and Identity, 6,* 101–117.

Self-Focused Attention

Much of the early work on self-focused attention derived from social psychological research published by Duval and Wicklund (1972) and Carver (1979). Carver (1979) defined self-focused attention in the following way: "When attention is self-directed, it sometimes takes the form of focus on internal perceptual events, that is, information from those sensory receptors that react to changes in bodily activity. Self-focus may also take the form of an enhanced awareness of one's present or past physical behavior, that is, a heightened cognizance of what one is doing or what one is like. Alternatively, self-attention can be an awareness of the more or less permanently encoded bits of information that comprise, for example, one's attitudes. It can even be an enhanced awareness of temporarily encoded bits of information that have been gleaned from previous focus on the environment; subjectively, this would be experienced as a recollection or impression of that past event" (p. 1255). Ingram (1990) has summarized this definition and suggested that self-focused attention constitutes "an awareness of self-referent, internally generated information, that stands in contrast to an awareness of externally generated information derived through sensory receptors" (p. 156).

Self-focused attention has been shown in numerous studies to be associated with depression. This link was first uncovered by Timothy Smith and Jeff Greenberg, then graduate students at the University of Kansas. Subsequent to this, two theoretical approaches to depression have emphasized an important role for self-focused attention in depression. Probably the first specific theoretical account was proposed in Lewinsohn's (1985) revised account of depression, which had previously relied almost exclusively on behavioral ideas. The revised model, however, gave a central role to a cognitive idea, self-focused attention. Specifically, Lewinsohn (1985) suggested that disruptions in a person's life alter self-schemas and initiate a heightened sense of self-awareness. This heightened awareness results in a reduction in the person's behavioral and social competencies that are needed to alleviate the effects of negative life events.

Pyszczynski and Greenberg (1987, 1992) also accorded a critical role to self-focused attention in their self-regulatory perseveration model. According to their model, when individuals experience a disruption in a life domain that is of central relevance for their conceptions of self-worth, individuals become inordinately self-focused. This process persists for depressed individuals, which results in the development of a self-focusing style affecting self-esteem, task performance, negative affect, and a host of other symptoms of depression. When subsequent events are negative, Pyszczynski and Greenberg (1987, 1992) propose that this style leads depressed individuals to increase their self-focus, but for positive events they reduce self-focus and are thus unable to reap the emotional benefits of these positive events.

A considerable amount of data have suggested that self-focused attention is not unique to depression (Ingram, 1990, 1991). Indeed, heightened self-focused attention appears so ubiquitous across a variety of disorders, so that it is perhaps best seen as a nonspecific or generalized psychopathology factor, that is, a factor that contributes to all psychological disorders. Even though this does not diminish the importance of self-focused attention, it does suggest that other factors are required to understand the relationship of this process to depression and such a wide variety of other dysfunctional states.

RICK E. INGRAM

See also

Attention
Automatic Thoughts
Rumination

References

Carver, C. S. (1979). A cybernenetic model of self-attention processes. *Journal of Personality and Social Psychology, 37,* 1186–1195.

Duval, S., & Wicklund, R. (1972). *A theory of objective self-awareness.* New York: Academic Press.

Ingram, R. E. (1990). Self-focused attention in clinical disorders: Review and a conceptual model. *Psychological Bulletin, 107,* 156–176.

Ingram, R. E. (1991). Tilting at windmills: A response to Pyszczynski, Greenberg, Hamilton, and Nix. *Psychological Bulletin, 110,* 544–550.

Lewinsohn, P. (1985). A behavioral approach to depression. In J. C. Coyne (Ed.), *Essential papers in depression.* New York: New York University Press.

Pyszczynski, T., & Greenberg, J. (1987). Self-regulatory perseveration and the depressive self-focusing style: A self-awareness theory of reactive depression. *Psychological Bulletin, 102,* 1–17.

Pyszczynski, T., & Greenberg, J. (1992). *Hanging on and letting go: Understanding the onset, progression, and remission of depression.* New York: Springer-Verlag.

Self-Regulation

Self-regulation refers to people's capacities to influence their own thoughts, feelings, and behaviors. Formerly, dominant behavioral perspectives had emphasized the power of stimulus control over behavior. Advances in psychological science, however, have led to a different view, one in which humans have the potential to overcome situational influences. We have self-control. This ability is made possible by a number of distinctive cognitive capacities, including the ability to cognitively represent future possibilities, to reflect on one's abilities, and to evaluate performances. These capacities enable us to pursue and accomplish valued goals. Although contemporary self-regulation theories differ in some ways, there is considerable consensus on the role of these basic cognitive capacities in self-regulation. Before describing self-regulatory functioning in depression, we first outline the major components of the human self-regulatory system.

Components of the Self-Regulatory System

Goal Representations

Nearly all self-regulatory theories emphasize the importance of goal representations (Baumeister & Vohs, 2004). These are cognitive representations of desired (or undesired) future states that serve as guides and motives for action. Goals function as benchmarks against which ongoing behavior is compared and evaluated.

Goal representations differ along both quantitative and qualitative dimensions. Quantitatively, goals can vary in their levels of challenge (e.g., "pass the class" or "get an A"), specificity (e.g., "volunteer at the soup kitchen" or "be good"), and proximity ("earn an A on tomorrow's exam" or "graduate college with a 3.5 or better GPA"). Structurally, goal representations can vary in the degree to which they conflict with one another. Generally, optimal self-regulation is characterized by goal representations that are challenging, specific, and proximal (or proximal goals linked to distal goals) and do not conflict with each other.

Qualitatively, goals can be framed as either future states to be approached or future states to be avoided (Higgins, 1997). Goals can be framed as ideals that represent the individual's hopes and aspirations or as oughts that represent the individual's responsibilities and obligations (Strauman, 2002). They can also be framed as activities to be learned (i.e., growth or learning goals) or as personal characteristics to be demonstrated (i.e., validation or performance goals) (Dweck, 2000). In general, optimal self-regulation is characterized by approach, ideal, and growth goal representations.

Evaluative Judgments

People also assess the relative successfulness of their performance in relation to adopted goals or standards. These evaluative judgments are affectively tinged. When performance is evaluated as falling short of goals or standards, people react with distress. This negative affective state can be motivating or disabling, depending partly on the size of the discrepancy between standard and performance. In general, large perceived discrepancies lead to feelings of futility, depression, and low motivation, and small perceived discrepancies spur positive affect, greater persistence, and eventual goal accomplishment (Locke & Latham, 1990). In a sense, these affective states of satisfaction or dissatisfaction with performance provide humans with their own source of reward and punishment. People also evaluate the rate at which they are reducing the discrepancy between goal representations and evaluative judgments of current performances (Carver & Scheier, 1998). Slow rates of discrepancy reduction are associated with more negative affect whereas faster rates of discrepancy reduction are associated with more positive affect.

Self-Efficacy Appraisals

Finally, people do not just act; they reflect on their abilities to act. Self-efficacy appraisals refer to people's assessments of their abilities to organize and execute specific behavioral performances (Bandura, 1997). When people judge themselves capable of performing goal-related activities, they may persevere even when their initial performance was substandard and dissatisfying. When people appraise themselves as not efficacious, even a small goal-performance discrepancy can lead to dysphoria and a slackening effort or even abandonment of effort altogether (Cervone & Scott, 1995).

Integrated Self-Regulatory System

Each of these cognitive components—goal representations, evaluative judgments of performances, self-efficacy appraisals—function in concert as an integrated self-regulatory system (Figure S.2). For instance, if performance is evaluated negatively, this can lower self-efficacy appraisals, which can lower the level of challenge of the goal representation (e.g., "I don't have the ability to perform graduate-level work, therefore I must lower my goals for a profession in psychology").

Goal Representations in Depression

Depressed individuals represent goals suboptimally along both quantitative and qualitative dimensions. Quantitatively, depressed individuals' goals are perfectionistic and overly challenging (Hewitt & Flett, 1991). Across a number of studies, depressed individuals have been found to hold relatively stringent performance goals in that the goal level adopted exceeds the performance level that participants judge they can achieve (Ahrens, 1987). Why do depressed people adopt more challenging goals? One possibility is that people learn early in development to adopt perfectionistic goals. However, several studies have found that the experience of negative affect in depression itself can sometimes lead to the construction of more perfectionistic goal representations (Tillema, Cervone, & Scott, 2001).

Depressed people have been found to possess goals that differ in two other quantitative dimensions. First, they appear to adopt goal representations that are less specific, or more abstract (Emmons, 1992). Representing goals in more broad and expansive terms (e.g., "ward off the ravages of time" instead of "stay out of the sun") causes people to

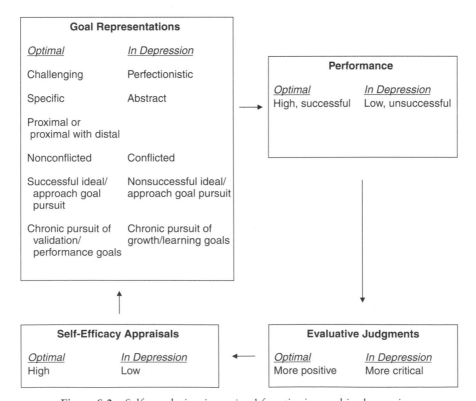

Figure S.2   Self-regulation in optimal functioning and in depression.

view goals as less likely to be accomplished (i.e., causes low self-efficacy). More abstract goals also fail to specify clear actions for goal attainment. Both of these consequences can lead to failed self-regulation and greater distress (Bandura, 1986). Finally, in depression, people are more likely to have multiple goals that conflict with each other (e.g., "appear attractive to opposite sex" and "please my spouse") (Emmons & King, 1988).

Depressed and nondepressed individuals also show several qualitative differences in goal representations. People who perceive that they are failing to achieve ideal goals are prone to depressive symptoms (Strauman, 2002). Relatedly, people who appear to have deficits in accomplishing approach or promotion goals are prone to depression (Higgins, 1997). In fact, a specific form of cognitive therapy that explicitly addresses deficits in approach and promotion goal orientation and goal pursuit has shown superior treatment effects compared to standard cognitive therapy for depressed individuals evidencing deficits in approach and promotion goal processes (Strauman et al., 2006).

Dykman (1998) argued that some people are prone to chronically pursuing validation goals. As a result of having this type of goal orientation, these individuals "continually mine the world for information relevant to their worth, competence, and likeability" (p. 153). For such individuals, then, performance situations are emotional minefields because self-esteem is always on the line, contingent on successful performance. Not succeeding translates into appraisals of low self-worth and increased depression. In contrast, other people tend to adopt growth-seeking goals and approach performance situations with a focus on developing potential and skill. For these individuals, poor performance does not call into question self-worth; rather, subpar performance is merely viewed as a learning experience that ultimately leads to self-betterment. According to this theory, these growth-oriented individuals should be more resilient and less likely to develop depression in response to poor performance. Initial findings have

generally supported the role of validation-seeking goal orientations in predicting changes in dysphoric symptoms, but only in the context of negative life events (Lindsay & Scott, 2005).

Other researchers have investigated the relationship between past, unfulfilled goals and depression (Lecci, Okun, & Karoly, 1994). In addition to current goal pursuits, people have representations of past goals that were unfulfilled. Referred to as regrets, these unfulfilled goals show an especially strong link with depression if the person had invested considerable time and effort trying to achieve the goal. Regrets may be particularly important as people age, as there is less opportunity to pursue the goal again and attain success after initial failure.

Evaluative Judgments in Depression

One of the most robust findings in the depression literature is the finding that depressed people are particularly self-critical in evaluating their performance (Rehm, 1988). However, recent work has suggested that depressed individuals are only less accurate in evaluating performance when performance is objectively successful (Dunn, Dalgleish, Lawrence, & Ogilvie, 2007). When evaluating objectively failed performances, however, depressed individuals appear to evaluate their performances more accurately, in line with depressive realism hypotheses (Alloy & Abramson, 1988). Nevertheless, for depressed individuals, successful performances are more likely to be evaluated critically. This pattern fosters the perception that one has failed to perform at a level required for goal accomplishment or that one is reducing the performance-to-goal discrepancy at too slow a rate. Both processes would further promote depressive symptoms.

Self-Efficacy in Depression

There is strong empirical support for a relationship between low self-efficacy judgments and depression in adults. For instance, low self-efficacy for parenting, coping, social skills, and activities of personal importance have all been related, either directly or indirectly, to depressive symptoms (Bandura, 1997). This relationship between low self-efficacy judgments and depression has also been documented in children and adolescents (Bandura, Pastorelli, Barbaranelli, & Caprara, 1999).

Conclusions

People possess the capacity to self-regulate through the exercise of cognitive abilities including setting goals, evaluating performances in relation to goals, and reflecting on abilities. Depressed individuals appear to exhibit a number of maladaptive self-regulation characteristics (see Figure S.2). They tend to frame goals in nonoptimal ways, think poorly of their abilities to perform goal-related tasks, and evaluate their performances more critically. Each of these processes would be associated with self-regulation failure and increased distress. To the extent that treatment approaches can improve these maladaptive self-regulation features, the depressed individual should experience greater self-control and consequently less depression.

WALTER D. SCOTT AND SUZANNA L. PENNINGROTH

See also

Self-Efficacy
Self-Esteem
Vulnerability

References

Ahrens, A. H. (1987). Theories of depression: The role of goals and the self-evaluation process. *Cognitive Therapy and Research, 11,* 665–680.

Alloy, L. B., & Abramson, L. Y. (1988). Depressive realism: Four theoretical perspectives. In L. B. Alloy (Ed.), *Cognitive processes in depression* (pp. 223–266). New York: Guilford Press.

Bandura, A. (1986). *Social foundations of thought and action: A social cognitive theory.* Englewood Cliffs, NJ: Prentice-Hall.

Bandura, A. (1997). *Self-efficacy: The exercise of control.* New York: W. H. Freeman and Co.

Bandura, A., Pastorelli, C., Barbaranelli, C., & Caprara, G. V. (1999). Self-efficacy pathways to child depression. *Journal of Personality and Social Psychology, 76,* 258–269.

Baumeister, R. F., & Vohs, K. D. (2004). *Handbook of self-regulation.* New York: Guilford Press.

Carver, C. S., & Scheier, M. F. (1998). *On the self-regulation of behavior.* Cambridge, England: Cambridge University Press.

Cervone, D., & Scott, W. D. (1995). Self-efficacy theory of behavioral change: Foundations, conceptual issues, and therapeutic implications. In W. O'Donohue & L. Krasner (Eds.), *Theories of behavior therapy: Exploring behavior change* (pp. 349–389). Washington, DC: American Psychological Association.

Dunn, B. D., Dalgleish, T., Lawrence, A. D., & Ogilvie, A. D. (2007). The accuracy of self-monitoring and its relationship to self-focused attention in dysphoria and clinical depression. *Journal of Abnormal Psychology, 116,* 1–15.

Dweck, C. S. (2000). *Self-theories: Their role in motivation, personality, and development.* New York: Psychology Press.

Dykman, B. M. (1998). Integrating cognitive and motivational factors in depression: Initial tests of a goal-orientation approach. *Journal of Personality and Social Psychology, 74,* 139–158.

Emmons, R. A. (1992). Abstract versus concrete goals: Personal striving level, physical illness, and psychological well-being. *Journal of Personality and Social Psychology, 62,* 292–300.

Emmons, R. A., & King, L. A. (1988). Conflict among personal strivings: Immediate and long-term implications for psychological and physical well-being. *Journal of Personality and Social Psychology, 54,* 1040–1048.

Hewitt, P. L., & Flett, G. L. (1991). Dimensions of perfectionism in unipolar depression. *Journal of Abnormal Psychology, 100,* 98–101.

Higgins, E. T. (1997). Beyond pleasure and pain. *American Psychologist, 52,* 1280–1300.

Lecci, L., Okun, M. A., & Karoly, P. (1994). Life regrets and current goals as predictors of psychological adjustment. *Journal of Personality and Social Psychology, 66,* 731–741.

Lindsay, J., & Scott, W. D. (2005). Dysphoria and self-esteem following an achievement event: Predictive validity of goal orientation and personality style theories of vulnerability. *Cognitive Therapy and Research, 29,* 769–785.

Locke, E. A., & Latham, G. P. (1990). *A theory of goal setting and task performance.* Englewood Cliffs, NJ: Prentice-Hall.

Rehm, L. P. (1988). Self-management and cognitive processes in depression. In L. B. Alloy (Ed.), *Cognitive processes in depression* (pp. 143–176). New York: Guilford Press.

Strauman, T. J. (2002). Self-regulation and depression. *Self and Identity, 1,* 151–157.

Strauman, T. J., Vieth, A. Z., Merrill, K. A., Papadakis, A. A., Kolden, G. G., Woods, T. E., et al. (2006). Self-system therapy as an intervention for self-regulatory dysfunction in depression: A randomized comparison with cognitive therapy. *Journal of Consulting and Clinical Psychology, 74,* 367–376.

Tillema, J. L., Cervone, D., & Scott, W. D. (2001). Dysphoric mood, perceived self-efficacy, and personal standards for performance: The effects of attributional cues on evaluative self-judgments. *Cognitive Therapy and Research, 25,* 535–549.

Self-Verification

Self-verification theory proposes that people expect and want others to see them as they see themselves. For example, just as those who see themselves as friendly want others to see them as friendly, so too do people who feel that they are shy want others to recognize them as shy. Firmly held self-views allow people to predict the responses of others and know how to act toward them. For example, a woman's belief that she is friendly allows her to predict that others will notice her friendliness. This prediction may motivate her to seek membership in social groups and involve herself in social activities. Her shy counterpart, however, will predict that others will notice her shyness. This prediction, in turn, may cause her to pursue more solitary activities or associate with other individuals who do not expect or require high levels of gregariousness. Because people's self-views play such a critical role in their lives, they become invested in maintaining them by obtaining self-verifying information. These activities are highly functional; by seeking information that confirms their own self-views, people are able to maintain the unity, integrity, and continuity of their own belief systems.

In the case of individuals with positive self-views, self-verification motivates the same behaviors as does another important motive: the desire for self-enhancing or positive evaluations. For example, those who view themselves as "worthwhile" will find that their desires for both self-verification and self-enhancement motivate them to seek feedback that others also perceive them as worthwhile. In contrast, people with negative self-views, such as those who are depressed, will find that the two motives conflict with each other. For example, those who see themselves as "worthless" will find that whereas their desire for self-verification motivates them to seek evidence that others perceive them as worthless, their desire for self-enhancement motivates them to seek evidence that others perceive them as worthwhile. As we will discuss later, this need for self-verification among depressed individuals may act as a factor in perpetuating their depressed state.

Self-verification strivings can manifest themselves in three distinct ways. First, people may construct self-verifying opportunity structures for themselves, or social environments that somehow meet their needs, by seeking and entering into relationships only with people who verify their own self-views. Swann, Wenzlaff, Krull, and Pelham (1992) found that in relation to nondepressed college students, depressed college students preferred interaction partners who viewed them unfavorably. Similarly, in relation to nondepressed students, depressed students preferred friends or dating partners who evaluated them unfavorably. This desire to select verifying social environments has been shown to be so strong that when given a choice between interacting with partners who evaluated them negatively versus participating in another experiment altogether, those who were dysphoric preferred to interact with the negative evaluator, whereas nondysphoric individuals preferred to opt out and participate in another experiment (Swann, Wenzlaff, & Tafarodi, 1992). Apparently, as this research suggests, people tend to prefer relationships and settings that provide them with evaluations that confirm their self-views, even when those evaluations are decidedly negative.

A second way in which people self-verify is by attempting to bring others to see them as they see themselves. One way people may attempt to do this is through the way in which they interact with others. Swann, Wenzlaff, Krull, and colleagues (1992) found that college students who were mildly depressed as compared to nondepressed were more likely to solicit negative evaluations from their roommates. Moreover, students' efforts to acquire negative feedback appear to eventually result in interpersonal rejection; the more unfavorable feedback they solicited in the middle of the semester, the more their roommates derogated them and planned to find another roommate at the semester's end. In addition, when people receive discrepant feedback about themselves and perceive that they are being misconstrued, they will redouble their efforts to bring others to see them as they see themselves. Swann, Wenzlaff, and Tafarodi (1992) found that upon receiving positive evaluations, dysphoric people attempted to reaffirm their negative self-views by seeking information regarding their limitations, whereas nondysphorics reacted to the positive evaluations by seeking information regarding their strengths. Therefore, people tend to intensify their efforts to obtain self-verification when they suspect that others' appraisals challenge their self-views.

Finally, the third way that people self-verify is by construing their worlds in ways that make them seem more verifying than they actually are. For example, when Giesler, Josephs, and Swann (1996) had participants rate the accuracy of feedback, they found that depressed individuals were unique in perceiving negative feedback as more accurate than positive feedback. Presumably, such a bias convinces depressed people that negative feedback should be taken seriously and positive feedback should be dismissed because it is off the mark.

This dominance of self-verification over self-enhancement in the mental processes of depressed people may unwittingly contribute to the perpetuation of their depressed states. For example, as mentioned in our discussion of Swann, Wenzlaff, Krull, and colleagues' work (1992), the more depressed individuals seek unfavorable feedback, the more their roommates derogate and reject them. Thus, even though their desire for coherence and predictability may be inherently adaptive, their tendency to use negative self-views to guide their search for coherence may trigger rejection, which will in turn further isolate them. Note however, that even though depressed people may, in effect, sow the seeds of their own rejection, their activities should not be considered masochistic. That is, although depressed people may succeed in maintaining cognitive order by creating self-verifying environments, when they receive negative evaluations they are every bit as unhappy as are people who have positive self-views (Swann, Wenzlaff, Krull, et al., 1992). Thus, by continuing to solicit this negative feedback, depressed individuals may deal repeated blows to their mood in the service of validating and shoring up their negative self-concepts.

Finally, the self-verification strivings of depressed people may cause them to resist efforts to lift them out of their depressed states. Of the existing psychotherapies to treat depression, cognitive behavioral therapy (CBT) is the most effective evidence-based method currently in practice. Because one primary goal of CBT is to challenge irrational thinking, such as unfounded negative self-views, depressed individuals who engage in constant self-verification of negative self-views may find it particularly difficult to change these firmly held self-views the more they act to confirm them.

Although self-verification may act as a complicating factor regarding the treatment of depression, it does not render successful treatment for depression unattainable by any means. Rather, a thorough understanding of the importance of coherence strivings to mental well-being suggests that any treatment program must be cognizant of these strivings. Self-verification requires that the individual continue to believe in the veracity of the overarching knowledge system even when maladaptive components of that knowledge system undergo change. Therapy must therefore be geared toward improving the self-view in small increments while simultaneously acknowledging positive as well as negative qualities of patients. Little by little, as the depressed individual can believe in these more positive self-views and seeks to verify them, self-verification can actually act as a tool for recovery.

CHRISTINE CHANG-SCHNEIDER
AND WILLIAM B. SWANN, JR.

See also

Reassurance-Seeking

References

Giesler, R. B., Josephs, R. A., & Swann, W. B., Jr. (1996). Self-verification in clinical depression: The desire for negative evaluation. *Journal of Abnormal Psychology, 105,* 358–368.

Swann, W. B., Jr., Wenzlaff, R. M., Krull, D. S., & Pelham, B. W. (1992). The allure of negative feedback: Self-verification strivings among depressed persons. *Journal of Abnormal Psychology, 101,* 293–306.

Swann, W. B., Jr., Wenzlaff, R. M., & Tafarodi, R. W. (1992). Depression and the search for negative evaluations: More evidence of the role of self-verification strivings. *Journal of Abnormal Psychology, 101,* 314–317.

Serotonin

Serotonin (also known as 5-hydroxytryptamine, or 5-HT) is a neurotransmitter, a chemical that transmits nerve impulses across a synapse (the gap between nerve cells or neurons). Most 5-HT-containing neurons are localized around the midline of the brain stem, with a wide distribution of receiving areas throughout the nervous system, from the spinal cord to the cortex. Serotonin has a key role in the regulation of mood and pain sensitivity; in the control of eating, sleep, arousal, and aggression; in sexual behaviors; and in learning. Disruption of serotonin has important effects in these basic functions and has been implicated in depression, anger, aggression, and suicide.

The serotonin transporter is a protein (also known as 5-HTT) that is found on the presynaptic membranes of serotonergic neurons (i.e., at the nerve endings between nerve cells involved in serotonin transmission). This protein "sucks up" or recycles excess serotonin after it has finished acting on neurons (and has been secreted in the synapse) and therefore has an important role in regulating the supply of serotonin at synapses.

There are clues about the importance of the transporter protein from observations of humans. The antidepressant group of specific selective serotonin-reuptake inhibitors or SSRIs (which includes fluoxetine, better known as Prozac) are now the most widely prescribed medications for depression and anxiety disorders and have been found to act by blocking this transporter protein. Ecstasy (MDMA) acts on the serotonin transporter by releasing serotonin into the brain, causing a period of elation followed by depressive feelings as the drug wears off.

The SLC6A promoter region of the gene (5-HTTLPR) acts like a dimmer switch, controlling the amount of serotonin available at the synapse. There is normally some variation in genes, leading to two known variants: the short allele (s) and the long allele (l). Put simply, the short variant reduces transcriptional efficiency (i.e., makes less protein), resulting in increased levels of serotonin in the synapse, and the situation is reversed for the long allele. At a cellular level, those people who have more of the short allele may be less efficient at stopping unwanted messages, and they seem to be more reactive to a range of life events.

Everyone inherits two copies (or alleles) of the serotonin transporter gene, one from each parent. As everyone has two copies of the gene, they may be homozygous for the two short alleles (i.e., have two short alleles, s/s) or two long alleles (l/l), or may have one of each type of allele (s/l), which is known as being heterozygous or having two different alleles in this case.

There have been links demonstrated between the serotonin transporter gene and certain personality traits such as anxiety and negative emotionality (Murphy et al., 2001). Brain imaging has revealed those with at least one short allele to have greater amygdala neuronal activity in response to fearful stimuli compared to those homozygous for the long allele. This differential excitability of the amygdala to emotional stimuli may contribute to the increased fear and anxiety typically associated with the short allele (Hariri et al., 2002).

It was hoped that the 5-HTT gene would provide a link between environmental stress and development of depression, but it is now thought that previous models simply linking the serotonin transporter genes and depression have been too simplistic, and that the key to psychiatric genetics involves the interplay between individuals and their environmental stressors. Evidence from studies in mice and monkeys suggest that the short variant is predisposed for depression via a gene-by-environment interaction. For example, when rhesus macaque monkeys were exposed to adverse early rearing (by peers rather than mothers), those with the s allele showed more distress, less activity, and more physiological signs of stress, while those with the l/l alleles developed more playful behavior.

In a longitudinal study of 847 Caucasian New Zealanders (Caspi et al., 2003), the short variant of 5-HTTLPR appeared to be linked to vulnerability to stress (such as loss of a job, breaking up with a partner, death of a loved one). Among people who suffered multiple stressful life events over 5 years, 43% of those with the s allele developed major depression, compared to only 17% with the l/l versions of the gene.

Effects of genes in complex disorders like psychiatric illnesses are most likely to be uncovered when such life stresses are measured, since the gene's effects may only be expressed, or turned on, in people exposed to the requisite environmental risks. Others have found increased reactivity in the period after stressful life events leading to depression (Kendler et al., 2005; Wilheim et al., 2006), while increased depressogenic effect in women can be accounted for by the effect of neuroticism (Jacobs et al., 2006). The stressful events led to onset of new episodes of clinical depression among people with one or two copies of the s allele who did not have depression before the events happened. There have now been a number of replications of this study, and the association is looking robust. A comprehensive review of these studies is available (Uher & McGuffin, 2007). As in the monkey study, Caspi's group also found that childhood adverse events had a greater effect on depression onset for those with the s allele. Some studies have suggested that the effects of the polymorphism may be greater in females, who tend to show greater reactivity to stress overall, particularly in the years of potential childrearing. There has also been a report of an association between the s allele and use of fewer problem-solving strategies, an effect that was greater for males (Wilhelm et al., 2007).

The interaction between genes and environment appears to continue into later life, as older people with the s allele have been found to be more likely to develop depression after an acute heart attack (Lenze et al., 2007) or a hip fracture (Nakatani et al., 2005).

Subsequently, high-expressing and low-expressing allelic variants of the 5-HTTLPR have been described. These variants may have implications for both gene expression and how individuals handle antidepressants related to serotonin function, particularly the SSRIs (Hu et al., 2007). The developments in this field have proved exciting and interesting, as they provide a possible window into mechanisms that show us how the emotional mind, genes, and the environment can interact.

KAY WILHELM

See also

Biological Models of Depression
Brain Circuitry
Dopamine

References

Caspi, A., Sugden, K., Moffitt, T. E., Taylor, A., Craig, I. W., Harrington, H., et al. (2003). Influence of life stress on depression: Moderation by a polymorphism in the 5-HTT gene. *Science, 301,* 386–389.

Hariri, A., Mattay, V., Tessitore, A., Kolachana, B., Fera, F., Goldman, D., et al. (2002). Serotonin transporter genetic variation and the response of the human amygdala. *Science, 297,* 400–403.

Hu, X. Z., Rush, A. J., Charney, D., Wilson, A. F., Sorant, A. J. M., Papanicolaou, G. J., et al. (2007). Association between a functional serotonin transporter promoter polymorphism and citalopram treatment in adult outpatients with major depression. *Archives of General Psychiatry, 64,* 783–792.

Jacobs, N., Kenis, P. G., Peeters, F., Derom C., Robert Vlietinck, R., & van Os, J. (2006). Stress-related negative affectivity and genetically altered serotonin transporter function: Evidence of synergism in shaping risk of depression. *Archives of General Psychiatry, 63,* 989–996.

Kendler, K. S., Kuhn, J. W., Vittum, J., Prescott, C. A., & Riley, B. (2005). The interaction of stressful life events and a serotonin transporter polymorphism in the prediction of episodes of major depression. *Archives of General Psychiatry, 62,* 529–535.

Lenze, E. J., Munin, M. C. Skidmore, E. R., Dew, M. A., Rogers, J. C., Whyte, E. M., et al. (2007). Onset of depression in elderly persons after hip fracture: Implications for prevention and early intervention of late-life depression. *Journal of the America Geriatric Society, 55,* 81–86.

Murphy, D., Li, Q., Engel, S., Wichems, C., Andrews, A., Lesch, K. P., et al. (2001). Genetic perspectives on the serotonin transporter. *Brain Research Bulletin, 56,* 487–494.

Nakatani, D., Sato, H., Sakata, Y., Shiotani, I., Kinjo, K., Mizuno, H., et al. (2005). Influence of serotonin transporter gene polymorphism on depressive symptoms and new cardiac events after acute myocardial infarction. *American Heart Journal, 159,* 652–658.

Uher, R., & McGuffin, P. (2007). The moderation by the serotonin transporter gene of environmental adversity in the aetiology of mental illness: Review and methodological analysis. *Molecular Psychiatry, 13,* 131–146.

Wilhelm, K., Mitchell, P. B., Niven, H., Finch, A., Wedgewood, L., et al. (2006). Life events, first depression onset and the serotonin transporter gene. *British Journal of Psychiatry, 188,* 210–215.

Wilhelm, K., Siegel, J., Finch, A. W., Hadzi-Pavlovic, D., Mitchell, P. B., Parker, G., et al. (2007). The long and the short of it: Associations between 5-HTT genotypes and coping with stress. *Psychosomatic Medicine, 69,* 614–620.

Shame

Shame is generally recognized as a particularly intense and often incapacitating negative emotion. Both clinical observation and phenomenological studies have characterized the experience of shame as involving feelings of inferiority, powerlessness, and self-consciousness, along with the desire to hide and conceal deficiencies. As inferiority and powerlessness are ubiquitous features of many theories of depression, it is not surprising that shame has been increasingly linked to depression. However, it is "the doubleness of experience" (Lewis, 1987, p. 16) inherent in shame, involving both self in one's own eyes and in the eyes of the other, that may offer additional insights into the understanding of depression. Existing knowledge of the role and relevant characteristics of shame in the onset and course of depression are outlined here.

Helen Lewis, one of the first theorists to discuss shame specifically in relation to depression, described it as a negative feeling involving the whole self. She distinguished it from guilt, which does not normally generalize beyond the specific behavior that provoked it (and which she believed was more characteristic of obsessionality and paranoia). These notions have been generally promoted in the shame literature and have received indirect support from a number of correlational studies conducted with student samples. In the main these have shown shame in the absence of guilt to be more highly correlated with depressive symptoms than guilt in the absence of shame. Some have discounted this evidence because it does not reflect the type of all-enveloping pathological guilt only encountered in depressed clinical samples, although shame-centered clinicians such as Lewis have argued that severe guilt is always fused with shame. Nevertheless, the two emotions in their severe form have distinctive characteristics that might link them independently to depression: shame being concerned with the anticipation of rejection, and guilt with the anticipation and deservingness of punishment (Andrews, 1998).

The emphasis in much of the shame literature is on shame in relation to guilt. However this covers only one focus for shame, namely on one's moral transgressions. Shame may also be experienced specifically in relation to physical and nonphysical aspects of the self, as well as being evoked by others' transgressions against the self, such as being put down or abused. When shame has been considered in relation to the body, for example, it has been shown to have dispositional, ever-present elements that may generalize only during depressive episodes (Andrews, 1995). This indicates the need to distinguish between specific and generalized forms of shame. The two different forms may have different origins, be related to different self-constructs, and need different types of therapeutic management.

Clinically oriented theorists have described shame as a central feature of a variety of mental disorders. Consideration of its functional role in particular disorders such as depression has been relatively neglected. While there is a wealth of evidence of an association between shame and depression from correlational studies in both student and clinical samples, there has been little discussion of what these associations might represent. One objection has been that because of the high reliance on negative and global self-referent items in most shame scales, correlations between shame and depression may be a consequence of a diffuse negative affectivity reflected in both measures. This begs the question of whether shame acts as a risk factor in the onset of depression, is concomitant with depression, or is a consequence of depression. The small amount of evidence there is suggests that shame is likely to function at all these levels.

Positive evidence for the role of shame in the onset of depression comes from three longitudinal studies using both interview and questionnaire methods. The samples have included children, undergraduate students, and adult women. In the one study to control for prior symptoms, the predictive effect of shame on subsequent depression symptoms varied according to the shame measure used (Andrews, Qian, & Valentine, 2002). The Experience of Shame Scale (ESS) had a significant predictive effect, but the Test of Self-conscious Affect (TOSCA), much used in correlational studies, did not. It was concluded that the reason for the differential performance of the two scales was that the ESS assesses specific areas of shame related to self and performance, whereas the TOSCA assesses general shame and may be more prone to mood-state effects.

Within a psychodynamic framework, Helen Lewis and others have proposed that a propensity to shame arises out of experiences of maternal loss and rejection. In contrast, Paul Gilbert's (1989) biosocial theory, informed by ethological studies of nonhuman primates, views shame as concerned with involuntary submission and defeat, ultimately leading to depression in humans. Common to both perspectives is the notion that shame can function as a mediating factor between prior adverse experiences and subsequent depression. In this regard there is increasing evidence of a link between early abusive and rejecting experiences and a propensity to shame in a variety of different samples and settings. Specific evidence of shame as a mediator between negative childhood experiences and depression is more elusive. However, one study has demonstrated the mediating effect of bodily shame in the relationship between childhood abuse (both sexual and physical) and subsequent chronic depression in adult women (Andrews, 1995). The mediating effect of shame

has also been demonstrated in other conditions such as eating disorders and posttraumatic stress disorder.

Shame has been shown to play a role in the course of depression in one in-depth interview study of 35 clinically depressed male and female patients. Patients whose depression had taken a chronic or recurrent course were distinguished from those who had experienced just one acute episode. After controlling for age, significantly higher levels of shame relating to personal qualities and behaviors were found in the chronic or recurrently depressed patients compared with patients with acute episodes (Andrews & Hunter, 1997). In a few cases it was apparent that shame may very well have been a consequence of persistent depressive and other symptomatology. For example, some patients reported feeling ashamed of their unkempt appearance and desire to withdraw from social interaction.

Central to the experience of shame is a wish to hide oneself and one's deficiencies, and Andrews and Hunter concluded that this may lead to a chronic course of depressive disorder by affecting disclosure of the issues involved. A number of studies investigating disclosure in therapy have reported relatively high rates of nondisclosure ranging from 41% to 54% in patients with a variety of conditions, and shame has featured highly in those that investigated the reasons why. In one study that investigated these issues in members of a depression self-help group, shame was the most frequent overall reason for nondisclosure in therapy (Hook & Andrews, 2005). Moreover, shame was shown to be a more frequent reason for nondisclosure of symptoms than distressing life experiences. Similarly, shame proneness was significantly related to nondisclosure of symptoms but not to nondisclosure of distressing experiences. Most importantly, among individuals no longer in therapy, nondisclosure of symptoms while in therapy predicted high levels of current depressive symptoms. These findings suggest that encouraging and facilitating the disclosure of shameful symptoms and related behaviors has positive implications for the effectiveness of treatment. The findings also highlight the importance of recognizing and dealing with clients' shame in an empathic and validating way as a component of treatment. To this end Gilbert and Irons have developed compassionate mind training to help clients with shame-based conditions, including difficult-to-treat depression (Gilbert & Irons, 2005). Its purpose is to work with clients' harsh inner dialogues using cognitive-emotional techniques and imagery to help them develop a compassionate inner voice.

In conclusion, over 20 years ago shame was termed the "sleeper" of psychopathology by Helen Lewis because of the relative lack of consideration it was afforded by theorists and researchers. Since then the theoretical literature has burgeoned, but the functional role of shame in depression and other disorders has only just started to be addressed. It is hoped that increasing research in this area will lead to a full awakening regarding this neglected emotion through the integration of theory and practice with research evidence.

BERNICE ANDREWS

See also

Guilt

References

Andrews, B. (1995). Bodily shame as a mediator between abusive experiences and depression. *Journal of Abnormal Psychology, 104,* 277–285.

Andrews, B. (1998). Shame and childhood abuse. In P. Gilbert & B. Andrews (Eds.), *Shame, interpersonal behaviour, psychopathology, and culture* (pp. 176–190). New York: Oxford University Press.

Andrews, B., & Hunter, E. (1997). Shame, early abuse and course of depression in a clinical sample: A preliminary study. *Cognition and Emotion, 11,* 373–381.

Andrews, B., Qian, M., & Valentine, J. D. (2002). Predicting depressive symptoms with a new measure of shame: The Experience of Shame Scale. *British Journal of Clinical Psychology, 41,* 29–42.

Gilbert, P. (1989). *Human nature and suffering.* Hove, UK: Erlbaum.

Gilbert, P., & Irons, C. (2005). Focused therapies and compassionate mind training for shame and self-attacking. In P. Gilbert (Ed.), *Compassion: Conceptualisations,*

research, and use in psychotherapy (pp. 263–325). London: Routledge.

Hook, A., & Andrews, B. (2005). The relationship of non-disclosure in therapy to shame and depression. *British Journal of Clinical Psychology, 44,* 425–438.

Lewis, H. B. (1987). Introduction: Shame—the "sleeper" in psychopathology. In H. B. Lewis (Ed.), *The role of shame in symptom formation* (pp. 1–28). Hillsdale, NJ: Erlbaum.

Smoking

In addition to the increased risk of morbidity and mortality experienced by cigarette smokers, research indicates that smokers may experience greater affective vulnerability compared with nonsmokers. The literature on the relationship between depression and smoking and treatment for depressed smokers is reviewed here.

Nearly two decades ago, Glassman and colleagues (1988) published a now classic report on the relationship between smoking and depression. During a clinical trial of clonidine for smoking cessation, they found 61% of their sample had a past history of major depressive disorder. Furthermore, such a history was found to have a strong negative influence on the ability to stop smoking. Since this initial report, literature has proliferated on both clinical and epidemiological studies examining this topic and indicates a strong and consistent association between current cigarette smoking and depression. In the National Comorbidity Study, Lasser and colleagues (2000) found that the rate of current smoking was 45% among individuals with a current (past month) diagnosis of major depressive disorder compared with 22% among individuals with no current psychiatric diagnosis. Studies based on clinical treatment samples indicate between 18% and 61% of smokers report a past history of major depressive disorder, which is much higher than the general population rate of about 17%. Also, smokers score higher than nonsmokers on measures of current depressive and negative affect symptoms, and depression proneness.

What is less well understood are the causal mechanisms that account for the relationship between smoking and depression. Three hypotheses have been tested: (a) smoking leads to development of depression; (b) depression leads to initiation of smoking; and (c) there are shared etiologies, including genetic, environmental, and psychosocial variables. Longitudinal, epidemiological studies conducted primarily among adolescents indicate smokers are more likely to develop depression than nonsmokers (e.g., Choi, Patten, Gillin, Kaplan, & Pierce, 1997). Other research found that individuals with elevated depressive symptoms are more likely to initiate or progress to regular smoking. Some, but not all, studies have shown evidence in both directions, indicating a reciprocal relationship. First, long-term exposure to nicotine itself or nicotine withdrawal may influence neurobiological systems that have an etiological role in depression. For instance, the nicotine withdrawal syndrome as defined by the *Diagnostic and Statistical Manual of Mental Disorders* (*DSM-IV*; American Psychiatric Association, 1994) criteria includes symptoms that may overlap with a depressive episode, such as irritability, dysphoria, difficulty concentrating, and appetite and sleep disturbance. Furthermore, individuals who smoke may be less likely to develop alternative coping skills in response to stress, which might lead to development of depression. Second, depression may increase the risk for smoking through a self-medication process, due to the mood-altering effects of nicotine. For example, nicotine may affect the dopaminergic and adrenergic systems through its impact on catecholamine release—a process similar to that found in antidepressant medications. Interestingly, among nonsmokers with current major depressive disorder, nicotine patch therapy alleviated depressive symptoms, indicating the potential antidepressant effects of nicotine. Other studies have focused on understanding genetic factors or comorbidities (e.g., conduct disorder) that may underlie vulnerability to both smoking and depression. Results from a study of adult female twins were consistent with a common genetic liability to major depressive disorder and lifetime smoking (Kendler et al., 1993). Moreover, genetic variation in certain neurotransmitter systems (e.g., dopamine receptors) may increase liability to both depression and nicotine use.

Depression and Smoking Cessation Outcomes

Research has examined whether smokers with depression are less likely to quit than nondepressed smokers. Since the Glassman (1988) report, the findings from numerous studies on this topic have been inconsistent. A meta-analysis examined outcomes in 15 studies, of which 14 were clinical trials of smokers treated with pharmacotherapy (e.g., bupropion) and/or behavioral treatment (Hitsman, Borelli, McChargue, Spring, & Niaura, 2003). Results indicated that prior major depressive disorder was not predictive of smoking cessation treatment outcomes at 3- to 6-month follow-ups. However, subsequent research found that smokers who have experienced recurrent major depressive disorder (two or more episodes) are less likely to quit smoking, which may reflect a substantial underlying vulnerability to the disorder. Moreover, the negative effect of any major depressive disorder history (single episode or recurrent) may be apparent in the more immediate (i.e., 1 week) postquit period, but not at follow-up periods that are well after the treatment has ended. In addition, smokers with prior major depressive disorder appear to report characteristics that may be associated with reduced success at quitting. Compared to individuals with no such history, major depressive disorder positive smokers report greater severity of nicotine dependence and symptoms of depression prior to treatment, less self-efficacy to quit smoking, and fewer coping skills for managing mood. Additional research indicates that smokers with prior major depressive disorder may experience more severe mood and other withdrawal symptoms during a quit attempt and are at increased risk for developing an episode of major depression during smoking cessation treatment.

In contrast to the inconsistent findings on major depressive disorder history, most studies have found that higher levels of depressive- or negative affect–type symptoms at baseline or during a quit attempt are associated with a reduced likelihood of future success. Similar to other addictive behaviors, negative mood states are the most frequently reported precipitants of smoking relapse episodes. Studies using real-time, daily recordings of mood states further indicate that precipitous increases in negative affect are associated with smoking relapse.

Treatment of Depressed Smokers

Given the relationship between smoking and depression, researchers have investigated whether an antidepressant medication or behavioral treatment focused on attenuating negative mood enhances outcome for depressed smokers. Studies have found that the antidepressant bupropion (Zyban) is effective for smoking cessation, irrespective of past history of major depressive disorder (Hayford et al., 1999). Interesting findings have been observed with the antidepressant fluoxetine. While this medication has not been found to be effective for smoking cessation overall, it may selectively benefit smokers who report elevated depressive symptoms prior to quitting.

With respect to behavioral treatment, researchers have found that supportive counseling may selectively benefit smokers with elevated negative affect scores prior to treatment. An example of this type of treatment is providing portable audiotape players to smokers that contain personalized and supportive therapist messages. Conversely, these approaches do not appear to be helpful to smokers with low negative affectivity scores. Researchers have theorized that while the addition of depression-specific therapy content is helpful for those who need it, affect regulation treatments may hinder cessation attempts for those without depressive symptoms by diluting the smoking-related content. Similarly, a number of studies have examined whether cognitive behavioral treatment (CBT) of the type used in the treatment of depression could enhance smoking treatment outcome for smokers with a past history of major depressive disorder. Results have been conflicting, with the current consensus being that CBT is not more effective than a standard behavioral smoking treatment for smokers with a single episode of prior major depressive disorder. However, CBT appears to be effective for smokers who have experienced recurrent depression.

Only three studies focused on individuals with current major depressive disorder or individuals taking an antidepressant medication; these smokers are usually excluded from clinical smoking cessation trials. One small study found that the nicotine patch was effective compared to placebo for smokers with current major depressive disorder. Moreover, those who were successful in quitting showed significant improvement in mood, whereas mood ratings deteriorated in those who resumed smoking. Another larger study found that an individualized, stepped care approach to treatment based on the patient's readiness to quit was more effective than self-help materials for smokers currently receiving outpatient treatment for major depressive disorder.

Clinical and Research Implications

This brief review of the literature on smoking and depression suggests several clinical implications and future directions for research. Depressive and negative affect symptoms are more predictive of smoking cessation outcome than is a previous disorder. Thus, depressive or negative affect symptoms should be assessed as part of routine clinical care for smokers, prior to treatment and during the quit attempt. Conversely, the assessment of smoking status history as part of the assessment and treatment of depression appears warranted.

The clinical practice guidelines on treatment of tobacco use indicate that the combination of behavioral treatment and pharmacotherapy is most effective for adult smoking cessation. Pharmacotherapy options (e.g., nicotine patch, buproprion) that are FDA approved for smoking cessation appear to be effective for smokers with or without depression history. The treatment could be augmented with CBT for smokers with recurrent major depressive disorder.

Future research is needed to determine the attributes that characterize the depression-vulnerable smokers who are at greatest risk for cessation failure. Potentially, more informative predictors that warrant investigation are major depressive disorder episode duration or recency. For example, remnant mood alterations from a recent episode (e.g., in the past 6 months) might place a smoker at increased risk for cessation failure compared with an episode that occurred 5 or more years ago. Although individuals with current major depressive disorder and/or who are taking an antidepressant medication are typically excluded from clinical trials of smoking cessation, providers are likely to see these types of patients in their practice. Thus, more research on best practices for this subgroup of smokers is warranted. Alternative behavioral treatments found to be effective in the treatment of depression, including exercise, warrant exploration in depressed smokers. Additional studies are also needed to understand the causal mechanisms underlying the smoking-depression relationship. Such research is important as each explanation has different and important implications for understanding nicotine dependence and depression, as well as the prevention of and treatment for each disorder.

CHRISTI A. PATTEN AND TABETHA BROCKMAN

See also

Heart Disease
Medical Conditions and Depression

References

American Psychiatric Association. (1994). *Diagnostic and statistical manual of mental disorders* (4th ed.). Washington, DC: Author.

Choi, W. S., Patten, C. A., Gillin, J. C., Kaplan, R. M., & Pierce, J. P. (1997). Cigarette smoking predicts development of depressive symptoms among U.S. adolescents. *Annals of Behavioral Medicine, 19*, 42–50.

Glassman, A. H., Stetner, F., Walsh, B. T., Raizman, P. S., Fleiss, J. L., Cooper, T. B., et al. (1988). Heavy smokers, smoking cessation, and clonidine: Results of a double-blind, randomized trial. *Journal of the American Medical Association, 269*, 2863–2866.

Hayford, K. E., Patten, C. A., Rummans, T. A., Schroeder, D. R., Offord, K. P., Croghan, I. T., et al. (1999). Efficacy of bupropion for smoking cessation in smokers with a former history of major depression or alcoholism. *British Journal of Psychiatry, 174*, 173–178.

Hitsman, B., Borelli, B., McChargue, D. E., Spring, B., & Niaura, R. (2003). History of depression and smoking cessation outcome: A meta-analysis. *Journal of Consulting and Clinical Psychology, 4*, 657–663.

Kendler, K. S., Neale, M. C., MacLean, C. J., Heath, A. C., Eaves, L. J., & Kessler, R. C. (1993). Smoking and major depression: A causal analysis. *Archives of General Psychiatry, 50*, 36–43.

Lasser, K., Boyd, J. W., Woolhandler, S., Himmelstein, D. U., McCormick, D., & Bor, D. H. (2000). Smoking and mental illness: a population-based prevalence study. *Journal of the American Medical Association, 284*, 2606–2610.

Social Support

Social support refers to the aid provided by others to those facing stressful events. This can include material aid, for example, financial assistance or help with daily tasks; relevant information intended to help the individual cope with current difficulties; or the opportunity for emotional expression and venting (e.g., House & Kahn, 1985). Typically, communal relationships within an individual's social network are the sources for social support. Support is typically measured with one of several self-report instruments or through structured interviews. It has been assessed in terms of both the support a person has received over a defined period, and the perception that social resources would be available if needed.

Research conducted over the last 40 years has consistently shown that lower levels of perceived social support are associated with increased symptoms and/or rates of depression. In contrast, the literature examining received social support has yielded either null findings or found increased depression with increased received support (Bolger, Zuckerman, & Kessler, 2000; Cohen & Wills, 1985). That received social support is sometimes associated with increased depression may merely indicate that it is those who are most in need (under stress, experiencing negative emotions) who actually mobilize their social networks.

The majority of studies examining perceived social support and depression are cross-sectional in design. Paykel and Cooper (1992) provide an in-depth review of 24 (of the now more than 30) cross-sectional studies. An association between lower levels of depression and reporting greater perceived social support has been found within both community and inpatient populations, across a wide range of ages, and for both men and women. This association is independent of whether support is assessed by self-report instruments or structured interviews. Inherent to the nature of cross-sectional designs, these investigations provide poor temporal resolution and do not provide information on the direction of causality. That is, while low levels of perceived support may result in more depression, it is just as likely that higher levels of depressive symptoms result in decreased ability to create and maintain a supportive social network, or a negative bias in interpreting and/or reporting whether support is available. Moreover, third (spurious) factors such as demographic differences or personality characteristics might actually be the causal factor influencing both depression and support.

By design, prospective studies addressing the role of support in depression eliminate the interpretation that an association is attributable to depression influencing social support. They accomplish this by assessing support first and predicting subsequent changes in depression. These studies also typically control for potentially confounding demographic and environmental factors such as age, sex, race or ethnicity, and socioeconomic status. The prospective literature suggests a similar positive influence of perceived support throughout the course of a depressive episode (reviewed by Paykel and Cooper, 1992; also see subsequent studies including Bruce & Hoff, 1994; Brummett, Barefoot, Siegler, & Steffens, 2000; Stice, Ragan, & Randall, 2004). At a subclinical level, lower perceived social support consistently predicts future elevated symptoms of depression within community samples. Clinically, lower social support is identified as a risk factor for the incidence of major depressive disorder. One investigation provides additional insight by demonstrating that lower parental social support and not lower peer social support yields elevated rates of onset for depression within adolescents (Stice et al., 2004). Within depressed individuals, lower baseline levels of social support predict subsequent increases in symptom severity, prolonged persistence of depressive episodes, and decreased responsiveness to pharmacotherapy.

The literature examining social support and depression continues to expand, in part, through studies considering this relationship within the context of various physical ailments. For example, within patients with type 2 diabetes (Connell, Davis, Gallant, & Sharpe, 1994; Zhang, Chen, & Chen, 2008) and breast (Koopman, Hermanson, Diamond, Angell, & Spiegel, 1998) and head and neck cancer (de Leeuw et al., 2000), higher levels of perceived social support are associated with decreased symptoms of depression.

Mechanistically, there are two potential pathways through which social support may influence depression: (a) a main effect mechanism and (b) an interactive (stress-buffering) mechanism (Cohen, 2004; Cohen & Wills, 1985). Stress-buffering suggests that social support protects persons from the potentially pathogenic influences of stressful events. For instance, social support enables individuals to acquire less-negative interpretations of potentially stressful events or to improve opinions of their abilities to overcome stressful events. In turn these changes allow for more beneficial emotional and physiological responses to events. In contrast, the main effect mechanism does not assume that one must be facing a stressful event to benefit from social support. The argument here is that social relations improve health-related behavior, increase positive psychological states, enhance emotional regulation, and promote beneficial functioning of the autonomic nervous system, hypothalamic-pituitary-adrenal axis, and immune system irrespective of whether someone is stressed (Cohen, 2004).

Although there is some evidence that perceived support operates as a stress-buffer in helping to prevent stress-elicited depression (Brown & Harris, 1978), in general, little attention has been paid to distinguishing between main effect and interactive mechanisms in this literature.

As a natural extension of the epidemiologic literature, researchers have evaluated interventions designed to increase perceived social support in hopes of decreasing depression. For instance, among chronically depressed individuals, a volunteer befriending intervention was associated with recovery from and improvement of depression (Harris, Brown, & Robinson, 1999). This randomized controlled trial utilized a waiting-list control design, and the intervention consisted of trained volunteers who met with and talked to the depressed individuals for a minimum of 1 hour per week over an 18-month period. Similarly, interpersonal psychotherapy (IPT) that is intended to enhance social skills and to minimize interpersonal deficits by fostering social support has become an accepted psychotherapeutic treatment for depressed individuals. De Mello, de Jesus Mari, Bacaltchuk, Verdeli, and Neugebauer (2005) provide a review of the 13 randomized controlled trials that examined the effectiveness of IPT in the treatment of depression. Consistently, IPT has proven to be more efficacious than either placebo or cognitive behavioral therapy, a more widely utilized psychotherapeutic technique.

For patients with coronary artery disease, however, the utility of social support intervention is less established both in regard to the treatment of depression and the depression-associated risk for cardiac morbidity and mortality. For instance, in an early randomized trial that facilitated social support for cardiac patients through repeated telephone calls and visits to the patients' homes by nurses (with no training in mental health), the intervention failed to reduce depression and for women fostered increased cardiac mortality (Frasure-Smith et al., 1997). This heightened mortality rate following the intervention may have resulted from increased distress associated with either home visits and/or the inability of patients to utilize denial as a coping method when faced with repeated reminders of their worsening coronary artery disease. Similarly, within a recent randomized control trial of cardiac patients with major depressive disorder, IPT lowered symptoms of depression but failed to yield significantly greater reductions than standard clinical management (Lesperance et al., 2007). One investigation, however, has utilized cognitive behavioral therapy as well as structured therapy sessions aimed at increasing perceived social support; it yielded decreased rates of depressive symptoms and increased reports of social support (Berkman et al., 2003). Unfortunately, the intervention did not change cardiac morbidity or mortality when compared to the control group. Overall, the mixed efficacy and potential harm of social support interventions in patients with coronary artery disease highlights the need for continued research that utilizes sound theoretical frameworks, interventionists with rigorous mental health training, and continuous assessments of the psychological well-being of the participants.

In sum, an extensive literature comprises both cross-sectional and prospective investigations and reveals that lower levels of perceived social support predict various aspects of depression from onset, through symptom severity, to remission and recurrence. This relation exists within community samples and inpatient populations, and in the context of various physical ailments. Mechanistically, social support may influence the various depression outcomes through both main-effect and stress-buffering pathways; the specific psychosocial, behavioral, and physiological pathways between social support and depression, however, remain poorly defined. The small but growing intervention literature demonstrates the potential ability to decrease depression through fostering social support. Future research should examine more closely the specific aspects of social support (i.e., instrumental, informative, and emotional) that are most predictive of depression and the precise mechanisms linking these two phenomena. This in-depth research would yield improved theoretical models that would further enhance and tailor social support interventions to decrease all aspects of the course of depression.

JEFFREY HORENSTEIN AND SHELDON COHEN

See also

Heart Disease
Medical Conditions and Depression
Risk
Stress and Coping
Stressful Life Events

References

Berkman, L. F., Blumenthal, J., Burg, M., Carney, R. M., Catellier, D., Cowan, M. J., et al. (2003). Effects of treating depression and low perceived social support on clinical events after myocardial infarction: The Enhancing Recovery in Coronary Heart Disease Patients (ENRICHD) Randomized Trial. *Journal of the American Medical Association, 289,* 3106–3116.

Bolger, N., Zuckerman, A., & Kessler, R. C. (2000). Invisible support and adjustment to stress. *Journal of Personality and Social Psychology, 79,* 953–961.

Brown, G. W., & Harris, T. (1978). *Social origins in depression: A study of psychiatric disorder in women.* New York: Free Press.

Bruce, M. L., & Hoff, R. A. (1994). Social and physical health risk factors for first-onset major depressive disorder in a community sample. *Social Psychiatry and Psychiatric Epidemiology, 29,* 165–171.

Brummett, B. H., Barefoot, J. C., Siegler, I. C., & Steffens, D. C. (2000). Relation of subjective and received social support to clinical and self-report assessments of depressive symptoms in an elderly population. *Journal of Affective Disorders, 61,* 41–50.

Cohen, S. (2004). Social relationships and health. *American Psychologist, 59,* 676–684.

Cohen, S., & Wills, T. A. (1985). Stress, social support, and the buffering hypothesis. *Psychological Bulletin, 98,* 310–357.

Connell, C. M., Davis, W. K., Gallant, M. P., & Sharpe, P. A. (1994). Impact of social support, social cognitive variables, and perceived threat on depression among adults with diabetes. *Health Psychology, 13,* 263–273.

de Leeuw, J. R., de Graeff, A., Ros, W. J., Blijham, G. H., Hordijk, G. J., & Winnubst, J. A. (2000). Prediction of depressive symptomatology after treatment of head and neck cancer: The influence of pre-treatment physical and depressive symptoms, coping, and social support. *Head and Neck, 22,* 799–807.

de Mello, M. F., de Jesus Mari, J., Bacaltchuk, J., Verdeli, H., & Neugebauer, R. (2005). A systematic review of research findings on the efficacy of interpersonal therapy for depressive disorders. *European Archives of Psychiatry and Clinical Neuroscience, 255,* 75–82.

Frasure-Smith, N., Lesperance, F., Prince, R. H., Verrier, P., Garber, R. A., Juneau, M., et al. (1997). Randomised trial of home-based psychosocial nursing intervention for patients recovering from myocardial infarction. *Lancet, 350,* 473–479.

Harris, T., Brown, G. W., & Robinson, R. (1999). Befriending as an intervention for chronic depression among women in an inner city, 1: Randomised controlled trial. *British Journal of Psychiatry, 174,* 219–224.

House, J. S., & Kahn, R. L. (1985). Measures and concepts of social support. In S. Cohen & S. L. Syme (Eds.), *Social support and health* (pp. 83–108). New York: Academic Press.

Koopman, C., Hermanson, K., Diamond, S., Angell, K., & Spiegel, D. (1998). Social support, life stress, pain, and emotional adjustment to advanced breast cancer. *Psychooncology, 7,* 101–111.

Lesperance, F., Frasure-Smith, N., Koszycki, D., Laliberte, M. A., van Zyl, L. T., Baker, B., et al. (2007). Effects of citalopram and interpersonal psychotherapy on depression in patients with coronary artery disease: The Canadian Cardiac Randomized Evaluation of Antidepressant and Psychotherapy Efficacy (CREATE) Trial. *Journal of the American Medical Association, 297,* 367–379.

Paykel, E. S., & Cooper, Z. C. (1992). Life events and social support. In E. S. Paykel (Ed.), *Handbook of affective disorders* (2nd ed.) (pp. 149–170). Edinburgh, Scotland: Churchill Livingstone.

Stice, E., Ragan, J., & Randall, P. (2004). Prospective relations between social support and depression: Differential direction of effects for parent and peer support? *Journal of Abnormal Psychology, 113,* 155–159.

Zhang, C. X., Chen, Y. M., & Chen, W. Q. (2008). Association of psychosocial factors with anxiety and depressive symptoms in Chinese patients with type 2 diabetes. *Diabetes Research and Clinical Practice, 9,* 523–530.

Stress and Coping

Responses to stress include a broad array of intertwined physiological, cognitive, emotional, and behavioral processes, which may be initiated automatically or volitionally. Automatic responses, rooted in biology or conditioned responses, may facilitate or disrupt effortful coping, and volitional coping responses are often geared toward regulation of involuntary stress reactivity. Early research on responses to stress emphasized dispositional responses and stable defense mechanisms, largely ignoring situational influences on coping. Coping research was transformed in the 1970s and 1980s with the transactional model developed by Richard Lazarus and Susan Folkman, who defined coping as "constantly changing cognitive and behavioral efforts to manage specific external and/or internal demands that are appraised as taxing or exceeding the resources of the person" (Lazarus & Folkman, 1984, p. 141). The transactional model emphasizes that coping is a volitional, goal-directed process, with responses expected to vary across stressors and over the course of a single stressor, depending on appraisals of the situation, contextual demands, and available resources.

Although most current models limit the definition of coping to conscious, volitional efforts to regulate thoughts, feelings, behaviors, or physiological arousal in stressful situations, consensus about optimal boundaries between such related concepts as self-regulation and stress reactivity has not yet been reached (Compas, Connor-Smith, Saltzman, Thomsen, & Wadsworth, 2001). In practical terms, it is often difficult to determine whether a response to stress is fully volitional (Skinner, Edge, Altman, & Sherwood, 2003), with ongoing disagreement about whether responses such as rumination represent involuntary processes or volitional strategies.

Key Coping Dimensions

The most commonly used higher-order coping dimensions are problem- or emotion-focused coping, engagement-disengagement coping, and primary- and secondary-control coping (see Compas et al., 2001; Skinner et al., 2003, for reviews). Less common distinctions include cognitive-behavioral, active-passive, beneficial-harmful, self-externally focused, and sensitization-repression coping. Coping dimensions have many areas of overlap, with problem solving classifiable as problem focused, primary control, engagement, active, or beneficial coping.

Problem- and Emotion-Focused Coping

This distinction emphasizes the target of the coping response and is the basis for the two most commonly used coping measures, the Ways of Coping Questionnaire and its variants (Folkman & Lazarus, 1985), and the COPE (Carver, Scheier, & Weintraub,

1989). Problem-focused responses, such as gathering information, planning, and implementing solutions, are intended to change the stressor directly, whereas emotion-focused responses, such as emotional expression, seeking support, and avoidance, are intended to minimize negative emotions. Although this distinction helped usher in the era of modern coping research, it is does not appear fundamental to the structure of coping, as many coping responses are simultaneously problem and emotion focused. For example, an individual may plan responses to a stressor both to resolve the problem and to decrease distress. The emotion-focused category is also quite broad and includes strategies that are negatively correlated with one another (Austenfeld & Stanton, 2004). Emotion-focused strategies such as relaxation and seeking support typically predict positive outcomes, whereas avoidance, venting, and aggression, may be symptoms or causes of distress (Compas et al., 2001).

Engagement-Disengagement Coping

Engagement-disengagement coping focuses on an individual's orientation to the stressor and is related to the narrower distinctions between approach-avoidance, and monitoring-blunting. Engagement coping involves orientation toward the stressor through active attempts to manage the situation or associated emotions, whereas disengagement coping involves distancing oneself from the stressor or related emotions through strategies such as avoidance, denial, and withdrawal. Although distraction has historically been considered a form of disengagement, confirmatory factor analyses consistently find superior fit for models placing it on an engagement factor, perhaps because distraction also involves active engagement with positive thoughts and activities (Skinner et al., 2003). The engagement-disengagement distinction has been criticized for ignoring the goal of coping, and for confounding engagement with "good" coping and disengagement with "bad" coping. Measures of engagement coping typically omit strategies likely to be harmful, such as confronting others, and measures of disengagement often include negative emotional expression items more appropriately categorized as engagement responses (Skinner et al., 2003).

Primary- and Secondary-Control Coping

Primary- and secondary-control coping emphasizes the goal of coping and is related assimilative-accommodative coping. Primary-control responses are efforts to directly influence the stressor or related emotions through strategies such as problem solving, emotional expression, or relaxation, whereas secondary-control coping responses are efforts to adapt to the stressor through strategies such as positive thinking or acceptance. Although secondary control was initially conceptualized as a means of maintaining perceived control in uncontrollable situations, more recent conceptualizations describe secondary control as a means of maximizing fit with the environment (Morling & Evered, 2006).

Hierarchical Models of Responses to Stress

All of the major higher-order coping dimensions have been critiqued for a failure to represent the full range of coping responses, and for grouping unrelated strategies together (Compas et al., 2001). Confirmatory factor analyses consistently indicate that no one dimension is sufficient to represent the structure of coping, and there is growing agreement that a hierarchical, multidimensional structure will best represent the structure of responses to stress. Compas and colleagues proposed a three-tiered model, with a primary distinction between involuntary stress responses and voluntary coping, a secondary distinction between engagement and disengagement responses, and a tertiary

distinction of voluntary engagement coping into primary- or secondary-control responses. This hierarchical model results in two broad involuntary stress response categories, and three broad coping categories. Involuntary engagement includes responses such as emotional and physiological arousal and intrusive thoughts; involuntary disengagement includes emotional numbing and uncontrolled flight. Primary-control engagement coping includes strategies such as problem solving, emotional expression, seeking support, and emotional regulation that involve active attempts to change the stressor or related emotions. Problem-focused coping fits within this broad family. Secondary-control engagement coping includes strategies such as acceptance, cognitive restructuring, humor, positive thinking, or distraction to aid adaptation to stress. Disengagement coping includes strategies such as avoidance, denial, wishful thinking, and withdrawal. Because emotion-focused coping includes a range of controlled and uncontrolled processes, specific emotion-focused strategies are distributed across all five stress-response categories. Confirmatory factor analyses of a measure designed to fit this hierarchical structure, and of other coping measures, show consistent support for this basic model across samples, stressors, and cultures (Connor-Smith, Compas, Wadsworth, Thomsen, & Saltzman, 2000; review by Skinner et al., 2003).

Issues in Coping Assessment

Our understanding of coping has been hampered by lack of consensus about the structure of coping, along with overreliance on cross-sectional self-report studies of dispositional coping. Currently, there are over 100 published coping categorization schemes, including more than 400 basic coping strategies (Skinner et al., 2003). Exploratory factor analyses of the most commonly used measures have produced several different sets of subscales and higher-order factors, leading to multiple scoring schemes for many measures (Compas et al., 2001). Because this lack of consistency makes it extremely difficult to compare findings across studies, the emphasis is shifting to theory-based measure development and confirmatory, rather than exploratory, factor analyses.

Study designs have also been a poor match with coping theory. Optimal coping is thought to involve matching coping strategy selection and timing to the specific demands of a stressor, but the coping literature consists mainly of cross-sectional studies of dispositional coping. Assessment of how people cope in general obscures relations between coping and adjustment because the risks and benefits of specific coping strategies depend on circumstances. A similar problem arises in studies of situation-specific coping in which each participant selects his or her own stressor. Aggregation of responses across stressors ranging from flat tires to bereavement is unlikely to provide a clear picture of relations between coping and adjustment. Assessing responses to a single stressor or domain of stress that is consistent across participants will best reveal relations between coping and adjustment. Cross-sectional designs are problematic because stress both prompts coping and causes distress, potentially leading to spurious correlations between coping and symptoms, and because short and long-term consequences of coping differ. For example, writing about negative emotions increases distress temporarily but produces emotional and physical health benefits over time (Lepore & Smyth, 2002).

Finally, few studies have assessed coping with observational or multiple-informant approaches, which is problematic, because self-reports of coping are biased by social desirability, poor recall, degree of problem resolution at the time of the report, omission of unsuccessful strategies, and difficulty aggregating responses over time and across stressors (see review by Compas et al., 2001). Further, self-reports indicate only that a strategy was used, not whether it was implemented skillfully. Findings based on prospective designs, daily or momentary reports, standardized laboratory stressors, observations, and multiple informants should be weighted more heavily than those from cross-sectional designs.

Influences on Coping

The selection, implementation, and impact of coping responses depend not only on the nature of the stressor, but also on factors such as age, gender, culture, and personality.

Age

In infants, responses to stress are simple, reflexive actions such as turning away or crying, which protect the child by limiting exposure to aversive stimuli or by enlisting adult help. More complex coping develops through experience, with behavioral strategies preceding cognitive strategies, which require more sophisticated language and metacognitive abilities. Although behavioral distraction and support-seeking begin in early childhood, cognitive distraction and cognitive problem solving are infrequent. These cognitive strategies increase in frequency and sophistication starting in middle childhood, with complex cognitive strategies such as proactive planning emerging in adolescence. The shape of coping responses also changes with age. Seeking adult support starts declining in early to middle childhood, as seeking peer support increases, along with the capacity to accurately match sources of support to the nature of the problem (see review by Skinner & Zimmer-Gembeck, 2007).

Culture

Across cultures, common stressors, available resources, event appraisals, and acceptability of various stress responses are likely to differ, potentially influencing coping. Although the structure of coping and core coping strategies appear relatively consistent across European and American samples (Connor-Smith & Calvete, 2004; Gelhaar et al., 2007), few studies have explored coping in Asian samples. Comparisons of coping structure across cultures are complicated by the fact that multiple coping dimensions and structures have been identified within each culture. Frequency and efficacy of coping strategy use may differ across cultures, with hints that secondary control coping may be more common and beneficial in collectivist cultures, and primary control more common and beneficial in individualistic cultures (Morling & Evered, 2006).

Personality

Personality may influence both the selection of coping strategies and the impact of those strategies. Meta-analytic findings link neuroticism to more wishful thinking, withdrawal, and emotion-focused coping, extraversion to problem solving and support-seeking, and conscientiousness to problem solving and cognitive restructuring (Connor-Smith & Flachsbart, 2007). Personality may also influence the quality of coping, with conscientious individuals more skilled at planning and implementing solutions, and extraverted individuals more skilled at obtaining support. Finally, personality may influence coping effectiveness, with the benefits of strategies differing across individuals. For example, daily report studies suggest that escape-avoidance increases depressed mood for individuals low in neuroticism but is unrelated to mood for those high in neuroticism (Bolger & Zuckerman, 1995).

Gender

Gender differences in coping may arise because men and women experience different stressors, appraise similar stressors differently, are socialized to use different responses, or experience different outcomes. Although gender differences in coping are small, females report using more of almost all strategies, in part due to higher appraisals of stress (Connor-Smith et al., 2000; Tamres, Janicki, & Helgeson, 2002). The largest gender differences are seen for strategies involving a focus on emotions, such as seeking emotional support, ruminating, and using positive self-talk. On measures of relative coping (amount of one strategy divided by total coping), which account for the tendency of females to report more total coping, women remain more likely than men to seek emotional support, but men are more likely to use active coping (Tamres et al., 2002). Some studies suggest that gender moderates relations between coping and adjustment, with women benefiting more than men from support-seeking, and men benefiting more than women from problem-focused coping, but these findings are not consistent (Austenfeld & Stanton, 2004; Tamres et al., 2002).

Impact of Coping on Adjustment

Thousands of studies have investigated the impact of responses to stress on anxiety, depression, externalizing behaviors, and physical health. A smaller number have explored relations with positive outcomes, such as social competence or life satisfaction. Because research on involuntary responses to stress has emphasized responses such as physiological arousal, intrusive thoughts, and emotional numbing, automatic stress responses are typically linked to risk for psychological symptoms. However, many automatic stress responses, such as orienting attention away from subliminal threat cues, are likely to be beneficial.

Meta-analyses indicate that direct effects of coping on adjustment are relatively modest, with coping having a stronger impact on psychological outcomes than on physical health outcomes (Clarke, 2006; Penley, Tomaka, & Wiebe, 2002). However, cross-sectional studies of dispositional coping are not well suited to revealing the nuances of relations between coping and adjustment, as the impact of coping is moderated by factors such as age, gender, personality, and the controllability, duration, and domain of the stressor (Clarke, 2006; Penley et al., 2002). For example, accepting responsibility for problems is unrelated to outcomes for controllable stressors but predicts greater distress for uncontrollable stressors (Penley et al., 2002).

Engagement Coping

In general, problem-focused, engagement, primary-control and secondary-control coping are associated with better psychological adjustment and social competence (Clarke, 2006; Compas et al., 2001; Penley et al., 2002). Stressor controllability moderates the impact of primary-control coping, which is beneficial in response to controllable stressors but harmful in response to uncontrollable stressors (Clarke, 2006). Age also moderates the impact of primary-control coping, which is unrelated to distress in children, but protects against internalizing problems in adolescents, perhaps because adolescents implement strategies more skillfully.

Secondary control is linked to lower levels of distress across samples and cultures, for stressors including parental depression, financial problems, homesickness, and consequences of aging (see review by Morling & Evered, 2006). Distraction predicts low levels of intrusive thoughts, anxiety, and depression in both naturalistic and laboratory studies (Compas et al., 2001). However, acceptance coping in the absence of other secondary-control strategies occasionally shows detrimental effects, perhaps because it reflects resignation and hopelessness, rather than maximizing fit with the environment (Morling & Evered, 2006).

Disengagement Coping

Disengagement strategies such as distancing, escape-avoidance, and wishful thinking are associated with physiological arousal, intrusive thoughts, anxiety, and depression in laboratory and naturalistic studies (Compas et al., 2001; Penley et al., 2002). Stressor duration may moderate the impact of disengagement, as avoidant responses appear to be more problematic for acute stressors than for chronic stressors (Penley et al., 2002). Personality may also moderate the impact of disengagement, which may have fewer short-term costs for individuals high in neuroticism (Bolger & Zuckerman, 1995), perhaps because turning away from stress helps to reduce involuntary arousal. However, sustained disengagement in the absence of primary- or secondary-control coping predicts poor outcomes across personality traits and stressors.

Emotion-Focused Coping

Emotion focused coping is strongly linked to poor outcomes (Compas et al., 2001), with strategies such as confrontive coping, self-control, avoidance, and accepting responsibility predicting greater emotional distress and poorer physical health (Penley et al., 2002). However, this link between emotion-focused coping and distress is a result of items reflecting uncontrolled emotional expression, self-criticism, aggression, and avoidance on the original measures of emotion-focused coping. Newer measures that assess controlled strategies for understanding, regulating, and expressing emotions predict higher levels of hope and physical health, and lower levels of depression, anxiety, and physical pain (Austenfeld & Stanton, 2004; Connor-Smith et al., 2000). Benefits of emotional expression and regulation strategies are greatest when the stressor is perceived as uncontrollable or involves an interpersonal component (Austenfeld & Stanton, 2004).

Coping Skills Interventions

Many interventions for anxiety and depression include coping components, teaching skills such as problem solving, cognitive restructuring, positive thinking, relaxation, and self-soothing. Current knowledge about the impact of coping on adjustment suggests that simply teaching a wide assortment of coping skills and encouraging all individuals to cope in the same way is unlikely to produce the maximum benefit. Instead, depression prevention and intervention programs should consider the influence of age, culture, gender, and developmental capacity and help individuals to match coping responses to external demands (e.g., stressor severity and controllability) and to internal demands (e.g., personality, emotional arousal). An extraverted adolescent girl low in involuntary stress-reactivity may benefit most from seeking emotional support from friends and immediate use of problem solving, whereas a young boy high in involuntary stress-reactivity may need to regulate arousal through behavioral distraction before attempting to solve the problem with adult support.

JENNIFER K. CONNOR-SMITH

See also

Social Support
Stress Assessment
Stressful Life Events
Stress Generation

References

Austenfeld, J. L., & Stanton, A. L. (2004). Coping through emotional approach: A new look at emotion, coping, and health-related outcomes. *Journal of Personality, 72,* 1335–1363.

Bolger, N., & Zuckerman, A. (1995). A framework for studying personality in the stress process. *Journal of Personality and Social Psychology, 69,* 890–902.

Carver, C. S., Scheier, M. F., & Weintraub, J. K. (1989). Assessing coping strategies: A theoretically based approach. *Journal of Personality and Social Psychology, 56,* 267–283.

Clarke, A. T. (2006). Coping with interpersonal stress and psychosocial health among children and adolescents: A meta-analysis. *Journal of Youth and Adolescence, 35,* 11–24.

Compas, B. E., Connor-Smith, J. K., Saltzman, H., Thomsen, A. H., & Wadsworth, M. E. (2001). Coping with stress during childhood and adolescence: Progress, problems, and potential in theory and research. *Psychological Bulletin, 127,* 87–127.

Connor-Smith, J. K., & Calvete, E. (2004). Cross-cultural equivalence of coping and involuntary responses to stress in Spain and the United States. *Anxiety, Stress, and Coping, 17,* 163–185.

Connor-Smith, J. K., Compas, B. E., Wadsworth, M. E., Thomsen, A. H., & Saltzman, H. (2000). Responses to stress in adolescence: Measurement of coping and involuntary stress responses. *Journal of Consulting and Clinical Psychology, 68,* 976–992.

Connor-Smith, J. K., & Flachsbart, C. (2007). Relations between personality and coping: A meta-analysis. *Journal of Personality and Social Psychology, 93,* 1080–1107.

Folkman, S., & Lazarus, R. S. (1985). If it changes it must be a process: A study of emotion and coping during three stages of a college examination. *Journal of Personality and Social Psychology, 48,* 150–170.

Gelhaar, T., Seiffge-Krenke, I., Borge, A., Cicognani, E., Cunha, M., Loncaric, D., et al. (2007). Adolescent coping with everyday stressors: A seven-nation study of youth from central, eastern, southern, and northern Europe. *European Journal of Developmental Psychology, 4,* 129–156.

Lazarus, R. S., & Folkman, S. (1984). *Stress, appraisal, and coping.* New York: Springer.

Lepore, S. J., & Smyth, J. M. (Eds.). (2002). *The writing cure: How expressive writing promotes health and emotional well-being.* Washington, DC: American Psychological Association.

Morling, B., & Evered, S. (2006). Secondary control reviewed and defined. *Psychological Bulletin, 132,* 269–296.

Penley, J. A., Tomaka, J., & Wiebe, J. S. (2002). The association of coping to physical and psychological health outcomes: A meta-analytic review. *Journal of Behavioral Medicine, 25,* 551–603.

Skinner, E. A., Edge, K., Altman, J., & Sherwood, H. (2003). Searching for the structure of coping: A review and critique of category systems for classifying ways of coping. *Psychological Bulletin, 129,* 216–269.

Skinner, E. A., & Zimmer-Gembeck, M. J. (2007). The development of coping. *Annual Review of Psychology, 58,* 119–144.

Tamres, L. K., Janicki, D., & Helgeson, V. S. (2002). Sex differences in coping behavior: A meta-analytic review and an examination of relative coping. *Personality and Social Psychology Review, 6,* 2–30.

Stress Assessment

The role of stress in depression is a key conceptual question in understanding the etiology and course of depressive disorders. In general, it is broadly recognized that life stress plays a role in mood disorders (e.g., Hammen, 2005; Kessler, 1997; Mazure, 1998), but this role is influenced by key mediators (e.g., cognitive style; Monroe, Slavich, Torres, & Gotlib, 2007) and moderators (e.g., genetic predisposition; Caspi et al., 2003). Understanding these relationships is complicated by the fact that measurement of life stress is a difficult task. Invariably, stress reporting is a retrospective activity, vulnerable to biases directly related to the topic at hand (e.g., mood-influenced recall) as well as idiosyncratic influences. The challenge of defining stress has also been noted, with some scholars emphasizing the stress response, as in Seyle's (1956) general adaptation syndrome. Thus, a crucial preliminary issue in life stress assessment is the clear distinction between external events or conditions and the resulting internal stress response. Our focus here is on the assessment of environmental stress, for clarity referred to as *stressors*. Precision in making this distinction is vital to avoid confounding the stressors, the mediating and moderating influences, and the outcome of interest (depression symptoms).

Initial research on stress in mood disorders developed from studies showing that recent life events predicted a number of negative health outcomes (e.g., Rahe, Meyer, Smith, Kjaer, & Holmes, 1964). These studies used self-report questionnaires (e.g., Holmes & Rahe, 1967; Miller & Rahe, 1997) to measure the number of negative stressors in a preceding time period and generally demonstrated that increased numbers of stressors preceded negative health outcomes. When these self-report methodologies were applied to major depression, a similar pattern was found, with increased numbers of life stressors preceding the onset of major depression. However, self-report assessments suffer several clear structural and theoretical limitations. Initial measures confounded depression symptoms and stressors (e.g., including "changes in sleep" as an event). They also leave decisions as to what experiences get reported to the respondent. Therefore individual differences may lead to different respondents interpreting the items in very different ways, reducing the reliability of the measure (Gorman, 1993). In addition, understanding the timing of an event is critical in relation to the onset of disorder, and it is frequently difficult with self-report instruments to get a good assessment of whether stress preceded or followed symptom change.

Self-report questionnaires tend to also be based on several implicit or explicit assumptions about stress. The first is an additive model of stress impact. Most use some form of total score, either counting number of events, or weighted scores (e.g., adding up the values of the weights; 200 for divorce, 50 for being fired, etc.). This implies that the effects of stress on the likelihood of depression are linear, when it is possible that there are important qualitative factors (e.g., traumatic events) that differentially influence depression. Additionally, standard measures have

typically treated chronic stress in a manner similar to acute stress.

Alternative approaches to stress assessment have been developed by several groups, including Brown & Harris (1989), Hammen, Marks, Mayol, and DeMayo (1985), and others (e.g., Paykel, 1997). These are generally referred to as investigator-based approaches, because the goal is to have the investigator have control over the key theoretical data collection points. These measures involve an investigator conducting a semistructured interview to assess a broad domain of stressors and then probing with follow-up questions to gather information regarding important components (e.g., severity, focus, duration, date). Objective stressor information from the interview is then presented to a panel, excluding information about how the individual responded to the stressor and excluding any affect expressed during recall in the assessment. Whereas the individual's response to the stressor and affect are not considered, investigator approaches do often incorporate the context in which the stressor occurred. This constitutes another significant improvement over checklist measures, providing the ability to distinguish between events occurring in supportive circumstances (e.g., a child born to a couple with adequate financial resources and the desire to start a family) and less favorable contexts (e.g., the birth of a child to an unmarried teenager without financial resources). The panel then uses standardized criteria to rate each stressor on theoretically relevant dimensions, taking into account the individual's circumstances. As an example, the Brown and Harris method utilizes an extensive manual with over 500 pages of stressor examples and ratings (Bifulco et al., 1989). These procedures provide greater standardization for coding of stressors and, therefore, improve the reliability and validity of the data.

In general, comparisons between investigator-based interview methods and self-report checklist methods have found the former superior in predicting outcomes, enhancing accuracy of dating stressors, and reducing bias (Gorman, 1993; Katschnig, 1986; McQuaid,

Monroe, Roberts, Kupfer, & Frank, 2000; Simons, Angell, Monroe, & Thase, 1993). Thus, investigator-based interview methodologies have come to be considered the gold standard for life-stress assessment (Hammen, 2005). However, the greater precision comes with a price: the investigator-based interview methods require training for both interviewers and rating panels and are more labor intensive for both the interview and rating procedures.

Using these validated approaches, life events have been shown to predict increased risk for major depressive disorder (e.g., Brown & Harris, 1989; Kessler, 1997). In particular, the presence of one or more severe events significantly increases the risk of major depression. In addition, recent findings indicate that for patients with a previous episode of depression, the presence of one or more undesirable events increases the risk for the recurrence of depression for patients treated with pharmacotherapy, while patients not taking medication were less likely to have a recurrence if they experienced undesirable life stress (Monroe et al., 2006). Research findings are beginning to clarify the nature of increased risk associated with stressors and initial onset, treatment response, and recurrence of major depressive episodes (Daley, Hammen, & Rao, 2000; Monroe, Kupfer, & Frank, 1992).

An additional advantage of the greater detail afforded by investigator-based assessments includes distinguishing stressful events with a discrete date of occurrence (e.g., marital separation, fired from a job) from chronic ongoing stressors that persist for extended time periods (e.g., chronic marital discord, chronic financial problems). As previously noted, extensive depression research has focused on stressful events but has largely ignored the role of chronic stressors, with a few exceptions (Brown & Harris, 1978; Daley, Hammen, & Rao, 2000; McGonagle & Kessler, 1990; Monroe et al., 2007). Results of these studies suggest that neglect of chronic stressors needs to be remedied. McGonagle and Kessler (1990) found that chronic stressors were generally more strongly related to

depressive symptoms than acute stressors. In this study, an interaction between chronic and acute stress was detected that suggested "that the joint occurrence of both stress types is associated with less depression than one would predict based on an additive model" (p. 691). Monroe and colleagues (2007) observed that severe events were more likely among individuals with fewer lifetime depressive episodes, whereas severe chronic difficulties were more likely among those with a history of more depressive episodes. In contrast, chronic difficulties were associated with initial onset, but not recurrence, of depressive episodes in a study of young women (Daley, Hammen, & Rao, 2000). Comparison across the limited investigations of chronic stressors is complicated by substantially differing lengths of time required for designation as chronic, with periods as short as 4 weeks and as long as 2 years utilized in different studies. Nevertheless, these intriguing results suggest that chronic stressors are an important area in need of replication and future research despite the associated challenges.

Stressor characteristics may play a role not only in depression onset and recurrence, but also in recovery from depressive episodes. Again, this literature is scant but worthy of consideration. In a small female sample, Brown, Adler, and Bifulco (1988) examined depression remission in relation to reductions in chronic difficulties or the experience of what they termed a "fresh start" event, defined as a stress event that either reduced a chronic difficulty level or "gave promise of a better future" (p. 490). As examples of fresh start events, they described a positive outcome of a serious surgery, and procuring a legal injunction against an abusive spouse. More women with a fresh start event or chronic difficulty reduction recovered from their depressive episode compared to women without these stressor experiences. These findings are consistent with another study reporting a modest depression remission effect in response to experiencing a neutralizing event, an event that neutralized the consequences of a prior event or difficulty (Tennant, Bebbington, & Hurry, 1981).

We have noted the importance of accurate dating of stressors in order to establish causal links between the experience of a stressor and subsequent depression symptoms. However, accurate assessment of the temporal relationship between stressors and depression also allows for examining whether depression increases the likelihood of experiencing subsequent stressors, termed *stress generation* (Hammen, 1991). Women with unipolar depression reported more interpersonal stress events (e.g., conflicts, changes in relationships) compared to women with no disorder, a medical disorder, or bipolar disorder (Hammen, 1991). Additionally, the stressors were rated for whether the individual contributed, at least in part, to the occurrence of the event, and the depression group reported more of these events. Other research has also supported this stress-generation hypothesis (Cui & Vaillant, 1997; Harkness & Luther, 2001; Harkness, Monroe, Simons, & Thase, 1999). Thus, the stressor-depression relationship appears to be bidirectional.

Stressor research findings are influenced by several important factors. A recent large epidemiological study demonstrated that the relationship of stress to depression was moderated by genotype (Caspi et al., 2003). In particular, the serotonin transporter gene has been associated with variability in stress reactivity. Individuals with two short alleles were found to have a higher likelihood of depression as level of stress increased, whereas for those with two long alleles the risk of depression did not vary with level of stress. Heterozygous individuals had a pattern between the two homozygous groups.

In summary, assessment of life stress is important for both researchers and clinicians in the depression field. Although well documented, the relationship between stressors and depression is complex, with specific characteristics of stressors tied to depression onset and recurrence, as well as remission. Stressor assessment using investigator-based interview approaches is suggested to better capture the detailed characteristics and temporal relationship of stressors to depression symptoms. Continued research is needed in this area to further elucidate the role of moderators and mediators impacting the life stress–depression relationship.

SUSAN R. TATE AND JOHN R. MCQUAID

See also

Stress and Coping
Stressful Life Events
Stress Generation

References

Bifulco, A., Brown, G. W., Edwards, A., Harris, T., Neilson, E., Richards, C., et al. (1989). *Bedford College Life Events and Difficulties Schedule*. London: Royal Holloway and Bedford New College.

Brown, G. W., Adler, Z., & Bifulco, A. (1988). Life events, difficulties and recovery from chronic depression. *British Journal of Psychiatry, 152*, 487–498.

Brown, G. W., & Harris, T. O. (1978). *Social origins of depression: A study of psychiatric disorder in women*. New York: Free Press.

Brown, G. W., & Harris, T. O. (1989). Life events and psychiatric illness: Depression. In G. W. Brown & T. O. Harris (Eds.), *Life events and illness* (pp. 49–93). New York: Guilford Press.

Caspi, A., Sugden, K., Moffitt, T. E., Taylor, A., Craig, I. W., Harrington, H., et al. (2003). Influence of life stress on depression: Moderation by a polymorphism in the 5-HTT gene. *Science, 301*, 386–389.

Cui, X.-J., & Vaillant, G. E. (1997). Does depression generate negative life events? *Journal of Nervous and Mental Disease, 185*, 145–150.

Daley, S. E., Hammen, C., & Rao, U. (2000). Predictors of first onset and recurrence of major depression in young women during the 5 years following high school graduation. *Journal of Abnormal Psychology, 109*, 525–533.

Gorman, D. M. (1993). A review of studies comparing checklist and interview methods of data collection in life event research. *Behavioral Medicine, 19*, 66–73.

Hammen, C. (1991). Generation of stress in the course of unipolar depression (1991). *Journal of Abnormal Psychology, 100*, 555–561.

Hammen, C. (2005). Stress and depression. *Annual Review of Clinical Psychology, 1*, 293–319.

Hammen, C., Marks, T., Mayol, A., & DeMayo, R. (1985). Depressive self-schemas, life stress, and vulnerability to depression. *Journal of Abnormal Psychology, 94*, 308–319.

Harkness, K. L., & Luther, J. (2001). Clinical risk factors for the generation of life events in major depression. *Journal of Abnormal Psychology, 110*, 564–572.

Harkness, K. L., Monroe, S. M., Simons, A. D., & Thase, M. (1999). The generation of life events in recurrent and non-recurrent depression. *Psychological Medicine, 29,* 135–144.

Holmes, T. H., & Rahe, R. H. (1967). The Social Readjustment Rating Scale. *Journal of Psychosomatic Research, 11,* 213–218.

Katschnig, H. (1986). Measuring life stress: A comparison of the checklist and the panel technique. In H. Katschnig (Ed.), *Life events and psychiatric disorders: Controversial issues* (pp. 74–106). Cambridge, England: Cambridge University Press.

Kessler, R. C. (1997). The effects of stressful life events on depression. *Annual Review of Psychology, 48,* 191–214.

Mazure, C. M. (1998). Life stressors as risk factors in depression. *Clinical Psychology, Science and Practice, 5,* 291–313.

McGonagle, K. A., & Kessler, R. C. (1990). Chronic stress, acute stress, and depressive symptoms. *American Journal of Community Psychology, 18,* 681–706.

McQuaid, J. R., Monroe, S. M., Roberts, J. E., Kupfer, D. J., & Frank, E. (2000). A comparison of two life stress assessment approaches: Prospective prediction of treatment outcome in recurrent depression. *Journal of Abnormal Psychology, 109,* 787–791.

Miller, M. A., & Rahe, R. H. (1997). Life changes scaling for the 1990s. *Journal of Psychosomatic Research, 43,* 279–292.

Monroe, S. M., Kupfer, D. J., & Frank, E. (1992). Life stress and treatment course of recurrent depression, 1: Response during index episode. *Journal of Consulting and Clinical Psychology, 60,* 718–724.

Monroe, S. M., Slavich, G. M., Torres, L. D., & Gotlib, I. H. (2007). Major life events and major chronic difficulties are differentially associated with history of major depressive episodes. *Journal of Abnormal Psychology, 116,* 116–124.

Monroe, S. M., Torres, L. D., Guillaumot, J., Harkness, K. L., Roberts, J. E., Frank, E., et al. (2006). Life stress and the long-term treatment course of recurrent depression, 3: Nonsevere life events predict recurrence for medicated patients over 3 years. *Journal of Consulting and Clinical Psychology, 74,* 112–120.

Paykel, E. S. (1997). The interview for recent life events. *Psychological Medicine, 27,* 301–310.

Rahe, R. H., Meyer, M., Smith, M., Kjaer, G., & Holmes, T. H. (1964). Social stress and illness onset. *Journal of Psychosomatic Research, 8,* 35–44.

Seyle, H. (1956). *The stress of life.* New York: McGraw-Hill.

Simons, A. D., Angell, K. L., Monroe, S. M., & Thase, M. E. (1993). Cognition and life stress in depression: Cognitive factors and the definition, ratings, and generation of negative life events. *Journal of Abnormal Psychology, 102,* 584–591.

Tennant, C., Bebbington, P., & Hurry, J. (1981). The short-term outcome of neurotic disorders in the community: The relation of remission to clinical factors and to "neutralising" life events. *British Journal of Psychiatry, 139,* 213–220.

Stressful Life Events

From the break-up of one's marriage or the loss of a close friend, to getting fired from one's job or losing one's home, to finding out one's partner has terminal cancer or experiencing the death of a parent, stressful life events tax our psychological and physical resources and can cause significant increases in sadness, anxiety, and irritability. In the long-term, most people are resilient in the face of even very severe stress and do not suffer lasting psychological effects. For a significant minority, however, stressful life events can trigger a downward spiral into major depression. Research on the role of life events in major depression has focused on the following three questions: (a) What are the characteristics of life events that are most strongly associated with major depression? (b) What are the characteristics of individuals that place them at risk for developing major depression in the face of life events? (c) What are the characteristics of individuals that confer resilience in the face of life events?

Characteristics of Life Events Associated With Major Depression

Life events are strongly related to major depression. A very large number of studies conducted over the last 40 years have consistently demonstrated that significantly more individuals with major depression have at least one negative life event, and have significantly more events, prior to onset than nondepressed individuals in a comparable time period. Indeed, summarizing across these studies, individuals with depression were nearly 3 times more likely than those without to have experienced a stressful life event prior to onset (Mazure, 1998).

Researchers have determined that (a) "severe" life events and (b) events involving themes of loss are of prime relevance to depression (Brown & Harris, 1989). Severe events are associated with a high degree of psychological threat, and their impact is still severe 2 weeks after the event. Examples of severe loss events include finding that one's spouse of 20 years has moved out, or learning that one's father has died suddenly of a heart attack. The importance of severe loss events is demonstrated powerfully in the results of a large study conducted in the United Kingdom (Brown & Harris, 1989): among individuals with no stressful life events, only 1% developed major depression in the subsequent 3 to 6 months, and among those with a nonseverely stressful event, only 6% developed depression. In contrast, among those with a severe loss event, over 5 times as many individuals (32%) subsequently developed depression. In this and similar studies, close to 75% of individuals with major depression have been found to have suffered at least one severe loss event in the 3 to 6 months prior to their depression onset. Therefore, nonseverely stressful life events (e.g., a friend moves away) and/ or events that do not involve themes of loss (e.g., notice of eviction), while arguably still very unpleasant, do not appear to pack the psychological punch necessary to precipitate major depression.

Characteristics That Confer Vulnerability to Stressful Life Events

Researchers have discovered that certain individuals possess characteristics that predispose them to be more sensitive to the effects of stressful life events. These risk characteristics, or diatheses, serve to moderate the effect of life events such that individuals with the diathesis (a) are more likely to develop major depression in the face of severe life events and (b) require a lower severity level of stress to trigger depression than those without (Monroe & Simons, 1991). In other words, these individuals' threshold for reacting to stress with depression is lowered by the presence of the diathesis. Three diatheses will be described here: genetics, personality, and depression history. It is important to note that this list of diatheses is not exhaustive, nor are the items mutually exclusive. Indeed, these three risk factors likely work together to promote a vulnerability to the effects of life events on depression.

Genetics

Family, twin, and adoption studies conducted over 50 years have provided strong evidence that major depression runs in families, and that much of its familial aggregation is due to genetic factors. Exciting new research has also provided evidence that at least part of the genetic link to depression may be caused by the effect of a genetic vulnerability for increasing individuals' sensitivity to stressful life events. For example, an important study looking at monozygotic (identical) and dizygotic (fraternal) twin pairs found that individuals at highest genetic risk for depression (i.e., a monozygotic twin whose co-twin was depressed) were more than twice as likely to develop depression in the face of a severe life event than those at lowest genetic risk (i.e., a monozygotic twin whose co-twin was not depressed) (Kendler et al., 1995).

Now that the human genome has been mapped, researchers are in the exciting position of specifying genetic risk at the chromosomal level. The serotonin (5-HT) system has received the most attention as a source of candidate genes for depression because it is the target of selective serotonin-reuptake inhibitor medications that are the standard pharmacotherapy for the disorder. The serotonin transporter gene (5-HTT), in particular, has been found in several studies to moderate the response to stress. Specifically, individuals who possess a particular variant of this gene have shown higher rates of major depression, more depressive symptoms, and higher levels of suicidality in response to stressful life events than those who do not (e.g., Caspi et al., 2003).

Personality

Several personality characteristics also have been implicated in promoting risk for major depression in the face of stressful life events. For example, individuals high in the trait neuroticism are characterized by a tendency to feel negative emotions, to be emotionally labile, and to be highly reactive to stress. Not surprisingly, these individuals are more likely to develop depression following severely stressful life events than individuals low in this trait (e.g., Ormel, Oldehinkel, & Brilman, 2001).

Other studies have defined personality vulnerability in terms of two traits believed to be central to the diathesis to major depression: sociotropy (or dependency), defined as a strong investment in, and valuation of, interpersonal relationships and intimacy; and autonomy (or self-criticism), defined as a strong investment in, and valuation of, independence and achievement (Beck, 1983). Individuals scoring high on one or the other of these traits are also more likely to show depression symptoms, and to develop major depression, in the face of stressful life events than those scoring low on these traits (see Clark & Beck, 1999).

Depression History

One of the most intriguing recent developments in life-stress research has been the discovery that depression itself may become a diathesis, thus changing the relation of stressful life events to future recurrent episodes. In particular, Post's (1992) stress sensitization (or kindling) hypothesis proposes that individuals become sensitized to the life events that precipitate depression, and to the episodes of depression themselves, such that less stress is required to precipitate recurrent episodes of depression than was required to precipitate the first onset. A large number of studies support Post's hypothesis (see Monroe & Harkness, 2005). In brief, severe life events are significantly more strongly related to the first episode of depression than to subsequent recurrent episodes. Furthermore, mild (nonsevere) life events are significantly more strongly related to depression recurrence than to the first onset. In other words, while severely stressful life events are required to trigger the initial onset of depression, as individuals' sensitivity to stress increases across recurrence, their threshold for reacting to

stress with a depressive episode decreases. Post's hypothesis goes a long way, therefore, to explaining why major depression is such a highly recurrent disorder.

A Further Effect of Depression History: Stressful Life Event Generation

Not only do stressful life events trigger depression; strong evidence now shows that a history of depression also serves to generate additional stressful life events (Hammen, 1991). In particular, several studies have now demonstrated that individuals with a history of recurrent depressive episodes are more likely than those with no depression history to experience events that are at least in part dependent upon their own behavior or characteristics (e.g., breaking up a relationship, getting fired from a job). By contrast, a history of depression does not increase the likelihood of experiencing independent, or "fateful," events that are outside of the individual's control (e.g., mother's cancer diagnosis, best friend moves away).

Studies confirming stress generation are important because they clarify the bidirectional relation between stress and depression. Hammen (1991) suggests that individuals with a history of depression generate stressful life events because the depression has compromised their coping and support resources. Furthermore, depressed individuals experience disruptions in occupational or interpersonal functioning (e.g., frequent work absences or avoidance of social contacts), which may eventually result in severe dependent life events (e.g., fired from job, break-up in relationship). It is important to note that the same risk factors that confer a diathesis to increased stressful life event sensitivity are also related to life event generation, namely a genetic predisposition to depression, negative personality characteristics, and a history of prior depressive episodes. As such, these risk factors may represent a double threat in promoting vulnerability to depression; that is, one of the reasons why these risk factors are so strongly related to depression may be because they work together to (a) increase the number of life events that these individuals encounter (event generation) and (b) increase the likelihood that individuals will react to these stressors with depression (event sensitization).

Characteristics That Confer Resilience in the Face of Stressful Life Events

Not everyone who experiences a severely stressful life event will develop major depression. Research on the characteristics that confer resilience is important because it can provide valuable targets for depression treatment. Many studies have focused on personality traits that show resistance to stress, such as hardiness, positive emotionality, and optimism (Bonanno, 2004). For example, hardy people turn the proverbial "lemons into lemonade" by viewing adversity as an opportunity for new learning and actively engaging with adversity to affect its outcome and avoid isolation. Therefore, in face of adversity hardy individuals are better able to use active coping and harness social support, two behaviors that are themselves strongly related to a reduced risk for major depression.

Specifically, active coping uses behavioral and/or psychological strategies to change the stressful life event itself or how one thinks about it. These strategies have been found to buffer the effects of stress. In contrast, avoidant coping strategies that keep people from directly addressing stressful life events (e.g., withdrawal, alcohol use) have been shown to predict depression (Holahan & Moos, 1987). In addition, perceived levels of social support buffer the effects of stress such that people who perceive their level of emotional and practical support from family and peers to be high are less likely to suffer distress in the face of stressful life events than individuals who have a low level of perceived social support (Cohen & Wills, 1985). Interestingly, when researchers look at the actual size of people's social support networks (e.g., number of friends), this variable does not buffer the effects of stress, although larger social networks are still related to a reduced risk for depression.

Conclusions

The role of stressful life events in the onset of depression is now well established. In particular, the experience of severely stressful loss events is associated with a threefold increase in the risk of developing depression in the subsequent 3 to 6 months. While stressful life events are the most direct triggers of depression, the relation of stress to depression is strongly influenced by biological and psychological risk factors that likely work together to increase individuals' sensitivity to stress. Furthermore, once the depression syndrome is underway, scars left over from the repeated experience of stress and depression serve to generate more stressful life events and to lower individuals' thresholds for reacting negatively to stress. Therefore, treatments that focus on stress early in the course of depression will likely show superior effects in preventing recurrence. Particularly useful may be cognitive and behavioral treatments that include the teaching of active coping strategies, as well as interpersonal therapies that increase individuals' perceptions of social connectedness and support. Continued development and refinement of treatments that recognize the important role of stressful life events in the onset and recurrence of depression are crucial to preventing what can become a lifelong pattern of illness.

KATE L. HARKNESS

See also

Anaclitic and Introjective Depression
Serotonin
Social Support
Stress and Coping

Stress Assessment
Stress Generation

References

Beck, A. T. (1983). Cognitive therapy of depression: New perspectives. In P. J. Clayton & J. E. Barrett (Eds.), *Treatment of depression: Old controversies and new approaches* (pp. 265–290). New York: Raven Press.

Bonanno, G. A. (2004). Loss, trauma, and human resilience: Have we underestimated the human capacity to thrive after extremely aversive events? *American Psychologist, 59*, 20–28.

Brown, G. W., & Harris, T. O. (1989). Depression. In G. W. Brown & T. O. Harris (Eds.), *Life events and illness* (pp. 49–93). New York: Guilford Press.

Caspi, A., Sudgen, K., Moffitt, T., Taylor, A., Craig, I., Harrington, H., et al. (2003). Influence of life stress on depression: Moderation by a polymorphism in the 5-HTT gene. *Science, 301*, 386–389.

Clark, D. A., & Beck, A. T. (1999). *Scientific foundations of cognitive theory and therapy of depression.* New York: John Wiley & Sons.

Cohen, S., & Wills, T. A. (1985). Stress, social support, and the buffering hypothesis. *Psychological Bulletin, 98*, 310–357.

Hammen, C. (1991). Generation of stress in the course of unipolar depression. *Journal of Abnormal Psychology, 101*, 45–52.

Holahan, C. J., & Moos, R. H. (1987). Risk, resistance, and psychological distress: A longitudinal analysis with adults and children. *Journal of Abnormal Psychology, 96*, 3–13.

Kendler, K. S., Kessler, R. C., Walters, E. E., MacLean, C., Neale, M. C., Heath, A. C., et al. (1995). Stressful life events, genetic liability, and onset of an episode of major depression in women. *American Journal of Psychiatry, 152*, 833–842.

Mazure, C. M. (1998). Life stressors as risk factors in depression. *Clinical Psychology: Science and Practice, 5*, 291–313.

Monroe, S. M., & Harkness, K. L. (2005). Life stress, the "kindling" hypothesis, and the recurrence of depression: Considerations from a life stress perspective. *Psychological Review, 112*, 417–445.

Monroe, S. M., & Simons, A. D. (1991). Diathesis-stress theories in the context of life stress research: Implications for the depressive disorders. *Psychological Bulletin, 110*, 406–425.

Ormel, J., Oldehinkel, A. J., & Brilman, E. I. (2001). The interplay and etiological continuity of neuroticism, difficulties, and life events in the etiology of major and subsyndromal, first and recurrent depressive episodes in later life. *American Journal of Psychiatry, 158*, 885–891.

Post, R. M. (1992). Transduction of psychosocial stress into the neurobiology of recurrent affective disorder. *American Journal of Psychiatry, 149*, 999–1010.

Stress Generation

Stress generation is defined as actively contributing to the occurrence of one's own negative life events. The relationship between depression and stress has long been established in the depression literature. In fact, much of the literature demonstrates a directional relationship in which stress or a stressful event can lead to later feelings of depression. Hammen (1991) coined the term *stress generation* when she proposed and supported the converse idea; depression at one point in time can actually lead to later stressful events. So as opposed to the historical relationship of stress predicting depression, stress generation research examines the directional relationship of depression predicting stress at a later point in time. Some theories suggest that people with symptoms of depression possess interpersonal attributes that lead them to respond to situations in a manner that creates additional life stress. These stressors can in turn lead to further depressive symptoms; creating a destructive cycle of depression and stress.

The stress generation hypothesis was first tested using a year-long longitudinal design that compared the stressful life events of female participants with unipolar depression, bipolar disorder, a chronic medical condition, and control participants. The results of this seminal study indicated that women with unipolar depression experienced more dependent stressful events (events they were at least partially responsible for) upon 1-year follow-up than women who were medically ill, those with bipolar disorder, and the control participants (Hammen, 1991).

The stress-generation effect is a robust finding. Since the initial inquiry, this effect has been replicated in numerous studies and has been supported across many research labs and in many populations that span age, sex, and ethnicity. The stress-generation effect has been extended to adult and adolescent children of mothers with depression, adolescents, African American adolescents and children, wives in married couples, undergraduate students, depressed individuals currently seeking treatment, and middle-aged individuals seeking general health care.

In addition to research that has replicated the stress-generation effect in various populations, many studies have examined possible mechanisms for this effect by exploring factors that mediate and/or moderate the relationship between depressive symptoms and later stress. Many different factors have been investigated, including problem-solving strategies, reassurance-seeking, social support, family history, diagnostic status, and attachment.

Several different personal styles have been investigated in relation to stress generation. For instance, one study investigated the role of interpersonal problem-solving strategies (IPS) in stress generation among adolescent women. IPS is the ability to recognize and effectively solve problems of an interpersonal nature. Results suggested that interpersonal stress mediated the relationship between initial depressive symptoms and later stressful events. Further, it suggests that if an individual has poor IPS she may be more likely to have interpersonal stress and depressive symptoms.

Another approach looked at the effect of excessive reassurance-seeking on stress generation. Depressed individuals often habitually seek reassurance about how others feel about them. Because they tend to do this often, and it is perceived as negative to others; excessive reassurance-seeking seldom results in the desired effect. In fact, it tends to alienate the depressed person from others. When examined in the context of stress generation it was found that small social stressors mediated the relationship between reassurance-seeking and depressive symptoms.

Attachment has also been found to affect stress generation in depression. Interpersonal stressful life events have been found to mediate the relationship between insecure attachment (avoidant and anxious) and depressive and anxiety symptoms. Taken together, these studies suggest that childhood experiences can have a significant impact on depressive symptomatology.

Other researchers have taken a developmental approach to studying stress generation. Findings suggested that adolescent and adult children of depressed women had higher levels of stressful life events than the comparison groups of children of medically ill or control mothers. Children of depressed mothers displayed higher levels of dependent stressful events such as problems in family conflict and peer conflict areas. Additionally, these children were exposed to both episodic (short-term) and chronic (long-term) stressful events.

Family history of depression and comorbidity has been shown to be related to depressive symptomatology in numerous studies. These factors have also been linked to stress generation. It has been found that family history of psychopathology was a predictive of personal pathology, which was in turn predictive of stress generation.

Additionally, the role of social support has been tested in married couples. Specifically, depressive symptoms significantly predicted stress generation in wives. Both perceptions of social support and social support behavior mediated the relationship between depressive symptoms and later stress. Thus, the manner in which wives with depressive symptoms asked for, received, and gave social support tended to generate additional stress in the marriage.

One study of stress generation among individuals with recurrent and nonrecurrent depression indicated that participants with recurrent depression had more dependent stressful events than those with nonrecurrent depression in the 12 months prior to their most recent episode. Additionally, the effect of diagnoses and comorbidity on the stress generation was investigated in individuals with a depression diagnosis, depression plus an additional diagnosis (comorbid depression), a nondepressive diagnosis, or no diagnosis. Individuals with a depression diagnosis were more significantly impacted by dependent events than individuals with no diagnosis. Also, individuals with a comorbid diagnosis later experienced more dependent and interpersonal conflict stress than those with only a depression diagnosis even after controlling for severity of depression. Lastly, the study found that chronic stress and psychopathology were predictive of future episodic stress.

Since the stress-generation effect has been replicated in numerous different samples, it is clear that this self-feeding cycle of depression and stress plays an important role in the exacerbation and continuation of depressive symptoms. It seems logical then to question whether individuals with other psychological disorders could also prospectively generate stress, or if there is something specific to depression that causes this effect to happen. This idea of specificity has been tested, and studies have found that stress generation is specific to depression. In other words, there is a specificity of the stress-generation effect, such that individuals with depression tend to create additional stress in their lives, but individuals with other psychological disorders do not. For instance, Hammen's (1991) seminal study found that the stress-generation effect was specific to depressed individuals as compared to those with bipolar disorder or a medical illness. A later study found that depression prospectively predicted stressful life events, whereas conduct disorder did not. Similarly, several studies found that the stress-generation effect was present for depressive symptoms but not anxiety symptoms. This is particularly interesting, as depression and anxiety tend to have a high rate of comorbidity and overlapping symptoms.

Another important distinction in the stress-generation literature is the difference between dependent events and independent events. Dependent events can be defined as situations the individual contributes to or participates in, such as an argument with a friend. Independent events are those that are typically seen as out of an individual's control, such as the death of a family member. The theory of stress generation posits that individuals with symptoms of depression tend to create additional dependent negative life events. Indeed, many studies have supported the hypothesis and found that individuals with depression tend to generate dependent stressful events, but not independent stressful events.

On the other hand, some studies have found support for the generation of independent stressful life events among individuals with depression. These findings are particularly surprising because it is difficult to understand how an individual could create independent stressful events, or events that are supposedly out of their control. Thus, many researchers do not expect to find these results, and some do not even examine independent stressful events. However, some researchers found that depressive symptoms predicted independent stressful events. In fact, some studies have found the stress-generation effect for independent events but not for dependent events. Upon first glance, these findings may appear to be counterintuitive because it seems unlikely that an individual could play an active role in causing a stressful life event such as fighting at home or the loss of a family member. However, it is possible that there is not a clear distinction between dependent and independent events. Stressful life events may occur on a continuum from events that are completely dependent to events that are completely independent. As events move on this continuum toward being more dependent, then that allows a greater possibility for stress-generation processes to occur. Any stressful event that has any dependent quality whatsoever may be subject to stress-generation processes. Further, individuals with depression may place themselves in more risky situations and thus make it more likely that supposedly independent events will occur in their lives. The idea of a continuum of stressful life events and the possibility that a person with depression can generate independent events are hypotheses that future research will have to address empirically.

Despite many stress-generation findings and implications, the main mechanism of the stress-generation effect remains unknown. Many studies have found that the variables investigated account for only a relatively small portion of variance in stress generation. In other words, there are likely additional factors that need to be evaluated in order to ensure that a more complete picture of the effect is obtained. It is possible that there is not simply one variable that accounts for the variance in stress generation. If researchers begin to approach stress generation through methods that allow the investigation of multiple variables simultaneously, there may be more likelihood of identifying the main mechanism of the stress-generation effect.

Another curious gap in the research is that the possible effect of stress generation on suicidality has not been studied. This would be ideal to investigate given the fact that depressed individuals are at increased risk of suicide and suicidal ideation is one of the possible diagnostic criterion for major depressive disorder in the *Diagnostic and Statistical Manual of Mental Disorders* (*DSM-IV-TR*; American Psychiatric Association, 2000).

Research on stress generation has grown significantly since Hammen's (1991) landmark study. Many important factors that influence stress generation have been identified, and the effect has been replicated time and time again in a myriad of populations. This research contains rich implications for the clinical treatment of depression. Findings suggest that clinicians should work with clients to identify stressful situations that the client is actively involved in creating. Proper identification of and intervention in these events could reduce depressive symptomatology and, thus, further reduce stress. The cognitive behavioral analysis system of psychotherapy (CBASP) is a treatment for chronic depression that specifically focuses on negative events and the client's involvement in the occurrence of those events. It may be possible that the effectiveness of CBASP, or situational analyses more generally, may help patients work through the process of disrupting the stress generation cycle.

LaRicka R. Wingate and Collin L. Davidson

See also

Social Support
Stress and Coping
Stress Assessment
Stressful Life Events

References

American Psychiatric Association. (2000). *Diagnostic and statistical manual of mental disorders* (4th ed., text revision). Washington, DC: Author.

Hammen, C. (1991). Generation of stress in the course of unipolar depression. *Journal of Abnormal Psychology, 100,* 555–561.

Suicidal Cognition

The term *suicidal cognition* refers to thoughts, images, and ideas about suicide and the underlying psychological processes that create and maintain them. The lifetime rate of such suicide ideation among the general population is around 16% with the lifetime rate of nonfatal suicidal behavior being 5% (Weissman et al., 1999). Although suicide itself is rarer (1% of all deaths are by suicide; Centers for Disease Control and Prevention, 2007), because it often occurs in young people, it is the third-highest contributor to life years lost (after coronary heart disease and cancer).

Suicide and Depression

Suicidal behavior is one of the most serious outcomes of psychiatric illness and is particularly associated with major depression. Standardized tools for classifying mental disorders (such as the *Diagnostic and Statistical Manual of Mental Disorders* [*DSM-IV*; American Psychiatric Association, 1994]) list suicidal cognitions as one of the key symptoms of depression. They can range in severity from "recurrent thoughts of death" or "thinking that you would be better off dead," to thoughts or images of suicide and/or having a detailed plan for a suicide attempt. Sometimes patients find their symptoms vary from one episode of depression to the next, but alongside the two core symptoms of depression (low mood and loss of interest), suicide ideation is the symptom most likely to recur across depressive episodes.

It is often supposed that if a person talks openly of suicide, then he or she is less likely to actually attempt or commit suicide, but the opposite is more generally the case. Most people who commit suicide have expressed a wish to die to someone and may have had a history of recurrent episodes of depression in which they experienced suicidal cognitions.

Table S.1   Example Items from the Suicide Ideation Scale (Beck & Steer, 1993)

People are instructed to answer as they feel now.

What is your current desire to make an active suicide attempt, to actively harm yourself, actively kill yourself? Is there no desire at all?

Today do you have any passive suicidal feelings? For instance, on the one hand would you, in fact, take precautions necessary to save your life? Would you take medicine to save your life if you needed it?

Clinically, suicidal ideation and planning is assessed by asking directly about the extent of such thoughts and plans. There is no evidence that talking openly about suicidal cognitions puts the "idea of suicide into people's heads." A common measure used to discuss the extent to which people are experiencing suicide ideation is the Scale for Suicide Ideation by Beck and Steer (1993). Example questions can be seen in Table S.1. An alternative version of this scale asking about past cognitions is also available, as it has been found that asking about the worst-ever point in the past—how close a person came at that point to suicide—is a better indicator of future risk of suicide than asking about a person's current suicide ideation (Beck, Brown, Steer, Dahlsgaard, & Grisham, 1999).

How Robust Is the Relationship Between Suicidality and Depression?

The association of suicide and suicidal behavior with depression is maintained even if someone has other psychiatric diagnoses. For example, suicidal feelings and behavior are common in people who have a diagnosis of schizophrenia, but unless there are specific auditory hallucinations that seem to command the patient to kill him- or herself (which is relatively rare), the suicidal feelings arise most commonly when the patient is depressed and hopeless, often in part created by a sense of despair about his or her own diagnosis. A similarly close link between suicidal ideation with depression can be seen in patients with a diagnosis of drug or alcohol dependence, and in those diagnosed with a personality disorder.

Why Are Suicidal Cognitions in Depression So Recurrent?

Suicide ideation is one of the most recurrent symptoms of depression (Williams, Crane, Barnhofer, Van der Does & Segal, 2006). This means that if people have felt suicidal during one episode of depression, they are likely to feel the same way if they become depressed again. This is important to know because depression itself carries a high risk of recurrence (an 80%–90% chance of recurrence in people with three or more previous episodes of depression). In this respect, suicidal cognitions act like other negative thought patterns that are associated with depression. It is known that, during earlier episodes of depression, certain thought patterns become associated together and become linked ever more strongly to depressed mood. Every time depression recurs, the associative links become stronger so that future episodes of depression require fewer and fewer triggers.

Eventually, because even mild negative mood can retrigger these catastrophic thinking patterns, later experiences of suicidal cognitions will require fewer external triggers and be more easily initiated. As suicidal ideas become more familiar, they are seen to represent reality—"how things really are"—rather than such familiarity being seen as simply a symptom of an old pattern that has been frequently reactivated.

Suicidal Cognitions: Focusing on Themes

The Suicide Cognitions Scale (Table S.2; Rudd, Joiner & Rajab, 2001) assesses the

Table S.2   Four Themes (With Examples) of Rudd's Suicidal Cognitions Scale

---

1. Perceived Burdensomeness

This world would be better off without me.

I am a burden to my family.

2. Unlovability

I can never be forgiven for the mistakes I have made.

I am completely unworthy of love.

3. Helplessness

No one can help solve my problems.

Suicide is my only option to solve my problems.

4. Poor Distress Tolerance

I can't stand this pain anymore.

I can't tolerate being this upset any longer.

---

presence of four themes that people commonly experience when they feel suicidal.

Other research has investigated more facets of suicidality. For example, the Mental Pain Scale (Orbach, Mikulincer, Gilboa-Schechtman, & Sirota, 2003) has nine factors: irreversibility (e.g., "I have lost something I will never find again"), loss of control ("I am completely helpless"), narcissist wounds ("I feel abandoned and lonely"), emotional flooding ("I feel an emotional turmoil inside me"), freezing ("I feel numb and not alive"), self-estrangement ("I feel I am not my old self anymore"), confusion ("I cannot concentrate"), social distancing ("I want to be left alone"), and emptiness ("I can't find meaning in my life"). Orbach and colleagues found that it was irreversibility, loss of control, and emptiness that discriminated suicidal from nonsuicidal people, but of these, only emptiness remained when hopelessness, depression, and anxiety were taken into account. Further work by Orbach has found that it is not just experience of mental pain that predicts suicidality, but the sense that the pain is uncontrollable and intolerable; that is, it is the combined sense that a person wants desperately to get rid of the pain, but also feels that he or she cannot get rid of or escape it. This is consistent with the theory that suicidal ideas and behavior arise from a "cry of pain"

arising from a blocking of an urgent tendency to escape following defeat and humiliation (Williams & Pollock, 2000).

Hopelessness and Positive Future Thinking

Hopelessness about the future plays a central role in suicidal ideation and behavior. Both British and American studies over many years have reported that hopelessness mediates the relationship between depression and suicidal intent. Hopelessness has also been found to predict repetition of nonfatal suicidal behavior over several months. It predicts suicides up to 10 years later in patients hospitalized because of suicidal ideation (Beck, Brown, & Steer, 1989).

Although hopelessness is clearly an important phenomenon, until recently little work had actually examined the psychological mechanisms underlying hopelessness: it could arise either from a reduced expectancy for positive events or an increased expectancy for negative events. Research has found that the main problem is that, when suicidal, people are less able to think of future positive events but show no difference from nonsuicidal controls in being able to think of future negative events. Moreover, this deficit in positive anticipation is true for the immediate future (the next day and week) as well as the long-term future (1 year and 10 years). These studies show that inability to access positive future events may be the critical aspect underlying hopelessness.

A particular form of positive future is assessed in the Reasons for Living Inventory (Linehan, Goodstein, Nielson, & Chiles, 1983), which is closely linked to hopelessness. Compared to both the general population and psychiatric controls, suicidal people have fewer reasons for living.

Interpersonal Problem Solving

The second determinant of whether suicidal thoughts escalate into suicidal impulses and behavior is the availability of alternative coping options. Many studies suggest that suicidal patients have real difficulties in interpersonal problem solving, and that these difficulties have the effect of reducing alternative options to suicide. The most commonly used method of assessing such deficits is the Means-End Problem Solving Test (MEPS). The MEPS provides subjects with a number of different social scenarios. For each scenario they are given an initial situation where a problem has to be solved (e.g., a person's friends are avoiding them) and a desired end point (e.g., the person's friends like him or her again). Their task is to complete the middle portion of the story, providing means whereby the initial situation becomes the desired end point. Studies have shown that even a long time after an episode of suicidal depression, and even when problem solving seems to be completely normal, patients react to small deteriorations in mood with impaired problem-solving ability (Williams, Barnhofer, Crane, & Beck, 2005).

Conclusions

Suicidal cognitions are closely associated with depression, and, in particular, with hopelessness about the future. At the point when other depressed people might look for alternative ways to solve problems, people vulnerable to suicidal cognition find that their problem-solving capacity narrows, and they can think of nothing else to do. If at this point they also feel they are unlovable, a burden to others, and experience mental pain that seems intolerable and uncontrollable, they may be at high risk for serious suicidal behavior.

J. Mark G. Williams and Danielle S. Duggan

See also

Hopelessness
Suicide in the Elderly
Suicide in Youths
Suicide Theories
Suicide Warning Signs

References

American Psychiatric Association. (1994). *Diagnostic and statistical manual of mental disorders* (4th ed.). Washington DC: Author.

Beck, A. T., Brown., G., & Steer, R. A. (1989). Prediction of eventual suicide in psychiatric inpatients by clinical ratings of hopelessness. *Journal of Consulting and Clinical Psychology, 57,* 309–310.

Beck, A. T., Brown, G. K., Steer, R. A., Dahlsgaard, K. K., & Grisham, J. R. (1999). Suicide ideation at its worst point: A predictor of eventual suicide in psychiatric outpatients. *Suicide and Life-Threatening Behavior, 29,* 1–9.

Beck, A. T., & Steer, R. A. (1993). *Manual for the Beck Scale for Suicide Ideation.* San Antonio, TX: Psychological Corporation.

Centers for Disease Control and Prevention. (2007). *Suicide data sheet.* Retrieved June 2008, from http://www.cdc.gov/ncipc/dvp/suicide/SuicideDataSheet.pdf

Linehan, M. M., Goodstein, J. L, Nielsen, S. L., & Chiles, J. A. (1983). Reasons for staying alive when you are thinking of killing yourself: The Reasons for Living Inventory. *Journal of Consulting and Clinical Psychology, 51,* 276–286.

Orbach, I., Mikulincer, M., Gilboa-Schechtman, E., & Sirota, P. (2003). Mental pain and its relationship to suicidality and life meaning. *Suicide and Life-Threatening Behavior, 33,* 231–241.

Rudd, M. D., Joiner, T., & Rajab, M. H. (2001). *Treating suicidal behaviour: An effective, time-limited approach.* New York: Guilford Press.

Weissman, M. M., Bland, R. C., Canino, G. J., Greenwald, S., Hwu, H. G., Joyce, P. R., et al. (1999). Prevalence of suicide ideation and suicide attempts in nine studies. *Psychological Medicine, 29,* 9–17.

Williams, J. M. G., Barnhofer, T., Crane, C., & Beck, A. T. (2005). Problem solving deteriorates following mood challenge in formerly depressed patients with a history of suicidal ideation. *Journal of Abnormal Psychology, 114,* 421–431.

Williams, J. M. G., Crane, C., Barnhofer, T., Van der Does, A. J. W., & Segal, Z. V. (2006). Recurrence of suicidal ideation across depressive episodes. *Journal of Affective Disorders, 91,* 189–194.

Williams, J. M. G., & Pollock, L. R. (2000). The psychology of suicidal behaviour. In K. Hawton & K. Van Heeringen (Eds.), *The international handbook of suicide and attempted suicide* (pp. 79–93). New York: Wiley.

Suicide in the Elderly

Research has found that the elderly are at the greatest risk for suicidal behavior compared to any other age groups, in both men and women worldwide (Pearson & Conwell, 1995). Comparable to other age groups, suicide rates in the elderly are higher in men than in women and higher in Whites than in non-Whites. In fact, the high rates of suicide in the elderly have been accounted for predominantly by the higher prevalence of older White men, in whom the suicide rate of 48.7/10,000 is over 4 times the overall age-adjusted suicide rate of 11.1/100,000 in the United States (Centers for Disease Control and Prevention, 2004).

The ratio of suicide attempts to completed suicides is also smaller in the elderly than in other age groups. In the general population, there have been 8 to 40 attempts reported for every completed suicide. In young adults, there are 200 attempts for every completed suicide. However, in older adults, the ratio of attempted suicides to completed suicides is 2 to 4:1. One reason for the lower ratio of attempted to completed suicides in the elderly is that older adults are in poorer health than younger adults and are therefore more likely to die from self-inflicted injuries. Also, a higher percentage of older adults live alone and therefore are less likely to be discovered after a self-inflicted injury compared to adults who live with others. Finally, older adults use more immediately lethal means of suicide than younger adults. In 2004, 52% of all suicide deaths in the United States were by firearm. In comparison, 72% of suicides among adults over age 60 were completed using a firearm.

Risk and Protective Factors for Suicidal Behavior in the Elderly

Researchers have identified multiple risk and protective factors for suicidal behavior in the elderly (Conwell, Duberstein, & Caine, 2002). Similar to other age groups, psychiatric illness is a potent risk factor for suicidal behavior in older adults. Psychological autopsy studies have repeatedly demonstrated that psychiatric illness exists in the large majority of older adults who die by suicide, and it is ordinarily undiagnosed prior to death. Major depressive disorder is the most common psychiatric diagnosis in older adults with suicidal behavior. Substance use, anxiety, and primary psychotic disorders have also been found to correlate with suicidal behavior in some studies.

Physical illness and functional impairment have also been associated with risk for suicide in older adults. Specific illnesses with an increased relative risk for suicide include multiple sclerosis, Huntington's disease, spinal cord injury, stroke, systemic lupus erythematosus, HIV/AIDS, malignant neoplasms, renal disease, and peptic ulcer disease. Studies are less consistent, however, about whether physical illness and functional impairment are independent risk factors for suicidal behavior or if their impact is mediated by depression.

Social factors shown to be associated with suicide in older adults include bereavement, financial stressors related to retirement and living on reduced means, family discord, and low levels of social support. In contrast, strong interpersonal relationships serve as a protective factor; that is, older adults with close friends and relatives in whom they can confide are less likely to die by suicide.

Personality traits that have been associated with suicide in the elderly include neuroticism, hypochondriasis, hostility, shy seclusiveness, and a rigid, independent style. Further research has reported that older individuals with more anxious and obsessive traits tend to be at higher risk for suicide. Also, hopelessness has been found to be a very strong predictor of suicidal behavior, specifically in older adults.

Finally, access to lethal means, specifically handguns, has been shown to place older adults at increased risk for suicide, and restricting access to firearms has been associated in ecological studies with reduced rates of suicide in the elderly.

Prevention of Late-Life Suicide

The high lethality of suicidal behavior in later life indicates that prevention efforts should target the older person at risk well before she or he enters a suicidal crisis (Conwell & Thompson, 2008). Two studies, the Prevention of Suicide in Primary Care Elderly: Collaborative Trial (PROSPECT) study (Bruce et al., 2004) and the Improving Mood—Promoting Access to Collaborative Treatment (IMPACT) study (Unützer et al., 2002), have addressed the needs of older adults with affective illness in primary care practices. Both used a randomized controlled trial design to compare usual care with an intervention that enabled depression care specialists to work with primary care physicians, patients, and their family members to optimize treatment of the subject's mood disorder. Intervention components could include psychotropic medications, brief psychotherapy, education, and family support. In both studies, suicidal ideation decreased significantly faster in intervention patients than those in usual care. Because of sample size limitations, neither trial was able to assess the effectiveness of their interventions on suicidal behavior. Also, since both study populations were approximately 70% women, the effectiveness of the interventions on that segment of the population at highest risk for completed suicide, older men, remains largely unknown.

The Telehelp/Telecheck study (De Leo, Dello Buono, & Dwyer, 2002), based in Padua, Italy, evaluated a telephone-based program serving over 18,000 functionally impaired and socially isolated elders. Specifically addressing the social needs of callers, this intervention resulted in significantly fewer than expected suicides in this region over an 11-year period. However, the intervention appeared to be effective in reducing suicide only among elderly women, with no effect on elderly men.

In summary, further development and implementation of preventive interventions for suicidal thoughts and behaviors in the elderly are needed. In particular, a focus on how to engage older men in interventions must be specifically considered. From a public health perspective, the proportion of the population that is over 65 years of age is increasing dramatically. Therefore, the need to find effective ways to prevent suicide in later adulthood is becoming ever more urgent.

CAITLIN THOMPSON AND YEATES CONWELL

See also

Geriatric Depression
Hopelessness
Suicidal Cognition
Suicide in Youths
Suicide Theories
Suicide Warning Signs

References

Bruce, M. L., Ten Have, T. R., Reynolds III, C. F., Katz, I. I., Schulberg, H. C., Mulsant, B. H., et al. (2004). Reducing suicidal ideation and depressive symptoms in depressed older primary care patients: A randomized controlled trial. *Journal of the American Medical Association, 291*, 1081–1091.

Centers for Disease Control and Prevention. (2004). *Web-based injury statistics query and reporting system.* Retrieved December 2, 2007, from http://www.cdc.gov/ncipc/wisqars/

Conwell, Y., Duberstein, P. R., & Caine, E. D. (2002). Risk factors for suicide in later life. *Biological Psychiatry, 52*, 193–204.

Conwell, Y., & Thompson, C. (2008). Suicidal behavior in elders. Suicidal behavior: A development perspective across the lifespan. *Psychiatric Clinics of North America, 31*, 333–356.

De Leo, D., Dello Buono, M., & Dwyer, J. (2002). Suicide among the elderly: The long-term impact of a telephone support and assessment intervention in northern Italy. *British Journal of Psychiatry, 181*, 226–229.

Pearson, J. L., & Conwell, Y. (1995). Suicide in late life: Challenges and opportunities for research. Introduction. *International Psychogeriatrics, 7*, 131–136.

Unützer, J., Katon, W., Callahan, C. M., Williams, J. W., Jr., Hunkeler, E., Harpole, L., et al. (2002). Collaborative care management of late-life depression in the primary care setting: A randomized controlled trial. *Journal of the American Medical Association, 288,* 2836–2845.

Suicide in Youths

Youth suicide is a tragedy of substantial public health significance throughout the world. According to the World Health Organization's global report on mental health (2001), suicide is one of the three leading causes of death among people aged 15 to 34 years in all countries. Although, traditionally, suicide rates have been highest among the male elderly, rates among young people have been increasing to such an extent that they are now the group at highest risk in approximately one-third of countries. A recent meta-analysis of 128 studies conducted internationally revealed that 10% of youths reported a suicide attempt, and 20% to 30% said they had thought about suicide at some point in their life (Evans, Hawton, & Rodham, 2005). Furthermore, the emotional distress, impairment, and health care costs associated with suicidal thoughts, behaviors, and deaths are substantial.

Terminology

The terminology used to describe suicidal behavior and suicidal death varies greatly both within and between countries, presenting significant challenges to researchers and clinicians who work with suicidal youths. In the United States, the terms *suicidal ideation, suicidal attempt,* and *death by suicide* are all commonly used, with suicide attempt being differentiated from nonsuicidal deliberate self-harm based on evidence of intent to die. However, in European countries, the term *deliberate self-harm* is used more broadly and includes suicide attempt (Evans et al., 2005). A universal, clear, consistent, and agreed-upon nomenclature of suicidal phenomenon is needed in order to ensure consistency across countries in their classification of suicidal phenomenon. Lastly, it is notable that as a field there has been a move away from using the term *committed suicide*

toward the use of a less pejorative *died by suicide.*

Prevalence and Gender Differences

Recent youth suicide statistics (aged 5–24 years) from selected countries that report mortality data to the World Health Organization indicate a high degree of variation in suicide rates across countries (Table S.3). For example, suicide rates in the Russian Federation and former Soviet states are especially high, as are those in Finland, New Zealand, and Ireland. Rapid cultural transition, assimilation, and loss of traditional cultural practices have been suggested as possible explanations for the high suicide rates among youths in these countries, which have rates of suicide two to three times higher than the United States. Countries with the lowest suicide rates include mainland China, Dominican Republic, Greece, Philippines, Spain, and Italy. There is a dearth of information about suicide rates from countries in Africa. While international suicide rates for youths vary greatly between countries, it is also important to note that suicide rates within countries also fluctuate significantly by race and ethnicity. For example, in the United States, American Indian and Alaskan Native youths have a suicide rate twice the national rate (Centers for Disease Control and Prevention [CDC], 2005). Furthermore, suicide rates among Inuit youths in Nunavut Territory are 6 times those of Canada's southern provinces (Tester & McNicoll, 2004).

It is interesting to note that while suicide rates are higher in young males than young females in North America, Western Europe, Australia, and New Zealand, they are equal in some Asian countries such as Singapore, and in China more young females die by suicide than young males (Gould, Greenberg, & Velting, 2003). The gender difference in youth suicide deaths in most countries is likely due to the greater likelihood of males having multiple risk factors such as comorbid mood and alcohol abuse disorders,

Table S.3   Youth Suicide Rates in Selected Countries by Age and Sex[a]

Country	Year	5–14 years			15–24 years		
		M	F	All	M	F	All
Russian Federation	2004	3.6	1.0	2.3	47.4	8.2	28.1
Lithuania	2004	2.7	0.5	1.6	42.9	7.4	25.5
Belarus	2003	1.8	0.5	1.2	34.6	5.8	20.5
Finland	2004	1.2	0.3	0.8	33.1	9.7	21.7
New Zealand	2000	1.0	0.3	0.7	30.4	5.7	18.2
Iceland	2004	0.0	0.0	0.0	27.3	4.7	16.2
Ireland	2005	0.7	0.4	0.5	20.4	3.2	11.9
Norway	2004	0.0	1.0	0.5	20.3	7.3	14.0
Argentina	2003	1.1	0.7	0.9	19.2	5.5	12.4
Belgium	1997	1.0	0.0	0.5	19.2	5.4	12.4
Canada	2002	0.9	0.9	0.9	17.5	5.2	11.5
Australia	2003	0.5	0.5	0.5	17.4	3.6	10.7
Chile	2003	1.4	0.3	0.8	17.3	4.0	10.8
Japan	2004	0.4	0.4	0.4	16.9	8.4	12.8
USA	2002	0.9	0.3	0.6	16.5	2.9	9.9
Austria	2005	0.6	0.2	0.4	15.7	3.6	9.8
Hong Kong	2004	0.5	0.8	0.6	15.4	9.0	12.2
Sweden	2002	0.7	0.5	0.6	14.6	4.5	9.7
Hungary	2003	1.4	0.0	0.7	14.4	3.4	9.0
Thailand	2002	0.6	0.5	0.6	13.8	3.8	8.9
Zimbabwe	1990	0.5	0.5	0.5	13.0	12.1	12.5
Colombia	1999	0.8	1.1	0.9	12.7	6.1	9.4
Denmark	2001	0.6	0.0	0.3	12.5	2.4	7.5
France	2003	0.7	0.2	0.4	12.5	3.7	8.1
Singapore	2003	0.8	0.8	0.8	12.2	8.9	10.5
Republic of Korea	2004	0.6	0.7	0.6	11.3	8.0	9.7
Mauritius	2004	0.0	0.0	0.0	11.2	5.2	8.2
Israel	2003	0.5	0.0	0.2	10.9	0.9	6.0
Germany	2004	0.4	0.2	0.3	10.5	2.7	6.7
Mexico	2003	0.8	0.5	0.7	10.1	2.8	6.4
United Kingdom & N. Ireland	2004	0.1	.00	0.1	8.0	2.3	5.2
Netherlands	2004	0.7	0.2	0.5	7.3	2.6	5.0
Brazil	2002	0.3	0.3	0.3	6.9	2.4	4.6
Italy	2002	0.2	0.2	0.2	6.5	1.5	4.1
Spain	2004	0.5	0.1	0.3	6.4	2.1	4.3
Albania	2003	1.3	0.0	0.7	5.5	4.9	5.2
Mainland China	1999	0.9	0.8	0.8	5.4	8.6	6.9
Dominican Republic	2001	0.0	0.0	0.0	3.4	0.9	2.2
Greece	2004	0.4	0.0	0.2	3.0	0.3	1.7
Philippines	1993	0.0	0.0	0.0	2.7	2.7	2.7

[a]*Rank-ordered by 15- to 24-year-old male suicide rates. Source of data: World Health Organization (2008).*

greater levels of aggression, and choice of more lethal suicide attempt methods. The higher rate of death by suicide among female youths in China is puzzling to researchers. Possible explanations have been suggested, such as the common presence of highly lethal insecticides and difficult access to treatment facilities, but this question requires further research.

This higher rate of death by suicide among adolescent males is in contrast with suicidal ideation and suicide attempts, where females have much higher rates than males after puberty. In the United States, girls are significantly more likely to have seriously considered attempting suicide (21.8% vs. 12%), made a specific plan (16.2% vs. 9.9%), attempted suicide than boys (10.8% vs. 6%), and made a medically injurious suicide attempt (2.9% vs. 1.8%) in the previous year (CDC, 2006).

Risk Factors

Primary risk factors for attempted and completed suicide among adolescents include a previous suicide attempt, suicidal ideation, depressive disorders, alcohol and drug use, and conduct-disordered or aggressive-impulsive behavior (Gould et al., 2003). Converging evidence from psychological autopsy studies, regardless of geographic region, indicates that 80% to 90% of adolescents who die by suicide suffer from a significant psychopathology. A history of suicide attempts is common among adolescents who complete suicide, and long-term outcome studies of adolescents hospitalized following suicide attempts indicate significant risk for suicide, particularly for males.

Cognitive factors (such as hopelessness, poor interpersonal and social problem-solving abilities), sexual orientation (being gay or bisexual), biological factors (abnormalities in serotonin functioning), a family history of psychopathology or suicide, physical and sexual abuse, and suicide contagion effects have also been shown to be related to increased risk for suicidal behavior and death. Finally, two types of stressful life events most

commonly precipitating a youth suicide are a romantic relationship ending and legal or disciplinary problems.

Due to the multiple risk factors and pathways to youth suicide, taking a biopsychosocial approach to both suicide risk assessment and treatment is warranted. Adolescent suicide can be best understood within a developmental psychopathology or transactional model, where there is an accumulation of risk factors that can exacerbate each other over time, creating a trajectory toward suicidality. Such a model can incorporate findings such as the high prevalence of mental and substance use disorders in youths who die by suicide, the role of social integration and relationships, and findings concerning known precipitators of suicide. Such a perspective is also consistent with a model of suicide that has been recently put forth by Joiner (2005). This theory posits that individuals die by suicide when thwarted belongingness and perceived burdensomeness are combined with the acquired ability to inflict self-harm.

Suicide Prevention and Treatment

Suicide prevention efforts are being developed and implemented around the world, with varying degrees of success (Gould et al., 2003). Education and awareness programs, suicide hotlines, gatekeeper training, mental health screening, peer helpers, and postvention and crisis intervention are the most common forms of suicide prevention programs. In addition to these interventions, evidence-based treatments exist for many of the conditions that elevate adolescents' risk for suicidal behavior and suicide (e.g., depression, alcohol and substance abuse, antisocial behavior); however, few controlled treatment or intervention studies have been conducted specifically with suicidal adolescents, and findings are mixed. Problem-solving interventions, multisystemic therapy, home-based family intervention, and social support intervention have all shown promising but mixed results on reductions in suicidal ideation and attempts.

Roisin O'Mara and Cheryl A. King

See also

Hopelessness
Suicidal Cognition
Suicide in the Elderly
Suicide Theories
Suicide Warning Signs

References

Centers for Disease Control and Prevention. (2005). *WISQARS injury mortality reports, 1999–2005*. Retrieved from http://www.cdc.gov/ncipc/wisqars/

Centers for Disease Control and Prevention. (2006). Youth risk behavior surveillance: Surveillance summaries. *Morbidity and Mortality Weekly Report, 55*, SS-5.

Evans, E., Hawton, K., & Rodham, K. (2005). The prevalence of suicidal phenomena in adolescents: A systematic review of population-based studies. *Suicide and Life-Threatening Behavior, 35*, 239–250.

Gould, M. S., Greenberg, T., & Velting, D. M. (2003). Youth suicide risk and preventive interventions: A review of the past 10 years. *Journal of the American Academy of Child and Adolescent Psychiatry, 42*, 386–405.

Joiner, T. (2005). *Why people die by suicide*. Cambridge, MA: Harvard University Press.

Tester, F. J., & McNicoll, P. (2004). Isumagijaksaq: Mindful of the state: Social constructions of Inuit suicide. *Social Science and Medicine, 58*, 2625–2636.

World Health Organization. (2001). *The world health report 2001—mental health: New understanding, new hope*. Retrieved from http://www.who.int/whr/2001/en/index.html

World Health Organization. (2008). *Mental health: Programs and projects*. Retrieved from http://www.who.int/mental_health/prevention/suicide/country_reports/en/index.html

Suicide Theories

Suicide is a global public health problem: according to the World Health Organization, one million individuals worldwide died from suicide in 2000. The vast majority of people who die by suicide suffer from mental disorders. Depression is a mental disorder that confers considerable risk for suicide in both adults and youths, with one estimate suggesting that the suicide rate among people with depression is approximately 20 times that of someone in the general population (Harris & Barraclough, 1997). Indeed, one of the symptoms of major depressive disorder according to the American Psychiatric Association is suicidal thoughts or behavior. However, it is also true that most people in the general population will not die by suicide; thus, even with a twentyfold increase in risk, most individuals with depression will not die by suicide. A study of a nationally representative sample of adults in the United States examined the prevalence of certain suicidal behaviors and found that nearly half of those with a lifetime history of depression experienced suicidal ideation, while fewer than 10% attempted suicide in their lifetime (Hasin, Goodwin, Stinson, & Grant, 2006).

These data indicate that depression is a significant risk factor for depression, but that it lacks specificity, as most individuals with depression will not die by suicide and not all individuals who die by suicide are depressed. Thus, a more comprehensive account of suicide than what can be provided by data on the relation between depression and suicide is needed to explain and predict suicide. Below, we provide a review of the major theoretical accounts of suicide.

Durkheim's Sociological Theory

One of the earliest theoretical accounts of suicide that remains prominent is Durkheim's (1897) sociological theory. Durkheim proposed that problematic levels of two social forces, social integration and moral integration, cause suicide. Too little social integration in society leads to an increase in egoistic suicides because individuals lack a life-saving connection that transcends themselves (i.e., a connection with society). Too much social integration in society leads to an increase in altruistic suicides because individuals sacrifice themselves for the larger good of society. Too little moral regulation (i.e., the degree to which society regulates the beliefs and behaviors of individuals through such means as societal norms and the legal system) results in anomic suicide—often through economic upheavals—because individuals' needs and abilities to achieve those means are thrown into a state of disequilibrium. Too much moral integration results in fatalistic suicide, the prototypical example being slaves who die by suicide.

Psychodynamic and Escape Theories

Psychodynamic theorists have also provided accounts of suicide, beginning with Freud's formulation of suicide as an act of aggression turned inward on the self, a view that was later elaborated by Menninger in his text *Man Against Himself* (Menninger, 1938). The conceptualization of suicide as a means of escape from psychological pain also figures prominently in psychodynamic accounts. In these accounts of suicide as escape, the act of self-harm is preceded by—and facilitated by—the breakdown of cognitive processes and the dissolution of the self.

A contemporary elaboration of the psychodynamic account, also informed by social and personality psychology theories and findings, was provided by Baumeister (1990). This theory describes a sequence of steps leading up to a suicide attempt as an escape from psychological pain. The first step in the sequence is the experience of a negative and severe discrepancy between personal expectations and actual outcomes (e.g., failures, unmet goals, disappointments). Second, the individual attributes this disappointment internally and blames him- or herself. Next, an aversive state of self-awareness develops, which produces negative affect. Next, the individual attempts to escape from this negative affect as well as from the aversive self-awareness by retreating into a numb state of cognitive deconstruction. In this state, meaningful thought about the self, including painful self-awareness and failed standards, is replaced by a lower-level awareness of concrete sensations and movements, and of immediate, proximal goals and tasks. This state of cognitive deconstruction results in reduced behavioral inhibition that contributes to lack

of impulse control in general and especially a lack of impulse control for suicidal behavior. According to Baumeister, when individuals are in a state of cognitive deconstruction, thinking becomes constricted and myopic and the ability to identify alternatives to suicide as an escape from pain is impaired, thus increasing the likelihood of suicide attempts.

Shneidman's Psychache Theory

Escape from psychological pain is the prominent feature of another theorist's account of suicide: Shneidman (1996, p. 4) wrote, "In almost every case, suicide is caused by pain, a certain kind of pain—psychological pain, which I call psychache. Furthermore, this psychache stems from thwarted or distorted psychological needs." For Shneidman, psychache—defined as general psychological and emotional pain that reaches intolerable intensity—is a proximal cause of suicide. That is, whatever earlier risk factors are at play, they operate through increasing psychache, which in turn, predisposes the individual to suicide. However, Shneidman (1985) also states, "What my research has taught me is that only a small minority of the cases of excessive psychological pain result in suicide, but every case of suicide stems from excessive psychache." This suggests that psychache is necessary but not sufficient for suicide to occur.

Beck's Hopelessness Theory

Beck, Brown, Berchick, and Stewart (1990) developed a cognitive theory of suicide that emphasizes the role of hopelessness. The theory proposes that hopelessness—beliefs that circumstances will not get better in the future—causes suicidal ideation. Hopelessness for Beck plays the role of psychache for Shneidman. Empirical evidence from a number of studies suggests that hopelessness is indeed a risk factor for death by suicide. In a large-scale prospective study of psychiatric outpatients, patients who scored high on a self-report measure of hopelessness were 4 times more likely to die by suicide in a given year than those who scored lower. Similarly, a large community study found that individuals who expressed hopelessness were 11.2 times more likely to die by suicide over a 13-year follow-up period.

Linehan's Emotion Dysregulation Theory

Linehan's (1993) theory proposes that emotion dysregulation is a core problem in suicidal behavior and that emotional dysregulation results from biological predispositions and invalidating environments. Further, the theory proposes that emotional dysregulation, when paired with the experience of negative emotional stimuli, results in high emotional sensitivity, an intense emotional experience, and a slow return to emotional baseline. Emotion dysregulation is further aggravated by invalidating environments—those environments in which communication of private experiences is met by erratic, inappropriate, and extreme responses. Self-injury (including suicide), according to Linehan, is an attempt to regulate emotions—an attempt that becomes necessary because more usual emotion regulation mechanisms have broken down or never developed adequately. She also presumes that suicide is the ultimate way for an individual to regulate negative affect, thus dovetailing with proposals of psychodynamic and escape theorists. Based on this theoretical framework Linehan (1993) developed dialectical behavior therapy, a treatment for suicidal behavior and borderline personality disorder. This therapy has been shown to be effective in six randomized controlled trials.

Joiner's Interpersonal Psychological Theory of Suicide

The interpersonal-psychological theory of suicide (Joiner, 2005) posits that an individual will not engage in serious suicidal behavior (i.e., self-injury with the intent to die) unless he or she has both the desire and the capability to do so. The theory further proposes

that suicidal desire results from the presence of two interpersonal constructs: thwarted belongingness and perceived burdensomeness. A thwarted sense of belongingness results from an unmet need to belong, whereas a sense of perceived burdensomeness results from an unmet need to contribute to the welfare of others. The theory also proposes that suicidal desire is not sufficient to result in death by suicide—individuals must also possess the capability to enact lethal self-injury. This capability can be acquired over time through exposure—and attendant habituation to—the fear and pain involved in self-injury.

The theory addresses the prevalence of suicidal behavior by proposing that the outcome of suicidal behavior depends on the presence of all three factors—thwarted belongingness, perceived burdensomeness, and acquired capability for lethal self-injury—such that each of the three factors is a necessary but not sufficient condition for suicidal behavior. The theory assumes that there are relatively large numbers of people who desire suicide and a modest number of those who have developed the capacity for suicide. Thus, the simultaneous presence of all three factors should be comparatively rare. This hypothesis is consistent with the relative rarity of suicide: many theories are inconsistent with the fact that only a small subset of those who think about suicide go on to attempt and fewer still die by suicide. A study specifically testing the theory in a sample of clinical outpatients found that, in line with the theory, individuals high on both perceived burdensomeness (cf., suicidal desire) and acquired capability were rated at highest risk for suicide by clinicians.

Conclusions

Each of the theories mentioned above has contributed to the field's understanding of suicidal behavior by generating hypotheses to be tested and/or creating ideas to be applied to clinical work. For example, the interpersonal-psychological theory rests on Durkheim's (1897) proposal of the integral role of social processes, social integration in particular. As another example, a structured and empirically supported suicide risk assessment framework, the Collaborative Assessment and Management of Suicidality (CAMS; Jobes, 2006), is grounded in Shneidman's (1985) psychache theory. Finally, Linehan's (1993) emotion dysregulation theory is the foundation for dialectical behavior therapy, the only treatment for suicidal behavior shown to be effective in more than one trial. Thus, the theories described above, designed to predict and prevent suicide, would surely support Kurt Lewin's claim that "there is nothing so practical as a good theory."

KIMBERLY A. VAN ORDEN AND THOMAS E. JOINER JR.

See also

Geriatric Depression
Hopelessness
Suicidal Cognition
Suicide in the Elderly
Suicide in Youths
Suicide Warning Signs

References

Baumeister, R. F. (1990). Suicide as escape from self. *Psychological Review, 97*, 90–113.

Beck, A. T., Brown, G., Berchick, R. J., & Stewart, B. L. (1990). Relationship between hopelessness and ultimate suicide: A replication with psychiatric outpatients. *American Journal of Psychiatry, 147*, 190–195.

Durkheim, E. (1897). *Le Suicide: Etude de socologie.* Paris, France: F. Alcan.

Harris, E. C., & Barraclough, B. (1997). Suicide as an outcome for mental disorders. *British Journal of Psychiatry, 170*, 205–228.

Hasin, D. S., Goodwin, R. D., Stinson, F. S., & Grant, B. F. (2006). Epidemiology of major depressive disorder: Results from the National Epidemiologic Survey on Alcoholism and Related Conditions. *Archives of General Psychiatry, 62*, 1097–1106.

Jobes, D. A. (2006). *Managing suicidal risk: A collaborative approach.* New York: Guilford Press.

Joiner, T. E., Jr. (2005). *Why people die by suicide.* Cambridge, MA: Harvard University Press.

Linehan, M. M. (1993). *Cognitive-behavioral treatment of borderline personality disorder.* New York: Guilford Press.

Menninger, K. A. (1938). *Man Against Himself.* New York: Harcourt, Brace and Company.

Shneidman, E. S. (1996). *Definition of suicide.* New York: Wiley.

Suicide Warning Signs

Warning signs have become relatively commonplace in health care over the last several decades, with broad public recognition of warning signs for heart attack, stroke, and diabetes. Only recently has the approach been applied to suicide (Rudd et al., 2006). Although warning signs for suicide are easily available to the public in a number of formats, including the Internet, there has been little and, arguably, no scientific oversight until the last few years. As a result, there has been a confusing array of messages, risk factors, and clinical recommendations. As an example, Mandrusiak and colleagues (2006) identified over 3,000 warning signs for suicide on the Internet, with the vast majority having no empirical support.

Differentiating warnings signs from risk factors is critical to understanding the role of warning signs in the process of suicide risk assessment. Warning signs in other health domains (e.g., heart attack, stroke, diabetes) include both signs (something observed by another) and symptoms (something reported to another). As has been discussed elsewhere (Rudd, 2006), the time frame over which most common suicide risk factors are studied has little, if any, relevance for clinical practice, ranging from a year to well over 20 years. What is important for practicing clinicians, first responders, gatekeepers, and anyone facing the challenge of someone at risk for suicide, are decisions about what to do in the next few minutes, hours, or days. Suicide warning signs have emerged in an effort to focus more precisely on clinically relevant time frames, with the goal of facilitating efficient and effective decision making and saving of lives.

There is certainly overlap between warning signs and risk factors for suicide. The primary distinguishing feature of a warning sign for suicide is that it characterizes current functioning. The relationship to suicidal behavior or suicide is proximal rather than distal in nature, something that is common for risk factors. Accordingly, suicide warning signs are associated with near-term risk (minutes, hours, days), rather than acute (days to weeks) or longer-term (years) risk. Warning signs help answer the question, "What is this individual doing (observable sign) or saying (reported symptom) that indicates elevated risk to die by suicide in the next few minutes, hours, or days?" Warning signs possess a few additional unique characteristics. Warning signs for suicide can also be differentiated from risk factors by definitional specificity, empirical foundation, nature of occurrence (static vs. episodic), application context, implications for clinical practice, and intended target group. More specifically, in contrast to risk factors, warning signs for suicide tend to be less well defined, have less empirical support, be episodic and variable in nature, be meaningful only as part of a constellation of signs and symptoms, and be generally intended for public consumption and use.

A suicide warning sign can be defined as the earliest detectable sign that indicates heightened risk for suicide in the near term (i.e., within minutes, hours, or days). A warning sign refers to some feature of the developing outcome of interest (suicide) rather than to a distinct construct (risk factor) that predicts or may be related to suicide (Rudd et al., 2006). As the focus of this definition makes clear, warning signs are associated with suicide attempts and death within short time periods.

Expert Consensus on Suicide Warning Signs

An expert consensus panel organized by the American Association of Suicidology agreed on two points about suicide warning signs. First, suicide warning signs need to be addressed in hierarchical fashion. Second, clear and detailed instructions need to be made available to the general public on how to respond when warning signs are recognized. With respect to the need for a hierarchical approach, the consensus panel recognized that one warning sign needed immediate attention and response and, accordingly, needed to be presented separately. The panel emphasized

that anyone threatening to hurt or kill him- or herself, someone looking for ways to kill him- or herself (seeking access to pills, weapons, or other means), and someone talking or writing about death, dying, or suicide needs immediate attention or help. It is recommended that if this warning sign is observed or reported, the following actions are indicated: calling 911, seeking help from a mental health provider, or calling the national crisis hotline (1-800-273-TALK). The second tier of suicide warning signs, not requiring immediate response, includes the following: hopelessness; rage, anger, and/or seeking revenge; acting reckless or engaging in risky activities seemingly without thinking; feeling trapped like there is no way out; increasing alcohol or drug use; withdrawing from family, friends, and society; anxiety, agitation, or the inability to sleep, or sleeping all the time; dramatic changes in mood; and seeing no reasons for living or no sense of purpose in life. Suicide warning signs wallet cards are available at no cost from the Substance Abuse Mental Health Services Administration at http://mentalhealth.samhsa.gov/disasterrelief/publications/allpubs/walletcard/engwalletcard.asp.

Clinical Application of Suicide Warning Signs

Although warning signs for suicide, for the most part, target the general public, they have clear implications for clinical practice and risk assessment. Most important, suicide warning signs indicate elevated risk over a short time period. In other words, they suggest imminent risk and, in clinical practice, demand immediate attention and a definitive response. From a clinical perspective, integrating warning signs into risk assessment models is most effective by thinking about mental status. All of the identified warning signs have a direct and meaningful impact on mental status, along with being both observable (signs) and reportable (symptoms) in nature. Any time a clinician recognizes and documents a suicide warning sign, some mention needs to be made about its relative impact on mental status. Risk increases in parallel fashion with mental status impairment. In short, it is a simple and straightforward way of answering the question, "How severe is the warning sign and how much impairment in individual functioning is observed or reported?" It is also important for clinicians to be aware that there are observable signs of hopelessness, not just a patient self-report of feeling hopeless. Observable signs of hopelessness include the following: noncompliance with treatment (therapy or medicines), refusal to access care during crises or emergencies, little engagement or involvement during sessions, refusal to complete homework, refusal to agree to a safety plan, detailed and specific suicidal thoughts, any preparation behaviors (letter or journal writing about suicide, organizing a will, purchasing life insurance), rehearsal behaviors (practicing for suicide), refusal to give up an available method, persistent reckless behavior, an inability to provide reasons for living, among a host of others.

In the clinical environment, it is important for clinicians to make use of warning signs when negotiating crisis response plans (i.e., directions on what to do in a crisis). More specifically, patients should be made aware of the warning signs for suicide, encouraged to monitor them closely, and be provided clear and specific steps to take should the various warning signs emerge. Such an approach lends itself nicely to role-playing and essential skill building for patients at risk for suicide, with a focus on the patient's unique warning sign profile.

The hope is that warning signs will not only facilitate greater public awareness about suicide and improved responses to those at risk, but they will also have clear implications for how risk assessment is conducted in clinical practice and how patients at risk for suicide are managed.

M. DAVID RUDD

See also

Geriatric Depression

Hopelessness
Suicidal Cognition
Suicide in the Elderly
Suicide in Youths
Suicide Theories

References

Mandrusiak, M., Rudd, M. D., Joiner, T. E., Berman, A. L., Witte, T., & VanOrden, K. (2006). Warning signs for suicide and the Internet: A descriptive study. *Suicide and Life-Threatening Behavior, 36,* 263–271.

Rudd, M. D. (2006). *Assessing and managing suicidality.* Sarasota, FL: Professional Resource Press.

Rudd, M. D., Berman, A. L., Joiner, T. E., Nock, M. K., Silverman, M., Mandrusiak, M., et al. (2006). Warning signs for suicide: Theory, research, and clinical application. *Suicide and Life-Threatening Behavior, 36,* 255–262.

Symptoms of Depression

Depressive disorders are classified as mood disorders. Depression is thus a disorder of affect and is often referred to as an affective disorder. Affect is usually viewed as synonymous with emotion and thus in the case of depression refers to feeling a sad mood. A sad mood is also thought of as dysphoria. Beyond dysphoria, however, a major depressive episode is characterized by a variety of symptoms. Some of these symptoms are codified in the *Diagnostic and Statistical Manual of Mental Disorders* (American Psychiatric Association, 2000) and are required for a formal diagnosis. These symptoms include (a) depressed mood, (b) diminished interest or pleasure in activities, (c) significant weight loss or gain, or changes in appetite, (d) insomnia (difficulty sleeping) or hypersomnia (sleeping too much), (e) psychomotor agitation or retardation, (f) fatigue or loss of energy, (g) feelings of worthlessness, (h) difficulty concentrating, and (i) suicidal ideation (thoughts) or a suicide attempt.

A formal diagnosis requires that at least five of these symptoms be present for at least 2 weeks. Additionally, at least one of the first two symptoms must also be present for a diagnosis. These are known as the cardinal symptoms of depression and are those that define it as a disorder and differentiate it from other disorders. The first is obvious; to be diagnosed with a mood disorder, depressed mood must be present. The second symptom, diminished interest, is referred to as anhedonia and is frequently seen in other disorders also. Depressed mood and anhedonia are usually both experienced, but some depressed individuals can experience one but not the other.

There are several situations that must also be observed for a formal diagnosis. In particular, to be diagnosed with a major depressive episode, these symptoms must cause significant distress or impair the person's ability to function. They also cannot be due to a medical condition, or because of the use of medication or substance abuse. Lastly, these symptoms cannot be due to bereavement, unless they last for longer than 2 months or markedly disrupt functioning.

Depressed individuals can experience other symptoms of depression, such as decreased interest in sex, but such symptoms are not part of the formal diagnostic criteria. Symptoms, whether part of a formal di-agnosis or not, can be grouped into clusters with similar features. Dysphoria features are those dealing with the mood, while vegetative symptoms are those that deal with physical functioning, such as sleep and appetite difficulties and diminished sex drive. Cognitive symptoms are those dealing with cognitive functioning, such as difficulty thinking, as well as the experience of negative thoughts. Some symptoms, such as apathy, fatigue, and lack of energy, fall under the general category of apathy.

RICK E. INGRAM

See also

Diagnostic and Statistical Manual of Mental Disorders

References

American Psychiatric Association. (2000). *Diagnostic and statistical manual of mental disorders* (4th ed., text revision). Washington, DC: Author.

T

Temperament

Temperament is a risk factor for the emergence of depression or depressive symptoms in children and adults. In particular, temperament characteristics of negative and positive affectivity, effortful control, and impulsivity have been shown to relate to depression, and individual differences in these characteristics appear to be vulnerabilities for depression.

Conceptual Models of Temperament

Several models for the role of temperament in the emergence of psychopathology have been suggested. In a diathesis-stress model, or vulnerability model, temperament represents a vulnerability for psychopathology when stressful or disruptive conditions are present. Such a model can be expanded to examine resilience, as well, in that some characteristics might be protective in the presence of other risk factors. Thus, the effects of other risk factors, such as stress, family context, parenting, and social relationships, on psychopathology might be exacerbated or mitigated depending on an individual's temperament characteristics.

In an evocative or transactional model, temperament characteristics might shape other risk or protective factors, which might, in turn, relate to the emergence of psychopathology. In this case, temperament characteristics might be related to stress appraisals, coping, cognitive styles, relationship quality, emotion regulation, selection of environment and experiences, and other factors that might result in symptoms or psychopathology. It is interesting to note that there is relatively little research examining the role of temperament in depression compared to the extent of research examining the role of temperament in other forms of psychopathology such as anxiety, externalizing, antisocial, and substance use problems. However, there is increasing attention to examining temperament as a risk factor for depression.

In the sections that follow, we provide a definition of temperament and identify temperament characteristics that appear to play a role in the emergence of depression. We also discuss evidence for potential mechanisms of those effects, focusing on support for the vulnerability-resilience and evocative effects models.

Definition of Temperament

Temperament is defined as the physiological basis for individual differences in reactivity and self-regulation, including motivation, affect, activity, and attention characteristics (Rothbart & Bates, 2006). Reactivity refers to responsiveness to change in the external and internal environments and includes physiological and emotional reactions. Commonly included in studies of temperament are indicators of fear (inhibition, withdrawal), frustration or anger, approach, pleasure, and positive affect. Self-regulation refers to orienting and executive control of attention and behavior that operates to modulate reactivity, facilitating or inhibiting the physiological or affective response. Self-regulation is commonly assessed with measure of attention focusing, attention shifting, and inhibitory control, which compose the construct effortful control.

Underlying these dimensions of reactivity and self-regulation are individual differences in motivational systems reflecting differential susceptibility to reward and punishment. Activation of the behavioral inhibition system (BIS), which is responsive to cues of punishment or threat, produces fear and anxiety, serving to inhibit approach behaviors in response to negative consequences and cues of aversive consequences. Activation of the behavioral activation system (BAS), which is responsive to cues of reward, motivates approach or behavioral activation toward an incentive or active avoidance of punishment and produces frustration when reward attainment is blocked (Gray, 1991). The balance of individuals' reward and punishment orientations influences their perceptions of a situation (e.g., threatening or enticing), their affective reactions to the situation (e.g., fear, frustration, excitement, or boredom), and their behavioral responses (e.g., avoidance, withdrawal, or approach).

A number of potential mechanisms might account for the relation between temperament and depression. Temperament is believed to have both direct effects on the development and expression of symptoms, increasing the likelihood of symptoms emerging, as well as indirect effects through selection or structuring of the environment, eliciting patterns of social interactions, biasing information processing and cognitive patterns, and shaping characteristic coping styles. Temperament also interacts with an individual's social and environmental experiences, exacerbating, or buffering the effects of those experiences.

Temperament and Depression

Negative Affectivity

Negative affectivity, which reflects a susceptibility to react to stress with a high degree of distress, is linked with internalizing disorders (Krueger & Markon, 2006) and depression, in particular (e.g., Lonigan, Phillips, & Hooe, 2003). In addition, the association between negative affectivity and depressed mood has been validated cross-culturally, and important mechanisms of its effects have been identified. For example, negative affectivity is related to increased self-focus, attention to negative events, and negative expectancies and has been shown to predict negative or depressogenic cognitive styles. Individuals high in negative affectivity have a propensity to perceive events as threatening and to use less-constructive coping strategies in response to stress (Lengua & Long, 2002). Negative affectivity also relates to lower perceived social support.

Researchers have also examined fear and frustration components of negative affectivity separately, as they are thought to stem from different motivational systems, that is, the BIS and BAS, respectively, and thus, may have differing patterns of association with depression and its predictors.

Fear and Inhibition

A substantial body of research has investigated the role that temperamental fear may play in the development of psychopathology. With regard to depression, much of this literature focuses on distinguishing between anxiety and depression at the etiological level, as well as identifying factors that predict the development and maintenance of symptoms. The common etiology hypothesis suggests that, because anxiety and depression co-occur at high rates, common underlying factors must represent vulnerabilities for both disorders. Limited support has been achieved for this hypothesis, as much of the research conducted has been cross-sectional and unable to clarify the specificity of effects. However, when studies have employed methods that allow for the clarification of specific associations by partitioning variance or using longitudinal methods, fear is consistently and robustly associated with anxiety symptoms, but not with initial levels or changes in depression. Fear may pose a risk for developing depression when contextual risk factors such as negative parenting or stressful life events are present (Kiff, Lengua, & Bush, 2009). However, it appears that the risk for depression conferred by higher fearfulness or inhibition is primarily through the co-occurrence of anxiety disorders with depression.

Although stressful and negative environmental factors have been linked to depression, researchers are beginning to understand how children's temperamental vulnerabilities may affect these associations. For example, research shows that children high in withdrawal negativity (high BIS) are vulnerable to developing a depressogenic cognitive style in response to the stress associated with negative life events. In addition, fear may moderate the effects of other risk factors. For example, individual differences in children's fearfulness appear to affect susceptibility to negative parenting (e.g., Lengua, 2008). It has also been found that high-fear boys, compared to low-fear boys, are more likely to demonstrate depressive symptoms in relation to parental overinvolvement and harsh discipline.

Frustration and Irritability

Frustration is characterized by high levels of negative affect in response to blocked goals. Research has generally noted an association between temperamental frustration and externalizing problems in children. Thus, frustration may represent a general vulnerability for the development of psychopathology or may serve as a risk for depression through the high co-occurrence of internalizing and externalizing disorders. In addition, researchers have identified that high levels of temperamental frustration is more common in boys, which may explain the association with externalizing problems. Nonetheless, some researchers have demonstrated that high levels of frustration present a vulnerability for the development of depression. In particular, temperamental frustration may be a risk factor for bipolar disorder.

Frustration might increase the risk for depression by rendering individuals more sensitive to the effects of negative relationships or experiences, or by engendering more negative social interactions. For example, easily frustrated children may be more sensitive to the effects of negative parenting; children's irritability increases their susceptibility to developing depression when coupled with low maternal warmth or high maternal overprotection. In addition, individuals who are high in frustration or irritability might evoke more negative reactions from others, including more negative parenting behavior, which in turn, might increase risk for depression.

Positive Affectivity

Positive affectivity reflects an individual's propensity to experience positive moods, inclination to be approach oriented, and high BAS activity in Gray's model. Individuals low in positive affectivity or BAS activity are less likely to recognize positive experiences and potential positive outcomes or expect positive events. Thus, lower levels of positive affectivity have been suggested to be a risk factor for depression. In particular, it has been suggested that vulnerability to depression is highest in individuals characterized by a high degree of negative affectivity and a low degree of positive affectivity. Indeed, evidence indicates that positive affectivity or BAS activity is related to lower levels of depression, and there is a particularly strong, negative correlation between positive affect or BAS activity and the anhedonia and depressed affect components of depression.

Low positive affectivity might present a risk for depression through its relation with depressive cognitive styles. For example, it has been found that lower levels of positive affectivity at age 3 contribute to depressotypic cognitive styles at age 7. Consistent with theories implicating the role of positive affectivity as a temperamental vulnerability for depression, this characteristic specifically predicted interpersonal helplessness and lower positive schematic processing at age 7. Research also suggests that children's depression symptoms are related to a probability bias against positive events, such that higher levels of depression are associated with lower probability estimates for future positive events. In addition, higher levels of positive affectivity may be protective, mitigating the effects of other risk factors. For example, positive affectivity moderates children's responses to maternal rejection, which predicts children's depressive symptoms for children low in positive affectivity but not for children high in positive affectivity.

Effortful Control

Effortful control reflects individual differences in the ability to regulate one's attention and inhibit dominant responses in an effort to initiate a subdominant action. The attention regulation and shifting components of effortful control are negatively related to negative affectivity, as individuals better at directing their attention can attenuate their distress. Much of the research regarding effortful control and psychopathology has been conducted in samples of children and has tended to examine internalizing more broadly rather than depression in particular. Researchers have generally found that individuals higher in effortful control may be less prone to developing internalizing problems. The few studies that have examined associations between effortful control and depression specifically suggest that effortful control is negatively related to depression. Also, effortful control is consistently and robustly related to externalizing problems. Thus, the association of lower effortful control to higher rates of depression may operate through the high co-occurrence of depression and externalizing problems in children and adolescents.

Effortful control might predict lower depression through the modulation of negative affect. It might also operate through the inhibition of initial impulses to avoid or withdraw from social or challenging situations, allowing the individual to engage in activities or social interactions despite reduced motivation to do so. Such activation might mitigate

depressive symptoms through increasing positive expectancies and reducing anhedonia. In addition, effortful control is related to greater use of active coping strategies, which might mitigate the impact of stressful life experiences on depression (Lengua & Long, 2002). Individuals higher in effortful control might also evoke fewer negative or conflictual interactions with others. For example, children higher in effortful control tend to elicit less harsh and rejecting parenting.

Researchers have also examined how effortful control may affect the association between environmental factors and depression symptoms. Accordingly, effortful control was found to moderate the effects of contextual risk on internalizing problems such that there were fewer adverse effects of contextual risk for children higher in effortful control (Lengua, 2008). Effortful control also moderated the effects of parenting on changes in depression symptoms. Children low in effortful control seemed to benefit from higher levels of maternal guidance and structuring as they reported decreases in depression symptoms across the study. Conversely, children low in effortful control whose mothers did not display a high degree of scaffolding did not report a decline in symptoms (Kiff et al., 2009). These results suggest that effortful control may be an important factor in determining how and when environmental stressors negatively impact adjustment.

Impulsivity

Impulsivity has been defined as the inability to wait for a desired goal and has been viewed as an indicator of behavioral undercontrol or disinhibition. Impulsivity is most often considered a vulnerability factor for externalizing problems, yet there is evidence that impulsivity is related to higher levels of depression. However, the evidence for the relation between impulsivity and depression is inconsistent with some evidence that impulsivity is inversely related to depression. Their research suggests that individuals higher in impulsivity are also higher in ego resilience, which relates to lower depression (Eisenberg et al., 2004).

It is important to consider that impulsivity is a temperamental characteristic that is highly correlated with other temperament dimensions including negative affectivity and effortful control, which are also related to depression. Thus, it is possible that impulsivity is related to depression as a result of its correlation with other variables. Also, impulsivity is an important factor in externalizing problems and thus might relate to depression as a result of the high degree of co-occurrence of depression with externalizing problems, particularly in children.

Conclusions

Temperament is an important factor to consider in the emergence of depression. Negative affectivity, irritability in particular, positive affectivity, effortful control, and impulsivity appear to directly predict depression through the expression of depressive symptoms. Further, these characteristics interact and transact with other risk factors for depression, including cognitive, behavioral, social, and environmental risk factors, eliciting them and exacerbating or mitigating the effects of other risk factors on depression.

LILIANA J. LENGUA AND CARA J. KIFF

See also

Automatic and Controlled Processing in Depression
Behavioral Activation System
Behavioral Inhibition System
Childhood Depression
Externalizing Disorders
Internalizing Disorders
Parenting

References

Eisenberg, N., Spinrad, T. L., Fabes, R. A., Reiser, M., Cumberland, A., Shepard, S. A., et al. (2004). The relations of effortful control and impulsivity to children's resiliency and adjustment. *Child Development, 75*, 25–46.
Gray, J. A. (1991). The neuropsychology of temperament. In J. Strelau & A. Angleitner (Eds.), *Explorations in temperament: International perspectives on theory and measurement* (pp. 105–128). New York: Plenum.
Kiff, C. J., Lengua, L. J., & Bush, N. R. (2009). *The interaction of maternal parenting and child temperament in predicting growth in depression and anxiety symptoms.* Unpublished manuscript, University of Washington, Seattle.
Krueger, R. F., & Markon, K. E. (2006). Understanding psychopathology. Melding behavior genetics, personality, and quantitative psychology to develop an empirically based model. *Current Directions in Psychological Science, 15*, 113–117.
Lengua, L. J. (2008). Anxiousness, frustration, and effortful control as moderators of the relation between parenting and adjustment problems in middle-childhood. *Social Development, 17*, 554–577.
Lengua, L. J., & Long, A. C. (2002). The role of emotionality and self-regulation in the appraisal-coping process: Tests of direct and moderating effects. *Applied Developmental Psychology, 23*, 471–493.
Lonigan, C. J., Phillips, B., & Hooe, E. S. (2003). Relations of positive and negative affectivity to anxiety and depression in children: Evidence from a latent variable longitudinal study. *Journal of Consulting and Clinical Psychology, 71*, 465–481.
Rothbart, M. K., & Bates, J. E. (2006). Temperament. In N. Eisenberg, W. Damon, & R. M. Lerner (Eds.), *Handbook of child psychology, Vol. 3: Social, emotional and personality development* (pp. 99–166). Hoboken, NJ: Wiley.

Therapeutic Lifestyle Change

Therapeutic lifestyle change (TLC) (Ilardi et al., 2005) is a 14-week behavioral intervention for depression based on a set of six principal lifestyle elements of established antidepressant efficacy: physical exercise, omega-3 fatty acid supplementation, bright light exposure, enhanced social connection, antiruminative activity, and adequate nightly sleep. Predicated on the assumption that the burgeoning depression epidemic in North America and Europe is attributable in part to the loss of key protective features that characterized life in the distant past, TLC has as its focus the reclamation and integration of these salubrious lifestyle elements into the fabric of modern life.

Theoretical Foundations of TLC

TLC is based upon the premise of evolutionary mismatch (Nesse & Williams, 1994), which posits a poor fit between the modern postindustrial milieu and the Pleistocene-era adaptations that still characterize the human brain. According to this conceptualization, the human brain—in particular, the neurological architecture underlying affect regulation, stress response, social behavior, and other depression-relevant systems—is still well adapted to the hunter-gatherer environment that prevailed for the great majority of human evolutionary history. During this premodern period of human existence, numerous environmental features helped protect people from spiraling into full-blown, maladaptive episodes of depressive illness. In the modern environment, however, such antidepressant contextual elements are assumed to exist at diminished levels. The theory is congruent with the environmental mutation model of mental disorders described by Cosmides and Tooby's (1999) taxonomy, and it views depression as a harmful consequence of changes in the environment having been inadequately met by concomitant neurological adaptations.

The TLC theoretical framework is supported by converging lines of epidemiological evidence. First, there is the puzzling observation that depression's prevalence in the United States and other industrialized nations has increased dramatically over the last 50 years—a period over which the aforementioned environmental mutations have grown exponentially—and these increases are largely attributable to increased risk in each generational cohort (Seligman, 1990). Additionally, there is the finding that rates of depression tend to be lower in developing countries than in industrialized nations (Weissman et al., 1996), and also lower in rural areas of developing nations in comparison with more urbanized areas (Colla, Buka, Harrington, & Murphy, 2006). A similar pattern has also emerged within the United States, where the Amish, who are insulated from mainstream technological and social mutations, appear similarly insulated from this depression "epidemic" (Egeland & Hostetter, 1983).

Strikingly, depression is less detectable among the few contemporary modern hunter-gatherer societies surveyed, such as the Kaluli of Papua New Guinea (Schieffelin, 1985) and the Toraja of Indonesia (Hollan, 1992)—a pattern that would be expected if the Pleistocenelike environments provided by the lifestyles of these modern hunter-gatherers conferred antidepressant qualities not similarly provided by industrialized (or even agrarian) lifestyles.

Components of TLC

TLC identifies six principal lifestyle elements that confer protection from depression, but that are no longer adequately present in the modern, postindustrial context. Although TLC draws heavily from anthropological records of contemporary and historical hunter-gathering societies, the elements themselves (and the corresponding "dosages" of each) are approximated, rather than strictly duplicated, by the intervention.

Omega-3 Fatty Acid Consumption

Polyunsaturated fatty acids (PUFAs) play an important role in the function of many neurological processes. Among these, the role of the omega-3 PUFAs has been most strongly implicated in the building and maintenance of neurological structures in the brain, with proposed mechanisms including increased membrane elasticity, potentiated neurotransmission, and anti-inflammatory cellular activities.

Abundant evidence suggests the modern human diet is remarkably deficient in omega-3 PUFAs. In the Pleistocene environment, long-chain forms of omega-3 PUFAs—namely, eicosapentaenoic acid (EPA) and docosahexaenoic acid (DHA)—would have been easily accessible through the widespread consumption of grazing animals, which would have metabolized these long-chain forms from shorter PUFAs in the green plants they consumed. In the Western diet, long-chain omega-3 sources have effectively been restricted to ocean-caught fish, as most farm-raised fish and livestock are fed with omega-3-deficient grains or animal by-products.

Omega-3 PUFAs have been directly implicated in the treatment and prevention of depression. In cross-national comparisons, Hibbeln (1999) found a substantial association between omega-3 PUFAs consumed in a population and corresponding rates of depression. In randomized controlled trials, omega-3 supplementation has also demonstrated efficacy in the treatment of depression, both as an adjuvant treatment and as a monotherapy (Ross, Seguin, & Sieswerda, 2007).

Accordingly, TLC promotes daily high-dose omega-3 supplementation. Drawing upon the extant clinical literature, the protocol directs clients to supplement their normal daily diets with 1,000 mg of EPA and 500 mg of DHA, supplied in the form of high-quality fish oil capsules.

Physical Exercise

Contemporary hunter-gatherers typically spend many hours each day engaged in vigorous physical activity. In gathering edible plants, tracking animals, collecting water, and scouting adjacent territories, they often travel on foot up to 10 miles daily. Modern Americans, in contrast, are notoriously sedentary, and the majority of adults now get no regular physical exercise at all.

Yet regular exercise confers a powerful protective benefit vis-à-vis depression. Numerous clinical trials also document the efficacy of physical exercise as a first-line treatment for depression. Aerobic exercise—just 90 minutes per week—has even been found as effective as selective serotonin-reuptake inhibitor medication in randomized controlled trials (Blumenthal et al., 2007). The TLC protocol includes an aerobic exercise component, under the direction of a trainer or consultant, at a recommended minimum "dosage" of 30 minutes, three times per week.

Light Exposure

Because the light of a sunny day is over 100 times brighter than that of a well-lit indoor room, modern Americans and Europeans—who spend the bulk of their time inside—get much less light exposure than did their distant hunter-gatherer ancestors. They even get considerably less light than their counterparts from a few generations ago, when people spent much less time indoors.

Circadian rhythm is heavily influenced by both the amount and the intensity of light that strikes the retinas each day, and insufficient light exposure is now recognized as a prime culprit in the disruption of circadian rhythms. Such disruption, in turn, frequently gives rise to dysregulated sleep, altered hormone secretion, and fatigue. Light exposure has also been found to play an important role in mood regulation, and extended sunlight deprivation has robust depressogenic effects.

Bright light therapy has been found to be of great benefit in the treatment of seasonal-onset depression, and even to exert a potent antidepressant effect with nonseasonal forms of depression, as well (e.g., Tuunainen, Kripke, & Endo, 2004). The TLC protocol incorporates a daily light exposure element—using either natural daylight or a broad-spectrum light box—at a recommended intensity of 10,000-lux (the brightness of a sunny morning) for approximately 30 minutes.

Social Connection

Hunter-gatherers typically live in close-knit social groups ranging in size from 50 to 100, characterized by a high level of social support and interdependency. Modern American society, in contrast, is notable for its growing social disengagement and isolation, and the steady erosion of social bonds. A recent large-scale longitudinal survey, for example, pointed to a sharp decline in the mean number of friendships among American adults since the mid-1980s (McPherson, Smith-Lovin, & Brashears, 2006). Sadly, the majority of adults now report the absence of a single close friendship outside of the immediate family.

This relentless disappearance of social ties is a troubling development, especially since social support serves as an important buffer against depression onset. Notably, psychotherapies that explicitly target the enhancement of social relationships are also efficacious in treating depression and in reducing the risk of depression recurrence. TLC, therefore, incorporates a prominent focus on increasing social interaction and the strengthening of interpersonal bonds—a process facilitated in part by the delivery of TLC in a group format that promotes a high level of social support.

Antiruminative Activity

Rumination—the tendency to dwell repetitively on negative thoughts—is a cognitive process that renders people vulnerable to depression. Accordingly, rumination has received considerable attention of late from depression researchers, both as an etiological factor and as a potential target of clinical intervention. Indeed, therapy approaches specifically designed to reduce or counteract rumination have shown great promise in the treatment of depression (Dimidjian et al., 2006).

Unlike life among our hunter-gatherer and agrarian ancestors, the contemporary Western lifestyle affords ample time and opportunity for rumination. The erosion of community bonds has brought in its wake a sharp increase in social isolation—the principal context in which rumination occurs. In addition, most workers now commute by themselves and spend hours each week sitting alone in traffic. The average American also spends over 30 hours each week watching television, a surprisingly nonengaging activity that serves as a prime occasion for rumination.

TLC teaches patients to identify their ruminative behavior in real time and to follow this detection by redirecting their energy to more adaptive activities. Whereas traditional cognitive behavioral therapy focuses upon modifying the *content* of depressive cognition (i.e., substituting negativistic ruminative thoughts with more rational ones), TLC targets the ruminative process itself. In a nutshell, the focus is a shift from thinking to doing.

Sleep

A century ago, before the widespread adoption of electric lighting, Americans slept an average of 9 hours each night. That nightly mean has fallen with each successive generation and now stands at a mere 6.8 hours, considerably below recommended norms. Hunter-gatherers, on the other hand, typically spend 10 to 12 hours each night in darkness, and may complain—if anything— of getting *too much* sleep.

Inadequate sleep may lead over time to a number of deleterious health consequences, ranging from impaired cognitive function to metabolic and hormonal disturbances. Chronic sleep loss also puts a person at markedly increased risk for depression, and interventions aimed at enhancing the quantity and quality of sleep have been shown to effectively reduce depressive symptoms.

Three elements of the TLC protocol— aerobic exercise, bright light exposure, and omega-3 supplementation—have a demonstrated ability to improve sleep quality. In addition, however, the TLC protocol includes an explicit focus on addressing sleep deficits through the integration of established behavioral techniques such as stimulus control, sleep restriction, and enhanced sleep hygiene.

Conclusions

Ilardi and colleagues are evaluating the acute efficacy of the TLC protocol for major depression by means of a randomized trial with a wait-list, treatment-as-usual community control condition. Among 81 TLC participants, 68% have achieved favorable treatment response in intent-to-treat analyses, in comparison with a 19% response rate among community controls (Jacobson et al., 2007). The protocol has also shown to be feasible for the majority of participants, with overall adherence to the six primary protocol elements averaging approximately 74%. The TLC protocol thus shows promise as both a treatment for depression, as well as an adjunctive treatment added to existing treatments.

STEVEN S. ILARDI

See also

Circadian Rhythms
Evolution
Exercise and Depression
Insomnia
Omega-3 Fatty Acids
Rumination
Seasonal Affective Disorder
Seasonal Affective Disorder: Light Treatment

References

Blumenthal, J. A., Babyak, M. A., Doraiswamy, P. M. W., Hoffman, B. M., Barbour, K. A., Herman, S., et al. (2007). Exercise and pharmacotherapy in the treatment of major depressive disorder. *Psychosomatic Medicine, 69,* 587–596.

Colla, J., Buka, S., Harrington, D., & Murphy, J. M. (2006). Depression and modernization: A cross-cultural study of women. *Social Psychiatry and Psychiatric Epidemiology, 41,* 271–279.

Cosmides, L., & Tooby, J. (1999). Toward an evolutionary taxonomy of treatable conditions. *Journal of Abnormal Psychology, 108,* 453–464.

Dimidjian, S., Hollon, S. D., Dobson, K. S., Schmaling, K. B., Kohlenberg, R. J., Addis, M. E., et al. (2006). Randomized trial of behavioral activation, cognitive therapy, and antidepressant medication in the acute treatment of adults with major depression. *Journal of Consulting and Clinical Psychology, 74,* 658–670.

Egeland, J. A., & Hostetter, A. M. (1983). Study 1: Affective disorders among the Amish, 1976–1980. *American Journal of Psychiatry, 140,* 56–61.

Hibbeln, J. R. (1999). Long-chain polyunsaturated fatty acids in depression and related conditions. In M. Peet, I. Glen, & D. F. Horrobin (Eds.), *Phospholipid spectrum disorder in psychiatry* (pp. 195–210). Carnforth, UK: Marius Press.

Hollan, D. W. (1992) Emotion, work and value of emotional equanimity among the Toraja. *Ethnology, 31,* 45–56.

Ilardi, S. S., Karwoski, L., Lehman, K. A., Minatrea, A., Prohaska, J., Steidtmann, D., et al. (2005). *Therapeutic lifestyle change for depression: Original treatment protocol.* Lawrence: University of Kansas.

Jacobson, J. D., Lehman, K. A., Stites, B. A., Karwoski, L., Stroupe, N. N., Steidtmann, D. K., et al. (2007, November). *Therapeutic lifestyle change for depression: Results of a randomized controlled trial.* Presented at the annual convention of the Association for Behavioral and Cognitive Therapies, Philadelphia.

McPherson, M., Smith-Lovin, L., & Brashears, M. (2006). Social isolation in America. *American Sociological Review, 71,* 353–375.

Nesse, R. M., & Williams, G. C. (1994). *Why we get sick: The new science of Darwinian medicine.* New York: Times Books.

Ross, B. M., Seguin, J., & Sieswerda, L. E. (2007). Omega-3 fatty acids as treatments for mental illness: Which disorder and which fatty acid? *Lipids in Health and Disease, 6,* 21.

Schieffelin, E. L. (1985). The cultural analysis of depressive affect: An example from Papua New Guinea. In A. M. Kleinman & B. Good (Eds.), *Culture and depression* (pp. 101–133). Berkeley: University of California Press.

Seligman, M. E. P. (1990). Why is there so much depression? The waxing of the individual and the waning of the commons. In R. E. Ingram (Ed.), *Contemporary psychological approaches to depression* (pp. 1–9). New York: Plenum Press.

Tuunainen, A., Kripke, D. F., & Endo, T. (2004). Light therapy for non-seasonal depression. *Cochrane Database System Review, 2,* CD004050.

Weissman, M. M., Bland, R. C., Canino, G. J., Faravelli, C., Greenwald, S., Hwu, H. G., et al. (1996). Cross-national epidemiology of major depression and bipolar disorder. *Journal of the American Medical Association, 276,* 293–299.

Thyroid Function

Although disorders of the thyroid gland are associated with many psychiatric manifestations, depressive symptoms are the most common. Conversely, among patients with primary depressive illness, there is a higher than expected prevalence of thyroid dysfunction compared to the general population. This bidirectional association between depression and the thyroid gland is our focus. In addition, thyroid hormones have a role in the treatment of depression in patients who are euthyroid. Evidence for the efficacy of thyroid hormones in depression and guidelines for their use are provided.

Thyroid Gland Function and Importance in Homeostasis

The thyroid gland is located at the front of the neck and consists of two lobes and a connecting isthmus. It is a highly vascular, soft tissue normally weighing 12 to 20 grams. It is composed of numerous thyroid follicular cells that enclose the colloid, a proteinaceous fluid containing the thyroid hormone precursor thyroglobulin. Upon demand for thyroid hormones in the body, the follicular cells process thyroglobulin and release the thyroid hormones, thyroxine (T_4) and triiodothyronine (T_3), into the circulation. Thyroid hormones influence the growth and maturation of tissues, cell respiration, energy expenditure, and the turnover of substrates. They are responsible for the maintenance of general homeostasis of the body. Nearly all systems are governed by these hormones, and their optimal function is dependent on normal thyroid function, known as the euthyroid state.

The thyroid axis is an example of a classic endocrine feedback loop. Hypothalamic thyrotropin releasing hormone (TRH) stimulates the production of pituitary thyrotropin (thyroid stimulating hormone, TSH) which in turn stimulates the thyroid gland to synthesize and secrete T_4 and T_3. Thyroid hormones feed back negatively to inhibit production of TRH and TSH. TSH level is the most sensitive and specific marker of thyroid function. T_4 is secreted in at least twentyfold excess over T_3 yet is considered to be a precursor for the more potent T_3. Eighty percent of T_3 production and concentration in the blood comes from extraglandular conversion of T_4 to T_3 by the deiodinase enzymes, and the remainder from thyroid secretion. T_3 has approximately 3 times the hormonal potency of T_4 due to its greater bioavailability in the plasma and 10 to 15 times greater affinity for thyroid receptors. Thyroid hormones act by binding to nuclear thyroid hormone receptors α and β and influence genomic expression.

Neuropsychiatric Manifestations of Thyroid Dysfunction

There are two common thyroid dysfunctions. Hyperthyroidism, excessive thyroid function, is usually due to the autoimmune Grave's disease or to an autonomous thyroid nodule. Hypothyroidism, deficient thyroid function, is usually due to the autoimmune disease Hashimoto's thyroiditis, or to destruction of the thyroid gland.

Primary thyroid disorders are associated with a variety of neuropsychiatric manifestations and may induce almost any psychiatric symptom or syndrome. Hyperthyroidism, can be associated with anxiety, fatigue, insomnia, irritability, restlessness, emotional instability, weight loss, and impairment of concentration and memory. It can even develop into full-blown mania, psychosis, or delirium. In some cases psychomotor retardation, apathy, and withdrawal are the predominant manifestations. Hypothyroidism can be associated with depression, fatigue, decreased libido, memory impairment, irritability, a dementia like state, psychosis, and suicidal ideation. Since depression is by far the most common psychiatric disorder associated with the thyroid, this association is considered further.

Depression and Thyroid Dysfunction

There is a bidirectional association between depression and thyroid hormones. Depressive symptoms can be found in many primary hypothyroid patients, and hypothyroidism can be found in approximately 10% to 15% of patients presenting with primary depression. Many of the disturbances in mood, quality of life, and neurocognitive function found in hypothyroidism improve as a result of replacement treatment with T_4. In more resistant cases, partial substitution of the daily T_4 allowance with T_3 has been reported to further improve mood and cognitive performance.

Although the majority are euthyroid, patients with major depressive disorder have a higher than anticipated rate of subclinical thyroid abnormalities. Most findings indicate subclinical hypothyroidism with high TSH. In addition depressed patients may show a reduced (blunted) TSH response to the TRH stimulation test. Some studies support an association between subclinical thyroid dysfunction, more severe depression, and a reduced response to treatment. There is some evidence to suggest that an autoimmune process may be occurring in some depressed patients even in the absence of overt thyroid dysfunction.

Elevated thyroid binding inhibitory immunoglobulin and thyroid microsomal antibody levels have been reported. Changes have been reported in the thyroid function of depressed patients treated with antidepressants. These changes are inconsistent and may be due to recovery rather than a direct effect of antidepressants.

In the case of bipolar disorder, marginal thyroid function may be associated with a greater frequency and severity of mood episodes. In bipolar depression, although within normal range, both lower values of free thyroxine index and higher values of TSH were associated with longer time needed to achieve remission.

The Therapeutic Use of Thyroid Hormones in Depression

Mode of Action

Thyroid hormones act at intracellular, nuclear thyroid receptors (TRs) that are ligand-regulated transcription factors and are members of the nuclear hormone receptor superfamily. These receptors are divided into two main kinds, TRα and TRβ, which in turn are divided into subtypes 1 and 2. Each of these receptors includes three domains: a ligand binding domain; a central DNA binding domain, which binds to specific sequences called thyroid response elements (TREs) in the promoters of target genes; and a transactivation domain that modulates the cell transcriptional mechanism. TRs bind to TREs either as a homodimer or as a heterodimer with the retinoic acid receptor. Unliganded TR is typically bound to corepressor molecules connected to other associated factors, which interfere with transactivation domain modulation of gene transcription. The binding of hormone molecules induces the release of copressor, the recruitment of coactivator molecules, and consequent active modulation of gene transcription by TRs.

The influence of thyroid hormones, via their nuclear receptors, on neurotransmitter systems that are linked to the pathophysiology

of depression, such as the serotonergic and noradrenergic systems, may provide the substrate for their involvement in depression and their effects as antidepressants (reviewed by Lifschytz et al., 2006; Newman, Agid, Gur, & Lerer, 2000). Hypothyroidism has been shown to be associated with differential changes in noradrenaline synthesis levels in different brain areas, with decreases in cortical, $\alpha 1$, $\alpha 2$, and β adrenoceptor density and a decrease in post-β-noradrenergic receptor cAMP production in some reports. Similar evidence exists for the serotonergic system: treatment-reversible increases in brain levels of the 5HT metabolite 5HIAA and cortical and hypothalamic 5HT1a receptor density were reported in hypothyroid animals. Research using the in vivo microdialysis technique, demonstrated a clear functional effect of T_3 causing a desensitization of presynaptic inhibitory serotonergic receptors of the 5HT1a, 5HT1b subtypes, supporting the hypothesis that such effect and an ensuing increase in serotonergic neurotransmission may underlie the antidepressant effects of T_3. The microdialysis findings have been corroborated by behavioral tests that demonstrate antidepressantlike effects of T_3. Gene expression studies suggest that the mechanism underlying 5HT1a and 5HT1b receptor desensitization by T_3 is a decrease in transcription levels (Lifschytz et al., 2006).

Clinical Studies

The thyroid hormones, T_4 and T_3, have long been used to potentiate antidepressant treatment. Research with T_3 has been more extensive and includes administration as a monotherapy but more usually as a supplement to standard antidepressants. Studies with T_3 have been of three types.

In acceleration paradigms, T_3 is administered from the outset of treatment or very early in the course in conjunction with an antidepressant to achieve more rapid onset of antidepressant effects. Altshuler and colleagues (2001) reported that in five of six randomized, double-blind, controlled studies T_3 was significantly more effective than placebo in accelerating clinical response (pooled, weighted effect size index was 0.58) when administered concurrently with tricyclic antidepressants to patients with major depression. To date, there are no published studies specifically designed to examine acceleration by T_3 of the more commonly used selective serotonin-reuptake inhibitor (SSRI) antidepressants.

In augmentation studies, T_3 is added to the therapeutic regimen of patients who have not responded to several weeks of treatment with a standard antidepressant. Aronson, Offman, Joffe, and Naylor (1996) aggregated eight studies (four of which were randomized, double-blind) that encompassed a total of 292 patients with treatment-resistant depression, in which T_3 was added to ongoing treatment with tricyclic antidepressants. The T_3-augmentation group had a relative response of 2.09 ($p = 0.002$) compared to controls, corresponding to a 23.2% absolute improvement in response rate. The quality of the studies was uneven, the number of participants was relatively small, and the findings were not statistically significant when the analysis was restricted to the double-blind studies. Nonetheless, the overall pattern suggested that T_3 might be an effective method of augmenting the antidepressant effects of TCAs in patients with treatment-resistant depression.

T_3 augmentation of SSRIs has been examined in five studies (reviewed by Cooper-Kazaz & Lerer, 2007). The three small open studies (11, 19, and 25 patients) that examined the effect of T_3 augmentation of SSRIs after nonresponse to 6 to 14 weeks of treatment yielded encouraging results. Response/remission rates were 40%/36%, 35%/30%, and 42%/25%. T_3 dose was up to 50 µg/day, and the duration of augmentation treatment was 2 to 4 weeks. The two randomized augmentation studies are very different in several respects and difficult to compare. The STAR*D study (Nierenberg et al., 2006) was single-blind, lasted up to 14 weeks, and compared T_3 and lithium (Li) augmentation in 142 patients who failed to remit on (or were intolerant of) at least two antidepressants or one antidepressant plus an augmentation

other than T_3 or Li. In only 57.7% of patients was an SSRI augmented. Remission rates were 15.9% for Li and 24.7% for T_3 but the difference was not statistically significant. In contrast, the study by Joffe, Sokolov, and Levitt (2006) was double-blind but lasted only 2 weeks and involved only 36 patients randomized to four treatment groups, rendering it clearly underpowered. An SSRI was augmented in 77.8% of the cases. Categorical response and remission rates were not given. There was no difference in effect of T_3, Li, Li plus T_3, or placebo augmentation on 17-item Hamilton depression scale scores. Overall, the data supporting efficacy of T_3 augmentation of SSRIs in nonresponsive patients are suggestive with remission rates of 25% to 36% but not definitive. Further well-controlled trials are needed to establish whether T_3 is an effective augmenting agent in patients treated with SSRIs who have not responded.

In enhancement studies, T_3 is administered concurrently with an antidepressant from the inception of treatment, and the outcome is examined after a treatment course of 4 weeks or (preferably) more. Depending on the frequency of clinical evaluations in the initial stages, enhancement studies may also yield information on acceleration. There are three SSRI enhancement studies, including two randomized double-blind, placebo-controlled trials (i.e., Appelhof et al., 2004; Cooper-Kazaz et al., 2007) and one randomized, double-blind, placebo-controlled effectiveness study (Posternak et al., 2007). The two efficacy studies reached opposite conclusions: the results of Appelhof and colleagues (2004) study did not support a role for T_3 addition to paroxetine, whereas Cooper-Kazaz and colleagues (2007) study showed significant enhancement of the effects of sertraline in terms of increased response and remission rates. The study by Posternak and colleagues (2007) found a nonsignificant trend for greater effectiveness of T_3 than placebo. It is interesting to note that the results for the placebo arms of all three studies were comparable, response/remission rates being 46%/36% (Appelhof et al., 2004), 50%/38% (Cooper-Kazaz et al., 2007), and 52%/37%

(Posternak et al., 2007). This could suggest that enhanced response and remission in the T_3 arm is unique to the addition of T_3, reflecting specific conditions or patient characteristics needed for T_3 to have an effect. Appelhof and colleagues (2004) and Cooper-Kazaz and colleagues (2007) studies were similar in inclusion and exclusion criteria, major depressive disorder recurrence rate, size of sample, depressive episode severity, length of study, and T_3 treatment. They differed in the SSRI administered (paroxetine versus sertraline), antidepressant dose (relatively higher for paroxetine [30 mg/day] than sertraline [100 mg/day]), chronicity of the depression (44% vs. 11.6%), and degree of resistance to antidepressant treatment (38% > Stage I vs. 8%). It is possible that a better response was observed in Cooper-Kazaz and colleagues' (2007) study because the patients were potentially more responsive to treatment and received a relatively lower antidepressant dose thus allowing more room for a therapeutic effect of T_3 to be demonstrated. It is more difficult to compare the results of these two studies with those of Posternak and colleagues (2007). Only 82% of the patients in Posternak and colleagues' (2007) study were suffering from nonpsychotic major depressive disorder (12% were suffering from bipolar depression and 6% from psychotic major depressive disorder). The degree of chronicity is not mentioned, the length of the study was 6 weeks, and only 52% of the patients were treated with SSRIs. Further studies are needed to establish whether T_3 is effective in enhancing the antidepressant effects of SSRIs.

T_4 has been studied less extensively than T_3 in the treatment of affective disorders. The addition of supraphysiological doses of T_4 to antidepressant–resistant unipolar and bipolar depression improved the outcome in a small open clinical study (Bauer et al., 1998). Supraphysiological doses of T_4 also improved bipolar disorder prophylaxis in a small prospective open study (Bauer et al. 2002). In a recent, small open study, moderate doses of T_4 successfully augmented serotonergic antidepressants in female patients with refractory unipolar or bipolar depression (Lojko & Ryba-kowski, 2007). Several studies indicate specific efficacy of the addition of T_4 in the treatment of rapid-cycling bipolar disorder, reducing both amplitude and frequency of manic and depressive phases (e.g., Bauer & Whybrow, 1990). Finally, in one study comparing T_4 and T_3 potentiation of TCA antidepressants, significantly more patients suffering from nonpsychotic, unipolar depression responded to T_3 as compared to T_4 (Joffe & Singer, 1990). The few studies that assessed the efficacy of T_4 in the treatment of resistant depression had several limitations: the studies were small and open, in some studies unipolar and bipolar depression were analyzed together and most of the responses were in bipolar patients, and in some the doses of T_4 were supraphysiological and in one study had serious adverse effects.

Adverse Effects

Clinicians hesitate to use thyroid hormone in the treatment of depressed patients with no primary thyroid dysfunction. In the majority of the studies T_3 was used at a dose no higher than 50 μg/day. This dose is lower than the physiological level of thyroid hormone, thus it is not expected to override and shut down the normal thyroid axis but rather to shift its set point to a new equilibrium. This new set point has higher T_3 levels, mainly from exogenous sources, lower T_4 levels due to reduced endogenous production, and within normal yet reduced TSH levels. The induction of hyperthyroidism is not expected nor desired for clinical effect; therefore, clinical and laboratory thyroid functions should be monitored and doses adapted accordingly.

The potential adverse effects of T_3 are tachycardia, nervousness, insomnia, tremor, diarrhea, headache, angina, weight loss, fatigue, diaphoresis, dry mouth, muscle pain, and in severe cases arrhythmias or cardiac decompensation. In contrast to the concerns of clinicians, the studies reviewed here indicate a paucity of adverse effects associated with use of T_3 as a supplement to SSRIs and other second-generation antidepressant agents. It is interesting to note that the study that showed the most T_3-associated adverse effects and no therapeutic advantage to the supplementation (Appelhof et al., 2004) employed the SSRI paroxetine, which has significant adrenergic effects (Frazer, 2001). Since thyroid hormone enhances adrenergic signaling, the combined use with paroxetine can explain the adrenergic side effects observed by Appelhof and colleagues.

Clinical Considerations

To date, there are no clear guidelines for the use of thyroid hormones in the treatment of depression. There is almost no evidence for the use of T_4 in nonbipolar depression, and that supporting its use in bipolar depression is limited. More data are available to support the use of T_3 in major depressive disorder. The studies cited here are of different quality and design. The evidence generally supports the use of T_3 for the augmentation of tricyclic antidepressants and, to lesser degree, SSRI antidepressants, after failure to induce remission. The role of T_3 as an enhancer needs to be studied further. It is not clear how long T_3 should be continued in patients who respond to it and whether longer-term administration has adverse consequences. Until this issue is addressed empirically, it would be prudent not to continue T_3 as a maintenance therapy in responding patients but to taper and stop the hormone within the phase of continuation treatment.

At the doses used (up to 50 μg/day) T_3 appears to be safe and well tolerated, and adverse effects need not be an impediment to clinical use provided that thyroid function is monitored. Potential adverse effects should be monitored but should not deter clinicians from using T_3. The appropriate timing of T_3 supplementation needs to be explored and the appropriate dose and length of treatment established. Further controlled studies are needed to definitively establish the use of T_3 as an effective supplement to SSRIs in patients with major depressive disorder.

RENA COOPER-KAZAZ, TZURI LISFSCHYTZ,
AND BERNARD LERER

See also

Dopamine
Hormones
Medical Conditions and Depression
Serotonin

References

Altshuler, L. L., Bauer, M., Frye, M. A., Gitlin, M. J., Mintz, J., Szuba, M. P., et al. (2001). Does thyroid supplementation accelerate tricyclic antidepressant response? A review and meta-analysis of the literature. *American Journal of Psychiatry, 15,* 1617–1622.

Appelhof, B. C., Brouwer, J. P., Van Dyck, R., Fliers, E., Hoogendijk, W. J. G., Huyser, J., et al. (2004). Triiodothyronine addition to paroxetine in the treatment of major depressive disorder. *Journal of Clinical Endocrinology and Metabolism, 89,* 6271–6276.

Aronson, R., Offman, H. J., Joffe, R. T., & Naylor, C. D. (1996). Triiodothyronin augmentation in the treatment of refractory depression. A meta-analysis. *Archives of General Psychiatry, 53,* 842–848.

Bauer, M. S., & Whybrow, P. C. (1990). Rapid cycling bipolar affective disorder, II: Treatment of refractory rapid cycling with high-dose levothyroxine: A preliminary study. *Archives of General Psychiatry, 47,* 435–440.

Cooper-Kazaz, R., Apter, J. T., Cohen, R., Karagichev, L., Moussa, S. M., & Grouper, D., et al. (2007). Combined treatment with sertraline and liothyronine in major depression: A randomized, double-blind, placebo-controlled trial. *Archives of General Psychiatry, 64,* 679–688.

Frazer, A. (2001). Serotonergic and noradrenergic reuptake inhibitors: Prediction of clinical effects from in vitro potencies. *Journal of Clinical Psychiatry, 63,* 16–23.

Joffe, R. T., & Singer, W. (1990). A comparison of triiodothyronine and thyroxine in potentiation of tricyclic antidepressants. *Psychiatry Research, 32,* 241–251.

Joffe, R. T., Sokolov, S. T. H., & Levitt, A. J. (2006). Lithium and triiodothyronine augmentation of antidepressants. *Canadian Journal of Psychiatry, 51,* 791–793.

Lifschytz, T., Segman, R., Shalom, G., Lerer, B., Gur, E., Golzer, T., et al. Basic mechanisms of augmentation of antidepressant effects with thyroid hormones. *Current Drug Targets, 7,* 203–210.

Lojko, D., & Rybakowski, J. K. (2007). L-thyroxine augmentation of serotonergic antidepressants in female patients with refractory depression. *Journal of Affective Disorders, 103,* 253–256.

Newman, M. E., Agid, O., Gur, E., & Lerer, B. (2000). Pharmacological mechanisms of T3 augmentation of antidepressant action. *International Journal of Neuropsychopharmacology, 3,* 187–191.

Nierenberg, A. A., Fava, M., Trivedi, M. H., Wisniewski, S. R., Thase, M. E., McGrath, P. J., et al. (2006). A comparison of lithium and T3 augmentation following two failed medication treatments for depression: A STAR*D report. *American Journal of Psychiatry, 163,* 1519–1530.

Posternak, M., Novak, S., Stern, R., Hennessey, J., Joffe, R., Prange, A., et al. (2007). A Pilot effectiveness study:

Placebo-controlled trial of adjunctive L-triiodothyronine (T3) used to accelerate and potentiate the antidepressant response. *International Journal of Neuropsychopharmacology, 10*, 1–11.

Transcranial Magnetic Stimulation

Transcranial magnetic stimulation (TMS) was introduced as a diagnostic tool by Barker and colleagues in 1985. Almost a decade later, Pascual-Leone, Valls-Sole, Wassermann, and Hallett (1994) demonstrated that applied in trains of repeated stimuli, TMS is able to modulate the brain activity beyond the duration of the train itself, and pioneered the exploration of TMS as a therapeutic tool in neuropsychiatric disorders. TMS is now well established as a tool to gain insights into the pathophysiology of brain disorders and is increasingly studied as a possible therapeutic intervention for a large number of neurologic and psychiatric diseases (Figure T.1). Therapeutic utility of TMS has been most extensively studied in medication-resistant depression.

TMS is based on Faraday's principle of electromagnetic induction; rapidly changing magnetic fields produce electrical currents, which in turn can induce a secondary current in a nearby conductor properly oriented to the plane of the current. A copper-wire coil, connected to a bank of capacitors, generates time-varying magnetic pulses that are able to penetrate the intact scalp and skull without attenuation or pain. The magnitude of the magnetic field generated can reach 2.5 tesla, but the pulse is very brief, around 200 μsec. These rapidly changing pulsed magnetic pulses induce focal electrical currents in the cortical area beneath the coil, which in turn depolarize cortical neuronal elements (axons and dendrites rather than

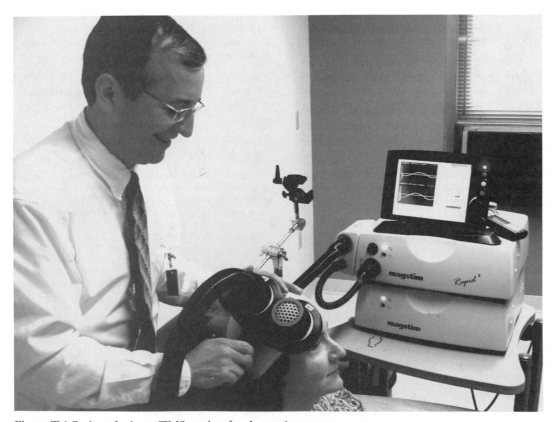

Figure T.1 Patient during a TMS session for depression.

cell bodies), generate action potentials, and affect brain activity.

What Does TMS Do to the Brain?

TMS can be applied in the form of single pulses, paired pulses with variable intervals to the same or different brain areas, or as trains of pulses (repetitive TMS or rTMS) with variable frequency. Repetitive administration of TMS enables modulation of the cortical activity that can last beyond the duration of the train itself by induction of synaptic plasticity. Depending on the number of sessions applied, the duration of the aftereffects (or off-line effects) may vary between hours and several days, and might allow a therapeutic utility in a variety of neuropsychiatric disorders that reveal alterations in brain function.

The nature of the modulation primarily depends on the location of stimulation and the stimulation parameters, which include the frequency and magnitude of the stimuli, duration of the trains and intertrain intervals, and total number of stimuli applied. Cortical excitability studies targeting the motor cortex revealed that stimulation with low frequencies (≤ 1 Hz) leads in most instances to a suppressive effect in the targeted cortical regions, whereas high frequencies (≥ 5 Hz) are principally facilitatory. Functional imaging studies (SPECT, PET) in humans and experiments in animal models confirm these differential effects of low- versus high-frequency rTMS. Importantly, stimulation of a given cortical area induces distant cortical and subcortical effects, within and across the hemispheres, by means of transsynaptic spread along functional networks. The local and distributed impact of TMS depends on the parameters of stimulation but also on the level of activity and connectivity of the modulated network.

The mechanisms that lead to these long-lasting modulatory effects of rTMS still remain to be elucidated. Synaptic plasticity in the form of long-term synaptic potentiation (LTP) or depression (LTD) is likely to be involved. Brain-derived neurotrophic factor (BDNF) polymorphisms and other genetic factors that play important roles in the expression of LTP and LTD likely contribute to interindividual differences in TMS impact.

What Is the Rationale for TMS Use in Depression?

Numerous studies on the pathophysiology of affective disorders reveal altered activity in the prefrontal cortex, especially in the left hemisphere, in patients with depression. This prefrontal dysfunction is expression of abnormal activity in a corticosubcortical network that includes also the subgenual cingulate cortex as a critical node. Given the capacity of rTMS to modulate activity in a distributed network, targeting the prefrontal cortex and normalizing the decreased activity on the left might provide an effective window for neuromodulation of this cortico-subcortical network in depression. Pascual-Leone et al. (2004) conducted the initial controlled study of efficacy of TMS and reported a significant improvement in depressive symptoms following five consecutive days of high-frequency (10 Hz) rTMS to the left (but not the right) dorsolateral prefrontal cortex (DLPFC). A number of studies have confirmed the antidepressant efficacy of high-frequency rTMS to the left DLPFC. Furthermore, low-frequency (1 Hz) rTMS to the right DLPFC has also been found to be effective. Recent studies comparing the antidepressant effects of left high frequency versus right low frequency found these two strategies similarly efficacious. It is conceivable that decreasing activity on the right side may increase activity on the left via transcallosal connections and may result in the equivalent physiological effects for the reestablishment of balance in malfunctioning bihemispheric networks. Combination of these two approaches, bilateral stimulation of right and left hemispheres, deserves further study. Finally, it is conceivable that different patients may respond better to targeting of the right or the left hemisphere.

Is There a Role of TMS in Clinical Treatment of Depression?

In the last decade, a large number of trials have been conducted to evaluate the potential clinical use of rTMS in depression. Several meta-analyses have been published supporting the antidepressant efficacy of rTMS over sham stimulation. However, the effect size has been small in many studies, and the clinical significance remains debatable. Recent rTMS trials reveal a greater clinical impact than the earlier studies, probably due to better study designs and more effective parameters of stimulation (e.g., number of sessions).

A multisite randomized controlled trial tested the efficacy and safety of rTMS in 301 medication-free patients with major depression who were moderately treatment resistant. Daily session of 3,000 stimuli at high frequency (10 Hz) were applied to the left DLPFC for 4 to 6 weeks. Active rTMS was significantly superior to sham and twice as likely to induce remission by the sixth week. The therapeutic efficacy of rTMS was similar to traditional antidepressants (as assessed by Hamilton Depression Scale), with a better tolerability profile.

Another important consideration is the impact of rTMS on the treatment of relapses, and maintenance of the achieved therapeutic effect. Data regarding this matter are currently very limited. We have demonstrated the reproducibility of the antidepressant effect of repeated rTMS applications for up to 4 years in medication-free patients with refractory depression who initially showed a clinically significant benefit to rTMS. Benefits from each rTMS course were sustained for a mean of nearly 5 months. For maintenance of the antidepressant effects, one to two sessions of weekly rTMS application was suggested.

Experience to date suggests that TMS might have a greater role in treatment of a subgroup of depressed patients. Young age, absence of psychotic features, lack of refractoriness to medications, and short durations of depressive episodes seem to predict a greater benefit from rTMS. Further studies are required to ascertain the patient characteristics that might predispose to a strong antidepressant response.

Safety

Overall, TMS appears to be very safe in the treatment of depression if the recommended guidelines are followed. The most serious adverse event related to TMS is induction of a seizure. This is a rare complication if the stimulation is applied according to the safety guidelines and the patients are screened for the risk of seizure. To date, seizures have occurred in only two patients with depression during high-frequency rTMS application, and stimulation parameters used were outside the recommended safety guidelines. It is important to note that none of these patients had further seizures or developed epilepsy. Low-frequency stimulation to the right prefrontal cortex is even less likely to induce a seizure and should probably be the choice while treating depression in patients with epilepsy or other significant risks.

Like many of the antidepressants, TMS has induced mania in a few bipolar patients. Apart from these, TMS has been reported to be well tolerated with minor or no side effects. The largest report regarding the safety and tolerability of rTMS in depression obtained data from 325 patients in over 10,000 cumulative treatment sessions. Most frequent side effects included mild headache and application site pain; no seizures occurred, no changes in auditory threshold or cognitive functions were detected. Discontinuation rate due to side effects was lower than for the classical antidepressants, 4.5% and 3.4% in real and sham groups, respectively. Given this adverse effect profile, TMS presents significant advantages over electroconvulsive therapy and might be worth trying in patients who are relatively stable.

What Future Developments Are Needed?

Overall, TMS is a novel promising modality for the treatment of depression. Further study of the exact mechanisms to the action of TMS is crucial. The effects of frequency, intensity, and conditioning on induction of LTP and LTD; the relation of genetic and individual variations to antidepressant response; interactions of metabolic factors (e.g., folic acid and vitamin B-12) with the antidepressant efficacy; and adjunct interventions, such as cognitive behavioral therapy and possible pharmacological augmentation strategies, should be studied. Combination of TMS with EEG and functional neuroimaging may allow practitioners to individually tailor the intervention and achieve greater efficacy. The efficacy of rTMS in patients who are not refractory to medications (drugs alone vs. TMS alone), its use in children and adolescents, maintenance of this therapy, and its long-term effects also remain to be clarified.

ASLI DEMIRTAS-TATLIDEDE AND
ALVARO PASCUAL-LEONE

See also

Affective Neuroscience
Functional Neuroimaging

References

Pascual-Leone, A., Rubio, B., Pallardo, F., Catala, M. D. (1996). Rapid-rate transcranial magnetic stimulation of left dorsolateral prefrontal cortex in drug-resistant depression. *Lancet, 348,* 233–237.

Wasserman, E. M., Epstein, C. H., Ziemann, U., Lisanby, S., Paus, T., & Walsh, V. (Eds.). (2008). *The Oxford Handbook of Transcranial Stimulation.* New York: Oxford University Press.

Twin Studies

Twin studies provide the best means of exploring the extent to which population variation of common complex disorders, such as depression, is explained by genetic or environmental factors, without necessarily requiring direct assessment of environments. By examining twin pairs reared together, we can infer what proportion of the variance is attributed to each of three components or factors:

- Additive genetics (heritability) (A): a measure of genetic effect size.
- Shared family environments (C): anything in the environment that makes one twin more similar to his or her co-twin. If childhood adversity affecting all offspring in a family contributes to the development of depression, it would be identified as C.
- Nonshared family environmental factors (E): anything environmental that makes twins dissimilar to one another. If things that happen to one twin but not the other, such as being made redundant, contribute to the development of depression, this would be identified as E. Error of measurement is also partitioned under E.

This partitioning of the variance is achieved by examining the similarity of depression diagnoses across pairs of twins reared together. We know the following:

- Monozygotic (MZ) twins share 100% of their genes.
- Dizygotic (DZ) twins on average share 50% of their segregating genes (i.e., the genes that vary in the population).
- Both sorts of twins share 100% of their shared environments and 0% of their nonshared environments, by definition.

We also have to make several assumptions. First, individual genetic (and environmental) factors operate independently and additively rather than interacting with one another. Second, the environments experienced by MZ pairs are no more similar than those experienced by DZ pairs (the equal environments assumption). This latter assumption has been tested, and although it has been found that young MZ pairs are sometimes and in certain situations treated more similarly than young DZ pairs, such as being dressed in similar clothes, these particular environmental exposures have been found to be unrelated to cognitive, personality, and psychiatric outcomes (Morris-Yates, Andrews, Howie, & Henderson, 1990).

Where MZ pairs have higher concordance than DZ pairs for an outcome such as depression, genetic influence on the outcome is indicated. Similarly, nonshared environmental influences are inferred by the extent to which MZ pairs are dissimilar. More precise estimates of genetic and environmental effects can be obtained using a simple set of equations that express the expected values of twin correlations (Falconer, 1960):

$$r_{MZ} = A + C$$
$$r_{DZ} = (\tfrac{1}{2} A) + C$$

where r_{MZ} is the correlation between MZ pairs, and r_{DZ} is the correlation between DZ twins.

Substituting and rearranging gives:

$$A = 2\,(r_{MZ} - r_{DZ})$$
$$C = r_{MZ} - A$$
$$E = 1 - r_{MZ}$$

These relationships can also be depicted in a path model (Figure T.2). Structural equation modeling programs such as Mx (Neale, Boker, Xie, & Maes, 2002) can be used to estimate the model parameters and their statistical significance.

The resulting heritability (and environmentality) estimates pertain to the population and time period from which the data

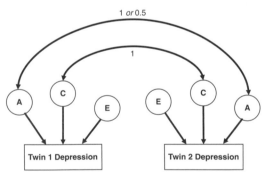

Figure T.2   Path diagram representing a univariate twin model. Measured traits (depression status) are depicted by rectangles; latent (unobserved) factors are depicted in circles. Single-headed arrows represent causal pathways; double-headed arrows represent correlations between latent factors. The correlation between the genetic influences is 1 for MZ twins and 0.5 for DZ twins because the latter share only half of their segregating genes.

were gathered. The implication is that a high heritability would not mean depression is irrevocably determined by genes, because if the environment were changed then environmental variations could become more heavily related to depression outcome, and so the heritability could be lowered.

Research Findings

Unipolar Depression

Numerous behavioral genetic studies of depression have been performed using populations from Western Europe, Australia, and America. Twin studies have consistently shown higher concordance for mood disorders in MZ than DZ pairs. Population-based studies have shown substantial genetic influences on adult depression (A), generally of 30% to 40%, with minimal influence from shared family environmental factors (C), and the remainder of the variance influenced by E. Higher heritabilities have been found in a more severely depressed, hospital-based sample, which might indicate that more severe forms of the disorder are more heritable, but alternatively it might reflect the greater reliability of measurement among more severe cases. This suggestion is supported by a community-based study that took unreliability of measurement into account in the model and found similarly high heritabilities.

It has also been suggested that earlier-onset cases of depression, which may be more severe than later-onset cases, have higher heritabilities (reflected in especially high concordance for depression in MZ pairs under age 30). However, this may be an artifact of not controlling for cohort effects, and other work does not support heritability differences at different ages of onset. Higher heritability with earlier onset seems plausible if one expects genes to have a constant effect from birth, meaning that people with a higher genetic loading will succumb earlier in their lives, but in reality genetic factors that influence depression may have varying salience at different stages in life (Nes, Roysamb, Reichbarn-Kjennerud, Harris, & Tambs, 2007).

unipolar depression and anxiety disorders such as generalized anxiety disorder. This again requires the use of cross-twin cross-disorder associations. A review of such studies showed that some of the genetic factors influencing depression are also involved in anxiety disorders, but that there is less overlap between the environmental influences (Middeldorp, Cath, Van Dyck, & Boomsma, 2005). That is, certain people are genetically susceptible to both types of disorder, but the particular environmental insults on a susceptible individual seem to influence whether anxiety or a depressive disorder develops.

Conclusions

Twin studies are a useful resource for research into mood disorders. They can tease apart the influences of genetics and environment, which otherwise are confounded within families. They can indicate the overall magnitude of genetic and environmental influences without having to measure these directly, and so without focusing research onto particular genes or environmental exposures that are currently in vogue. Twin studies have shown that both unipolar and bipolar disorders are substantially heritable, and they have illuminated some mechanisms through which environments operate in combination with genes.

Twin studies also have limitations. Their results can be generalized only as far as the population from which they have been sampled. When studying discrete disorders rather than continuously measured traits such as personality scales, many affected individuals are required, necessitating large sample sizes for community studies. The results are easily misinterpreted, and it is often necessary to delve deeper than an initial univariate analysis in order to understand the ways in which genes and environments are involved in the development of psychiatric disorders.

HARRIET A. BALL AND PETER MCGUFFIN

See also

Family Transmission of Depression
Genetics of Depression
Genetic Transmission of Depression
Molecular Genetics

References

Bertelsen, A., Harvald, B., & Hauge, M. (1977). A Danish twin study of manic-depressive disorders. *British Journal of Psychiatry, 130,* 330.

Falconer, D. S. (1960). *Introduction to quantitative genetics.* Edinburgh/London: Oliver & Boyd. Essex, England.

Jones, I., Kent, L., & Craddock, N. (2004). Genetics of affective disorders. In P. McGuffin, M. Owen, & I. Gottesman (Eds.), *Psychiatric genetics and genomics* (pp. 211–246). Oxford, UK: Oxford University Press.

Kendler, K. S., Gatz, M., Gardner, C. O., & Pedersen, N. L. (2006). Swedish national twin study of lifetime major depression. *American Journal of Psychiatry, 163,* 109–114.

Kendler, K. S., Kessler, R. C., Walters, E. E., MacLean, C., Neale, M. C., & Heath, A. C. (1995). Stressful life events, genetic liability, and onset of an episode of major depression in women. *American Journal of Psychiatry, 152,* 833–842.

Kessler, R. C. (1997). The effects of stressful life events on depression. *Annual Review of Psychology, 48,* 191–214.

McGuffin, P., Rijsdijk, F. V., Andrew, M., Sham, P., Katz, R., & Cardno, A. (2003). The heritability of bipolar affective disorder and the genetic relationship to unipolar depression. *Archive of General Psychiatry, 60,* 497–502.

Middeldorp, C. M., Cath, D. C., Van Dyck, R., & Boomsma, D. I. (2005). The co-morbidity of anxiety and depression in the perspective of genetic epidemiology. A review of twin and family studies. *Psychological Medicine, 35,* 11–24.

Morris-Yates, A., Andrews, G., Howie, P., & Henderson, S. (1990). Twins: A test of the equal environments assumption. *Acta Psychiatrica Scandinavica, 81,* 322–326.

Neale, M. C., Boker, S. M., Xie, G., & Maes, H. H. (2002). *Mx: Statistical modelling* (6th ed.)., Richmond, VA: Department of Psychiatry.

Nes, R. B., Roysamb, E., Reichbarn-Kjennerud, T., Harris, J. R., & Tambs K. (2007). Symptoms of anxiety and depression in young adults: Genetic and environmental influences on stability and change. *Twin Research and Human Genetics, 10,* 450.

Rice, F., Harold, G., & Thapar, A. (2002). The genetic aetiology of childhood depression: A review. *Journal of Child Psychology and Psychiatry, 43,* 65–79.

Sullivan, P. F., Neale, M. C., & Kendler, K. S. (2000). Genetic epidemiology of major depression: Review and meta-analysis. *American Journal of Psychiatry, 157,* 1552–1562.

Thapar, A., & McGuffin, P. (1994). A twin study of depressive symptoms in childhood. *British Journal of Psychiatry, 165,* 259.

Although genetic influences and nonshared environmental influences are important in adulthood, and a similar pattern is seen in adolescence, a slightly different etiology is seen in childhood. Twin studies examining depressive symptoms have suggested age differences in heritability, with symptoms being more heritable in older children and adolescents than in young children (Thapar & McGuffin, 1994), but again the evidence is mixed (Rice, Harold, & Thapar, 2002). Although there is evidence of shared environmental influences on depression in childhood, such influences seem not to be involved in symptoms or diagnoses of depression in later life.

In addition, twin studies provide evidence of large nonshared environmental influences on depression. These are likely to include recent stressful life events (Kendler et al., 1995) and may also include lower-level, chronic forms of stress, although the long-term nature of chronic problems often makes it hard to assess whether the stress or depression came first and was causal (Kessler, 1997). The influence of measurement error is also partitioned into the E parameter, which could include recall bias, and the extent to which screening questionnaires detect true cases of psychiatric disorders.

The lack of an influence of C on depression in adulthood, as shown in a literature review (Sullivan, Neale, & Kendler, 2000) and in a subsequent analysis of over 15,000 Swedish twin pairs (Kendler, Gatz, Gardner, & Pedersen, 2006) appears to suggest that factors such as family income level in childhood and parenting ability are not causal risk factors. Actually, there are still several ways in which family factors might be involved. Many exposures that we may think count as C may at root be influenced by E or even A. For example, one child may have a difficult relationship with his mother while his siblings do not experience this negative environmental exposure. The reason for this difference may be due to the child's genetically influenced temperament (A) or may be due to chance factors in the environment (E). An example of a (partly) heritable environmental exposure is negative

life events: it appears that genetics as other factors) influence personality in turn influences the selection of in— als into particular environments. The g susceptibility to life events may accoun some of the heritability of depression. O complications arise when particular genes occur with particular environments (know as gene-environment correlation, or r_{GE}). F example, overanxious parenting may covar with anxiety in offspring, but the child's anxiety might be a reflection of heritable anxious tendencies that pass genetically to offspring, not a direct effect of parenting on offspring anxiety. Thus care needs to be taken when interpreting the results of twin studies.

Bipolar Disorder

Several twin studies have been conducted to examine the etiology of bipolar disorder, but most had small sample sizes (Jones, Kent, & Craddock, 2004). The two largest studies were of hospital-based twin registers in Denmark (Bertelsen, Harvald, & Hauge, 1977) and the UK (McGuffin et al., 2003). Both studies suggested high heritabilities for both unipolar and bipolar disorders (approximately 70% and 80%, respectively), and also that there is genetic overlap between the two. In other words, some of the genes that make people susceptible to unipolar disorder are the same genes that make people susceptible to bipolar disorder. This is inferred by examining cross-twin cross-disorder associations; in the twin studies mentioned, there was an elevated chance of a twin having unipolar disorder if the co-twin had bipolar disorder (and vice versa), and these associations were stronger among MZ pairs than among DZ pairs. However, in exploring this further, McGuffin and colleagues (2003) found that much of the genetic liability to bipolar disorder is specific to the manic syndrome.

Comorbidity With Anxiety

Further studies have examined the etiological factors underlying the comorbidity between

V

Vulnerability

Ideas about vulnerability are several decades old, although its conceptual appeal has increased recently. Despite how widespread the concept is, few precise definitions of vulnerability have been offered. Ingram, Miranda, and Segal (1998) summarized what appear, based on the available literature, to be core characteristics of the construct, and those characteristics are used here as a basis for discussing the idea of vulnerability.

Vulnerability Is Stable

Zubin and Spring (1977), pioneers of the vulnerability idea, are very specific about the trait nature of vulnerability: "We regard [vulnerability] as a relatively permanent, enduring trait" (p. 109). Although other investigators have not been quite as specific, the enduring nature of vulnerability is implicit in many discussions of vulnerability. Hence, little change in vulnerability is theoretically possible, which is particularly the case for models that suggest that vulnerability is genetic.

The enduring nature of vulnerability is clearly seen in contrast to the state or episodic nature of psychological disorders. Zubin and Spring (1977), for instance, differentiate between an enduring vulnerability trait, and episodes of schizophrenia that "are waxing and waning states" (p. 109). Hollon and Cobb (1993) also distinguish between stable vulnerability traits that predispose individuals to the depression, and state variables that represent the onset of the symptoms. Depression can therefore emerge and fade as episodes cycle between occurrence and remission, but the traits that give rise to vulnerability for depression remain.

Although vulnerability is assumed by many to be permanent, this need not always be the case. For example, if vulnerability is psychological rather than genetic in nature, it is theoretically possible to alter vulnerability factors; vulnerability levels, for example, may fluctuate as a function of new learning experiences. In this regard, data suggest that depressed patients treated with cognitive therapy, or combined cognitive therapy and pharmacotherapy, are less likely than patients treated with pharmacotherapy to experience relapses and recurrences. It is possible that factors other than vulnerability reduction may be at work in these results, but this example does illustrate how, at least in principle, vulnerability levels might be altered.

Stability Versus Permanence

The possibility that psychological vulnerability can be altered suggests a subtle but important distinction between stability and permanence. Even though the idea of stability suggests a resistance to change, it does not suggest that change is never possible. Indeed, the entire notion of psychotherapy is based on the premise that, under the right circumstances and with the application of efficacious therapy methods, changes in an otherwise stable variable can occur. Without significant life experiences or intervention, however, little change in a stable variable should be seen. Hence, when considering a psychological level of analysis, it seems reasonable to think of vulnerability as stable, but not immutable.

The Endogenous Nature of Vulnerability

Vulnerability is endogenous; whether stemming from genetic characteristics, acquired biological or neuroanatomical dysfunction, or through learning processes, vulnerability resides within the person. This can be contrasted to other approaches to depression that focus on environmental or external sources of stress that initiate a disorder, or perhaps that focus on interactions. External processes are clearly important, but the vulnerability part of depression processes are typically viewed as emanating from within the person.

Stress

In a very general way, stress can be understood as falling into several broad categories. One major category of stress is seen as the occurrence of significant life events that are interpreted by the person as undesirable. Another type of stress can be seen as the accumulation of minor events (or hassles). Although descriptions of stress are varied, a common way to view it is as the life events (major or minor) that disrupt the stability of an individual's physiology, emotion, and cognition. In the original description of stress, Selye (1936) noted that such events represent a strain on adaptive capability that initiate an interruption of routines. Hence, stress interferes with the system's psychological and physiological homeostasis and is thus seen as a critical variable in a multitude of models of depression, regardless of whether these models focus explicitly on vulnerability factors.

Stress is typically seen as reflecting factors operating externally to the individual. An external locus, however, does not imply that individuals play no role in creating stress. While negative events do simply befall people, researchers have agued that some negative events are the result of a person's own actions, a process known as stress generation. For instance, the person who is inappropriately critical of others may engender tumultuous relationships with acquaintances, coworkers, and romantic partners that result in the generation of significant levels of stress. At-risk people may therefore play a role in creating their own stresses that precipitate depression.

Investigators have pointed out that it is extremely difficult to disentangle external stress from the cognitive appraisal processes. The person who is experiencing depression may appraise an event as much more negative than would a nondepressed person who experiences the same negative event. The commingling of events and the appraisals of these events have made the objective measurement of stress quite difficult. It can also be quite difficult to distinguish between stressful events that precede and are perhaps linked to the onset of depression, from those that follow and are the result of a depression (e.g., stress generation). Indeed some investigators have argued that even attempting to separate stress from a person's life is artificial.

The Diathesis-Stress Relationship

As noted, vulnerability is defined as an internal factor, while stress is an external factor. How then can stress be a part of vulnerability? The answer to this question is rooted in the idea of a diathesis-stress relationship. The term *diathesis* can be used interchangeably with *vulnerability*, and as Monroe and Simons (1991) note, the concept dates back to the ancient Greek, and to the late 1800s in psychiatric vernacular. A diathesis is seen as a predisposition to illness and has evolved from its original focus on constitutional, biological factors to presently also encompassing psychological variables such as cognitive and interpersonal susceptibilities. Many models of depression and vulnerability are explicitly diathesis-stress models; while there is general agreement that vulnerability constitutes an endogenous processes, these models also recognize that events perceived as stressful acts do trigger the vulnerability processes. Depression, in this conception, is thus the interactive effect of the diatheses and events perceived as stressful. When seen from this viewpoint, stress is integral to virtually all extant conceptualizations of vulnerability.

The Latent Nature of Vulnerability

Many vulnerability investigators have categorized vulnerability as a latent process that is not easily observable. From a research perspective, this can be seen in an empirical search for observable markers of vulnerability; investigators have sought to find reliable indicators of the presence of the vulnerability. A variety of strategies for identifying markers have been used, but in each case they operate under the assumption that (a) vulnerability processes are present in individuals who have few or no outward signs of the disorder, (b) they are causally linked to the appearance of symptoms, and (c) they are not easily observable. This is particularly true for investigations that rely on some kind of stressful or challenging event to make detection of the vulnerability factor possible. A search for vulnerability markers is thus an empirical strategy reflecting the judgment that vulnerability is present and stable, but latent.

Summary of the Features of Vulnerability

In sum, the literature on vulnerability suggests a number of essential features that characterize the idea of vulnerability. A fundamental core feature of vulnerability is that it is considered a trait as opposed to the kind of state that characterizes the appearance of depression. It is important to note in this vein, however, that while vulnerability is seen as a trait, and that psychological vulnerability may be stable and relatively resistant to change, it is not necessarily permanent; experiences can

occur that may attenuate the vulnerability. In addition, vulnerability is viewed as an endogenous process that is typically viewed as latent. Lastly, while distinct from vulnerability, stress is a critical aspect of vulnerability in that vulnerability cannot be realized without stress, at least according to many models. This idea about vulnerability represents the essence of the diathesis-stress approach that is common among models of depression.

The Relationship Between Vulnerability and Resilience

The flip side to vulnerability has been labeled *invulnerability, competence, protective factors,* or *resilience,* all terms that suggest invulnerability to depression in response to stress. Each of these terms can reasonably be used interchangeably, but some subtle distinctions do exist. Some researchers prefer the term *resilience* over other terms because it implies a diminished but not zero possibility of depression (see Ingram et al., 1998). A term such as *invulnerability,* on the other hand, suggests an all-or-none quality; people are either vulnerable or they are invulnerable, and to the extent that individuals are characterized as invulnerable, this implies that they will never experience depression.

One way to view the relationship between resilience and vulnerability is that they represent different ends of a continuum that interacts with stress to produce the possibility of depression. Thus, at the high-vulnerability end of the continuum, little life stress would be necessary to produce depression. At the resilient end of the continuum, depression is still possible, but a great deal of stress would be needed before depression results. Hence, with enough stress, even the most resilient of people can develop symptoms sufficient to meet criteria for depression, although these symptoms might be milder and briefer than those of the vulnerable person who experiences low or moderate stress, and almost certainly milder than those of the vulnerable person under significant stress. Resilience thus implies a resistance to disorder, but not an immunity.

Summary

In sum, while explicit definitions of vulnerability are difficult to come by, vulnerability can be reasonably defined by examining the various features that have been attributed in the literature to vulnerability. In this regard, vulnerability is seen as a process that places the person at risk for depression and that is stable and internal to the person. An external part of this process is stress, which, when considered within a diathesis-stress framework, becomes an integral part of risk. The flip side of vulnerability is resilience, which is seen as a resistance to depression, but not as invulnerability.

RICK E. INGRAM

See also

Diatheses-Stress Models of Depression
Risk
Stress Assessment
Stress Generation

References

Hollon, S. D., & Cobb, R. (1993). Relapse and recurrence in psychopathological disorders. In C. G. Costello (Ed.), *Basic issues in psychopathology* (pp. 377–402). New York: Guilford Press.

Ingram, R. E., Miranda, J., & Segal, Z. V. (1998). *Cognitive vulnerability to depression*. New York: Guilford Press.

Monroe, S. M., & Simons, A. D. (1991). Diathesis-stress theories in the context of life stress research: Implications for the depressive disorders. *Psychological Bulletin, 110,* 406–425.

Zubin, J., & Spring, B. (1977). Vulnerability: A new view of schizophrenia. *Journal of Abnormal Psychology, 86,* 103–126.

AUTHOR INDEX

Subject Index